THE CAMBRIDGE MEDIEVAL HISTORY

VOLUME VI

SOLD

THE CAMBRIDGE MEDIEVAL HISTORY

PLANNED BY

J.B.BURY

EDITED BY

J.R.TANNER

C.W.PREVITÉ-ORTON

Z.N.BROOKE

VOLUME VI

VICTORY OF THE PAPACY

CAMBRIDGE

AT THE UNIVERSITY PRESS

1968

Published by the Syndics of the Cambridge University Press
Bentley House, 200 Euston Road, London, N.W.1
American Branch: 32 East 57th Street, New York, N.Y. 10022

Standard Book Number: 521 04538 x

First Edition 1929
Reprinted 1936 1957 1964
1968

Printed in Great Britain
at the University Printing House, Cambridge
(Brooke Crutchley, University Printer)

PREFACE.

THREE of the contributors to the present volume died before its publication: M. Louis Leger, Member of the Institute of France, who wrote on Hungary, 1000–1301; Dr Hastings Rashdall, Dean of Carlisle, who contributed the chapter on Medieval Universities; and Miss Jessie Laidlay Weston, who wrote on Legendary Cycles of the Middle Ages. The *Cambridge Medieval History* has also sustained a great loss by the death of its architect, Professor Bury. Fortunately his plan for the work had long ago been completed, but the Editors will greatly miss his ready help in difficulties and the wise counsel which was so freely at their disposal.

They wish to thank Dr G. R. Potter for help in revising the chapter on Medieval Universities; Mr G. R. Crone and Mr H. Rothwell for assistance in the compilation of the maps; and Professor T. F. T. Plucknett and Miss M. S. Maris for compiling the index. They also desire to express their gratitude to Mr C. C. Scott, Sub-Librarian of St John's College, for invaluable help in preparing the bibliographies for the press.

J. R. T.
C. W. P.-O.
Z. N. B.

July, 1929.

INTRODUCTION.

It is an almost necessary consequence of publishing an historical work in a series of volumes, each of which deals with a separate chronological fraction of the whole, that there are a number of general chapters covering aspects of all or most of the period which yet can only be allotted a place in one volume. And in this sixth volume of the *Cambridge Medieval History*, the greater part of which deals with the thirteenth century, there accordingly appear chapters on Trade and Commerce, Warfare and Architecture, Religion and Learning, whose themes far transcend that limit of time. But there is an alleviation to this disparity of aim between the volume as a whole and certain of its most important constituents; for the thirteenth century was not (save in the most useless meaning of the phrase) an "age of transition," but one of completion. Themes common to all the Middle Ages find their fullest expression in it. It saw no rapid transformation making the time before it archaic in thought and life, and giving the time that came after it the aspect of a new-fashioned world. We may admit, indeed, that it held within it, as all ages must, the germs and symptoms of the decay of its most impressive embodiments; that it held no less in some of its humbler growths the obscure seeds of very different times. But as a whole the century was not an age of dissolution of an old order, but of the old order's full perfection.

Almost, we might say, from the dissolution of the Roman Empire in the West, certainly from the dissolution of Charlemagne's Empire in the ninth century, the peoples of Western Europe had been slowly refashioning, or rather remaking, their civilisation and their institutions, the whole fabric of their thought and life. Roman and barbarian had been melted down in the furnace of the Dark Ages to a common unity, a barbarism of harmonious and life-filled elements capable of growth and unborrowed progress. The new peoples were full of creative vigour; they dimly realised that they possessed a heritage both Roman and Teutonic, and as they advanced partially and gradually in the understanding of that heritage and applied it to the existing world, they moulded it anew in a multitude of original forms and devices, elementary, barbaric, and at times childlike, but all alike instinct with life and the power to change and grow. Whether they acted or they dreamed, this faculty of living growth was in them. The dreams became more rational and more real; the actions more purposeful and more restrained.

This progress from the ninth century to the thirteenth took many forms and has many aspects, but in every country of the West they are expressions of a civilisation fundamentally one and of a growth essentially harmonious. As the chapters on Scandinavia and Spain, on Bohemia and Poland, in this volume shew, there is an intrinsic likeness in their most aberrant shapes. The material conditions and problems that had to be met were in the gross the same; the human temperament and capacity, as well as the cultural equipment, which met them were specifically similar. European civilisation, in fact, rested and rests on a fundamental kinship of modes of action and modes of thought; and in that kinship the common language of educated men—Latin—the common institution to which all belonged—the Church—played their part along with mingled blood and a common elementary stock of legal and moral ideas. In a later age Europe could dispense with these formal bonds, not because its real unity had grown weaker, but because it had become indestructibly strong. The common fund of ideas had become more patent in its elaboration than in its primitive simplicity.

To give an exhaustive list of the forms and aspects which characterised medieval civilisation from the ninth to the thirteenth century would be an impossible and needless task. In the sphere of institutions they included the Universal Church and the sovereign Papacy, feudalism and the feudal monarchy, the ambiguous Empire which had kinship with both Church and feudalism, and also those voluntary associations which as monastery, order, university, commune, or gild, provided perhaps the most highly developed life of the age. In what may be called the more material sphere we may reckon travel and commerce, manufacture and agriculture, weapons and architecture. These lead us to the intellectual advance indissociable in fact from either institutions or material civilisation. We find the jurisprudence which explained and developed, adapted and expanded the Civil, the Canon, and the local customary Law; the imagination and craftsmanship which built cathedral and castle and informed both peaceful and warlike arts; the acute and fecund thought which explored theology and philosophy; and the creative fancy and insight which brought into being saga, epic, lyric, and romance, with power to make those forgotten generations live to us still.

In all these aspects of medieval life—to call them departments is to disguise their interpenetration and interdependence—the decisive ply was given long before the thirteenth century. Without raising formidable questions of necessity and free-will, of development or catastrophe, we may say that given the antecedent events and conditions, given the particular stimuli of actions and personalities that worked on them in succession, the civilisation of the thirteenth century was an eminently natural product of that of the ninth and tenth. Even the marvellous "renaissance" of the twelfth century caused no change of direction, only an immense advance in efficiency and elaboration. And it may even be claimed that so faithful had been that advance to the inspiration of the preceding centuries that it had raised their ideas and ideals almost to their perfection, a perfection from which further growth indeed came, but by exaggeration, inner discord, and decay, which were the signs of the approach of a true "age of transition." The thirteenth century sees Innocent III, St Louis, Magna Carta, the *Primo Popolo* of Florence, St Francis and St Thomas Aquinas, the Sainte Chapelle and the castle of Coucy, Gregory IX's *Decretals* and Bracton, Matthew Paris, the Icelandic Sagas, and the *Parzival* of Wolfram von Eschenbach. The fourteenth century, for all its glories, sees the Babylonish Captivity, the Hundred Years' War, the artisans' and peasants' revolts, the Italian tyrannies; its great names and achievements—and they are very great—look forward to modern times for which they pave the way; save Dante, whose youth belongs to the earlier period, and who has a double front, they do not complete, they beget and forecast.

If we take the leading features, the embodied ideas, of thirteenth-century society singly, the impression of reaching the highest pitch in a characteristic form is deepened. First, the Catholic Church—Christendom—which was given a semi-political meaning by Charlemagne, the organised, hierarchical fellowship of Christian men for salvation, found its ruler in the Papacy under Nicholas I and Gregory VII, its accessible code of law in Gratian, its corporate effort in the Crusades. Innocent III and his immediate successors continued and made in some sort effective this institution. They organised, guided, legislated for, and endeavoured to rule Christendom. Under them, the idea they inherited reached, so to say, its limits of successful working; and as it exceeds these in its centralised despotism and its elaborate machinery, it tends towards decay. The history of the Church and the Papacy from Leo IX onwards may be from this point of view described as a progress towards solidarity, order, and central control. Local rulers and primates and their synods restored law and discipline in the local Churches, but the Popes established contact and central control over these provincial efforts, and provided in fact the common law which all held to exist and the court of appeal by which it could be brought into daily effect. Their trained bureaucracy, concentrated at the Roman Curia, spread its tentacles over the West. In the Popes of the thirteenth century this *plenitudo potestatis*, legislative, administrative, financial, and almost doctrinal, was undenied; and in their omnicompetence, so long striven for, they had the opportunity of making their gravest errors.

The reform and solidifying of the Church was in a sense the victory of unity, order, and legal method over anarchy, of sovereignty and government over insubordination. The Popes did not issue from the traditional organisation of the Church; they dominated and used it by their own prerogative, which had long formed a part of the traditional conception. Not widely different was the contemporaneous progress of the secular monarchies and the development of feudalism, although here we may guess that naked principles were less firmly grasped and extreme conclusions not only rarely reached, save by Frederick II, but in general hardly suspected to exist. The logic of feudalism demanded a king, a supreme suzerain, the source of feudal powers; and feudal custom gave to the king in theory the most stringent rights over his vassals, contingent indeed on his performing his less exacting duties to them. His rights as suzerain, moreover, harmonised with his prerogatives as king, to whom the charge of governing and defending his people, of giving them justice and peace, was committed by God. It was the realisation of this feudalised monarchy which had been the endeavour of the western kings. More and more, even in France, the great insubordinate vassals had been brought to heel, and, where their rights seemed to exclude the king, abolished. It is significant of the true force of feudal theory that this was often done with their own connivance; Henry II, as Duke of Normandy, could aid his dangerous suzerain Philip Augustus, and the league against Blanche of Castile shattered on its own convictions as well as on its disunited selfishness. In conjunction with the enforcement of his suzerain rights, the king deployed his royal prerogative. He formed his non-feudal bureaucracy; he enforced and expanded his justice; he insisted on his claim to obedience, on his central control; both through and by the side of his feudal vassals he permeated his land with his authority. As in the Papacy, record and routine, specialisation, legalism and officialdom, had become the norm of the thirteenth-century monarchy. The process is seen most completely in England, France, and Sicily, but the type is European. The Royal Curia, ever merging into the Great Council, the Court of Justice, and the Household, typifies not only the growth of law and method and State unity but also the blended character of the feudal kingship that was living up to its mission. But here again the limits of the conception were being reached. Was the king to continue to live of his own, to depend on feudal levies, to work through feudal means? Advance meant quitting the feudal circle for the national sphere, and as in Sicily for the despotic sphere. Were the subjects to be content to render feudal submission and to receive feudal reciprocity, one by one? Advance meant the corporate action of estates of men and the claim to guide or limit the prerogative. Feudalism, no doubt, was to remain as a fashion, an ethos, but as the principle of State structure it was to go.

The great exception to this process of completion may be seen in the fate of the Empire, but while the exception is of vast importance, there were special reasons to account for it which only enforce the more general tendencies of development. In its highest theory—as Christendom—the Empire was inevitably the rival of the Papacy, whatever varying interpretation of "the two swords" might be adopted: even Dante has practically to forget his praises of unity when he places the Emperor by the side of the Pope. There was not room for two absolute exponents of the unity of Christendom. As ruler of Christendom the feudal, localised Emperor with his disjointed dominions was hopelessly at a disadvantage with the ecumenic Pope. If he tried to develop an hereditary feudal, yet bureaucratic State, like his brother monarchs, he was discarding the conservative attitude which was his main support against the radical Papacy. For the Empire looked back to Charlemagne and Otto the Great, and struggled against the tide. From the practical side, too, the Emperor was helplessly conservative. He could not unify, either separately or as a whole, his three disparate kingdoms of Germany, Italy, and Burgundy, and the struggle to hold all three had prevented him even attempting to do so. Partly as a consequence of this uncongenial personal union, partly on account of divergent original conditions[1], full-grown feudalism only came to Germany when the monarchy was in swift decay, and never really came to Italy, the *Regnum Italicum*, at all—there primitive feudalism was superseded by the communes, and the surviving fragments developed in contorted forms. Thus the Empire shews us versions of feudal and post-feudal development with the monarchy sterilised. We watch its disintegration under Frederick II. It was after all a condition of the most splendid history of the age.

The society whose greatest manifestations were the feudal monarchies and the mystical body of the Church was not formed on an individualistic basis. Although great personalities were as striking and effective then as at any time, and although personal passions were less checked than in more civilised periods, men with rare exceptions acted as groups and communities. The most advanced of these were non-feudal. The monasteries and the Military Orders, indeed, had seen their best days, though the finishing touches to their organisation may be claimed in principle for the thirteenth century[2]; but the Orders of Friars took their place in the van, and the universities shewed the freest form of self-governing communities.

[1] See the Introduction to Vol. v, pp. xviii, xix.
[2] See *supra*, Vol. v, Chap. xx, pp. 685 ff.

The intellectual Dominicans devised a representative system of remarkable consistency, while the communes and gilds applied the most complicated and ingenious methods of self-government to all affairs: war, justice, legislation, administration, and trade. And it is significant that none of these institutions were able to improve on their methods of the thirteenth century. How they achieved them may be seen in the appropriate chapters of this and the preceding volume.

We should not expect to find a similar stage in the ascent of material civilisation. Manufacture, the exploitation of the land, the methods of commerce, shew an unresting course. Yet even here in certain aspects signs of a completion of an evolution may be detected. Gothic architecture reaches its supreme expression in the thirteenth century, to lose itself later in ingenuity and skill. In even more striking fashion the castle and fortified town reach their zenith. And at any rate the commerce with the Levant had outgrown its more experimental period, and the chief European manufactures had become firmly established in fixed habitats and a mature routine. The augustal and then the florin of the West supersede the gold bezant as the one unimpeachable currency. The centre of European trade left Constantinople for Italy in 1204. The epoch-making capture of Constantinople in the Fourth Crusade and the subsequent clashes of East and West in the Levant have been told perforce in earlier volumes to avoid a break in the narrative, but the chapters which follow should be read in their light: that Western Europe has now won precedence of Eastern and that the movement to control the Mediterranean which began in the eleventh century has now reached its terminus, while the necessity to defend it from the Ottoman Turks has yet to come.

That precedence is a sign of the less ponderable intellectual and moral advance made by the West in working out its special civilisation, and here again the thirteenth century bears the marks of a completing age. It would be over-venturesome to define too closely the change by which generations in succession grow more mature, more expert in life and nature; but such a process is an obvious fact (as is also its counterpart—decadence), and in particular spheres something of its course may be seen. Two studies were largely responsible for training the "European mind." One was jurisprudence. The continual study of Roman Law[1], followed by that of the imitative Canon Law, was of incalculable benefit from 1100 to 1300. It is hard to overrate the importance of the revival of Justinian's Code at Bologna, and of Gratian's compilation of his *Decretum*[2], the latter really

[1] See *supra*, Vol. v, Chap. xxi.

[2] *Concordantia Discordantium Canonum.* The proper title expresses its place in development. The general law of the Church could now be clearly known.

the result of codifying efforts during a century and a half. They each provided at last an accepted Statute-book of universal law. From the Civil Law, above all, men learned how to criticise texts, how to explore the sources of knowledge with critical induction, how to apply logical principles to the inexhaustible contingencies of life, even how to create new law and remould custom on grounds of fitness, expediency, and equity. The very formalism of the Law made this racial education the more congenial and effective to these still uncouth centuries. Meanwhile men's conceptions were widened and deepened and their reasoning faculties ever sharpened and tempered by the dialectics and metaphysics of scholasticism. When—again following the capture of Constantinople in 1204, but due also to the long efforts of translators in the twelfth century[1]—the works of Aristotle, now rendered more and more, however roughly, direct from the Greek, became the staple exercise of the universities, the habits of mind engendered in law and scholasticism joined forces[2]. We see their completed development in the thirteenth century: the glossator Accursius, the decretalist Hostiensis, and the schoolman Aquinas are contemporaries. And in both cases a break-away, something like disorder and revolution, is observable in the succeeding time—the beginning, it has already been suggested, of an age of transition.

These somewhat arid pursuits happily did not monopolise the speculative intellect of the West. As in plastic art, so in literature it ran its course. In France, in Scandinavia, in Germany, in that other country, the Church, we see the same ripening faculties, the growth of a whole literature. The Sagas achieve the utmost realism and vividness in the portraiture of character and the stresses of life; the ethos of two widely divergent national societies appears in the wild legends and fantastic exaggerations of the Northern and the Charlemagne cycles of romance; the fairyland of Arthurian chivalry comes to our ears like a distant chime—"the horns of Elfland faintly blowing"—and the deeper music of the Latin hymns, or the fiery eloquence of St Bernard, drones solemnly beside them. Later times could only repeat and imitate these; Dante and the "dolce stil nuovo" begin a new current.

As men's knowledge and reasonableness slowly grew, as some beginnings of peace and legal right succeeded unabashed violence[3], as the incessant efforts of the Church, contaminated and spasmodic as they might be, con-

[1] See Haskins, *Studies in the History of Mediaeval Science*, 1924.

[2] Earlier and less complete instances of this amalgamation in a less developed time may be seen in Lanfranc and more especially in St Anselm, *Cur Deus homo?*

[3] We may use Henry II's Assize of Novel Disseisin, forbidding "self-help," as a too favourable symbol of the change. We must of course allow for the ineffectiveness of formal law.

tinually impressed Christian motives and standards on inborn heathenism, it was natural that there should be a steady if languid rise in the ideals and standards of life. Here again we may note that these standards were raised upon lines long laid down and by institutions typical of these centuries. First, there was the ascetic ideal of Christian perfection which dominated religious life. The history of monks and friars from St Benedict of Aniane to St Francis of Assisi may from one angle be truly viewed as a series of baffled reforms; it may also be as truly looked on as a successive deepening and widening of a particular conception of Christian duty and renunciation. The prosaic quietism of Cluny is mingled with the propaganda of Church reform, its quasi-comfort is followed by the lyrical austerity of the Cistercians, and the supreme limit of the ascetic ideal is reached by St Francis and his early friars practising utter renunciation in touch with the full life of the world, and including in it an active duty of charity among men. Here, too, completion is reached in the thirteenth century. Repetition or decline may follow, but the conception of a corporate ascetic life under a Rule will not further expand, and in course of time will find other interpretations of the highest Christian life beside it.

Meantime as a social force this effort of centuries had not gone for nothing. The influence of a fervent or even a tepidly respectable monastery or brotherhood, living by law, preferring peaceful means, recognising obligations to humanity, not merely to special kindred, feudal, or class groups, maintaining a standard somewhat higher than their surroundings, had its natural effect in producing a wish for better things than contemporary practice. Perhaps it was the ubiquitous friars who first brought home Christian ethics to the mass of the medieval populations. But the raising of ideals was not due to the religious alone, nor was their asceticism the only type of life held up to the admiration of the time. A similar rise in standards, of a more mundane nature, and like asceticism, it may perhaps be said, on somewhat narrow lines, may be seen in the growth of chivalry, another characteristic embodiment of the age. The knight becomes chivalrous in the eleventh century. To unflinching courage and fierce loyalty to kindred and to lord, is added a fierce championship of the Christian faith, and later, courtesy and fair play to the combatant; protection of women and the weak, inculcated by the Church first rather as a check, becomes slowly enough part of the necessary ideal; it is a far cry from Roland and William of Orange to Perceval and Galahad, a journey that takes the *amour courtois* with all its elements of strength and weakness on the way. And the change indicated in the romances is paralleled in real life: we journey from William the Conqueror and Godfrey of Bouillon past Frederick Barbarossa and Earl William Marshall to St Louis. The highest ideal of secular chivalry was reached in literature and in life in the thirteenth century. It becomes more showy and conventional later, while more wide-spread. It, too, had to break the mould of caste and profession to make a transition to later times.

The emphasis, however, on this aspect of completion in the thirteenth century does not imply that it was a static age incapable of progress, or on the other hand that it contained the golden times, *semper cedentia retro*, of the human race. Not then, more than at any other epoch, did men make even a near approach to their own ideals. The evils they fought against, anarchy, oppression, reckless impulse, and crass ignorance and savagery, were but little mitigated by the advance, which yet is very visible. Not only so; those forms of society, that advance in knowledge, that intellectual training, which the feudal age had devised and experienced, were shewing their limitations the more they seemed to progress. A structure of centralised absolutism, of pedantic legalism, of innumerable tenurial contracts, of a thought both inexperienced and rash and incongruously fettered, confident of packing the hearsay universe into a nutshell, an art that knew no measure or probability, and that reached true greatness—as indeed it did—only where the inescapable facts of engineering forced perfection on its creative instinct: all these could not give a final solution to human problems or assuage the ills that flesh is heir to. Their inadequacy and their defects were seen in their decadence and decline so near at hand. They became subject—so we may interpret events—to a law of diminishing returns. The field was overcropped, the overwrought principle became a barren sophism.

Yet the feudal age was preparing and protecting the beginnings of its eventual successor, and these preludes and portents derive a prophetic magnitude from their later growth. Amid those covert beginnings under the shadow of Papacy and Empire we may count the dim origins of national States and national consciousness. England, France, and Castile, and the Scandinavian kingdoms, are on the way to become consolidated States by 1300, and national antipathies at any rate are affecting politics: in splintered Germany and Italy there is at least a national tradition. The English Parliament and the Spanish Cortes are national assemblies as well as outgrowths of a feudal curia; and the nation of estates, feudal in a way as it is, begins to disregard the strictly feudal bond in favour of a simpler grouping of men by function rather than by terms of a contract. In a similar manner we may trace, although still shrouded under various aliases and unconscious of itself, the advent of a middle class in essence neither feudal nor hierarchic. The bourgeois of commune or borough, the teeming bureaucracies of the kings, the swarms of clerks who learned and taught at the universities, all foreshadowed that stratum of society neither limited by the highly specialised code of the feudal magnate nor like the peasants practically tied to the soil on which they grew. They might be wealthy, they might be travelled. Expanding commerce, expanding administration, expanding learning brought them in touch with all the new ideas there were, and made them more supple and more original in their outlook on life. A mentality of business and efficiency was diffused among them, whether they came from minor gentry, from commerce, or from handicrafts. If in England they were to shew the greatest sense of common interest, in all the West they existed in more exclusive groups; and they were to bring a matter-of-fact sobriety, a political moderation, and an instinct to appreciate and use the realities of life, into European civilisation. This, however, was to come. In the thirteenth century one can only say that they were beginning to be freed from the inherited conventions of the reigning feudal and ecclesiastical framework of society. They were given a neatly-plotted place in it by its theory, but they were not of it, and in spite of theory they were, in a way, to pervade eventually all its parts, and perhaps already to corrode its ideals. A sardonic, practical, yet sentimental and poetic, bourgeois literature begins to appear (in France) in the thirteenth century, just as a homely, realistic grotesque peers out from the foliated capitals and under the misericords of Gothic churches. The interest in the personalities and daily habits of men which meets us in Gerald of Wales, in Matthew Paris, and in Fra Salimbene, the personal vagaries of thought of so many half-heretical clerks, and the taste for an almost scientific observation of nature which appears in scattered scholars and finds a temporary apogee in Frederick II and Roger Bacon, all portend, though from afar, a new age; and before that murky, long-delaying dawn the gorgeous starlit sky of the Middle Ages was to lose its lustre.

These beginnings, however, were but a small part of the background of great events. The thirteenth century began with the sudden paralysis of the Empire, and the triumphant pontificate of Innocent III. Its early years saw the dissolution of the great Angevin dominion, and the unawaited bridling of the English kingship. The weak French monarchy suddenly took a leading place in Europe. The capture of Constantinople abased the preeminence of the Levant. The Christians of Spain finally gained the upper hand at Las Navas de Tolosa. The Papacy then puts out its strength: the Albigensian heresy goes down before it; its henchmen the Friars permeate all the activities of the West; it begins once more its duel with the obsolescent Empire strangely championed by a pioneer of intellectual revolt and innovation in Frederick II. The Empire falls; Germany and

Italy change their feature; but the Papacy is left deeply infected, deeply distrusted, and enslaved to its own political schemes and alliances. Meantime, Europe has seen the face of Asia changed by the Mongol conquest, and herself is only saved perhaps because the wave of invasion is exhausted. The strange experiment of the Latin Empire fails, and the Crusades peter out with the defeats of St Louis and the loss of Acre. And amid the clash of arms and revolutions the merchants throng the ways of traffic by land and sea, scholars trudge beside them, Florence becomes the clearing-house of Europe, waves of art pass from Palermo to Milan, from Paris to Westminster, and in churches rising out of the turmoil of peace and war those potent generations put their hearts in stone and make the figments of the brain their most lasting memorial.

CORRIGENDA.

Vol. I.

p. 204, l. 5 from bottom. *For* vasting *read* wasting.
p. 259, l. 18. *For* Isonza *read* Isonzo.
p. 323, l. 12. *Delete* Chu.
p. 439, l. 5. *For* Lombardy *read* Transpadana.
p. 475, l. 10 from bottom. *For* Scampia *read* Scampa.

Index.

p. 711, col. 2. *Delete* Chu, River, 323.
p. 726, col. 2. *For* Isonza *read* Isonzo.
p. 730, col. 2. *Delete* Lombardy, held by Theodoric, 439.
p. 743, col. 2. *For* Scampia *read* Scampa.
p. 750, col. 2. *Insert* Transpadane (Gaul), held by Theodoric, 439.

Vol. V.

p. viii, l. 6. *For* Anastasius *read* Anacletus.
p. xii, l. 2 from bottom. *For* Anastasius *read* Anacletus.
p. 4, l. 7. *For* Břatislav *read* Vratislav II.
p. 4, ll. 10, 16, 23. *For* Břatislav *read* Vratislav.
p. 13, n. 2. *Read* Ulrich (Udalrich) of Augsburg (923–973) is sometimes said to be an exception, but his letter *De continentia clericorum* is now held to be a forgery. So etc.
p. 54, l. 13 from bottom. *For* Carmel *read* Horeb.
p. 88, l. 21. *For* promoted to the archbishopric *read* promoted to be cardinal (1095) and later archbishop.
p. 106, l. 6 from bottom. *For* he later *read* Pope Honorius II.
p. 174, l. 22. *For* Stephen II *read* Stephen IX.
p. 186, l. 17. *Read* "Whosoever maketh himself king in Sicily speaketh against Caesar."
p. 230, l. 22. Read *Bononia*.
p. 346, l. 15. *Read* 7 March 1138.
p. 505, ll. 13–10 from bottom. Additional note. Since Mr Corbett's death, documents recording grants of land under William the Conqueror have been signalized, one made by Baldwin, Abbot of Bury St Edmunds (ed. Douglas, D. C., EHR. xlii (1927), pp. 245 sqq.), and the other by Robert, Bishop of Hereford (ed. Galbraith, V. H., EHR. xliv (1929)).
p. 510, ll. 11–14. *Read* Stigand occupied...Domesday as having held till his death a personal barony...he ranked.
p. 517, ll. 10 and 12. *For* Azo *read* Azzo.
p. 541, l. 6. *Read* Lyons-la-Forêt.
p. 668, l. 6 from bottom. *Read* Hadrian IV.
p. 769, l. 19 and ll. 8 and 12 from bottom. *For* "mater ecclesiae" *read* "matrix ecclesiae."
p. 779, l. 10 from bottom. *For* prebendinants *read* perhendinants.
p. 795, l. 2. *Read* separata a sensibilibus an in sensibilibus posita.

Index.

p. 952, col. 2. *Delete* Azo, an Italian marquess, lays claim to the county of Maine, 517.

" " *Add to* Azzo, marquess of Este, "lays claim to the county of Maine, 517."

p. 956, col. 1. *Delete entry* Břatislav.

p. 974, col. 2. *Insert* Hugh Bardolf, 583.

p. 979, col. 2. *Delete* Lions-le-Forêt, 541.

p. 981, col. 1. *Insert* Lyons-la-Forêt, 541.

p. 986, col. 1. *Under* Octavian, anti-pope *delete* 368.

p. 991, col. 1. *Under* Ranulf, earl of Chester, *for* 449 *read* 549.

p. 997, col. 1. *Insert* Simon Grim, 588.

p. 1002, col. 1. *Add to entry* Vratislav II, "founds see at Olmütz, 4; ecclesiastical policy of, *ib.*"

p. 1004, col. 2. *Insert* William de S. Mariae Ecclesiae, 583.

Vol. VI.

p. 72, l. 9 from bottom. *For* Duke of Moravia *read* Margrave of Moravia.

p. 128, last line.
p. 129, l. 2. } *For* Masovia *read* Mazovia.

p. 129, l. 11 from bottom. *For* Gothland *read* Gotland.

p. 139, l. 8. *For* Leopold *read* Lupold.

p. 159, ll. 10–11 from bottom. *For* Archbishop-elect *read* Bishop-elect.

p. 176, l. 24. *For* Philip della Fontana *read* Philip da Pistoia.

p. 266, l. 9 from bottom. *For* 1242 *read* 1249.

p. 292, line 15. *For* Alfonso I *read* Affonso I.

p. 391, l. 24. *For* Gothland *read* Gotland.

p. 405, l. 6. *For* Alfonso Enriquez *read* Affonso Enriques.

TABLE OF CONTENTS

INTRODUCTION.

CHAPTER I.

INNOCENT III.

By E. F. Jacob, D.Phil., Professor of Mediaeval History in the Victoria University of Manchester, late Student of Christ Church, Oxford.

CHAPTER II.

PHILIP OF SWABIA AND OTTO IV.

By Austin Lane Poole, M.A., Fellow and Tutor of St John's College, Oxford.

CHAPTER III.

GERMANY IN THE REIGN OF FREDERICK II.

By Austin Lane Poole, M.A.

CHAPTER IV.

THE INTERREGNUM IN GERMANY.

By Austin Lane Poole, M.A.

CHAPTER V.

ITALY AND SICILY UNDER FREDERICK II.

By Dr Michelangelo Schipa, Knight Grand Cross of the Order of the Crown of Italy, Professor of Modern History in the University of Naples.

CHAPTER VI.

ITALY, 1250—1290.

By C. W. Previté-Orton, Litt.D., F.B.A., Fellow and Librarian of St John's College.

CHAPTER VII.

ENGLAND: RICHARD I AND JOHN.

By Frederick Maurice Powicke, M.A., Hon. D.Litt., F.B.A., Fellow of Oriel College and Regius Professor of Modern History in the University of Oxford.

CHAPTER VIII.

ENGLAND: HENRY III.

By Professor E. F. Jacob, D.Phil.

CHAPTER IX.

THE REIGNS OF PHILIP AUGUSTUS AND LOUIS VIII OF FRANCE.

By Professor F. M. Powicke, F.B.A.

CHAPTER X.

SAINT LOUIS.

By Charles Petit-Dutaillis, Dr-ès-Lettres, Director of the National Office of French Universities and Schools.

CHAPTER XI.

THE SCANDINAVIAN KINGDOMS UNTIL THE END OF THE THIRTEENTH CENTURY.

By Dr Halvdan Koht, Professor of History in the University of Oslo.

CHAPTER XII.

SPAIN, 1031—1248.

By Dr RAFAEL ALTAMIRA, Judge in the permanent Court of International Justice at the Hague; late Professor of Jurisprudence in the University of Oviedo.

CHAPTER XIII.

(A)

BOHEMIA TO THE EXTINCTION OF THE PŘEMYSLIDS.

By Dr KAMIL KROFTA, Professor of Bohemian History in the University of Prague, Vice-Minister of Foreign Affairs in Czecho-Slovakia.

(B)

POLAND, 1050—1303.

By ALEXANDER BRUCE-BOSWELL, M.A., Bowes Professor of Russian History, Language, and Literature in the University of Liverpool.

(C)

HUNGARY, 1000—1301.

By the late LOUIS LEGER, Member of the Institute.

CHAPTER XIV.

COMMERCE AND INDUSTRY IN THE MIDDLE AGES.

By JOHN HAROLD CLAPHAM, Litt.D., C.B.E., F.B.A., Fellow of King's College, and Professor of Economic History.

CHAPTER XV.

NORTHERN TOWNS AND THEIR COMMERCE.

By HENRI PIRENNE, Professor of Medieval and Belgian History in the University of Ghent.

CHAPTER XVI.

THE DEVELOPMENT OF ECCLESIASTICAL ORGANISATION AND ITS FINANCIAL BASIS.

By the Rev. E. W. WATSON, D.D., Canon of Christ Church and Regius Professor of Ecclesiastical History in the University of Oxford.

CHAPTER XVII.

THE MEDIEVAL UNIVERSITIES.

By the late Very Rev. HASTINGS RASHDALL, D.D., D.Litt., F.B.A., Dean of Carlisle, sometime Fellow of New College and Hertford College, Oxford.

CHAPTER XVIII.

POLITICAL THEORY TO *c.* 1300.

By W. H. V. Reade, M.A., Sub-Warden and Tutor of Keble College, Oxford.

CHAPTER XIX.

MEDIEVAL DOCTRINE TO THE LATERAN COUNCIL OF 1215.

By Alexander Hamilton Thompson, M.A., Hon. D.Litt., F.B.A., F.S.A., St John's College, Cambridge, Professor of History in the University of Leeds.

CHAPTER XX.

HERESIES AND THE INQUISITION IN THE MIDDLE AGES, *c.* 1000—1305.

By A. S. Turberville, M.A., B.Litt., formerly Scholar of New College, Oxford, Professor of Modern History in the University of Leeds.

CHAPTER XXI.

THE MENDICANT ORDERS.

By A. G. Little, M.A., Hon. D.Litt., F.B.A., Balliol College, Oxford, late Reader in Palaeography in the University of Manchester.

CHAPTER XXII.

(A)

ECCLESIASTICAL ARCHITECTURE.

By the Very Rev. D. H. S. Cranage, Litt.D., F.S.A.,
King's College, Cambridge, Dean of Norwich.

(B)

MILITARY ARCHITECTURE

By Professor A. Hamilton Thompson, F.B.A.

CHAPTER XXIII.

THE ART OF WAR TO 1400.

By Professor A. HAMILTON THOMPSON, F.B.A.

CHAPTER XXIV.

CHIVALRY.

By Miss A. ABRAM, D.Sc.

CHAPTER XXV.

LEGENDARY CYCLES OF THE MIDDLE AGES.

By the late Miss JESSIE LAIDLAY WESTON, Hon. D.Litt.

LIST OF BIBLIOGRAPHIES.

LIST OF MAPS.

VOLUME VI

CHAPTER I.

INNOCENT III.

I.

Shortly before he died the aged Celestine III proposed that John Colonna, better known as Cardinal Giovanni of St Paul, should be his successor. Roger Howden relates that he even suggested abdicating in John's favour, but the cardinals would not hear of it. If devoted piety and respect for poverty and self-abnegation had been all that was required of the new pontiff, they would have chosen the monk who laid the foundations of the Papal Penitentiary, the humble spirit who befriended Francis of Assisi. They took instead a deacon of the college, Lothar of the Conti family, lords of Segni, thirty-seven years to succeed ninety-one. They wanted a statesman rather than a religious genius, and Lothar seemed the man to restore the political power of the Papacy in Italy and beyond the Alps, to protect the religious orders against secular encroachment[1], to combat the danger of heresy. The Curia had indeed shewn its hand when it supported Tancred of Lecce against Henry VI for the Sicilian kingdom, and there was to be no departure from its political path. Thus far Innocent III—under that name he was consecrated on 23 February 1198—found his lines determined for him. The cardinals knew that he was full of energy and ambition. They could not have foreseen, even dimly, what was to be the effect of his personality and will: the use made of every shifting of fortune to increase the spiritual authority and the temporal possessions of the Holy See; the comprehensive vision that subordinated each detail, however small, to the general execution of his aim; the power of adaptive recovery after defeat, the inexorable genius of order and method and lucid expression. Within the larger framework of that policy they were to see strange fluctuations and unexpected collapses: grandeur of conception jeopardised by unscrupulous agents, splendour of design obscured by faulty understanding and uncertain handling of men. Yet the general result was to stand above all controversy. The religious life of Western Europe was organised and directed as never before; the rivers emptied themselves into the Mediterranean, the roads led to Rome; and the believer could pray *Adveniat regnum tuum*, more certain at heart that the mirror of the heavenly Kingdom was to be found in the Church-State militant here in earth.

[1] The position at Canterbury, where Richard I and his archbishop had come into collision with Christ Church over the projected foundation for secular canons at Lambeth, probably influenced the election considerably. See Karl Wenck, *Die Römischen Päpste zwischen Alexander III und Innocenz III* (*Papsttum und Kaisertum*, Festschrift Paul Kehr), pp. 460–63.

Lothar's ancestors were German settlers in Latium. In the twelfth century the family was of such standing that his father, Thrasamund, could marry a daughter of the Roman house of Scotta. A young man of some means, Lothar had studied theology at Paris under Peter of Corbeil, law at Bologna under Uguccio of Ferrara, the most celebrated of Italian decretists. He was first actively connected with the Curia during the pontificate of Lucius III, thanks, no doubt, to his uncle, the future Clement III. During the short reign of Gregory VIII he was made sub-deacon, and later on in the time of Clement III Cardinal-deacon of SS. Sergius and Bacchus (1187). Celestine III's elevation brought the Orsini, enemies of the Scotta, into prominence, and Lothar suffered temporary eclipse, during which he wrote the famous, but in all respects conventional, treatise *De contemptu mundi*[1]—a string of biblical citations connected by a commentary. In the Curia he was probably then the young radical who had to be suppressed for advocating drastic measures as against the caution of older heads. In appearance he was small, but his presence was distinguished and commanding. The early mosaic portrait of him from the apse of St Peter's, now preserved in the Capella Conti (Villa Catena), shews a young face, stern, dark, and alert[2]. His personality was dynamic rather than magnetic, a man to be admired more than loved. He was an accomplished speaker, had a fine ear for the sound of a period, and his work in the Chancery added considerably to the practice of the Roman *cursus*. He was a preacher and expositor rather than a philosopher, though he could wield the syllogism with the best. A thorough knowledge of the Old Testament and the Apocrypha provided him with a constant store of allegory and symbolism wherein, like any theologian of his time, he delighted, while for secular quotations he drew largely upon the *Epistles* and *Ars Poetica* of Horace. Fully four thousand eight hundred of his letters survive, yet it is not easy to form a personal judgment of him from them, so formidable, often so exasperating is the façade of words built by himself or the clerks of his Chancery. The impressive phrase fell easily, a little too easily, from Innocent's pen. But on a point of law or administration there is no trace of verbiage: all is as clean-cut as an Anglo-Norman writ. Innocent's rescripts and decretals are classical models of legal judgment. In patient deliberation, in minute examination of every relevant point, he excelled. Thrice a week, we are told, he held a public consistory, "in which he heard the complaints of individuals. The smaller cases he examined through judges delegate, the more important he set forth himself with such refinement of skill and wisdom that all were amazed at these qualities, and many learned men and jurisconsults would frequent the Roman Church

[1] One may recall von Ranke's judgment, *Weltgeschichte*, VIII, p. 274: "Innocenz verachtete die Welt nur soweit, als sich mit der Absicht und der Fähigkeit vertrug, sie zu beherrschen."

[2] Reproduction in Fedor Schneider, *Rom und Romgedanke im Mittelalter*, p. 30.

simply to listen to him, and learned more in his consistories than they would have in the schools, especially when they heard him giving judgment; for so subtle was his statement of the case on either side that each party hoped for victory when it heard his presentment of its position; and no advocate, however skilful, appeared before him but did not acutely dread his objections to the points pleaded."[1] "Solomon III" was the name given him by one of his household in a humorously satirical account of his summer quarters at Subiaco[2], and the writer may well have heard from his own lips his favourite remark that he was a debtor, to fools as to the wise, to do justice. So too with administration. His keen business-like mind overlooked nothing. He has left us a picture of himself writing indignantly to rebuke the Archbishop of Antivari for accepting as genuine a surreptitious papal letter that made Innocent address him as "Beloved *son* in Christ" instead of "Venerable *brother*," and employ the plural when the singular was the invariable usage. "Wherefore we would have you in like cases take such care that you will no more be circumvented or deceived, but will scrutinise the apostolic letters more diligently in seal and thread, parchment and style, that henceforth you will not take true for false, or false for true."[3] *Tam in bulla quam in filo, tam eciam in carta quam stylo*: the Chancery rhyme, transformed to curial prose, typifies the cautious administrator. But this archivist's attention to significant minutiae was but a small part of an equipment devoted to the service of the greatest of medieval ideals and one never relaxed: the supremacy of Christ's Vicar on earth.

"Petro non solum universam ecclesiam, sed totum reliquit saeculum gubernandum." The claim advanced by Nicholas I, pushed further by Gregory VII in the *Dictatus papae*, and re-stated by Alexander III, is asserted more fully and strongly than before. Christendom is one community, the garment of Christ without seam: one, not merely in the sense of a moral unity, but a visible, concrete world-state under clerical guidance, its rulers the governors of their various territorial areas, each recognising the supremacy of the Roman See and admitting the Pope's plenitude of power. The foundation of this Society is unity of faith and obedience to the successor of Peter; for the Pope, that successor, has no equal upon earth. He is the representative of Christ. The Holy See is "set in the midst between God and man, below God, but above man." At his consecration Innocent preached on the text: "See, I have this day set thee over the nations and over the kingdoms, to pluck up and to break down, to destroy and to overthrow, to build and to plant." This view was grounded not merely upon Christ's command to Peter and the

[1] *Gesta Innocentii*, c. 41. MPL, CCXIV, LXXX–I.

[2] Cf. K. Hampe, *Eine Schilderung des Sommeraufenthaltes der römischen Kurie unter Innocenz III in Subiaco*, 1202, HVJ, 1905, 509–535.

[3] *Reg.* III, XXXVII. MPL, CCXIV, 920. Cf. R. L. Poole, *The Papal Chancery*, p. 137. The reforms in the papal secretariat are briefly considered on pp. 75–79.

Donation of Constantine, but upon a hierarchical reading of Old Testament history which he never tired of repeating. In the answer to the ambassadors of King Philip of Swabia given in consistory (1199 or 1200) his essential thought is expressed: Melchisedech, King of Salem and priest of the Most High, foreshadows and typifies the priesthood in its relation to the world, the superiority of spiritual over temporal power, "praeeminentiam quam sacerdotium habet ad regnum," because the two were united in the priest-king. Melchisedech is the figure he used in an early letter to the spiritual and lay princes of Germany (3 May 1198) to represent the majesty of Christ as King of Kings and Lord of Lords. This combination of a divine and human order in a single person descends through history to Peter's representative.

It is easy to multiply instances of this deeply-felt historical mysticism, and what follows here constitutes no denial of the fundamental idea[1]. Yet in spite of these and other high utterances, his canonist's caution and vivid sense of the practical kept Innocent from trying to give constant effect to a doctrine of Petrine authority such as glossators and later commentators on his decretals were disposed to put into his mouth. Personally he was no rigid doctrinaire, but a man with a great ideal before him, alive to the facts of the situation, often bowing to the inevitable and reacting to pressure. His spirit was never dismayed by the gulf lying between the high Petrine theory of sovereignty and the historical and more limited practice of the Roman bishop. It could be bridged, if one went carefully enough. It never affected him as strongly as it had affected Gregory VII, with his finer intuition and darker sense of conflict. There were no tears, no spiritual wrestlings, at Lothar's elevation. He could speak of the Papacy as "the most glorious position on earth," where Hildebrand had felt only "bitterness of grief and great anxiety" encompassing him. He believed in the power of organisation and the magic of diplomacy, and was never left helpless by the pride and hardness that seemed invincible. A tough patrician, unlike the legal maniac Boniface VIII he could bend without breaking. Whatever he may have felt, the moment he had before him a concrete problem involving principle or had to make a decision constituting a precedent, he became cautious and deliberate, though never purely traditionalist or conservative. When he claimed as the successor of Peter to intervene in temporal matters, it was to provide peace or justice, to help widows, orphans, or crusaders, to punish sin. It was in compliance with his duty to preach peace that he wrote in 1203 to Philip Augustus calling on him to make terms with John Lackland and drawing a picture of the disastrous consequences of

[1] Dr Konrad Burdach's interpretation of Innocent's theory, *Vom Mittelalter zur Reformation*, II, 1, pp. 240–295 is accepted here; but one may emphasise the caution underlying several of Innocent's classic utterances, *e.g.* the decretal *Per venerabilem*, without underestimating the magnitude of the theocratic claim.

war. When he received the answer that he had no business to interfere in a matter between lord and vassal, he shifted his ground, disavowed the intention of interfering with feudal relations, and maintained that he had rightly intervened *ratione peccati*, for no one of sound mind could fail to recognise that it was his duty to snatch every Christian from mortal sin. This famous definition of the ground of papal intervention forms one of his decretals: the canonist Hostiensis, however, commenting upon the passage, hastened to point out that the text did not imply that the two jurisdictions, spiritual and temporal, were distinct; nay rather that they both had a single source; that the Papacy possessed the two swords—a doctrine that Innocent did not maintain with absolute consistency.

A similar use was made of the letter which he wrote in 1206 to the Bishop of Vercelli on behalf of the authorities of the commune. Here he directed that papal letters which dealt with matters properly belonging to the secular authorities should be disregarded; but that persons who considered that they had been wronged in the secular courts might appeal to the bishop, or, if they so preferred, to the Pope, particularly at a time when the Empire was vacant and there was no secular judge to whom they could resort. This ruling led Innocent IV in his *Apparatus* to the Decretals of Gregory IX to enter in great detail into cases of "denial of justice" where the Church might legitimately intervene, and the conclusion is drawn that the Emperor is *advocatus* of the Pope. But Innocent III was neither laying down rules of justice to be regularly observed during an imperial vacancy, nor transferring into the canonical sphere the consequences of *deni de justice* in customary law. How cautious an innovator he was in matters on the border line between spiritual and secular jurisdiction can be seen in the great decretal *Per venerabilem*, his reply to the Count of Montpellier's application for the legitimising of his children. The count had pointed, as a precedent, to Innocent's order removing illegitimacy from the children born to Philip Augustus by Agnes of Meran. Innocent maintained that for temporal purposes legitimisation was a matter for temporal powers to deal with, and the count had a superior. Philip, on the other hand, had no superior and thus wronged no one by submitting to papal jurisdiction. Within the patrimony the Pope had jurisdiction as a temporal lord; without, he could in certain cases exercise it[1], on the ground that in Deuteronomy provision was made for reference on doubtful matters to the Levites, and their jurisdiction under New Testament dispensation belonged to the Pope. These "certain cases" Innocent defined according to the Decalogue as falling within three categories: *inter sanguinem et sanguinem* (criminal law in a civil process), *inter causam et causam* (ecclesiastical and civil law alike), and *inter lepram et lepram* (the Church's criminal law)[2]. The first and second must come

1 "Certis causis inspectis jurisdictionem casualiter exercemus." The reading "causaliter" is less substantiated.

2 The last is, of course, perfectly normal.

into operation in a case of difficulty or doubt. The condition should be noted, as well as the respect shewn for the rights of the overlord. In these cases the apostolic jurisdiction is exercised as a last resort; the Christian law always can, and sometimes must, supply the desired solution. There can be no mistaking the general tendency of the decretal. The priest-king, the Pope, is also the supreme judge in Christendom; the Levites, his Cardinals, are his court. Their jurisdiction resembles the *dominium eminens* of the Roman Emperors. Potentially supreme in spiritual and temporal causes alike, it is in practice self-limited. It is there, yet not necessarily insisted upon. But nothing can limit it when once it has been called into action upon specific matters where feudal law or national custom cannot avail.

The same mixture of audacity and circumspection is evident in the most far-reaching of his diplomatic dealings, the business of the Empire[1]. He took his stand upon the claim of Gregory VII to confirm the choice of the electors and to approve the person of the elected; conversely, therefore, to reject the other competitor or competitors. Now Gregory VII justified his attitude by announcing the supremacy of the papal power over all worldly authority. Innocent, on the other hand, less theoretically and very characteristically took as his justification the so-called historical fact of the *translatio imperii* from the Greeks to the Romans through the medium of the Papacy. In the famous judgment (not however meant for publication) which he delivered in Consistory upon the claims of the three candidates, he upheld the right of the Holy See to deal with the matter on the ground that the Roman Empire belonged to it *principaliter* and *finaliter*; *principaliter*, because the Papacy was the origin and cause of the transference; *finaliter*, because the Emperor received the last laying-on of hands from the supreme pontiff, was blessed, crowned, and invested by him with the Empire. The argument is from history and historical ceremony. The right to elect none the less rested firmly with the princes of the Empire, and Innocent repeatedly stated that he had no desire to deprive them of it. It is hard to decide whether he was sincere in these assertions; whether his exhortations to unity and concord addressed to the lay and spiritual nobility of Germany between 1199 and 1201 were not disingenuous; whether he was right, when charged with intervening through his legate in the dispute between Otto and Philip, in denying that he had ever exceeded his three-fold right of *confirmatio*, *approbatio*, *reprobatio*. It is not difficult to shew that in this and in many other transactions strong reasons of expediency governed him consciously or sub-consciously; but the real point of importance is that his method was always a legal one, and by this deliberate procedure, step by step, he was able to enforce more extreme measures and sentences than any of his predecessors and to do so with remarkable frequency. Yet the very legality of his mind and methods

[1] For his relations with Otto and Philip of Swabia see *infra*, Chap. II.

seems to have brought with it a corresponding deficiency in probing character or in understanding local atmosphere and local conditions, and a lawyer's readiness to seize upon a formal point to the exclusion of other considerations. Once he had set a train of events in movement, he did his utmost to be fair, took nothing for granted, examined every representation made to him and in so doing was liable to see not the wood but only the trees; to lose, as in the Albigensian Crusade, the general control of things and to be forced to rely on his extraordinary resilience and recuperative power to make the best of a bad situation. And he did not always choose the instruments of his policy well. From his subordinates and his allies he often expected more than they could give or failed to fathom their weaknesses. He thought that they were filled with the same kind of impersonal ardour as himself; that the dignity of their offices or commissions would carry them to success. Upon the personal element he frequently set curiously little value.

He had a noble conception of his office, a keen sense of his responsibility. His favourite metaphor was the Fisherman's boat on Gennesaret. "By Peter's boat is figured the Church," he wrote in 1199 to the Greek Patriarch; "Peter, then, according to our Lord's command launched out his ship into the deep, letting down his net for the draught, and thus placed the supreme command (*principatum*) of the Church in the region where temporal power flourished at its highest, the home of the imperial monarchy to which the various nations at fixed times paid their tribute, as the waves go to make up the sea." Here spoke the religious legatee of Rome to the schismatic claimant of the estate. More interesting, because more self-revealing, a use of the imagery came from him five years later after the fall of the Patriarch's city. Writing on the text Luke v, 3–6, to the crusading clergy at Constantinople a vindication of the primacy of the Roman Church in converting and teaching the world, he said: "Jesus in fact went up into the ship of Simon, when He caused the Church of Peter to rise, a fact clearly apparent from the time of Constantine onwards.... *And sitting down He taught the multitudes from the vessel*, for thenceforward He caused Peter to be firmly seated, whether in the Lateran or in the Vatican, and made him teach, since from now onwards doctors began to multiply in the Church, Leo, Gregory, Gelasius, Innocent, and many others after them. But for a time He ceased to speak, when the word of preaching ceased in the Church, not so much because of the unworthiness of its pontiffs as on account of the evil lives of its subjects.... And therefore He said to Simon, when He ceased to speak, *Launch out into the deep and let down the net for a draught.* Then is the ship launched into the deep when the Church is lifted up on high by lofty doctrine or advanced to better estate. But whether in these days the ship was launched into the deep, I prefer not to say, lest I might appear to commend myself; but one thing I affirm with confidence, that I let down the net for the draught."[1] Innocent launched out in very truth. The deep, he said in one of his sermons, was Rome, preaching the net of many threads and strings that typified the authorities used and the methods of address. He was speaking here as one exercising *praelatio*, the care of souls, whose first duty is to instruct; and throughout his intensely political life his pastoral task was ever before him. In his sermon at the opening of the Lateran Council he emphasised the Pope's duty of scrutinising every activity in the Church. "The supreme pontiff, who is watcher over Israel, must traverse (*transire*) the whole Church...investigating and inquiring into the merits of each and all." No reader of his Register can fail to be astonished at the rapidity with which he turns from the highest matters of statesmanship to cases involving tiresome and minute detail from the outskirts of Christendom or even to the subtlest points of theology; at the extraordinary versatility of his organising power, and the immense gravity of his judgments.

He was a diplomat and an opportunist, ready to seize the immediate advantage, but never losing sight of the goal. He had no hesitation in playing upon discreditable motives, when he could gain by so doing. He was not above inventing situations that did not exist or even telling deliberate falsehoods. No man in that age could entangle himself in international politics without endangering his honesty, and he quoted most appositely the saying that the man who handles pitch defiles himself. For this lack of scruple—and the very fact proclaims the great advance of the Papacy to temporal power since the days of Alexander III—he has been taken severely to task[2]. Yet he can only be judged as a man of his age. He was convinced that the Papacy alone could guarantee a richer ethical and religious life to the world, and that it must therefore govern men's lives by means of an organised divine society, the Church. He realised to the full the splendour of her continuity, he felt at one with her saints. A peculiar trend of circumstances gave him some of the gravest of European issues to determine, some of the noblest of opportunities in European politics to handle. Elected as he was, believing what he did, he could never stand aside or remain an occasional arbiter. For among pontiffs of international mind with the interest of Christendom at heart none of such practical ability joined with such consciousness of his position had appeared since the days of the first Gregory.

[1] *Reg.* VII, CCIII; MPL, CCXV, 512–14.

[2] "Er kannte für die Politik nur ein Gebot, das der Zweckmässigkeit": Hauck, *Kirchengeschichte Deutschlands*, IV, p. 719. I agree with Dr Erich Meyer (*Staatstheorien Papst Innocenz III*, p. 7) in thinking this verdict too extreme. See also the observations of Prof. Hampe, *Deutsche Kaisergeschichte*, 2[e] Aufl., p. 199.

II.

We shall confine our account of Innocent's activities to the part he played outside Germany in limiting and fettering the over-mighty Hohenstaufen Empire—that Empire which, in the eyes of the Curia, was the utter negative of the Hildebrandine ideal of an autonomous Church; to the efforts he made to establish the unity of the faith and of Christian worship, both as regards the Eastern Empire as well as the heresy that threatened the West; and to his largely successful attempt to assert the feudal suzerainty of St Peter over the younger kingdoms. We shall then turn to the main characteristic of his pontificate, the increased centralisation of the papal monarchy, and survey the principal organs of administration which gave effect to it. Finally we shall consider certain particular directions in which Innocent's legislation was of vital effect in moulding the canonical system of the Church.

In Rome and Italy the situation in 1198 was critical, but full of possibilities. The City lay under the direction of an official who had sworn fealty to Henry VI and of a senate over which the Papacy had no control. In addition, a part of the Roman nobility was not readily disposed to accept the rule of one connected with the Scotta clan. Outside Rome, before Henry VI's death, his officials had reduced the State of the Church to the boundaries of the Roman Duchy; his seneschal, Markward of Anweiler, had been invested with the March of Ancona and was Duke of Ravenna; Conrad of Urslingen was in possession of Spoleto, and Henry's younger brother, Philip of Swabia, had been created Duke of Tuscany. But everywhere the tide had turned against the imperial vicars and the cities were rising to their opportunity of independence. Henry VI's endeavour had been to strengthen the Empire with the solid monarchy of Sicily by bringing about the succession of his son Frederick to the combined territories; but the widowed Constance stood in need of a protector, and there was a good chance of reforming the feudal compact of 1059 and of gaining more advantages than the Treaty of Benevento (1156) had permitted to the Papacy.

The City prefecture, which Henry had reduced to the position of vassalage under the Empire, had in the twelfth century become a papal office, exercising criminal and civil jurisdiction over the city, and, in theory at all events, over the surrounding country to a distance of a hundred miles around Rome. The prefect was invested with the purple mantle of office by the Pope, rode by his side in processions, and swore to maintain the rights of the Church. The dignity was in process of becoming hereditary in the Vico family (Viterbese by origin) which possessed considerable estates in Tuscany. By Henry's death Piero, the present prefect, lost his patron, and Innocent took advantage of the fact to restore the old relation of dependency by making him take the oath of vassalage (22 February 1198). He was at first likewise successful with the Senate. This body during the last fifty years had varied in numbers from fifty-six to a single person. The senators were not papal officials; they represented the Roman municipality, the Republic on the Capitol, and single senators like Benedict Carushomo, who had made themselves independent of the Holy See, had appointed rectors in the Roman country towns and had even sent communal judges into the Sabina and the Marittima. Innocent induced Scottus Paparone, the single existing senator (who had shewn himself submissive to Henry VI), to abdicate; but it was essential for him to control the system of election. Accordingly, instead of allowing the whole body of citizens to use their right to vote, he succeeded in nominating a special body of electors, *mediani* or mediators between the Pope and the citizens, to appoint the new senators. In the present case, as a single senator only was to be nominated, one *medianus* only was selected. The choice of the new official had however to go before the assembly of citizens for approval, and the Pope's liberty of choice was therefore restricted. But Innocent got what he wanted, and by means of the newly appointed candidate secured throughout civic territory the replacement by papal judges of the justices appointed by the Capitol. These changes did not involve the abdication by the Romans of their position or the subjugation of the City. In helping the populace in their war against Viterbo (1199) and in dictating terms to that city when defeated (January 1200), Innocent recognised the Roman people as a sovereign power. The subjugation of the Viterbese was made not to him but to the Roman commune. Nor was the problem of the senate by any means settled. In the course of 1202 certain measures taken by Innocent's brother Richard against Count Odo of the house of Poli caused popular hatred of the Conti, already fostered by their Orsini enemies, to flame out. The Poli, an impoverished noble family, out of enmity to the Conti offered their estates, which were already mortgaged to Richard, to the Roman People on the Capitol. The People accepted them, but Innocent in support of his brother claimed the lands as fiefs of the Church, invested his brother with them, and soon afterwards secured their transference entire to the Conti. This piece of so-called nepotism was to cause fighting between the papal party, led by the Senator Pandulf of the Subura, and the democratic party, and inevitably to raise the question of another form of senate. The city became so dangerous, feeling against the Conti so strong, that in 1203 Innocent had to leave Rome for Palestrina. During the very days when the Latin crusaders were conquering Constantinople, the Pope was forced by the petty feuds of the Roman barons to leave the Eternal City. In the autumn, when Constantinople fell, the irony of the position brought him to such physical weakness that his death was rumoured. At Rome the old senate of fifty-six was tried. In the November elections the cardinals whose duty it was to elect the *mediani* were forced to swear that they would choose at least two candidates from the faction hostile to the Pope. The new body when elected was sharply divided on the question of the Poli estates, and civil war broke out in Rome. In March 1204 Innocent saw his chance to return and put the senate in order by restoring the single senator. Once back again, he appointed as his *medianus* John Pierleone, a man acceptable to both parties, to make the choice; but Pierleone's choice for the senatorship fell upon a noble, and the democrats, ranged under the demagogue John Capocci, Innocent's most energetic enemy, proceeded to elect an opposition senate under the title "Good men of the Commune." The strife was finally settled by the appointment of four umpires to decide the question of the Poli lands and the manner of electing the senate. These adjudged to Innocent the right of electing, for John Capocci's methods did not appeal to them. The Pope used his success moderately. At first he allowed fifty-six to be chosen; then, six months later, he returned to the plan of a single senator and selected Pandulf, now captain of the papal party in Rome. Peace was finally made between the Pope and the City in 1205. One monument of the struggle survives, the Conti tower, relic of the splendid bastion built by Innocent to overlook the Forum and the Subura. It bears witness to the influence of a family feud upon the constitution of Rome as well as to the local dangers that beset the pontiff.

In central Italy Innocent rode the full flood of reaction that followed immediately upon the Emperor's death. In the weakness of the imperial power he saw the opportunity to recreate a powerful patrimony of St Peter; but he must do it at first as an Italian patriot, heading the Guelf opposition against the Hohenstaufen Empire. Conrad of Urslingen was overcome without difficulty, and the valley of the upper Tiber together with the important Duchy of Spoleto (which meant the greater part of Umbria) was freed from its fealty to the German dukes. Its cities, Assisi, Foligno, Gubbio, Todi, and even Perugia did homage and had their communal franchises confirmed in return. In Tuscany an anti-imperial league of cities was already in being, established (November 1197) with the co-operation of Celestine III. This confederation Innocent sought to direct. The negotiations which led up to a renewal of the original agreement with the Papacy (October 1198) shew clearly that he was aiming at the recovery of the Matildine estates which had fallen into the hands of Florence, Siena, Lucca, and other cities. These he never succeeded in obtaining, and his failure to do so contributed to the future greatness and independence of the Tuscan cities; on the other hand, he was successful in securing such Matildine estates as had been monopolised by Henry VI and Philip of Swabia. The recovered territories were secured by the establishment of a series of castellanies distributed over the Campagna, the Marittima, the "Patrimony of St Peter in Tuscany," the Duchy of Spoleto, and the bishoprics of Spoleto and Narni. The cities of Romagna and the March of Ancona, when Markward had been ejected, present the same kind of problem as those of the Tuscan league. After the first flush of liberation they formed alliance with the manifest aim of ridding themselves of all external control. They refused to obey the legates of the Holy See, and some, like Ascoli and Camerino, remained subject to the Empire, while others like Sinigaglia allied themselves with the nobility that was friendly to Markward. The final solution of the problem in this district was the contract which Innocent made with Azzo VI of Este in 1212 enfeoffing him with the March of Ancona in return for preservation of the rights of the Church. The administration of the other territories was placed in the hands of papal legates or laymen of standing. This, as a recently discovered constitution of Gregory IX has shewn, did not in the long run prove satisfactory, as the *rectores extranei* did not scruple to help themselves from the goods of the Church, and it was finally, after Innocent's death, found advisable to put the whole patrimony in the charge of a committee of cardinals acting with papal support[1].

The most formidable opponent was Markward of Anweiler. Innocent's dealings with this remarkable man and with his German allies in the south are bound up with the regency exercised by the Church over Sicily. Before his death Henry VI had given Markward a series of last instructions for his future dealings with the Curia. These or part of them were found in a box in his baggage captured (1200) after his defeat between Monreale and Palermo, and we owe the account of them to Innocent's biographer. They are fully in the spirit of the very large concessions which Henry VI had tried to get the Papacy to accept in return for its recognition of the hereditary character of the imperial crown and the right of the young Frederick of Sicily to succeed. The widowed Empress Constance and her son Frederick were to hold Sicily in fee of the Pope and the Roman Church; in case the young king died without heir, the kingdom was to become the property of the Holy See. In return for the Pope's admission of Frederick's right of succession, the Matildine lands and the whole Patrimony together with Montefiascone were to be handed over to the Pope, while Markward was to hold the duchy of Ravenna, the territory of Bertinoro, and the March of Ancona from the Papacy. If Markward died without heirs, these fiefs were to become the property of the Roman Church. It is probable that, shortly after Innocent's elevation and before the news of the election of Philip of Swabia (6 March 1198) arrived, Markward attempted to come to an understanding with Innocent upon these terms, but with no result. Whether he revealed their whole content it is hard to say; but it is not just to charge him with a total refusal to carry out the deceased Emperor's wishes, or, simply on the strength of the curial account, to condemn him for disavowing the promises made by his representatives. It may well be that Innocent was using the anti-German reaction that followed Henry's death and the uncertainty existing among the Hohenstaufen supporters in Italy whether to uphold Frederick or

[1] K. Hampe, *Eine unbekannte Konstitution Gregors IX*, ZKG, XLV (Neue Folge VIII), Heft II, pp. 190–97.

not, to demand more than Markward was authorised to concede[1]. At any rate the negotiations failed; Markward was excommunicated, deprived of his duchy of Ravenna and the March of Ancona, and in 1199 left for the Sicilian kingdom to enforce his claim to the tutelage of Frederick in accordance with the permission given him by Philip of Swabia whom he had recognised as Emperor-elect in August 1198.

After the death of her husband, Constance had sought Innocent's protection for herself and her three-year-old boy[2]. It was the Pope's opportunity to divide Sicily from the Empire and to recover for the Holy See the ecclesiastical privileges wielded by the Norman kings of Sicily in virtue of their position as hereditary legates of the Church. Innocent only granted Constance the kingdom in fee on condition that she recognised the right of the Papacy to hear appeals, call synods, send legates, and have a considerable say in elections. When she died in November 1198, she left Innocent, as suzerain, the guardianship of her son. The Pope, while exercising a general supervision, placed the government of Sicily in the hands of a council consisting of the Archbishops of Palermo, Capua, and Monreale, and of the Bishop of Troja, Walter of Palear, the most influential as well as the most difficult of councillors to handle, already smarting under a previous dismissal from his chancellorship and ready to take offence. On the mainland there confronted them the particularly difficult task of driving the German nobles from their strongholds. Diepold of Vohburg, Count of Acerra, held Rocca d'Arce in the frontier lands of the Liris; Conrad of Marlenheim was in possession of Sora and the Castle of Sorella. These had made common cause with Markward, who was now (1199) from the vicinity of Naples threatening to descend upon Sicily, while his depredations struck terror into the south. Innocent—it was characteristic of him—both raised an army and opened negotiations; but no agreement was possible when Markward was determined to be regent of Sicily. With the support of Pisan merchants and of a section of the nobility Markward landed in Sicily and prepared to besiege Palermo. A papal army sent by Innocent under the command of his cousin, the Marshal Giacopo, defeated him 21 July 1200, but none the less he succeeded step by step. His progress was largely due to the alienation of the selfish and greedy Walter of Palear from the Pope. In these straits Innocent decided to call in to his help Walter, Count of Brienne, husband of Alberia, a daughter of Tancred, the last Norman king. Walter now appeared at the Curia to demand Lecce and Taranto as his wife's inheritance. There was no escaping the fact that through her he had also pretensions to the Sicilian Crown, and here the danger lay. Upon taking him into the service of the Church Innocent recognised the justice of his claims to the fiefs, but bound him by oath never to infringe Frederick's

[1] On this difficult point see F. Baethgen, *Die Regentschaft Papst Innocenz III im Königreich Sizilien*, pp. 119–24.

[2] See *infra*, Chap. IV.

rights as King of Sicily. Walter was nothing more to him than a useful instrument, who could be discarded for a better, if a better presented himself. But the fact that Walter represented the dispossessed dynasty aroused deep distrust at the court of Palermo. It drove the Chancellor into Markward's arms.

Walter de Brienne was at first successful on the mainland. But the island and, in November 1201, the capital Palermo, fell to Markward. Innocent could not get Walter to leave Taranto and attack Markward in the island. The Frenchman may very reasonably have doubted whether the Sicilian supporters of Frederick would receive him, and we have proof of their suspicions in the fact that Innocent delegated his authority, when Walter's army should arrive in Sicily, to the Abbot Roffred of Monte Cassino and to Giacopo the Marshal. However, in September 1202 Markward died, and Innocent was transported with joy. "I saw the ungodly flourishing like a cedar of Lebanon: I went by, and lo, his place was nowhere to be found." It was a fine testimonial, but the joy was a little premature. Walter of Palear came back to Innocent's side, yet Frederick was still in the hands of Markward's successor, William Capparone, where he was to remain till Diepold of Vohburg, after having defeated and slain Walter de Brienne (1205), came over to the papal party and restored the boy to the papal legate and Walter of Palear (1206). In 1204, when Peter II of Aragon was in Rome, Innocent had negotiated for his ward a match with Peter's sister Constance. But it was not until 1208 that the opposition in southern Italy was satisfactorily subdued by Conrad of Marlenheim's surrender of Sora and Sorella. Then indeed the way was open for a settlement of the Sicilian kingdom. In June 1208 at a great assembly held at San Germano Innocent placed the administration of the mainland in the hands of the Counts of Fondi and Celano as *magistri capitanei*; and later in the year the regency was brought to an end.

Both now and two years later when Frederick was summoned to the Empire Innocent could feel that he had done his best for Sicily[1]. He had strenuously resisted the alienation of the demesne; he had consistently fought the imperial interest in the kingdom; he had, as far as was possible, maintained the rights and the possessions of the Sicilian clergy. But for his ward it had been a legal, not a personal relationship. Innocent only once saw Frederick. He expressed interest in his studies, pleasure at his progress; but it was a bitter childhood for the young king. When he was of age he gave short shrift to the canons of Palermo when they

[1] "Hinc est utique, quod pro tua justitia defendenda saepe duximus noctes insomnes, et prandium in coenam convertimus.... O quoties euntium et redeuntium nuntiorum examina sibi invicem obviarunt, qui per varias orbis partes pacis tuae procuratrices litteras detulere! Quoties epistolae, pro tua tuique regni tranquillitate mittendae, notariorum fatigavere calamos, et scribarum atramenta siccarunt!" *Reg.* IX. CCXLIX, MPL, CCXV, 1081–2.

besought Innocent to elect upon the vacancy of the see[1]; he dismissed Walter of Palear for a time at least from the chancellorship. He had become a prince determined to recover every lost Crown right, and to restore the power of the central government. In a sense the regentship of Sicily had begotten the greatest future menace to the Papacy.

But to Innocent Sicily was only part of a larger whole defined and guaranteed in the three successive concessions made to him by Otto IV at Neuss (1201) and at Spires (1209) and by Frederick at Eger (July 1213). By them the State of the Church was declared to be the whole territory between Radicofani and Ceprano, the March of Ancona, the Duchy of Spoleto, the land of the Countess Matilda, the county of Bertinoro, the Exarchate of Ravenna, and the Pentapolis with adjacent lands contained in earlier imperial privileges. That there was real need from the papal point of view to have these territories publicly and repeatedly confirmed to the Holy See it will be easily realised. During the contest in Germany the Italian city-states lost no opportunity of securing privileges from whosoever was in the ascendant. Before Philip of Swabia was released from the ban, in the Duchy of Spoleto itself, Assisi had secured from him the liberty of electing consuls. After his release from the ban, he appeared in Italy in the spring of 1208 as King of the Romans and demanded through Wolfger of Aquileia the rights of the Empire from the Tuscan cities which had appropriated them during the interregnum. A treaty between Philip and the commune of Siena (23 May 1208) shews the demand conceded in the stipulation that all citizens between the ages of fifteen and seventy were to swear fealty to the king and that all property belonging to the Empire at the death of Henry VI should be restored. Treaties of this type were dangerous to the claims of the Church, and Otto's disregard of his solemn promises in the wholesale granting of the Church land in fee to his supporters after his coronation reinforced Innocent's determination to have the papal territories once more acknowledged and confirmed. The boundaries of the Papal State are drawn at their fullest.

From the first to the last day of his pontificate Innocent had the idea of the Crusade uppermost in his mind. Some of his finest sermons were preached on the sufferings of the martyrs who had dared all for Christ, and he was oppressed by the love of ease among Christian princes and the unfulfilled vows which, as he said, had delayed the mercy of God. His encyclicals and proclamations of a plenary indulgence made in 1198 with the co-operation of Cistercians and Benedictines shew him eagerly concerned with the expedition which was to restore the Christian kingdom in Palestine. A clerical fortieth was demanded, collecting-boxes were ordered to be placed in churches, creditors were bidden to defer their demands for payment from all who took the Cross. Innocent told the

[1] See Innocent's protest in *Historia Diplomatica Friderici Secundi*, ed. Huillard-Bréholles, t. I, pars i, 140–2.

Patriarch of Jerusalem, the Bishop of Lydda, and the Grand Masters of the Military Orders to keep him informed of the situation in the Holy Land, and entered into friendly relations with the King of Little Armenia, who recognised him as universal bishop. While prepared to deal on ordinary diplomatic terms with the enemy and to better the conditions of Christians in Muslim areas—and here we may remark the foundation in 1199 of the Order of Trinitarii for redemption of captives—he was the whole time preparing to call the West to the recovery of Jerusalem. In so doing he was bound to face the Eastern question in its contemporary setting; he could not avoid the problem of Constantinople. The general opinion of Western Europe was that the Eastern Empire had hitherto displayed a malevolent neutrality in the matter of the Crusade. Henry VI had tried to cut the knot by planning the capture of the Eastern capital; but this project had made the menace of the Hohenstaufen appear so formidable that Celestine III had not hesitated to enter into friendly relations with Alexius III. It was now Innocent's policy to secure the reunion of the Greek and Latin Churches (the predominance lying with the Latin), and to make Alexius one of the principal helpers in the Holy War. In thinking that the usurper who had dethroned his brother and ousted that brother's son from the succession was in a position to be of use either from a military or financial point of view he was undoubtedly mistaken; but it was still more unfortunate that the negotiations for reunion could not be made to keep pace with the preparations for the Crusade[1]. While he was lecturing the Greek Patriarch on the primacy of the Roman See and urging the Greek Emperor to deliberate on the matter at a General Council, the host was collecting, the Hohenstaufen plan for the capture of Constantinople was being revived, and the control of the expedition had been placed in the hands of Boniface of Montferrat, an intimate friend of Philip of Swabia, son-in-law of the dethroned Isaac Angelus. Not only was Innocent not consulted about the supreme command of the expedition, but he was forced to accept as an accomplished fact and to make the best of the terms dictated to the Crusaders by the Venetians, upon whom depended the conveying of the force. He ratified the agreement of 8 May 1201 on condition that a legate should follow the expedition and that no wrong should be done to any Christian people, unless in a case of actual obstruction. It is impossible to say how much Innocent knew then of the Hohenstaufen plan, but it is clear that by November he had heard of the proposal, for in the meantime the young Alexius had visited Rome and in audience with him held out the promise of a union of the Churches, if the legitimate family was restored to the Byzantine throne. Alexius III got wind of this and sent to Innocent to implore him to prevent the danger. In a remarkable reply dated 16 November 1201 Innocent stated that he had discouraged the idea, but that the Emperor should use not words but deeds, and hasten "to extinguish the fire while

[1] For the Fourth Crusade and its results cf. *supra*, Vol. IV, Chaps. XIV, XV, and XIX.

it was still far away" lest it should reach his own country. He was using as a threat to stimulate the Emperor into action the very danger which he himself must have dreaded and have tried to avert. If he realised its imminence, this conduct was not creditable to him. If he did not, Zara was soon to shew him that the fire was not to be played with. The capture of the sea-port in the realms of his Hungarian "vassal" caused him acute distress; it also reduced excommunication to the verge of absurdity, for unless the whole enterprise was to be cancelled—the heroic, but impolitic course—the Crusaders must be conveyed by the excommunicate Venetians. Innocent decided to continue the expedition, and in absolving the Crusaders through his legate issued to them an express prohibition not to violate Greek territory. How that prohibition was observed has been related elsewhere.

The change of tone between his communications of the beginning of February and those of early November 1204 is very marked. In the first instance he was frigidly addressing leaders who had again incurred excommunication for infringing his express command; in the latter he was warmly congratulating Baldwin for acting as the medium of the divine justice in translating the Greek kingdom from schismatics to the Catholics. The change was not only due to his recognition of an accomplished fact, the taking of Constantinople, which he spoke of as a "miraculous event" for the union of the Churches which it promised; he had genuinely convinced himself that Constantinople was a necessary stage in the delivery of Jerusalem. But he was to be disillusioned. He had allowed the Crusaders a year to establish themselves in the city and its surrounding country; unfortunately, in June 1205, Cardinal Peter of Capua absolved from their vows all Crusaders who remained in Constantinople till March 1206. This was not Peter's first misdemeanour, and he was sharply rebuked and sent back to Palestine. In the autumn of 1205 the Pope rebuked Boniface of Montferrat for neglecting his vow and antagonising the Greek Church by the plunder of its treasuries. March 1207 saw him still hopefully addressing the Latins in the Empire as *crucesignati*; but the army which had been collected by the Bishop of Soissons to strengthen the force in Constantinople lost its chief at Bari, and thenceforward Innocent's hopes began to fail. He bitterly reproached Venice as the cause of the diversion, and his belief was to be strengthened by her purely selfish expedition for the reduction of Crete in 1209. The year before he finally despaired of further progress and began efforts for a totally new enterprise.

Yet disappointment was outweighed by the interest of reorganising the Greek Church, and Innocent threw himself wholeheartedly into the task. The Latin occupation did not automatically bring with it the desired union. Outside the newly appropriated territories were formidable centres of resistance, the Empire of Theodore Lascaris in Bithynia, the lordship of the Princes Alexius and David in Trebizond and Heraclea (Pontus), and the Epirote despotism of Michael Angelus. Within, the conduct of the Latins at Constantinople had not advantaged Rome, and the Greeks were sullen and suspicious. It was Innocent's desire at first to Latinise the Greek rite; but the mission of Cardinal Benedict of Santa Susanna (May 1205) led to wiser counsels. Benedict concentrated principally on questions of dogma, and did his work with moderation and humanity. He entered into relations with the independent Greeks of Nicaea, represented by the Metropolitan of Ephesus; at Constantinople, Thessalonica, and Athens he assembled the principal doctors of the Greek Church, let them defend their position, and expounded to them Latin doctrine. At Athens he conducted a series of formal disputations on the Procession of the Holy Ghost with its great archbishop, the early humanist Michael Acominatus. He told Innocent that he was not in favour of making the question of leavened or unleavened bread in the Eucharist the ground for rupture or the exercise of compulsion, and the Pope agreed with him. Innocent saw that more could be done by propaganda than by force, and from France and Germany called for a band of regular clergy armed with missals and breviaries, and for volunteers from the masters and scholars of the University of Paris. The real stumbling-block was the oath of canonical obedience which Innocent and the legate made a *sine qua non*. This was the test that led to the voluntary exile of Acominatus to Ceos, of Manuel of Thebes to Andros, and of the Archbishop of Crete to Nicaea. The oath was a double one taken both to the Latin superior and to the Pope. A great number of clergy swore obedience to Innocent, though they did it with bad grace. "They declare and believe that the Pope is not the successor of Peter, but Peter himself," was their acute remark about the Latins. But the Venetian Patriarch of Constantinople, Thomas Morosini, did not inspire confidence. Appointed over again by Innocent on grounds of the initial illegality of his choice, and consecrated at Rome (20 March 1201), Morosini had received the pallium and large privileges, including that of nominating Latin clerks to benefices vacated by Greeks. The Orthodox knew that he was very amenable to Venetian pressure, that the Doge Dandolo had made him swear to allow only Venetians to be appointed canons of Santa Sophia, that when he got badly into debt he was forced to hand over certain of the churches to his creditors in payment; they knew that he was not above despoiling the treasure of his own cathedral, and that he was so little regarded by his fellow Latins that two years after the conquest Innocent had to instruct the Emperor and the Latin leaders at Constantinople to pay him due respect in order that the recalcitrant Greek clergy might follow their example. Had Cardinal Benedict been in Morosini's place, the oath of obedience might have proved easier. As it was, the only temporary *rapprochement* between Greeks and Latins was brought about by the mission of the intolerably pompous Cardinal Pelagius in 1213–14, when the Greek clergy clamoured to the Latin Emperor for protection against the invader. The description given by the Metropolitan of Ephesus of the negotiations with the court of Theodore Lascaris reveals with bitterly sarcastic humour the gulf that lay between the mind of Nicaea and the mind of Rome.

The financial settlement of the new Latin Church was set forth in a triangular agreement which Innocent ratified between his representative Cardinal Benedict, the Patriarch Morosini, and the Emperor and barons. The conquerors promised to give the Church a fifteenth of all possessions in land or on the coast outside Constantinople, and a fifteenth of all merchandise coming from without, the distribution to be made by a committee of assessors. The Latins were to pay tithes of all fruits and crops, even if the Greeks were finally induced to pay also; and all Church property and its inhabitants were to be free from lay jurisdiction. The Church was to be the first recipient of a fifteenth of any lands won by future conquest. Later, Innocent ruled that the Emperor was to receive the oath of fealty from the bishops for any temporalities which they might hold from him. When the conquest and partition of northern Greece and the Morea had been effected, Achaea, the metropolis of which was Patras, was divided into six suffragan bishoprics, the archbishop holding from Geoffrey Villehardouin eight knights' fees and his diocesans one apiece, the quota of the Teutonic Knights, the Hospitallers, and the Templars respectively. In place of Archbishop Acominatus, whose cathedral was the still unruined Parthenon, "Our Lady of Athens," a Frenchman was installed. "The renewal of the divine grace," wrote Innocent, "suffers not the ancient glory of the city of Athens to grow old." Innocent granted the request of the archbishop and chapter (whose members proved scandalously non-resident) that the Athenian Church should be governed by the custom of the Church of Paris. She had under her eleven sees. To Corinth Innocent allotted seven. These arrangements were found unworkable owing to poverty, and the provinces of Patras and Corinth were later reduced to four sees each. Internally, there was much friction. The primate of Achaea was restive under a Venetian patriarch, and the Franks were for the most part hostile to their own Latin clergy. Tithe was hardly forthcoming, and the nobles had no hesitation in appropriating it. In vain Innocent wrote to the Emperor asking him to enforce its payment. There were amazing disorders in the quarrel between Villehardouin and the Archbishop of Patras: the confiscation of the archbishop's fee, the singular course adopted by Villehardouin of releasing the Greek priests and monks from the jurisdiction of the Church of Patras, and of preventing Greek serfs from shewing obedience to the Roman Church. Innocent's formal triumph resulted in a feudalised Church, poor and in peril of secular encroachment, in a muddle of doctrinal compromise or in sullen and suspecting isolation. Orthodoxy had a racial and political past that could not be effaced, and the Councils of Ferrara and Florence were later to prove that even agreement at a representative congress of the two Churches was not a sufficient guarantee of union.

But within the Western Church itself all was not well. It is difficult to realise that at the zenith of her power maintenance of the unity of the faith was the most urgent spiritual task incumbent upon each pontiff. Innocent had to restore rather than to maintain. The heresy that increasingly threatened the Church throughout the second half of the twelfth century was not academic unorthodoxy, but various forms of attack on the foundations of the hierarchical system coming from the adherents of men of deep spiritual life like Peter de Bruys, Henry of Lausanne, and the followers of Peter Waldo. Innocent—and, indeed, his predecessors—had no lack of sympathy for the desire for poverty and simplicity; the example of St Bernard had not been for nothing. Innocent could understand, though he might not condone, the anti-sacerdotalism provoked by the wealth and worldliness of the higher clergy, and he never failed to castigate negligence and luxury; but when the assault on the hierarchy was the outcome of a theory of mind and matter impossible from a philosophical and a social point of view alike, a theory that attracted both by the intensity of its contrast with prevalent conditions as well as by its permitted laxities[1], resistance on the part of the Church was inevitable. Besides the territorial wealth and state of prelates, ignorance was responsible for much. The laity were but poorly educated in matters of doctrine and religious organisation. There was urgent need of popular explanations of the tenets of the faith in non-technical language. Country priests were often too simple and unlearned, and the upper ranks too aloof and occupied in the politics of their convents or sees, to attend to the pastoral duty of exposition. Innocent first encountered the problem in Lorraine. Men and women of the laity in the diocese of Metz had been holding private group-meetings for the purpose of reading a French translation of certain books of the Bible, and when admonished by their parish priests disdainfully refused to desist. This lay usurpation of the preacher's office led Innocent to expound in an encyclical the Catholic view that preaching was essentially an act of public instruction to be performed by priests, seeing that the mysteries of the faith were not for all men. "For such is the depth of Holy Scripture that not only the simple and illiterate, but even the wise and learned are not of themselves sufficient to understand them." Even professional teachers must not depreciate simple priests, but rather honour them for their ministry. If the priest went wrong, the only person to apply correction was his bishop. Innocent's gentle reproof of the laity for despising the *simplicitas sacerdotum* did not, however, conceal his anxiety. The insistence laid in his correspondence upon the need for good instruction and the provisions made by the Lateran Council for the supply of theologians in cathedral churches indicate his views on the matter. But it should be noted that the permissions to preach given by him in 1201 to the Humiliati, in 1207 to Durand de Huesca, and in 1210 to St Francis himself had a moral, not a doctrinal end in view. The *arcana fidei* were for ordained ministers alone to expound.

[1] On the Catharist doctrine, see *infra*, Chap. XXI.

Elsewhere it was not unorganised piety, but local paganism and political anarchy which encouraged heresy. In Hungary and the Balkans the Church was miserably weak[1]. The Latin convents drew their novices principally from Germany and Italy; Slavonic monks disliked Latin ritual and turned longingly to Byzantium. The Archbishops of Gran and Kalocsa were engaged in perpetual strife. There was only one see in Bosnia, and both here and in Dalmatia the Catharist Church was strong. The Ban Kulin, the vassal of King Emeric of Hungary, had been converted together with his family to Catharism, and was an active proselytiser. In October 1200 Innocent brought pressure to bear upon Emeric, whom he considered as his vassal, to order the ban to persecute the heretics, or, in the event of his refusal, to take possession of his domains—the authorisation he was later to give to Philip Augustus in respect of the lands of Raymond VI of Toulouse—and communicated to him the statute made against the Cathari at Viterbo. Though Kulin yielded to a papal mission in 1202, Catharism, as Honorius III was to find, was by no means stamped out among the Southern Slavs. In Italy the secularist attitude of many communal authorities encouraged a rich crop of tares. Besides the Cathari proper, whose organisation was very strong and complete, there were Patarines, "Poor" Lombards, and Waldensians proper of the Lyons congregation, distributed among the Lombard cities and in Tuscany. The chronicler Stephen de Belleville tells of the chief men of seven different sects engaged in a public dispute held in one of the churches of a town in Lombardy, and relates elsewhere that a Waldensian of eighteen years' residence in Milan informed him that as many as seventeen sects were to be found there, *a se invicem diversae et adversae.* The strongest centres of Catharism itself were Verona, Viterbo, Ferrara, Florence, Prato, Orvieto, Rimini, Como, Parma, Cremona, and Piacenza, while there were important churches at Desenzano on Lake Garda and in the March of Treviso, where the licentiousness and turbulence of the local clergy brought into relief the more austere conversation of the heretics[2]. Innocent's chief efforts were directed to keeping them out of the town magistracies, where, as consuls or chamberlains, they had ample opportunity to squeeze contributions for civic purposes out of the bishops and local clergy. In 1198 he instructed his legate in Lombardy to exact an oath from all municipal officials not to admit heretics to office. To Orvieto he sent at the request of the Catholics (1199) a young Roman noble Peter Parenzo as podestà, but so strong was the heretical opposition that the unfortunate man was dragged outside the walls and beaten to death. To Viterbo he issued strict injunctions that no heretic was to be allowed office nor enjoy power of devise or right of succession; if he was

[1] See the account of Catharism in the Balkans in C. Schmidt: *Histoire de la doctrine et de la Secte des Cathares ou Albigeois.*

[2] For Treviso, see *Reg.* III. epp. VI, XXXIX; VI. epp. XLV–VI; X. ep. LIV, and G Volpe, *Movimenti religiosi e sette ereticali nella società medievale italiana*, pp. 83–97.

a judge, his sentences were to be null; if an advocate, he must not be permitted to plead in court; if a notary, his authentication was to be invalid. Within the patrimony, the temporal goods of heretics were to pass into the hands of the Church; without, they were to be at the disposal of the (faithful) municipal authorities. These instructions Viterbo disregarded. Not until Innocent came in person to the town in 1207 were the principal *perfecti* and *credentes* of the Viterbese Cathari compelled to leave the town, their goods confiscated, and their homes demolished. We shall observe the importance of the issue in considering the 46th clause of the Lateran Council's decrees.

But the inveterate problem was that of Southern France, which not even St Bernard's eloquence had been able to move. The home of the Catharist church was the county of Toulouse, the diocese of Carcassonne, and the county of Foix, though throughout Languedoc the nobility had allowed themselves to be won by Catharism, and many families openly practised "adoration" of the *perfecti*. In 1177 Raymond V of Toulouse had lamented the impossibility of extirpating heresy from his domains: his son Raymond VI favoured it openly. He was accompanied everywhere by two *perfecti* so as not to die without receiving the *consolamentum*. This example led to a general carelessness of, and often hostility to, the rights of the Church. Heretics were allowed to preach in the villages and to act as doctors; *perfecti* received legacies for the good of their Church. The lords of the south thrust Cathari superiors upon the convents in their gift, and high dignitaries of the Catholic community either encouraged or did not oppose the sect. Raymond de Roquefort, Bishop of Carcassonne, secretly encouraged it; Raymond, Bishop of Toulouse, deposed in 1206 on grounds of simony, was suspected of the same offence, and the Archbishop of Narbonne did not trouble himself about their activities. In Berengar, a natural son of Raymond Berengar, Count of Barcelona, we have a typical southern ecclesiastic, of whom Innocent might justly complain that his example corrupted the Church. This prelate, "the shadow of a great name" (*stans magni nominis umbra*), as Innocent happily described him, lived luxuriously quiescent in his abbey of Mont Aragón, which he had failed to surrender when made archbishop, never visiting his diocese, sometimes not going to church for a fortnight at a time, refusing to fill the vacant stalls in his chapter and dispensing with the awkward presence of an archdeacon. The heretic might perhaps have smiled more bitterly at the troubadour Folquet of Marseilles, the Genoese, who left his elegies and indiscretions for the Cistercian habit and later the bishopric of Toulouse: where, in the acid description of the author of the *Chanson de la Croisade*, "there was lit such a fire that no water could ever extinguish it; for he deprived more than five hundred thousand people, great and small, of life, body, and soul. By the honesty I owe you, in deed and in word, he is more like anti-Christ than a messenger of Rome." The figures are exaggerated, the facts are not. In that environment paganism turned as quickly to

Christianity as Christianity to paganism. Yet the greatest of medieval poets forgot the butchery and set Folquet in the Heaven of Venus amongst those who had been lovers upon earth.

Until 1204 Innocent tried the weapon of evangelism, and used small groups of Cistercian missioners whose executive powers were gradually increased as resistance stiffened. They were badly received, for it was known that Peter de Castelnau, archdeacon of Maguelonne, their leader and legate of the Holy See after 1203, was armed with powers of deprivation, and the retinue and pomp displayed by the Cistercian abbots, who joined and accompanied them on their journeys, antagonised the devotees of a simpler sect. New tactics were introduced by Diego, Bishop of Osma, and his sub-prior Dominic, who went bare-foot into the towns and villages, to discuss with the Cathari the principles of the Catholic faith. Debates were held in Catharist strongholds: at Pamiers, Diego came to argue before the family of the Count of Foix; at Montréal, discussions lasted a fortnight, and the best Catharist speakers appeared. But the soundness of the Catholic position could not be allowed to depend upon the verdict of arbiters often prejudiced in favour of heresy. By 1204 it had become plain to the legates that neither argument nor example were of any use. A drastic purging of the Church was needed: loyal clergy would have to be substituted for those suspected of heresy; and, above all, pressure would have to be brought to bear upon the chief supporters of the Catharist Church, the Count of Toulouse and his vassals and the communal authorities, to expel all heretics from their territories. This conclusion was impressed upon Innocent by the firmly convinced Arnaud Amalric, Abbot of Cîteaux, now Peter de Castelnau's colleague in Provence, with the result that at the end of May 1204 the legates received commissions in very general terms to extirpate heresy in Provence and Languedoc, and to ask for the help of Philip Augustus and his vassals against the lords of the south. At the end of his letter Innocent cautioned Arnaud and Peter to proceed moderately and give no occasion for reproof. He must have felt that the legates saw the issue more clearly and decidedly than he did, and that, while giving them general support, he must leave room for contingencies. The fact became clear when the legates came to deal with Berengar of Narbonne. They called insistently for his deposition; but Berengar appealed, appeared personally in Rome, and by clever manoeuvring succeeded in delaying till 1210 the penalty he deserved. Innocent was ready to give the man a chance to shew his penitence. He never prejudged this or any other case. If information was brought to him, he was prepared to have inquiry made at once, and the new facts would be weighed with the old before action was taken. The contrast between this cautious legality and the hard, opinionated, and (until his quarrel with Simon de Montfort) perfectly consistent attitude of Arnaud Amalric comes out in the way in which the parties faced the crux of the whole matter, Raymond VI of Toulouse. The process of deposing suspected ecclesiastics (1204–6) was not so difficult as that of inducing Raymond to enforce Innocent's sentence calling upon lords to expel heretics from their fiefs. For this purpose the legate Peter formed a league of the count's vassals which he invited Raymond to join. On the latter's refusal, the legate excommunicated him, laid his lands under interdict, and turned the league of vassals against their over-lord. Menaced both by Innocent and by the confederation, Raymond yielded and promised adhesion; but he could scarcely forgive the legate for his action. In January 1208 Peter de Castelnau was murdered by some unknown person.

It was probably a case similar to Becket's, a deed done by some underling who thought to rid the count of his principal enemy. Opinion set definitely against Raymond, and Arnaud was not slow to use the suspicion (which he proclaimed as a fact) and the emotions roused by the event. Its main result was to unite Innocent and his legates in method as well as in aim. Doubtless at their suggestion the Pope in May 1204 and February 1205 had made his first requests to Philip Augustus for aid in extirpating Catharism in the south. After gaining nothing he had waited more than two years and then (November 1207) had written again, on this occasion holding out to the king and his vassals indulgences similar to those granted for the Holy Land, thereby turning an expedition within the bounds of Western Christendom into a crusade. Philip had replied that he was engaged in a struggle with John Lackland and could not divide his forces; if the Holy See would guarantee him a firm truce with England, he would make war for a year; but he would not expend more than a certain sum. After the legate's death Innocent, having declared the Count of Toulouse excommunicate and absolved his vassals from their oaths of obedience, sounded the call to arms more urgently, and had the crusade preached throughout northern France. A special mission headed by Cardinal Guala di Beccaria was sent to make a great effort with Philip Augustus. Innocent saw clearly the danger of 1203 repeating itself; divided counsels and the pressure of over-powerful or irresponsible elements on the course of the Crusade would be avoided if the sovereign of the greatest Christian community in the West took the lead or nominated a deputy to act on his behalf and thereby made the crusade his own. Philip would do neither. He would allow his vassals to participate, but they must take their own under-tenants and their supporters, not the competent mercenaries whom he needed against the "two great lions" on his flanks, John and Otto. Many lords of the Île-de-France, the Orléanais, and Picardy answered the summons, and a number of prelates, including the Archbishops of Bourges, Bordeaux, Rheims, and Rouen. Peter de Vaux-Cernay puts the numbers of the crusading host before Carcassonne at 50,000 men, probably an extreme figure. These forces the legate Arnaud assembled at Lyons before the end of June 1209.

Meanwhile the tragi-comedy of the Count of Toulouse had started. Raymond first tried to raise a coalition against the crusading army, when it should arrive. When this failed, he pressed forward the negotiations which he had already begun with Rome. At the end of 1208 he had sent the Archbishop of Auch and the deposed Bishop of Toulouse to complain of the hostility shewn him by Arnaud. He was willing, he said, to make complete submission before any other legate. Innocent, reasonable and judicial as ever, promised to examine his justification, and sent into Provence for the purpose a new legate, the apostolic notary Milo. Raymond was accordingly cited to Valence, where he promised to obey the legate's orders; his absolution took place in front of the porch of St Gilles (17 June 1209), and next day he was given the requirements of the Church: among other terms, the complete banishment of all heretics from his domains and his active and personal support for the Crusade. He took the Cross on 20 June; and on 26 July Innocent sent him a letter of congratulation and promised him his protection. Four days before that letter was written the awful carnage of Béziers had taken place, the systematic dispossession of the southern nobility begun. Narbonne and many other towns surrendered in sheer terror, Carcassonne capitulated on 15 August and its viscount, Raymond Roger, was made a prisoner and died during the following winter. Simon de Montfort, who had accepted command of the expedition after the Duke of Burgundy and the Counts of Nevers and St Pol had refused it, became Viscount of Béziers and Carcassonne and organiser of the occupation. There was complete understanding between him and the legate. Both saw that Innocent had not considered ahead what was to be the permanent fate of the acquired territories, though he had offered them to Philip Augustus. But Philip had refused to play, and the way was open before the ambitious Simon. Both had taken the measure of Raymond and knew him to be very uncomfortable in his present false position and thoroughly untrustworthy; they would at first isolate him (they had Innocent's approval for this course), conquer up to the borders of his demesne, then provoke him by excommunication and interdict to actions of definite hostility which would justify a general assault upon his lands and his capital. Both realised that, to counteract the trickling back to the north of the crusaders who came for forty days' service only, a permanent garrison must be established at strategic points in the country, especially in the Black Mountain (the high ground between Carcassonne and Albi) and along the river Agout, while to secure the strongholds in the foot-hills of the Pyrenees north and north-east of Foix would prevent its count from giving trouble. It was the reduction of this territory by the acquisition in 1210 of Bram and Montréal and in 1212 of Lavaur that brought the crusaders to the borders of Raymond's direct dominion.

Ever since he had left the crusading army after the taking of Carcassonne, Raymond's relations with Simon de Montfort and the legate Arnaud had become more and more strained. When summoned to give literal execution to the promises made at St Gilles and to surrender to the crusaders a number of burgesses of Toulouse suspected of heresy, he had refused, and the refusal had brought renewed excommunication and the interdict upon Toulouse. This time Raymond was not content with an embassy, but went in person to Rome. He saw what the encirclement and the excommunication were aimed at—his own disinheritance. Whether his case satisfied Innocent or not (and there is no evidence that it did), the Pope cautiously decided that non-fulfilment of the "contract" made at St Gilles was not legitimate ground for dispossession; and he referred the question of his guilt to a council at which a third assessor besides the two legates was to be present. At the same time he told Arnaud to go carefully, as everything depended on his action. There is no need to assume any opposition between Innocent and Arnaud at this time. The Pope, however, was a lawyer; Arnaud and Simon were not. The subtle pupil of Uguccio had no sympathy with summary justice. The Church would lose incalculably by a false step in so vital a matter as the dispossession of a great feudatory of the French Crown, and the King of Aragon, the Pope's vassal, would feel justly aggrieved if his Pyrenean vassals, the Counts of Foix and Comminges, were disinherited. Yet as evidence against Raymond accumulated, Innocent veered towards the legate's idea of dispossessing him. He had to take the opinion of his representatives on the spot, and as the purification of the Church became more complete, petitions and letters against the count streamed into Rome from the newly-established clergy. He could not have resisted so strong a body of loyal opinion without making his representatives look foolish and creating antagonism. At the same time it was quite clear from Simon de Montfort's progress in Languedoc and settlement of the crusading army on the conquered lands that the motive of territorial annexation was indissolubly linked with the zeal for the principle of Catholicism. The establishment of a *droit coutumier* for the new territories at Pamiers organising the confiscation on a permanent legal basis raised the question of the finality of the settlement. Philip Augustus disputed it actively; and now at the end of 1212 Peter II of Aragon sent to Rome a strong protest against the usurpations committed by Simon de Montfort against Raymond and his own vassals[1]. Innocent recognised the weight of this plea, and himself pointed out to the legates that Raymond had never been allowed to clear himself of the murder of Peter de Castelnau, and that even if he failed in that justification, the sentence would not involve Raymond's son. The legates disposed of the situation very simply. A council met at Lavaur, heard Raymond's justification, and rejected it; shortly afterwards they rejected the King of Aragon's demand for restitution of his lands (which had now been overrun) to Raymond, and Peter appealed to Rome; but before the plaint was lodged, Innocent had realised how fast matters were moving and commanded Arnaud, now Archbishop of Narbonne, to stop the Crusade and to direct the Christian effort against the Moors in Spain.

[1] For the intervention of Aragon, cf. *infra*, Chap. XII.

It was too late. Threatened with excommunication by the council for taking Raymond's part, Peter at the end of his patience formed a league consisting of the Counts of Toulouse, Foix, Comminges, the Viscount of Béarn, the knights of Toulouse and Carcassonne, and the consuls of Toulouse, and recklessly challenged Simon de Montfort. The southern opposition had crystallised. Innocent might send the legate Robert de Courçon to establish peace in Languedoc and turn the Crusade to the Holy Land, but the battle of Muret (12 September 1213) settled for the time being the question of the occupation. The death of Peter and the utter defeat of the coalition opened Provence and the lower Rhone Valley also to Simon. That born leader won over both Courçon and Cardinal Peter of Benevento, whom Innocent sent in 1214 to reconcile the citizens of Toulouse and the southern lords to the Church and to protect their property; and the war of acquisition blazed again fiercely throughout Languedoc. Innocent's policy of pacification was completely overborne. Even when Philip Augustus thought it time to intervene and sent his son Louis to the south under commission to protect the lordship of Montpellier and the interest of Peter of Aragon's heir, Simon and the legate succeeded in winning him to their designs and, thanks to Louis, the count was proclaimed Duke of Narbonne. From the Rhone to the Garonne, from Albi to the Pyrenees, Simon de Montfort was master. The acts of his chancery entitled him Count of Toulouse and Leicester, Viscount of Béziers and Carcassonne, and Duke of Narbonne.

Yet Innocent had the last word. By declaring the property of lay heretics confiscate and extending the penalty to all supporters who did not within a year seek absolution from the excommunication imposed upon them, the Lateran Council of 1215 appeared to Simon de Montfort and his friends to sanction the fall of Raymond and his allies. But the Count of Toulouse, accompanied by the Counts of Foix and Comminges, appeared before the Council to defend his interests and a legal contest between his party and the representatives of Simon de Montfort followed. Innocent's decision attempted to conciliate both parties. He did not venture to disavow his legates. Raymond had been guilty and justly deprived of his estates; the Pope however assigned him an annuity of 400 silver marks. The Countess of Toulouse was declared a faithful Catholic and her dower was maintained. The lands conquered by the crusaders, especially Montauban and Toulouse, were to remain in the hands of Simon de Montfort and other grantees; but those not yet occupied were to be guarded in the name of the Church for the son of Raymond VI when he came of age. The question of Foix was treated in the same spirit. The count's territories were to be guarded by the Church pending an inquiry into his conduct, and Foix itself was to be restored to him as soon as he had obtained absolution. It is probable that the Count of Comminges was treated in the same way. A sentence of total disinheritance, of doubtful validity in feudal law, would not have pleased the court of France, and the relations between the secular and ecclesiastical authorities in regard to the lands of heretics were still very ill-defined.

In his relations with the temporal powers[1] Innocent was governed by the thought of Gregory VII: the Pope is responsible to God for the salvation of kings just as much as of ecclesiastics. It is his business to exhort them to righteousness and peaceful conduct towards each other and to respect for the rights of the Church. Much of his effort was directed to preserving among the newer or less securely based monarchies the forces of order that favoured reforming canonical ideas. Where he could, he continued the Gregorian policy of binding them to the Roman See by the feudal contract; where he could not, he intervened by remonstrance or excommunication and interdict to defend the *ius canonicum* against the conflicting claims of national custom or individual interest.

As a civilising force spreading religion and learning the care of the Papacy was unquestionably valuable in the less integrated communities, but in its relations with the local religious situation the Holy See was brought into opposition with powerful interests, and local upholders of the papal point of view found themselves involved in some phase of the great ecumenical struggle between Church and State. This was especially the case in Scandinavia[2]. The Norwegian Church settlement dated from 1152 when Nidaros was separated from Lund and erected into a metropolis with eleven dependent sees. Under the arrangement made by Cardinal Nicholas Breakspeare the choice of bishops had passed from the king to the cathedral chapters, and bishops had been given the right to appoint to parishes, while a change in the law of bequests had permitted a proportion of both real and personal property to be devised upon the Church. During the weakness of the kingdom before the coming of King Sverre (1184), King Magnus (V) had been forced to purchase the support of the powerful reformer, Archbishop Eystein, by still further grants of immunity, including a large measure of Church influence in determining the succession to the Crown; and during the same period, "God's law," the *ius canonicum*, was drawn up for the Norwegian kingdom, and administered in the Church Courts. When Sverre the priest fought his way to the Crown, it was a question whether the old law of the kingdom of Norway and the ecclesiastical arrangements of St Olaf should stand, or whether the recent compact between the feebler kings in the days of Cardinal Nicholas and Archbishop Eystein should supplant them. Sverre had acted as the champion of ancient custom; he had upheld against the metropolitan the rights of private patrons over the *Eigenkirchen*, and had refused to accept Eystein's codification of Church Law. For his exile of Archbishop Eric of Nidaros (Eystein's successor) and his vigorous opposition to Bishop Nicholas of Stafanger and the party of the Bagals, he

[1] For the relations of Innocent with Germany and the Empire, cf. *infra*, Chaps. II, III, and IV; with England, cf. *infra*, Chaps. VII and VIII; with France, cf. *infra*, Chap. IX.

[2] Cf. *infra*, Chap. XI.

had been declared excommunicate and had issued a defiant apology of his own conduct[1]. Innocent, on his accession, paid no heed to the arguments drawn from ancient custom or from the *Decretum* of Gratian, which Sverre strikingly used in his defence, but laid the interdict upon Norway. He wrote warning the Icelandic Bishops of Skaalholt and Hole to use every weapon against the king's party; he bade Archbishop Eric from his refuge with Archbishop Absalon in Denmark excommunicate the Bishop of Bergen for favouring Sverre, and ordered the whole body of prelates in Norway to abstain from any dealings with the man. He begged the Kings of Denmark and Sweden to gird themselves and overthrow "that limb of the devil." The interdict was not enforced with the same rigour as in England, for the position of the monarchy was even more absolute in Norway, and Sverre was standing upon ancient custom while John tended to defy it. Before his death, however, the great Viking relaxed somewhat, and suggested a more peaceful policy to his son Hakon. This was to recall the fugitive bishops, and accordingly upon the new king's accession Eric and his colleagues returned. Hakon held out as a compromise the terms of the settlement of 1152. Although Sverre himself had regarded the burning question of the appointment of bishops by the Crown as unaffected by the settlement of Cardinal Nicholas, the archbishop accepted, took the excommunication off Sverre's adherents, and removed the restrictions consequent upon the interdict. It was probably a wise policy, but Innocent's point of view was very different. In a letter of 1204 exulting over the late king's death, he severely rebuked the archbishop for removing the sentence in usurpation of papal right, and compared him to an ape that imitates human actions which it is unable to perform. Innocent's dealings with Norway make it clear that he gave no thought to the position of the dynasty, threatened as it was by the understanding between its opponents the Bagals and reforming churchmen. No Norwegian monarch could have adopted the full Church programme without endangering his throne; but Innocent never took such considerations into account, unless the relation between the monarch and the Papacy was a feudal one. Then, as in the case of King Emeric of Hungary and of King John, a measure of protection against rebellious rivals or subjects was freely given, as feudal custom demanded. It is, however, only fair to remember that pressure upon temporal rulers regardless of their internal political situation was sometimes necessary in order to guarantee continuity of religious life in the country, as is shewn by the case of Vladislav and the Polish dukes excommunicated by the Archbishop of Gnesen[2]; or in support of the fundamental principles of the Canon Law, though here the strength of that pressure might be varied in accordance with the measure and quality of the opposition likely to be encountered—a point borne out by the course of Innocent's remonstrances with Philip Augustus over his long maltreatment of Ingeborg.

[1] Cf. *infra*, Chap. XI. [2] Potthast, *Regesta* I. Nos. 2948–2960.

In the time of Gregory VII the idea of grouping the various Christian states under the suzerainty of Rome was favoured by the Curia chiefly in the interests of the clerical reform which would be diffused thereby. The ends were largely moral and religious. But as the Church's organisation developed, the possibility of having at one's back so powerful and universal an instrument made an increasing appeal to the rulers of smaller kingdoms who wished to guarantee their conquests (often at the expense of their neighbours)[1], and the Curia for its part began to see the temporal as well as the spiritual advantage in the tribute which in certain cases was paid in addition to the customary Peter's Pence. In Mediterranean politics the aid of Aragon, for the time being one of the most loyal of tributary feudal kingdoms, was a valuable asset, as we have seen in the case of Sicily; and from the point of view of relations with the Eastern Empire it was important that Hungary and the newly-formed Bulgarian kingdom should be centres of Latin influence among peoples by nature more inclined to the Orthodox than to the Western rite.

The history of the Spanish kingdoms provides good illustration of the way in which the contract was interpreted. Innocent doubtless had before him in the original Register of Gregory VII the Pope's letter declaring that in virtue of ancient customs (by which the Donation of Constantine was probably intended) the kingdom of Spain was delivered to St Peter *in ius et proprietatem*, but that the service (*servitium*) had been interrupted by the Saracens, and calling upon the princes to help St Peter to recover "his justice and his honour."[2] That there lay in the Gregorian use of the terms *servitium*, *fidelitas*, a perhaps not unintentional ambiguity is suggested by the tactics of the Curia at the time in attempting to make Peter's Pence a sign of feudal subjection to Rome. Innocent, on the other hand, thought more clearly. Both in the case of Spain and elsewhere he made a distinction between such annual payments and the tribute paid in virtue of the direct feudal concession of a kingdom to the Papacy: *salvis per omnia denariis Sancti Petri*, as was stipulated in the terms of King John's contract. Castile and Leon did not fall within this category, and it was in defence of the law of marriage that Innocent intervened to annul the marriage (on grounds of consanguinity) of Berenguela, daughter of Alfonso VIII, with Alfonso IX of Leon, and laid the interdict on the countries when he could not get the parties to separate. But over Portugal and Aragon he claimed and exercised definite feudal rights. From the former he demanded, and, after resisting King Sancho's attempts to bargain, received the annual payment of 100 gold bezants; from the latter he got 250 gold obols per

[1] Apart from the case of Sancho of Portugal (see below), one may instance those of Othon de la Roche, lord of Athens, who did homage for the castle of Levada (21 June 1214); of the town of Montpellier (April 1215); and of Vladislav of Poland, anxious to preserve the share of his inheritance which he had recovered (1211). Cf. Paul Fabre, *Étude sur le Liber Censuum de l'Église Romaine*, p. 127.

[2] Gregory VII, *Registrum* IV. 28; ed. Caspar, I, 345–6.

annum. In 1204, Peter II of Aragon came to be anointed and crowned in San Pancrazio, and swore to be the obedient feudatory of his lord, Pope Innocent; to maintain his realm in that obedience, to defend the Catholic faith, persecute heresy, and respect the liberties of the Church[1]. Innocent's reciprocal duties to his Spanish vassals took shape not only in confirming important acts of the Portuguese and Aragonese Chanceries, but in co-ordinating and placing under the leadership of Aragon the Christian effort to wipe out the Almohad reconquest, which proved successful at the great victory of Las Navas de Tolosa. We have already seen how Innocent carried out his obligations of guardianship towards Sicily. In England the legate for the time being played a vital part in English administration from 1213 onwards. Guala was in a very real sense a defender of the country against the attacks of Prince Louis both before and after Henry III's accession. For in April he had gone at Innocent's bidding to the Council of Melun to dissuade the King of France from conquering England, the property of the Roman Church in virtue of its right of lordship—a doctrine which Philip Augustus, in view of the condemnation of John by his own court, denied. After John's death he played a most important part[2]. The advantages of the feudal relation to the nascent state as well as to Rome may be read in Innocent's relations with the Bulgaro-Wallachian kingdom comprising Bulgaria, Roumania, and a part of what was Roumelia. Johannitsa, the ruling tsar, had inherited the anti-Byzantine traditions of the first Bulgarian empire, which he had made it his intent to revive at the expense both of Hungary and of Constantinople[3]. To secure this, he asked Innocent for coronation and unction, promising to hold the kingdom from St Peter. Innocent saw the advantage of having a friendly power along the great crusading route from central Europe; but to him the enfeoffment of Johannitsa was dependent upon the Bulgarian's readiness to allow the complete dependence of the clergy upon the Roman Church and his permission to the Archbishop of Trnovo to receive the pallium from the Pope alone. Johannitsa's aims were frankly political, but he could afford the conditions demanded; Innocent, as he expressed the hope to his future vassal, saw a Romanised dynasty and a Latinised Church. *Petrus sicut plenitudine, sic latitudine.*

III.

Innocent's immense diplomatic and pastoral activity was alone made possible by a very highly organised Curia containing within itself a Chancery, a Camera or Exchequer, and judicial organs. Before we pass to his legislation, we must speak briefly of the secretariat and the system of justice over which he presided.

[1] See *infra*, Chap. XII. [2] See *infra*, Chap. VIII.

[3] Cf. *supra*, Vol. IV, Chap. XVII. Johannitsa is also called Kalojan.

The coming of Innocent, as M. Delisle pointed out, marks a new era in the history of the Papal Chancery. Its traditional usages crystallise, and a system of minute rules for the conduct of business, regular formulae for the different kinds of letters, and a more exact science of documentary criticism appear. At the head of the organisation stood the Chancellor or Vice-Chancellor. The Chancellor, by tradition the regular datary of the Apostolic letters, had ceased to be Librarian when the Archives and the Library were separated (1144). Up till 1187, with a single exception, he was a Cardinal-priest or Cardinal-deacon holding his post for life or until he was made Pope. As he had to autograph all letters, deputies *vices cancellarii gerentes* were frequently employed, and out of this practice grew the vice-chancellorship, though the formal title was frequently avoided in order to benefit the papal coffers[1]. These deputies were not necessarily cardinals. Under the anti-Pope Calixtus III and under Urban III persons of lower dignity had been employed; Gregory VIII and Clement III used the services of Moyses, a canon of the Lateran, and Innocent himself, at the beginning of his pontificate, permitted three notaries in succession, Raymond, Blasius, and John, to sign as Vice-Chancellors[2]. In 1205 he returned to the old system and had John, Cardinal-deacon of Santa Maria in Cosmedin, as Chancellor till 1213; John was the last of the line, for after his death Innocent put in deputies. Dr Poole has pointed out that the significance of this change lay in the fact that henceforward the Vice-Chancellor, who had become the real head of the Chancery, was appointed from outside the ranks of the cardinals, and was chosen not for dignity, but for competence. He might be some-one who had risen from the lower offices of the Chancery. These were four in number, each directed by a notary of the Sacred Palace, part of whose business was to submit to the Pope the petitions forwarded to the Holy See. There was the office of the minutes, staffed by the *abbreviatores*, who drew up in a shortened form minutes of the papal acts called by Innocent *litterae notatae*; there was the office of engrossment, where, according to the tenour of the minute made, the papal letter was written out in full (*in grossam litteram*); the gross, it may be noted, frequently passed under the eye of the Pope; thirdly, there was the office of the Registers, wherein the *registratores* or *scriptores registri* copied from the minutes the papal acts into the official archives. With Innocent's pontificate begins the great continuous series of thirteenth-century Papal Registers; with the exception of the *Registrum de negotio Imperii* the volumes that we possess of Innocent's records are not the original registers, but books compiled from

[1] "The Vice-Chancellor received the fees due to the Chancellor, whereas, if his duties were performed by another officer, the fees were paid into the Pope's chest." R. L. Poole, *The Papal Chancery*, p. 139.

[2] The reason was probably that he wished to eliminate the influence of the acting Chancellor Cencius, who under Celestine III had amalgamated part of the Chancery with the *Camera*: cf. M. Tangl, *Die päpstlichen Kanzleiordnungen von* 1200–1500, p. xiii.

the finished documents after they had been got ready for despatch, a more elaborate form of procedure than had been hitherto in use. Lastly, there was the office of the Bull, where the *bullarii* applied the papal seal by attaching it in the manner prescribed for the various categories of documents.

The documents which emanated from Innocent's Chancery were, in the language of diplomatic, either Great or Little Bulls. Great Bulls or "Privileges," as Delisle called them, were solemn acts containing the Rota and the monogram and the full Chancery Date, subscribed by a certain number of Cardinals, issued to confirm the liberties and possessions of Churches. Little Bulls or "Letters" may be classified as either Letters of Grace or Letters of Justice, the one being Licences or Indults, the other Mandates or Commissions[1]. The former were sealed on silk with the Pope's name written in capitals; the latter were sealed on hemp and have only the initial letter in capitals. The character of a letter conferring a favour differed in the ornateness of its script and style from one containing a judgment or a command. Most minute care was taken over the *bulla.* Innocent once repudiated as false a document said to be his "because it lacked one point." The points were dots round the circumference and dots framing the heads (on one side of the seal) of the Apostles Peter and Paul; St Peter's hair and beard were entirely composed of them. Innocent's bulls, as Delisle shewed, had 73 round the circumference, 25 round St Paul, 26 round St Peter, while St Peter's hair had 25 and his beard 28. A genuine bull must have all these, otherwise the matrix was spurious and it could be rejected. Innocent greatly improved the science of diplomatic. He drew up a set of rules for the detection of forgeries. Not only were the seals examined, but also their attachment to the string and that of the string to the document. In difficult cases one must look further to the *modus dictaminis,* that is the correct observance of the cursus, the curial rule of rhythm, and to the *forma scripturae,* the correctness of the document in its form. Innocent was by no means infallible as a detector of forgery, as it appears when he took for genuine two gross forgeries purporting to be indults of Pope Constantine in 709 and 710 written on parchment, which, of course, was not used at that period. But the science of diplomatic could not yet embrace documents five hundred years old, and within these limitations the Curia must have been acute at detecting the spurious and the supposititious letter. This was essential, for into the papal court streamed the causes of Christendom, the litigants in numerous cases supporting themselves by earlier grants, privileges, and concessions of the Holy See not all discoverable in the Registers. A large proportion of the chapter *De fide instrumentorum* in the *Decretales* of Gregory IX was supplied by Innocent.

The majority of cases, tried originally before the bishops, which were taken by way of appeal to Rome, came before the Pope as *iudex ordinarius*

[1] Poole, *op. cit.* p. 115.

singulorum and were decided in consistory, that is, the judicial session of the Pope and those of his cardinals for the time being in Rome. Once submitted to him, they might be sent for hearing to judges delegate in the country whence they came, the Pope reserving to himself the final pronouncement of the sentence, or they might be dealt with in Rome itself. In the latter case he frequently deputed one or more of his cardinals or chaplains skilled in law as *auditores* to hear and examine the evidence and come to a conclusion on a specific point of fact, which had to be cleared up before he could pronounce in consistory a definite sentence in the suit. Sometimes he committed the whole case to them and gave judgment on the basis of their findings; sometimes he dealt with the matter in his own auditory. The beginning of the thirteenth century is too early a period in which to speak of a definite college of auditors, the Rota[1], for in Innocent's time the auditors are not yet *generales*, as they became under Gregory IX and Innocent IV, not yet permanent officials, but persons appointed under special commission. A great deal of the argument of the advocates (standing counsel at the Curia), and of the proctors or representatives of the parties, took place before them, for no Pope could attend personally to such a mass of business throughout the length of its course.

Two examples, one purely legal, the other a *cause célèbre* into which political consideration entered, will illustrate the phases of a case in the Roman Curia. Two citizens of Viterbo are disputing before the local ecclesiastical judges a contract made at the church door over the purchase of a house. The judges condemn the detainer of the premises, who appeals on the ground that the sale was conditional, not free. Innocent submits the case to a papal sub-deacon and chaplain, as auditor, making it his duty to find out the relative value of the evidence of written instruments and of witnesses present at the contract. When the Pope has satisfied himself on this point (*his ergo et aliis tam coram nobis, quam coram dicto capellano propositis et plenius intellectis*), he pronounces judgment in consistory that the sale was conditional[2]. Here the judges of first instance are judges ordinary. The case of Gerald de Barri, besides illustrating procedure at Rome, displays the action of judges delegate appointed by the Papacy during the course of an appeal, very much in the capacity of auditors at the Roman court. On the death of Bishop Peter de Leia the chapter of St Davids nominated their effervescent and inimitable archdeacon Gerald foremost along with three others for their bishop. Hubert Walter, the Archbishop and Justiciar, was determined on political grounds that no Welshman should become bishop, especially as the Church of St Davids had claims to be metropolitan and independent of Canterbury, and did all he could to prevent the canons being given royal permission to elect

[1] The view followed here is that of G. Phillips, *Kirchenrecht*, VI, pp. 449–471, and accepted by J. B. Sägmuller, *Die Entwicklung der Rota bis zur Bulle Johanns XXII "Ratio iuris" a.* 1326, *Theologische Quartalschrift*, LXXVII (1895), p. 97 sq.

[2] *Decretal. Gregor. IX.* II, xxii, De fide instrumentorum, c. x.

Gerald. Owing to John's accession he did not at first succeed, the election was made, and Gerald left England to receive consecration from Innocent in order to obtain the dignity of a metropolitan. Hubert, well knowing the nature of the Welshman's claim, did all he could to impugn the validity of the election, and Gerald was forced to pay in all three visits to the Roman Court between 1199 and 1202. On the first (November 1 to middle of March 1199–1200) the archbishop forestalled him by writing to the Pope and cardinals, and Innocent refused to consecrate, though he had raised Gerald's hopes by calling him "Menevensis electe," and had received in return a copy of the most painful laudatory elegiacs[1]. He referred the matter of the election to judges delegate in England, and when Gerald asked for another commission to decide the status of the Church of St Davids, he would not accord it. He evidently did not think that Gerald's answers to the gentle and crafty questions about St Davids, which he had asked one evening in his room[2], were satisfactory, and what he must have thought of Gerald's memorandum on the history of the see, a document full of historical howlers, one can only imagine. Nothing daunted, Gerald entered the registry, and with the clerk looking on turned up the registers and found a decision of Eugenius III to submit the claim of St Davids to a commission. This was precedent, and Innocent consented to have this question also investigated by judges delegate. Gerald returned to Wales, unearthed fresh evidence at St Davids, and prepared to appear before the judges delegate in England. But King John refused to grant him a safe conduct, and the Pope transferred the hearing to Rome. Arriving there for the second time (March 1201) Gerald found two clerks sent by the archbishop already there to oppose him. The case of the status of St Davids was heard in public consistory, while that of his own election was taken before two auditors before going before the Pope. But the archbishop's representatives asked for a delay which was accorded them, and the papal judgment in consistory could therefore only deal with the costs of the case. The next hearing was appointed at Rome for November 1201, and Gerald returned to Wales to find the chapter bribed against him and the Justiciar Geoffrey Fitz Peter issuing writs for the confiscation of his rents. It seems, however, that before November the judges delegate in England summoned him to appear, but that the trial could get no further because the Bishop of Ely, one of the chief judges, was away. Losing patience, Gerald took the false step of excommunicating

[1] *De jure et statu Menevensis Ecclesiae*, p. 176. The verses (p. 94) contain the couplet

"Omnia cum possit qui praeminet omnibus Inno-
Centius, innocuus est tamen atque pius."

[2] During the conversation Innocent looked up the address-book of the Chancery, an earlier list than that printed by M. Tangl, which enabled Gerald to point out that Menevens*is* Ecclesi*a* was mentioned in the nominative (a sign of independence), not the accusative, and the Pope to confirm by shewing that a rubric intervened between Canterbury and Wales in the enumeration of sees. *De jure et statu M.E.* pp. 165–6. Cf. M. Spaethen in *Neu. Arch.* XXXI, pp. 597–629.

two of his principal opponents, and was therefore cited to appear before judges delegate of the Papacy for such an action taken *pendente lite*. He appealed to Rome, and, although every conceivable form of pressure was exerted to make him come to terms with the archbishop, prepared once more for the journey. He succeeded in defying the king's prohibition for him to cross, reached St Omer (November 1201), and arrived at Rome just before Christmas. In consistory he made the doubtful move of impeaching the character of the archbishop's witnesses (he said they were suborned men who had never seen St Davids) before dealing with the validity of their evidence, and had to suffer in return the ridiculous charge of horse-stealing, which entertained Innocent greatly. Not till April 1202 did the Pope give sentence, then only to quash the elections both of Gerald and of the archbishop's candidate. The instance shews the limitations of papal judges delegate in the realms of a man like King John and the strength of political pressure in a case where election was complicated by other considerations. For Llewelyn of Wales was in the background, and to Hubert Walter Gerald was, unfortunately, Gerald.

Criticise it as we may, and as most contemporaries did, for its delays and venality, in the Roman Curia men moved in a different world to that of the State: a world where subtle distinctions were heard, and delicately shaded opinions expressed, the spiritual home of educated and intelligent humanity. Moulded by this atmosphere, Innocent set himself to ensure the supremacy throughout Christendom of that cultured life in all the ranges of its activity, art and ceremony, law, philosophy, and literature, welded together in the synthesis of religion. The community that by its wealth of institutions and its group-life alone could make spiritual activity possible must conquer; the mind of the Church must prevail in society. But that community could only achieve this by setting its own house in order, by a perfect system of organisation, canons regulating in every detail the life and position of each member of the hierarchy and reducing the laity to a state of passive obedience.

To this order Innocent made a powerful and many-sided contribution, developing the legal logic of his immediate predecessors, himself the vehicle of a progressive tradition. For just as it is impossible to think of Edward I apart from Bracton, so Innocent can scarcely be considered apart from the later commentators on the *Decretum* of Gratian, and without reference to the general tendency of papal legislation from Alexander III onwards. Like Edward I he came to codify and to define. His canons are to be found in two compilations of a series of five, the *compilatio tertia* and *quarta*. The "third" contains his decretals up to 1210, the "fourth" includes the canons of the Fourth Lateran Council. An earlier selection was made from Innocent's Registers by Bernard of Compostella, archdeacon of the Roman Church, called by Bologna students the *Romana Compilatio*; but, finding that it contained certain decretals objected to by the Curia, Innocent got his notary, Peter of Benevento, to make the "third" for the Bologna law school. Walter von der Vogelweide spoke of it like a loyal German episcopalian as Innocent's "swarzes buoch daz ime der hellemôr hât gegeben." From a national point of view he was right: the book was in many respects diabolical. The *novum ius*, the papal decretals from the time of Alexander III, bore marked contrast to Gratian's academic moderation, the *vetus ius*, as Bernard of Pavia called the famous *Decretum*. The new decretals were not a text-book, as was Gratian's, but authoritative canons of a centralising order that constituted the ground-work of the first collection with the force of universal law, the *Decretals* of Gregory IX. The Lateran Council of 1179 is the starting-point of the new tendency, and Innocent in the great assembly of 1215 took as his basis, and re-enacted, a number of its most important canons. Any tendency, therefore, to treat the Council of 1215 in isolation must be avoided. Yet it was in many ways unique: since the early days of Nicaea and Ephesus and Chalcedon no such assembly had been seen. Four hundred and twelve bishops, eight hundred abbots and priors, and numerous representatives of absent bishops and of chapters crowded close upon each other, and ambassadors were sent by Frederick II, by the Latin Emperor of Constantinople, the Kings of France, England, Jerusalem, Aragon, and Hungary. A note alike of climax and of expectation was struck by Innocent's sermon on the text: "With desire have I desired to eat this Passover with you before I suffer." It was in a sense the highest point of his career. Passover, he explained, meant a transition, a temporal passage of the crusaders to Jerusalem and the deliverance of the Holy Places, a spiritual passage to the Reform of the Church, and it was to this double end that the Council had been summoned.

The depth and scope of these and of his earlier canons, their historical background, their reception and effect, cannot be analysed in a few paragraphs. We can but present very simply some of their more constructive aspects, using not the proper legal classification, but a more arbitrary division into decretals concerned with the sacramental doctrine of the Church, the personnel, organisation, and discipline of the clergy.

The Church is declared to be one and universal, the only means to salvation; her sacraments are the channel by which grace is communicated to men. Chief among them is the Eucharist, wherein the body and blood of Christ "are really contained in the Sacrament of the altar under the species of bread and wine, the bread being transubstantiated into the body and the wine into the blood by the power of God, so that, to effect the mystery of unity we ourselves receive of that which is His what He himself received of that which is ours." Only a priest duly ordained according to the Church's power of binding and loosing might celebrate this mystery. It was a wide and moderate declaration suitable for acceptance as a matter of faith, as it contained no precise statement on the nature of the presence in the sacrament and was agreeable alike to those who held a carnal view and to those who followed the twelfth-century theologians in emphasising the spiritual character of Christ's Body there present[1]. For the historian the emphasis should, however, lie on the sacramental function of the priesthood; this, as Troeltsch rightly said, "bound the organism together and is the essential factor of importance in the Church's encircling miraculous power."[2] The point is borne out by the canon of the council (c. 21) ordaining that all who had come to years of discretion should confess their sins at least once a year to their own priests, fulfil the penance imposed, and receive the sacrament of the Eucharist at least once a year, at Easter, unless counselled by their own priest to refrain for a time; anyone wishing to confess to some other priest must first obtain the leave of his own to do so. The effect of this canon, in conjunction with the first, was to strengthen the position of the parish priest. But it also laid stress upon the importance and necessity of absolution for the forgiveness of sins and helped to make clearer the inter-relation of the different elements in the sacrament of penance. For while confession to priests had been practised for centuries, the doctrine of its place in the penitential system was still not very precise. Gratian in his *Decretum* had balanced and compared the views of those who said that contrition alone was necessary and confession to a priest merely the attestation of pardon, and of those who maintained that complete remission could not take place before confession and satisfaction[3]; and although he determined in favour of the latter view, the very fact that he reproduced so carefully the theory of a number of theologians who laid the greatest possible stress on contrition is significant. Furthermore, Innocent's own canonist master, Uguccio of Ferrara, definitely came down upon the side of those who maintained that sin was remitted by contrition alone without confession or satisfaction, though he admitted that confession of faults was necessary in order to give public effect to penitence. Innocent's view was more like that of Hugh of St Victor and Peter Lombard, who felt that exaggerated emphasis on contrition tended to restrict the effects of absolution[4].

If such were to be the priest's powers and responsibilities, the matter of his selection was of the highest importance. At the top of the scale, the supreme authority in the province and in the diocese must be "freely and lawfully" elected, as Gratian had prescribed. In all parts of Europe elections of the higher clergy presented the most complicated issues owing to the pressure exerted by the secular power and to dissensions in cathedral and other chapters; for, in the case of bishops, throughout the second half of

[1] Darwell Stone, *A History of the Doctrine of the Holy Eucharist*, I, p. 313.

[2] *Soziallehren der Christlichen Kirchen und Gruppen*, p. 218. We should beware, however, of seeing in canons 1 and 21 of the Fourth Lateran Council an attempt of the priestly order to vindicate its exclusive supremacy over the conscience. The need, in certain cases, of confession to lay persons continued to be taught by theologians.

[3] Pars II, Causa XXXIII, Quaestio III, De Penitentia, Dist. I.

[4] For the views of twelfth-century theologians (especially those of Peter the Chanter) on this important matter, see Fr. A. Teetaert, *La Confession aux Laïques dans l'Église latine depuis le VIIIe jusqu'au XIVe siècle*, pp. 85–102. For Uguccio of Ferrara, *op. cit.* pp. 222–3.

the twelfth century the cathedral chapter was gradually taking the place of the original electing body, the clergy and people of the cathedral centre. The qualifications for office had been determined by the Third Lateran Council. The candidate for a bishopric must be at least thirty, for other offices with the care of souls at least twenty-five years of age, and of upright character and a good standard of education (c. 3). Though in disputed elections both greater merit and numerical majority were required to enable a candidate to succeed (c. 17), the methods of choice varied considerably, and in 1215 it was time that they should be still further defined. In the twenty-third canon of the Council three forms were admitted, election by scrutiny, by inspiration, and by compromise, *i.e.* in cases of disagreement by a committee chosen from the opposing parties. In election by scrutiny there was to be a secret ballot, and the choice was to fall upon the man on whom the votes of all or of the *maior vel sanior pars* concurred. The *sanior* was a necessary qualification; and if a majority candidate was found unworthy, a minority candidate worthy, Innocent would confirm the election of the latter[1]. It was his object to get men of the best character, and, when possible, of learning and experience. He regularly and carefully exercised his right to examine the person of the elect and the method followed in the election, before he confirmed the chapter's choice. The canons had to be observed. An illegitimate person might be asked for, but could not be elected by the chapter: the election of Mauger to the see of Worcester was quashed in 1200 because the chapter had not humbly prayed for a dispensation on his behalf[2]. In 1208 there was a disputed election to the archbishopric of Tours: one side had elected the chanter of Paris, the other their own dean. Innocent confirmed the choice of the side *auctoritate et numero maior*, but after ascertaining that the elected was well commended[3]. Not only did Innocent quash elections and make it his rule to punish chapters guilty of irregular practice and ecclesiastical superiors who permitted it, but he held that failure to elect within a fixed time might lead, in the case of a metropolis, to the election passing to the Papacy. The principles of the right of devolution (the word itself seems to have been first used by Innocent)[4] were laid down in the General Council of 1179 (cc. 3, 8, 17). Collation to higher ecclesiastical offices must take place within six months, in default of which it was to pass to the immediate higher authority. In 1215 the principle was confirmed and its application was extended to benefices compulsorily vacated by clerks who had more than one cure of souls, if the patron did not appoint within three months (c. 29). It is noteworthy that the task of examining how benefices were distributed by the bishop and chapter was particularly entrusted to provincial synods (c. 30).

[1] *Decretal. Gregor. IX.* Lib. I, Tit. vi, De Electione, c. xxii; cf. c. xvii.

[2] *Ibid.* c. xx.

[3] *Reg. XI,* CXLIX. MPL, CCXV, 1465.

[4] G. J. Ebers, *Das Devolutionsrecht vornehmlich nach Katholischem Kirchenrecht,* p. 180 sq. shews that the expression dates from early in his pontificate.

In two other cases the Papacy might intervene. The Pope alone authorised translation of bishops[1]. Innocent suspended Conrad of Hildesheim for accepting the bishopric of Würzburg, and, when William of Chimay with the connivance of his metropolitan left Avranches for Angers, he threatened the bishop with suspension. In the second place, he had the right and, as he expressed it, the duty in virtue of his plenitude of power to provide for necessitous clergy: as he said to the chapter of Harlebeke (Flanders), "we are bound to occupy ourselves in securing to poor clerks means of existence." He was prepared to step in and collate to prebends literate and unbeneficed clerks of good reputation[2]. He asked the King of England and Richard of York to intervene with the canons of York on behalf of his old Paris teacher, Peter of Corbeil. Though benefices were sometimes conferred by him on clerks of the Curia, the right was exercised with moderation. He was always clear about the principle underlying his right to provide.

In the sphere of organisation Innocent gave a vigorous impulse to synodal and capitular activity. No less than sixteen councils were held by his legates in different countries before the great assembly of 1215. The Lateran Council ordered provincial councils to be celebrated yearly by metropolitans and the "canonical rules" had to be read aloud. In every province there was to be a triennial chapter of religious orders and regular canons which had not held such meetings previously. Abbots and priors were to attend and two abbots of the Cistercians were to be present to instruct in the rules of procedure followed by their order. The aim of these gatherings was to be reform and the observation of the rule. In these chapters visitors of the monasteries and nunneries of the order throughout the province were to be appointed; they were to go in the Pope's name to exempt as well as to non-exempt houses, and to report irregularities to the diocesan, and, in case of difficulty, to the Holy See. This order was not popular with English Benedictines. Its effect was to generalise representation throughout the religious orders and to provide a greater system of surveillance and discipline. To make the circle of uniformity complete, the thirteenth canon of the Council forbade the establishment of any new religious order.

Great stress was laid on the need for instructing the clergy and laity and on the duty of preaching. Many bishops, observed the Council, were hindered from that duty by the size of their dioceses, by sickness, hostile incursion, or (a scandal henceforth not to be tolerated) lack of knowledge. In such cases they must appoint and ordain in cathedral and other churches preachers and confessors to supply the need. In conformity with the eighteenth canon of the Third Lateran Council, each cathedral and other church that can afford it must spare a prebend to support a master to

[1] *Decretal. Gregor. IX*, Lib. I, Tit. vii, De translatione episcopi, c. ii.

[2] See examples given by E. Roland, *Les Chanoines et les Élections Épiscopales du XIe au XIVe siècle* (Aurillac, 1909), pp. 124–5.

teach clerks and other poor scholars literature and composition, and each metropolitan church should sustain a theologian also to instruct its priests and others in Holy Scripture and the care of souls. In these canons Innocent had his eye upon the nascent universities, whose activities he greatly encouraged; for it was he who had backed the party of the future by recognising the society of Paris masters as a legal corporation (1210–11) and by placing upon the chancellor restrictions which prohibited, in Dr Rashdall's words, "the efforts of a local hierarchy to keep education in leading-strings" (1212); it was the policy of his legate, Nicholas of Tusculum, through the ordinance of 1214, to encourage the autonomy of the masters of Oxford in their struggle for corporate existence against the local burgesses.

In the canons upon the sacrament of marriage and the immunity of clerical property from lay taxation Innocent's legislation had special effect upon the relations between Church and laity. In marriage the Church exercised the greatest influence upon social life, for, as is well known, by Innocent's time she had acquired exclusive right of legislation in matrimonial matters and most cognate questions. In the thirteenth century the canonists who turned their attention to the subject were chiefly engaged in determining the conditions necessary to make the act of consent a valid one, and in working out a theory of impediments characterised by common sense and leniency. For the Church found herself compelled to give up the "exogamic" system (as M. Le Bras has termed it) by which marriages between relations of the seventh degree were prohibited, especially in view of the conditions in rural communities where the inhabitants were largely interrelated. Innocent now had the prohibition on grounds of consanguinity confined to the first four degrees only, and a similar simplification made for cases of affinity. Clandestine marriages were forbidden, and the intention of the parties had to be publicly announced by the priest. The Church courts were directed only in very exceptional cases to admit hearsay evidence of impediment; the witnesses giving it must be grave and responsible persons and the sources of their information must be carefully indicated.

Around the claim of the Church to hold her lands independent of lay exactions a battle had raged ever since the apparently indefinite increase in her possessions began to threaten secular lords with expropriation or the withholding of services. In the twelfth century it was the communes which with their egalitarian principles and peculiar needs had most of all denied this claim to "real immunity," and had called upon the bishops and clergy in the cities to contribute to the cost of expeditions and the upkeep of defensive works. The principle followed by the Church was that laid down in the *Decretum* for the bishop who wished to raise any contribution from his clerks: any subsidy from clerical immovables must be *caritativum*, a voluntary gift, and made there only for "just and reasonable cause."[1] It was in this spirit that the Third Lateran Council, after deploring secular

[1] Causa x, Quaest. III, c. 7.

extortions and anathematising those that made them, forbade the communal authorities to levy such exactions unless the bishop and clergy saw that there was real need for it and the contributions of the laity were not sufficient for the purpose (c. 19, *non minus*). The canon had little effect. After Alexander III's death the situation grew worse. Throughout Italy the demands of the secular authorities to tax clerical property increased, and led to excommunication and frequently to a state of war within the city or the eviction of the clergy[1]. Innocent constituted himself the defender of clerical property, as Lucius III and Clement III had done; he got provincial synods to use the interdict freely against the wicked consuls and rectors. The forty-sixth clause of the Fourth Lateran Council strengthened the canon of 1179 and opened up a new avenue of intervention. It covered the private property of clerks as well as the goods of the Church; and it added to the conditions upon which the subsidy might be granted the stipulation that the Papacy should be asked by the local clergy to give its authorisation before the grant was made, because in the past some of the contributions had been made unwisely.

The canons on ecclesiastical discipline issued in 1215 followed in some respects the lines laid down by the legate Robert de Courçon at Paris in 1212 (or 1213) and at Rouen in 1214. The Paris assembly was, however, remarkable for the very detailed instructions it issued on the life and morals of the clergy and the conduct of monasteries and nunneries. The Lateran Council, while ordering penalties for incontinency and drunkenness and regulating the dress and conduct of religious and secular clergy alike, was occupied with the larger administrative questions of the tenure of benefices, jurisdiction, and ecclesiastical censure. There must be no fraudulent resignations; pluralities are forbidden; sons and illegitimate sons of canons must not succeed to prebends in their fathers' churches. Rectors must pay their vicars a *portio sufficiens* and not keep them on starvation-wages, and those in charge of parish churches must administer them in person and not by vicars, unless the church is annexed to a prebend or an office, in which case a properly paid vicar must be put in. Procurations may only be exacted when archdeacons or papal legates come in person, and these visitors must not exceed the tariff of entertainment laid down by the Third Lateran Council, nor should prelates exact from their subordinates more than they are bound to furnish in such payments. In judicial matters, no clerk may extend his jurisdiction to the prejudice of secular justice. Appeals to a higher court should only be made for serious reasons which must be submitted to, and considered valid by, the judge of first instance, and bringers of frivolous appeals must pay the costs of the action—this without prejudice to the right of the Papacy to try the "greater causes." No one may abuse the good faith of the Holy See and obtain letters citing his opponent before a court Christian more than two days journey from his own natal

[1] For examples see G. Le Bras, *L'Immunité réelle* (Rennes, 1920) pp. 64–69, and his treatment of Cl. XLVI of the Fourth Lateran, pp. 72 sq.

diocese, unless both parties agree. Very careful rules were made for the examination of clerks charged with misconduct: no accusation involving degradation of the defendant may be made unless the accuser is willing to undergo a similar penalty in the event of his case being unfounded, and the methods of prosecuting notorious evil-doers were defined. A properly attested record of every case must be drawn up for the benefit of each party, a copy being kept by the court to prevent disputes arising out of the judgment. In cases of spoliation, the plaintiff who gets the judgment shall not lose his property by prescription, *i.e.* by not being able to enter into possession of it within the specified year, but shall be put into possession of it even after a year's delay. No sentence of excommunication may be uttered without due canonical admonition, and never without certain and valid reason; in cases where the sentence was unfounded and the utterer refused to withdraw it, complaint to a superior judge was permitted.

Upon foundations such as we have tried to depict rather than upon the half-successful, half-baffled effort to win temporal power rested the papal theocracy. Its dogma, its rite, its organisation, its system of justice—these, as Innocent knew, were its abiding possessions. Yet a material and temporal superstructure had to be built in a rough age in which respect for power and acquisition competed, and often successfully, with reverence for law and right, an age in some respects extraordinarily materialist and extraordinarily devoted to tradition. That tradition was not of the Rome whither the Christ of legend turned again to be crucified, Rome red with the blood of martyrs or bewildering with her churches, but of the city of the earlier Emperors, marble-white and mighty, the tamer of the East, the terror of the farthest West. The magic of this Pagan past wrought silently in the lives of the greatest Italian Popes of the Middle Ages. At its best it gave them their genius for uniformity and discipline, their large and splendid solicitude for their subjects. It was Innocent III who in a sermon on an anniversary of his consecration gave noblest expression to their ideal: "Nam ceteri vocati sunt in partem sollicitudinis, solus autem Petrus assumptus est in plenitudinem potestatis. In signum spiritualium contulit mihi mitram, in signum temporalium dedit mihi coronam; mitram pro sacerdotio, coronam pro regno, illius me constituens vicarium, qui habet in vestimento et in femore suo scriptum, "*Rex regum et Dominus dominantium: Sacerdos in aeternum, secundum ordinem Melchisedech.*""

CHAPTER II

PHILIP OF SWABIA AND OTTO IV.

With the death of the Emperor Henry VI the great schemes of the House of Hohenstaufen for universal dominion and hereditary rule collapsed completely. The chaos that followed reveals the slenderness of the foundations on which Frederick Barbarossa and his son had built; when the master hand and the master mind were taken away, the whole edifice crumbled. It is not to be supposed, however, that a statesman so acute and so far-sighted as Henry VI was blind to the dangers of the future. Indeed his last acts, his release of Richard I of England from his feudal obligations[1] and his testament, were clearly intended to minimise the disaster which his death before he had completed his task would inevitably bring. During the last years of his life he had spent much time and effort in the attempt to secure the friendship of those powers which were his natural enemies—the Papacy and England—both so nearly allied with his opponents at home, the Welfs. With England he had been successful; but Celestine III had stubbornly resisted all his advances, had uncompromisingly rejected the very big concessions Henry had been prepared to make in order to obtain a lasting peace with the Curia. Nevertheless, what he had failed to bring to pass in his lifetime, Henry hoped might be achieved after his death. This clearly was the intention of the testament. It was his hope that by making substantial concessions to the Pope he would save what he deemed essential for his son—the Empire and Sicily. These concessions amounted to the recognition of the feudal relationship of the kingdom of Sicily to the Papacy and the restoration of the lands of the Countess Matilda. It was further stipulated that Markward of Anweiler should hold his extensive possessions in Central Italy, the dukedom of Ravenna and the March of Ancona, in fee from the Pope. This is the substance of the fragment of the original document which the author of the *Gesta Innocentii III* has thought fit to record[2]. That the testament did not affect the situation was due to the fact that the man to whom it was entrusted, Markward, did not disclose it, and it only

[1] On the interpretation of the two passages of Hoveden (Rolls Series, ed. Stubbs, III, 203 and IV, 30) which supply the evidence for this fact, see Winkelmann, *Philipp von Schwaben*, pp. 488 sqq. The release from vassalage was probably included in the testament.

[2] c. 27, reprinted in MGH, *Const.* I, 530 sq. Its genuineness has frequently been called in question. Ficker, *Über das Testament Kaiser Heinrichs VI*, contends that it was forged or at any rate tampered with by Markward; Gerlich, *Das Testament Heinrichs VI*, that it was a papal forgery. But the arguments of Winkelmann, *op. cit.* pp. 483 sqq. in favour of its genuine character are now generally accepted. Cf. Hampe, *Deutsche Kaisergeschichte*, p. 201, n. 1.

accidentally came to light in July 1200 when the victorious papal troops rifled his baggage after the battle of Monreale and discovered it. By this time the whole position was altered by three years of civil disturbances.

It may however be doubted whether, even if the document had been made public immediately after Henry's death, it would have proved acceptable to the parties concerned. Frederick, it is true, had been elected King of the Romans during his father's lifetime; but there was a strong feeling among some of the princes that this practice savoured too much of hereditary succession, that it prejudiced their right of free election, and at any rate that an infant of two years old was not the appropriate person to set at the head of affairs at so critical a moment in German history. Moreover there was the Pope to reckon with. Celestine, despite his ninety years, had battled manfully against the aggressive policy of Henry VI and had refused many tempting offers in his efforts to maintain the independence of the Curia. Would not the acceptance of the will entail the sacrifice of much that he had been fighting for? It would mean at least the union of Sicily with the Empire. Celestine outlived his opponent but a few months, and the interests of the Church passed into younger, abler, and more energetic hands.

Of the five sons of Frederick Barbarossa three were already dead[1]. Of the two survivors, Otto, Count Palatine of Burgundy, was too inefficient and too much occupied with the concerns of his county to be seriously thought of. Philip, the youngest and in character the most attractive of the family, though trained for the Church and even elected while still a boy to the see of Würzburg, had subsequently renounced his orders; in 1195 he had been enfeoffed with the duchy of Tuscany and with the lands of Matilda, and on the death of his brother Conrad in the following year he had succeeded to the family duchy of Swabia. He was now a handsome young man of some 22 years of age, with fair hair and a comely and pleasing expression; his mild, kindly, and generous disposition won for him the affection of his friends, the respect of his opponents. Arnold of Lübeck, whose sympathies were on the side of the Welfs, does not stint his praise: "he was a man endowed with many virtues, for he was gentle, humble, and courteous." But perhaps his very virtues made him less fitted to cope with the difficulties of his position: he was too refined, too much of a gentleman for the rude times in which he lived; he was not a great statesman or a great soldier; he lacked judgment, the power of decision, the gift of leadership; he could command the affection but not the discipline of his supporters. But even before Henry's death his good qualities had marked him out as the future champion of the fortunes of his house. He had been closely in the confidence of the Emperor, who early in 1197 had entrusted him with the task of conducting his son from Foligno to Germany for his coronation; he had already crossed the Alps

[1] The second son, Frederick, had succumbed to the pestilence at Acre in 1191 and the third, Conrad, had been killed in a feud with Berthold of Zähringen in 1196.

and had reached Montefiascone in the neighbourhood of Rome on his way to meet the boy when he heard the news of his brother's death. The event was heralded by risings against German rule in all parts of Italy. Philip, in danger for his life, was compelled hastily to retrace his steps, and not without difficulty regained Germany in safety[1].

There everything was already in a state of anarchy and confusion. To the obvious causes for such a state of things was added the misery created by the failure of the harvest in two successive years and the consequent high price of corn. It was not a time to set a child on the throne; Frederick had not been baptised when he was elected King of the Romans; this was excuse enough for nullifying an election to which scarcely anyone wished to adhere. However honestly Philip may have wished to promote the cause of his young nephew—and there is no reason to doubt that he sincerely tried to do so[2]—he must soon have been persuaded that the interests of his country no less than those of his house required him to abandon a course of action which it would have been sheer madness to pursue. At a meeting of his supporters held at Christmas at Hagenau he was adopted as a candidate; at Ichtershausen in Thuringia on 6 March 1198 he gave a reluctant consent, and two days later at Mühlhausen near Erfurt he was duly elected by a large and representative gathering of princes.

But in the meanwhile the opponents of the house of Hohenstaufen, a powerful group of nobles in Westphalia and the district of the lower Rhine, had not been idle. Their leader, Adolf of Altena, Archbishop of Cologne, was, in the absence of the Archbishop of Mayence, who was away on crusade, the chief primate in Germany. Both in his private and in his official capacity he was a man of much consequence. The family had almost secured the great see as an appanage of their house, for no less than five of its members held the archbishopric in the course of a hundred years[3]. The family possessions, which included the counties of Berg, Altena, Mark, and Isenburg, surrounded the city of Cologne on the right

[1] It was probably during his short stay in Italy on this occasion that Celestine III published the sentence of excommunication against him for his earlier attacks on papal territory. See Winkelmann, *op. cit.* pp. 31 and 493 sq.

[2] See especially Philip's letter to Innocent in 1206 (MGH. *Const.* II. 10 sq.) in which he says that he tried to induce the princes by letters and envoys to accept Frederick.

[3]

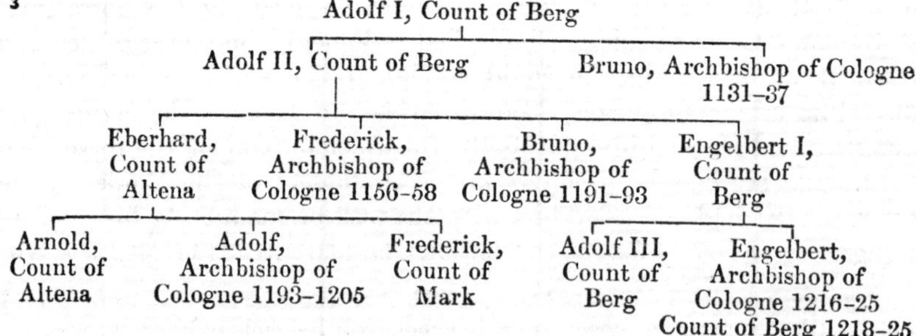

bank of the Rhine, the rich fiefs attached to the see enclosed it on the left; by the partition of the Welf estates on the fall of Henry the Lion, the Archbishops of Cologne had acquired ducal authority over Westphalia. Archbishop Adolf was therefore in a strong position. Already he had taken a prominent part in opposing the ambitious policy of the Hohenstaufen when he had resisted successfully the plan of Henry VI of making the German kingship hereditary. Then, as now in the present crisis, his importance was enhanced by the fact that long custom had attached to his office the function of crowning the king-elect.

About Christmas 1197 he called together his party at Andernach to consider possible candidates; many names were suggested and canvassed before a suitable person could be found to accept the expensive and hazardous honour of becoming the chosen rival of the Hohenstaufen. It was even said that the Kings of England and France were considered and rejected[1]. Duke Bernard of Saxony was approached, but he gave a peremptory refusal: it would cost, he said, too much money and bloodshed, besides he was too fat to undertake so energetic a rôle; so he drifted away to the other side and took a prominent part in the election of Philip. Berthold of Zähringen, to whom the crown was next offered, was at first prepared to consider the idea; but he found it altogether beyond his means to satisfy the exorbitant demands of his supporters; moreover, he seems on second thoughts to have had some care for the interests of his country, for he declared that for his part he would not be the cause of a schism in the kingdom. So he withdrew his candidature, and he too crossed over to Philip who was ready with his purse to recoup him for the large sums of money he had already incurred on his abortive election.

The English ambassadors were present at the adjourned meeting of the anti-Hohenstaufen party which met at Cologne in February, and it was their influence that brought Richard's nephews, the sons of Henry the Lion, into the field[2]. The eldest, Henry, Count Palatine of the Rhine, was away on crusade[3], and so was passed over in favour of his younger brother, Otto. Born about 1175, Otto was almost an exact contemporary of his rival; he had spent his boyhood chiefly at the English court, whither he had followed his exiled father in 1182, in England itself, in Normandy, or in Aquitaine. His uncle Richard, whom in character he somewhat resembled, had from the beginning of his reign shewn a marked interest in the boy's fortunes. As early as 1190 he had given him the earldom of York, but owing to resistance on the part of the Yorkshiremen to their new lord, he had changed the gift to the county of La Marche. In 1194 Otto was one of the hostages at the court of the Emperor

[1] Gervase of Canterbury, ed. Stubbs (Rolls Series), I, 545.

[2] See Philip's account of the election, MGH, *Const.* II, p. 12: "recepta multa pecunia a rege Anglie, qua magni viri sepe corrupti sunt, consanguineum nostrum Oddonem comitem Pictavie elegerunt."

[3] But Buchner, *Der Pfalzgraf bei Rhein,...und die Doppelwahl...* 1198 (*Festgabe Grauert*, 1910), maintains that he was present and promoted his brother's candidature.

Henry VI for the payment of his uncle's ransom. Released from captivity, Richard continued to promote his nephew's welfare; a project was set on foot to secure for him the succession to the Scottish throne by marrying him to Margaret, the daughter and heiress of William the Lion, and when this fell through he was enfeoffed with the county of Poitou (1196). It would be a great stroke of policy if Richard could now secure for his nephew the imperial throne; for it would strengthen enormously his position against Philip Augustus. He was prepared to spend much money and labour to carry a project so much to his advantage to a successful conclusion.

Personally Otto was not a man to attract supporters. To the gentle Hohenstaufen, the rather boorish Welf presents a striking contrast. He was a tall, powerfully built, athletic young man; like his uncle, King Richard, a brave, dashing, impetuous soldier who "roaring like a lion's whelp, incited by the desire of plunder, eager for the battle, fought for victory or death."[1] But this is all that can be said for him. He had no intellectual gifts; he was proud and stupid, obstinate and lacking in diplomatic skill. In this regard he may seem strangely unsuited for the position he had been chosen to fill; but other and more obvious men had been approached without success, for it was not altogether an enviable task to lead a small group of malcontents against the great power that the Hohenstaufen could command in Germany. Otto was something of a *pis aller*, and as such he had much to commend him; the money which was forthcoming from England appealed strongly to the German princes, and the close commercial connexion between England and Cologne assured him a welcome in that city, which had long been prominent as the centre of anti-Hohenstaufen feeling. So at an adjourned meeting held at Andernach about Easter time his candidature was definitely adopted; Count Emich of Leiningen was despatched to fetch him from Poitou. On 17 May he was at Liège whence, accompanied by Archbishop Adolf, he proceeded to Cologne.

From the arrival at Cologne events moved rapidly. Immediately after his formal election on 9 June he marched on Aix-la-Chapelle; the handful of knights that Philip had thrown into the town could offer no effective resistance to the large forces Otto brought against it. After a short siege it fell into his hands (10 July). On the 11th he strengthened his position among the princes of the Netherlands by betrothing himself to the daughter of the Duke of Brabant; on the 12th he was crowned by the Archbishop of Cologne in the great church at Aix-la-Chapelle. However irregular and unrepresentative his election might be, the fact that he had been crowned in the traditional place of coronation and at the hands of the man whose right to perform it was sanctioned by the custom of two

[1] Arnold of Lübeck, VI, 2, "rugiens ut catulus leonis," an allusion to the family name Welf (whelp). See Pertz' note to his edition of Arnold, SGUS, p. 220. Perhaps there is also an allusion to his father Henricus *Leo*.

centuries weighed heavily in his favour[1]. It was nearly two months later, 8 September, that Philip was crowned, and then not at Aix but at Mayence, not by the Archbishop of Cologne but by the Archbishop of Tarantaise.

The circumstances of the coronation, however, were the only real asset in Otto's favour; the position of parties shewed an overwhelming preponderance on the side of his opponent. Outside his narrow sphere in the north-west of Germany Otto could count only on two princes, the Bishop of Strasbourg and the Count of Dagsburg, who happened to be at feud with the house of Hohenstaufen. "While only Cologne and part of Westphalia favoured Otto," Arnold of Lübeck tells us[2], "the whole strength of the Empire supported Philip," and he mentions the princes of Franconia, Saxony, Swabia, Bavaria, and Thuringia; Ottokar of Bohemia was won for his cause by the judicious grant of a royal title. Even Innocent III himself was bound to admit that Philip was elected by the majority and the more dignified of the princes[3]; the powerful body of imperial *ministeriales*, the court officials, so numerous they were, Philip tells us, that he can scarcely count them, were ranged on the same side. Even in that part of Germany—the north-west—where Otto's influence was strongest, Philip could rely upon some support, on the Bishop of Liège, for example, on Walram, son of the Duke of Limburg, and on the Archbishop of Trèves; for although the latter had been associated with Adolf in the negotiations with Berthold of Zähringen, he had changed over to the side of Philip before the election of Otto. While Philip had the wide and rich personal estates of the Hohenstaufen family and the great treasure amassed by the late Emperor at his disposal, Otto had merely the relatively small estates of the Welfs round Brunswick and Lüneburg and but a slender income. He was indeed financed almost entirely by his uncle, the King of England. This reliance of Otto on a foreign power made the question an international one; for in consequence of it Philip hastened to revive the old Hohenstaufen-Capetian alliance which Henry VI had broken off. The compact with Philip Augustus was made a few days after the election of Otto (29 June) and was directed not only against Otto and the King of England, but against their ally, Baldwin of Flanders, whose lands within the Empire (imperial Flanders) the French king was given permission to plunder and occupy[4].

[1] Emphasis is given to these points in the letter of Otto's electors to the Pope (MGH, *Const.* II, 24) and of Otto himself (*Reg. de neg. imp.* no. 20). It is often urged by Innocent III, especially in the *deliberatio*. Cf. also *Ann. Marbac.* ed. Bloch, p. 72; Otto de S. Blasio, ed. Hofmeister, c. 46; Burchard of Ursperg, ed. Holder-Egger and von Simson, p. 82, "properant electi reges, uterque ut occupet sedem regni Aquisgrani." Both Philip and Frederick II thought it wise to repeat the coronation ceremony at Aix when they captured the town.

[2] VI. 2.

[3] In the *Deliberatio*, *Reg. de neg. imp.* no. 29.

[4] MGH, *Const.* II, 1.

At the critical time of the elections many of the German princes were still absent in Syria; their gradual return in the course of the following year was therefore a matter of the keenest interest to the two combatants. Archbishop Hartwig of Bremen, Count Adolf of Holstein, Dietrich, Margrave of Meissen, who brought with him the whole weight of the family of Wettin, added considerably to the strength of Philip's position in the north and east of Germany; for Otto, on the other hand, the return of his brother, the Count Palatine, and of his intended father-in-law Henry, Duke of Brabant, counterbalanced the gains of his rival. Then Herman, the Landgrave of Thuringia, returned, ready now, as at all times during the civil war, to place his services in the hands of the highest bidder; and he was promptly bought by Otto[1]. Almost last of all to arrive was the man who, had he been on the spot at the critical moment, might have saved the situation, Conrad, Archbishop of Mayence, the Arch-Chancellor, who threw in his lot with neither side, but hoped to retrieve the position by maintaining the legality of the election of Frederick in 1196.

An interval of about three months separated the elections of the two kings. It is a remarkable fact that no attempt was made by Philip to use this valuable time to crush his opponents in the Rhineland. On the contrary, it was not until well on in the summer of 1198 that he struck the first blow. This was an unsuccessful attempt to bring to submission the two supporters of the Welf cause in Alsace, the Bishop of Strasbourg and the Count of Dagsburg, who, from the geographical position of their lands, were a constant menace to Philip's own family estates in Swabia. The attack was characteristic of the warfare which intermittently for some sixteen years spread desolation and ruin throughout Germany: the country was devastated, the towns pillaged and burnt, the inhabitants subjected to the most loathsome ignominies[2]. Little can be said for the conduct of any of the armies that shared in this wanton work of destruction, but the most brutal, the most revolting atrocities, if we may believe contemporary accounts, were perpetrated by the Bohemian soldiers fighting under the standard of King Ottokar, who, we are told, "would never undertake a campaign unless they were given free licence of plundering."[3]

The raid against Strasbourg took place before his coronation. After that event Philip pushed northward down the Rhine, and, with only a little fighting at the crossing of the Moselle, managed to get within a couple of

[1] According to Burchard (p. 83) Herman himself hoped to acquire the crown.

[2] See, *e.g. Chron. Reg. Colon.* ed. Waitz, SGUS, p. 165: "Sanctimonialem quandam omnibus indumentis spoliatam oleo perungentes, in plumis lectualibus volutabant, sicque monstruose hirsutam caballo imposuerunt, versa eius facie ad caudam caballi." A medieval form of tarring and feathering.

[3] Arnold of Lübeck, VI, 5. Cf. *Chron. Reinhardsbrunn.* MGH. *Script.* XXX, p. 560: "Ubicumque [Ottokar] castrametatus est, ibi virginum defloracio, matrimonii separacio, sanctimonialium et viduarum nefanda ab eis corruptio perpetrata est. Denique civitates deflagrarunt, emunitatibus ecclesiarum et monasteriorum minime parcentes, sacra profanis miscuerunt."

miles of Cologne itself. He might then and there, thought the historian of Trèves, have taken the city, whose ruined walls offered no obstacle to an assault, and so have ended the civil war in the year of its outbreak. But the advance of the Duke of Brabant made Philip cautious, and the opportunity was lost, for soon the news from Thuringia brought the rival kings hurrying eastward to this new theatre of war. Here the Landgrave Herman was trying to get possession of the two imperial towns, Nordhausen and Saalfeld, which had been granted him as part of the bribe which had secured his services for Otto. Both were captured before the end of the year, and Goslar was only saved by the timely appearance of Philip (5 January 1199).

Neither side had gained any decisive advantage by the fighting of 1198, and each seemed reluctant to renew hostilities in the next year; the first six months, from the military point of view, were a blank. At last in June Otto attempted an advance up the Rhine, but he could get no farther than Boppard, a few miles south of Coblenz which he had burnt on his march—the only recorded incident in this otherwise uneventful campaign. Nevertheless, uneventful as it was, it had serious consequences for Otto: it displayed his weakness to the world; the confidence of his supporters was shaken, and even the burghers of Cologne entertained doubts of the wisdom of their archbishop in promoting a rival to the Hohenstaufen[1].

Philip's fortunes rose as rapidly as Otto's declined. On his second expedition against Strasbourg, the Bishop, Conrad, and his ally, the Count of Dagsburg, made their submission. In Alsace he was joined by Henry of Kalden, Marshal of the Empire, and Conrad of Urslingen, Duke of Spoleto, two of the finest soldiers of their day, trained in the Italian wars of the Emperor Henry VI. These successes and the obvious waning of Otto's cause were sufficient to bring the Landgrave of Thuringia to Philip's side. Herman by his numerous tergiversations[2] amassed a great treasure in money and estates; but in justice it should be said of him that he made better use of his perhaps misgotten gains than many a noble who acquired wealth out of the civil wars. He was a great patron of art and literature; minnesingers thronged his hospitable court; Walther von der Vogelweide, Wolfram von Eschenbach, and many others enjoyed his liberal patronage. The magnificent halls of the Wartburg, the scene of the part-legendary, part-historical contest of minstrels, the *Wartburgkrieg*, still stand to commemorate perhaps the greatest among the promoters of the arts in the thirteenth century[3].

By the end of the year Philip's position in the north-east of Germany was assured. The Bishops of Halberstadt and Osnabrück, who had hitherto remained neutral, now definitely declared for him; and the Christmas

[1] *Chron. Reg. Colon.* p. 168.

[2] He changed sides in 1198, 1199, 1202, 1204, 1208, and 1210.

[3] The period of the Civil War is conspicuous for its literary activity. It is the greatest epoch of German medieval lyric and epic poetry. In these years were produced not only the best work of the minnesingers, but also the great epics, the *Niebelungenlied*, the *Parsifal* of Wolfram of Eschenbach, the *Tristan and Isolde* of Gottfried of Strasbourg.

festival, when he rode crowned with his queen Irene through the streets of Magdeburg, marks the official recognition of his title in Saxony[1]. It closed for Philip a year of conspicuous success.

Otto on the other hand, who spent Christmas in the neighbourhood of Goslar, could look back on the events of the year with anything but satisfaction. He had lost ground steadily; his allies in Alsace and Thuringia had deserted him, and, most calamitous of all, King Richard, to whose energy and financial aid he largely owed his election, died of an arrow wound while besieging the castle of Chaluz on 6 April. He could expect little from John. There is evidence for the payment of certain sums in the summer of 1199[2], but in the following January the preliminaries were arranged for the treaty with Philip Augustus which was finally concluded at Le Goulet in May; by the terms of that treaty John bound himself to withdraw his support from Otto. When therefore the latter sent his brothers Henry and William to England in September for the legacy in jewels bequeathed to him by Richard, John refused to hand it over, taking his stand on his agreement with the King of France. If Otto meant to continue the contest, he must seek for allies elsewhere; he must get the Pope to declare openly in his favour.

In Italy a strong reaction against German domination had followed immediately on Henry VI's death. Everywhere the German officials were attacked and driven out, the German garrisons were expelled from their fortresses. The Papacy was not slow to take advantage of these general rebellions. Celestine III in his last days had begun the work of annexation which his successor Innocent III carried on with characteristic energy. Papal legates fomented and made use of the prevalent anti-German feeling. In his duchy of Spoleto Conrad of Urslingen made what resistance he could, but he was isolated and could expect no help from Germany; he tried to save his position by attempting unsuccessfully to bribe the Pope; then he submitted unconditionally at Narni in April 1198, and retired a little later across the Alps to the camp of Philip. A papal rector superseded an imperial duke in Spoleto. Markward of Anweiler, after struggling vainly against the adverse forces, was driven from the March of Ancona which, like Spoleto, was annexed to the Papal States. Markward withdrew to the south, to Apulia and Sicily, where he and Diepold of Acerra, despite the efforts of Innocent, were long able to hold their own.

In Lombardy and Tuscany anti-imperialist leagues were revived under papal influence. But though they were anxious enough to throw off German domination, to cast out German officials, they were not prepared to submit

[1] See the poem of Walther von der Vogelweide (ed. Paul, 68) and also the graphic account in the *Gesta Episcoporum Halberstadensium* (MGH. *Script.* XXIII, p. 113). The author was probably an eyewitness. Cf. Böhmer. *Reg.* v. no. 32 a.

[2] See Kienast, *Die deutschen Fürsten im Dienste der Westmächte*, p. 156; but his interpretation of the entries in the *Charter Rolls* ed. Hardy, I, pt. i, pp. 11 and 31, is disputed by Haller, *Innocenz III und Otto IV*, in *Papsttum und Kaisertum*, (*Paul Kehr zum 65 Geburtstag dargebracht*), p. 486 n. 2.

to papal domination or papal officials in their place. Innocent, not content with the annexation of southern Tuscany and of the long-disputed bequest of Matilda, claimed the whole of Tuscany as an integral part of the domain of the Church of Rome (21 February 1198), and to this claim the Tuscan towns offered a stubborn resistance.

But the success that Innocent had achieved in Italy was in no small measure due to the civil war in Germany, and the prolongation of the war while he was consolidating his gains would be of inestimable service to him. This fact accounts for the attitude of neutrality which he adopted in the opening phase of the struggle. But that he must ultimately be involved was obvious; with the election of the King of the Romans the Pope had properly nothing to do—that was an affair of the German princes alone—but it was admitted on all sides that only the Pope could confer the imperial title and dignity. Accordingly both parties addressed letters to Innocent announcing their respective elections and soliciting what he alone could give—the imperial crown.

Otto in a letter written probably in the late summer of 1198[1] reminded Innocent of the services his father had rendered to the Holy See by championing its cause against the Hohenstaufen; he tells of his coronation and how he had then sworn to maintain the rights and possessions of the Church of Rome and of the other churches of the Empire, and finally how he would renounce for the future "the detestable custom" of the *ius spolii*. In return he asks that the Pope will grant him the imperial crown, excommunicate the electors of Philip, absolve his partisans from their oath of allegiance, and lastly publish broadcast through Germany the sentence of excommunication against Philip himself. Here there was nothing derogatory to the position and prerogatives of the king: a mere formal oath to maintain the rights and possessions of the Church and the renunciation of an admitted abuse. Not so with his electors. In the letter signed by Archbishop Adolf, the Duke of Brabant, and six other princes, not only imperial coronation but papal confirmation of the election is requested. This was admitting a dangerous claim of the Pope, and one which led directly to papal interference in the election itself[2].

Philip, in the letter which he addressed to the Pope either on the day of his coronation or soon after, makes no other allusion to the event than in styling himself *Dei gratia Romanorum rex et semper augustus*; it simply contains an excuse for having retained the Pope's legate, the Bishop of Sutri, so long at his court, and the first real intimation of the facts was made in the impressive declaration of his supporters at Spires on 28 May 1199. It was signed by twenty-six princes, and twenty-four others, who were not present at the diet, intimated their consent in writing. The two

[1] But W. M. Peitz, HJ. XLVI (1926) argues for the spring of 1199.

[2] The demand for confirmation is also made in the individual letters of Adolf, the Count of Flanders, the Count of Dagsburg, the King of England, and the podestà of Milan. The letters are included in Innocent's *Registrum de negotio imperii*, nos. 3–10.

lists, taken together, reveal the overwhelming strength of the Hohenstaufen party in Germany. They include the Patriarch of Aquileia, the Archbishops of Magdeburg, Trèves, Bremen, and Besançon, and twenty-three bishops, among them three out of the five suffragans of the diocese of Cologne. The secular princes were represented by the King of Bohemia and his brother the Margrave of Moravia; the Dukes of Saxony, Bavaria, Austria, Meran, Lorraine, Zähringen, and Carinthia; Philip's brother, the Count Palatine of Burgundy, and the Margraves of Meissen and Brandenburg. After informing the Pope that they have lawfully elected Philip *in imperatorem Romani solii* they explain how, on account of the resistance of a few princes, they met together in the preceding January at Nuremberg, and there unanimously promised to give him their support against all who opposed his authority "in the Empire and in the lands which his most serene brother held"; they request the Pope not to interfere in any way with the rights of the Empire, while they for their part will see that the rights of the Church are not diminished or infringed; they beg him further to lend his support to Markward, Marquess of Ancona, Duke of Ravenna, and *procurator* of the kingdom of Sicily—an array of titles which could scarcely fail to arouse the anger of Innocent. They close by announcing a speedy expedition to Italy for the imperial coronation. The letter may rank with the best efforts of the chancery of Frederick Barbarossa and Henry VI. It is a bold, unequivocal assertion of the Hohenstaufen policy as maintained by these two Emperors. There is no request for confirmation; the lawfulness of the election is taken for granted; so too is the right to the imperial crown. Innocent is merely asked not to interfere in matters that do not concern him, but to render assistance to the imperial representative in Italy, Innocent's greatest enemy, Markward.

But before this uncompromising letter had been dispatched, Innocent had already abandoned his neutrality. The death of Richard I (6 April 1199), on whom Otto staked all his hopes, meant the almost inevitable victory of the Hohenstaufen. Innocent, who had no illusions about the character of Richard's successor, might now expect to see the victorious Philip marching through Italy, re-establishing as he went the imperial control in those lands which he, Innocent, had so recently annexed to the Papal States, but where papal authority was as yet but infirmly rooted. The civil war in Germany must continue for a while longer, and Innocent must provide the support which hitherto Richard had rendered to maintain the cause of the Welf; the attitude of neutrality must be given up[1].

Conrad of Wittelsbach, Archbishop of Mayence, was, at the time of the double election, absent from Europe, crusading in Syria. His views on the question that was convulsing Germany, when they came to be known, were likely to be listened to by the two parties, for he commanded

[1] That Richard's death was the probable cause of Innocent's change of attitude has been shown by Professor Haller, *op. cit.* p. 486.

the respect of both[1]. His natural inclination one might expect would be to resist the Hohenstaufen candidate. For in the course of his chequered career he had been deprived of his archbishopric by Frederick Barbarossa in consequence of his recognition of Pope Alexander III (Würzburg, 1165). Alexander had rewarded him for his loyalty by creating him Cardinal-bishop of Sabina, and after the peace of Venice he acquired the archbishopric of Salzburg which he held till, in 1183, a fresh vacancy occasioned his return once more to his former primacy at Mayence.

To this old but influential and highly esteemed statesman, Innocent addressed on 3 May 1199 the letter with which he opened his campaign of intervention in the German dispute. After outlining the situation as he saw it, Innocent asks the archbishop to send in writing a statement to the effect that he will consider as binding whatever decision he, the Pope, might make; he is further to instruct all who are in obedience to him to recognise as king and give their support to him whose nomination is approved by the apostolic see. On the same day he wrote to the German princes claiming the right of the Curia to decide the question. There is at present no hint as to which side he means to support; and even the letter written to the electors of Otto two or three weeks later (20 May), the long-awaited answer to their letters of the previous summer in which they had informed the Pope of Otto's election, contains no more than a general promise that he would shew Otto his favour provided that he persevered in the devotion which his family had hitherto shewn to the Church. But Otto wanted more than this. His position was becoming every day more desperate; the campaign of the summer of 1199 had, as we have seen, gone ill with him; and he confessed to Innocent that since the death of Richard he, the Pope, was "his sole comfort and support.' He prayed him therefore to declare openly for him.

A diversion in the diplomatic negotiations with the Curia was introduced by the return of Archbishop Conrad. He landed in Apulia in July, occupied himself for a time in a fruitless endeavour to bring about an understanding between Markward and the Pope with regard to the southern kingdom, and then journeyed north to Rome where he spent the autumn. Innocent's attempt to wring from him a pledge to abide by his ruling on the German dispute had not been conceded. The archbishop had his own views on the matter, and proposed to keep his hands free to try what he could do to solve the problem by mediation. Neither of the rivals was, in his opinion, a lawful king; both should stand aside in favour of Frederick whose election he regarded as binding. But things had already gone too far to draw back; all that he could accomplish, as a result of an interview with Philip at Nuremberg, was a truce for the

[1] Cf. Innocent's letter to him (*Reg. de neg. imp.* no. 22): "non est qui post Romanum pontificem vel in ecclesia Romana vel in imperio Romano tantum locum obtineat quantum obtines in utroque." See also *Chron. Reinhardsbrunn.* MGH, *Script.* xxx, 562: "Deoque dilectus et hominibus."

Rhineland to last until 11 November of the same year. In the meanwhile a court of arbitration composed of eight representatives of each party under his presidency was to meet near Coblenz on 28 July to decide the question.

Otto was not a little alarmed. He could not conceal from himself the fact that a representative body of arbitrators would inevitably give a verdict against him; his only hope was to get the Pope to forestall such a decision by deciding himself for Otto. So in desperation he wrote once more to Innocent (April 1200), imploring him to recognise him openly as king and to write to the sixteen arbitrators bidding them to do likewise. In return he expressed his readiness to agree to the conditions which his ambassadors had already arranged with the Pope nearly a year before (May 1199). For a long time Otto had stood out against these humiliating terms—they were the terms to which he subsequently set his seal at Neuss—but the trend of events in Germany, the ill success of his campaigns, and more than anything else the arbitration scheme of the Archbishop of Mayence, allowed him no choice but to yield. This promise was what the Pope was waiting for. Once assured of Otto's submission to his conditions, which amounted to the sacrifice of the imperial position in Italy, he proceeded with the course of action he had already planned. He wrote to the German princes declaring that, while he had no wish to infringe their rights, they must choose a king whom he could and ought to crown; at the same time he intimated quite plainly that Philip was not such a person but that Otto was. He sent an emissary to Germany to further his plans; he canvassed the princes by promising to use his influence with the successful candidate to insure the inviolability of their lands and positions. This was as far as he was able to go at the moment, for there was still an obstacle in his path.

Conrad of Mayence, on whom he had at first relied to second his efforts, so far from doing so, was working independently on different lines. Conrad's influence among the German princes was very great; it might well happen that his and not Innocent's plan might prevail, and Innocent's intervention would result only in loss of prestige. He wished to avoid this at all costs; and so he delayed until the archbishop's plan of arbitration had failed. Conrad, weary of the whole business, went off to Hungary to settle a dispute between the sons of the late king Béla and to promote a crusade; and on his return to Germany in the autumn he died, leaving Innocent free to pursue his course unimpeded.

Innocent, however, did not take the important step of recognising Otto openly without first fully considering the question in all its aspects in a secret consistory held probably at the close of the year 1200. In the opening sentence of the *Deliberatio de facto imperii super tribus electis* he claims the right of providing an Emperor on the ground that the Empire *principaliter et finaliter* belongs to the apostolic see: *principaliter* by reason of the supposed translation of the Empire from the Greeks to the Franks by Leo III—a fiction now for the first time officially expressed—*finaliter* by reason of the fact that by the Pope the Emperor is crowned and invested with the Empire. He then proceeds to examine the individual claims of the three candidates—for Frederick's interests are not overlooked—from the three points of view of legality, suitability, and expediency. The frankness with which the points for and against each candidate are discussed is conclusive evidence of the strict secrecy of the debate[1].

Against the otherwise lawful election of Frederick it was urged that he was manifestly unsuitable on the ground of age; for he who himself is in need of a guardian surely is incapable of governing others. Moreover it is certainly inexpedient, for it would involve the union of Sicily with the Empire, which would be disastrous to the Church. The legality of Philip's election must be admitted, since *a pluribus et dignioribus sit electus*, and further it would be most inexpedient to make an enemy of a man so powerful in land, wealth, and supporters. On the other hand, he was at the time of his election under sentence of excommunication, and that a brother should succeed a brother might appear too much like hereditary succession. Innocent closes his case against Philip by declaring that he was obviously unsuitable because he was a persecutor of the Church and comes from a race of persecutors; and in a long passage he enumerates the attacks made against the Church by the Emperors from the time of Henry V onwards, concluding with the invasion of papal territory by Philip himself as Duke of Tuscany.

The case for Otto was manifestly the weakest and occupies a very small space in the long document; the only real argument in his favour was that it suited papal policy, but this Innocent would like to disguise. He therefore, while admitting that but few of the princes participated in his election, argues that among those few were "the majority of those who have the right to elect." We cannot here enter into the history of the development of the College of Electors; suffice it to say that by 1198 but four of the later seven can claim any sort of right to "be first in the election"—the three Rhenish archbishops and the Count Palatine of the Rhine who represented the ancient right attached to the extinct dukedom of Franconia; and of these four, two—the Archbishop of Mayence and the Count Palatine—were at the time of the election out of Germany, while the Archbishop of Trèves was not a promoter of Otto but on the contrary was present at the coronation of Philip and a signatory of the Spires declaration. Only the Archbishop of Cologne represented those to whose votes special significance was attached. But Otto in contrast to Philip is not only himself devoted to the interests of the Church but comes from families on both sides similarly devoted. So Innocent argued, and so gave his verdict in Otto's favour.

The decision at which Innocent had arrived was not immediately put into effect nor even published. In his letters to the German princes of

[1] See Tangl, *Die Deliberatio Innocenz' III*. SPAW, LIII (1919), p. 1018.

5 January 1201, after explaining the grounds for his assumption of the right to decide the question in terms similar to those used in the *Deliberatio*, he merely requests them to agree upon a king whom he might properly crown Emperor or to leave the decision to him[1]; he then informs them of his intention to send a legate to Germany, Guy, Cardinal-bishop of Palestrina. Guy was to co-operate with Octavian, Cardinal-bishop of Ostia, who was already in France, engaged, among other things, in trying to persuade Philip Augustus to give up Philip and to espouse the cause of Otto.

Armed with a mass of letters dated from the papal chancery on 1 March[2], the legate, travelling through France in order to confer at Troyes with his colleague Cardinal Octavian, reached Aix-la-Chapelle about the middle of June. Here he was met by Otto, who had in the meantime, at Neuss on 8 June, set his seal to the terms which Innocent demanded. These amounted to no less than a complete surrender of the imperial position in Italy. Not only was he obliged to recognise the conquests and annexations which Innocent had already made, but he was further required to assist in the acquisition of the remainder of the lands to which the Holy See laid claim. These are then defined: all the land from Radicofani to Ceprano, that is to say, the Patrimony, the Exarchate of Ravenna, the Pentapolis, the March of Ancona, the Duchy of Spoleto, the land of the Countess Matilda, the County of Bertinoro, with other adjacent territory mentioned in many privileges of the Emperors from the time of Louis the Pious. He further agreed to assist in defending the kingdom of Sicily for the Church. By another clause his relations with France were to be controlled by the Pope; and at the end of the document he pledged himself to repeat these same promises when he had been crowned Emperor. Otto made desperate efforts to free himself from these last two conditions. Freedom of action in his relations with Philip Augustus he regarded as essential, while, if he could but manage to omit the last clause referring to the confirmation of the promises after his imperial coronation, he might render the whole document so much waste paper. For he thought that what he had sworn as king he might renounce as Emperor. To this end he did not hesitate, it seems, to tamper with the document in such a way that these two last clauses might be suppressed; the attempt failed, and a new draft was made[3].

[1] His object was to prepare the way for the publication of his verdict. He knew that the time had passed for any agreement among the princes, but it might strengthen his hand if he gave them a last opportunity for doing so, and they failed to avail themselves of it. See Bloch, *Kaiserwahlen*, pp. 35–6.

[2] *Reg. de neg. imp.* nos. 32–49. Otto is addressed in the first of these *illustri regi Ottoni in Romanorum imperatorem electo.*

[3] See Haller, *op. cit.* pp. 475 sqq. The document from which Otto attempted to exclude these two clauses is printed in MGH, *Const.* II, p. 20, and wrongly attributed to the year 1198, *i.e.* as concessions made to the Pope at the time of his election; it seems clear however that Otto made no such bid for papal support until forced to do so owing to the critical state of his fortunes. The second draft, which includes the two conditions which he tried to evade, is that printed in MGH, *Const.* II, p. 27.

The fact that Otto's most influential supporter, the Duke of Brabant, was wavering in his loyalty probably more than anything else determined him to subscribe to the Pope's conditions and to implore the legate to recognise him publicly as king. Together they proceeded to Cologne, where a meeting of the princes had been arranged. There on the appointed day, 3 July, Otto was proclaimed king "by the grace of God and of the Pope" as he came to style himself, and Philip and his partisans were excommunicated. But the gathering was an insignificant one: few of the princes had answered the summons of the legate; the messengers who carried them were received with hostility; often they were refused admission into the towns, and sometimes, Cardinal Guy tells in reporting these events to Innocent[1], they ended their lives on the nearest gallows. This was not encouraging. The proclamation was repeated at Maastricht and again at Corvey—an attempt to win over the Saxon bishops—but we have no evidence to shew that the attendance at these meetings was better than that at Cologne. Only at Rome do we hear of anything like enthusiasm. There, if we may believe Hoveden, who may have been at Rome at the time, Otto was proclaimed on the Capitol and throughout the city, "Vivat imperator noster Otho."

The princes of the Hohenstaufen party, undaunted by the sentence of excommunication pronounced against them by the legate, renewed their oath to Philip at Bamberg on 8 September, and at the same time prepared a vigorous protest against papal interference which was ultimately dispatched to Rome from the diet of Halle early in the next year[2]. In his reply, which he addressed to the Duke of Zähringen, Innocent, besides recapitulating much that he had recorded in the secret *Deliberatio*, explained fully what he regarded to be the position of the Pope in the matter of the election of the King of the Romans. The particular interest and importance of the Bull *Venerabilem* is that it later found a place among the *Decretals* of Gregory IX, and so became embodied in Canon Law[3]. Again, as in the *Deliberatio*, Innocent sets out from the argument for the dependence of the Empire on the Papacy based upon the fictitious *translatio*. He does not dispute the right of those princes "to whom by law and ancient custom it is known to belong" of choosing the king; for this right came to them from the apostolic see when it transferred the Empire from the Greeks to the Germans. But as the man they choose is afterwards crowned Emperor by the Pope, he, the Pope, must have the power of scrutinising the person elected to see that he is a man worthy of the dignity; for they might choose an obviously unsuitable person, an imbecile, an excommunicate, a heretic. Surely, Innocent asks, we ought not to anoint, consecrate, and crown a man of this sort? *Absit omnino!* He must therefore have the *ius et auctoritas examinandi personam electam*, from which clearly follows

[1] *Reg. de neg. imp.* no. 51.
[2] MGH, *Const.* II, p. 5.
[3] *Corpus iuris canonici, Decr. Greg. IX.* c. 34, 1, 6.

the power of rejecting the unsuitable. Philip, on examination, proved unsuitable; hence Innocent has rejected him and confirmed the election of Otto.

In some aspects the course of events in Germany might encourage Innocent to hope that his verdict might ultimately meet with acceptance there. For Otto's prospects had perceptibly brightened in the latter part of the year 1200. Even in the field he had met with some success: Saxony had not been covered by the truce arranged by Archbishop Conrad for the seven months from April to November; that had been restricted to the Rhineland. So in August Philip took the opportunity to attack the home of the Welfs—Brunswick. The Count Palatine, who was engaged in the siege of Hildesheim, hastened to defend it, and held it against all the assaults of the besiegers. At last Philip was constrained through lack of supplies to relinquish the siege and to agree to a brief truce[1].

This was the first real set-back that he had hitherto encountered; but it was not the only one of this year. The constant quarrels between the Count of Holstein and Canute VI of Denmark finally led to the entry of the latter into the war on the side of Otto. It had come about by Count Adolf's capture of the Welf town of Lauenburg, and his subsequent attack on Ditmarschen which was subject to Denmark (1201). Canute retaliated: Adolf himself was defeated and captured; Holstein was overrun and occupied by the Danes. This alliance was cemented a year later by two marriages between the Welfs and the Danish royal house. The connexion however brought little credit and not much real assistance to Otto. Neither Canute nor his brother Waldemar, who succeeded him in December 1202, had any serious interest in Otto's cause; they entered the war for their own political advantage and devoted their efforts to establishing their control over Nordalbingia, which they did with such success that when in August 1203 Waldemar entered Lübeck he was hailed, Arnold tells us, joyously as "King of the Danes and the Slavs and lord of Nordalbingia"; and this frontier territory remained for many years subject to Danish rule.

Philip's position in the north and east, already weakened by his failure at Brunswick and by the Welf-Danish alliance, was further damaged by the outbreak of a violent family quarrel among his supporters. Ottokar of Bohemia divorced his wife Adela, the sister of Dietrich of Meissen, and thereby gave offence to the whole house of Wettin and their powerful connexions, the Duke of Saxony and the Margrave of Brandenburg. The feud was the cause of Ottokar's desertion to Otto in 1202.

But Otto found his own party by no means easy to manage. He was prevented from taking advantage of the weakened position of his rival in the north-east of Germany by feuds in the ranks of his own supporters:

[1] Otto, who was certainly not present when the siege began, is said by Hoveden (IV, 116) to have come to the help of his brother, and this also is implied in the detailed account of Arnold of Lübeck (VI, 4). Winkelmann (*op. cit.* p. 184, n. 1) thinks it improbable that Otto took part in any of the fighting at Brunswick.

the Duke of Brabant, the Count of Guelders, the Count of Holland, were all quarrelling among themselves. Adolf of Cologne himself was shewing signs of wavering. The restoration of the head of the Welf family, the Count Palatine, in the county of Stade and in the Bremen fiefs, and his assumption of the title of Duke of Saxony, had alarmed those princes who had grown rich out of the spoils of Henry the Lion hardly twenty years before; and the Archbishop of Cologne had been the greatest gainer of them all. The Count Palatine might have ambitions to recover in their entirety the great estates his father had once held. There were other grievances as well: Otto had promised at the time of his election large rewards to Archbishop Adolf, and they had not yet been paid. The loyalty of the citizens however saved Otto from the importunity of his creditor; they realised the value to the city of the trade connexion with England. Otto they deemed more essential to their prosperity than their archbishop. So, in the agreement of September 1202, the four orders in the town, the priors of the church, the nobles, the *ministeriales*, and the burghers, not only swore allegiance to Otto, but also declared that their obedience to the archbishop was dependent upon his continued adherence to the same side. Adolf was satisfied in the matter of the promised payments and the burghers were rewarded by privileges in respect of mints and tolls. Again all Cologne was united in support of the Welfs.

The towns of Germany, which at this period were rapidly growing in wealth and importance, were eagerly bargained for by the rival kings. The pact with Cologne is not an isolated instance. In the same year Philip made a substantial grant of trading privileges to the city of Trèves. He had already done so even before his actual election (January 1198) to Spires; after his coronation at Aix-la-Chapelle in 1205 he made grants to Cambrai (whose bishop was a strong partisan of the Welfs) and to Strasbourg, and in 1207 to Ratisbon. Such concessions of privileges made to acquire or maintain the allegiance of towns are not without their importance in municipal history; but more important still was the very injurious effect of the sacrifice of the royal right of markets and tolls on the financial position of the Crown. For with the great development of trade and commerce in the twelfth century these rights had become one of the most lucrative sources of royal revenue.

Elections to vacant sees also affected the position of parties in Germany. "Scarcely was there a bishopric, an ecclesiastical dignity, even a parish church that did not become litigious," Burchard of Ursperg remarks with pardonable exaggeration. These disputes on the whole improved the position of Otto. The death of Archbishop Conrad of Mayence in the autumn of 1200 gave rise to a schism. The majority, acting, we may imagine, under the influence of Philip who presented himself at the electoral meeting, chose Lupold, Bishop of Worms, a strong Hohenstaufen partisan, but a man of secular rather than spiritual interests; and Philip, without waiting for papal confirmation, immediately invested him with the regalia of the see. The minority—three or four at the most, if we may believe Philip's account of the affair—protesting against the king's presence, went off to Bingen, where they elected the provost of the cathedral, Siegfried of Eppstein. In spite of the great popular acclamation with which Lupold's election was at first received, Siegfried seems soon to have gained the ascendancy in the city, and was the means whereby Otto succeeded in gaining a footing within the walls of what had hitherto been a stronghold of Hohenstaufen interest (Christmas 1200). He managed also to intercept Philip's treasure as it was being taken from the city, a material gain to his impoverished resources. But Otto's influence here was only transient; for in the next summer we hear that the citizens closed their gates against the emissaries of Innocent III.

In a contested election at Liège, Hugh of Pierrepont, a not very reputable person who had nothing but his Welf sympathies to recommend him, was recognised and consecrated by Cardinal Guy (April 1202). Recognition of Otto was a necessary condition of the confirmation of the appointment of Eberhard to the archbishopric of Salzburg; but this amounted to little more than a public pronouncement; in his heart he remained anti-Welf, and was the bearer of the Hohenstaufen protest sent to the Pope from Halle. The position of parties was more seriously affected by the conduct of Conrad of Querfurt, who had been Bishop of Hildesheim since 1194 and Chancellor to Henry VI since 1195, and was translated by Philip to the see of Würzburg without papal license in 1198. Deprived of both bishoprics by the Pope, he remained obdurate, and for a time styled himself in Philip's documents as Bishop of Hildesheim and Bishop-elect of Würzburg. But by 1201 he had submitted to the Pope, was confirmed in the see of Würzburg, and while retaining the chancellorship and outwardly the friendship of Philip, secretly worked in the interests of Otto for the downfall of his master. On him mainly rests the responsibility for the lack of decision and enterprise which at this time characterised Philip's movements. He was in close correspondence with Ottokar of Bohemia and with Herman of Thuringia, both of whom largely through his agency deserted to Otto. His career of duplicity was cut short by assassination in December 1202.

It cannot be denied that in these ecclesiastical disputes the Pope and his legate were guided in their decisions by political rather than by spiritual motives. But, in spite of their efforts, the German Church clung to the side of the Hohenstaufen with striking solidarity. Two archbishops and eleven bishops put their names to the Halle protest; one—the Bishop of Halberstadt—rather than give way to Innocent, left Germany and went on a pilgrimage to the East. A few, under threat of deprivation, submitted so far as to take the oath to obey the Pope in the matter of the German kingship; but their oaths were insincere, wrung from them by duress, and little affected their real political attitude[1].

[1] See Hauck, *Kirchengeschichte Deutschlands* IV, p. 740, n. 3.

This staunch attitude of the German episcopate may be partly accountable for that curious episode of the war, Innocent's negotiations with Philip in the year 1203. The Pope feared, it seems, that he might be backing a losing side. So with that astuteness which marks all his diplomacy he prepared himself to meet either eventuality. Without in any way breaking with Otto, in fact while continuing publicly and vigorously to support him, he secretly admitted overtures from Philip. It was not merely the position in Germany that caused him anxiety; it was also Philip's connexion with the Fourth Crusade. In the winter of 1201 Philip had received at his court both his brother-in-law, Alexius IV, who, having escaped from Constantinople, was seeking assistance against his usurping uncle, Alexius III, and Boniface of Montferrat, the chosen leader of the Crusade. It is on the whole probable that at his court at Hagenau in December the plan of diverting the Crusade to Constantinople was formed[1]. Philip negotiated with the Venetians and with the crusading army at Zara; there is no doubt that he was deeply involved in the movement. Innocent, little as he liked the idea of the expedition against the Greek capital, could not shut his eyes to the fact that it might lead to the much desired union of the Greek with the Latin Church. This indeed was one of the inducements which Philip instructed his ambassador, Otto of Salem, to hold out to the Pope. Innocent, without in any way committing himself, allowed the Prior of Camaldoli, a man much employed in papal business, to accompany the monk of Salem back to Germany, where their conversations with Philip resulted in the drafting of a formal document containing the concessions which the latter was prepared to make. These included the restoration of all lands which he or his predecessors had taken from the Church, the renunciation of the *ius spolii*, the canonical election of bishops and other prelates, the reform of monasteries; he repeated his crusading vow; he promised to introduce a law by which anyone who should be excommunicated by the Pope should also fall under the ban of the Empire; he offered to cement the compact by marrying his daughter to a nephew of the Pope. But on the crucial question of the lands in central Italy nothing was said. It is evident that Philip was not prepared, as Otto had been at Neuss, to sacrifice the imperial interests south of the Alps[2]. Nevertheless his offers were not to be despised; and had it not been for the turn of events in Germany they might have anticipated the reconciliation between Philip and the Pope four years later.

Otto, aided by the transference to his side of Herman and Ottokar, and

[1] See *Chron. Reg. Colon.* p. 199; *Gesta Innocentii,* c. 83. For the whole question of Philip's connexion with the crusade see *supra,* vol. IV, 416 sq. and 603 sq.

[2] Perhaps some arrangement which would satisfy Innocent in this respect was contemplated in connexion with the proposed marriage. Such a plan formed part of the proposed settlement between Innocent and Philip arranged shortly before the latter's death. See *infra,* p. 71.

by Philip's own mismanagement of the campaign, was gaining ground rapidly. At the court at Ratisbon in May Philip had planned to take the field against Herman; at first he seems to have been successful; but with incredible lack of judgment he granted the landgrave a week's truce, which gave time for the latter's allies, the Count Palatine and the King of Bohemia, to come up. The odds were now against him; he was driven into Erfurt, besieged, and forced secretly to escape to the friendly shelter of the Margrave of Meissen. He returned once more to Erfurt where his army was besieged for a month, but with no better success; he was again compelled to withdraw, this time to Swabia. This Thuringian campaign is particularly conspicuous for that relentless cruelty, that wanton destruction of life and property, which characterised the whole war. Arnold of Lübeck records that no less than sixteen monasteries and three hundred and fifty parish churches were destroyed by the Bohemian army in a campaign that lasted little more than a month.

In August Otto, accompanied by the legate, joined his allies in Thuringia; at Merseburg Herman renewed his homage and Ottokar was crowned by the Pope's legate King of Bohemia[1]. The remainder of the campaign was less successful, and the attempts to win Halle, Halberstadt, and Goslar, were unavailing. But the work of the summer of 1203 taken as a whole was a marked success for the Welfs. For the first time in the course of the war the superiority was on Otto's side. No longer was his influence confined within the narrow limits of the lower Rhine. He had sufficient confidence in the strength of his position to make preparations to carry the war into the heart of the enemy's country, for he proposed at his court at Soest to open the next campaigning season by an attack on Swabia. In November he wrote hopefully to the Pope that his position was improving from day to day[2]. Without undue optimism the Pope might now think that his policy was triumphing; at any rate there was no longer any need to dally with Philip's envoys.

The projected attack on Swabia never matured. Otto had overestimated the strength of his position. The weakness lay in the lack of any real bond to unite his party. Philip could rely on the tradition of his house, which had undeniably done great things for Germany; on the personal attachment and loyalty of the mass of Germans to his family and more especially to himself, for he, perhaps more than any of the Hohenstaufen, was an attractive and even lovable character. Otto could look for no such sentiments towards himself among the German people. Jealousy of the Hohenstaufen, personal gain, petty rivalries, by such slender ties

[1] It appears that Ottokar's other demand, that the bishopric of Prague should be dependent on his kingdom, was also tacitly recognised. See Hauck, *Kirchengeschichte Deutschlands*, IV, 736, n. 4.

[2] That the opposition in southern Germany was breaking up, that the Archbishop of Salzburg, the Dukes of Austria and Bavaria were ready to join him, as he says in this letter (*Reg. de neg. imp.* no. 106), there is little evidence to justify us in believing.

was his party attached to him, and the year 1204 witnesses their unloosing.

A dispute over the inheritance of Count Dietrich of Holland, who died in February, dislocated the Welf party in the Netherlands. The nobility, more interested in the local than in the national quarrel, ranged themselves on the side of one or the other of the disputants and ceased to be concerned in the fortunes of Otto. More serious still was the defection of his own brother Henry. The latter had suffered heavily through the war; he had lost the Palatinate of the Rhine, and not unnaturally expected compensation; but his demands were greater than Otto could afford to satisfy, for they comprised the best part of what remained of the Welf inheritance —Brunswick and the castle of Lichtenberg. Otto refused, and at Burgdorf, near Goslar, when the rival armies were preparing for battle, Henry crossed over to Philip, who rewarded him not only by restoring to him the Palatinate but by giving him in addition the valuable imperial stewardship of Goslar.

This was the first of a series of desertions. Herman and Ottokar came next. Philip devoted the summer to the subjection of Thuringia; the siege of Weissensee, which held out for some six weeks, was the only notable incident in the campaign; Ottokar came to its relief, but the sight of Philip's formidable army daunted him; he left his camp and stole back by night to Bohemia. Herman in despair made his submission (17 September), and it is worthy of remark that on this occasion alone he gained nothing by his changing of sides; indeed he had to give up the fiefs he had acquired by his previous tergiversations. The King of Bohemia was not long in following his example; the payment of a substantial fine brought him again into Philip's good graces.

The desertion of the Landgrave and the Bohemian king from one side or the other had become such a common occurrence that we may believe that little confidence can have been placed in their loyalty; their action in September 1204 can hardly have been a matter for surprise. The desertion of the Rhine princes, the promoters of Otto, in November, although not altogether unexpected, was a much more serious affair. Both the Duke of Brabant and the Archbishop of Cologne had before now shewn signs of wavering in their loyalty, the one in 1201, the other a year later; but in each case the danger had for the time been averted. Nevertheless their grievances had remained, and they made little attempt to conceal their growing discontent. They only awaited a suitable moment for desertion, and that moment came with Otto's misfortunes in the summer of 1204. The success of Philip and the success of Philip's ally, the King of France, over Otto's ally, the King of England, made the time opportune. There was also in the case of the Duke of Brabant the question of Otto's marriage; since 1198 he had been betrothed to the Duke's daughter, and the pledge had been solemnly renewed at the court at Maastricht in 1201, when the papal legate had proclaimed Otto as king. But unaccountably, as it seems to us, Otto had not taken, nor was he apparently proposing to take, any steps to fulfil his engagement. The duke began to entertain other ideas for his daughter's future; a marriage in the other camp might be arranged; Philip's nephew, Frederick of Sicily, was spoken of as a possible and suitable alliance[1]. Philip was prepared to offer very attractive terms to these two; for their desertion would practically complete the ruin of Otto, and besides the confirmation of existing privileges and rich rewards, Philip, perhaps having in mind the possibility of a family alliance, granted to the Duke of Brabant the exceptional privilege that his fiefs might descend in the female line. The Archbishop of Trèves and the Bishops of Constance and Spires acted as mediators, and on 12 November the Archbishop of Cologne and the Duke of Brabant took the oath to Philip at Coblenz. The suffragan bishops of the Cologne diocese followed the example of their metropolitan; the bishops of Münster, Liège, and Osnabrück passed over to the side of Philip. Innocent was enraged at this wholesale desertion. Particularly he vented his wrath on Archbishop Adolf, that son of Belial who had deprived him of victory, who had ruined his hopes of making the Curia the arbiter of the affairs of Europe. Innocent might heap his vituperation upon the deserters, might thunder against them his excommunications, might lay their lands under interdict; he might encourage the few remaining supporters of Otto. But his anathemas and his exhortations were alike unavailing. The position of the Welf party was past retrieving. Only in his native Brunswick and in the city of Cologne was Otto's cause still maintained.

Cologne did not follow the example of its archbishop. They held to their agreement of 1202. If for no other reasons, commercial considerations imperatively demanded that they should remain firm in their loyalty to Otto; for this very year King John had written that the safe-conduct afforded to merchants of Cologne only held good so long as they supported his nephew. So they hounded out their archbishop and gave themselves strenuously to the rebuilding of their walls against Philip's attack, which for the next two years was to be concentrated against their city. As Adolf failed to respond to the threats and to the summons of Innocent, a new archbishop, Bruno of Sayn, the Provost of Bonn, was elected in his place[2].

[1] The suggestion for a marriage with Frederick of Sicily was particularly displeasing to the Pope, who was at that time planning a marriage for his ward with Constance, the widow of Emeric of Hungary and sister of the King of Aragon. See *Reg. de neg. imp.* no. 111. Eventually, in 1207, a marriage was arranged between the duke's son, named like his father Henry, and Philip's daughter Mary (MGH, *Const.* II, p. 15). A long while after, in 1214, Otto did fulfil his early engagement and married Mary, the daughter of the Duke of Brabant; but he had married Philip's daughter Beatrix of Swabia in the interval. She died in 1212.

[2] No German bishop could be found to assist Archbishop Siegfried of Mayence at the consecration, and two bishops had to be summoned from England by the Pope. *Chron. Reg. Colon.* pp. 179, 223.

But the schism thus created only added to the existing troubles; for though Bruno was gratefully welcomed in the city, in the diocese at large Adolf continued to be recognised.

To complete his triumphs, Philip was crowned with his wife Irene at Aix-la-Chapelle by Archbishop Adolf on 6 January 1205—this time by the right man at the right place. His opponents could no longer use the irregularity of his previous coronation by the Archbishop of Tarantaise at Mayence as an excuse for refusing him recognition. His position in Germany had by this second coronation been regularised.

The greater part of the year 1205 was taken up with preparations for the great attack upon Cologne, where the remnant of the Welf faction, the Duke of Limburg and his son Walram, Archbishop Siegfried of Mayence, and the Bishop of Cambrai, were collected. The Rhine was blocked above and below the city to prevent supplies from reaching the garrison; Adolf, whose influence in the neighbourhood of Cologne was very strong, was left to harass it; while Philip himself withdrew to the south to muster his forces. The Dukes of Austria and Bavaria and the Count Palatine of the Rhine joined him with their levies. In September everything was in readiness; the Moselle was crossed, and the army passed without encountering any opposition through Andernach and Bonn. Between Bonn and Cologne Philip halted to refresh his troops and to await the coming of the Duke of Brabant. His camp stretched, we are told, over the better part of two miles, a fact which affords us some idea of the strength of the force considered necessary to wear down the obstinate resistance of the burghers of Cologne. The Duke of Brabant at last made his appearance, immediately quarrelled with his chief, and only agreed to give his services at the price of five hundred marks a week—an illuminating example of the mercenary attitude adopted by the greater number of princes during the civil war.

On 29 September Philip's army was before Cologne, and the attack began. The assault led by the Dukes of Austria and Bavaria lasted five days and resulted in huge losses to both sides. On one occasion Otto, with that impetuous courage which was one of his few redeeming features, sallied from the town, was met by the marshal, Henry of Kalden, and was unhorsed, wounded, and only saved from capture by the bravery of Walram of Limburg. But the main attack failed. For another year the city held out, and the only result of this elaborately planned campaign was the capture of the small town of Neuss in the beginning of October. The season for campaigning was already far advanced; and it had been a bad season, for we hear that even on Philip's march on Cologne in September his troops had suffered terribly from exposure; many horses and some men had perished through the inclemency of the weather; since then they had been through some hard fighting, and the Rhine fleet, left behind at Bonn, with food supplies, munitions, money, and stores of all kinds, had been destroyed by the enemy. It would have been useless to prolong the campaign further. Philip therefore again withdrew to the south in order to make fresh preparation for another attack on the stubborn city in the following year.

This took place in July and, owing to the treason of Duke Henry of Limburg, was decisive. The latter, who was in command at Cologne, instead of keeping his troops within the strongly fortified city, led them out into the open country. Unprepared for the attack and hopelessly outnumbered, they were overwhelmed by Henry of Kalden near the castle of Wassenberg; the bulk of the army was killed or captured; Bruno, the newly consecrated Archbishop of Cologne, was among the prisoners and was thrown in chains into the castle of Trifels; Otto with Walram of Limburg, who, unlike his father, remained loyal, escaped by devious paths to Cologne. This was really the end. Further resistance was clearly useless. Shortly after the battle the two kings had for the first time a personal interview in Philip's camp between Bonn and Cologne; but Otto still obstinately clung to his pretensions and nothing came of it. But if Otto failed to realise that his cause was irretrievably lost, the people of Cologne admitted it. An influential party in the town was favourable to peace with the Hohenstaufen. Their town was practically in a state of blockade; the Rhine and the principal roads leading to the city were closed. The Duke of Brabant acted as mediator, and at Coblenz on 11 November the preliminaries were agreed to. Philip was not vindictive, for the terms which were finally settled in January 1207 were certainly lenient. The main difficulty was what to do about Archbishop Adolf. He had been excommunicated and deprived of his see by the Pope; he had been thrown out of the city by the burghers; but he had made himself extremely useful to Philip during the past two years, and Philip was therefore not prepared to sacrifice him in the moment of victory. It was arranged that the citizens should use their influence with the Pope on Adolf's behalf; but if the Pope would not restore him, they were to accept a bishop of Philip's choosing. Before the capitulation Otto left the city. He betook himself first to Brunswick, whence by the help of Waldemar of Denmark early in 1207 he reached Ripen on the Schleswig coast, and so to his uncle in England.

Innocent had done his best for Otto. But he had his own difficulties to contend with in Italy. The weakness of his position in the lands he had annexed, in Ancona and Spoleto, was revealed when in the autumn of 1204 Lupold, the Hohenstaufen Archbishop of Mayence, had suddenly appeared there with an armed force in the capacity of imperial legate. Philip, flushed with the successes of that year, was, it seems, contemplating an attempt to revive the imperial power in Italy. His legate passed unmolested through Lombardy; for the Lombards had no desire to interfere with the present state of things in Germany which gave them the opportunity they needed to strengthen their political independence. He was welcomed at Ferrara, at Ancona, and at Assisi, to the last of which he granted a charter subsequently confirmed by Philip. Innocent was infuriated not only by the presumption of Philip in sending an imperial legate to Italy at all, but also by the person he sent, a man whom he had excommunicated and deprived of his see. He can scarcely find seemly language with which to refer to this intruder of Mayence, the diabolical Lupold, this pestilent fellow. Lupold was some time in the late summer of 1205 defeated by the papal troops, and made his way back to Germany with but a remnant of his army. But Innocent never forgot the outrage, and when in 1206 he received once more the overtures of Philip, he made the sacrifice of Lupold an indispensable condition.

Innocent's attempt to browbeat the German bishops had signally failed. It was clearly necessary to relax to some extent the unbending attitude he had hitherto adopted. Ludolf of Magdeburg, the loyalest supporter of Philip and the leader of the Hohenstaufen party in Saxony, was in 1205 reconciled with the Pope, and, after his death in August of the same year, his successor, a man of strong Hohenstaufen sympathies, was, after some delay and demur, accepted by the Pope. Conrad, Bishop of Halberstadt, who, rather than take the oath that Innocent had required of him, had gone off to the east, now returned, and though still a staunch adherent of Philip, he too was reconciled with the Pope. A similar change of attitude is perceptible in his relations with Philip himself. In June 1206 he dispatched Wolfger, the Patriarch of Aquileia, to Germany to request Philip to give up Lupold. Philip answered in a long letter, addressed to the Pope himself, remarkable for its sincerity and for its conciliatory tone[1]. It opens with a detailed account, perhaps the most interesting that we possess, of the circumstances that led to his own election and to that of his opponent. He then comes to the crucial question of the moment, the schism in the diocese of Mayence. His proposal is an eminently reasonable one: he will give up Lupold, if Innocent will give up Siegfried; and he is prepared to provide for the latter out of his own revenues until a place of suitable dignity can be found for him. But he cannot agree to having the foremost metropolitan see in Germany in the hands of his avowed enemy. He sees difficulties in the way of a truce with Otto, but on the main point, as he regards it, *pro reformanda pace et concordia inter vos et nos, inter sacerdotium et imperium*, he makes the very sensible suggestion that it should be submitted to a court of arbitration composed of cardinals and German princes.

Innocent in his answer rejected the proposal for the solution of the Mayence difficulty, and continued to press for a truce with Otto. In this last phase of the struggle—the phase of negotiation—it was Innocent rather than Otto that impeded the re-establishment of law and order, for Otto was now almost a negligible factor. Innocent's German policy was anything but disinterested, anything but highminded; it was detrimental alike to the Church and to the people of Germany. It was he who span

[1] MGH, *Const.* II, p. 10 sqq.

out the negotiations, who played for time in the vain hope that, if a long truce could be arranged, Otto might sufficiently recover his resources and with foreign help might even yet come out victorious. Of the three principals concerned, Philip alone sincerely wished to put an end to the business, and with this object was prepared to make any concessions consistent with his dignity and his position as acknowledged King of Germany. So in February 1207 he sent again to the Pope. His ambassadors, Wolfger of Aquileia at their head, were given plenipotentiary powers to settle the questions at issue. But this attempt to hasten matters to a conclusion only led to the dispatch of legates and more tedious delays and more wearisome negotiations. The legates, Ugolino, Cardinal-bishop of Ostia, afterwards Pope Gregory IX, and Leo, Cardinal-priest of Santa Croce, did however accomplish something: they disposed of some of the difficulties that obstructed the path to peace. Philip was released from the papal ban, Bruno of Sayn was liberated from the castle at Trifels, Lupold was virtually abandoned, and Siegfried in effect was recognised by Philip as Archbishop of Mayence. But no progress was made on the main issue between Philip and Otto. The latter was approached to no purpose, for he thought to renew the struggle with the help of foreign powers—England and Denmark. In this he was encouraged by Innocent, who repeatedly urged King John to take more active steps on his nephew's behalf.

In the truce concluded between England and France in the autumn of 1206 the clause of the previous truce forbidding John to assist Otto was omitted. John therefore was at liberty to give what help he would to his defeated nephew when the latter visited the English court early in 1207; he did in fact receive a sum of six thousand marks from the English exchequer on account of Richard's bequest. From the side of Denmark there were also encouraging signs: the conflict of German and Danish interests in Livonia had led Waldemar once more to take an active part on Otto's side, and his enmity to Philip was increased when the Hohenstaufen party at Bremen elected in succession to Archbishop Hartwig in November 1207 Waldemar, Bishop of Schleswig, a most determined enemy of the Danish king. Although therefore with Wassenberg and the capitulation of Cologne the Welf party in Germany may be said to have been practically annihilated, yet there was still a chance that Otto, furnished with foreign gold and foreign troops—there was already a Danish garrison at Brunswick—might at least make Philip's position uncomfortable. So Otto obstinately refused to entertain the idea of renouncing his pretensions. Philip was at Quedlinburg and Otto near Goslar[1]; two interviews took place between them and the legates, at which Philip made handsome offers to compensate his rival; he should marry one of his daughters and have the duchy of Swabia or the kingdom of Arles. But it was to no purpose.

[1] Goslar had been captured by Otto's brother William and Gunzelin of Wolfenbüttel in June 1206. It was the last success of Otto's party during Philip's lifetime.

All that was accomplished was a truce to last till June in the following year.

The legates, and with them Philip's envoys, returned to Rome early in the next year (1208) to report such progress as they had made. Then it was that Innocent capitulated: he recognised Philip as king and promised him the imperial crown. In a moment he threw up the claims upon which he had been so insistent, of being the arbiter in the German election and of examining the fitness of the person elected. He even yielded his claim to the lands he had annexed in central Italy—Tuscany, the March of Ancona, the Duchy of Spoleto. To what was this sudden and extraordinary reversal of policy due? Was it indignation at the obstinacy of Otto or was it the effect of a personal bribe? for among the conditions of peace it was agreed that Philip's daughter Beatrix should marry the Pope's nephew, and this nephew should be enfeoffed with these disputed lands in Central Italy[1]. The legates once more set out for Germany in order to clear up the few outstanding difficulties that yet remained; they were still on their journey when the news of Philip's death reached them.

Philip was at Bamberg, where his army had been mobilised, awaiting the expiration of the truce (24 June) to deal a decisive blow against his rival. On the 21st he attended the wedding of his niece Beatrix and the Duke of Meran; he had retired to his quarters in the bishop's palace to rest after the fatigues of the morning when he was struck down in revenge for a private grievance by Otto of Wittelsbach, Count Palatine of Bavaria. The murderer escaped; but it is to the credit of Otto that one of his first acts as undisputed king was the punishment of his late opponent's assassin. He was put under the ban of the Empire, hunted down in a barn near Ratisbon, and slain by that most faithful of Hohenstaufen *ministeriales*, Henry of Kalden (March 1209).

The German princes were wearied of wars. To raise Frederick to the throne would have made a continuance of the civil war inevitable. It would also involve them in difficulties with Innocent, who would go to almost any lengths to avoid the union of Sicily with the Empire, and who wrote at once on hearing the news of Philip's death to the bishops bidding them under no circumstances to permit the election of a new candidate. Innocent would be interfering once more in German affairs, causing schisms in the dioceses, throwing broadcast his excommunications, besieging the princes with letters. They had had enough of this sort of thing, they longed for a little peace and quiet. Otto's course, if he behaved sensibly, was an easy one. The first step was taken only a week or so after Philip's murder by Albert, Archbishop of Magdeburg, the leader of the Hohenstaufen party in Saxony; he visited Otto in his camp at Sommerschenburg and came to terms with him, much to the advantage of his church, his diocese, his family, and himself[2]. But apart from this personal reconciliation he gained

[1] Burchard, p. 88. He qualifies his statement with the words "ut retulerunt nobis viri veridici." Cf. the clause in the proposed terms of 1203, *supra*, p. 63.

[2] MGH, *Const.* II, p. 30 sq.

his main object, for he persuaded Otto not to thrust his way to the throne by force of arms, taking his stand on the validity of his election in 1197, but to submit himself peaceably to a fresh election and to trust to the diplomacy and the conciliatory endeavours of the archbishop to induce the princes to accept him. To this point the princes attached great weight, and in fact Otto, in a compliant mood, dated his documents for a week or two after his election at Frankfort as in the first year of his reign. But he soon gave it up; the end of the year 1208 is in his documents no longer the first but the eleventh year of his reign[1].

In the north-east of Germany Otto's position was a strong one. The influential Wettin and Ascanian families even before Philip's death had shewn some inclination to join him; the promise to abandon the Danish alliance and to re-establish Count Adolf in Holstein brought the rest of the border nobles to his side; and a gathering of Saxons and Thuringians summoned by Archbishop Albert to Halberstadt on 22 September[2] accepted him unanimously. The Count Palatine reverted again to his brother. The two Welf Archbishops of Mayence and Cologne, Siegfried and Bruno, who were at the time of Philip's murder at Rome prosecuting their claims against their respective anti-bishops, immediately hastened home and were able to use their influence on behalf of Otto, to whom, at least indirectly, they owed their promotion. The Hohenstaufen *ministeriales* were brought over in a body by their leader Henry of Kalden, and even the strongest supporter and intimate friend of Philip, Conrad, Bishop of Spires, adopted the same course. Louis of Bavaria, who hesitated for some time, was finally won by the grant of the confiscated fiefs of Philip's murderer. The betrothal of Otto to Philip's daughter Beatrix, formally carried out in the following May when the legates brought the papal dispensation for a marriage within the prohibited degrees, did much to reconcile the Hohenstaufen party to the idea of a Welf king. The only real opposition came from France. Philip Augustus, who had a dread of a Welf on the throne of Germany, supported by Philip's widow Irene, put up Henry of Brabant. But Irene died in August, and the nobles of the lower Rhine did not fall in with the proposal, which was accordingly dropped. The few princes, the King of Bohemia and his brother, the Duke of Moravia, the Dukes of Zähringen, Lorraine, and Brabant, who still hung back, offered no resistance, and indeed accepted the *fait accompli* at the diet of Würzburg (24 May 1209).

There could have been little doubt what the result of the election at Frankfurt on 11 November would be. The fifty-five princes who attended were unanimous. The Franconians, Bavarians, and Swabians who had not been present at the meeting at Halberstadt now formally recognised Otto. The business was concluded by the promulgation of a general land peace,

[1] Böhmer, *Regesta*, v. nos. 244, 245, 246.

[2] On the disputed date of this meeting see Böhmer, *Regesta*, v. no. 240 c. Winkelmann, *Otto IV*, p. 111, n. 4 accepts the date given in the *Magdeburger Schöppenchronik*, 25 July.

"all the princes swore to keep the peace by land and sea," and, wrote Otto of St Blaise, "the troubled kingdom enjoyed a rest for a little while."

Innocent III regarded the murder of Philip as the judgment of God, and worked busily for Otto in these months, encouraging his supporters, exhorting those who hesitated, threatening those who opposed. Otto was deeply grateful to the Pope and humbly submissive: *quod hactenus fuimus*, he wrote to him in July, *quod sumus aut erimus, quantum ad regni pertinet promotionem, totum vobis et ecclesie Romane post Deum debentes, quod et gratantissime recognoscimus*[1]. The Pope could not wish for fuller acknowledgment of his services. But he intended to profit by the favourable opportunity to increase permanently the influence of the Curia and its authority over the German Church, and at least on paper he got what he wanted. On 22 March 1209 from Spires Otto issued a diploma by which he acknowledged the territorial claims of the Papacy in their widest extent; further he permitted unrestricted appeals to Rome in ecclesiastical causes; he renounced not only the right of appropriating the moveable property of a deceased bishop (*Spolienrecht*) as he had done in 1198 and 1201, but also the right to the revenues of vacant churches (*Regalienrecht*). As regards ecclesiastical elections, he practically surrendered all those rights which had been preserved for the Emperor by the Concordat of Worms. Briefly, he resigned that control over the German Church which his predecessors, and particularly Frederick I and Henry VI, had exercised, on the whole to the mutual advantage of Church and State alike, since the days of Otto the Great.

What is remarkable is that this document made far wider concessions than that issued at Neuss at the moment of Otto's deepest abasement, when the Pope's help alone could save him. He was now king without a rival, and king not "by the grace of the Pope" as he used to style himself, but by the unanimous election of the German princes. There was no need in 1209 as there had been in 1201 to make an abject submission to the Pope. Innocent was, however, soon to learn the value of such promises. It is more than probable that Otto never seriously intended to abide by them. It was easy enough to say, as he did say later, that they were not binding on the ground that they had not received the sanction of the princes. There are indications during the months in which he was making his preparations for the expedition to Rome that he was contemplating the re-establishment of imperial power in Italy, that he, the Welf, was purposing to adopt the Hohenstaufen policy. In his relations with Italy he was guided by the Patriarch of Aquileia, whole-heartedly Hohenstaufen in outlook, whom he made imperial legate with the widest powers[2] and sent across the Alps to prepare the ground for his own coming to Italy.

In August he led the army which had assembled at Augsburg across

[1] MGH, *Const.* II, p. 32.

[2] See the royal encyclical to the Italians announcing his appointment, MGH, *Const.* II, p. 33.

the Brenner; in October he received the imperial crown[1]. His actions even before the coronation clearly reveal his intention to pursue, despite his promises, the policy of Henry VI in central Italy. As time went on his design became more ambitious and more aggressive. Before the end of the year 1209 he was planning with Diepold, whom he appointed Duke of Spoleto (February 1210), with the Pisans, and with the disaffected barons of Apulia, the conquest of Sicily; and it is clear from a letter Innocent wrote to the Sicilian chancellor, Walter of Palear, which may perhaps be dated as early as December 1209, that he, Innocent, knew of the Emperor's intentions[2]. It was the cause of the quarrel. Already in January 1210 Innocent wrote to the Bishop of Ratisbon complaining of Otto's ingratitude, and of his persecution of the Church and of the orphaned Frederick; for against Frederick also Otto entertained a strong and growing antipathy, which was not lessened by the fact that Frederick shewed that he did not regard himself merely as King of Sicily but as Duke of Swabia and the heir to the Hohenstaufen family possessions[3]. Innocent shewed on the whole greater forbearance than might have been expected under such provocative circumstances. For a time he contented himself with complaints, warnings, and threats; and with quietly stirring up agitation against him in Germany and the Italian cities[4]. But Otto paid no heed; he only became more aggressive. In August he launched his attack against the Tuscan patrimony, and in November began his conquest of Apulia. Then it was that Innocent carried out his threats, published the sentence of excommunication against the Emperor and released his subjects from their oath of allegiance.

From the beginning of the year the Pope had been in close correspondence with Philip Augustus who, for his part, had been energetically engaged in working up discontent among the princes of Germany. But their aims were not quite similar. Innocent, it would seem, had grave misgiving about bringing forward the only alternative to Otto, Frederick; for it would mean the sacrifice of all that he had been fighting for, the separation of Sicily and the Empire. He still therefore clung to the idea of a reconciliation with Otto. Innocent's hope was that a rebellion in Germany would merely force Otto to abandon his campaign against Sicily. But this was not at all the view of Philip Augustus and of the group of princes associated with him; they wanted to get rid of Otto once and for

[1] For the details of Otto's Italian campaign see *infra,* Chap v, pp. 137–8.

[2] See Hampe, *Beiträge zur Geschichte Kaiser Friedrichs II,* HVJS (1901), pp. 172 sq. The letter is printed *ibid.* p. 193.

[3] *Ibid.* p. 173. Böhmer, *Regesta,* nos. 622, 623. Frederick was prepared to give up his claim to the family inheritance in Swabia according to a passage in the Continuation of the Annals of Admont, MGH, *Script.* IX, 591, *sub anno* 1210 (September 29? Böhmer, *Regesta,* no. 439 sq.) if Otto would leave him in undisturbed possession of Sicily.

[4] On 28 February 1210 Perugia agreed to give armed support to the Pope against the Emperor. Böhmer, *Regesta,* no. 6082 a.

all; they were ready to rebel, but only if the Pope would agree to their conditions: namely, that he would never make peace with Otto, that he would pronounce their release from their oath of allegiance, and finally consent to the election of a new king. Innocent, however, was not yet prepared to take so decided a step; he tried once more to negotiate with Otto, and only when this failed did he repeat the sentence of excommunication (March 1211). In the meantime opinion in Germany was tending more and more in the direction of revolt. Philip of France had found a ready agent in the Landgrave of Thuringia[1], and with him was soon associated the scarcely less shifty King of Bohemia. These two with Siegfried of Mayence appear to have taken the lead at the diet of Bamberg where Frederick's election was for the first time openly proposed; but the meeting was divided; more canvassing and more negotiating were required before the proposal was accepted at the diet of Nuremberg in September 1211.

The news of the rebellion determined Otto, who had conquered Apulia, to desist from the attack on Sicily and to return home. But he can have scarcely realised the full extent of the danger, for he did not hurry his journey. He set out from Calabria in the beginning of November; he did not reach Germany till the following March. *Gravis Italicis, Alamannis gravior, suis ingratus fines attigit Alamannie; a nullo sibi principe occurritur; nulli gratus excipitur.* Such, according to the contemporary monk of St Gall, Conrad of Fabaria, was the gloomy welcome Otto met with on his return to his native land. He was never popular, he had never gained the affections of his subjects. Nevertheless his presence in Germany did to some extent check the tide of revolt. At Frankfort in March the Duke of Bavaria and the Margrave of Meissen joined him; the Duke of Austria followed their example shortly after. The Duke of Brabant and the Count Palatine were still loyal, and a number of the smaller nobility attended his court during the first months after his return. Dietrich of Cologne, who in spite of the papal ban continued to support Otto, was deposed by Siegfried of Mayence in virtue of his legatine authority; and the former archbishop Adolf was re-established in his place. But Cologne, true to its Welf tradition, clung to its Welf archbishop, and would have nothing to do with Adolf; only the clergy accepted him.

Otto himself acted swiftly against the leaders of the rebellion. He deprived Ottokar of his kingdom (March) and he led his army against Herman (July). He had taken several Thuringian strongholds and was besieging Weissensee when he heard the news that Frederick, the priests' king (*rex presbyterorum*)[2] as he contemptuously called him, was on his way to Germany. With the hope of retaining the support of at least some of the Hohenstaufen party, he now hurriedly married Beatrix, to whom he

[1] Philip Augustus agreed to marry the Landgrave's daughter provided that the Pope could be induced to grant a divorce from Ingeborg. See Hampe, *op. cit.* p. 190, n. 4.

[2] This was one of the counts brought against Otto at the Lateran Council.

had been betrothed since 1209. But it failed in its purpose, for she died within three weeks of her marriage (August 11). Swabia and Bavaria declared for Frederick, and Otto in alarm threw up the siege of Weissensee and turned southward to meet his new rival.

Frederick, after some hesitation and against the advice of his wife Constance and many of his Sicilian councillors, had accepted the offer of the German crown made by the princes at the diet of Nuremberg. In the spring he set out on his journey, and travelling by way of Rome and Genoa, and thence across Lombardy, he reached Trent only to find the Brenner barred against him. Turning north-west along the valley of the Adige, he made his way, probably over the Ofen and Flüela passes[1], to Chur and so down the Rhine to Constance. He arrived there in the nick of time, three hours before Otto, who by forced marches had hastened from Thuringia to prevent his entering Germany. Arriving too late, Otto retired down the Rhine, and tried again to check his advance at Breisach. But the citizens there revolted and he had to save himself by a rapid retreat to the friendly shelter of Cologne. Frederick too moved from Constance slowly down the Rhine, the number of his supporters continually increasing as he went; even Louis of Bavaria, who had so recently made a solemn compact with Otto, was among these new adherents. He reached Frankfort, where he was formally elected on 5 December. Four days later he was crowned by Archbishop Siegfried in the Cathedral of Mayence.

The parties were fairly evenly divided: Frederick was the accepted king in South Germany, in Bohemia—for he had reinstated Ottokar in his kingdom (Basle, 26 September)—and in Thuringia. He held the Palatinate which Henry resigned in favour of his son and namesake; the son joined Frederick, while the father withdrew northward to defend the family estates round Brunswick for his brother. The lower Rhine districts and the greater part of North Germany, and especially the north-east, still stood by the Emperor; for the Ascanian house in Saxony and Brandenburg and the Wettin in Meissen and the East Mark remained loyal. The campaigning of the summer of 1213 was on the whole uneventful and indecisive. In June Otto took the offensive against the Archbishop of Magdeburg, who once again headed the Hohenstaufen party in Saxony, won a victory over him (Remkersleben, 11 June), and for a brief moment held him a prisoner. But it seldom came to an engagement in the open field; the campaign for the most part consisted of the usual ineffective plundering raids, devastations of property, sieges, but rarely captures, of castles. Frederick, who joined in the fighting in September, did achieve one success: he managed to detach the powerful Margrave Dietrich from the side of Otto.

But the result of this somewhat dreary warfare left the position of parties very little altered. More important, more interesting, and in the

[1] Or, more probably, Coolidge thinks, by the Tonale, Aprica, and Septimer passes (*The Alps in Nature and History*, pp. 185, 189 sq.).

end more decisive, was the international aspect of the struggle. In the first place there was the Pope who required from Frederick what he had required from Otto, but this time with some kind of guarantee that the concessions granted would be carried out. The importance of the Golden Bull of Eger (12 July 1213) which *mutatis mutandis* is a verbal transcript of Otto's grant made at Spires in 1209, lies in the fact that unlike its prototype it received the sanction of a large number of distinguished and influential princes. Three archbishops, four bishops, the King of Bohemia, the Dukes of Bavaria and Austria, the Landgrave of Thuringia, and several counts and *ministeriales* set their signatures to the document, which thus became a properly executed law of the Empire. By its terms the territorial aspirations of the Papacy were recognised in their fullest extent; the German Church was emancipated from imperial control[1].

Innocent, however, was hampered in his diplomatic relations by the fact that Otto, his bitterest enemy, was allied with King John who, after his submission in May 1213, was his feudal dependant; he was forced to do what he could to curb the efforts of Frederick's ally, Philip, to crush Frederick's enemy, John. In this Innocent failed, and in the end John, his protégé, was involved in the ruin of Otto, his enemy, at the hands of Philip of France.

Frederick, who owed his promotion mainly to the zealous intrigues of Philip, had, before his coronation at Frankfort, held an interview with Louis, the French king's heir, at Vaucouleurs (19 November 1212) and concluded an alliance with him and received a substantial subsidy. Likewise, similarity of circumstances and of interests drew John of England into closer alliance with his nephew; before May 1213, when John submitted to the Pope, it was only natural that the two excommunicated sovereigns should make common cause against their common enemies. English subsidies poured into Germany during the year 1212. Both sides indeed depended mainly on their allies for financial support, for neither could rely to any extent on the resources of the kingdom, so chaotic had become the financial organisation after sixteen years of civil war[2]. Both sides were busy buying the support of the venal princes of Germany, Frederick with French, Otto with English money.

Frederick had made less headway than his initial successes would have led one to anticipate. The French fleet for the invasion of England had been destroyed in a harbour on the Flemish coast near Bruges. Otto was confident, and planned with John a joint attack against their common enemy Philip Augustus. In the spring of 1214 he was busily engaged with preparations, trying to introduce some harmony among the quarrelsome nobles of the Netherlands; in May, in order to bind the restless and

[1] MGH, *Const.* II, pp. 57 sqq. The renunciation of the *ius spolii* and the *ius regaliae* was repeated in 1216. *Ibid.* pp. 67 sqq.

[2] Otto in 1212 even considered making brothels a source of state revenue. *Chron. Reinhardsbrunn.* MGH, *Script.* XXX, 583.

unstable Duke Henry of Brabant more firmly to his side, he married his daughter Mary, and so at this eleventh hour carried out the engagement into which he had entered seventeen years before. His efforts to make the princes of the lower Rhine work together were successful. Nearly all of them brought their levies in July to Nivelles, south of Brussels, which had been fixed as the starting point of the campaign[1]. This army, despite the advantage of numbers and position, despite the reckless bravery which Otto himself displayed, was almost annihilated on the field of Bouvines near Lille on 27 July 1214.

The battle was decisive. Otto with the remnant of his army made his way to Cologne. Frederick, who had taken no part in the campaign, was not slow to take advantage of the discomfiture of his rival; soon after the battle he crossed the Moselle and received the submission of the princes of the Netherlands. The Welf interest in the Palatinate had also in this year become extinct with the death of the younger Henry. It was granted to the Duke of Bavaria, and his son Otto, who, by marrying Agnes, the daughter of the elder Henry, Count Palatine, acquired too the allodial estates of the Welfs in that neighbourhood. In this manner the Palatinate as well as the dukedom of Bavaria came into the hands of the powerful house of Wittelsbach.

The whole Rhineland was now Frederick's but for Cologne, Aix-la-Chapelle, and the imperial palace at Kaiserswerth. These too fell into his hands in the campaign of the following summer. He entered Aix-la-Chapelle on 4 July 1215, and on the next day, adopting the precedent of Philip, was crowned a second time in the traditional place of coronations. He also on this occasion, to the surprise of his court and to his own lasting regret, took the crusading vow, which, while it satisfied Innocent of the good intentions of his former ward, was to cause all manner of trouble between the Emperor and Innocent's successors. With the surrender of Kaiserswerth on 24 July and of Cologne on 4 August the Welf resistance in the west was at an end.

Before the capitulation of Cologne Otto had betaken himself to Saxony, where he could still reckon on substantial support: there was his brother Henry at Brunswick and a powerful group of nobles on the north-east frontier who strongly resented the attitude Frederick adopted in German-Danish politics; for in December 1214 he had ceded to Waldemar Nordalbingia, that is to say, the country north of the rivers Elbe and Elde, a district in which many of these border nobles had important interests. Frederick's campaign in the beginning of 1215 had done nothing to break down this opposition. So for a time the struggle dragged on in this region, Albert, Archbishop of Magdeburg, and Waldemar of Denmark on the one side, Otto, his brother Henry, and the Ascanian family on the other. The long-continued fighting, however, wore down the strength of the Welf armies; the widespread devastations of the country caused a serious

[1] For the details of the campaign and of the battle of Bouvines, see *infra*, chap. IX.

shortage of supplies; no foreign power was prepared to waste its energies on a cause already lost. The Lateran Council, which confirmed the result of the German civil war by the formal deposition of Otto and recognition of Frederick, hastened the end and brought many waverers to the winning side. When Frederick in September 1217 again took the field in person he found his opponent too weak to risk a battle in the open. But a decisive action was not needed; Frederick's presence was in itself sufficient to break down further serious resistance.

Otto himself fought on with dogged perseverance and unfailing courage, still claiming to be Emperor, but an Emperor almost without subjects and without land, till an over-dose of medicine prematurely ended his life at the Harzburg on 19 May 1218. Henry complied with his brother's request expressed in his will executed the day before he died and retained in his possession the imperial insignia for a period of twenty weeks. He then delivered them over to Frederick. With the submission of Henry and of the Duke of Saxony, who alone among the leading nobility had remained true to Otto to the last, the opposition to the Hohenstaufen was at an end. The family estates of the Welfs passed to Otto, son of the Emperor's younger brother William, who regained the confidence of the rival family, was created Duke of Brunswick-Lüneburg by Frederick, and was the ancestor of the long line of Welfs, who eventually in the twelfth generation acquired the throne of England.

CHAPTER III.

GERMANY IN THE REIGN OF FREDERICK II.

The civil war had had disastrous results for Germany. Philip, Otto, and Frederick, in order to win the support of powerful nobles, churches, towns, had granted away lands, privileges, rights, prerogatives, all that had in the past meant the strength of the German kingdom and of the Holy Roman Empire. The Church had been emancipated from royal control; the princes of the Empire were becoming more and more independent, they were rapidly changing into territorial sovereigns, *domini terrae* as they are designated in the famous privilege of 1231; the towns had come to realise their strength, had proved themselves to be a power to be reckoned with. Slowly but surely Germany was moving along the path of dissolution, was becoming a conglomeration of semi-independent princedoms instead of a unified State. Frederick's German policy, as we shall see, far from checking it, all tended to hasten the course of this movement. He alienated with a lavish hand the royal rights in favour of the princes, and especially the ecclesiastical princes on whose support during the greater part of his reign he principally relied. Such a policy, however unfortunate in its results, was perhaps inevitable when there were two rival kings, each of whom could only gain or keep the adherence of powerful lords by outbidding his opponent. But when with the death of Otto in 1218 the real need for it had passed, the number of grants of privileges, instead of diminishing, enormously increased. So we find Frederick in these years moving about his kingdom conciliating his subjects to his rule, rewarding the loyalty of some, buying the favour of others, settling disputes, and attempting to restore some semblance of order in the land—always by the expensive and disastrous method of sacrificing the regalian rights. When the business of the Empire did not require his presence elsewhere, he would take up his residence at Spires or Nuremberg which had always been conspicuous for their attachment to the house of Hohenstaufen, or still more frequently at Hagenau in Alsace; the fine palace there, built by his grandfather, was his favourite home north of the Alps, *inter alia patrimonialia cariorem*, and there he would spend months at a time busily engaged in granting away the lands and rights of the Empire.

The compliant, we might almost say weak, attitude that Frederick adopted towards the princes is exemplified early in his reign at the diet of Würzburg on 15 May 1216 when he issued the *Sententia de non alienandis principatibus*. By an arrangement with the Bishop of Ratisbon, Frederick had alienated by exchange the two imperial abbeys of Ober- and

Niedermünster. The abbesses, who were not consulted in the transaction, made their complaint at the diet of Würzburg. The princes, who regarded the precedent as a dangerous one, not only got the exchange annulled, but forced Frederick to make a general declaration against such alienations in the future, "that no principality could or ought to be exchanged or alienated from the Empire or be transferred to another prince against the will of the prince of that principality and without the full consent of the *ministeriales*." The same fear of irritating and so losing the support of the ecclesiastical princes is perceptible in his policy towards the towns. As regards the imperial towns he acted with his customary liberality; so Aix-la-Chapelle (1215), Goslar and Nuremberg (1219), Dortmund (1220) received very ample charters of privileges. He would have liked to adopt the same policy towards the seignorial towns if the lords would have let him; but when he tried it, he met with a rebuff. In 1215 he was obliged at the instance of the bishop to deprive the citizens of Cambrai of the privileges they had received from him only a year before; again, in 1218 he recognised the *rath* set up by the citizens of Basle, but the bishop complained, and the recognition had to be withdrawn.

It may be argued in excuse of Frederick's policy that the princes had grown over-powerful during the civil war, they were already past controlling, and they had learnt how to use their strength to their own advantage; but in this Otto's death made a difference. For although for the last two years of his life Otto had not been a serious menace to Frederick's position, his very existence had given opportunities to discontented nobles to rise in rebellion. Herman, the Landgrave of Thuringia, was, it seems, contemplating yet another desertion, notwithstanding the fact that it was his own intrigues which were largely responsible for Frederick's summons to Germany, when death, on 25 April 1217, happily removed him from the field of politics. Perhaps the most conspicuous, but also one of the most treacherous characters in the civil war, he had by his repeated changes from one side to the other profoundly influenced the fortunes of the parties; he was dangerous as an opponent, but almost equally so as an ally. One could wish that he had kept out of politics and devoted himself altogether to patronage of the arts, to minstrels' contests, and to the entertainment of the somewhat indiscriminate collection of artistic and literary men that Walther von der Vogelweide tells us gathered together at the Wartburg. For in these things he was without a master. His son Louis was a more stable character, a loyal friend, not obsessed with a love of intrigue and gain, the husband of the austere St Elizabeth, at whose inspiration he was led to follow a life of piety and good works.

Another prominent figure of the civil war, the man first chosen to contest the crown with Philip, Berthold V of Zähringen, died a month or two before Otto (18 February 1218). But after giving up his candidature for the throne he had joined Philip, and, except for the short period of Otto's uncontested power, he had been a fairly steady adherent of the

Hohenstaufen party. His death was the cause of trouble and confusion, for he left sisters and cousins but no children. The inheritance was a rich one, comprising large tracts of Jurane Burgundy[1] and Swabia, and was keenly sought after by the relatives and by Frederick himself, who, in his anxiety to get what he could out of it, went so far as to buy out the claim of one of the collaterals, the Duke of Teck. A partition of the estate satisfactory to the parties concerned was ultimately arranged at Ulm in September 1219: the lands on the right bank of the Aar fell to one brother-in-law of the late duke, the Count of Kyburg, while those mainly situated north of the Rhine, the district of the Black Forest and Breisgau, went to the other, Egeno Count of Urach; Frederick's share was considerable; it included much of what is now northern Switzerland and the towns of Bern, Zürich, Schaffhausen, and Solothurn, which were soon raised to the position of imperial cities. The extinction of the house of Zähringen had another important consequence: it broke one of the real ties between Germany and the kingdom of Burgundy, over which the Dukes of Zähringen had intermittently exercised authority in the capacity of rectors. This title was later conferred upon the young King Henry[2]; but in the hands of a boy of nine years old it could have been little more than a title. From the point of view of German influence in the Arelate, the childless death of Berthold of Zähringen was a serious loss[3].

There had been troubles also in Bohemia, which, in consequence of a quarrel between King Ottokar and the Bishop of Prague, had been laid under interdict, and in Lorraine where Duke Theobald, by an unjustifiable interference in a dispute in the neighbouring Champagne, had gravely endangered the Franco-German alliance. It led in fact to a quarrel with Frederick, and Theobald declared for Otto (1216). The king took arms against him, occupied his duchy, and ultimately brought him to submission (June 1218). Nevertheless the enmity continued, and when, a little more than a year later, this prince met his end by poison administered by a harlot, common report attributed the instigation of the act to Frederick[4].

Although Frederick was recognised as king throughout Germany he was still without the symbols of his office, the royal insignia; these Otto's brother, the ex-Count Palatine Henry, obstinately clung to even after the

[1] Now part of Switzerland.

[2] He first used the title in a document of 4 January 1220, Böhmer, *Regesta*, v, no. 1081.

[3] Frederick had certainly paid more attention to the affairs of Burgundy than many of his predecessors. In November 1214 he had spent five busy days at Basle dealing with Burgundian matters, and in January of the following year he had tried the expedient of setting up an under-king in the person of William of Baux, Prince of Orange, over the *regnum Vienense, quod et Arelatense dicitur*; but this too was but an empty title, for William seems to have exercised no influence as king, and died two years after his appointment.

[4] Richer, *Gesta Senonensis Ecclesiae*, MGH, *Script.* xxv, p. 300.

period of twenty weeks fixed for their retention by Otto in his testament. Pope Honorius, anxious to remove every obstacle to Frederick's departure for the Crusade, was urgent with entreaties and threats which at last had the desired result. At Goslar in July 1219 Henry accepted the advantageous conditions Frederick was prepared to offer: he surrendered the insignia in return for 11,000 marks and the office of imperial vicar in the lands between the Weser and the Elbe. This was the end of the long struggle between the families of Welf and Hohenstaufen which had begun far back in the twelfth century with the rivalry of Henry the Proud and the first Hohenstaufen king Conrad. The people of Germany could once more devote themselves to the occupations of peace; they could, as the Magdeburg chronicle puts it, again begin to work the land and sow corn[1].

But with the establishment of peace the question of the Crusade had to be faced. There can be no doubt that, when at his coronation at Aix-la-Chapelle in 1215 Frederick had taken the crusading vow, he had done so in all sincerity. Nor had he been urged to it by an importunate legate; he had taken the vow of his own free will. The early postponements were the necessary results of the political situation in Germany. It was imperative that he should restore some sort of order into the country which had just passed through nearly twenty years of civil war before setting out for a prolonged absence in the East. On 1 June 1216, the date appointed by the Lateran Council for departure, his rival was still living and the affairs of Germany were in chaos. There was no question of Frederick going. So in the summer of 1217 the Crusade started without him. But on 24 June 1218, the date to which his departure had been deferred, although Otto was dead, Frederick had, as we have seen, other difficulties to deal with before he could safely set out upon his journey, and particularly the resistance of Otto's brother Henry; this was put forward as the need for a further delay, in which Honorius acquiesced without much demur. It was postponed for a year, and then once more on the same grounds for another three months—till Michaelmas 1219. But after this the excuses became more slender, and Honorius correspondingly was more loth to accept them. When in October, in response to Frederick's renewed request for delay, he fixed a third term for March 1220, he threw out a hint of excommunication in the event of the non-fulfilment of his vow[2].

Honorius, wholly absorbed with the idea of carrying through the Crusade, was anxious to avoid doing anything which might hinder its accomplishment; and of this attitude Frederick took the fullest advantage in the matter of Sicily and the election of his son Henry as King of the Romans. It was these things that occupied his attention during the last months of his stay in Germany. On 1 July 1216 he had taken a solemn oath to Innocent III that as soon as he should be crowned Emperor he

[1] *Magdeburger Schöppenchronik* (*Chroniken der deutschen Städte,* VII, p. 143) quoted by Jastrow and Winter, II, p. 263.

[2] MGH, *Epistolae Saec. XIII,* i, nos. 95, 97, 106, and 112.

would altogether resign the kingdom of Sicily to his son Henry, who had already been crowned king in 1212; he was to hold it of the Roman Church, be released from all paternal control, and due provision was made for its government during his minority. The object of this arrangement was to avoid the union of Sicily and the Empire in the hands of Frederick; a union in the hands of his son, not contemplated at the time, without being opposed to the actual wording of the oath, was none the less opposed to its intention. But Frederick could not lightly renounce the home of his childhood, his hereditary kingdom, the one spot in Europe perhaps where his astonishing character was really understood. His plan was somewhat to reverse the parts; he was to rule Sicily, his son Germany. We find him pleading with Honorius for a relaxation of the conditions of his oath to Innocent. On 10 February 1220 he repeated the promise with the proviso that he might succeed his son on the throne of Sicily in the event of the latter predeceasing him without children; on the 19 February he begged the Pope to allow him to retain the kingdom of Sicily during his own lifetime. That it was his intention to root his son in Germany is equally unmistakeable. In 1216 the boy with his mother, Queen Constance, was brought to Germany. He was created Duke of Swabia in 1217 and Rector of Burgundy in 1220[1]. Frederick now meant, if he could manage it, to get him elected King of the Romans.

His intention was apparently known and complained of at the papal court early in 1219, for in May Frederick wrote stating his motives: they were to ensure the good government of the Empire during his absence on crusade and to secure for his son the possessions of his house in the event of anything befalling him in the East. But the anxiety at Rome was not allayed, and after the election, which took place at the diet of Frankfort in April 1220, Frederick wrote his excuses to Honorius, protesting his entire ignorance of the whole affair, *nobis insciis et absentibus*, and that it had been done by the princes owing to a dispute between the Archbishop of Mayence and the Landgrave of Thuringia which threatened to lead to civil war; he even professed that he had refused his consent until it had been ratified by the Pope[2]. That the election of a child could avert civil disturbances was of course absurd, moreover it was wholly untrue that he refused his consent, for it was in grateful acknowledgement of their act that he made on 26 April the famous *privilegium in favorem principum ecclesiasticorum*, which indeed was framed with the very object of inducing the ecclesiastical princes to permit that to which they were naturally keenly opposed. They were opposed to it both on he ground that it implied that the kingship was in fact hereditary, and because it ran counter to the whole trend of papal

[1] Böhmer, *Regesta*, nos. 892 and 1081. After 1218 his title of King of Sicily no longer appears in documents, *ibid.* no. 3346 g.

[2] Winkelmann, *Acta imperii*, I, p. 156. Cf. also the letter of the Chancellor Conrad, Bishop of Metz, MGH, *Epp. Saec. XIII*, I, p. 92.

policy. Only the most far-reaching concessions could tempt them to ignore the remonstrances of Rome; but Frederick to gain his end was prepared to grant them far-reaching concessions, and they yielded.

Frederick, after repeating his former renunciation of the *ius spolii*, granted to the ecclesiastical princes free testamentary power; he renounced the right of imposing new tolls and mints within their territories and jurisdictions without their consent, while he recognised all tolls and rights of coinage which had already been conceded to them; he denied to the serf of the ecclesiastical prince the method of gaining his freedom by residence in a city for a year and a day. The abuse of power by the steward (*advocatus*, *vogt*) was checked by making him liable to a fine of 100 marks for damage done to the property of churches[1], and the jurisdiction of royal officials in episcopal cities was restricted to eight days preceding and following the holding of a diet. He placed the man excommunicated by the Church beyond the pale of the courts; he may neither act as witness or plaintiff; he may only appear as the defendant to charges brought against him, and then he is denied the assistance of an advocate; if after six weeks he has failed to get absolution, he falls under the ban of the Empire, *quia gladius materialis constitutus est in subsidium gladii spiritualis*. So too Frederick surrendered the right of erecting castles and cities on church lands[2].

By the Bull of Eger the German Church had been emancipated from the imperial control; the old influence exercised by the Crown over elections was no more; disputed elections came to be decided at Rome; only the bare formal investiture with the regalia remained to the king. By the *privilegium* of 1220 and subsequent additions made by Frederick and his son, the ecclesiastical princes became territorial sovereigns. By a clause in the constitution issued at the time of his coronation at Rome Frederick exempted the clergy altogether from secular jurisdiction both in civil and criminal causes[3]. Moreover, as the influence of the Crown in ecclesiastical matters diminished, the influence of the Papacy proportionately increased. Papal legates and papal agents were constantly resident in Germany, exercising authority over the Church in all kinds of ways, especially over matters of discipline and heresy[4], developing by this means the papal policy of centralisation. Frederick was led to adopt this policy so injurious to the position of the Crown, not because he was particularly interested in the welfare of the Church, but because it served, or at least he thought it served, his purpose; he was anxious to devote his attention to Italy and to Sicily, and for this it was essential that Germany should remain at peace, which he believed could be most easily

[1] The abuse of power by stewards of churches was effectively dealt with in 1234 by the *Sententia in favorem ecclesiarum*, MGH, *Const.* II, pp. 228 sq.

[2] MGH, *Const.* II, pp. 86 sqq.

[3] MGH, *Const.* II, p. 108, § 4.

[4] See for their activities the itineraries in Böhmer, *Regesta*, v. 3, pp. 1521 sqq.

secured by an alliance with the princes, and especially with the ecclesiastical princes. Similar motives led him to select one of the most powerful of their number, Engelbert, Archbishop of Cologne, as the guardian of his son and his vicegerent in Germany during his absence. The arrangements for the Italian expedition were made at the diet of Frankfort; at the end of August he set out to cross the Brenner for his imperial coronation.

These first eight years (1212–1220) form the only protracted stay that Frederick made in Germany. He returned in the summer of 1235 to deal with the situation created by the rebellion of his son, and except for a break of a few months spent in north Italy in the latter part of 1236 he remained north of the Alps till August 1237. He then departed never to return. So in his long reign of nearly forty years he gave but eight in all to Germany; and when he came, he came as a stranger into a foreign land, neither understanding nor much caring for the country, its people, or its institutions; hating the climate and the, to him, dreary scenery. This Norman-Italian-Oriental southerner, this *puer Apulus*, who travelled with a harem and a menagerie, was an exotic in Germany, incomprehensible to his German subjects who understood him even less than he understood them. Moreover, not only did he not come to Germany, but he did not repose his complete confidence in those men in whose hands he left the government of the country. His representatives were continually hampered in their administration by inconvenient instructions from the absent Emperor.

In the first period he placed his chief reliance on the ecclesiastical princes whose firm support he had secured before his departure for Italy by the *privilegium* of 1220, and the Hohenstaufen *ministeriales* who exercised a marked influence on the upbringing of the young King Henry. That Germany enjoyed a period of comparative peace was almost wholly due to the wise statesmanship of Engelbert, who was placed at the head of the administration. He was the fifth of his house to occupy the see of Cologne; through family influence he had at an early age obtained high preferment in the Church; at fourteen he was provost of the cathedral, and he was only just over thirty when in 1216 he was consecrated archbishop. During the civil war he had followed the fortunes of his uncle Archbishop Adolf, first as a zealous supporter of Otto, then as a deserter to Philip; for this last act he fell with Adolf under the Pope's displeasure, was excommunicated, and only reconciled with the Church on performing the penance of taking part in the Albigensian Crusade. In 1215 he joined Frederick and remained henceforth a firm adherent of the house of Hohenstaufen. The civil war had left Cologne heavily encumbered with debt. His careful and thrifty handling of the finances removed the burden and proved his ability as an administrator. Towards the nobility and especially towards the lay stewards, whose oppressions and exactions had become an intolerable abuse, he took a firm line; he put down "the insubordination of the counts, nobles, *ministeriales*, and burghers of his diocese," wrote his biographer, Caesarius of Heisterbach, "so that no one dared oppose him." In his city, his diocese, and his duchy of Westphalia he made his authority felt effectively; elsewhere he could not exercise such a direct control; the independent sovereignty of the princes had already become too firmly established. He did what he could by a policy of maintaining the *landfrieden*, and the years of his administration are remarkable for the absence of any serious feuds. *Pacem firmissimam elaboravit.*

In his foreign policy Engelbert was less successful; this was chiefly due to the fact that Frederick took a more lively interest in the relations of the Empire with her neighbours than he did in her purely domestic concerns, and his views frequently did not coincide with those of his representative in Germany. The power of Denmark under Waldemar II had increased to an alarming extent; she had occupied the German territory north of the Elbe including the two important towns of Hamburg and Lübeck, and her conquests were recognised by treaty in 1214; the whole area of German colonisation along the Baltic coast was threatened. By a bold but treacherous stroke the Count of Schwerin succeeded in capturing the Danish king and his son in the island of Lyöe near Fünen (6 May 1223) and thrust them into prison at Danneberg. Although the method of capture was generally disapproved, the opportunity of using it to the advantage of the Empire was too good to be neglected. The government therefore immediately took steps to induce the count to hand over the royal prisoners. This was achieved at Nordhausen in September. Frederick had already intimated in a letter to the Bishop of Hildesheim his general consent to the policy of using the occasion for the recovery of the lands beyond the Elbe; but difficulties arose owing to the intervention of the Pope, to whom the Danes had appealed. He ordered the count to release his prisoners unconditionally under pain of excommunication. The attitude of Honorius seems to have modified Frederick's views, for Herman of Salza, who acted as his representative in the matter, ultimately negotiated a treaty (July 1224), the terms of which were far more lenient than those contemplated in the preliminaries at Nordhausen; they were however rejected by the Danes, and Waldemar remained a prisoner, while Nordalbingia was slowly reconquered by the counts of the district. The Danish leader, Albert of Orlamünde, was defeated at Mölln, Hamburg and Lübeck were recovered, and Waldemar was forced to submit to the terms demanded by the Count of Schwerin: the lands north of the Elbe were surrendered unconditionally and the king's ransom was fixed at 45,000 marks of silver. But Waldemar was no sooner at liberty than he appealed to the Pope to release him from the terms to which he had agreed. The Pope promptly complied with the request, with the inevitable result that war once more broke out between Denmark and the princes of north Germany. Waldemar, aided by his nephew, the Welf Otto of Brunswick, invaded Holstein in the autumn of 1226. But after some initial success he was decisively defeated at Bornhövede between Kiel and Lübeck (22 July 1227).

The overthrow of the Danish power on the southern shore of the Baltic opened the way for the further development of German colonisation and missionary enterprise. The work of the Knights of the Sword in Livonia and Esthonia proceeded uninterrupted by Danish rivalry. The year before the final settlement of the entanglement with Denmark Frederick had confirmed the grant of Prussia made by the Polish Duke Conrad of Masovia to the Teutonic Knights. This was the beginning of the conquest and colonisation of that region which centuries later gave its name to the dominating power in Germany.

In his attitude towards the western kingdoms, France and England, Engelbert found himself acutely at variance with his master. After the death of Philip Augustus war again broke out between England and France, and Louis VIII approached Frederick with the object of renewing the alliance concluded at Vaucouleurs in 1212; he succeeded so far as to obtain from the Emperor a promise that neither he nor any of his subjects should conclude any alliance with England (Catania, November 1223). This was merely continuing the traditional and natural Hohenstaufen policy. Engelbert on the other hand adopted a different course, and he may be accused of acting in this matter too much as the representative of Cologne, too little as the statesman of the Hohenstaufen. The commercial interests of Cologne were inseparably bound up with those of England, and the archbishop had much at heart the welfare of his city; he had done much to foster its economic prosperity, and so greatly did it flourish that already in his day it became a common saying "wer Köln nicht gesehen hat, hat Deutschland nicht gesehen."[1] He set to work therefore to bring about an alliance with England, which he hoped to seal by the marriage of the young Henry, whom he had crowned king at Aix-la-Chapelle on 8 May 1222, with Princess Isabella, the sister of Henry III.

He was successful in quashing a counter-proposal for a marriage of the young king with a French princess, which seems to have been put forward at an interview with Louis VIII near Toul in November 1224. But he could make no headway with his own project. An embassy headed by Walter Mauclerc, Bishop of Carlisle, did indeed visit Germany to negotiate the business, but the ambassadors found opinion in Germany decisively against the match, and they returned home without accomplishing anything[2]. Neither an English nor a French marriage commended itself to the princes, for they had a candidate of their own, the daughter of Ottokar, King of Bohemia, with whom an enormous dowry was offered as an inducement to the Emperor. Duke Leopold of Austria was dispatched to San Germano to gain the Emperor's consent; but it was not Ottokar's but Leopold's own daughter Margaret whom Frederick selected

[1] Quoted Jastrow and Winter, p. 361.

[2] The alliance with France concluded by Frederick in 1223 was, after Engelbert's death, ratified by King Henry at Trent, 11 June 1226.

as the bride for his son. The marriage took place at Nuremberg on 29 November 1225.

Three weeks earlier Engelbert had been assassinated by his cousin Frederick of Isenburg, near the town of Schwelm. The actual motive for the murder was Engelbert's action in checking the oppressive conduct of his nephew towards the convent of Essen of which he was steward; but there is no doubt that the archbishop's stern measures in putting down the lawlessness that prevailed at the end of the civil war had met with fierce and widespread resentment among the local nobility. It was not a spontaneous act, but a premeditated conspiracy in which many persons of high rank and influence were involved. Count Frederick was put under the ban of the Empire and excommunicated by the Church; after nearly a year he was rounded up, confessed his guilt, and was broken on the wheel; his brothers the Bishops of Münster and Osnabrück, his chief accomplices, were deprived of their sees.

It was easy to avenge the murder, not so easy to deal with the situation which resulted from it. There was no one fitted by position and ability to fill the place at the head of the government that Engelbert had occupied. Many of those ecclesiastical princes who had enjoyed the Emperor's confidence when he left Germany in 1220 had since died: Otto of Würzburg, for example, in 1223 and Conrad the Chancellor, Bishop of Metz and Spires, in 1224. The administration passed into the hands not of one of the leading churchmen but into those of a secular prince, Louis, Duke of Bavaria, a man who had neither the strength of character nor the gift of statesmanship possessed in such a marked degree by Engelbert. Moreover the position of regent was becoming every year a more difficult one; for as he grew up the young king began to weary of tutelage and to develope ideas and a policy of his own which did not always conform to those of his guardian. Unlike his predecessor, who made the maintenance of the *landfrieden* the central feature of his domestic policy, Louis took no steps to check or to intervene in the numerous feuds which broke out in all parts of the country. On the rare occasions when he departed from this policy of non-intervention or perhaps what is better described as impolitic inactivity, he did so from motives of self-interest rather than from reasons of state, as when he and King Henry disputed the inheritance of Otto of Brunswick-Lüneburg to the Welf estates on the death of Henry, the Count Palatine of the Rhine. They both raised counter-claims of the slenderest description, and together made an expedition against Brunswick; but they achieved nothing and were compelled ignominiously to retreat.

In the autumn of 1227 the news of the Emperor's excommunication reached Germany, but it made little or no impression on the country at large: neither the ecclesiastical nor the secular princes availed themselves of the Pope's release from their oaths of fealty; only one bishop, the Bishop of Strasbourg, published the sentence against Frederick, and he did so rather from private motives[1] than from any sincere belief in the justice of the papal cause. The excommunication of Frederick may have influenced to some extent the conduct of Louis of Bavaria, who quarrelled with his master towards the end of the year 1228. The cause of the rupture is obscure; it was probably chiefly due to the natural desire of King Henry, who was now seventeen years old, to have a more independent position in the government of the country. Friction was the inevitable result; at the Christmas court at Hagenau it came to an open quarrel, and the duke joined the papal side and went off to Bavaria to raise a rebellion. Pope Gregory, in the meanwhile, was doing all in his power to undermine the imperial government in Germany. In pursuance of this object he dispatched in February 1229 Otto, Cardinal-deacon of St Nicholas in Carcere. But the legate was unable to enter the heart of Germany; he spent months of enforced inactivity at Valenciennes; the councils which he summoned were prevented from taking place; his attempts to set up an anti-king met with little encouragement. Otto of Brunswick was invited to undertake the part, as his uncle Otto IV had done before him; but although urged to do so by Henry III of England, he, after some hesitation, wisely declined. The rebellion raised by the Duke of Bavaria was crushed without difficulty; Strasbourg, the other centre of resistance, was blockaded, and through the mediation of the Abbot of St Gall was brought to terms (August 1229). Frederick had in the meanwhile returned from his successful if unorthodox Crusade (June 1229) and had made short work of the opposition stirred up against him in Italy by Gregory IX. In July 1230 peace was made at San Germano, and in August Frederick was released from the sentence of excommunication. Both in Italy and in Germany the Pope's efforts to undermine the power of the Hohenstaufen had signally failed.

The German towns during the first half of the thirteenth century presented a difficult problem to the government. In spite of the resistance of their feudal superiors, they were always growing more powerful and more independent. A group of towns on the middle Rhine even ventured to form a league, and this just at the moment when the second Lombard league had been established and had had the audacity to prevent King Henry from crossing the Alps to attend the diet of Cremona at his father's summons in the summer of 1226. The Rhine league was quickly suppressed at the instance of the Archbishop of Mayence against whom it was primarily directed (Würzburg, 27 November 1226)[2]. Normally, as in this case, the Duke of Bavaria continued the policy of Engelbert, and indeed of Frederick himself, of supporting the bishops against their aspiring

[1] He was occupied in disputing the inheritance of the Count of Dagsburg with the Count of Pfirt, and King Henry gave his support to the latter.

[2] This is the first known league of the Rhine towns; it was composed of the towns of Mayence, Bingen, Worms, Spires, Frankfort, Gelnhausen, and Friedberg. See MGH, *Const.* II, p. 409.

townsmen; but once at any rate he diverged from it with unfortunate consequences. This was the case of Verdun. At the end of March 1227, on the occasion of the coronation of the queen, Margaret of Austria, he granted to the city in the name of the young king a constitution which was permitted to carry out its functions even despite the opposition of the bishop. A week later, 6 April, the king was forced to revoke the charter in the most humiliating manner "at the request of the envoys of the bishop" on the ground that he had no right to grant it without first consulting the bishop[1]. It was only granted, he explained in a subsequent letter, because of the importunity of the burghers and in the press of business. This forced revocation might indeed have been expected, for the ecclesiastical interest was exceedingly strong, and even Frederick had suffered similar reverses on the rare occasions when he had ventured upon a course of action in opposition to the bishops. But this was not the end of the Verdun affair; scarcely more than two months later the king and his minister again changed their policy, and once more granted the charter to the city[2].

This action is symptomatic of the attitude which Henry adopted when he came to be freed from the control of a guardian; and he vigorously pursued it in the face of the formidable opposition not only of the princes but of the Emperor himself. It was the main cause of the friction and ultimately of the quarrel between father and son; for the father had learnt to rely for support on the princes of Germany whose interest it was to check the development of municipal power. The strikingly different political outlook of the two accounts to a large extent for the different attitude they adopted towards these conflicting elements of German society—the princes and the burghers. Frederick's was imperial; Henry's national. The latter held the princes in suspicion; their independence within their dominions, their acquisition of what had been royal prerogatives, altogether their over-mighty power he regarded, and rightly so, as a very serious menace to the position of the Crown. The towns, on the other hand, whose economic prosperity benefited the country, might, with due encouragement, come to act, as in England and France, as a valuable check on the dangers inherent in an uncontrolled feudal society. Unfortunately Henry had neither the character nor the ability to carry through such a policy, and the forces against him were too great. His attempts were defeated, and the victory of the princes was on each occasion marked by fresh concessions of prerogatives and privileges at the expense of the Crown.

Many of the princes joined the Emperor in Italy on his return from the Crusade and took an active part in the negotiations which led to the peace of San Germano. Their absence from Germany provided Henry with an excellent opportunity to set on foot his new policy. He was supported

[1] Winkelmann, *Acta*, p. 391.
[2] Böhmer, *Acta*, p. 281.

by a number of the smaller nobility and *ministeriales* and also by Duke Louis of Bavaria, with whom he was now completely reconciled and who had during his regency shown a slight inclination in the same direction. In April the king confirmed a former charter in favour of Liège, in June he recognised a league of Netherland towns with Liège at its head[1]. A few months later he went even farther: he would enter into no engagement with the Bishop of Liège without reserving the inviolability of the rights and privileges of the league. He conferred on the burghers of Nijmegen all the liberties and customs enjoyed by Aix-la-Chapelle and other imperial towns, and the right to carry their merchandise free of toll by land and water throughout the Empire; they might also receive whomsoever they would as burghers.

The return of the princes to Germany quickly put an end to his work. At Worms in January he was forced to issue a general edict against town leagues: no city or town was permitted to form *communiones, constitutiones, colligationes, confederationes vel coniurationes aliquas*[2]. Then in the following May the princes wrung from him the famous *constitutio in favorem principum*[3]. It practically made the prince the absolute authority within his domain to the exclusion of the rights of the Crown; he became, as indeed he is described in the document, the *dominus terrae*. Some of the clauses were direct limitations of the power of the Crown. Such for instance is that which binds the king to construct no new fortress or city to the prejudice of the princes (cl. 1), or those which impose restrictions on the royal rights of establishing markets and mints (cl. 2 and 17) and on jurisdiction. The *Centumgravius* (Schultheiss), who was responsible for local justice, was to receive his office no longer from the king but from the lord of the land (cl. 7). Others again were directed especially against the power of the towns: so the *pfahlburgers*, that is, citizens who did not reside within the walls, but nevertheless acquired the protection and the rights of the city, were suppressed (cl. 10)[4]; escaped serfs were no longer to be received in imperial towns (cl. 12); the jurisdiction of the town was confined (cl. 18). Some of the privileges contained in this document were not entirely new; some of them had been granted or had been assumed before in individual cases. But the constitution of 1231 made them general and made them statutory; together with the *privilegium in favorem principum ecclesiasticorum* of 1220, it provides the legal foundation for the territorial sovereignty of the princes. To prevent the worst results that might follow from this position, a safe-

[1] It comprised the towns of Liège, Huy, Dinant, Fosse, St Trond, Maastricht, and Tongres.

[2] MGH, *Const.* II, p. 413.

[3] *Ibid.* p. 418 sq.; it was confirmed, with slight modifications, by Frederick a year later at Cividale, *ibid.* p. 211.

[4] The fact that this clause was repeated more emphatically in the Peace of Mayence four years later (MGH, *Const.* II, p. 244, cl. 13) implies that the towns were strong enough to continue the practice of admitting them in spite of this prohibition.

guard in the form of a royal edict was published the same day: it forbade the princes from making new laws on their own account; the consent of the *meliorum et maiorum terrae* must first be obtained[1].

In the meanwhile the relations between the Emperor and his son were growing more and more strained. It was not only in the different attitude that he adopted towards the towns that Henry earned his father's displeasure and distrust; it was his whole manner of life. "Ve terre, ubi rex puer est!" the chronicler of Ebersheim quotes not ineptly in recounting the events of these years. He relied upon advisers, especially the lower nobility and the *ministeriales*, in whom the Emperor had little confidence; he consorted with poets and actors; his court was luxurious and prodigal; his married life was anything but successful, and he made some efforts to obtain a divorce from Margaret of Austria with a view to marrying Agnes of Bohemia. In all these respects his conduct met with the severe disapproval of Frederick. Then the mysterious and unaccountable murder of Duke Louis of Bavaria added to the difficulties of the political situation in Germany; it nearly caused an outbreak of civil war. He was killed on 16 September 1231 at Kelheim near Worms by a hired assassin—a Saracen emissary of the Old Man of the Mountains (Vetulus de Montanis) who was in league with the Emperor, as the story went in Germany. There is no doubt that it was widely believed, though without adequate foundation, that Frederick had a hand in the deed[2]. The state of things in Germany had become so strained that it was imperative that the Emperor should come to an understanding with his son. For this purpose he summoned Henry and the German princes to attend the diet at Ravenna.

The diet of Ravenna had been first arranged for November to deal with the affairs of Lombardy; but the Lombards in July had renewed their league at Mantua, and they again, as in 1226, closed the Alpine passes to prevent the ingress of King Henry and the princes into Italy. The diet had to be postponed till Christmas when some of the Germans managed to put in an appearance, having travelled thither by way of Aquileia and the sea. But the barring of the routes through the Alps provided Henry, who had no wish for the meeting with his father, with a tolerable excuse for remaining in Germany, and the work of the diet proceeded without him. Frederick, embittered by the obstinate resistance of the Lombard cities, and fearing perhaps that the example might be followed in Germany, issued a sweeping edict against all communes, councils, civic magistrates or rectors or other officials set up without the leave of the bishop; he similarly annulled all gilds, *artificii confraternitates seu societates*. To the princes on the other hand he was, as usual, bountiful; they were to enjoy their liberties in the widest interpretation (*latissima interpretacione*

[1] On the constitutional importance of this edict see Schröder, *Lehrbuch der deutschen Rechtsgeschichte*, 6th edn, p. 670.

[2] See *Chron. Reg. Colon.* p. 263. The contemporary notices are briefly collected in Böhmer, *Regesta*, no. 11104, a. See also Winkelmann in MIOGF, XVII (1896).

gaudeant)[1]. But Frederick was legislating against a power already too strongly established; the position of the German towns could not be shaken by a general edict issued from Italy by an absent Emperor. In spite of the anti-municipal legislation, the towns continued to prosper, to grow more powerful, and to defy both Frederick and the ecclesiastical princes. Indeed, at this very time, notwithstanding the Constitution in favour of the princes, Henry had reverted to his policy of befriending the towns and was issuing edicts to their advantage[2]. The Emperor adjourned the diet of Ravenna to Aquileia to give another opportunity to his disobedient son to render himself before him; there could now be no excuse on the ground of the closing of the Alpine passes to justify his non-appearance, and Henry allowed himself to be persuaded by the imperial chancellor, Siegfried, Bishop of Ratisbon, to comply. He was reconciled with his father, but only under the most humiliating conditions: he not only promised on oath to obey the imperial commands and especially to bestow his favour upon the princes[3], but these were *ipso facto* to be released from their oaths of fealty in the event of his breaking his promise. It appears that Frederick contemplated stronger measures, even deposition, but the princes, now assured of their position, intervened in his favour, and bound themselves to support the Emperor should Henry revert to his evil ways (Cividale, April 1232).

The outstanding feature of German history during the two years following Henry's submission to his father was that remarkable wave of persecution of heresy which spread through the country and which was carried out with an almost unparalleled fanaticism and ferocity. Little had been done in this respect in the earlier years of Frederick's reign. Occasionally we hear of the condemnation of a heretic: a certain Henry Minnike of Goslar was burnt for heresy in 1225; a wealthy citizen of Strasbourg in 1229. But it was not till 1231 that energetic steps were taken to root out the evil: in that year Gregory IX commissioned the Dominicans and also Conrad of Marburg with the task of tracking down heretics and bringing about their condemnation; that they might the more effectually accomplish this work they were further granted judicial authority. So the trial of heretics passed from the control of the bishops into the power of the inquisition. The harsh edict against heretics published by

[1] MGH, *Const.* II, p. 193.

[2] *e.g.* on 15 January 1232 he recognised indirectly an association formed by the towns of Frankfort, Wetzlar, Friedberg, and Gelnhausen (Böhmer, *Regesta*, no. 4225), and on 17 March he confirmed the rights and liberties and the *rath* of Worms (*ibid.* no. 4228). At the complaint of the bishop Frederick ordered in May the destruction of the town hall "pulcherrima domus totius terre." The citizens, rather than leave it to the bishop, demolished it themselves. Ultimately, in February 1233, a compromise was reached between the burghers and the bishop, and the *rath* was restored.

[3] Frederick's manifesto of January 1235 (MGH, *Const.* II, pp. 237 sqq.): "egerimus ...iuratoriam cautionem: quod mandata et beneplacita nostra penitus observaret et precipue principes nostros speciali diligeret et prosequeretur honore."

Frederick at the diet of Ravenna in March 1232 added the imperial authority to the inquisition which had been set working in Germany by the decrees of Gregory IX. All heretics throughout the Empire were to be condemned and handed over to the secular arm to suffer death at the stake; even those who repented and were willing to return to the faith were to be thrust into prison, there to serve out a life-sentence. The Dominicans were taken under the special protection of the Emperor. An orgy of killing followed. In the centre of it all was Conrad of Marburg, the *iudex sine misericordia*, a secular priest of Mayence, who had already been much employed both by Gregory and by his predecessor Honorius first as a preacher of the Crusade, then as an instrument for the suppression of heresy. He had been the confessor of St Elizabeth who, after the death of her husband, the Landgrave Louis, at Brindisi in 1227, had been driven from the Thuringian court by Henry Raspe and had taken refuge at Marburg, where, submitting herself wholly to the influence of Conrad, she soon wore out her strength by asceticism and good works (1231). It was after this that heretic-hunting became an all-absorbing passion, indeed almost a disease, with Conrad. He and his satellites grossly misused the judicial power entrusted to them; "on the same day that anyone was accused," wrote the chronicler of Cologne, "whether justly or unjustly, without the power of appeal or the opportunity of defence being afforded him, he was condemned and thrown to the cruel flames."[1] In answer to protests made at this slaughter of innocents they are reported to have said "We would willingly burn a hundred innocent persons so long as there is one guilty one among them."[2] The first victims were the humbler folk; but flushed with success the inquisitors soon began to attack the upper classes, and it led to their undoing. The atrocity of their proceedings and their total disregard of the elements of justice had by this time aroused the disgust and the hostility not only of laymen but of the clergy. With the exception of the Bishop of Hildesheim, whose sincere but misguided zeal for the faith had induced him to take a prominent part in the persecution, the bishops were unanimous in their opposition. The end came when the Count of Sayn, a man of blameless character and apparently perfectly orthodox, was charged with heresy. The case was brought before the court at Mayence in July 1233 and, in spite of the pleadings of Conrad of Marburg, was adjourned for a further hearing; this took place at Frankfort in February of the next year and his innocence was proved up to the hilt, no less than eight bishops besides many other clergy supporting him as oath-helpers. Conrad was dead; he had been murdered in the neighbourhood of Marburg on his way from the court of Mayence in the previous summer. The movement died down as rapidly as it had arisen. The efforts of the Pope to stir up a crusade for the eradication of heresy met with little

[1] *Chron. Reg. Colon.* sub. anno 1233, p. 264.
[2] *Ann. Wormat.*, MGH, *Script.* XVII, p. 39.

success[1]. A clause was introduced into the Peace Constitution published at Frankfort in February 1234 according to which heretics were to be dealt with by the properly constituted judges who were to have regard to the principles of equity[2]. A reflexion of the movement against heresy may be seen in the wholly selfish and unwarranted attack upon the unfortunate peasant-community dwelling to the west of the mouth of the Weser—the Stedingers. Their only faults appear to have been their independence of the neighbouring lords and their refusal to pay tithes to the Archbishop of Bremen. They were proceeded against as heretics; a crusade was proclaimed; and in the summer of 1234 they were all but annihilated by the princes of the Low Countries in a battle fought at Oldenesche.

King Henry had little sympathy for the extreme violence of the measures taken for the suppression of heresy. The charge made by the Annalist of Worms[3] that the inquisitors won Henry's support for their ruthless proceedings by their proposal that the property of a burnt heretic should be shared between the king and the bishop concerned, seems quite without foundation. For, far from acceding to such a suggestion, he issued in June 1231 an edict whereby the family property of a condemned heretic was to go to the heirs, the fiefs were to revert to the lord who was also to have the moveables[4]. It is to Henry's credit that throughout he adopted a temperate attitude; he was prepared to deal with heretics by proper judicial methods, but he did nothing to favour the wild excesses of Conrad of Marburg and his fellow inquisitors[5]. While his moderation in this respect brought him undoubtedly into better relations with the bishops, it added a new cause for dissatisfaction with his father who, perhaps rather to please Gregory with whom he was at this time on the most friendly terms than from any great zeal on his own part, was actively engaged in the suppression of heresy in Italy.

Henry was a wayward son, thoughtless, unsteady, injudicious; he was also ill advised by men who themselves had received little of the Emperor's favour, though they and their like had in former times been the chief prop of the house of Hohenstaufen, the smaller nobility and the *ministeriales*, Anselm of Justingen, Henry of Neiffen, Conrad of Winterstettin[6]. Not-

[1] See the letter of Gregory addressed to the Archbishop of Mayence, the Bishop of Hildesheim, and the provincial prior of the Dominicans, MGH, *Epp. Saec. XIII*, I, pp. 455 sqq. Persons taking part in the suppression of heresy were to receive the same indulgences as those going to the Holy Land.

[2] MGH, *Const.* II, p. 428: "Ad hec universis iudiciariam potestatem habentibus auctoritate regia precipimus, quatinus ad reprimendam hereticorum perfidiam toto nisu solerter intendant ac iniuste persecutioni iudicii preferant equitatem."

[3] *Ann. Wormat.*, MGH, *Script.* XVII, p. 39.

[4] MGH, *Const.* II, p. 422. But the expenses of the burning were to be deducted from the estate.

[5] See H. Köhler, *Die Ketzerpolitik der deutschen Kaiser und Könige in den Jahren* 1152–1254. (Jenaer Hist. Arbeiten. Heft 6.) 1913.

[6] That Frederick held them responsible for the rebellion may be deduced from clause 18 of the Mayence Peace Constitution, MGH, *Const.* II, p. 245.

withstanding the oath by which he had bound himself at Aquileia in 1232, despite the repeated warnings sent by Frederick from Italy, Henry had soon reverted to his old practices and to his old associates. Although by his attitude towards heresy he had to some extent improved his relations with the higher clergy, he had quarrelled with most of the lay princes, and with some irretrievably: with Duke Otto of Bavaria against whom he made an unwarranted attack in 1233, with the Margrave of Baden, and with Godfrey of Hohenlohe. Feuds among the princes themselves broke out and continued unchecked and uncontrolled. Matters were fast moving to a crisis. In September 1234 he issued a manifesto addressed to Conrad, Bishop of Hildesheim, in which he justified his past conduct and especially emphasised the services he had rendered to his father while the latter was under sentence of excommunication[1]. The letter clearly reveals how fundamentally Henry's view of his own position differed from that of Frederick: the Emperor regarded his son merely as his representative in Germany, there to carry out implicitly his own commands; Henry considered himself as an independent ruler, free to act or to follow what line of policy he chose. A few days later at an assembly held at Boppard he made the first preparations for revolt; there "by threats, prayers, and money," he began to canvass for supporters against his father, "and he found," adds the Cologne chronicle, "not a few."[2] As a matter of fact, outside his intimate circle of *ministeriales* and lesser nobles he had not many adherents of any value. He had exacted an extraordinary oath of allegiance from several towns to aid him against every man, not excepting the Emperor himself; but when the time came not a single town put up the least show of resistance to Frederick's advance. He had on his side a few bishops, those of Spires, Würzburg, Worms, and Strasbourg, but not one secular prince except perhaps the quarrelsome Duke Frederick of Austria, and even he was ready to sell himself to the Emperor if the latter would supply him with money for his feud with the King of Bohemia. Henry also intrigued with foreign powers. He sent Henry of Neiffen and the Bishop of Würzburg to attempt to detach Louis IX from his alliance with Frederick. The fact that the Emperor was at this time negotiating his marriage with Isabella, sister of Henry III of England, might indeed give him grounds for hope in this quarter. But thanks to the mediation of Pope Gregory, the marriage proposal did not affect the political relations between France and the Empire, and Henry's plan failed. With better success he made overtures to the Lombard cities. On 17 December the Marshal, Anselm of Justingen, to whom the business was entrusted, arranged a treaty with them for ten years. This was the unforgiveable sin, an act of open treason whereby Henry placed himself on the side of the most determined enemies of the Empire, and its object too was outrageous: it was to prevent Frederick reaching Germany by getting the Lombards once more to bar the passes of the Alps.

[1] MGH, *Const.* II, pp. 431 sqq. [2] *Chron. Reg. Colon.* p. 266.

The moment for rebellion was ill-chosen. Frederick was now at the height of his power and at peace with the Church; for the Pope, who resented Henry's lack of zeal in the matter of the German heretics, energetically supported the father against the son. He wrote letters of admonition, he threatened excommunication, he released the princes from the oaths of fealty they had taken to him. Frederick, confident in his own strength and his son's weakness, was completely unconcerned by the turn events had taken. He did not even take an army with him when he set out by ship to Aquileia on his way to Germany. He merely took his court in all its glory and splendour, which duly impressed his German subjects with a sense of the greatness of their lord, his collection of wild animals, and a handful of soldiers[1]. He had prepared the way for his coming by an encyclical letter addressed to the princes from Barletta. He flattered them, called them "the pupils of his eyes," and declared that it was Henry's oppressive measures against their class that made his presence in Germany imperative[2]. Frederick was not disappointed in the trust he had imposed in them; they readily responded to his summons, and a large number of them met him when he appeared in Styria in May 1235. The rebellion crumpled up with surprising speed; Henry's attack on Worms, which maintained the imperial cause against its bishop, failed completely; his supporters deserted in large numbers as Frederick advanced; he was prevailed upon by Herman of Salza, who always acted as mediator in quarrels in which the Emperor was concerned, to make his submission at Wimpfen, on the Neckar, where the Emperor held his court. Henry's fate was not immediately decided; the question was postponed to the great diet held at Worms in July. Frederick was at first, it seems, inclined to a lenient course: Henry might have at least his liberty if he performed certain conditions, among them the surrender of the strong castle of Trifels; but failing to comply with the terms, he was thrust into prison first at Heidelberg, then at Alerheim near Nördlingen, and finally in Apulia, whither he was conducted by the Patriarch of Aquileia. There in one prison or another he eked out a wretched existence till 1242, when he died from either a premeditated or accidental fall from his horse while journeying to the castle of Martorano.

The diet of Worms which terminated the unhappy reign of Henry (VII) witnessed also a very different scene. For there was carried out, with all the pomp and gala celebrations for which Frederick's court was famous, his third marriage with Isabella, the sister of Henry III of England.

[1] "procedens in magna gloria cum quadrigis plurimis auro argentoque onustis, bysso et purpura, gemmis atque preciosa suppellectili, cum camelis mulis atque dromedis, Sarracenos quoque multos et Ethyopes diversarum arcium noticiam habentes cum symiis et leopardis, pecunias et thesauros suos custodientes secum adducens, in multitudine copiosa principum et exercitus Wimpiam usque pervenit." Godfredi Viterbiensis *Cont. Eberbacensis*. MGH, *Script.* XXII, p. 348.

[2] MGH, *Const.* II, pp. 236 sqq.

The negotiations for this had begun some time before: in November of the previous year Peter della Vigna had been dispatched to England; on 22 February the formalities were arranged at London. In May, accompanied by the Archbishop of Cologne, the Duke of Brabant, and the Bishop of Exeter, the princess sailed from Sandwich to Antwerp; thence she proceeded to Cologne, where she was welcomed amid great rejoicings and magnificent decorations. There she remained till six weeks later she was summoned to Worms for the marriage ceremony. Her brilliant reception was in tragic contrast to the grimness of her married life; she was soon to undergo the treatment which had worn out the youth and spirit of her predecessor, the Empress Yolande; she was placed under the close custody of Moorish eunuchs.

Besides the obvious political consequence of bringing the Empire into closer and better relations with England, the marriage had another effect scarcely less important: it improved very greatly Frederick's position in the north-west of Germany, in those districts of the lower Rhine which were so nearly bound to England by political and economic ties, and which had since the time of Frederick Barbarossa been the centre of revolts against the house of Hohenstaufen. It was a step towards the final reconciliation of the great family feud of the Welfs and the Hohenstaufen. The present representative of the former house, Otto of Brunswick-Lüneburg, had had the good sense not only to refuse the papal offer of the German crown at the time of the Emperor's excommunication, but also to abstain from involving himself in the quarrel between Henry and his father. At the great diet at Mayence in August he had his reward: he yielded up his possessions to the Emperor and received them back as the duchy of Brunswick-Lüneburg with the much prized privilege of hereditary succession in the male and female line.

The diet of Mayence, which took place a month after Frederick's marriage with Isabella, was attended by nearly all the princes of Germany. Its object was the restoration of peace and order after the confusion and lawlessness which had prevailed almost unceasingly since the death of Engelbert of Cologne. The famous peace ordinance, which was promulgated both in Latin and in the vernacular language[1], was intended to secure as far as possible the maintenance of order and the regulation of justice even in the absence of the Emperor. It embodied much that had already been established in earlier constitutions, especially the Frankfort *Landfriede* issued by King Henry in 1234; but it also contained a great deal of new legislation. Severe punishments were prescribed for breach of the peace; private war might only be resorted to under certain circumstances, self-defence for example, and even then it must follow a carefully

[1] *Chron. Reg. Colon.* p. 267: "Pax iuratur, vetera iura stabiliuntur, nova statuuntur et Teutonico sermone in membrana scripta omnibus publicantur." K. Zeumer has proved that the German version, unfortunately lost, was the original, and he has reconstructed the text. *Neu. Arch.* XXVIII, pp. 435 sqq. 1903.

regulated procedure. For the better and more expeditious execution of the law a chief justice (*iusticiarius curiae*) was set up as the head of a central court of judicature[1]. The Emperor reserved to himself jurisdiction over princes and in other very important cases (*de causis maximis*); he also kept in his hands the power of imposing the ban of the Empire and of removing it; but for the rest the justiciar was to be supreme. He was to be a freeman, and he was to hold office for at least a year, *si bene et iuste se gesserit*. At his side was placed a lay notary whose duty it was to receive indictments, and to record sentences and rulings of the court to serve as precedents for the future. The Peace of Mayence was frequently confirmed by later kings; it became indeed not only the basis of all future peace legislation, but the starting point of the later development of the law of the Empire.

The ecclesiastical princes were still the pillar of Frederick's strength in Germany; twelve bishops had attended his entrance at the gates of Worms on 4 June. In the Peace of Mayence the liberties of the Church were confirmed; the oppression of the stewards (*advocati*, *vögte*) restrained; tolls and mints and other regalian rights of the princes defended against usurpation. Nevertheless the towns, in spite of the severe measures taken against them in the Privilege of the Princes of 1231 and in the edict of Ravenna of 1232, in spite also of the vigorous attempts of King Henry to win their support for his rebellion, had remained loyal to the Emperor, and received their reward in more sympathetic treatment. The Mayence Constitution contains few restrictions affecting them, and only one clause—the prohibition of the *pfahlburgari* and *muntmanni* (clause 13)—imposes a direct limitation on their power of development. During his stay in Germany between 1235 and 1237 the Emperor was more generous in his charters to towns, especially of course to the imperial, such as Nuremberg and Oppenheim, but also to the episcopal towns; in the latter cases usually with the concurrence of the bishops, who were beginning to realise that it was not to their interest to struggle against the inevitable constitutional and economic advance of their cities.

The Emperor spent the months before setting out on the campaign against the Lombards, which had been arranged at the diet of Mayence, in ordering the affairs of the kingdom, in making arrangements for the maintenance of peace, and in strengthening his territorial position. At Augsburg in the autumn of 1235 he bought out the claim of the King of Bohemia through his wife Cunigunda, daughter of King Philip, to a part of the Hohenstaufen estates in Swabia. Among his multifarious duties he found time to attend on 1 May 1236 the great ceremony of the translation of the bones of Elizabeth of Hungary, who had been canonised by Pope Gregory in 1234, to the church of Marburg.

[1] His position and functions are in some respects analogous to those of the Grand Justiciar whom Frederick had established in Sicily. The influence of the Sicilian organisation is also unmistakable in some of the other clauses.

In the following June the army assembled in the Lechfeld for the conquest of Lombardy. The Emperor was, however, unable to lead his full strength across the Alps, for there remained in Germany one rebel whom he had not succeeded in reducing to obedience. This was Frederick, Duke of Austria, the last of the Babenberg dukes, a violent, quarrelsome, impetuous man, who had persistently disobeyed the Emperor's summons, and whose conduct in the revolt of Henry (VII) had been very dubious; he had in fact after the collapse of the rebellion welcomed at his court one of the ringleaders, Anselm of Justingen. At Augsburg in June 1236 he was placed under the ban of the Empire, and the princes of the south-east of Germany, the King of Bohemia, the Duke of Bavaria, and several bishops, were entrusted with its execution. This they accomplished with remarkable ease: the greater part of Austria and Styria, including Vienna itself, fell into their hands; so satisfied were they with their success that they returned home, leaving the Burgrave of Nuremberg in charge of their conquests. Duke Frederick immediately took the field, defeated the burgrave at Steinfeld to the south of Neustadt, captured the Bishops of Freising and Passau, and recovered the greater part of his possessions. The news of these events brought the Emperor back to Germany; he spent Christmas at Graz; in January 1237 he was in Vienna, which in April he made an imperial city. At the same time he made Styria directly dependent on the Empire. But his intention to do the same with Austria was too ambitious; preoccupied as he was with the affairs of Lombardy, he had not the time nor the military strength to spare for the undertaking. No sooner was his back turned than the duke again managed to establish his authority in the greater part of his duchy.

The influence which Frederick had gained over the princes of Germany is shewn by the ease with which he succeeded in inducing them to elect his son Conrad, then nine years old, as King of the Romans and future Emperor. This was done at Vienna in February and confirmed at Spires in July 1237. Born in Apulia in 1228, he had as an infant been recognised as King of Jerusalem (1229). He had accompanied his father to Germany in 1235 and might have been elected king at the great diet of Mayence had it not been for the opposition of the Pope. As it was, he was left as the nominal regent when Frederick recrossed the Alps in the summer of 1236. He now succeeded his imprisoned brother as king, and when the Emperor departed from Germany once more in August 1237, never to revisit it, Conrad remained behind as his representative under the guardianship of Siegfried, Archbishop of Mayence, who stood by him both in a personal and in a public capacity: he was his *magister et amicus*, but he issued his documents as *sacri imperii per Germaniam archicancellarius et procurator*[1]; he occupied, that is to say, a position similar to that once held by Archbishop Engelbert during the boyhood of King Henry. But, like his brother, the young king soon surrounded himself with the official

[1] Böhmer, *Regesta*, nos. 4390 and 11212.

class, the Swabian and Franconian *ministeriales*, of whom Conrad of Winterstettin and Godfrey of Hohenlohe were the most prominent. It was men from this class who were chiefly responsible for his education, who became his intimate circle, who acted as his advisers[1]. But Frederick, warned by bitter experience, kept a watchful eye on his son's upbringing; he would frequently write letters to him full of fatherly counsel and of advice respecting the duties of a king.

The uncompromising attitude adopted by the Emperor towards the Duke of Austria had unfortunate consequences. Neither the Duke of Bavaria nor the King of Bohemia, who had been the most urgent in pressing the Emperor to impose the ban and who had been among the foremost of those charged with its execution, desired to push matters to extremes. So much did they dislike Frederick's plan of absorbing the duchy into the Empire that they not only ceased to take any active part in the war against the duke, but early in 1238 (7 March) they actually entered into an alliance with him against the Emperor. This was partly at any rate contrived by Pope Gregory, who intended to use the three princes of the south-east as instruments to work the ruin of Frederick in Germany[2]. When on Palm Sunday (20 March) 1239 Frederick was for the second time excommunicated, these princes at the instigation of the Pope broke out into open rebellion. They tried to raise up an anti-king to Frederick; but neither Abel, the second son of King Waldemar of Denmark, nor Robert of Artois, the brother of King Louis IX of France, who was approached later, were prepared to entertain the project. The general feeling in the country seems to have been that the sentence of excommunication was unjustified and occasioned by political motives; indeed not a bishop could be found to publish the sentence; the Landgrave of Thuringia and the Margrave of Meissen who had inclined towards the papal side were won back by the efforts of the Archbishop of Mayence; the three princes of Bohemia, Bavaria, and Austria stood alone. However much the other princes might differ in their views of the respective merits of the causes of Pope and Emperor—and they certainly differed very materially[3]—they were at least unanimous in desiring peace, and at Eger on 1 June they agreed to entrust the task of mediation to Conrad of Thuringia, who had just succeeded Herman of Salza as Grand Master of the Teutonic Order; he died at Rome in June 1240 without having accomplished anything. However, the failure to do so was due to no fault of his own, but solely to the stubborn obstinacy of Gregory who wanted

[1] See Winkelmann, *Geschichte Kaiser Friedrichs II und seiner Reiche*, II, 1 abt. (1865), p. 57 sq.

[2] "Ad instantiam suam," "iussu pape," see Böhmer, *Regesta*, no. 11215 a. Frederick of Austria appears to have won over the King of Bohemia by the promise of ceding to him the parts of Austria north of the Danube. *Ibid.*

[3] See Hauck, *Kirchengeschichte Deutschlands*, IV, p. 830, n. 7, and Böhmer, *Regesta*, nos. 11250 and 11251. The Archbishops of Cologne and Bremen and the Bishops of Strasbourg and Liège inclined towards the papal side.

no peace. For him it was a fight to the death. Nevertheless he was disappointed in his hopes from Germany. He thought he would be able to rouse German sympathy for the papal cause; instead he found princes who wanted peace and people who were definitely hostile; the towns of South Germany sent contingents to fight Frederick's battles in Lombardy; the clergy, especially in Bavaria, paid not the slightest regard to the excommunication; the Teutonic Order, to which Frederick had always been particularly generous in grants of lands and privileges, was solid in its support of its patron. And not the least shattering blow, the Duke of Austria in the autumn of 1239 was reconciled with the Emperor and reinstated in his dukedom; his example was soon followed by the King of Bohemia, and Otto of Bavaria alone remained to represent the papal party. But Gregory only redoubled his efforts to raise Germany against its Emperor: in November he instructed the bishops to publish the sentence of excommunication in all towns and villages with ringing of bells and burning of lights; he threatened to excommunicate all who gave their support to the Emperor; then early in 1240 he ordered a crusade to be preached against "the son of perdition." But the more violent his methods became, the more stubbornly were they resisted. Moreover Gregory was singularly unfortunate in his choice of an agent. Albert Behaim, Archdeacon of Passau, enthusiastic to fanaticism as he was in his devotion to the Holy See, was tactless and injudicious, and he only embittered his opponents by his wholesale and unauthorised excommunications and interdicts. Not unlike Conrad of Marburg a few years earlier, he ruined a papal policy by excess of zeal. In the spring of 1240 he excommunicated half the bishops of Germany, including the chancellor, Siegfried, Bishop of Ratisbon, the Archbishops of Mayence, Trèves, and Salzburg; he excommunicated the Duke of Austria, the Landgrave of Thuringia, the Margrave of Meissen; he excommunicated many cathedral chapters and abbots; he laid Austria under interdict and meted out the same treatment to those towns which had sent troops to assist the Emperor in Lombardy. The Archbishop of Salzburg and the Bishop of Brixen became so exasperated that they closed the passes of the Alps to prevent him from communicating with the Pope. Even the Duke of Bavaria grew tired of the extravagant conduct of the papal agent, and it was he who ultimately expelled him from Bavaria.

While the Pope was devoting all the forces at his command, excommunications, crusades, intrigues, to crush the Emperor, and was refusing even to entertain overtures for peace, a real danger was threatening the whole Christian world. The Mongols, who during the early years of the thirteenth century had spread over the greater part of Asia, were now under Batu Khan pressing farther and farther westward. They had subdued the Cumans on the north-west shore of the Black Sea. They had overrun southern Russia: Moscow and Vladímir fell in 1238; Kiev in 1240. They had pushed on into Poland, seized Cracow (March 1241), crossed the Oder, and defeated and killed Duke Henry of Silesia, who attempted to check their advance, at Liegnitz (9 April 1241). Simultaneously another swarm under Batu himself had crossed the Carpathians and attacked Hungary; the army of King Béla was surprised and annihilated, and the king fled to Austria for help. There was no doubt of the seriousness of the peril. The vast Mongolian army was not a mere horde of undisciplined barbarians; it was well organised, well trained, and well led. Frederick protested with some justice that he was himself unable to leave Italy, but he wrote to all the kings of Europe urging them to prepare to meet the common danger by united action[1]. The bishops of Germany preached a crusade, King Conrad himself took the cross at Esslingen (19 May), and the army was to assemble for the campaign at Nuremberg on 1 July. But by then the imminent danger had passed. The Mongolian attacks on Bohemia and Austria had been successfully repulsed; then came the news of the death of the Great Khan Ogdai, and of the political disturbances in central Asia resulting from it. The Mongols withdrew eastward, and Germany was freed from the threat of invasion.

During the last eight years of Frederick's reign the Pope waged a relentless war for the extermination of the house of Hohenstaufen, a war which threw the whole of Germany into confusion and anarchy. Innocent IV, who was elected to the pontificate on 25 June 1243, was more successful as a politician and as an agitator than Gregory IX had been, and he had better material to work upon; for no less a person than Siegfried, Archbishop of Mayence, Frederick's vicegerent in Germany, deserted his post and turned papalist. He may have been influenced by the Emperor's neglect of his country in the hour of need, for the latter had remained in Italy during the Mongolian invasion; it was even whispered, though of course without a particle of truth, that Frederick had himself invited in the Asiatic hordes[2]. He may have considered the measures taken by Frederick against Pope Gregory, such as the seizure of the cardinals and bishops who were proceeding to the council at Rome in May 1241, as too violent to be honestly approved. It is enough that on 10 September 1241 he had an interview with Conrad, Archbishop of Cologne, who all along had had leanings towards the papal side, and concluded with him an alliance which was definitely directed against the Emperor. Shortly after, they were joined by Arnold of Isenburg, who after a disputed election became Archbishop of Trèves. The three Rhenish archbishops with several of their suffragans formed a very powerful nucleus of an anti-Hohenstaufen party in Germany.

The desertion of the Archbishop of Mayence necessitated fresh arrangements for the government of Germany, for Conrad was still but a boy, not yet fourteen years old. The changes carried out in 1242 mark

[1] See his letter to Henry III in Matthew Paris, *Chron. maj.* (ed. Luard), IV, pp. 112 sqq.

[2] *Ibid.* p. 119.

a complete reversal of Frederick's previous policy[1]. He could no longer rely on the great churchmen in whom he had hitherto reposed his confidence and whom he had singled out for exceptionally generous treatment in the way of grants of lands and privileges; they had failed him. In the spring Henry Raspe, Landgrave of Thuringia, and Wenceslas, King of Bohemia, were named his deputies in Germany, each with the title *sacri per Germaniam imperii procurator*[2]. But the appointment of two prominent lay princes was not the only indication that the Emperor had ceased to count upon the higher clergy. He now turned to the cities of Germany, not only to the imperial towns which he had generally patronised, but to the bishops' towns which, in order to please their ecclesiastical masters, he had usually downtrodden, and he found that, with few exceptions, they rewarded his confidence and his bounty by staunch loyalty. Cologne itself was largely imperialist, influenced no doubt by the English alliance which resulted from the marriage of Frederick with Isabella; the burghers took part in the campaign which ended in the capture and imprisonment of their papalist archbishop (February 1242); it was only by granting extraordinary privileges that William of Holland ultimately gained admittance into the city (October 1247).

Worms enthusiastically supported Conrad, and in the fighting in the region of the upper Rhine in 1242–1243 they rendered him great service, especially with their fleet of boats which on one occasion sailed down the river and relieved the fortress of Castel which the Archbishop of Mayence was besieging. Erfurt suffered the imposition of an interdict rather than desert their king; the burghers of Ratisbon drove out their disloyal bishop, Siegfried, once the trusted chancellor of Frederick, and, when he died shortly after, they refused him burial within their city; Frederick handsomely rewarded them by expressly exempting them from the terms of the edict of Ravenna of 1232 and by permitting them to set up a town council with a burgomaster and civic officials independent of their bishop (November 1245)[3]. The financial support supplied by the towns compensated to some extent for the serious losses caused by the alienation and pawning of crown and personal property to which the Hohenstaufen were compelled to resort in order to gain assistance in other quarters.

With the formal deposition of the Emperor at the Council of Lyons in July 1245 we enter on the last and the most deplorable phase of the war. In the autumn of the same year Innocent sent Philip of Ferrara as legate to Germany; he was the first of a series of legates commissioned

[1] That Frederick himself visited Germany in the early part of the year 1242 for the purpose of reorganising the government, as suggested by a passage in Matthew Paris (IV, p. 268) and accepted by Schirrmacher, *Friedrich II*, IV, pp. 499 sqq., and more recently by Schirmer, *Beiträge zur Geschichte Kaiser Friedrichs II*, 1904, has been set aside on the ground of insufficiency of evidence. See Hampe, *Kaisergeschichte*, p. 266, n. 1.

[2] Böhmer, *Regesta*, nos. 4457 and 11390.

[3] *Ibid.* no. 3516.

with almost unlimited powers to carry out the Pope's political aim—the overthrow of the Hohenstaufen and the election and recognition of an anti-king. The election of an anti-king was achieved without much difficulty: Henry Raspe, Landgrave of Thuringia, had joined the papal side in April 1244; he was really the only lay prince available, and he was chosen "at the Pope's command" at Veitshochheim near Würzburg on 22 May 1246, by the archbishops of the Rhineland and a few other bishops. Not a lay prince was present; it was merely an affair of the Church party; Henry was, as Albert of Stade justly calls him, *rex clericorum*[1]. Indeed there was a strong feeling in the country, as the same author records, that the Pope was meddling in matters that were no business of his: the Pope was not concerned in the institution or in the deposition of an Emperor, but only in his coronation[2]. Henry so far acknowledged that he was the instrument and the champion of Rome as to have the heads of SS. Peter and Paul engraved on the obverse of his seal[3].

Nevertheless it was easier to bring about the election of an anti-king than to win for him recognition. This had already been proved when Innocent III had tried to force Germany to accept Otto IV. Innocent IV was if possible more determined and certainly far less scrupulous in his methods than any of his predecessors. He and his agents stopped short at nothing; nothing was too dishonourable, too undignified, too unchristian, so long as it served their ends[4]. Excommunication was pronounced against the supporters of the Hohenstaufen and their lands were laid under interdict. Masses ceased to be said in many churches throughout the country and in consequence large numbers were cut off from the exercise of their religion; their marriages were not recognised by the Church; their children went unbaptised; they were denied Christian burial. A crusade was proclaimed against Frederick and his son, and was actively preached by the mendicant orders in the villages and towns of Germany; those who had taken the cross for the redemption of the Holy Land were persuaded to perform their vow in the war against the Hohenstaufen. Every inducement was offered to entice imperialist clergy to turn papalist; while entrance into Holy Orders was denied not only to the actual partisans of Frederick but also to their sons and their grandsons, it was permitted even to the natural sons of the clergy who supported the Pope; the irregularities and crimes of the latter were connived at, and their sins were covered by dispensations. Bribery was practised on an enormous scale, and to provide the necessary money the Church, not only in Germany and Italy but in England, was taxed to

[1] MGH, *Script.* XVI, p. 370.

[2] *Ibid.* p. 369: "Ad papam non pertinere, imperatorem eis vel instituere vel destituere, sed electum a principibus coronare."

[3] Hampe, *Kaisergeschichte*, p. 272.

[4] For the methods employed by Innocent IV see Hauck, *Kirchengeschichte Deutschlands*, IV, pp. 863 sqq. on which the following summary is largely based.

the limit of its resources. Benefices were granted by papal provision as rewards for zeal in the cause of Rome; indeed in Germany practically all Church appointments were at this time controlled by the Pope's agents. No chapter could proceed to the election of a bishop without first obtaining the advice and consent of the Pope or his legate; Innocent even stooped so low as to nominate a layman, Henry of Guelders, to the see of Liège and to dispense him from the obligation of consecration (1247), and he held his bishopric as a layman till his deposition in 1273[1].

Henry Raspe at first met with success. King Conrad, who tried to prevent him holding his first diet which had been summoned to Frankfort, was defeated on 5 August 1246, mainly owing to the treachery of the Counts of Wurtemberg and Grüningen who, bribed by the Pope with seven hundred marks of silver, deserted with two thousand Swabians. Henry was therefore able to hold his diet; but the fact that the legate, Philip of Ferrara, excommunicated and summoned to Rome no less than two archbishops, those of Salzburg and Bremen, ten bishops, and four abbots for non-attendance there, shews that even among the higher clergy there was still a preponderance that favoured the Hohenstaufen. The efforts of the anti-king were now directed to an attempt to subdue Swabia, the home of his opponents. At Frankfort he formally deprived Conrad both of the duchy and of his family possessions; some Swabian counts and nobles had already joined him; and in the winter 1246–7 he ventured to embark upon a campaign. He made however little headway; in January he laid siege to Ulm, but the stubborn resistance of the inhabitants and the severity of the weather forced him to abandon it. The winter campaign had seriously affected his health; he withdrew to the Wartburg near Eisenach, where he died in February 1247. He was the last of his house, which had ruled Thuringia for nearly a century and a half. It now escheated to the Empire and was in course of time granted by Frederick to Henry, Margrave of Meissen, who was connected by marriage with the last landgrave[2].

The Thuringian landgraves had on many occasions during the civil disturbances of the last fifty years given trouble to the ruling house, which gained considerably by their end. Not many months before (June 1246) Duke Frederick of Austria died fighting against Hungary, and another of the great German families became extinct; for this turbulent prince was the last of the Babenbergs in the male line. Austria, like Thuringia, fell in to the Empire, but contrary to feudal custom it was not regranted after the lapse of a year and a day, but was retained in the hands of the Crown and ruled by a captain-general (*capitaneus et procurator*). The arrangement, though it caused much internal discord, on the whole strengthened the Hohenstaufen position in the south-east. Indeed, this region, which had stood out prominently as the centre of papal influence in the crisis of 1239, was in 1246 a stronghold of the imperialists. Duke

[1] MGH, *Epp. Select.* II, pp. 325 sqq.; *Ann. S. Jacobi Leodiensis,* MGH, *Script.* XVI, p. 643.

[2] See *infra,* p. 125 n. 1.

Otto of Bavaria, who on the former occasion had been the German champion of the papal cause, was now not only the ally but the father-in-law of Conrad IV. For the latter married the duke's daughter Elizabeth in September 1246 at Vohburg. How seriously this alliance was regarded at the papal court may be judged from the letter written shortly before the marriage took place to Duke Otto by his former friend, Albert of Passau, who was at the time at Lyons with Innocent IV. He was willing to contrive that the Pope should annul the betrothal and arrange a better match for his (the duke's) daughter; he would procure a reconciliation with Henry Raspe and the removal of the sentences of excommunication and interdict which the legate had imposed upon him and his dominions. He then made an alternative suggestion: he would get the Pope to confirm the marriage, and permit Conrad to retain Sicily and the kingdom of Jerusalem, provided that he would desert his father; Henry Raspe in this case would keep Germany and the Empire. That these proposals were made with the approval of Innocent there can be little doubt. Besides shewing the importance the Pope attached to the friendship of Bavaria, it reveals the lengths he was prepared to go, the sacrifices he was prepared to make, to achieve the ruin of Frederick.

The Bavarian marriage and the death of Henry Raspe were serious blows to Innocent's policy. Moreover, among the powers of Europe the Pope had not met with the sympathy he had hoped for; the Kings of England and France ignored the sentence of deposition pronounced at the Council of Lyons, and continued to regard and to address Frederick as Emperor. If the Pope's arbitrary methods of appointing papalists to German bishoprics gave him the controlling hand over the higher clergy, he failed completely to shake the loyalty of the lay princes. It was not an easy matter to find a suitable successor to Henry Raspe; and the choice finally fell on a young man who was not even of princely rank, William, the Count of Holland. He was elected in the presence of Peter Capocci, the legate who had taken the place of Philip of Ferrara, at Worringen near Cologne on 3 October. Besides the ecclesiastics, he was supported by one layman of a substantial position, his uncle the Duke of Brabant. But essentially he was another *rex clericorum.* Although by his family connexions he had influence in the districts of the lower Rhine, he nevertheless found it by no means easy to gain access to the principal towns. He won Cologne by a quite exceptional charter: besides granting privileges in the way of tolls and jurisdiction, he bound himself to lead no army into the city, to hold no diet within its walls, to build no fortress on its territory, to impose no taxation upon its inhabitants; he resigned in fact all royal prerogatives in its favour. In consequence of this we find him seldom in the chief town of the lower Rhine, and then only on peaceable business; he was present at the ceremony of laying the foundation stone of the new cathedral (July 1248), and there also he was received at the house of the Dominicans by the schoolman Albertus Magnus (January 1249). But it was not, as it had been under

Otto IV, the political and military centre of this Netherland king. It took him several months to force his way into Aix-la-Chapelle where, a little more than a year after his election, he was crowned by Archbishop Conrad of Cologne in the presence of two legates (1 November 1248). The royal fortress of Kaiserswerth was only starved into submission after a siege lasting a whole year. Boppard held out against three separate attacks and only succumbed when besieged for the fourth time in August 1251. In these first years he was kept fully occupied in improving his position in those parts where his kingship was more or less acknowledged, by making grants and confirming charters and by a judicious use of the papal money placed at his disposal; in this way Duke Matthew of Lorraine was brought over to his side. He was also engaged in feuds in his own country—one particularly long and troublesome with Margaret of Flanders. So he seldom ventured far afield during Frederick's lifetime. He made however two expeditions up the Rhine; on the first of these, in 1249, he captured Ingelheim, where he confirmed the old Eger Bull of Frederick II in favour of the Pope. But during the siege he suffered a severe blow: his most powerful supporter, Archbishop Siegfried of Mayence, fell ill and was taken to Bingen where he died. His successor, Archbishop Christian, was a peaceable person and altogether disinclined to fight for the papal cause by the means prescribed by Innocent IV; he was indeed deposed from his see for his inactivity in this respect in July 1251. With Siegfried of Mayence, William of Holland and the Pope lost their greatest champion in Germany. The capture of Ingelheim was the only result of the campaign; William attacked but failed to capture Frankfort in July; but by the autumn he was back in the Low Countries without having struck a serious blow at his opponents. The second campaign up the Rhine in the summer of the next year was still less eventful. Conrad was also in the field, and on one occasion the two rivals were encamped within a few miles of each other in the neighbourhood of Oppenheim; but William would not risk a pitched battle and withdrew. At the end of the year he was still only king in the district of the Lower Rhine; in the east of Germany he was ignored; in the south he was bitterly opposed. Up to the time of the Emperor's death at Fiorentino in December 1250 the policy of Innocent IV in Germany had met with little real success. He had set up two anti-kings, but neither had been recognised outside a comparatively small area; all he had achieved was to introduce chaos and anarchy, civil war and bloodshed, into the whole of Germany.

CHAPTER IV

THE INTERREGNUM IN GERMANY

In the autumn of 1251 Conrad IV crossed the Alps to take up his father's place in Italy, leaving his interests in Germany under the care of his father-in-law, Duke Otto of Bavaria. The Pope, after a cordial interview with his protégé, William of Holland, departed from Lyons to take up his residence at Perugia. The struggle between the Pope and the Hohenstaufen was again transferred to Italian soil, and William of Holland was left alone in Germany to make what he could out of its chaotic condition. Indeed, with the removal of so many obstacles from his path he might now reasonably hope to extend his authority beyond the limits of the Low Countries. With this object in view he approached the princes of the north-east of Germany, who had taken little part in the turmoil of the last few years. The way was prepared by the king's marriage with Elizabeth, the daughter of the Duke of Brunswick, on 25 January 1252. Both princes and towns of Germany received letters from the Pope bidding them recognise his king; this they were not unwilling to do, but they were dissatisfied with the form of the election of 1247; it was undoubtedly not in accordance with German constitutional practice. William's position was similar to that of Otto IV after the murder of Philip of Swabia: both had been properly crowned by the Archbishop of Cologne at Aix-la-Chapelle; both had been accepted by the Pope; but neither had been elected by a representative body of the princes of Germany. As Otto had been obliged to submit in 1208 to a fresh election, so William consented to a like procedure at Brunswick on 25 March 1252.[1] It was "certain towns and cities," and notably Lübeck, that excused themselves from recognising William as king on the ground that "the noble princes, the Duke of Saxony and the Margrave of Brandenburg, who have a voice in the election, had not consented to the election".[2] These towns were insisting on the doctrine of the *Sachsenspiegel* written some years earlier, according to which the electoral right belonged to the three Rhenish archbishops and the three great titular officials of the imperial household, the steward, the marshal, and the chamberlain, whose offices were attached respectively to the Count Palatine of the Rhine, the Duke of Saxony, and the Margrave of Brandenburg. The archbishops had been responsible for the election of William of Holland, but the lay electors had taken no part in it. The ceremony at Brunswick was intended to rectify this defect.[3] The Electors of Saxony and

[1] See Bloch, *Die Staufischen Kaiserwahlen und die Entstehung des Kurfürstentums*, pp. 237 sqq.

[2] MGH, *Const.* II, p. 631.

[3] The Count Palatine, who was also Duke of Bavaria, was excluded from taking part in it on the ground that, as a supporter of Conrad IV, he was under sentence of excommunication. Bloch, *op. cit.* p. 247.

Brandenburg were richly rewarded for their acceptance of William, the one by the grant of the right of investiture of the bishoprics of Lübeck, Ratzeburg, and Schwerin, the other by the city of Lübeck itself.

The effect of this second election at Brunswick on the position of King William was instantaneous: he was received with royal honours in the Saxon towns he visited in April, in Goslar, Halle, and Merseburg; the Archbishop of Magdeburg and the Margrave of Meissen acknowledged him and received their fiefs from his hands; the King of Bohemia sent ambassadors conveying his consent to the election. Nevertheless in the south and centre of Germany there were still many who clung to the Hohenstaufen. William in July summoned a diet to Frankfort which was to give public recognition to his position as King of the Romans, but the burghers closed the gates of their city against him and this important meeting had to be held in the fields outside the walls. Among those there assembled were the Archbishops of Mayence and Cologne and several other bishops; of the lay princes, Albert, the new Duke of Brunswick —his father, Duke Otto, had died as he was about to start for the diet— alone is mentioned by name; there were also a number of abbots, counts, and nobles. But in spite of the somewhat meagre attendance of the lay nobility, the diet transacted important business: Conrad IV was again formally deprived of his dukedom of Swabia and of his family estates; a phase of the long feud in which William from the beginning of his reign had been involved with the Countess Margaret of Flanders[1] was concluded by the confiscation of her imperial fiefs, which were handed over to her bastard son, the king's brother-in-law, John of Avesnes. The validity of William's election was solemnly declared, and all the imperial cities, castles, and property were accordingly assigned to him; within a year and a day all princes, nobles, and *ministeriales* were required to take up their principalities and fiefs from him under pain of forfeiture.[2] The measures taken at the diet of Frankfort gave the impression that William was now firmly established as King in Germany. But this was far from being the case. No sooner had he improved his position in the north-east than he began to lose ground in the Rhine country; in the autumn of the same year he irretrievably quarrelled with the Archbishop of Trèves, whom he rightly or wrongly accused of instigating an attack upon him at Coblenz, and by 1254 he was at enmity with all three Rhenish archbishops, the very men who had taken the leading part in setting him up as king. Indeed, Conrad of Hochstaden, Archbishop of Cologne, became the most active of all his opponents; he allied himself with the king's lifelong antagonist, Margaret of Flanders, and her supporter, Charles of Anjou; he set fire to the house in which the king and the legate, Peter Capocci, were lodged at Neuss, hoping to burn them to death. There were other significant indications of the king's unpopularity: a large stone was hurled at his

[1] For the importance of this feud see below, p. 127 sq.

[2] MGH, *Const.* II, p. 465 sq.

head at Utrecht; his queen was robbed and taken prisoner in the neighbourhood of Worms. Although after the death of Conrad IV in May 1254 a number of the towns, such as Worms and Spires, which, so long as there had been a Hohenstaufen king, had firmly refused to recognise any other, now acknowledged him, William failed altogether to make his authority felt as a reality in Germany. It was becoming more and more evident that the territorial lords did not want a strong king and a strong central government. A puppet ruler suited their ends better; they were wholly occupied in making themselves supreme within their own lands, in reaping the advantages they had won in the great *privilegia* of 1220 and 1231; absorbed in their particularist interests, they ceased to care about or concern themselves with the affairs of the Empire.

In these circumstances it is not surprising that for a time the administration of the kingdom was dominated not by a king, by a bishop, or by a great lay prince, but by a group of towns. Nothing is more remarkable than the rapid constitutional and economic development of the towns of Germany during the first half of the thirteenth century; they advanced steadily in the midst of the political confusion, often in the face of opposition from the central government, nearly always in spite of fierce resistance from the territorial lords. Gradually they succeeded in freeing themselves from seignorial domination, acquired the control of their own affairs, and developed their trade and commerce. Peace, security of the highways, and the suppression of tolls arbitrarily raised by the local lords were of primary importance to these flourishing communities of traders. The towns therefore banded together to perform the duties in which the weak and ineffective government signally failed—the maintenance of the *landfrieden.* For some years past towns had grouped themselves to promote their political or economic aims by common action. In 1226, in the lawless period which followed the death of Engelbert of Cologne, a number of Rhine towns had formed a league, but this and similar attempts were quickly crushed by Frederick, who had learnt in Lombardy the power such combinations might exert. During the last years of his reign, however, when the towns became the most solid support on which the Hohenstaufen could rely, the formation of leagues was not obstructed. So in 1241 Lübeck and Hamburg joined together to suppress robbery and other crimes perpetrated on the stretch of coast between the mouth of the Trave and the city of Hamburg and along the river Elbe; from this small beginning perhaps may be dated the most famous of all leagues—that of the Hanse towns. In 1246 Münster and Osnabrück bound themselves to protect all markets held within the two dioceses. Others had a more political intent: Metz and Toul, and a more important group of some twelve towns in Swabia and Alsace, allied themselves in support of the Hohenstaufen against the anti-king.

The idea of a league embracing a large number of towns with the avowed object of maintaining order was first conceived by a burgher of Mayence, a certain Walpode, in 1254. His efforts resulted first in local agreements between a few towns in the immediate neighbourhood: Mayence, Worms, and Oppenheim; Mayence and Bingen. Then on 13 July of that year the great confederation of the Rhine towns came into being. Among the original members were Mayence, Cologne, Worms, Spires, Strasbourg, and Basle; and their object, as set forth in the covenant of foundation, was the restoration of order, to prevent "the dangers which for a long time had pervaded the land and the risks encountered on the highways." It differed from the earlier leagues in that it included the bishops and the local nobility; the members bound themselves to protect all classes, *minores cum maioribus*, the clergy, the peasantry, and even the Jews, and to proceed with their joint forces against disturbers of the peace; the lords agreed to remove all unauthorised tolls both by land and by water. Provision was made for the settlement of disputes which might arise among the members of the league. It soon came to embrace all the towns of the Upper and Middle Rhine. At the meeting of the members of the league held at Worms on 6 October an edict was issued which contained elaborate regulations for the preservation of order and for dealing with violators of the peace; all those sworn of the peace were required to keep arms in readiness to take measures against wrong-doers; the Rhine towns were to provide armed vessels: those above the junction of the Moselle as far as Basle were to furnish a hundred, those below fifty.

William of Holland had encouraged the commercial aspirations of the towns both before his election in his own county and after, in those parts that had acknowledged his rule. Very soon after its foundation he began to identify himself with the policy of the Rhine League: at the meeting in October 1254 he was solemnly recognised as king by the confederate towns; he was present at Worms in February 1255 where the members of the league met to swear the peace; and a month later at Hagenau he not only confirmed this peace in his own name but actually became the head of the league and used it as the machinery for the maintenance of the peace; he nominated a chief Justiciar whose duty it was to deal with complaints of breach of the peace; all such complaints must first be brought before the king or his Justiciar, and only with their counsel and consent might the league take action against the violators[1]. An important result of the association of the king with the league was that the members of the latter came to take part in the business of the State. At the diet of Worms in February 1255 delegates of the towns took their place beside the bishops, princes, counts, nobles, and *ministeriales* in the passing of royal ordinances; it is the first hint of representation of German towns in a legislative assembly[2]. In the course of the year the league widely extended

[1] By a later enactment of 10 November the *Schultheissen* of the royal cities of Boppard, Frankfort, Oppenheim, Hagenau, and Colmar might also deal with such complaints, MGH, *Const.* II, p. 478.

[2] See the *sententiae de bonis naufragantium et de falsis monetis*, MGH, *Const.* II, p. 473: "Ad notitiam universorum volumus pervenire, quod nobis apud Wormaciam

its influence: it spread into the Lower Rhine; in May the towns of Westphalia came in; from a letter addressed to the king in July it appears that more than seventy towns of South Germany took part in the assembly held under the presidency of the Justiciar, Count Adolf of Waldeck, at Mayence. With its increase in size and influence the need arose for a more settled system of conducting its affairs. At first, meetings of the league were summoned as occasion demanded, usually at Mayence or Worms, the two towns who had taken the initiative in its formation; in October it was decided to hold stated meetings at definite places and intervals: at Cologne at Epiphany, at Mayence in the octave of Easter, at Worms on the feast of St Peter and St Paul, at Strasbourg on the Nativity of the Blessed Virgin.

Nevertheless the inclusion of territorial lords in what was essentially a league of towns led very soon to difficulties; the old antagonism between the two elements sprang up again; the lords would often hamper the work of the league; the Count of Leiningen on one occasion seized the deputies of Mayence and Worms on their way to a league meeting at Strasbourg, and thrust them into prison. Some of the grievances of the lords were allayed by the conciliatory policy of the towns, who for instance renounced the hated *pfahlbürger*; but the friction continued. The difficulty of maintaining peace was further aggravated by the serious feud between the king himself and the Archbishop of Cologne. The latter in the summer of 1255 was trying to bring about the deposition of William and the election of Ottokar of Bohemia in his place. But the warnings of the new Pope, Alexander IV, effectively put an end to the conspiracy. However, William's position was so much strengthened by the league that he began to make preparations for a journey to Italy for his imperial coronation in the near future. But he had first to deal with an insurrection in West Frisia. Riding over the ice-covered marshes in mid-winter, his horse slipped; he was thrown to the ground and killed by some Frisians near Medemblik (28 January 1256).

The premature death of William of Holland was a misfortune for Germany. He was making headway, and might, had he lived, eventually have succeeded in restoring some sort of order in the country. His death threw everything again into confusion; there was no prince of outstanding position and merit upon whom the electors were likely to agree; and unanimity of certain princes was now the rule of electoral procedure. This was definitely established by the Brunswick decree of 1252, and it was emphasised by the towns, which had come during the last few years to exercise a predominant influence in German politics, when they informed

pro tribunali sedentibus et presentibus venerabilibus G. Moguntino archiepiscopo et R. Wormaciensi episcopo, dilectis principibus nostris, quam pluribus comitibus, nobilibus, et ministerialibus imperii nec non et sollempnibus nuntiis omnium civitatum pacis federe coniunctarum de Basilea inferius et pacem communiter generalem iurantibus, ..."

the princes *ad quos spectat regis electio* that they would only recognise a unanimously elected king. The method of choosing a king had completely changed in the course of the first half of the thirteenth century. At the double election of 1198 all the princes were deemed to be qualified to take part; at the double election of 1257 the right was confined to a group of seven princes. The elections of 1257 mark a definite stage in the development of the College of Electors. How that group came to be constituted is a matter of the acutest controversy. Long before the thirteenth century the Rhenish archbishops had taken a prominent part in the election of the German king: one summoned the meeting, another crowned the elect, and the third, the Archbishop of Trèves, without having any definite rôle assigned to him, had usually exercised considerable influence, and in the election of Conrad III in 1138, when the see of Mayence was vacant, his influence was decisive. The title of the ecclesiastical electors was quite independent of the offices they held, the archchancellorships of Germany, Italy, and Burgundy; for until well on in the thirteenth century the archchancellorship of Burgundy was in the hands not of the Archbishop of Trèves but of the Archbishop of Vienne. Eike of Repgau, however, who in the *Sachsenspiegel* first mentions the seven electors, clearly associates the right of the lay electors to vote first with the ministerial offices they occupied, and he excludes the King of Bohemia, the cupbearer, on the ground that he was not a German[1]. But there were certainly other reasons for singling out these four. The Count Palatine represented the extinct duchy of Franconia in which the election ought always to take place, and from the latter part of the twelfth century his influence at elections is recognised. For the rest, since the splitting up of the old tribal duchies it was long a matter of uncertainty who among the new body of princes were the most eminent. Sometimes one, sometimes another came to the front, and it was only gradually in the course of the thirteenth century that the Duke of Saxony, the Margrave of Brandenburg, and the King of Bohemia came to be singled out as the leading princes of Germany[2], and the great offices of the Crown came naturally to be attached to them.

In the election of Conrad IV in 1237 we find two of the archbishops, those of Mayence and Trèves, participating, and with them the Count Palatine and the King of Bohemia; in that of William of Holland only the three Rhenish archbishops took part. But for this very reason the election was regarded as incomplete and the supplementary election at

[1] *Vide supra*, p. 110.

[2] The position of the Duke of Bavaria is anomalous. At the election of 1257 he exercised a joint vote with his brother the Elector Palatine; for on the death of Otto II of Bavaria, the inheritance was divided between the two sons, Louis who received the Palatinate and Upper Bavaria, and his brother Henry who had Lower Bavaria. But the independent Bavarian claim was frequently asserted till the end of the thirteenth century.

Brunswick was considered necessary before William could gain any general recognition. Then on 13 January, 1257, in letters addressed by two of the electors themselves, the Archbishop of Cologne and the Count Palatine, to Richard of Cornwall, we have the first documentary evidence of the college of seven[1].

Notwithstanding the insistence on the principle of unanimity, it was almost certain that in the existing state of German politics no agreement was possible; for Germany itself was little by little losing its national unity and was breaking up into a number of more or less independent principalities. The good of the country as a whole was being sacrificed to the selfish aims of the princes; it was fairly evident that to the majority of these a weak rather than a strong, an absent rather than a resident king would be preferable, for such a man would interfere the less with their particularist ambitions. It is these facts that account for the international character of the events of 1256–7.

The powers of western Europe soon became active in the matter. As early as March, before there had been any meeting of the electors, Henry III wrote to William Bonquer, his agent at Rome, expressing his desire that a man should be chosen who was pleasing to him and that the Pope should send a legate to Germany to further his wishes. Henry's interest in the business was largely dictated by his Sicilian policy, for the success of his son Edmund might stand or fall by the result of the imperial election. But it was just the election of Edmund as King of Sicily that determined Alexander IV to oppose the election of Richard of Cornwall as King of the Romans, for this would mean the union of Sicily and the Empire, not indeed in the hands of one man but in the hands of one family. The Pope therefore and the King of France, who was actuated chiefly by his antagonism to England, threw their weight in support of another foreign candidate, Alfonso X of Castile, who through his mother Beatrix was the grandson of Philip of Swabia and who had on that account already put forward a claim to the family estates of the Hohenstaufen. Pope Alexander in 1255 had on his behalf appealed to the Swabian nobles to support his pretensions to the dukedom of Swabia; but in fact it was Italy and not Germany that Alfonso cared about, and it was by envoys from the always strongly Hohenstaufen city of Pisa that he was chosen King of the Romans in March 1256 at Soria in Castile[2]. Needless to say, Pisa had no sort of right to take upon itself the duty of filling the vacant throne, and, except in Marseilles which was allied with Pisa, the election was disregarded. In Rome the candidature of Alfonso was taken up in July; in Germany it was not seriously considered until much later.

[1] It is preserved in the *Additamenta* of Matthew Paris, *Chron. Majora*, VI, pp. 341 sq.; MGH, *Const.* II, p. 484; cf. K. Zeumer, HZ, XCIV, p. 215 sq.

[2] From the point of view of the Curia this claim through the Hohenstaufen was dangerous; it opened the way for a further claim on Sicily: the election of Alfonso by the Pisans was significant. See Hauck, V, p. 29.

The electors themselves were extraordinarily dilatory in the matter. This was no doubt partly due to the fact that Gerhard, Archbishop of Mayence, whose duty it was to summon the electors, was a prisoner in the hands of the Duke of Brunswick. It fell, therefore, to the Archbishop of Cologne to take the initiative, and he, it seems, was not prepared to hurry; an electoral meeting appears to have been summoned to Frankfort on 23 June, but we do not know whether it took place, and certainly nothing came of it. The group of princes in the north-east of Germany, and particularly Duke Albert of Saxony and the Margraves John and Otto of Brandenburg, were more active; they disliked the interference of foreign powers and were anxious to put forward a German candidate; their views were shared by the towns of the Rhenish League, with whom they were in close communication. But the difficulty was to find a suitable man. The Hohenstaufen, Conradin, was too young; so too was the late king's son Florence; Ottokar of Bohemia, in some respects an obvious person, was too powerful and too unpopular; Louis, the Count Palatine and Duke of Bavaria, was in disfavour, having this year (January 1256) murdered his wife on an ill-founded suspicion of infidelity. Finally, at Wolmirstadt on 5 August they agreed upon one of themselves, the Margrave Otto of Brandenburg. But they failed to carry his election at the formal meeting summoned to Frankfort on 8 September. The intrigues of their opponents frustrated it.

It was in the spring of 1256 that Henry III began to entertain the idea of securing the throne for his brother Richard of Cornwall. He was in his forty-seventh year, one of the wealthiest men of his time, and well known on the continent. His sister Isabella's marriage with Frederick II had brought him into close touch with the Hohenstaufen; on his return from the Crusade in 1241 he had spent some time with his brother-in-law in Sicily, and had even visited Rome on his behalf in the vain hope of effecting a reconciliation with Gregory IX. On the death of Henry Raspe, Richard was among those, if we may believe Matthew Paris, to whom the German crown was offered by the papal legate; but in deference to his friendship for Frederick he had declined it. Again it was loyalty to the Hohenstaufen, perhaps, that induced him to refuse the Pope's offer of the Sicilian crown which was subsequently accepted by Henry III for his second son Edmund. But there was now no Hohenstaufen in the way to cause him serious scruples. In June an embassy composed of Richard Clare, Earl of Gloucester, Robert Walerand, and John Mansel was dispatched from England to negotiate with the German princes. Much money was spent and the votes of three of the seven electors were won. From motives somewhat similar to those which had actuated Adolf of Altena in promoting the candidature of Otto IV, Conrad of Hochstaden, Archbishop of Cologne, placed himself at the head of the party which favoured Richard of Cornwall. Otto IV was half English by birth and wholly English in upbringing; in both cases the economic relations which bound the Lower Rhine country, and especially the city of Cologne itself, to England played no small part. The Archbishop secured the vote of his imprisoned colleague, the Archbishop of Mayence. Each received 8000 marks, and the third ecclesiastical elector, Arnold of Trèves, might have had almost twice that sum had he been willing to vote against his conscience. Of the lay electors, it was clearly useless to attempt to win over those of Saxony and Brandenburg; they had from the first adopted a different course; but Louis, the Count Palatine and Duke of Bavaria, brother-in-law of the last Hohenstaufen king, Conrad IV, and first in precedence of the lay electors, was open to a bargain. The compact was made at Bacharach in November: in return for his support Richard agreed among other things to pay him 12,000 marks and, after his election, to make over to Louis' nephew Conradin the duchy of Swabia and the allodial possessions of the Hohenstaufen. The seventh elector, Ottokar King of Bohemia, hesitated long; the Archbishop of Cologne paid him a visit at Prague in the summer, but he still hung back, and it was only after the election of Richard that he sent his envoys to signify his consent (22 January). The formal election took place outside the gates of Frankfort—for the electors were refused entrance into the city itself—on 13 January 1257.

The candidature of Alfonso of Castile had been warmly taken up in France and also at the Curia; in Germany he found a champion in Arnold, Archbishop of Trèves, who duly elected him at Frankfort on 1 April, the Electors of Saxony and Brandenburg, though not present, being consenting parties. Ottokar, who by Eike in the *Sachsenspiegel* had been denied the electoral right on the ground that he was not a German, in fact voted twice. He had gone back on his decision of 22 January and had temporarily thrown his weight on the side of Alfonso.

The official intimation of Richard's election was brought to England by a deputation consisting of the Archbishop of Cologne, the Bishops of Utrecht and Liège, Florence Count of Holland, Otto Count of Guelders, and others. They arrived shortly after the Great Council held at London on 18 March, at which Richard had made arrangements for the administration of his English affairs during his absence in Germany. They rendered their homage and were rewarded with rich presents; the Archbishop of Cologne, upon whom was bestowed a handsome mitre wrought with gold and precious stones, received his gift with the gracious reply: "mitravit me et ego eum coronabo." Richard, accompanied by his wife and two sons, by the German envoys, and by forty-seven English nobles, set out from London on 10 April. He took with him also great sums of money, raised partly from his estates, partly by cutting and selling the timber in his forests and by borrowing from the Jews. Money indeed was his chief asset, and he used it unsparingly; the Hamburg chronicler relates how "he scattered it like water at the feet of the princes," and Matthew Paris records the saying of a contemporary satirist: "it is for my sake, cries Money, that Cornwall is wedded to Rome."

The party was delayed some time at Yarmouth by a contrary wind; but by the end of the month of April they were able to cross to Dordrecht, and proceeded thence through Holland and Guelders to Aix-la-Chapelle. The way had been well prepared by the Earl of Gloucester and John Mansel, who visited Germany a second time in the winter of 1256–7. No attempt was made by the rival party, which was represented in the Low Countries by so powerful a prince as the Duke of Brabant, to check Richard's advance. Notwithstanding the declaration made by the towns of the Rhine League at Mayence in March and at Würzburg in August 1256, that they would only recognise a unanimously elected king, a declaration to which Aix-la-Chapelle was itself a party, that city not only opened its gates to Richard but gave him a magnificent welcome; and there he was crowned with his wife Sancia by Archbishop Conrad of Cologne on 17 May 1257.

Richard now had two great advantages over his rival: he was in Germany and had been crowned at Aix. Alfonso so far from being crowned had not set foot in Germany, nor did he appear to have any intention of so doing. This considerably cooled the ardour of his adherents. The princes of the north-east, Saxony, Brandenburg, and Brunswick, did not lift a finger on his behalf; they ceased to concern themselves in the matter. On the Rhine some influential persons and a few towns had declared for Alfonso, notably the Archbishop of Trèves, the Bishops of Worms and Spires, the Duke of Brabant, and the towns of Worms, Spires, and Oppenheim; but the success which attended Richard's progress through the Rhineland after his coronation is sufficient evidence to prove that the partisans of the Spanish king were not prepared to exert themselves greatly unless he took the trouble to visit the country. In fact, the success of Richard during the first months of his reign was certainly remarkable. The novel circumstance of a foreign prince, a stranger to the country with only a full purse to recommend him, marching peaceably up the Rhine and receiving the submission and homage of the towns and lords almost without striking a blow, was indeed astonishing. The fact that this happened shews that the political power and organisation of the Rhenish League was at an end; it had been unable to abide by its resolution only to recognise a king that had gained the votes of all the electors; each town followed its own independent course and made its individual bargain with Richard. Cologne, Bonn, Andernach, Oberwesel, and Bingen opened their gates without hesitation; only Boppard put up some resistance and withstood a siege of about seven weeks before it was captured. At the end of August Richard reached Mayence, where he held on 8 September his first diet. Through the energy of Archbishop Gerhard of Mayence and Bishop Henry of Strasbourg many more towns accepted him: Frankfort, Gelnhausen, Wetzlar, Friedberg, and finally, after some negotiating, Oppenheim; and even more distant towns, Hagenau, the favourite residence of the Hohenstaufen in Alsace, the strong castle of

Trifels where the imperial insignia were guarded, and the distant Swabian town of Nuremberg. From Mayence he pushed on to Oppenheim and thence to Weissenburg. Here his progress was interrupted; he had to abandon his plan of a farther advance southward owing apparently to the danger that his communications with the Netherlands and with England might be cut off by his opponent Arnold of Trèves[1], and he withdrew to the friendly regions of the Lower Rhine. Writing to Henry of Lexinton, Bishop of Lincoln, from Neuss in October on the results of his first expedition, he claims that the nobles and great men of Alsace, Swabia, Franconia, Saxony, and Upper Burgundy had done him homage, excepting only the towns of Worms and Spires; this was certainly rather more than the truth. Nevertheless his success was undoubted; even if he had gained little authority over his new subjects, he had at least been recognised by many of them as their king. When he returned to Mayence and its neighbourhood in the following summer, the two cities, Worms and Spires, which had refused to accept him on his previous visit, made their submission. Bishop John of Lübeck could without exaggeration write in June or July 1258[2] to the burghers of his city that Richard's power extended "from Berne to the sea."

But the towns of the centre and south of Germany had only been won after patient and often prolonged negotiation; they had not, like the cities of the Lower Rhine, been content with a mere confirmation of existing privileges; they generally expected and gained additional concessions, and made their submission conditional upon the Pope's confirmation of Richard's election. If the Pope approved the election of another king, their oath of allegiance to Richard became void. For this if for no other reason the attitude adopted by Pope Alexander was of the first importance to Richard; actually, however, Richard made it clear from the outset that he did not mean to be content with the mere title of King of the Romans; he intended to go to Italy and to wear the imperial crown.

Alexander IV was not, like Innocent IV, a fighting Pope, wholly absorbed in a bitter unchristian hatred for the House of Hohenstaufen; he was on the contrary of a spiritual turn of mind, and disliked politics; he regarded with aversion the unscrupulous and degrading methods employed by his predecessor to advance the papal policy, and indeed perhaps the most noteworthy acts of his pontificate from the point of view of Germany were those which nullified the most outrageous measures of Innocent IV. These were contained in three bulls issued on 5 April 1255. By the first of these, appointments to canonries by papal provision in excess of four in number were cancelled; by the second, those appointments which Innocent had made to bishoprics, abbacies, and priorates before the vacancies had actually occurred were made void; by

[1] Lemcke, *Beiträge zur Geschichte König Richards von Cornwall,* p. 42.

[2] *Ibid.* pp. 68 sq.; cf. also Bappert, *Richard von Cornwall,* Excurs II.

the third, it was made incumbent on a bishop-elect to undergo consecration within six months of his election. This last injunction was badly needed, for many of the bishops appointed in Innocent's time had forgone the obligation and held their offices without performing the duties attached to them; Henry of Leiningen had occupied the see of Spires for more than ten years without being consecrated, and Henry of Guelders, who had been appointed Bishop of Liège in 1247, was still a layman. Many ecclesiastics had enjoyed under Innocent's dispensation comfortable security from interdict, excommunication, and suspension; these immunities were now withdrawn. Undoubtedly some confusion must necessarily have resulted from this sudden reversal of policy; but in consequence of it the German Church recovered some of its old freedom, its prestige, and gradually came once more to some sort of order. Bishops were normally elected by the chapters, and regard was paid to their spiritual fitness not only to their political opinions.

But although Alexander IV did much towards the revival of religious life and discipline in the German Church, his lack of political insight made him unfitted to deal successfully with the problem of the German kingship. In the months preceding the elections of the rival kings the Pope, partly because of his friendship for France, partly because of the complication of the Sicilian question, had tended to favour the Spanish rather than the English candidate. But since then a turn of events had inclined him to alter his position. Alfonso had allied himself with Ezzelin da Romano and the Ghibelline interest, and even proposed to make an armed expedition to Italy had he not been prevented by the threatened attack of the Moors on Cordova. The towns of the Guelf faction naturally therefore took the side of his opponent; for the same reason the Pope dropped his neutrality and began openly to favour the cause of Richard. Before the end of the year 1257 the latter had through the Patriarch of Aquileia made overtures to Alexander on the subject of the imperial coronation, and early in 1258 he was informed, probably by Master Arlotus, the envoy sent from Rome to the English court on the business of Sicily, that the Pope was well disposed towards him and was prepared to grant him the imperial crown[1]. But Alexander still shrank from taking the decisive step; the official summons to Rome which Richard was eagerly awaiting did not come, for Alexander was unwilling to break off his friendly relations with Louis IX, the ally of Alfonso. It was under these circumstances that Richard in the summer of 1258 threw himself with energy into the movement for the establishment of peace between England and France, the negotiations for which had already been in progress for some time, but had up till now met with no result. The terms of the treaty, ratified in Paris in December, were arranged in February 1259, and their effect on the Pope's attitude was decisive. In April Alexander

[1] Lemcke, p. 60 and n. 25.

openly declared for Richard and empowered his envoy Walter of Rogate to invite him to come to Italy for his imperial coronation[1].

But by this time Richard had returned to England, partly in order to hasten on the peace negotiations, partly on account of the baronial crisis and the unsettled state of things resulting from the king's misgovernment and the Provisions of Oxford, partly too to replenish his purse, the real source of such power as he had managed to acquire. Though he visited Germany on three subsequent occasions, in 1260, 1262, and 1268, he never recovered the influence that he had won at the time of his departure in January 1259. This was never great: outside the Rhineland he was ignored; the German chroniclers are not interested in writing of his movements; his authority was never felt. None the less, for a foreigner with no ties and no property in Germany he had done well to have gained even mere recognition on the whole length of the Rhine. Had he succeeded in wringing from the Pope a more definite confirmation of his title and had he divorced himself entirely from English politics to devote himself to the affairs of his kingdom, he might perhaps have become a real ruler instead of a mere titular King of the Romans. As it was, he became deeply involved in the political disturbances of the latter part of the reign of Henry III, and was captured at the battle of Lewes and imprisoned for a year in Kenilworth Castle, while his position in Germany was ignored and forgotten.

When he landed at Dover on 27 January 1259, he certainly intended to return at the earliest opportunity and to make the expedition to Rome for the imperial crown. Innocent III had claimed for the Holy See the right of deciding in a disputed election to the German throne; it was incumbent therefore on Alexander to make a decision. Nevertheless the position was an embarrassing one, for although neither Richard nor Alfonso was obnoxious to the Curia, neither was entirely satisfactory. So he delayed until in May 1261 death relieved him of the necessity of making up his mind. His successor Urban IV was a man of a different stamp. James of Troyes owed his advancement in the Church to Innocent IV who had employed him frequently in papal business, and like his patron he was a politician. Though by birth a Frenchman, he had spent the greater part of his active life in Germany, especially in the east, in the newly colonised areas of Pomerania and Prussia; he had been archdeacon of Liège and subsequently in 1253 Bishop of Verdun; two years later Alexander IV had appointed him Patriarch of Jerusalem. He was therefore a man of wide experience and one who was familiar with Germany and her problems. Yet in spite of his many qualifications, his handling of the question of the disputed election was quite ineffectual. By bestowing the crown of Sicily upon his countryman, Charles of Anjou, he removed one objection that might be raised against Richard's candidature; for as

[1] Bappert, *Richard von Cornwall*, p. 39 sq.

long as the offer of the Sicilian crown remained open to Edmund there was the danger that Germany and the kingdom might be in the hands of one family. But for the rest he made little headway; he refused the request of Alfonso for imperial coronation on the ground that both he and Richard had declined to submit their claims to papal arbitration. When in response to this letter the two kings conceded the right of the Pope to decide between them, Urban gave the title of King-elect of the Romans to both, explaining in a letter written to Richard a few days later that he did not attach any importance to the title until he had issued his verdict; and he fixed 2 May 1264 for hearing the case[1]. But for one reason or another the hearing was postponed and postponed. Urban died in October 1264 and was succeeded by another French Pope, Clement IV, a lawyer, but one who regarded himself as above the law[2]. Indeed, though in general he followed the policy of his predecessor, he set his pretensions higher: he not only claimed the right to decide a contested election but also the control of affairs of the Empire in the time pending the decision[3]. However, he had neither the strength nor the energy to put these claims into practice; he only fixed dates for hearing the case, which through the failure of one party or the other to send representatives was never heard. He tried to get the rival kings to abdicate voluntarily, but neither would give way; and when he died in 1268 the German problem was no nearer a solution. After this it could not be settled from Rome, for there was no Pope to settle it: an interregnum of nearly three years followed the death of Clement IV.

In the meanwhile the Germans were tiring of their virtually kingless condition. There was a not insignificant party that wished to see the traditional strong monarchy of the Hohenstaufen revived in the person of the boy Conradin, who was being brought up at the court of his uncle, the Duke of Bavaria. His election as king was often threatened, and once at least, in April 1262, an electoral meeting was actually summoned by Werner, Archbishop of Mayence, for the purpose of carrying it through. But these attempts were always frustrated by King Ottokar of Bohemia, who had taken advantage of the anarchical state of the country to make himself the most powerful prince in the Empire[4]; he had added to his Bohemian kingdom Austria and Styria, and in August 1262 gained King Richard's confirmation of these acquisitions. The present condition of things in Germany was admirably suited to the development of his power,

[1] Urban's letter of 27 August, which is printed in MGH, *Const.* II, pp. 522 sqq., is of interest in the history of the disputed election and of the College of Electors; for it contains the first official recognition by the Curia of the seven electors: "circa electionem novi regis Romanorum in imperatorem postea promovendi apud principes vocem in huiusmodi electione habentes, qui sunt septem numero."

[2] Hauck, v, p. 41, n. 3. "quamquam nos supra ius providentia divina statuerit."

[3] *Ibid.* p. 42, and n. 3.

[4] See *infra.* ch. XIII A. pp. 438–9.

and, when there was danger of a resuscitation of the Hohenstaufen monarchy, he sent urgent messages to the two people whose interests, besides his own, were most nearly affected—the Pope and Richard of Cornwall; and both were roused to action. The Pope wrote letters threatening with excommunication anyone who ventured to take part in the election of Conradin, and Richard came hurrying back to Germany, hoping by his presence to put an end to the idea of promoting Conradin to the German crown (1262); but the danger was revived more than once, and was not even entirely dispelled by the execution of Conradin after the battle of Tagliacozzo in October 1268. For a pretender, a son of a blacksmith at Ochsenfurt, a university student, came forward at Pavia asserting that he was Conradin, and found many people to believe in him until his case was investigated by Bishop Everard of Constance and the Abbot of St Gall, and the fraud was exposed.

The German escort which accompanied Richard to England in January 1259 were surprised to find how little he was esteemed among his own people. "How can we treat with honour," they said, "a man whom even his fellow-countrymen do not respect"; and they went on to say that, if they could get from him what money he had left, they would gladly dispense with his personal presence; they thereupon returned to Germany in disgust. Matthew Paris' story probably represents fairly accurately the opinion in Germany with regard to Richard. When his stock of money was exhausted they had no further use for him. On his subsequent visits he made little impression on his subjects and exercised scarcely any influence. His stay from June till October 1260 was quite uneventful: we find him at Cambrai, at Worms where he spent most of the summer, at Mayence, and at Boppard; he granted a few charters, he settled a dispute which for three years past had disturbed the peace of the city of Worms. His next journey was both longer and more important; it lasted from July 1262 until February 1263, and he traversed the whole length of the Rhine as far as Basle. It was on this occasion that he confirmed King Ottokar, as already mentioned, in his recent acquisitions of Austria and Styria; he was also with some difficulty reconciled with Ottokar's opponent, Archbishop Werner of Mayence, the promoter of Conradin. He was less successful in his attempt to restore order. A fierce feud had raged for some time between the Bishop and the townsmen of Strasbourg, a war called after Bishop Walter of Geroldseck the "Bellum Waltherianum," in which not only Alsace but a large part of Swabia was involved. It came ultimately to a pitched battle at Hausbergen in March 1262; but notwithstanding the defeat of the bishop's party and the attempted mediation of King Richard, the quarrel continued till after Bishop Walter's death in February 1263. Nor was this by any means an isolated instance. The inevitable result of the almost total absence of a central government was that feuds broke out and were waged unchecked all over the country; there were struggles like that at Strasbourg between bishops and towns; private wars between neighbouring princes; disputes over succession like that which prevailed incessantly in Thuringia over the inheritance of the last of the line of landgraves[1].

Richard sometimes made arrangements for carrying on the government during his absence. When he returned to England after his brief visit in 1260[2], he appointed Philip of Falkenstein, his chamberlain, as his representative in the Wetterau; Bishop Werner of Strasbourg in Alsace; Philip of Hohenfels in Boppard and Oberwesel. But "they worked everything to their own advantage, and nowhere was peace to be found."[3] Some years later, when the danger from the Hohenstaufen party was acute, the imperial lands on the right bank of the Rhine were entrusted to the care of Ottokar of Bohemia, those on the left bank to the Archbishop of Mayence (1266). But no one man was ever made responsible for the administration; no prince was entrusted with a position such as Engelbert of Cologne or Louis of Bavaria had occupied in the long absences of Frederick II from his kingdom. The result was that certain of the stronger princes took upon themselves the duty of restoring some sort of order by means of local *landfrieden* sworn usually for a period of years. Archbishop Conrad of Cologne, acting perhaps as the representative of King Richard, issued such a one for the district of the Lower Rhine (November 1259); another issued in 1265 covered the diocese of Paderborn and the landgraviate of Hesse. Archbishop Werner of Mayence was particularly active in trying to improve the wretched state of the country by this method: in 1264 he united with the Count Palatine of the Rhine in a *landfrieden* embracing their own territories; the next year he arranged a peace which was sworn by a number of counts and nobles of the neighbourhood of Mayence and by the towns of the Wetterau; and it was largely his influence that induced King Richard during his visit to Germany in 1269 to publish a general land-peace to be enforced throughout the whole Rhineland.

This last visit of Richard, made in August 1268, was more eventful than either of the two which had preceded it. He spent the summer at Cambrai and Aix-la-Chapelle; in December he was at Cologne; in the spring at Worms. There about the middle of April he held a diet at which the Archbishops of Mayence and Trèves, three other bishops, the Count Palatine, and a number of counts and lesser nobles presented themselves. They belonged, it is true, exclusively to the Rhine district, for beyond it his influence was entirely negligible; none the less it is significant, for never since the first year of his reign had he been attended by so many German

[1] It was finally settled in 1263 by a partition of the old landgraviate between the two claimants: Thuringia itself fell to Henry the Illustrious, Margrave of Meissen, whose mother Jutta was the daughter of Landgrave Herman; Hesse passed to Henry the child, the grandson of Landgrave Louis and St Elizabeth, who was raised to the rank of prince of the Empire by Adolf of Nassau in 1292.

[2] Böhmer, *Reg.* 5356*a* and Bappert, p. 33 sq. wrongly attribute this arrangement to the year 1258. See Lemcke, p. 81, n. 26.

[3] *Ann. Wormat.*, MGH, *Script.* XVII, p. 60.

princes. The diet also transacted important business: "here," wrote Thomas Wykes[1], "he began to consider how more beneficially and effectually he might deal with the evils that oppressed the unhappy country, that the stubborn violence of the footpads being overcome, the longed-for peace might return to the Rhine and the requisites of life might reach the inhabitants unimpeded." This passage concisely sums up the work of the diet of Worms. Here the Rhenish land-peace was sworn; here unlawful tolls, except the ancient imperial tolls levied at Boppard and Kaiserswerth, were removed; here the *ungelt*, a kind of excise on wine and food-stuffs, was abolished. The same writer records the universal rejoicing with which these measures were received, and the revival of trade and the cheapening of prices which resulted from it.

It was on the occasion of this visit that, with the object of ingratiating himself with his subjects, he married on 5 June as his third wife the daughter of a prominent German noble, Beatrix of Falkenburg, a woman reported to be remarkable for her beauty. However, the marriage had no effect upon his position in Germany, for, some six weeks afterwards, he crossed with her to England, where he spent the remainder of his life. He died of paralysis on 2 April 1272, and was buried by the side of his second wife Sancia in the great Cistercian abbey which he had founded at Hailes.

France, with the encouragement of the Popes, took every advantage of the political confusion which prevailed in the Empire during the last years of the Hohenstaufen and during the interregnum to encroach upon the imperial frontiers both in the north and in the south, in the valley of the Rhone and in the Low Countries. In the kingdom of Arles there were, as in Germany, the same feuds between towns and their feudal superiors, and to this was added a further cause of disturbance, religious dissension. It was the heresy prevalent in Provence which afforded to the Pope and to France the opportunity to strike a blow at the authority, slight as it was, held by the Emperor over that district. At the Lateran Council in 1215 the imperial fiefs, which included Vivarais, of Count Raymond VI of Toulouse, the favourer of the Albigenses, were assigned without consulting the lawful suzerain, the Emperor, to the leader of the crusade, Simon de Montfort; and by a clause in the treaty concluded at Paris in 1229 Raymond was required to cede to the Church for ever the land which he held of the Empire beyond the Rhone. In 1226 Louis VIII mustered an army at Lyons in imperial territory and marched against the imperial town of Avignon, which capitulated after a three months' siege. The feud between Raymond VII of Toulouse and Raymond Berengar IV of Provence, who was supported by his son-in-law Louis IX, led in 1239 to a further weakening of the imperial and a corresponding strengthening of the French influence. Then in 1246 the decisive blow fell. Raymond Berengar died in 1245 leaving no sons, but four daughters. The three elder were already well

[1] *Annales Monastici*, ed. Luard (Rolls Series), iv, pp. 222 sqq.; cf. also *Ann. Wormat. sub anno* 1269, p. 68.

provided for; they had married respectively the King of France, the King of England, and Richard of Cornwall who was soon to become King of the Romans. He therefore bequeathed his lands to the youngest and still unmarried daughter, Beatrix. The hand of this valuable heiress was eagerly sought after by the neighbouring princes, by the Count of Toulouse and by the King of Aragon; but the prize was won by Charles of Anjou, the brother of Louis IX. He entered Provence with a French army, liberated Beatrix who was being besieged by King James of Aragon, and married her in January 1246. The anarchy which reigned in Germany and the struggle between the Pope and Emperor in Italy prevented any imperial interference, and the French occupation of Provence was allowed to take firm root. The barrier which severed France from Italy was broken down, and the penetration of French influence in Italian politics was made easy. It opened the way for Charles of Anjou's expedition and for his acquisition of the Sicilian crown.

A somewhat similar encroachment was also being made by France on her north-east frontier. Freed since the battle of Bouvines from interference both from the Empire and from England, she began to intervene more and more in the affairs of her neighbours, to influence the politics of the Low Countries, and to extend her power there at the expense of the Empire. In this development the feud between the house of Avesnes and that of Dampierre played a very important part. Margaret, the heiress of Flanders and Hainault, married in 1212 Burchard of Avesnes, who had entered the Church, and on this ground the marriage was declared void. Margaret however continued for ten years to live with him and bore him two sons. She then regretted her past conduct, left him, married William of Dampierre, and developed a violent hatred for the sons by her first marriage. When in 1244 she entered upon her inheritance, the question of succession became acute. Gregory IX had declared her sons by her first husband bastards; Frederick II had declared them legitimate. The question was referred to the arbitration of the Pope and Louis IX, who in 1246 granted Hainault to John of Avesnes, Flanders to William of Dampierre. The award seemed just; Louis, however, though acting in the matter with scrupulous equity, had in fact greatly promoted the interests of France, for William of Dampierre was a French vassal, a noble of Champagne, and upon him Louis had bestowed not only French, but imperial Flanders. But French diplomacy had done more than this; it had made the Count of Flanders entirely dependent on French assistance to defeat the claims of his rival John of Avesnes, who took his stand as the champion of imperialist interests. The position of the latter was greatly strengthened when William of Holland was elected King of the Romans in 1247, for the Counts of Holland were also threatened by the power of Flanders, which exercised suzerainty over the southern part of Zeeland, over the mouth of the Scheldt, and even claimed rights over the mouth of the Meuse and the Rhine. The reign of William of Holland was almost wholly absorbed with the great feud with Flanders. The treaty in 1256 which ended the war was altogether in the French interest: John certainly retained Hainault, yet he was compelled not only to renounce Namur which had been granted him by William of Holland, but also to acknowledge the Flemish over-lordship of Zeeland. By a vigorous support of the candidature of Richard of Cornwall, John tried to arrange a formidable alliance between Germany and England directed against France; but all to no purpose. France steadily extended her influence. Guy, the son of William of Dampierre, purchased from Baldwin, the Latin Emperor of Constantinople, the county of Namur (1263), and, after the death of his mother Margaret in 1280, succeeded peacefully to the Flemish inheritance. As a result of the long feud France had supplanted the Empire in imperial Flanders (east of the Scheldt) and in Namur, and was in a fair way to gain a decisive influence in the extensive dominions attached to the see of Liège, which stretched to the south and to the north-east of the county of Namur. The Low Countries at the end of the thirteenth century appeared to be no more than an appendage of the Capetian monarchy[1].

But if the boundaries and the sphere of influence of Germany had seriously receded in the west, the loss was more than compensated by its rapid expansion in the east. The thirteenth century is the most flourishing and vigorous period of German colonisation in the Slavonic lands. The movement had always gone forward independently of the Emperors, and was therefore little or not at all affected by the weakness or lack of central government. It had been promoted by the border princes, by Henry the Lion, Albert the Bear, and the Babenberg dukes of Austria; by active missionary bishops and by monastic orders, especially by the Cistercians and the Premonstratensians. The nobles and missionaries of the Church in the east of Germany continued their work, ignoring or oblivious of the political confusion which prevailed in the west. The brothers John and Otto of Brandenburg pushed forward their frontier to the Oder and beyond it, and founded Frankfort on the Oder (1250). Silesia was peaceably occupied and settled by German colonists, and no less than fifteen hundred villages are reckoned to have been planted there during the twelfth and thirteenth centuries[2]; Germans were settling and opening up the great tracts of virgin forest in Bohemia and farther to the south-east in Moravia, and even as far as Transylvania German colonies were to be found. More important still was the slow but steady advance of the Teutonic Knights in Prussia and Livonia. The attempt to introduce Christianity among the heathen Prussians had been begun early in the century by a Cistercian monk, Christian, from the monastery of Oliva near Danzig. He appears to have been granted by Innocent III about 1215 the rank of bishop, and with the help of the Polish duke, Conrad of Masovia, he made some

[1] Pirenne, *Histoire de Belgique*, I, p. 232.

[2] Jastrow und Winter, *Die Hohenstaufen*, II, p. 637.

progress in Kulmerland and Prussia; but his work was almost undone by a heathen reaction in 1223. The Duke of Masovia turned for help to Herman of Salza, who sent the Teutonic Order to recover the lost ground; Kulmerland was granted to the Order and the arrangement was sanctioned by the Emperor Frederick at Rimini in March 1226. In 1230 the Knights began the conquest, and in spite of frequent checks advanced steadily. Their progress is marked by the erection of fortresses which developed into towns: Thorn in 1231, Kulm in 1232, Marienwerder in 1233, Elbing in 1237. In that year the Order incorporated the Order of the Knights of the Sword, which had for some years past been actively working for the conquest and conversion of Livonia and Esthonia. An advance in 1251 led to the founding of Memel on the coast at the extreme north of East Prussia, and after a campaign in 1254 Königsberg was founded and named after King Ottokar of Bohemia who had taken part in the campaign.

The German people made excellent colonists in the Middle Ages, enterprising, industrious, and not easily discouraged by the difficulties which they encountered. Nobles and peasants migrated from the more thickly-populated areas of the old country to settle in the newly-won lands. They opened up the country, made clearings in the dense forests which covered the plain of central Europe, and started a thriving agriculture. And side by side with this great territorial expansion, trade and commerce developed. This was due to the energetic policy pursued by the towns. After the break-up of the great Rhenish League in 1257 small groups of towns, like those which had preceded the greater league, again formed themselves for the mutual protection of their commercial interests and for their defence. The three towns of Mayence, Worms, and Oppenheim, the original members of the League of the Rhine, formed one; the Westphalian towns another; Lübeck, Rostock, and Wismar a third (September 1259). This last in the light of later developments is the most interesting of the three, for it was the nucleus of the "Wendish group" in the Hanseatic League.

Through the activity and vigour of the towns and the enterprise of the merchants, Germany was rapidly gaining the predominant influence in the trade of the North Sea and of the Baltic. From early in the century the German merchants had acquired equal rights and privileges with the Swedish inhabitants at Wisby on the island of Gothland, which had for a long while been the centre of the Baltic trade; they established a trading association at Novgorod and by degrees ousted the Scandinavian merchants who had before almost monopolised the trade with Russia. Soon Lübeck supplanted Wisby as the directing influence in the Baltic. The legate Albert, Archbishop of Livonia, Esthonia, and Prussia, in acknowledgement of the great services they had rendered to the missionary work among the Slavs, granted the merchants of Lübeck freedom from all imposts and tolls in his extensive province (1256); the city received trading privileges in all the Scandinavian countries, from Hakon of Norway (1247), from Eric King of Denmark (1259), and from Earl Berger, uncle and regent of

King Waldemar of Sweden (1261). On the other side of the Danish peninsula, in close alliance with Hamburg, Lübeck was making similar developments as the rival to Cologne in the trade of the North Sea. In recognition of her support of the candidature of Richard of Cornwall, she had received trading privileges in England in 1257. Ten years later, in 1266 and 1267, Hamburg and Lübeck received the right to have their own hanse in England and became serious rivals to the merchants of the Cologne "Steelyard." They had acquired also from Margaret of Flanders trading rights in the Flemish towns. To the energy and enterprise of these two cities is due mainly the rise of the Hanseatic League.

The Great Interregnum had afforded the princes of Germany the opportunity to consolidate their position as practically independent territorial lords; it had struck a deadly blow at central government in Germany. Nevertheless it had left enduring marks on the course of German history in the definite establishment of the College of Electors, in the constitutional and commercial development of the towns, and above all in the great wave of expansion eastward where was firmly planted the seed of Germany's future power.

CHAPTER V.

ITALY AND SICILY UNDER FREDERICK II.

THE history of Italy and Sicily[1] in the time of Frederick II consists of the tragic vicissitudes of a great idea, the unity of Italy within the Empire. But, attacked on all sides, by the Papacy, by the communes, this idea came to ruin. The political life of Italy, still styled a kingdom, was parcelled amid numberless units, living each for itself and to itself; their exuberant energy was directed only to their own separate interests, and therefore they were as a rule the more bitterly hostile to one another when they were neighbours[2]. This permanent conflict of interests was suspended indeed by many communes when the Emperor Frederick I threatened their very existence. Then was formed for the first time the Lombard League[3], although even then not a few communes supported the German sovereign. At the Peace of Constance Frederick was compelled to recognise the legal existence of the communes, and their right of self-administration, of exercising jurisdiction, and of contracting alliances, in return for their fealty and certain prescribed duties. Soon these obligations of the communes fell into oblivion, and Italy dissolved amid surviving feudal lords and republics, guided and torn by local passions and local interests in a perpetual strife of little leagues and counter-leagues.

With an inverse evolution Southern Italy, splintered in the tenth century, had been consolidated by the Normans under the house of Hauteville and had been formed by Roger II into the kingdom of Sicily, then the richest and most civilised state in Europe, with its capital in the splendid city of Palermo. Here in contrast to the North was a unity identified with the monarchy which governed it[4].

Almost at the junction of these two divergent territories, in the little city of Jesi in the March of Ancona, the Empress Constance, the daughter of Roger II, gave birth on 26 December 1194 to Frederick-Roger, who as Frederick II was to be the greatest personality of the thirteenth century. His father, the Emperor Henry VI, was then erecting a personal and German domination from the Alps to the African sea. By

[1] The Italy and Sicily of the thirteenth century bear a different sense from that of to-day. Italy is the *Regnum Italicum* of the Holy Roman Empire, the northern half of the peninsula; Sicily is the Norman kingdom including Apulia and Capua from the Tronto and the Garigliano as well as the island of Sicily.

[2] See *supra*, Vol. v, Chapter v.

[3] See *supra*, Vol. v, Chapter XIII.

[4] See *supra*, Vol. v, Chapter IV.

policy rather than by arms he was controlling Lombardy; Central Italy was placed under three German dukes; he even obtained an oath of fealty from the prefect and senator of Rome. Meanwhile he at last conquered Sicily, suppressing revolts with pitiless ferocity and causing his Sicilian, even more than his Italian, subjects to look on his early death (28 September 1197) as a liberation.

As had happened three years before[1], Sicily came into the hands of a woman and a child, of Constance who had already rejoined her husband in the island, and of Frederick whom his father had had elected King of the Romans at the diet of Ratisbon. By his imperial brother's order Philip, Duke of Swabia, was on his way from Germany to conduct his nephew to be crowned at Aix-la-Chapelle, when on the Emperor's death a revolt of the Tuscans and the political situation in Germany compelled him to return and fight for the German crown[2]. The Empress had Frederick brought from Foligno to Palermo, where the strife of parties produced an extremely difficult situation. The German soldiers of fortune domineered as conquerors; the conquered Normans, with the mass of the population, demanded the expulsion of the foreigners, including the son of the "pitiless" Henry. Of the Saracens, some had withdrawn to the hills to make ready for insurrection, others, remaining as artisans in the cities or cultivators in the plains, feigned conversion to Christianity while filled with rancour against the Christians. Amid these clashing elements there appeared Markward, the seneschal, already disliked by Constance as the adviser of Henry VI's fierce policy. Being expelled from the March of Ancona by a popular outburst, like Philip from Tuscany and Conrad of Urslingen from Spoleto, he now demanded the regency of Sicily as the executor of the Emperor's testament.

Constance had already sent to the Pope to request her son's investiture with Sicily and permission to bury her husband in the cathedral in Palermo. Confronted with the demands of the seneschal, she now declared him a public enemy, dismissed all Germans and adherents of their party such as Walter of Palear, Bishop of Troia, Henry's chancellor, and surrounded herself with counsellors of the Norman faction. Meanwhile Pope Celestine III died at the age of ninety-one, and was immediately replaced by Innocent III, energetic, ambitious, and in the prime of life (8 January 1198). Hence the Empress was obliged to send to the new Pope another more solemn embassy, while she had her son anointed and crowned with great pomp in the cathedral of Palermo (Whitsunday, 17 May 1198).

Like Henry VI, Constance claimed for the Crown those rights which Tancred had given up—the apostolic legateship, the control over appeals to the Papacy, the holding of synods, and the election of prelates. Now

[1] It should here be mentioned that the limits of this chapter forbid the treatment of intellectual and economic development.

[2] See *supra*, Chapter II.

Innocent firmly insisted on their surrender, and Constance in her strait was compelled to surrender the first three, while retaining only in part the control of ecclesiastical elections. Another danger was produced by the Pope's equity. He commanded the liberation of Tancred's family and of the other Sicilian captives in Germany; and the ex-Queen Sibylla was released or escaped along with her daughters, the eldest of whom found a French husband, Walter, Count of Brienne, who, though poor, was related to the royal houses of France and England, and proved a formidable champion of the dispossessed dynasty.

At the Pope's command Constance restored Walter of Palear to the chancellorship, and promised to pay annually the accustomed tribute of 600 *schifati* for Apulia and 400 for Marsica (equal together to 270 ounces of gold); and thus obtained the investiture of the kingdom of Sicily for herself and her son. In her fears for the boy's future, she provided by her will that on her death the Pope himself should become his guardian with the handsome yearly recompense of 3750 *schifati* besides the reimbursement of expenses incurred for the defence of the state. She also set up a Council of Regency, consisting of the Chancellor Palear and the Archbishops of Palermo, Monreale, and Capua. Not long after she expired (27 November 1198).

Innocent III declared that he accepted the guardianship in right of his pastoral office, his suzerainty of the kingdom, and the last will of the dead Empress. He confirmed the Council of Regency, but despatched Gregory of Galcano, Cardinal of Santa Maria in Portico, as Vicar Apostolic to take over the guardianship and direct the Council. The deaths, however, of two of the Council and the weakness of Caro of Monreale gave all its powers to the aspiring Bishop of Troia. Master of the capital and the person of the little king, the Chancellor sought only his personal aggrandisement, and, disregarding the Legate, alienated royal demesnes and rights in order to gain a following. Since the supreme authority was weakened by discord, the secondary powers were unbridled, whether prelates, barons, townsmen, German soldiers of fortune reappearing at the death of the Empress, or the Genoese. The last, privileged throughout the island and lords of Syracuse, behaved like an independent power; but their enemies, the Pisans, were roused against them. Markward, after an attempt to conquer the kingdom from the north, neutralised Innocent by a feigned repentance, and, leaving the mainland war to Count Diepold, was transported by a Pisan fleet from Salerno to Trapani (October 1199). There he raised in revolt all the Val di Mazzara and the Muslims, and prepared to besiege Palermo.

The Chancellor Walter, lacking both troops and money, was forced to make common cause with the Pope. With troops under Innocent's cousin, the Marshal Giacopo, he severely defeated the rebels before Palermo (21 July 1200), and raised the siege. This was enough to make the Pope recall his forces and reward his cousin with the county of Andria. On the mainland his instrument was the Count of Brienne, who claimed with his approval his wife's inheritance of Lecce and Taranto. At the head of French troops, levied with the help of papal money, Count Walter overthrew the German Count Diepold of Vohburg near Capua (10 June 1201), and proceeded to King Tancred's lands in Apulia. But this success of the rival dynasty alarmed the Chancellor, who was already enraged by the Pope's strict control and the quashing by Innocent of his election to the see of Palermo; and he closed with the less domineering partner and adversary. He ceded to Markward the government of the island and the custody of Frederick, and took for himself the rule of the mainland, all in open defiance of the Pope. Innocent responded by excommunicating the Chancellor and depriving him of his bishopric of Troia, while he admonished the seven-year-old king (3 July 1201) and thus provoked (from whose initiative we do not know) the first circular appeal to the princes of the world for help against unjust attack among the many such manifestoes which were a character of his reign.

The clumsy surgeon who caused Markward's death in an operation for the stone did not change the situation in the island, for another German, William Capparone, usurped power with the title of Captain-general (September 1202). On the mainland Diepold, lord of Salerno and much of Campania, warred against Walter of Brienne, master of a great part of Apulia. The native baronage was divided between the two; Walter of Palear obdurately refused pardon and held by Diepold. But when in a surprise attack on the historic plain of Canne the Count of Vohburg was put to flight by the Count of Brienne, the pride of Walter was humbled. After an interval of concealment he submitted to the Pope, was restored to the chancellorship, and later was compensated for the loss of the see of Troia by that of Catania.

In the island, where events were diversified by a sharp war between the Pisans and the Genoese, in which the latter were victorious and retained their city of Syracuse, the papal party continually advanced, until Capparone himself sent ambassadors to recognise the papal suzerainty (October 1204). The work was completed by two events, which, in themselves misfortunes, yet gave Innocent the final victory. The Pope fell ill at Anagni, and the rumour of his death lured almost all Apulia into insurrection against Walter of Brienne. The count recovered ground and renewed the war with Diepold, whom he besieged in the castle of Sarno. But in his arrogance he did not keep the requisite watch, was surprised in his camp, and died of his wounds (June 1205). With the disappearance of the champion of the Hautevilles, the opposition to the Pope grew weaker; Diepold himself submitted and was sent to Palermo to induce Capparone to consign King Frederick into the hands of the Legate, Cardinal Gherardo of Sant' Adriano, Innocent's nephew, towards the close of the year 1206. The Pope later reckoned his expenses in all at 12,800 gold ounces, Frederick's first debt.

Two years had yet to run before the king attained his majority, fixed by the Pope at fourteen. They were years of turbulence: there was a Muslim revolt with its centre at Corleone; Diepold, embroiled with the Chancellor, joined the German bands who plundered the Terra di Lavoro; the native barons usurped jurisdiction, built illegal castles, carried on their feuds, and tormented the population. Innocent did more than exhort: he drove out one German adventurer, and gave his county of Sora to his own brother Richard; at a congress in San Germano (June 1208) he set up a fresh regency for the mainland. But when the kingdom was consigned to Frederick the demesne was depleted, and the revenues were so exhausted that the most pressing daily needs of the king were only provided for by the loyal gifts of the townsmen of the greater cities.

Secluded in the palace and its gardens, Frederick had grown up amid adversities. Even so he had been able to develope his marvellous natural powers, training assiduously his strong and active body, and enriching his mind with every kind of profitable study. He said himself later that in his youth, before taking up the burden of government, he had sought after knowledge and loved her beauty without ceasing, and had always breathed her balsamic perfumes. Two months after his majority there landed at Palermo the wife chosen for him by the Pope, Constance, sister of Peter II of Aragon and widow of Emeric, King of Hungary (February 1209). She was accompanied by her brother Alfonso, Count of Provence, and a brilliant train of Aragonese, Catalan, and Provençal knights, and 400 lances for her husband's service. But when, already provoked by the insolence of the Sicilian barons, Frederick marched eastwards "to conquer the land," his foreign forces were dissipated by an epidemic, and he "remained at Messina with his townsmen, for there were no other knights with him." Secret conspiracy and open insolence were rife among the nobles. The king succeeded in cajoling them, and then suddenly arrested a number of them and confiscated their usurped domains. Other energetic acts followed, such as the dismissal of the Chancellor; the canons of Palermo, on their refusing to elect a nominee as archbishop, were exiled. But here Frederick found himself still in trammels. The Pope rated him for the sentence on the canons, and commanded the reinstatement of Walter of Palear as Chancellor (25 January 1210). Frederick characteristically justified his treatment of the barons by a manifesto; at this moment, however, he and his suzerain were in dire need of one another's aid.

If the possession of Sicily by his son confirmed in some measure the work of Henry VI, the peace he had given Italy collapsed at his death. The three duchies he had formed in the centre fell to pieces as we have seen, and everywhere the intestine war burst out more furiously than ever. The Pope himself was an aggressive, if not warlike, power. Immediately on his accession he secured control of the prefect and the senator of Rome, only to lose it again when the Romans, against his command, insisted on waging a victorious war with wealthy Viterbo. Worse still, the single senator was again replaced by the senate of fifty-three members, which compelled the Pope to quit Rome for a year. But the disorders of a new election induced the Romans to recall him and to restore to him the right of nominating the senator. Meantime he had gained a nominal accession of territory. By the diploma of Neuss (8 June 1201), the Guelf claimant Otto IV ceded to the Church the country between Radicofani and Ceprano, the Exarchate, the Pentapolis, the March of Ancona, the Duchy of Spoleto, and Matilda's lands, in short all and more than all the territory which was to form the Papal State up to 1860. But it was not until the autumn of 1207 that the enlarged papal dominion was acknowledged in a congress of petty rulers at Viterbo.

Tuscany made an attempt at providing for peace with curious speed. On Henry VI's death the Tuscan cities and lords formed at San Genesio a "Tuscan League" under the patronage of the Pope: they would recognise neither emperor nor king without the Pope's consent, and would aid the Roman Church against any one who, not being a member of the league, disturbed its possessions. The league indeed broke down, for the allies, among them Florence, attacked one another. Pisa, who had held aloof from the movement, was meanwhile carrying on her war with Genoa, and lost a point to her rival when her *protégé* Marquess William of Massa was driven out of his two Judicates in Sardinia.

In the March of Verona and Friuli there reigned perpetual strife, both between the great nobles among themselves and between them and the communes, but there were clear signs of the nobles gaining clients and leading parties in the latter. In Piedmont the communes were in the ascendant, and new communes, like Cuneo, were formed on the lands of the Marquess of Saluzzo and the Bishop of Asti. In central Lombardy a Lombard league headed by Milan fought Cremona and her allies during the abeyance of the Empire; and this was typical. The external wars fostered internal strife, which caused too often the exile of a defeated faction among the enemies of their native city[1].

Into this land of discord came Otto IV, the surviving claimant of the Empire. On renewing at Spires the donation of Neuss he had been promised by Innocent III the imperial crown; and in 1209 he came urging peace and protesting himself rigidly impartial. But his actions belied him. Ezzelin II, lord of Bassano, received Vicenza; Salinguerra not only kept Ferrara but was made Count of Romagna. Genoa, on the other hand, was forced to renounce the dominion of Albenga and Savona;

[1] It was in this period that the names of Guelf and Ghibelline arose in Tuscany for the rival factions which favoured Otto and Philip. They were derived from the war-cries (*Hie Welf; Hie Waiblingen*) used in Germany by the adherents of the rival houses. See *supra*, Vol. v, Chapter x.

Asti that of Annone, centre indeed of the imperial demesne in Piedmont. Meanwhile Otto at an assembly at Bologna demanded the fealty of communes and feudal lords, with their contingents for his march to Rome and the long arrears of tribute. Passing through Tuscany, he met the Pope at Viterbo; there he pledged himself never to invade the kingdom of Sicily, a sign perhaps of the likelihood of the invasion, and on 4 October 1209 the coronation at St Peter's was peaceably performed. But the Senator, indignant at the commune of Rome being ignored, had already barred the bridges of the Tiber, and in the evening the Romans rose in insurrection. The Emperor in disgust made his way back to Lombardy. At Piacenza he let his designs be seen; he was reverting to the policy of Henry VI and would unite Sicily to the Empire. His pledges, perhaps, were too many and too onerous to keep; and the Empire's need of demesnes and revenues was more crying than ever before.

Otto IV began by reconciling for the nonce Pisa and Genoa, and then invited both to furnish him with ships for the passage to Sicily. Though Genoa refused, Pisa agreed and equipped forty galleys. But when his intrigues were extended to Sicily, the German captains of Henry VI preferred their compatriot to Henry's Sicilian son, and drew to their side the more turbulent barons, the prelates, discontented townsmen, and the Saracens of the island; the Guelf banner was hoisted at Naples and elsewhere. To the Pope Otto practically threw down the gauntlet. His distant kinsman, Azzo VI, Marquess of Este in the Veneto, had been invested by Innocent III with the March of Ancona. The Emperor now annulled this grant and himself invested Azzo with the March, and the traitorous Count Diepold with the Duchy of Spoleto, as his own lieutenants. Finally, advancing southwards once more with a powerful army composed of Germans, Lombards, and Tuscans, he entered Marsica from Rieti in November 1210, to be met obsequiously by the Abbot of Monte Cassino and all the lords of the Terra di Lavoro save the Count of Aquino. He halted to winter at Capua, and the same fate seemed to hang over the head of the young Hohenstaufen as had been inflicted by Henry VI on the last child-king of the Norman line.

This time the saviour of the Sicilian monarchy and of the liberty of Italy was the Pope. When he saw that his exhortations and threats (March 1210) were in vain, he excommunicated the perjured Emperor and his supporters, and placed Capua and Naples under interdict (November 1210). When Otto subdued Apulia and much of Calabria, Innocent solemnly renewed the excommunication on Holy Thursday (30 March) 1211, and called all his partisans and all enemies of the Emperor to arms. More effective still was his summons to the German princes to depose Otto and to elect in his stead Frederick of Sicily, "as young in years as old in wisdom." This bold move had immediate success; the ancient adherents of the Hohenstaufen in Italy, the Marquesses of Este and Montferrat, the communes of Genoa, Pavia, Cremona, and

Verona, rose in Frederick's favour; those in Germany invited him to come to lead them.

Otto IV with his communications being cut and Germany revolting had no choice but to retreat. Scarcely had he recrossed the Alps before his lieutenants were driven out of Spoleto and Brescia, while Azzo VI secured the rule of Ferrara. But Innocent's main purpose had been to save the States of the Church and papal independence. He was determined to maintain the separation of Sicily from the *Regnum Italicum*, and he hoped to render the victory of his Hohenstaufen *protégé* innocuous by the stringent obligations to which Frederick submitted at Messina in February 1212. Not only were the tribute and fealty for Sicily renewed, not only did the Pope enforce the cession to himself of the royal rights over Monte Cassino, and the counties of Sora, Aquino, and Fondi, but he constrained Frederick to declare that directly he should be crowned Emperor he would emancipate his son Henry and cede to him the Sicilian kingdom, that during Henry's minority the kingdom should be governed by a person approved by the Pope, and that it should for ever be divided from the Empire and Italy. With what feelings Frederick subscribed can be imagined when we remember what place in his heart was held by "his precious heritage," "his very own possession," "the apple of his eye," which gave him what he felt to be his most glorious title, and which, during all his life, amid all his dominions was his elected home.

Meanwhile the infant Henry was crowned at Palermo, the regency of Sicily being entrusted to Queen Constance. Then, embarking at Messina, Frederick landed at Gaeta on 17 March 1212. After a stay of about a month, under blockade by Pisan galleys, he proceeded to Rome by land, and thence by sea to Genoa in May. The Ottonian Lombards held the usual routes, but in July with the help of his partisans he slipped through to Trent by unknown, tortuous, and difficult ways. He was not to return for eight years.

During this time Sicily was ruled by Constance, but the royal authority declined more and more through persistent rebellions and agitations. In the island, the Muslims sallied forth from the mountainous centre of the Val di Mazzara to plunder, to seize other places, and to make prisoners whom they held to ransom. Both in the island and on the mainland turbulent nobles were in arms. A famine came to aggravate these evils, in which it is said that mothers ate their own children[1]. Meanwhile Frederick could do little save obtain papal letters with their sonorous platitudes and counsels.

In Italy conditions were little better; the local struggles were rekindled and were not extinguished either by the definitive defeat or by the death of Otto IV. Frederick at Ratisbon constituted (16 February 1213) his relative Frederick, Bishop of Trent, imperial legate for "all Italy," the

[1] Sicardus Cremon.

first instance of such an appointment. Under the legate were placed then or later vicars of the separate regions. Among these was Aldrovandino of Este, vicar of the Romagna, who had already been appointed to the March of Ancona by the Pope in succession to his father Azzo VI, and was influential in Verona, in Padua, and in Ferrara. The young marquess overcame the Ottonians in the March, and invested with the office of vicar of Sicily was entering the kingdom when he died suddenly, it was said by poison. His successor as vicar of Sicily, Leopold, Bishop of Worms, was restoring order and repressing abuses, when he too was prevented by death from completing his work (1217). In the north the Estensi's rival, Salinguerra, not only gained the upper hand at Ferrara but obtained from the Pope investiture of Matilda's lands with Modena, Reggio, Parma, Bologna, and Imola (7 September 1215).

In the meantime Innocent III was fortifying the State of the Church by further guarantees and as he hoped barring the way from the Empire to Sicily more effectually than ever. By the two treaties of Eger (12 July 1213) and Spires (11 October 1215) Frederick, reproducing the charter of Neuss, confirmed Otto's grants, and pledged himself to conquer for the Roman see what had yet escaped it, and to defend its rights over Sicily and the islands of Corsica and Sardinia; while he ceded the pledged county of Sora to the Papal States. Further, he renewed his promises to allow free ecclesiastical elections, free appeals to the Pope, free ecclesiastical courts, free ecclesiastical administration of vacant sees, and he bound himself to punish heretics and to take the cross. His recompense for these enormous concessions was a precedent as fatal: the Fourth Lateran Council (11–30 November 1215) sanctioned the deposition of his Guelf rival and his own elevation.

The crusading peace imposed by the Council was not observed either by Milan and Piacenza, or by Genoa and Pisa. While they fought Innocent III died at Perugia on 16 July 1216, and was succeeded by his very opposite, Honorius III. To the born autocrat with his bluff adroitness and daring strategy succeeded the tried official who as the Chamberlain Cencio Savelli had tabulated in his *Liber Censuum* the revenues of the Papacy. And this ex-minister was an elderly man, loving peace and justice, forgiving, willingly credulous. But if he could be overreached, his policy would not be deflected, for it was that of the Papacy and the Curia; this was the fatal obstacle to Frederick's schemes, the relentless perseverance not of a man but of an institution.

Things took a better turn in Lombardy after the arrival in 1218 of a new papal legate, the energetic Ugolino dei Conti, Cardinal-Bishop of Ostia. He induced Genoa to make peace both with Pisa, who had just secured the fealty of the Judge of Cagliari, and with Venice. Genoa was rewarded largely for her support of Frederick; to a confirmation of all imperial grants and of her rights over her two Rivieras was added (1218) a confirmation of her possessions and privileges in Sicily. Not only was she grateful, but emulous Pisa began to imitate her enemy's profitable devotion. Meanwhile, under the working of a papal interdict, Milan submitted to peace with Pavia (1218), and other reconciliations followed. It was in Rome that the Pope failed; the people restored the commune and forced him to take refuge at Rieti and later at Viterbo.

In these years Pope and Emperor were in harmony. Honorius allowed Frederick's queen and son to rejoin him in Germany; and now Frederick summoned to him the ecclesiastical and lay lords of Italy and the deputies of the communes to swear fealty and deliberate on their country. Few came, but they were rewarded, especially the prelates. Giacopo, Bishop of Turin, succeeded the dead Frederick of Trent as General Legate, and quickly found that Bologna would not make peace with Imola at his command. The ban of the Empire on the offending city displayed his anger and his impotence (May 1219).

At this very time the first skirmish of the coming duel between Empire and Papacy took place. Honorius summoned Frederick to his Crusade. The reasons, however, which Frederick pleaded to justify postponement were too strong to be denied by the Pope, although excommunication was already threatened. Other grievances Honorius had: that Frederick was planning the election of his son King Henry as King of the Romans; that he interfered in ecclesiastical elections; that he allowed Rainald, son of Conrad of Urslingen, to entitle himself Duke of the now papal Spoleto. On these counts Frederick, in need of his imperial coronation, made a humble, temporising reply. When Honorius demanded the solemn renewal of all his pledges, and especially that of the perpetual separation of Sicily and the Empire, Frederick obeyed at the Diet of Hagenau before the papal legate under the guarantee of the princes (September 1219). Meantime he devised evasion. He promised to abdicate the Sicilian throne, but reserved his right of hereditary succession to his son in that papal fief, if he predeceased him without heirs (10 February 1220). Then as a further sop to the Pope and as a dexterous piece of courtship of the Romans, hitherto unwisely flouted by the Emperors, he announced his approaching coronation to the Senate and people, and begged them to recall the Pope. For once a King of the Romans was popular in his capital; the Senator Parenzio assured him of Rome's joy, and of her obedience to the Pontiff. Then Honorius could return to the Lateran; and Frederick begged as a favour to be allowed to keep the kingdom of Sicily for his lifetime. Further, at the Diet of Frankfort (April 1220) his concessions to the Roman Church were once more ratified, and his routes to Rome for the coronation and to the East for the Crusade were fixed. But at the same diet his hardest pledge was broken. A garbled version of the facts was later given to Honorius: that without Frederick's knowledge, in order to provide for the safety of the State during his absence in Rome and the East, the German princes had elected Henry King of the Romans and had sworn fealty to him. Innocent III's device of separation was for the time at an end; and Frederick, leaving his son in Germany with a council of regency, crossed the Brenner with a strong German force (September 1220).

Italy was in a state of unusual tranquillity; and Frederick was able to advance from Verona without fighting. He must have already conceived the division of the *Regnum Italicum* into five vicariates under the General Legate (now Conrad, Bishop of Metz). These vicariates were: from Trent to the river Oglio; from Pavia upwards (with Piedmont and the Milanese); from Pavia downwards (with Genoa); the Romagna; and Tuscany. Subordinate to the vicars were the captains of great cities named by the Emperor, and judges appointed by the vicars. In each province there were imperialist lords and communes: Azzo VII of Este, the Marquess of Montferrat, the Count of Biandrate, the four sons of Guido Guerra in Tuscany, and the cities of Pavia, Cremona, Parma, Pisa, and Siena. Frederick's wish to conciliate the Church was obvious throughout. He notified (24 September 1220) all communes that he had annulled whatever in their laws in an heretical spirit injured ecclesiastical liberties. He invested the Pope's delegates with Matilda's lands. From near Bologna he wrote to Honorius hoping "that you will gather the fruit of that tree planted and tended by the Church." But when he invited his Sicilian magnates to the coronation the Pope's suspicions were aroused, and he demanded that the Emperor's coronation-constitution should contain a safeguard of the Church's rights and a condemnation of heresy. Frederick promised that it should, and explicitly acknowledged that Sicily was no part of the Empire, but held by him as a fief of the Church, declaring that he would only appoint natives to office therein. At last on 22 November 1220 he with his consort received the imperial crown in St Peter's without the customary tumults, and then took the cross again, promising immediate help for the crusade in Egypt and to sail himself within nine months. He promulgated the desired constitution, and, to prove his cooperation with the Pope, appointed Ugolino of Ostia, the papal legate, his own legate in Italy along with Conrad of Metz.

But in spite of the two legates the politics of Italy took their normal course of discord and war. In Tuscany, which had been for some time at peace, Pisa, Siena, Pistoia, and other communes fought endlessly from 1221 with Florence, Lucca, Arezzo, and their minor allies. Bologna and Faenza conquered and filled up the moats of Imola; the Ravennates slaughtered Ugolino, Count of the Romagna; the Estense faction fought Salinguerra over Ferrara. As to Milan, where the popular party prevailed, the nobles with the archbishop emigrated and ravaged the country-side. There was no preventing the faction and inter-city strife that provoked a Franciscan friar, himself a Lombard and a Guelf, to describe his countrymen as "a race most tortuous and changeable, speaking in one way and acting in another, like eels that the more they cling the quicker they slip away."

But to them autonomy, however turbid, was the supreme good. The new Emperor on the contrary, determined to give peace and order to his dominions, was resolved that this liberty should not last. It was the second fatal antagonism of the reign.

Frederick's first and most necessary task was to consolidate his hereditary realm on lines laid down by the Norman dynasty, but far more developed. First of all, he must restore the demesne, squandered by his father and guardians, and usurped under forged diplomas, and he must extirpate rebellion. Two men who now entered his service were to serve him well: Roffredo of Benevento, an eminent professor of law first at Bologna, then at Arezzo, whom he made a judge of the Great Curia; and a low-born Capuan, Peter della Vigna, now made a royal notary. A series of revendications formed the first step: Sora was taken from Richard dei Conti; the Abbot of Monte Cassino lost his criminal jurisdiction; Siegfried, Diepold's brother, lost his fiefs and was sent with him to Germany. At Capua in December 1220 Frederick held the first General Court of the kingdom, and promulgated twenty chapters of assizes or constitutions, dealing with fiefs, the demolition of "adulterine" castles, the construction and administration of royal castles, the investigation into the validity of titles to lands, and the reform of the Norman judicial system. "We," said the Emperor, "who have received from the hand of the Lord the sceptre of the Empire and the rule of the kingdom of Sicily, announce to all our faithful subjects of the aforesaid kingdom what is our will and pleasure." In a General Court at Messina (May–July 1221) this autocrat added some censorial constitutions against dicers, blasphemers, Jews (for whom a distinctive garb was prescribed), prostitutes, and scurrilous *jongleurs*. These were the first nucleus of the Frederician legislation. During the next ten years other less precisely known laws were issued; they probably included the ten years' freedom from taxation for immigrants, the stricter regulation of notaries and advocates, the duty of officials to denounce corruption in the administration, the prohibition of pledging plough-oxen or agricultural implements, the just price to be paid tailors, cobblers, and carpenters, the punishment of false coining and fraudulent goods. The reform of abuses public and private is the obvious aim of this legislative activity.

Meanwhile Frederick was attacking open rebels like Thomas, Count of Molise and Celano, on the mainland and Morabit with his Saracens in the island. The rebel count held out for three years, and then went into exile through papal mediation; during his absence Frederick confiscated his lands. The Saracens, supplied with munitions by the Genoese who were indignant at the loss of their special privileges in Sicily, at first repelled the Count of Malta. In 1222 the Emperor himself entered the Val di Mazzara and captured the fortress of Giato with Morabit, whom he hanged at Palermo. Next summer he attacked the Muslims on several sides, and compelled numbers of them to surrender. With them he repeopled the ancient Lucera in the Capitanata on the mainland, not far from his favourite residences and hunting-grounds in Apulia. They were formed into a military and agricultural colony, specially favoured, and they ended in being most useful and faithful clients, impervious to interdict and excommunication. In the Muslim war Frederick not only imposed fresh taxes but called out the feudal array. The latter measure had a subsidiary use, for three notably disloyal counts were imprisoned when they appeared and their fiefs were confiscated.

In February 1223 Frederick continued his reforms by fresh constitutions issued in a court at Capua: they organised the administration, prevented the alienation of Church lands, ordered an inquest into the validity of grants made since William II's reign, and introduced a new silver coin, the "imperial," to replace the Amalfitan *tari*. The royal castles were repaired, and the new palace at Foggia was begun. Soon after he planned a more lasting foundation. The only higher education in the kingdom was given by the School of Medicine at Salerno. Frederick, himself learned, a philosopher, and an author, would not endure that his subjects in a land so fertile and happy should beg elsewhere the bread of knowledge. From Syracuse on 5 June 1224 he announced that he had founded in the enchanting city of Naples, abounding in every gift of God, a Studium Universale, "fountain of knowledge and seed-plot of learning." Outside of Spain this was the only university founded by the secular state alone in the Middle Ages. He called thither from all sides lectors in all arts and sciences with the promise of high salaries; he forbade his Sicilian subjects to study outside the kingdom, while endowing the new university with all kinds of facilities material and moral, and assigning subsidies for poor students. Poverty and humble birth were never demerits in his eyes. He only considered personal capacity and fidelity in the choice of his fellow-workers and ministers. Indeed, from these he formed a new nobility. A year or two earlier a Frederick of Arco and his two nephews received for their services the title of counts, "as if they descended from ancient nobles and ancient counts."

In this way Frederick raised the intellectual level of his kingdom, while by the consolidation of the supreme power and the repression of feudal abuses he reorganised the administration, and placed all his subjects under the same uniform and equal laws with as much liberty as did not disturb order and peace. And at the same time he revived the fleet, protected commerce, agriculture, and industry, and multiplied the sources of public and private wealth.

But such a strengthening of Sicily, whose king was also Emperor and ruled to north and south of the Papal States, early alarmed the Pope. To patronise Frederick's domestic enemies became the policy of the papal Curia. Frederick's interference in ecclesiastical elections, his punishment of prelates, his anti-feudal laws, all met with papal protest. But

Honorius' chief demand was that Frederick should quit his task as king to launch on the adventure of the crusade. Frederick had transported crusaders and had sent forty galleys to relieve Damietta; but the place fell (8 September 1221) before their arrival, and the old Chancellor Walter of Palear who was in command of them dared not face the wrath of his sovereign. He fled to Venice, was despoiled of his possessions, and died in poverty. But Honorius laid all the blame on Frederick's tardiness. At a meeting with the Pope at Veroli Frederick again swore to start, but no date was yet fixed. Meanwhile, an awkward incident took place. Gunzelin of Wolfenbüttel, imperial vicar in Tuscany, came to the rescue of Viterbo again assailed by the Romans, and usurped the rule of the duchy of Spoleto. The Emperor, however, completely disavowed the vicar, sent him to Honorius to make his peace, and replaced him in Tuscany by the "Duke of Spoleto." The Pope, on his side, thought of a lure to the crusade. When the solemn congress for it met at Ferentino in March 1223, Frederick undertook at the Pope's instance a twofold obligation. The Empress Constance had died on 23 June 1222. The widower now promised to start for the Holy Land before 24 June 1225, and to marry Isabella (or Yolande), the only daughter of King John of Brienne and, through her mother, heiress of the kingdom of Jerusalem.

It seemed that the Emperor was now in earnest. While he sent to fetch the bride from Syria, he prepared a strong fleet, and provided for the government of Sicily during his absence. But the reorganisation of Sicily was not complete; the Saracens were not wholly subdued. He had not yet been free to take personal action in the *Regnum Italicum*, where the new quiet of Sicily was thought an intolerable despotism, the representatives of the Emperor were distrusted, and the increase of his authority was dreaded as a peril for the liberty so hardly won. For these reasons Frederick asked for a fresh delay; and for this his ambassadors, who came to the Pope at Rieti, whither he had fled from Rome, seemed themselves a warrant—they were King John of Brienne, the Patriarch of Jerusalem, and the Grand Master of the Teutonic Order, Herman of Salza. The Pope consented; it was the only way of avoiding an immediate rupture due to the irremediable opposition of the two points of view. At San Germano on 25 July 1225 two cardinals fixed Frederick's departure for August 1227, but he was obliged to renew his oath, to send 1000 knights at once to the Holy Land, and to deposit 100,000 ounces of gold to be forfeited for God's service if he broke his pledge. Frederick indemnified himself on his marriage with Yolande (9 November 1225); John of Brienne, suspect himself and the uncle of King Tancred's heir, Walter, was forced to abdicate the throne of Jerusalem, and the Emperor received the fealty of his new wife's vassals. For the time Honorius pensioned the aggrieved ex-king with the government of the Tuscan Patrimony; later he became Latin Emperor of Constantinople.

But Frederick's main objective was to assert the imperial authority in

Italy, and to link the Empire with Sicily. Not only to deliberate on the preparations for the crusade and on the extirpation of heresy, but also to provide "for the honour and reform of the state of the Empire," he convoked to a General Diet at Cremona for Easter 1226 his son King Henry with the German princes, the Italian vassals, and the deputies of the communes. On his way thither he flouted the Pope and shewed his hand: besides the Sicilian vassals he ordered the knights and city-deputies of the duchy of Spoleto to join him at Pescara on 6 March 1226. The Pope forbade them to obey, and an angry correspondence followed, violent enough for an open breach had either party wished it. Meanwhile the Lombards more than took up the challenge. Instead of attending the diet, the Milanese, Bolognese, Brescians, Mantuans, Bergamese, Turinese, Vicentines, Paduans, and Trevisans, formed at Mosio near Mantua on 6 March 1226 the second Lombard League, an offensive and defensive alliance for twenty-five years. Other communes, such as Piacenza, Verona, Faenza, Vercelli, Lodi, Alessandria, hastened to join, and the Piedmontese Peter della Carovana chanted in the fashionable Provençal his song of defiance: "Behold our Emperor who gathers great forces. Lombards, beware lest he make you worse than slaves, if you stand not firm.... Remember the valiant barons of Apulia who now have naught but grief in their dwellings. Love not the folk of Germany; far, far from you be these mad dogs. God save Lombardy, Bologna, and Milan, and their allies, and Brescia, and the Mantuans, and the good men of the March [of Verona], so that none of them be a slave." Thirty years before, Peter Vidal had raised the same war-chant against the German conqueror, Henry VI. But Frederick came from Sicily to give order and peace to the chaotic north; for him William Figueira and Peter Cardinal prayed that the Milanese might be overthrown by the puissant, wise, and learned Emperor.

Frederick rebuilt the walls of Imola, and awaited his son at Parma (June 1226). But the Lombards seized the *Chiuse* of Verona, and demanded as the price of Henry's passage that the Emperor during his stay in Lombardy should renounce the right of putting to the ban of the Empire and dismiss his army; that he and his son should submit to the jurisdiction of the papal legate; and that King Henry should not bring more than 1200 knights to Cremona. In spite of his indignation, Frederick prudently laid the dispute before the papal legate, who proposed a compromise accepted by the Emperor and rejected by the League, while fresh adherents—Crema, Ferrara, the Counts of Biandrate, and the Marquess of Montferrat—joined the allies. Thus the diet was a mere shadow of the decisive assembly intended; neither the Emperor's ban, nor the interdicts and excommunications of the Bishop of Hildesheim, who preached the crusade on the Pope's behalf, had any effect; Frederick's Italian schemes were checked for the time. Genoa was against him owing to the revolt from her of the Riviera di Ponente; in Tuscany only Pisa was loyal. It was absolutely necessary for him to gain the support of the Papacy to recover his prestige. He succeeded by his energetic measures in satisfying Honorius of his zeal for the crusade, and the Pope at last acceded to his requests for mediation. The Bishop of Hildesheim's anathemas were annulled, and early in 1227 an accord was drafted, which bound both parties to abandon hostilities, the Emperor to revoke his sentences, and the League to maintain 400 knights for two years in the crusade. The Emperor accepted it, but by the time the League's acceptance came Honorius was already dead (18 March 1227), and the new Pope, Gregory IX, had already threateningly demanded Frederick's prompt departure on the crusade.

Ugolino dei Conti, Cardinal-Bishop of Ostia, was a kinsman of Innocent III, to whom he owed his promotion, and had abundantly proved his capacity and strength of character. His was a fiery nature of inextinguishable passion, which made him at once the fervent ascetic beloved of St Francis, the enthusiast for the ideal of the Papacy as set forth by Gregory VII, and the hater of the secular genius in whom he discerned its greatest enemy. His insight was greater than his diplomacy, and, indomitable as the old Pope was, Frederick outplayed him to the end. All the same, in sheer ability he stands very high among the wearers of the tiara. A firm grasp of principles in their application to the variety of life made him a great canonist, the five books of whose Decretals are worthy of the Gratian they extend, and an intuitive reformer of ritual which should appeal to the devout imagination. He saw only too clearly in Frederick's schemes the subjection of the Papacy to the Empire; the conquest of Lombardy must not happen; the Sicilian monarchy must no longer be a compact despotism over layman and clerk.

While the new Pope sojourned in Anagni, the crusaders concentrated in Apulia were decimated by southern heat and malaria. Yet 40,000 are said to have sailed from Brindisi in August. The Emperor himself, with the Landgrave Louis of Thuringia, embarked on 8 September. But the landgrave's fatal illness forced them to anchor at Otranto, and Frederick fell ill himself. He sent on the rest of the fleet under the Patriarch of Jerusalem, and went to Pozzuoli to drink the waters. His envoys excused him to the Pope at Anagni, but Gregory IX was in no mood to listen; he at once excommunicated the Emperor for breach of his vow (29 September), and renewed the sentence in St Peter's on 18 November 1227. He had forced the inevitable issue prematurely.

Frederick on his recovery renewed his preparations; but he also issued (6 December 1227) a notable manifesto to the crusaders and princes of Europe, denouncing the secular pretensions of the Papacy, which, having reduced the King of England and others to vassalage, desired to place the Empire under its feet. It was a common danger:

"Tunc tua res agitur paries cum proximus ardet."

He ordered the Sicilian clergy to disregard the interdict. Although a proposed diet at Ravenna could not be held owing to the Lombards' enmity, the court the Emperor held at Easter 1228 at Barletta was thronged, and all arrangements were made for his absence. At this same time the birth of an heir, Conrad, to the kingdom of Jerusalem cost the Empress Yolande her life. On 28 June Frederick sailed for Palestine.

Gregory IX on his side on Holy Thursday (23 March) renewed the excommunication and interdict, and threatened to deprive Frederick of Sicily; but the Romans did not love his absolutism, and when on Easter Monday he preached against the crusading Emperor he was driven from St Peter's and forced to quit Rome for nearly two years. War was now in progress; Frederick's Vicar of Sicily, Rainald, "Duke of Spoleto," invaded the March of Ancona of which the Emperor had already made him "Imperial Vicar"; Gregory begged for money and men from France, Lombardy, Spain, and England, and let loose on Sicily an army under Cardinal John Colonna. John dei Conti, Count of Fondi, alone resisted the ravages of this horde in the Terra di Lavoro. The Pope exacted taxes, gave and confiscated fiefs, dispensed town-charters, and fomented insurrections—Gaeta came over, and Messina, Syracuse, and other towns rebelled. And it was falsely rumoured that Frederick was dead.

In this turmoil, increased by the intestine wars of North Italy, Frederick, now the regainer of Jerusalem[1], returned to Brindisi (10 June 1229) to find the gates of Foggia and other papalist towns closed against him. He at once sued for peace, but Gregory only denounced the "execrable pact" he had made with the Sultan as an insult to the Saviour. Thus forced to war, Frederick mustered his army at Naples and marched to raise the siege of Caiazzo in the Terra di Lavoro. As he advanced, the papalist troops could only recoil into the State of the Church, and he recovered the province almost without a blow. But he was hoping for a speedy accommodation with the Pope discouraged by his reverses. Herman of Salza undertook the task, which proved long and arduous. The Pope was exacting and determined to remain in concert with the Lombards; Frederick, who punished the rebel cities in Apulia, was resolved to recover revolted Gaeta and Sant' Agata. A flood of the Tiber followed by a pestilence, however, strengthened the Pope's position by bringing him back to repentant Rome in February 1230. The treaty was at last signed on 23 July at San Germano; on 28 August Frederick was absolved at Ceprano, and after a visit to the Pope at Anagni returned to Sicily to heal the wounds of the war. But the terms were hard. The Pope, indeed, recognised Frederick's simultaneous reign in the Empire and Sicily; Gaeta and Sant' Agata were to be his within a year. But the Emperor remitted all offences, restored the lands he had seized, and bound himself neither to tax the Sicilian clergy, nor to

[1] See *supra*, Vol. v, Chapter VIII.

interfere in the election of their prelates, nor to try them in secular courts. The Sicilian monarchy had lost a part of its powers.

Frederick made it his first task to recover rights and lands lost during his absence, and in this he had occasion to besiege and banish his unsuccessful deputy Rainald of Spoleto. In 1233 he followed up his reconquest by subduing and harshly punishing Messina, Syracuse, and other island towns. But he engaged also in a larger design. He was not only king but Caesar, and he determined like Justinian and Theodoric to promulgate a new body of law, to reform his distracted kingdom. The former laws, "rusty from disuse," were to be fused with his own into a new code, and to form a complete system of law and government. The work, completed in two months, was entitled *Liber* or *Lex Augustalis* and promulgated at Melfi in a solemn consistory. It became law on 1 September[1] 1231, and was immediately translated into Greek, still a living language in Sicily. One of the chief compilers was Giacomo, Archbishop of Capua, in spite of Gregory IX's prohibition of making laws *destitutivas salutis et institutivas enormium scandalorum*; but the greatest merit belongs to Peter della Vigna. The work consisted of 217 constitutions grouped in three books, (I) of public law, (II) of procedure, and (III) of feudal and private law, and of punishments. Later, 61 *constitutiones novellae* were from time to time added; thus in 1234 was issued *De corrigendis et compescendis excessibus officialium*, establishing annual provincial *curiae* or parliaments to review the conduct of magistrates. The whole formed the first medieval code clearly inspired by the principles of Roman jurisprudence replacing customary and feudal law, and is a monument of the civilisation of Sicily. Even admitting its absolutism and its Draconian penalties, the enlightened spirit of its promulgator, far in advance of his century, is attested by the intention to prevent rather than punish crime; the guarantees for personal liberty, and encroachments on serfdom; the monopoly of criminal jurisdiction for the Crown; the protection of the vassal against the baron and of the weak against the strong; the organisation of magistracies and offices; the abolition of the ordeal and rights of wreck; the protection of foreigners; and the admission of female inheritance. The administrative system preludes the civilised monarchy of modern times; the king and his councillors ruled the state through efficient local officials. The work of Roger II[2] was completed by his grandson in this land compact of diverse, jarring elements, which were combined and dominated without the supremacy or destruction of any. Here as elsewhere in the West was a feudal organisation, but it was restricted and subordinated to that of the State. Beside and above the barons were the officials, paid and protected by the State, yet watched by the government

[1] The beginning of the Indiction and of the year by the Greek reckoning, still in use in Sicily.

[2] See *supra*, Vol. v, Chapter iv.

and kept in line by general courts where all could utter their grievances. A special register was maintained of the bureaucracy. Each functionary had to present two annual reports, one on matters entrusted to subordinates, one on his own activities. But offences against the official class were more heavily punished than those against private persons.

Frederick's ministers were recruited from jurists and notaries, provincial officials from the knights. Save for four prelates (the Archbishops of Palermo and Capua, and the Bishops of Melfi and Rapallo), and two great nobles, allied to him by marriage, the Counts of Acerra and Caserta, he left the aristocracy aside. As under the Norman kings, there were seven great officers, chosen by the sovereign. The Grand Chancellor kept the great seal, drafted laws, and watched over their working. The Grand Constable commanded the army and presided over the court of barons. The Grand Admiral commanded the fleet, and dealt with naval causes. The Grand Justiciar was minister of justice and appeals; the Grand Chamberlain of finance and the demesne—under him were the two Secreta (Treasuries) for the mainland and the island. The Grand Seneschal supervised the palaces, forests, and the household. The Grand Protonotary or Logothete was a secretary of state for non-judicial business. These officers, often with the addition of trusted prelates and barons, formed the Council of the Crown.

The kingdom was divided into two captaincies-general, one of the mainland to Roseto, the other of most of Calabria and of Sicily proper; but the Captain and Master Justiciar of each were only appointed for special emergencies. The eleven provinces, however, represented permanent needs. In each of them was a Justiciar, annual but renewable, who exercised criminal jurisdiction and kept order; his staff of judges and notaries was nominated by the king, and he could not be a native of his province or an ecclesiastic. Civil justice was dispensed by bailiffs and judges under the Master Chamberlain. For the poor justice was gratuitous, and widows and orphans were even subsidised in their causes by the State. In finance, the provincial authority was the Master Chamberlain (or the *Secreto* in the south), who administered demesnes, customs, and tolls, and paid the expenses of administration. The same system was in use for direct taxes and the Justiciar; and the surpluses, if any, were paid to the royal treasury at Naples. A kind of Exchequer, the *Curia magistri rationum*, audited the State accounts.

The revenue was large. At first feudal tenants, ecclesiastical or lay, paid only the feudal obligations (defence, coronation-gift, knighting the king's son, marriage of his daughter, *auberge* or entertainment, and relief); but Frederick after his crusade introduced provisionally the *collecta*, a hearth-tax, which became annual as the *collecta ordinaria* and was intensely unpopular. To the Norman indirect taxation he added the *nova statuta*. In spite, however, of heavy taxation, the government paid with difficulty its Saracen and German mercenaries, and was forced to borrow.

The loans grew enormous in the troubles of Frederick's later years, and were the more burdensome from being raised from foreign merchants. Frederick attempted a remedy for this by counter-measures. He was most severe in punishing official extortion; he fostered industry and commerce —in 1234 he established annual general fairs; he combined the economic knowledge of the Saracens with the Norman instinct for organisation. If the State kept up old monopolies (salt, iron and steel, silk, etc.) and instituted new (slaughter-houses, money-changing, etc.), they were regulated so as not to fetter industry. Prohibition was only applied to siege-machines and war-horses. The tax on exported grain was lowered from a third to a fifth and even to a sixth, and the Emperor explained to remonstrants that freedom of commerce leads to its increase and to that of public prosperity. He suppressed internal customs as a check on intercourse; he winked at the presence of enemy Genoese and Venetians who were solely engaged *salubriter et quiete* in their commerce. Not least of these beneficial measures was the coining in 1231 of *augustals*—in imitation of the East Roman bezant—which initiated the West in a pure and stable gold coinage, to be copied and outlived by the Florentine florin.

In like manner he encouraged agriculture: he forbade the seizure of oxen and implements for debt; he created model farms; he exterminated injurious animals; he fostered the cultivation of cotton and the sugar-cane, and the plantation of the date-palm; he sought to acclimatise the indigo-plant; he allowed the clearing of demesne-forest for vineyards. If he forbade for a time intermarriage with foreigners, it was due to the Sicilian rebellion; and he favoured immigration, founding, like the Norman kings, Lombard colonies in the island. New cities, Augusta, Monteleone, Aquila, were built by him, as well as his royal castles. He sank wells and constructed bridges; he renewed the Roman outlets of Lago Fucino.

The depression of the barons did not mean the political elevation of the communes—a term which in Sicily was equivalent to the English "borough," not to the Italian or French commune. Their ancient privileges were rather a collection of customs than real charters; and Frederick abolished the elective *strategoti* and *compalazzi* who ruled, and insisted on appointing bailiffs in their place: citizens lost the privilege of being only tried in their own commune; they, like the barons, were to be under the general law. But this unifying system, along with the checks on oppression, was in itself an elevation of the bourgeoisie. The most striking decrees are those of 1232 and 1240, by which every city and fortified town (*castello*) was to send two deputies to treat with the Emperor on the common weal. With this was conjoined an even more important ordinance (1233): every year on 1 May and 1 November there were to assemble in five cities solemn courts of the neighbouring prelates and barons with four deputies of each greater city and two of each lesser city and *castello*. These were to sit eight or fifteen days to receive complaints. The president—a special royal commissioner—and two assessors were to investigate the cases, and to send those involving higher officials to the king, those involving lower officials to the local justiciar. Here we see Frederick calling the Third Estate to his parliament, hitherto composed solely of prelates and barons, and although it was merely as an instrument and for consultation, the growing importance of the bourgeoisie is none the less clear.

To sum up, whatever the Popes declaimed on Frederick's unbearable despotism, it is undeniable that the new resources he created and applied to great designs were beneficial to the nation. Under his vigorous, and up to a certain point liberal administration, the kingdom of Sicily was raised to a state of prosperity and civilisation not reached as yet by any other country of Europe.

After the reconciliation with Gregory IX, the Emperor thought it best to proceed in Italian affairs in concert with the Pope. Attempts were made by both to end the universal strife; more effectual were the Emperor's vain demand for the cities' fealty and his summons of the German princes to a general diet at Ravenna for 1 November 1231. Instantly the League was renewed and, in spite of the Pope's assurance that he was arbitrator in their dispute with Frederick, the Lombards closed the Alpine passes. When the Emperor reached Ravenna towards Christmas he found only faithful Italian lords and the rulers of a few loyal communes such as Parma, Cremona, and Pavia. To continue the diet with the Germans he had to advance himself to Aquileia. Meanwhile the Pope's efforts at a solution of the Lombard deadlock resulted in an arrangement to discuss it before him on 1 November 1232; but this meeting was prevented by a new train of events.

One embarrassment of the Popes was the hatred subsisting between Rome and Viterbo, which was usually loyal to them, and a success of the Viterbese caused the Romans, even under John Conti of Poli, the Pope's kinsman, to force Gregory once more to exile. In spite, however, of Frederick's evasion of his demands for armed help, the Pope secured his recall by negotiation, and then adopted a new method with the Lombards. This time he employed a celebrated Dominican friar, John of Vicenza, who by his preaching had acquired an extraordinary ascendency over the people both in the cause of peace and in the persecution of heresy. John in June 1233 proposed an agreement by which the Lombards should only furnish the Emperor with 500 knights once in every two years. The League accepted these terms, and even Frederick, although wroth at receiving no compensation for the past, consented to them when the Pope threatened to abandon his mediation. But the sacrifice became useless as soon as Friar John's eclipse allowed the League to break the treaty. Though Florence had turned a deaf ear to the friar from the first, the people of his native Veneto were strangely obedient; he changed their statutes, he freed prisoners, he absolved from excommunication, and gave a summons for an assembly in the plain of Pagnara near Verona on 28 August. It is said that there came over 400,000 persons of all ranks, unarmed and barefoot. Deputies of communes and feudal lords wept at his eloquence and bowed to his decisions. But the execution of these caused disillusion; unhealthy exaltation gave way to the permanent motives of strife, and John's own extravagances discredited and overthrew him. He returned with greater zeal to the renunciant's life he had elected.

Meanwhile the Romans, since Gregory would not help them to destroy Viterbo, forced him to flee once more, and as a crowning act their Senator, Luca Savelli, declared both the Tuscan and the Roman patrimonies part of the dominion of the commune of Rome. Gregory, enraged, proclaimed a crusade against the city, and once more drew near to the Emperor in an interview at Rieti. He begged the Lombard League to allow German troops to pass for his defence, and he was again admitted as arbitrator between the League and the Emperor. Frederick in return was already attacking the Roman *castello* of Rispampano when there came the terrible news of his son Henry's rebellion. The Pope promptly censured the unnatural son, but sent no word of reproach to the Lombards, who had enticed him on by the offer of the Iron Crown. Frederick perforce embarked at Rimini in April 1235 for Germany with his second son Conrad. Sicilian reinforcements helped to win the Pope a victory near Viterbo, and a new Senator, Angelo Malabranca, welcomed him back to Rome in May. Thus restored to power, in the Emperor's absence, Gregory gained a series of diplomatic successes: he reconciled Florence to Siena; he annexed Massa-Carrara on the death of its Marquess; his legate made peace between the Judges of Arborea and Cagliari in Sardinia, and received their fealty; Adalasia, heiress of the Judicates of Torres and Gallura and consort of the Judge of Cagliari, even promised her inheritance to the Papacy if she died childless.

In Germany, Frederick dethroned his son, and on 15 July 1235 wedded Isabella, sister of Henry III of England, an alliance favoured by the Pope. The proposal of a campaign in Lombardy with German troops was already causing friction with Gregory, who urged his rights as arbitrator and attributed the ineffectual character of his efforts to an innovation—the submission of the Veronese to Ezzelin III da Romano, that terrifying figure of a city-tyrant; he also reiterated the grievances, new and old, of the Church. Frederick, however, proceeded. In a circular of capital importance he summoned a general diet at Piacenza. Italy was "to re-enter the unity of the Empire"; and not only rebel Lombardy but the lands he had ceded to the Church were to be subjugated, and the gift was to be revoked, for the beneficiary had proved ungrateful and its agents were contriving his ruin to please the Milanese. He was Italian by birth and native sovereign of Sicily; thence he had conquered beyond the Alps and beyond the sea. These singular expressions, which disregard the old imperial and theocratic formulae, overturned the traditional basis of Italian political life and suggest the newer monarchies.

To this striking novelty Gregory IX opposed the imprescriptible rights of the Church in their highest form: God reserved for himself alone the power to judge the Holy See, under whose sentence he placed the world in all hidden and open things. He cited the legend of the Donation of Constantine in its most exaggerated form, and added that of the translation of the Empire: from Greece the Holy See transferred the Empire to the Germans in the person of Charlemagne; but the Pope renounced nothing of his right of supreme dominion.

But Frederick had already crossed the Mincio with the words: "Pilgrims and travellers can go freely everywhere, and shall not I, the Emperor, venture on the lands of the Empire?" He burnt Vicenza (November 1236), and his lieutenants, Count Gebhard of Arnstein and others, subdued the whole Trevisan March; but he was called back to Germany to subdue the rebel Duke of Austria, and to effect the election of his son Conrad as King of the Romans. He did not rebut the Pope's renewed efforts at mediation, but when the resultant congress met at Brescia in May 1237 Herman of Salza declared that, unless a peace honourable to the Empire were concluded before the Emperor's return, war would be resumed *à l'outrance*. On 12 September Frederick re-crossed the Alps before an agreement was attained, and the die was cast. Refusing further papal mediation, he besieged Goito on the Mincio in full force; Mantua then submitted, and Montechiaro, the key of Brescia, was captured; some Lombard imperialists, fleeing the war, were even transported to Corleone in Sicily. Frederick then encamped on the Oglio near Pontevico, while on the opposite western bank were the Lombards under the Venetian Peter Tiepolo, then *podestà* of Milan. When the Emperor bridged the river at Soncino, the army of the League began to retreat northwards towards Palazzolo; but they were overtaken unawares near Cortenuova. Their rout was complete; large numbers were slain; many prisoners, including Tiepolo, the *carroccio*, and the *castello* of Cortenuova fell into the Emperor's hands (27 November 1237). In terror Lodi opened her gates, and Milan and Piacenza begged for peace, Milan offering every renunciation and indemnity if she might keep her *fidanza* and *contado*. Frederick may not have intended to abuse his victory, but on the advice of the Cremonese and Pavese he insisted on unconditional surrender. It was the fatal mistake of his reign: the Milanese resolved to perish with arms in their hands rather than submit to so great a disgrace, and their example fired their allies. To isolate them, Frederick advanced westward. From Pavia he sent to the Romans the Milanese *carroccio*, saying it appertained to the city, the source of the Empire, to guard the imperial trophy. He received the submission of Vercelli and Novara, and later of Turin; to all such towns their privileges were confirmed. He then left Manfred Lancia, his vicar, to reduce Alessandria and other rebels with the aid of the loyalists, while he himself prepared the final blow against Milan.

For this purpose he held at Verona on 1 May 1238 a general diet, which this time the German princes could attend. He demanded once more men and money from Sicily, and troops from Hungary, Germany, and Provence. Ezzelin, the tyrant of Verona, married his illegitimate daughter Selvaggia, and Genoa once more submitted. Then in full force he began the siege of Brescia, hoping by its capture to blockade Milan on every side. But Brescia for two months frustrated all attacks, and Frederick, losing hope as the autumn passed, burnt his siege-engines at dawn on 9 October and retreated to Cremona. This heroic resistance of Brescia turned the scales against the Emperor: his enemies took the offensive; his doubtful friends, like Genoa, broke faith; and the Pope gained courage to add to his former grievances the renewed attack on the peace-wishing Lombards. Frederick replied in kind, but also completely exasperated Gregory by a not too profitable diplomatic success. He obtained the hand of the widowed Adalasia of Torres for his illegitimate son Henry or Enzo, born of a Cremonese mistress and very closely resembling him. The youth, only fifteen, was knighted, given the title of king, sometimes of Torres and Gallura, sometimes of Sardinia, and was sent to the island. This was enough; Gregory resolved to renew the death-struggle between the Papacy and the rejuvenated Empire. He concluded a secret treaty (30 November) with Genoa and Venice—they were not to make peace with the Emperor for nine years without his consent, and were to be given privileges by "the future king of Sicily." Frederick indeed was weaker than he seemed; his debts amounted to 24,653 ounces of gold, a burden on Sicily not wholly compensated for by the very large share Sicilians enjoyed of offices in Italy. He sent a threatening protest to the cardinals; but on Palm Sunday (20 March) 1239 Gregory IX launched the expected excommunication from the Lateran.

Each side appealed to Christendom. In an encyclical the Pope demonstrated the grievous faults of the heretic Frederick. In his circular the Emperor denounced the Church's ingratitude and declared himself ready to prove his orthodoxy to competent judges; and in fact, whatever he thought in his heart, his public conduct and his harsh legislation against heresy were unimpeachable. Inspired pamphlets seconded the Emperor's efforts, but in his own age in vain. Two bishops sent to the cardinals to urge the convocation of a general council were thrown into prison; the sovereigns of Europe held aloof; while the conduct of the subdeacon Gregory of Montelongo as papal legate in Lombardy made public the strict alliance of the Pope with Milan, "the cesspool of the Patarines." The Pope obtained the sinews of war by raising a tribute of 15,000 marks of silver from the Lombard League, besides contributions from all Christendom and burdensome loans from bankers. Frederick on his side withheld the Sicilian tribute of 1000 *schifati*; he expelled Lombard friars from Sicily, and confiscated the possessions of foreigners; he levied an "aid" from cathedrals and monasteries, and forbade journeys to Rome without a licence as well as the entrance of anti-imperialist writings.

Frederick had some success in winning over the States of the Church, for at his command Foligno, Viterbo, Tivoli, and other cities swore fealty to his son King Enzo, now his General Legate in Italy; but farther north he lost ground. Azzo VII of Este, a temporary convert, and Alberic da Romano, Ezzelin's brother and tyrant of Treviso, revolted on the imprisonment of their children. Frederick vainly attacked Treviso and Bologna, while Ravenna turned against him under Paolo Traversari, and Venice promised the Pope twenty-five galleys against Sicily in return for future cessions. After failing in the Romagna the Emperor laid siege to Milan (September 1239). His forces included contingents from Bergamo, Lodi, Mantua, Pavia, Asti, Tortona, Vercelli, and Novara; but, as usual in the siege of great cities in the Middle Ages, the defence, protracted for a month and a half, had the victory, and Frederick retreated to Piacenza, and then amid autumnal floods into Tuscany. The League, left free to act, captured Ferrara by a piece of treachery devised by the papal legate, and with it the aged faction-chief Salinguerra who held it for the Emperor. As a result of the campaign Frederick lost to the League two important strategic points for operations in Lombardy especially from the south—Ferrara commanding the lower Po, and Ravenna his port and base of supplies.

In Tuscany the Emperor had better fortune. He compelled the Bishops of Luni and Volterra, as earlier the Bishop of Arezzo, to surrender to him their counties; he garrisoned Pontremoli, which with Massa-Carrara and other confiscated papal land he formed into the vicariate of the Lunigiana under Marquess Oberto Pelavicini—thus the great western road, the Via Francigena, was wholly under his control where it spanned the Apennines. Tuscany itself was almost all in his obedience. Now he would strike at the chief and inspirer of his enemies —the only means of a secure victory. Entering the Duchy of Spoleto, he held a diet at Foligno and, refusing further mediation, formed a new vicariate out of the States of the Church. Most, though not all, of the towns declared for him; there remained Rome, where part of the nobles were imperialist, the rest not papalist. From Viterbo he marched toward the city. It was a decisive moment (22 February 1240). But from the Lateran a mournful procession, bearing the heads of the two Apostles, crossed the city to St Peter's amid an immense throng. To it the venerable Pope addressed a fiery harangue describing the wrongs of the Church and calling on his hearers to take the cross in its defence. The effect was immediate; the Romans rushed to arms with a fury that daunted the imperial faction. Frederick waited a fortnight, and then returned through Antrodoco to Sicily (19 March 1240). He there held his second general parliament at Foggia, to which forty-eight cities of the demesne each sent two deputies. The beleaguering of Benevento and Ascoli, and the foundation of the new frontier town of Aquila shewed perhaps his premonitions of a future defensive war.

A new turn of events now ushered in a new diplomatic struggle. At the beginning of the war Louis IX of France had interceded with the Pope, and the ecclesiastical princes of Germany had sent an embassy to defend the Emperor. Now they despatched to Gregory the new Grand Master of the Teutonic Order, Conrad of Thuringia, with urgent petitions for the end of a war so pernicious to Christendom. The Pope in response opened negotiations through Cardinal John Colonna, his legate in the Romagna, and Frederick, taught by the last year, at once accepted the invitation. But then Gregory surprised the Emperor by a sudden move: he convoked to Rome for the following Easter a general council to decide on the great dispute. At this Cardinal Colonna was so wroth as to revolt himself, and Frederick denounced the Pope's duplicity in circulars to sovereigns and the cardinals. But this did not diminish the formidable danger of the council. Certain military successes the Emperor obtained—the capture of Ravenna after Traversari's death, and of Faenza and Benevento in April 1241. Twenty-five Venetian galleys, however, defeated twelve Sicilian and ravaged the coast of the Capitanata (autumn 1240); and it was a poor revenge to hang the Tiepolo captured at Cortenuova, the son of the Doge. Frederick was in such straits for money that he issued from his camp at Faenza stamped pieces of leather with the compulsory value of a gold *augustal*. None the less he grappled with the ubiquitous Church. He banished all friars, his persistent enemies, from Sicily save two natives for the care of each convent; he refused safe-conduct to, and ordered his subjects to capture, prelates journeying to the council.

Meanwhile Genoa was welcoming the prelates on their way to Rome; they set sail, but between the Pisan islands of Giglio and Montecristo they were attacked on 3 May 1241 by King Enzo and the Sicilian Admiral Ansaldo de Mari; some escaped, some (among them two cardinals) were captured and imprisoned in Sicilian castles. Eight days after, the Pavese defeated the Milanese at Le Ginestre. Under the impression of these calamities, Gregory IX again offered to absolve Frederick "if he agreed to what the honour of God and of the apostolic see demanded." Frederick once more accepted the offer, and approaching Rome declared he came as a friend; but the Earl of Cornwall, his brother-in-law and envoy with full powers, was astonished to receive a summons for the unconditional surrender of the Emperor. The war was renewed. In Rome the Senator Matteo Rosso Orsini, a papalist, captured Lagosta (the mausoleum of Augustus), the Colonna stronghold, while outside Cardinal Colonna seized Tivoli and Frederick from Grottaferrata laid waste the Campagna. At this juncture the aged Pope breathed his last on 21 August 1241. The future was to justify his intuition of victory and resistance.

On Gregory's death the Emperor at once withdrew to his kingdom, while the few and discordant cardinals were forced by the Senator to elect a Pope. They chose Celestine IV (Goffredo Castiglione), an infirm old man who died seventeen days after (17 November 1241); and then they fled from the city to different refuges. For eighteen months, while his vicars subdued the remnants of the Papal States, and a mighty fleet was prepared against Venice and Genoa, Frederick laboured to obtain a Pope in his interests. He sent embassies and letters, with petitions, with exhortations, and with menaces; three times he encamped on the Alban Hills devastating the Campagna; and he left the Romans at last in peace and liberated the two captive cardinals only on a promise from the Sacred College that an election would take place at Anagni.

The election proved a disaster to Frederick, for Cardinal Sinibaldo de' Fieschi, who on 25 June 1243 became Pope Innocent IV, was the most formidable of all his adversaries. Diplomatic gifts far beyond the average were in this Genoese jurist at the service of an audacious firmness and perspicacity. The Emperor, however, made public demonstrations of joy, and sent an embassy with congratulations and offers of obedience, saving the rights and honour of the Empire. Through a return embassy the Pope replied that he too desired peace provided that all the prisoners taken at Giglio were released, and all the grievances which had provoked the excommunication (in especial the invasion of the Papal States) were remedied; that the Church, on those points on which it had acted unjustly, was ready to make amends at the arbitration of a commission of lay and ecclesiastical princes; but that all its adherents, above all the Lombards of the League, must be included in the peace. In the negotiations that followed, Frederick was under a fatal illusion of his own power and of the pliability of the Papacy. He refused to pardon the Lombards, and proposed as a compromise on the question of the papal lands to receive them as a fief at a tribute higher than their revenue. This was to re-announce his intention of unifying Italy, the chief dread of the Papacy, and Innocent resumed the fierce hostility of Gregory IX. A papal army under Cardinal Ranieri Capocci entered Viterbo suddenly by treachery (August 1243), and closely besieged the imperial garrison in the citadel. Gregory of Montelongo, legate in Lombardy, was ordered to rekindle opposition, and the Pope by means of his own brothers-in-law and other kinsmen in Parma founded a new papalist faction there called the Rossi, which undermined the hitherto firm imperialism of the city. In Tuscany, the young Guido Guerra, of the imperialist Counts Guidi, was induced to revolt to the Guelfs, as in Tuscany the papalists were called. In Sardinia, Adalasia's marriage to Enzo was annulled. Finally, at the petition of the Romans Innocent made a triumphal entry into Rome in November 1243.

The Emperor replied by laying siege to Viterbo and attempting to gain over the Romans. But the general desire among the exhausted population was for peace; the failure of the harvest produced famine; in Tuscany there were earthquakes, in Lombardy a pestilence. Frederick himself began to vacillate, and more and more to wish for absolution. He gave up the siege of Viterbo on terms which were not all kept. He asked for the King of England's mediation, and then appointed the Count of Toulouse, and his own judges Peter della Vigna and Taddeo da Sessa, his plenipotentiaries. On Holy Thursday (31 March) 1244 they swore in the Lateran on the Emperor's soul to a peace which he had accepted. But the terms were such as shewed that he could only be admitting them as a temporary expedient to obtain absolution, for they would have destroyed his life-work. He was to restore to the Church and its adherents his conquests; to set free his prisoners and hostages; to annul bans and confiscations, with compensation to be awarded by the Pope; to receive into favour rebels both old and new; to submit the dispute with the Lombard League to the decision of the Pope and that with the Romans to the Pope and cardinals; to exempt the barons from service in person; to declare to the sovereigns that only a formal defect in its notification, not contempt of the Church, had caused him to disregard his excommunication, and that he would now fast and give alms till the day of absolution; to put knights at the Pope's disposal; and finally to give satisfaction for every papal grievance. Henry IV at Canossa had not been more humiliated.

Perhaps it was due to the incredibility of this surrender that Frederick, in spite of his disavowal, was thought to have incited the seditions which broke out in Rome. Innocent accused him of withdrawing from the treaty, and urged the Landgrave of Thuringia to revolt in Germany. In June the Pope left Rome for Civita Castellana. Frederick, it is true, soon gave signs of reversing his policy. His delegates demanded that his absolution should take place first, the Pope's the restitution of papal territory and the Lombard arbitration. A personal interview of Pope and Emperor was arranged for at Rieti, but in the meantime Frederick demanded that the Pope's arbitration should be based not on the Peace of Constance but on the Lombards' offers at the time of his victory of Cortenuova, and that the Pope should abandon his alliance with the League; he also claimed that the services due to the Emperor from the Papal States should be defined before he restored them to the Pope. To these demands Innocent made no reply; but he strengthened the Sacred College by nine new cardinals and wrote secretly to his Genoese countrymen to send him a squadron to Civitavecchia. Then he moved not to Rieti but in the opposite direction to Sutri (27 June); and thence he went by night disguised as a soldier over by-ways to Civitavecchia. There the ships awaited him, and he reached Genoa by sea on 7 July 1244. It was a master-stroke. The astonished Frederick hastened into Tuscany and despatched the Count of Toulouse to renew negotiations, at the same time appealing to the cardinals. But the Pope, unheeding his suppliant messages, was seeking an absolutely secure refuge. Received with devotion by Boniface of Montferrat, he gained over the commune of Asti and Amadeus IV, Count of Savoy. He crossed the Alps through Savoyard territory, and established his court at Lyons (2 December), where he was still nominally in the Empire yet under the protection of the King of France. There he summoned a General Council for 24 June 1245; he ordered the publication of the ban on Frederick throughout France, and on Holy Thursday (13 April) 1245 renewed it solemnly, including in it Enzo and Manfred Lancia. On 18 April he cited the Emperor before the Council.

Frederick's counter-moves were partly military. To cut off Italian aid from the Pope, he ordered the Alpine passes to be closed. Marching once more from Sicily, he devastated the countryside of Viterbo, and sent a force against Piacenza. But modern as his spirit was, the medieval atmosphere in which he moved strongly influenced him, and he sent to Lyons the Patriarch of Antioch only to find the Pope firm on his original terms. The Emperor made Taddeo da Sessa his proctor at the Council; but fearing the result under Innocent's influence, and, as if the papal enmity were due to personal causes, hoping that with another Pope he might achieve his dreams, he announced to the cardinals that he would appeal from Innocent to God, to the future supreme Pontiff, to a universal council, to the princes of the Empire, and the rulers of the world. Taddeo reported that the prelates of the Council were all hostile to him, yet he despatched a more solemn embassy consisting of the Grand Master of the Teutonic Order, the Bishop of Freising, and Peter della Vigna. They came too late. Already the Pope had ordered a crusade to be preached in Germany against the sometime (*olim*) Emperor, and on 17 July 1245 the Council had declared Frederick of Swabia deposed as a relapsed violator of the peace with the Church, as guilty of sacrilege and suspected of heresy.

At the Pope's command some German princes elected Henry, Landgrave of Thuringia, as King of the Romans, and in April 1246 Philip, Archbishop-elect of Ferrara, was sent to Germany as legate for the rebellious crusade. Meanwhile Innocent treated Sicily as a vacant fief, annulling all the acts of the deposed sovereign and summoning his subjects to "liberty." Two cardinals, furnished with plentiful funds collected in all quarters by every means, were charged to rouse to rebellion the population of central Italy and Sicily. As subordinate agents fanatical friars, who with some openness wandered through Italy exciting hatred against the Emperor and his officials, also, disguised as pilgrims or traders, worked secretly in Sicily against the despot who despoiled the nobility and oppressed the population. The remaining Muslims of the island also made common cause with the Pope and rose in revolt.

Frederick again attempted to justify his cause to princes and peoples. In circulars he shewed that the Council's sentence was inequitable and illegal, and that his cause was theirs. But this was a premature truth; the reason he invoked was not the reason of his age. Louis IX, who alone responded to his appeal, only obtained the Pope's consent to a fruitless double conference at Cluny (November 1245, April 1246). Frederick's resources, too, were unequal to the situation. If wherever he came with his army obedience was enforced, when he departed there was insurrection or conspiracy. When he was in Piedmont, Alessandria, the marquesses, and the Count of Savoy all submitted; on his departure, Alessandria, Novara, and Boniface of Montferrat reverted to the Lombard League. At Parma he discovered the conspiracy hatching there, but the Rossi leaders got away to papalist Piacenza. Meantime in September 1245 he held a diet at Parma, which authorised the levy of a heavy *collecta* from ecclesiastics, forbade political prosecutions for heresy, and arranged a new attack on Milan.

The Sicilian, Italian, and German troops under the Emperor passed through Pavia to Abbiategrasso on the Ticinello (Naviglio Grande), whilst Enzo and Ezzelin of Verona advanced from the east. But the Milanese under Gregory of Montelongo on the opposite bank of the Ticinello after three weeks' waiting repelled two attempts of Frederick to cross (at Buffalora and Casterno, 1 and 4 November 1245). Enzo indeed forded the Adda at Cassano, and defeated the enemy at Gorgonzola on 8 November, when he was momentarily taken prisoner and exchanged. Then he was rejoined at Lodi by his baffled father, whose wrath was shewn in depriving his Genoese prisoners of their right eye and right hand.

The Emperor wintered at Grosseto in Tuscany, and King Enzo in Cremona. A plot of the Reggian exiles was suppressed, but a far more important conspiracy was revealed to Frederick by a courier despatched in haste by his son-in-law Thomas d'Aquino, Count of Caserta (February 1246). Tebaldo Francisco, the Apulian *podestà* of Parma, had been lured to join the Rossi by nothing less than a promise in the Pope's name of the Sicilian crown. With him were leagued the powerful house of Sanseverino, Andrea Cicala, captain-general from the Tronto to Roseto, Pandolf di Fasanella, once vicar in Tuscany, the sons of the dead Henry de Morra, Frederick's faithful minister, and others who owed everything to him. Frederick and Enzo were to be murdered, and then a general insurrection was to break out. So sure of success were the plotters that the report of Frederick's death was already bruited abroad when he unexpectedly landed at Salerno. They fled in panic: Pandolf and others to Rome to receive the Pope's praise for their efforts; others again to castles. But of these Sala was captured at once by Thomas, Count of Acerra, and Capaccio surrendered after a four months' siege. Tebaldo and five others were first paraded from town to town with the papal bull which induced their treason on their foreheads, and then put to death. The rest, too, expiated their crime by ferocious punishments; they were blinded, mutilated, thrown into the sea in sacks, burnt alive. Their property was confiscated; the houses and towers of the Rossi at Parma were demolished. The Saracens in Sicily were next forced to beg for mercy by the Count of Caserta, and were deported to Lucera; and after four centuries the island was emptied of its Muslim inhabitants.

The death of the anti-Caesar Henry on 17 February 1247 gave Frederick new hopes of peace. He left Sicily and Calabria in charge of Peter Ruffo, the Grand Marshal in the name of his grandson Henry, son of the now dead rebel King Henry, and Apulia in that of the Count of Caserta. Out of deference to the Pope he did not, as he wished, attack the hostile Romans. At Cremona he held a diet of his partisans. He now strengthened himself by intermarriages. He had already given a fresh grievance to the Pope by marrying his child daughter to the Emperor John Vatatzes of Nicaea, the enemy of the Latins of Constantinople. To the fifteen year old Manfred, born to him by the much-beloved Bianca Lancia, he wedded Beatrice, daughter of Count Amadeus IV of Savoy, and widow of the Marquess of Saluzzo. One of his daughters he married to Marquess Giacomino del Carretto. At the same time he appointed Manfred vicar "from Pavia downwards."

Frederick was hopeful of putting pressure on the Pope. He sent to Lyons a solemn embassy of prelates with a clear confession of his faith. But he was told in reply that his request for its examination was temerarious and illusory unless he came in person unarmed and under safe-conduct (23 May 1247). Undeterred, he advanced in arms towards Lyons. Sending on his baggage through Savoy, he announced his approaching arrival to Louis IX, and invited many French magnates to a meeting at Chambéry.

But he never crossed the Alps. While he wandered after the mirage of peace, the exiles of Parma, collecting at Piacenza under the command of Ugo di San Vitale, defeated at Borghetto on the Taro the Parmesan army led by the *podestà*, Henry Testa of Arezzo, who with many others was slain. The victors re-entered Parma on 16 June. Papalists streamed in from all round, among them Count Richard of Sanbonifacio, the legate Gregory of Montelongo, Azzo of Este, and Alberic of Romano—so many that it was difficult to feed them. Parma was by its position on the cross-roads an indispensable link in the Emperor's communications. At the news Enzo abandoned the siege of the Brescian fortress of Quinzano, and hurrying to the river Taro recalled his father. The journey to Lyons ended abruptly. Frederick joined forces with Ezzelin at Cremona and encamped with his son outside the revolted city. With the reinforcements he had gathered 38,000 men, whom he too found it difficult to supply, and he swore to raze to the ground and sow with salt the city which had thwarted him. Beside Parma he built his new town of Vittoria (Victory), and ravaged the *contado*. All over Lombardy from Genoa to Bologna the war flamed up with increased ferocity. Turin was won and lost by the papalist Marquess of Montferrat. Thomas of Savoy, brother of Amadeus IV and late Count-consort of Flanders, changed from papalist to imperialist in return for the grant of Turin, Ivrea, and the vicariate "from Pavia upwards." Cardinal Octavian degli Ubaldini, legate in the Romagna, plotted with the Florentine Guelfs to subject Florence to Bologna, but the Emperor's bastard, Frederick of Antioch the vicar of Tuscany, discovering the intrigue, hastily expelled the Guelfs from Tuscany and secured the city (31 January 1248). In the March of Ancona, despite a brilliant imperialist victory, Cardinal Ranieri Capocci, the legate, succeeded by bribes and concessions in recovering almost all the country for the Pope.

Amid these vicissitudes the Emperor fell ill, and during his convalescence spent his mornings hawking. He was three miles from Vittoria at dawn on 18 February 1248 when the Parmesans unexpectedly assaulted it at the point farthest from Parma and least defended, and broke in after a brief resistance. Taddeo da Sessa was among the slain; about 3000 were made prisoners; the immense imperial treasure was captured; and the new town was given to the flames. The ringing of the alarm-bell recalled Frederick, who cut his way through sword in hand, but too late. Followed by a few knights he withdrew from the smoking ruins through Borgo San Donnino to Cremona, whence he despatched orders to Sicily for fresh armaments.

He was still determined to detach the Pope from the rebels, but Innocent on Holy Thursday (18 April) 1248 once more renewed the excommunication, and nine days later extended it to the sons, the grandsons, and all the adherents of the *quondam* Emperor. All papal legates were enjoined to proclaim the crusade against the reprobate Swabian. They had some success. Cardinal Ubaldini occupied most of the Romagna including Ravenna and Rimini. Cardinal Ranieri Capocci (who was empowered to absolve from simony rebels against Frederick) penetrated into Sicily fulminating interdict and excommunication, giving and taking away churches, fiefs, offices, and privileges, and throwing the country into wretched disorder. Faced by this war, Frederick renewed his proposals for peace. From Asti he sent ambassadors to the King of France to entreat his intercession and offer himself, his dominions, and his subjects, all to the war against the infidels; but to Louis' envoys Innocent IV refused to negotiate until Frederick had renounced the Empire for himself and all his descendants (July 1248). He then absolutely denied in an encyclical to all princes the current rumours of an accommodation. Frederick, however, persevered in a peace-policy. In a diet at Casale, at which the Marquess of Montferrat, bribed with the *castello* of Verrua, was present, he granted to Tortona the right of coining money to be current everywhere, to Lucca the Garfagnana, to Pisa the Lunigiana—the communes were worth wooing. Fresh ambassadors, Amadeus IV of Savoy and his brother Thomas, were sent to the Pope with a new scheme of reconciliation. It is doubtful if they reached him; but in any case Innocent on 8 December 1248 abolished by a bull the treaty of 1198 between Pope

Innocent III and the Empress Constance: he declared the Church in Sicily independent of the lay power; the king was not to intervene in the appointment of prelates or cite ecclesiastics to his courts; the clergy were not to swear fealty to the sovereign; they could fortify castles, rebuild cities, repopulate towns without regard to the royal authority. Ranieri Capocci's successor as legate in Sicily, Cardinal Peter Capocci, was instructed to declare in April 1249 that peace would never be granted Frederick so long as he or any of his sons remained Emperor or king.

In spite of these attacks it was not till the discovery of a new plot in which rightly or wrongly Peter della Vigna, protonotary of the Empire and logothete of Sicily, was accused of complicity, that Frederick was disillusioned of his hopes of reconciliation. Returning from Piedmont to Cremona, he suddenly ordered the arrest of the all-powerful logothete who had betrayed him. The Cremonese mob wished to lynch the ingrate, but he was taken in chains by night to Borgo San Donnino (February 1249). Then Frederick, awaking from his dream of peace, denounced to all princes the crime of the Pope, who had induced his physician to give him a poisonous drug, and urged them to resist the temerity of the priesthood, who claimed to add temporal to their spiritual dominion, while he was endeavouring to limit them to their true sphere and reform Holy Church by giving it worthier ministers. Owing to his alliances with Ezzelin and others, and to the increase of the power of Marquess Pelavicini round Cremona, Parma, and Piacenza, he considered the position of King Enzo, his general legate, secure in North Italy, and himself moved to secure the south. He commissioned the Count of Caserta to investigate the disorders in Sicily, and especially to punish, even with the stake, the friars and those who dared bring papal missives across the frontier. In Tuscany he was met by the levies of the Ghibelline or imperialist towns, such as Arezzo, and cruelly punished an abortive conspiracy at San Miniato. Meanwhile Frederick of Antioch captured Capraia, the headquarters of the Florentine Guelf exiles (25 April 1249); the garrison were either executed or immured in Sicilian dungeons. The unhappy Peter della Vigna too was blinded, but he escaped further punishment by the suicide made famous by Dante[1]. Leaving Tuscany quiet, the Emperor then sailed from Pisa to Naples, which he reached on 25 May 1249.

A terrible misfortune befel him the day after. Modena being threatened by the Bolognese and others of the League, Enzo with the Cremonese faction-chief Buoso da Dovara hastened to defend the city. But at La Fossalta, two miles away, he was defeated and led a prisoner to Bologna. In vain Frederick threateningly demanded his son's liberation; the Bolognese answered with scoffing humility:

"A cane non magno saepe tenetur aper."

And in fact the Modenese, assailed by Bologna and her allies under

[1] *Inferno,* Canto XIII.

Cardinal Ubaldini, after three months' brave resistance were forced to surrender on 15 December, and to join the League. King Enzo was never to recover his freedom; after twenty-two years, the most attractive of Frederick's sons, king and troubadour, died in his Bolognese prison on 14 March 1272.

Yet the disaster of La Fossalta, however bitter to Frederick's personal feelings, did not arrest the general improvement in his fortunes which was setting in. While he was raising money and men to "crush the rebels" next spring, the redoubtable Ezzelin was seizing Belluno from the Da Camino, and Este and other towns from Marquess Azzo VII, who was then *podestà* in Ferrara. The Manfredi recovered Faenza, and the Counts of Bagnacavallo Ravenna. Walter of Palear, Count of Manopello, Frederick's vicar in the March of Ancona, followed up a decisive victory over the papalists by forcing Fermo to surrender. Piacenza, seeing the hated Parma Guelf, went over to the Ghibellines. And then Marquess Oberto Pelavicini, *podestà* of Cremona, avenged the defeat of Vittoria by driving the Guelfs from Parma with the aid of the exiled faction. Thus the links of the imperial chain which bound North Italy seemed to be restored. Even the Bolognese, in discouragement, begged for peace; while the Genoese suffered a defeat at sea by Savona. When the new German anti-Caesar, William of Holland, prepared to cross the Alps, King Conrad of Swabia defeated him and prevented his departure. On all sides fortune seemed to smile on the Emperor. But it was an illusory hope. For some time he had suffered from intestinal fevers, and, on going from Foggia to Lucera, he was so ill with dysentery that he was obliged to halt at the castle of Fiorentino. There he dictated his will, inspired by the deepest religious feeling and devotion to Holy Church. Three days later, on 13 December 1250, he expired "in most Christian fashion," as Manfred announced to his brother King Conrad IV.

With Frederick II there descended to the tomb the power to unite in a single state the Italian nation by cancelling the temporal power of the Popes. Over his grave communal liberty was again unchained in the north, with the clash of passions, of petty ambitions, of local interests, to be exhausted in the tyranny of the *signorie* which maintained particularism and its selfish conflicts. The tyrannies destroyed all sense of a common fatherland founded on race and language, and opened the era of foreign invasions. In the south, rebellions and anarchy ran their course once more, bringing in new dynasties and at last the fatal servitude for centuries to the alien power of Spain.

With Frederick, moreover, the Holy Roman Empire as a living system of government came also to an end. Its practical working had already altered under him. Barbarossa had attempted to revivify it and give it sufficient material resources of wealth and royal domain, first by asserting obsolete rights over the *Regnum Italicum*, later perhaps by the acquisition of the centralised kingdom of Sicily. But under Barbarossa and Henry VI the Empire's centre had ever been in Germany; with Frederick II Italy came first. And this change, which made even more patent the irreconcilable conflict of interest with the Papacy, brought about the long duel of his reign and the virtual dissolution of the Empire save as an aspiration and a dream.

But the man himself, "the wonder of the world and marvellous innovator," cannot be measured either by the dying ideals for which he mainly fought or by the modern state which he half consciously adumbrated. There is something demonic about him. To his contemporaries indeed, if we except impassioned controversialists, the Emperor seemed no monster, but splendid, infinitely attractive and dangerous. In the middle-sized, fat, red-haired man, witty and fluent in six languages, the only thing terrible was the snake-like gleam of his eyes. No monarch was ever less of a figure-head: amid the pomp and circumstance of his daily ceremonial, the luxury, half oriental, half western, of his harem and court, with his eunuchs and Saracen guard, amid his hunting and knightly exercises, amid the eager inquisitiveness and penetrating thought which made him the friend and correspondent of the philosophers and savants of his day, whether Christian, Muslim, or Jew, and which make his treatise on hawking the first modern natural history, he was his own chief counsellor and directed his government by his personal decisions. Peter della Vigna may have held the keys of his heart, but none could say that he enriched or led it. It is not difficult to make a list of Frederick's astonishing qualities: how this Italian Hohenstaufen was the heir and embodiment of three civilisations—Saracenic, Byzantine, western medieval—how his talents ranged in mastery over law, administration, war, diplomacy, philosophy, precocious science, poetry, and art. Nor is it very difficult to offer some palliation for his faults—the oriental harem-life that he inherited from the Norman Kings of Sicily, the faithlessness with which he met the paternal enmity of the Papacy, the irreverent wit which made Europe shudder, or the abominable cruelty only too much shared by his contemporaries, and provoked by black and ingrate treason. It is easy, too, to sum up his achievements: that by his all but successful resistance and his constant appeal to public opinion in manifestoes and letters he undermined the political prestige of the Papacy; that in the verse-making of his courtiers and himself Italian literature took its rise, and in his building and magnificence lay for the fine arts the fertile seeds of a new era; and that with his Byzantine and Norman inheritance he created "the state as a work of art." But these lists seem pettifogging besides the creative spirit that brought order and form where it passed, and inspired and compelled obedience. The power, which in the rout of able and illustrious men shines through crannies, in him pours out as through a rift in nature. Among the rulers in the centuries between Charlemagne and Napoleon he has no equal.

CHAPTER VI

ITALY, 1250–1290

At the moment of Frederick II's death, his power shewed little decline in Italy. He held the Regno (*i.e.* the kingdom of Sicily and its provinces on the mainland[1]) in undiminished submission. In the March of Ancona and Duchy of Spoleto, which owed allegiance to the Holy See, his partisans had the upper hand: the legate, Cardinal Peter Capocci, could only act on the defensive. In North Italy the imperialists seemed still more predominant. The house of Savoy was his ally, its chief, Count Amadeus IV, commanding the north-western passes, while its cadet, Thomas, ex-Count of Flanders, ruled Turin and his appanage of Piedmont; and the great city of Asti was firmly imperialist, so that in the west the only powerful papalist was Boniface IV, Marquess of Montferrat and regent of Saluzzo for his young kinsman, Marquess Thomas I. If Genoa, a greater state than these, was for the Pope, her Italian interests were mainly confined to her Riviera, and there she was busily occupied in subjugating her lesser neighbours, who of course were imperialist for the nonce. Farther to the east, Marquess Manfred Lancia was imperial vicar between the river Lambro and the western Alps; he was *podestà* of Pavia and Lodi, while Vercelli, Tortona, and Alessandria also admitted his authority. Whereas Lancia possessed little personal importance, his fellow-vicar and rival between the Lambro and the Mincio was the wielder of a kind of tyranny. This personage was the Marquess Oberto Pelavicini, co-tyrant of Cremona with its faction-chief Buoso da Dovara. Although the only other imperialist cities really in his vicariate were Bergamo and Reggio, his warlike prowess and his German mercenaries made him superior at the moment to his antagonists. The leaders of the papalist cities were the two warlike Cardinal-deacons, Octavian degli Ubaldini and Gregory of Montelongo, both indefatigable, but hampered by the divergent aims of the towns which, headed by Milan, were on their side. Piacenza hesitated between Pope and Emperor. Bologna, in concert with Cardinal Octavian, was preoccupied in establishing her own supremacy in Romagna on the basis of the reconciliation of both factions, although she lent a helping hand to the Church's efforts in Lombardy. Lastly, in the Trevisan March, the grim Ezzelin da Romano held sway from his capital at Verona. He was not imperial vicar for the March, an office which was held by Ansedisio de' Guidotti, his lieutenant at Padua, but over Verona, Padua, Vicenza, and Trent he ruled with absolute power. The only enemy

[1] The Italian terms of *Regno* for the realm and *Regnicoli* for its inhabitants have the advantage of avoiding on the one hand the ambiguity of "Sicily," leaving that to refer to the island only, and on the other the inconvenience of cumbrous descriptions and periphrases.

he had to fear was Marquess Azzo VII of Este, tyrant of Ferrara, for his brother Alberic da Romano, tyrant of Treviso, was but a nominal papalist, and, in spite of a seeming quarrel, a tepid adversary. Thus in northern Italy Frederick's star was in the ascendant; it was in Tuscany that his position was doubtful. His vicar in the south, indeed, Marquess Galvano Lancia, could depend on its principal city, Siena; but his son Frederick of Antioch, vicar in the north, had ill success and saw the Ghibelline nobles of Florence obliged to share power with the traders under the new constitution of the *Primo Popolo*.

On this promising outlook the news of Frederick's death worked a sudden change. The loss of his commanding personality not only dispirited the imperialists, it disunited them; and the common action we find among them subsequently is rather the compromise of separate ambitions than any true harmony of purpose. With the disappearance of the last true Emperor, the Empire itself seems to dissolve. Frederick's own testament recognised something of this kind. Besides the bid for popularity contained in its re-establishment of the customs of the Regno as they were under William the Good, he tried to conciliate the clashing ambitions of his sons. The Regno—it was the fatal necessity of Staufen policy—was devised to his eldest son, Conrad IV, King of the Romans, with succession to his next son, Henry; but the bastard Manfred was not only called to the throne in case the legitimate line became extinct; he was also given a vast appanage which included the principality of Taranto, and was nominated *Balio* or regent of the Regno and all Italy till the absent Conrad could reach his realm. It was a difficult task which required the harmonising of four divergent groups of interests. First, there were the discontented towns and barons of the Regno, irked by the strong centralised government and harassed by heavy taxation; their disaffection was to be crushed or cajoled. Then, the national dislike of the German connexion was to be dealt with; Frederick's armed strength consisted in German and Saracen soldiery, and the Regnicoli were averse to the Germans at any rate, and perhaps wished to be free from the burden of the Empire. With this desire Manfred's own ambition to supplant his brothers, bound up as they were with Germany and the Empire, only too well coincided, and his uncles, Galvano and Frederick Lancia, spurred him on. Lastly, there were the loyal counsellors of Frederick II, firm partisans of Conrad IV and the Staufen policy. At their head stood the seneschal, Margrave Berthold of Hohenburg, who had the confidence of the German troops, the marshal, Peter Ruffo, and the chamberlain, John the Moor, who disposed of the treasure and the Saracens. They all were quickly alienated from the young *Balio*.

For the moment there was little difficulty in taking over the reins of government. The boy-prince Henry was sent in charge of Peter Ruffo to rule Sicily and Calabria. Manfred himself started for the Terra di Lavoro in order to hold that most disaffected portion of the Regno in check. But he did not long succeed. Scarcely was the Emperor's death known when the imperialist towns in the March of Ancona and Duchy of Spoleto submitted to Cardinal Peter Capocci, Florence recalled the exiled Guelfs, and a conspiracy was soon afoot in the Regno itself. Early in March 1251 the Terra di Lavoro, led by the cities of Naples and Capua and the Counts of Acerra and Caserta, broke into revolt, while the frontier town of Ascoli in the Abruzzi submitted to the cardinal.

The strings of all these movements were held by the Pope. "Let the heavens rejoice and let the earth be glad!"[1] Innocent IV wrote jubilantly when the news came of the Emperor's death. No one knew better how much Frederick had meant to the imperial cause, and he gave way to triumphant hopes. He would not only sever the Regno from the Empire; he would annex it to the Holy See; and a lax combination of communes and nobles should rule southern, if not all, Italy under the guidance of the Papacy. His first act, on 25 January 1251, shewed his confidence. He somewhat airily ordered his legate Peter to make terms with the magnates of the Regno. Probably Innocent knew well the character of Margrave Berthold, suspicious of Manfred and fond of an inept diplomacy, and underrated the inexperienced *Balio*. As for King Conrad, he hoped to detain him in Germany. North Italy should be won over and brought to peace by himself in person on his way to Rome and his new realm. Even when the Pope heard of Manfred's vigorous proceedings against the rebels in the Regno, he only added a victorious invasion to his programme.

His preparations were gradually made. On 15 March he announced his return to Italy and summoned the northern cities to a conference at his native city of Genoa. On 19 April, after an interview with the anti-Caesar William, he left Lyons, and proceeded down the Rhone and by sea to Genoa, which he reached on 18 May. There the Lombard congress was held, and Innocent's disillusionment began. Instead of crossing straight to Rome, he decided to make a progress through Lombardy to gain adherents. Some success he had. Alessandria declared for him; Thomas of Savoy-Piedmont adroitly changed sides and secured his possessions by marrying the kindred-loving Pope's niece. But the politics of Lombardy were decided, not by the claims of Pope or Emperor, but by the rivalries of the cities and the strife of factions and classes within them. When Innocent arrived at Milan on 7 July, his long stay there was embittered by the demands of his hosts for the payment of their war-expenses, and each papalist town had its terms to make. The subjection of Lodi by Milan which occurred in August was thus of little profit to the Pope, while on 24 March Piacenza had gone over to Pelavicini. Nor was Innocent's farther journey to Perugia, where he fixed his headquarters from 5 November, marked by success. He quarrelled with Bologna, and had the mortification of seeing her set Buoso

[1] *Psalm* XCVI (Vulgate, XCV), 11.

da Dovara, the co-tyrant of Cremona, at liberty. The fact was that the power of Ezzelin and of Pelavicini was increasing, not diminishing, for the loss of Lodi and Alessandria was a blow to Manfred Lancia, not to them; while even in west Lombardy the progress that Asti made in subduing her smaller neighbours counterbalanced the party-change of Thomas of Savoy. Innocent's perception of facts is, perhaps, shewn in his nomination of a single moderate agent on reaching Perugia. Octavian degli Ubaldini was reappointed sole legate for Lombardy and Romagna, while Gregory of Montelongo received the patriarchate of Aquileia, so that he could control Friuli in the papal interest.

In the meantime the favourable moment had passed in the Regno. On the outbreak of the revolt in the Terra di Lavoro, Manfred had retired to Apulia, only to meet and to suppress an ephemeral rebellion of the towns there. Then he joined forces with Margrave Berthold, and they invaded the Terra di Lavoro. Here, however, though Nola was captured, Naples and the rest resisted his efforts. His position grew more insecure, for Cardinal Peter had incited the Abruzzan coastland to insurrection. His own ambition had further weakened Manfred. Peter Ruffo had refused to execute his grants in favour of the Lancia in Sicily, and had driven off Galvano Lancia who was sent to replace him. So Manfred and Berthold towards the end of June turned to the Pope, with what ulterior purpose on the part of either or both it is impossible to say. In any case Innocent's offers were too low, and Manfred in September retired to Apulia to await his brother's coming. The youth had at least checked the papal progress. Innocent's means were exhausted, and he confined himself to keeping the revolt alive. His dreams of conquest had been thwarted by the strongly organised bureaucracy left by Frederick II, and by his own lack of troops and money.

Frederick's heir, Conrad IV, now came to give unity to his party. In November he held a congress of the imperialist tyrants and cities at Goito near Cremona, and then crossed by sea to Siponto in the Regno in mid-January 1252. Conrad had the great advantage of knowing exactly his own views. He worked for the traditional Staufen policy: he would rule the Regno, and use its wealth to rule the Empire. On this basis he was anxious for an accord with the Pope, and on no other. In the Regno, too, he was strong, since the officials, and the Germans and Saracens, were for him, and there was no conflict of wills. Margrave Berthold had met him in Istria and gained, perhaps justifiably, his ear. He soon shewed his disapproval of his brother Manfred's conduct as *Balio*, while Berthold's share in the negotiations with the Pope was forgiven or explained. So Manfred was deprived of part of his appanage, and during the rest of the reign he was under suspicion. His relatives, the Lancia, were deprived of his lavish grants, but Berthold and Peter Ruffo received fresh donations. A parliament was held at Foggia, in which the abolition of the hated general tax, the *collecta*, was used to gain favour for the

German king; and then Conrad set to work. In February he opened negotiations with the Pope, but their result was utter failure, for Innocent would not hear of a union of the Regno with the Empire. Meantime Conrad was warring down the rebellion in the Terra di Lavoro, which, a significant fact, had spread since his arrival. Gradually he conquered the rebels, Capua surrendering in January and Naples on 10 October 1253. As the Abruzzi were slowly won back during these operations, Conrad was now at last master of his kingdom.

Outside the Regno the omens were also in favour of the Staufen. Rome itself had become imperialist. Wearied of the anarchy of the nobles, the *popolo*, led by the Colonna, adopted a constitution on the Lombard model with a foreign *podestà*, in Roman style a Senator. In November 1252 they obtained for the post one of the most eminent Italians of the day, Brancaleone degli Andalò. He was a Bolognese, one of the chief of the imperialist faction in his native city, and came of a family already noted for its energetic *podestàs*. His safety secured by hostages, his rule was a righteous tyranny. Stern justice was dealt to the disturbers of the public peace, and so powerful did the Senator become that he was able to take a haughty tone to the Pope, while he also negotiated with Conrad.

Meanwhile Innocent, who vainly attempted to counteract the Senator by spending the winter in Rome, did not prosper in Lombardy either. He was naturally anxious to isolate Conrad and cut off his communications with Germany. For that the ruin or the party-change of Oberto Pelavicini and of Ezzelin was necessary. A league of the papalist cities seemed the most feasible plan, and it was carried through at Brescia by Cardinal Octavian on 8 March 1252, but it remained almost a dead letter. Bologna, the only really prosperous commune, although she sent occasional aid, was absorbed in her Romagnol policy. Milan and the rest were crippled by financial embarrassment due to long years of war. Still more fatal to the scheme was the prevalence of heresy, which Innocent was seriously determined to suppress.[1] On 19 April the Dominican inquisitor, Peter Martyr, was slaughtered at Milan, and the murderer went free. Brescia and Mantua were other centres of heretical opinions, and the influence of the sects, together with the toleration they enjoyed under Ezzelin and Pelavicini, tended to make the cities where they had many adherents disinclined to proceed against the two imperialist tyrants. Ezzelin was too savage to attract fresh communes to his rule, but the milder Pelavicini profited. The two despots quickly replied to the new papal league by one of their own on 31 March, and soon scored an important success by the subjugation of the Piacenzan papalists who held out in the countryside. Cardinal Octavian, whose military incapacity and reconciling tendency made him suspected as an imperialist, although lack of means and men was the main cause of his failure, was recalled; but matters were not mended thereby. Parma was isolated by the submission of the Piacenzan papalists. She

[1] See *infra*, Chap. xx.

accepted a native tyrant, and on 20 May 1253 made peace with Pelavicini. Innocent IV's only consolation was that the imperial vicar gained merely a suspicious ally. Yet Pelavicini's direct domain was increasing. Manfred Lancia's loyalty to Conrad had been dubious ever since his nephew Prince Manfred and his other relatives had been disgraced. His cities, west of the River Lambro, had held aloof from the league of Ezzelin and Pelavicini. Finally, he changed sides and in 1253 became *podestà* of Milan. Conrad at once declared all the Lancia traitors, and made Pelavicini sole vicar of Lombardy on 22 February 1253. He even hunted his new foes from Constantinople where they took refuge. It was soon seen, however, that Manfred Lancia's slackness was partly due to the lassitude of his cities. Even with Pelavicini as lord, Pavia carried on the weary petty warfare languidly, and shewed her anxiety for peace. Further west, again, the outlook was little more encouraging for Innocent. Boniface IV of Montferrat did not long endure being on the same side as his rival Thomas of Savoy-Piedmont, and joined the imperialists in 1252. Thomas, indeed, grew more powerful: in 1253 he became regent of Savoy on the death of his brother, Amadeus IV. But Asti continually increased her dominion, and even Thomas became her vassal on 28 July 1252 as the price of peace.

Only in Tuscany could the Pope look for better things, and that, curiously enough, was against his will. In Tuscany there were no dreaded tyrants who were indissolubly connected with the Staufen, and perpetuated the might of the Empire by linking Germany with Italy and the Regno. There were republics fighting for their own territorial and commercial interests, which at this time had little effect on the main struggle of Pope and Emperor. Here Frederick II's officials faded away on his death, and the domains he had collected were promptly annexed by the cities. Here therefore Innocent appears as a fatherly pontiff and short-sighted politician. He did not realise the importance of Florence for the Papacy. Florence had readmitted her exiled Guelfs on 7 January 1251, immediately on the news of Frederick's death, and her leading Ghibellines went into exile in July. War had already broken out with the still Ghibelline cities, Pisa, Siena, and their allies, and in the conflict Florence, seconded by her natural Guelf allies, Lucca, Genoa, and Umbrian Orvieto, was emerging triumphant. The Pope's attempts at mediation did not hamper her; a series of victories marked the year 1252, and on 1 February 1254 Pistoia surrendered and became a Guelf town.

In spite of the poor success that crowned his efforts, and the steadily growing danger that surrounded him in the papal lands, Innocent IV pursued the policy he had most at heart with an admirable tenacity. But it was clear that neither his temporal nor his spiritual resources were equal to the uprooting of the Staufen from the Regno, and his petty efforts to keep alive the rebellion among the Regnicoli only emphasised his impotence. If he wished to conquer, he must find a champion. After a suggestion that Conrad's brother Henry should take the Regno and marry the Pope's niece had been firmly refused by Conrad in June 1252, he took the final decision to call in a new dynasty for the Regno, which in the end was to bring so many troubles on Italy. At the end of August he obtained the consent of the cardinals to offer the Regno to Richard, Earl of Cornwall, the wealthy younger brother of King Henry III of England, if he would come and conquer it at his own expense. Charles, Count of Anjou and Provence, the youngest brother of King Louis IX of France, was to be approached if Richard refused. Accordingly the Pope's envoy, Master Albert of Parma, reached England in November 1252 to negotiate; but Richard was cautious and haggled shrewdly, and the Pope could not meet his reasonable demands. So by March 1253 the Earl had finally refused. Unlike his brother, however, Henry III greedily swallowed the bait and begged the crown for his own younger son Edmund. For the moment his proffer seems to have come too late, since Master Albert crossed to France and began to angle for the second candidate, Charles of Anjou. Charles, too, was ready to snatch the crown; but he also was shrewd, and Innocent's terms were high. His relatives were against the scheme, the dangers of which were obvious while Conrad's success continued; and, in spite of the bargain being all but struck in July 1253, Charles had withdrawn his candidature by 30 October. It was then that Henry III's folly renewed Edmund's candidature. On 20 December Innocent authorised Master Albert to treat again, and on 6 March 1254 an arrangement was made at Vendôme, although some revision of it was necessary before Innocent would ratify it on 14 May. This ratification, however, was not imparted by Master Albert, and Conrad's death caused it to be withheld altogether[1].

Henry III's scruples at attacking his own kith and kin had been alleviated by the death in December 1253 of his nephew Henry of Staufen, which was at once attributed by rumour and the Pope to poison at the hands of his jealous elder brother King Conrad. Conrad on his part had not ceased to hope for an accommodation with his adversary. He was probably willing to give all but Innocent's indispensable condition, the separation of the Regno and the Empire. He knew that reconciliation with the Papacy was needful if he were to recover Germany, and Innocent's position seemed so hazardous that he might after all give way. In October 1253 he made fresh overtures to the Pope, perhaps on the suggestion of his ally, the Roman Senator Brancaleone. Innocent, whose negotiations with Charles of Anjou were just collapsing and who dreaded an immediate attack, gave favourable ear, and envoys met at Rome. But Innocent probably never intended to do more than win time and appear placable to the world. He deceived his blunt antagonist and held him in hand through the winter. No real progress was made, and Conrad was answering a series of flimsy charges, such as heresy and usurpation, in January 1254. Then he must have discovered the Pope's negotiations with Henry III, for

[1] Cf. for the terms with Henry, *infra*, Chap. VIII.

on 4 February Innocent IV gave him till 22 March to appear in Rome to exculpate himself, and thus broke off the parley. Conrad, excommunicated anew on 9 April, could only look for war.

He did so, however, with confidence. He had a fine army; his exhausted treasure was replenished by heavy taxes on the Regno; and he was prepared to march north to reconquer Germany. Then it was that his luck gave out. He had become infected, like so many German invaders, with a southern fever, most naturally malaria, and, although at one time his recovery seemed certain, he relapsed. On 21 May 1254 he died in his camp at Lavello. There is something attractive in the indomitable courage with which the last Staufen King of the Romans endeavoured to revivify the obsolete. Yet Conrad was opposing the necessary march of events. Frederick II at least had aspired to unite Italy by German and Saracen arms and the Regno's subsidies, which perhaps was practicable. Conrad looked on the ecumenical idea of the Empire from another side: Italy was a subject province and source of revenue, which should enable him to maintain the Empire in Germany and elsewhere. That it could not be done in the long run, that it gave the Popes a continuous support in Italy for their struggles for independence, he never saw. He had little alternative under the circumstances of his accession, needing as he did the Regno's wealth to overcome his foes in Germany; and the heir of the Staufen could hardly be the forerunner of Rudolf of Habsburg.

How much Conrad's German outlook and his exactions had alienated the Regnicoli from his house appeared immediately after his death. He dreaded a usurpation of the Regno by its native, Manfred, and almost in despair recommended his infant son, the ill-fated Conrad II or Conradin as he was universally called, to the Pope's protection. For *Balio* or regent he named the German, Margrave Berthold of Hohenburg, the chief of all who desired the German connexion. An obvious ruin now impended over the Staufen. Disloyalty had grown among the Regnicoli, and such favour as existed for the royal house was mostly engrossed by Prince Manfred. The child Conradin was far away in Germany, and even the Saracens of Lucera, though controlled by the loyal chamberlain, John the Moor, really preferred the brilliant youth whom they knew. Manfred himself desired at least the regency, but what with towns and nobles hankering after the liberty promised by the Pope, with the fighting force and the chiefs of the bureaucracy siding with the *Balio*, he only headed the strongest faction among three.

The elated Innocent was master of the game. He was urging the unready Henry III to immediate action when the news of Conrad's death arrived. Thereat he hastened to Anagni by 9 June 1254 to be near the frontier, and all his old hopes revived. Disunion and treason were sapping his adversaries' strength, and in July Prince Manfred appeared to treat for peace on behalf of the *Balio*. A treaty was all but made, which included an adjudication on Conradin's rights when, years later, he should come of age. But the Pope was wily and demanded immediate possession of the Regno; and this was refused. It seems as if Berthold was willing to take the risk of papal rule on the chance of restoring Conradin at the last; Manfred on the other hand held out, while the party which desired annexation to the Papal State gained ground. Berthold accordingly resigned and Manfred was declared *Balio*; but he was as weak as Berthold, and, unlike Berthold, could not depend on the soldiery. Meantime Innocent raked together an army with all haste, pledging Henry III's credit and disregarding his son's claims on the Regno. On 8 September he could besiege San Germano on the frontier. Manfred was helpless, and on 27 September accepted the Pope's terms: Innocent was to be ruler, saving the future adjudication on Conradin's rights; Manfred obtained his appanage under his father's will, and was made vicar of the mainland south of the rivers Sele and Trigno; the Lancias, now again beside him, recovered the grants he had made them.

Innocent seemed at the goal for which he had striven through so many anxious years. But the same faithlessness which made him ignore the claims of Henry III led to his downfall. He knew—and events proved him right—that no Staufen could abandon the imperial dream. He meant to annex the Regno once for all: Manfred was far too powerful a subject and a possible claimant; his power should be diminished. When the Pope's army preceded him into the Regno, its commander, his nephew, Cardinal-deacon William de' Fieschi, began to demand oaths of allegiance without the stipulated *salvo* in Conradin's favour; on 7 October the Pope himself offered to Peter Ruffo, vicar of Sicily and Calabria since 1252, to make his Calabrian property an immediate fief of the Holy See, thus exempting it from Manfred's vicariate. None the less Manfred met his future suzerain at the frontier and led his horse over the Garigliano on 11 October. But when Innocent reached Teano, the inevitable discord broke out. Manfred found that his rights over his barony of Monte Sant' Angelo were to be brought in question, and left the town to consult Berthold. Scarcely was he out of Teano, when he met his supplanter in Monte Sant' Angelo, Borrello d'Anglona, and in the chance affray Borrello was killed. It was unfortunate for Innocent, since the event and the impossibility of trusting himself to the Pope steeled Manfred's wavering decision to resist. He had no other chance even of safety, for Berthold renounced him and made full submission to the Pope at Capua on 19 October; and next day Innocent came to final terms with Peter Ruffo, by which he was made vicar of Sicily and Calabria, now formally annexed to the Papal State. Thus both Conradin's claims and Manfred's treaty rights of 27 September were put aside. The desperate prince fled to Apulia, still perhaps hoping to bargain through John the Moor who ruled Lucera and its Saracens. But John was deciding for the Pope; Berthold's brothers were holding Apulia; and Cardinal William had already reached Ariano with the papal army on his way to occupy Lucera. Among romantic adventures Manfred's spirit awoke. On 2 November 1254 he entered Lucera, which John the Moor had quitted, seized the royal treasure, rallied the Saracens, and began a revolt. On the same day Berthold returned to Foggia and Cardinal William and his army encamped at Troia.

The tables were now suddenly turned. Innocent IV could still depend on the towns to which he granted communal autonomy and on a few ambitious nobles; but, by his breach of the treaty with regard to Conradin, he had united the cause of the rightful king with that of Manfred in one national and loyalist movement. Berthold might still persist in his blundering plan of submitting to the Pope in order to help Conradin another day; he could not now carry with him the German soldiery, since he could not pay them, and his jealousy of Manfred and his greed were manifest. Manfred was Conradin's only hope; he had the treasure, and the Germans flocked to him. The Saracens, too, were all for the tolerant Staufen they knew, while the barons, irrespective of former party-divisions, proceeded to go over to the native prince. The decisive action soon came. Berthold loved negotiating, and he was fully aware of the wretched quality of the cardinal's hireling troops. During long *pourparlers*—no truce is mentioned—Manfred routed Berthold's brother Otto and his detachment near Foggia on 2 December. The moment the news reached Troia, both the cardinal and his men fled in wild panic across the snow-covered hills to Ariano. In a few days Manfred ruled Apulia save a few towns, the Lancia and other barons had joined him, and even Peter Ruffo, in spite of justifiable suspicions, accepted him as Conradin's *Balio*, on condition, however, of his own independent regency in Sicily and Calabria.

When the news reached Innocent, the Pope was on his death-bed. He had fallen ill at Teano, but none the less he had kept at work during his residence at Capua, and on 27 October had entered Naples in triumph. He perceived gradually that his expectation of annexing the Regno was vain, and coolly began again to treat with Henry III, whom he yet hoped to cheat of some or all of the booty. Henry's slackness, indeed, might fairly be held to diminish his gains under the treaty. Meantime the parliament that had been summoned was put off, for the Pope was confined to his bed. Then the news of the cardinal's rout came as a parting stroke. The sick man's conscience smote him; he was continually murmuring: "Domine, propter iniquitatem corripuisti hominem."[1] On 7 December 1254 he died.

It is hardly a just reproach to Innocent IV that he introduced foreign rule into Italy by his negotiations with Henry III, for the foreigner was already there. The Staufen and their subsidiary tyrants depended on

[1] *Psalm* XXXIX (Vulgate XXXVIII), 11. The prayerbook version is: "When thou with rebukes dost chasten man for sin."

German or Saracen levies. And, in defence of his policy, it is true that he stood for a milder rule against often ferocious tyrants. The free communes, with all allowance made, were juster and more humane than Ezzelin and Pelavicini or even than the Staufen. Innocent was profoundly convinced that the independence of the Papacy was impossible so long as the Empire and the Regno were under the same sovereign, and indeed so long as the Emperor claimed a real dominion in North Italy. The solution of his choice was to make all Italy a land of petty states, to the south in subordination to the Roman See, to the north in allegiance to the Empire, yet really also guided by the Pope. Then the Papacy would be free and could direct Europe through obedient kings and magistrates. And his conception of the Papacy was more secular than any Pope's before him. He viewed his weakness as political and his remedies were political. He used his spiritual powers constantly to raise money, buy friends, injure foes, and by his unscrupulousness he roused a disrespectful hostility to the Papacy everywhere. His dispensations were a scandal. In contempt of his spiritual duties and of local rights, he used the endowments of the Church as papal revenue and means of political rewards: there would be four papal nominees waiting one after another for a benefice. Bad appointments were a natural consequence of such a system; and, further, legates chosen for war and diplomacy would more likely than not be thoroughly worldly in character, like such Cardinal-deacons as Octavian and Gregory of Montelongo, or the truculent elect of Ravenna, Philip della Fontana. Of the loss of prestige and spiritual influence occasioned by him Innocent was unconscious. He had good intentions but not good principles. Endowed with courage, with invincible resolution, with astuteness, his cold equanimity was seldom shaken by disaster or good-fortune, and he patiently pursued his ends with a cunning faithlessness which lowered the standards of the Church. His influence on events was enormous. He wrecked the Empire; he started the Papacy on its decline; he moulded the destinies of Italy.

The election of a new Pope followed quickly. The natural desire of the cardinals was for some one without Innocent's faults, and on 12 December 1254 they concurred in the promotion of Gregory IX's nephew Rinaldo Conti, Cardinal-bishop of Ostia. Alexander IV was, indeed, the opposite of his predecessor. He was a pious, learned prelate, protector of the Franciscan Friars, easy-tempered and easily led. "He did not care for the affairs of princes and kingdoms," but would select a manager for a business and then leave all to him. He was honestly anxious for peace and right, the suppression of heresy, and the reform of abuses in the Church; yet his weakness threw him into the hands of Innocent's advisers, and he tremblingly followed his ways. In the matter of the Regno Cardinal Octavian, able and moderate, became his oracle, being appointed legate in January 1255, with the dubious Berthold by his side. It was resolved to carry through the treaty with Henry III, after overtures to

Conradin's German guardian, Duke Louis of Bavaria, had come to nothing, and Manfred had kept firm to his demand for the recognition of Conradin and his own regency. Edmund's investiture was now confirmed on 9 April 1255, and Henry's envoy agreed that Innocent's expenditure should be paid, and that an army should come by Michaelmas 1256.

Active preparations, meanwhile, were made to crush Manfred. By a curious combination he had ousted Ruffo from Calabria, while the Sicilian towns had gone over to the Pope. But the prince was finding it hard to subdue the papalist Apulian communes. The time seemed propitious for a vigorous effort, and at the end of May 1255 Cardinal Octavian marched on Lucera with a large and inefficient army. He was advised by Berthold, and this was his ruin, for the news came that Conradin's guardian had allied with Manfred. It seems most likely that Berthold could not endure to fight against the heir of the Staufen, and lured on the legate to break a temporary truce with Manfred and to march on to Foggia. There during the deadly summer months he was blockaded by the prince, while Berthold with the best of his troops was making a long tour for supplies in Apulia. At last the margrave drew near, letting Manfred know his movements. One night he tried, or feigned to try, to break through the blockading lines, and was utterly defeated. The legate and his starving army could hold out no longer. Early in September he made a treaty with the victor, by which Conradin's and Manfred's rights were acknowledged, while all papalists, including the Hohenburg brothers, were restored, and the Terra di Lavoro was ceded to the Pope. Then he was allowed to retreat to Alexander IV, who disowned the bargain.

Manfred could now gather the fruits of victory. Most of the Regno went over to his side. In 1256 he conquered the Terra di Lavoro, while his adherents won Sicily for him. The last embers of revolt were stamped out in 1257, and he could then pursue his own ambitions. Already in 1256 he had blinded his enemies, the Hohenburgs, and had procured the murder of Peter Ruffo in exile. It only remained to usurp the throne. A false report of Conradin's death was spread, whereat the *Balio* held a Parliament at Palermo, and of course was begged to assume the crown, which he did on 10 August 1258. Perhaps he might have founded a lasting dynasty if he could have kept up a policy of non-intervention in Northern Italy. He was secure in the Regno with the support of the bureaucracy; his German and Saracen troops were good and loyal; his own indolent temper made inaction pleasant. But the son of Frederick II could with difficulty renounce the Emperor's projects and the attempt to unite all Italy under his sway, while his Lombard kinsmen urged him on and were ready to take the trouble of business off his hands. They might argue that it was necessary to establish barriers against a fresh invasion, for Alexander IV persisted in his refusal to ratify Cardinal Octavian's treaty. The Pope, in fact, perseveringly attempted to bring Henry III with an army against the Regno, although the English king, weary of his bargain and tethered by his Parliaments, broke his promises and endeavoured to escape from the expedition altogether. Even so, however, the weak Pope, crippled by debts, could be dangerous. He had done his part in diminishing the power of Ezzelin and Pelavicini. The Romans, whose countryman he was, had expelled the imperialist Brancaleone from office in November 1255, and he could now reside alternately in Anagni and at the Lateran. His allies and faithful creditors, the Guelfs of Florence, ruled Pistoia, Arezzo, and Volterra, had brought Siena to unwelcome terms, and had twice overthrown the rival Ghibelline city of Pisa, in 1254 and 1256. Their commerce had taken on a vast extension through the banking business of the indebted Papacy and Innocent IV's financial expedients. Lastly, on the death of King William, once anti-Caesar to Frederick II, on 28 January 1256, two rival Kings of the Romans had been elected, Richard, Earl of Cornwall, and Alfonso X, King of Castile; and Conradin's indignant guardian, Louis of Bavaria, had acknowledged Richard, whose imperial claims in Italy seemed a possible danger to Manfred.

In 1257 Manfred began his policy of expansion, which was a combination of Frederick II's designs for dominion over all Italy and of the old oriental schemes of the Norman dynasty. While remaining neutral in the war in progress between Venice and Genoa in the Levant, he renewed their ancient privileges in the Regno and thus gained their friendship. We can hardly doubt that he also had a share in the new revolution in May 1257 at Rome, where Brancaleone was reinstated and ruled as strongly as ever. An alliance was at once made between the Senator and Manfred, whose treasure began to flow in Rome. He also negotiated with the Central Italian towns, and drew many to his side. In October 1258 he was able to appoint a vicar for the March of Ancona and Duchy of Spoleto, who acquired most of the March. In Tuscany, Siena declared for King Manfred in 1259. Events in western Lombardy, too, were in his favour. Thomas of Savoy had tried conclusions with Asti, and after a defeat had been captured by his revolted city of Turin in 1255. Although he was released in 1257, he died in February 1259 restricted to his ancient appanage of Piedmont, and imperialist Asti was momentarily predominant.

In east Lombardy, however, Manfred's intervention was necessary if he wished to lead the imperialists, for the power both of Ezzelin and of Pelavicini was shaken, although for very different reasons. Pelavicini did certainly represent one of the factors of the Italian city-tyranny which was coming into existence in his day. He was a warlike noble to whom his imperial vicariate gave influence and, what was more important, a body of German troops. But he had no real root in any of his cities, and shared his authority with the local faction-chiefs who had called him in and could drive him out. His own native city of Parma never admitted him. These faction-chiefs, like Buoso da Dovara at Cremona, were the product of the rise of the middle-class of traders to power in the towns. Amid endless divergencies of detail the main lines of development were the same. The middle-class in their gilds had claimed and were obtaining a separate organisation as the *popolo* alongside of the older governing body, the Commune, where the nobles were preponderant. The *popolani*, as they were called, were usually abetted by a minority of the nobles who were at faction-strife with the others of their order. Unfortunately in the Lombard towns the *popolo* as a rule proved incapable of working their organisation so as to secure internal peace and to govern their city, or even to overcome the main body of the city's nobles. For one thing, they had neither sufficient support from nor control of the petty tradesmen and employés beneath them. Part of their failure was due to the struggle of Pope and Emperor. The factions of the nobles took sides as papalists or imperialists, for which as the thirteenth century drew to its close the Tuscan names of Guelf and Ghibelline became general. The struggle rarely appealed to the *popolani*, who were far more influenced in their action by the rivalry of city with city and the attitude of their nobles towards themselves. Thus a multitude of cross-currents prevented all stability. If Bergamo became papalist, the *popolo* of Brescia would veer round to the imperialist faction of its nobles. The whole strife was embittered by the custom of exiling the defeated faction of nobles, which was a consequence of their irreconcilable feuds, and was almost rendered necessary to a victorious *popolo* if any sort of peace was to be kept within the city. Sometimes, indeed, a well-knit *popolo*, like that of Bologna, could keep both factions of nobles in check for a term of years and pursue a consistent practical policy within and without. But as a rule the distracted *popolani* would entrust the government for longer or shorter periods to a noble faction-chief, generally the chief of the smaller faction, whether papalist or imperialist. He would hold, at first, however absolute his real power, one or more of the city-offices, usually *podestà* as head of the Commune or Captain as head of the *popolo*, or sometimes Captain of the militia. As time wore on, new enactments would increase his powers, especially after he had been elected for life, till at length he would be Captain-General with absolute authority, and *signore* or lord, *i.e.* no longer an official, and finally an hereditary sovran. Each city indeed had its own series of changes, its own variations from the type, but in the gross the development was in curious parallel to Roman history with its co-ordinate assemblies of the centuries and tribes and its evolution of the Principate.

Such a variation was Ezzelin. In essence his position resembled that of the full-fledged tyrant, in that he was a local faction-chief of Verona allied with the *popolo*. He was akin, also, to Pelavicini, in that he owed his absolutism to German troops, obtained at first through his alliance with Frederick II. But he was singular in that his power was extralegal and he held no office. None the less he was despot of his territory:

the imperial vicar, Ansedisio de' Guidotti, was his humble instrument to rule Padua; the magistrates of Verona and Vicenza were his creatures. He fell, however, not owing to his usurpations, but owing to the streak of insanity in his character. His German guards lifted him above public opinion. Harshness towards faction-rivals became mad cruelty in him, and his thirst for blood was mingled with a perverse hatred of his species, which perhaps was the real ground of the intangible reputation for heresy which clung to him. Thus lashed with scorpions, his *popolani* grew disaffected, especially in the miserable city of Padua. Innocent IV had coolly parleyed with him, but the kindly Alexander IV really acted against him. In December 1255 he appointed the adventurous and more than secular Philip da Pistoia, the elect of Ravenna, legate to lead a crusade against the tyrant who was also the mainstay of the imperialists in Lombardy. It was a task far beyond the power of the Lombard papalists, disunited and preoccupied with their own city-interests, but Philip gained the aid of Venice, who added to his exiles and crusading riff-raff soldiers, ships, and victuals. On 20 June 1256 he captured Padua, while Ezzelin was ravaging the Mantuan *contado*. Ezzelin could not recover the town, and this first intervention of Venice in her hinterland was an unalloyed success. Ezzelin, however, if mad, was both a ruler and a general. In spite of the slow weakening of the Lombard imperialists, he seized Brescia in 1258 with the aid of Pelavicini, after they had defeated and captured Philip of Ravenna at Gambara. But he cheated his ally of his share in the conquest, and thus produced a temporary league against himself of all his neighbours, including Azzo of Este, Milan, and Bologna, led by Pelavicini, who in 1258 had become Manfred's representative. Ezzelin took the offensive in August 1259 by invading the Milanese; he was outgeneralled, outnumbered, defeated, and taken prisoner at Cassano by the passage of the river Adda, to die by tearing the bandages from his wounds on October 1. His brother Alberic of Treviso, latterly his ally, next year was horribly put to death. In many ways Ezzelin had been a prototype of the degenerate despots of the fourteenth century; but his maniacal cruelty had been wreaked on a wider circle than those of his imitators: he had held an army of opponents in his prisons.

By this victory of Pelavicini, Manfred, at least by proxy, had become powerful in Lombardy. Mastino della Scala, an imperialist, obtained the tyranny of Verona; and the papalist Martin della Torre, since 1258 tyrant of Milan, was for the time being Pelavicini's ally. Year after year the royal vicar's power increased: he directed the politics of most of central Lombardy, and he began to plan out a commercial policy which should further the recovery of the cities after so many broils. Yet he was bound to continue war to maintain his position. In the end his strength decayed, not from misgovernment, but owing to the death of his ally, Martin della Torre.

The establishment of a tyranny was not the only way out from the strife of the *popolo* with the nobles. In Genoa the nobles were also the chief shipowners and capitalists, and thus doubly entrenched in power and identified with the city's prosperity. When even there a dictatorial Captain of the *popolo*, William Boccanera, was placed in power by a revolution in 1257, he gained no lasting support, and his ill-conduct of the naval war—Genoa being driven from the Syrian coast and from Sardinia by Venice and Pisa—in spite of the all-important Treaty of Nymphaeum with Michael Palaeologus in 1261, which was to give Genoa almost a monopoly of the Black Sea trade[1], led to a renewal of aristocratic government in 1262. Feuds then led to a resurgence of the *popolo* in 1270; yet the two joint Captains, a Doria and a Spinola, were Ghibellines and aristocrats and their strong government, supported by the yearly plebeian "Abbot of the *popolo*," was in no way akin to a Lombard tyranny. The most successful constitution, however, was that of Tuscan Florence. In the *Primo Popolo*, as it was later called, which was set up in 1250, the *popolo* was organised in a militia of local companies. It was commanded by the Captain of the *popolo*, who, roughly speaking, possessed coordinate powers with the *podestà* of the commune, and advised with Councils of his own, corresponding to those of the *podestà*. By his side, too, stood the twelve *anziani* (ancients) who supervised finance. In spite of its cumbrousness and the mutual suspicion which pervaded it, this constitution worked well in practice, for the rich bankers and merchants who controlled it were well backed by the general opinion of the *popolo*. Their ability was shewn in the prosperous wars by which Pisa was vanquished and their small neighbour-towns subjugated. Finance, however, shewed them at their best, as it was the source of their predominance. In 1252 they usurped an imperial prerogative by coining the famous gold florin, and their wisdom kept it undebased, so that it became the standard coin of Western Europe. They were chief bankers to the Pope, and his and Henry III's debts increased their trade, especially in England, where the wool export was largely pledged to them. They were strong enough to defeat in 1258 an attempt of their countryman, Cardinal Octavian, to seize a tyranny over Florence in concert with the exiled Ghibellines, and they were dreaming of a mid-Italian dominion for their city when they were overthrown by Manfred's intervention.

It was Siena, the steady foe of Florence, who opened the way for the Sicilian king. In May 1259 she accepted his overlordship, and Manfred sent in return bodies of German horse to her aid. This was the decisive factor in the struggle that followed. True, Pisa's recent recovery as against Genoa in the Levant and Sardinia counted for something; true, that the repulse of the ambitious reconciler, Cardinal Octavian, had alienated the Curia—it was then, not earlier, that he "lost his soul for the Ghibellines." But Florence was strong and well led; her defect lay in the fact that the

[1] See *supra*, Vol. IV, p. 510 sq.

burghers, excellent against like troops to themselves, had neither the training nor the delight in sword-play which could resist the German men-at-arms in the open field. The nobles of the countryside were more capable of fighting the Transalpines, but they were largely Ghibelline and at war with their native city. So on 4 September 1260 the Florentine host was overthrown with fearful slaughter, 10,000 out of 33,000, at Montaperto. Submission followed at once; the Guelf nobles and some leading *popolani* went into exile, and Florence herself might have been rased to the ground, had not her Ghibelline leader, Farinata degli Uberti, withstood her envenomed foes *a viso aperto*.

Thus Manfred through his vicar at the head of a Ghibelline league of cities ruled all Tuscany, even Lucca submitting in 1264. It was not a harsh government, although the *Primo Popolo* in Florence was abolished, and the Ghibelline nobles controlled the Commune; the *popolo* still had to be humoured, if made subordinate. The king's weakness partly lay in the restiveness of the cities, all pressing their separate interests which were not his, and still more in economic circumstances. The bankers and merchants of Florence and Siena were irretrievably bound up with the Popes, whose bankers and creditors they were, and whose revenues they largely collected. The Popes, too, wielded a deadly weapon; they could forbid the overjoyed debtors of the bankers abroad to pay their debts. Hence Siena lost, for instance, the English trade. Subterfuges, like a concealed partnership with Guelf firms, were of no avail in the long run, and one by one the leading bankers, secretly or openly, became Guelfs, as the new Pope, Urban IV, put steady pressure upon them. They had watched without flinching the tragic procession of the Flagellants, who in 1260 pervaded Italy. That melancholy spasm of revivalism—city after city stirred by the nameless self-scourging penitents and adding to their number, unless a stern despot like Pelavicini warded off the infection—did not indeed create a return to godliness. It was only, as was said by Gregorovius, the funeral dirge over the magnificent conceptions of the Empire and the Papacy. Men did not, save in the mystic expectations of Joachism, recognise the beginnings of a newer world.

We may guess that the policy of Cardinal Octavian, who led the Curia, was not unlike that of the later Pope, Nicholas III: that he wished a strictly local King of Sicily, and a peaceable Papal State in Central Italy, within which the old factions should be reconciled. But the scheme had failed. Although Rome had again become uncertainly papalist in 1259 some months after Brancaleone's death, Manfred conquered Tuscany and made progress in the papal lands. Naturally, when the Pope died on 25 May 1261 at Viterbo, the Cardinals recurred to a more worldly pontiff. On 29 August they elected James Pantaléon, Patriarch of Jerusalem, the son of a shoemaker of Troyes, who took the name of Urban IV. A born despot, who "did what he willed," he was the first non-Italian, now that national feeling was strongly developed, to sit in St Peter's chair, and he at once gave the papal policy a pro-French direction. Fourteen new cardinals, several of them French, created for him a majority in the Sacred College, and increased his freedom of action. Vigorous measures and new men did much to restore his authority in the papal lands and to alleviate the papal debts. Like Innocent IV he saw that Staufen rulers in Empire or Regno must aim at a unification of Italy, since even Manfred openly claimed the Empire. A champion, then, must be called in to fight against them, and Urban was resolved that the champion should be French. First, however, he must convert the righteous Louis IX of France to aggression on the Regno; for that Conradin's claims must be dismissed and Manfred must be proved an irreconcilable enemy. A further complication was introduced by the efforts of the ex-Emperor Baldwin of Constantinople to obtain the restoration of the Latin Empire and the expulsion of the schismatic Palaeologus by means of Manfred as champion, an object sure to appeal to the crusading French king. Manfred must then be proved useless to Christendom. So negotiations were opened with him which lasted through 1262, and in which Urban contrived to make demands such as the Sicilian king would not grant. On 29 March 1263 Manfred was excommunicated anew, this time with Louis IX's approval[1].

Urban IV had never intended a reconciliation. He had long been in treaty with Charles of Anjou, once the alternative candidate of Innocent, Edmund of England being deservedly cashiered. A prolonged haggling took place over the terms of the agreement, for Urban had no intention of founding a new prepotent dynasty in Italy, and Charles meant to be no catspaw. In March 1264 matters were furthered by Charles finally taking over the senatorship of Rome, offered him since August by the papalist faction there, and sending a deputy. The Pope may not have been pleased at seeing his hand forced, but was too hard-pressed by Manfred to be unbending to Charles, and the bargain was all but concluded when he died worn out at Perugia on 2 October 1264. The strong-willed, keen-sighted Frenchman had set on foot a great work, the exclusion of the Germans from Italy and the introduction of the French. His successor was to see the accomplishment of the design and to feel its effect, the renewed subjugation of the Papacy to a lay power, this time French.

His successor after a four months' conclave was another Frenchman, an ex-chancellor of Louis IX. This was Guy Foulquoi "le Gros," a native of Languedoc and Cardinal-bishop of Sabina; he was an exemplar of the pagan virtues, with asceticism added. Clement IV, as he was styled, was crowned on 15 February, and at last concluded the treaty with Charles in April 1265. Its principal provisions were: the separation of the Regno from the Empire; the Sicilian king was to hold no office nor land in the papal territory, nor any dominion in Lombardy or Tuscany; for three years, however, Charles might be Senator of Rome, unless he obtained the Regno in a shorter period; Charles was to pay 50,000 marks down on

[1] Cf. for St Louis' attitude, *infra*, Chap. x.

conquest, and a tribute of 8000 gold ounces yearly, and was to furnish 300 knights for three months yearly, if called upon to do so; the clergy were to be tax-free and subject to ecclesiastical tribunals only; the Regnicoli were to enjoy their customs as under William the Good. Both allies were in desperate need of money. Still they borrowed, begged, and taxed; the affair was a crusade, and the French clergy gave a tenth of their possessions to it. The Tuscan Guelf bankers were cajoled and coerced to lend with the prospect of the exploitation of the Regno to requite them. Charles had equipped a fleet from his county of Provence, and crusaders flocked together from all France, eager for booty and spiritual benefits.

The leading characteristic of Charles of Anjou, who thus became the Pope's champion, was a devouring ambition, which stopped at no obstacle and was never satisfied. He was a statesman strong and cold, ruthless and crafty. Unweariedly active, he had no liking for any sort of diversion, and with this dour activity went a love of despotic rule. Of an orthodox nature, heresy vanished before him. Without being in any way a monster, he was singularly unloveable, and the narrowness of his sympathies, confined to Frenchmen who were noble, made him a harsh governor. In 1246 he had obtained the county of Provence in the Arelate by his marriage with Beatrice, youngest daughter and heiress of Raymond Berengar IV, Count of Provence, who died in 1245. In spite of revolts, he had succeeded in turning his dominion there into a complete despotism and had begun fresh conquests. Between 1258 and 1264 he had made himself lord or count of southern Piedmont, composed of the little communes which had recently been subject to Asti, and thus he had a foothold in Italy. Now he was to be the defender of Holy Church, and doubted neither the righteousness of his hire nor that of any of his subsequent proceedings. He convinced himself that his own exaltation was the chief need of Christendom.

By 1265 immediate action was essential. Manfred was head of a great confederation, made victorious by his Germans and Saracens. He ruled Tuscany; his ally Pelavicini was the greatest power in Lombardy; he had much authority in the papal March of Ancona where his vicar had won a victory in 1264; the Trevisan March was at least neutral; and Venice and Genoa were his friends. Tunis was his tributary; his father-in-law was Despot of Epirus; his son-in-law was heir to Aragon. He seemed to aim at uniting Italy, seizing the Empire, and keeping a supremacy in the East. But the wielder of this dominion was himself weak. In spite of his courage and ability and his many adventures, Manfred yet remained a child of the harem, which Frederick II, like his Norman predecessors, had fatally adopted. Indolent and undecided, prone to act through confidential officials, and loving the imagination of his own greatness, the "Sultan of Lucera," as his insulting enemies called him, spent his days in his delicious country-palaces among the Apennines, dictating his adroit, vainglorious manifestoes, and unable to brace himself up to the pleasureless activity necessary for his ambitions and even for his safety. He now shewed the same oriental mixture of self-confidence and enervation. James de Gantelme, a Provençal, came to Rome as Charles' vicar in the spring of 1264. It was necessary to expel him, if Charles was not to have a basis of operations. But Manfred only made two ineffective, if clever, campaigns which left things as they were. He could not resolve to press the attack home in person, and seized the occasion of Pope Urban's death to give up the enterprise. Very different were the actions of his adversaries. Penniless and surrounded, the Pope and Gantelme held out dauntlessly in Perugia and Rome.

Charles' plan was simple. He would go himself to Rome to hold and prepare his base. His crusading army, unable to cross the sea which Manfred commanded, should take a circuit through Lombardy and Romagna and so reach him. This scheme was possible owing to the change which had occurred in Lombardy. In December 1264 Philip della Torre succeeded his brother Martin as tyrant of Milan. He at once broke with Pelavicini, and formed in February 1265 in concert with Marquess Obizzo of Este a new papalist league, which in its turn allied with Charles, and kept gaining over fresh cities, while Pelavicini lost Modena and Parma. To its progress the succession of Napoleon della Torre in October 1265 made no difference. In November 1265 Charles' crusading army crossed the Alps and assembled at his town of Alba. It consisted of 5000 French men-at-arms and 25,000 foot, and was of fine fighting quality. By Vercelli, which a revolution took from Pelavicini and gave to the Torriani, through Milan, Mantua, and Bologna they went—Pelavicini, now much diminished in power, not daring to attack—gained the Flaminian Way, and reached Rome in January 1266. Meanwhile Charles with a smaller force had taken ship on 14 May 1265, and favoured by the weather and the general paralysis of Manfred's side, had entered Rome. He was invested as king and crusading chief on 28 June.

Manfred was awaking to his danger. After a further unreal campaign against Rome in the summer of 1265, during which Charles seemed to offer battle in vain, he made earnest preparations for defence. He recalled his Germans from the north, he massed his Saracens, he summoned in December the feudal levies. Treason, however, was already at work. The Norman barons of the Regno had never submitted willingly to their kings, and the German conquest had further alienated them. Heavy taxation, also, made the Regnicoli only too ready to listen to the Pope's glowing prophecies. Manfred knew it, and shewed too late the energy of despair. Charles stormed the frontier town of San Germano on 10 February 1266, and the Terra di Lavoro began to declare for him; so Manfred retreated to the inner line of defence in the pass of the Apennines, and encamped at Benevento, whither Charles followed. They joined battle on 26 February with nearly equal forces, but the French troopers were too strong for Manfred's fighting men, Germans, Lombards, and Saracens, and the Regnicoli fled without a blow. Manfred saw his fate and charged into the fray to fall by an unknown hand. With him the glory of the Regno departed. Like Frederick II he had fostered its rich culture, the most advanced in Europe; he was himself an author. In spite of indolence, revengefulness, and faithlessness, he had been a merciful, indulgent prince. Now the Regnicoli were to fall under an utterly selfish, greedy ruler, and to expiate their own fickle treason. True it is, that it was time that European civilisation should find its centre to the north away from the semi-oriental influences of Sicily. It was time, too, that the now unfruitful connexion of Italy and Germany should give place to independent development. And these necessities were effected by the victory of the French knights over German and Saracen at Benevento.

A kaleidoscopic change took place all over Italy on Manfred's fall. The Regno accepted its new master. Almost all the March of Ancona submitted to the Pope. At Florence, after an intricate series of compromises, the Ghibelline nobles left the town, and the *popolo* was revived; the Guelfs of course came back throughout Tuscany and took the lead. In Lombardy there followed a number of revolutions, as the imperialist towns turned papalist. Pelavicini lost all his dominions and retired to his estates, where he died in 1269; Buoso da Dovara was similarly relegated to his possessions in the Cremonese *contado.* Societies were formed in many towns to secure peace and orthodoxy, and they soon became actively papalist bodies. Of all the cities, only tyrant-ruled Verona and republican Pavia retained their imperial party standpoint.

It seemed for a moment as if the aims of the Popes were fully brought about. That they were not, was due partly to King Charles' ambition and partly to his necessities, but also to the rivalries of the north Italian towns, the policy of which was only partially and unwillingly concerned with the strife of Pope and Emperor, and not at all fulfilled by the mere victory of Clement IV. Charles' government of the Regno rapidly became a public scandal. The Staufen had ruled through the Regnicoli themselves; but Charles, who had seen their treason and who knew that such loyalty as existed was for the Staufen, governed them as he governed the Provençals, by foreigners. Only the tax-farmers were native, and these men soon earned a hatred which their predecessors had avoided. The French officials, on their side, were oppressive aliens. The Tuscan merchants and bankers absorbed the country's trade, once in native hands. The promised Parliament was not held. The taxes themselves were as heavy as of old, and harder to bear, for the general *collectae* were still levied, in spite of Charles' promises to the Pope, and the clergy were now exempt from them, Charles' promise being kept on that head. Charles might justly claim that he could not abolish the *collectae* had he wished, since the bureaucratic State needed heavy taxes for its support, and he had soldiers and debts to pay, among which the debt and tribute to the Pope were prominent. This argument, however, did not convince the Pope, and no wonder, for Charles embarked at once on great schemes which meant costly preparations. "What do you wish me to rejoice at?" he said after Benevento; "to a valiant man the whole world would not suffice." The capture of Constantinople in 1261 by the Greek Emperor Michael VIII gave him a pretext for subduing the schismatic Greeks, and he formed a comprehensive maritime policy like that of the Norman kings, which included the conquest of the Balkans and the supremacy in the trade of the Levant. The Regnicoli, thus made his stepping-stones, became eager for revolt, and looked in their turn for a champion.

Clement IV was well-informed, and his angry reproaches were justified, but his own measures did little good. He insisted on Charles resigning the senatorship of Rome according to the treaty; but the subsequent rule of the papalist nobility roused the Romans to revolution, and in June 1267 a new Senator was appointed, Don Henry of Castile. Although a younger brother of Alfonso X, he was practically a wealthy adventurer, and he had recently become mortal enemy to Charles over his disappointed hopes for a kingdom in Sardinia. Once Senator, he soon fell out with the Pope and joined the imperialist faction. In Tuscany Clement's intervention had been equally unhappy. He was an aristocrat and disliked the rule of the *popolo*; he wished his dependents, the Guelf nobles and bankers, to be untrammelled masters of Florence; he was jealous for the papal authority, and he dreaded with reason a new storm coming from Germany, to which even a partly Ghibelline Florence might give free ingress, for the exiled Ghibellines kept their ground in the *contado*, as was usual with a defeated city-faction, and possessed a formidable force of German troopers. When the Florentine *popolo* pursued a reconciling system and disregarded the Pope's wishes, the angry Clement resolved to abandon a main security of the Papacy and bring King Charles into Tuscany. With remarkable blindness he shewed himself more patient to Ghibelline Pisa, and attempted to make her peace with Charles, who had abolished her toll-freedom in the Regno and was aggrieved by her consequent hostile attitude to him.

The main reason for all these Tuscan proceedings was the imminent invasion of Italy by Conradin. The last heir of the Staufen was in 1267 a boy of fifteen, precocious, bold, and ambitious; he was the only hope of the malcontent Regnicoli and the Italian imperialists. Early in the year relatives of Manfred and ex-officials, like the Lancia, came flocking to his court in Swabia; and a plan was struck out by which he should march to Tuscany and thence invade the Regno, while the Regnicolo, Conrad Capece, should attack Sicily from Tunis. Some vague notion of the scheme must have been known to the Pope and Charles, and they resolved to gain Tuscany first.

Charles met Clement at Viterbo in April 1267. However unwillingly, the Pope appointed him *Paciarius*—pacifier—of Tuscany for three years, a grant which enabled him shortly after to usurp the vicariate of the Holy Roman Empire in that province. The king's troops preceded him to Florence, whence the remaining Ghibellines fled. He was at once made *Signore* and *Podestà*, with a vicar to represent him. In a new constitution the *popolo's* organisation and Captain were abolished, and the Guelf nobles and bankers placed in exclusive power. A new magistracy was recognised, that of the Parte Guelfa, governed by the usual apparatus of Captains and Councils; and its function was to keep the Guelfs in power, analogously to the action of the peace-societies in Lombardy. For this purpose one-third of the confiscated property of the Ghibelline exiles was handed over to it. Not all of Tuscany, however, shewed the submissiveness of Florence; Siena and Pisa, the latter now at open war with Charles, held out along with the Ghibellines in the Florentine *contado*. In the course of the war 800 Ghibellines and Germans were shut up in Poggibonsi, and Charles who came north in August 1267 set about its siege. The task was hard, for the town only surrendered on 30 November, and this delay gave the Ghibellines their chance. Pisa allied with Conradin, who also gained over Don Henry and Rome; while Conrad Capece obtained the alliance of the Emir of Tunis, and with Don Frederick, brother to Don Henry, raised a formidable revolt in Sicily at the end of August 1267.

Meanwhile Conradin entered Verona with a German army on 21 October. Now excommunicated by the Pope, he gained no result from his diplomacy in Lombardy, and he decided to make a dash for Tuscany. By a circuit southward he reached Pavia safely with 3000 troopers on 20 January 1268. Charles intended to march to fight him, but his better judgment was overruled by the Pope—his treasure was exhausted and Clement was paymaster. On 2 February the Saracens of Lucera had revolted, and the Pope insisted on Charles' return to quell them and hold the Regno. So the king moved south and began another weary unsuccessful siege. Conradin immediately slipped to Pisa by sea, and his army, avoiding the customary Via Francigena, blocked by Charles at Pontremoli, was adroitly led over the unguarded westerly pass of Cento Croci above Varese to the same point on 2 May. The Sienese *popolo* had come to power in March and were ardent Ghibellines. Thus supported, the young Staufen, who took the attitude, half of Sicilian King and half of Emperor, could march south, routing Charles' lieutenants on his way. Rome was reached on 24 July and the Regno entered at Carsoli on 20 August. Conradin was avoiding the Terra di Lavoro and aiming by the unguarded northerly route, the Via Valeria, at Lucera, but Charles met him ready for battle. He had abandoned the siege of Lucera and awaited the invader in the Campi Palentini. Behind him the Regno rose in rebellion, barons and townsmen together over two-thirds of the land; only French-garrisoned towns and the Staufen-hating Terra di Lavoro and Principato stood on his side. The two armies fought their battle on 23 August 1268 close to

Albe[1]; Conradin's 7000 horse were composed of Germans, Don Henry's Spaniards, and Italians; Charles' much inferior force, hurried north in haste, was French and Italian only. It was Charles' generalship in employing a reserve in ambush and the staunchness of his French knights which won the day; even the unyielding Spaniards were routed, and the devout conqueror could write to the Pope "to arise and eat of his son's venison." It was, indeed, a feast of vengeance, which eclipsed Conradin's unchivalrous murder of his prisoner, Charles' Tuscan vicar, John de Braiselve. Executions, mutilations, burning alive, were the order of the day. Don Henry was soon captured, to suffer imprisonment for many years; Conradin all but escaped by sea from the Roman Campagna, to be brought to a mock and formal trial at Naples. He was beheaded with his boy-friend, Frederick of Austria, on 29 October 1268, although European opinion was shocked by the slaughter of a royal rival in cold blood. Charles' motives were those of policy; he could not reign securely while the rightful heir survived. The Pope gave consent by silence; his aims at least were achieved, for, despite later transitory changes, any real intervention of Germany in Italy, or danger to the Papacy from the Empire, came to an end. The prepotence he had now to fear was that of his French countrymen.

It remained to gather in the spoils. Charles promptly re-obtained the Senatorship of Rome, although his tenure of the office was limited to ten years by the Pope. As for the rebels in the Regno, they largely submitted at once, while the obstinate were warred down. On 27 August 1269 Lucera surrendered, and the revolt in Sicily came to an end with the capture and execution of Conrad Capece in July 1270. Sporadic risings indeed took place almost yearly, but their importance was slight save as an indication of Charles' misrule. The king's methods were thorough: the rebel baronage was replaced by a loyal French nobility by means of wholesale confiscation. Otherwise, after the first vengeance, only ringleaders and obstinate rebels were put to death. He moved the capital to loyal Naples in the Terra di Lavoro, no great grievance to Palermo, for the Staufen, too, had preferred the mainland; but his absolutism was more pronounced than theirs, since he ceased to assemble the Parliaments which they had occasionally convoked, and the burden of his taxation steadily grew, since he needed money to realise his ambitious dreams.

For those dreams his hands had been freed by the death of Pope Clement IV on 29 November 1268. Although the Pope had been all in his favour during the war with Conradin, and had even on 17 April 1268 appointed him indefinitely imperial vicar of Tuscany, it was not likely that he would suffer Charles' continued intervention in the north for long. Charles too obviously was imitating the Staufen scheme of rule

[1] The classical Alba Fucina; the battle is usually named after Tagliacozzo, the nearest town on Conradin's line of march.

over all Italy. Then, like all Popes, he must press on the project of a genuine crusade in Palestine, while Charles was bent on the conquest of the schismatic Greeks of Constantinople and on peace with the Mamlūk Sultan Baibars, ruler of Palestine, while he effected it. Now that the Holy See was vacant, Charles knew that the papalist—Guelf we may now say—majority of the cardinals by no means desired a new lay and French master, however convinced they might be that Ghibellinism was to be suppressed and the Germans and their Emperor practically excluded from Italy. It was his cue, therefore, to exploit the political, national, and personal divisions among the cardinals so as to prevent the formation of the two-thirds majority which would suffice to elect a fresh Pope. He could thus utilise the interval to affirm his power in Italy, and to take irremediable action in the East.

In Italy success on the whole awaited him. After a year's warfare in Tuscany he forced Pisa to a peace in 1270, and the same year Siena made submission, became Guelf, and expelled the Ghibellines. Save in Pisa, Charles acted in concert with the Guelf nobles and bankers to whom he was so closely bound. His rule was mild and, so to say, constitutional; he gave the harassed country peace and prosperity. In Lombardy he extended his Piedmontese territory by the submission of Turin and Alessandria in 1270, while further east he became Signore of Brescia in 1270, and attempted to gain the like position in the other Guelf cities. But his demand was refused in 1269, although he obtained a kind of oath of allegiance. It was a serious mistake to claim it, for the house of Della Torre, which held the tyranny of Milan and its dependent towns, was alarmed and inclined to look for new allies.

Charles' attention, however, during the vacancy of the papal see was mainly directed to his brother King Louis' unwelcome crusade. Had he been able, perhaps, he would have stopped it altogether; yet he at least managed to make it less harmful than it might have been. Time, indeed, in which he hoped to master Constantinople, was wasted, but money was got. In August 1269 he had refused to re-establish the Staufens' treaty with Mustanṣir, the Emir of Tunis, and the latter's envoys had gone on to Paris. An idea of beginning his crusade at Tunis appears thenceforward to have taken root in the French king's mind, although it was not finally decided to do so until the crusading fleet reached Cagliari in Sardinia by 11 July 1270. Charles' share in this decision remains doubtful; yet he was due to meet his brother in Sicily, and seems to have planned to join in the Tunisian expedition, take his profit out of it, and then proceed with his Grecian war[1]. He never met Louis IX either in

[1] See Sternfeld, *Ludwigs des heiligen Kreuzzug nach Tunis*, Chaps. x to xiii. The facts Sternfeld gives seem to me to suggest more desire on Charles' part for the attack on Tunis than he considers probable. Any crusade was unwelcome; that to Tunis might increase the tribute. Charles would not share Louis' illusions as to the conversion of Mustanṣir, which might abolish the tribute.

Sicily or Tunis; for, when he had wrung out of the Regnicoli sufficient means to arrive at Carthage on 25 August 1270, he found his brother just dead. He at once became leader of the Crusade, and used it for his interest. On 1 November a treaty was made with the Emir. By it Charles obtained the ancient *status quo* under the Staufen, but with doubled tribute, payment of some arrears, and a large share of the war indemnity which the Emir had to pay. Another important clause prescribed the expulsion from Tunis of the dangerous fugitive Regnicoli. The genuine crusaders might be wroth, but Charles, with debts paid and a little money in hand, could proceed with his oriental project. He had long prepared for it. In 1269 his alliance with Baldwin, the Latin ex-Emperor, was cemented by a marriage arranged between his daughter and Baldwin's heir, Philip. In the same year a further match, carried out in 1271, between Charles' own son Philip and the heiress of William de Villehardouin, Prince of Achaia, gave Charles a prospect of direct dominion in the Morea[1]. Already in 1267 he had gained possession of Corfù and of the dowry of Manfred's captured queen in Epirus, which in 1272 was to grow into a kingdom of Albania. If Venice in 1269 refused her co-operation, he secured the friendship of Hungary by a double marriage-treaty, owing to which his grandson, Charles Martel, long after mounted the Hungarian throne. In short, all seemed going well, in spite of the delay over the Tunisian Crusade, till Charles on 22 November 1270 landed at Trapani. The next day a sudden hurricane arose and shattered the fleet in harbour. The ships and treasure for the Greek war went to the bottom; possible troops, from Charles' point of view, were lost in the thousands of drowned crusaders; and the conquest of New Rome was fatally deferred.

It was now clear that the election of a Pope could no longer be avoided. Not only was the outcry of Western Christendom against the vacancy growing, but the Ghibellines were using the time to work in Lombardy. King Richard of Cornwall had long ceased to pay attention to Italy; his rival Alfonso X of Castile seemed at last to be taking his title of King of the Romans in earnest, and the Lombard Ghibellines with little hesitation turned to him. A Pope was required to resist him, if possible a French Pope. Charles, therefore, accompanied his docile nephew, Philip III of France, to the unending conclave at Viterbo; but their joint efforts to obtain the election of a French Pope were unavailing. When the cardinals some months after agreed to accept the nomination of six of their number, it was found that the moderates had triumphed. An Italian, not a Frenchman, was chosen, a friend of Charles, who was yet no puppet, and chiefly—what would satisfy the Ghibellines—a man who believed in the old order of Papacy and Empire and who longed to unite all Christendom for a crusade. Tedald Visconti of Piacenza, Archdeacon of Liège, was far away in Palestine when he became Pope Gregory X on 1 September 1271. He only reached Rome on 13 March 1272, accom-

[1] Cf. *supra*, Vol. IV, pp. 444, 446.

panied by his disillusioned royal vassal. He saw his policy with perfect clearness: there was to be a real Emperor, now that he could only be useful and not dangerous; and the reunion with the schismatic Greek Church should be carried through as the indispensable preliminary for a crusade in the Holy Land. While reunion was aimed at, Charles' war of conquest in Greece must remain in abeyance; he was the Pope's creature, and could not resist an obviously justified command. But he should not be uncompensated. Within due limits he should be supported in his Italian greatness, which was after all his first interest.

For the Union with the Greek Church and the settlement of the new order of things in the West, a General Council was necessary, which should seal the treaty of peace after the war begun between Papacy and Empire at the Council of Lyons in 1245. Gregory's Council was summoned for Lyons also, and in June 1273 the Pope set out from his residence at Orvieto. He hoped to leave reconciled factions behind him in Italy, but in this he was thwarted. The accord he decreed in Florence on his journey was wrecked by Charles, to whom its execution fell, and no better success attended him in Lombardy. Charles' behaviour was due to his estrangement from his suzerain. On the death of Richard of Cornwall on 2 April 1272, the election of a new King of the Romans loomed nearer, Alfonso X being impossible from a German or a papal point of view. Charles quickly schemed to utilise the election. The French were now the leading nation; his nephew, the colourless Philip III, should obtain the Empire and the titular leadership of Europe, and this would settle at once the matter of Charles' position in North Italy, where his nephew would certainly not oppose him. Here Gregory put his foot down. While exerting strong pressure on the German Electors to create a new King of the Romans, he refused, in spite of Charles' wrath, to recommend Philip III for their choice. The result was that Rudolf of Habsburg was elected on 1 October 1273. He sent his envoys to the Council of Lyons when it was opened on 7 May 1274, and was gladly recognised. In return, he accepted the moderate Guelf views: he renounced all rights over the papal territory; and he admitted the permanent separation of the Regno and the Empire. The good Pope's object was thus attained, and he could undertake the pious task of promoting friendship between Charles and Rudolf.

A still greater triumph rewarded Gregory's brilliant diplomacy on the Reunion question. He used Charles' ambitions for the conquest of Constantinople as pressure to induce the Greek Emperor Michael Palaeologus to submit to the Roman see and Western creed. At the same time he made it clear that Charles would not be allowed to attack the Eastern Empire, if the schism were healed in time. Michael's convictions took rapid shape under these threats and promises. A Greek Synod gave a forced approval, and accredited Greek envoys accepted the Western "Filioque" and the papal supremacy at the Council on 6 July. It was only a screen spread over the chasm of dissidence; but it sufficed to baffle Charles, and Gregory could hope for a true crusade of all Christendom[1].

One more decree, passed on 16 July, was to prevent the scandal of a long vacancy in the Popedom. After ten days of ineffectual conclave the hesitating cardinals were to be placed under progressive austerities. Only with a Pope elected could they return to even tolerable comfort. It was an honest endeavour to meet a public need, yet it marked Gregory's weakness: he put all his trust in the appearances of things, and thought that, with an Emperor, with some sort of Pope, with a nominal Union, all would go well; but the heavy feet of his contemporaries soon trod through his painted panorama.

The good intentions, however, of an able, highminded man bore fruit, humbler, perhaps, but more useful than his world-wide schemes. The Spanish danger in North Italy had increased. Marquess William VII of Montferrat had become the son-in-law of Alfonso X, and could begin a revolt from Charles in Piedmont and a Ghibelline resurgence all over Lombardy. More important was a consequence of Charles' own aggressive ambition. The revolution of 1270 in Genoa had placed in power the Ghibelline nobles supported by the *popolo*. Charles needed the city and its fleet, and therefore allied with the exiled Guelfs. He then forced on a war in 1273, but by sea and land was signally defeated. Now Genoa could admit the Spaniards into Lombardy, and she used her opportunity. She allied on 26 October 1274 with the west Lombard Ghibellines, William VII of Montferrat and Asti, who were losing to Charles' attacks, and transported 1000 Spanish troopers to Lombardy. All the Ghibelline cities promptly acknowledged Alfonso X's title, and their number grew. Finally, the victory of Marquess Thomas of Saluzzo over Charles' seneschal at Roccavione on 10 November 1275 caused the Sicilian king to lose Piedmont. His allies, the Della Torre, had been at least luke-warm, and his supremacy in North Italy was vanishing and being replaced by a less effectual dominion of Alfonso.

But Gregory X resolved that the Spanish dominion should not be. In May 1275 he intercepted Alfonso, who was coming to lead his Lombard partisans, at Beaucaire at the frontier of Provence, and, after months of negotiation, obtained in August his renunciation of the Roman kingship. It was a great surrender, but Alfonso's deserted realm of Castile was becoming restive, and the difficulty of reaching Italy by the route he had chosen was manifest. That done, the Pope could meet King Rudolf at Lausanne in October 1275. The King of the Romans, too, was pliable. He again confirmed all his concessions; he at once sent German troopers to Milan to resist the Alfonsist Ghibellines; he himself would come to be crowned Emperor next year. Gregory could re-enter Italy full of hope for an interview with Charles, who as well as Alfonso was

[1] Cf. *supra*, Vol. IV, pp. 610–12.

checkmated in Lombardy. In December he learnt that Rudolf's envoys were demanding the oaths of allegiance not only from the Lombard cities but also from Romagna, according to ancient custom. The Pope, however, was determined to require the literal observance of the ancient charters which secured Romagna to the Papacy, and he demanded at once the renunciation of Romagna from the king. The answer never reached him, for he died at Arezzo on 12 January 1276.

Two ephemeral Popes succeeded Gregory X. The Savoyard Innocent V, who reigned from 21 January to 22 June 1276, did little save refuse to sanction Charles' Grecian war and to arrange a peace between him and Genoa. The Genoese Hadrian V, who reigned from 11 July to 18 August, had only time to suspend Gregory's conclave decree, which had worked havoc on the cardinals in the conclave at Rome which elected him. Charles thus lost not only two favourable Popes but their and others' votes in the next conclave. Accordingly, on 15 September 1276 Peter Juliani, a Portuguese cardinal, was elected at Viterbo as John XXI. He was a cheerful dilettante and left the conduct of affairs to the leading moderate Guelf in the Sacred College, Cardinal John Gaetan Orsini. Charles in vain urged the Pope to induce the rupture of the Union, which might indeed be justified on account of its proved unreality. He only obtained the Pope's sanction for his acquisition of the shadowy kingdom of Jerusalem, now confined to Acre. Then John XXI, too, died suddenly on 20 May 1277. A prolonged struggle began in the conclave between the moderate Guelfs and the pro-French party, in which the moderate Guelfs won by the election on 25 November of Cardinal John Gaetan as Nicholas III.

Like so many of the Popes of Roman birth, Nicholas possessed that ruler's nature, statesmanlike, patient, and masterful, which seemed to revive the ancient Roman spirit. His temperament was thoroughly secular; he was splendour-loving and a great builder. His most patent fault was nepotism, which led him easily to simony. Although special favour to his own relatives was natural to a Pope when each cardinal belonged to a political party and was prone to independent action, and although Innocent IV and Gregory X had set him an example, Nicholas III's desire to exalt the Orsini went far beyond older limits and has branded him as the introducer of a new disease in the Western Church. It affected the schemes he inherited from Gregory X: the checking, yet the compensation of, Charles of Sicily, the alliance with, yet the precautions against, the King of the Romans, the neutral independent Papal State. For these aims the clearsighted, nepotistic Pope struck out his plan of the four kingdoms. Charles was to keep the Regno and be allied to Rudolf, but was to be excluded from the rest of Italy and to receive the kingdom of Arles for his grandson Charles Martel in exchange. Rudolf, likewise, was to lose North Italy and Arles, but in return Germany and the imperial title should be made hereditary in the Habsburgs. The kingdom of North Italy should be conferred on the house of Orsini. Thus the principle of nationality would be in a way admitted. In this secular interpretation of Gregory's ideas, the crusade of course took a subordinate place, although the Pope had no notion of giving up the ecumenical activities of his office.

The first step was to make sure of Romagna for the Papal State. He at once demanded from Rudolf the renunciation of dominion there. The king made no resistance. He was fighting for his kingship with Ottokar of Bohemia, and, as we shall see, his Lombard protégés were fallen. But he found it difficult to make the renunciation formal and irrevocable enough to satisfy the Pope, who remembered that the ancient donation had been treated as unmeaning for three hundred years, and it was not till February 1279 that every possible guarantee was given. Still Nicholas was convinced of the reality of the surrender in May 1278, and could proceed with his further design of ousting Charles from Rome and Tuscany and of making him the ally of Rudolf. In addition to the power any strong-willed Pope was bound to have over Charles, Nicholas enjoyed other advantages. He had mastered the cardinals by a large creation, and was thus freer than most recent Popes; he was a native Roman, and could rely on his fellow-countrymen; imperialism in the old sense was extinct as a political force; and lastly, Charles' power had waned after his loss of Piedmont and his defeat by Genoa.

Lombardy, in fact, had at last become independent with the fall of the house of Della Torre which had ruled Milan. The Ghibellines had regained much favour in their cities, now that they were dissociated from any foreign ruler, while the Della Torre, who employed King Rudolf's Germans, had made themselves hateful by misgovernment. The lead against the Milanese tyrant was taken by the Archbishop of Milan, Otto Visconti, whom he had always kept in exile. The Archbishop rallied the Ghibelline exiles who formed the majority of the Milanese nobility, and, in spite of a defeat, seized on Como in November 1277. Thence he attacked his foes with the support of most of the countryside, and overthrew them on 21 January 1278 at Desio. The tyrant Napoleon and many of his kin fell into Otto's hands, and next day Milan received the Archbishop as her despot. A new grouping of towns at once followed, in which Milan headed the Ghibelline, and Cremona the Guelf, league, and indecisive fighting continued for some years, chiefly concerning the possession of Lodi, which the remaining Della Torre made their headquarters. It was dangerous enough to induce the archbishop to submit to call in William VII of Montferrat in 1278 as Captain-General of Milan for four years.

With Lombardy really lost, Charles was weaker than before in Tuscany. He had, against his wish, helped his Guelf allies to reconquer and further depress Pisa in 1275–6; he had also seen in Florence a new single Captain instituted for the Parte Guelfa, who had in practice equal powers with Charles' vicar, while the feuds springing up among the Guelfs were impairing the stability of the whole *régime*. Nicholas had thus the opportunity to insist on mediating. On 24 May 1278 in a personal interview he ordered Charles to quit the Roman senatorship on 16 September when his term of office expired, and also to resign the vicariate of Tuscany eight days later. His commands were obeyed, and, in reward, the Pope took up the question of Charles' alliance with Rudolf with such zeal that in the summer of 1280 the treaty was all but ready.

Meanwhile Nicholas was eagerly contriving peace, papal suzerainty, and Orsini domination in Central Italy. At Rome his action was immediate and characteristic. He issued a new constitution forbidding a non-Roman Senator; he obtained from his countrymen the direct rule of the Eternal City for life, becoming in this way both suzerain and grantee; and then he promoted his brother to the senatorial office. This had been an easy task, but that of reconciling the Tuscan factions and of annexing Romagna was hard. Formally, indeed, Bologna and the Romagnol towns made no great objection to the oath of allegiance to the Pope, but they were not anxious for his effective government and were torn by faction. The days had gone by when Bologna had dominated Romagna and compelled the factions to endure one another. Her trade was rapidly declining and she had lost in a three years' war with Venice. Then her nobles got out of hand, and in 1274 the Guelfs or Geremei had driven out the Ghibellines or Lambertazzi. War broke out over all Romagna, in which the Ghibellines led by Count Guido of Montefeltro had a decided advantage over the Guelfs in spite of the aid given to the latter by Guelfic Florence. Matters were in this stage when on 25 September 1278 Nicholas appointed one nephew, the worthy Cardinal Latino Malabranca, legate for Tuscany and Romagna, and another nephew, Bertold Orsini, Rector or "Count" of Romagna under him. The two patched up a general peace with infinite trouble, and on 8 October 1279 Cardinal Latino was able to arrive at Florence for his mission there. But in December the Ghibellines were again driven from Bologna, and neither Bertold nor Latino had been able to quench the resulting war or to restore the short-lived papal rule, when Nicholas III died on 22 August 1280.

In Florence, however, Cardinal Latino ameliorated the state of the city permanently, although, curiously enough, his actual scheme proved a fleeting mirage. Nicholas was made Signore on 19 November 1279, and a general reconciliation and a new constitution were promulgated on 18 January 1280. Almost all the Ghibellines returned and re-obtained a portion of their lost property. The *popolo* again received an organisation and a Captain. The Parte Guelfa and its Captain remained as a partisan body, while the Ghibellines were given a similar status. If the Ghibellines were soon edged out of political power, they had been repatriated for good. Further, a Council of Fourteen was set up for general supervision and finance. In 1282 they were replaced by the Priors of the Arts, who, being based on the gilds, were far more successful and became the true rulers of the city. Thus Florence passed under the control of the wealthy middle-class. She, at any rate, produced a government by the *popolo* which could work. As if to signalise the new era, shrewd King Rudolf sent a vicar to Tuscany, whose vain efforts ended in small payments to his exchequer. The destruction of the Empire in Italy was illustrated by the trifling price which its claims could fetch.

Nicholas filled a small place in history compared with his ambitions. His four kingdoms' scheme, nebulous always, quite vanished at his death. Still he had helped to wind up several insolvent ideals, and had maintained the Papacy in complete independence. His successor was to lose that independence, and to declare an open bankruptcy.

After his recent experience, Charles was determined to secure a pro-French Pope. A timely riot of the Viterbans terrorised the moderate Guelf cardinals, and on 22 February 1281 the college elected Cardinal Simon de Brie Pope as Martin IV. Their choice was a representative of the rising national feeling of his day. This ancient councillor of St Louis and negotiator between Charles and Urban IV hated Germans and loved his French countrymen. He was both able and irresolute, and thus a fit tool for Charles. His pontificate was a foretaste of Avignon. His subservience, indeed, proved the ruin of Charles, who had the rein given to his passionate ambition, for he immediately threw himself into the king's arms. On obtaining the direct rule of Rome for life, he made his patron Senator for that period in contempt of Nicholas III's constitution; and the whole Papal State was quickly officered by Charles' functionaries. In Romagna some success was gained by this method, for, in spite of the crushing defeat of the papal representative, John d'Eppe, at the head of the Guelfs, on 1 May 1282 at Forlì, the outwearied Ghibellines laid down their arms in 1283. It seemed as if Italy was safe, although on 25 May 1281, near Vaprio, Archbishop Otto Visconti overthrew the Della Torre for a generation, and soon recaptured Lodi. Lombardy might after all be left to itself, with Milan, William VII, Asti, and the other states to quarrel as they would.

But Charles' chief wish was freedom of action in the East. Under Nicholas III the unreality of the Union and the insincerity of Michael VIII's adherence to it had grown very clear, but the Pope held Charles firmly in leash, while himself unbending in his demands on Constantinople. The more pliant Martin, however, immediately declared a breach by excommunicating the Greeks on 10 April 1281. No doubt he destroyed a sham; yet his motive was chiefly to open the way for Charles' resurrection of the Franco-Latin Empire. The Papacy in his hands had lost its ecumenical spirit. Charles could now prepare in earnest once more. He gained the alliance of Venice for a campaign in 1283, and the Regno was astir with the coming war. In the long desultory border conflict with Michael in Albania and Greece, he had on the whole been a loser, but victory seemed sure now that he could bend all his powers to its attainment.

The knowledge of his plans roused his foes to strike in time. Charles' rule in the Regno had been a bitter experience for its population. His foreign officials and troops were insolent, his native tax-farmers uncontrollably extortionate. His attempts at remedies were fruitless, for he kept adding to the burden of taxation, and was bound to foster the French and such as would serve them. Besides, he had no sympathy with the commonalty, and thought that, if he gave them peace and order, and endeavoured, as he truly endeavoured, to dispense justice, he had done. The occasional Parliaments were no longer assembled, the *collectae* he had sworn to abolish were yearly levied. Not only so, but in spite of clerical exemption the amount raised in each *collecta* was nearly doubled by 1282. And all was for an undesired war.

The long-gathering storm burst from Aragon. Its king, Peter III, was the husband of Manfred's daughter Constance, and had long nourished plans for reconquering her inheritance. He knew of the hatred felt by the Regnicoli against Charles, and the withdrawal of Alfonso X and the independence of Lombardy and Tuscany all increased his chances. He had for advisers two exiles from the Regno of commanding ability, John of Procida and Roger Loria. A wealthy ally, the chief need of the moneyless warrior-king, was at hand in the person of Michael VIII, now in the utmost danger, and John of Procida contrived the treaty between the two at Constantinople late in 1281. So King Peter proclaimed a crusade against Africa and feverishly pushed on his armaments. He was in close touch with the malcontents in the Regno, and especially in Sicily, where he meant to land. Then in 1282 he heard that he had been anticipated by a popular explosion. The Sicilian Vespers had taken place on 30 March, and Charles, his great schemes blown to air, had lost Sicily, as it turned out, for ever.

It was on Easter Monday that the Sicilian revolution, more singular perhaps in its successful sequel and its historical significance than in its immediate circumstance, began. Long sufferance had confirmed the French soldiery in the island in their opinion of the fatalistic submission and only fitful wrath of the Sicilians, and men-at-arms mingled with coarse insolence among the festival-makers before the church of Santo Spirito built by the English Archbishop Offamil outside Palermo. A crowning insult, the mishandling of a young married woman on her way with her family to the church, roused a bystander to strike the culprit down. On all sides arose the cry of "Death to the French!"; the riot spread to the city and continued through the night; no one who spoke French, man, woman or child, was spared. The insurrection and the massacre travelled with extraordinary speed and with the same atrocious vengeance throughout the island, and some 3000 to 4000 of the hated foreigners were slaughtered. Before the end of the month Messina had joined the revolt and compelled the royal vicar to leave the island. A curious experiment followed; the general wish was not to receive another ruler, but to copy Innocent IV's idea of vassal communes subject to the Papacy. Such were set up in Palermo, Messina, and elsewhere, ranged in an embryonic federation. But their envoys and prayers were sternly repulsed by Pope Martin, and Charles, astounded and enraged, diverted his armament of conquest to suppress this domestic revolt.

On 25 July the king crossed to Sicily and began the siege of Messina, the key to the island. The same exaltation of hatred which had produced the Vespers now led the untrained townsmen under Alaimo da Lentini to repair their ruinous walls and to repulse again and again Charles' attacks. But the failure of the mediation of the cardinal-legate Gerard of Cremona, Bishop of Sabina, shewed that there was no choice between conquest and foreign aid. This was ready; for Peter III had landed in Barbary on his simular crusade on 18 June, and was demanding tithes and the like concessions from the wary Pope. In his African camp envoys from Sicily offered him the crown he had plotted for, and on 30 August he landed at Trapani with 600 men-at-arms and 8000 *almugaveri*, the guerilla infantry whose courage and cruelty were to be known far and wide. His arrival and his fleet, one of the best in the Mediterranean, rendered Charles' position untenable. After a last vain assault the Angevin abandoned the siege of Messina and crossed to Calabria about 26 September 1282.

Beyond carrying the war into Calabria, which was to suffer for years from the guerilla exploits of the *almugaveri*, soon a mixed force of Catalans and Sicilians, Peter I of Sicily did little in the local war. His rule was arbitrary and unpopular, and he left for Aragon in May 1283 to arrange for the singular ordeal by battle with 100 knights a side, in which Charles and he had pledged themselves to engage at Bordeaux on 1 June. Obvious insincerity marked both the exponents of this histrionic chivalry, and a *beau geste* of chicanery was all that they seemed to achieve. But probably to gain time was their strongest motive: Charles was gathering fresh forces from France; Peter wished to stave off a French invasion of Aragon and to win ground in the Regno during the delay. He had left his queen Constance regent in Sicily and Roger Loria as admiral of the joint Sicilian and Catalan fleet. In Roger he possessed a born naval commander, a tactician and a hard-bitten fighter, a victor in every battle he engaged. It was Loria who deferred a new Angevin invasion by destroying a part of their fleet at Malta in July 1283. The new invasion, however, was to be most formidable, nor was the war to be in Sicily alone. Pope Martin deposed Peter from Aragon, proclaimed a crusade and interdict against him, declared Charles of Valois, the younger son of Philip III of France, King of Aragon, and arranged for the conquest of the country by the French king in 1285. Meantime he poured money into Charles of Anjou's hands and relentlessly used his spiritual weapons in the crusade against Sicily: Venice was placed under interdict for refusing to hire out her ships. Every resource was drained for this in

1284: a motley army of French and Italians was gathered; some 30 galleys at Naples, others from Brindisi, were to meet at Ustica and convoy the transports; to lead them Charles himself set sail from Provence. But now came the unexpected. His son and heir, Charles the Lame, Prince of Salerno, left as regent in the Regno, had busily carried out the preparations there, but was not to move till his father came. On 5 June 1284, however, Loria appeared with seemingly few galleys in the Bay of Naples, ravaging the islands and tempting an attack. Salerno fell into the trap and rowed out to fight a stronger fleet. The battle ended in his capture with many nobles, and Charles of Anjou arrived at Gaeta to find an immediate invasion impossible and Naples rioting. He could call his son "a cowardly priest, a fool who always chose the worse part," but he could not undo the event. Indeed he himself wasted men and money in a vain siege of Reggio, and then withdrew, with forces disaffected and thinned by desertions, to Apulia for fresh preparations and exactions, blended with schemes of reform to gain the loyalty of what we may now call the kingdom of Naples. His days, however, were numbered; his strength was exhausted by a slow fever, and he died on 7 January 1285 at Foggia. He appointed his kinsman Robert, Count of Artois, as *Balio*, to whom the Pope gave as colleague Cardinal Gerard of Cremona.

Charles of Anjou had failed not only in his wider ambitions of an Eastern Empire, but in his attempt to rule or guide Italy as a papal champion, to be a kind of inverted Hohenstaufen, and in the mere maintenance of his conquest of Sicily. His failure was perhaps not merely his own fault; for it was not in the power of man, not of Frederick II, to unite the Italy of the thirteenth century, and the national evolution was working towards another end. Yet his fame has suffered irredeemably and deservedly. He had prospered only when his own way was in some degree denied him, and fell a victim to his overweening ambition and inconsiderate pride. A bold knight and a forceful autocrat, his immense efforts to subdue Sicily all miscarried largely through the disaffection and desertion which his government of the Regno had provoked, and he was unaware or contemptuous of national feeling outside France and of the strength of the bourgeois trader. He exhausted the Regno; in North Italy he had ruled by faction and violence; his attempt to found a Mediterranean empire was a greed-begotten chimaera. Thus, in spite of many great qualities, his lasting work, fit for the grim face of his effigy on the Capitol, was that of a destroyer. He ruined the Hohenstaufen; he crippled the Papacy. In South Italy he only left a new dynasty, a worse government, and a degenerating people.

Although Charles II was in captivity, and soon transferred to the safer imprisonment of Aragon, the two regents took firm hold of the government. The insurrectionary movements on the mainland never amounted to much, and the guerilla warfare in the south made little progress beyond Calabria. The two colleagues were steadily upheld by the

Pope, for when Martin IV died at Perugia on 28 March 1285 his successor, the Roman Cardinal-deacon Jacopo Savelli, now Honorius IV, continued inevitably the fixed policy of the Curia. Sicily was to return to submission; the reforms in the Regno, promised and enacted by Charles the Lame in 1283, were confirmed; the *collectae* beyond the four feudal aids were forbidden in September 1285. These concessions were perhaps the more ample owing to the events of the war. In May the great French invasion of Aragon began, and it seemed that Peter, at odds with his own people, must go down before it. Yet it proved a miserable failure. The crusading army was smitten by pestilence in the long summer siege of Girona, while the fleet was completely disabled by a victory of Roger Loria. Philip III retreated to die on 6 October 1285 at Perpignan. His adversary, however, did not long outlive him, for Peter the Great died too on 11 November. His eldest son Alfonso III succeeded to Aragon, while his second son James became King of Sicily. The change was momentous, for though the two brothers remained allied their interests drifted apart, and it became clearer every year that the Sicilians must save themselves. Fortunately they held the sea; a surprise invasion which captured Agosta in May 1287 could be stifled by King James on 23 June, the same day on which the admiral Loria with smaller forces routed the Angevin fleet at Castellammare and bore off 42 captured galleys. What with truce and exhaustion, the war lapsed now for two years in spite of the renewed ban from Pope Nicholas IV. It flamed up again on the return of Charles the Lame. By the mediation of Edward I of England, Alfonso of Aragon at last bought peace and security by releasing him. A first bargain made at Oléron in 1287 was quashed by the Pope because it ceded Sicily to James; a vaguer second treaty at Canfranc on 27 October 1288 was allowed, and, leaving three sons as hostages, Charles returned to be crowned by the Pope at Rieti on 19 June 1289, to the joy, the very transitory joy, of the Guelfs, who thought they had gained a leader. Even the inconvenient obligations of Canfranc had been annulled by the Pope, and war had been renewed in the Regno by James. It was only the imminent danger of Acre from the Mamlūks which induced the combatants to a two years' truce in August 1289; and even that excepted Calabria and the *almugaveri*. Thus no question was settled, although much was foreshadowed; the Regno in fact was split up into two hostile kingdoms whose separate character remained until 1816. That of Sicily enjoyed a parting gleam of prosperity before it fell into turbid isolation. James' brief rule was good; sea-power gave wealth; the circumstances of the revolution and the influence of Aragon provided a remarkable stimulus to the island parliament, with its three estates, and the *Statuti di Giacomo* formed a basis for national liberties which were in the future to prove barren. As for Naples, ravaged, oppressed, and overtaxed, with foreign nobles, foreign troops, and the combined evils of excessive feudalism and corrupt bureaucracy, all exacerbated by the incurable ambitions of its dynasty, it was leaving the days of Frederick II further and further behind.

It is a testimony to the failure of Charles of Anjou that it is not his death but the Sicilian Vespers which mark an epoch. His predominance and his alliance with the Popes had given some sort of unity to Italian history, but now each province seems to work out its own destiny with little effective influence, if much interference, from the others. Rome itself soon slipped from Charles' grasp owing to a revolt of the Orsini in January 1284, which led to the appointment of Roman senators. Pope Honorius IV could keep order because he was a native Roman, but when he died on 3 April 1287 the apostolic see remained vacant for a year owing to dissensions among the cardinals in conclave, due perhaps more to the mutual hatred of the Orsini and Colonna factions who dominated the election than because they had settled policies to promote. Their eventual choice on 22 February 1288 was a pious, unselfish friar. Jerome of Ascoli, the Cardinal-bishop of Palestrina, and once General of the Franciscans, now Nicholas IV, had dared and survived the Roman fever which had struck down six of his colleagues and put to flight the rest, but brave as he was, he was soon notoriously in the hands of the Colonna, who under him ruled, in name at least, the congeries of towns and nobles which formed the Papal States. The Papacy, with its ecumenic claims as vigorously asserted as ever, was getting once more dangerously entangled in purely local broils and family interests.

If disunion was the chief characteristic of the Papal States, signs of future consolidation were visible in the next natural area to the north, in Tuscany. Immediately after the peace of Cardinal Latino, when Charles of Anjou was preparing to concentrate all his efforts in the East, Florence and her friends assured their safety and trade by putting the Tuscan Guelf League on a permanent basis. Florence and Lucca were the chiefs; Siena, Volterra, and others the secondary allies. On the military side the League maintained a permanent force of 500 professional and non-Italian men-at-arms to replace the occasional assistance of Charles' troopers. This was a notable step in the decline of the citizen soldier and the citizen nobility, for they were out-classed and in the end replaced by these trained competitors. In matters of trade, goods destined for, or coming from, any ally passed toll-free through the territory of the others. Here was a customs' union of a sort, from which industrial Florence gained most. But Martin IV increased the prosperity of all by the financial arrangements which bound the Papacy to Tuscany, for the collection of papal tithes was carefully apportioned among the Tuscan banking firms. It was the question of free transit which first led the League to join Genoa in harrying defeated Pisa; Pisan concessions made it languid and obedient to a papal prohibition; complete free transit was a chief condition of the peace of Fucecchio in 1293. So, too, one motive for the war over Arezzo was the security of the road to Rome.

Pisa was fatally hampered by her situation in Tuscany, but her true interests were seaward, and her deadliest enemy Genoa, whom she had the misfortune to rival not only in the Levant but in the rich islands they wished to exploit at their doors. Neither city wished to do more than stand profitably neutral in the war of the Vespers; in these years they fought their own quarrel to a finish. Genoa under her two aristocratic Ghibelline Captains was more united, less exposed to attack, and won. On 6 August 1284 the Captain Oberto Doria lured out the Pisan fleet to fight against odds by the island of Meloria, and there destroyed it. Over 9000 prisoners were taken to Genoese dungeons; Pisa was ruined, for, if fresh galleys could be built, the loss in men was irreplaceable. None the less she fought gallantly against the ring of foes. The bitter terms of peace wrung from her semi-tyrant, Count Ugolino, were among the causes in 1288 of his fall and tragic end. The temporary autocracy of Count Guido of Montefeltro which followed could shew his brilliant talents, but could not avert the inevitable loss of Sardinia and decline. Thus the third competitor among the maritime states fell out of the running, and Venice and Genoa were left to struggle, while Italy was the poorer of a centre of her civilisation.

The tendency to form larger territorial units, dictated in some degree by geography, and the ever-growing inclination to tyranny, which might give peace, efficiency, and equality, were clearly visible among the Lombard cities, which wished for liberty and autonomy but could neither keep nor give them. The first instance of composite dominions had been given by the *soi-disant* imperial deputies like Pelavicini, followed by the smaller coagulation of towns under the Della Torre; now we find a great independent war-lord attempting the same thing. William VII "Longsword" of Montferrat was much in request and much dreaded for his force of warlike vassals; and with the fall of the Torriani in 1278, combined with the fact that they remained strong and dangerous, his day seemed to have come. He ruled Ivrea, Turin, Alessandria, Tortona, Acqui, and Casale in his native West Lombardy; he became Captain-General of Milan, Pavia, Vercelli, Novara, Como, Verona, and Mantua. But this dominion was more apparent than real. He was a baron with no roots even in his own towns, while in most he was merely an ally of the true tyrant or native faction. Add to this that he was more of an intriguer than a warrior, and that his campaigns were games of bluff, and the temporary character of his state becomes clear. In 1280 he was kidnapped by Thomas, the heir of Savoy, in the course of an attempt to partition the Savoyard lands in Piedmont, and was forced to surrender Turin to his captor. At Christmas 1282 the Archbishop Otto Visconti suddenly turned him out of Milan, and the eastern cities followed suit. In the consequent hostilities the Torriani played a fighting part, but not so the marquess, who preferred raids on the powerful coalition of Milan, Pavia, Brescia, Piacenza, Cremona, Genoa, and Asti arrayed against him.

His most striking success was the acquisition of Pavia in 1289 by ingeniously gaining over her army to his side. Then in 1290 he himself was treacherously seized by the Alessandrians, and like Napoleon della Torre was only released by death from the iron cage which was his prison. His dominion at once broke up and his young son was deprived of Montferrat by Matteo Visconti. City-tyrannies were now the order of the day, yet with a tendency of Milan, the natural metropolis, to encroach on and overawe the others. At Milan itself the Archbishop contrived the election of his great-nephew, the wise Matteo, as Captain of the *popolo*, and Novara and Vercelli gave him the same office. Alberto Scotti ruled over Piacenza; Pinamonte Bonaccolsi over Mantua. Incurable faction-strife induced first Modena and then Reggio to elect the tyrant of Ferrara, Obizzo, Marquess of Este, as their *signore*; thus the natural outlets of the Po valley to the east were altogether in the same hands. It was beginning to need exceptional circumstances to maintain a city free.

Italy thus presented in 1290 a mosaic of diverse states. The efforts of the Emperors, of Manfred, and of Charles of Anjou to unite the land had all alike failed. That of the Popes to divide and supervise it was likewise no success, although defeat was yet to come; and this political enterprise was proving ever more disastrous to their spiritual influence over Europe. The Sicilians had given an example of revolt against their secular pretensions, and for the time the prestige of the Papacy was bound up with the dubious subjection of the island. Meantime anarchic communes in the Papal State, prosperous republics in Tuscany, city-tyrants in Lombardy, feudal monarchies in Naples and beneath the Western Alps, European sea-powers in Venice and Genoa, all jostled one another. The last period of the Italian Middle Age, that of independent national development round sharply differentiated provincial centres, had begun.

CHAPTER VII

ENGLAND: RICHARD I AND JOHN

England shared the influence of the great changes which marked the age of Innocent III and Philip Augustus. A period of adventure passed into a period of order. In spite of his regard for custom, Henry II was a constructive statesman; but during the reigns of his sons his bold experiments underwent the process of development, definition, and tentative change. On the one hand, the power of the central government increased: judicial, military, and financial measures brought the resources of feudalism under the control of the Crown; a series of elaborate inquiries into the distribution of property and income added to the information possessed by the officers of the Exchequer; departmental business became more specialised and official records were both more numerous and better preserved. The accession of Richard I was accepted later as the limit of legal memory. On the other hand, during the quarter of a century which preceded the Great Charter, the theory of royal responsibility received practical expression. The separation of England from Normandy and Anjou brought the king face to face with forces which henceforward were to have a national significance. The king was now not king of the English, but king of England, the great vassals were English barons; feudal custom, the adjustments between secular and spiritual authority, the writs and practices of the Curia Regis combined to become the law of England. When King John strained the instrument of government and disregarded custom, he was met by an opposition which, although it was feudal in form and temper, gave expression for the first time since the conquest to English opinion.

John's self-confidence was doubtless strengthened by the events of his brother's reign. During the life-time of Richard I the work of Henry II was submitted to a severe test. It survived the civil disturbances of the opening years, enabled the government to collect an enormous ransom, and to respond to the incessant demands for men, stores, and supplies during the later war between Richard and Philip Augustus. The success of English administration was the more remarkable from the fact that, four or five months excepted, the king was absent from England throughout his reign. The history of England between 1189 and 1199 is really concerned with the activities in the first place of William Longchamp, and afterwards of Hubert Walter. The latter was the ruler of England during the French war, and, while he was assisting Richard to hold his own, developed Henry II's machinery in every part.

Richard was crowned king on 3 September 1189, at Westminster. The order of the stately ceremony, which seems to have become a precedent, was afterwards preserved among the documents in the treasury, and is reported by the chronicler of the "deeds of King Richard." Richard was of a free and impetuous disposition in all his ways. He loved magnificence, was generous and magnanimous when he desired to reward or to please, made his plans on a large reckless scale, plundered boldly, and was openly avaricious. He had a passion for organisation, building, and fighting, but he had little foresight or stability. The act of arrangement, of putting things into order, interested him more than the maintenance of order. Within a few months of his accession he had overhauled the administration of his dominions, settled his relations with the King of Scotland and the princes of Wales, made several bargains with Philip Augustus, collected a fleet, issued codes of regulations for the crusaders, and ordered an equitable change in the English custom with regard to wreckage. The organisation of England was commenced before Richard had arrived. His mother, Queen Eleanor, who was acting probably under the direction of William the Marshal, issued a proclamation of amnesty for those who had been illegally imprisoned[1] and ordered all free men to take the oath of allegiance to Richard. In Normandy Richard endowed his brother John with the county of Mortain and large English estates[2]. After his coronation, in a series of great councils held at the abbey of Pipewell (near the hunting lodge at Geddington in Northamptonshire), London, or Canterbury, and at Bur in Normandy, he filled the vacant bishoprics and abbeys, appointed sheriffs, received the homage of William of Scotland, and provided for the regency in England during his absence on crusade.

Throughout his English progress with its pomp and display Richard had made it clear that his immediate object was the Crusade. He had come to England to be crowned, and he stayed only long enough to collect a vast treasure and to make arrangements for the government. On the lowest computation the treasure left by Henry amounted to 100,000 marks, or about three times the annual revenue. Richard increased this sum by his exactions from the retiring, as well as the new officials and sheriffs. Henry II's great justiciar, Ranulf Glanvil, was plundered on giving up the justiciarship and the county of Yorkshire. Bishop Hugh of Durham bought the former office and the county of Northumberland. William Longchamp, the new Bishop of Ely, paid three thousand marks for the chancery, and Godfrey de Lucy, the new Bishop of Winchester, got the treasures of his church, the custody of the castle, and the sheriffdom of Hampshire for three thousand pounds. Other sheriffs paid similar sums. For the relaxation of the hard terms

[1] *Gesta Henrici et Ricardi,* ed. Stubbs, II, pp. 74–5; cf. *Magna Carta Commemoration Essays*, pp. 114–5.

[2] The Pipe Roll of 1 Richard I shews that John received the revenues of the baronies of Gloucester and of Lancaster for the last quarter of the year ending Michaelmas 1189. *The Great Roll of the Pipe for the first year of King Richard the First,* ed. Hunter, pp. 7, 18.

made in 1175 the King of Scots paid £10,000. Richard's settlement of his kingdom was based, therefore, upon a series of financial bargains, and suffered in consequence. The king had hardly turned his back before all sorts of local feuds and conflicting interests began to reveal themselves. During his slow journey to the East, he was forced to compose difficulties which at a distance he could hardly understand. His instructions were so hypothetical and conflicting that they have been the despair of historians. In October 1192 the news from home made him decide to return.

At first sight the arrangements for the government of England during the king's absence seem statesmanlike. The Crusade withdrew from England some of its ablest and most prominent men, including Glanvil and Baldwin the Archbishop of Canterbury; but Richard left behind a large number of his father's trained servants. By his first arrangement the Earl of Essex and the Bishop of Durham were to be justiciars, supported by a small group of advisers. All these men, together with the sheriffs in the midland and south-eastern counties, the barons of the Exchequer, and the justices, were experienced administrators. After the death of the Earl of Essex, William Longchamp the new chancellor was associated with the Bishop of Durham, and finally, when the two bishops were seen to be ill-mated colleagues, Richard gave the supreme position to the chancellor. The chancellor was to act as justiciar, while Bishop Hugh was to be justiciar in the north of England and castellan of Windsor in the south. The colleagues of the chancellor, forming with him a council of state, were the marshal, now Earl of Pembroke, Geoffrey Fitz Peter, Hugh Bardolf, and William Brewer. In one of his letters the king describes them as *appares*, and they were evidently intended to occupy a position above the other justices and officials of the Exchequer. It is clear, however, that the Exchequer was regarded as the seat of government[1]. In the absence of the Archbishop of Canterbury the chancellor was, at the king's request, created papal legate by Pope Clement III. Upstart though he was, Longchamp was thus placed in a position to control, in addition to the secular administration, the powerful episcopate which now existed in England. As a last precaution, Richard imposed an oath upon his brothers John and Geoffrey that they would not enter England for three years. Unfortunately John was released almost immediately from this obligation.

The position allowed to Count John was, indeed, the chief cause of danger, and illustrates the defects of Richard's policy. Richard and his mother were strange to English administration and dealt with English needs according to Poitevin rather than Anglo-Norman tradition. As Duke of Aquitaine Richard had achieved some success by a combination of strong administrative measures, such as the appointment of vigorous

[1] See Richard of Devizes, in Howlett, *Chronicles of the reigns of Stephen, Henry II and Richard I*, III, pp. 389, 390; cf. Howden, III, p. 141.

officials, castle-building, and a reform of the coinage, with the old policy of playing off one local interest against another. In England, so long as he had a good central administration, he saw nothing impolitic in the formation of strong local interests. He allowed his brother to form a state within a state, for he was accustomed to independent vassals like the Counts of La Marche and Angoulême. John had his own administration, which was a counterpart to that of the English chancery and exchequer. The royal officials and judges did not enter his shires, Derby and Nottingham, Somerset, Dorset, Devon and Cornwall, nor the county and honour of Lancaster, nor the honours of Peverel, the Peak, Tickhill on the borders of Nottinghamshire and Yorkshire, Marlborough and Ludgershall in Wiltshire, nor the great honour of Glamorgan which pertained to the Gloucester inheritance. These jurisdictions were, until 1194, exempted from the direction of the central government. In addition, John was lord of the lands and rights of the earldom of Gloucester, of the honour of Wallingford in Berkshire, and Eye in Suffolk, and many other lands in the midlands. He also held the revenue of the forests of Andover and Sherwood. It is true that Richard had taken the precaution to retain in his own hands some of the most important castles in this demesne. The grant of the shires included financial and judicial rights, but not the wardenship of the castles of Nottingham, Exeter, and Launceston. The castles of Tickhill, Gloucester, Eye, and Wallingford were also reserved. On the other hand, the king had sold many counties, including the custody of his most important castles, to great local personages who would be tempted to take sides with John in the event of a dispute. When the chancellor was placed at the head of affairs, the close connexion, so carefully elaborated by Henry II, between central and local government hardly existed beyond the home counties. Moreover, the Church in England was disturbed by serious disputes.

William Longchamp, in spite of his triple position as legate, chancellor, and justiciar, was not equal to the task which Richard had given him. His father was not of noble origin, and in spite of his English connexions and lands, he was regarded as an outsider. His appearance was by no means impressive, while his demeanour was overbearing and his style of living extravagant. He openly expressed his contempt for provincial English society, and he neglected to take the advice of his colleagues. As legate, he annoyed the English clergy by his autocratic bearing and his excessive demands upon their hospitality; as chancellor, in possession of the king's seal, he claimed to control the executive and the disposition of the revenue[1]. Not unnaturally he speedily found himself opposed by clergy and barons alike. His considerable ability and foresight were disregarded by men who, stirred by political annoyance and social prejudice, saw in him only an ugly distorted foreigner of

[1] Cf. the phrase *iure cancellariae nostrae* in his letter of August 1190 to Walter of Coutances (Diceto II, 93).

servile origin and bad manners. His earliest actions illustrate both his insight and his imprudence. He was determined that there should be no dual government. Sure of the king's confidence, he decided to secure without delay as much power as possible. The castles were the strategic points. Richard had entrusted the Tower of London to him, and he had ordered a deep fosse to be dug about it. The chief royal strongholds outside London were Winchester, Windsor, York, Lincoln, and Dover. The last named was under the control of his brother-in-law, but the rest were held by officials who were either dangerous or had ceased to be in close touch with the central government. The chancellor took Winchester from the bishop, Windsor from Bishop Hugh of Durham, and York from its castellan. The Bishop of Durham, in spite of the king's grants, was further deprived of his political power and detained in his manor of Howden. The sheriff of York shared the fate of the castellan on the ground that they had both been implicated in the recent massacre of the Jews.

By these measures the chancellor had widened the area under the direct control of his administration; and, if he had acted with more caution, he might have firmly established himself, for at first he seems to have had his colleagues with him. But his semi-regal progresses, and his style of arrogant self-confidence, rapidly forced opposition to express itself. Complaints went to Richard before the end of 1190, and early in 1191 his enemies found a basis for attack. Queen Eleanor left England in order to negotiate and prepare for Richard's marriage to Berengaria of Navarre; and John arrived shortly before her departure. The count immediately became a centre of intrigue. The unscrupulous Hugh of Nonant, Bishop of Coventry, who was sheriff of the three counties of Leicester, Stafford, and Warwick, lying between John's honours in Gloucester and Derby, became his furious partisan. The sheriff of Lincolnshire, Gerard of Camville, was a still more useful ally. Gerard had bought his shire and was permitted to retain the custody of the castle of Lincoln which was hereditary in the family of his wife, Nicolaa of La Haye. After the check given to the Bishop of Durham and the downfall of the sheriff and castellan in York, he was the obvious leader of independent action in the north of England. In the days of King Stephen, the building of unlicensed castles and the abuse and usurpation of official power had been the main activities of the lawless element among the baronage; and the chancellor had good reason to believe that these anarchical tendencies were reviving. He struck at Gerard as the most prominent official among the suspected party. According to the charges brought against him after the king's return, Gerard had allowed Lincoln Castle to become a refuge for highwaymen who robbed the merchants on their way to Stamford fair; and had afterwards been guilty of treason in refusing, on the ground that he had done homage to John, to appear before the king's justices. Early in July 1191 the chancellor marched to take possession of Lincoln.

The move against Lincoln was the signal for open conflict between John and the chancellor. During the spring of this year several great issues had been raised. The news had reached England that, through the death of Archbishop Baldwin before Acre, the see of Canterbury was vacant. The succession immediately became the chief concern of the English clergy: if the chancellor became archbishop, his position would be greatly strengthened; if he did not, his position as legate might be seriously weakened. The dangerous question of the succession to the throne had also been reopened. Since his accession Richard had gradually declared his preference for Arthur, the son of his dead brother Geoffrey of Brittany, and in his treaties with Tancred of Sicily and Philip of France at Messina he definitely put him forward as his heir. But John could not be expected to acquiesce in this arrangement. It is significant that about this time the chancellor secured the adhesion of the King of Scots to Arthur's succession, and before his advance on Lincoln had suppressed a mysterious rising in Herefordshire, where Roger of Mortimer, lord of Wigmore, a neighbour of John in the Welsh March, had been intriguing with the Welsh princes. Disputes had also arisen between John and the government with regard to the castles and revenues claimed by John as part of his demesne. When the chancellor struck at Gerard of Camville, John shewed his power by securing from their castellans the surrender of Nottingham and Tickhill. Longchamp had to turn aside, and, after some angry exchanges of defiance, temporary agreement was reached at Winchester on 28 July, by the arbitration of barons and knights chosen from each side. The most important clause in this agreement was the chancellor's promise that he would do his best to secure the succession for John in the event of the king's death.

Up to a point the chancellor had been able to pose as the champion of order against rebellion and treachery; but from the spring of 1191 his authority rapidly decreased. On 27 April, before the crisis had come to a head, Walter of Coutances, the Archbishop of Rouen, landed in England. He had been released from his crusading vows and sent back by Richard from Messina to watch affairs and if necessary to act. The king had no desire to displace the chancellor, and for some time the archbishop used his large experience as an administrator to encourage good relations between Longchamp and John. On 28 July, after a revival of the dispute about Gerard of Camville, he assisted in the settlement made at Winchester. Yet there is no doubt that his presence gave confidence to the large number of bishops and barons whose sympathies were with John, but whose fears and sense of loyalty gave strength to an authorised government. By general consent John was the rightful heir of Richard, and if his influence in the cause of order could be secured by the recognition of his claim, the barons were prepared to recognise him. The chancellor's record was by no means unblemished; he had favoured his kinsmen, disregarded his colleagues, and squandered the revenue which came from ecclesiastical sources[1]. The history of the negotiations prior to the end of July shews that in the opinion of his own supporters he had acted rashly, if not unjustly. He was losing the support even of the financial interests in London. Amongst the clergy it was soon known that the Archbishop of Rouen had powers from the king to proceed with the election to the see of Canterbury. The recent death of the Pope had put an end to the chancellor's legatine authority, and the lead was now taken by Walter of Coutances.

The opportunity of getting rid of the chancellor was given by his sister Richenda, wife of the castellan of Dover. In September 1191 Archbishop Geoffrey, the half-brother of King Richard and John, came to England. Like Walter of Coutances, Geoffrey had in his time been head of the chancery, and immediately after his father's death the king had secured his election as Archbishop of York. The election had raised a violent storm of opposition, led by Hugh of Durham, and Geoffrey had only recently succeeded in obtaining papal recognition. In August he was consecrated at Tours; in September he boldly came to England, relying perhaps on the friendship of his old servant, the chancellor, whom he had introduced to official life. But the chancellor had no desire to see in England yet another element of discord, and ordered the castellan of Dover to prevent his entry. In the absence of her husband, Richenda, who would seem to have exceeded her instructions, had the archbishop dragged from the priory church of St Martin and imprisoned in the castle of Dover. The consequences of this outrage were rapid and dramatic. The saintly Hugh of Lincoln and the intriguing Hugh of Coventry joined in denunciation of the act of sacrilege. A pamphlet warfare was opened against the chancellor, who in vain repudiated his sister's action. His colleagues deserted their shires to join John at Reading. Longchamp, after some shuffling, agreed to submit himself to trial, but hearing that John's forces were preparing to occupy London, he turned back from the meeting-place and took refuge in the Tower. He found that all resistance would be useless and, after a series of ignominious adventures, left the country at the end of October.

Longchamp's career in England deserves attention because it shews how easily the system of government, through which Henry II had been able to concentrate his power, could be undermined. The events which followed the chancellor's flight are significant because they reveal the Great Council acting alone for the first time in English political history. Under the guidance of administrators trained in the ideas of Henry II, it assumed the direction of affairs in the interest of the State.

Count John, the Archbishop of Rouen, the Marshal, and the citizens of London had combined to depose the chancellor. They found the authority for their action in a letter, dated from Messina on 20 February,

[1] Howden, III, p. 193. There is a suggestion of judicial abuses in the compact of July 1191 (*ibid.* III, p. 136).

which was produced by the archbishop in a Great Council held at St Paul's. In this letter the king authorised the marshal and his colleagues to recognise the archbishop as justiciar in case of necessity. All parties benefited by the new settlement. The barons, it would seem, took an oath of allegiance to John and recognised his right to succeed his brother. The archbishop became justiciar and was careful to act with the advice of the marshal and his colleagues. The citizens of London secured general recognition for their commune, the rights of self-government which they had asserted some time before. The recognition of John and the commune is open to criticism; but the government established by the Great Council administered England with success during two very critical years. The services rendered at this time by the archbishop's colleagues should not be underrated. It is not surprising that they hesitated long before they joined in the attack upon the chancellor and allowed him to be deprived of the great seal. Longchamp had been invested with very great powers, his loyalty to Richard was unquestioned, and he had a considerable following. Although, according to Roger of Howden, his deposition was approved by the king, he did not lose royal favour. Later, he was mainly responsible for the arrangement with the Emperor by which Richard was released; and he was entrusted with important work until his death. It is significant, therefore, that Richard did not blame the marshal and his colleagues for their action. They had kept the peace between the various English interests, directed the verdict of the Great Council, and rehabilitated the justiciarship. The offices of justiciar and chancellor were never again combined, nor did the chancellor resume the chief place among the great officers of state until the end of the next century[1].

Returning pilgrims brought news at the end of 1192 that King Richard was on his way home. They had seen his ships arrive at Brindisi. If he had arrived safely, he would have found that the crisis which had hurried his return was over. He would have been welcomed by a united family and a successful administration, which, both in England and Normandy, had held its own against the intrigues of Philip Augustus. The news of his capture by the Duke of Austria at once disturbed the apparent harmony. All the latent anxieties of John were revealed. In his treacherous nature his reason was always at the mercy of his passions. At one time cynical and lethargic, at another full of impatient energy, he was the instant victim of suspicion. He had hoped that his brother would not return; now at the last moment he might prevent him. He had feared lest his claims to the succession might not be recognised; now he would end his fears. As he hurried to confer with the King of France, he was invited by the seneschal and barons of Normandy to deliberate with them

[1] Longchamp ceased to have control of the seal in July 1194 (EHR, xxiii, p. 226). All his earlier *appares* remained faithful to Richard and the new government, with the possible exception of Hugh Bardolf. (Cf. Howden, iii, p. 241.)

upon means of defending the duchy. He insisted upon an oath of fealty which they properly refused. He agreed with Philip upon the division of his future dominions, returned to England with a band of mercenaries, collected a body of Welshmen, occupied Windsor and Wallingford, and claimed recognition as King of England. Richard, he said, was dead. The Archbishop of Rouen stood firm. The coasts were carefully guarded against the invasion prepared by the King of France, and in England John's forces soon began to give way. In April 1193 the strain was released. Hubert Walter, the Bishop of Salisbury, arrived with the news that Richard was alive, in the custody of the Emperor Henry VI. John had to make the best terms that he could, and when, early in July, he heard that "the devil was loosed," fear assailed him and he fled to Philip again.

Richard, however, was not yet free, although the terms of his release had been arranged. If John had shewn the slightest loyalty to his brother, he would have been perfectly safe, for, as late as 9 July, Richard's envoys arranged a treaty with Philip at Mantes which included in its terms the restoration of John to the dignified appanage granted to him before the king had left for the East. Now the count had gone too far. The Normans would have nothing to do with him, and he became the eager accomplice of Philip, who, encouraged by the delay of Richard's release, strove his utmost to induce the Emperor to keep the King of England in captivity. John decided to hold his own in England, but his plans were revealed through the boastings of a confidential clerk. By this time, early in the year 1194, Richard was on his way home. When he arrived, he found that Hubert Walter, the Bishop of Durham, and their colleagues had stifled all danger. Of John's castles only Tickhill and Nottingham held out. Tickhill was surrendered in a few days, and on 28 March Richard, fighting, unknown to the besieged, in a coat of light mail and an iron cap, had the pleasure of sharing in the capture of Nottingham.

After the surrender of the castle of Nottingham, Richard held a Great Council, at which he began to deal with the pressing business of the State. On 17 April, the Sunday after Easter, he wore his crown with peculiar ceremony in the cathedral of Winchester, and received the blessing of the new Archbishop of Canterbury, Hubert Walter. This ceremony, "intermediate between a coronation and a crown-wearing," was intended to emphasise the complete restoration of the royal dignity after the humiliation of imprisonment; and it followed the order observed on a similar occasion in 1141 after Stephen's captivity. If it is true that Richard had acknowledged the lordship of the Emperor and that there was some doubt whether England was not a vassal-state, the re-coronation was particularly necessary. Between the ceremony and his departure, which was delayed by contrary winds until 12 May, the king continued his arrangement for the government of England. On the second day of the council at Nottingham (31 March), John and the Bishop of Coventry had been cited to appear within forty days. According to some authorities John was actually disinherited and his possessions were retained in the king's hands; if, however, these measures were taken, they soon lost effect. But the king's chief concern was to collect men and money for his war against Philip Augustus. A great part of his ransom had just been collected in order to secure his release; the government had levied an aid of twenty shillings on the knight's fee and had taken a fourth of all lay and ecclesiastical revenues, the wool of the Cistercians and of the Order of Sempringham for one year, and the treasures of the churches. But the country had still to make up her full share of the total 150,000 marks exacted by the Emperor. At the same time, the danger from Philip was pressing, and at Nottingham Richard demanded a land-tax of two shillings on the carucate, another contribution from the Cistercians, and a third of the knight-service owed by his tenants. Money was also raised by the sale of offices, fines, and ransoms from John's supporters and by "gifts" paid "for joy at the king's return." Hence it happened that the Bishop of Coventry, scoundrel though he was, Gerard of Camville, and most of the other rebels had soon bought their pardons. John himself was the chief sufferer, for it would have been both expensive and impolitic to reinstate him completely. A personal reconciliation between the brothers in Normandy was followed in the autumn of 1195 by the restoration to John of the honours of Mortain, Gloucester, and Eye; but he was not permitted to control a single castle, and the Exchequer recovered its authority in the English shires which had been granted to him in 1189.

Richard had resumed control of English affairs even in his irksome captivity. He held his court at the various places, Spires, Trifels, Hagenau, Worms, where he was detained; and the Germans were astonished at the number of his visitors. Richard shewed no special favour to the Archbishop of Rouen and his English colleagues. The archbishop was summoned to Germany at the end of 1193, and was succeeded by Hubert Walter, who had shortly before been elected Archbishop of Canterbury. About the same time, the other justices ceased to exercise their authority as *appares*. Their last act was the collection of the royal ransom[1]. On his departure for Normandy in 1194, England was left in charge of Hubert Walter, and the traditional system of government, by which a chief justiciar executed the commands of an absent but accessible king and supervised the administration of justice and finance, was restored.

[1] Howden, III, p. 225. William Brewer had already joined the king in June (*ibid.* p. 215). In a letter of 19 April 1193, Richard wrote, not to the Archbishop of Rouen, but to Queen Eleanor and the justices (*ibid.* p. 208), but the archbishop did not cease to receive impatient orders from him (*Hist. de G. le Maréchal*, l. 10003). There seems to be no ground for the view of Stubbs that, by changes in the sheriffdoms, Richard desired to express disapproval of the justices (*Const. History*, I, p. 542; contrast *Hist. de G. le Maréchal*, ll. 10092 ff.).

The greatness of Hubert Walter is not yet fully recognised. Papal legate from 1195, justiciar until the middle of 1198, he possessed most of the powers at which William Longchamp had aimed. His strength of character, ingenuity, and a natural insight into detail which his legal training had quickened, made him more than equal to his position. He had been trained in the household of the justiciar Ranulf Glanvil, whose wife was Hubert's aunt. In 1186 he became dean of York and seems to have passed before 1189 to more direct attendance upon the king in the chancery. If, as a high authority suggested, he was the author of the tract upon the laws of England (*leges Anglicanae*) usually ascribed to Glanvil, he had acquired in his uncle's service a profound and orderly understanding of Anglo-Norman administration, a clear concise style, and some knowledge of Roman law. As Bishop of Salisbury, he preceded Richard on the crusade and speedily became the most useful if not the most important person in the English camp. Among other services he devised a system of poor relief for the benefit of needy crusaders. His appointment as archbishop and afterwards as justiciar proves Richard's admiration for him. He was not a particularly religious man, not very learned, nor of strict moral life. He was fond of power and wealth. His secular outlook was the despair of that unyielding ecclesiastic, St Hugh of Lincoln; his indifference to the new culture and his suspicion of the cosmopolitan tendencies in the law and practice of the Church stirred the hatred of such men as Gerald of Wales. He was a great administrator in Church and State, proud of his office, eager to do things well, and, like Lanfranc, impatient of the logic which insisted on formulating the political dilemmas of the age.

The justiciar made the assertion of his authority his first task. As archbishop he had already claimed the office of legate and protested against the legatine authority of Longchamp. As archbishop also he had asserted his superiority to the Archbishop of York, and soon after Richard's departure he took an opportunity, as justiciar, of humiliating his chief rival. In his quarrels with his canons, Archbishop Geoffrey had laid himself open to civil as well as canonical proceedings; and, while the Pope was deciding against his ecclesiastical claims, a commission of inquiry, appointed by the justiciar, found his agents guilty of robbery. On Geoffrey's refusal to accept legal liability, he was dispossessed of nearly all his estates. The shrievalty of Yorkshire, for which he had paid no less than £2000, was entrusted to two wardens (*custodes*). The aged Bishop of Durham was dispossessed of the shrievalty of Northumberland in a still more summary manner. By September the justiciar had got control of the north and had turned his attention to more general matters. The well-known judicial inquiry ordered in this month was a kind of national stock-taking. The king, doubtless by Hubert's advice, had already revised the distribution of the shires, partly for the sake of financial profit, partly, perhaps, in order to break the connexion between particular shires and sheriffs who had been powerful during his absence. It is worthy of note that, although the justiciar recognised the judicial experience of the justices who had ruled England in the previous years and placed three of them upon the important commission of 1194, he ordered them and their colleagues to withdraw from the bench when they came to counties in which they ruled or, since Richard's first coronation, had ruled as sheriffs. The elaborate inquiries of the justices were to be unprejudiced. These inquiries dealt both with unfinished judicial or financial business, and with the escheats, wardships, and demesnes of the king, the last of which were to be inventoried in a very elaborate manner. In addition, the justices were instructed to put into operation a careful scheme for preserving the record of all debts owing to Jews. They were to exact a tallage from the boroughs and the royal demesne. Finally, the practice of entrusting the record of pleas of the Crown to special officials at the time of their first presentment or detection was made general by the commission of 1194. Three knights and a clerk were to be elected in each shire court to act as *custodes placitorum coronae.* In 1195 the justiciar revised the local machinery for the preservation of the peace. His edict, although partly a statement of custom, also contains matter which was new in English practice.

As justiciar Hubert Walter was president of the Exchequer, and his chief work was done in this great centre of orderly activity. He attempted the revision of taxation and of the existing system of military service. The land-tax, or Danegeld, had long ceased to be a regular charge upon the community, although its exaction was still regarded as a possible necessity[1]. Richard had recourse to it in 1194, before he left for Normandy[2]. In 1198 Hubert Walter felt that the time had come for a systematic return to the principle of a land-tax upon a new assessment. He sent two commissioners to each shire, who, in co-operation with the sheriff and certain elected knights, inquired into the amount of arable land (*carucarum wannagia*) from representatives of each vill[3], and levied a tax, first of two, afterwards of three shillings upon each ploughland. The ploughland, or parcel which could be reckoned to a single plough, was estimated to be one hundred acres. A few returns, contained in the Exchequer record known as the *Testa de Nevill*, prove that this inquiry was seriously attempted, if not completed; but the justiciar ceased to rule England in this year, and the scheme for a new Domesday Book was apparently abandoned. During the minority of Henry III "carucages and hidages" were occasionally levied, but it is probable that they were levied on the old assessment, if not according to the simpler method of 1200 and 1220 when the expedient was adopted of counting the ploughs

[1] *Dialogus de Scaccario,* Book I, ch. II; and the note in the Oxford Edition, p. 197.

[2] The so-called carucage of 1194 (Howden, III, p. 242) apparently required no new assessment, and is simply a return to the old Danegeld.

[3] That this is the meaning of wainage here (Howden, IV, p. 46) seems clear from the context, from the returns in the Testa (see Round, EHR, III, pp. 502–5; *Book of Fees,* I, pp. 1–14), and from the similar returns of 1222 in the Domesday of St Paul's (ed. Hale), e.g. p. 99. On the various meanings of wainage see Tait, EHR, XXVII, p. 722.

actually in use and charging two or three shillings on each. As in Ireland during the eighteenth century, the symmetrical assessment of ploughlands broke down. Indeed in England the idea of a general land-tax was discarded after 1235, save for the fixed sum paid as a local rate under the names of hidage and sheriff's aid.

The justiciar's reorganisation of military service was undertaken in close co-operation with the king, and although equally transitory was more immediately successful than the attempt to revive the land-tax. The Norman wars required the presence of a small long-service force of knights in addition to the mercenaries and the local levies and garrisons. Between 1194 and 1198 Richard made three or four attempts to raise such a force from his English fiefs. In 1194 he demanded a third of the knight-service of England, in 1196 he ordered each lay baron to cross the Channel with a few picked men, in 1198 he tried to raise a force of 300 knights from the whole body of English vassals, and, as this plan seems to have broken down owing to the opposition of the Bishops of Lincoln and Salisbury, he finally demanded a tenth of all knight-service. In these various demands two objects were made increasingly clear: the king desired to insist upon the duty of the English vassals to equip and pay for a small long-service army; and he ultimately made no distinction between the liability of lay and of ecclesiastical fiefs. The demand of 1198 that the military obligations of the vassals should be treated as a whole by the levy of a tax to pay 300 knights, and the consequent debate in the Great Council at Oxford, suggest that Hubert Walter was preparing to go farther still. The opposition of Bishop Herbert of Salisbury suggests, as Stubbs pointed out, that the archbishop was going beyond what the *Dialogus de Scaccario* terms the fixed rules of the Exchequer. His proposal involved a considerable change in the relations between the Crown and the military tenants; the direct, limited, and personal liability of each vassal would have been merged in the liability to a general tax on the knight's fee; and in course of time such a tax might well have provided the king with a standing army. If this view is correct, Hubert's failure is very important. Future events were to shew how far succeeding kings could go within the framework of feudal organisation. John turned Richard's expedients into a system. Scutages, or taxes on the knight's fee, were levied regularly, and the vassals who served in person had to secure their "writs of scutage," or right to appropriate the tax from their fees, as best they could. Additional fines were levied on those who failed to cross the sea or bargained for exemption from personal service. Careful investigations were made into the services due to the king in England. Although Henry III was unable to levy scutage at will, he adopted, so far as was possible, the policy of his father, and Edward I deliberately collected scutage as a tax independent of considerations of service. Yet neither John nor Henry III nor Edward I seems to have tried to go so far as Hubert Walter nearly succeeded in going. In 1201 and again in 1205 John summoned his vassals and their knights to Portsmouth, and there made his selection and decided upon his exactions. In the latter year he ordered, as part of a larger scheme of national defence, every tenth knight to be equipped for service by his fellows. Although the military tenants, lay and clerical, seemed to be completely under royal control, they were still immediately concerned in the equipment of the host; their legal quota of knight-service (*servitium debitum*) was in most cases less, often ludicrously less, than the service which their estates could have provided. In their eyes an aid or scutage on all knights' fees was illegal, unless it were levied in connexion with a definite military enterprise, and unless those who served could recover it. And when the northerners refused foreign service, John's absolutism was brought to an end.

King Richard never saw England again after 1194 and, five years later, he died in Aquitaine from the results of a wound (6 April 1199). His successor was crowned, after taking the usual oath, on Ascension Day. Archbishop Hubert had resigned the office of justiciar to Geoffrey Fitz Peter in 1198, but he did not sever his connexion with the administration. He was John's chancellor until his death in 1205; and it is impossible to dissociate him from the developments of John's early reign, or indeed to consider the reigns of Richard and John apart from each other. King John, in fact, felt with much truth that he was not his own master so long as his great minister was alive. Hubert Walter held the view, natural to an ecclesiastical statesman, that the kingship was an office invested with solemn duties. Royal power must be inseparable from the law. And the archbishop's prestige was so great that a word from him upon the interpretation of the law could set aside the opinion of the king and his advisers[1]. Under his eye and in the hands of Geoffrey Fitz Peter, the hardworking experienced baron who succeeded him as justiciar—*regni columna, legum peritus*—the administrative system continued unshaken. For this reason, before we consider the new king's quarrels with the Church and the baronage, we may say something here about the general tendencies in John's reign and connect them with a survey of developments in English government and society.

The reign of King John is, to a degree found in no period of previous history, a commentary upon the development of the *Curia Regis*. The growth of the court, and notably of the Exchequer, both displayed and consolidated the strength of the royal power. The Crown was able to strengthen its hold over local administration and to profit by the increasing prosperity of the country. On the other hand, the disasters of the time, the loss of Normandy and the quarrel with Pope Innocent III,

[1] A royal writ to the justiciar forbade Ralf de Clere, a minor, to plead—"et dominus archiepiscopus, cujus custodie Radulfus predictus est, dicit quod non est contra consuetudinem regni si loqui procedat. Ideo habent diem," etc. (*Curia Regis Rolls*, I, 279).

threw the king's unstable personality into strong relief against the background of administrative routine and social activity. The baronage was disillusioned. The generation which came to manhood after the great rebellion of 1173 had lived through a time of great experiences. Its spirit had been fed on a new literature, in which the expression of the cruder passions was refined by a suggestion of the beauty of self-restraint and idealism in life; its eyes had rejoiced in new forms of art, a marvellous activity in the building of churches, monasteries, castles, bridges, whose austerity was consistent with the reception of new devices or luxuries. Some of these young nobles had brought back from the East ineffaceable memories of a crusade under the greatest leader of his time, and had shared in his counsels during the stiff contests with Philip Augustus on the Norman frontier. They had seen Château Gaillard rise with the rapidity of a miracle and had heard the bitter news of its capture. Some had worked beside Hubert Walter and Geoffrey Fitz Peter and, if the intricacies of the abacus or the technicality of the common law might be somewhat beyond their comprehension, they had learned that the new administrative system could be as interesting as a tournament, and was far more closely related to the problems presented in the management of their own estates. The experience of all had impressed upon them the duty of loyalty; and the inclinations of few would be towards sympathy with the ecclesiastics who scurried out of England in the days of the Interdict; but they could not fail to feel the contrast between their king—who had so often disappointed them in the past—and a man like Stephen Langton, in whom, as in the great and well-remembered Hugh of Lincoln, loyalty was devotion, not to a man, but to a system of law and order which he believed to be a reflection of the law and order of the universe. Whether they continued to cling to the king or not, the more serious men among the baronage must have learned to interpret the traditions of personal loyalty and the feudal contract in a larger way, to have been conscious of deeper implication in the favourite distinction of political thought—a distinction as profound as it was simple—between the *rex* and the *tyrannus*. Beneath all the violence and impulsiveness of society in this time, the hatred of some, the lethargy or selfishness of others, we can feel at work the impulse to a new adventure in response to the idea that administration is a public, not merely a personal, task.

John's character hastened both the development in his Curia and the interpretation by his vassals of the royal power. He was not lacking in energy or insight. After his withdrawal from the continent, he renewed his acquaintance with England to much purpose and probably knew it better than any other English ruler prior to Edward VII and George V. In discussion he was shrewd, though sophistical. His biting tongue, which can occasionally be heard even beneath the forms of his official correspondence, could wound the more because it was informed by wit and observation. As the Plea Rolls shew, he was not neglectful of business, and, although he preferred a trial by combat to a legal discussion, he could intervene effectively in a dispute. We shall never know the extent of his personal responsibility for the measures of his reign, such as the great inquiry of 1212, but it is clear that he was always a real force, never a nonentity. His decisions were formed rapidly and for a time executed ruthlessly. During the period of the interdict he was in an excited state, varying from vindictive irritability to far-reaching schemes for the reduction of Wales, the Isle of Man, Ireland. At the same time he chafed under discipline. He liked his ease and he took his ease when he liked. At the most critical time in the history of his house he won for himself the nickname of "soft sword," and his enemies welcomed his succession because he was a lover of quiet; not the rest of the soul, but the indolence of the self-indulgent. If the report by the Marshal's biographer of the conversation between the Earl Marshal and Archbishop Hubert Walter after Richard's death can be trusted—and there is no reason to doubt its general accuracy—the archbishop agreed with reluctance and foreboding to the recognition of John. The Marshal preferred John to Arthur on legal grounds (he quoted a Norman custom) and because Arthur had bad friends, was proud and passionate, and disliked the English. The archbishop told him that he would never regret anything as much as this decision. The king's peculiar temperament, indeed, which was unbalanced and erotic, put him at the mercy of fits of anger, cruelty, and lethargy; and, more than this, made him quite indifferent to those principles of harmony in life and nature which underlay all the current belief in justice and responsibility. He was, as William of Newburgh well said, an enemy to nature (*hostis naturae*), a fool, in the Scriptural sense, who says in his heart that there is no God. Habits of decorum and respect for the views of other people were impossible to him. He rejoiced in the death of his greatest ministers. He far outstripped his father and brothers, whose feelings of reverence were not highly developed, in his indifference to the claims of his Church upon the conscience; not that he was a free-thinker, so much as that loyalty meant nothing to him. Hence he saw treachery everywhere and was happiest in the company of boon companions, who doubtless found much amusement in his irresponsible humour and his cynical jibes at the serious and pedantic. He was a clever, amusing, unreliable, distrustful, and thoroughly bad man.

His saving quality was that he was an Angevin, of the race of Fulk Nerra. His energy might fail, but he could never forget that he had succeeded to a great inheritance. In his youth he had intrigued for it, and in manhood he clung to it. In his irresponsibility he was ambitious; in his moods of lethargy he could plan great enterprises, to which his vitality was not unequal. Hence his reign was rich in achievement, of which he was never a mere spectator.

In this period systematic records begin to be kept in the royal chancery and before the royal justices. Although it is now hardly possible to define the extent to which records of letters and proceedings were kept in the reign of Henry II, Archbishop Hubert certainly developed the practice greatly and it cannot be an accident that the earliest extant Chancery Rolls belong to his time, and that the references to earlier Plea Rolls of proceedings in the Curia Regis are casual and doubtful. We know the precise date—15 July 1195—on which a final concord was first written in triplicate, and its foot (*pes*) filed in the Treasury. The elaborate system of recording the financial operations of the Jews, instituted by the archbishop in 1194, shows his orderly mind at work soon after his appointment as justiciar. The "Exchequer of the Jews," which appears soon afterwards, was not a new financial department; it was a piece of permanent machinery with justices, clerks, and records, dependent upon the Exchequer at Westminster, for the supervision of Jewish business and the settlement of disputes to which the financial transactions of Jews, especially with Christians, gave rise; and it was an expression of the general development at this time of judicial activity, and of the systematic registration of judicial business. As a financial body the Exchequer itself had behind it long experience in the keeping of records. Domesday Book was still the "Book of Winchester," but was probably now kept at Westminster. At all events the Treasury at Westminster was a great record office, with its Pipe Rolls, returns of knights' fees, records of old inquiries such as the Inquest of Sheriffs (1170), and the investigations of wardships, heiresses in the king's gift, escheats, and the like. Here Hubert Walter, and in John's reign the great treasurer William of Ely, were content to define and improve. To Hubert was due the exhaustive stocktaking of 1194 and the survey of ploughlands four years later, fragments of which still survive. William of Ely in the Red Book of the Exchequer[1] saved the returns of knights' fees of 1166; he was doubtless partly responsible also for the great enquiry of this reign recorded in the Book of Fees. The Exchequer officials by 1215 must have had access to an almost unmanageable mass of material relating to tenures of every kind.

It is customary to divide the records of current business into the two series of Exchequer and Chancery records, the former consisting of membranes fastened together at the head, the latter of membranes sewed, the foot of one to the head of the next, to form a continuous roll. The distinction is a real one: thus, the Plea Rolls, which are Exchequer records in form, were actually Exchequer rather than Chancery documents; judges sat in the Exchequer to hear common pleas and all judicial rolls were returned, or were supposed to return, to the Treasury. Yet it would be misleading to make the distinction between Chancery and Exchequer the starting-point in the analysis of English administration at this time. Both were activities, inseparable in practice, of the royal Curia and, taken together, did not exhaust the functions of the Curia, either as a financial or as a secretarial body.

[1] Alexander Swereford entered the returns of 1166 in the Red Book *sub prefato Willelmo Elyensi* (I, 5).

The king was the source of order and justice. His court was the seat of government. In John's reign the judicial, financial, and secretarial elements in the royal household were well developed, and through them the Crown kept in touch with, and controlled, the whole country. The two marks of the household were a capacity for indefinite expansion and a tendency to differentiation. No logical line can be drawn between the groups of men, the furniture and wagons which followed the king from place to place, and the Great Council of ecclesiastics, magnates, officials who gathered about him on solemn occasions; we cannot say where the household ceased to comprise the activities of his subjects. A great baron who had the right to carry the sword or hold the cup when the king sat in state, and the humble tenant who held his land by the serjeanty of carrying the king's letters to Newcastle or providing bread for his kitchen, were alike involved in the business of the household. Wherever the king came, a score of latent duties might leap into activity, in the stable or the kitchen, at the gate or in the forest; and all would be under the supervision of the royal Chamber. Every kind of activity, from matters of State to the trivial details of domestic life, were within the cognisance of the Chamber, and of its financial department, the Wardrobe. They come before us in the records of expenditure (*Misae* rolls) which can definitely be described in John's reign as rolls of the Wardrobe. The almoner who periodically feeds a crowd of poor folk is paid in the Wardrobe. The candles burnt before the holy relics and the royal gambling debts are alike charged there. If the king takes a bath, his *aquarius* draws his fee at the Wardrobe; if huntsmen and dogs are summoned or sent into temporary seclusion, the expense of their maintenance is entered on the roll of the Wardrobe. A messenger arrives carrying a gruesome burden, the heads of some treacherous Welshmen; another departs bearing a fragrant garland of roses from Geoffrey Fitz Peter's gardens at Ditton to the King's mistress; both are paid in the Wardrobe. The rolls reflect national as well as domestic interests. The Wardrobe has its chests for important documents, the charters or receipts of great nobles, the correspondence of foreign princes[1], its sacks of money, its chequered cloth for the reckoning of accounts, its clerks with wax, ink, and parchment. It handles the money which the Chamber can draw at will upon the royal treasure. Normally the outlay is not large; it meets current expenses, presented to the Chamber by various departments or individuals. These bring their *computi*, which are sometimes examined by one or two officials—for example, Richard Marsh, Keeper of the Seal. Their accounts, if of any length, are entered on the *dorso* of the *Misae* roll. But when a great expedition is on foot, the roll shews that large sums are involved—long lists of pensions are paid to foreign allies, wages to hundreds of Welsh

[1] In due course most of these found their way to the treasury at Westminster, the chief record office, where similar documents were, quite as frequently, directly deposited.

mercenaries. The Wardrobe and Chamber are working with the Marshalsea as a War Office.

Naturally, the growth of business involved differentiation. Some officers of the Chamber were always with the king, for they had the small seal, which operated the whole machinery of state. The Wardrobe was generally with the king but not always. It was still literally a wardrobe, as well as a financial department—the royal tailor (*scissor*) was a prominent person in it—and when the king was a guest, as of the justiciar in his manor at Ditton, the furniture of his bedroom was not required; the carts and horses carrying the wardrobe waited for the king elsewhere. The Chancery, so far as it was independent of the Chamber, might or might not be with the king, and if the keeper of the seal were in the Chamber, the presence of the chancellor was not necessary. Sometimes, when John was making a rapid tour far away from London, Chancery and seal, chancellor and keeper, all stayed behind. Letters under the great seal were issued under a writ of small or privy seal, and a note to this effect was inserted in the Patent or Close or Charter roll[1]. Departmental officers were empowered to authorise letters affecting their departmental business, just as the Exchequer issued writs under the Exchequer seal, which was a facsimile of the great seal, without reference to the king. Indeed, it would seem that public documents of the highest importance might pass the great seal without a royal writ of authorisation, for King Richard deprived Longchamp of his great seal on the ground that he had affixed it to a treaty which infringed the customs of Poitou. The same possibility of temporary detachment from the king existed in the case of the judges and barons in his train; when we are told that the king was in one place and the Curia in another, we may probably see a distinction between the domestic and the non-domestic elements in the household.

These facts shew that the tendency to specialisation was due to the expansion of business in a feudal household which had a kingdom for its province. The Chancery, the Wardrobe, and the court of justices were the links between the royal chamber and the country. They were extensions of function, which kept the Crown in touch with earlier localised expressions of the royal power and which were destined to produce intricate developments in their turn. Let us take, for example, the relations between the Wardrobe and the Exchequer. As spending departments they are hardly distinguishable. If the Chamber were short of ready money and no one was at hand to lend it, the Chancery would be ordered to send the bills of the royal huntsman and tailor to the Exchequer in a writ of "liberate," which would be entered upon the Close Roll. The earliest Close Rolls indeed were records of such letters, although in a few years (by 1206) they became registers of miscellaneous correspondence issued

[1] For example, when John was in the North of England in the summer of 1212, he had his Chamber, Wardrobe, and privy seal with him; but the Chancery remained in the South. Richard Marsh, the keeper, joined him later at Nottingham.

under the great and small seal[1]. In such a case the Exchequer, through the medium of the Chancery, would stand in precisely the same relation to the Chamber as the Wardrobe did. We may regard the various chancery rolls of letters patent and close, of charters, and oblations or fines, together with the wardrobe accounts of loans (*prestita*) and expenses (*misae*), as developments of the chamber rolls which, though now lost, are known to have existed from the middle of the twelfth century. They were devised, perhaps by Hubert Walter himself, to keep a systematic record of the complicated relations between the Chamber and the administrative machine.

The frequent and sometimes prolonged absence of Henry II and Richard I in their continental fiefs had naturally had much influence on English government. The justiciar was the king's deputy during these periods of absence. He transmitted or executed royal commands under his own seal and presided over the King's Court. He was inevitably less independent and self-contained than the king; he required a base; and the evidence suggests that this base was the Exchequer, just as the Exchequer at Caen was the base of the Norman seneschal. Longchamp, who combined the functions of justiciar and chancellor and therefore issued letters under the great seal, made the Exchequer his head-quarters. When he was justiciar, Hubert Walter was constantly concerned with Exchequer business. Geoffrey Fitz Peter, though frequently on circuit or in John's company, had his head-quarters at Westminster, where he presided over the Bench or Court of Common Pleas and supervised the agreements known as final concords. At Westminster the justiciar found the treasurer, barons, and officials of the Exchequer as well as the judges. He was in the chief palace of the kingdom, a home of routine and orderly tradition. The royal treasure was there, or at the Temple on the way to London, or in the Tower on the other side of the city. The records of judicial proceedings could be examined there. The activities of Westminster, although in fact no less than in theory an extension of the activities of the wandering court, were the expression of official as distinct from arbitrary power. The Exchequer was the seat of public law, the home of a professional civil service linked up with the administration of the shires, the collection of taxes, and the work of the justices; it expressed the fact that, whether the king was at hand or not, the king's government always went on. By this time it sat almost continuously throughout the year, and the two terms of Michaelmas and Easter were merely periods of concentrated business and audit.

Henry II's judicial reforms had started a similar development of judicial officialism, whose rules, practices, precedents were rapidly giving shape to

[1] Letters close and the Close Roll are mentioned before the close rolls begin (e.g. *Rot. litt. pat.*, 25, 35). The so-called Liberate Roll of 3 John was at one time described as a close roll, although the description was afterwards changed (*Rotuli de Liberate*, etc. p. 108). This roll was also known as the English Roll (cf. *Rotuli Normanniae*, p. 107 with *Rotuli de Liberate*, pp. 67-8).

the body of common law. The king usually had in his train a group of justices who heard pleas. In theory the king was present; the proceedings were recorded on a roll of pleas before the king. In fact also the king was present as often as not, and, if some great tenant-in-chief were concerned, or some knotty point had been referred to him, or some new ordinance had to be sanctioned, the Curia Regis became a council of prelates and barons as well as judges. At this date there was no distinction between the Council as a future parliament and the Council as a future King's Bench, nor between equity and common law. John, who took his judicial work seriously, dealt with all sorts of matters, sometimes as an arbitrator, more frequently as a judge. Yet the differentiation of judicial business in the technical sense can already be traced. If we read the story of the wrangles, the abusive give and take, between John and his barons, described by the biographer of William the Marshal, we find it hard to draw the line between a family quarrel and the pleadings in a court of justice; if on the other hand we read the cases which the clerks of John's justices thought it wise to record, we breathe a rarefied air. There is less formality, less specialism than there is at Westminster, but most of the cases are very similar.

The later history of England is the history of the conflict of various tendencies within this great royal household which we have tried to describe in the preceding pages—a system so simple in principle, yet so complicated in structure, concentrated here, diffused there, in one place a thing of routine, in another almost anarchical in its irresponsibility. During the first few years of John's reign these tendencies were in equilibrium. The king had in his justiciar, chancellor, and treasurer three of the most efficient men of the age. His justices, sheriffs, castellans, and more intimate officials and companions were, on the whole, men who had been trained in the service of his father and brother. The baronage supported him loyally in his conflict with Philip Augustus. The change for the worse was gradual, and the loyalty of the majority of the administrative officers and of an influential minority of his barons was remarkable to the very end. It stood the strain of his frequent fits of petulance, suspicion, and treachery. Yet under the demoralising conditions of the interdict, the breach between the king and the mass of the baronage became marked. The influence of the coterie of domestic clerks, knights, bachelors, and mercenaries about him grew, until at last all the efforts of men of stability and moderation to maintain peace were in vain.

During the earlier years, however, the Crown strengthened its hold over local administration and profited by the increasing prosperity of the country. Hubert Walter's policy was continued and extended by John's ministers.

Far-reaching reforms were made in the organization of local finance under the supervision of the Exchequer. It has been noted that during this period the sheriffs frequently acted, not as *firmarii* but as *custodes*, and although the exact bearing of this change cannot be satisfactorily explained, it was doubtless connected with the enormous increase in the profits of the shires—an increase so onerous and involving so much extortion that it was attacked in one of the clauses of the Great Charter. Again, by the introduction of the grouping of debts under the sheriff's name and the contrivance of the dividend tally or single receipt for a variety of small payments, the Exchequer began to meet the problems of book-keeping caused by the innumerable fines and amercements. These reforms involved important changes in Exchequer administration and increased the efficiency of the sheriff's departments, for the sheriff was made more directly responsible for the collection of local debts. His extended powers gave him opportunities for exaction to which both the Charter and subsequent complaints bear witness[1].

The Exchequer, indeed, was in touch continuously with every section of the community. The great inquiry of 1212 into tenures was no isolated, although it was an impressive and comprehensive, achievement. The very rapidity with which it was carried through proves that the data were easily acquired, and comparison between the returns and the parallel compilation in the Red Book of the Exchequer shews that the Exchequer was already in possession of much classified material[2]. For example, the resumption of alienated demesne, which the Waverley annalist erroneously supposed to be the main object of the great inquiry, had begun several years before, *e.g.* in the honour of Lancaster. The revenues from the royal estates increased, sometimes by fifty or a hundred per cent. Bensington in Oxfordshire, which in 1189 was farmed at £57. 8*s*., was valued at £100 in 1199, and in 1208 was expected to bring £149. 2*s*. into the Exchequer. The constant tallages to which the demesne was liable pressed hardly upon the boroughs, the Jews, and the estates of bishops, chapters, and monasteries which came into the king's hands during the Interdict. A Gloucester writer complains that the tallage of 1210 affected all the churches of England, rich and poor, so that not even the lepers escaped. Among the scores of municipal charters granted or confirmed by John, only about half-a-dozen contain a clause of exemption from tallage. John took the Jews under his special care. Hubert Walter had established government supervision of Jewish transactions at the Exchequer. In 1201 their position was confirmed in an elaborate charter. They were safe-guarded, so far as was possible, from such savage outbreaks as had disgraced Richard's accession; they lived in special quarters under the protection of royal castellans, and had the right to be tried by their peers. This was probably the period of their greatest activity, for every baron turned to them in his embarrassments, and their wealth helped to build more

[1] See especially Miss Mill's paper, TRHS, Fourth Series, VIII, pp. 151 ff. (1925). For other changes cf. Turner, *ibid.*, Second Series, XII, pp. 121 ff. (1898) and XVIII, pp. 289, 290 (1904); and Poole, *The Exchequer in the Twelfth Century*, p. 130.

[2] *The Book of Fees* (London, 1920), I, pp. 52 ff.

than one noble monastery; but their privileges isolated them and were useless against the king. John took 4000 marks for the Charter of 1201; in 1210 he laid hands upon them and demanded a tallage of 66,000 marks. His knowledge of their transactions was used to exploit them as well as their debtors, while in times of political excitement, as in 1215, they were exposed to attack as the king's creatures.

Society as a whole was hardly less responsive to official discipline. Heavy scutages were levied annually, there was a plough tax in 1200, a seventh on barons' movable property in 1203, a thirteenth on the value of chattels in 1207. The opposition, even of the clergy, was slight, for although the Church forced the king to confine the thirteenth to the laity, it found it advisable to subscribe. At this time of war and anticipation of French attack on England, the spirit of the people seems to have been as docile as the administration of Geoffrey Fitz Peter and William of Ely was efficient. A sum of nearly £60,000 was raised from the thirteenth within a few months, and in the following year the justices on eyre were ordered to inquire into the arrears which were still unpaid[1]. The recruiting of mercenaries in Wales and the March, the collection of stores and material, the arrangements for transport in the earlier years, involved elaborate organisation and implied general acquiescence. The ease with which the Angevin kings could bring together a large fleet by uniting the resources of the ports is revealed for the first time in the letters of this reign, and there is an element of truth in the exaggeration that King John was one of the founders of the English navy. The plan, made in 1205, for the military organisation of the country is an even more impressive witness to the administrative unity of England: every group of nine knights was to equip a tenth; the population was to be formed into a vast sworn commune under a hierarchy of constables, who in shire and hundred, city and borough, were to enforce the obligation of every male of twelve years of age and upwards to defend his country.

The baronial movement, which led to the first political struggle in English history, was closely connected with the social development, the growing capacity for corporate self-discipline, which was the counterpart to the development in administrative unity and bureaucratic control. The rebellion of 1215 was separated from the rebellion of 1173 by over forty years of political experiment and social advance. Prelates, barons, lawyers, clerks, knights, and burgesses had behind them a record of concerted endeavour. They were capable of thinking intelligently and critically Beneath the rule of the royal court, of sheriffs and justices, in hall and chapter and cloister, in the courts of the bishop and the archdeacon, of shire, hundred, and manor, in the borough and the market, a self-reliant life was actively at work. The dominating issues of the reign have too often diverted attention from the organic developments in English society. The intensity of local and class interests breaks through

[1] *Rotuli finium*, p. 459; Brit. Mus. Addit. MS. 14252, f. 117 (EHR, XVII, 710).

the records of bishopric, abbey, and borough. The bishop disputes with his chapter, bishop and chapter with the neighbouring monasteries, the Benedictine with the Cistercian, and the orgy of passion is full of dialectic concerned with endless technicalities, involving constant reference to Rome. All parties were conscious of being bound up with a great legal system which they were helping to define; and the energy and purpose in the life common to them all were enshrined in the buildings—so intricate and beautiful in their austerity—which have survived to this day. The main part of Wells Cathedral, the choir of Lincoln, the western bays of the nave at Peterborough, the retrochoir of Chichester were built or finished in Richard's reign. When John died the galilee at Ely and the choir at Lichfield had been completed; and the masons were at work upon the transept and nave of Lincoln, the choirs of Fountains and Rochester, the west front of Peterborough, the retrochoirs of Winchester and Worcester, and the church of St Saviour's, Southwark. Around some of these and other marvels in stone, the burgesses were adjusting their secular affairs; for the reign of John marks the climax of the vigorous municipal movement of the twelfth century. He granted more than seventy known charters to from fifty to sixty boroughs. These charters were not extorted by the pressure of new circumstances; the great majority of them confirm or develop existing privileges and date from the early years of his reign—nine from 1199, eighteen from 1200, fourteen from 1201, six from 1204, eight from 1205. In Normandy and Aquitaine his generosity had a political motive, in England it was probably bought by the large sums which, as the oblate rolls shew, he received in return. In our municipal history the foundation of Liverpool is his only act of distinction, just as the foundation of Beaulieu was his main achievement as a patron of monasteries. The absence of a royal policy, as indeed of a determined communal movement, increases the significance of the boroughs in the quiet economic development of England. The boroughs were gradually and in very various degrees acquiring certain notes or characteristics which distinguished them from other groups or areas; all had tenurial privileges, many had the right to appoint their own officials, control their courts, and, through a gild merchant, protect their trade. John's charter to Dunwich refers to the representation of the borough by twelve men before the justices—a privilege which every sheriff could feel to be distinctive. The phrase "free borough" (*liber burgus*) which is common in charters of this reign, was used as a convenient and elastic formula by which a place was recognised to possess a status different from that of a manor but which did not "tie the grantee to a particular model." "Thus the connotation of 'free borough' varied from the privileges of London or Winchester to the mere burgage tenure of the humblest seignorial borough."[1] The arrangements for the defence of England in

[1] Tait, *Liber Burgus* in *Essays in Medieval History presented to Thomas Frederick Tout*, p. 93. Cf. the *Chronicle* of Jocelin of Brakelonde (ed. Camden

1205 shew how the borough was regarded as a type of 'commune' fitting into the structure of the whole community.

The interests of most of these small societies were doubtless insignificant. With the exception of London, they could exercise little, if any, pressure as separate bodies, and they had no opportunity of joint action, except on the few occasions on which the king summoned representatives of selected towns for some definite and fleeting purpose. Yet the significance of these centres of continuous and organised activity is very great. They were proud of their traditions, tenacious of their customs, able to bargain with their lords. The story of Abbot Samson's relations with his borough of Bury St Edmunds is not only a typical piece of municipal history; it is also a picture in miniature of efforts which were made in all classes and communities towards self-assertion and definite understandings. The insistence upon customary procedure, the definition of the competence in jurisdiction of the monastic cellarer and the borough reeve, the wrangles about reapsilver and other dues, the substitution of fixed payments for vexatious assessments, the charge that rich burgesses were favoured at the expense of the poor, the wise adjustments made by the abbot, help us to understand the dual character of English rule. At every turn the administration co-operated with local bodies; it extended the traditional system of the sworn inquiry, and trained knights and burgesses in the service of the whole body politic. The local juries summoned by the sheriff to give evidence on any matter upon which the justices might require local information, or to assess taxation or view expenditure, had very great public responsibility. They might be called upon by the Crown to justify their evidence, and if they were negligent they fell into the king's mercy. The practice of calling up knights from the shires to report, with authoritative testimony (*recordatio*), upon judicial proceedings in local courts, was firmly established at this time; and the non-existence of any clear line of division between juries in judicial and administrative matters made it easy to call upon local representatives for conference as well as for testimony. For example, it would be hard to draw any line of principle between the twelve burgesses who went to the justices on eyre and, let us say, the "duodecim de melioribus et discretioribus hominibus" of Bristol, whom King John summoned on one occasion to Marlborough to hear his commands[1]; and from this it was an easy step to a conference of representatives from various towns with a royal official on such business as the defence of the land. The employment of local people in public administration within their own areas had naturally gone much further. In 1194 Hubert Walter ordered the indirect election of knights or other law-worthy men who should report upon the escheats, wardships, and demesne of the Crown. The

Society), p. 73—"a tempore quo villa Sancti Aedmundi nomen et libertatem burgi accepit."

[1] *Rot. lit. claus.* I, 116 a, writ of 14 May 1211.

survey of wainages in 1198 was made by knights elected for the purpose. The Assize of Measures was executed by local wardens. The collection of a fifteenth on merchandise in 1205 was entrusted to six or seven of the more substantial men who were to be elected in each port. Among the writs which prepared the way for the great concentration of forces at Nottingham in September 1212, preliminary to the projected attack on Wales, there is a letter dated 18 August ordering each sheriff to summon all those who were in debt to the Jews to appear before the king, and also to appear himself with all haste "et adducas tecum sex de legalioribus et discretioribus militibus balliae tuae ad faciendum hoc quod eis dixerimus."[1] In the following year John summoned four men from each shire to discuss the affairs of the realm (*ad loquendum nobiscum de negotiis regni nostri*). The investigation into abuses which were denounced in the Great Charter was entrusted in each shire to twelve sworn knights, who were to be elected in the Shire Court; and, if civil war had not broken out, these local commissions would probably have been brought together, as similar bodies were in 1258 and subsequent years. In the light of all these instances of the practice of representation, the puzzling passage in Roger of Wendover's chronicle on the assembling of local juries at St Albans in 1213 loses much of its significance[2].

The gradual extension of the representative principle was a necessary stage in the development which led to the parliamentary system, for the peculiar tenacity of this system was due, not to an organisation which had many continental parallels, but to the fact that the knights and good men of the shires had already become inextricably involved in the government of England. The developments of the twelfth century had done much to prevent the formation in later times of a rigid system of privileged classes, mutually exclusive of each other. The distinctions between different classes of men were, indeed, recognised by English law, but England was not to contain clearly defined *estates*. The unity of English society, at least in its administrative capacity, explains the fact that, once the baronial opposition to John had been formed, its demands were more than a class manifesto.

The growth of trade had done something to strengthen the community of interests. Two clauses of the Great Charter (Caps. 35, 41) define important principles of commercial policy. One re-enacts an assize of 1197 which ordered that throughout the kingdom the same weights and the same measures of wine, ale, and corn should prevail, and that cloth should be woven of the same width; the other abolishes maltolts or new customs charged on merchandise and, repeating an order of the year 1200, gave all merchants, except those from lands at war with the king, the right of free entry and exit from the country. The Assize of Measures had always

[1] *Rot. lit. claus.* I, 132 a.

[2] For the controversy on this passage (*Roger of Wendover*, ed. Coxe, III, p. 261) see the Bibliography.

been difficult to enforce, and numerous letters of exemption had been sold. The policy of freedom to trade involved innumerable modifications in practice; each borough insisted upon its exclusive privileges or monopolies, each landholder would continue to exact the customary tolls, but the prosperity of both depended to an increasing degree upon the presence of the merchant class. London for a long time had had close connexions with the traders from Cologne and the Meuse valley, for through the Lorrainers they had the benefit of merchandise which came by way of Ratisbon from Constantinople, the market for gold and silver and precious stones. The relations of the South and East of England with the Low Countries and Germany had grown rapidly during the later years of the twelfth century. The men of Boston, Yarmouth, Lynn, Sandwich, and the southern ports exchanged wool, cheese, and tin for wine and cloth. The traders of Brabant came from Antwerp, Louvain, and Brussels, the Frisians from Emden and Stavoren; Saxon merchandise was imported from the Westphalian towns, or through Bremen by way of the river valleys of Brunswick. The men of Cologne, now a great city whose political sympathies were with the English kings and their nephew Otto of Brunswick, came through Utrecht or by the toll station at Geervliet at the mouth of the Meuse. Elsewhere the movement which involved England in the ecclesiastical life and political adventures of Europe had brought commercial relations, notably with Aquitaine, Portugal, and Lombardy. Two important measures taken by John, with the counsel and consent of the magnates, ten years before the Great Charter was granted, illustrate the growing appreciation of the value of these commercial ties[1]. In June 1204 he laid down rules for the conduct of trade between England and the lands of Philip Augustus. Although the bitterly resented conquests of Philip were hardly completed in Normandy, trade, except in food-stuffs, was by no means forbidden; but a small host of local elected officials was created under three commissioners to levy a fifteenth upon all merchandise carried to or from the lands subject to the French king. Six months later, in January 1205, another measure provided for the gradual withdrawal of the old coinage and the issue of new money. Jews, goldsmiths, and foreign traders were permitted to buy food and clothing with the old money, but were required to use the new in their main commercial dealings and when they arranged loans.

This study of English society during the reigns of Henry II's sons may now be completed by a short survey of the reign of King John in England. The outstanding events are the quarrel with the Church with its consequence, the interdict, and the struggle for the Charter.

Archbishop Hubert died in the middle of the night of 12–13 July 1205. His knowledge of the law and his past service in the highest positions in the State gave him a personal authority which, at any rate in the ad-

[1] *Rot. lit. pat.* 42–3, 54 b.

ministration of every day, exceeded that of John himself; and his influence upon policy was revealed in a very puzzling way during the last months of his life. In the spring of 1205, while the king was collecting a great host at Portsmouth and the fate of Rouen and the last Norman strongholds was still undecided, the archbishop had intervened to interrupt negotiations between the King of France and John's envoys, William the Marshal and the royal clerk, Hugh of Wells, who kept the great seal. The Marshal's biographer interpreted this act as a treacherous intrusion by a jealous man; yet, if the Coggeshall chronicler was rightly informed, the Marshal and the archbishop joined shortly afterwards in dissuading the king from his intended campaign in Poitou. Whatever manoeuvres lay behind these actions, it is significant that the archbishop was still able to get his way, and it is still more significant that he seems to have insisted, as archbishop or chancellor or in both capacities, on his right to be consulted and to add his authorisation to important negotiations. It is unlikely that he acted merely on his own behalf; we may perhaps read in this intervention by a dying man an attempt to define a view which, in the next reign, was to become a constitutional principle of the baronial party: namely, the responsibility of the chancellor to the king and his advisers for the use of the great seal which authorises royal acts.

However this may be, the king was greatly relieved by the archbishop's death. He was free to press on his grandiose schemes, the first of which was the abortive French campaign which occupied him during the summer and autumn of 1206. In 1207 he got rid of his half-brother Geoffrey, Archbishop of York, who had resisted the collection of the thirteenth from tenants of the Church[1]. The secular administration of the great northern see was, like that of so many other sees in this reign, placed under the control of royal officials. King Richard is said, during a dispute with Hugh of Lincoln in the last year of his reign, to have raved against the timid scrupulosity of the English officials and to have threatened to send his mercenary Mercadier to deal with the stiffnecked saint. John was now in a position to put his brother's hot speech into cold practice.

The opportunity was improved by the quarrel with Rome. The king set his mind, Roger of Wendover informs us, on having as archbishop a man who had been trained in the royal service under his eye and was familiar with his affairs (*magna sibi familiaritate conjunctum...secretorum suorum conscium*). From his point of view the obvious man was the Bishop of Norwich, John de Grey, whom John persuaded the monks of Christ Church, Canterbury, to elect in December 1205. But the situation was complicated by two very important facts. In the first place every election to the archbishopric, at least since 1162, had raised the question of the fit and customary electorate. The monks had persistently refused to allow the co-operation of the bishops of the southern province; the

[1] The bishops as a rule compounded by granting *dona*, and the religious paid fines. See Mitchell, *Studies in Taxation under John and Henry III*, p. 89.

bishops had insisted upon their right to a voice in the election. In order to steal a march upon them, some of the monks, in the night when Archbishop Hubert died, had hurriedly and, so it was decided afterwards, uncanonically elected their sub-prior, Reginald, and had sent him off to Rome to receive the pallium. Reginald could not keep the occasion of his journey secret, and the bishops had discovered it. The disputes and appeals to Rome which ensued added significance to the second complicating fact—the well-known attitude of Pope Innocent III. Innocent, frequently and persistently, tried to supervise the election of bishops in Normandy and England, in order to bring them into conformity with the decrees of the Lateran Council of 1179[1]. His sagacious decision in a difficult case in 1199–1200, when Mauger, Bishop of Worcester, a good man of illegitimate birth, had been chosen, was later to be included in the *Corpus Iuris Canonici* (the decretal *Innotuit nobis olim*). He detested the delays in appointment, and the method, still generally adopted, of election by representatives of the chapter in the king's chamber; and he had seized any chance of submitting the process in particular elections to the test of the canons. Hitherto, a breach between Pope and king or between Pope and clergy had been avoided; but the situation created by the double election of Reginald and John de Grey raised fundamental issues. The validity of the recent elections and the case between the bishops and the monks were clearly matters for decision at Rome, and, after Innocent had quashed the second election, the king consented to a fresh election before the Pope by sixteen accredited electors from the monastic chapter. He promised to abide by the election of any Englishman, but privately extorted an oath from the majority of the monks that they would again choose John de Grey. In December the various parties—proctors of king and bishops, with the representatives from Canterbury—urged their various causes, and Innocent in full consistory decided that the suffragans had no right to interfere in the election of an archbishop, but also that the sub-prior's election was, like John de Grey's, invalid. He brushed aside the oath extorted by the king, and called their attention to the claims of the Englishman Stephen Langton, a cardinal who had won fame as a scholar at Paris. The electors, with one exception, were persuaded, and King John must have heard of Langton's election early in January 1207, three or four weeks after his return from Poitou.

John was a master in dilatory negotiations, and the great interdict was not published by the three bishops, London, Ely, and Worcester, to whom Innocent had entrusted the conduct of the affair, until 24 March 1208. In spite of royal opposition Langton had been consecrated by the Pope at Viterbo in June 1207. John had retaliated by refusing to receive him and by ejecting the monks of Christ Church. Proposals for a settlement came to a head in January 1208, when the king informed the three bishops that he was ready to come to terms, "saving his royal rights and liberties.'

[1] See the essays of Gutschow and Packard, mentioned in the Bibliography.

On 12 March, in the presence of all the existing bishops, he met Simon Langton, the archbishop's brother, at Winchester. Simon, speaking from instructions, insisted upon full and absolute obedience. John's fury broke loose, and the negotiations ended abruptly. He immediately proceeded to appoint royal bailiffs for the administration of the dioceses. The Bishop of London and his two colleagues published the interdict, and with one or two other bishops, fled from the country.

The view which the archbishop took of the quarrel is illuminating. In a letter addressed to the English he argued the case, not so much as a papalist, but rather as an exponent of feudal custom in the light of those high principles of law to which all human law should conform. John's position was not so strong as Henry II's had been, for Christendom, which was now firmly united under Innocent III, was divided in the days of Alexander III. By putting himself against the will of the Church, canonically expressed, by refusing to honour his own promises, John was imposing upon his vassals an obligation which made them traitors to the supreme lord, the King of Kings, God himself. Even a slave is not bound to his lord in everything (*secundum enim leges humanas in atrocioribus etiam servus domino non tenetur*). And Langton was writing to free men, to men who understood the legal and moral implications of lordship. Any vassal who broke his obligations to the king at the will or command of inferior lords was regarded as a traitor, for he had done homage to his lord "salva fide domini regis." John had placed his vassals exactly in this position, for they owed him obedience "salva fide Domini superioris, scilicet Regis aeterni." The time was to come when the archbishop would be ready to maintain his doctrine of feudal freedom and feudal responsibility against the Pope himself. The king's attitude, on the other hand, was frankly conservative and separatist. He undoubtedly reflected the views of administrators who thought of English custom in non-feudal terms, and had breathed that historical atmosphere which was so prevalent in the court of Henry II. It is curious to find him appealing to English practice in the reign of Edward the Confessor, and linking the story of St Wulfstan's appointment to the bishopric of Worcester with the argument that English prelates were by custom elected in the royal Chamber[1]. We know that he had men about him who were ready to argue on behalf of royal rights against the claims of the Papacy in the manner of the Anonymous of York a century earlier[2]. That John of all people should compare himself to the Confessor and take St Wulfstan, to whose protection at Worcester he was later to submit his body for burial, as a patron saint is sufficiently strange. The fact helps us to understand the mood of men like Geoffrey Fitz Peter and Hubert de Burgh, and to realise in some degree the influences under which Henry III, the devotee of Edward the Confessor, passed his childhood.

[1] *Annales Monastici* I, pp. 211–213.

[2] See Wendover on Alexander the Mason (ed. Coxe, III, pp. 229, 230).

The years of the great interdict were years of demoralisation, not because the king did not have the general will behind him, but because he gradually lost all sense of restraint in a situation which, however men might endure it, was fraught with daily inconvenience and humiliation and involved a continuous strain upon the conscience. The administration, which was probably more efficient at this time than it had ever been, found little difficulty in coping with the actual facts. The interdict was an opportunity no less than a menace, and even before it was pronounced John's plans were ready. The policy adopted was the seizure into the king's hands of all ecclesiastical property, spiritualities as well as temporalities. Wardens, generally the sheriffs, were appointed in each shire. The amount of extra work which had to be done in the offices of local administrators must have been severe, and it was fortunate that important reforms in the presentation of accounts had recently been made by the Exchequer. Prelates, religious houses, and parish clergy were alike submitted to this régime and were provided with a subsistence allowance (*estuvium*) in the performance of their attenuated duties. It appears that in each parish this allowance was made under the supervision of four lawful men[1]. The revenues, with this deduction, were destined for the royal treasury, at any rate so far as they came from churches on the king's demesne. Many barons received royal permission to assume the control of the monastic houses and churches on their estates and to have the rents drawn by clerks from their domain. The Earl of Norfolk, for example, got the custody of the rents and property of churches in his gift, and of the abbots of his fief, "si alicuius crociam habent de dono suo." To what extent custody involved the right to retain the proceeds in such cases requires investigation. An estimate of the loss suffered by the clergy during the next five years is impossible, for there was inevitably much extortion and destruction of property; but the Exchequer admitted that John had received £105,000, and the king himself was prepared to compound the sums due in compensation at 100,000 marks. Some of the bishops got fairly large payments in 1213 and 1214 by way of compensation; the clergy as a whole had to write off most of their loss. Finally, the king extorted from the clergy charters of quit-claim of his extortions[2].

Such was the general character of John's reply to the interdict. The plan was not observed universally, for modifications or exemptions were numerous. The author of the *Life* of St Hugh of Lincoln, referring to a certain Reymund, afterwards Archdeacon of Leicester, breaks off his narrative to observe that, in the days of the interdict, Reymund was one

[1] See letters to H. de Nevill in *Rotuli litt. claus.* I, 109 b. This goes far to explain the summons to St Albans in 1213 (*Roger of Wendover,* ed. Coxe, III, p. 261).

[2] The *Misae* Roll of his fourteenth year contains a reference to the purchase of two coffers to contain these charters. Cole, *Documents illustrative of English history in the thirteenth and fourteenth centuries* (1844), p. 242. The charters were of course invalidated, but John continued to extract quit-claims as late as 1215 (e.g. *Rot. litt. pat.* p. 140 b).

of the few "ecclesiarum rectores" who refused to reach an accommodation with the king. Certainly it was to the interest of any ecclesiastic, at a time when, in spite of a proclamation of April 1208, churchmen were regarded as almost outside the law and were liable to suffer personal indignity, violence, and loss, to pay something in return for protection and the control of his property. Acquiescence on the part of the lower clergy was inevitable, and for six years Englishmen had all around them a Church which did not function, closed buildings, unused cemeteries, silent bells, disconsolate dignitaries, and parsons whose only duties were the baptism of infants in private houses or the celebration of mass for the dying. If they had bought control of their estates, they would suffer from the heavy tallage of 1210; if they had not, they lived on pittances provided by the wardens—royal officials, their landlords, or a group of their own parishioners. The orders of regular clergy, if they obeyed the papal decree, were debarred from the spiritual exercises in choir which were a necessary counterpart to their daily tasks and private devotions. The Cistercian monks, it is true, acted for some time in disregard of the papal injunctions, and in obedience to the Abbot of Cîteaux continued their services on the ground that no authentic copies of the papal bull had reached the Order; but they were compelled to submit, and, on the other hand, though they got control of their lands[1], they were pillaged unmercifully by the king, notably after their refusal to finance his expedition to Ireland in 1210.

It would be tedious to analyse the negotiations which continued at intervals before John's definite promise of submission in May 1213. Peace hovered on the horizon in October 1209, but its fugitive appearance was followed by the personal excommunication of the king. From this time all leadership of the Church in England disappeared. John could rely on only two bishops, his friends Peter des Roches, of Winchester, and John de Grey, of Norwich. His servants, the two brothers Jocelin and Hugh of Wells, the one now Bishop of Wells, the other of Lincoln, withdrew after the act of excommunication. Another ally, Philip, Bishop of Durham, had died in 1208. As the Bishop of Norwich was justiciar in Ireland from 1209 to 1213, the king had the Bishop of Winchester alone of all the bishops by his side during these years, "ad computandum impiger, piger ad evangelium." The sees of Lichfield, Exeter, and Chichester were vacant; Archbishop Geoffrey of York was already in exile and died in 1212. The rest had joined Stephen Langton and, with the exception of the Bishop of Worcester, who died in exile, returned with him. Many of the great abbeys by this time were also without a head, and some, like Waverley, had been deserted by brethren unable to hold on any longer. Unless agreement were reached, dissolution threatened the ecclesiastical system. The credit of averting this disaster lay with the papal legate, Pandulf, a skilful exponent of the directions of the bold and clear-sighted

[1] This was arranged during a visit of John to Waverley in April 1208.

Pope Innocent. Experience shewed that personal discussion with John, though it was not shirked, was futile; but early in 1213 the political situation abroad—the embarrassment of John's allies, Otto IV of Brunswick and Raymond VI of Toulouse, and the alliance between Innocent and Philip Augustus—gave the Pope his opportunity. John had to decide between submission to the Church and a life and death struggle against a French invasion, with a disheartened and restless people behind him. He was wise enough to choose the former alternative.

The situation which developed during the next three years was a strange and paradoxical one. In the spring of 1213 John had been an excommunicate, his kingdom declared forfeit by the Pope, his foreign enemies ready to attack him with the privileges of crusaders. He had posed as the champion of ancient English customs against alien interference in Church and State. His justiciar and the officers of his administration were on his side, and he had extracted promises of support from his people, first at Marlborough in September 1209, when all freemen were ordered to swear fealty, and again in 1212–13, when the magnates of England and Ireland approved of his resistance to the Pope[1]. Three years later, in the spring of 1216, he was fighting as a vassal of the Pope, as a crusader protected by his vows, against excommunicated rebels backed by the foreign power whom Innocent had used against him in 1213. The archbishop, whose election had caused all the trouble before 1213, was now suspended from his office because he had failed to support the papal policy against the rebels. The clergy who had suffered in the days of the interdict for the cause of ecclesiastical law and unity now saw their local liberties threatened by the encroachments of papal emissaries working hand-in-glove with John.

The attitude of Innocent is not hard to explain. He had got his way and had reconciled an erring son to the Church. The time had come for peace, not for wrangling about details. The cardinal-legate Nicholas was sent to measure justice with prudence. When the bishops grumbled that the terms arranged in a series of councils for the repayment of their losses (*ablata*) were neither adequate nor properly guaranteed, Innocent doubtless reflected that he had not been fighting on their behalf so much as for principles which were now assured. The archbishop and his colleagues, faced with the task of setting their dioceses in order, naturally took a more insular view, and in any case the archbishop's belief in papal authority was bound up with a belief in law and custom which he could not but interpret, as no Pope or legate was able to do, in the light of local tradition. The successful assertion of the Pope's *plenitudo potestatis* saved the unity of the Church, but it put the local clergy in that equivocal position from which they were at last violently extricated by King Henry VIII. The later history of Archbishop Stephen is the first and perhaps the best example. The scholar, cardinal, persecuted prelate were merged in the

[1] Norgate, *John Lackland*, pp. 172–3.

English primate, the chief adviser of the Crown. As such he found that duty and inclination led him to support, at the risk of papal disapproval, the vassals against their lord. Just as a few years earlier he had exhorted them to place their allegiance to the Lord of Lords above their allegiance to the king, so now he exhorts the king to remember that their loyalty to him is only a conditional loyalty.

To all appearance John was in a very strong position. He had got large sums from the property of the Church, from tallages and scutages; the Exchequer was working smoothly and had recently carried through its great inquiry of 1212–13. He had fierce, able, well-paid mercenaries at his service, the ports and shipping had been organised by William of Wrotham, the feudal levies had not been allowed to forget their military duties. During the interdict expeditions had been led against Wales and Ireland and had threatened Scotland.

With Scotland John's relations had been friendly. William the Lion did homage to him at Lincoln in 1200 and was able by a series of concessions to avert invasion in 1209. He had made a show of claiming the three northern counties of England, but was really concerned to keep his frontiers intact. In 1209 a castle was rising at Tweedmouth to threaten Berwick, and after abortive negotiations John gathered a host with which to enforce a claim to the possession of three castles on the borders. In August William made peace at Norham. He agreed to pay 13,000 marks by instalments—a promise on the whole faithfully performed—to give hostages, send his two daughters to John who was to have the feudal right of finding husbands for them, and to authorise his young son Alexander to take an oath of fealty for the disputed castles. In return the fortifications at Tweedmouth were abandoned. The Scottish King, indeed, stood to gain by an English alliance. He was a feudal lord, hard-pressed at times by native pretenders and hemmed in by the Norse Kings of the Isles. It was better to have the English King at his back, even at the cost of vassalage, than to face his displeasure. So William bought John's "benevolence" in 1209 and again in 1212. In this latter year mercenaries from the south helped him against the rising of Guthred son of MacWilliam, while on his side King William surrendered to John the right of arranging Alexander's marriage. The young man, a small red-haired lad of attractive bearing, was knighted by the English king. His sisters and his father's hostages, some of whom were sons of great English barons in the north, remained in John's keeping, and in the same year John received the homage of Reginald, King of the Isles.

Alexander, "the little red fox," as John later called him, was to cause trouble after he became king, when some of the northern barons rose in rebellion; but in the meanwhile the understanding between the two countries was helpful. Indeed William is said to have warned John of the treachery around him while he was collecting a large host at Northampton for an attack upon Wales (September 1212). This expedition, for which very extensive preparations had been made, was intended to put an end to the restless activity of Llywelyn ap Iorwerth, the king of Snowdonia. Fleets were sent along the Welsh coasts from Bristol and Chester and the advance by land was to start from the latter place. The adventure was hurriedly abandoned, the forces summoned from England, Ireland, and Galloway had to return; but Llywelyn was not in a position to press his advantage. He was John's man, for he had done him homage in 1209, his wife was John's illegitimate daughter, his son was a hostage, and John had shewn that he was quite ruthless in the execution of hostages and prisoners. Moreover Llywelyn's alliance with the other princes of Wales was not secure, and the English garrisons in the castles of Deganwy and Rhuddlan were on the watch, while the well-organised palatinate of Earl Ranulf of Chester lay behind. It was in John's reign, as we may learn from numerous entries on the chancery rolls, that the cordon, which his grandson was to draw tight, was first placed around the lairs of the Welsh princes.

John's attitude to the Welsh princes was in part dictated by his position as a great Marcher lord, for during the greater part of his reign he had direct control of the Gloucester inheritance. Similarly his relations with Scotland were influenced by the complex of feudal ties which deprived the border between England and Scotland of most of its reality. His Irish policy was even more directly the outcome of feudal problems, and reacted upon his position in England[1]. John de Courcy, Earl of Ulster, whom he overthrew with the help of the Lacys in 1205, was a brother-in-law of Reginald, King of the Isles. Hugh de Lacy, the next earl, and Walter de Lacy, Earl of Meath, had important English connexions, and were overthrown in their turn with the aid of the lords of Galloway and Carrick. Their downfall was mainly the result of their understanding with William de Braiose, the lord of Gower in South Wales and of the great honour of Limerick. It was natural for men with such vast opportunities and privileges to regard themselves as immune from those trammels by which they and their peers were bound in England, yet, if they were unchecked, they were natural centres of intrigue with the king's enemies. William the Marshal himself, who esteemed loyalty as the chief virtue, found it hard to submit his privileges as lord of Leinster to the interference of the royal justiciar, just as he had found it hard to accept John's decision that he must choose between himself and the King of France, and not try to serve both. The results of John's imposing and drastic intervention in 1210 were felt at once in England. The Lacys had fallen, William de Braiose was a fugitive, the Angevin administration had been effectively imposed upon the Anglo-Irish lords, and the native Irish rulers had for the time been fitted into the system of vassal relations. During the next few years John could rely upon the support of his men in Ireland. They backed him in his resistance to the Pope, and they sent a strong force under their justiciar, the Bishop of Norwich, to swell the host which gathered on

[1] For its importance in Irish history, see *infra*, Vol. VII.

Barham Down to protect England against France in the spring of 1213.

It must indeed have seemed to John, as it seemed to contemporaries, that during these years no man dared withstand him. He had received the homage of princes throughout the British Isles. And when he in his turn submitted himself to Rome and knew that the danger of French invasion had passed, he might well renew the conflict across the Channel with confidence. The very difficulties of his foreign friends, of which the Pope had taken advantage, now gave him new prestige, for he could rely on their steady support in his stand against the growing might of Philip Augustus. During the last few months he had taken into his pay practically all the lords and very many knights in the Low Countries, including the Count of Flanders, and the Count of Boulogne, who with Hugh de Boves, an adventurer from Picardy, acted as his agent[1]. He was in close touch with some of his old Poitevin vassals, with the Kings of Aragon and Portugal, and especially with his relative Raymond VI of Toulouse. He had learned how to play upon the sympathies of the towns of Flanders and the Rhineland. In short he built up a coalition which all who felt themselves to be in danger from France or who, like John's nephew, the Emperor Otto IV, realised that France was the main obstacle in their path, could not but join. Just before Whitsuntide 1213, an English fleet surprised and destroyed Philip's ships in the Flemish harbour at Damme. Early in the following year, the king was ready to put the elaborate plans of the coalition into effect. His northern allies struck their blow through Flanders, while he moved northwards from La Rochelle. As he marched towards the Loire, his friends and vassals around him, he played not with his own destinies alone but with those of Western Europe. No member of his house, not even the great Richard himself, had ever cut such a figure in the world.

As is well known, John came back to England in October foiled and disappointed. His own campaign had been inglorious, and in July, away to the north-east, his rival had scattered his allies at Bouvines. A year later he was fighting for his kingdom against the most terrible rebellion that any King of England had yet had to face.

The disasters which began in France and continued after his return were due in large measure to John's irresponsible optimism in 1213. We have seen him, apparently at the height of his power, launching out into great schemes. We have seen him, a few months earlier, a man suddenly conscious of realities, making a surrender to the Pope as complete as his defiance had been. Both confidence and despair were rooted in the experiences of the interdict and excommunication; and the annalists who grudgingly recognised his power testify to the facts which

[1] The chief text is the *Misae* Roll, 14 John, in Cole, *Illustrative Documents*. The details are skilfully discussed by Henri Malo, *Un grand feudataire, Renaud de Dammartin, et la coalition de Bouvines* (Paris, 1898), chap. IX. See *infra*, chap. IX.

were undermining it. But John rarely saw the writing on the wall, and, when he did see it, he immediately forgot it.

The Great Charter is a carefully drawn document, and a careful examination of the events of the years 1213 to 1215 is required if its various parts are to be given their due significance. In its general form and in its insistence upon the return to good customs, it marks the culmination of the policy which the archbishop had tried to impose upon John ever since his return. The association of a large body of barons with this policy was due to John's aggression after the refusal of many to follow him abroad and to pay the scutage demanded on his return. The comprehensive nature of the baronial demands, the result of their association with Langton, reflected that change in the position of the baronage which has already been discussed. The guarantees demanded from John, including the expulsion of the mercenaries and the imposition of a controlling body of twenty-five, were a later development, fostered by distrust and the heat of dissension.

It is clear that the archbishop's view of the price which John had to pay for reconciliation to the Church was administrative reform. Since his excommunication the king had been very powerful, and his ministers very efficient, but they had borne very hardly on the people. Suspicion, to which the exaction of hostages from so many of the royal vassals bore witness, had bred recklessness and tyranny. The enormous weight attached to the prophecies and sermons of the hermit Peter of Wakefield in 1212 shews that king and people were nervously excited. It is significant that John began early in 1213 to issue commissions of inquiry into the misdeeds of local officials; and, before the archbishop absolved him at Winchester in July, he made him swear to bring back the good laws of his predecessors, especially those of the Confessor, abolish bad laws, do justice to all men according to the judgment of his Court, and render to every man his rights. In the following month, at St Albans, came a still more explicit anticipation of the Charter. If Wendover's narrative can be trusted, the proceedings at this council were very significant. The king was absent on an abortive cruise which, if his men had followed him, he had intended to be the beginning of his Poitevin campaign. The justiciar, with the Bishop of Winchester, the primate, and bishops and magnates, declared in the king's name that the laws of Henry I should be observed and bad laws be done away; and sheriffs, foresters, and other royal officials were commanded to cease from all injuries and extortion. If Geoffrey Fitz Peter was really acting in conjunction with the hated archbishop in forcing a policy of reform, one can well understand that his death in October was a relief to the king. The justiciar had supported John well, but he must have seen much to justify his disapproval. The return of the archbishop meant a return to the normal as it was in the time of Hubert Walter, when justiciar and archbishop worked together as chief advisers to the Crown. A story current later at St Albans said that John, when he heard of Geoffrey's death, grimly remarked: "Let him go to greet Hubert Walter in hell." In the meanwhile the archbishop worked away steadily on earth. At the end of August he faced the king's fury and dissuaded him from proceeding "vi et armis" against the men who had refused to follow him abroad. They were to be summoned to trial according to law in the King's Court. As we hear no more of this quarrel for the time being, it is probable that an understanding was reached on the issue of foreign service and legal procedure[1]. It was at this time, during a council at St Paul's, that the archbishop is said to have produced Henry I's Charter of Liberties and to have explained privately to some of the barons the lines upon which they should proceed.

At all events John was able to take a considerable force to Poitou. It comprised many barons and knights, as well as Welsh mercenaries, and, although some of the great men and practically all the barons north of the Humber failed to appear, it was by no means unrepresentative of English feudalism. During the king's absence the Bishop of Winchester, with the archbishop as chief counsellor, presided over the administration. The legate arranged a settlement about compensation due to the Church, the interdict was removed, and, shortly after his return, John formally ratified his promise to allow canonical elections (21 November 1214). But he was now discredited by military failure, and the baronial party which desired to see a comprehensive settlement of abuses and disputed questions had been formed. The demand, made in the summer, for a scutage of three marks on the knight's fee, a tax from which only those who had served in the expedition could claim exemption, had brought matters to a head. The Exchequer was able to collect only about one-fifth of the payments due[2]. Early in November the opposition formed a conspiracy at Bury St Edmunds. They took their stand on Henry I's Charter and swore to force the king, if necessary by arms, to observe the promises which he had made. The terms of their resolution shew that they deliberately associated themselves with the policy upon which the archbishop had acted since he absolved John in the summer of 1213. Early in January they appeared at court in the New Temple and called on John to fulfil the oath which he had sworn at Winchester.

John had one characteristic in common with better men—he could be most alert in times of crisis. He staved off the baronial demand by pledging himself, with the archbishop, the Bishop of Ely, and William the Marshal as sureties, to give satisfaction at Easter. He used the

[1] The "Unknown Charter of Liberties" (see the Bibliography) may quite well record such an understanding. Henry I's Charter is copied out and followed by a list of royal concessions on the very points at issue during July and August. It includes a provision about foreign service not dealt with in any other document.

[2] See especially S. K. Mitchell, *Studies in Taxation under John and Henry III*, pp. 109–118.

breathing space to secure his position. He began a campaign of propaganda in the shires, ordered a renewal of the oath of allegiance, summoned aid from Ireland and Poitou, and took the last step in self-protection by assuming the cross. Both sides set out their position before the Pope, who, while urging John to give lawful satisfaction, admonished the barons for their conspiracies and contumacy and ordered them to pay the scutage. The barons were forced into the open and in Easter week, instead of seeking the royal promises again, came together in force at Stamford.

It was the fashion at the time to describe the rebels as the Northerners. This was nothing more than a recognition of the fact that the original nucleus of resistance was among the barons across the Humber, notably in Yorkshire, who had refused foreign service and the payment of scutage. The centre of the opposition was in reality Essex and East Anglia. The North was equally divided and the northerners owed much of their strength to their understanding with the new King of Scots, the young Alexander II. The temporary prominence of Eustace de Vescy was due to the fact that he had been associated with Robert Fitz Walter in the plot which had so disturbed John in 1212. The two barons had fled and their return and restoration to their lands had been part of the terms imposed on John by the Pope. Robert Fitz Walter was a very powerful man. Lord of Dunmow in Essex, and of Baynard Castle, outside London wall on the river to the west of the city, he was in right of his wife in possession of the lands, also mainly in Essex, of the house of Valognes. It has been reckoned that his service must have amounted to a hundred knights[1]. There was no greater man in the south-east of England, and his position gave him peculiar significance in London. He had been a strenuous, if at times unsuccessful and suspected, servant of John, and had fought for him in Normandy along with Saer de Quincy, lord of Leuchars in Fife, and husband of one of the heiresses of the house of Leicester. Saer de Quincy, in order that his position in England might be duly recognised, had been invested by the king with the title Earl of Winchester. About these two men the rebellious barons of the south-east were grouped. The adhesion of the Clares to the party gave it a dignity and following which it could hardly have maintained without them. Richard, Earl of Clare and Hertford, had entered by inheritance upon the English lands of the families of Giffard and Saint-Hilaire. In right of his wife, one of the Gloucester co-heiresses, he had expectations which were fulfilled when in 1217 his son Gilbert became Earl of Gloucester as well as of Hertford. His kindred were to be found throughout the higher baronage, and it may well have been the influence of kinship which brought the young William the Marshal to desert his father and join the rebels. The party were strengthened also by the adhesion of the Earls of Norfolk and Hereford, of Fulk Fitz Warin and

[1] Round, J.H. in EHR, XIX, pp. 709–710.

John Fitz Alan from Shropshire, William Malet from Somerset and, after some hesitation, William d'Aubigny, the powerful lord of Belvoir in the Midlands.

It is impossible to estimate the motives which inspired these men. That there were causes of cohesion due to kinship, neighbourhood, and the memories of outrage and injustice is clear. Some of the younger men had suffered from the king's greed and caprice when they entered upon their inheritance. Others had been wronged by interference with their domestic peace, and doubtless many bitter recollections, unknown to a later age, were stirred by incidents which seem colourless or trivial as they are recorded on the rolls of Chancery and Exchequer. We do not know, for example, the dark story which lay behind the enmity of the Earl of Essex, the son of Geoffrey Fitz Peter; but we do know that his first wife had been the daughter of Robert Fitz Walter and that Robert had complained of the king's attentions to her; and we know that in 1214 the Earl had been compelled to pay or promise an enormous fine on his marriage, possibly an enforced marriage, with John's discarded wife, Isabella of Gloucester. It is certain, moreover, that the cruel vendetta which John had waged against the family of his old friend William de Braiose had moved the English to indignation. William was lord of Bramber in Sussex, of Totnes and Barnstaple in the west country, of Gower, Radnor, and Brecon in South Wales, of Limerick in Ireland. His fall in 1210 was attributed by the king to a refusal to pay a debt, and was glossed over by the royal council; but it was almost certainly due to his and his wife's knowledge of the fate of Arthur of Brittany. The story was beginning to leak out. William had to flee and his wife and heir, captured during the Irish campaign, were starved to death in Windsor Castle. After this no man who incurred John's hostility could feel safe.

Such was the composition of the baronial party which met at Stamford in the Easter week of 1215. The king was prevailed upon to ask for the demands of the insurgents in writing. When the archbishop and the Marshal brought the document to John, he refused the conditions with indignation. "Why not ask for my kingdom?" Thereupon the rebels formally renounced their homage and chose as their leader, "Marshal of the army of God and Holy Church," Robert Fitz Walter. On 9 May John offered arbitration by four men from each side with the Pope as supreme arbitrator, and repeated his former undertakings to proceed against no one except in accordance with the law of the land and the judgment of his peers in the royal court—an anticipation of a famous clause inserted in a more general form in the Charter (c. 39). But the barons were rapidly gaining control of the home counties, and although John had some success in the West, notably at Exeter, he had to submit to meet them at Staines with a view to a formal treaty of peace.

On 17 May the baronial forces had entered London. The great city had been steadily favoured and fleeced by the king since in 1191 he had made friends with its leading citizens and encouraged it to form itself into a commune. The commune, in any technical sense of the word, had not lasted, but during the reigns of Richard and his brother the city had thriven. It was now ruled by a mayor—John's last attempt to placate it shortly before its rebellion had taken the form of a charter in which he recognised its right to elect this official every year—it appointed its own sheriffs and collected its own rates and taxes. Its chief court was the husting, composed of the mayor, the elected aldermen of the wards, and the "good men" or barons of London who sat with them on the four benches. On two occasions, once under the leadership of William Fitz Osbert in 1194 and again in 1205–6, the lesser citizens had tried to overthrow the civic aristocracy which governed, or, as they said, misgoverned them, and on the latter occasion the king had sent a special commission to hear Crown pleas and to supervise a reconstitution of the council. From this time the governing body, which held the Hustings Court and had charge of the financial administration, consisted of the mayor and twenty-four sworn councillors elected by the community[1]. The duties of watch and ward and the rules for the collection of rates and tallages were about this time carefully defined, and a strong sense of corporate life prevailed throughout the sokes and parishes, and in the artisan quarters of the city. Progress naturally produced the desire for greater freedom for more far-reaching reforms which would restrain the king's habit of demanding heavy tallages and would distribute power within the city more generally. The Londoners wanted more control of the river, security against Jews and foreign merchants, reforms in the customs and exchange. They wanted the mayor to be elected, not by the ruling class, but in the folk-moot which was fast becoming obsolete. Robert Fitz Walter, who, as lord of Baynard's castle, bore the title of "signifer et procurator" of the city, saw his chance. If any were hostile they were unheard. The barons occupied the city and proceeded to strengthen the walls. When they marched up the valley of the Thames to meet the king, they had the mayor of London with them.

The real history of the Great Charter, which was drafted and redrafted during the discussions at Runnymede, belongs to a later age. That as a whole it reflected the best and most stable feeling of Englishmen—of the moderate barons, the bishops, and the trained administrators—is clear from the fact that in its revised form it was issued after John's death by the legate, William the Marshal, Hubert de Burgh, and other royalists. In the form given to it in 1225 it was regarded as a definite settlement of the law which regulated the relations between the Crown and the vassals, and the administration of justice and finance. In this

[1] Unless, as Miss Bateson thought, this body was a reconstituted body of aldermen.

form, much of it was old, some a mere restatement of administrative policy[1], adjustments and reforms disputed by none in local and judicial administration, and reaffirmations, suited to the time, of feudal custom. Since the days of Hubert Walter royal prerogative could not be synonymous, in any healthy mind, with arbitrary rule. The acceptance of the Charter had been urged upon John by the archbishop and by his more responsible advisers, and from this point of view it was in fact an elaboration of the oath taken by John in 1213 at Winchester; just as the oath was an elaboration of promises which he had declared at his accession. Even the clause which forbade the tendency to undermine the judicial immunities of private courts by frequent use of the writ *praecipe* was not so much an act of violent reaction extorted by a self-seeking baronage as an attempt to strike the balance between traditional rights and the encroachments of the Curia Regis. What wrecked the settlement from the outset was the rising temper of the king on the one hand, and of the rebels—many of whom were young and inexperienced men or ambitious *frondeurs*—on the other. Robert Fitz Walter and his companions had adopted in the name of God and the Church the programme which the archbishop had originally outlined for them, but they had no intention of following ecclesiastical guidance when power was once in their hands. The shrewd observers, such as the author of the so-called *Histoire des ducs de Normandie*, who saw in the struggle a fight for franchises and power, or who, like the Marshal's biographer, dismissed it tersely as an act of folly, took a very natural view; but they were thinking of the men, not of the document. Until John was dead and passion had cooled and the opportunity for enjoying the sweets of power and revenge had gone, the only clauses of the Charter which mattered were those which transferred the control of affairs to the barons themselves.

For a while John had to wait on events. He did his part, and issued the necessary orders for the investigation of local abuses with the aid of twelve knights from each shire, and for changing local officials. He had protested that his feudal lord, the Pope, must have a say in the matter, and he saw to it that Innocent got his version of affairs. He was a crusader under the protection of the Church, and, so long as he could send messages abroad, he could be sure of buying support from his friends on the continent. He was powerless for the time, and ill in body, but he could carry his oath lightly. Everything indeed depended upon the way in which the barons, and especially the body of twenty-five who were chosen to protect the settlement and see that the royal grant was observed, interpreted their opportunity. For some years the king had depended in the main upon a select band of men like-minded with himself, English lords like

[1] *E.g.* the clause (no. 41) about the rights of foreign merchants simply expands an order made in April 1200, circulated to the cities of London and Winchester, the barons of the Cinque Ports, the bailiffs of Southampton and Lynn, and the sheriffs of the maritime counties on the south and east coasts (*Rotuli Chartarum*, p. 60 b).

Robert of Vieuxpont, the Bassets, and William Brewer, administrators like Philip of Ulecot and Henry of Cornhill, a crowd of obscure "bachelors" or lesser landholders and household followers, and the powerful foreign adventurers, such as Faukes de Breauté, the low-born Norman who was sheriff of Glamorgan, Hugh de Boves, who acted as his agent abroad, and mercenaries from Touraine, several of whom had charge of shires or castles or both. Gerard of Athée, the chief of the latter, was no longer alive in 1215, but the memory of his evil rule in the Severn valley, at Gloucester and Bristol and Hereford, was still fresh, and Engelard of Cigogné had succeeded him in Gloucestershire. All of them were fearless and ruthless soldiers, upon whom John could depend. According to the Charter they and their broods were to be expelled, and if wise counsels had prevailed among the barons, it is unlikely that John's friends in England would have done anything to prevent their departure. But the twenty-five did nothing to win the approval of the moderate section, and the consequence was that men who looked upon the rebellion with dislike or misgiving either rallied to the king or took as little part in affairs as they could. Among those who definitely threw in their lot with John were some of the chief earls and barons in the country. In addition to the Earl Marshal, the Earls of Salisbury, Arundel, Warenne, and Chester were on his side. William Longsword, Earl of Salisbury was the king's half-brother and had been his chief support in recent years. He had ruled Gascony, been Warden of Dover and the Cinque Ports, led the royal army to Ireland and, in 1214, in Flanders. As lord of Eye in Suffolk he was a neighbour of many of the rebels. William, Earl of Arundel, held a great honour owing the service of eighty knights' fees in Sussex and another nearly as great in East Anglia, where his seat was Castle Rising. He was the brother-in-law of the mighty Ranulf, Earl of Chester, who from the almost independent shire of Chester dominated the middle west and had control of the honours of Leicester, and, with the exception of the castle, of Richmond, where he was in touch with the royalists Robert of Vieuxpont at Appleby and Hugh of Balliol at Barnard Castle. William, Earl Warenne, was like the Earl of Arundel a relative of the king—his father was an illegitimate brother of Henry II—and, like the Earl of Chester, a figure in the North. He had Conisburgh in Yorkshire, Stamford and Grantham in Lincolnshire, and Castle Acre in Norfolk, in addition to his fiefs in Surrey.

John, supported by the Pope and by many of the English bishops with Pandulf the papal legate by their side, would in any case be a formidable foe. He had his mercenaries, and could draw freely for men upon the Low Countries, South Wales, and Ireland, where he lavished favours upon the Anglo-Irish barons of all parties. His emissaries were busy in Poitou and Brittany. By alienating the loyalists in England the opposition made their own position untenable without foreign aid, and by bringing in foreign aid and a French claimant to the throne they won a present success at the risk of almost inevitable failure in the future. Distrust of John was natural and proper, but from the outset they shewed an arrogant implacability which soon degenerated into the short-sighted egotism characteristic of earlier baronial revolts. The twenty-five, if one prejudiced but generally reliable authority can be trusted, acted not as watchful guardians but as rulers of the kingdom. John's mercenaries styled them the "twenty-five kings." After the conference at Runnymede an attempt had apparently been made to place the maintenance of the peace under a mixed body of barons chosen from each side, and the archbishop had vainly tried to secure some undertaking from the rebels of allegiance to the king. He had hoped to find in the Charter a real concordat, maintained by a joint effort as the Provisions of Oxford were to be in 1258. The body of twenty-five was to be, not a governing body, but a guarantee held in reserve, in case the Marshal and his colleagues should fail to secure the enforcement of reforms. It may be that the opposition had more justification for their disregard of this policy than we know; it is at least significant that the archbishop refused to acquiesce in the execution of the papal letters authorising their excommunication. Yet when John's advisers saw the administration disorganised, the Exchequer at a stand, the shires so far as was possible placed under the military control of particular baronial leaders and the sheriffs disregarded, their rally to his side is not surprising. They could indeed do nothing less after the failure of all attempts of the bishops to effect a compromise, and the promulgation at the end of August of the excommunication by name of the leading rebels. About the same time the Pope, as over-lord of England, annulled the Charter and forbade its observance under penalty of excommunication. Shortly afterwards the legate and the Bishop of Winchester, as Innocent's commissioners, suspended the archbishop from his functions. His heart could not be in this holy war, and, with most of the other bishops, he was glad to leave the country to attend the great council which was gathering at the Lateran.

After his first acquiescence the king, needless to say, had shewn no desire for a settlement. He avoided all opportunities of arbitration, and kept to the south coast. Foreign mercenaries were gathering and he had only to await their arrival. He established himself at Dover and prepared his plans against the rebels, who had made London their headquarters. His rapid success is one of the most remarkable episodes in English history, a striking commentary on the poverty of leadership and military enterprise among the feudal gentry of England. In those days of elaborate sieges and mercenary troops, warfare had become a profession, and the barons in London had neither the inclination nor the ability to plan a campaign or face John's foreign soldiers. Many of them had seen service in France, but none had experience of leadership sufficient to cope with such men as Faukes de Breauté and the Earl of Salisbury, or with the demonic energy of John in his fits of vigour. They wasted their time in

London, efficient only in hate, while the king overran the whole country and cooped them up in the City and a few eastern fortresses. Until the arrival of Louis of France at the end of May 1216, the country west of Watling Street was practically untouched by the war; while on the other side of it John did as he pleased. The one notable incident of the war was the heroic defence of Rochester in November by William d'Aubigny of Belvoir, and after its surrender on St Andrew's day baronial castles fell like ninepins. London was invested from Windsor, Hertford, Berkhamsted, and Bedford, the last of which had been taken by Faukes de Breauté, and while Faukes and his colleagues proceeded against one fortress after another in East Anglia and Essex, the king secured the whole of the North. Belvoir and Pontefract fell without a struggle; the northerners who were not in London sought the protection of Alexander, who was punished for his raids into Northumberland by the destruction of Berwick and the ravaging of the eastern Lowlands. In March John was back again in the South, and hemmed in London still more closely by the capture of Colchester and the castle of the Earl of Oxford at Hedingham. By this time the rebellion was practically confined to London, strong in the protection of its walls and the Tower, and in the spirit of its citizens. The Pope had declared the city to be under an interdict and had ratified the excommunication by name of the rebel leaders.

If the barons could not wage war, they could pursue negotiations. The Thames and the eastern ports were open, and from the outset intercourse between London and the court of the King of France was continuous. The rebels early approached Louis, the son of Philip Augustus, offering him the throne in return for aid. The enterprise was a hazardous one and Louis matured his plans deliberately. But at least three contingents of French knights were sent to England during the winter and early spring of 1215–16. Some of them were employed, not without signs of racial friction, to strengthen the baronial garrisons in the neighbourhood. Philip waited for the arrival of a papal legate, Guala, before reaching a final decision, for he realised that he must make out a strong case for intervention in the face of papal disapproval. The discussion took place in a great assembly at Melun at the end of April. Louis, it was decided, was to make the attempt on his own behalf, but with his father's approval. He would claim the English throne as the husband of Blanche of Castile, the grand-daughter of Henry II, against a king who had forfeited his rights, firstly, by the murder of Arthur, for which he had been condemned in the French court, secondly, by granting away his kingdom to the Pope without the consent of his vassals. In the view of most modern scholars the first reason for forfeiture has little or no historical validity, and it is clear that the second has even less. But, in spite of the legate's protests, the argument served, and by the third week in May Louis was in Kent. A great storm had dispersed the fleet which John had collected to protect the south-eastern coast, and the king, unwilling to pit his foreign mercenaries against their fellows, withdrew to Winchester. The legate landed about the same time to play a political rôle which was to become increasingly important in what he regarded as a papal fief.

It would be unprofitable to describe the events of the next six months. Louis' arrival was sufficient to restore the confidence of the opposition but insufficient to prevent general disorder. At first his success was striking. He retook Rochester and occupied Winchester. Insurgents who had begun parleys with John renewed the attack, and John was at last deserted by the Earls of Arundel and Warenne, whose lands were in danger, and, for a time, even by the Earl of Salisbury and William of Aumale. But the military position soon reached a deadlock. John had reorganised his forces in the south-western counties and left them sufficiently strong to enable him to harry the northern midlands. Apart from fugitive successes at Exeter and Worcester, Louis' efforts were confined to the south-east, and the efforts of the northern and East Anglian barons to haphazard local attacks. Alexander of Scotland braved the risks of a journey to join the invader, to whom he did homage, but gave little effective help, and was kept in check in the north by Robert of Vieuxpont in Westmorland and Cumberland, and Hugh of Balliol and Philip of Ulecot at Durham. In the midlands the great royal castles Windsor, Nottingham, Newark stood firm, and when John died at Newark, Hubert de Burgh was still holding Dover, "the Key of England," against the prolonged siege by Louis. The king's last days were spent in an orgy of reckless ferocity in the fenlands and Lincolnshire. His energy was still as great as ever, but his self-control had gone. At Lynn he was seized with an acute attack of dysentery, and, a sick man, insisted on crossing the Wash without waiting for the tide to recede. Although he managed to struggle to the Cistercian abbey of Swineshead, his baggage-train and treasure were lost in the quicksands. He died at Newark on 19 October 1216, after making an edifying will on a dignified deathbed; and his body was taken for burial to Worcester to lie under the protection of St Wulfstan. The leadership against the excommunicated invaders and rebels came to the more temperate and capable hands of the legate and the Marshal.

They faced a country full of disorder, in which the only signs of capacity, if we except the conduct of Hubert de Burgh at Dover, were shewn by isolated confederacies of knights or burgesses and by mercenary captains who had no ideas beyond the maintenance of the strongholds entrusted to them and the satisfaction of their desires. The administration had broken down, the records of the Exchequer, including the Charter of Liberties, were in the possession of Louis. The last audit of the reign, recorded on the Pipe Roll of 16 John, began in the autumn of 1214, and the last royal mandate to the barons of the Exchequer was issued on 3 September 1215, just before hostilities began. It is unlikely that there was anyone to act upon it. The efficient treasurer, William of Ely, seems to have ceased duty a month earlier. During the war, the King's Wardrobe took the place of the Exchequer[1]. Corfe Castle, which is mentioned as a royal treasury in 1212, seems to have become the repository of such records and revenue as were not immediately required. But what local dues were collected were generally paid to the nearest magnate who had any claim to authority.

Few kings have left their mark on English history as John did. He was never a nonentity; his vices were the exaggerated vices of his virile race. Distorted recollections of him were passed on for centuries in places which he had visited with his attentions, and later writers found no story about him too extravagant for belief. He left several illegitimate children, of whom two, Richard and Oliver, distinguished themselves in the civil war, and another, Joan, was the wife of Llywelyn of Wales. By his vigorous and passionate wife, Isabella of Angoulême, whom he had stolen from Hugh, son of Hugh IX, Count of La Marche, he had five children. In 1216 Henry, the eldest of these, was only nine years of age; he and Richard, King of the Romans, are inseparable from later English history; so is Eleanor, the youngest, the wife of Simon de Montfort. The others died young, but not too young to be, one an Empress, the other a queen. Their mother in due course married her former lover, Hugh; and their undisciplined sons were destined to be occasions of strife after they found a refuge at the court of their half-brother in England.

[1] All the fines made after August provide that instalments shall be paid direct to the king.

CHAPTER VIII

ENGLAND: HENRY III

The long reign of John Lackland's son, which began in disturbance and ended amid bitter memories, was to leave its constructive mark on nearly every branch of English life. The names of Grosseteste, Matthew Paris, Roger Bacon, Simon de Montfort, Bracton, and the young Gilbert de Clare alone would lend it distinction; and even more than its personalities, the growth of the communities of the land, the development of the common law and of legal theory, the creation of many of the precedents and forms of later English administration, combine to make it a period of first-rate historical importance. In religious matters a conflict of loyalties, the king's filial devotion and gratitude to Rome for help rendered in the dark early days set against local feeling for diocesan and parochial welfare, determines the relations of Church and State in this country for many succeeding years. In literature, the writers of St Albans provide an example of monastic historiography scarcely equalled by later medieval generations. In art, an English school of craftsmen emerges, and architecture reaches a brief climax of restrained perfection. Above all, the loss of the northern French provinces in John's reign is now having the effect of concentrating in the hands of the servants of the English Crown the resources of a dominion more compact and unitary than before, so that in spite of powerful cosmopolitan influences in social and governmental life we can trace during Henry's reign, even in the baronage itself, the beginnings of English sentiment and self-sufficiency. Our polity was to prove not unlike the choir of St Peter's Abbey at Westminster: the architect, the exemplars, may have been French, but the idiom and the crowning result were our own.

The loyal supporters of King John who gathered at Gloucester to crown a nine-year-old boy (28 October 1216) had resolved in common with many humbler ranks throughout England that the son should not suffer for his father's sins. Those sins, or what people took for them, had given Louis of France (now besieging Dover Castle) and his supporters London and the principal fortresses of Surrey and Hampshire, in the Midlands and the North the great de Quincy bastion of Mountsorel and most of the Yorkshire castles, and in the East considerable tracts of the maritime counties and part of Cambridgeshire. Of the opposing baronage the Earls of Salisbury, Winchester, Arundel, Norfolk, Essex, Clare, and Warenne, the eldest son of William Marshal, and Peter Fitz Herbert were among the chief partisans of Louis. But the loyalists had three great assets. The foreign mercenary captains retained by John were men of experience and determination. In the hands of two soldiers of Touraine, Engelard d'Athée and Andrew Chanceaux, stood Windsor, blocking the Thames Valley, while the castles and shires of Northampton, Oxford, Buckingham, Bedford, Hertford, and Cambridge were held by the fiery little Norman, Faukes de Breauté, called "the rod of the Lord's fury" by the indignant chronicler of the abbey which he had despoiled. Peter de Mauley, sheriff of Somerset and Dorset, Savary de Mauléon, sheriff of Hampshire, Philip Marc, sheriff of Nottingham and Derby, were, like their colleagues, the able and ruthless men demanded by an emergency. Secondly, in Earl William Marshal of Pembroke, hoary and splendid embodiment of loyal knighthood, the king's party had a man strong enough to command the respect of the two most powerful and independent personalities in the country, Earl Ranulf of Chester and the Bishop of Winchester, Peter des Roches. To the Marshal, John on his deathbed had committed the future king, and his appointment as *rector regis et regni* by the loyal barons in a Council held on 29 October commanded general confidence. In the third place, perhaps most important of all, Honorius III and his legate in England, Guala, left no stone unturned to support the ward of the Papacy against an excommunicated invader. Guala was given wide powers of censure and even of degradation in the case of clerks supporting Louis, and threw all his influence into making Henry's cause the cause of the Cross, while Honorius brought pressure to bear upon Philip Augustus to withdraw his son, protected English interests in Gascony, and exhorted and expostulated with English magnates in Henry's interests. Striking testimony to this effective aid was given in a letter which the Marshal wrote in the king's name when the worst was over (6 November 1217), acknowledging that he had been raised "from weeping to laughter, from darkness to light, from the confinement of the cradle to the spaciousness of the kingdom."[1] It was no exaggeration; and Henry never forgot to be grateful.

The first act of the regency was to reissue the Great Charter (12 November 1216). Wisely under the circumstances the royal councillors refused to tie their hands by re-enacting the clauses about scutage (*M.C.* J. 12, 14), or by renewing the article enjoining that the farms of shires, wapentakes, and hundreds should be reduced to their old figures (*M.C.* J. 25). The unpopular foreign soldiers specified by name in the earlier document (cl. 50) were naturally enough retained, and a number of John's promised restitutions and re-instatements had to go by the board. The eviction of Louis and the recovery of the lost areas were the paramount tasks. By truces made in December 1216 and January 1217, the government first concentrated its forces by withdrawing the garrisons of a number of castles in Essex and East Anglia, which stood as isolated posts in hostile territory. Louis was unable to reap the full benefit of a sacrifice so surprising at first appearances, for owing to the loyalty of the Cinque Ports he had to watch his communications, nor did he help his interests

[1] *Royal Letters*, ed. Shirley, I, p. 6.

by his return to France at the end of February 1217 at his father's summons. In March the Wiltshire and Hampshire strongholds of Marlborough, Winchester, Farnham, Odiham, and Southampton were recaptured, and it was possible to begin the siege of Mountsorel. Generous terms were offered to all who would secede, and defections from the French side began in earnest; so much so that when Louis returned on 23 April 1217, he found the young Marshal and William Longespee, Earl of Salisbury, fled from his cause, and the garrison of Mountsorel calling for assistance. He could not go north, as there was lost ground to recover in Hampshire and Sussex, and the mischievous activities of the Ports to be neutralised; but, in order to relieve Mountsorel, he despatched a column which was diverted eastwards to Lincoln at the request of Hugh of Arras, who from within the city was besieging the heroic dame Nicolaa in the castle, for months a lonely beacon of the royal cause. It was the Marshal's opportunity. Counselled by Guala and Peter des Roches, he summoned all loyal castellans and knights to Newark (15 May 1217), whence, in hope of eternal salvation, the royalists marched to Lincoln, to force an entry and catch the beleaguerers within the walls. Ingress was effected at several points, and the fight that lasted from early morning till three in the afternoon proved a victory for the king, who at his headquarters in Nottingham had the satisfaction of learning on 19 May that Mountsorel had fallen. Mere events and the failure of his fleet to bring reinforcements led Louis to concentrate his forces in London. He was not beaten yet; sea-power, rather than land armaments, was to defeat him. A great battle in the Channel, in which Philip d'Aubigny and Hubert de Burgh destroyed the French fleet under Eustace the Monk off Sandwich, settled the issue, and Louis in London awaited inevitable siege. The Marshal, however, was prepared to treat. Negotiations, begun at Lambeth, reached their end at Kingston (12 September 1217). By the terms then agreed upon, it was stipulated that prisoners should be released and English subjects who had fought against John should do homage to Henry; that the supporters of each party should recover the lands they held before the war, though at the instance of the legate this provision was not to extend to clerks who had supported Louis; that Louis should release all his English followers from their oaths of fealty to him; and (a secret provision) that the king should indemnify the French prince for his invasion in 10,000 marks—a heavy sum when the state of the country is considered[1]. Louis was thereupon

[1] M. Petit-Dutaillis is probably justified in his scepticism (*La Vie et le règne de Louis VIII*, pp. 175–6) about the serious nature of Louis' promise, narrated by Roger of Wendover, and repeated by Miss Norgate (*The Minority of Henry III*, p. 59), that he would do his best to induce his father to restore to Henry his rights beyond the sea. How the story grew can be seen from Matthew Paris' insertion of the apocryphal "et cum rex foret (sc. Lodovicus), ipse in pace dimitteret" (omnia iura sua) in the Wendover section of the Corpus Christi MS. of the *Chronica Majora* (cf. *Chron. Maj.* II, p. 31).

absolved by Guala, and a little later left England (28 September 1217), the recipient of honourable terms.

It will be well to consider the period of the Minority and the Justiciarship of Hubert de Burgh (1216–32) as a whole. During the ten years from 1217 to 1227 the formal executive passed through several stages proportionately with the king's growth to manhood. The Marshal, acting as regent until his death in May 1219, exercised many of the functions of king, attested royal letters in his own name, and used his own seal as the seal of the kingdom, *quia sigillum non habuimus*, as Henry was made to say. With him, coadjutor but in some sense his superior[1], stood the legate, the representative of Henry's papal guardian. Evidence shews that except in very important matters of State he very sensibly did not intervene to enforce his own rights, but that a division of labour existed between himself and the Marshal. Peter des Roches had special charge of Henry, whose mother Isabella went back to Angoulême in the summer of 1217; and Hubert de Burgh, made Justiciar by John in 1215, retained at that king's death the office granted him during pleasure, and occupied himself largely with administration. Attestations of letters close and patent by the two latter become more frequent after November 1218, and they seem to have risen to prominence as the Marshal's health declined. In September 1218 Guala was succeeded by Pandulf, papal chamberlain and Bishop-elect of Norwich, who had boldly stood up to John on Innocent III's behalf in 1211. On the decease of the Marshal, therefore, the government became a sort of triumvirate. The earl on his deathbed had, in spite of the Bishop of Winchester's protests, left Henry to the care of "God and St Peter"; thus Pandulf, theoretically speaking, combined in himself both regency and legation. What his power could be, if he chose to exercise it, we may infer from the careful instructions about the custody of the great seal, which he sent, when the Marshal was dying, to the vice-chancellor, Ralph Neville, in order to secure the collection of the revenue. But, as a matter of ordinary practice, he shared the work with the Justiciar and Peter des Roches. For nearly three years he remained, living part of the year at his Gloucestershire manor, a wise and cautious administrator, dealing tactfully with fractious barons like the Count of Aumale, arranging the details of a marriage alliance between Alexander II of Scotland and the Princess Joan, and interesting himself so much in the affairs of Poitou that after he had ceased from office he undertook a mission there on behalf of this country. On his departure in 1221 the Justiciar's influence gradually became paramount, till by means of Henry's partial coming of age in 1223 he had very largely superseded the episcopal tutor. Thenceforward from 1223 to 1227, and after the king's full coming of age till 1232, Henry and Hubert jointly managed affairs, with the indignant

[1] G. J. Turner, *The Minority of Henry III*, TRHS, New Series, XVIII, p. 268.

bishop, whether on crusade or in his native Poitou, thrust into the background and awaiting the day of retribution. It is important to note that till Henry's full majority in 1227, when the Charter Roll begins, the king and his ministers could make no grant in perpetuity. In 1218, when the first Great Seal of Henry's reign began to run, this limitation was expressly stated: and the partial coming of age in 1223, which gave Henry the free disposal of his castles and wardships, did not remove the disability. The latter point suggests that the first or partial majority was declared for political objects, in order to recover royal rights and lands in the hands of those from whom it would normally have been difficult to extract them. Herein lies a detail of some significance when the rebellious movements of the Minority and the influence of Hubert de Burgh are considered; for the passing of the Justiciarship marks the end of the first period of the reign.

A country long disturbed is not easily brought back to peaceful ways. The government was forced to rely during 1216–17 upon John's sheriffs and castellans who remained for the most part undisturbed in their bailiwicks. Whether they were left there out of policy or whether the ministers recognised any claim, tacit or expressed, on their part to continuity of office appears doubtful; the former seems the more likely alternative. But the return to the *status quo* prescribed in the Treaty of Kingston meant that many private strongholds had to change hands, and not a few loyalists were thus deprived of expected rewards. Moreover a castle was the administrative centre of a district, whether county or barony, where continuity of command and defensive organisation were often essential to the maintenance of peace. The government that ordered its resumption did not always appreciate this necessity, and there were other causes of a personal or a fiscal nature, such as the status of the new keeper or castellan, or the necessity of an account (in the case of a royal castle) between the present holder and the king, that made the transaction a difficult one. Much of the discontent, many of the acts of recalcitrancy, which culminated in the movements of 1223–4, arose from the orders of surrender. While selfish motives played their part, it is worth observing that the opposition thus engendered came from men who had done King John good service and held no specially anarchical theory of government[1]. The Count of Aumale, Hugh de Balliol, Brian de Lisle, Robert of Vieuxpont cannot be dismissed in Wendover's phrase as men "who found it sweet to live on rapine." The sympathies of Ranulf of Chester in the rebellion of Faukes de Breauté were not alienated without some potent cause. Early outbreaks were not serious. Hugh de Balliol's detention of the Mesnill castle of Whorlton and the Northumberland strongholds of Mitford, Robert de Gouy's refusal to hand over Newark and Sleaford to Bishop Hugh of Lincoln, or the Count of Aumale's obstinacy when bidden to

[1] G. J. Turner, *The Minority of Henry III* (II), TRHS, Third Series, I, p. 216.

give up the midland forest castles of Sauvey and Rockingham (1218–19) and the fortress of Bytham (1217–20), were instances of individual insubordination only; but there was something more than sensitiveness or the prickings of ambition behind the risings of Earl Ranulf, Earl Gilbert of Gloucester, and Walter de Lacy in 1223 or the defiance of the de Breauté brothers next year. These were partly the consequences of a manoeuvre of Peter des Roches, partly due to the drastic methods of the Justiciar. In proportion as Hubert de Burgh's power grew after Pandulf's departure, it became clear to the bishop that the only way to assert his own influence was to give Henry power in his own Council and to allow him to make himself felt in the government of his own realm. This accomplished, the Justiciar could only then maintain his supremacy by means of his personal influence over the young king, and Peter might step in, undermine that influence, and overthrow the Justiciar. The suggestion for the partial termination of the Minority seems to have been made to Honorius III by the bishop, who sent also a request that the Pope would issue instructions concerning the royal castles[1]. It was cunning, but dangerous diplomacy. The move to secure the restoration of the castles, gratified by the papal command for their surrender (April 1223), was attributed, as had been maliciously intended, to Hubert de Burgh, particularly in view of an unpopular inquest which the Justiciar launched in the king's name (January 1223) in order to ascertain what customs and liberties were held by King John before war with the barons broke out. But his conduct subsequently did not allay suspicions of self-seeking. Two barons, Walter de Lacy and Ralph Musard, were summoned to Court to surrender the royal property in their hands; on their arrival they were made to assign to the Justiciar the castles of Hereford and Gloucester, and the unwarrantable action proved sufficient to provoke first the remonstrances and later the armed defiance of Ranulf of Chester and his confederates, who, when brought to terms, explained that their action had been directed against the Justiciar, not against the king. The other part of the bishop's plan, however, failed, for Hubert was strong enough to survive the unpopularity created by the appointment of new custodians of the royal castles, and his influence was to last nearly ten years more, if ultimately its very prolongation was to make certain the abolition of the justiciarship in England.

Though Hubert had been unable to humiliate the Earls of Chester and Gloucester, he was at least able to strike down a disturbing force ranged in 1223 on their side. No sooner had the reconciliation of the discontented

[1] "Episcopus Wintoniensis misit Romam W. de Sancto Albano (*sic* for S. Albino) pro dicto negotio": "Responsiones Huberti de Burgo" in *Chron. Maj.* VI (*Additamenta*), p. 69. This follows Miss Norgate's interpretation, *op. cit.* pp. 200–1. Hubert's attestation of the credentials of William de St Aubin (*Cal. Patent Rolls*, 1216–1224, p. 328) does not seem an insuperable objection; the commission is quite generally worded, "pro negotiis nostris in curia promovendis."

earls with the government taken place than Faukes de Breauté was charged with capital crime and sixteen additional pleas of disseisin brought against him before the Justices of Assize at Dunstable. "The great disseisor," as Maitland called him, was a fine soldier, but a bad neighbour. His conduct when in command of the midland shires had been autocratic in the extreme. The religious he had alienated by soiling his hands with the plunder of St Albans; in 1217 he had fallen foul of the young William Marshal, and through his custody of the great de Redvers estates in the west had claimed a standing which many magnates resented. He was undoubtedly a nuisance, but 1224 was no time for the government to turn upon him, as events were to prove. The excuse for armed action was the capture by William de Breauté, Faukes' brother and castellan of Bedford, of one of the Justices of Assize who had condemned Faukes by default at Dunstable. Faukes was outlawed, Bedford besieged, and the whole activities of the government were bent upon its capture—while Louis VIII overran Poitou. The energies spent on taking Bedford and hounding Faukes out of the country might have been expended in defending English possessions overseas. But the Justiciar could not wait. At home, his conduct was criticised in dignified letters from Ranulf of Chester and more outspoken comments from Llywelyn of Wales; abroad, his action had the unfortunate effect of strengthening French propaganda against England at the Curia and creating doubt and dismay in the minds of Pope and Cardinals. When late in 1224 Geoffrey Craucumb and Stephen Lucy, Henry's proctors, came to Rome, they found extraordinary stories about the state of England in circulation, one in particular to the effect that the English magnates were offering the throne to John de Brienne, whenever he cared to come over and take it[1].

The rebellion of Faukes de Breauté might have had less repercussion abroad, had not English interests in Poitou and Gascony been for some time in a serious position. Their rectification was to occupy the activities of Henry and the Justiciar for some years after 1225. On the death of John, all that remained of Poitou after the partial carrying out of the sentence of total confiscation in the period following its announcement by the French *Curia Regis* (28 April 1202)[2] was La Rochelle and its environs

[1] See their letter in *Royal Letters*, I, pp. 240–3: "Dominum papam quidem et cardinales non solum commotos circa statum regis et regni ipsius perpendimus, verum penitus se desperatos unanimiter fatebantur. Nam rex Jerosolyme et dicti Gallici predicabant omnibus, quod majores Anglie obsides offerebant usque ad quinquaginta, de reddendo sibi terram, cum primo venire curaret ad illam."

[2] I accept the important conclusion of M. Ch. Petit-Dutaillis, *Le Déshéritement de Jean Sans Terre*, *Revue historique*, t. CXLV. pp. 161–178, esp. 178: "En resumé," he remarks, "l'an 1202, avant qu' Arthur tombat entre ses mains, Jean fut condamné par la cour de Philippe Auguste à perdre *tous ses fiefs français*. Par ce jugement, par le défi et les actes d'hostilité qui le suivirent, tout lien féodal était brisé entre eux. L'exécution de la sentence ne sera pas complète et, malgré les conquêtes de Philippe Auguste et de Louis VIII, les rois d'Angleterre, restant en guerre avec les rois de France, garderont d'importants domaines sur le continent; mais c'est seulement par le traité de paix de 1259 qu'ils redeviendront hommes liges des rois de France."

corresponding with the modern prefecture of Aunis, Niort and the southern half of the present department of Deux-Sèvres, and Saintonge. English Gascony was roughly the duchy of Aquitaine, south of Blaye; it approximately comprised the territories on the maritime side of the administrative boundary separating the modern departments of the Dordogne and Lot et Garonne from that of the Gironde, and of Gers from that of the Landes, while the Pyrenean fiefs of Soule, Béarn, Bigorre, Quatre Vallées, and Cominges formed its mountainous extremities. Over these combined territories, bristling with internal strifes of local nobles against the towns of the littoral, and of one commune against another, was the English seneschal of Gascony and Poitou, the military and administrative governor, whose headquarters was Bordeaux and who sat as justice in the courts held there and at Bazas, Dax, and St Sever. This official, whose salary was 1000 marks per annum, had under him, as his treasurer and paymaster, the constable of Bordeaux, and below him a group of constables, *baillis*, and *prévôts*, mostly drawn from the local nobility. Preservation of the peace and collection of the Gascon tolls occupied most of the attention of the seneschal, who was often too poor and generally too busy to deal adequately with the northern province. Upon the English remnant of this area Louis VIII on his accession fixed his eyes. Owing to the truce which Honorius III arranged between Philip Augustus and Henry to last for four years from 1220, direct aggression was impossible; the towns of La Rochelle, Niort, and St Jean d'Angely held firmly to the power that favoured communal liberties, the English Crown; but in the bitter feud of the Poitevin nobles, Hugh de Lusignan Count of La Marche, the Viscount of Thouars, William Maingot, and William l'Archevêque, against these once prosperous communities, a way might be opened notwithstanding. The English government did not support its seneschals adequately. Vigorous remonstrances of Geoffrey de Neville, complaining that these ruffianly gentry were treating him like a little boy and threatening to leave unless energetic steps were taken, passed unheeded. The miserable towns were forced to write deprecatory letters on behalf of their oppressors, and the pathetic appeals of Niort for a strong governor fell on deaf ears. When, therefore, the truce was over, Louis had no difficulty in capturing the enfeebled outposts.

English apathy had been due partly to financial poverty, partly to the genuine difficulty of dealing with the shifty and attractive Hugh de Lusignan, whose family had never loved the Angevins. The situation had been greatly complicated by the vociferous appeals of the Queen-Mother for the dower-lands in southern Poitou assigned to her by King John but not restored to her on her return to France. To have given them back immediately would have been to incur the displeasure of Count Hugh, the most powerful of the Poitevin magnates; and English policy was to keep Hugh friendly as a counterpoise to the encroachments of Louis. Isabella through her claims first fell out with her old fiancé, and then, on the shallow pretext of saving him from taking a wife "in the North" (*in Francia*), solved the question by falling into his arms (1220). The alliance was to bring the union of La Marche and Angoulême; the continued reluctance of Hubert de Burgh to pay the dowry was to cause an alliance between Louis VIII and Hugh that, when the hour arrived, was to settle the fate of the territories which the French king and the Lusignan couple were coveting. Moreover, as Hugh and Isabella were holding Henry's eldest sister Joan practically as a hostage for the dowry, there was nothing for it but to disgorge the lands. The right policy for Hubert de Burgh between 1221 and 1224 was to strengthen the English seneschal at all costs, but it is clear that the way was blocked by his desire to conciliate the Lusignan and the hope that negotiations undertaken by Honorius with the French Crown for the restoration of the confiscated lands would succeed. After the loss of Poitou a commercial warfare was opened between England and France, while Hubert de Burgh manœuvred for position. The initiative was not taken till 1229. At Christmas 1228 came a letter from the Duke of Brittany offering Henry the sovereignty of the former possessions of the Angevins in the north in return for his help in a league of Breton, Norman, and Poitevin nobles against Louis. The government, as a draft memorandum of the Council shews[1], took the bait seriously. The insufficient preparations made at first (Michaelmas 1229) for the expedition need not argue the Justiciar's apathy in the matter. Henry's angry charge of treason was beside the point, for the postponement of the sailing was as a matter of fact urged a little later by the Duke of Brittany himself, who came over in the winter to arrange further details and receive appropriate honours. In May 1230 the force set out. Its success was compromised by the landing in, and connexion with, Brittany. A descent upon La Rochelle, a quick march into Poitou, would have won the Viscount of Thouars and perhaps stabilised the unstable Hugh de Lusignan himself. As it was, Henry could not enter Poitou, owing to the movements of the French army, till June, and by that time the heroic Blanche of Castile had taken the sting out of her opponents. All Henry could do was to make a demonstration march through Gascony and thence return to Nantes, where he spent his time elegantly till his passage home on 27 October 1230.

The Justiciar's conduct of French affairs gave a handle to his opponents[2] and doubtless aroused the king's suspicions, upon which the household was not slow to play. Till 1230 Henry had no personal seal of his own. On his return from France a privy seal makes its appearance for the first time in the reign, and the fact is significant. It marks the beginning of the separation of the Chancery and the Court. Whilst abroad, the royal household had conducted the administration of the expedition;

[1] *Royal Letters*, I, pp. 350–1.

[2] See the complaints in Matthew Paris, *Chron. Maj.* VI (*Additamenta*), pp. 66–7. His creation of himself as Earl of Kent (1227) would scarcely be forgotten.

more and more Henry came to rely upon it as the organ of his personal government and upon the new seal as the instrument of his private designs. It is perhaps a little early to distinguish clearly between the "national" offices of Chancery and Exchequer and the private or personal office of the king's *hospitium*; yet the distinction was soon to be realised. The central administrative fact of the Minority is the growth of the king's domestic treasury, his Wardrobe, with its staff of clerks and its own traditions and methods. Their system of account did not conflict with that of the Exchequer; normally, considerable block grants were made to the Wardrobe by the other office on receipt of a bill (*billa de Garderoba*), and the Exchequer would not inquire how the money was spent. But the Wardrobe was capable of overlapping the Exchequer by attracting into itself the farms of cities and boroughs, drawing upon the sheriffs for provisions, or making anticipatory drafts upon the revenues of counties. The claim made in 1258, and again later, that into the Exchequer should go "all the issues of the land" points to the absence of what to-day would be called "Treasury control," as a check on the Wardrobe's expenditure. But there was a political side to this activity. By the revival of the Privy Seal the Wardrobe, in Professor Tout's words, "became also a household Chancery, the more so since the Great Chancery was ceasing to be merely a court office."[1] The attempt to administer the country primarily through the primitive curial organism, strengthened and made efficient by clerks independent of the greater offices that were frequently in the hands of magnates, and strictly dependent on the royal will, is the groundwork of Henry's policy. The first stage of that attempt was to be an effort to unify the domestic and public treasuries under a single household clerk by first getting rid of that tutelary anachronism, the Justiciar. The latter, the subsidiary aim, was accomplished; the former, dictated perhaps by the example of the *grande Chancellerie royale* or the Papal Curia, was to fail, and its failure was to perpetuate the dualism of household and national offices which underlies many of the struggles between baronage and Crown.

Two other factors may have helped the Bishop of Winchester (who returned to the fray in 1231) and his Poitevin followers to pull the Justiciar down. One turns on a point of Exchequer administration, the other concerns Anglo-Welsh relations. During John's reign there had been a steady increase in the farm demanded from the shires, the extra payments being known as the profits. The Charter of 1215 put an end to this increment; and although the clause forbidding the profits was dropped in Henry III's reissues, only profits from demesne manors appear on the Pipe Rolls at the beginning of the reign. At the same time an important change in the method of collecting the summonses, which began with the invention in 1207 of the "dividend tally,"[2] whereby various individual accounts

[1] *Chapters in Medieval Administrative History*, I, p. 214.

[2] Miss M. H. Mills, *The Pipe Roll for* 1295. *Surrey Membrane* (Surrey Record Soc.), Introd. p. x.

could be grouped under the sheriff's name—a welcome simplification and a landmark in the progress from accounting by individuals to collective accounting by the shrievalty—continued to be adopted during these early years. It can hardly be a coincidence that in 1223, the date of Hubert's rise to power and the banishment of the bishop's protégé, Peter de Rivaux, from the Wardrobe, the profits were suddenly restored and the new method of summons dropped[1]. The reaction lasted till the Poitevin influence began to trickle back, in 1229–30. It is clear that the methods of Hubert and the Poitevins were very different; and as it was the latter that were to become the basis of the reorganisation of the shire accounts and of their collection until the middle of the fourteenth century, it would appear that the Justiciar's more conservative way did not commend itself as practicable. Secondly, Hubert's policy in Wales was unsuccessful. In 1228 an English expedition against Llywelyn had failed dismally at Kerry and humiliating terms had to be made. Nor did the Justiciar's personal ambitions make for quiet. Foreshadowing the younger Despenser in Edward II's time, he attempted to build up for himself a great territorial power in the south. Since the beginning of the reign he had held the three castles of Grosmont, Skenefrith, and Whitecastle, and in 1223 had acquired in addition the castle and honour of Montgomery. In 1227 he secured Archenfield in Herefordshire, and in 1229 the lordships of Cardigan and Carmarthen, now created into a new marcher holding by the service of five knights. At the end of 1230 the lordship of Gower was subordinated to this fee, and in the same year, on the death of Earl Gilbert of Gloucester in Brittany, he was granted the custody of the lands and the heir, and thus became virtual lord of Glamorgan. In April 1231 the Earl Marshal died suddenly, and the custody of the Braiose lands in the March, which the late earl had received from the Crown, was set free and in a little time was conferred upon Hubert. These encroachments on the pride of Llywelyn the Great produced the formidable Welsh raid of 1231, in which the Justiciar and king were quite out-generalled. The unwelcome failure was pointed by the barons' refusal of an aid for the Welsh war at a Council held at Westminster in March 1232—the second refusal within a year, for in March 1231 they had denied him money for a French expedition. Bishop Peter could now deal a fatal blow to the Justiciar by alleging his connivance in a series of attacks made on the property and persons of papal tax-collectors in England, which had excited Gregory IX's indignation. Henry decided upon a change of régime. Peter de Rivaux, the Poitevin clerk who seems to have hailed from Airvault (Deux-Sèvres), had been Keeper of the Wardrobe before 1223, and was probably the nephew of Peter des Roches, now received the keeping of the Wardrobe, Chamber, and Treasury of the King's household for life

[1] M. H. Mills, *Experiments in Exchequer Procedure*, 1200–1232, TRHS, Fourth Series, VIII, pp. 166–69.

(11 June 1232), the chamberlainship of London, the custody of the King's Jewry and of the ports and coasts of England (except Dover), and the keeping of all escheats and wardships throughout England (28 June). By 17 July he had been made sheriff for life of twenty-one counties, answering for all but two (Surrey and Sussex) at the "ancient farms," and had received the Forest of England in keeping for life. The grant of twenty-five important English and Irish castles, and the extension of these great powers to Ireland, completed the amazing elevation. Most of these offices were exercised by deputy; but the unitary tendency is clear. Court official had triumphed over baronial minister. The Wardrobe became solitary and supreme; for Peter had received the custody of the small seal, and with that grant it had been provided that he should have "a clerk faithful to the King" as his representative in the Exchequer, to which he was exempted from rendering account. It was perhaps the misuse of this very seal in authenticating to certain magnates of Ireland the famous "blood-stained letter" declaring Richard Marshal a traitor and enjoining his capture—a letter which brought the unfortunate man to his death—that in 1234 decisively strengthened the reaction against the Poitevins, headed by Edmund Rich, the new Archbishop of Canterbury; for it was not long before the outlawry of Hubert de Burgh, his extraction from sanctuary at Brentwood, and his imprisonment at Devizes, raised indignation against the success of the Poitevins. This was expressed by the mouth of a Dominican at a Council at Oxford in June 1233, while tidings of the picturesque but distressing incidents of the months when Hubert was a fugitive or prisoner threatened to spread serious disturbance, especially in the West, where Marshal intervention and Marcher aid had set the Welsh border on fire. For a second time within living memory the Church combined with the baronage against the Crown, and Henry was forced to restore Hubert's lands and honours—but not his office. There is little reason to exalt the Justiciar's policy, as did the chronicler of the friendly convent of St Albans in annotating the history written by his predecessor; there is still less reason to undervalue it, for Hubert had been a strong repressor of disorder, had, in the words of a litigant *coram rege*, "held the whole kingdom in his hand"[1]; but some sympathy is due to the victim of personal hatreds and of the colder and more inhuman ruthlessness of fiscal reorganisation. With him passed the old vice-regal justiciarship; for the revival of the office in 1258 made the Justiciars Hugh Bigod and Hugh le Despenser strictly dependent upon the revolutionary Council.

Before we pass on to the period of Henry's personal government, we may pause to regard the man round whom, little as he grasped their full significance, great events were to turn. Henry III has suffered much at the hands of political historians, chiefly as a foil to the virtues of

[1] *Bracton's Notebook*, ed. Maitland, case 1221.

Simon de Montfort. His fate has been largely the work of a conventual patriot with a genius for barbed and malicious anecdote, whose acidulated comments have not failed to produce their desired effect. One can hardly expect impartiality from a man who, he tells us, saw with his own eyes Henry and Geoffrey de Lusignan, as they strolled in the abbey orchard at St Albans, being pelted with stones, turves, and green apples by a miserable Poitevin clerk newly presented to the Crown living of Preston. To Matthew Paris the king was a self-contradictory mixture of caprice, craftiness, and childish simplicity, a subject for many an admirable story, though it was perhaps too cruel to make St Louis after the failure of the Taillebourg campaign restrain the Gascons from deriding him, with the contemptuous words: "let him alone, let him alone...his alms and masses will deliver him from all danger." Yet in fact one artist failed to understand another. There was little in common between the robust *raconteur* and the refined, distinguished figure represented upon Peter Cosmati's lovely tomb at Westminster. Henry's great passion was for building, decorating, and the collection of beautiful things of every kind. Probably the first king of finely educated taste since Alfred of Wessex, a connoisseur to the finger-tips, he enjoyed nothing so much as buying or getting made in considerable quantities images, jewels, plate, relics, pictures, and rich stuffs of all kinds. The nature of the cloth, the setting of the jewel, the style of the ornamentation he would specify with minute care[1]. These treasures did not go, as might be thought, solely to decorate the households or persons of his relatives; they were for the most part destined as gifts for the shrine of St Edward the Confessor, the focus of his ardent religious life; for the former ward of the Papacy by his genuine devotion merited a better place in Dante's vision than the delectable valley of the late-repentant. He built madly, to his own impoverishment and our perpetual gain. In the twenty-five years between 1245 and 1270 he had erected the fabric of Westminster Abbey (excluding the seven western bays of the nave), the chapter house, that portion of the cloister that leads to it and those of its bays that are attached to the south aisle of the early part of the church. Within, he had built the shrine of St Edward with its wonderful decorations, had brought to breathing life the beautiful figure sculpture in the arcades, introduced the Cosmatesque mosaic into the floor of the presbytery, tiled the chapter house with the finest pavement of the kind now extant, and probably ordered the painting of the splendid re-table now shown in the southern

[1] *E.g. Close Rolls*, 1242–1247, p. 293: "*De leopardis et gradibus faciendis.*—Rex Edwardo de Westm', salutem. Quia reducimus ad memoriam quod nobis dixistis quod parum plus erit sumptuosum facere duos leopardos eneos qui erunt ex utraque parti sedis nostre de Westm' quam eos facere ex marmore insciso vel sculpto, vobis mandamus quod eos fieri faciatis ex metallo sicut dixistis et gradus ante sedem predictam fieri faciatis ex petra inscisa...." Cf. p. 370, for the setting of a precious emerald which is to be bought "quicquid custare debeat."

ambulatory of the choir. On the river-bank he had amplified and transformed the Palace buildings, and had beautified St Stephen's Chapel, the Westminster parallel of the Sainte Chapelle which he had longed to carry off to England "tout droit." Windsor Castle he had greatly magnified and strengthened, and had carried out structural alterations in seventy-five per cent. of the royal manors throughout the country. Work on such a scale could only be conducted through a large staff, both clerical and technical, and under Henry III there emerges for the first time in our records an organisation which, as Mr Lethaby has observed, it would be no anachronism to call a firm working under royal direction. The craftsmen, who were the masons and carpenters attached to the Palace, were directed by a clerk of the works, at first by Odo the Goldsmith, later by Odo's son, the more famous Edward of Westminster, who, aided by William of Haverhill, acted as the administrative head of a little school of art. Edward and William were not only "Keepers of the Works at Westminster," they were also—a significant point—Treasurers of the Exchequer. It seems that a special board or "Exchequer" was established at Westminster[1], and there is evidence that the money from fines was devoted to the expenses of the fabric and perhaps paid in to the separate abbey account kept there. This special accounting fell upon the keepers in addition to their ordinary Exchequer duties, and when it is remembered that the senior colleague was responsible for the Windsor operations as well as for the fabric of royal castles and manors, and that all instructions to workmen went through him, it will be realised what a weight lay upon his shoulders. It is pleasant indeed to read of the king ordering his favourite flower, the rose of Provins, to be painted on the dealbated walls of the queen's chamber, or carved in the exquisite spandrels of the eastern wall arcade in the abbey; giving instructions on the colour of wainscoting, ordering stars to be stencilled on backgrounds of azure or vert, or specifying the motet to be sung at Christmas. No other medieval monarch has revealed himself so intimately in the records of his Chancery; but there was another side to these aesthetic activities, and judgments of taste are no substitute for wise and equable authority or the keeping of plighted word. Ingenuous and trusting, taking things at their decorative value, Henry plunged into transactions which would have horrified his grandfather and doubtless were to sharpen the critical faculty of his eldest son; then, in order to extricate himself, he had to temporise, sometimes even to prevaricate, and often in the end to call in his farther-sighted brother, Richard of Cornwall, to get him out of the mess by some convenient compromise.

[1] *Cal. of Patent Rolls,* 1232–1247, p. 478. "Grant to God and St Edward and the Church of Westminster, for the fabric of the said Church, of £2,591...the king wills that this money be paid at the New Exchequer which he has established for this at Westminster."

Piety and magnificence are stamped upon the years of his personal government. Both brought him, scarcely foreseeing, into the storms of European politics. Already in 1225 his marriage had been in contemplation. Overtures for a suitable daughter had been made to the Duke of Brittany, to Leopold VI of Austria, to the King of Bohemia, but without result. In 1235 he asked Count Amadeus IV of Savoy for his niece Eleanor, the daughter of Raymond Berengar IV, Count of Provence, and sister-in-law of Louis IX. The marriage took place in 1236 with far-reaching results. A special Wardrobe, a subordinate household, was organised for the new-comer, whose expenses grew as time went on; more important, the Savoy connexion introduced to England Eleanor's two uncles, Boniface, who was to become Archbishop of Canterbury in 1245, and Peter, his brother, who was to play a useful part in public life. With another uncle, William, the elect of the see of Valence (*ob.* 1238), came the able clerk Peter d'Aigueblanche, a cadet of the house of Briançon, who in many ways epitomises the "alien" in thirteenth-century England. For several years the Keeper of the Wardrobe, then Bishop of Hereford, negotiator of the marriage of Richard of Cornwall with Sanchia of Provence, collector of papal taxes, diplomatist sent on missions to Louis IX and Alfonso X of Castile, administrator in Gascony, liberal benefactor of his cathedral and staunch upholder of the liberties of his see against the citizens of Hereford, who cordially disliked him, the Savoyard succeeded through that sheer, ruthless vitality and address which was always effective with the king. But on the whole Savoy brought little discredit on Henry, except in so far as it transmitted papal demands during three difficult years of poverty. Archbishop Boniface, whom the chronicler of the superbly exempt St Albans disliked because he did not always respect conventual liberties, was a moderate man, anxious for reform. Peter, although he may have extracted more than was his due in getting the earldom of Richmond (1240), the wardenship of the Cinque Ports (1241), and the honours of Tickhill and Hastings (1249) together with several lucrative wardships, was the colleague of Simon de Montfort on missions in 1254 and 1257, took part in the action of the Barons against the Poitevins, and joined in their letter to the Pope against Aymer de Valence (1258). It was otherwise with the children of Isabella and Hugh le Brun. After their mother's decease in 1246 (Hugh died in 1242) William de Valence, Geoffrey, Guy, and Aymer de Lusignan accepted Henry's hospitable invitation to make their home in England, and came over, William, Guy, and Geoffrey to get allowances of £500 a year at the Exchequer, Aymer to be first educated at Oxford, and then, through an intrigue with the Papacy, foisted upon the monks of St Swithin as Bishop-elect of Winchester. Records of grants in Charter and Patent Rolls shew that William was the only one to acquire in perpetuity really large territorial interests, the chief being the castle and lordship of Pembroke which he got through his wife, Joan de Mountchesney, whose mother was one of the Marshal co-heiresses. What alienated the English magnates was the way in which the Poitevin brothers absorbed wardships, marriages, and escheats, or in Aymer's case, benefices, and so accumulated sufficient funds to buy themselves a place among the nobility. The best example of this tendency was the purchase in 1255 jointly by William and Aymer for 5000 marks of the marriage of young Gilbert de Clare, Earl Richard of Gloucester's son, with their niece Alice[1]. The de Clares were bigger game than anything to be found in Poitou.

But if Henry was an admirable relative, he was still more ambitious for those nearest to him. Dynastically, European rulers formed a single family of wide ramifications, and the maintenance of the balance of power against his French relations was the guiding principle in Henry's match-making. The marriage of his sister Isabella to the Emperor Frederick II (1235) was the first step in this direction; the next the attaching of Brabant by the projected union of prince Edward with the daughter of its duke. The proposal (1247–8) failed, but the need of securing the re-nouncement of Castilian claims upon Gascony, and perhaps (after the first attempt at an alliance) the weaning of Alfonso X's mind from the project of the Empire, led Henry to make sure of his southern neighbour, and Eleanor of Castile became Edward's wife (1254). The crowning move was towards the very throne of Caesar, which that prince of negotiators and confidential clerks, John Mansel, and the Earl of Gloucester secured for Richard of Cornwall from the electors at a high price. To provide Edmund with the crown of Sicily, offered to and refused by the cautious Richard, seemed worth a debt entered with a few strokes on the papal merchants' ledgers. Henry's relations with St Louis are an interesting example of his mentality and policy. Till 1258 he never gave up the idea of recovering Normandy and Anjou; he was easily enticed into the unsuccessful coalition against Louis headed by Hugh and Isabella de Lusignan as a protest against the homage exacted by Alphonse of Poitiers in his new appanage of Poitou and Auvergne (1242). Forced to a truce in 1243, he made no attempt to conclude any sort of peace until 1250[2], but the proposal seems to have been quickly dropped and the régime of truces continued. At first his humiliation in 1242 rankled, and he warned Boniface of Savoy to have no friendly dealings with the French king[3]; but it was impossible to bear personal resentment for long against that fountain of courtesy, whose court foreshadowed in a distant way that of Louis XIV in the leadership of contemporary chivalry and

[1] *Cal. of Charter Rolls*, I, pp. 438–9. Cf. p. 403, for the purchase (for 1000 marks) by William de Valence of the inheritance of Robert Pont de l'Arche.

[2] *Foedera* (1816), I, 272.

[3] See Boniface's amusing letter, *Royal Letters*, II, pp. 35–6, in which he replied that he had avoided entering France in order not to be asked to stand god-father to the royal child that was expected.

literature. In 1253 Henry asked to be allowed to pass through French territory, and the benign Louis, in acceding to the request, came to meet him and laid the blame for any estrangement that might exist between them upon his barons. The graceful act was followed next year by the substantial present of an elephant, that drew large crowds to see it in London; Henry doubtless preferred the jewelled brooch in the form of a peacock which Queen Margaret more appropriately sent. A curious by-path of Henry's diplomatic relationships were the negotiations with Duke Sculius of Norway about compensation for losses suffered by Norwegian traders at the hands of English pirates during John's reign. The friendly interchange of notes may have indirectly led to the English Benedictine mission to Norway, of which Matthew Paris was himself a member.

Europe, from the monarch's point of view, was a family system and marriage the way to prominence; she was also one Church which Henry was pledged by his feudal contract to aid and counsel against the worst enemy, secularism. In judging the crisis in the Church in England which the ecumenical struggle of Pope and Emperor was to provoke, it is essential to avoid exaggeration. Englishmen have seldom had a true notion of the meaning and purpose of the papal monarchy, and in the thirteenth century monastic chroniclers were no exception. Matthew Paris, who spoke slightingly of the work of the Friars, could not fully grasp the needs of the universal Church-State. Many of its abuses he castigates sternly and well. With incomparable verve he would attack incompetent papal presentees, the usurious transactions of papal merchants in England, the *non-obstante* clause in papal bulls; but his outlook never comprehended the fiscal implications of Innocent III's great ideal, nor grasped the necessity (from the curial point of view) of supporting the central organisation which alone could give it practical form. Henry, though he had become Frederick's brother-in-law, viewed it with sympathy, while at times disapproving of the new methods of the Curia during the critical pontificate of Innocent IV. But his gratitude for indispensable help in the past did not make his disapproval whole-hearted enough to be effective; he lacked the power of loyal and respectful remonstrance which enabled Louis IX to keep the Gallican Church above the oncoming tide; and the suspicion of his compliance with papal demands in order to secure his own nominees to the episcopate was strongly founded. By 1240 it was becoming clear that parochial welfare and the rights of patrons—the two, it must be allowed, not always synonymous—were seriously threatened, whether by the contributions demanded for the war against Frederick, which formed the subject of the Berkshire rectors' protest that year (1240) and of the letter of the English bishops to Innocent IV in 1247, or by Innocent's licences to hold in plurality, exemptions from residence, and provisions, the recurring theme of Bishop Grosseteste's indignation. The tension with the Curia was all the more painful because in Rome lay the only hope of purification and reform in a Church which stood sorely in need of a periodical tonic. In 1236 the Legate Otto had held a Council at London for this end, and its salutary canons against the immorality and ignorance of the lower clergy and the lack of proper procedure in the Courts Christian, attacked abuses which find frequent mention in English diocesan canons of the early thirteenth century. Ottobono's constitutions of 1268 envisaged similar deficiencies. Their reform was the aim of all pastoral spirits who, like Robert Grosseteste, combined devotion to Rome with the conviction that the care of souls was the mainspring of the Church's life.

Yet practical reforming activity was outweighed by the constant drain of subsidy and tithe, and by the treatment of the benefice with cure of souls as a source of emolument like an exhibition or scholarship. In 1226 patrons had been put on their guard by the request, transmitted by the Legate Romanus, for two prebends from every diocese and a monk's share from every monastery, in order to subvent curial needs and to stop the system of gratuities in suits at Rome. The magnates, following the French example at the Council of Bourges, refused with misplaced hilarity; for the poverty of the Curia was to make itself felt far more severely later on. Before 1245 there was clerical taxation in plenty and reluctance felt to contribute against a man for whom people had much sympathy in England; but taxation alone would not have provoked the protests of the crucial years (1245–57). Letters of expostulation to Innocent IV in 1246 stated that the promised action had not been taken to remedy the English grievances presented at Lyons alleging that Provisions up to "60,000 marks a year" were being made, in return for which a twentieth had been granted by the prelates. The protest drew from Innocent IV the threat of excommunication upon the prelates, whereupon the king, pacified by a papal grant of the commutation of crusaders' vows, gave way, and the twentieth was levied. Pressure was brought to bear upon Archbishop Boniface, who owed his position largely to papal influence, to take a year's revenue of all churches vacant within the province, and, in addition to this and the collection of the annual tribute of 1000 marks, the system of Provisions continued unabated. Although Innocent in a moment of difficulty was prepared to relax the *amount* of Provisions[1], the alliance of Curia and King, which cemented itself after 1249, effectively prevented any steps being taken. The *condominium* of Pope and King in the English Church was sealed by the grant to Henry in 1250 of the crusading tithe for three years, to be paid when the king was ready to start. Henry was not prepared to move till 1252[2], and in the meantime he received the commutation of vows which amounted to a large sum. In 1250 came Frederick II's death, which revived at the

[1] Cf. *Chron. Maj.* VI (*Additamenta*), pp. 133–4.
[2] See the documents printed in *Foedera*, I, 285–7.

Curia the old plan of uniting Sicily to the papal dominions. This underlay the offer of the Sicilian Crown, which Henry accepted for Edmund, and for this the taxation of the clergy was extended from three years to five, while in return for a highly problematical payment of £100,000 from the Curia when Henry started on the expedition of recovery, the English king was to stand surety for the immediate debts of the Holy See, reckoned at 134,541 marks. The next Pope, Alexander IV, made Henry renounce the claim to the £100,000. If ever a man was in the grip of an impossible bargain, it was Henry III; and meanwhile Westminster had to be continued, the expenses of the Gascon expedition of 1253 met, and a Welsh campaign paid for. We have emphasised these demands because the taxation of clerical spiritualities has an important effect on the procuratorial representation of the clergy. From 1226, the year when convents and chapters were represented, through 1237, 1240 when the bishops pressed for the presence of archdeacons, 1254 when representatives of the diocesan clergy were summoned, 1255, 1257, to 1258, the convent and the diocese are becoming articulate, and the secular church borrows and adopts the capitular impulse in the religious orders, that started with Cîteaux and Prémontré and was generalised by the decree of the Lateran Council of 1215. From Benedictines and Austin Canons[1] as much as from the mendicant orders this constitutional development may have been transmitted, till it culminated in a fully representative Convocation.

Under grievances partly administrative, partly financial, the magnates, too, were uniting. From 1240 to 1258 the Wardrobe was in foreign keeping. Owing to the campaigns of 1242–3 and 1253–4, receipts and expenses had almost doubled since the period of its English custodians, Walter of Kirkham and Geoffrey of the Temple (1234–40). Once more it was tending to confuse with its own operations the work of both Chancery and Exchequer. Royal employees like Edward of Westminster and William of Haverhill, whose activities we noticed above, were not men to draw the line carefully. It has been pointed out that the succession of Chancellors who held office from 1244 to 1258 were not persons of high ecclesiastical dignity or aristocratic standing[2]. They were efficient servants under Henry's thumb. It was perhaps the desire to avoid this type of official just as much as their grievance at the way in which money grants were spent that led the magnates in 1244, the year of Ralph Neville's death, to make the grant of a subsidy after the Gascon expedition the occasion of a demand for a new Chancellor who was to be chosen with their assent. What Stubbs called "the demand of a ministry" was the embodiment of this spirit. Henry complied with the letter of their request, but not with the intention; and the result was the complaint of

[1] See the account of early Chapters of the Augustinian Canons in H. E. Salter *Chapters of the Augustinian Canons*, pp. ix–xii and 1–8.

[2] Tout, *op. cit.* I, p. 285.

1248 that the offices of State as well as the Chancery were in the hands of unworthy servants of the Crown, removable at pleasure. Henry promised to make their offices permanent, but the arrangements for a yearly-appointed Chancellor, and for the scrutiny of his office, made in the Oxford Parliament of 1258, suggest that the promise was not kept. Behind these demands lay, naturally enough, common reluctance to grant the subsidies required in 1238, 1242, and at the other times, in addition to the normal feudal taxation. The king's farms, escheats, and wardships, the whole bundle of rights later known as the *praerogativa regis*, were enough, it was argued, to support the king; and it may be remembered that the tenth and fifteenth were not yet established as a fully regular institution in return for which redress of grievances was automatically granted. But there were more far-reaching causes of complaint binding together the magnates, which till 1258 could only find expression in the demand for the confirmation of the Great Charter, a shadowy advantage in general, however much particular clauses of the 1225 reissue might benefit individual litigants in the courts. Then, in the Petition of the Barons at Oxford, just as in the articles of the Church Synod at Merton the same year, were formulated specific complaints, beside which the grumbling against aliens, against gracious aids and papal collectors, was of little account. The simple tenor of these was that a great bureaucracy was getting out of hand, the creation of Angevin method and experience over-reaching itself; and the attempt was made to capture the whole mechanism of government, to bring back the aristocratic régime of great officials, in this instance made responsible to the baronial Council, and to put the household system in a subordinate place. The magnates at last saw that force was needed, and decided that that force should be a sworn association into which the king together with his relations must enter by oath in order to restrain his own servants and be guided by the community of his people. For while Henry had been emulating the Sainte Chapelle or dreaming of Sicily and the Holy War, profound developments in the organisation of society and in the relation of the law to these developments had been taking place. These, the legal and constitutional changes which they demanded, and the result of the attempts to make them effective, constitute the interest of the years 1258–72.

To attribute, in common with several monastic chroniclers, the baronial movement of 1258 to 1267 to the desire to expel the alien, to secure office for the king's "natural" councillors whom he had forsaken, and to curtail extravagant expenditure, would be to neglect deeper causes arising primarily from the greater articulation of community life and from the fact that the social groups now realising themselves were finding a voice and, to a limited extent, a policy. These potent forces, evoked by the increasing contact of government with society, operated on the side of a party many members of which would have denied their efficacy or their existence. That they did so operate was due partly to the genius of one section, perhaps of one leader, in the baronial ranks, partly to the influence of contemporary lawyers and jurists who had no intention of putting back the clock to the hour of rigid feudalism. The liberal school of constitutional historians has seen in the movement the first steps taken towards representative government by Parliament. At the present, emphasis tends rather to be laid upon the drastic and revolutionary character of the new control, and upon the positive efforts made in the direction of reforming local government and of ameliorating the tenant's relation to his lord. Neither, at the one extreme, representation in the three annual parliaments projected, nor, at the other, mere feudal loyalty to an alien adventurer would have kept England in turmoil for four years—for research has shewn that the battle of Evesham did not end the struggle—or have produced the Statute of Marlborough, and, through that enactment, the Statutes of Westminster I and of Gloucester in Edward I's reign. The older view needs a new orientation.

Throughout the century the contact between individuals, whether persons or groups, and the governmental machine was being organised in many new directions. As administrative technique grows, that contact is expressed in new formulae which tend to crystallise and consolidate the bodies that make use of them. A new record, perhaps, or a new division or heading in the already existing record, makes its appearance, and the novelty at once betrays some change in the methods or personnel of the central or local authority. The great consolidating factor of the first forty years of Henry III's reign is the steady increase in the number of the original writs. In Glanvil's treatise thirty-nine were to be found; in a list contained in a Cambridge manuscript of the early years of Henry's reign, which Maitland summarised, there are fifty-eight; and in a later register, also at Cambridge, dating before the Provisions of Westminster (1259) but later than 1236, one hundred and twenty-one. It is the great time of judicial invention, and the learned clerk, trained *in utroque jure*, is beginning to make himself felt. The great contemporary jurist Bracton laid down that full effect should be given to a writ, even if its form was unusual, as long as it was not directly contrary to law; and even then, if by special favour an unusual form was devised, the judges must uphold it, provided that the Council had not expressly dissented[1]. The procedure of the *Curia Regis* throughout its various expressions—the court *coram rege*, where are heard the pleas that follow the king, the bench, where pleas of land and many conveyances take place, and the courts of the justices on General Eyre and other business—hardens under the need of dealing discriminately with the various writs of the Chancery, which now, with the increase of judicial remedies, becomes every day more departmentalised,

[1] *De legibus Angliae*, f. 414 b.

as the creation of the Hanaper in 1244 bears witness. In the early part of John's reign the judges of the various curial bodies were re-absorbed among the king's *familiares*; the distinction between the *placita coram rege* and the *placita in banco* was in its essence neither one of personnel, nor of the forms of action, nor even of superiority and inferiority. The *coram rege* court differed in its atmosphere[1], was the older and more primitive organism, more equitable and so more authoritative, for the Council was close in the background, and the king himself was the fountain of justice. But the clause of the Charter forbidding common pleas from following "our court" and the multiplication of writs, emphasised the distinction between it and the other body, a distinction that comes into being before 1234 when special rolls headed *placita coram rege* appear, while the king's minority and the primarily administrative character of the Justiciarship sent the pleas into the hands of professionals who found it necessary to discriminate between the forms of action. A prominent factor in the crystallising process was the extension of the writ of trespass. More and more cases of which the fiction of violence (*vi et armis*) could be predicated came to be taken *coram rege*, and after the rebellion of 1263–7, when suits for recovery of lands under a special writ called *talem qualem* and innumerable cases of personal injury were heard, the land pleas were very largely sent into the bench. Not that *Assise et jurate* could not be heard *coram rege*—so late as 1268 we have a roll with this particular heading[2]—but the *coram rege* jurisdiction extended primarily to such cases when evoked from other courts, unless they directly touched some right of the Crown or were brought by prominent tenants-in-chief. The rise to supremacy of the *coram rege* tribunal in Henry's reign is marked, perhaps sealed, by the extension after 1265 of the writs of *certiorari* calling up to the king's judges the processes of suits heard locally. Hand in hand with this centralising development went a marked increase of judicial visitation in the counties. The questions asked on the General Eyre multiply; the chapters cover not only felony and the proprietary rights of the Crown, but also details of local administration[3]. A stream of questions, to be settled by local recognition, pours forth from the Courts and the Exchequer. Domesday Book and the Black and Red Books of the Exchequer are not enough; material is being accumulated, by feudal collections and by local inquests, for that amazing Edwardian anthology of fees, the *Liber Feodorum*, and the Exchequer Court, though its investigations are strictly concerned with the claims of Pipe Roll accountants from year to year, has by 1236 started a record of its own, to which administrators can refer. All this great activity involving local response has, just as much as the well-known expedients for the assessment and

[1] F. M. Powicke in EHR, xxxix, pp. 265–6.

[2] Curia Regis Roll, 182.

[3] See Miss H. M. Cam's *Studies in the Hundred Rolls* (*Oxford Studies in Social and Legal History*, vol. vi), pp. 9–29.

collection of taxes on movables and for the defence of localities[1], brought to the fore the County Court, with its two great public assemblies (*magni comitatus*) and its ordinary monthly meetings, its juries which, in Maitland's words, "distill the *fama publica*," and, most of all, its committee of four, sometimes six, knights who scrutinise the presentments of the hundreds at the Eyre, bear its record[2] to Westminster when summoned there, and are supported by contributions from the townships as a permanent, not a mere temporary institution. It has brought, not indeed to his decline, but to new professional status, the county knight of local standing who fills the office of sheriff, presiding over his deputy and a staff of literate and often calligraphic clerks. The military defender of the shire now sits in an office in the castle, surrounded by rolls, tally-bundles, and chests. The Exchequer has made him responsible for all the debts owed to the king in his shire saving those of towns or liberties in his bailiwick that account directly at the Exchequer. In his hands, fuller than any other man's, is the execution of all writs from the Courts and from the Exchequer, with again the exception of those franchise-holders that possess the *retornum*. His is the duty of proclaiming and publishing royal charters and commands, the summoning of all juries, the collections of fines and amercements, the enforcement of the payment of feudal dues. But the great responsibility laid upon his shoulders and on his bailiffs and officers has brought again the problems of 1170 in acuter form. The shrievalty was indispensable; but by the middle of the thirteenth century it was riddled with grave abuses. We have only to go to the *capitula itineris*, the Petition of the Barons in 1258, or to the questions and solitary return of the Inquest of that year[3], to see what these abuses could be. Against this royal specialist poor men had little chance of local action. The appeal was formidable, only a last resort; and the General Eyre came too infrequently.

No less conscious and articulate a community was the borough. The great early period of charter-giving was over; but the transference of fiscal and commercial privileges to new urban centres, the great multiplication of seignorial boroughs and the grant of the return of writs, carry on the advance. Most valued of all were the privileges of being able to exclude the Sheriff. The *non-intromittat* clause in borough charters forbade him to interfere in urban affairs; the clause conferring the *retornum brevium* gave the borough the right to execute the precepts of the king's writs. The first communities to receive this were Canterbury and Colchester

[1] See the series of writs printed in Stubbs, *Select Charters*, 9th ed., pp. 351–66.

[2] Apart from sending the record of a process before Justices in Eyre (the meaning here), the County Court, in the thirteenth century, is evidently a court of record. See Hilary Jenkinson, *Plea Rolls of Mediaeval County Courts* (*Cambridge Historical Journal*, I, pp. 103–7, esp. p. 105).

[3] Discovered by Miss Cam, and printed in E. F. Jacob, *Studies in the Period of Baronial Reform and Rebellion* (*Oxford Studies in Social and Legal History*, vol. VIII), pp. 337–44.

in 1252; and, in the time of the king's worst need (1256–7), the privilege was sold to no less than seventeen boroughs. These and earlier grants had brought with them the institution, generally unmentioned in the charters, but implicitly recognised in the address of the royal writs sent to cities and boroughs, of a mayor and "good" men or councillors. Though before 1215 London alone was authorised by charter to elect a mayor, in nine other leading cities and boroughs the right had been assumed and was taken for granted. Other towns followed quickly. But burghal growth had brought its social evils. The essence of a borough was, as Professor Tait has explained, burgage tenure, "tenements held by low quit rents and freely transferable." Ease of conveyance and considerable freedom of devise (except where the *retrait lignager* was customary) led to the accumulation of burgages in the hands of rich families, and commercial privileges. especially those of the gild merchant, gave rise to divergent interpretations of the share of taxation to be borne by various elements in the community. We find, from the middle to the end of the thirteenth century, movements of the "poor" and "lesser" or "middle" (*mediocres*) men against the "rich" or the "old legal men," in explanation of which Dr Unwin pointed to the forced loans on account of taxation through which the leading burgesses had become creditors of the rest. "The movement of resistance to this kind of oppression," he observed, "was combined with an attempt to maintain or re-establish the gild principle of equal shares in the monopolies and privileges of local trade, which the enterprise and capital of the richer gildsmen had set aside."[1] It is significant that the baronial movement under Simon de Montfort should have roused the lesser gildsmen in London, whose example spread to other towns and involved, as Wykes tells us, almost all the *communia mediocris populi regni Angliae.*

Change was invading the feudal groupings of society. Of the three types of private jurisdiction, baronial (the court of the honour or barony), franchisal (the private hundred court), and domanial (the court of the manor), the first was now definitely on the decline. The military tenants of the honour were more and more tending to hold directly of the king military service in person was becoming increasingly harder to enforce and in honour courts, like that of Ramsey, the attendance of suitors had seriously fallen off. The more the subdivision of the fees, the greater the difficulty of regulating the repartition of suit and of exacting payments in lieu of service. The history of scutage in Henry's reign witnesses to the growing weakness of the power of feudal lords over their military tenants. New avocations and distributions of fees had made the levy so complicated and the reduction of the *servitium debitum* which had taken place in John's reign had caused such great loss to the Crown, that fining tended to become the normal procedure of the Crown vassal; and after 1257, from which date onwards no further scutage was taken by Henry III, it became

[1] *History,* IX, Oct. 1924, p. 234.

the sole alternative to service[1]. The honour, divided and subdivided, still hangs together, even though it may escheat to the Crown, but only because the Exchequer, on the look-out for extra burdens, will have it so. Perhaps the only real remnant of the old personal service is found in the organisation of the staffs, the *familiae*, of great magnates, consisting of knights valets, bachelors, esquires, and clerks, often men of standing and experience in their counties, who are enfeoffed with lands in the honour, and, unable to fly their own pennons like the bannerets, adhere to the persons of the great, from whom they have received or will receive the dignity of knighthood. The failure of the central baronial authority to solve the problems of suit is leaving for revision by royal provision and ordinance much in feudal custom that is tangled and obsolete. On the other hand franchisal rights—both view of frankpledge and the three-weekly court—are living realities, because they are profitable. It is these that the Crown, as the Inquiry of 1255 indicates, is beginning to regard with watchful eye. Even within the private hundred the king is claiming certain rights, so that ultimately the jurisdiction of the territory attaching to the immediate centre of the liberty, the *banlieu*, will become, as at Ramsey and Glastonbury, the only sphere from which he may be excluded. Within liberties, as without, the problem of administrative misgovernment is growing serious. The liberty is a financial asset more than a moral liability, and the bailiffs of the alien franchise-holder are no better and no worse than the officials of English barons like Richard de Clare. Once more, as in the case of the royal officers, a supervising authority is lacking, and to plead against the very convener of the private hundred is a practical impossibility.

The change in the old feudal relations, the product of peace, commercialism, and education—for we are on the threshold of an age when, owing to new collegiate institutions, education becomes more downspread —is registered in the growth of the common law built up upon the practice of the King's Court. The system in its transition is described for us by Henry de Bracton, who collected in his Note-book leading cases from the rolls of Martin de Pateshull and William de Raleigh, and in his work on the laws of England wrote our first standard text-book of English litigation. His portrayal emphasises the importance of the writ and the dependence of English law on decided cases. He shews that the remedies given by English law are not yet limited; to meet new cases in which it was thought advisable that an action should be granted, the Chancery clerks could issue *brevia magistralia*. The same inventive faculty has been at work filling up the gaps between the earlier possessory and proprietary Assizes. *Novel disseisin* and *Mort d'Ancestor* cannot cover contingencies now arising from leases and succession. The law is moving away from the rigidities of feudalism, and its pilots are the judges of the King's Court. Termors have claimed and won a new protection; to evade the rule that litigation about

[1] Miss H. M. Chew, *Scutage under Edward I*, EHR, XXXVII, pp. 324–5.

proprietary rights must begin in the lord's court, the writs of entry, suggesting a flaw in the present tenant's title, have been devised. To supplement *Mort d'Ancestor*, the actions of Aiel, Besaiel, and Cosinage have come into being; new forms have been found to protect the lands of minors from waste; and litigants are flocking to the new trespass actions where the jury decides on a point of fact raised in the pleading rather than on the question put to the recognitors in the writ that started the process. It should not surprise us to find the author of this great treatise among the justices specially employed by the reformers of 1259, or mitigating the rigours of the treatment meted out to those reformers after the fall of Kenilworth in 1266. It is natural that those who had most contact with representative forces in the counties should not be bound by oligarchical prejudice, nor, in an age when divine right was growing, bow down before the image of Godhead upon earth.

In fine, conditions were ripe for the rise of a middle element in society. Could it make its influence felt upon the government which had unknowingly called it into being? Paradoxically enough, the baronial movement was to provide an answer. There was everything that was oligarchic about its inception. At the Easter Parliament that met at London from 9 April till 5 May 1258, the king, who had asked for relief in his bankruptcy after an unsuccessful expedition in Wales, was confronted by Roger Bigod on behalf of the baronage with the demand for the banishment of the Poitevins and the appointment of a commission of reform as the one and only condition of a grant. Henry perforce accepted, and a Council of Twenty-four, half royal, half baronial nominees, was appointed, which evidently set to work before the adjourned Parliament assembled at Oxford at the beginning of June. Their report and an account of the action taken in accordance with it are embodied in the memorandum of the Council known as the Provisions of Oxford, shewing what their plans were. At the immediate moment, the appointment and swearing-in of an official Justiciar, Treasurer, and Chancellor, and of new native-born guardians of the royal castles; for the future, an inquest into the misdeeds of local officials, regulations on the conduct of newly-appointed administrators and of nominees to the shrievalty and escheatorships, and recommendations for a series of reforms in the household and the Change of London, and for three annual parliaments. Most important of all, the baronial Twelve had overcome the Poitevin resistance on the Council to the extent of recommending the election of a body of fifteen as a standing organ of government, who were to meet at the three annual assemblies of Michaelmas, the Purification, and the first of June, another body of twelve chosen by the barons on behalf of the whole community. Another committee of twenty-four was chosen to treat of an aid. This new arrangement, which gave the dominating voice to the barons (they had nine representatives on the fifteen), was set in motion on 26 June, when four electors appointed by the Twenty-four were to make their choice. By 4 August the new arrangements had been made and the king issued letters patent promising to observe whatever the Council of Fifteen might decide. That body some time in July adjourned to London and met daily at the New Temple as a sort of statutory commission. On 18 October the king issued in French and English the decree calling upon all men to swear that they would hold and defend the arrangements made by the Council. It is important to realise what these arrangements or "establishments" (*isetnesses*) were. The Council was not a body of the old type, but a new, all-controlling, revolutionary committee. It controlled the Great Seal, through the Justices kept in close touch with the Exchequer, and was the authority that authorised the payment of debts or of important grants and the appointment of financial custodians. It took the task of local reform very seriously. The Justiciar Hugh Bigod was sent out into the counties to follow up the Inquest into administrative grievances taken by the four knights in each county, and both before and after Michaelmas heard complaints, presented probably by written petition, of royal and seignorial misgovernment. At the Michaelmas Parliament the Sheriffs were changed and the new personnel was chosen uniformly from the knights who conducted the Inquiry of the autumn. They were appointed "in the manner provided by the magnates of the Council": that is, they each took an oath to avoid extortions, and to act in effect as *custodes* or "keepers," not as *firmarii*, *i.e.* persons who farmed out the hundreds or wapentakes and had the sums calculated to be so obtained reckoned in their account by the Exchequer as part of the *proficuum*. This prohibition of the letting of bailiwicks became a reality in 1264, as a sheriff, charged in 1267 with more than he could pay, was to claim[1]. In Hilary term, 1259, we find the four knights electing one of their number to be sheriff. The new form of election was to be a vital issue in the forthcoming struggle with Henry.

In the spring of 1259 occurred the first serious difference of opinion in the Council. The returns of the Inquest of 1258 and the records of the Justiciar's circuit must have made it clear that abuses in baronial liberties still needed amendment. Outside the liberties, the king had taken the steps prescribed; within, no measures had been taken. This was evidently the reason for the passionate charge made by Simon de Montfort against Richard de Clare, that the latter was not carrying out a policy of common agreement. The outburst led his friends to remonstrate with the Earl of Gloucester, and the magnates issued an undertaking (March 1259) to allow the abuses of their own officials to be corrected. But the slowness of the magnates to set their own houses in order was in all probability the factor that provided in the autumn of 1259 the protest of a body termed by the

[1] Giles de Gousle, sheriff of Lincolnshire, who complained that he was 200 marks down "because the bailiffs of the Wapentakes were elected according to the Provisions of Oxford and did not pay farms as in times of peace." Exchequer Plea Roll, 1 e, m. 2 d. Cf. Jacob, *op. cit.* p. 266.

Burton Annalist the "Community of the bachelery of England," an association of lesser country landowners serving on the staffs of the great magnates and now attending them at Westminster, whose aims were clearly in harmony with those of Simon de Montfort in the spring[1]. In accordance with this pressure there was added to the enactment which the Council had for long, probably ever since August 1258, been preparing, a number of administrative clauses, which were published as an integral part of the Provisions of October 1259 (commonly known as the Provisions of Westminster, but called by contemporaries "The Provisions of Oxford" as they completed the work of the Oxford Parliament). These clauses, so far from weakening, strengthened the control of the Council over the King[2] by establishing a financial committee with strong judicial representation to sell the wardships, to consider questions of tallage, and to help the Justiciar and Exchequer in the appointment of sheriffs for the coming year. The Council was to delegate two or three of its members to be with the king in the intervals between its plenary sessions. In local government the committee of four knights was to be used to observe and inquire into the conduct of royal and seignorial officials, and to form a reserve for the shrievalty, the personnel of which was to consist of members of the Vavasour class. The administrative clauses were largely conceived in the interest of this grade. In addition an Eyre of grievances was to be undertaken by visiting commissions of two justices and a member of the Council in each one of six areas, and procedure by complaint was once more to be adopted. The records of this circuit, till it was cancelled in June 1260. bear full witness of the need for reform that existed. The legal clauses of the Provisions completed and added to an already published interim enactment of the Barons called the *Providentia baronum Angliae* (March 1259). They aimed at simplifying, and relieving some of the burdens connected with, suit to the lord's court, at protecting the rights of minors, determining the frequency of pleas of dower and advowson, and dealing with the problems of distraint and grievances arising from the sheriff's tourn. A composite measure, like the earlier Statute of Merton, many of its clauses were based on previous rulings or *determinationes*; it gathered together the various tentatives towards legal advance, and, as we see from the Plea Rolls, was eagerly resorted to by litigants.

The next three years were to mark the rise to definite leadership in the baronial party of an already prominent member. His memorial cross at Evesham to-day terms him, in the words of a contemporary poet, *Protector gentis Angliae.* Simon de Montfort embodied so fully the spirit of the Provisions, that their survival seemed to hang upon his success or failure. Yet in 1258, and perhaps the early part of 1259, Richard de Clare

[1] Jacob, *op. cit.* pp. 126–34.

[2] F. M. Powicke, *Some Observations on the Baronial Council* (1258–1260) *and the Provisions at Westminster* (in *Essays in Medieval History presented to T. F. Tout*, p. 128).

and the Earl Marshal, Roger Bigod, stood equal with him in the Council. He represents the turning away of the movement from oligarchy, whose aim was simply the restriction of the Crown, to constructive aristocracy based upon more deeply sunk foundations. He was great and heroic because of his sympathy with all that was best in the political thought of his day—the constitutionalism of Grosseteste, the later and maturer reflections of Bracton—and because he saw the possibilities of self-government latent in English local institutions. Stubbs' magnificent dictum that he "had had genius to interpret the mind of the nation" scarcely over-states the truth. This local sympathy evidently underlay his quarrel with Richard de Clare, though personal reasons doubtless contributed, for, while attracting the devotion of his inferiors, Simon antagonised his equals. His relations with Henry III had cast a shadow on the lives of both men. He was feared above all others by the king who had sent him to govern Gascony and failed to support his too drastic policy (1248–52), who, by uncertain handling of affairs in that province, had endangered his interests in the south of France, who had, he thought, denied his wife the full dowry due to her, and by his evasions of the Charter was threatening his rights in the honour of Leicester. Private motives mingled with public, but public were uppermost in his mind. By 1260 the new constitution had begun to fail. Henry started the fight against the Provisions, in which he succeeded first in shaking off the central control of the baronial nominees (1260–1) and then in getting rid of the Justiciar and the locally-appointed sheriffs. The Peace of Paris (to which we shall refer later) had brought support to his cause; the Curia listened to his complaints and granted him absolution from his oath to the Provisions (13 April 1261). He was strong enough to publish his freedom from all restraint in May 1262; but the Provisions, the bone of the whole contention, were reissued in January or February 1263, and not till 1264, when their repudiation by the Court had become an established fact for more than six months, were they submitted to the decision of Louis IX and proclaimed by him derogatory to the royal dignity. The reason for this long interval of obstinate bargaining and manœuvre is to be found partly in the strong local appeal of the administrative provisions, partly in the rift in the baronial ranks which carried one section, anxious for compromise and no rupture, gradually over to the point of view of Henry and Edward, partly in the desire of the government not to cross the new Earl of Gloucester, young Gilbert de Clare, who was on Leicester's side. But by May 1263 Simon de Montfort had seen that war was inevitable and Edward had won over powerful support in the Welsh Marches. The story of the recourse to arms and the baronial victory of Lewes (14 May 1264) we need not tell, but shall pass immediately to the acts of de Montfort's administration (1264–5).

These are in harmony with the steps taken at the instance of the lesser landowners in 1259, rather than with the Acts of the Parliament of

1258 before Simon's supremacy had become unchallenged. For immediate security, guardians of the peace were appointed in each shire, and four knights, after the precedents of 1254 and 1261, were summoned to meet the king in Parliament on 22 June. In that assembly the king was placed under the tutelage of a Council of Government of nine persons, nominated by three electors chosen by the barons. Three Councillors were to be in constant attendance (here there is an echo of 1259) and by their advice the ministers and wardens of royal castles were to be appointed. The Provisions were confirmed and later (13 December 1264) issued at Worcester as "The Charter made to the Community of England." They contained, it is important to observe, additional clauses that later made their way into the Statute of Marlborough. The immediate task of the government was that of defence against the queen, who was threatening an invasion from France; hence it was not till 20 January 1265 that it was possible to hold a prolonged parliament in which the affairs of the disturbed March could be settled, the position of Edward (still in confinement) determined, and the legality of the new settlement provided for. The writs for this gathering were sent to fifty-five abbots, twenty-six priors, five earls, and eighteen barons; and general summonses went to the Sheriffs for two knights from each county, and to boroughs for two of the "more discreet, lawful, and worthy burgesses." Legal records of the time leave no doubt as to the sympathy of many prominent urban centres with the earl's movement. This great step formed a precedent for the Council of 1268 held just before the legatine Assembly, when a selected group of cities and boroughs sent representatives. The new form of government was strictly dependent upon harmony among the *electores*, and this was not to be. Personal friction, as his later conduct was to shew, rather than grounds of policy divided Gilbert de Clare, one of the *electores* with the Bishop of Chichester and Simon, from his great colleague. In the early months of 1265 the young earl intrigued with the Marchers, and in May 1265 Edward saw his chance. Raising his adherents in Cheshire and Shropshire while Simon de Montfort was engaged in Wales, he took Gloucester by the promise of pardon to its garrison if they surrendered. Simon's summons of his eldest son from Pevensey to Kenilworth was not in time to be of aid. Edward forestalled him, marched on Kenilworth and crushed the younger Simon, then turned to defeat and slay the father at Evesham (4 August 1265).

But the baronial movement was by no means dead. The reckless and extraordinarily haphazard granting away of the confiscated lands of the rebels after Evesham provoked the bitter resistance of the Disinherited, and the formation of independent centres of resistance at Kenilworth, Axeholm, and Ely, that pillaged the countryside in sullen despair. That the government was brought to a better mind and to a recognition of the magnitude of the problem caused by the grants was due in part to the pacific intervention of the Legate Ottobono after Kenilworth had fallen (1266), in part to the fine, if impulsive, action of Gilbert de Clare. After the siege of Kenilworth the legate was prominent in securing the terms of the *Dictum* which laid down the principle "no disherison, but re-purchase." Rebels were allowed to buy back their lands from loyalist grantees at a rate proportionate to their degree of guilt, which had to be judicially determined. But the terms were very hard, and recourse was not generally had to the process till the autumn of 1267. By that time a new step had been taken. In 1265 and 1266 Gilbert de Clare had shewn his sympathy for the rebels—he had been one himself—by restoring without fines or re-purchase many of the lands of Simon de Montfort's supporters which his bailiffs had confiscated after Evesham. After the *Dictum* had been published he entered into an understanding with John d'Eyvill, the soul of the defence of Ely, and concerted with him a rebellion which brought the government to its senses. While the king was at Cambridge, Gloucester seized London, whither the Disinherited came flocking to him *quasi ad tutorem*, and John d'Eyvill slipped out of Ely to join him. Held up at Stratford (Essex) the king was in a serious quandary, as his frantic calls for help from overseas shew; but King Richard 'of Almain' succeeded in bringing the parties together, and a pardon for all Gloucester's very large mesnée was granted, together with protection for all Disinherited (virtually exiles before) coming to make their peace with the king. Then and only then was it possible to send out into the counties a special Eyre to apply the terms of the *Dictum* equitably and mercifully. Surviving records of this circuit testify to the widespread nature of the disturbance, to the fact that locally the rebellion (as was the case in 1381) had been largely directed against the official classes loyal to the king, that it had been supported by large numbers of the lower clergy and not a few abbots and priors, and that a considerable following of county gentry, not bound to the baronial side by feudal ties, had thrown in their support on the side of their great upholder.

If Simon de Montfort's action had failed, it had at any rate brought English local government a step further along its path. The discoveries made in the inquests and trials to which, directly or indirectly, it had given rise, formed an essential preliminary to the great investigations of Edward I. The action of the country knights, the earl's sympathy with their grievances and reliance upon their co-operation, pointed the way to that most characteristic of English regional institutions, the Justice of the Peace. Legally, the advance made was of high importance. The inseparable connexion that must exist between administrative inquiry and legislative enactment had been demonstrated. The clauses of the Provisions of October 1259 dealing with suit, the sheriff's tourn, fines for *beaupleder*, and distresses, were the outcome of the experience of enlightened lawyers like Roger de Thurkelby, Gilbert de Preston, and Henry de Bracton, whose sympathy for the movement is clearly apparent. It was through them that the Statute of Marlborough, reasserting the principles of 1259, became an enactment which, in Maitland's words, "in many ways marks the end of feudalism." In foreign affairs the baronial Council had, largely through the work of Simon de Montfort, concluded the active negotiations which had been going on for five years with France (1254–9). The Treaty of Paris (December 1259), which is largely his work, terminated the English claim, that *damnosa haereditas*, upon Normandy, Anjou, Touraine, Maine, and Poitou; the French king ceded to Henry his rights in the bishoprics and cities of Limoges, Cahors, and Périgord; the Agenais was to remain provisionally in French hands while Henry was to receive the revenues of the province in the form of an annual rent; and the restored rights as well as the already existing English possessions in Gascony were to be held as fiefs from the French Crown. In addition, Louis undertook to pay Henry the upkeep of five hundred knights for two years. The second and third of these stipulations were to lead to trouble in later reigns, and a satisfactory settlement of them was never reached; in a sense the Hundred Years' War dates from the disputes arising out of these promised restorations. But the surrender of the claim to the northern territories helped to complete for England the nationalising process which their loss had begun; and the definition of the position of the English King in regard to the French Crown constituted, from a French point of view, an "acte de haute politique," as the late M. Auguste Longnon termed it, an essential step in the formation of French national unity. Both carried the two countries forward to the time when their community of institutions and culture weakened and each was to make its characteristic contribution to the European order.

CHAPTER IX.

THE REIGNS OF PHILIP AUGUSTUS AND LOUIS VIII OF FRANCE.

The long reign of Philip Augustus (1180–1223), of which the brief rule of his son Louis VIII may be regarded as a continuation, was the most striking period in the history of the Capetian kings.

Philip, it is true, only laid the foundations of a larger France. He did not, for example, build up a widespread centralised state, whose officials administered a common law subject to the correction of the royal court. In his day France, although in conventional speech it could, as we shall see, be given a wider interpretation, was still, as it long remained, an ill-defined narrow area around the cities of Paris and Orleans, stretching from the district of Senlis in a south-westerly direction to the borders of Berri. It was ill-defined because, although the extent of the royal domain was known, France was not sharply distinguished from districts with which, at any particular point, it might have social or geographical affinities, and this uncertainty was reflected in common speech by the varying usage of a term which had no legal validity. No legal validity, for within this political "France" local custom varied, just as it varied throughout the outlying fiefs, great and small, of the French Crown. In this period the existence of local customs was generally recognised, and within France we find the customs of Senlis and of Orleans, as well as of Paris. And it was the customs of Paris—of the area around Paris—which came to be known in the Middle Ages as the customs of France. They had grown up unaffected by conscious legislation, which is first found in the reign of St Louis. The decrees issued by his grandfather Philip were administrative—a law against blasphemy, an assize of arms, financial measures, an order for the paving of the streets of Paris, and so on[1]. Similarly, we must look forward to St Louis' reign to find a system of appeal by which the local administration of law could be supervised by the *curia regis*. Even then men thought with difficulty of the realm of France as a whole, and if lawyers occasionally spoke of a "consuetudo Francie" in the sense of juristic facts common to the whole kingdom, they were normally concerned with the interpretation of local custom.

What King Philip did was to put himself over large stretches of modern France in the same position as he occupied in this narrower medieval France. Needless to say, he was not merely a conqueror, seizing fiefs in which he had no interest. He was the overlord, availing himself of one

[1] The Ordinance of 1209 suppressing parage and that of 1214 on dower are exceptions, but their obligatory character should not be emphasised. Cf. the observation of Olivier Martin, *Histoire de la coutume de la prévôté et vicomté de Paris*, II, i, p. 269 (1926).

opportunity after another to take the place of vassals who were weak or dangerous. Thus he gave a content to the traditions of a monarchy which had a Carolingian origin, he made the style used in his charters, "Francorum rex," mean something, he shewed that the feudal ties which connected him with the princes west of the imperial fiefs and north of the Pyrenees had a reality in the nature of things.

Philip was a well-built, fresh-complexioned man. In youth he had, like his natural son, Philip Hurepel, a shock of untidy hair, but in later life he was bald. He is said to have had the effective use of only one eye, a defect of which his enemies were quick to take note. There is a story that a drawing of Philip, depicted with one eye, adorned the wall of King John's chamber; John shewed it one day to Philip's jester, temporarily a refugee from his master's wrath, who promptly forfeited all claim to favour by the remark: "No wonder that you all run away from him.' Philip was fond of good living, was very choleric, and by no means a man of strict morals; but he was moderate in his tastes—for example, he disliked display or extravagance in dress—and rapidly recovered from his outbursts of violent temper. Indeed he was, in many ways, a conventional level-headed Frenchman, energetic, practical, observant, a faithful son of the Church, and, though sometimes dominated by passion, rarely swayed by sentiment. He was the master of his household, and the memory of his sayings and little ways lingered long in the family circle. Judged by the standards of the age, Philip's household must have been an orderly community, perhaps rather dull and austere under the guidance of its observant master. An old man, who in St Louis' time was still attached to the service of the chamber, had rueful memories of the day on which he had put damp crackling logs upon the fire, and how Philip had in his anger promptly turned him out. Yet the careless fellow returned. On the great festal occasions display was allowed, and the king gave full rein to his natural feelings of generosity to the poor.

On the outside world Philip made a similar impression. In the eyes of some, it is true, he was the model of a glorious and successful King—Philip the Conqueror. The title *Augustus*, coined for him by his chaplain, William the Breton, was not current in the Middle Ages, but was popularised by the patriotic historians of a later age. In the eyes of others, such as the moralist Giles of Paris, he was a great man spoiled by hardness, avarice, and lust, but yet a real king, preferable to a man like Richard of England. But in general opinion he was a man of great practical wisdom and of apt pithy speech, terrible to the proud and the evil-doer, generous to the poor, always ready to discuss problems of Church or State without prejudice. Not specially cultivated or interested in learning and the arts, he recognised their value to society, and took the trouble to make the acquaintance of leading spirits, a Peter the Chanter or a Stephen Langton. He had an unusual dislike of blasphemy, and his favourite oath was "by the lance of St James." His sagacity was not the sagacity of a patient, far-sighted, self-restrained man, for he was impulsive and hot in temper; it was the quality of a man whose energies were always well directed and whose mind was always on the alert. It is remarkable that, in spite of his passionate nature, he was very careful for his personal safety. There was a lack of generosity in him, which made him a hard bargainer and, except at Bouvines, a bad leader in battle. He shrank from death, as he shrank from all sorts of waste and extravagance. And, just as he was a master of political intrigue, so he loved the science of military engineering, and preferred to undermine a fortress rather than to take it by assault.

The story of Philip's domestic life and of the marriage alliances in which he was concerned, is a good illustration both of his character and of the close relations which existed, in the life of a powerful medieval ruler, between his private affairs, the extension of his domain, and the course of his public or foreign policy. Through his mother Adela of Champagne, he was closely connected with the great family which impinged on either side upon the royal domain. When he was associated with his father Louis VII a few months before the latter's death (1 November 1179–18 September 1180), the lad of fourteen seemed likely to fall under the control of his four uncles, William, Archbishop of Rheims, Henry I, Count of Champagne, Theobald V, Count of Blois and Chartres, the last of the Seneschals of France, and Stephen, Count of Sancerre. The rich valleys of the middle Loire and of the upper Seine and its tributaries, with their noble churches, prosperous towns, and busy fairs were firmly held by a single house, whose closely-knit interests might well stifle those of the Crown. As we shall see, Philip from the outset shewed that he had other ideas. Family solidarity was maintained and lasted well into the next century, but Philip, like Saint Louis, was always sufficiently sure of himself to take his own line. He was indeed too much of a realist to be swayed by the influences of kinship. So far as is known, he was quite indifferent, for example, to the fortunes of his sister Agnes of France, who, in the year of his accession, was sent off, a child of eight years of age, to begin her troubled and romantic career in the East.

Philip's own marriages were as much dictated by political prudence as were his sister's, while his domestic life was even more chequered by passion; yet the astuteness of the man was unfailing, so that the stormiest episodes of his private life are inseparable from the grave interplay of the interests of Church and State and the relations between the Papacy and the Empire. His first marriage, which took place in April 1180, lasted ten years, until 1190, when his wife Isabella of Hainault, the mother of the later Louis VIII, died at the age of nineteen. The history of this marriage, Philip of France's earliest effort in self-emancipation, is the main theme in the history of the early years of the reign, and the agreements to which it gave rise affected the course of Franco-Flemish relations until 1226. Directly or indirectly it added to the French domain Artois,

Valois, and Vermandois. Philip's second marriage, with Ingeborg of Denmark, was inspired by less realistic political considerations, while its unhappy outcome involved him in a very serious conflict with Pope Innocent III. The story cuts across the main themes of our narrative and, at the risk of some loss in chronological sequence, may be told at once. In 1193 Philip had in hand a great attack upon Normandy. As part of a wider plan, he had also collected a fleet for the invasion of England. His alliance at this time with Canute VI, King of Denmark, was inspired by a desire for Danish aid. In return for a marriage alliance he is said to have asked for the transference to himself of the traditional claims of the successors of the great Canute to the English throne and for the assistance of the Danish forces for a year. The prospect of an understanding was not unattractive to Canute; French fashions and French culture had become the vogue, and the dismemberment of the great Saxon duchy in north Germany had not entirely relieved Denmark from its fears of German interference. But he was not prepared to go so far as Philip wished. He consented to send his sister Ingeborg, a beautiful girl of eighteen, with a dowry of 10,000 marks of silver, and the marriage took place in August at Amiens[1]. The king's pleasure in his bride changed in a few hours to a strong feeling of aversion, which he did not conceal during her coronation on the following day. The long agony of Ingeborg, which is fully revealed in the voluminous correspondence between king, queen, relatives, and the papal court, lasted for twenty years. It is clear that Philip was affected by a physical repugnance which he could only attribute to some evil agency (*maleficium*). He was in this regard no longer the politician, but a man whose sense of desperation in an intolerable situation rendered him, now reckless and cruel, now treacherously complaisant. The goodness of Ingeborg was not seriously in question, and her helplessness in a strange country among people whose language she did not understand stirred widespread sympathy. At one time she would be treated with a measure of consideration, at other times she was taken from convent to convent, or kept prisoner in a royal castle. During the worst period, some ten years after her marriage, she complained to the Pope that she was denied all society, denied too all the consolations of religion save an occasional mass and an occasional visit from some monk. She could have with her no congenial companions, could not choose her own confessor, was given bad food, and was deprived, not only of the comforts which befitted her station, but even of the necessary aids to a life of decency. But throughout she shewed herself as determined to insist upon her rights as Philip was to refuse them. The Popes to whom she appealed for justice were in a painful position. The octogenarian Celestine III did his best for her, but he had his own difficulties. Innocent III shewed his usual persistence, but

1 Philip, on the eve of the marriage, gave her as dowry (*in dotalicium*) the proceeds of the prévôté of Orleans, with Chécy, Châteauneuf, and Neuville (Delaborde, *Actes*, I. 552, no. 456).

Philip withstood him for fifteen years. This was a matter in which, so long as Ingeborg was not definitely repudiated as queen, only moral pressure could be exerted, and in which—as public affairs must outweigh domestic concerns—the wisest policy was a policy of patience.

At first Philip put himself clearly in the wrong. He persuaded a council of bishops and magnates at Compiègne that Ingeborg and he were related within the prohibited degrees; and the French bishops, headed by the Archbishop of Rheims, dissolved the marriage. The queen and her brother appealed to the Pope, Celestine III, who, after an examination of the evidence, annulled the decision (May 1195). Disregarding the papal injunctions, Philip took a more irrevocable step in defiance of the Church and, after approaching several ladies in vain, took as his wife in June 1196 Agnes, the daughter of the Duke of Meran or Merania, the great fief recently carved out of Bavaria by the Hohenstaufen for the Counts of Andechs. In the face of these facts the strong-minded Innocent, who succeeded to the Papacy in 1198, could not hesitate. The relations between Philip and Ingeborg might cause perplexity, but there could be no doubt what his duty was so long as Philip flouted a papal decree and lived with an intruder. Kings must be taught that they were not exempted from the duties of the ordinary Christian. The legate, Peter of Capua, was instructed to lay France under an interdict unless Philip would take back his lawful wife. After a fruitless council at Dijon in December 1199 the legate withdrew to Vienne, in imperial territory, and there, in another council, published the interdict on 13 January 1200[1].

France was not unfamiliar with the interdict, a favourite means of ecclesiastical pressure; but the terms of this particular suspension of spiritual gifts were severe, the occasion had been solemnly advertised, and feeling on both sides ran high. At first acquiescence was general, but soon the French clergy were strangely divided, and while some bishops, including the Archbishop of Sens and the Bishop of Paris, braved the displeasure of the king and the temporary alienation from their sees, many rallied to him. But on the whole, as the effects of the interdict made themselves felt, feeling turned against the king. During these months France was at peace, and popular enthusiasm was being aroused by preachers and papal propaganda for a new crusade. Innocent, without abating his demands, prepared for a settlement. He sent a new legate, Cardinal Octavian of Ostia, a member of his own family and a relative of the king. If Philip would repudiate Agnes and recognise Ingeborg, proceedings for a new trial might be opened. By this time Philip also was ready to compromise. The bishops, however friendly, were wavering and unhappy; there were some active men who, we may be fairly certain, stood out for peace, men like the outspoken Giles of Paris and Peter of Corbeil, the new Bishop of Beauvais, an old master in the Schools of Paris, who had at one time had the Pope among his pupils. Obstinacy

[1] The terms are printed in Hefele-Leclerq, v, pp. 1226–7.

would bring excommunication upon the king. So at another great council of the great men of the kingdom Philip met Ingeborg, for the first time since the Council at Compiègne, in the presence of the legate. He undertook to recognise her as his wife until the legal issue was decided in six months' time, and, on the strength of this understanding, the interdict was raised (7 September 1200). Agnes of Meran was separated from the king, but Ingeborg was placed in irksome confinement in the castle of Étampes.

So long as Philip did not persist in his repudiation of Ingeborg he was free to act as he pleased. He availed himself fully of this advantage at the council which met at Soissons in the following March. Elaborate preparations had been made for the trial. A second legate, the Benedictine John, cardinal-priest of St Paul, was on the way. Philip came with a band of jurists, the defenders of Ingeborg with their evidence and genealogies. As the cardinal Octavian was regarded with suspicion by the Danish party, the council was adjourned until his colleague arrived. At first the king had the advantage, and the most impressive defence of Ingeborg was made by an unknown cleric; but the arrival of John of St Paul changed the outlook. Philip decided that it was time for him to assume a dramatic part; early one spring morning he rode away with Ingeborg as his lawful wife; and the council was dissolved with nothing decided. In July Agnes of Meran—whose lot cannot have been a happy one—did Philip a last service by dying. The king established a nunnery in her memory and secured from the Pope the legitimation of her children. Ingeborg had to suffer twelve more years of neglect, humiliation, and cruelty, while the paper warfare went on interminably. At last in April 1213, in the midst of his arrangements for the invasion of England as the champion of an outraged Church, Philip took back his queen as suddenly as twenty years before he had rejected her. Everything was put right, all criticism was stilled, and everybody was or pretended to be happy. Ingeborg survived her husband for many years.

Agnes of Meran left two children, who were legitimated by the Pope. Mary, the elder, was used by her father with characteristic skill as a pawn in his political intrigues. She was betrothed to Arthur of Brittany, and, after the disappearance of that unfortunate young man, to Philip, Margrave of Namur, the brother of Baldwin of Flanders. Baldwin's absence on crusade, and his subsequent desertion of his western fief for the glories of empire in Constantinople, gave Philip of Namur additional importance. In 1206 the King of France attached him to his side, and the betrothal to Mary was part of the bargain. The pair were married in January 1211, but Philip of Namur died in the next year, and at the Great Assembly of Soissons in 1213 his young widow—a girl of sixteen or so—was given to her father's Rhenish ally, Henry of Brabant. The marriage was part of the elaborate compact by which the Duke of Brabant was bound to the side of Philip Augustus and Frederick of Hohenstaufen, and undertook to help the former in the projected invasion of England. Mary's brother, the second child of Agnes of Meran, was destined, almost from his birth, for an equally important rôle. He was named Philip after his father, and like his father was conspicuous by the shock of disorderly hair which gave him the nickname, Hurepel. In 1201, while a baby in the castle of Poissy, he was betrothed to Matilda, the heiress of Boulogne. The compact was renewed in 1209, when Philip Augustus began to suspect the fidelity of the Count of Boulogne, Renaud of Dammartin; and it was carried through after Renaud's fall in 1214. Nine years later, in 1223, Philip Hurepel was invested with the fief of Boulogne, and, as one of the great magnates of France, bore the sword at the coronation of his nephew, Louis IX.

The story of Ingeborg and of the interdict of 1200 throws much incidental light upon France and French society at the end of the twelfth century. The disputes with the Pope revealed the strength of the ties between the Crown and the clergy, and the possibilities of the independent temper which was to develop the Gallicanism of later days. The limitation of the interdict to a definite area, which did not correspond with diocesan but with feudal boundaries, raised legal difficulties whose settlement was to be an important precedent[1]. The interdict, according to the choniclers, was laid upon the whole of France (*Francia tota*), a phrase which gives us the current as distinct from the strict definition of France, for the country affected was, in the Pope's words, *terra quae regi tunc temporis adhaerebat*, and the list of bishops involved shews that France in this sense included the lands of Champagne, Blois, Burgundy, Nevers, and the fiefs of the north-east to the English Channel, but not the great fiefs of the north and west and south[2]. Normandy and Aquitaine were clearly not regarded as "adhering" to Philip, although their lord had done homage. It was a curious result of this distinction between France and the fiefs of the Plantagenets that the marriage between the twelve-year-old Louis and his twelve-year-old bride, Blanche of Castile, was celebrated within the Norman frontier, by the Archbishop of Bordeaux (May 1200). This marriage, so fraught with consequences, was part of an undertaking with Blanche's uncle, King John of England, and it took place in Normandy because the interdict prevented its celebration in France.

Such was Philip Augustus, a man who was able, through his steady waiting on circumstance, to turn even his passions and domestic errors to political advantage. The story of his reign has a threefold interest: first, the advance to the north-east, with the accompanying assertion of his mastery over his powerful relatives and vassals; secondly, his successful contest with the great house of Anjou; thirdly, his steady consolidation

[1] See Innocent's letter to the dean and chapter of Sens in the Decretals, lib. 1, tit. v, *de postulatione praelatorum*, c. 1 (Potthast n. 1043).

[2] The bishop of Auxerre sought to justify his opposition to the papal action by the plea that, as the successor of St Germanus, he was feudally independent of the King of France.

of his victories by the rounding off and administration of his vast new domain. Or, in other words, it is the story of the assertion of the supremacy, within a wider France, of the overlord in Paris and Orleans of the narrow *Francia*.

Philip was born in August 1165 and was only fourteen years of age when he was associated with Louis VII as King of France. His marriage in the following April, some months before his father's death, was his first act of self-assertion, for it was a declaration of alliance with Philip of Alsace, the Count of Flanders, against the family of his mother, Adela of Champagne. Philip of Alsace was the sort of man—brilliant, adventurous, astute, successful—to appeal to any boy of spirit, beset by a group of uncles who regarded their power as a matter of course. The pair disregarded the prejudices of the family. The young king married the count's niece Isabella of Hainault; and, early one morning, the queen was crowned in the abbey of Saint Denis, not by the Archbishop of Rheims, but by the Archbishop of Sens. Her dowry, the lands known in later days by the name of Artois, but at this time a group of fiefs in western Flanders, was retained for the present by Philip of Alsace, who, with her father Baldwin V of Hainault, doubtless expected to step into the place of the queen-mother and her brothers as chief advisers of the Crown.

Philip would seem to have scented the danger which lay in his alliance with Philip of Alsace, as soon as he had incurred it. Within a few weeks of his marriage he came to an understanding with his most powerful neighbour and vassal, King Henry. Henry, perhaps warned by the king's relatives, had crossed to Normandy, for the Counts of Flanders and Hainault were prepared to join their new ally in a fresh adventure—this time in pursuit of the rights against Henry which Philip had inherited, as a trust from his father, in Berry. It is probable that at this stage his paternal uncles, the Count of Dreux and Peter of Courtenai, pointed out to Philip what risks he ran, possible also that Theobald of Blois, the most pacific and wary of his mother's brothers, became uneasy. At all events Philip and Henry met near Gisors in June 1180 and, renewing the arrangement made at Nonancourt in 1177, agreed to submit their dispute in Berry to arbitration. And it is also clear that the Count of Flanders was disillusioned; during the next few years, in alliance with various members of the house of Champagne and Blois, notably Stephen of Sancerre, he was engaged in a feud with his boy-suzerain. This feud was the expression of a continuous sense of hostility or suspicion, not a sustained war; its history is a record of manœuvres, of a purely opportunist kind. Philip of Alsace could not rely upon a definite group of allies, bound together by identical interests. He soon lost the united support, if he ever had it, of the king's maternal uncles. Theobald V of Blois stood aloof, Henry of Champagne died, the Archbishop of Rheims returned to his nephew's side to become for many years his right-hand man, the protector, as Philip expressed it in 1184, of youth against faithless adversaries, "in consiliis nostris oculus vigilans, in negociis dextra manus." The Count of Flanders probably set more hope upon his Rhenish connexion, and upon the Emperor Frederick Barbarossa, who was on the look-out for support for his son, afterwards the Emperor Henry VI; but the princes of the Low Countries could never combine for long, and Frederick was far too busy elsewhere to do more than give temporary undertakings, exchange embassies, and send parties of knights.

The interest of these alliances lies in the light which they throw upon local politics, and in the possibilities which they suggested. They did something, no doubt, to prepare the way for the combinations formed later by Richard and John of England. The closest ally of Philip of Alsace was his brother-in-law, Baldwin V of Hainault, the father of the young Queen of France, but even this connexion was shaken by his marriage, shortly after the death of his first wife, Isabella of Vermandois, to a daughter of Alfonso I, King of Portugal. At this time (1182) Philip was about forty years of age and might well have an heir; and, if he did, the prospects, which were in fact realised later, of a union between Flanders and Hainault would vanish. The danger which beset his daughter, as a result of his military demonstrations against the King of France, weighed still more heavily upon Baldwin. The situation was an unnatural one; and at last the eighteen-year-old king shewed his resentment (and revealed his character) by threatening to repudiate the queen. A great Council of the realm gathered at Senlis in March 1184, and only the expostulations of his advisers deterred Philip from his foolish purpose. Yet the threat had effect, for, during the absence of Philip of Alsace on a visit to the tomb of St Thomas at Canterbury, Baldwin V came to a definite understanding with his formidable son-in-law. It seemed at last that war would be waged in earnest. An alliance between a King of France and Hainault, an imperial fief, was a dangerous thing. Hainault was attacked and ravaged by the forces of Flanders, Brabant, and Cologne, while Baldwin looked on, helpless, if safe, in Mons. The king prepared a host—the first great military achievement of his reign—for the invasion of Vermandois and Flanders. In the early summer of 1185 he moved northwards from Compiègne towards Amiens and encamped at Boves, at the junction of the Somme and the Avre. The Count of Flanders, after seeking in vain for help from King Henry II and the Emperor, came to terms, and in July a treaty was concluded which enlarged the French domain as it had never been enlarged since the accession of Hugh Capet.

When Isabella of Vermandois and Valois, Countess of Flanders, died in 1182, the problem of the succession to Vermandois had been raised; and the manœuvres of the next three years were dictated by the natural desire of Philip of Alsace to retain this valuable fief and of Philip of France to secure it. The country of Vermandois, extending over the valleys of the Somme and the Oise, comprised Vermandois proper (Péronne, St Quentin, etc.), Amiens, and Montdidier with their *chatellénies*. The Count of

Flanders asserted that, although it was the fief of his late wife, he had acquired lawful right to it. Eleanor, wife of the Chamberlain of France, Matthew III Count of Beaumont-sur-Oise, claimed to succeed as the sister of Isabella. The king, while favouring the heiress, based his own claim on kinship in the seventh degree with Isabella to the exclusion of all collateral heirs. Leaving Valois to Eleanor, he strove from the outset to gain effective control of Vermandois. In consequence of the settlement with the Count of Flanders in July 1185 Vermandois was divided. Philip took Amiens, Montdidier, and numerous other fiefs in the west, Philip of Alsace was allowed Vermandois proper, *i.e.* Péronne, St Quentin, and Ham, with the proviso that his suzerain had the power of *rachat*. Baldwin V of Hainault was to be indemnified for his losses in war, and the alliance with Flanders was to be renewed.

By this treaty Philip of Alsace lost control of the city of Amiens and of over sixty castles. All that he retained in Vermandois was the title of count and a life interest in the eastern part of the county. After his death in Palestine (1191) Philip Augustus secured Péronne by the treaty of Arras (March 1192), while Eleanor was granted a life interest in St Quentin. On her death, in June 1213, the king took the last step in this piecemeal absorption of her sister's inheritance, and added Valois and St Quentin, with their dependencies, to the Crown. He was thus immediate lord of a line of cities and fiefs which lay continuously from Paris to Montreuil-sur-Mer. In due course he would be able to take over the lands of Artois which he claimed in right of his wife[1].

The failure of Philip of Alsace in 1185 put an end to the lofty ambitions, but not to the restless activity, of this brilliant and versatile prince. Henry II and the Emperor combined to reconcile him to Philip of France. In March 1186 he was at Amiens, when the alliance with Philip and Baldwin of Hainault was firmly established. For the rest of his life he was faithful to the king. He helped him to strengthen his position in view of the inevitable conflict with the house of Anjou, and accompanied him on his crusade.

Hence, when Philip Augustus, ten years after his marriage to Isabella of Hainault, made his arrangements for the government of France during his absence in the East, he had cleared the way for the second great achievement of his reign. He had become master in his own house; he could rely upon the great families, all closely related to his own, of Champagne, Flanders, and Hainault. His domain extended from the Loire to the English Channel. He was on friendly terms with Pope and Emperor and, a young man of twenty-five, strong, wary, and rich in experience, was inferior to no European prince in prestige and ability.

[1] In 1187 he secured from the bishop the lordship over Tournai and its district, in south-eastern Flanders, north of Cambrai—an area which, in spite of its geographical isolation, was generally attached in later times to the bailliage of Vermandois.

And, as we must now see, he had already shewn his intention of asserting his authority in the West, and of availing himself to the full of the opportunities opened up to him by the discords in the family life of the house of Anjou.

In 1180 the relations between the houses of France, Blois, and Anjou were close. The daughters of Louis VII and Eleanor of Aquitaine, Philip's half-sisters and Henry's step-daughters, had married the Counts of Champagne and Blois. Philip's sister Margaret was the wife of the young Henry, Henry II's eldest surviving son. Henry and his brother Geoffrey, Count of Brittany, were present at Philip's coronation and became his personal friends as well as his vassals. When their father protected his young relative in the dangerous time, 1180–1182, during which he was threatened by the combined power of Champagne, Burgundy, and Flanders, these young men abandoned themselves with zest to the war against the allies, especially against the Count of Sancerre. The old king doubtless regarded Philip, much as he regarded his sons, with the mingled feelings of grim affection, tolerance, and suspicion; and it is beside the mark to regard Henry as an imperial statesman and to try to trace in his acts a far-seeing, elaborate, and consistent foreign policy, quite unnatural in the atmosphere of western feudalism. His restless ability, asserted by a series of dramatic accidents, had made the head of the house of Anjou the greatest figure, with the exception of the Emperor, in Europe. As such he was called in 1185 to the rescue of his Angevin kinsman in Palestine and to take control of the kingdom of Jerusalem. But, as a wise householder, he took counsel with his magnates and refused the invitation. His responsibilities in England, Normandy, Anjou, Aquitaine were far too pressing to give room for adventures of this kind. His numerous interventions in European affairs were not directed by logical policy; they were the natural result of his position, the undertakings of every-day sagacity, or the flashes of royal splendour. Thus, during the controversy with Archbishop Thomas of Canterbury, Henry naturally cultivated the goodwill of the Emperor; his envoys were present at Würzburg in 1165, and three years later his eldest daughter married the most powerful of Frederick's vassals, Henry the Lion, Duke of Saxony and Bavaria. During the same time Henry sought the friendship of William of Sicily and of the north Italian cities and came to an understanding with his neighbour Alfonso VIII of Castile, who in 1169 married his second daughter, Eleanor. When the dispute with the Church was over, Henry continued to extend his influence in the south, with Raymond V of Toulouse and Humbert III of Savoy. Early in 1173 he met the leading princes of the south at Montferrand in Auvergne; the marriage-treaty was made, which, if it had been carried out, would have given Henry's son John the control of the Alpine passes and the succession to Savoy; and Raymond V of Toulouse did homage. It is possible that the Italian cities offered him the crown of Italy. In 1176, the year of the imperial defeat at Legnano, the project for a marriage between William II of Sicily and Henry's youngest daughter, Joan, was resumed with the strong support of Alexander III. Joan was married at Palermo in February 1177. There was no deep-rooted hostility to the Emperor, with whom Henry seems always to have been on friendly terms; there was no conscious plan for the "encirclement of France." If William of Sicily and Joan had left an heir, the Hohenstaufen would not have succeeded to Sicily and the whole history of Europe would have been profoundly changed; but it is not more likely that Henry desired to avert imperialist designs in Sicily than that he expected, through Henry the Lion, to create a new imperialist house in Germany, or, through Alfonso of Castile, to become the great-grandfather of St Ferdinand and St Louis.

Henry had no desire to upset the French kingdom, just as he had no desire to reject the imperial tradition[1]. He was too firmly established and powerful to be alarmed by Philip's success in 1185, and, with the Emperor, took a hand in reconciling him with the Count of Flanders. A statesman of the twelfth century did not plan to revise the system of feudal relations which composed what, in modern speech, is grandly termed the public law of Europe; and so long as Henry, as was second nature with him, controlled the administration of his dominions and kept the Norman frontier well fortified, he could feel secure. His danger lay in the needless, grasping, treacherous ambitions of his quarrelsome sons. As Philip grew to manhood he realised the opportunity which their domestic passions gave him, not only to settle outstanding disputes with the Angevin house, but also to give reality to his position as the overlord of the Angevin fiefs on the continent. During the twenty years which followed the treaty of Boves, he seized every chance, accustomed his vassals to the idea of a traditional conflict with his neighbour, and then, with a rapidity which must have surprised himself, added the greater part of the Angevin inheritance to his French domain.

In the autumn of 1177, at Nonancourt, Henry II and Louis VII had agreed to go together on crusade and to submit to arbitration their disputes over Auvergne, Berry, and the Norman Vexin. Not long afterwards they had their last interview at Graçai-en-Berri, presumably to deal with the arbitrators' award. Whatever this may have been—and it would seem that Henry's rights of possession at this time suffered no interference—King Louis was bitterly chagrined, for according to the story told many years later by Gerald of Wales, he upbraided Henry for his usurpations, of which the plainest, the most flagrant, was the unjust occupation of Auvergne, and solemnly entrusted the maintenance of his cause to God, his heir, and the barons of the Crown. Indeed, in this year, Henry must have seemed at the height of his power. Since the great rebellion of 1173 he had firmly established his control. In 1175 he

[1] See H. W. C. Davis's review of Hardegen's *Imperialpolitik Heinrichs II von England* (1905) in the *Eng. Hist. Review*, XXI (1906), pp. 361–7.

revised his arrangements for his sons, and those youthful warriors, Richard and Geoffrey, after doing homage, had been sent to prove their valour and statesmanship in their future fiefs of Aquitaine and Brittany. In Normandy, searching inquiries were made into encroachments upon the demesne, and Richard of Ilchester restored the Exchequer to activity and the finances to order. In 1177, after the treaty of Nonancourt, Henry held his court at Verneuil, where he issued an administrative order, to be observed everywhere in his dominions (*potestates*), relating to the debts of crusaders. In the same year, in all his continental lands, he took peculiar and systematic care in the appointment of the higher officials (*iustitiae et rectores*). The pious journey, for which these acts were a preparation, was never made, and when Philip came to the throne, he found Henry still busily at work. The subjugation of Aquitaine had been completed, for the moment, by Richard, whose amazing courage, energy, and perseverance in conquest had already made him famous, and whose determination to build up an orderly centralised state far outweighed his glaring weaknesses in the eyes of the observant ecclesiastics of his time. He helped his father to vindicate feudal right to the wardship of the rich heiress of Châteauroux and Déols in Berry. He demonstrated the extent of ducal power in the Limousin and the recesses of Gascony. And by the dramatic siege of the great fortress of Taillebourg, which surrendered on Ascension Day 1179, he broke the long rebellion of the Count of Angoulême and Geoffrey of Rançon in the heart of the duchy. Henry had already bought out the rights of the Count of La Marche, and had for the time being added it to the domain. By the end of 1179 Richard, now definitely recognised by Henry as Count of Poitou, was supreme from the valley of the Loire to the Pyrenees. In the same year the last Breton revolt, that of Guiomarc'h of Léon, was crushed, and the definite establishment of Geoffrey was followed in 1181 by his marriage, arranged many years before, to Constance, the heiress of Conan IV. In 1180 Henry kept Christmas at Le Mans, and issued an assize of arms—afterwards extended to England, and adopted by the King of France and the Count of Flanders—to be observed "throughout the lands across the sea." However limited its observance was, this act is striking testimony to the unity of the Angevin dominions. It is not surprising that Philip, after a tentative demonstration against him, decided to postpone the settlement of his grievances and, in 1181, renewed the treaty of 1177.

It would be easy to exaggerate the cohesion of Henry's vast lordship. The customs of Brittany were not identical with those of Poitou; between Normandy and Gascony the difference was almost incalculable. The common element in administration was provided by Henry's wandering court, with its chancery and household, and by a group of high officials who executed his writs and acted in his name, not in the name of the provinces which they ruled. Their centres were the castles of the domain, and the castles were the centres of fiscal areas (*praepositurae*). As time went on, and the series of lordships (excluding Brittany) fell under the rule of one man, first Richard, then John, each great province was administered by a seneschal, who presided over the local exchequer, and was responsible for the lord's judicial pleas. The official, even the military, element was not necessarily native to the district. Seneschals, castellans, bailiffs, mercenaries might be sent from other Angevin fiefs. They were, so to speak, extensions of the Angevin household, were directed by one will, and were maintained, if need be, from a common fund. Apart from this simple machinery, provincial traditions were upheld. Any disregard of feudal usage was fiercely resented[1]. Legislation, like the Assize of Arms, common to all the Angevin lands was rare and cannot be described as a change in feudal custom. The main effects of union were probably seen in the wider opportunity for trade and social intercourse, a certain measure of uniformity in financial method and in military engineering, and especially in the grant to communes, in their charters, of the customs and privileges of distant places.

The contrasts which underlay the superficial unity of Henry's *dominium* were revealed during the quarter of a century which succeeded the accession of Philip of France. In 1180 Normandy, and the area which included the counties of Maine, Anjou, Touraine, and the district round Poitiers and Bordeaux, were firmly administered, while the fragile ties which bound the greater part of Aquitaine and Gascony to Henry seemed unlikely to endure. In 1205 Philip had secured nearly all the former lands, while John depended upon the Aquitanian nobles for support. The change was not so paradoxical as it appears; for the comparative peace and prosperity of Normandy and Anjou were maintained by a system of government which penetrated the whole of society and would disappear if this system were shattered. A change of rulers was infinitely preferable, in the eyes of the inhabitants, to a state of chaos. When a breach was once made in its defences it was easier to hold a well-organised than a disorganised community. In Normandy Henry had been able to build upon strong foundations, and during the last two decades of the century England and the duchy were better administered than any state to the west of the Byzantine Empire, with the possible exceptions of Sicily and Venice. Under the control of seneschal and bailiffs Normandy had an uninterrupted life which, as was seen during Richard's absence on crusade, could hold its own against external interference. Its legal customs were well understood, and, although the earliest Norman custumal dates from about the year 1200, some of them had probably been written down before our period begins. The seneschal presided over a financial and judicial system, with its headquarters at Caen, similar to the English system.

The "pleas of the sword" comprised the more important criminal jurisdiction as well as the administrative rights of the duke, and were held by

[1] Count Geoffrey's assize on the indivisibility of baronies and knights' fees (1185) was issued after consultation with the Breton barons.

"seneschal and justices" throughout the duchy, in the franchises[1] no less than the bailiwicks; and the ducal monopoly of a great number of civil pleas had been secured by a development of writs under a series of assizes almost identical with those which regulated civil jurisdiction in England. Before 1180 the older administrative divisions, the *vicecomitatus* and the *praeposíturae*, had been worked into a system of commands known as *bailliae* or bailiwicks, whose officers were responsible to the Norman exchequer with duties similar to those of the English sheriff. The bailiffs were frequently castellans, farming the *praepositura* of the ducal castles within their areas of jurisdiction, but sometimes they co-operated with castellans who were financially responsible or with paid castellans who were not. Henry had overhauled the whole of the Norman defences, especially on the border, and had devised plans whereby he could, if he desired, group the series of castles along the valley of the Eure or of the Epte under a great single military command. In short, while the sense of unity, deep-rooted in tradition, was expressed in feudal custom and a far-reaching administration based upon that of the Franks, the power of the duke was great enough to permit of much conscious artifice and change. The bailiwicks shewed the influence of the old ecclesiastical and secular divisions, but were not slavishly defined by them. They were creations of convenience and could be grouped, as they were in John's short reign, under the control of a few hands, while the castles were distributed among few or many vassals or mercenaries[2].

Owing to lack of material it is not possible to estimate the extent to which this administrative system operated in the other Angevin fiefs. There were provincial seneschals, who were regarded as deputies of the lord and invested, under him, with full powers, provincial exchequers, treasuries in the castles of the domain, and machinery for the farming of revenue and the execution of writs. The system was probably very similar in the fiefs of the great vassals, such as the Count of Angoulême. But naturally, the farther one penetrated from the neighbourhood of Tours and Chinon, of Poitiers, Saintes, and Bordeaux, the less one could rely upon the protection of the overlord. The greater part of Aquitaine and Gascony was in the hands of lords who in their irresponsibility were indistinguishable from the barons in central France as a whole. They belonged to the feudal society of Auvergne and Burgundy. Their attitude to life was voiced by the poet baron, Bertrand of Born, the claimant of the castle and fief of Hautefort in the Limousin, on the border of Périgord. Life, as we see it in Bertrand's *sirventes*, was a succession of fierce, joyous impressions; of love and fighting, delightful intrigue and splendid hatred. He looked back with the liveliest distaste upon an unwilling holiday which

[1] Some lords of franchises had the profits of their pleas, but could not hold them except under supervision.

[2] For the particular bailiwicks and other details of this system see Powicke, *Loss of Normandy*, pp. 103 sqq. (1913).

he had spent with Richard at Henry's court in Argentan; it was so dull, so incapable of sparkling gibes and laughter; only the presence of Henry's daughter, the charming Duchess of Saxony, had made it tolerable. Yet Bertrand was a realist. He began by hating Richard, then, as his intrigues came to naught, was forced to a reluctant but frank admiration, and in the end became his willing servant. The change can be traced in the songs which are a running comment upon the great rebellion which he helped to plan in 1182. This rebellion, which grew out of the endemic unrest of the time, found a rallying-point in the young King Henry, Richard's elder brother. The story illustrates to perfection the strange quality of twelfth-century feudalism, of these men who professed "gentility," the mother of " largesse," despised " covetousness," quoted the *Chansons de geste* to each other as a scholar quoted Virgil, and fought like cunning wild-cats over their feudal rights. This spirit affected the Court and even won the grudging acquiescence of the old Henry, but it infected his sons and the nobility of Aquitaine. After the settlement of the years 1177–1181, the king had tried to keep his sons about him, and to prepare for a peaceful and legal succession after his death. He and the younger Henry came to the support of Richard in the summer of 1182, when the league of the Counts of Limoges, his half-brother of Angoulême, the Count of Périgord, and their barons and allies, was temporarily destroyed[1]. But, probably during the campaign, the younger Henry was played off by the barons of Aquitaine against his brother, and his anger was further stirred when Richard built a castle, which he called Clairvaux, just within the borders of Anjou. This irregularity was put right in the course of the Christmas festivities at Caen, but Henry was alarmed and tried to reach a final agreement between the brothers shortly afterwards at Le Mans. The brothers swore to keep peace among themselves, Geoffrey did liege-homage to the young Henry for Brittany, and Richard, after discussion, undertook to do the same for Aquitaine. Then the discovery was made that the young king was pledged to the barons of Aquitaine, who must first be consulted. The consultation never took place. Richard hurried off to prepare for war, and the king, reflecting perhaps that they had better fight then than later, angrily encouraged the young Henry to subdue his pride.

The old king soon found that the danger was much greater than he had supposed. He had expected that, after some rough-and-tumble fighting, the barons of Aquitaine would be induced to submit to the arbitration of his court; but the chance given by the young Henry's interference was not to be missed, and a genuine rising spread rapidly throughout the south. Philip of France had already accepted the homage of Ademar of Angoulême, and now with a good face could send help to his friend and brother-in-law of Anjou. Geoffrey, with the aid of his vassals and mercenaries from Brittany, threw himself eagerly into the fight. The lords of the viscounties and baronies of Gascony and Auvergne joined

[1] For the story of these wars see Norgate, *Richard the Lion Heart,* c. 2.

with those of the Limousin. The Duke of Burgundy and the Count of Toulouse came in on the side of the young Henry, Alfonso of Aragon on the side of Richard. From all directions the young king's companions-in-arms (*bachelors*) flocked to his side, for this adventure was better than any tournament. And, worst of all, the dreaded mercenary bands (*routiers*), growing as they came, turned out from their lairs—Sancho from the hills of Serannes, Curbaran, who had adopted the name of a Saracen prince in the *Chanson d'Antioche*, Raymond, and other leaders of "Tartarean legions." The famous Mercadier, who was to be Richard's favourite captain, was also there. Beyond the pale of society, and even of the Church, these bands were well armed and disciplined; they recognised no obligation to the helpless folk whose lands and goods they devastated; they grew rich not merely on their pay, but on the spoils of churches and monasteries, cities and villages. For a few months it seemed as though the Angevin power, and with it whatever existed of social order in Aquitaine, would disappear. The old king came hurrying to the rescue of Richard, and Richard, as usual, was everywhere, doing marvellous deeds of speed, skill, valour, and ruthlessness; but the sudden death, in June 1183, of the young king did more than the fighting could do to end the crisis. The league broke up, the forces of Burgundy and Toulouse slipped away, and in the course of the next year Richard was once more in control.

The history of the revolt shewed how difficult it was to arrange for the future government of Henry II's possessions on the basis of feudal relations between his sons. It revealed the latent danger from a conflict of feudal claims between the King of France and the Duke of Aquitaine —a source of trouble which was to develop during the next two centuries. Moreover it illustrated the dilemmas created by personal ideas of loyalty. One of the young king's bachelors was William the Marshal, who was reconciled with his master at this time, and went to him protected by the benevolent assurances both of Philip of France and the old king. The latter is alleged to have encouraged William to do his duty although it involved resistance to himself[1]. On the other hand, when the young king's seneschal excused himself from service on the ground that he was the liege man of Henry the elder, who at the time was approaching Limoges, he was contemptuously allowed to go. The history of this period, notably of the conquest of Normandy, provides many examples of this conflict of loyalties, so difficult to reconcile with the conception of a self-contained state. It was the unhappy lot of Aquitaine and the adjoining lands to suffer from all the evils of unregulated feudalism. The effects of war did not end with the peace-making of the feudal chiefs. On this particular occasion the havoc and misery were spread far beyond the original home of the disputes, and the wretched people throughout central France themselves sought a remedy from their calamities. During the early part of 1183 the brotherhood of the white-caped friends of peace (*capuciati*) was

[1] *Histoire de Guillaume le Maréchal* (ed. Meyer), II, 6657–6660.

spreading rapidly. The movement had begun in Puy-en-Velay with a band of persons gathered together by a carpenter, Durand Dujardin. It aroused universal interest and the story of its origin and development is full of inconsistencies. A sceptical chronicler of Laon says that the carpenter was tricked by a wily canon who desired to keep open the roads for pilgrims to the relics in the cathedral of Puy. The general view was that he was a pious visionary, a kind of St Francis. However this may be, the movement was at first an expression of generous feeling, in which men of all ranks took part. It began as an association of persons who swore to seek peace, it developed into a society for the violent suppression and massacre of the mercenaries[1]; it seems to have changed into a revolutionary sect, seeking to throw off the evils of bondage and to preach the equality of man, and within two or three years of its birth it disappeared, execrated by clergy and laity alike. Many lords called in against it the very mercenaries whom at one time it had helped them to suppress.

The story of the extension of the royal power over the greater part of the Angevin dominions has frequently been told. Here we can only deal with the main tendencies and results; detailed narratives are easily accessible elsewhere[2].

Henry was not at his best in the years which followed the death of his eldest son. He allowed himself to be distracted from a sensible policy by his affection for his youngest son, John. Richard was by no means unmanageable; though fitful, he was generous, and on more than one occasion during these years he submitted himself impulsively and wholeheartedly to his father's will. But he refused to be party to any scheme for the surrender of Aquitaine to John, still less to a drastic division of the Angevin inheritance. The situation became acute in 1187 and the mutual suspicion of Henry and Richard gave Philip his opportunity. The growing strength of the French monarchy was patent to all, and before Henry's death shrewd observers, like Ranulf de Glanville the justiciar, had realized that the advantage lay with Philip rather than with his neighbour.

Henry had never done homage to Philip. The last occasion on which he had solemnly recognised the overlordship of the French King had been in January 1169, during the Becket controversy, when, as we learn from the letters of John of Salisbury, he did homage to Louis VII. But, after the death of the young Henry, an understanding with Philip was necessary; for the Norman Vexin legally returned to Philip's sister, the widowed Margaret, and, moreover, new plans for the succession to the

[1] The extent to which the confraternity of the *capuciati* or *pacifici* spread is seen from the facts that Raymond Brun was slain by them in Châteauneuf (Angoumôis) and Curbaran at Châteaudun (Orléanais). Mercadier was taken into Richard's service, and "Le Bar" or Louvrecaire, who appears at this time, was later high in John's service.

[2] See the Bibliography for the works of Luchaire, Norgate, Cartellieri, etc.

Angevin fiefs required Philip's sanction. At the end of 1183 Henry did homage to Philip for all his continental lands and agreed that the Norman Vexin should be regarded henceforth as the dowry of Margaret's sister, Alice, who should marry one of his sons. In March 1186, at Gisors, this arrangement was confirmed and Richard—in spite of his devotion to Berengaria, the daughter of the King of Navarre—promised to marry Alice. When Geoffrey of Brittany died at Paris in August, the way seemed to be clear, for Geoffrey had always been a disturber of peace. But Philip, with his relatives of the house of Blois and Philip of Flanders now united in his support, saw that the time for strong action had come. Richard had spent the summer in a war with Raymond of Toulouse, wresting from him the turbulent province of Quercy. Philip intervened as overlord, then claimed the wardship of Geoffrey's child, Arthur, and finally, in April 1187, demanded back the Norman Vexin and the unhappy Alice, who was still unmarried. He followed up this diplomatic attack by a quick and successful campaign in central France. In eastern Berry, Graçai and Issoudun were seized, and Châteauroux was besieged. Henry and Richard joined forces for the protection of Châteauroux, and this first military demonstration ended in June with a truce which was to last for two years; but the great contest had begun, and, in spite of numerous reverses and delays, Philip never rested until he had turned his rights as suzerain—rights of which he availed himself at every turn—into the rights of immediate lordship over Normandy, Anjou, and the greater part of Poitou.

Two very different considerations—the one making for peace, the other for war—complicated the position at this time. The one was the danger in Syria, the other Henry's plans for John. The truce of June 1187 was followed, later in the year, by the news of Saladin's dramatic successes in the East. Richard characteristically took the Cross at once, and when he had to crush another rising, headed by Geoffrey of Lusignan, in 1188, insisted among the conditions of peace that his rebellious vassals should go on crusade. Early in 1188 the two kings, moved by the eloquence of the Archbishop of Tyre, also agreed to do the same. The excitement was widespread among the magnates on each side, and in the face of such a crisis, domestic quarrel was seen in its true light, as a piece of criminal folly. During the preparations neither side was to countenance attacks on the other. Unhappily, emotional exaltation cannot remove the natural passions of undisciplined men; unhappily also, the temper of the South was not like that of the North. A series of incidents stirred the dispute between Raymond of Toulouse and Richard to a fierce renewal of war. On the whole, right seems to have been on Richard's side, and Philip's earliest remonstrances were not unfriendly. But he did not wish Richard and his mercenaries, who took one town and stronghold after another, to add yet another great fief to Aquitaine, and, when the arbitration of his Court was refused, he threatened to renew his attack. The threat was carried out; Châteauroux fell in June, the Auvergne was overrun, and Philip began operations in Touraine and Maine. Once more Henry and Richard joined forces, once more the desultory fighting was interrupted by negotiations. It was at this stage that the misunderstanding—the outcome of four years of intrigue and suspicion—between Henry and his son enabled Philip to divide them. Richard was doubtless affected by his desire to go on crusade and by the influence of the Count of Flanders, and his vacillation turned to fury against Henry at a fateful meeting which took place between them and Philip at Bonmoulins, in Normandy, on 11 November. In the previous year there had been rumours that Henry was planning to grant to John all the continental fiefs except Normandy; and now, when Henry shewed reluctance to recognise Richard as his successor and to proceed with the marriage between him and Alice, Richard's passion carried him away. He had come to the meeting in Philip's company, and his father, doubtless seeing that they had arrived at an understanding, refused to confirm under constraint the settlement to which he had himself agreed in 1186. The bystanders saw Richard suddenly kneel down, and perform the act of homage to Philip. The colloquy ended, and father and son went their several ways. By this act Richard was recognised by Philip as his vassal for all continental fiefs, saving Henry's rights during his lifetime. They stood by each other during the next few months; all Henry's attempts at compromise, all proposals of ecclesiastical mediation or threat of interdict and excommunication, failed to move them. At a meeting in Whitsuntide 1189, Henry went so far as to offer Philip everything he wanted, if he would substitute John for Richard. This was the end. The allies invaded Normandy and Maine, seized Le Mans, and surrounded Tours. Henry, a dying man, came from Chinon to a last meeting held at Colombières, between Tours and Azai-le-Rideau. He surrendered on all points and, returning to Chinon, died two days later (6 July). He lived long enough to receive from Philip, as he had stipulated, the list of those who had joined the alliance against him, and to hear that the first name upon it was that of his youngest son.

By the treaty of Colombières Richard was recognised as Henry's successor. The Norman Vexin was to be retained as the dowry of Richard's future wife Alice. Philip gave back Châteauroux, but received a large indemnity and kept the rest of his conquests in Berry and the immediate suzerainty over Auvergne. Thus he had performed the task with which his father had entrusted him and had prepared the way for the extension of the royal domain in the heart of France.

Philip and Richard resumed their companionship in July 1190, exactly a year after the treaty of Colombières. They joined forces at Vézelai, on their way to the Crusade. They were better matched as foes than as friends. Richard, now thirty-three years of age, was in the full glory of his manhood, Philip was twenty-five. The one was engaged on a great adventure, arrogant in his sense of strength, revelling in his freedom, susceptible to any distraction. The other was far-sighted, reluctant, uncertain in his physical health, the suzerain of a vassal who took and held a higher place in the opinion of the crusading hosts. In short, they were incompatible, and Philip was at a disadvantage. At Messina Richard refused to fulfil his promise to marry Alice. He was now his own master, he was in love with Berengaria of Navarre, and there was a very ugly story abroad about relations which his father had had with the French princess. So Berengaria came to Sicily and was married, and Philip acquiesced in a revision of the treaty[1]. Alice was to be sent back to her brother as soon as Richard returned, the Norman Vexin was to remain as part of Normandy, unless Richard had no male heirs, and if Richard had two sons, both were to hold their lands in chief of the French Crown, the younger having either Normandy, or Maine and Anjou, or Aquitaine and Poitou. It is noteworthy that Philip foreshadowed a division of the Angevin inheritance. Raymond of Toulouse was to be forced to submit to the judgment of Philip's court, Philip was to keep Issoudun and Graçai and the overlordship of Auvergne, Richard was to keep Quercy, pay 10,000 marks of silver, and be Philip's liege man (*ligius homo*).

By the end of the year the King of France was back again, celebrating Christmas at Fontainebleau. During the Crusade, the Count of Flanders, Philip of Alsace, had died and, in accordance with the treaty of 1185, the king could recover eastern Vermandois (Péronne and St Quentin). He had also nourished a lively hatred of Richard and the time for revenge had come. It would seem that no copy of the treaty of Messina had reached Normandy, and Philip produced a charter in which Richard ordered the return of Alice *and* the Norman Vexin. The Seneschal of Normandy, William Fitz Ralf, refused to act upon it without independent instructions, and, as decency forbade at this early stage an attack upon the lands of a crusader, Philip had to wait his time. The news of Richard's capture in December 1192 on his way home revived his chances. He had already entered upon the possession of Péronne and St Quentin in the Vermandois, and had renewed the ultimate rights of his house over Artois by an arrangement (*iure uxoris*) with the new Count of Flanders, Baldwin V (VIII) of Hainault, the brother-in-law of the late count and the father of Philip's late wife Isabella. He seized Gisors and the Norman Vexin, allied himself with Canute of Denmark, and prepared for an invasion of England. With John as his ally, he tried to secure Normandy and to bribe the Emperor not to execute his treaty with Richard. But again he over-reached himself. The officials and magnates resisted John's wiles in England and Normandy, and Philip's rapid in-

[1] March, 1191. The only text is a later copy in the English archives (Exch. T.R. Diplomatic Doc. 6). The best edition is in Delaborde, *Actes*, I, pp. 464–6, no. 376. For the significance of liege-homage at this time, see Lot, *Fidèles ou Vassaux?* (1904), pp. 237–240, and for the treaty, Powicke, *Loss of Normandy*, pp. 126 sqq.

trigues weakened rather than strengthened his influence at the imperial court. Richard was set free early in February 1194, and on his way home succeeded in straining the alliance between Philip and Baldwin of Hainault and in forming a confederacy of pensioners in the Rhineland. When he landed in Normandy, in May 1194, he was at least able to face Philip on equal terms.

Although he had failed in his main intention[1], Philip had been very busy during the previous months. In Aquitaine King Sancho of Navarre, Berengaria's brother, and the seneschal of Poitou had to face (1192–3) a rebellion, and Ademar of Angoulême had, with John's consent, been received by Philip as his direct vassal for nearly all his fiefs. In Normandy many of the great fortresses of the frontier, in addition to Gisors, were in Philip's hands. In July 1193 Richard's chancellor, William Longchamp, in order to avoid further molestation, had agreed as Richard's agent to the surrender of Arques and Drincourt in eastern Normandy, of Loches and Châtillon-sur-Indre in Touraine, as sureties for the payment of a large sum of money. This cession with additions was confirmed by John in a later treaty with Philip in January 1194. When Richard arrived, Philip was actually in possession of Vaudreuil, near the junction of the Eure with the Seine, had captured Évreux, and after a demonstration before Rouen was threatening Verneuil.

For five years Normandy was the scene of as much activity as had been known since the foundation of the duchy. One of the greatest soldiers in history brought to its salvation all the experience, the skill in fortification, the reckless abandonment which he had learned or shewn in Aquitaine and the Holy Land. Within a few weeks of the rejoicings which greeted his arrival, Verneuil, the fortress on the Avre, was relieved, Loches, one of the noblest castles in Touraine, was recovered, and Philip, caught suddenly at Fréteval, between Châteaudun and Vendôme, fled back to safety, leaving behind him his treasury and chapel, his engines of war, and the furniture of his tents. Among the booty Richard found the charters by which those who had played him false during his absence had bound themselves to Philip's service. In July he was in Aquitaine, bringing Ademar of Angoulême and Geoffrey of Rançon once more to heel. Then came the first lull in the storm. A papal legate and the Abbot of Cîteaux were striving for peace, and on 23 July a truce until 1 November 1195 was made. War broke out again in the summer of 1195, and Philip, suspecting, it would seem, that he would not be allowed to keep Vaudreuil, began to destroy it during a conference in the neighbourhood. The noise made by the falling stones reached Richard's ears, the conference became a fight, and Vaudreuil was retaken. But the agents of peace resumed their work, and what was meant to be a definitive peace was made in January 1196 at Louviers, south of Vaudreuil. The promise of imperial support and a successful demonstration against Philip in Berry had enabled

[1] In the summer of 1193 Rouen, under the Earl of Leicester, who had returned from the Crusade, successfully resisted a very energetic siege.

Richard to exact satisfactory terms[1]. Philip kept the south-eastern March, from Vernon to Nonancourt. Nothing was said about the Vexin, but he surrendered his other conquests east of the Seine. The castles on the Eure would protect his domains, the retention of Gisors and the Norman Vexin satisfied a very old grievance and brought him near to Rouen. On the other hand the Angevin power was more compactly united under Richard than it had ever been under Henry II, and through his alliances Richard was protected from attack from without. Later in the year he strengthened himself still further by an alliance with his old enemy, Raymond VI of Toulouse, who married Joan, the widow of William II of Sicily and Richard's favourite sister.

The treaty could not ensure a lasting peace; the more firmly Richard established himself, the more Philip had to fear. The roll of the Norman Exchequer for 1195 shews that, during the truce, Richard had spent large sums on the fortification of the castles, and in April 1196 in a letter to the justiciar in England he expressed the opinion that Philip intended war rather than peace, and instructed him to send to Normandy all the barons whose chief seats lay in the duchy, and the English barons with a small number of their knights prepared for a long period of service. In June Philip was, in fact, making headway again in the north. He had given his sister Alice to the Count of Ponthieu, and now he secured the support of the young Baldwin IX of Flanders (the future Eastern Emperor) and the able Count of Boulogne, Renaud of Dammartin, who was later to be so useful to the Angevin cause. In July Philip seized Aumale, lately granted with its countess to Richard's loyal friend Baldwin of Béthune, but never again to be ruled by the family which bore the title. But his successes were few. Richard's forces overran a great part of the Norman Vexin, and, by the persuasive tongue of Earl William the Marshal, that hero of tournaments, the Counts of Flanders and Boulogne were won back again. Philip invaded Flanders in vain and in September 1197 a truce was arranged, so that a new treaty might be made. On this occasion the parties applied for the assistance of the new Pope, Innocent III, who never ceased henceforward to work for peace.

Richard's position at this time was a strong one. The great crusader had won the lively admiration of the new Pope. In Germany and the Low Countries he exercised much influence at the election of his nephew, Otto of Brunswick (whom he had enfeoffed with the county of Poitou), as King of the Romans in March 1198. In the South, since his alliance with Raymond VI of Toulouse, he had little to fear. Brittany was under his control, Flanders his ally, and England his reservoir of men and treasure. He was served in Normandy and Anjou by capable administrators and castellans, and had a powerful force of mercenaries at his back. And in 1197–8 he crowned the rock at Andeli with the magnificent Château

[1] The text of this treaty, which is of great interest for feudal geography, is in Teulet, *Layettes* II, pp. 182–4, no. 431, and *Cartulaire Normand*, pp. 276–7, no. 1057.

Gaillard, henceforward the centre of a system of strong defences in the valley of the Seine, over against Philip's castles at Vernon and Gaillon. For this purpose it was necessary to invade the rights of the Archbishop of Rouen, his old adviser Walter of Coutances, in his manor of Andeli, but the Pope arranged a liberal settlement with the infuriated ecclesiastic. Apart from the advantage of its impregnable site, the new castle was a natural starting-point for the recovery of the Norman Vexin. When the war began again in the autumn of 1198, the short campaign was disastrous for Philip. He was driven from nearly the whole of the Vexin, and when a truce was made in November, was in effective control only of the valleys of the Seine and the Epte. A treaty was to be made under the mediation of the papal legate, Peter of Capua, who had been sent with large powers in 1196 to preach a crusade and decide the fate of Philip's wife, Ingeborg of Denmark. But the treaty was not made. In its stead, a truce for five years was arranged early in 1199 and was in force when the news arrived in April that Richard had met his death in Aquitaine. He was killed in his forty-fourth year, in pursuit of a trivial quarrel about a non-existent treasure.

Philip leaped to take advantage of the confusion which ensued, and when the treaty was at last concluded in May 1200 at his new castle of Le Goulet, the possession of Gisors and the Vexin was confirmed. By the terms of this treaty, the frontier of France was pushed forward to a strip of neutral country round Andeli, and west of the Seine to include the city and district of Évreux. John definitely surrendered Issoudun and Graçai in Berry, this time as a dowry for his niece Blanche of Castile on her marriage with Philip's son Louis. He undertook not to countenance any hostile acts by the Count of Flanders against his suzerain. Philip on his side recognised John as lord of all the Angevin lands, but, before doing so, he had taken a long step forward in the assertion of his powers as suzerain. For on the news of Richard's death the Angevin dominion had, for a time, fallen asunder. While the magnates of England and Normandy acknowledged John, and Aquitaine rallied to the aged Eleanor, the barons of the western lands in Maine, Anjou, and Touraine turned, in local sympathy, to the boy Arthur of Brittany. Just as Eleanor, though nearer eighty than seventy years of age, found new energy in this crisis, so Constance of Brittany was stirred to avenge her own wrongs and vindicate her son's claims. The Angevin barons were won over, and national feeling aroused in Brittany. Fortunately for John, Chinon and other castles had been handed over to him, and, although Philip hurried to Tours, Eleanor was able, with the aid of the Poitevins, to check the dangerous movement. William des Roches, Arthur's seneschal in Maine and Anjou, deserted him. The disputed succession was referred to Philip's court, and it was by a judgment of this court that John's rights were secured. Further, John undertook that he would do nothing to prejudice Arthur's rights in Brittany without a judgment of his own court, and, as an additional safeguard, Arthur was consigned for the time being to Philip's care. Eleanor, before handing Aquitaine over to John, had already done homage to the French King. Thus, while the integrity of the succession was maintained, Philip had given reality, as none of his predecessors had been able to do, to his overlordship, and had definitely secured the Norman Vexin, the district of Évreux, and eastern Berry.

Fortune soon gave him the chance of pressing home his feudal advantage. Within two years of the treaty of Le Goulet, his court—by a judgment of great importance in the history of the "peers of France"—declared John a contumacious vassal. The King of England was condemned to lose all the lands held of the French Crown, and in execution of this sentence Philip, in May 1202, began the war which ended in the addition of most of the Angevin fiefs to the French domain. The occasion had been provided by a quarrel between John and the house of Lusignan. The story of this famous family is obscure, but by 1199 the head of the house, Hugh IX, had, in spite of claims put forward by Ademar of Angoulême, secured the county of La Marche. Hugh had several brothers, including Geoffrey and Ralph, lord of Exoudun in Poitou, and in right of his wife Count of Eu in the north-east corner of Normandy. Good relations with this powerful trio were advisable, if John was to hold his widespread inheritance in peace. At first the outlook was hopeful. The barons of Aquitaine and Gascony accepted the new duke, and by July 1200 Hugh of Lusignan and Ademar of Angoulême were reconciled; the former kept La Marche, and betrothed his son, the later Hugh X, to Isabella, Ademar's daughter, a girl of fourteen. John had busied himself in this settlement, but the sight of Isabella immediately diverted his unstable mind. He had recently divorced his wife, Hawisia, the heiress of the Gloucester lands, and had been in treaty with the King of Portugal for a marriage with one of his daughters. Now everything was changed. He made an end of the old feud with Angoulême, married Isabella at Chinon on 30 August, and took her away to England, where she was crowned as queen on 8 October. The anger which this triumphant courtship caused in the family of Lusignan was the immediate occasion of the loss of the Angevin possessions.

In earlier days the incident would not have been serious. The marriage was in many ways an advantageous one. John secured the succession to Angoulême, a compact lordship which the French King had hitherto used as a means of breaking the unity of Aquitaine. The hostility of the house of Lusignan was nothing new, and as events shewed, was not implacable. He checked the first attacks of the Lusignan brothers without difficulty, and in the following spring even took over the administration of La Marche. The danger really lay in the opportunity given to Philip of France. Philip waited his time and received John at Paris in June 1201 with a magnificent hospitality. But, when John in the following autumn began to push home his success against the Poitevin rebels, Philip was ready to make himself felt. Their lands were in John's custody and in

October he summoned them to answer for their treachery both to Richard and himself. His plan was to pit them against professional champions (*viros arte bellandi in duello doctos*). They demanded to be tried by their peers, and appealed to Philip. Philip matured his designs during the winter, and when John very naturally refused to appear before his court in Paris, began hostilities in the end of April 1202.

In 1202 the minds of men were restless and divided. Many had resented John's succession, many more were alienated by his caprice or by the contrast between his querulous vacillation, his unregulated energy or unintelligible sloth, and the resolute compelling personality of his brother. The system of administration could offer no rallying-point, as perhaps had been the case during Richard's absence, for it was not a means of expression for provincial patriotism, but a machine which would work as well under one lord as under another. Moreover John had no claims upon and felt no obligation to the trained administrator. He changed the seneschal of Normandy twice in three years, made the ambitious William des Roches hereditary seneschal of Anjou and Touraine, concentrated the bailiwicks in a few hands, and submitted the countryside to mercenary garrisons under upstart or alien leaders. Philip was able to proceed bit by bit, confirming charters and customs, setting up trustworthy officials, at the worst only substituting for one irresponsible mercenary chief (*routier*) another who was more responsible. He had organised the Évrécin in this way before the war began, and he continued the patient policy as the war proceeded. As a last resort John scattered grants of communal government among the towns and called up the *arrière-ban* or general levy; but he could not appeal to any spirit of passionate popular resistance, for no such spirit existed. The real resistance to Philip was shewn by great castles, like Château Gaillard, under the command of men such as the Constable of Chester or the mercenary Girard d'Athée, whose interests were not local at all.

Hence when Philip began to move, he was able to move quickly. He had no external danger to fear. The Count of Flanders and many of his neighbours had gone on crusade and, after Richard's death, were glad to go. The Count of Toulouse deserted the Angevin alliance, and in Aquitaine the Count of Limoges joined the house of Lusignan. John's one great success, which gave him possession of Arthur and many of his enemies, turned to his undoing, for it was followed by an epidemic of disloyalty.

In a letter of 11 May John compared his own humility and moderation with the overweening insolence of his suzerain, and in a later letter he refers to Philip's efforts to deprive him of his inheritance. By the end of July Philip had secured the outer ring of castles in eastern Normandy from Lions-le-Forêt to Eu, and, with Ralph of Exoudun, had laid siege to Arques, south of Dieppe. He had invested Arthur with Brittany, Aquiraine, Touraine, Anjou, and Maine and had sent him off to join the rebellious barons of Poitou at Tours. Arthur, with the brothers Hugh and Geoffrey of Lusignan, the Count of Limoges and others, intercepted the old Queen Eleanor at Mirebeau on her way south from her retreat at Fontevrault. His force occupied the town and laid siege to the castle; but he was caught unawares at dawn on 1 August, and with many of his chief allies was captured by his uncle. His vassals never saw him again. He was taken to Falaise, then to Rouen. There is no evidence that he was dealt with by John's Court, although the Pope was apparently satisfied by representations made in later years that he deserved his fate. Modern students of feudal law have not endorsed this opinion, and to contemporaries the murder of Arthur seemed a most shameful crime. According to the most probable story, John made away with his nephew on 3 April 1203, the day before Good Friday; but suspicion was rife many months before this date, and uncertainty prevailed many months later. Acting on their suspicion the Bretons had risen, and, through John's folly in alienating William des Roches, they had with them the nobles of Maine, Anjou, and Touraine. Philip was able to detach these provinces from John's control. He entered into identical agreements with the barons of each area, and shortly after Easter 1203—a few days in fact after the unknown tragedy at Rouen—made a voyage down the Loire as far as Saumur. By the middle of the year only Loches and Chinon, with the citadel of Tours, still held out. The last named fell in 1204, the others in 1205. Thus owing to the solidarity which Philip's policy and Arthur's disappearance had imposed upon the central provinces of the Angevin dominions, Normandy and Aquitaine were separated.

In the meanwhile defection had been rife in Normandy, and especially in the west, where the influence of events in Maine and Brittany was most easily felt. Robert, Count of Alençon or Séez, led the movement in January 1203, and the Norman records of this year are full of entries about the confiscated lands of the *tournés*, as the Marshal's biographer terms the deserters. Their conduct was a sign that the morale of the Normans was breaking down, but it did not at first affect the military administration. During 1203 treasure and material poured in from England, and the strong defences in western Normandy were carefully organised in case Philip should break through the lines of castles in the valleys of the Eure and the Risle, or the Bretons and their allies close in upon them. If John had not lost his head and left the country at the end of the year, after some savage and ineffective raids into the Chartrain and Brittany, he might have held out for some time, keeping the Cotentin, if not Caen, as the base for reinforcements from England. But his nerve failed him as Philip captured one fortress after another in central Normandy; and the Normans, not altogether unwilling to find an excuse, made English indifference the justification for their surrender.

By the autumn of 1203 Philip had opened the way to Rouen. In June two English barons, Robert Fitz Walter and Saer de Quincy, in later years leaders in the fight for the Charter, surrendered Vaudreuil; in September Radepont on the Andelle, which guarded the approach from the south-east, was taken; and the investment of Château Gaillard began. It must have been at this time that John realised the firmness of his adversary. As late as 29 July he was writing as though a truce for two or three years was in sight. He had for some time been in touch with Otto and the Pope and in negotiation with Philip; but Philip was determined to push his advantage to the end. In June, July, and August the vassals of France, including Burgundy, Champagne, Blois, and Renaud of Dammartin, Count of Boulogne, formally counselled Philip not to make peace at papal instigation. The exhortations of Innocent and the attempted mediation of his legate, the Cistercian Abbot of Casamari, were in vain; and at a great feudal assembly at Mantes in August Philip laid down the famous principle that matters of feudal law, as distinct from moral issues, were not matters for papal competence. The disinheritance of John in Normandy was completed in 1204. Roger de Laci's heroic defence of Château Gaillard ended in March, and Philip, leaving Rouen on one side, marched across the Risle, to occupy Argentan, Falaise, and Caen. At Caen he was joined by the Bretons under Guy of Thouars, who had been recognised by John as lord of Brittany as being the last husband of Constance (*ob.* August 1201). Guy came from a successful campaign in the west, where he had captured Mont St Michel and Avranches, and he was sent back with the Count of Boulogne to complete his work. Disregarding all John's efforts for peace, Philip went calmly on; he settled the affairs of the occupied territory, and invested Rouen, where refugees had gathered from all sides. The citizens had formed a kind of league with Arques and Verneuil, the only great fortresses which still held out; but circumstances were too strong for them. They realised their impotence, and the end came on St John's Day, 24 June. Normandy, although claimed by the Kings of England until the definitive treaty of Paris in 1259, was never again, except for a couple of decades in the fifteenth century, to be separated from France. Philip preserved provincial customs, lay and ecclesiastical; the latter especially were the subject of careful enquiry; he accepted the homage of the Norman barons who desired to throw in their lot with him and to risk the loss of their English lands. The Exchequer under a board of French commissioners became the centre of provincial administration and justice, the local administrative areas were regrouped under French bailiffs at Rouen, Gisors, Pont Audemer, Verneuil, Caen, Bayeux, and in Caux and the Cotentin. Most of the castles and the lands of many great English barons were added to the domain.

Philip, however, did not rest content. During Richard's captivity he had meditated an invasion of England as John's ally; now he began to plan an invasion of England as John's enemy—a project which was ultimately attempted in 1216. If the barons whose chief seats were in England hoped to recover their Norman lands, Philip's new vassals also had their eyes on their English estates. Renaud of Dammartin, Count of Boulogne in right of his wife, was especially eager to secure the Boulogne inheritance across the Channel; and there was now no Anglo-Flemish alliance to stand in the way of further adventure.

Nothing came of the project of invasion for the present, and soon Renaud of Dammartin had gone over to John's side. Philip's immediate preoccupations in 1205–6 were the capture of Chinon and Loches, the settlement of Brittany under Guy of Thouars, and the assertion of his claims as overlord in Flanders. While he was before Chinon in June 1205 he heard that Baldwin of Flanders, the Emperor of Constantinople, had been captured by the Bulgarians at Adrianople two months before; and a year later he entered into a close agreement with Baldwin's brother and regent, Philip of Namur. After the fall of Chinon Philip had made it his headquarters, under the control of the Duke of Burgundy, for an advance into Aquitaine. John and his administrators in England had been very busy. In 1205 England had been organised for defence, and when the fear of invasion passed a great naval expedition had been gathered at Portsmouth. John reached la Rochelle on 7 June 1206, and turned southwards to the stronghold of Montauban, where the Garonne and the Dordogne meet. Like Richard, John seems to have been more at home in his mother's country than in Normandy, and it was characteristic of the difference between the two duchies that the barons of Aquitaine, however uncertain and rebellious in their relations with their duke, however willing to avail themselves of the protection offered by the French Court, would not submit themselves, as the barons of Normandy did, to any steady course. At Montauban the turbulent lords of Gascony had gathered around the seneschal of Castile, who represented John's brother-in-law Alfonso VIII. Alfonso had seized the opportunity offered by John's misfortunes to assert his claims to Gascony. In 1204 he had won the support of the chief bishops and feudatories of the land. But at Montauban his pretensions were scattered to the winds. In epic literature the castle was famous as the place which Charlemagne had vainly tried for seven years to take. John's English soldiers took it in a fortnight, and with it the leaders of the Gascon rebellion. John could turn northwards with safety. In Poitou he was joined by Aimeri, viscount of Thouars, the great fief which lay to the south of Brittany, now ruled by his brother Guy, and, with the viscount, John invaded the cradle of his race and reached Angers and the borders of Maine. But on Philip's approach towards Poitou, a truce for two years was made at Thouars (October 13). Neither side was prepared to put to the test the divided allegiance of the Poitevin barons. During the following years the west of Poitou, under the viscount of Thouars and Savaric of Mauléon, stood by John and successfully resisted attack in 1208, in spite of the defection to Philip of the house of Lusignan and La Marche. Moreover, the Albigensian wars began in 1209 and Raymond VI of Toulouse looked to John for aid; and John, in his turn, amidst the troubles of the interdict and his quarrel with the Pope, looked confidently to his nephew Otto, who came under the ban of the Church at the end of 1210. So a step was taken towards the great campaign of 1214.

Attempts to reduce the diplomatic history of Western Europe during these years to a system are vain and misleading. The position of affairs changed from year to year, almost from month to month. In the mind of Philip Augustus the only clear issue had come to be his hostility to the Angevin house and the danger of the alliance between it and the Emperor Otto. It is sometimes supposed that the King of France was a consistent friend to the Hohenstaufen, but the consistency lay only in his fear of Otto. In his youth he had had to face the prospect of the intervention of Frederick Barbarossa on the side of the widespread confederacy which Philip of Flanders had formed against him; and although he had managed to maintain friendly relations with the great Emperor, so on the whole did Henry II. Later he intrigued with the Emperor Henry VI against Richard, but Richard had been stronger than he and won the favour of his captor. During the contest between the rivals, Otto of Brunswick and Philip of Swabia, he had naturally used all his influence in support of his namesake, for he was hard pressed by Otto's uncle and benefactor, Richard, and involved in a harassing dispute with the Papacy on account of his repudiation of his wife Ingeborg; but as soon as Richard was dead, peace made with John, and a settlement with Pope Innocent in sight, he wavered. Philip's firm and oft-expressed conviction that Otto's success would spell danger to himself and his realm made any arrangement impossible, save as a transitory expedient, and the expropriation of John, with the prospect of an invasion of England, must have widened the breach between them. Misfortune on the other hand drew John and Otto together. In 1207, after John's return from Poitou, and when Otto's isolation in Germany was most intense, the Emperor-elect came to England to seek his uncle's support. The two princes held conference in Essex, in the chamber of the famous Samson, Abbot of Bury, in his manor of Stapleford. At this time John was only entering on his quarrel with Innocent, and Otto was still under the Pope's hesitating protection. Yet it is significant that, as Otto's power waned in Germany and that of his rival, Philip of Swabia, grew, Philip Augustus grew cooler in the latter's support, while, when Philip of Swabia was murdered in June 1208 and Otto's fortunes revived, the French king looked around for a new anti-king. The expansion of France, in fact, was displeasing to the German court, whatever its political complexion, just as the prospect of unity in Germany was a cause of alarm to Philip. His attempt to put forward the Duke of Brabant as king failed; Otto received the imperial crown from Innocent in October 1209 and for a short time seemed likely to restore the Empire to its ancient glory. He was in close touch with John. Philip's allies in the north of France were beginning to waver, and it was necessary to anticipate attack by resuming the offensive.

The rash ambition of Otto, lured on by his new sense of power to break his engagement with the Pope, made the way clear for Philip. In November 1210 the Emperor was excommunicated, in the next year the young Frederick of Sicily was put forward against him and civil strife revived in Germany. Philip exerted himself busily on Frederick's behalf. French envoys negotiated with the German princes, were present at his election in December 1212, and a few days earlier, at Vaucouleurs in Lorraine, had arranged an offensive alliance with him against Otto and John of England. English gold helped Otto, French gold helped Frederick. Yet the realistic independence of Philip is very striking during these years. He was at last working, not against, but with the papal candidate of Empire. His two enemies were under the ban of the Church. But, in marked contrast with Otto, he did not for a moment lose sight of his main objective. Innocent's ideals were not his ideals; just as his policy was inspired by no generous affection for the Hohenstaufen, so he was quite unmoved by any ecclesiastical considerations. For some time he had met Innocent's call to a crusade against the Albigensian heretics in Languedoc with polite equivocation. Papal agents had helped to arrange the truce with John in 1206 and had worked for its renewal, in the hope that Philip would come to the aid of the faith in the South. Philip felt no call to interfere with persons who were not his vassals; and until his vassal, the Count of Toulouse, was convicted of heresy, he would not attack him, much though he had suffered at his hands. If Raymond were convicted, then, he said, he would know what to do. The crusade of 1209 was not his, but the work of ecclesiastics and knightly adventurers. Similarly, Philip refused to be diverted into a military attack on Otto's German allies. To this holy war also the clergy should contribute—he would acquiesce in a papal tax—but active intervention was another matter. This was his attitude in 1210, before Frederick had appeared. He had prepared the way for rebellion against Otto, but, while tireless in intrigue and lavish with financial help, he would not scatter his strength. He would use his forces against John and Otto in his own way, for the consolidation of his great domain, and, if possible, its extension across the Channel. It is characteristic that the Atlantic and Mediterranean coasts had no glamour for him. They could wait. He wished to be sure of the well-organised provinces of the Loire and the Seine, the Somme and the Meuse, with their cities, their wealth and administrative systems. And, if he were to keep these safe, he must be free to strike at England and at Flanders.

Whether Philip's policy was the outcome of deep reflection may perhaps be doubted; it was certainly urged by hate. But his instinct was a sound one. His safety, no less than his power, depended on the control of Vermandois, Artois, and Normandy; and, so long as John was able to follow up his intrigues, the fidelity of the new domain could not be assured. At the same time, strongly entrenched though John was, he was not impregnable. If he was wealthy with the spoils of the Church, he was outside the pale as an excommunicated king (November 1209), and he had made many enemies. Philip was in correspondence with disaffected English barons, and had probably learned by 1210 from the lips of a very distinguished refugee, William de Braiose, the detailed story of Arthur's death. If there be any truth in the report which he afterwards circulated, that John had been condemned in his court for the murder of his nephew[1], this may well have been the time of judgment. But, before he could attack England, he found that he had to reckon with the influence of John upon his own vassals. By far the most important of these was the Count of Boulogne, Renaud of Dammartin. Renaud had become a very important person. He had, in addition to his wife's rich county, with its ports of Calais and Boulogne, received from Philip the great Norman fief of Mortain, and, in exchange for Mortemer-sur-Mer, Aumale and Domfront. He had betrothed his daughter to Philip's son by Agnes of Meran, and he had married his brother Simon to Philip's niece, the heiress of Ponthieu. A typical chevalier, a patron of letters, a builder, and a statesman with a keen sense of the value of commerce, he held a position in the north very like that which Philip of Alsace had held twenty years earlier. Unhappily he could not stand aside and avail himself of the quarrel between John and Philip; he had to choose between one and the other, and in 1211 Philip discovered that he had been seduced by John and the Emperor. Renaud's position on the Breton frontier and on the north-eastern coast was so strong that he perhaps anticipated, as an ally of Otto and John in the recovery of Normandy and the ruin of Philip's prestige in north-eastern France, a greater future than he could expect as a powerful vassal of the French crown. Philip acted with his usual promptitude. Mortain was taken by siege, Domfront surrendered, the counties of Aumale and Boulogne were overrun. Renaud and his brother took to flight, and were henceforth the chief agents in the formation of the Anglo-German alliance.

The occupation of Boulogne and Calais brought Philip nearer to his goal; but John and his allies found unexpected support in the new Count of Flanders, Ferrand of Portugal. In order to understand Ferrand's attitude, we must go back to the settlement made twelve years before (2 January, 1200) after the death of King Richard, in the second treaty of Péronne. Philip's position in Vermandois, in the county proper (St Quentin and Péronne) no less than in Amiens, was no longer in question; but he made some concessions regarding the lands in Artois, as it was now called, which had been the dowry of his first wife and which he had in trust for

[1] The general consensus of learned opinion is strongly against the "second trial" of John, although Cartellieri, who dates it in the spring of 1204, has accepted it. See the elaborate essay, in which the evidence is exhaustively reviewed, by Petit-Dutaillis, *Le déshéritement de Jean sans terre et le meurtre d'Arthur de Bretagne*. Paris. 1925.

his son Louis. His direct suzerainty over this area—practically identical with the modern department of Pas-de-Calais, and comprising Arras and the fiefs of Boulogne, Saint-Pol, and Béthune—was recognised, with two important qualifications. Baldwin IX's lordship was to include a strip of territory containing the communes of Saint-Omer and Aire along the eastern border; and, in the second place, if Louis should die without heirs, the whole of the remainder of Artois was to return to Flanders[1]. Baldwin's counties of Flanders and Hainault—the one a French, the other an imperial fief—stretched therefore from the Scheldt behind Bruges and Ghent to a line in front of Saint-Omer, Aire, and Mons. On the other hand, by his occupation of Boulogne, in northern Artois, and his close relationship with his brother-in-law William of Ponthieu (in the lower Somme valley), Philip by 1212 had extended his power to the Channel in the whole of the gap between Flanders and Normandy. Now in 1212 the hand of Joanna, the elder daughter of the Emperor Baldwin, was bestowed on Ferrand, the younger son of Sancho I of Portugal, a young man of twenty-four. The marriage took place in the king's chapel in Paris, and Ferrand set out with his bride to take possession of Flanders. On his arrival he found that Louis of France had stolen a march upon him. The young prince was determined to allow no strong and independent Flanders on the flank of his province of Artois, and began by seizing Saint-Omer and Aire. Ferrand, busy enough in securing the succession to Flanders, which had been ruled by local officials for so many years, was forced to acquiesce (February 1212). But the young southerner never forgave the insult. Before many months had gone by, he was in touch with King John, and when Philip, early in 1213, refused to give back the two towns without a judgment of his court, he joined the great alliance against him.

The English records shew that John's emissaries were to be found far afield at this time, in Portugal, Aragon, and Toulouse, in the cities of the middle Rhine, and of course at Otto's court. The accession of Ferrand and his aunt, the dowager Countess Matilda, and of the neighbouring princes of the Empire gave strength to the party and made a more ambitious programme possible. On his side Philip had realised that he must strike hard; the invasion of England even troubled his dreams. The appearance at his court of Robert Fitz Walter, and his understanding with other English barons, shewed him that the time had come. He would see to Flanders, while Louis attacked England. The solemn decision was definitely reached when Pope Innocent, unable to bring Otto and John to terms, came wholeheartedly into line with Philip for the first and last time. They regarded the issues of their day with very different eyes; but if a holy war was to be preached against John, as well as against Otto and the heretics of Languedoc, Philip was clearly the man to undertake it, and about this venture Philip

[1] This is the reason why Artois was finally added to the French domain only on the accession of Louis' son, Louis IX (1226).

would feel no hesitation. In November 1212 Philip made his treaty with Frederick of Sicily; two months later, he received from the legate Pandulf Innocent's injunction to deprive the excommunicated and obdurate King of England of his crown. On 8 April 1213 a great council gathered at Soissons, the papal mandate was read and accepted, and Philip ordered a fleet to gather at Boulogne, and his men to meet him at Rouen on 21 April. He had his ally Henry of Brabant beside him, and bound him down by a marriage with his daughter Mary, the widow of Philip of Namur. And, above all, he shewed his whole-hearted desire to remove all obstacles to an understanding with the Church by a final reconciliation with his wife Ingeborg of Denmark.

Philip decided to make Gravelines, on the Flemish border, his starting-point. So the great fleet and army, got together at the expense, so English chroniclers say, of from forty to sixty thousand pounds, moved on from Boulogne in the second week of May. But on 22 May, the day of Philip's arrival at Gravelines, he was forbidden in the Pope's name to proceed. Innocent had urged Philip to the adventure, but in his plans the invasion was intended to bring John to reason, and the legate who brought the papal letters to Philip had also been empowered to treat with John. John's surrender, more abject even than he had expected, at once changed the position. During the next few days events moved very quickly. On 24 May Philip forced Count Ferrand to a decision. The count had adopted a waiting policy: he was Philip's liege man, yet had refused to submit his grievances to the judgment of Philip's court; he was in John's pay, yet he had not yet gone over to him. In a stormy interview he refused to join in the invasion, and was declared to be the king's enemy. Acting throughout on the advice of his vassals, Ferrand called for help from England. Philip had moved his fleet to the Swine, which was the harbour of the rich mercantile entrepôt, Damme, and was connected by canal with Bruges. He hastened to secure the Flemish towns—Bruges, Ghent, Ypres, and the rest. Bruges and Ypres were already in his hands and Ghent under siege when the English surprised him. On 30 May an English fleet, under the command of John's half-brother, the Earl of Salisbury, attacked the French ships in the Swine. Four hundred of the smaller ships anchored there were brought out to sea. Over eighty larger vessels, beached by Damme, were captured or burnt. The earl had with him the Counts of Boulogne and Holland, and on the following day, after a landing, Count Ferrand formally joined the alliance. Philip, a few miles away at Bruges, was strong and rapid enough to save Damme, with its treasure and merchandise, and to defeat the land attack. The earl and the counts withdrew to the island of Walcheren; but the plans for an invasion of England were frustrated and Philip destroyed the remainder of his unfortunate fleet.

The importance of this revolution in affairs was great. By distracting Philip from a risky invasion of England, it forced him to concentrate upon Flanders, and to bring all the casual tendencies of the time to a definite issue. The persistence of King John during the last two or three years had debauched the chivalry of Flanders, Holland, Brabant, and the neighbouring lands, and had strengthened the independence of the Flemish towns. As early as 1208 the latter, whose self-government on the lines of the constitution of Arras, had been secured under the rule of Philip of Alsace, had come to an understanding with John. They had learned to act together and had already adopted the anti-French policy which was to become a fixed tradition. Far beyond their borders English money had percolated steadily. By 1213 John's pensioners, paid so much a day, were to be found all over the Low Countries, and many were actually in his service. It has been said that they included so many Brabançons that the Duke of Brabant had to resort to mercenaries in order to fill his depleted ranks. However this may be, Philip found himself faced by a very strong alliance. The Emperor Otto realised that he could best secure his own interests by putting himself at the head of it, and his resolution brought other powerful adherents, including Henry of Brabant, Philip's ally and former candidate for the Empire. During 1213 and the first half of 1214 Flanders was the scene of devastating, if desultory, warfare—a war of sieges, in which towns, notably Lille, were taken and retaken; by the spring of 1214 the long-matured plans for an invasion of France, by way of Vermandois, came to a head. While John made his last great attempt in Poitou, the Emperor and his allies, the Dukes of Brabant, Lorraine, and Limburg, the Counts of Holland, Flanders, and Boulogne, with a few French deserters of whom the Count of Nevers was the most conspicuous, concentrated their forces at Valenciennes in Hainault. Otto had his Saxon chivalry with him, the Earl of Salisbury was at the head of an English contingent, Renaud of Boulogne and Hugh of Boves brought the rest of the adventurers collected by them with the aid of John's treasure. Historians have failed to agree upon the size of this host[1], but that the allies were superior in number to the French would seem to be certain. Philip, after his Poitevin campaign, had come to Péronne and was separated from his foes by the imperial bishopric of Cambrai. He decided to put himself between Valenciennes and the Channel, marched northwards through Douai to Lille (at this time in his hands), then eastwards along the Roman road over the marshy country between Lille and Tournai. The allies had turned north and came to halt at a strong position where the Scheldt and the Scarpe meet, a few miles south of Tournai. They were sure of an easy victory, and when they heard that Philip had decided to turn back to Lille and choose a more favourable battleground, they decided, in spite of Renaud of Boulogne's opposition, to pursue him. Philip, to his surprise,

[1] See Cartellieri, IV, pp. 608–620, on the number of knights at Bouvines. He quotes all the texts and refers to modern literature. It is unlikely that there were more than three thousand knights altogether; and the total numbers in the two armies must have been far below the 80,000 (allies) and 25,000 (French) estimated by Delpech.

was caught up at Bouvines, a village on a plateau just to the east of the solitary bridge over the river Marcq, which had already been crossed by the infantry of the communes. He had just time to draw up in order of battle and to bring back the communal lines, and on a hot Sunday afternoon (27 July) won the great victory which destroyed the power of Otto and secured for the future the new France. When the great dragon on a thirty-foot pole was torn from its wagon and hacked to pieces, Otto's empire fell with it. Henry of Brabant was one of the first to flee from the field; Count Ferrand and Renaud of Boulogne were taken prisoner and lingered in prison—Renaud until his death—for thirteen years. Flanders was ruled by the Countess Joanna under Philip's watchful scrutiny, Boulogne came to his son Philip Hurepel. The unusual concentration of forces, the anxious uncertainty, and the dramatic triumph alike stirred a new sense of unity and power within the kingdom of France. The demesne was no longer to be a collection of fiefs and cities, backed by a semi-independent Champagne or Burgundy, but a centralised state, in which the provincial customs of Normandy, Vermandois, or the Beauvaisis, and the communal privileges of Amiens, Arras, Compiègne, Rouen, and the rest, were subordinated to a uniform administration. Philip came back to Paris amidst scenes of popular and academic enthusiasm. Most of the prisoners, drawn perhaps in the wagons of the victorious communes, were brought to the capital to grace his triumph and were confined in the Grand and the Petit Châtelet.

Before the battle of Bouvines was fought King John had failed in his last attempt to reconquer his lost dominions; perhaps, if the campaigns had more nearly synchronised, the issue would have been different, although it is not clear that the forces which had been with Louis in Poitou were seriously diverted to join his father. John, after his reconciliation with the Church, had immediately turned his thoughts to the expedition which had been prepared in 1212; but, in spite of his energetic preparations, he was unable to sail until February 1214. A few weeks earlier he had received in England the personal homage of Ferrand of Flanders and Raymond VI of Toulouse, the former buoyed up by lively hopes, the latter in desperate straits. For three months John doubled backwards and forwards in Aquitaine—now here, now there; the ways of such a trickster, said William the Breton, are as mysterious as those of a serpent or of a feather in the wind. Philip came into Poitou to cut off his advance, and even to hold him off by suggestions for a marriage treaty, but John was so elusive that he had to withdraw for his northern campaign with nothing accomplished. John had a definite reason for his erratic movements. He secured his hold of one province after another, he was deep in negotiations with the family of Lusignan, and above all, he had to await the development of his allies' plans in Flanders and Hainault. But by the end of May he was ready. At Parthenai on 25 May the three brothers, Hugh of La Marche, Ralph of Eu, and Geoffrey of

Lusignan did him homage and fealty, and John's daughter Joan was promised in marriage to Hugh's son[1]. At last, the king wrote, he could carry his attack beyond the limits of Poitou. He was at first rapid and successful. By the middle of June he was in Angers, and on 19 June laid siege to a new castle built by the seneschal of Anjou, William des Roches, between Angers and Nantes at Roche-au-Moine; but the approach of Louis from Chinon brought the ever latent spirit of disaffection to light. John's presence was always a strain on the personal loyalty of some people, and an open battle against the French overlord might have dangerous consequences. He had to withdraw to the South (2 July), and before he could re-establish his position the news of Bouvines had come. A month later Philip himself was in northern Poitou, and on 18 September, after some days of negotiation with John's envoys, he made a truce to last for five years after Easter 1215. It would have been foolish in either king to seek a fight to a finish, for in Aquitaine fighting could never be finished. Philip wished to consolidate his success in the north-east, and, in spite of his great advantage, could hardly expect to prevent the retention by John of the maritime districts of Aquitaine, or to cut off La Marche or Angoulême from English reinforcements. John was still less in a position to fight; he had lost countless treasure in the last few years and could make no headway in Poitou. Finally the papal legate, the English Cardinal Robert Curzon (de Courçon), who had been in France since the previous autumn preaching a crusade, was active in negotiation. The Pope had striven for peace throughout the year; after the disaster at Bouvines, the call to the Crusade might be heard. At all events a truce was made, and in 1220, when it expired, it was renewed for four years.

Philip lived for nine years after the truce of Chinon. He was then nearing his fiftieth year and his work was done. There is a touch of weariness in his negotiations about the Albigensian Crusade to which he rallied on his death-bed, and even in his handling of the English invasion in 1216. Modern historians have scoffed at the statement of contemporaries that Philip was reluctant to allow his son to attempt a conquest of England, but his attitude at the famous assembly at Melun in April 1216 is not inconsistent with this view. He had set his heart on the enterprise in the years gone by, and nothing had ever come of it. Louis went at his own risk, in support of a claim based partly on a legal case, now generally believed to have been fabricated and in any event irrelevant, partly on his wife's descent from Henry II, partly on the urgent invitation of the English rebels. Philip held the balance even, and characteristically swept aside the papal claim that, as a fief of the Church, England should be regarded as immune from attack.

[1] The later Hugh X, who afterwards married, not Joan, but her mother, John's widow, Isabella of Angoulême.

Similarly the intervention in the Albigensian Crusade and the gradual penetration of Aquitaine, though they began before Philip's death, were not pressed until afterwards. The king's main achievements, apart from the subjection of the north, were the ordering of his demesne, the accumulation of a large treasure, carefully disposed of by will, and the assertion of royal right in the county of Auvergne. In the summer of 1223 he summoned a great council for the consideration of the policy to be pursued with regard to the Albigensian Crusade, but before he could meet his vassals he died at Mantes, on the way from Paci to Paris (14 July 1223).

His successor was at this time about thirty-six years of age—a slight "little man of poor physique, pious, determined and shrewd," the father of a family of small children who were to cut a great figure in the world. Louis had been given his independence in 1209 at the age of twenty-two, when he was knighted by his father. From this time he took an increasing share in the affairs of state. His sharp practice in 1212, when he seized Saint-Omer and Aire, had, by throwing the young Ferrand of Flanders into opposition, precipitated the definitive struggle of 1213–14. He had checked John in Poitou, invaded England, and shared in the general enthusiasm for the crusade against the Albigensian heretics. When he died in the Auvergne in October 1226 he had brought Poitou, the Atlantic ports, and part of Gascony either under his immediate lordship or into his domain, and had entered upon the conquests of Simon de Montfort in Languedoc. Thus he had rounded off his father's work and also had prepared the way for that system of appanages, in his own Artois, in Anjou, Poitou, and Toulouse, by which the new France was largely administered in the thirteenth century.

Louis' success in the west was due to the inability of the administration, badly supported from England, to maintain control in the face of the great barons, and especially the Count of La Marche, Hugh X, who had married John's widow, Isabella of Angoulême, and, through her, was the greatest man in Aquitaine[1]. Many efforts were made during the second period of truce with France (1220–24) to bring peace and unity on the basis of an accommodation with Hugh. Louis was prepared to renew the truce for ten years, but the English government could not tie the hands of the young king for so long a time. Hence when the truce expired it was not renewed. Louis came to terms with Hugh of La Marche and gathered together a great French host at Tours in June 1224. Within a few months the whole of Poitou and several of the towns of Gascony around Bordeaux were won. La Rochelle, Saint-Jean-d'Angeli, Niort, and the other cities were confirmed in their privileges under the French crown. The dominion of Henry III was confined to the areas of Bordeaux and Bazas and the lowlands to the south of the Garonne.

[1] For the conquest of Poitou by Louis see *supra*, Ch. VIII, pp. 258 sqq.

The elimination of Plantagenet influence removed the last hindrance in the way of the French exploitation of Languedoc. Throughout his royal dominions, the last years of Philip Augustus had seen the removal of intermediate lords between the Crown and the local vassals, and even the appearance of new little islets of royal domain. The history of Auvergne provides an excellent case in point. Philip had first secured from Henry II and Richard I the acknowledgment of his rights as direct overlord; he then seized every chance of recognising the immediate dependence upon himself, to the exclusion of the Count of Auvergne, of the bishops of Clermont and Le Puy, the abbeys, and secular lords. This process had already gone far when in 1213 Philip turned upon Count Guy II on account of his molestations of bishops and abbots and his understanding with King John of England. A sharp brutal campaign brought the long period of absorption to an end. The Counts of Auvergne were confined to their *chatellénie* of Vic-le-Comte, the Bishop of Clermont became the legal lord of the city of Clermont, while some 120 small fiefs were added to the royal domain. Now, on a larger scale, this process had begun in Aquitaine, and was to be continued piecemeal so long as the kings of England had any rights on French soil. It was going on nearly every year in all directions—thus, in 1218 the county of Clermont in the Beauvaisis fell to the Crown, in 1219 the county of Alençon in Normandy, in 1221 the seigneury of Nogent, in 1221 that of Issoudun in Berry, in 1223 the county of Beaumont-sur-Oise[1]. The impetus given by Philip's early successes seemed to be gathering an effortless speed, and one can understand why, during the last enterprise of this period—the royal expedition to Languedoc—the reaction which endangered the first years of St Louis can first be traced in the reluctant service and the envious forebodings of those great vassals who were most closely allied with the royal house, the heads of the families of Champagne and Dreux.

Until Louis VIII stamped it with the marks of royal aggrandisement, the terrible warfare against the heretics of Languedoc had all the characteristics of a crusade. The Crown played a permissive part. The Crusade was led by a papal legate, followed by sworn volunteers of all ranks—nobles, knights, burgesses—and was maintained on the whole from ecclesiastical taxation. For nearly twenty years it distracted the attention of the north, and at one time or another most of Philip's vassals and nearly all the great ecclesiastics took part. The king's annoyance at this disturbance during the most critical years of his reign must have been intense. Louis had first succumbed in February 1213, when the appeals of King Peter of Aragon against French interference were set on one side; but he was not able to go south until 1215, and then only on a short and, one might say, unofficial journey. His visit is said to have

[1] This list is given by Longnon, *La formation de l'unité française*, p. 112.

been that of a pilgrim and to have lasted for the usual period of a pilgrimage, forty days, after his arrival at Lyons on Easter Day (19 April). The ecclesiastical chiefs did not desire to see royal intervention as an expression of the feudal claims of France over Toulouse—as Philip was alone prepared to contemplate. They would prefer to welcome it as assistance in a religious warfare, and the more successful the wholehearted crusaders, above all Simon de Montfort, were, the more anxious the legate and his colleagues became about the future. In this, as in other matters, the policy of the Church differed widely from that of the French King. The failure of the attempted conquest of England intensified the religious character of French participation in the Crusade, for Louis had attacked a king under papal protection, and when he made peace at Kingston in 1218, had to submit to the judgment of the Church. He was a penitent, and his penance took the form of special financial contributions to the war against the heretics. Pope Honorius III liked to regard France as a land dedicated to a mission, taxed heavily for this purpose, and under special papal protection. When Simon de Montfort fell before Toulouse in 1218 leaving a young son, Amaury, to succeed him, the Pope was concerned to prevent independent negotiations between Philip Augustus and the heretics to the detriment of the Crusade, and to urge upon the French to come to the rescue to carry on the good work in the old way. Philip was well content to wait; he would acquiesce in the papal policy, but he would not put all his strength at the service of the Church. Louis, as in duty bound, made his military pilgrimage. He took part in the dreadful massacre at Marmande, besieged Toulouse without success, and returned to the north (August 1219). Time was working on his and his father's side. Amaury was no match for the Count of Toulouse, and at last, at the end of 1221, sent his chancellor to Philip, urging him to take over the lands of the heretics as part of his domain. The Crusade as a crusade had collapsed, and the legate joined with the bishops of Languedoc in the appeal to France. When Philip died, both the orthodox party and Raymond VII of Toulouse were competing for his support. His successor had every advantage on his side: he was a loyal son of the Church, a friend of the legate, a champion of orthodoxy, yet in full control of the situation. The Crusade was given a national character in the great councils of Paris and Bourges in 1226. Success was assured before the expedition had started; and by the time that Louis had reached his goal by way of Avignon, Béziers, and Carcassonne, the whole country was at his feet. At Pamiers in October he declared that lands confiscated from heretics belonged by right to the royal domain, and during his short stay in the South he organised Languedoc as its lawful lord. In fact the situation was not so simple as it seemed to be, and after his death the conflicting interests of the Church, the Count of Toulouse, and the French Crown had to be adjusted by the treaty of 1229. But the events of 1226 shewed that the

Albigensian Crusade in the South had prepared the unity of France as effectively as the conquest of Normandy in the North.

The Crusade of 1226 did more than this. As the champion of the Church, Louis did not hesitate to approach Languedoc from Lyons along the left bank of the Rhone. He came to the imperial city of Avignon by way of imperial territory. At the command of the ecclesiastical leaders he did not hesitate to attack Avignon—at this time a refuge for heretics—when the city closed its gates against him. The siege of Avignon was the only serious military incident of the campaign, and its surrender broke what spirit of resistance remained in the South. One action of Louis was full of significance for the future. In order to overcome Avignon he made a treaty of parage with the Benedictines of Saint-André, an abbey whose site dominated the new town. In return for a fixed revenue, the monks allowed the king to build a castle at Saint-André, and to place a garrison there, and to receive the oath of fidelity from the inhabitants. Just as his father, by his policy in the North, began to penetrate with French influence the imperial fiefs on the borders of Flanders and Vermandois, so his son made the first small step towards the penetration of the imperial kingdom of Arles.

The reign of Philip Augustus put the King of France in a position which could give full scope both to the magnanimity of Saint Louis and to the relentless legalism of Philip the Fair. Force and law had never been combined to such skilful purpose. Every victory was followed up until its results were made secure, so that the history of the development of French institutions is the history of the expansion of France regarded from the other or interior side.

At every stage Philip gave a new reality to his feudal position. By the end of his reign his supremacy was too great for legal expression, and the victor of Bouvines becomes the "Carolin," the successor of Charles the Great, whose blood ran in the veins of his first wife[1]. Although it is clear that Philip made conscious use of the Carolingian tradition, and was not unwilling to merge the attributes of a feudal chief in the attributes of royalty, his own importance lies in the fact that he gave new meaning to kingship by his insistence upon his rights as suzerain. He was influential enough to impose important modifications of the feudal law of succession—notably the rule which made all the sharers in a divided inheritance directly dependent upon the overlord—upon the lands of his great vassals as well as within his domain. By his insistence upon the implications of the homage due to himself—the emphasis upon it as liege-homage, recognising in him a claim to prior personal service—he put an end to the perplexing casuistry to which a multiplicity of claims

[1] The writer of the *Registrum Guarini* of 1222 associates Philip, as the victor of Bouvines, with his Carolingian predecessors. The *Chroniques de France* later commented upon the descent of Louis VIII through his mother from Charles the Great. See the passages of Delaborde, *Actes*, I, pp. xxxiv–v.

so constantly gave rise. Thus he would not tolerate the double position of the Count of Flanders, Ferrand of Portugal, who tried to serve King John of England while remaining his vassal. Again, the English barons, who like William the Marshal would have kept their Norman lands by doing him homage, had also to promise not to serve against him; in other words, they put themselves in an impossible position. These are technical examples of a general policy, firmly and consistently applied. The trial of John for his treatment of his Poitevin vassals, the insistence that the royal court was the proper tribunal to settle the difference between Richard of Aquitaine and Raymond VI of Toulouse, the proceedings against the Counts of Flanders and Boulogne, the maintenance of the rights of John as against those of Arthur to Anjou in 1199, shew how the treatment of the most important issues was never divorced from legality. And the casual opportunities of every day were never allowed to slip: great vassals who had been wont to succeed to their lordships as a matter of course were forced to pay *rachat* for recognition; the exercise of the wardship and marriage of their heirs was made a matter of careful definition under royal control; and all over the France of to-day, especially in Auvergne, the Cévennes, and the outlying provinces of Aquitaine, vague feudal relationships were given a precise form in explicit treaties or contracts of parage or joint control, often at the expense of the local lord. It should be remembered, in this connexion, that in virtue of traditions not clearly feudal in character the kings of France exercised scattered rights within all the great fiefs, and upon these a strong king could build. The commune of Châteauneuf at Tours, for example, was only to a slight degree under the control of the Count of Anjou; its administration was under the control of a royal official known as the treasurer, its charter was granted by the French King (1181), its judicial system, which in 1190 was the subject of a careful joint inquiry, was most strictly defined. Similarly, when Philip recognised Richard's rights in Quercy he excepted, as a matter of course, the two royal abbeys which were dependent upon himself.

Yet, as it has been the main object of this chapter to shew, the real strength of the kingdom lay in the France of the royal domain; and the development of the administrative system followed the extension of the domain. As King of Paris and Orleans, Philip at the beginning of his reign had a very limited power. His influence outside his domain was largely due to the close ties between the Crown and the bishoprics—which, with the exception of the Norman bishoprics, were almost independent of the great local feudatories. Hence the *curia regis*, in its narrower sense, was mainly concerned with local affairs, and in its widest form, as a council of the magnates, was as likely to become a deliberative assembly of equals as the advisory body of a king. The rapid extension of the domain changed all this. When Vermandois, Artois, then Normandy itself were successively brought under royal control, and the resources of the Crown were doubled, the prestige of the court was greatly enhanced. It was fortunate, moreover, that, except during the early years of his reign, the magnates of the realm were not numerous or strong enough to overshadow Philip. A circle of great vassals as ambitious and energetic as was Philip of Alsace or Renaud of Dammartin would have embarrassed him at every turn. But Champagne for over twenty years, and Flanders for over ten years, in the new century were in the hands of regents. The Countess Blanche of Champagne, ruling for her son, depended upon the king, and Flanders suffered through the absence and, later, the death of Count Baldwin IX. The duchy of Burgundy also was for several years in the hands of a woman. In consequence Philip's control over the lands which, in the phrase of Innocent III, recognised his lordship (as distinguished from an almost empty suzerainty) was almost as great as it was in his domain. In 1210 for example, when Philip seems to have feared an attack by the Emperor Otto through Champagne, he was energetic in securing its defences, and throughout the young Count Theobald's minority his consent was required before new castles could be built.

Under these circumstances the *curia regis*, as a body of counsellors, jurists, and officials, became an instrument of national government and the centre of a more intricate administrative system. The great feudal councils of magnates and ecclesiastics were of course frequently summoned to support the king in his assertion of principle or in grave political decisions. They were called during the dispute with the Pope regarding Ingeborg, and supported Philip in his proceedings against John and also against Innocent's intervention in feudal issues. Similarly the great vassals, lay and clerical, were invited individually to emphasise their approval of Philip's refusal to make peace when the conquest of Normandy was in sight. Again, it was during the reigns of Philip and his son that the distinction between the peers of the realm and the other bishops and barons of the King's Court was made. King John was condemned in 1202 by his peers and by other barons; in 1216 a case was judged by "the peers of our realm," the Archbishop of Rheims, the Bishops of Langres, Châlons, Beauvais, and Noyon, and the Duke of Burgundy, "and by many other bishops and barons." The peers did not as yet constitute a separate court, and any claim of this kind was repudiated in 1224. The "twelve peers of France," as a distinct body, have not yet appeared; but, perhaps in order to define a competent tribunal for the trial of the greatest vassals of the Crown, and to make the *curia* an indisputably valid engine for the assertion of royal rights, some of the most exalted vassals were distinguished as an integral element of the court. The tendency was a repetition—in a more closely knit kingdom—of the development of courts of peers in Flanders, Vermandois, Champagne, and many other fiefs.

Yet the mainspring of royal administration, and of justice also, was to be found in the royal household, in the *curia* as an organised expression of the *familia*. It is probable that even the peers of France owed their distinction to a traditional connexion with the royal palace[1]. Philip Augustus was strong enough to work through his chosen advisers and officials, and to avail himself just so far as he wished of traditional forms and assemblies. The great officers of state, the seneschal, the butler, the chamberlain, the constable, standing around the king in his palace, might be called upon to attest a solemn act of state, but they played only a small part in daily affairs. The two most important offices, those of seneschal and chancellor, lapsed in Philip's reign, so that no great personage intervened between the king and the administration. The king's uncle, the Archbishop of Rheims, was the only eminent figure among Philip's administrators, and then only in the early years of the reign. Philip relied on his chamberlains, particularly Walter of Nemours and his son, and, later, Bartholomew of Roye, on his marshals and constables. Walter of Nemours was in control of the chancery during the early years, the sagacious Brother Guérin, Bishop of Senlis, towards the end of the reign. Important negotiations were entrusted to them, and they even advised the king on the field of battle. The Bishop of Senlis, for example, drew up the order of battle on part of the field of Bouvines, with the same sureness of touch with which he arranged the records of the chancery. The numerous records of Philip's reign have unfortunately disappeared almost entirely. The earlier series were lost at Fréteval in 1194 during the flight before King Richard, and although the younger Walter of Nemours carefully reconstructed their contents during the next twenty years, the only guide to the arrangements and contents of the royal archives, early and late, is the series of *Registers*, three in number, which contain copies of important royal and private charters, letters, statements of service, manumissions, and the like. The first comprises acts prior to 1212, the second acts prior to 1220, the third—which was the most elaborate and was drawn up in 1222 by Stephen of Gallardon, a chancery clerk, under the direction of Bishop Guérin—acts after 1220. The *Registers* are not exhaustive and were probably memoranda books which could be carried about. The archives, secretarial and financial, were arranged in the royal palace in Paris. The financial records were the outcome of the supervision of local administration by the royal Chamber, and of the treasure in the Temple by Brother Aimard, the Templar.

Although the *Registers* contain many important documents such as the record of military service, with its financial equivalent, due from royal abbeys, communes, and estates (*prisia servientium*), and statements of the arms and armour stored in the royal castles[2], it is significant that the two most illuminating documents of the reign are known through incidental

[1] The bishops of Noyon and Beauvais were "comites palatini." See Viollet, *Institutions politiques*, II, p. 105. For the Counts of Toulouse and Champagne as counts-palatine, see Lot, *Fidèles ou Vassaux?* pp. 126, 139, 152.

[2] Both are reprinted, with careful commentary, in Audouin, *L'armée royale au temps de Philippe Auguste* (1913).

survivals in other quarters. Of these, one, the arrangements made in June 1190 for the government of France during Philip's absence on the Crusade, was inserted by Rigord, the monk of Saint Denis, in his chronicle; the other, an isolated statement of the accounts of the realm for the years 1202–3, was printed, from a text now lost, by Brussel in the eighteenth century. In 1190 Philip entrusted the kingdom to his mother and the Archbishop of Rheims; and it is clear from his careful instructions that the domain was by this date divided into administrative areas under bailiffs. The original bailiwicks were coincident with the older administrative divisions (*in terris nostris que propriis nominibus distincte sunt baillivos nostros posuimus*). Commissions of two or more persons, trained in the royal household, were at first sent round; then large and vague areas were allotted to particular officials; finally, by the end of the reign, distinct areas begin to be mentioned, named from the centres of the domain, Orleans, Paris, Amiens, etc. In 1190, moreover, the bailiffs were instructed to hold assizes once a month and to exercise control over each *prévôté* in their areas with the counsel of four trustworthy men of the locality. Every quarter the regents were to hear complaints (*clamores*) at Paris, and on this occasion the bailiffs were to be in attendance to report upon the affairs of the kingdom. The importance of Paris is shewn by the appointment by name of six burgesses (instead of the four to be chosen in other places) who were not only to act as advisers to the local administrator, but also to receive the royal revenues three times a year and, after they had been recorded in writing, deposit them in the Temple. This render of accounts three times a year is reflected in the three terminal accounts from the *baillivae* and *praepositurae* in the only surviving balance sheet, that for 1202–3. We may infer, therefore, that the financial system, operated after Philip's return by the royal Chamber, was connected with the reorganisation of the local administration.

The accounts for 1202–3 are obviously a war budget, for the expenditure noted, about £95,000, was almost all incurred on the Marches, that is to say, the fortified and garrisoned areas on the Norman frontier. The total receipts—after deduction of probable double entries—were close upon £100,000 in excess of the recorded expenditure, and the balance represents the normal revenue which was required for the normal administration (household, wardrobe, chamber etc.). It has been suggested that the extraordinary revenue expended in the Marches was drawn from the savings of previous years accumulated in the Temple[1]. As a sum equivalent to about £50,000 in the same currency was brought from England in this year to supplement the normal Norman revenue of £20,000, it will be seen that Philip's resources during the last stages of the war against John compare very favourably with those of the duchy. And, if in the middle of his reign, before the great conquests, Philip's normal revenue from his

[1] We are indebted to M. Ferdinand Lot for this interpretation of the accounts of 1202–3. For other figures see the references in Cartellieri, IV, p. 597.

domains was about £100,000, we may safely assume that the resources of Louis VIII were two or three times as much, though not so great as the £1200 a day calculated by the royal officials in their well-known conversation with the provost of Lausanne.

The organisation of the Marches in 1202–3 is a very striking illustration of the efficiency of the administration under such men as Walter of Nemours, Bartholomew of Roye, and Aimard the Templar. Over a long front, and working on exterior lines in provinces which did not possess the unity of Normandy, Philip was able to protect his dominions, prepare a great plan of invasion, and allocate a treasure more than comparable to that expended by Richard in 1197–8 (when he spent over £50,000 on Château Gaillard) and by John. The later records of the reign reveal Philip in control of a still more elaborate organisation prepared to meet the threatened attack by the Emperor. In 1210 and 1211 he was especially active in all the lands between Orleans and the north-east frontier. The castles were rebuilt or restored, the towns walled, sometimes as at Arques under his personal supervision; and a careful inventory was kept of the equipment of war in the towns and strongholds of the realm. He depended for his garrisons and armies mainly upon his heavy-armed knights—some 2000 in number—and the troops of mercenaries under Cadoc and other leaders, also upon the mounted serjeants (*servientes*) provided by the domain, but, like Richard, he substituted a permanent paid force for a feudal levy which owed only a short period of service, and, therefore, he raised money to pay for his mercenaries and engineers and the long-service knights and serjeants by commuting the service due from the abbeys and towns to an equivalent in money. Only a few communes actually sent men to the campaign of Bouvines.

It is not easy to define the sources of royal revenue apart from the proceeds of the domain administered by provosts and bailiffs—the rents, tallages, profits of justice. Philip was able to dispose of large sums in Germany and elsewhere, just as Richard and John of England could; on the other hand he received large sums by the terms of treaties or in return for favours and pardons. The only extraordinary taxation of a general kind was levied for purposes of the Crusades in the East or Languedoc in co-operation with the Church. At various times he extorted money from the clergy, notably the abbeys; he regulated, with great financial advantage to the Crown, the transactions of the Jews, whom earlier in his reign he had temporarily expelled; the *auxilium exercitus*, paid instead of the military duties of serjeants (*prisia servientium*), amounted to about £12,000 in 1194 and to over £26,000 in 1202–3. Other sources were the standardised money equivalents of various ancient dues and the increased annual farms of chartered communities. Indeed, the wealth of Philip Augustus was due to careful exploitation of a prosperous and better ordered state, in which the domain was constantly increasing. Philip was a practical man served by able men. He realised the importance of stability in financial affairs, and, as administrative control became closer, he could afford to encourage stability and self-government in the rural and municipal areas and in the communes. He departed from precedent by granting communal charters in the old domain on the Norman frontiers, he developed the communal movement largely in his new acquisitions, Vermandois and Artois, and he confirmed it in Normandy and Poitou. He was vigilant in the protection of the trading community, including the merchants who travelled to the great fairs of Champagne and the subjects of his enemies. Numerous passages in the literature of the time, especially in the *Chansons de geste*, reveal a curiously intimate feeling of affection for the sweet land of France, which one entered at Orleans. It was a rich and pleasant land, stretching northwards to Beauvais, a land to look back upon with regretful eyes and to dream about. And in the heart of it lay Paris, with its great monasteries and churches, its wonderful island with the new cathedral of Our Lady and the great royal palace, its bridges and fortresses and busy quays and harbours, its streets full of pilgrims and merchants and students. In Philip's time, the privileges of the Parisian merchant *hansa* were confirmed and extended, its monopoly and relations with the merchants of other trading centres, like Rouen, defined. The leading burgesses took part in royal administration, and the merchant body already had certain rights of jurisdiction. Many of the craft-gilds dated their privileges from the days of Philip Augustus. It was his aim to make the city more than a half-rural centre of a large administrative area (the *prévôté* and *vicomté* of Paris). He ordered the burgesses in 1190 to build the walls on the right bank, and in 1209 he himself built the walls on the left bank of the Seine, and ordered the owners of fields and vineyards within the enclosure to let their lands for building. At the weakest point in the fortifications on the right bank he built the great Tower—soon called the Louvre—which had a position in Paris like that of the Tower in London. Nothing is more characteristic of Philip than the picture of him walking up and down in the chamber of his island palace, meditating on the affairs of his kingdom, and then pausing to gaze out of the window over the fair and busy scene, whose complex life owed so much to his guidance. It was the beginning of a new age, not less brilliant but more ordered than the old. Henceforth the life of chivalry, of commerce, and even of learning, was not to expend itself in numerous centres of competing energy, but to be subdued to the influence of a common ideal which at last had found expression in permanent institutions.

CHAPTER X

SAINT LOUIS

From 1226 to 1270 the crown of France was worn by a saint, whose actions, public and private alike, were governed by moral and religious principles, and whose aim was the salvation of souls. It is therefore essential to begin by considering the king's psychology, which explains most things in his reign. It is, moreover, of extraordinary interest in attaining an intimate understanding of the Middle Ages, and we are enabled to follow it closely, as there are trustworthy documents extant, notably the valuable memoirs dictated by the Sire de Joinville, who accompanied the king on his first Crusade. Louis IX and Louis XI are the two medieval French kings about whom we know most. After ascertaining the principles which guided his policy, we shall try to discover whether his court and servants were animated by a like spirit, and what were the instruments and resources at his disposal. Then we shall observe his conduct, first while defending himself successfully against his rebellious vassals, and later, during the second half of his reign, when he endeavoured to realise his ideals in his internal government and external policy.

The figure of his mother, Blanche of Castile, is inseparable from his. He was 12 years of age, and she 38, when Louis VIII died. It was she who educated and formed the young king; she governed during his minority, never ceased to take a part in public affairs, and, at the end of her life, she was again regent from 1248 to 1252 during his absence in the East. Through her mother, she was a grand-daughter of the imperious Eleanor of Aquitaine and the great English King Henry II; and her father was Alfonso the Noble, one of the most valiant Kings of Castile. Blanche possessed a commanding character, great energy, and a taste and talent for politics. She was a virtuous woman full of ardent piety, who brought up her children in the practice of an enthusiastic and uncompromising devotion. Louis IX, in particular, was educated as though destined for the Church, austerely, and none too gently. An anecdote told by Joinville shews that Philip Augustus also took a share in his grandson's education, counselling him to be strict to those about him.

Physically Louis was unlike his mother. He took after his paternal grandmother, the blonde Isabella of Hainault, and his father, the delicate Louis VIII. Fra Salimbene, who saw Louis IX in 1248 before his departure for the Holy Land, says, "the king was thin, slender, lean, and tall; he had an angelic countenance and a gracious person." Even at this time his health was wretched. He suffered from chronic attacks of erysipelas which caused him intense pain. Moreover in 1242, while fighting the English in the marshy district of Saintonge, he had contracted a malarial infection which brought on pernicious anaemia, and he nearly died of it in 1244. His ascetic life and self-imposed mortifications tended to enfeeble him yet further. In Egypt he was again seriously ill. By the time he returned to France he was bald and bent; and by the end of his life he was a mere shadow.

Constantly subject to illness and of a nervous and irritable temperament, he had achieved a remarkable mastery over himself. He must not be represented as a sanctimonious devotee. His character was energetic and decided, nay even obstinate; he was a brave knight and a king who knew how to punish. He was not devoid of a certain hardness; he complained to his confessor that, when praying, he had no tears "to water the aridity of his heart." In dealing with his courtiers he always maintained a certain distance, and never spoke familiarly to any one[1]. And yet there radiated from him a singular charm. The friendly intercourse, full of naturalness and delicate humour, which he daily extended to those whom he esteemed, exercised on them so great an attraction that never was king more dearly loved. His simple manners blending with a truly kingly majesty, his perfect good-faith, his aversion to lying and hypocrisy, inspired affectionate admiration, and he was venerated for his temperance, chastity, and the fervour of his piety. On this last point there is a large amount of evidence, which was collected shortly after his death for the purpose of his canonisation, and which was faithfully summarised by William of St Pathus, confessor to Queen Margaret. Like all great saints, Louis IX spent much time both by day and by night in the exercises of prayer and meditation, depriving himself of bodily enjoyments, practising mortification, having himself scourged with little iron chains, and tending the poor and sick, especially those suffering from the more loathsome diseases. But it must be remembered above all that he was a mystic and a moralist. "This saintly man loved God with all his heart," says Joinville; he sought to attain the state of ecstasy, and, face downwards on the ground, he became absorbed in prayer from which he emerged dazed and murmuring, "Where am I?" He was tormented by the thought that God, Who had died on the cross for men, was not loved and served as He deserved, that there were lukewarm Christians (among whom he included his friend the Sire de Joinville), blasphemers, and infidels, and that he himself did not love his Saviour enough, nor suffer enough for His sake. But he was not one of those mystics to whom the love of God is all-sufficing and all-excusing. Sin horrified him. Few saints who mixed in the life of the world so clearly discerned, in the Middle Ages, the essential principles of Christianity. His devotion was enlightened and his faith grounded on a deep knowledge of the Holy Scriptures. He took greater pleasure in sermons, the study of passages of Scripture, conversations with theologians, and discussions on morality with the people round

[1] *Guillaume de St Pathus*, pp. 19, 55.

him, than in hearing an endless succession of masses, like his pious cousin Henry III.

We can therefore comprehend the attitude which he assumed to his family, his counsellors, and his subjects. In his eyes his first duty was to guide them all to Heaven. He believed that in this respect he possessed a right which none could dispute. So great in these matters was his authority as head of the family, that once his wife, in danger of death, refused to vow a pilgrimage, because he was not near her and could not give his permission. His idea of the royal power, and the principles of his internal and external policy, were in perfect conformity with his perpetual pre-occupation for the salvation of souls. He did indeed succeed in avoiding vain-glory, had no love of power, and even contemplated abdication; he only retained the crown from a sense of duty. But he believed firmly that his sacring conferred on him very extensive rights, and that, when his conscience pointed out to him clearly a course to be taken, he might then resort to arbitrary actions and ignore all counsel. This just and moderate king was one of the founders of the absolute monarchy in France. But he shewed to his subjects the devotion of a father, going so far as to risk his life for them, and he respected established rights and privileges whenever they were not absolutely opposed to his moral ideal. Towards the neighbouring kingdoms he displayed scrupulous justice, and he was a peacemaker. On the other hand, as was inevitable, this saint had no feelings of tolerance either towards heresy among his subjects, or towards the Muslims. The figure of Louis IX offers a violent contrast to that of his contemporary, Frederick II.

Although St Louis was so firm, his internal and external policy was occasionally swayed by the influence of his court and his officials, and this must be recognised. Margaret, daughter of the Count of Provence, whom he married in 1234, was of an arrogant[1] and restless nature; she did not succeed, like her sister Eleanor, wife of Henry III, in filling the court of her husband with natives of Provence, but Louis had to keep a close watch on her, and he allowed himself to be somewhat influenced by her in his relations with England. Of the king's three brothers, the eldest, Robert of Artois, was imprudent and unruly, as he amply proved during the Egyptian Crusade. The next, Alphonse of Poitiers, was a reasonable person, who resembled Louis IX, though with fewer virtues. But the youngest, the proud and ambitious Charles of Anjou, involved the king in a very risky Mediterranean policy.

At first Louis IX's chief counsellors were experienced and wise survivors from the reign of Philip Augustus. Those whom he subsequently selected for himself were for the most part churchmen, such as Eude Rigaud, Archbishop of Rouen, William of Auvergne, Bishop of Paris,

[1] "Humiliter incedit (rex) et gerit se; uxor autem ejus alio modo." B. Hauréau, *Les Propos de Maître Robert de Sorbon*, p. 7 (extr. from the *Mém. de l'Acad. des Inscriptions*, Vol. XXXI, 2nd pt., 1884).

Matthew of Vendôme, Abbot of St Denis, Guy Foulquoi (the future Pope Clement IV), and the famous Robert of Sorbon, founder of the College of the Sorbonne. Or else they were petty nobles such as his beloved chamberlain and secretary, Peter of Villebéon. His counsellors were mostly Frenchmen from the Orléanais, the Île de France, Picardy, and Champagne, who retained the traditions and ideas of the old Capetian monarchy. We do not yet find in the *Curia Regis* those lawyers of the Midi, politicians devoid of scruples, who later, under Philip the Fair, imported subversive principles and revolutionary methods into the central government. The officials round Louis IX, although they laboured ardently for the advantage and power of the king, were conservative. It was chiefly the officers in charge of the bailiwicks and seneschalships far from the king's eye who were dangerous to the nobility, the clergy, and the privileged bourgeoisie. The division of France into bailiwicks (in the north) and seneschalships (in the Midi) was now an accomplished fact, and the important persons placed over them possessed unlimited powers; they managed the royal demesnes and farmed them out to agents, who guaranteed payment of the revenues; they represented the king in districts where the comital powers were his as well, and even in the great fiefs adjoining their circumscriptions which belonged to some count or duke. They laboured, with a zeal often excessive and unjust, to extend the judicial rights and the possessions of the king; they undermined the seignorial privileges of the nobles and prelates; while the petty officials under their orders tyrannised over the peasants and the bourgeois. It was in vain that St Louis strove to oppose these methods; in spite of his fairmindedness and his scruples, the corrosive action of the administration created by Philip Augustus still continued.

The conservative character of the government contemplated by St Louis, as also the monarchical progress achieved under the influence of the king's servants, can clearly be seen in the history of the *Curia Regis* during this reign.

If we except the great constitutional struggles then going on in England, with which there is no analogy in France, the Capetian *Curia Regis* presents certain great resemblances to that of the Plantagenets. The term and the institution both remained vague. The *Curia* assisted the king to govern; it was formed from those who had been summoned for some special object, or who chanced to be residing at court, or who held office there and were in receipt of a regular salary. Sometimes they formed great and very numerous assemblies, summoned by the king, and similar to those of previous centuries; sometimes they were little meetings of men competent to deal with politics, law, or finance: officers of the Crown, the "clercs du roi," the "chevaliers du roi."

During the reign of St Louis, however, the work of subdivision and specialisation, which had begun long before, became accelerated, and the rational organisation of the central government made great strides. As far as we can judge from very inadequate documents, there was as yet no distinct political Council; the word *Consilium* was applied to every kind of meeting of the *Curia*. On the other hand, the commissions of legal officials and of financial officials were taking shape; their traditions were becoming established, and their methods of work were improving.

We know the dates when the Courts of King's Bench and Common Pleas were established in England; it is impossible to assign a date to the Parlement de Paris which in France corresponds with these. If, however, it were absolutely necessary to decide at which period the *Curia Regis* gave birth to the Parlement de Paris, we should select the reign of St Louis. In the first place, it was towards the middle of the thirteenth century that the word *parlamentum*, although still often applied to general courts, began to assume the special meaning which it retained throughout five centuries and to describe the *Curia* in its judicial sittings. In the second place the itinerant character of the commissions of judges was disappearing more and more. Their establishment in Paris had become inevitable owing to the new character of the procedure. At the beginning of the thirteenth century a large number of judgments, even of great importance, were given verbally, without any written document, and their substance could only be established by means of *record*, *i.e.* by witnesses. After the annexation of Normandy to the royal domain, and under the influence of Norman methods, written proceedings superseded the system of *record*. Judgments began to be entered on rolls, certainly not later than 1254, and by 1263 the more interesting were being registered (Collection des *Olim*). In short, a Record Office was definitely established, which necessitated fixed premises, as the piles of documents very quickly assumed enormous proportions; to ensure the swift transaction of business, it became necessary for the legal staff to remain in Paris, although the king and his court still made frequent changes of residence. Finally, and this was the chief sign of a great transformation, this legal staff gradually eliminated the non-professional element. Twenty or thirty individuals, who had studied customary law and who spent their lives in examining cases and giving decisions, formed the "parlement." In each case, one of them presided and pronounced judgment. They were called "conseillers," "maîtres," "chevaliers du roi," or "clercs du roi." Bailiffs were also very often to be found among the judges. There were among the bailiffs of St Louis some professional jurists who spent part of their career as *maîtres* in the Parlement; such was, for instance, Peter of Fontaines, bailiff of Vermandois in 1253, who, by desire of Louis IX, wrote a treatise for the legal instruction of the princes. But those who appear under this title in the list of judges were bailiffs still acting as such, who sat either because they happened to be in Paris with the king, or because they were concerned in the case. In like manner bishops were summoned when a prelate was involved in a case. For the same reason it was recognised that the magnates had a right to be tried by the "peers of France," who on such occasions sat with the legal officers of the king; but (on this point as on many others we must not accept every statement made by Matthew Paris) there was no "court of twelve peers." The real royal judges, those who presided over all the cases of which the king took cognisance, were professional lawyers, often of obscure birth, whom he had chosen for their talents and their uprightness. These ancestors of the proud Parlement de Paris, which played so important a part throughout the whole existence of the French monarchy, became established as a body in the reign of St Louis[1]. Moreover they could sit in other sections of the *Curia*, and in the solemn assemblies, and might be political counsellors as well as judges; and for this reason the Parlement, or *Curia Regis* sitting to try cases, would never renounce its political claims.

The origins of the *Chambre des Comptes*[2] are even more obscure than those of the Parlement de Paris. The financial documents of the thirteenth century have almost disappeared, and we have no treatise of this ancient time comparable with the *Dialogus de Scaccario*. But the organisation of the *Curia Regis* sitting to receive the accounts rendered by the bailiffs, and to prepare in advance for the audit, is certainly much older than that of the Parlement; it was only perfected during the reign of St Louis. Here also there is no doubt that the annexation of Normandy tended to aid the progress of monarchical administration. Borelli de Serres, who has displayed so much penetration in studying the origin of public finance in France, has discovered an account dealing with the bailiwicks of Normandy in 1229–1230; it is much more methodical and regular than the accounts of the bailiwicks of "France" in the same period. Evidently the king's servants deputed to sit at the Exchequers of Rouen and Caen brought thence better rules—not only for legal but also for financial administration. From a comparison of the few rolls that remain, it is evident that greater order and precision had gradually been introduced into the classification of receipts and expenditure. But the great reforms in the financial services and in the Treasury did not take place until the reigns of Philip the Fair and his sons.

A budget founded on the same methods as those obtaining in the time of his father and grandfather was indeed congenial to the conservative tastes, the simplicity, and the pacific policy of St Louis. It is impossible to estimate the king's total revenues at this period; the documents are not sufficiently coherent. But we can at least say that the character of the royal revenues had not changed. Most of the resources were still derived from the royal demesne. Besides this, the officials still continued to collect profitable fines, sums paid in lieu of military service, donations

[1] See the list of the members of the Court in 1254, 1256, 1259, 1261, in the *Textes relatifs à l'histoire du Parlement*, published by Ch. V. Langlois, 1888, pp. 40, 44, 49, 63.

[2] This term first appeared at the beginning of the fourteenth century. The word "Échiquier" in France only existed in Normandy, which even after the annexation retained its judicial and financial Exchequer.

voluntary only in name which were demanded from towns and which tended more and more to their financial ruin, and finally heavy tallages imposed from time to time on the Italian bankers and the Jews. On the occasions of the two crusades of St Louis and the Sicilian expedition of Charles of Anjou, the clergy had to pay very heavy taxes. In all this there was nothing really new.

Nor was there any essential modification in the methods by which the royal revenues were collected. The provostship of Paris had, indeed, been reformed, but this reform did not bear the character which has been assigned to it by historians up to our day. Relying on references in the *Grandes Chroniques de France* and in Joinville, it was believed that this office had been farmed out at the beginning of the reign to various unscrupulous bourgeois, who were supposed to have oppressed the population to the grave detriment of the royal treasury; St Louis, "having," says Joinville, "learned the whole truth,...would not allow the provostship of Paris any longer to be farmed," and entrusted it with good pay to an honest man named Stephen Boileau[1], who did justice without bias, and was so careful that the Treasury's receipts were doubled. In reality the reform had neither these motives nor these results. Stephen Boileau's predecessors were prominent and honest merchants. Boileau himself had at first farmed the provostship. But after about 1265 it is probable that neither he nor any one else would have accepted the office on these terms, for it threatened to become ruinous. The revenues indeed remained the same, while the expenses charged to the provostship were daily increasing. About this time the king decided that Stephen Boileau should cease to farm the office and should become a mere agent; the receipts became increasingly inadequate, but the deficit was henceforth borne by the Treasury. The population was no less oppressed than heretofore, because, in order to bring in the various revenues of the demesne within the provostship of Paris, Stephen Boileau entrusted their collection to numerous farmers, so that the inconveniences which the former system had imposed on the subjects were retained[2]. This is a characteristic example; even in Paris there was no attempt to suppress the system by which the royal demesne was exploited, so as to supersede it by a system of direct collection.

Louis IX had many opportunities of adding considerably to his resources by acquiring new domains. His scrupulous honesty prevented this. The tale of acquisitions during his reign is quickly told. By the treaty of

[1] He was the author of the famous *Livre des Métiers* (edited by Lespinasse and Bonnardot, Paris, 1879).

[2] Borelli de Serres, *Une Légende administrative, La Réforme de la Prévôté de Paris et Étienne Boileau*, in *Recherches sur divers services publics, Notices relatives au XIIIe siècle*. Was there any connexion between this reform (which dated from 1265) and the appearance (in 1263) of the title of Provost of the Merchants and Échevins bestowed on the provost and *jurés* of the *Marchands de l'Eau*, who henceforth formed a kind of municipality? Personally, we doubt it. Cf. Georges Huisman, *La juridiction de la Municipalité parisienne de St Louis à Charles VII*, 1912, pp. 20 sq.

Paris which in 1229 ended the Crusade against the Albigenses, the Count of Toulouse was deprived of the duchy of Narbonne, *i.e.* Lower Languedoc; everything within this district which had belonged in demesne to the count, especially the viscounty of Nîmes, henceforth formed part of the royal demesne; the rest passed from the suzerainty of the count into that of the king. In 1239 the Count and Countess of Mâcon, who were childless, sold their county to the king. Finally, after the death of the king's uncle, Philip Hurepel, the counties of Clermont-en-Beauvaisis and Mortain, and the castellany of Domfront, accrued to the royal domain. On the other hand, Louis IX formed for his younger sons appanages which almost counterbalanced the above-mentioned annexations; thus Peter received the counties of Alençon and Perche, and Robert that of Clermont-en-Beauvaisis. These appanages awarded to his sons were, however, very modest compared to those which he conferred on his three brothers, in obedience to the will of his father Louis VIII. On attaining their majority, one of them, Robert, received Artois (1237); to another, Alphonse, were given Poitou, Saintonge, and Auvergne (1241), to which was added, after his marriage to Joan of Toulouse, the heritage of Raymond VII, Count of Toulouse, who died in 1249; finally the youngest, Charles, received Anjou and Maine (1246). If these magnificent provinces had not been assigned to the princes of the royal family, over half the kingdom would have formed part of the royal domain. But possibly the unification of France rather gained than lost from this policy of appanages. In particular, it seems that the very careful administration of Alphonse of Poitiers contributed to the rapid assimilation of the provinces of the Midi.

The advantages which the monarchy reaped from the moderation and uprightness of Louis IX can clearly be seen in the monetary history of the reign. The king was loth to make excessive profits on the Mint, or to make arbitrary changes in the relation between the coins and the money of account; neither did he, at his own good pleasure, modify the ratio between gold and silver coins. The king's currency inspired so much confidence that he was enabled to restrict to his advantage the circulation of the seignorial currencies, without arousing excessive indignation. He did not claim, as did later Philip the Fair, that he held the exclusive right of coining, or of authorising the coining of money, but he prohibited the use of any currency other than his in all places where there was no seignorial mint, and he ordained that the royal currency should be accepted *per totum regnum*. His officials, of course, went farther than he did, and often attempted unduly to prevent the currency of seignorial money. But the next generation experienced much graver abuses and looked back regretfully to the good coinage of St Louis.

Such as they were, the financial resources of the monarchy enabled him to defend himself when attacked, to carry out two crusades, and finally to establish peace throughout the kingdom. This was achieved without any alteration in the old military system. In case of danger, he had recourse to feudal service, and the service of the communes in the royal demesne. The right of summoning to the host all the common people of the demesne was exercised, but almost solely to permit the levying of taxes in lieu of service. On the other hand, regular troops consisting of knights, cross-bowmen, and serjeants, were engaged and paid, who could be employed at will and depended on with safety. The enemies of France found themselves confronted with a sound and efficiently-led army.

In a word, under St Louis the French monarchy displayed no inordinate ambition, and did not possess the new resources which would have been necessary to satisfy it. But it perfected the earlier means of action, and, as will be seen, Louis knew how to reap full advantage from his twofold character as a supreme suzerain and the possessor of divine right bestowed by the sacring. During the childhood and youth of the king, the monarchy experienced some hard blows, which it succeeded in parrying; after 1243, or thereabouts, its triumph was assured, and it enjoyed an incomparable prestige. We must first study it on the defensive.

When Louis VIII died, he entrusted the care of the kingdom and of his son to Blanche of Castile. The barons were annoyed by this decision, and there were significant and alarming abstentions from the coronation of the young Louis IX on 29 November 1226. Blanche's somewhat harsh methods left the barons no hope of dividing among themselves the rich heritage of Philip Augustus and his son. They immediately announced that they were unwilling to be governed by a woman and a stranger, who was sending the royal money to Spain, was teaching her son to dislike the nobles and to surround himself with priests, and was preventing him from being liberal with his possessions. They called her by the name which in the *Roman de Renard* is given to the she-wolf: *Dame Hersent.* And in the winter of 1226–7 a feudal coalition was formed.

But the protagonists of the feudal opposition were of poor metal. The old members of the League which Philip Augustus had overthrown at Bouvines were no longer formidable; Ferrand, Count of Flanders, who had been set free on 6 January 1227, remained inert, and his accomplice, Renaud de Dammartin, Count of Boulogne, died soon after in prison. Philip Hurepel, the king's uncle, a negligible and inefficient person, whom the barons would have liked as regent so that they might have a free field, was incapable of playing the part of a leader. The Count of Champagne, Thibaud le Chansonnier, was a great noble given to poetry, versatile and inconstant; he professed a platonic love for Blanche of Castile, which she turned to account; in his vacillations, he was formidable neither to the monarchy nor to the allies whom he betrayed. The nobles of Poitou, such as the Count of La Marche, were perpetual busy-bodies, troublesome rather than dangerous, always ready to yield to force and to start fresh and useless intrigues the next day. Blanche's most dangerous enemy was Peter of Dreux, great-grandson of Louis VI, who held the county of

Brittany as guardian for his son, who was still a minor. He was a harsh and ambitious man, dissatisfied with his precarious position and with his temporary title of Count of Brittany. He was nicknamed Mauclerc, because of the brutality with which he treated the Breton clergy. Finally, the coalition could reckon on the Count of Toulouse, who had not yet made his submission, and on the King of England, who regretted the French possessions which had been wrested from John Lackland.

The struggle was confused and uninteresting; as intricate and as useless as, in later days, was the Fronde during the minority of Louis XIV; as full of childish intrigues and betrayals; as disastrous for the hard-working populations of certain provinces, such as Champagne which was laid waste by the soldiers. The first coalition concluded between Peter Mauclerc, Thibaud of Champagne, the Poitevin nobles, and the King of England, was easily foiled by means of a few concessions, the most serious of which was the grant of Bellême and St James de Beuvron, important fortresses on the borders of Normandy and Brittany, which Peter Mauclerc demanded (February—March 1227). In the same year the nobles all but captured the young king. "All the barons" says Joinville, "were assembled at Corbeil. And the sainted king once told me that neither he nor his mother, who were at Montlhéry, durst return to Paris, until the people of Paris came armed to fetch them. And he told me that from Montlhéry onward the roads were full of men armed and unarmed as far as Paris, and that all prayed to Our Lord that He would grant to the king a good life and a long, and that He would defend and guard him from his enemies." These vivid impressions of childhood must have made a deep mark on the mind of Louis IX; in such days he conceived a great horror of feudal disorder and vowed that he would restore peace to France.

During the years 1228–9, the nobles continued to agitate and to conspire; but Blanche of Castile, skilfully aided by an Italian prelate, the Cardinal-legate, Romano Frangipani, succeeded in partially disorganising the forces of her enemies. The cruel war between the Albigensian heretics and the royal troops, which had been going on in the county of Toulouse since 1226, came to an end, after a systematic devastation of the Toulousain district. The legate forced Count Raymond VII to submit and to accept very severe terms. Raymond was only allowed to retain the district of Toulouse, Agenais, Rouergue, Quercy, and the north of Albigeois (Treaty of Paris, 11 April 1229). In the north, Thibaud of Champagne was almost completely won over to the monarchical cause. The good towns in the royal domain between the Seine and Flanders, thirty-four in number, swore to serve faithfully the king and his mother. A heavy blow was struck at the prestige of Peter Mauclerc by the capture of his castle of Bellême, which was held to be one of the strongest fortresses in the kingdom. This was a strenuous operation of war, carried on absolutely ruthlessly in the heart of winter (January 1229) by the Marshal John Clément, in the presence of Louis IX and Blanche.

Peter Mauclerc then resolved on open treason, and on 9 October in the same year he landed in England. A few days later, he did homage for Brittany to Henry III. In the month of January he sent to bid defiance to the King of France. The year 1230 was particularly critical. The King of England, after having made considerable preparations and requisitioned several hundred vessels, landed at St Malo on 3 May. Meanwhile Champagne was invaded: Philip Hurepel, the Duke of Burgundy, and the other conspiring barons could not forgive Count Thibaud for having deserted to the queen's party; it was asserted that he had poisoned Louis VIII and that he was Blanche of Castile's lover. Fortunately for her, the inert Henry III had not sufficient energy to seize so good an opportunity; and, moreover, the French barons hesitated to betray their king openly and disobey the Pope, who was supporting Blanche of Castile. When they received their summons to the host to repel the English invasion, they did not refuse their service of forty days, and contributed their quotas to the royal army which invaded Brittany; they allowed the *Curia Regis*, assembled in the camp outside Ancenis, to declare that Peter Mauclerc had forfeited the guardianship of Brittany (June 1230). At the end of the forty days, they went back to their spoliation of Champagne; but Blanche of Castile, now free from anxiety in the west, was in a position to help her vassal. The enemies of the Count of Champagne dared not attack the army in which the young king was present in person, and, when Philip Hurepel concluded with the Queen Regent a peace favourable to himself, the coalition of nobles became disorganised (September). Meanwhile Henry III was feebly carrying out a useless military advance as far as Bordeaux; then, uneasy at the attitude of certain Poitevin barons, and unwell, he retraced his steps and returned to England (28 October). His subjects were very resentful at this wretched expedition, and for over ten years his financial embarrassments obliged him to postpone his plan of reconquering the fiefs lost by John Lackland. In 1234 Peter Mauclerc, counting on his support, again took up arms. As the King of England only sent some 60 knights and a body of Welsh bowmen, Peter was unable to resist the royal army, made his submission, and informed Henry III that he renounced his allegiance.

In the same year, 1234, on 25 April, Louis IX attained his majority. His mother, who still continued to play a great part in politics, had well defended the interests of the Crown during his minority. No foreign prince had succeeded in lessening its glory. By the marriage between Louis and Margaret of Provence, French influence was extended beyond the Rhone, which then served as frontier. Internally the royal domain had been increased by the addition of a part of the county of Toulouse. The lands which had for a time been granted to Peter Mauclerc had been recovered. Thibaud le Chansonnier, in return for the services rendered to him by the king[1], had ceded to him the direct suzerainty of the counties of Blois, Chartres, Sancerre, and Châteaudun. One by one all the great barons who had caused the disturbances had disappeared, or were about to do so. Philip Hurepel was dead. Peter Mauclerc, after renewed attempts at disorder, soon relinquished Brittany to his son, John the Red, who had attained his majority. As to the versatile Count of Champagne, his part in the history of France ended in ridicule and humiliation; in 1236, after conspiring with Peter Mauclerc, he was made to come and sue for pardon at court; and the king's young brother, Robert of Artois, arranged for ordure to be thrown on his head. Thibaud left for Navarre, of which he had become king, and Louis IX was rid of this troublesome and very undependable person.

The last uprising of the malcontents occurred between 1240 and 1243. It might have had serious results, as the whole of the west and south of France was affected. In 1240, owing to causes which we shall consider later, the Albigenses again became active, and there were armed risings in Languedoc. In the following year Alphonse, the king's brother, was invested with his appanage, and went to Poitou to receive the homage of his vassals. The most powerful of these was Hugh of Lusignan, Count of La Marche, who had married Isabella of Angoulême, widow of John Lackland and mother of Henry III, the very person whose marriage to the King of England had caused the appeal of the Poitevin barons and the sentence of disinheritance pronounced by the Court of France against John in 1202. She was a woman with an imperious and violent temper, before whom Hugh trembled. We learn from a very interesting letter written by a bourgeois of La Rochelle to Blanche of Castile[2], that Isabella could not bear the thought that her husband was vassal to Alphonse of Poitiers. She roundly declared to Hugh of Lusignan that he should never again share her bed if he consented to abase himself in this manner. Hugh, who would have preferred a policy of bargaining and small profits, resigned himself to the task of forming a conspiracy. Conditions were favourable. The Poitevin barons were proverbially addicted to treason. They held meetings, first among themselves, then with the Gascon barons and the mayors of Bordeaux, Bayonne, St Émilion, and La Réole. The "French," they said, wish to enslave us; it were better to come to terms with the King of England, who is a long way off, and will not take from us our lands. And, in fact, they did come to terms with the King of England, and also with the King of Aragon, who was lord of Montpellier, and with the Count of Toulouse. At the court held at Poitiers on Christmas Day, Hugh of Lusignan defied his lord, the Count Alphonse, and war was prepared.

[1] Blanche of Castile and Louis IX had supported him against Alix, Queen of Cyprus, who was advancing claims to Champagne; and the royal Treasury supplied the 40,000 *livres* necessary to buy her out.

[2] Discovered and published by Leopold Delisle, BEC, Series IV, Vol. II.

In the spring of 1242 the royal army very quickly captured the Poitevin strongholds. Henry III vainly demanded from his Parliament the resources necessary for a fresh invasion of France. He landed at Royan on 12 May 1242, with a small expedition consisting only of seven earls and 300 knights. Isabella welcomed her son warmly and thanked him for coming to succour his mother, "whom the sons of Blanche of Spain so wickedly wished to tread underfoot." But when the armies of the two kings met near the bridge of Taillebourg on 21 July, there was no battle; alarmed at the sight of the French camp, which looked like a "large and populous city," Henry's scanty troops retired within the walls of Saintes. On the morrow, however, the English and the Gascons made a sortie. But Henry III gave the signal for flight. The Poitevins submitted; Hugh of Lusignan, Isabella, and their children presented themselves before Louis IX, and kneeling begged for mercy. Mad with anger, Isabella became a nun and retired to Fontevrault, where she died in 1246, quickly followed to the grave by her husband. Meanwhile Henry III retired to England two months after his defeat at Saintes, with yet another failure to his account.

This was the last English invasion during the reign of St Louis. It was also the end of the feudal anarchy in Poitou for many a day; order was established by the administration of Alphonse of Poitiers and later by that of the king's officials.

But the Midi was not yet pacified. In that region, Louis IX reaped what the severity of his officials and the inquisitors had sown. The treaty of 1229 had not put an end to the persecutions from which Languedoc suffered. In the seigniory retained by Raymond VII, Count of Toulouse, who was personally inclined to a tolerant and kindly policy, he was under the supervision of the legates and the bishops, who rained excommunications on him whenever he shewed any signs of lukewarmness in religious affairs. In 1233 he was obliged to publish statutes against heresy, and to allow the Inquisition to be organised within his States. The persecution was ruthless, and it ruined, decimated, dispersed on distant pilgrimages, or terrorised by frequent auto-da-fes, a large number of families. Tolerant Catholics were prosecuted and heretics were offered a choice between conversion or death. "Behold," said the Inquisitor, "the consuming fire which devours thy companions. Answer me quickly; either thou shalt burn in the fire, or thou shalt conform.... See, how the people crowd to see thee burn."[1]

In the new royal seneschalships of Beaucaire and Carcassonne, religious persecution was not the only evil. The seneschals and *viguiers* who administered them were knights from northern France; they treated their

[1] Paul Meyer, *Le débat d'Izarn et de Sicart de Figueiras, Annuaire Bull. S.H.F.*, 1879, pp. 249, 260. Paul Meyer thinks that this curious poem is a little later than 1244.

districts as conquered country[1]. The seneschals, once they were appointed by the king, lived like great independent barons, and profiting by the difficulties of the monarchy, they enjoyed absolute authority. Peter of Athies, who was seneschal of Beaucaire from 1239 to 1241, abused his position shamefully; greedy and licentious, he governed by fear, and refused to obey the orders sent by the king. "I would," he said, "gladly give a hundred silver marks if I might hear nothing more of the king and queen." William of les Ormes, seneschal of Carcassonne, imprisoned some burgesses who, crippled by the taxes he had imposed, ventured to appeal to the king. Each seneschal had for lieutenants several *viguiers* (*vicarii*). These purchased their appointments, and meant to derive great profits therefrom; they disobeyed the seneschal even as he disobeyed the king. Finally, in each parish of the demesne, there was a *baile* (*baiulus*) to manage the king's property and arrest delinquents. The *bailes* were recruited from among the natives of the province, but were none the less violent and tyrannical. Thus the inhabitants were, in one way or the other, crushed beneath the weight of vexations, fines contrary to custom, arrests on false pretences, requisitions without payment, forced labour, injury to property, and, finally, arbitrary taxation.

During the early part of St Louis' reign, it frequently happened that similar abuses were suffered elsewhere, and there were complaints in the Midi about the officers of the Count of Toulouse, before the Albigensian crusade. But the oppression had become aggravated in the two seneschalships, because it was not easy to lodge a complaint at the king's court, which was so far away. Moreover, it had assumed a much more destructive character, because the repression of heresy was an excuse for violent methods, and because the privileges of the lay and ecclesiastical aristocracy and of the bourgeoisie, which had been respected by the Counts of Toulouse, were now bitterly opposed by the king's officials. Not only were those inhabitants convicted of heresy, the *faidits*, punished and dispossessed, but very often the goods of those whom the Inquisition recognised as victims of false accusations were not returned to their owners, and the Catholic relatives of the *faidits* were persecuted and robbed. Finally, the seneschals, under pretext of restoring order and defending the king's rights, were above all intent on destroying strongholds, preventing the exercise of seignorial and municipal jurisdiction, and extending the royal demesne properly so called to the limits of their seneschalships. They engaged in a bitter struggle with the nobles of the Cévennes in the mountainous districts of Gevaudan and Velay, and even in Vivarais, which was still territory of the Empire. The Albigensian crusade, which had ruined so many southern families, had left two powerful houses in the Cévennes—the Pelet, and the lords of Anduze—who were allowed to remain after promising fidelity and orthodoxy. Round these two

[1] All the facts which follow are taken from the inquests published in *Recueil des Historiens de France*, Vol. XXIV.

families there existed a horde of brigand barons, poverty-stricken but formidable warriors, who passed their lives in quarrelling but would not brook foreign domination. Peter of Athies succeeded in taking and demolishing a large number of strongholds, and in establishing royal *bailes* here and there in Gevaudan. His struggle with Dame Tiburge, widow of Bernard Pelet, was famous. He was not always victorious, but he destroyed five of the castles which had belonged to the Pelet family and shattered their prestige. In like manner, Peter Bermond of Anduze was partially dispossessed. Finally the towns, which had gradually obtained the right of forming "consulats" with important privileges with regard to administration, justice, and taxation, went back to their former insecurity. At Beaucaire, for instance, the consulate was suppressed, and the judicial and financial privileges of the town were persistently violated.

An outlaw, Raymond Trencavel, resolved to use the popular discontent to revive the Albigensian resistance. He was the son of Raymond Roger, Viscount of Béziers and Carcassonne, one of Simon de Montfort's victims. Raymond Trencavel, who had been excommunicated in 1227 and deprived of his possessions, had taken refuge at the court of the King of Aragon, a centre of intrigues against France. Without waiting for substantial support from the enemies of Louis IX, he appeared in Languedoc in 1240 with a band of exiles and of Catalan knights, persuaded part of the population in the seneschalship of Carcassonne to espouse his cause, and seized a few places. The seneschal William of les Ormes, the Archbishop of Narbonne, and the Bishop of Toulouse organised the defence of Carcassonne, and called for help from the Count of Toulouse, who however preserved a doubtful neutrality. In reality he was counting on Trencavel's success, but did not wish to compromise himself immediately. Trencavel occupied the open *bourg* of Carcassonne, and 33 Catholic priests were massacred there. But the fortified *cité* resisted Trencavel's furious assaults (17 September—11 October 1240), and he made off when he learnt that royal troops were approaching. Blanche of Castile, who seems at this time once more to have assumed control of affairs in the Midi, had entrusted a strong army to an efficient leader, the Chamberlain John of Beaumont, who was notorious for his brutality. Trencavel retreated across the Pyrenees.

Many of his partisans were hanged; many old families round Carcassonne were deprived of their possessions, and the land passed finally to new owners. But the Count of Toulouse, encouraged by the King of Aragon, the Count of Foix, and other Pyrenean seigneurs, secretly prepared a revolt. In 1241 he negotiated with Hugh of Lusignan, who was prepared to defy Alphonse of Poitiers. Meanwhile the Inquisitors, at this most untimely moment, redoubled their zeal, and even attacked Catholics who had merely kept up relations of friendship and neighbourliness with the Cathari. Exasperation increased, and the news spread that the English and the barons of the west were about to drive the

French back to the Île de France. A fortnight after Henry III's landing at Royan, the two inquisitors who had just arrived at Avignonet[1] to try heretics were assassinated with their suite. It seemed as though the whole of the Midi was about to revolt. Raymond VII seized Narbonne and Béziers. But Louis IX's victory at Saintes demoralised the Southerners. Abandoned by the Count of Foix, and threatened by a new crusade which would deprive him of his possessions, on 20 October 1242 Raymond VII sent suppliant letters to Louis IX and Blanche. Soon after he obtained peace, in return for a promise to observe the treaty of Paris and to destroy heresy within his dominions. The remaining strongholds, which served as habitual refuges for the heretics, very soon fell. The provincial nobles were decimated and ruined, and heresy, which depended on them, gradually disappeared.

The disturbances whose history we have just summarised, marked alike the close of the Albigensian resistance and the end of the dangers which had threatened the monarchy ever since the coalition of Bouvines. Henceforward Louis IX could devote himself to the salvation of his soul and the good government of his kingdom.

The dominant pre-occupation in St Louis' mind was to lead men heavenward in his company. Therefore the Christian education of his subjects in every rank of life was his chief interest. Every evening, at bed-time, he personally gave religious instruction to his children. He wrote for their use with his own hand the *Enseignements*[2], which are chiefly pious precepts. Vincent of Beauvais, the famous author of the *Speculum*, tells us that St Louis charged him to give moral and religious instruction to "princes, knights, counsellors, ministers and others, who were resident at court or administering public affairs elsewhere."[3] The king liked to arrange sermons for the edification of his barons, for the common people, or even for the clergy. He considered that there were never enough houses dedicated to prayer. "And so," says Joinville, "even as the writer who has written a book illuminates it with gold and azure, the said king illuminated his kingdom with beautiful abbeys." One of the most perfect gems of Gothic art, the Sainte Chapelle in Paris, was built at his order (1246–8) to provide a worthy abode for the relics of the Passion, which he purchased from the needy Emperor Baldwin. What may be termed the social policy of St Louis was definitely religious in character. When he founded in Paris the famous lay congregation of the Quinze-

[1] A *bourg* situated near Villefranche in Lauraguais, about thirty miles from Toulouse.

[2] On these remarkable documents, see H. F. Delaborde, *Le texte primitif des Enseignements de St Louis à son fils*, BEC, 1912, and the bibliography given by A. Molinier, No. 2657.

[3] Quétif and Échard, *Scriptores ordinis praedicatorum*, Vol. I, 1719, p. 213.

Vingts, to provide an asylum for 300 blind folk[1], when he sent succour to provinces threatened with famine, when he personally attended the poor and sick, he was applying the precepts of his religion with intelligence and love, but he was far from possessing any of our modern ideas. For this same man, still with the intention of securing his own salvation and that of others, shewed himself capable of cruel fanaticism.

He indeed punished blasphemers and persecuted heretics with great harshness. It was owing to his active co-operation that Popes Gregory IX and Innocent IV were enabled to establish the Inquisition in France, when in most countries of Europe it was repulsed by the secular clergy. And especially from 1233 onwards the persecution became systematically organised, and spread almost throughout France, because of the resistance offered by the Cathari in the South and infection from the Albigensian heresy in the Northern provinces. Louis and his mother defrayed the expenses of the inquisitors, and supplied them with a guard for their protection. The secular clergy had abandoned their ancient prerogative at the request of the Pope and the king; while councils at Béziers, Albi, and Tours established the tribunals of the Inquisition and their terrible secret procedure, which was to exert so sinister an influence on French criminal law. The officials of St Louis offered no opposition to prosecutions which enabled them, by means of confiscations tending to the king's advantage, to enrich the treasury and round off the demesne.

The prevailing credulity is shewn by the belief accorded to Brother Robert, who between 1233 and 1239 terrorised the Île de France, Burgundy, Champagne, and Flanders. He was a converted Patarine, and was therefore nicknamed the *Bougre* or Bulgar. After a holocaust of 183 heretics, or so-called heretics, who were burned before an immense throng at Mont-Aimé in Champagne, men realised that this maniac was condemning Orthodox and Cathari alike; he died in prison. We have seen how in the Midi the Albigensian resistance ended in the final submission of Raymond VII. But the persecution continued, and the Count of Toulouse helped therein, in accordance with his promise. He shewed great zeal. In the year of his death (1249) he burned near Agen 80 Cathari who had recanted their errors, and whom an inquisitor would not have handed over to the secular arm for execution. After him came the greedy Alphonse of Poitiers, who married his daughter and took possession of the country; he was less barbarous, but gave his support to prosecutions from which the king allowed him to benefit.

Personally Louis IX would certainly not have ordered the burning of repentant heretics, for one of his great desires was for conversions. Just as at his abbey of Royaumont he educated Saracen children whom he had brought from the East, so by his generous gifts he succeeded in

[1] These were poor Paris folk, and not, as told by legend, three hundred knights blinded in the Crusade. See L. Legrand, *Les Quinze-Vingts* (*Mémoires de la Société de l'Histoire de Paris*, 1886, pp. 107 sq.).

persuading a certain number of Jews to be baptised. But all toleration was foreign to his mind, and it was only with great difficulty that he was persuaded to allow the presence of Jews in his kingdom for financial reasons which his counsellors urged on him. Joinville tells us that he allowed that "very good clerks," capable by their attainments of converting infidels, might argue with the Jews, but that the only possible attitude for a layman, if he heard them decrying the Christian law, was "to plunge his sword into their bellies, as far as it would go."

Nowhere was the rigidity of Louis IX's principles in the internal government of his kingdom more forcibly shewn than in the exercise of his duties as a judge. There he applied the theory of monarchy rendered divine by the sacring to its full extent. He regarded himself as God's delegate. He was pre-eminently the king justiciar. No doubt many of the events in the judicial history of his reign—which has scarcely begun to be written—are manifestations of the tenacious activity of his counsellors sitting in the Parlement, and of the enterprising spirit shewn by his bailiffs and seneschals. But it seems possible to trace the king's share, which was no small one. In the first place, he liked to try cases himself, according to his conscience. In several great criminal cases he imposed his will. He also liked to set the over-litigious on the "right and straight" path. Joinville depicts him at the foot of an oak at Vincennes, or else seated in his garden in Paris, superintending the exercise of justice by his counsellors, and altering the sentence when it did not please him. Moreover he took care that justice should be equal for all. Neither the most noble families, nor the members of his household, could expect any favour from him. Charles of Anjou, who was selfish and vainglorious, was slow to understand that the king's brother must pay his debts and consider other people. Louis IX did not spare him.

The old barbarous customs of vengeance, of private war, of judicial duels, horrified Louis. The judicial duel was used either as a method of proof against a witness accused of falsehood, or a means of recourse against a judge appealed against for false judgment. Influenced obviously by Canon Law, which did not admit the duel, Louis IX forbade its use before the royal judges. This was one cause for the enormous multiplication of appeals brought before the Parlement of Paris. The king went still farther, when he attacked the old right of vengeance which was practised by the bourgeois and the peasants as well as the nobles, but which had specially terrible results when it caused war between two great feudal families. The remedies which had been found, a truce or surety between families at feud, a "paix à partie," *i.e.* "peace between the parties," terminating the blood-feud and accompanied by a penance for the guilty, all this did not content St Louis. He established, or at least revived, the Quarantaine-le-Roi, a truce of 40 days imposed on those of the relatives who had not taken part in the original affray.

He revised those "paix à partie" which did not seem to him to impose severe enough penances on the murderers. Finally, about January 1258, he decided to forbid "all private wars, all incendiarism, all disturbance caused to husbandry" throughout his kingdom, and the carrying of arms was strictly prohibited. Family feuds did not absolutely cease, but they were effectively checked by the interdict against carrying arms; in the Midi, even outside the royal domain, cognisance of any infraction of this law was one of the cases reserved for trial at the royal courts.

It was not enough to impose on others order and justice, and a respect for persons and property. St Louis realised that for the last fifty years the monarchy had been committing crimes of violence and injustice, alike in the old domain and the new. When he was on the point of departure for the Egyptian Crusade, he felt scruples over leaving unanswered the complaints he had received, and he determined to entrust a mission of reparation to certain trustworthy men. Hence the system of circuits of *enquêteurs*, which began in 1247, and which, after the king returned from Palestine, took place every year. Before and after the days of St Louis, it sometimes happened that the Kings of France sent counsellors to make distant circuits; but this was intended, in the narrowest sense of the word, to serve the king's interests, to compel obedience from his officials, to make peculators disgorge their ill-gotten gains, or to restore the tranquillity which had been disturbed. St Louis, in his letters of January 1247, declared that the mission of the *enquêteurs* was to "receive in writing and to examine the grievances which may be brought against us and our ancestors, as also allegations of the injustices and exactions of which our bailiffs, provosts, foresters, sergeants, and their subordinates may have been guilty." Thus the king wished to repair the sins which had been committed; the inquests had a moral and religious character. Moreover, the *enquêteurs* were almost always Franciscan friars, especially at first. Gradually there were introduced among them some counsellors from the Court, who presided over the commissions, because it was recognised that the religious lacked experience and frequently allowed themselves to be deceived. But until the end of the reign, the people regarded the circuits of *enquêteurs* as intended "to give justice to everyone, the poor as well as the rich." After the death of St Louis, the character of these missions completely changed.

Only a small part of the depositions collected has survived. Nevertheless it fills a folio volume of the *Recueil des Historiens de France.* Sometimes we find complaints classed according to a geographical plan, and relating to all kinds of subjects, often futile and trivial. Sometimes we find a wide inquest concerning the administration of some bailiff or provost, and occasionally the emptiness of the accusations proves that the official was an honest man. But very many abuses, violent actions, and arbitrary proceedings, are freely denounced. This enormous mass of documents was not collected in vain; the *enquêteurs* possessed most extensive powers to right wrongs. Moreover the statements received gave rise to *ordonnances*, such as that of 1254 on the administration of bailiffs and seneschals.

By means of the Inquests of St Louis, his letters and *ordonnances*, and other documents, we can form some idea of his attitude towards the clergy, the nobles, the privileged towns, and the common people.

The traditional defensive attitude of the Capetian monarchy and lay society towards the Church was not interrupted by St Louis. Astonishment has been expressed because so pious a king, albeit shewing the greatest theoretical respect towards any wearer of the tonsure, and exercising the greatest care in the disposal of any benefices to which he held the nomination, should yet have proved so energetic a "layman." He did not question either the spiritual supremacy of the Church, nor the old alliance which bound it to the monarchy. He only aimed at repressing the abuses which threatened the temporal power, and, in this sphere as elsewhere, he wished to preserve every one's rights. His mother Blanche of Castile had set him an example. She had had violent conflicts with the Bishop of Beauvais, with the Archbishop of Rouen, and with the masters and students of the University of Paris, whose courses were interrupted for two years (1229–31).

Joinville records interviews between the king and certain bishops about temporal matters. St Louis spoke to them very sharply, and did not hesitate to accuse them of covetousness and disloyalty. In like manner, the Inquests prove that his officials insisted that the clergy should shew them respect; thus a *viguier* once condemned some monks to be fined because they had not left their refectory and come in a body to receive him. St Louis repressed his officials when they exceeded their powers, but did not permit their legitimate authority and their independence to be questioned. If they refused to seize the goods of excommunicated persons, the king upheld them; he considered that in such cases the Church should not call for his support. As regards jurisdiction, he preserved the same attitude as his grandfather Philip Augustus. As certain prelates offered a stubborn resistance to the jurisdiction of the royal and seignorial judges, an assembly was held at St Denis in 1235, and the king joined the barons in sending a protest to Pope Gregory IX against the proceedings of the clergy.

In other circumstances he made common cause with his clergy against the Holy See, or even, towards the end of his reign, with the Holy See against his clergy. Relations between Church and State in France as well as in England, during the last three centuries of the Middle Ages, were affected by the greed and favouritism of the Popes, who claimed to dispose of the benefices and property of the churches, while the governments did not wish foreigners to monopolise appointments to bishoprics and abbeys, nor gold to be taken out of the kingdom. The first great *ordonnance* prohibiting irregular appointments to benefices, and the levying of taxes for the benefit of the Roman *Curia*, was for long attributed to

St Louis; this pretended "Pragmatic Sanction" is a forgery, which was fabricated by the counsellors of Charles VII in 1438. But in his youth St Louis would not have been disinclined to favour such an edict. In 1247 the demands for money made by the Popes, who claimed the right of taxing the clergy in France to maintain the struggle with the Emperor Frederick, provoked a manifestation with which St Louis associated himself. Ambassadors from the king and clergy were sent to Rome to make solemn complaint that benefices were being bestowed on foreigners, and that the French Church was being robbed by the Roman *Curia.* But after his crusade in Egypt and Palestine, St Louis changed his tone, and was inclined to side with the Holy See against the clergy. He became bent only on the deliverance of the Holy Land, and the conquest of Sicily, so ardently desired by the Popes, seemed to him the first stage of this deliverance. Willingly or unwillingly, the clergy of France had to pay and to borrow in support of these great schemes.

Thus the relations of St Louis with the clergy were, as was natural, determined by the traditional policy of the monarchy and by circumstances. As regards the nobles, it is equally impossible to describe his attitude in a single phrase. As further documents are published, and the provincial history better known, the impression is rendered more complex.

Personally Louis IX was conservative. If we consider his decisions, or study carefully the *Life* of Joinville, who composed his memoirs, or at least put the finishing touches to them, in the days of Philip the Fair and noted the changes that had taken place, we feel that Louis had a great idea of the sacred rights of the monarchy, but that he still adhered to the feudal point of view. He did not use the victories achieved by himself and his mother to destroy the turbulent dynasties of Brittany or Poitou, and the motive force in his negotiations with the King of England was, as will be seen, to resume correct feudal relations with him. When he suppressed the judicial duel, it was only in the royal domain. It is a mistake to talk of the extension in his reign of "royal cases," *i.e.* cases in which the royal justice, as such, reserved for itself the trial[1]. When we examine the facts, it will be found that these so-called royal cases, in the time of St Louis, can almost all be explained by feudal law. The multiplication of the "bourgeois du roi," who escaped the law-courts of their feudal lords, does not seem to have been systematically intended by Louis IX, nor by the Parlement of Paris. The king carried his respect for the independence of his barons so far that, in 1246, he allowed those in the north and west, under the influence of the anti-clerical agitation of Frederick II, to organise a league to oppose the temporal claims and the excessive enrichment of the clergy and the Pope[2]; it had a directing

[1] Compare the analogous "Pleas of the Crown" in England.

[2] The party in favour of the Crusade was also indignant at seeing the conflict with the Hohenstaufen absorbing the efforts of the Papacy. The four commissaries elected by the league were Hugh IV, Duke of Burgundy, who went to Palestine from 1239 to

committee, subscriptions, and statutes. For twelve years we find the Holy See fulminating vainly against the *statutarii*; the king was not disturbed, and remained neutral, both because he shared some of the opinions held by the leaguers, and because he did not feel for his nobles the meddlesome mistrust of a Philip Augustus or a Louis XI.

Nevertheless the nobles—even in the ancient domain, and even after the troubles which we have described had been allayed—complained and grumbled, and Louis' reign was not regarded as a Golden Age until later, in retrospect, when the violent methods of his successors were being experienced. This was because Louis IX considered that, as supreme suzerain and as king, he had a right to repress injustices and brutalities with severity. He frequently punished barons who had executed accused men without a trial or by a wrongful judgment. He attempted to stop tournaments, which were the favourite pastime of the nobles. His prohibitions of carrying arms, and of vengeance, although in practice they had to be modified, caused great irritation. But above all the nobles were exasperated by the slow, steady, and irresistible progress of the monarchical administration, which was assisted in its work by the king's brothers in their appanages. Appeals to the *Curia Regis* became multiplied; the encroachments of the bailiffs and seneschals of the king and his brothers on seignorial jurisdictions, even when disavowed, created precedents which were not forgotten.

A similar picture is supplied by the documents concerning municipal history. In theory the alliance between the monarchy and the towns continued. "Preserve," writes Louis IX in his *Enseignements* to his son, "the good towns and communes of thy kingdom in the state and in the franchises in which thy predecessors preserved them; and if there is aught to amend, amend and redress it. And keep them in thy favour and thy love, for if thou art strong in the friendship and wealth of the great towns, thy subjects and foreigners will fear to act ill towards thee, especially thy peers and thy barons." The fidelity of the great towns of the ancient domain had indeed been precious during the troubles of the regency, and Louis IX granted many confirmations of their liberties. It is none the less true that it was during his reign that the decay of urban liberties began in France. This tendency to decline was inevitable. Owing to economic progress, there had arisen capitalist oligarchies which had seized municipal power, which governed to their own advantage, kept wages low, and crushed the poorer people with heavy taxes. The "mediocres" formed leagues, and insurrections took place. The towns, unquiet and ill-administered, were unable to pay the heavy sums which the monarchy demanded from them. Ballads made by the petty bourgeois of Arras about the great defrauders and their false declarations of properties and

1241, and from 1248 to 1250; Peter Mauclerc, who accompanied Louis IX to Egypt; Hugh of Lusignan and Hugh of Châtillon, Count of Saint-Pol, both of whom were crusaders.

incomes have been found[1]. Then the king took serious measures. In 1262 there appeared two *ordonnances* which were designed to put the king's officials in a position to know exactly the state of the towns' finances, and to organise monarchical control; every year the municipalities were to be re-elected on the same day—29 October—and the accounts for the last year were to be brought to Paris by the outgoing *échevins* and their successors on 17 November. These *ordonnances* were carried out only in "France" and in Normandy, and only for some 20 years. But thus there began an administrative superintendence which never again slackened. Moreover, it did not lead the monarchy to moderate its fiscal demands. The towns, faced with constantly increasing exactions, were deeply in debt by the end of the reign.

Outside the "great towns," the common people in the *bourgs* and country districts of the royal domain suffered, as is proved by the Inquests, from plundering by subordinate officers, and from fines inflicted rightly or wrongly by the provosts. They were rigorously held in hand, and brawls were severely punished. But they were also protected, wherever the monarchy possessed any effective power.

As a whole the French peasants owed to St Louis and his mother a period of tranquillity such as they had not enjoyed since time immemorial. Therefore when they learned of Louis IX's misfortunes in the Holy Land, they were more deeply affected than the nobles and the clergy; in 1251, throughout the north-east of the kingdom, the shepherds and peasants, the "pastoureaux," rose to join the king at the bidding of a visionary. This "Crusade of the Pastoureaux" ended badly; they took to pillaging churches and the houses of bourgeois. After much hesitation, Blanche of Castile decided to order its repression. She had thought that these unfortunate men would really go to deliver her son. This was not the only proof she gave of her sympathy with the poor. In the following year (1252) she went herself to deliver the peasants whom the Chapter of Notre Dame at Paris had caused to be arrested wholesale for refusing to pay the *taille*, and whom they had cruelly thrust into stifling prisons.

In order really to understand and grasp, in a definite and limited field, the attitude of the monarchy towards the various classes in the nation, it is well to examine the king's policy in the seneschalships of Beaucaire and Carcassonne, and that of his brother Alphonse of Poitiers in the county of Toulouse during the last years of the reign.

During the quarter of a century which preceded his death, Louis IX, without relinquishing the repression of heresy, healed the wounds of his southern provinces. He undertook the administration himself, with the help of his mother, his brother Alphonse, the Parlement of Paris, and the *enquêteurs*. The royal seneschals and *viguiers* of Languedoc no longer enjoyed the dangerous independence which they had been granted during the early years of his reign. After 1254, the seneschals only

[1] H. Guy, *Adan de le Hale*, 1898, pp. 87 sq.

remained in office for one or two years, four at the most. They were supervised by the *enquêteurs*, and occasionally the Parlement of Paris reversed their decisions as improper. The *iudex senescalli*, who helped them to try cases, gradually absorbed their judicial functions; he became the *iudex maior* (*juge mage*, senior judge); he alone was allowed to condemn any one to imprisonment in grave cases. The old custom of summoning the great landowners to give their opinion on the advisability of exporting wheat was restored, and these small assemblies in the seneschalships[1] had sometimes to discuss other questions. And finally, by the famous *ordonnances* of 1254 and 1259, these seneschals, so carefully counselled and supervised, received instructions breathing the very spirit of St Louis; the king was bent on forcing them to execute righteous judgment, on preventing them from extorting money by fraudulent means, or making the taxes heavier; in certain specified cases, the confiscations imposed under pretext of heresy were to be cancelled; the king's officers were to repress vice, and to set a good example. At least in their administrative clauses, these *ordonnances* were useful, as the *enquêteurs* could ensure their being carried out.

In the county of Toulouse, Alphonse of Poitiers pursued a similar course. It is obvious that St Louis exercised very great influence on his brother, as on the rest of the family. It is noteworthy that Alphonse of Poitiers did not settle at Toulouse after the death of his father-in-law, Raymond VII; he lived near his brother in Paris or thereabouts, and accompanied him on his two Crusades. He was a lover of red-tape, careful, avaricious, and fond of prolonging business. But the *ordonnances* on administrative reform published by the two brothers prove satisfactorily by their date and their contents how well they agreed. The general results of their administration were alike.

Throughout Languedoc, the history of the lay and the ecclesiastical aristocracy at this period is only a story of decadence. The old families were ruined; the new-comers from the North, except the Lévis family, were of no account. Louis IX and Alphonse of Poitiers moderated the excessive zeal of the seneschals and *bailes*, and curbed, not without difficulty, their tendency to usurp lands, rights, and jurisdictions, even within the territory of bishops and abbots. They put a stop to the more scandalous conflicts arising therefrom. Both of them insisted on the strict observance of the *ordonnances* against carrying arms, and to the best of their ability they repressed the deep-rooted habits of private war. The towns and country districts of the Midi began to expand and to prosper during these happy days at the end of the reign. Louis IX, even though he repressed the abuse of power by urban oligarchies, shewed favour to the bourgeoisie,

[1] That of 1259 at Beaucaire included three bishops, three abbots, three nobles, and the consuls of seven towns. These meetings of "prudhommes" to express their opinion on the exportation of food-stuffs had been recommended to all the bailiffs and seneschals by the *Ordonnance* of 1254.

restoring some of the old liberties, for instance reinstating the consulate at Nîmes. When he created the town of Aigues-Mortes, so as to have a port of his own on the Mediterranean, he conferred on it great privileges, which attracted a crowd of immigrants (1246). Carcassonne, which had been completely deserted for seven years after Trencavel's revolt, was repopulated. Alphonse of Poitiers, who was more meddlesome than his brother, and was in constant conflict with the town of Toulouse, was nevertheless a great builder of *villes neuves*. In a word, the two brothers pacified the Midi. The brilliant seignorial life of the twelfth century had disappeared, but the bourgeois and the peasants regained security under the Capetian government.

With those differences and distinctions which provincial and local history record, but which cannot here be mentioned, France, during the peaceful period which ended St Louis' reign, presented a spectacle of order, steady work, and development. The land was well cultivated, and the wastes and the forests were being put under cultivation. The economic and social condition of the peasants was improving; the day of wholesale enfranchisements was dawning. The towns were developing in spite of the precarious condition of the municipal finances. Merchants and students travelled in security. Great artists, such as Peter of Montreuil, had brought Gothic architecture to a pitch of perfection which was never surpassed. The most celebrated poem, perhaps, of the Middle Ages, the *Roman de la Rose*, dates from this period. French prose was being created; we have a model in Primat's *Grandes Chroniques de France*, which were commissioned by the king. The racy language of French writers seemed to the neighbouring peoples the most delightful of all. The monarchy greatly contributed to the prosperity of the nation by its wisdom, and its prestige gained thereby. France and her monarchy became great at the same time.

We have pointed out some shadows in this brilliant picture. The king sincerely desired to recognise, to reveal, to efface these. But his bailiffs and seneschals were often too strong for him. The Inquests and the *ordonnances* could not succeed in restoring the France of fifty years back, and the ground gained by the king's servants was seldom lost. Owing to the very fact that Louis IX was a saint, their proceedings were even more dangerous to the institutions and customs of the past, for the king, the upright man, retained the love of his subjects; against his own will, and without losing his halo, he profited by the abuses of power committed by his servants. In this reign, monarchical progress was the complex result of the sanctity of a revered ruler, and the patient and obstinately aggressive policy of the king's servants.

In foreign policy, Louis IX was more his own master. He did not go to war with Christians unless he was attacked, and, when his safety was assured, he imposed on his counsellors a pacific and conciliatory policy toward the Western States. "Avoid," he wrote in his *Enseignements* to his heir, "making war on Christians. If thou art wronged, try sundry means of seeing whether thou canst retrieve thy rights before having recourse to arms." On the other hand, he organised two offensive expeditions with the object of reconquering the Holy Land and converting the Infidels, or exterminating them if they resisted. The Crusade was his chief aim in foreign policy.

He lamented the conflict between the Holy See and the Empire, which was a great obstacle to the deliverance of Jerusalem, but he did nothing to weigh down the balance. To understand his attitude, he must not be considered from the standpoint of a Catholic of to-day. In his eyes the imperial power and the papal power were equally legitimate and ought to remain intact. On the other hand, the independence and neutrality of the kingdom of France had to be maintained. He did not wish his brother Robert of Artois to accept the imperial crown, offered him by Gregory IX (1240); but he obliged Frederick II to release the French prelates who had been captured at sea on their way to the council at Rome (1241). When Innocent IV was in peril in Rome and crossed the Alps, Louis IX did not offer him refuge in France, and the Pope stopped at the frontier at Lyons, which was still an imperial city. The representatives of Louis in the Council of Lyons begged the Pope to be conciliatory; for was not Frederick II offering to submit to the arbitration of the Kings of France and England? Innocent IV rejected all compromise, and declared his enemy to have forfeited his kingdoms (1245). Louis IX remained neutral. He might have seized the opportunity of extending the frontiers of his kingdom beyond the Rhone. He did not seek to fish in troubled waters. The only advantage he sought from the Pope's critical position was to obtain his favour for the marriage of Charles of Anjou to the heiress of Provence (1246). But he continued to treat Frederick II amicably. He even allowed him to issue a proclamation to the French barons, and to correspond with those who in 1246 founded, as we have seen, a league against the encroachments of the Church. Only when Frederick II invited the leaguers to join him in marching on Lyons and seizing the Pope, St Louis informed Innocent IV that he would protect him. Frederick abandoned his plan (1247).

Without waiting for the close of this tragic conflict, which was by no means ended by the death of Frederick II (1250), Louis left for the East. He had ceased to count on the reconciliation of the two adversaries, or on their co-operation. In 1246 the Pope himself had given secret orders that the preaching of the expedition to the Holy Land was to be stopped in Germany; he was bent only on securing partisans against Frederick. Now it was in the month of December 1244 that Louis had taken the Cross, for reasons which have been given elsewhere[1]. At the time when the capture of Jerusalem by the Khwārazmian Turks, and the victory of

[1] See *supra*, Vol. v, Chap. viii, p. 315.

the Emir Baibars Bunduqdārī at Gaza became known in France, Louis was in the clutches of malarial fever, and his death was expected; as soon as he was strong enough to speak, he took the Cross. The expedition, which was to be so imprudently conducted, was prepared with the greatest care, and at enormous cost. Heavy subsidies were demanded from the clergy and the towns. The town and port of Aigues-Mortes were constructed to ensure the safe departure of the fleet. The island of Cyprus was chosen as the base for supplies, and St Louis stayed there for eight months to concentrate his army. Unfortunately, these great preparations were not supplemented by reliable information concerning the country about to be invaded. Louis IX had decided, not without good reason, to attack in his own country Ayyūb, the Sultan of Egypt, who, as we have seen, could be considered the author of the defeats sustained by the Christians in 1244. There was, however, no exact information about Egypt or the Nile. The disasters of the Crusade in 1218–21 had taught the crusaders no lessons, and they were to be repeated.

Sailing from Cyprus on 15 May 1249, Louis IX arrived at the Damietta mouth of the Nile on 5 June, only a few days before the annual rise of the river began. Damietta was easily taken, but it was six months before the flood abated. Meanwhile resources failed and discipline waned in the army. When the crusaders started to march on Cairo, and found themselves opposed by the army of the new Sultan, Tūrān-Shāh, Ayyūb's son, the signal for disobedience was given by the king's own brother, Robert of Artois. His rashness, for which he paid with his life, caused the defeat of Manṣūrah (19 December). A halt had to be called. The lack of fresh and sound food caused epidemics of scurvy and dysentery which decimated the army, still mercilessly harried by the Saracens. Joinville's graphic account should be read. From his pages it is easy to picture the atrocious sufferings undergone by the crusaders, and the exploits they accomplished. Moreover many of them were earnestly aspiring to gain the martyr's crown. When Guy of Château-Porcien, Bishop of Soissons, learned that a return to Damietta was inevitable, Joinville tells us that "he, having a great desire to go to God, did not wish to return to the land where he was born; he spurred his steed, and attacked the Turks single-handed, who killed him and placed him in the company of God, in the army of martyrs." During this retreat, which ended in the capture of the army, Louis IX also nearly "went to God"; he was suffering from dysentery and almost at the point of death when he was captured (5 April 1250); an Arab physician tended him and cured him. He displayed his usual energy in negotiating his release. Brutally threatened with torture by the counsellors of Tūrān-Shāh, then, when the latter was killed in a revolt of the Mamlūks, threatened with death by the emirs and obliged to be present at the torture of the Patriarch of Jerusalem, he would not cede to the Sultan any of the Syrian strongholds, and refused to take the oath demanded by the Emirs, which seemed to him impious. He finally obtained his own release by restoring Damietta, and freed the remnants of his army by the payment of ransoms[1]. He went on to Syria (May 1250) to fortify the strongholds which were still in Christian hands, and remained four years, in spite of the appeals of his mother and the advice of many of his faithful counsellors. Negotiations with the Tartars which had been begun at Cyprus were now resumed; he cherished the idle dream of converting them to Christianity; he despatched the Franciscan William of Rubruquis to the Great Khan, and, as before, received only an insolent invitation to make his submission.

The tidings of his mother's death (27 November 1252) ought to have decided him to return to France, but he did not set sail until 24 April 1254. Now civil war was raging in Flanders, and Henry III had again demanded from Blanche of Castile the fiefs forfeited by John Lackland. Opinions were much divided both in France and in England on the subject of the conquests of Philip Augustus and Louis VIII. In England, the party of the barons and the national Church wished to see the State relieved of the continental question, and considered that the people should not be expected to make fresh sacrifices for a matter of private interest; but his Poitevin and Gascon counsellors urged Henry III to reclaim the lost fiefs. In France, the counsellors of the monarchy were bent on resisting this claim with energy. Louis IX was inclined to follow an intermediate course. He did not question the lawfulness of the sentence of 1202, but he admired the piety of Henry III, and was moved by family feelings. Finally the position seemed to him ambiguous and dangerous; Henry III had retained in France only the duchy of Guyenne, but all ties of vassalship had been severed between the two kings, and Henry had recently concluded a treaty of alliance with the King of Castile (22 April 1254). As soon as he returned from Palestine, Louis IX entered on peace negotiations with Henry III. They dragged out their weary length. Finally, urged by his barons, who were assuming an increasingly disquieting attitude, Henry III yielded. Peace was concluded on 28 May 1258, and ratified at Paris in December 1259.

By the Treaty of Paris Henry III once more became the liegeman of the King of France, and renounced his claim to Normandy, Anjou, Touraine, Maine, and Poitou; but Louis IX restored to him all that he held in fiefs or in demesne in the dioceses of Limoges, Cahors, and Périgueux, as well as the succession to all that Alphonse of Poitiers held in Agenais and Saintonge, to the south of the Charente, should Alphonse die childless. As Henry III could not obtain money from his Parliament for his Sicilian scheme, he also demanded the sum necessary for the support of five hundred knights for two years.

Louis IX was convinced that he had served the interests of the Crown well. "He was not my man, and he enters into homage to me," he said

[1] A sum of 167,103 *livres* of Tours was paid. The other half of the ransom was never paid, as the Saracens violated the treaty by massacring the sick captives.

in answer to all objections. A few counsellors regretted this peace, but we have no solid grounds for supposing that this was the general opinion in France. In like manner, the troubadour Sordello accused the king of cowardice and folly, because he did not use his rights as son of Queen Blanche to seize Castile. Louis IX paid no attention to idle bluster, and preferred to live on good terms with his cousin Alfonso X and consolidate this friendship by means of marriages. On the other hand, in Languedoc, he wished to settle every one's rights by concluding the treaty of Corbeil with the King of Aragon (11 May 1258). The Kings of Aragon had for long claimed suzerainty over Languedoc and the county of Toulouse. King James I renounced this claim, but still retained the troublesome seigniory of Montpellier. On his side Louis IX abandoned all rights over Catalonia and Roussillon. The heir to the throne, Philip, married Isabella of Aragon.

During the years which followed his return from Syria, Louis IX devoted himself to the task of making peace between Christians. His most important achievement was in Flanders. Already in 1246 he had tried to act as arbitrator in order to settle the quarrel between the two sons whom Margaret, Countess of Flanders, had had by her marriage with Bouchard of Avesnes, and the children of her second marriage with William of Dampierre; during the Crusade war had broken out, and Margaret, rather than yield Hainault to her son John of Avesnes, whom she hated, had offered this county and the guardianship of Flanders to Charles of Anjou. The King of the Romans, William of Holland, supported John of Avesnes, and the ambition of Charles of Anjou threatened to kindle a serious conflict. On his return, Louis insisted on acting as arbitrator (*Dit* [award] of Peronne, 24 September 1256). John d'Avesnes renounced some fiefs and became the vassal of Charles of Anjou for Hainault.

Such was the influence of the King of France that, from the north to the south, foreigners took him as judge of their differences; the King of Navarre and his sister, the Count of Burgundy and the Count of Chalon, the Duke of Bar and his neighbours, the Count of Luxemburg and the Duke of Lorraine, Guigues, Dauphin of Viennois, and his neighbours, the Count of Savoy and Charles of Anjou, the inhabitants of Lyons and the canons of the cathedral church, all had recourse to him. The English barons and Henry III entrusted to him the task of pronouncing on the validity of the Provisions of Oxford; the "Mise of Amiens" (24 January 1264) bears the very characteristic marks of his political ideas. He would not admit that a king should be prevented from choosing his own counsellors and officials. He annulled the Provisions, while ordering that old charters and customs were to be respected and all quarrels to be forgotten. The issues at stake were too serious; his decision was nugatory.

Louis IX, whose health was becoming more and more precarious, was ill again that year. And yet he had not relinquished his Eastern plans, and meant to execute them at last, although late. The convention referring to the Sicilian expedition of Charles of Anjou was certainly in his eyes only a stage on the way to a new Crusade. We have already[1] seen on what conditions Charles of Anjou became the champion of the Papacy against the Hohenstaufen. Here it will be enough to shew what was St Louis' attitude.

The death of Frederick II had not modified his desire for preserving the balance of power and his respect for established rights; on his return from the Holy Land, he at first remained neutral, considering Conradin as the legitimate heir. But the aversion which he felt for Manfred, who did not hesitate to negotiate with the Muslims, and the emotion caused by the tragic events which disturbed the East in 1260–61, altered his views. In 1261 a Frenchman of energetic and obstinate character, Urban IV, became Pope; after his accession he appointed to the cardinalate Guy Foulquoi and two other counsellors of St Louis; he gradually induced the king to regard the question of Sicily as linked with the pacification of Christendom and the deliverance of the Holy Land. He offered the crown of Sicily to the Count of Provence, Charles of Anjou, who ever since 1258 had not ceased to intervene in the quarrels of the Piedmontese seigneuries, and who had inordinate ambitions. Louis IX, greatly respected by his family, could easily have put an end to it all by his veto. Charles of Anjou evidently succeeded in persuading him that fertile Sicily would be a good base of supplies, which would facilitate the crusade. Louis IX therefore undertook the negotiations, obtained from the Pope better conditions for his brother, and the convention of 15 August 1264 was in part his work. He allowed his subjects to enter Charles' service in large numbers, and the Holy See to levy crushing taxes on the Church of France.

Having become master of Sicily, which is some 90 miles from Tunisia, Charles of Anjou was evidently among those who persuaded his brother that the first objective of the Crusade should be Tunis. Louis IX ceased to exercise a clear judgment where the Crusade and the Muslims were involved. He really believed that the Ḥafṣid emir Mustanṣir, who frequently entered into negotiations with the Christian rulers, was disposed for conversion. North Africa would again become a great centre of Christianity. Should this plan fail, Tunis, an easy prey to seize, would at least furnish vast resources for a fresh expedition on Egypt. Consequently the very burdensome preparations which he had been making since 1267 for the deliverance of the Holy Land were at the last moment diverted to Barbary. On 1 July 1270, at the very height of the dog-days, Louis embarked. His weakness was steadily increasing. When Joinville, who refused to accompany him on this mad expedition, bade him farewell, the king was unable to sit on a horse, and Joinville had to

[1] See *supra*, Chap. VI.

carry him in his arms for a short distance. He was in quest of martyrdom and he obtained it. A malignant fever and dysentery decimated his army as soon as it landed, and he was one of the victims. He died on 25 August. A few hours before his death, he was heard to murmur: "O Jerusalem, Jerusalem."

Louis IX was lamented and praised throughout Christendom, and almost immediately there were tales of miracles wrought by his relics. He was canonised a few years later (1297). From a thousand proofs of the pure glory which surrounded his name in the Middle Ages, we will quote the following versicles and responses from an "Office of St Louis" composed in the fourteenth century:

"Happy the kingdom governed by a king foreseeing, pious, refined in his character, courageous in adversity. He used his riches to succour the poor, he despised the soft things of life. He loved labour and defended the churches. He established the throne on justice. He caused France to enjoy peace. The Church owes to him her prosperity, and the whole of France the honour wherewith she is surrounded."[1]

[1] Published by L. Delisle, BEC, 1905, pp. 521 sqq.

CHAPTER XI

THE SCANDINAVIAN KINGDOMS UNTIL THE END OF THE THIRTEENTH CENTURY

The peoples and countries of the Scandinavian North were late in stepping forward into the light of history. As pirates they began to be known by the natives of Western Europe from the end of the eighth century, and, shortly after, foreign chronicles give small glimpses of their circumstances at home. But their own historical monuments do not date farther back than the beginning of the tenth century, when court poets began to celebrate the heroic exploits and the proud lineage of their kings. Their traditional and customary laws were not put into writing earlier than the end of the eleventh century. Historical research and the collecting of traditions from the past began only in the course of the twelfth century, and flourished in the thirteenth. The result is that our knowledge of the first centuries of Scandinavian evolution is often very uncertain and full of gaps. We are able to compile complete lists of the rulers of all three kingdoms from the tenth century onwards; but the chronology of the first kings is rather doubtful, and their real history is interwoven with legend. The fundamental structure of society in many respects is only a matter of hypothesis, and we cannot clearly discern the development of political institutions.

Nevertheless, there is something enthralling in the study of those olden times, not only because the birth of nations is always an interesting phenomenon, but still more because of the poetry that so deeply colours the life and the events of that youthful society. Here we come into contact with a powerful race of state-builders, nations endowed with a strong social instinct and at the same time exhibiting a force of individualism that makes us see the single man in his full personality. When asked for their chief, the Vikings of Rollo proudly answered: "We have no chief, we are all equals." In the same way the sagas of the North give the impression of a society made up of chiefs, of strong and independent individuals, and these men are not only warriors and wild barbarians, they are also jurists, refined poets, and artists. They are capable of adapting themselves to Western civilisation without surrendering their national character and institutions.

At the beginning of historic times, in the course of the tenth century, we see the Scandinavian peoples constituting themselves as three separate kingdoms, and in that way defining themselves for ever as three independent nationalities. Of course, the making of those kingdoms and the formation of the corresponding nations was a work of long evolution; but we are not able to follow in detail the history of their founding.

In general, we may discern the geographical conditions that made for the separation into the three nations. The provinces of Denmark in particular were knit together by the strong tie of sea-ways; but the big land-blocks of Norway and Sweden, divided by pathless mountains and forests, might have grown up into two or three more kingdoms, were it not for the appearance of new forces of development.

The Scandinavian kingdoms, such as history knows them, were created by war, although commerce, law, and language contributed mightily to the result. By runic inscriptions we are taught that the Scandinavian language, at least as early as the ninth century, had divided into two separate branches, the Norwegian to the west, the Dano-Swedish to the south and east. Archaeological discoveries, as well as the information given by King Alfred's translation of Orosius, shew that, in the south-eastern part of Norway, in the province of Vestfold, a centre of commerce was in existence from the end of the ninth century, and that from thence trade-routes led by sea around the whole coast of Norway, by land deep into the valleys of the east. Long continuous stretches of dense forest separated Norway from Sweden, whereas Danish and Norwegian traders were sailing yearly between Vestfold and the Danish ports of the Baltic, those of Schleswig on the west and Scania on the east. At the same time, another centre of commerce was arising in Upland in Sweden, also in lively communication with the ports of Denmark. As a result, Vestfold and Upland became the centres of political unity for Norway and Sweden, although, for a while, it seemed uncertain whether they would not rather join with Denmark.

The political basis of the kingdoms as they ultimately took shape is to be discovered in a legal foundation, the binding together of groups of provinces around a common *thing* or court administered under common law. Just before the opening of history, we see the whole of Denmark thus organised; three great law districts, the chief provinces of Norway, were also constituted about three law *things*; and in Sweden most of the provinces already possessed their separate laws. The constituent force that made its way through all the state-forming elements of law, commerce, language, and geography, and led on to greater kingdoms, was war—the struggles of conqueror kings.

The whole period of the Migrations and the Vikings, the centuries between A.D. 500 and 1000, is a period at once of expansion and of warfare. This is the time when folk-chiefs rise against each other, battling for power, and, incessantly, kingdoms are made and unmade. The age itself felt strongly the unity of the two great movements it saw going on, the conquests of the Vikings abroad and the building up of kingdoms at home. A North German scholar of the eleventh century, Adam of Bremen, describes the peoples of those times as living *in tanta regnorum mutatione vel excursione barbarorum.* About the year 900, in particular, the Scandinavians are vigorously engaged in founding new kingdoms, as well by their excursions abroad as by their wars at home. The Norwegians discover Iceland, where, in the course of half a century, they organise an aristocratic republic of considerable wealth and endowed with high qualities of intellectual character; a little earlier they had already established a small commonwealth in the Faroe Islands, an earldom in the Orkney and Shetland Islands, a kingdom in the Hebrides and Man, and other kingdoms in Ireland, particularly one at Dublin. Here they were compelled to fight against the Danes, whereas in England they placed themselves at the service of the Danish chiefs who conquered the Danelaw. In France and the Netherlands, undoubtedly, the Danes were in the majority amongst the Vikings, whilst the chief who became the founder of Normandy, Rollo, was probably a Norwegian. At the same time, the Swedes were founding the Russian kingdom of Novgorod and Kiev[1].

The establishment of the kingdoms in Scandinavia dates from exactly the same period. The struggle for the union of the Danish provinces seems to have lasted for about two centuries, the kingdom of Denmark during this time being repeatedly united and dissolved, until a mighty warrior took it firmly under his control. We are able to give the approximate date of the event, as we still possess the richly decorated runic stone on which Harold Bluetooth (*c.* 950–985) proudly announces that he was the king who won the whole of Denmark.

In Norway, the work of unification did not begin until the end of the ninth century. It was one of the Vestfold kings, Harold Fairhair, heir to a group of provinces in the east of the country, with whom originated the idea of a Norwegian kingdom. He allied himself with the Earl of Throndheim in the north, and conquered the west; we are still able to enjoy the picturesque verses by one of his skalds which tell of the great battle in Hafrsfjord (*c.* 900) where he struck down his last opponents. The kingdom did not remain unshaken; for more than a hundred years it was a prey to rival pretenders of the line of King Harold or of the Earl of Throndheim, or even to foreign conquerors. But the whole country was again united in resolute independence by the saintly King Olaf (1016–1028), and when his son Magnus was elected king in the year 1035, the kingdom of Norway was finally established.

The origin of the Swedish kingdom is shrouded in deeper darkness; for in reality we know nothing about the origins of the country. At the beginning of historic times we see Swedish territory divided between two relatively ancient kingdoms, Sweden (Svealand) proper north of the great lakes, with a king seated in Upland, and Gautland (Gothland) in the south, possibly ruled over by an earl. But about the year 1000 we find the King of Sweden, the mighty Olaf the Tax-king, master of Gautland too, and from that time the whole country is virtually a single kingdom, whether the union was effected by King Olaf himself or by his renowned father Eric (Erik) the Victorious.

[1] See *supra*, Vol. IV, Chap. VII, pp. 204 sqq.

From the beginning of the eleventh century, then, the Scandinavian nations had established themselves as three separate kingdoms, and it is precisely from that time that we notice in court poetry and in folk tradition the first signs of a national self-consciousness in the form of mutual antagonism. There are three nations as well as three kingdoms, and each of them has its own history. In recent as well as in olden times, it has been usual to write their history, often with express intention, on separate lines; and for a detailed account of national development it is not possible to do otherwise. But in tracing the chief lines only of social and political history, it seems profitable, at least for the Middle Ages, to keep all the three nations within a common narrative, so as to bring into view the essential parallels as well as the minor differences of their development.

It is moreover the case that the history of the three nations from their very origin is so closely interwoven that it is impossible to disentangle their several strands. We are told, indeed, that the ancestors of King Harold Fairhair, six generations earlier, arrived in Norway from Sweden; we know that he himself took his queen from Denmark, a fact that is celebrated by his court skald, and that the son of this marriage, King Eric Bloodyaxe, married the sister of King Harold Bluetooth, who, in his turn, adopted the sons of King Eric and made them his vassals. On the other hand, we know that about A.D. 900 Swedish kings for a time made themselves masters of Denmark, or at least of Southern Jutland, and we are told that the grandfather of Harold Bluetooth, the liberator of Denmark, was of Norwegian origin. The son of this Harold, the great viking, King Svein Forkbeard, married the mother of King Olaf the Tax-king of Sweden, whose daughter was afterwards married to St Olaf, King of Norway.

The relations of the three kingdoms were nevertheless not altogether peaceful, for if it was a duty inherent in every king to keep the peace at home, it was no less his duty to go conquering abroad. During the tenth century we constantly find the Norwegian kings harrying Gautland and Denmark, and about the year 1000 the Kings of Denmark and Sweden ally themselves against Norway. King Harold Bluetooth had already reckoned himself master of Norway as well as of Denmark; now, in the year 1000, Norway is for a time really conquered by Denmark. The growing Danish imperialism, impersonated particularly by the great King Canute (Knut), the conqueror of England, makes Sweden and Norway turn to each other for assistance, and success in war keeps swinging from the one side to the other. Norway is liberated, reconquered, and lastly (1035) liberated again; and the time arrives when the King of Norway even makes himself for some years King of Denmark. From about 1050 the three kingdoms of the North are compelled to respect one another's independence, and from that time, too, political considerations displace the mere policy of conquest in the relationship of the kingdoms.

In estimating the absolute and relative strength of the northern kingdoms at the time of their establishment, it should be observed that although the main area of each country is just the same as to-day, the frontiers did not then follow exactly the same lines. Denmark certainly was, then as now, the smallest country in area, but it was much larger in earlier times than it is to-day. Whereas now it has an area of about 40,000 square km., it may be reckoned to have comprised in those times at least 65,000 square km.; Jutland was Danish as far south as the river Eyder, and east of the Sound Denmark included the rich province of Scania with Halland and Blekinge. Sweden, in our times by far the largest of the three countries and before the losses of a hundred years ago yet larger, at its establishment possessed a rather modest area that may be calculated at about 330,000 square km., just a little more than Great Britain and Ireland. It had not yet begun to win the Lapmarks in the north and Finland in the east, and it was essentially a Baltic state, being barred from the North Sea by Denmark and Norway, and having but a single outlet to the west through the Göta Elf. For many centuries the three kingdoms met at this point, and it was a matter of great importance to have the mastery here, the more so as the province north of the river, the old Ranrike, now Bohuslän, was one of the richest provinces of the whole of Scandinavia. As the possessor of this province, Norway for a long time had the upper hand, and, on the whole, from the final attainment of her independence, Norway more than the other two countries had the appearance of a great power. It is not easy to make an exact calculation of her extent at that time, the frontiers to the north being extremely ill-defined. It is possible that, as early as this, some of the northern Swedish provinces were considered as part of the Norwegian kingdom, as they certainly were two centuries later. But then the King of Norway was the master of all the wandering tribes in the far north, those peoples that the Norwegians themselves called by the name of Finns, now generally referred to as Lapps. Thus Norway from its origin was the only Scandinavian country that had as its subjects people of another race, and we know that from the eleventh century the limit of the Norwegian kingdom was set as far as the eastern point of the Kola Peninsula. Taking all this into consideration, the area of Norway at that time may be estimated at considerably more than 400,000 square km. It was also an important feature in the character of the Norwegian kingdom that it, alone of the Scandinavian countries, possessed colonies beyond the sea; for, during the reign of Olaf the Saint, the chiefs of the Faroe Islands and the Earl of the Orkneys and Shetlands had accepted the dominion of Norway.

The one purely Scandinavian country that still lay outside the three kingdoms was the commonwealth of Iceland; but its inhabitants knew perfectly well that they had come from Norwegian stock. In Norway they had the rights of natives; with Norway they had their chief commerce; their literature exercised a strong influence upon Norwegian civilisation; and, lastly, they acknowledged the dominion of the King of Norway. Farther away, the small Norwegian colony of Greenland, struggling for life on a narrow coast-line between ice and sea, was of little importance to Scandinavian society as a whole.

What has been said here about the areas of the three kingdoms does not give a true impression of their intrinsic strength. Indeed, the great forests, mountains, and heaths of Norway and Sweden very materially diminished their inhabitable territory. There are many indications that, from the Viking age and during the centuries that followed it, much new land was cleared and cultivated in Norwegian and Swedish woods. But there is no doubt that little Denmark, with its fertile plains, especially in the eastern provinces, outnumbered in population the other two kingdoms. It is not possible to give approximate figures for the eleventh century, except by a guess from very uncertain material, but even a conjectural estimate may serve to indicate the real strength of the Scandinavian kingdoms at that time. Norway, the largest in area, may have possessed about 200,000 inhabitants, exclusive of some 25,000 upon the western islands, whilst about 50,000 Norwegians lived in Iceland. In Sweden, the population may be reckoned at about 300,000, in Denmark certainly at more than 500,000. From these figures Denmark easily appears as the greatest power in the north, all the more as its population was concentrated in a relatively small area, and while Norway and Iceland produced the highest work in literature at that period, Denmark undoubtedly stood foremost in political evolution.

The Migrations and the age of the Vikings had meant for the Scandinavian peoples a period of great activity in intellect and thought. At first from the south, later from the west, new ferments of religion and art had spread to the north and given a new physiognomy to the Scandinavian civilisation, certainly to that of the upper classes. Their artistic imagination was stimulated by the animal ornamentation which their natural joy of embellishment took hold of and transformed into a true national art; entangled limbs and wings and heads of imaginary beasts began to appear upon the hitherto plain sides of weapons or tools, and on trinkets. Undoubtedly there was something of magic in this decorative art; for instance, when the Scandinavians adorned the stems of their ships with a dragon's head, they certainly did it in order to frighten away the protecting spirits of their enemies; and therefore it was forbidden to sail along the shore of one's own country with the prow-head exposed, so as not to frighten the home spirits. Other elements, too, of foreign civilisation here entered into the great realm of religion. So, when their letters were modelled on the Greek and Latin alphabets, for many centuries these runes were only used as instruments of magic, and the writing of them was an occult art. On the other hand, during those ages, religion itself rose from mere magic and nature-cult up to higher levels of belief in more human gods; the myths began to break off from mere cult and transformed themselves into pure poetry. The result of this process we only know from the series of Norwegian songs, chiefly composed in the tenth century, which have come down to us under the name of the *Edda.* In contrast to the old Anglo-Saxon and German epics, these are brief lays, composed in short strophes, of an impressionistic, vividly dramatic art which makes them more congenial to modern taste; there is in these verses at once concentrated energy and exquisite refinement. Along with the mythic songs about the gods, the *Edda* contains another series of lays about heroes and heroic deeds, and as the themes of these hero-songs are mostly taken from the German traditions of the Nibelungs, the influence from abroad is plainly manifest; but in this case, too, the form is throughout independent, truly national, in full accordance with the energetic strophes that we know from the contemporary poems about the kings and their battles.

The *Edda* songs in the Norse language are the highest product of the heathen civilisation of Scandinavia, and even they are engendered by the collaboration of native and foreign forces. Soon after, foreign civilisation won a still greater victory in Scandinavian spiritual, moral, and even social life, by the introduction of Christianity. German monks had come to preach the Gospel in Denmark and Sweden as early as the beginning of the ninth century; since that time, Vikings and merchants had spread the knowledge of the Christian faith through their countries; the Viking states in England, Ireland, and France had at an early date to accept Christianity. The new national kings established it at home. Harold Bluetooth made Denmark a Christian kingdom in the middle of the tenth century; this was the natural result of the elevation of the country to membership of European society and civilisation, and the royal power sufficed to effect a conversion without arousing serious opposition. In Sweden also the change from heathendom to Christianity was relatively easy. Here, Olaf the Tax-king settled the matter about the year 1000, and perhaps it was not a mere coincidence that the daughter-realm in the east, the Russian kingdom, just at that time was Christianised from Byzantium; the Great Prince Yaroslav married a daughter of King Olaf. In Norway, the struggle of heathendom was short, but dramatic; coming from England, King Olaf Trygveson (995–1000) forced Christianity upon the chiefs and the people by the sword, and he came to live in folk-lore as the great vanquisher of ghosts and trolls.

Dramatically enough, but in quite another way, Christianity triumphed in Iceland. When a Christian party formed itself there and stood in arms against the heathen party in the general *thing* (1000), so that the commonwealth was on the point of breaking up, the heathen lawman declared Christianity to be the common law of all Icelanders, but on condition that the right of secret sacrifices to the heathen gods should be retained. Obviously Christianity was everywhere accepted from merely worldly considerations, and of course the old folk-superstitions, the magic arts and customs, were kept alive. But later on the heathen myths vanished before the light of the Gospel; the religion of the Scandinavian peoples passed to a still higher level, and real Christian ardour began to animate life as well as poetry.

The religion and the poetry of the Eddic lays evidently belong to an upper class and not to the common people. One of the songs gives a poetic paraphrase of the organisation of society, and here we meet with a leisured class which maintains the higher civilisation, while slaves and peasants are compelled to do the hard work. In recent times there have been contending opinions about the social conditions amongst the old Scandinavian peoples, and for want of sources we are reduced to making inferences from rather vague indications. Nor is there any certainty that the conditions were the same everywhere; in many respects we know that they were not. The whole population was rural; it is more than doubtful whether there was, at some two or three market-places, possibly a small settled town-population. The people lived by farming, in the forests of Sweden and Norway supplemented by hunting, on the coasts by fishing. In Denmark and most of Sweden, the farming was carried on by village communities; in Norway and Iceland, each man had his individual farm. In both cases, individual ownership was only in embryo; the virtual owner of the land was the family or the kindred, and the head of the household had no right of alienating any part of the farm. The first encroachment upon this family right came through the Canon Law; but already before the introduction of Christianity there had appeared a tendency towards economic individualism in connexion with the aristocratic development of society.

It seems to be beyond doubt that in the whole of Scandinavia, from the Viking age onwards, the aristocracy made an immense advance; war as well as commerce brought wealth into single hands, and so there grew up a class of estate-owners. From olden times, there existed the great difference between slaves and freemen; but the class of slaves never seems to have been very numerous in the Scandinavian countries, and the freeman always had to work on his farm. Now arose a new class-difference of more far-reaching consequences: a landed nobility formed itself above the common farmers, and these to a great extent became the lease-holders of the noble proprietors. This development did not go on evenly in all parts of the three countries; in some parts, particularly in the forest lands of eastern Norway and northern Sweden, it was counteracted by individual clearing on the waste lands. But, whether slowly or fast, the aristocratic tendency asserted itself everywhere and could not be stopped. It must be noticed, however, that the peasant class did not lose their liberty with their property; they remained freemen, and as such they still were the typical basis of society.

Every free farmer, whether copyholder or freeholder, had the right or even the duty of attending the court of his district, the *thing* or *althing*, where the law was proclaimed and cases were tried. Formally, we might speak of a democracy, and the force of traditional law and general opinion was irresistible; but, even by virtue of law and opinion, the people found it natural to follow their chief, and insensibly their right of judging became a right of assent. At first, it was the law that spoke through the lawman; later it was the chief, the guardian of the law.

The class of landed proprietors that in this way took hold of political as well as economic power, from its very origin and for a couple of centuries after, was throughout a rural aristocracy. In the history of Scandinavian political organisation, it is a very important fact that, long after the establishment of united kingdoms, the effective political life of the people was restricted to territories of a much smaller extent. The spirit of society and law asserted itself most strongly inside the circle of the parish, in the hundred or *herad*, where all were bound together by economic and social interests. Above the herad, the *land* or *fylki*, the county, united wider circles of the people for legal purposes; but in Sweden, the judicial organisation did not in fact go farther than this, and here the kingdom remained divided into not less than sixteen separate law-districts or lands. It was not until the fourteenth century that unity of law was established for the Swedish kingdom.

In Denmark and Norway, the unification had already reached a higher level before the establishment of the kingdom. From the beginning of historic times, we find Denmark organised in only three law-districts, Scania, Sealand, and Jutland; but, curiously enough, this division of the country was kept in existence until the end of the seventeenth century, and the special Jutland law, indeed, was in force in southern Jutland even until the year 1900. In Norway, from the eleventh century, partly through the concurrence of the kings, the whole country was organised in five law-districts, two in the east, one in the west, and two in the north, the last two however following the same law; here complete unity of law was established as early as the thirteenth century. But notwithstanding such unity of law, there did not exist in any one of the three kingdoms a popular court of a wider circuit than the circumscribed *law-thing*; no national organisation of the people was called into life by the king. Only the little commonwealth of Iceland was a living unity, and its *althing*, or general court, established in the year 930, is to-day beyond comparison the oldest national assembly of the world.

Of course, the aristocracy did not feel restricted in this way to local activity; indeed, it may be said that the consummation of the kingdom was partially prepared by the family alliances of the county aristocracy from the several parts of each country. Nevertheless, it remained essentially bound to its county sphere, where it was economically rooted, and only through its service to the king was it an instrument of national administration. Indeed, in those times, the king might truly say: "L'Etat, c'est moi." He was from the first the only national institution. His power was founded upon the sword and conquest, and his original aim did not go further than that of the Vikings, the winning of honour and wealth. But the acquisition of power itself had its consequences; in order to preserve it, it was necessary to have it organised, and, quite naturally, the kingship became an economic, military, administrative, and lastly even a spiritual power in the national life.

It must be confessed that we really know very little about the exact organisation of the oldest state institutions of the Scandinavian kingdoms. Some facts, however, stand out with relative clearness. It is certain that the king obtained his chief income from his patrimonial estates, increased by those he confiscated from his opponents by conquest. We happen to have contemporary evidence that the first King of Norway, Harold Fairhair, came from Vestfold in eastern Norway, and was in possession of large royal domains in the western part of the country. But the king could not be content to live only on his private income; he was surrounded by a numerous guard that asked for board and valuable gifts, and he had to contrive that all his subjects should assist in the maintenance of his power.

In this connexion it is remarkable that the first king whom we certainly know to have reigned over the whole of Sweden is given the sobriquet of Tax-king. The Scandinavian word here translated by tax (*skot*, English *scot*) originally had the meaning of contribution or grant; we may combine this with the name of the oldest tax in Denmark, the *stud* or assistance, and we see the origin of the tax in an old Norwegian custom, called *veizla*, a word that means grant or entertainment or fee, as the case may be. From olden times, we see the king, in typical medieval fashion, passing from one of his estates to another, everywhere taking his *veizla*; he had to receive all his income in kind, as money was extremely scarce, and so he had to come and seek his dues himself, instead of having them sent into a central treasury; in fact, he had to eat them on the spot, and when he received his entertainment at his own farm, it seems to have been the custom for the steward of that domain at the same time to demand assistance in kind from the whole surrounding district. This was the basis of the earliest taxation[1].

Then the king had his natural task as the defender of peace at home and on the frontier, and from the duty arose a power. Law and justice were administered by the popular court, but the king had to see that the judgment was executed, and therefore he received a fixed part of the fine that was the regular redemption of the guilty. It appears as if, in this arrangement, the king of the realm was the heir of the county kings; at any rate, through the collection of the law-fines by his servants,

[1] The *veizla* thus corresponded to the feudal right known as *albergaria,* which in England decayed into *purveyance.*

he was a steadily working factor in the social life of his subjects and made himself more effective in this way than by any other means. On the other hand, the establishment of the complete kingdom seems to have been the occasion for an increase of the royal power in the same sphere, the new king imposing upon his subjects a special and heavy fine for disobedience to royal commands.

For the security of his person and for the general administration of the country, it sufficed for the king to retain a household guard, which was called by the Anglo-Saxon name *hird*. But when the kingdom was menaced by foreign war, it was necessary to set up a stronger defensive force, and for war purposes the king had to organise a military service of the people. Here again, the king of the realm was able to take over an inheritance from the old county-kingdoms, namely, the institution of *leidang*. Originally this institution was developed in Denmark, perhaps as early as the sixth century. From its origin it was, and it always remained, an organisation for war by sea, since only by sea could troop movements be undertaken, and even war by land was nothing but ravaging the coast. The *leidang*, then, was the conscription of mariners, both as rowers and as warriors, and the organisation of it consisted in the division of the country into ship-districts, each of which furnished one warship with the necessary crew. From Denmark, this system very early spread to Gautland (Gothland) and to south-eastern Norway, where Danish kings ruled about the year 800. Very early also we find it in Swedish Upland, where the name of *Roslag*, *i.e.* rowing-law district, seems to bear witness to its existence from the ninth century and is supposed to be the origin of the national name of Russians. At the same time, the custom was adopted in England, and the Norwegian kings of the tenth century established it for all the coast-lands of their country. In this way the king of each Scandinavian land obtained a navy at his disposal, and the kingdom acquired a military organisation of a national character. As the royal power was essentially a military power, it was very fitting that the first national institution created by the king should be military also.

Besides the king, there came into existence another national power, the Church. It is indeed a remarkable coincidence that, in the Scandinavian countries, the introduction of Christianity and the establishment of a national Church were contemporary with the final victory of the national kingship and were even brought about by the victorious kings. This fact strongly points to the conclusion that the struggle for national unity must have been influenced by foreign ideas and models; but the Christian Church is the only institution that may be regarded as a foreign product. Christianity not only meant a new spiritual and moral life; still more, it was a fact of social importance. Heathen religion at its height did not reach beyond a more or less narrow local worship, evidently somewhat different in different places. With Christianity there came unity of religion and, at the same time, unity of ecclesiastical organisation.

The Catholic conception, which of course was current in the northern countries as well as elsewhere in Europe, was not that of a national Church but of a world-Church. But, as a matter of fact, the Church powerfully helped to organise the peoples as nations. The first laws that were really national laws were those regulating Christianity and the duties of the people in respect to the clergy and churches; and, from the first, the Church of each country was administered by bishops who were in the direct service of the king. By papal bulls of the tenth century, the German Archbishop of Hamburg, residing at Bremen, was installed as the ecclesiastical ruler of the whole Scandinavian North; but he met with great difficulties in trying to establish his power in this part of his province, and never succeeded in making it a solid fact. The political dissensions of the three kingdoms seriously affected their ecclesiastical relations; when one kingdom adhered to the Hamburg metropolitan, at least one other was almost certain to hold aloof and to look to England for its ecclesiastical relations.

The ambitious Archbishop Adalbert (1043–1072) made great exertions to obtain an effective acknowledgment from all the northern countries and, indeed, went far toward his goal; but when his emissaries came to the Norwegian king Harold Hardradi (the Hardruler, 1047–1066), who had formerly been in the service of the Byzantine Emperors and was dominated by autocratic ideas, the king wrathfully turned the men away from his presence, crying that he knew of no other archbishop or lord in Norway except Harold alone. In this outburst we see the primitive expression of national self-assertion even in ecclesiastical matters, just as the court poets of King Harold were eager to celebrate Norwegian bravery as contrasted with the cowardice of the neighbour nations. Thus in each country the Church was felt to be a national institution, and this feeling was strengthened by the canonisation of national saints, who gathered around them the faith and the veneration of the people; they were elevated into symbols of national organisation, both political and ecclesiastical, and they could be used in this way because they were taken from amongst the kings of the country.

The national character of this saint-making clearly appears in the history of the first and most important of them, King Olaf of Norway. At the moment when England was in revolt against her Danish conquerors, he succeeded in liberating his country from Danish dominion (1016) and made himself king of the whole country as well as of the western islands; and he became the real organiser of the kingdom and the Church of Norway. But after twelve years of hard fighting he had to flee before the overwhelming power of King Canute (Knut) the Great, who had won over the chiefs of the country by golden promises, and, when Olaf came to reconquer his kingdom with Swedish assistance, he fell beneath the weapons of his fellow-countrymen in the battle of Stiklestad (29 July 1030). The new Danish dominion, however, did not prove as beneficent as had been promised, and, whether the cause was the imposition of new taxes or merely bad years by land and sea, the Norwegians grew discontented. The first sign of national opposition was the recognition of King Olaf as martyr and saint in the year following his death, and a church was built for his relics at the town of Nidaros. The cult of St Olaf quickly spread over the whole of Norway and even beyond the frontiers; he even became a national saint in Sweden; he was venerated in Denmark, and churches were built in his honour across the Baltic and in England. But to the people of Norway he was more than a saint, he became a national hero, attracting to himself the popular legends originally formed round the first King Olaf and the heathen god Thor. Everywhere in the country people told of his fights with the trolls or showed the holy fountains which he had caused to break forth, and, at the same time, he was the eternal king of the country. His burial-church at Nidaros gave the nation a spiritual centre; in his name kings and bishops fought for the power of State and Church, and the customary laws of Norway were hallowed as St Olaf's laws.

In Denmark, half a century later, one of the kings became a martyr, not of national independence but of national organisation. For some years after the death of Canute (Knut) the Great, Denmark lay under the rule of the Norwegian king Magnus the Good, the son of St Olaf; but after his death (1047) Canute's sister's son, Svein Estridson, succeeded in defending the independence of Denmark against the attacks of King Harold Hardradi, and he was the founder of a new Danish dynasty. Five of his sons, one after the other, followed him upon the throne, and now the organisation of government was seriously taken in hand. The first of the sons of Svein, King Harold Whetstone (1074–1080), is mentioned as a reformer of the criminal law, and he accomplished an extension of governmental activity in the control of the coinage. The next king, Canute, pushed forward more vigorously, and consequently came into open conflict with his subjects. He wanted to create a fixed system of taxation as well for state purposes as for the maintenance of the Church; he imposed heavy services upon the peasants, demanded a poll-tax of the whole people, and required everyone to pay tithes to the clergy. All this was felt as slavery by the people; a rebellion broke out, and King Canute was killed before the altar of the church where he had sought safety (10 July 1086). But the years that followed were marked by such dearth that his successor, King Olaf, was nicknamed Hunger, and the clergy did not omit to persuade the people that this was the judgment of God because of their rebellion. After a few years King Canute was recognised as a saint and even canonised by the Pope, and his second successor, King Eric the Evergood (1095–1103), was able to enforce the tithe. Thus the people grew accustomed to pay regular taxes, and the martyrdom of St Canute was a gain to the State as well as to the Church.

By this time the Scandinavian Churches were beginning to develop into separate organisations independent of the State. It should be noticed that this development did not proceed in opposition to the government; on the contrary, it was directly favoured by the kings. As a general rule, we have to acknowledge that the Church took charge of social tasks that the king was as yet unable to undertake, and, while the State power was still relatively weak, there could be no question of a general opposition between Church and State. It was St Canute himself who granted to the Church of Denmark an independent jurisdiction in ecclesiastical affairs, and his father, King Svein Estridson, had already begun to agitate the question of a separate Scandinavian metropolitan. In Denmark, we find the whole country organised in dioceses, eight in number, at least as early as the reign of Svein (1047–1074), and soon the other Scandinavian countries followed its example. The commonwealth of Iceland got its first fixed bishop's see in the year 1056, its second exactly half-a-century later. In Norway, King Olaf the Peace-king (1067–1093) organised four bishoprics with fixed sees; in Sweden, we find five bishoprics firmly established before the year 1120, probably owing to the action of King Inge Stenkilsson. The second Icelandic bishop induced the *althing* to adopt the tithe in the year 1097; it was introduced into Norway by King Sigurd, 'the pilgrim to Jerusalem,' shortly after 1110; and possibly at the same time King Inge established it in Sweden.

After the foundation of bishoprics and the introduction of tithes, the Church was far better equipped than before for acquiring land and wealth, and, from the beginning of the twelfth century, it won a steadily stronger economic basis for its social and moral activity. At the same time, the religious and ecclesiastical movements of Western Europe spread vigorously into the northern countries and introduced strong forces into their church life; pilgrims and crusaders departed for the Holy Land, missionaries set out to work amongst the neighbouring heathen, monasteries were founded on every side. The effect was twofold: the northern Churches became more intimately connected with the whole Catholic Church of Europe, and at the same time their national position grew stronger. The kings were still leading in the movement, and it was the work of King Eric the Evergood to organise the whole of Scandinavia into an independent ecclesiastical province. He went in person to Rome to obtain the papal authorisation, and the first Scandinavian archbishop was consecrated at Lund in Scania in the year 1104.

But national politics as well as ecclesiastical development soon demanded a division of the province; the Cistercian revival made for a more effective supervision of the actions of the clergy, and the bishops of Norway united with the kings in asking from the Pope a national archbishop. In the year 1152 the Englishman Nicholas Breakspeare (later Pope Hadrian IV) arrived in Norway as a papal legate, and an archbishop was installed at Nidaros as metropolitan of eleven dioceses, five in Norway and six in the western islands. Some years later, in 1164, Sweden obtained an archbishop of her own at Upsala, and about the same time one of the Swedish kings, Eric, who had been recently (18 May 1160) killed in civil war, was elevated to the position of the national saint. Thus each of the Scandinavian kingdoms had acquired complete national organisation of its Church, and contemporary with the establishment of national archbishoprics in Norway and Sweden was the acknowledgment of independent ecclesiastical jurisdiction—in other words, the elevation of the clergy into a separate order of the nation. In all the three countries, the papal acceptance of the new organisation was accompanied by the demand for a special Rome-scot, the Peter's pence, by which the people were more firmly tied to the mother Church, and also learned the habit of paying taxes in money.

The progressive organisation of State and Church necessarily reacted upon the social relations of the people. The chief task of kings and clergy was to institute peace and law among the subjects; the clergy introducing into the new provinces of the Church the general Christian penitential regulations, and the kings enforcing the national penal laws. In contemporary poems, St Olaf is praised because he used his kingly power to mutilate thieves and decapitate vikings, in this way protecting the property of men, and we hear a strange note from those fighting times: "now," says the poet, "the subjects rejoice at peace." The chief theme of the court poets had been battles and victories of their kings; but from this time onward again and again the poems are full of the word "law."

Evidence of the growing importance of public law is to be found in the fact that the laws were put in writing. The oldest trustworthy notice of an enterprise of this kind comes from the commonwealth of Iceland, the land of jurists and lawsuits. In the year 1117, the *althing* decided to introduce a commission of jurisconsults for the recording and the reform of the laws of the country, and in the next year their completed work was presented to the *althing* which gave its consent by a majority. In the other Scandinavian countries, the compiling of law-books was mainly a private enterprise, undertaken by the law-men of the provinces (as in Norway and Sweden) or by other lawyers. The Norwegian provincial laws seem to have been put into writing as early as the end of the eleventh century, during the reign of Olaf the Peace-king; but they have not come down to us in a form older than the end of the twelfth century. The oldest Danish law-books still preserved are dated from about 1200, although they are evidently founded upon an earlier work; the Swedish provincial laws were only arranged and written in the course of the thirteenth century.

All these laws without exception indicate a change in the structure of society compared with earlier times. Originally, the strength of society lay in the kindred, the union of a wide range of kinsmen, and the earlier laws still shew us each individual protected in his rights by his kindred. The kinsmen may swear him free of a crime, they participate in paying his fines as well as in demanding damages due to him; they have a right of pre-emption upon his land in case he is obliged to give it up. But, at the time of the law-books, we observe a decline of the kindred; its range has been decidedly narrowed. Behind the laws we catch glimpses of an epoch when kinship to the tenth and even to the fifteenth degree had a social meaning; in the laws themselves the really effective kinship appears restricted to the nearest kinsmen, the cousins and second-cousins, or even to what is virtually the family household. This development is most conspicuous in the economic field; landed property has become a family estate instead of a possession of the kindred. But even in the matter of social security, the individual has lost many of his former connexions. There were several causes for this change: the migrations of the Viking age had helped to dissolve and dislodge the kindreds; still more important was the effect of the increase of aristocracy, the people gathering around a chief who undertook their protection; in economic relations, the advance of the Canon Law tended to make property more of a personal matter than before. But the essential fact was the displacing of the kindred by the new social forces, particularly the State and its representatives.

Meanwhile, there is to be noticed an intermediate form of organisation, taking up the task of social protection in an epoch when the kindred had loosened its hold upon the individual and the State was not yet able fully to replace it. This organisation was the *gild*. There has been a good deal of dispute about the origin and antiquity of the Scandinavian gilds, whether they have grown from a foreign or a domestic root. The discussion of the question has certainly shewn that there are some quite important national elements in the institution, just as the word itself is genuine Scandinavian. Nevertheless, it is a well-established fact that the typical perfect gild is older in the Netherlands and in England than in the Scandinavian countries, and that the first-known Scandinavian gild is found among the Danes in England early in the eleventh century. Later in the century we find gilds in Norway and Sweden, and from the beginning of the twelfth century in Denmark as well. Everywhere they are plainly Christian organisations, in Norway often dedicated to St Olaf, in Denmark to St Canute, and their aim is to gather the neighbours together for economic and legal protection. They flourished for a couple of centuries and, during this time, performed a task that, to its full extent, was as yet above the power of the State. But it is unmistakable that the chief tendency of evolution was the steady strengthening of State power.

The ascendancy of the State found its expression in external politics also; the viking raids were replaced by the wars of the kings. The first King of Norway, Harold Fairhair, even formed an alliance with King Aethelstan of England for subduing the vikings, and one of his sons, Hakon, who afterwards became King of Norway and extended the system of *leidang* there for the defence of the country, was known to posterity as the "foster-son of Aethelstan." The Danish kings, on the contrary, made themselves leaders of the viking hosts; Svein Forkbeard and Canute the Great even conquered the whole of England. Seeing the irresistible strength of Denmark in this direction, it is strange to notice its weakness towards the south; the Danish kings had more than once to bow to the lordship of the Germanic Emperors, and the Wendish pirates were never prevented from ravaging the Danish coasts. This was evidently one of the causes which made Svein Estridson and his sons give up their plans for re-conquering England; these plans were, however, inherited by the Norwegian kings, Magnus the Good and Harold Hardradi, but resulted only in the fall of King Harold at Stamford Bridge (25 September 1066).

After the conquest of England by Norman dukes who traced their lineage back to Norwegian and Danish vikings, the hostile relations with England came to an end. Denmark turned against the Wends and expanded its territory towards the Elbe and south of the Baltic. Norway re-enforced its dominion over the western islands, and King Magnus Bareleg (1093–1103), so named from his Scottish dress, determined to conquer the rest of the Norwegian colonies of the West. His fighting prowess made him live in Gaelic folk-songs until recent times as King Manus with the lion, and he succeeded in making Man and the Hebrides a part of the Norwegian kingdom; but in Ireland he met his death, and his enterprise only prepared the way for the Norman conquest of the island.

During his reign there was held a three kings' meeting at the junction of the frontiers of the three Scandinavian kingdoms, in the town of Konungahella, *i.e.* the Kings' Landing-place. Thither came Eric the Evergood of Denmark, Inge of Sweden, and Magnus Bareleg of Norway, and the Norwegian saga has preserved the popular talk that never were seen more chieftainlike men, King Inge bigger, stouter, and worthier than the other two, King Magnus brisker and more sportsmanlike, King Eric the fairest of complexion, but all three distinguished and gallant men. At this meeting (1101) they agreed upon perpetual peace and amicable co-operation between their kingdoms, and, as a pledge of the agreement, the daughter of King Inge was betrothed to King Magnus; from that time she bore the name of Margaret the Peace-maid. After the fall of King Magnus she married the Danish King Nicholas (1104–1134), the last son of Svein Estridson, and so she became a living expression of Scandinavian policy. Indeed, from this time, the politics of the Scandinavian kingdoms were more intimately interwoven than ever before, although the relations between them did not remain any too peaceable.

From about 1130, in all three kingdoms, there came a period that has been named the Civil Wars by later historians, but is more truly described as the Wars of Pretenders. Primarily, it was a conflict between the purely dynastic interests and the idea of political unity. In each country the dynasty was originally a conquering power, the kingdom was regarded as a kind of private estate of the royal house, and every descendant of the conqueror thought himself entitled to participate in the heritage. In Norway and Sweden, at various times, two or even more sons of a king had ruled the kingdom together. In Denmark, the idea of political unity was older and stronger; but, even there, personal interests came into opposition with the natural policy of the kingship, and, from 1131, the sons and grandsons of the last kings fought about the possession of the throne for more than twenty-five years. At the same time, royal pretenders fought each other in Norway and Sweden, and the civil war of each country immediately reacted upon the wars of the other two. This was the natural outcome of the policy of intermarrying that, particularly since the end of the eleventh century, had been adopted by the Scandinavian royal families; and now the royal marriages had become a means of obtaining influence in the neighbour countries. In this way, every pretender was able to secure a point of support abroad, and the Wars of Pretenders grew into not only national wars but even Scandinavian wars.

In Denmark, the unity of the kingdom was restored comparatively soon; after a series of bloody battles and treacherous murders, one of the pretenders, in the year 1157, succeeded in removing all his rivals and making himself master of the kingdom. This was Waldemar the Great (1157–1182), a grandson of King Eric the Evergood, and himself the founder of the Waldemarian dynasty. His personality was an unusually powerful one which dominated all who surrounded him, but his qualities were essentially those of a heavy-handed warrior who struck down all his enemies. Happily for him, he had at his side a counsellor who was at the same time a military commander and a real statesman—the nobleman-bishop Absalon, who was still the virtual leader in Danish politics for twenty years after the death of King Waldemar. From the accession of Waldemar, Denmark was again the dominating power of the Scandinavian North, as it had been from Harold Bluetooth to Canute the Great, and its influence made itself effectively felt in both the other countries.

It so happened that just at the time when dissension and rebellion were brought to an end in Denmark, the Wars of Pretenders in Norway and Sweden flared up more hotly than ever before, and raged in both countries with but short interruptions from about 1155 until towards 1230. The general Scandinavian character of these wars clearly appears from the fact that we may speak of Danish and Swedish parties in Norway, and of Danish and Norwegian parties in Sweden. But the Danish power in both countries was by far the most important one; from Denmark rebellious pretenders often received effective support of men and weapons, and Waldemar the Great for some years was even acknowledged as the overlord of eastern Norway.

But the support of Denmark was not given to rebels indiscriminately. What makes the Wars of Pretenders important in history is the fact that they developed more and more into wars of principle, conflicts between opposite political ideas. The State power itself was at stake in these wars; clericalism and feudalism arose with new demands for political and local government; and from the wars a new society emerged.

Upon closer research it appears manifest that, in Norway as well as in Sweden, the Danish kings always supported the clerical party. This is not to say that in Denmark clericalism unconditionally ruled the State. Here too, kings had belonged to opposite parties, and, in the decade after 1130, one of the kings had even abolished the archbishopric of Lund. But, as a matter of fact, the Church became a deciding factor in the civil wars, and, by the victory of Waldemar the Great, the alliance between archbishop and king was sealed. Conflicts might still arise, although mostly about personal questions. The king did not surrender his influence in ecclesiastical affairs, but he acknowledged the Church as an independent body in society, and his political system received the imprint of ecclesiastical ideals.

In Norway and Sweden it took a far longer time before the conflict between king and Church was settled. In both countries, as in Denmark, the national metropolitan became the natural rallying-point for the clerical party; he was the standard-bearer of advancing ecclesiastical policy. But changing kings adopted different attitudes to the demands of the Church for independence and influence. In Sweden, two dynasties fought over the kingdom, and as the one or the other was victorious, the Church was gaining or losing. So, at least, it was in appearance; in truth, however, the power of the Church was steadily growing, economically, politically, and morally. It is a significant fact that an anti-clerical dynasty gave to Sweden its national saint, King Eric (1160), and when his grandson, another Eric, won the kingdom from his opponent (1210), he compromised with the Church by receiving his crown from the hands of the Archbishop of Upsala; he was the first anointed King of Sweden, and, a few years after, the act was confirmed by Pope Innocent III.

In Norway, the conflict had a far more fundamental character and was signalised by a more dramatic course of events. This was due as well to the strongly national development of the kingship which made it more hostile to foreign ideas, as to the remarkable personalities who took the leadership in the conflict. The clerical view of politics came to the front when one of the fighting parties set up as its king a child of five years, Magnus (1161). He was a descendant of the royal house through his mother only, and so had no legal right of inheritance. To remedy this deficiency, his mighty and cunning father, the Earl Erling Crooked-neck, had him anointed and crowned by the Archbishop of Nidaros (1163) —that Eystein or Augustine who, two years before, had obtained his pallium from the hands of Pope Alexander III, and who made himself the faithful champion of the papal policy. He did not bestow consecration upon the young king for nothing, but required him to confirm and extend the privileges of the metropolitan Church, and even—a thing unprecedented in Scandinavia—to hold his kingdom as a fief of St Olaf, offering up his crown on the altar of the cathedral of Nidaros. Acts similar, although not exactly correspondent, are to be found in the history of several European countries, and, particularly, in the holy kingdom of Jerusalem. The chief significance of this proceeding was the intimate alliance of State and Church; at the same time, Eystein tried to consolidate his work by means of a law that, in future, only the eldest legitimate son of the king might inherit the throne; and, failing him, the bishops of the kingdom were given the deciding voice in the election of a new king. Nowhere had the Church obtained such a victory as this.

But only a few years later the parts were reversed, and the Church had to yield to a new king who became the most violent opponent of her secular power. This was King Sverre, perhaps the most extraordinary figure of Scandinavian medieval history. It may fairly be doubted whether he was really a king's son or simply an impostor; but his genius as a leader of men is beyond any doubt. Educated as a cleric, he came to Norway from the far-off Faroe Islands and conquered the kingdom. His qualities were not those of a mere warrior, but he was a military tactician who, at sea as well as by land, made his forces more mobile than had hitherto been the case, and he roused the enthusiasm of his men to the point of devotion. Beginning as the chief of a small and weak band (1177) supported from Sweden, he quickly succeeded in getting a stronghold in the northern counties, where the social development and the political traditions were most strongly conservative. To the recent idea of kingship by divine right, exemplified by King Magnus, he opposed the old-fashioned national kingship by popular assent, and he got the upper hand: Magnus fell (1184); Archbishop Eystein had to take refuge in England (1180); his successor fled to Denmark (1190); and the other bishops soon followed. King Sverre was excommunicated by the Pope, but nevertheless retained his power until his death (1202), and from his chancery he published a polemical pamphlet against the bishops, defending the supremacy of the royal power in the country by quotations from Holy Scripture and from the Canon Law. It is an interesting fact that, in this Norwegian treatise, we find again the argument put forward by the jurisconsults of Bologna in favour of the imperial power of Frederick Barbarossa forty years before; but nowhere, at so early an epoch as this, do we find the principle of secular supremacy so sharply defined as here. Starting from conservatism, King Sverre became a precursor of the great innovators of royal power and its theory in the thirteenth and fourteenth centuries.

Although he could frustrate the attempt at raising the ecclesiastical power above the king, he was not able to stop the natural progress of the Church, even in political affairs. After his death, his son and successor made his peace with the bishops, declaring that all the calamities of the country were due to the quarrel with them, and confirming all the privileges that were bestowed upon the Church by the founding of the archbishopric. By this act the bishops of Norway re-acquired their position as counsellors of the king as well as independent administrators of ecclesiastical affairs, and the Norwegian Church was organised on an equal footing with the Churches of Denmark and Sweden.

In all three kingdoms, the ecclesiastical conflict was really a link in the general political development of society, the feudalising of the State. Everywhere, in process of organising the political functions of society, the royal power was taking the lead, but, in the course of this process, the kingship itself produced forces that reacted upon its position with a dissolving influence. The primary cause of this seeming paradox was the economic structure of society, which gave but small opportunity for the centralisation of financial power. The more the king strove to establish a royal administration in all parts of his kingdom, the more he was compelled to give up his power to his local representatives; he simply had no means of remunerating his officers except by entrusting to them the fiscal profits of the local government. Now the Church not only constituted a particular branch of social administration, but her officers were among the first to take over the royal functions and profits in the districts. It cannot be an accident that in Scandinavia, as in the rest of Western Europe, the first immunities certified by royal charters are those given to ecclesiastical dignitaries, to bishops or to abbots. In truth, the Church plays an important part in the progress of feudalism, as well because of her administrative functions as by virtue of her increasing landed wealth.

The chief element of feudalism, however, is, of course, in the Scandinavian countries as in medieval Europe generally, the combining of military service with administrative power, and in this field of development Denmark again was in the van. The Wars of Pretenders usher in the new epoch. It is reported that in the year 1134 one of the Danish pretenders marched into battle with a body of horse, and the party of this pretender constantly appears in connexion with Germany; its hero, "Lord" Canute, the father of King Waldemar the Great, was even a vassal of the Germanic Emperor. Evidently, German influence is partly responsible for the introduction of the new arm; but the appearance of cavalry in the royal service meant new demands for military and financial organisation, and the gradual dissolution of the old popular levy. The frequent wars with the Baltic Slavs, the Wends, waged by King Waldemar and his sons, accelerated this development, and the Waldemarian century (1157–1241) is characterised both by the strength of the kingship and by the establishment of feudalism.

To Waldemar the Great and his two successors, Canute (1182–1202) and Waldemar the Victorious (1202–1241), fell the task of establishing the military reorganisation of the kingdom upon a new basis. More pressingly than ever before the king felt the need of a military force that should be more effective and more easily available than was the old *leidang*; he sought for men who were able and willing to be at his service at any time and with the complete equipment of the time. For this purpose a new group of king's men began to separate from the large class of farm proprietors. Originally they were not necessarily the richest men of the class; but, in compensation for their service they were freed from taxes, and as tax-free they constituted a new nobility.

On the other members of this class the result was exactly the opposite. Before the end of the twelfth century, the *leidang* was transformed into a tax, assessed upon farm values; from this time conscription was no longer a personal duty common to all freemen, but a burden belonging to real estate, imposed upon the non-nobles of the society. Thus an important change occurred in the position of the subject: formerly his relation to the king was essentially a personal one; henceforward he became a taxpayer. From a political point of view, this might be called progress, a step towards greater independence of the government. But in the change there was involved an accentuation of the class differences in society. The king's man, the new nobleman, alone remained in an entirely personal relation to the king; he became the *miles* of the king, bound to him by oath, and he was the man to be charged with the duties of government, civil as well as military. The taxes were still paid in kind and could not be gathered into the king's residence; and as he now ceased to receive them personally and consume them on the spot, they had to be used for the support of his local officials. The royal nobility now began to function as the governing class; the local offices became a part of their remuneration for military service; offices and their territorial circumscriptions began to be regarded as fiefs and were granted as such; the nobility assumed the feudal character. It even began to combine as an estate of the realm and, when summoned by the king, met in the general courts of the country, the Dane-courts. The highest class of the nobility, dukes and counts, and together with them even the bishops, had the right of taking knights into their service, and so they appeared in law almost as the equals of the king.

Apparently in the same way as in Denmark, a feudal nobility developed in Sweden. The sources of the period are still very poor for this country;

but in many respects the conditions are similar to those of Denmark, only with the difference that the political evolution of Sweden is always accomplished about half a century or more after that of Denmark. The Wars of Pretenders there also worked for new military demands, and, as in Denmark, foreign wars accelerated the movement. Since the middle of the twelfth century, the Swedish kings were frequently fighting for the conversion and the conquest of the inhabitants of Finland, and, finally, in the year 1249, the great Earl Birger succeeded in subduing the whole of western Finland, which from that time remained a part of the Swedish kingdom. In the course of this century, a royal and feudal nobility formed itself in Sweden also, and, after Earl Birger had been able to put his son upon the throne (1250) and so had founded the dynasty of the Folkungs, the nobility came forward as a real privileged class. His second son, King Magnus Barn-lock (1275–1290), became the organiser of the new society; he made his court the centre of chivalrous splendour, he granted immunities and fiefs, and, above all, by a law of 1280, he laid down the rule that anybody who served the king, the barons, or the bishops as a horseman was to be free from taxes. So the horse-service was made the foundation of tax-freedom, and the nobility was marked out as the free class in the sense of tax-free.

In Norway, the development of feudalism took place along different lines and did not lead to exactly the same results as in Denmark and Sweden. Just as in the conflict between State and Church, the new feudal society worked its way through dramatic events and came into existence almost by a revolution. Here again we meet with the energetic personality of King Sverre, and here his victory was more complete than with regard to the Church. It is a peculiar fact that his ideas about the new administration of the kingdom seem to have been a heritage from his opponent, King Magnus, who in this matter was the disciple of the Church. After the foundation of the Norwegian archbishopric, Magnus began to nominate royal sheriffs as his representatives in the counties beside the hereditary chiefs, and it was this beginning that was systematised by Sverre. In his fight for power, he almost literally decimated the old county nobility, and, whether on principle or by necessity, he did in fact put the whole country under the administration of his own sheriffs; they were paid from the incomes of their respective districts, and they were even said to hold their offices as fiefs. The remnant of the old aristocracy continued their agitation against the new dynasty even after the death of Sverre, until the bishops succeeded in mediating a compromise between the parties (1208), and from that time the county aristocracy consented to undertake the office of sheriff along with the king's men. Very soon the two classes were fused together in a new royal nobility, the barons of the king, and a selection of them formed the King's Council, whose assistance and assent became indispensable to the passing of royal decrees.

As far as we are able to follow this development in Norway, it seems to be founded wholly upon royal measures, the desire of the king to put his own officers in the place of independent nobles, and there does not seem to be any military reason for the change. Nevertheless, at the same time, the military organisation of the country was passing through a remodelling that helped to strengthen the feudal growth. The nature of Norway, its lack of wide plains, such as are found in Denmark and Sweden, did not afford any reason for establishing a cavalry force, and so there was but little need for imposing heavier military burdens upon a wealthy minority. But, along with the extension of royal government, the need of new taxes made itselt felt, and, from the end of the twelfth century, probably as early as the reign of King Magnus (1161-1184), just as in Denmark, the king began to demand payment of the *leidang* contributions as an annual tax. In the course of the thirteenth century the *leidang* became the chief tax of the country and was assessed upon the farms by a fixed valuation. Necessarily, then, the common people were only exceptionally called out for war service; and so the sheriffs acquired a still more feudal character than their administrative position alone could give them.

It has been the general opinion of historians that the kingdom of Sverre and his successors was essentially an absolute monarchy, and so the political development of Norway has been considered to be quite opposite to that of Denmark and Sweden. When later, in the fourteenth century, a feudal aristocracy manifestly takes hold of the government of Norway, this has been regarded as the result of a revolution, to a great extent brought about by influence from the neighbour kingdoms. This view of Norwegian history seems founded upon an illusion. There is this element of truth in it, that the feudalising of Norway obviously made slower progress than that of Denmark and Sweden, because the military system did not work with equal force in that direction, and because in Norway the office-holders were kept more strongly under the control of the king. It is a sign of the greater strength of the monarchy there that the Norwegian kings succeeded in securing by law the strictly hereditary character of the kingdom, whilst in Denmark and Sweden the principle of election was gradually established. But research into the whole administrative system of Norway seems to give the evidence of a steadily progressing feudalism, in the main of the same character as in the two other Scandinavian countries. In none of the three countries could feudalism reach the same degree of perfection as it did in the rest of western Europe; on the one hand, there remained too much peasant freedom, and, on the other hand, the central power of the king was never extinguished. But, during the twelfth and thirteenth centuries, the Scandinavian kingdoms were steadily approximating to the social and political system of the rest of Western Europe.

The great convulsion of Scandinavian society during the twelfth century could not but exercise a notable effect upon the spiritual activity of the peoples. Sweden still lagged behind; from that country no contribution was as yet made to the new movement. But, in Denmark and Norway, the national feeling was stimulated into a conscious life that made for a new kind of literary production; the sense of history awakened, the research into and composition of national history began.

It is a remarkable circumstance that, in this kind of achievement, the leading part was taken by the little nation of Iceland. In truth, the Icelanders were the real possessors of the literary traditions of the north. They had, as it were, monopolised the art and business of royal poetry; as court poets (*skalds*) they composed their artificial poems in honour of the kings, and particularly of the Kings of Norway, to whom the community of language made their involved verses more easily comprehensible, but also of the kings of Denmark and Sweden; and the difficult rules of metre and metaphor were handed down from master to pupil. The heroic age of the skalds endured through the tenth and eleventh centuries; but from that time the art of versification degenerated into an elaborate craftsmanship, fatal to the spirit of poetry, and, on the other hand, the kings ceased to appreciate the celebrating of merely warlike achievements; they became real statesmen and anxious to be the subjects of political history. Thus the Icelanders grew to be historians.

The social conditions of Iceland furthered this transformation. The old aristocratic families from the squatter times were tenacious in conserving the memories of their own past, and, in the solitary homes of the thinly peopled island, the taste for listening to story-telling developed almost into a passion. The story-teller became a professional man; short stories were combined into cycles; the *saga* was born, at the same time pointed and picturesque, imaginative and realistic, dramatic in its events, rich in contrasting psychology. The ecclesiastical erudition of the twelfth century added the element of scientific research that was needed for making history out of the story, and, before 1130, the great annalists Saemund and Ari became the fathers of Icelandic and Norwegian historical writing. In Iceland, more than elsewhere, the clergy, in spite of their learning, were tied to the conditions and traditions of the country and took an active part in the national life; very often, indeed, the priests, bishops, and abbots belonged to the established aristocracy, and their ecclesiastical education only made them more effective instruments of saga-composing in the national language. From the last decades of the twelfth century, and throughout the whole of the thirteenth, there went on an industrious writing and collecting of family and hero sagas which constitute a literature quite by itself, distinct from the rest of medieval production. The sagas were originally founded upon real history, or at least upon popular tradition; but they conformed themselves more and more to the demands of art. Dramatic excitement or the picturing of peculiar characters seemed more important than the truth, and at last even the heroes and the events of the romance were freely invented; although the high art of story-telling maintained a continuous existence.

This art of saga-writing was taken into their service by the Kings of Norway, and it even influenced the historical writing of Denmark. In Norway as well as in Denmark, the first historical works from the end of the twelfth century were written in Latin, and in Denmark the strength of ecclesiastical civilisation manifested itself by retaining Latin as the only literary language. Here, shortly after 1200, the cleric Saxo Grammaticus, a servant of the famous Bishop Absalon, wrote his great work *Gesta Danorum* in vigorous Latin of the French school; but his history is a truly national achievement, not only because it is built upon a foundation of rich Danish tradition, with an infiltration of traditions from Iceland and Norway, but also because it is dominated by a national spirit, near akin to the political work of his master Absalon. Saxo Grammaticus appears as the champion of royal power and national unity against popular will and county particularism; in social status he is an aristocrat, yet nevertheless he sees in the development of royal government a struggle against the old nobility; his work bears witness to the feudalising of contemporary ideas.

Saxo Grammaticus stands out as the one great author of thirteenth-century Denmark, and his work represents almost the whole of Danish literature of the Middle Ages. In the history of Norway, the place of Latin was taken by sagas in the Norse language, and here a real literature came into existence. Its founder was the revolutionary statesman King Sverre, who about 1185 began dictating his own history to an Icelandic abbot with the manifest purpose of defending his policy. His successors of the thirteenth century followed his example, placing the records of the royal chancery at the disposal of Icelandic authors. The earlier history was written partly by Norwegians, but chiefly by Icelanders, those too very often in the royal service; and here again the spirit of the age appears through the apparently objective narrative. The great master of the Norwegian saga was the Icelander Snorri Sturluson (1179–1241), himself a leader in the politics of his native island and not an outsider in those of Norway either. Being a lover of the arts and traditions of the past, he compiled a copious manual for poets, the celebrated *Younger Edda*, and then wrote the history of the Norwegian kings from the beginning until the appearance of Sverre. In combining therein the faculties of a keen critic, a vivid story-teller, a shrewd psychologist, and a pragmatic reasoner, he created a work surpassing anything else that the Middle Ages have left us of historical literature. Like the history of Saxo, the saga-book of Snorri is dominated by the idea of national unity and royal power, both institutions advancing towards victory against the strong opposition of a particularist aristocracy; such a work was more than history, it was instrumental in gathering the nation around her kings.

The spiritual co-operation of Norway and Iceland which found its highest expression in the sagas had its political pendant in the union of the two countries under the kings of Norway. The plans for such a union were at first formulated at the royal court; but they reached their realisation by the development of Icelandic conditions proper. The aristocracy of Iceland very early consolidated itself, dividing the political power among some fifty noble families, and, through the natural effort of maintaining their power as well as their nobility, the number of these families was steadily shrinking until, at the beginning of the thirteenth century, not more than a fifth of them were left. These few families filled the country with their bloody wars, and the power of Norway could not escape being dragged into the conflict, the poor peasants appealing for peace to the metropolitan of Nidaros, the grandees themselves appealing for assistance to the king. Peace was finally restored by the submission of the country to the king, embodied in a treaty of union (1262) which made the grandees of Iceland the vassals of the Norwegian king. The year before, the colonists of Greenland had put themselves under the dominion of Norway, and so, at this time, all peoples of Norwegian descent were united in one kingdom. Only a few years after, by the treaty of Perth (1266), Norway was compelled to renounce its dominion over Man and the Hebrides in favour of Scotland. But, still, the bulk of Norwegians obeyed the King of Norway, and the western islands were tied to the mother country very effectively by their need of Norwegian articles of export.

During the Middle Ages there was no period when the three Scandinavian kingdoms appeared more vigorous and powerful than they did in the thirteenth century. The population was fast increasing, land and woods were cleared, fields and pastures gave good returns, the wealth of kings and clergy manifested itself by the building of costly palaces and churches, the arts of architecture, sculpture, and painting followed the lines of European evolution and in many cases equalled their models, the Icelandic sagas spread their glory over the whole of Scandinavia, and everywhere there appeared a vivid spiritual activity. The three kingdoms were eagerly expanding their frontiers, and in all of them the organisation of government and society was effectively progressing.

In their political development, conflicting tendencies seemed to assert themselves. In all three kingdoms the royal power was evidently on the rise, although in somewhat varying phases. Everywhere, the king stood in the centre of the legislative power, formally restricted by the right of the local assemblies to sanction his ordinances, in reality more restricted by the powers of the royal court. Everywhere, the king had got his fixed taxes, and he had an army and a navy at his disposal. In all three countries, he was the executor of the law, and in Denmark and Sweden, since the thirteenth century, he had become the supreme judge of the kingdom, while in Norway, since the reign of King Sverre, royal representatives presided in the popular courts. Since, in Denmark and Sweden, the judicial power found its head in the king, it followed that, from this time onward, every judgment became valid for the whole kingdom; and in Norway, where this principle was already in force, King Magnus the

Law-mender in the year 1276 succeeded in creating a common law for the whole country.

But, besides the king, other political forces were coming to the front, rivalling him or even pushing him aside. These were the Church and the new feudal nobility, and with them conflicts were inevitable. As a matter of course, the Church maintained her old ecclesiastical ideals of self-government, and, in principle, the royal government did not disown them. But the balance of power between king and metropolitan was still an unstable one, and the feudalising of society prompted the Church to demand independence even in secular affairs, and particularly as to economic matters. Very naturally, therefore, the conflict this time became most acute in Denmark, where it endured from about 1245 for more than half a century. That unyielding dogmatiser, Archbishop Jacob Erlandson of Lund (1254–1274), did not hesitate to proclaim the superiority of the spiritual over the secular sword; the real point of conflict, however, was the question whether the king was entitled to demand the duty of *leidang* from the lands and men of the Church, and this question involved the whole question of the relations between king and Church. There was a series of acts of violence, of legal proceedings, of appeals to the Pope; archbishop and bishops were imprisoned or exiled, the king was excommunicated, the country laid under interdict. After the death of Archbishop Jacob there was peace for twenty years; but with Archbishop Jens Grand (1289–1302) all the scenes of the former conflict reappeared in almost identical forms. In the whole struggle it was a matter of great importance that there was no absolute concord within the Church; some bishops always held to the king, and even the Pope could not approve of all the acts of the archbishop. Finally, the king humbly submitted his case to Pope Boniface VIII and, by this act, obtained the removal of Archbishop Jens to a foreign see; afterwards, in a General Court (1303), the privileges of the Danish Church were solemnly confirmed, especially in respect to jurisdiction and patronage, but the king's right of *leidang* was maintained. By this compromise the peace between King and Church was restored for two centuries; the Church succeeded in strengthening her independent power in ecclesiastical affairs, but she had to submit to the king in the matter of taxes.

The like result was attained in the other Scandinavian countries. In Norway, matters came to a conflict exactly during the decades of truce in Denmark. The Archbishop of Nidaros, John the Red (1268–1282), had the idea of recovering the forfeited privileges which Archbishop Eystein had once wrung from King Magnus, and, after some years of negotiation, he only resigned them on condition that the general privileges of the Norwegian Church should be confirmed by an explicit document, issued by King Magnus the Law-mender (1277). This document remained, for more than two centuries, the basis of ecclesiastical independence in Norway. At the same time, Archbishop John obtained other privileges from the king, extending the tithes of the Church and exempting her from much of the *leidang* duty. But, after the death of King Magnus (1280), when a boy king mounted the throne, the barons of the kingdom engaged in a fight for the repeal of those economic privileges. The archbishop, unwilling to submit, had to flee the country and died in exile, and for six years the metropolitan see of Nidaros remained vacant. Finally, the successor of John made his peace with the king (1290), and the additional privileges of 1277 were abandoned. At the same date, without any fighting, the same principles were established with regard to the Church of Sweden. But in Sweden and Denmark, it must be added, the principles did not always correspond with the facts, as the individual bishops to a great extent obtained the liberties that were denied to the Church as a whole; this was the natural consequence of the progress of feudalisation, for the Church could not stand outside.

The compromise in Norway reacted upon the position of the Church in Iceland, where, until this time, the clergy were essentially a part of the secular society, and in subordination to the aristocracy of the country; several of the bishops had tried to constitute the Church as an independent body, and, after hard conflicts and varying successes, in 1297 a compromise was effected by which Canon Law was established in Iceland as well.

In the period in which the rivalry of king and Church was brought to an end, the conflict between king and nobility began shaping itself as an increasing movement in political life. The development of feudalism having proceeded farthest in Denmark, the conflict here presented itself earlier and raged with more violence than it did in the other two countries. During the reign of Eric Clipping (1259–1286), the grandson of Waldemar the Victorious, at a General Court in the year 1282, the nobles of the kingdom compelled him to sign a charter which has been rightly called the Magna Carta of Denmark, and which was the first of a long series of written obligations destined to restrict the power of the kings. By the charter of 1282, King Eric bound himself to call the General Court, or parliament, of the grandees every year; he promised that nobody should be imprisoned or fined without legal judgment or against the law, and that he never would issue his royal sentences against anyone except after legal summons. In this way the king was to be made constitutionally dependent upon the will of the nobles, and, when he did not conform himself to their wishes, he was treacherously murdered by a coalition of them (1286). The immediate consequence was a protracted struggle between the king and a powerful party of nobles, a fight which spread to Norway and Sweden as well, and from that time the opposition of king and nobility became a chief factor of Danish history.

A similar opposition did not manifest itself in Sweden and Norway until the beginning of the fourteenth century. But the foundations of it were laid by the commanding position secured by the nobility. In Norway, by laws of 1273 adopted in parliament, the sheriffs were formally constituted as royal vassals, their military duties exactly defined, and by a law of 1277, following an English model, the titles of baron and knight were established; shortly after, they are found in use in Sweden and Denmark also. In Norway and Sweden we find no law prescribing the convocation of parliaments of the nobles; but, in fact, such parliaments regularly assembled, and the king could not act without them. In both countries, as in Denmark, the nobility was becoming the dominant political power, ever more in opposition to the king.

As to the future development, it is an interesting fact that, at the same epoch, the class formed itself that was destined, in later centuries, to gain ascendancy over the nobility, namely, the burgher class. The thirteenth century, in fact, marks the entrance of the Scandinavian countries into European commerce and, as a consequence, the building-up of real cities. Of course, small towns existed from earlier times and had a certain commerce with foreign countries as well as with the home districts. But the great change brought about by the thirteenth century was the introduction into commerce of big staple articles. These articles were the herring of Scania and the cod of Norway. The herring-fisheries off Scania made the neighbour towns of Skanör and Falsterbo in summer-time two of the liveliest ports of northern Europe, and the cod-fisheries of northern Norway made Bergen a city of European size. When Wisby in Gothland, in the year 1285, submitted to the Crown of Sweden, it was already a powerful town that had won its wealth as an intermediate station for the commerce of the Baltic. But the burghers of Wisby were chiefly Germans, and, as a matter of fact, the export of the Danish herring as well as of the Norwegian cod was monopolised by German merchants, particularly those of Lübeck. In the second half of the thirteenth century German capital and German merchants took the lead in Scandinavian commerce, and, to Norway, the import of German grain became actually a vital necessity. In all the three countries, the kings granted privileges to the German merchants, and the first treaties of commerce were concluded with them; from this time we may speak of a commercial policy of the Scandinavian governments.

The general progress of commerce made itself felt in all parts of the three countries, and, everywhere, the towns, old and new, advanced towards greater importance. In Denmark, one town after another, in the course of the thirteenth century, got its charter for the regulation of its self-government; in Norway, a common law-book for all the towns was issued in the year 1276. Mostly, the towns were on Crown lands, and the king had his sheriff in each of them; but they had their own aldermen and councils, in Denmark often named *consules* as in Germany, and the special town courts were instrumental in making innovations in the practice of law and justice. For the purposes of trade the townsmen united into gilds, and so, in law and in fact, a real burgher class developed.

Yet this commercial class was not numerous nor very rich, and it had not won any political position at all. The privileged classes were the nobility and the clergy only, and their rivalry with the king will make up the substance of the history of the centuries that follow.

CHAPTER XII

SPAIN, 1031–1248

The period of Spanish history between 1031 (the date when the Caliphate of Cordova fell) and 1248 (when Seville was taken by Ferdinand III, King of Castile) is marked by such distinctive characteristics as to warrant its separation from the ages which preceded it, and such as gave a new bent to the political and social life of the Peninsula.

Up to 1031[1] the Muslims were in the ascendant and took the lead in Spain in political and economic life and in civilisation. Subsequently these advantages passed for the most part to the Christian States to their great benefit. This change is accounted for by two fundamental causes. The Western Caliphate was destroyed by the action of internal elements of disintegration; but its strength had lain chiefly in that unity which, when opposed by the military power of the Christians, had presented a united front rich in resources and directed by skilful and energetic leaders. When unity of action and co-operation were lost, not only was the power of attack gone, but also that of resistance to the blows of the enemy. On the other hand, the Christians had gained by the natural accumulation of strength in the course of time (the three centuries after the Arab invasion), the gradual establishment of security in a great part of the reconquered territory, and the development of economic resources resulting from the increase in population, agriculture, and commerce. Moreover, in the literature of the period and in actual social conditions there is evident an intensification of religious sentiment and of political opposition, both tending to stimulate the struggle against the Muslims and heighten the work of reconquest.

These two causes combined to render the period we are considering that of decisive victories for the Christian States. In spite of reverses, some of them severe, Toledo, Valencia, Las Navas, Murcia, the Balearic Islands, Cordova, Jaen, and Seville mark the rapid successive stages of the Christian advance towards the South, and as numerous factors of civilisation and wealth became absorbed into the life of the Spanish States thus augmented in territory, population, and resources, there appeared (at the close of the period under consideration and in that immediately following) splendid expressions of the Spanish genius, now so enhanced.

It is therefore strictly in consonance with the facts to shift the centre of interest in the history of the Peninsula from the Muslim to the Christian States, which were henceforth predominant and in which the different parts (kingdoms or independent counties) combined to form larger and mightier political groups.

[1] See *supra*, Vol. III, Chap. XVII.

Six years after the extinction of the Caliphate of Cordova in name and in fact, Ferdinand I of Castile united in his person the two crowns of Leon and Castile (1037); a little later, in accordance with a tendency which is very marked in Spanish history, and which perhaps originated in a subconscious realisation of the diversity of races and of their destinies, he refused to add to his dominions the kingdom of Navarre, notwithstanding the defeat he had inflicted at Atapuerca (1054) on his brother Garcia, King of Navarre, who fell on the battlefield. This war had, indeed, been provoked not by the ambition of Ferdinand but by that of Garcia, who wished to deprive his brother of the crown of Castile-Leon; but it is none the less singular to find a medieval monarch refusing to accept so tempting a prize. On the other hand, it is obvious that Ferdinand was concerned because the success of his reign was menaced by the opposition of the Leonese, occasioned not only by the defeat of their former king, Bermudo, but also, and probably still more, by the persistent feelings of hostility which had always separated the Castilians from the Leonese, and which are reflected in contemporary popular literature. Ferdinand's chief political significance may be found in his policy against the Muslims. He was above all a chieftain of the Reconquest, and circumstances favoured him.

The collapse of the Caliphate of Cordova had given rise by subdivision to several independent kingdoms governed by the most prominent personages of the army and of the Muslim aristocracy in the various regions. There were as many as twenty-three of these kingdoms, extending over a wide area from Aragon in the north and Valencia in the east to Andalusia and Murcia in the south and the former Lusitania in the west. They were called the kingdoms of the *Taifas*, from an Arabic word equivalent to "people" or "tribe." The natural ambition of each of these chiefs was to restore under his own rule the unity of the fallen Caliphate; which, in conjunction with the old political and social enmity between the Slaves and Berbers, gave rise to desperate struggles between them, more especially between the Kings of Granada, Málaga, and Seville, who were among the most powerful.

At Seville, the political power had been seized, under the outward form of a republic, by the Cadi Abū'l-Qāsim Muḥammad of the family of the 'Abbādites, a man possessing all the necessary qualities for obtaining ascendancy. He was first of all successful over his colleagues of the aristocratic Committee or Senate which governed the city and territory of Seville; then he made use of a stratagem often resorted to in the Muslim world, which consisted in the presentation of a false Hishām II as a refugee in Seville, claiming the supreme power as rightfully his. The fraud was successful in Seville, and the Muslim Kings of Valencia, Denia, Tortosa, Carmona, and even the aristocratic republic of Cordova, were also duped. This enabled Abū'l-Qāsim, who had been appointed Prime Minister by the false Hishām, to open hostilities against Yaḥyà, King of Málaga, chief of the Berbers, whom he crushed, and against Bādīs, King of Granada, who succeeded Yaḥyà as leader of the Berber party.

Abū'l-Qāsim died in 1042, and his son 'Abbād, surnamed Mu'taḍid, (still as minister to the false Hishām) continued the policy of territorial expansion by the capture of several cities and territories bordering on modern Portugal (Mertola, Niebla, Santa Maria de Algarve), and near Málaga and Cadiz (Ronda, Moron, Arcos, Jerez, Algeciras), meanwhile still prosecuting the war with Bādīs and greatly reducing the power of the King of Badajoz. By these means in 1058 Mu'taḍid was master of all the south-western portion of the former Caliphate, and was supported by his alliance with the Kings of Valencia and Denia.

It was, nevertheless, evident that the military power of the Muslims was much enfeebled. On the other hand, the union of Castile, Leon, and Galicia under Ferdinand I had increased the power of this king, who with his warlike disposition and desire for conquest did not fail to seize the opportunity. He first attacked the northern regions of modern Portugal, *i.e.* those farthest from Seville, quickly seizing Viseu and Lamego (1057). He next turned eastward and advanced on the territory of the Muslims of Aragon, taking some fortresses south of the Douro which belonged to the King of Saragossa. Finally, he advanced to the south against the King of Toledo, his troops penetrating as far as Alcalá de Henares, along the line of the Henares, a tributary of the Tagus. The result of these victories, combined with an offensive on Andalusian territory towards Seville (1063), was that Mu'taḍid and the Kings of Badajoz, Toledo, and Saragossa became Ferdinand's tributaries, thus recognising his military ascendancy. The situation of the time of Almanzor was exactly reversed. Moreover, Ferdinand's campaigns continued. In 1064 he captured the city of Coimbra to the south of Viseu, where he took over five thousand prisoners, and he waged war on the King of Valencia, whom he vanquished at Paterna, almost at the gates of the Muslim capital in the east. He only failed to capture the city itself owing to an illness which compelled him to withdraw. Shortly afterwards he died at Leon (1065), having smitten the Muslim power on all his frontiers, which he extended in all directions.

About the same time the new kingdom of Aragon, whose first king, Ramiro, had enlarged his dominions by the addition of Sobrarbe and Ribagorza on the death of his brother Gonzalo, also began the work of reconquest at the expense of the Kings of Huesca and Saragossa. The first assault on Gráus, to the north-east of Barbastro, was a failure and Ramiro was killed. But his son Sancho Ramirez (1065) continued the campaign, seized Barbastro, a strongly fortified town, with the help of a band of Normans recently arrived from France under the command of William de Montreuil, captured Monzón (farther south along the line of the river Cinca), and finally took Gráus itself.

In spite of the fact that Mu'taḍid had been obliged to recognise the political supremacy of the Castilian king, the kingdom of Seville continued to grow in power among the Muslim States. Mu'taḍid seized the first favourable occasion to do away with the fiction invented by his father, and announced that the false Hishām had recently died, appointing him as heir to the throne. He himself died in 1069, but his son Mu'tamid extended his dominions to the north and east, seizing Cordova and the kingdoms of Murcia. Seville thus became the most important political centre of Muslim Spain, while at the same time the intellectual tastes of Mu'tamid and his minister, Ibn'Ammār, rendered the city a refuge to the scientists and men of letters of their race, thereby recalling the splendours of Cordova under the Caliphate.

The reign of Mu'tamid coincided to a great extent with a temporary enfeeblement of the Christian kingdom of Castile and Leon, due to the inexplicable will of Ferdinand I, who, notwithstanding the grievous consequences due to the division of his states made by his father Sancho, and his experience of the power gained by their reunion under a single king, divided them anew between his sons: Castile went to the eldest, Sancho II, Leon to Alfonso VI, Galicia to Garcia. To his two daughters, Urraca and Elvira, he gave the territories of Zamora and Toro respectively. War very soon broke out between the brothers. Sancho, aspiring to be the sole ruler over the dominions of Ferdinand, attacked his brothers of Leon and Galicia, vanquished them, and obliged them to take refuge with the Muslims, Alfonso fleeing to Toledo, whose king was still a tributary of Castile, Garcia to Seville, which was in the same position with regard to Galicia. In these circumstances, no advantage was gained from Ferdinand's successful campaigns. Possibly Sancho might have achieved the end he had in view; but, not content with the great spoils of his brothers' kingdoms, he wished also to seize the modest possessions of his sisters; and during his siege of the town of Zamora, he was treacherously assassinated (1072) by a partisan of the princess Urraca, whose name is traditionally said to have been Bellido Dolfos. In this tragedy was involved the name of a Castilian knight who had already won renown during Ferdinand's last years, and whom we shall meet again in notable wise—the Cid.

Sancho's death reversed the international political situation with regard to the Muslims. Alfonso returned to Leon, and not only recovered his own kingdom but was recognised by the Castilians as heir to his brother Sancho. Not content with this unlooked-for addition to his possessions, Alfonso coveted Galicia, which he wrested from his brother Garcia, who had likewise returned from Seville with some auxiliary Arab troops. Garcia was vanquished, captured by Alfonso, and imprisoned in a castle; thus for a second time a single monarch ruled over the territories of central and western Spain, north of the line of the Tagus.

The conquest started again under Alfonso VI; the chief figures in it were the king himself and the Cid. Together they might possibly have finished the work of political reintegration so gallantly begun by Ferdinand I. But their dissensions, and above all the suspicious and resentful character of Alfonso, caused each of them to fight for his own hand in different parts of Spain to the detriment of the decisive success of their efforts. But each of them inflicted deadly injury to the power of the Muslims.

Alfonso was bound to the Muslim King of Toledo by a pact dating from the hospitality extended to the Christian prince when a fugitive from Leon. As regards his other tributary, the King of Seville, matters were very different. Mu'tamid had given military assistance to Garcia in his struggle with Alfonso, who now in revenge invaded his dominions; the Muslim ruler was only permitted to retain his kingdom at the intercession of his minister, Ibn 'Ammār, who was a personal friend of Alfonso. The King of Castile consented to be satisfied with the doubling of the tribute paid by Mu'tamid. Irregularities in its payment led to a second attack on Seville by Alfonso, and a military advance as far as Tarifa, in which many prisoners and much booty were secured (1082). Yet once again the Muslim king was allowed to retain his throne.

Shortly afterwards, a political revolt in Toledo, resulting in the expulsion of King Qādir, Alfonso's ally, afforded the latter a pretext for seizing the city. He began by restoring Qādir to his throne in return for increased tribute and certain fortresses (1084); but presently he demanded the city itself, and to attain this object he laid siege to it. The shortness of the siege betrayed the political weakness of the Muslims in a striking manner. On 25 May 1085, Alfonso made his entry into Toledo, thus securing the effective possession of a great part of the line of the Tagus, and a formidable base of operations for farther advances into Andalusia, in view of the strategic situation of the city. The consequences of this event were: firstly, the capture of Valencia by the Castilian troops to establish Qādir there as king, in compensation for his lost throne of Toledo, a step which placed the city and its surrounding territory (*i.e.* part of the eastern coast) in the power of the Castilian king, and enlarged the reconquered zone along the same parallel from the east to the west, from the Tagus to the Turia; secondly, the capture of the castle of Aledo farther south, which commanded the region of Murcia; finally, the submission of all the kings of the Taifas in the east and the south, from whom Alfonso exacted tribute and advantageous treaties.

The little kingdom of Aragon, whose beginnings we have noted, was not yet in a position to lend great assistance to Alfonso's victorious advance, but the latter prosecuted his efforts also to the east, and for some time laid siege to the city of Saragossa, the capital of one of the strongest Arab kingdoms in the north-east of Spain.

In their turn the Counts of Barcelona, successors of Raymond-Berengar I, waged war against the Muslim Kings of Saragossa and Tarragona, thus seeking to extend their dominions to the west and south. They failed in the west, but, probably in 1091, Berengar-Raymond II, son of Raymond-

Berengar I, captured the city of Tarragona, and so almost reached the line of the Ebro, near its mouth; he thus secured the peaceful possession of the territories to the north of the river, the former counties of Barcelona, Manresa, Gerona, and others, as also of the region named Panadés. The rulers of Barcelona also increased their domains and feudal suzerainty towards Roussillon and the country round Toulouse by means of family ties resulting from their marriages.

The Muslim world was not unnaturally perturbed by the Christian victories. The kings of the Andalusian Taifas were convinced that they were powerless to stem the forces of the Castilians and Leonese. But the spirit of nationality awoke in them, and also a feeling of responsibility towards their people. Therefore, though not without hesitation, they resolved to appeal for help to the nearest and most formidable Muslim political power; this was the empire of the Murābiṭīn Berbers (Almorávides), which extended over north-eastern Africa from Senegal to Algeria, and which was ruled over at this time by Yūsuf ibn Tāshfīn. The kings of the Taifas were well aware of the danger they were incurring when they invited a conqueror such as Ibn Tāshfīn to come to Spain. Mu'tamid realised it better than any of the others, but the shame of being so quickly driven out by the Christians decided them to send Ibn Tāshfīn an embassy consisting of envoys from the Kings of Badajoz, Seville, Granada, and Cordova.

Ibn Tāshfīn agreed to a clause binding him to respect the Spanish possessions of his co-religionists, but demanded the town of Algeciras. The ambassadors had no power to accede to this, and they received no definite promise of the required assistance. But Ibn Tāshfīn did not wait for a second invitation. As soon as the ambassadors had departed, he set out for Spain, seized Algeciras, and continued his military advance as far as Seville. The invasion of the Almorávides had become an accomplished fact without the formality of a treaty, and the kings of the Taifas were obliged to accept it. When Ibn Tāshfīn's troops were reinforced by the armies of the Kings of Seville, Málaga, Granada, Almería, and Badajoz, they constituted a formidable army. Alfonso bravely awaited their onslaught. The encounter took place in the fields round Azagal (Zalaca) near Badajoz, and the Christians were defeated with heavy losses (October 1086).

The military consequences of this reverse were that the Castilians were forced to retreat from the region of Valencia and to raise the siege of Saragossa; but the Muslim offensive was not pushed forward, and gained no advantage from the victory of Zalaca, because Ibn Tāshfīn was summoned from Spain to Africa by the death of his eldest son. Most of his soldiers followed him, those who remained being under the command of Mu'tamid. The Muslim attack became paralysed. The Christian troops even succeeded in making some advance towards Murcia and Almería, and a Muslim expedition against the castle of Aledo failed.

Thereupon Ibn Tāshfīn was again summoned, and returned to Spain in 1090. He commenced operations with the siege of Aledo, which he did not indeed succeed in taking. But the castle was in so battered a condition as the result of the siege that Alfonso abandoned it after rasing it to the ground. Practically therefore this strong military base was lost to the Christians.

There was accordingly every prospect of a formidable attack by the Almorávides in conjunction with the Spanish Muslims against the territory of Castile and the other Christian States. But this invasion did not in fact take place. The explanation for this must be sought in the real state of weakness of the Muslim military forces, arising not from lack of numbers or of fighting spirit, but from the fact that their military organisation was less coherent and efficient than that of the Christians, and also possibly from a want of clearness as to the real objective. This last hypothesis is founded on the speedy abandonment by Ibn Tāshfīn of the championship of Islām represented by the struggle with the Christians, in favour of destroying the independence of the Taifas to his own advantage. Ibn Tāshfīn was indeed urged thereto by the intrigues of the intolerant *faqīhs*, who complained of the wide religious liberty granted by the kings of the Taifas, but he was not less moved by greed of the wealth of his co-religionists, and the lure of the Spanish lands, which differed so greatly from those of North Africa and the Sahara. The result was the destruction of the Taifa kingdoms, and the reconstruction of Muslim political unity by Ibn Tāshfīn (1091) and his successor 'Alī (1111); but this in no way improved the political situation of the Muslims in Spain. In spite of continual war during the early years of the twelfth century, the frontiers gained by the Christians were not adversely affected On the contrary, they were advanced on the side of Aragon when Huesca was captured by King Peter I, Sancho's son (1096), and Saragossa by Peter's son Alfonso I (in 1118), resulting in the domination of a large tract south of the Ebro in which there were important cities, including Tarazona, Calatayud, Daroca.

Owing to the military character of the age, the representative figures of contemporary Spanish society must be sought among the warriors. But although among these there were kings such as Alfonso VI of Castile and Alfonso I of Aragon, the most adequate and lofty expression of Spain at the close of the eleventh and the opening of the twelfth century is found in the person of a Castilian noble, who became enshrined in so truly human a manner in the literature of the people that his name has been permanently impressed on the imagination of the European world. This noble was Rodrigo or Ruy Diaz de Vivar, the Cid. He united in his own person the characteristic qualities of the Castilian nobility of the day, whether from the political, military, or legal point of view, together with the ideal of national reconquest so dear to the hearts of the kings and their peoples.

We are now beginning to know the historical character of the Cid, whose very existence was for a while denied by modern historians. We know that he was born at Burgos, or else in the village of Vivar, in the immediate neighbourhood of the Castilian capital. During the last years of Ferdinand I's reign he was already a notable figure at court. He served in the army of King Sancho II, by whose side he fought in the battle of Golpejar and in the siege of Zamora. At Sancho's death, the Cid, like all the other Castilian nobles, recognised Alfonso VI as king, and was highly valued by the latter in the early years of his reign. This esteem was proved by Rodrigo's marriage to Jimena Diaz, daughter of the Count of Oviedo, Alfonso's cousin, which was arranged by the king himself. A little later the king shewed his confidence in the Cid by sending him to Seville to fetch the tribute due from King Mu'tamid. Mu'tamid was then at war with the King of Granada, who was supported by Count Garcia Ordoñez and other Castilian nobles. As this support was in contravention of Alfonso's alliance with Mu'tamid, the Cid attacked these nobles and made them prisoners. But a little later he himself engaged in a warlike raid against the King of Toledo, an ally of Alfonso, who as a punishment exiled the Cid from Castile (1081). With this event begins the characteristic phase of the Cid's career.

His exile released him from all dependence on the King of Castile, and left him free to offer his services as a soldier in any quarter. The Cid, however, never forgot either the general trend of the external policy of his nation, or his love of the country which he had been forced to leave. As the King of Castile was the ally and protector of the Muslim kings of the south, the Cid was for many years the ally and protector of the King of Saragossa—a proof of the strength and efficiency of his personal military power and that of the friends and adherents who had followed him into exile. On the other hand, the Muslim King of Lérida was an ally of Berengar-Raymond II, Count of Barcelona, and of Sancho Ramirez, King of Aragon. Consequently the Cid, in defence of his protégé who had been attacked by the King of Lérida, was obliged to fight against the Aragonese and Catalan troops engaged in the siege of the castle of Almenar. Rodrigo was victorious and the Count of Barcelona himself was for a while his prisoner (1082). An incident of this campaign was the entry of the Cid into the *comarca* of Morella near Valencia, which a few years later was the goal and centre of his military plans.

During the years 1087 and 1088 Rodrigo was once more at the Castilian court, having been restored to royal favour. But in 1089 Alfonso was again won over by the accusations of Rodrigo's enemies, who gave a malicious explanation of the fact that the Cid had made a belated appearance in the Aledo campaign against Ibn Tāshfīn in 1090. This time the king was not content with exiling the Cid, but confiscated all his property and imprisoned Jimena and their children. Rodrigo offered to submit himself to the ordinary judicial procedure of the time and to clear himself on oath, but Alfonso would not consent; and the Cid had to leave his country for the second time, fortunate in being able to take with him his wife and children, whom the king released.

Once again Rodrigo entered the service of the Muslim King of Saragossa, and waged war against the King of Lérida, who was still being supported by the King of Aragon and the Count of Barcelona. Once again the Cid was victorious and took Berengar-Raymond prisoner. One result of this fresh victory and of the generosity of Rodrigo towards the Catalan count, whom he set at liberty, was the friendship which the latter vowed to the Cid, and which he proved by the marriage of his nephew (the future Count of Barcelona, Raymond-Berengar III, called the Great) to Maria, the Cid's daughter. Moreover, Rodrigo was granted the protectorate over the Muslim provinces south-west of Catalonia, in place of the Catalan count who had been so unfortunate in war (1090–1091). Hereby all the territory south of the little kingdom of Aragon up to the frontiers of Valencia, Toledo, and Murcia was actually in the hands of the Cid, although the nominal sovereignty remained with the Kings of Saragossa and Lérida. Rodrigo, however, was anxious to return to his native land, in response to the overtures made to him by the Queen of Castile. To please Alfonso, the Cid co-operated with him in a military expedition he had undertaken against the Almorávid Muslims of Andalusia; but Alfonso remained obdurate (1092).

For the third time Rodrigo was driven from Castile, and this time he did what he had never previously done, although contemporary feudal law permitted such a course to a noble at enmity with the king and treated unjustly by him: he laid waste the Castilian district of Rioja, and sent a formal defiance to his old enemy, Garcia Ordoñez, Count of Nájera, who did not answer to the challenge.

Until 1092 the Cid had kept up political relations with the Muslim kingdom of Valencia. We have already seen that Alfonso of Castile had placed Qādir, his former ally in Toledo, on the throne of the great city of the east coast (1085–1086). When the Castilian troops left in support of the new King of Valencia were obliged to retire to Castile after the defeat of Zalaca (1086), Qādir felt so insecure on his throne that he sought an alliance with the Muslim King of Saragossa, which was in effect alliance with the Cid. The latter accordingly arrived at Valencia at the head of a mixed army of Muslims and Christians, established Qādir on the throne, defeated the kings and chiefs of Tortosa, Albarracín, Alpuente, and other places close to the Valencian *comarca.* He then concluded a treaty with Qādir, by the terms of which the Muslim monarch paid tribute to him.

In 1092 an event of a nature very common in the kingdoms of the Taifas again brought the Cid into action at Valencia. An insurrection led by the Cadi Ibn-Jahhāf resulted in the capture of the city and the murder of Qādir. Rodrigo intervened, and after many vicissitudes which it is unnecessary to mention here, he captured the city (1094), and for six years retained it as a Christian stronghold and a personal and independent lordship. Under the firm rule and able government of the Cid, Valencia became the impregnable rampart of Spanish power against the attacks of the monarch of the Almorávides, Ibn Tāshfīn, who, had he succeeded in overcoming the Cid's resistance, would have invaded the provinces of Aragon and Catalonia, thus endangering anew the north-east of Spain. But victory always accompanied the Cid, who was not content to remain on the defensive but attacked also, and was constantly intent on strengthening his military situation. For this purpose in 1098 he carried out the conquest of Murviedro (the ancient Saguntum) and Almenara, a little farther to the north, in the present province of Castellón. The petty Muslim kings of the neighbouring districts (Albarracín, Alpuente, etc.) were his tributaries, and the King of Aragon, against whom he had previously fought, and who, as we have seen, had taken the city of Huesca in 1096, now sought an alliance with the Castilian knight.

Rodrigo died in 1099, adored by his soldiers and honoured by the Christian sovereigns of Spain in spite of the ill-will of Alfonso of Castile; by his enemies he was alike feared and praised. He was connected with the Castilian royal family through his wife Jimena; with the house of the Counts of Barcelona by the marriage of his younger daughter, Maria, as we have already seen; and with the Kings of Navarre by the marriage of his elder daughter, Christina, to the Infante Ramiro, lord of Monzón, whence sprang the future King of Navarre (1134), Garcia Ramirez.

In spite of her widowed state, Jimena—an admirable example of moral force not uncommon among the women of medieval Spain—continued to hold Valencia and to repel the repeated attacks of the Almorávides. After three years of struggle, however, she realised that her military situation was becoming precarious, and therefore appealed for help to her cousin King Alfonso. He marched to Valencia with his army; but as he considered the city untenable and required all his forces to repulse the attacks of the Almorávides on Castile, he abandoned it, first setting it on fire (1102), and returned to Castile. He was accompanied by Jimena and her soldiers, bearing with them the body of the Cid, which was buried at San Pedro de Cardeña (Burgos); there too Jimena was interred a few years later. In 1842 their remains were discovered at Burgos, where a monument was erected in 1922.

These, omitting certain non-essential details, are the historical facts of the Cid's life. A great number of legends have sprung up round his name, partly from popular literature beginning with the poem of *Cantar de mio Cid* (the earliest of the poetical works dedicated to Rodrigo now extant, dating from about 1140, *i.e.* forty years after his death) down to the romances of the fifteenth century; their growth has been fostered by the credulity of medieval historians, and the bias shewn by most modern critics. The result has been the creation of a fantastic figure, sometimes adorned with qualities and deeds which were not his, and which are often absolutely foreign to the age in which he lived; at other times blackened by accusations of disloyalty, cruelty, and avarice which do not seem to be warranted either by documents or by historic sources, whether of his own time or a little later. We are beginning to study the actual biography of the man, now that the evolution of the poetic and historical sources has been worked out, and the actual text of the primitive poem settled. The Cid remains the most typical figure of the Spanish warrior in the eleventh century, and the only example in Spanish history of a noble who in his time enjoyed greater political power and military prestige than any contemporary king, notwithstanding the strong personality of Alfonso VI. He was alike a vigorous champion of the work of reconquest so gallantly undertaken by Ferdinand and Alfonso, and a striking proof of the military strength to which the Christians had now attained, and which the Muslims were henceforward unable to destroy.

Although Valencia was lost, Toledo was still in the hands of the Castilians, who continued to repel the incessant attacks of Yūsuf ibn Tāshfīn and his successor 'Alī; and it is indeed surprising that, in spite of several victories won by the Almorávid troops, Castilian territory was never invaded and conquered. In one of these victories, obtained by 'Alī's soldiers in 1108 at Uclés (near Tarancón, in the region of Cuenca, not far from Toledo and Madrid), Alfonso's son Sancho was killed as well as several of the Castilian leaders, and it seemed as though this must be the decisive blow to Castile. Nothing came of it, however, as the King of the Almorávides did not know how to make use of his victory; or perhaps once more his actual forces were capable of winning a single battle but not of effective conquest. There was no panic in Toledo; and most of the Castilian territory including its new frontier lands suffered no injury.

In the following year Alfonso died at Uclés (30 June 1109). This event gave rise to a grave political problem in Castile. The king left as heiress his daughter Urraca, widow of Count Raymond of Franche-Comté (one of the French nobles who had helped in the conquest of Toledo), and mother of a little Alfonso, too young to assume the government of a kingdom. However, custom in Castile and the other Spanish kingdoms recognised the right of a woman to the crown, and from this point of view Urraca would have had no difficulty in ascending the throne. But circumstances called for a warlike king, capable of resisting the redoubled attacks of the Muslims, now that the Cid and Alfonso were dead. The Castilian nobles could find no other solution than to arrange a marriage for Urraca; and in spite of the queen's opposition, they chose as her second husband Alfonso I, King of Aragon. From the military point of view they had chosen well. Alfonso was a valiant warrior, and the union of the Castilian and Aragonese monarchies must necessarily be of assistance in repelling the Almorávides and even in forwarding the task of reconquest. But once again in history, matters of trivial importance brought about the failure of a plan so wisely conceived. In the first place, the characters of the newly-wedded pair were absolutely incompatible, and this in itself was enough to prevent harmonious co-operation. In the second place, Alfonso wished to interfere in the internal government of Castile, and ruffled the patriotic feelings of the Castilians by appointing natives of Aragon and Navarre as commanders of fortresses in the territories belonging to Urraca. Finally, the queen was not a model of conjugal fidelity. Discord culminated in a declaration of the nullity of the marriage by the Pope. The final consequence was that, instead of an increase in the Christian power, there was war, almost a civil war in character, between the Castilians and Aragonese. The situation was rendered more serious by the insurrection of part of the Galician nobility under the leadership of Diego Gelmirez, Bishop of Santiago and lord of a territory of considerable importance, to maintain the cause of Urraca's son, the Infante Alfonso, whom they declared King of Galicia, as had been the wish of his grandfather Alfonso VI. They also tried to crown him King of Leon (1110). A period of absolute anarchy followed. The political and social forces of Castile were profoundly divided and were not only fighting amongst themselves; they were struggling against foreign interference, represented both by the King of Aragon, and by Teresa, Urraca's sister, who was married to Count Henry, a cadet of the Dukes of Burgundy; the latter wished to fish in these troubled waters and so to enlarge the county of Portucale, or Portugal, given to him by Alfonso VI, the history of which will be narrated in another volume of this work.

In this state of anarchy, which persisted until Urraca's death in 1126, we may perceive the expression of the unsettled condition of a society in travail with the evolution of its future unity. This was only achieved, after the removal and absorption of the different factors which had gradually been created by human necessities, by the military effort of reconquest, and by the reconstruction of Christian Spain. In these circumstances it was inevitable that the most characteristic figure in this crisis should be the bishop already referred to, Gelmirez, who, in addition to his high ecclesiastical importance, which the pilgrimages to Compostella are enough to prove, was almost a feudal lord, with a history full of dramatic interest.

The most striking proof of the state of anarchy is presented by the historical obscurity in which Urraca's last years are buried. The lack of documents, and the contradictory accounts given in the few extant, speak volumes as to the troubled condition of the kingdom. On the death of the queen, there was a natural concentration of most of the Castilian forces round prince Alfonso, the sole legitimate heir to the throne, on which he was the seventh of his name.

But the upheaval had been too complete for peace to come at once.

For some time yet Alfonso had difficulties with the Castilian and Galician nobles, who wished to assert their absolute independence; with his step-father, Alfonso of Aragon, with whom he came to terms which cost Castile the territory of Villorado and Calahorra (to the north-east of the present province of Logroño), and the provinces of Guipuzcoa and Alava; and with the Countess Teresa and her son and heir, Alfonso Enriquez, who finally submitted and renewed the feudal oath to Castile (1137).

Three years before this last date, Alfonso I of Aragon died without leaving any direct heir. The Castilian king put forward claims to the Aragonese throne, and invaded first Navarre and the Basque provinces, and later Aragon, seizing the capital, Saragossa (1136); but he relinquished it in 1140, having come to an agreement with the husband of Petronilla, the new Queen of Aragon, that he should be recognised as feudal overlord of the Aragonese kingdom, and that Castile should retain the north-eastern territory up to the Ebro, which thus became the boundary between the two kingdoms on that side.

Alfonso VII now renewed the war against the Muslims, who had naturally benefited from the internal troubles of the Christian kingdoms. Fortunately for the latter, the causes of weakness among the Almorávides and the Arab kingdoms of the north and east which still retained their independence were becoming more and more accentuated. The kings of the Almorávides had become demoralised by the wealth and the mild climate of Southern Spain; they had given up their former hardy and warlike habits, thus producing profound and general discontent among the Muslims, which found expression in constant insurrections and wide-spread anarchy, soon seized on by some bold leaders as an opportunity for declaring themselves independent of 'Alī and his successor Tāshfīn (1143–1145). There was now practically another period of disintegration such as that which followed the fall of the Caliphate of Cordova. At the same time the African possessions of the Almorávides were threatened by a fresh uprising of African tribes, coming this time from the Atlas, who rallied round the banner of religious reform and set up a powerful state. They took the name of Almohades (Muwaḥḥid), which in Arabic means Unitarians, and they demolished the empire of the Almorávides (1125), in spite of the assistance of troops sent to Africa by the monarch resident in Spain.

This new period of decomposition in the Muslim power coincided as regards Castile with the anarchy of Urraca's reign and the early days of Alfonso VII. In Aragon, on the other hand, it corresponded with the reign of Alfonso I, whom his contemporaries surnamed the Warrior (Batallador), and favoured him in his capture of Saragossa (1118) and the neighbouring regions of the north, west, and south. The Muslims tried to recapture Saragossa, but were defeated by Alfonso at Cutanda (1120). This victory emboldened the king, who entered on a campaign of invasion towards Valencia, Murcia, and eastern Andalusia (1125) with few political results; however, he reached the sea at Salobreña (Granada), in 1126 he gained a great battle at Arinsol near Lucena (to the south of the region of Cordova), and he brought back with him 14,000 Mozarabs with whom to people the conquered territory south of the Ebro. Shortly after, he transferred his military effort to the east of his kingdom with the object of conquering the Ebro up to its mouth and securing certain important cities to the north of the river which were not yet in his possession. In 1133 he took Mequinenza and its strong castle (to the south of the district of Lérida), and then moved a little northward to besiege Fraga. The troops which held the place having been reinforced by contingents sent from Cordova, the Aragonese were defeated (July 1134). Alfonso raised the siege and turned to attack the castle of Lizana (Lérida). Here death overtook him on 7 September 1134.

Almost exactly contemporaneous with Alfonso I of Aragon was Raymond-Berengar III, Count of Barcelona, son-in-law of the Cid, and, like him, a bold and fortunate warrior. He too contributed greatly to the work of reconquest and to the enfeeblement of Muslim power. His personal gifts as a conqueror were assisted by the enormous increase in his dominions in Catalonia and the south of France, due to his family relationships with other independent counts, and to his second marriage with Douce of Provence. As a result, by 1123, of all the former Catalan counties there remained none free of the sovereignty of Barcelona, except those of Urgel and Peralada, for that of Ampuria had recognised its vassalage. And, beyond the Pyrenees, the county of Provence had just been joined to the State of Barcelona (1112).

But peaceful gains were not enough for Raymond-Berengar III. In 1106 he wrested the town of Balaguer and its castles from the Muslims. In 1115, in alliance with the republic of Pisa, he made a military expedition to the islands of Majorca and Iviza, by which he gained the vassalage of the Arab governor, and a Balearic poem was composed in praise of his exploits; a little later he invaded the territory of Lérida and Tortosa, where certain dominions were still in the hands of the Muslims, and even entered part of Valencia, but here he did not succeed in making permanent conquests.

The Almorávides did not fail to retaliate, and once even penetrated to the suburbs of Barcelona, but they were defeated in 1114 and 1115. At the death of Raymond-Berengar III, the county of Barcelona was a very strong State by land and by sea, which entertained diplomatic and commercial relations with Italy, and played a part in the politics of Southern France and the Mediterranean. His son, and successor in the Spanish part of his possessions, Raymond-Berengar IV, some years later married Petronilla, Queen of Aragon, as has already been said. This event brought him into contact with Alfonso VII of Castile, who was just resuming the struggle with the Muslims of Andalusia and Estremadura.

After some military expeditions which placed him temporarily in possession of Cordova (1144) and the fortresses of Aurelia (near Ocaña) and Coria, Alfonso laid siege to the city of Almería (1147); in this enterprise he was assisted by the Count of Barcelona and the Genoese navy. A few years before he had secured the castle of Rueda belonging to the Muslim chief Mustanṣir, who was his ally and associate in these expeditions.

These advantages obtained by the various Christian sovereigns provoked a fresh African invasion of Spain. This time it was the Almohades, who, having conquered the Almorávides in Africa, now seemed to offer to the Spanish Muslims, still alive to the claims of their race and religion, the same hope as had formerly been offered by Ibn Tāshfīn. The Almohades arrived in Spain in 1146 at the urgent summons of one of those chiefs who had declared themselves independent of 'Alī, and by 1172 they had already restored unity to the Muslim States by means of the subjection of all the new kings of the Taifas. The last of these to resist the new dependence on the Africans was Ibn Mardanish (Ibn Ṣā'ad), King of Valencia and Murcia (the Wolf King), an ally of the Count of Barcelona, whom he joined against the Almohades; however, the son of Ibn Mardanish submitted to them in 1172. War broke out afresh between the two powers which were intent on contesting the possession of Spain. The chief events of this war took place in the reigns of Alfonso VII's successors.

Alfonso died in 1157. To medieval historians he is known under the surname of Emperor; and indeed he took this title and was crowned as such at Leon in 1135. But he was not the first Spanish monarch who combined the title of Emperor with that of king. Previous to his day, Ferdinand I had been honoured with this dignity, which to Spanish sovereigns represented the same political ideals as it did to those of France and Germany. In Spain, "Empire" also meant a protest and a kind of safeguard against the possibility of a claim to superiority by the German Emperors. Within the limits of Spanish political life, Alfonso had earned the title by the military ascendancy which had brought him the vassalage of, or the recognition of his superiority by, the Kings of Navarre and Aragon, the Counts of Barcelona and Toulouse, and other lords in Southern France, and the already mentioned Muslim chiefs and kings of the Taifas.

Unfortunately for the accomplishment of political unity in Christian Spain, the idea of Empire had as yet no permanency. Emperor was still a personal title, and not a name expressing the highest conception of political unity. Alfonso VII himself hindered the cause by his will, in which he divided his States between his two sons, Sancho and Ferdinand, who became respectively the Kings of Castile and Leon. The final and definitive reunion of the two crowns was thus postponed for sixty-three years, during which there were frequent struggles caused by the ambition of the two sovereigns.

Sancho III, the new King of Castile, whose reign was very short (only a year), spent almost the whole of the time at war with his brother Ferdinand II who wished to seize Castile, and with the Kings of Navarre and Aragon who were upholding their claims as to frontiers.

The political situation became further involved by the death of Sancho. He left a son, Alfonso VIII, aged three years. On this young king were focused the greed of the Christian monarchs neighbouring on Castile, and the rivalries of the Castilian nobles who aspired to hold the office of royal guardian and consequently to exercise political hegemony in the kingdom. The aristocratic forces of Castile and many adventurers and mercenaries collected round two great rival families, the Castro and the Lara. And while bloody civil war was devastating town and country, as usual to the injury of the peaceful population, the King of Leon seized several Castilian cities and fortresses, and the King of Navarre invaded the district of Rioja. This situation of serious danger for Castile lasted for eight years. At last Alfonso VIII succeeded in escaping from the city of Soria, where the Lara were keeping him practically as a prisoner, and, supported by several Castilian nobles who were partisans of neither great rival house, he began a melancholy journey round the free communes to secure their recognition of his sole authority. In 1166 he reached Toledo, where he was acclaimed king when only eleven years of age. This was decisive. Day by day his adherents increased in number, finally enabling him to subdue the unruly nobles, the Castro, the Lara, and others who wished to live in absolute independence. The points at dispute with Aragon were settled by agreement (1170—1177), and the Aragonese king (Alfonso II) helped Alfonso to recover the cities and lands which the King of Navarre had seized in Rioja. Finally in 1180 Alfonso came to terms with his uncle, Ferdinand of Leon. However, the restless character of the men of that day and the ambition of the kings presently caused fresh wars between the Christian kingdoms, particularly on the part of the Kings of Navarre and Leon against Castile; but the support of the King of Aragon (then Peter II) led to a second treaty of peace with the Leonese king (Alfonso IX, son of Ferdinand II) and to the defeat of the King of Navarre, who lost to Castile much territory in the region of the Basque provinces. This considerably reduced the extent of the kingdom of Navarre (1200), and led to the colonisation of several towns on the Cantabrian side (Castro Urdiales, San Vicente de la Barquera, Santander, Laredo, San Sebastian, Fuenterrabia, etc.) by Castilian families. Castile and Leon became allied by the marriage of Berenguela, daughter of Alfonso VIII, with the Leonese King, Alfonso IX.

This long period of strife and warfare between the Christians could not have occurred at a worse time. The Spanish Muslims had been strengthened by African troops of the Almohades and by a fresh concentration of effort, and were attacking the reconquered territory on every side. Almería and Cordova were recaptured and in the west the wave of conquest advanced as far as Alcántara (Estremadura), a stronghold which was only saved by the heroism of the Abbot of Fitero and the monk Fray Diego Velázquez, who preached a successful Castilian crusade. This was the origin of the Military Order of Calatrava, founded in 1164 by Alfonso VIII.

Alfonso had inherited the patriotic and warlike spirit of his grandfather. Even before he had settled the perplexities and difficulties of the internal policy of his kingdom, or his disagreements with his Christian neighbours, he undertook campaigns against the Muslims. To the east, this time with the aid of his namesake of Aragon, Alfonso attacked the stronghold of Cuenca, and took it after a long siege (1177), while simultaneously the Leonese king was making war towards Estremadura and advancing his frontiers on that side of his kingdom. After the success at Cuenca, the Archbishop of Toledo, who like many others was a warrior as well as a prince of the Church, led the recently-formed Knights of Alcántara on an incursion into the districts of Cordova and Jaen, and inflicted heavy loss in life and property on the Muslims; whereupon Ya'qūb, Emperor of the Almohades, wishing to avenge these defeats, sent over a strong contingent of African troops. On the news Alfonso summoned the Cortes to obtain the necessary supplies for the approaching campaign. He also appealed for help to the Leonese and Navarrese. Although this did not come, and the full military resources of Castile had not yet been collected, Alfonso was too impatient to wait, and accepted battle with the powerful army of the Almohades at Alarcos (a little west of the present Ciudad Real) on 18 July 1196, with the result that the Christian army received a crushing defeat. The chronicles speak of 25,000 Spaniards killed or severely wounded. The king himself was forcibly hurried from the field of battle by his faithful followers. The Almohades were free to spread northward and westward; Toledo, Madrid, Alcalá, Cuenca, and other cities were besieged by the conquerors. Seizing their opportunity while Alfonso was in these difficulties, the Kings of Leon and Navarre invaded Castilian territory. Alfonso was obliged to ask the Muslims for a truce; but as soon as the matters in dispute with his neighbours had been settled in 1197 and 1200, he resumed hostilities against the Almohades.

Both sides realised that a critical hour was at hand. The Almohades collected all their available troops. Alfonso VIII appealed for aid to all the Spanish sovereigns, and even to the Count of Portugal and the Holy See. The Pope ordered a Crusade to be preached, whereby many foreign knights and adventurers were attracted to Spain; these, however, almost all deserted soon after the campaign started. There remained with Alfonso only the Spanish forces (except those of Leon), and the Archbishop of Narbonne, who was a native of the Peninsula and had brought with him 150 soldiers. The army left Toledo on 20 June 1212, and after some victories in the course of its march southward—at Malagón, Calatrava,

Alarcos, Piedrabuena, and other places—the Christian troops crossed the Sierra Morena by the pass of Muradal. On the other side, at Las Navas de Tolosa, there awaited them the army of the Almohades led by their emperor himself. The battle took place on 16 July and resulted in a complete victory for the Christians, who secured enormous booty. The road to the south now being clear, the army proceeded to take the castles and towns of Vilches, Ferral, Baños, Tolosa, Ubeda, and Baeza. This triumphant advance towards southern Andalusia was only arrested by the plague, which broke out among the troops; but the Muslim forces had been sufficiently enfeebled by this decisive action. Thus an invasion of Estremadura attempted with some initial success by the Almohade general, Abū Sa'īd, in 1213, was stayed by the defeat of Febragaen. The King of Leon, who had taken no part at Las Navas, profited by this victory to attack in his turn, seizing the important towns of Cáceres, Mérida, and Badajoz (1229).

Alfonso VIII did not live to enjoy all the results of his victory, for he died two years after Las Navas (October 1214); but he had already seen the effects of the Muslim defeat in the beginnings of a fresh disintegration of the Muslim State, which was greatly hastened by the death of the Emperor Yūsuf II ten years later.

In Castile there was likewise a fresh period of dynastic and civil upheaval. Henry I, Alfonso's son, only reigned three troubled years, full of dissensions arising over the guardianship of the king, who was a minor. The crown passed to Berenguela, daughter of Alfonso VIII and divorced wife of Alfonso IX of Leon. Of this marriage was born a son, Ferdinand, to whom Berenguela ceded the throne, but his father Alfonso protested, alleging his own superior rights, as Ferdinand was the son of a marriage which had been dissolved by the Pope. Fortunately the new King of Castile was backed by a very strong party, consisting of all the nobles opposed to the Lara family (which supported Alfonso IX) and most of the communes. In the end he overcame the opposition of the Lara, repelled his father's intervention, and subdued a few nobles who had revolted against the royal authority from a spirit of independence.

Internal peace having been attained, Ferdinand (the third of this name) resumed the war with the Muslims. Circumstances were propitious. The union of the kingdom of Aragon and the principality of Catalonia in the person of Alfonso II of Aragon, son of Queen Petronilla and Count Raymond-Berengar IV, had created a very strong Christian State in the east and north-east of the Peninsula. This already strong power had been augmented by the inheritances of the Counts of Provence (1167–1168) and Roussillon (1217), as well as by the suzerainty acquired over Béarn and Bigorre (1187). In these ways the kingdom of Aragon was gravitating as an international power towards Southern France; and this presently led to important political consequences.

We have already seen that, save for short intervals, Alfonso II had been the ally of Alfonso VIII of Castile during the difficulties which disturbed the latter's reign. He aided him also in the work of reconquest, not only by the support given to the Castilian arms in the attack on the town of Cuenca and other places, but also in the campaigns which he personally undertook and in which he gained the towns of Caspe and Teruel (1170) and secured the districts of Albarracín and Tarragona (outside the city). By his assistance at Cuenca the King of Aragon obtained at the hands of Alfonso VIII his release from the vassalage which bound him to Castile. In 1179 the two monarchs signed a treaty fixing the respective limits of their future conquests in Muslim territory. Aragon was awarded the district of Valencia up to the port of Biar (almost in the centre of the present province of Alicante), a precedent for the frontier agreed on a few years later between Ferdinand III and James I, grandson of Alfonso II.

Alfonso died in April 1196, and his son and successor, Peter II, made yet another addition to his father's States in the shape of the county of Urgel, ceded to him by Countess Elvira (1205), and that of Montpellier, which came to him through his marriage with its heiress, Maria. These additions only served to complicate yet further the political problem created by the possessions of the crown of Aragon north of the Pyrenees. This problem was caused by the proximity of the French kingdom, whose rulers aimed at the mastery of southern France. An occasion of rupture soon offered itself in connexion with the religious situation in this territory, then permeated by the Albigensian doctrines, which were considered heretical by the Catholic Church. Peter was a Catholic, but he was also feudal overlord of the land in which the Albigenses lived and spread their doctrines. Thus, while from a religious point of view he was bound to combat the heretics, from the political point of view he was bound to protect them from all attack, especially if sentiments other than religious were involved; and this was to be feared on the part of the King of France and certain Catholic French nobles. It is thought that the consideration of this danger contributed to a very extraordinary political action on the part of Peter II when he went to Rome to be crowned by the Pope in November 1204. On this occasion the king promised to be the defender of the Catholic Faith, to guard the churches and their immunities, and to prosecute heretics, at the same time acknowledging himself vassal of the Pope, from whom Peter offered to hold in feudal vassalage the States of Aragon and Catalonia, with payment to the Holy See of an annual tribute, in return for the support the Pope would always give to the rulers of Aragon. If, as has also been suggested, the reason for Peter's liberality was merely to secure aid from the Pope and the Genoese and Pisans in his enterprise of conquering the Balearic Isles, it must be owned that the price paid was excessive.

This was certainly the opinion held by most of Peter's Spanish subjects. Nobles and communes alike demanded that the king should cancel the grant made to the Pope, and the king was obliged to yield; but Rome continued to regard the infeudation as valid, and the tribute to the Holy See was paid. Peter II and his vassals in Southern France reaped, however, no advantage from this feudal relationship. Certain Catholic elements proved irreconcilable, and the nobles of Toulouse and Provence resisted all enterprises against their Albigensian vassals, other than the preaching undertaken at this time in Provence by Dominic de Guzman, a Spanish monk who was the founder of the Dominican Order. Matters ended in the organisation of a crusade against the heretics, which was commanded and led by Count Simon de Montfort. The crusaders, who assembled at Lyons and consisted of French troops, advanced into the territory of the Count of Toulouse, then into Provence, and treated the people with unparalleled cruelty, especially the inhabitants of Béziers and Carcassonne, who offered a heroic resistance. No one was spared, no respect being paid to age or sex, and even Catholics fell victims to the fury of the assailants, who were severely blamed by Dominic.

The King of Aragon intervened as peacemaker in defence of his subjects; and although he was powerless to avert the slaughter, his mediation and that of the papal legate succeeded in arranging a convention which ended the war. Peter recognised Simon de Montfort as Lord of Béziers and Carcassonne, in vassalage to him, and a marriage was arranged between his son James and Simon's daughter.

Peace lasted only a very short time. Peter made use of the interval to join in the crusade against the Muslims which resulted in the victory of Las Navas. In 1213 war broke out again in the Toulousain territory, especially against the Count of Toulouse, who was Peter's brother-in-law. Peter again attempted to settle the quarrel by peaceful means, and to this end approached the Pope and the Council which had assembled at Lavaur for the precise purpose of deciding on the claims of the King of Aragon, and which was presided over by the Archbishop of Narbonne. The Council rejected Peter's appeal, and he thereupon declared war against Simon de Montfort in defence of the Count of Toulouse and other Toulousain and Provençal nobles who were his vassals. The only battle took place at Muret (12 September 1213), and in it the king lost his life.

His premature death occasioned a situation of great difficulty for the Spanish kingdom. Peter's only son James was still a child and was in the hands of Simon de Montfort, pending his projected marriage. At first Simon was not disposed to liberate the prince, but the energetic action of the Pope obliged him to give up their legitimate sovereign to the Aragonese and Catalans (1214). The minority of this prince (James I of Aragon and Catalonia) was disturbed by the ambitions of various nobles and members of the royal family. The former wished to assert their independence, the latter to seize the crown. It is unnecessary to mention the numerous vicissitudes of James and his partisans between 1216 and 1227, when a convention with the nobles was signed, terminating the strife which was dislocating the internal life of the kingdom. The personal character of the king, who was brave, energetic and discreet, contributed to increase gradually the number of his adherents, to settle many critical situations, and to ensure his complete success. This result attained, James found himself in a position to take his full share in the work of reconquest. It was about the same time that Ferdinand III of Castile, having overcome political difficulties similar to those of James, also resumed the all-important task of the Christian people of Spain. The two kings worked hand in hand for this object, as had formerly Alfonso VIII of Castile and Alfonso II of Aragon.

Ferdinand's first campaign in 1225 was directed against the territory of Cordova. He seized Andujar and other towns, in preparation for an attack on the capital. With an eye to the future, Ferdinand, who had formed an alliance with Ma'mūn, Emperor of the Almohades, when the latter was dethroned by a successful insurrection, sent an army to Africa to succour him. Ma'mūn was reinstated on his throne (1229), and out of gratitude to the Christian monarch he allowed the Castilians to settle at Marrakash; it appears they did this on the lines of a former emigration which had begun in the ninth century, and the influence of which had been long-lasting. This also served as the base of the Franciscan missions in Morocco.

In 1230, at the death of Alfonso IX of Leon, the two crowns became united in the hands of Ferdinand III, after some difficulties caused by Alfonso's will. Henceforward, Ferdinand could dispose of the military forces of the two great kingdoms in the centre and west of Spain. The day of decisive victory had now dawned and the task was facilitated by the subdivision of the Muslim States. After the death of Yūsuf, indeed, the personal ambitions of the emperor's relatives and captains revived, and several kingdoms arose out of the fragments of the former Almohade State in Spain: one at Valencia of short duration; another in Murcia (1228–1241), which under its king, Ibn Hūd, for a few years comprised most of the territory remaining to the Muslims; a third at Arjona (north-west of Jaen, near Andujar), founded in 1230 by Muḥammad Abū-'Abdallāh al-Ahmar, and increased later by the addition of Jaen, Baza, Guadix, and Granada. This last town was converted by al-Ahmar into the capital of the kingdom (1238), which eventually became the last representative of the al-Ahmar Muslim power, in the hands of the Naṣrid or Naṣrite dynasty, of which al-Ahmar was the founder.

His enemies being thus weakened, Ferdinand III determined to aim at the conquest of Cordova, which he realised in 1236. A few years later, the Muslim King of Murcia, Muḥammad ibn 'Alī, sought for the help of Ferdinand and, in return, offered him vassalage and half the contents of the royal treasury. The Castilian king accepted the offer, as a result of which the kingdom of Murcia, which included the territory of the south-east from Alicante to Alhama, became subject to the crown of Castile (1241). This political success was doubled five years later by the alliance of Muḥammad al-Ahmar of Granada, who, to ensure the safety of his kingdom, ceded to Ferdinand III the city of Jaen (1246), and bound himself to send Muslim troops to assist in carrying on the campaign in Andalusia. Ferdinand next advanced on Seville, where there existed one of the independent kingdoms which had arisen on the disintegration of the Almohade Empire. He took Carmona in 1247, and the Christian squadron commanded by the first Castilian admiral, Raymond de Bonifaz, having destroyed the Muslim fleet which was guarding the Guadalquivir, Seville was invested without any hope of relief. The city surrendered to Ferdinand after fifteen months' resistance, on 22 December 1248, and its surrender occasioned that of Medina-Sidonia, Arcos, Cadiz, Sanlucar, and other cities to the south of the capital. Notwithstanding this great success, which left him master of the whole of southern Spain except Granada and a small tract of territory in the south-west near Huelva, Ferdinand did not consider his task ended. Like all those who have thoroughly understood the danger to Spanish independence presented by the existence of an important political power in northern Africa, the King of Castile wished to prosecute the war beyond the Straits of Gibraltar, so as to destroy the possibility of a reaction of Muslim elements against Spain. But before he was able to realise the projected expedition, he died at Seville on 30 May 1252. With him there ended the period of great Castilian conquests in the Muslim dominions, only to be resumed two centuries later.

At the same time that Ferdinand III was attacking the south and south-east, James I of Aragon was carrying on the work of reconquest to the east. His first objective was the Balearic Isles. Majorca was famous for the fertility of its soil, and feared as a nest of pirates which rendered navigation in the western Mediterranean dangerous. James appealed to the nobles of his Aragonese States, but they did not look with favour on the expedition; the king, however, firmly convinced of the political and economic advantages to be gained, persisted and secured the co-operation of certain nobles and cities in Catalonia and Southern France. The Cortes which assembled in Barcelona in 1228 decided on the conquest of Majorca, which was quickly achieved, as James entered the capital of the island on 31 December 1229. In view of this success of the Christians, the Muslims of Minorca capitulated (1232), and in 1235 Iviza was conquered by the Archbishop of Tarragona and some Catalan nobles. The possession of the Balearic Islands secured for Barcelona a large share of Mediterranean commerce, and prepared the way for future military and economic exploits by Catalonia in the south of Europe. The territories of the islands were divided between the leaders of the expedition and colonised by settlers from the Peninsula, especially from the north of

Catalonia (Ampurdan), who brought with them their language, their civilisation, and their commercial spirit.

In the same year that Majorca was taken, an Aragonese noble, Blasco de Alagon, undertook an expedition on his own account into the mountainous territory north-west of Valencia, and captured the stronghold of Morella. James, who had likewise started an enterprise against the Muslims of Valencia in the direction of Ares, did not approve of this dangerous kind of independence, and betook himself to Morella with the intention of making Blasco give up the town, which should belong to no one but the king. Blasco was obliged to yield, whereupon James bestowed the town on him as a fief. The king prosecuted the campaign with the help of only a few of the lords and cities of Catalonia; but as his victories in the direction of Valencia continued, and the city itself was besieged (1238), most of the nobles and communes of Aragon and Catalonia finally joined in sending troops and militia. The capital surrendered in September of the same year, and this triumph was followed by the capture of Xativa, a very strong place, Alcira, and other towns in the plain of Valencia. The king divided the territory between the nobles who had helped in the campaign. The Muslim population remained in the country districts; but there were two revolts in the course of a few years, especially in the mountainous regions to the south and west, and their suppression necessitated much military effort.

When he had secured the Valencian region as far as Biar (Villena was conquered in 1240), James' share in the work of reconquest was ended, as the old convention of 1179 was ratified at Almizra in 1244. This established a frontier starting at the confluence of the rivers Jucar and Cavriel near the town of Cofrentes, bent to the south between Xativa, which remained in James' hands, and Enguera, then passed near the dry port of Biar in the district of Alicante, and ended at the Mediterranean, a little south of the *comarca* of Denia. But in 1261 the Muslims of Murcia revolted against the Castilian yoke, which had weighed on them since the pact of 1241. Then King Alfonso X of Castile, son and successor of Ferdinand III and son-in-law of James, appealed to the latter for help against the Murcians, who with the support of the Muslims of Granada were threatening the territory belonging to the King of Aragon. James sent the required help, and, while Alfonso was fighting the Murcian Muslims on one side, James crossed the frontiers fixed in 1244 and seized the cities of Alicante, Elche, and in 1266 Murcia itself, thus securing all the Murcian region for the Castilian crown. The Muslims now only retained the new kingdom of Granada, which included the province of that name and those of Almería and Málaga as far as Gibraltar. The reconquest of Spain was virtually accomplished. James could now venture to take part in a crusade to Palestine (1269), which was a failure, although a part of the expedition which reached Acre gave valuable help to the Christians who were defending the city against the Muslims. In another expedition, the Catalan fleet captured the town of Ceuta, but its possession was not maintained.

The natural development of the kingdoms of Castile and Aragon to the south blocked the path of Navarre and kept it isolated in the Pyrenees. In spite of the constant effort of many of her kings to increase their states at the expense of Castilian territory, Navarre saw her political power in the Peninsula steadily on the wane. From 1076 to 1134 she was united to Aragon, but regained her independence on the death of Alfonso I. During the remainder of the twelfth and early years of the thirteenth century, her monarchs continued, with some intervals of peace, their struggles with Castile and Aragon. The last Spanish King of Navarre, Sancho VII, at first pursued the same policy as his predecessors; but afterwards he helped Alfonso VIII in the Andalusian campaign (at the battle of Las Navas), and in the agreement of Tudela (February 1231) with James I of Aragon he betrayed a desire to appoint the latter heir to the Navarrese throne. But James did not take advantage of this opportunity, and the Navarrese chose as their king Sancho's nephew Theobald IV, Count of Champagne (1234). Henceforth, for many years the history of Navarre falls out of the main current of Spanish history.

The period between 1034 and 1248 is as important from the point of view of the history of institutions, wealth, and general civilisation in Spain, as it is from the military point of view and that of the reconquest which we have hitherto been considering. Great progress was made in all departments of social life, while simultaneously were being revealed more and more clearly the bases of the future greatness of the Spanish people, and of the originality of its legal, literary, and artistic achievement. In this process of settlement of the new elements of life created by the special circumstances of the time, by the effort to reconstruct a Western and Christian society, and by the Eastern influences emanating from the Arabs and the Jews, the different provinces of Spain followed diverse paths, and according to their character developed special qualities and institutions. But the movement of progress was not rhythmical and equal in all these provinces.

Thus the evolution of Castile and Leon was much more democratic and advanced, taken as a whole, than that of other parts of Spain. In the first place, the noble class became increased by the development of its lower grade, the secondary nobility, through the enlargement of the class of the former *Infanzones*, to whom was applied the new name of *Fijosdalgo* (whence the term *Hidalgo*), and by the admission to the rank of knight of every freeman who was able to keep a horse, *i.e.* able to become a military factor of the first class in the warfare of the period. Secondly, the repopulation of the lands taken from the Muslims, the security for a settled existence acquired as the frontiers advanced southward, and the increased possibility every year of cultivating the soil and establishing the industries necessary for the economic needs of the new or enlarged towns, served to re-create a middle class, as well as a class of free workmen and industrial employees who were to form the backbone of society in the communes snatched from the former seignorial jurisdiction. Finally, the rural Christian serfs who were the basis of agricultural life, and who until the end of the twelfth century represented a large and socially subject class, gradually became released from many of the bonds limiting their personal freedom, and developed into free workers, whence there soon emerged a rural democracy. A document of 1215 signed by Alfonso IX of Leon marks the beginning of this legal evolution, which, by the close of the thirteenth century, had generally bestowed on the former serfs the right of leaving the estates of their lords and of not being sold along with the land, had established the validity of their marriages without the necessity of obtaining their lord's consent, and had fixed the exact amount of dues in kind, in money, or in labour owed to their masters. The frequent revolts of serfs in lay and ecclesiastical lordships, and even of the free population in seignorial towns, shew very clearly the painful and sustained effort to obtain these improvements. Only, as is to be seen in all the legal documents of the period, the servitude of Muslim prisoners of war was still very hard, in contrast to the liberties granted to the Arab populations admitted into the Christian social structure, as will presently be shewn.

Conditions were different in Aragon and Catalonia. In Aragon during the thirteenth century there was a reaction which kept long depressed the condition of rural labourers, whether Christian or Muslim (*exaricos*). A document emanating from the Cortes of Huesca in 1245 shews that the lords enjoyed very harsh rights, extending to the absolute power of killing their serfs by starvation or cold. In Catalonia the serfs (*payeses*) were crushed by dues and personal services, to which were given the name of "evil usages." By the thirteenth century they had only obtained the possibility of purchasing their liberty by paying a sum of money (*redimentia* or *remensa*). In Catalonia the total liberation of this social class did not come about until the fifteenth century, and in Aragon later still.

On the other hand, the middle class enjoyed a greater development and a higher importance in Catalonia than elsewhere. This was the result of both the industrial and the commercial progress of the country, and naturally was mainly found on the coast, where the most prosperous towns were situated. It was this class that gave birth to the great Catalan expansion of future centuries. In Catalonia there was also an intermediate class between the serfs and the bourgeois of the communes, consisting of men who were free in law but who were dependents of noble landowners (*homes de paratje*), which was eventually to form a kind of agrarian middle class and to play a very important part.

Gradually, as Christian territory increased, two new elements of population were added to the original stock: the Mozarabs, who became incorporated in the Christian society by the conquest of the cities they inhabited (*e.g.* Toledo) or by emigration (*e.g.* those brought to Aragon by Alfonso I), and the free Muslims (*mudéjares*), whose personal and fundamental rights were respected by the conquerors in the treaties of capitulations of cities. The autonomous rights which these two kinds of population for centuries enjoyed are a very characteristic feature of Spanish life in the Middle Ages. Both alike brought very marked influences of civilisation and manners.

A third foreign element was also imported by the reconquest, which created so many fresh needs. This was the Jewish element. The Jews were very numerous and very prosperous in Muslim districts until the end of the twelfth century, when there was an outbreak of religious fanaticism against them, especially after the arrival of the Almohades in Spain; and this policy, ruthlessly applied during the later years of the period under consideration, caused a flood of Jewish emigration to the Christian kingdoms, into which they had already been introduced by the reconquest of several towns where they formed important communities. Christian society in Spain did not reject them. On the contrary, they were received very cordially and were granted legal and religious autonomy similar to that enjoyed by the *mudéjares*. This liberty, which continued until the beginning of the fourteenth century, attracted the Jews in vast numbers. In Toledo there were as many as 12,000. Alfonso VI allowed them to become eligible for public offices. They played a great part in commerce, in certain industries, and, above all, in intellectual life, as intermediaries between Oriental science and literature and European civilisation, which was still in a backward condition. They were thus the natural intermediaries between Christians and Muslims in treaties, alliances, and the like, and they were often found in the armies of Castile and other Spanish kingdoms.

In the political world, the struggle between the monarchy, now frankly hereditary, and the nobles still continued. Various instances of this struggle have been referred to in the history of several of the kings. The power represented by the nobles is reflected in the legislation which particularly concerns them, such as the code of the Usages (*Usatici*) of Catalonia, which is to a great extent a feudal code. Leon, Castile, and Navarre all have laws belonging to the same category.

On the other hand, the development of the communes, which was favoured by the kings, gave birth to a political element opposed to the nobles; this in one way made the State more democratic, in another furthered the triumph of the monarchy and thus paved the way for despotism. The solid autonomy of the communes and the important rights acquired by the townsmen are very well expressed in their special legislation of charters (*fueros*), of which some are complete codes (Cuenca, Cáceres, Teruel, Valencia). At the same time there were compilations of local customs (Lérida, Tortosa), and of those common to whole provinces (Aragon, Catalonia). Some very important communes had their private legislation, consisting of a body of various laws and customs, though not codified till later. Gradually there also began to appear the regulations issued by the communal assemblies, which constituted a considerable addition to the *fueros* issued by the kings or other lords.

The political importance acquired by the communes is expressed above all in two institutions, of which one was peculiar to them, and the other received its particular character from the intervention in it of the bourgeois element. These were the local Confraternities (*Hermandades* and *Comunidades*) formed by the towns against the nobles and against evil-doers, who were often soldiers thrown out of employment by the cessation of war, and the *Cortes* of the realm. The *Hermandades* or *Comunidades* existed in all parts of the Peninsula. In the first place they were the expression of the political sense of the communes, who recognised the advantage of co-operation in guaranteeing and defending their rights; in the second place, they provided a police force in days when the central authority had not enough power to enforce respect for the lives and property of its subjects.

The *Cortes* were formed by the old nucleus of the assemblies (*conventus, curiae, concilia*) of nobles and ecclesiastics, summoned by the king, with the addition of delegates from the communes. This took place for the first time in Leon, in the reign of Alfonso IX (1188). At this period in no other country of Europe did the townsmen thus participate in one of the most important political functions of the State. This innovation was paralleled in Aragon (1163?), Catalonia (1218), Castile (1250?), and Valencia (1283). Navarre had no democratic *Cortes* at this time. The *Cortes* prove not only how much political importance already attached in the twelfth century to the middle class which inhabited the towns, but also its social and economic importance. Indeed, the principal and most characteristic duty of the *Cortes* was the voting of the taxes demanded by the king—the first beginnings of the financial function of parliaments. They also possessed the right of demanding from the king the enactment of new laws or the repeal of existing ones, and they intervened at certain grave moments in political history, such as the succession to the crown, the appointment of Councils of Regency, the oath of new sovereigns, and the like. In practice, political circumstances presented opportunities of still more extended intervention to the *Cortes*, and especially to the bourgeois element.

Nevertheless, the communal power tended to encourage privilege, as each city aimed at having a statute to itself, the most favourable possible, and local codes of law. But in the thirteenth century the influence of Roman law intervened to arrest this disintegration of legal life. This influence found expression in a tendency to issue codes or compilations of law of general application. In Castile, Ferdinand III ordered the issue of a code (*Sentenario*) which did not acquire the force of law, but which paved the way for the great reforms of his son, Alfonso X. In Aragon, James I issued a compilation (*Compilación de Canellas*, or *de Huesca*), which, in addition to a summary of the legal principles of traditional Aragonese law, gave as supplementary sources natural sense and equity, which, in view of the university education of the jurists, meant Roman law. At the royal court the *Compilación* was regarded as the source of jurisprudence, but it did not abrogate the *fueros* of the cities. In Catalonia Roman law, as it existed previous to Justinian, was traditionally applied as supplementary. In spite of the lively opposition to Romanism, especially by the nobles (laws of 1243 and 1251), Roman law gradually assumed greater importance, which led to the unification of legislation. The new Justinianean law of the jurists is reflected in the code of the Customs of Tortosa.

By the side of the monarchy, the nobles, and the communes, the Church appears as one of the strongest moral and social forces. She was no more so in Spain than in the other countries of Europe. It is even noteworthy that the unifying and centralising movement of the Papacy, represented in south-western Europe by the Order of Cluny, was met in Spain by a strong national resistance, especially in the provinces of Castile and Leon. The very picturesque episode of the changing of the traditional Mozarabic rite for the Roman is a good demonstration of this resistance. The establishment of the Inquisition in the kingdom of Aragon was, moreover, only an episode in the movement of intolerance which was sweeping gradually over the Christian world. The name and personality of Dominic de Guzman so closely associated with it are much more characteristic of the period than of the nation. Perhaps the most characteristic feature in the social life of the Church in Spain was the growth of the immunities or privileges, personal and real (as regards taxes and landed property), which strengthened the economic and political power of the clergy.

Any picture of Spain in these ages would be incomplete without an examination of its intellectual life, in the particularly original spheres of literature, the plastic arts, philosophy, and law. But these points will be dealt with in the various chapters devoted to the general history of medieval civilisation. We shall then see the important part played in almost all these spheres by the influence of the East, which had so strong a centre in Spain, and among the Muslims and Jews there.

For this reason Spain played a very important part in Europe in assimilating and spreading to other Christian countries the civilisation of the East, which in its turn enshrined many classical elements gained by contact with the vestiges of the Greek and Latin world in Asia and Egypt. It was thanks to Christian Spain and the liberal hospitality she extended to Arab and Jewish philosophers, physicians, and writers, that Europe received the first impulses of her intellectual renaissance. Meanwhile, the Spain of the reconquest, by continual crusades against the

Muslims, was the strongest rampart for the rest of Europe, and saved the Christian world from an invasion which would otherwise have been easier on the Western side. The answer given by one of the Castilian kings to some one who sought his co-operation in the crusades in the East, was therefore justified: "We are always on crusade here, and so we do our share."

CHAPTER XIII.

(A.)

BOHEMIA TO THE EXTINCTION OF THE PŘEMYSLIDS.

At the time when the medieval Empire was gradually crumbling into small territorial states, a new state, situated as one might say in the heart of Europe, comes into the foreground of central European history. Distinguished from its more easterly neighbours, Poland and Hungary, by its close legal relations with the German Empire, it yet differs from all the principalities of that Empire in its characteristic nationality and its almost complete independence in internal affairs. This is the kingdom of Bohemia, which from the beginning of the eleventh century is indissolubly united with its neighbour Moravia, and in the fourteenth century extends its boundaries to include even Silesia and both the Lusatias.

At the period in which Bohemia begins to play a considerable part in central European history, and indeed long before this, we find in Bohemia and Moravia, if we disregard the not unimportant German minority, a Slav population very closely related to the Poles. The Slavs were, however, by no means the first inhabitants of these countries; for we learn, partly from the discoveries of archaeologists, partly from the writings of old chroniclers, that both lands were inhabited centuries before the immigration of the Slavs. Of the various peoples who had succeeded each other in Bohemia and Moravia before the advent of the Slavs, none of whom are of any importance for the later development of the country, we need only mention the Celtic Boii and the Germanic Marcomanni and Quadi. Of these, the Celts inhabited both the countries which later became Slavonic, or at any rate a large part of them, for about five hundred years before, the Germans for about five hundred years after the birth of Christ. Although recent archaeological discoveries seem to shew with ever increasing certainty that there were Slavs dwelling in Bohemia and Moravia at least as early as the time of Christ, if not before, still it is only after the beginning of the sixth century that we have historical proof of their presence in Bohemia. Towards the end of that century they fell under the dominion of the Avars, whose rule, however, cruel though it was, did not last for long. They shook off the Avar rule about the year 623, under the leadership of a Frankish merchant named Samo, who became king of the liberated Slavs. Samo's kingdom was not limited to Bohemia; but its extent cannot be accurately determined, and we know little of its internal affairs. On Samo's death (about 658) his great kingdom also collapsed.

In the following centuries, it is only by much later popular tradition, and, after the end of the eighth century, by occasional references in the writings of Frankish chroniclers, that any light is thrown upon Bohemia and Moravia. From these, we see no sign that the country was in any way a unitary state. The Slavs who had settled in Bohemia are certainly mentioned in Frankish sources, from the end of the eighth century, under the general name of "Beehaimi," "Boemani," and the like, denoting clearly the inhabitants of "Behaim" or "Boihaemum," that is, the land formerly settled by the Boii. But it is none the less certain that neither at that time nor for long after did the Slavs create a united kingdom in Bohemia, but they were split up into a considerable number of small tribes each ruled by its own prince. In the centre of Bohemia, round about the later capital, Prague, dwelt the race of true Bohemians (in Slavonic Čechs), who were destined later to combine all the tribes which had settled in the land into one state and one nation, and were to give it their name. This name the old legend derived from a certain Čech, first progenitor of the race, who is said to have led his people out of the east to their new home. Later, according to the legend, there appears at the head of the race the wise Libuša, whose chosen husband, the farmer Přemysl, was founder of the princely house of the Přemyslids, the house which, as time went on, gathered into its hands the overlordship of all Bohemia and Moravia, and ruled both countries until its extinction in 1306.

The union of the small Slavonic tribes in Bohemia and Moravia was indeed only gradually achieved, and required the co-operation of many different factors. In Moravia, the progress towards unification was more rapid than in Bohemia proper. As early as the first half of the ninth century, we find a united kingdom of Moravia, with prince Mojmír at its head. It included, besides Moravia, probably the northern portion of the later Austria, and certainly the western portion of the modern Slovakia. Mojmír's successor, Rastiz or Rostislav (about 846 onward), under whose rule the power of the Great Moravian kingdom was still further increased, won an important place in history through his services in the conversion of his people to Christianity. The Christian faith had indeed been known before this to the Slavs who inhabited Bohemia and Moravia, chiefly through German, and more particularly Bavarian, priests. From a contemporary source we learn, for instance, that in 845 certain Bohemian princes, with their followers, were baptised at Ratisbon. Rostislav himself also was a Christian. But among the people generally the new faith, preached as it was in a foreign tongue by German priests, was little comprehended. Accordingly Prince Rostislav, who was clearly actuated by the desire not only to establish the Christian faith in his dominions, but also to shake himself free from dependence upon the episcopate of Bavaria, turned, about 860, to Pope Nicholas I, and requested him to send teachers of the Christian faith competent to explain its leading principles in a way which the people might understand. When Rome, probably for the reason that no such teachers could be found, failed to comply with this request, Prince Rostislav caused the same petition to be laid before the Greek Emperor Michael at Constantinople.

So it came about that the Slavs of Bohemia and Moravia were brought into relations with the Greek East; relations which, though only transitory, were of the highest importance.

At Constantinople the desired teachers were in fact discovered in the persons of the two brothers, Constantine, later called Cyril, and Methodius[1]. Though Greek by birth, both were masters of the Slavonic tongue, for it was at that time spoken in Thessalonica, their native town, and in the districts round. To equip himself adequately for his labours in Moravia, Constantine, whose wide erudition had gained him the name of the "Philosopher," constructed, before he left Constantinople, a purely Slavonic alphabet—the so-called Glagolitic script—and translated the chief liturgical texts into Slavonic. After these preparations the brothers Constantine and Methodius journeyed to Moravia, about the year 863, there to begin the successful labours which won for them the honourable title of the apostles of the Slavs. By their means Moravia was completely Christianised, and its neighbour Bohemia, following its example, was also won over permanently to the Christian faith. But the exceptional importance of the brothers' efforts lies in the fact that, while they introduced Christianity, they, at the same time, brought the Gospels in the Slavonic tongue. Constantine and Methodius were thus the founders of the Slavonic church literature which, if in Bohemia and Moravia it soon died out, bore more abundant fruit among other Slavonic peoples.

At the papal court the activity of the two brothers met, in the first instance, with full approval. When Constantine, who had retired to a monastery in Rome and had adopted the name of Cyril, died during his residence there (869), Methodius was appointed first bishop, later archbishop, and was made head of a province which was considered as a revival of the old metropolitan see of Sirmium, and included, besides, the whole of Moravia. The clergy of Bavaria, who felt that their rights were thus curtailed and their material interests threatened, violently opposed the new archbishop. He was in fact for two and a half years held prisoner in Germany; but he succeeded none the less in maintaining his position.

The lordship of Moravia passed meanwhile from Rostislav to his nephew, the energetic Svatopluk (Zwentibold), in 870, who soon subdued to himself both the Bohemians in the west and the Slavonic Sorbs in the north, and enjoyed such great prestige among his contemporaries that he is often referred to as king. With Archbishop Methodius, Svatopluk maintained at first complete accord, and for political reasons, with a view to making his dominions independent of Germany in ecclesiastical affairs, supported him in all his struggles. But, as time went on, relations between them became strained, for Svatopluk inclined more and more to the archbishop's opponents, the Frankish priests, who made use of the Latin

[1] See *supra*, Vol. IV, chap. VII (B).

liturgy. The enmity between the supporters of the Latin and the Slavonic liturgies, which was inflamed also by disputes on matters of dogma arising out of the antagonism then beginning between Rome and Constantinople, did not cease even after the death of Methodius (885). When, however, in the same year, Pope Stephen V issued an edict by which the use of the Slavonic liturgy, expressly approved by his predecessors, was absolutely forbidden, and, as a result, a bitter persecution of the followers of Methodius was begun, with the full support of Svatopluk, and they were banished from the country, the last hope of establishing the Slavonic liturgy was gone. But the Great Moravian kingdom itself had no long life. Immediately after Svatopluk's death (894), it began to fall to pieces, and after a few years was destroyed by the Magyars (about 906).

The downfall of the Great Moravian kingdom was an event of the highest importance for the whole future history of Bohemia and Moravia. Above all, as a result, the connexion of the Slavonic peoples of those countries with Constantinople, established by the summons of the brothers Constantine and Methodius to Moravia, was entirely severed, and they were definitely and permanently brought within the sphere of West European civilisation. This is shewn most clearly in the further development of the Church in Bohemia and Moravia. The whole administration of the Church fell now under Western, and German, influence, and the Latin liturgy consequently won a complete victory. The Slavonic liturgy did not, it is true, disappear all at once; yet it held its ground only in a few monasteries, and even from them it was entirely expelled before the end of the eleventh century. It is true that in the fourteenth century the great King of Bohemia, the Emperor Charles IV, did establish in Prague a special monastery for the Slavonic liturgy, but the activities of this monastery, artificial in their inception, had no deep-seated connexion with earlier ages, nor had they any considerable influence upon the contemporary development of Bohemian civilisation.

Through the fall of the Great Moravian kingdom, the orientation of the political history of Bohemia and Moravia was changed. Its earlier development seemed to be leading up to a federation of the Slavs in Bohemia and Moravia, and also of the Slovaks, into a Slavonic kingdom of which the modern Moravia would have formed the centre; but such a development was henceforth permanently out of the question. The Slovaks were severed for centuries from political union with Bohemia and Moravia, and if the federation of these last two countries was certainly soon re-established, the centre of gravity of this new Bohemian-Moravian kingdom lay no longer in Moravia but in Bohemia. Here, in the course of the tenth century, is built up, by the subjection of all the old races under the rule of the Přemyslids, a homogeneous state, into which, in the first half of the following century (about 1029), Moravia also is permanently incorporated.

But another result of the collapse of the Great Moravian kingdom was that Bohemia and Moravia were brought into more intimate relations with the Romano-German Empire. As early as the reign of Charles the Great, probably about 805, Bohemia, or a part of it, fell under the overlordship of the Frankish kingdom, and was forced, apparently, to pay a yearly tribute (120 oxen and 500 silver marks). Soon after, Moravia also fell into complete dependence upon the East Frankish kingdom. The mighty Svatopluk himself was forced after long struggles, not only to swear life-long allegiance, but also to submit to the payment of an annual tribute (874). Still neither Bohemia nor Moravia was incorporated in the administrative organisation of the East Frankish realm; they kept their own princes who had full control of internal affairs. In the last years of Svatopluk, when Bohemia was a part of his kingdom, German overlordship in both lands lost practically all its significance. After Svatopluk's death, the Bohemian dukes broke away from his kingdom and gave in their allegiance to King Arnulf (895), yet, on the speedy collapse of the East Frankish kingdom, Bohemia was freed from its position of dependence.

However, as soon as the efforts of King Henry I had established a new German kingdom, Bohemia fell once more into its former dependence upon it. King Henry, by marching on Prague, forced the Bohemian Duke, St Wenceslas, to acknowledge his suzerainty (929). Wenceslas' brother and successor, Boleslav I (929–967), who had attained the throne by his murder, tried in vain to shake off the German over-lordship. After several years of resistance, he was compelled, when the Emperor Otto I invaded Bohemia, to agree to pay the old tribute and to recognise the suzerainty of the German Empire (950). From that time Bohemia became a fief of the German Empire and the Bohemian dukes became its vassals, bound to take part in the Emperor's campaigns and to attend the royal court.[1]

About a hundred years after the subjection of Boleslav I, the brave Duke Břatislav I (1034–1055), who during the reign of his father Oldřich (Udalrich) had succeeded in permanently uniting Moravia and Bohemia, and had later rendered himself for a time even master of part of Poland, made a fresh attempt to free himself from Germany; but he too was compelled by King Henry III once more to swear allegiance (1041). From that time the Dukes of Bohemia never again tried to shake off German overlordship; they fulfilled without resistance their obligations towards the Empire, and their relations with the German kings and emperors were for the most part friendly.[2] Břatislav's son, Duke Vratislav II (1061–1092), was a loyal supporter of King Henry IV in his frequent campaigns in Germany and Italy; in 1081 three hundred Bohemian men-at-arms distinguished themselves by their courage at the siege of Rome. As a reward

[1] For the relations of Bohemia with Germany from 919 to 1056 see *supra*, Vol. III, Chaps. VIII, IX, X, XI, XII.

[2] See *supra* Vol. V, chap. III.

for his loyal services the Emperor Henry, at a Diet of the Empire at Mayence in 1085, granted him the title of King of Bohemia, although only as a personal privilege. In connexion with this, but probably a few years earlier (about 1081), the German Emperor seems to have remitted the old tribute due from the King of Bohemia, in consideration of his sending three hundred fully-equipped men-at-arms to join in the Emperor's expedition to Rome.

On the death of the first King of Bohemia, Vratislav, the dignity of kingship was indeed lost to the country, but even then the Bohemian rulers were considered as among the most important of the princes of the Empire. From the beginning of the twelfth century (for the first time in the year 1114), we find the Dukes of Bohemia in hereditary possession of the office of cupbearer to the Emperor (*summus pincerna*), an office which procured for them an ever-increasing influence on the affairs of the Empire. Duke Vladislav II (1140–1173), in particular, acquired great authority. Following the example of King Vratislav, he zealously supported the German Emperor Frederick I Barbarossa in his warlike undertakings. In 1158 he descended in person with a large army into Italy, to give assistance to the Emperor against the North Italian towns, and took a prominent part in the capture of Milan. Even before this campaign, in which the reckless valour of Vladislav's Bohemian army performed wonders, the Duke of Bohemia had been crowned king by the Emperor at a Diet at Ratisbon (January 1158). He obtained thereby an honourable privilege by which not only he, but also his successors, were granted the right to wear the royal crown. Bohemia should thus have become an hereditary monarchy, but struggles for the succession broke out even in Vladislav's lifetime, and the Bohemian monarchy once more lapsed. Not until a quarter of a century had passed was it to be restored (1198) to a new and this time lasting existence.[1]

If Bohemia was, from the tenth century, a fief of the German Empire, yet its position differed in many and important particulars from that of other vassals. While with other vassals the right of heredity was only a gradual development, the Bohemian ducal office was considered from the very beginning to be the hereditary possession of a single princely family the Přemyslids. There was, however, no clearly-settled law of succession. In the earliest times of the united Bohemian state, in the tenth century, the dukedom passed in succession from the father to his eldest son, who at that time happened to be the oldest male member of the family Later the principle obtained that the oldest male member of the family should always ascend the throne. But this principle, which was hardly ever considered to have the authority of a formal law—the old view that Břatislav I had, in 1055, promulgated such a law, the so-called Law of

[1] For the relations of Bohemia with Germany from 1125 to 1190 see *supra*, Vol. v, Chaps x and xii.

Seniority, is entirely without foundation—was not adhered to in practice. There was bound to be, therefore, in every separate case, a difference of opinion as to which of the Přemyslids should succeed to the throne. The first word on this matter lay with the Bohemian nobles, particularly those who, as governors of the ducal castles, ruled the land with armed force to back them. The Kings of Germany were accustomed only to confirm the election and to invest the new duke with the fief of Bohemia. But the struggles for the throne, which usually arose owing to the lack of a definite ordinance regulating the succession, gave the German kings very frequently the opportunity of exercising a directly decisive influence upon the election. This influence reached its highest point during the struggles for the succession after the death of King Vladislav I. At that time, the Emperor Frederick I granted Bohemia as a fief now to one, now to another of the Přemyslids, according as they succeeded in winning his favour by gifts of money or by other means, and acted as if he alone had the right to decide who should occupy the throne of Bohemia. Matters came to such a point that in 1182 the Emperor ordered the Dukes Frederick and Conrad Otto, two claimants of the throne who were at the time in the field against one another, to appear before his tribunal at Ratisbon; and there he declared the former to be Duke of Bohemia, but granted to the latter Moravia as a margravate independent of Bohemia, and owing allegiance directly to the Empire. Until that time Bohemia and Moravia formed a single state, even though by old custom separate domains, especially in Moravia, had been allotted to the younger princes of the ruling family; but now they were to be transformed into two principalities of the Empire independent of each other. The Emperor's policy, however, did not attain its end. Moravia, after 1182, certainly always remained a margravate, and even its direct dependence on the Empire, established by the Emperor Frederick, did not very quickly fall into oblivion; yet in practice, even before the end of the twelfth century, it became once more an integral part of the unified kingdom of Bohemia and Moravia. It still, indeed, retained its own margraves—often the King of Bohemia himself held the title of margrave—but at the same time it always recognised the overlordship of the Bohemian king. Nor did the German kings retain the influence over the appointment to the Bohemian throne which had been won in the time of Frederick Barbarossa. The ruinous struggles for the throne in Bohemia ceased at the end of the twelfth century; and from this very fact the imperial influence in the election henceforward lost its importance. Soon after, the German kings themselves were compelled formally to renounce it.

The independence of the Empire which Bohemia displayed in the matter of the appointment of its rulers, an independence greater than that enjoyed by any other imperial princedom, is reflected clearly in the whole character of the Bohemian principality and in the internal organisation of the Bohemian State. Although a fief of the Empire, Bohemia was never directly part of the imperial organisation. The Frankish, and later the German, system never extended to Bohemia, which was never a mere administrative district governed by imperial officials. The Bohemian dukes were vassals of the German Emperor, but not his officials. Their power was not derived from the higher authority of the Emperor, but originated in themselves. It was neither limited by the interference of his higher imperial authority in the internal organisation of the land, nor was it weakened by the exemption from their rule of certain classes of people, or certain domains, directly subordinated to the Empire. They held sway over the whole land and over all their subjects, without distinction. In internal affairs, the Bohemian dukes were entirely independent rulers; they exercised freely, from the first, all those prerogatives of sovereignty which other princes of the Empire won for themselves only after many a year.

But further, in the period which immediately followed the foundation of a united Bohemian State, there was no man, even in the land itself, whose rights might limit the power of the duke. His authority was there legally unlimited. His was the sole decision over war and peace; he called out the troops equally for home defence and for a campaign abroad, and exacted obedience by force of arms. To the duke belonged also the supreme judicial power in the land; and to it all the inhabitants of the country without exception—including even the clergy—were subject. In this the duke found naturally a rich source of income, through fines, confiscation of goods, and the like. From his subjects he exacted at his will and pleasure various services and forced labours (for the construction and repair of castles, bridges, and roads, for the lodging and victualling of the royal household, etc.) as well as divers taxes in money and in kind. In addition to an annual "peace tax" (*tributum pacis*, Bohemian *mír*), levied in money, which from the time of the foundation of the united Bohemian State was probably paid by all free landowners, the duke exacted also exceptional taxes of his own authority. So too the establishment of tolls, customs, and markets, as well as the coining of money, was the privilege of the duke alone. He also possessed very extensive domains, which were cultivated by his numerous slaves, and he was considered to be lord of all uncultivated ground; of this he had free disposal.

For the exercise of these wide powers the duke was bound to appoint various officials. The most important of these were the governors of the royal castles, the castellans (*castellani*, *comites*, *praefecti urbis*), who in the duke's name governed the castles assigned to them, and the surrounding country with the population settled on it. In this way the whole land was divided into smaller administrative districts which resembled the Frankish counties, and probably were to some extent modelled on them, although they differed from them in the complete concentration of the public authority in the castles: an arrangement which we find also among other Slavonic peoples. For this reason, we may rightly speak of a castle organisation in this first period of the Bohemian State. Within the limits of their jurisdiction the castellans had considerable power, for they possessed almost full authority as representatives of the duke; but they were, on the other hand, completely dependent on the duke, who appointed and dismissed them at his pleasure. Since the duke, with his household, travelled about the country, and stopped now at one castle, now at another, he ensured the obedience of the castellans, and through them of the whole land. If the throne was vacant, or held by a prince who was not universally recognised, these castellans became the most important factor in the country. In the election of a ruler, and when there were rival candidates in the field, the decision lay usually in the castellans' hands. But once the duke had established himself on the throne and had occupied the castles with his followers, his rule was again unrestricted, for he was supported by his own followers and by the castellans. It depended on his own personal energy whether he ruled over these followers and over the castellans, or whether he was perhaps himself ruled by them. But we can find no evidence of any legal limitation of the power of the Bohemian dukes in these times; since the very people who, besides the duke, had a regular influence on the government of the country, the duke's followers and the officials of the court and of the castles, had no authority of their own independent of the duke.

This primitive patriarchal absolutism of the royal authority in Bohemia was made possible by the fact that, in the first centuries after the founding of a united State, there were no firmly established higher classes whose own clearly settled rights might have placed them in a position to impose definite limits upon the power of the duke. Among the Bohemians, as with other Slavs, in the days in which they were split up into little clans, there existed indeed a class of what might be called nobles by birth; but after the federation of the clans under the leadership of the Přemyslids, the old nobility, among whom are to be reckoned more especially the families of the different princes of the clans, either entirely disappeared—some of them were violently extirpated—or lost their former importance. Only little by little did a new nobility develop, and then, as it seems, on an entirely new basis. This new nobility falls very distinctly into two classes. The more numerous class was composed of warriors or knights (*milites*), that is, of those who were compelled to give personal service in war, as a rule, in all probability, on horseback. We soon find these warriors forming a distinct class, separate from the rest of the free population, and often intervening with considerable effect in the administration of the government. In the twelfth century they were usually designated nobles (*nobiles*). Above these warriors, however, stood a class of higher nobility, the true nobles (*nobiles*). These were composed at first chiefly of the higher ducal officials (castellans and others), and afterwards of those families to whose members the ducal offices were usually entrusted. But the Bohemian dukes were at this time in no way bound to choose their officers from particular families. There was, therefore, in Bohemia no real hereditary nobility whose closed ranks were sharply divided from the rest of the population. A nobility of this kind was not formed until certain families acquired large estates through the favour of the duke, and succeeded also in keeping them entirely in their own hands, so that their power was independent of the will of the sovereign and of the possession of a princely office. This did not take place to any considerable extent until the thirteenth century, and it was then that this great landed nobility first acquired a distinct and firmly established position, with authority of their own, that is, independent of the sovereign. Their members later were called simply barons (Bohemian *páni*, Latin *domini*, *barones*), while the lesser nobles were known as knights (Bohemian *rytíři*, *vladykové*).

Among the rest of the people, not of noble rank, there also grew up later many distinctions of social and legal position. In essentials, however, they fell into two great classes: the slaves and the free. We find slaves among the Bohemian and Moravian Slavs certainly before the foundation of a unified Bohemian State. Originally for the most part an article of export, they were later employed in great measure as farm-labourers or artisans on the large estates of the sovereign or of monasteries. Not until about the turning-point of the twelfth and thirteenth centuries do slaves disappear in Bohemia, when they are merged in the lowest classes of the agricultural and town population. Besides the slaves, the non-noble population of Bohemia was originally composed of small free landowners, peasants (*rustici*, *pauperes*, *heredes*). Their freedom consisted in their being dependent upon no one except the sovereign and his officers. They were certainly bound to give various compulsory services on the land, and to pay various duties, of which the chief was the "peace-tax." These public duties, which were in themselves by no means light, were made still more oppressive by the arbitrary actions of the ducal officers, and especially of the castellans. In order to escape from such arbitrary oppression, many of the original free-born peasants divested themselves of their freedom of their own accord, by placing themselves and their goods under the protection of ecclesiastical or lay authority, and thus became dependent on them. The dependency of the subject peasants referred to in the sources as "heirs" (*heredes*, Bohemian *dědicové*) seems to have come about in this way. Another part of the peasant population fell into dependence in the following manner: many personally free men settled on estates which were not their own, accepted the burden of various taxes and duties in return for the use of the land, and thus came into a position of dependence under the overlordship of the landlords. Such peasants, personally free but settled on land which did not belong to them, are called in the sources of the eleventh and twelfth centuries "strangers" (*hospites*). Thus, before the end of the twelfth century, the greater part of the once free peasant population had become dependent upon ecclesiastical and lay authorities, while the former slaves raised themselves indeed to a position of greater freedom than they had enjoyed before, but were still extremely dependent.

There was from the first another class of the community, composed of the clergy, although it was not so sharply divided from the rest of the people as it became in the later Middle Ages. The Christian faith was brought into Bohemia in the first half of the ninth century; and from the end of that century, after the Bohemian prince Bořivoj had received baptism at the hands of the Moravian Archbishop Methodius (about 880), it has at least the exterior semblance of a Christian country. Most of the members of the royal family were distinguished above all others for their zeal for Christianity: Bořivoj's wife, Saint Ludmila (*ob.* 921), and their grandson, Prince Wenceslas the Saint (*ob.* 929), are especially notable for this. So in the beginning of the tenth century the first Christian churches sprang up in Bohemia, and foreign priests sent from the neighbouring German dioceses came to spread the Christian faith among the people. Bohemia was first raised to the position of an independent diocese by the foundation of the bishopric of Prague (973–974), which was the joint work of the Bohemian Duke Boleslav II (967–999) and of the German Emperors Otto I and Otto II. Besides Bohemia, a considerable part of Poland, which was at that time united to Bohemia, and probably Moravia and western Slovakia also, formed a part of this new bishopric, which was placed under the jurisdiction of the Archbishop of Mayence. When, however, all Polish territory was severed, not only from Bohemia but also from the diocese of Prague, while a separate bishopric was set up at Olomouc (Olmütz) (about 1063) for Moravia, soon after that country had been finally united with Bohemia by Duke, afterwards King Vratislav, the ecclesiastical authority of the Bishop of Prague was in future confined to Bohemia alone. About the time of the foundation of the bishopric of Prague, there appear in Bohemia the two first monasteries of the Benedictine Order, one for women (St George at Prague about 967), the other for men (in Břevnov near Prague about 992); and these were followed by a number of other monasteries in Bohemia and Moravia. Endowed with rich estates, these old monasteries were among the most important economic factors in the country. Bohemia has to thank them above all for the knowledge of large-scale agriculture as it was carried on in Western Europe.

The position of these ecclesiastical establishments and of the clergy generally was originally by no means so independent and so self-sufficient as it became in the later Middle Ages. The Church was, on the contrary, entirely dependent on the lay authority. The will of the sovereign decided appointments to both the sees, even though the bishops received consecration from the Archbishop of Mayence and investiture from the Emperor. Similarly, too, the abbots of the monasteries founded by the sovereign were often appointed solely by him. The smaller churches, even when they had the character of the later parish churches, were considered to be, with all their appurtenances, the property of the founders and their heirs, who, as a result, were accustomed to appoint and dismiss the ecclesiastical incumbents of these churches entirely on their responsibility without any consultation of the bishop, and to treat them as their own nominees. The influence of the bishop on the administration of the Church was thus only very slight, and the action of the papal Curia upon ecclesiastical affairs in Bohemia was even slighter.

If the relationship of the Bohemian Church of that time with Rome was of only theoretical importance, its connexion with the secular world around it was all the more intimate. The priests were, as a rule, married, and neither in public administration nor in judicial matters was there any distinction between clerical and lay persons. From the point of view of nationality indeed, a considerable part of the clergy, especially of the monks, was distinguished from its surroundings; in particular there were among them certainly very many Germans. But there was also a large and influential Bohemian section. Not only were the two outstanding champions of ecclesiastical freedom, St Adalbert, Bishop of Prague (who met with a martyr's death as a missionary to the heathen Prussians in 997), and Henry Zdík, Bishop of Olomouc (*ob.* 1151), of Bohemian nationality, but the writers of the most important Bohemian legends and chronicles of that time (though it is true that they were written in Latin) were also Bohemian. We need only mention here, as the most outstanding of them, Cosmas, dean of Prague (*ob.* 1125), whose *Chronica Bohemorum* is among the best works of medieval historiography.

Although the missionary St Adalbert, the Bishop of Prague, had striven to win greater independence for the Church in Bohemia, and although the papal Curia, during the great investiture struggle, made an attempt to reform the administration of the Church in Bohemia in the spirit of the Gregorian ideal, it was not until about the middle of the twelfth century that, by a papal legate sent to Bohemia in 1143, the Church's rule as to celibacy of the clergy was, at least in certain cases, enforced. From that time the scheme of a reformation of the Bohemian Church was never dropped. King Vladislav I (II) himself was in favour of it, as well as the distinguished Bishop of Olomouc, Henry Zdík; yet reform made little headway. Celibacy of the clergy did not become the rule until the thirteenth century, and up to the end of the twelfth century the relations of the parish churches and their owners were hardly at all modified. Thus it came about that, in the second half of the twelfth century, the chief ecclesiastical establishments of Bohemia, especially the bishoprics of Prague and Olomouc, sought to obtain an exceptional position for their estates by means of a privilege of immunity from the Bohemian rulers. The peasantry settled on these estates were in this way freed from public services and taxes, and from the jurisdiction of the ducal castellans, and were placed directly under that of the officials of the royal household.

The growing power and importance of the Church in Bohemia led speedily to conflicts between its leaders and the rulers of the country. One such conflict between the Bohemian Duke Frederick and Henry Břetislav, Bishop of Prague, a member of the Přemyslid family, gave the German Emperor Frederick Barbarossa the welcome opportunity of declaring the Bishop of Prague an 'immediate' prince of the Empire (1187). Since Moravia, too, had been made into an 'immediate' margravate a short time before, the authority of the Bohemian duke, heretofore complete, was at the end of the twelfth century, so to speak, torn into shreds. This collapse of the power of the Bohemian dukes, due partly to the crafty policy of Barbarossa, partly to the pernicious struggles for the throne among the Přemyslids, was, however, not of long duration. Even before the end of the twelfth century, the cessation of the internecine feuds and the simultaneous collapse of the power of the German Emperor brought about a change for the better in this respect.

After the death, which occurred in 1197, of Henry Břetislav, Bishop of Prague, who four years before had become Duke of Bohemia and had also conquered Moravia, two sons of King Vladislav I, Přemysl Ottokar I and Vladislav Henry, came forward as candidates for the throne. The younger, Vladislav, was first raised to the throne by the Bohemians, but in the same year he came to an agreement with his elder brother, by which Přemysl Ottokar became duke in Bohemia and Vladislav Henry margrave of Moravia. Přemysl Ottokar I ruled thereafter in Bohemia until his death (1230) in complete harmony with his brother Vladislav (*ob.* 1222), and all his successors up till the end of the Přemyslid dynasty ascended the throne unopposed. This was a fact of the greatest importance for the further development of Bohemia, both in foreign and in home affairs.

Above all, an end was put once and for all to the dismemberment of the Bohemian State caused by the recognition of the margravate of Moravia and of the bishopric of Prague as direct principalities of the Empire. The agreement of 1197 had already restored the real unity of Moravia and Bohemia, and in the years that followed this union became ever more firmly cemented. The 'immediacy' of the bishopric of Prague was still more rapidly and decisively abolished. During his short reign Přemysl's brother Vladislav on his own authority appointed a new bishop in place of Henry Břetislav, and himself bestowed investiture upon him. By this action he made it clear, not only that he did not recognise the 'immediate' position of the bishopric of Prague, but that he was determined also to put an end to the bishop's former dependence on the German Emperor, formal though it was, which was expressed by the conferring of investiture by the Emperor. In the path indicated in this momentous action of Vladislav, the object of which was to make Bohemia more independent of the Empire, Přemysl Ottokar also persevered. As a result of the struggles for the throne which arose after the death of the Emperor Henry VI, Přemysl Ottokar achieved important successes in this direction. As early as 1198 he was raised to the dignity of king, and the dukedom of Bohemia was made a kingdom, by King Philip of Swabia, with whom he at first joined forces. When afterwards the new king, at the instance of Pope Innocent III, was persuaded to desert Philip and declare himself for the anti-king, Otto of Brunswick, Přemysl's royal title was confirmed to himself and his successors, not only by Otto but also by the Pope (1207). But Přemysl's friendship with Otto did not last long. The King of Bohemia soon entered again into friendly relations with Philip, and only the latter's murder (1207) prevented his defection from Otto. When, however, soon afterwards the Pope himself deserted Otto and began to support Frederick II, the young son of the Emperor Henry VI, the King of Bohemia allowed himself easily to be won over to Frederick. As a reward for this, he obtained from King Frederick in 1212, by a Golden Bull, an important privilege which for many years regulated the legal relationship of Bohemia to the German Empire. By the main provisions of this bull the royal dignity of Přemysl and his heirs is confirmed, but at the same time the old right of the Bohemians to choose their ruler for themselves is clearly recognised, although the Emperor's right to confer the *regalia* upon the elected king is reserved. In addition, the King of Bohemia is granted the right to confer investiture upon the bishops of his kingdom, not only in the case of Prague, but evidently in that of Olomouc also. Finally, it is decreed that the Kings of Bohemia are to be bound to attend the Court only when it is held at Bamberg, Nuremberg, or Merseburg, and, on the occasions of the Emperor's journeys to Rome, they are to have the choice of either sending three hundred armed men or paying three hundred silver marks.

Even after the Golden Bull of 1212, Bohemia remained a fief of the German Empire, but the bull considerably strengthened her peculiar position in regard to the Empire. In this respect the definite recognition of the Bohemian right of election is especially important. The value of this right had, it is true, been much diminished by the hereditary right of the Přemyslids to the crown, and it lost almost all its significance so soon as there was only one candidate for the throne. A no less important event, therefore, was the preparation by Přemysl Ottokar of a precise law of succession. It is true that he issued no decree on the subject, yet he succeeded in securing the election by the Bohemians of his eldest son Wenceslas as king, during his own lifetime, and in obtaining confirmation of this from the Emperor Frederick (1216). In this imperial confirmation, and even more clearly in another published (in 1231) after the death of Přemysl, emphasis is strongly laid upon the fact that Wenceslas was elected as the king's eldest son. From this time until the fall of the Přemyslids the rule of primogeniture in the succession was definitely maintained. This was certainly made possible by the fact that, on the death of the remaining Přemyslid kings, their sons were always the sole male members of the royal house. But in this way the election of the king became only a more solemn recognition and acceptance of the only legitimate heir.

If the duties of the Bohemian king towards the Empire were diminished by the Golden Bull of 1212, as time went on they became ever less. Though the King of Bohemia in 1212 was only released from personal participation in the actual 'journeys to Rome,' in after years, as the power of the German Empire was broken, the compulsion under which he lay to participate in the Emperor's campaigns generally ceased as it were of its own accord. Rudolf I certainly extorted from the Bohemian King Přemysl Ottokar II, after the latter's defeat in 1276, an acknowledgement that the king was bound to assist the Emperor in time of war in the same manner as other princes of the Empire, but after some years, in 1298, Rudolf's son, Albert I, promised King Wenceslas II, son of Přemysl Ottokar II, that provided he was elected King of the Romans he would exact no armed assistance from Wenceslas. Later, in 1314, the Bohemian King John of Luxemburg obtained a similar promise from the German King Louis of Bavaria, and so little by little Bohemian participation in the Emperor's campaigns came to an end.

While the obligations of the Bohemian kings towards the Empire grew steadily less and less after the beginning of the thirteenth century, on the other hand their rights in the Empire and their influence upon imperial affairs increased in importance. Even in the eleventh century the Bohemian dukes appear at the election of the German king, and after the end of the twelfth century especially they were accustomed to play a more important part on these occasions. When, in the thirteenth century, the theory began to be established that the right to elect the German king belonged only to the three Rhenish archbishops and to the holders of the so-called arch-offices of the Empire, the King of Bohemia, as hereditary holder of the office of cupbearer, was also counted as an Elector, and thus attained very high authority in the Empire. It is true that the first advocate of this theory, Eike von Repgow, the author of the famous *Sachsenspiegel*, wished from the first to deprive the King of Bohemia of his right of election, on the ground that he was not a German, 'umme dat he nicht düdesch n'is,' but his opinion was not heeded. Only at the election of Rudolf I of Habsburg (1273) was the Bohemian king's right of election denied, and the seventh electoral chair was adjudged to the dukedom of Bavaria; but King Rudolf himself later (1289 and 1290) restored to the King of Bohemia the office of cupbearer and the dignity of Elector.

The great increase in the power of the Kings of Bohemia, to which the accession of Přemysl Ottokar I opened the way, was also not without influence upon the foreign policy of Bohemia. This had formerly been regulated almost exclusively by the personal inclinations of the individual rulers, and thus almost entirely lacked consistency; but henceforth it begins to follow a clearly-conceived and consistent aim, so that as time goes on we can speak of definite traditions of Bohemian policy. In this connexion the relations of Bohemia with Austria must first be considered. Even in the last years of Přemysl Ottokar I, hostilities arose between Bohemia and Austria. Their origin lay in the fact that Henry, the eldest son of the Emperor Frederick II, married a daughter of the Austrian Duke Leopold VI, of the house of Babenberg, instead of the daughter of the King of Bohemia, to whom he had been betrothed since childhood. But it was only under Přemysl's successor, King Wenceslas I (1230–1253), that open war broke out on this account. In his attack upon the Duke of Austria, Frederick II the Valiant, the last Babenberger, the King of Bohemia was joined by his two neighbours, Béla IV, King of Hungary, and Otto, Duke of Bavaria, and after some time the Emperor Frederick II himself joined this coalition. As executor of the ban pronounced by the Emperor against the Duke of Austria, King Wenceslas together with other princes of the Empire invaded his territory and brought it almost under the Emperor's power (1237). But soon after, King Wenceslas, at the instigation of the papal Curia, broke away from the Emperor and reconciled himself with the Duke of Austria, whose niece Gertrude, to mark the occasion, was betrothed to Wenceslas' eldest son Vladislav (1239). Hostilities broke out again between Bohemia and Austria immediately after this, but were stopped by the common danger which threatened both lands in the approach of the Mongols. Wenceslas' kingdom was entered by these terrible foes. After the northern Tartar horde had crushingly defeated the Duke of Silesia (1241) at Liegnitz, it invaded Moravia also. While Bohemia was saved from the Mongols, owing largely to the exertions of King Wenceslas, who took up a position on the borders with a strong army to face the foe, Moravia was utterly laid waste, and not until their retreat from Europe was it freed from this torment.[1]

Hardly was the danger from the Mongols over before hostilities broke out once more between Bohemia and Austria; and these, in so far as they were involved in the great contemporary struggle between the Papacy and the Empire, were also of importance for the general history of that time. An important change in the relations between Bohemia and Austria came about on the death of Duke Frederick of Austria (1246). Only then did the long-arranged marriage between his niece Gertrude and Vladislav, son of the King of Bohemia, actually take place. Through this marriage the royal house of Bohemia saw open before it the brilliant prospect of a widening of its realms through the Babenberg

[1] Of a great defeat said to have been inflicted upon the Mongols near Olomouc, we hear first from a later tradition, of which use was made in the famous forgery of the nineteenth century, the so-called *Königinhofer* MS (*Královdvorský rukopis*).

succession. For when Duke Frederick had died childless, Vladislav, as husband of his niece Gertrude, became the most important candidate for the lands left vacant by his death. But only a few months after his marriage, Vladislav, whom the contemporary Austrian sources actually call "Duke of Austria," died, and so for the present the Bohemian royal house lost all hope of the Babenberg succession.

However, after the death of the Emperor Frederick II and that of Herman of Baden, Gertrude of Babenberg's second husband, in 1250, as soon as the position of affairs in Austria had become more favourable to the claims of Bohemia, hostilities again broke out. Přemysl Ottokar II, who, after the death of his elder brother Vladislav, was King Wenceslas' only surviving son, and had already been appointed Margrave of Moravia by his father, led an army into Austria, on the invitation of a section of the Austrian nobility with the support of the papal Curia and of the clergy, and subdued a considerable part of the country without meeting any opposition (1251). To strengthen his position, the young Přemysl married the sister of the last Babenberger, Margaret, who was more than fifty years of age. But immediately afterwards the powerful King of Hungary, Béla IV, came up against him, and in a short time by force of arms made himself master of Styria, a part of the Babenberg possessions.

The struggle between the two claimants to the former Babenberg lands was not yet at an end when Přemysl Ottokar II, on the death of his father, ascended the Bohemian throne, which he held for a full quarter of a century (1253–1278). In the next year, through the intervention of the papal Curia, which rightly regarded the young King of Bohemia as its true supporter, a peace was negotiated between Přemysl Ottokar and Hungary, by which Přemysl kept Austria while Béla retained Styria (1254). But when, some four years later, the Styrian nobles supported by Bohemia raised a rebellion against Hungarian rule, a new war broke out, which, after the King of Bohemia had won a brilliant victory at the battle of Kroissenbrunn, ended with the cession of Styria to him (1260). Afterwards he obtained from the German King Richard of Cornwall the investiture of both the newly-acquired lands, Austria and Styria.

The King of Bohemia had already, two years after his accession to the throne (1255), shewn his gratitude for the support extended to him by the papal Curia in these successful struggles for the Babenberg inheritance, by undertaking a crusade to assist the Teutonic Order against the heathen Prussians. At that time a part of Samland was conquered by the German Knights, and, to establish their rule in those regions, they founded the town named Königsberg (*Mons Regius*) in honour of the King of Bohemia. Soon after, Přemysl Ottokar pledged himself to the papal Curia to undertake another crusade, which, however, did not take place for several years (1268). This crusade, too, was to assist the Teutonic Order, but its special objective was the heathen Lithuania. This country, with some of the neighbouring lands, was to be converted to Christianity, but was at the same time to be placed under the rule of the King of Bohemia, and a newly-created archbishopric was to be founded, at the head of which was to be set the Bishop of Olomouc as archbishop. Without waiting for the papal decision on this plan, Přemysl Ottokar II started on his second crusade (in the winter of 1267–68); but when the Curia would not consent to his audacious design, he turned back without effecting anything.

While thus Přemysl Ottokar's plan to annex to his kingdom new provinces in the north miscarried, he soon after acquired an extension of it in the south. His kinsman Ulrich, the childless Duke of Carinthia, had appointed him his heir, and after Ulrich's death he obtained possession of Carinthia with the county of Carniola which was united to it (1269). Thus the kingdom of Přemysl Ottokar reached its greatest extent. Besides Bohemia and Moravia, it included Austria, Styria, Carinthia, and Carniola, in addition to some smaller possessions on the Adriatic. It thus stretched from the mountain ranges in the north of Bohemia to the Adriatic Sea, and was a forerunner of the later Habsburg monarchy, excluding Hungary.

The establishment of so powerful a kingdom, which threatened to be a dangerous competitor to the power of the Holy Roman Empire in Central Europe, was made possible by contemporary events in Germany, where there was, during the whole of this time, no generally recognised ruler—it is the period of the Interregnum. The continuance of the kingdom might possibly have been secured, had the King of Bohemia himself attained the German crown. Přemysl Ottokar, after the death of Richard of Cornwall (1272) if not before, did become a candidate for the Empire. The election of Rudolf of Habsburg as the German King (1273) inflicted a serious check on his policy, all the more so in that Rudolf was elected by evading the electoral rights of Bohemia, and in spite of the protest of Přemysl Ottokar. Since the new German King, whose royal power had been greatly diminished by the course of events in preceding years, aimed at establishing a strong position for himself by extending the power of his own house, he naturally took as his objective those territories of the Empire which during the Interregnum had fallen into the possession of Přemysl Ottokar, and which from the point of view of imperial law might be considered to have been illegally acquired. So it came about that at the diet of Nuremberg, a year after Rudolf's election, the King of Bohemia was deprived of all rights to these lands and was himself summoned to shew cause for his actions (1274). When Přemysl Ottokar heeded neither this nor yet a second summons, he was outlawed and was declared to be deprived of his own hereditary possessions (1276). At the same time a campaign in which the whole Empire joined was begun against the King of Bohemia. While Rudolf's allies, the brothers Meinhard of the Tyrol and Albert of Görz, attacked Carinthia, Carniola, and Styria, he himself invaded Austria. Weakened by the revolt of a powerful body of nobles in Bohemia, Přemysl Ottokar was soon compelled to sue for a truce. By a peace concluded with Rudolf at Vienna, he ceded Austria, Styria, Carinthia, and Carniola, and in return was invested by the German King with Bohemia and Moravia (November 1276). However, a new war against Rudolf, who was this time assisted by Hungary also, soon broke out; and Přemysl Ottokar was again unsuccessful. His army was annihilated at Dürnkrut in Austria, and there the king, once so glorious, met with a miserable death (26 August 1278).

Immediately after the battle, King Rudolf led his army into Moravia, and, since Přemysl Ottokar's only son, who became king as Wenceslas II (1278–1305), was only seven years old, for five years he kept the administration of the margravate in his own hands, while he had to entrust the administration of Bohemia for the same period to Přemysl Ottokar's nephew, Otto of Brandenburg, as Wenceslas' guardian. These five years were for Bohemia a real reign of terror, owing to the cruelty and avarice of Otto of Brandenburg and to the disorders caused by internecine feuds among the nobles; but then young Wenceslas, whom Otto only released from his guardianship on payment of a large sum, entered upon his father's possessions.

Soon after this, a prominent Bohemian noble, Záviš of Falkenstein, who had formerly been among the opponents of Přemysl Ottokar, but after his death married his widow, Wenceslas' mother, became the true director of Bohemian policy. When, however, the young king, under Záviš's influence, began to lay claim to the lands of which his father had been deprived, a part of which had already been bestowed upon Rudolf's sons, King Rudolf contrived that Záviš should be removed from the court; he was later imprisoned, and finally beheaded (1290). After some time, King Wenceslas indeed renewed his efforts to recover his father's kingdom—with this object his policy was specially directed against Albert of Habsburg. But later he gave up this attempt and turned his attention ever more towards the east. He had already entered into friendly relations with certain Silesian princes, and, during a dispute over the succession, had taken possession of the Polish county of Cracow; in 1300 he brought Greater Poland also under his sway, and had himself crowned King of Poland at Gnesen.

Immediately after this, an opportunity for a farther extension of his kingdom was offered to King Wenceslas. After the death of Andrew III, the last Hungarian king of the line of Árpád, the Hungarian nobles who were dissatisfied with Charles Robert, the candidate of the papal Curia, offered the crown of Hungary to the King of Bohemia. The latter did not, indeed, accept it himself, but he induced his Hungarian supporters to elect his twelve-year-old son, Wenceslas III, King of Hungary. The young prince, after adopting the Hungarian national name of Ladislas (László), was crowned and installed as king in the capital, Buda (1301). However, Pope Boniface VIII and the German King Albert, who naturally felt that their interests were threatened, bitterly opposed the Bohemian rule in Hungary. King Wenceslas, on his side, formed an alliance with King Philip IV of France (1303), and also entered into relations with England. But on the death of Pope Boniface (1304), the hostility between France and the Papacy came to an end, and with it the main reason for the French alliance with Bohemia. In Hungary, too, the position of affairs changed to the detriment of Bohemia, when the nobles began to fall away from her. Then King Wenceslas of Bohemia invaded Hungary with a large army, but soon beat a retreat without engaging battle, and brought back his son to Bohemia, together with the Hungarian royal insignia. On the other hand, King Albert, who with his allies invaded Bohemia and besieged the town of Kutná Hora (Kuttenberg), famous for its silver mines which were then at the height of their prosperity, had also to retire without gaining any success. A new campaign against Bohemia, which had been planned for the next year, was averted by the sudden death of King Wenceslas, who was only thirty-four years old (June 1305).

The new King of Bohemia, Wenceslas III (1305–1306), the only son of the late king, was hardly seventeen years old. He concluded a peace with King Albert soon after his father's death; in return for the cession of certain disputed provinces (Eger, Meissen), he received a solemn confirmation of the old liberties and rights of Bohemia. In Hungary, too, Wenceslas III gave up the hopeless struggle, for he handed over his claims upon Hungary, and the Hungarian royal insignia, to his cousin Otto of Bavaria. On the other hand he began to make preparations with great ardour for a campaign in Poland, in order to obtain possession of his father's seriously imperilled lands. But when, in the summer of 1306, he was staying at Olomouc, where his army was to concentrate, he was murdered in the dean's house by an unknown assailant (4 August 1306). At his death the male line of the Přemyslids was extinguished; and this was in itself an important turning-point in the history of Bohemia.

The time of the rule of the last Přemyslid kings is of significance, not only for the great external expansion of the power of the Bohemian throne, but also for important changes in the internal conditions of the lands beneath its sway. The disruption of the old constitution of the State and of society, a disruption which had been approaching even in earlier times, was fulfilled in this period. For in this period various special rights were acquired by single social classes, which thus withdrew themselves from the old organisation of the State and cut themselves off from the rest of the population and also from each other. In the forefront stand the clergy. The development, for which the way was prepared even in the twelfth century by the introduction of the celibacy of the clergy and the privilege of immunity granted to certain ecclesiastical establishments, was continued in the thirteenth century by the gradual emancipation of the Church in Bohemia from lay authority. In the very first years of the thirteenth century the chapters of both the cathedrals of Bohemia, at Prague and Olomouc, obtained the right of free election to their bishoprics. And soon after, Andrew, Bishop of Prague, entered upon a great struggle for ecclesiastical freedom against Přemysl Ottokar I, whom he, with the support of Rome, compelled to grant noteworthy concessions. By the agreements of 1219 and 1221, the bishop obtained the definite recognition of his right to appoint and dismiss the incumbents of all churches in his diocese, although the right of presentation of the patrons (*patroni*) was reserved; beyond this, he obtained the right to exercise jurisdiction over clerical persons in ecclesiastical matters, that is, particularly, in matters of discipline. The independence of the clergy in spiritual matters (*in spiritualibus*) as regards the secular authority, thus recognised in principle, was not realised at once in all its implications, but little by little it obtained real value. In secular matters, however, the clergy remained even after this subject to secular authority. Quarrels between clerical persons or corporations, in which landed property was concerned, were even at a later date decided by the ruler or by the competent secular court. Also the Bohemian kings never ceased to regard the possessions of the old monasteries, and other ecclesiastical establishments founded by their predecessors, as their own property, and to demand from them special contributions in addition to the regular taxes. On the other hand, these establishments had the right to obtain for all those who dwelt upon their estates complete exemption from the authority of the state officials, and to take upon themselves the full exercise of this authority. After the end of the great struggle with Bishop Andrew, King Přemysl Ottokar I by an important grant in 1222 confirmed to all the clergy of his country the right which had actually been possessed before by a large number of ecclesiastical establishments. The inhabitants of their property were exempted from the jurisdiction of the castle or provincial officials, and were placed directly under that of the king and of his chief court officials. But even in the thirteenth century it came about that, in the majority of the ecclesiastical establishments of Bohemia, the jurisdiction over their dependents, which by the privilege of 1222 was vested in the king, was abandoned to the clergy and to their officers.

Like the clergy, the nobles, especially those of highest rank, obtained at this time various rights for themselves and for the vassals settled on their estates. Even in the second half of the twelfth century, disputes between nobles, especially those which concerned landed property, were decided at great general judicial assemblies (*communia colloquia, iudicia generalia*), and in the second half of the thirteenth century a special court (*zemský soud*), composed only of the members of the highest nobility, the Lords, assumed this jurisdiction. But, following the example of the clergy, the nobles too obtained for their vassals, by placing them under their own authority, a similar exemption from the authority of the State. In this manner the peasants settled on the property of ecclesiastical and lay landlords first became their true vassals, bound not only to pay definite private services, but also to serve them in all such matters as were formerly regulated by the authority of the State, that is, of the ruler and his officials.

The legal position of the vassal peasant population also underwent at this time a fundamental change, due to German colonisation and the introduction of German law. The immigration of German colonists into Bohemia begins even in the twelfth century. They received from their new overlords, as a rule in return for a clearly determined yearly payment, only portions of untilled land, chiefly in the wooded and formerly uninhabited regions of the country, but on the other hand they enjoyed a more favourable legal position in regard to their landlords than that in which the native peasant population found itself. The main privilege of this new law in Bohemia, which was there known as the German Law (*ius teutonicum*), lay in this: it secured to the peasant the hereditary possession of his land and thus made him an hereditary or emphiteutic tenant (hence it is also called *ius emphiteuticum*), and, more than this, settled his duties towards the overlord by a firm and precise agreement. For the overlords themselves it was profitable, because it secured to them a fixed yearly income from their lands. Thus is explained the rapid spread of this "German Law" in Bohemia and Moravia, not only among the new colonists but also among the older peasant population, which for the most part was gradually brought into a relationship with its overlords similar to that of the colonists.

In this manner, in the course of the thirteenth and fourteenth centuries, the various classes of the dependent peasant population were fused into one tolerably united class of peasant vassals, who occupied their land as hereditary tenants in return for a definite yearly rent and for other precisely settled duties, and were exempt from the authority of the state officials, but, on the other hand, were subject to the authority of their overlords and were represented at the king's court only by them.

During this time a new class grew up in Bohemia and Moravia through the rise of a number of towns, of which there had been none before the thirteenth century. They developed partly out of older colonies of foreign, chiefly German, traders, which had early been formed here and there, and enjoyed special rights and immunities; in Prague we find as early as the eleventh century such a community of traders, with a considerable measure of autonomy; it was not till the first half of the thirteenth century that this community was transformed into the "Old Town" of Prague. In part, they were entirely new foundations of the kings and also of other overlords. At the end of the Přemyslid era there were in Bohemia alone not less than thirty-two royal towns, of which the greater part owed their foundation to Kings Přemysl Ottokar II and Wenceslas II.

Through the exemption of the clergy and the higher nobility, together with their vassals, from the authority of the old castellans, as well as through the establishment of the towns, whose inhabitants from the first stood outside the range of this authority, the old castle administration was completely undermined. Since the loss of most of their old authority had rendered the great number of old castle districts superfluous, the ancient smaller districts gradually, in the course of the thirteenth century, were replaced by larger spheres of administration; but these had, however, for the present, by no means so great an importance from the constitutional point of view as those old districts, since they possessed no permanent fully-equipped organ of administration, nor had they wide powers extending over the whole population, such as the erstwhile castle-administration had possessed.

As the old castle-administration decayed, so the importance of the central administration increased, and in the second half of the thirteenth century this becomes a truly national administration. The most important of the central institutions, the court of which we have spoken above, had, at the same time, the character of a permanent representative assembly of the higher nobility, of the great landed proprietors. This was particularly important for the reason that the court constituted at the same time the royal council, which assisted the king in deciding important national affairs. In this way the Bohemian landed proprietors gained a permanent and regular influence, not only upon the administration of justice, but also upon the political conduct of the country. The lower nobility, too, the higher clergy, and even the burghers, often exercised in those times an important influence upon national affairs, but this influence was neither so wide, nor so regular as that of the great proprietors. It made itself felt mainly at great assemblies, which we may call diets, though we must remember that they were substantially different from the later diets. Even in earlier times, in the eleventh and twelfth centuries, such general assemblies of the nobles and the higher clergy were held in certain exceptional cases; however, these did not pass resolutions, but limited themselves to taking cognisance of the decisions of the king which were presented to them. Also, at the general judicial assemblies mentioned above, which used to be held regularly from about the middle of the twelfth century, there must occasionally have arisen questions affecting national affairs. In the second half of the thirteenth century, these regular and general judicial assemblies cease, since they were supplanted by the newly organised court. Only exceptionally are general assemblies held after this, and then they are no longer judicial, but assume the functions of real diets, which not only deliberate upon important public affairs, but also decide upon them. In the first years after the tragic death of King Přemysl Ottokar II, particularly, there were held several such diets, at which the nobility, the clergy, and the representatives of the burghers decided upon important affairs which concerned the whole country: for instance, on the question of a general tax for the payment of the sums expended by Margrave Otto of Brandenburg as guardian of the young king. These decisions, however, took the form rather of agreements, similar to the German *Landfrieden*, which the participants bound themselves to observe, than of real decrees of a diet, universally binding in and for themselves. When, after the accession of Wenceslas II, normal conditions were re-established in the land, the necessity for such extraordinary diets ceased, and their further development only begins after the fall of the Přemyslid dynasty.

The great changes in the interior structure of the Bohemian State, which took place under the last Přemyslids, also affected the ethnographic aspect of the country. Even in earlier times there were in Bohemia and Moravia certainly many Germans, above all among the clergy, and especially in the monasteries; and they were also to be found at the court of the Bohemian rulers, whose wives, belonging for the most part to German princely families, brought their German retinue with them to Bohemia. Also most of the colonies of merchants, and those the most important, were composed of Germans, and, finally, there was probably a sprinkling of German immigrants among the peasant population too. But it was not until the second half of the twelfth century that a considerable immigration of German colonists to Bohemia took place. Whole districts, especially on the borderland, were then settled by Germans, and preserved their German character, in part, up to the present day. The first burghers of the Bohemian towns were almost exclusively German, and their German character in most respects outlasted the Přemyslid epoch by more than a century, and in some cases, especially in Moravia, preserved it until the present time. Besides this, both in early and in later times, the whole public and social life of Bohemia was exposed to the strong influence of her neighbour Germany. The Bohemian court was, in the thirteenth century, from time to time a place of resort for German minstrels, and had assumed an apparently strong German complexion. The Bohemian nobles, too, after the end of the twelfth century, adopted not only German customs but even German surnames. Not until the end of the Přemyslid epoch do we find a strong national consciousness among the Bohemian nobles, and then it was due partly to the conduct of Otto of Brandenburg in Bohemia, partly to their detestation of the German burgherdom which had sprung into existence and was attaining a steadily increasing importance in the country.

Besides the considerable influence of Germany upon the whole development of Bohemia, other influences of the highest importance were asserting themselves during this time. The great and successful struggle, previously mentioned, for the freedom of the Church, which begins in the time of Henry Zdík, Bishop of Olomouc, and reached its highest point under Bishop Andrew of Prague, was called into existence through the direct influence of Rome, and was brought to a victorious conclusion with the support of Rome, without any assistance from the neighbouring German prelates, indeed at times in spite of their opposition. The important reforming activities of the greatest of the Přemyslids, Přemysl Ottokar II and his son Wenceslas II, on the other hand, were influenced very powerfully by Italy. At the court of Přemysl Ottokar II the important position of royal protonotary was held by an Italian named Henry (*Henricus Italicus*), who seems to have exercised great influence upon the Bohemian Chancery and official documents. Another Italian (*Henricus de Isernia*) kept, at the same period, a school of rhetoric in Prague for the education of notaries, which was also remarkable as being the first school in Bohemia that was not controlled by priests. When King Wenceslas II contemplated causing a written code of laws to be drawn up for his kingdom, he summoned to Prague in 1294 a famous Italian jurisconsult, Gozzo of Orvieto, who actually carried out a part of the task, since he compiled the famous mining code of King Wenceslas (*Ius regale montanorum*), which became the model for the mining laws of several neighbouring countries, for instance Hungary.

As in King Wenceslas' efforts towards a codification of Bohemian law, so in his plan (which indeed was never carried into effect) to found a university in Bohemia, we see a noble aim towards a higher civilisation for his country. In regard to the economic improvement of his kingdom, Wenceslas deserves credit for a reform of the coinage, especially the issue in 1300 of the famous *groschen* of Prague. This reform was made possible mainly by the rich silver mines at Kutná Hora in eastern Bohemia, which at this time were a great financial support of the Bohemian throne.

Thus by the end of the Přemyslid epoch, Bohemia and Moravia, through the favourable development of their external and internal affairs and through the prudent rule of the last Přemyslids, reached so high a position in politics, in civilisation, and in economic affairs, that the kingdom of Bohemia began to play the leading rôle among the states of Central Europe. This brilliant development of Bohemia was checked for some time by the extinction of the Přemyslid dynasty and by the disorders which followed. Soon, however, it begins afresh, to reach its highest point, on the one hand in the reign of the Emperor Charles IV of the house of Luxemburg, and, on the other, in the great Hussite movement.

(B.)

POLAND, 1050-1303.

Although the Slav empire of Boleslav the Great (992–1025)[1] had been dissolved, the consolidation of a number of West Slav tribes under the Piast dynasty had lasted long enough to form a permanent Polish State, owing a theoretic allegiance to the Papacy and the Empire, but forming in practice an independent national entity—a State which was a bulwark of Slav resistance to German expansion, the representative to Orthodox Russia of the "Latinism" of the West, and a competitor with both Germany and Russia in the conquest and conversion of the pagan tribes of the Baltic region. Casimir the Restorer (1038–1058) had failed to regain for Poland the Slavs of Slovakia, Meissen, and Pomerania, the Prussians, or the Russians of the Bug and San, but he had reunited under firm monarchical rule his own tribe the Polanie of the Warta, the Kujawianie further East, the Mazowszanie or Mazovians on the Middle Vistula, the Wiślanie or Vistulans on the Upper Vistula, and the Slenżanie or Silesians of the Upper Oder. The archbishopric in the capital Gniezno (Gnesen) strove to assert metropolitan rights against Magdeburg over the bishoprics of Poznań (Posen), Wroclaw or Breslau, Cracow, and Kujawia. The Pomeranian bishopric at Kolberg had not survived, but a new see at Plock was established for Mazovia. By the prestige of the Piast dynasty and by ecclesiastical and administrative centralisation, the prince had temporarily overcome the provincialism of the tribes, but he had to carry on an incessant struggle against the local strength of the clans. From the clans the Court had attracted a number of individual magnates who constituted the official class and served the prince as his "comites," filling the various posts which had been established on the model of the Bohemian system, itself derived from Frankish institutions. The chief official, the prince's deputy in military and judicial affairs, was the Comes Palatinus, who came to be called in Polish the *Wojewoda.* The Succamerarius or *Podkomorzy* was in charge of the royal domain, the *Skarbnik* of the treasury, the *Kanclerz* of the chancery, while the provincial administration was carried out in the castles by the Comites Castellani or *Kasztelanie.* In place of the *comitatus* or drużyna, which had been so important under Boleslav, the prince drew his soldiers from a new class of *milites*, who were rewarded with estates which tended to become hereditary. This ecclesiastical and civil hierarchy superimposed on the clan system, together with the powerful position of the prince as supreme administrator and judge, chief landowner and sole commander of the army,

[1] For the earlier history of Poland, *see supra* Vol. III, references in the Index, and especially Chap. x.

formed the basis of the Polish State and gave it resources with which to maintain its position against the claims of the Empire and to compete with Bohemia, Hungary, and the Russian principalities. Its weakness lay in the smallness of the class that was influenced by Western ideas and institutions; in the fact that Christianity was a mere veneer and its chief exponents foreigners who were disliked by the natives; in the separatism of the tribes, which had different laws and few common interests; and in the local strength of the clans, which offered a solid, obstinate resistance to the new religious and political institutions. Fortunately, the Piast dynasty produced a series of rulers competent to overcome for a time these centrifugal forces.

Casimir I was succeeded in 1058 by his son Boleslav II the Bold, who possessed many of the qualities of his great-grandfather, and was able to enhance the power of the Polish State. In the interests of the Papacy he interfered in Czech, Hungarian, and German affairs with such success that he felt strong enough to have himself crowned as king in 1076. Secure against his western and southern neighbours, Boleslav emulated his great namesake by embarking on a Russian expedition. In support of the exiled prince Izyaslav, he invaded Russia in 1069 and captured Kiev, and, though his high-handed conduct and immorality led to his expulsion after ten months' residence there, he occupied on his way home the border provinces of Chervien and Przemysl which had formerly belonged to Poland. In domestic matters, however, Boleslav acted so despotically as to arouse strong discontent. A quarrel with the Church, which was led by Stanislas, Bishop of Cracow, ended in the assassination of the prelate by the infuriated king, who was forced to retire into exile where he shortly after died. Boleslav II is an enigmatic figure in history. Universally condemned by the chroniclers as the murderer of St Stanislas, he was undoubtedly the strong type of ruler which the country needed. The real weakness of his reign was the vagueness of plan which led him to adventurous interference in Hungary and Russia when it was open to him, by taking advantage of the quarrel between the Empire and the Papacy, to secure more solid gains west of the Oder. By his exile the prestige of the monarchy was dangerously lowered, the more so as his brother and successor, Vladyslav I Herman (1079–1102), was an incapable ruler who soon lost the recent Russian conquests and allowed the Russian prince Volodar to form at Przemysl a principality which was destined to be a dangerous neighbour to Poland. Apart from a campaign against the Pomeranians, his reign was marked by civil war in which the princely power was supported by the energetic but violent Palatine Sieciech against Vladyslav's natural son Zbigniev, to whom at his death he was forced to bequeath a part of his principality.

Boleslav III, surnamed Wrymouth (1102–1138), combined the valour and military skill of his ancestors with high qualities of statesmanship and the spirit of ascetic Christianity. He judiciously refrained from rash expeditions to Russia, and after a short war with Svyatopolk of Kiev, he married his daughter and maintained peace with Russia for sixteen years. Although the jealousy of his half-brother Zbigniev involved him in a war with Bohemia, he refused to be distracted from the principal object of his policy, which was to strengthen the position of Poland in the West by a stout resistance to imperial pretensions and by a forward policy against the tribes on his western frontier. Burning with zeal for the conversion of the infidel, he found a field for his crusading ardour among the heathen Slavs. The Pomeranians, who occupied the territory from the Lower Oder to the Lower Vistula under the rule of their native princes, were still obstinately pagan. Not only did their land separate Poland from the Baltic sea, but it was a field for Danish and German aggression. The attempts of Boleslav I to convert these pagans had been as fruitless as his conquest of their land had been transitory, and since his time the almost impenetrable marshes of the Noteć had isolated them. The young Polish prince, at the dictates of policy and religion, determined to anticipate the Germans in the conquest of this important territory whose inhabitants were in language and customs so near to the Poles. In 1102 he crossed the Noteć and overcame the princes of the south; then, gradually occupying the northern territory, he penetrated as far as the sea and captured the towns of Belgard, Kolberg, Wollin, and Stettin. The victory of Naklo in 1109 completed the Polish conquest and left Boleslav in possession of all Pomerania from the Vistula to the Oder. The South Pomeranians were converted to Christianity but were left to be ruled by their own princes as vassals of the Polish prince. During the campaign Boleslav was embarrassed by the hostility of Zbigniev, who not only called in the Czechs, but intrigued with the pagans against his brother. On being exiled he sought the assistance of the Emperor Henry V, who was anxious to reassert his power over his eastern neighbours in order to restore the imperial prestige lost by his father, and was ready to take advantage of any opportunity to interfere in the domestic affairs of Poland, Bohemia, and Hungary. Allying himself with Svatopluk of Moravia, therefore, Henry attacked the Hungarians. But while King Koloman held his own in Pressburg, Boleslav compelled Svatopluk to make peace, whereupon Henry turned against him and demanded the cession of half Poland to Zbigniev and the payment of an annual tribute by Poland to the Empire. On Boleslav's refusal, Henry invaded Silesia and, after besieging Bytom (Beuthen) and Glogów (Glogau) without success, attempted to capture Wroclaw (Breslau). Harassed continually by the attacks of the Polish prince, he was forced to abandon the siege and retired with great loss. When Zbigniev, persisting in his opposition, obtained the support of the Czech prince Vladislav I, Boleslav, after two campaigns in 1109–1110 in which he forced the Czechs to make peace, at length lost patience and caused his brother to be blinded and exiled—a necessary act of violence which he expiated by severe penances and long pilgrimages. The peace with Russia was broken in 1118, and, though war dragged on till 1123, Boleslav wisely refused to take an active part in it, and in 1120 decided to resume his campaign against the Western Slavs. The cause for the renewal of war was the revolt of the chief prince in South Pomerania, who negotiated with Russia and with the fierce Prussian tribes for assistance. Boleslav defeated him in two campaigns and annexed to Greater Poland the southern strip of Pomerania, including Naklo, Santok, and Czarnków, which remained an integral part of Poland. He then turned against the Prince of Stettin who had been privy to the rebellion, and not only forced him to submit, but invaded the lands west of the Oder, conquered the seaboard as far as the island of Rügen, and finally compelled the untamed Lyutitzi to do him homage. In order to complete the conversion of the conquered tribes, Boleslav called to his assistance Otto, Bishop of Bamberg, who, though a German, had learned Polish during his residence as chaplain at the Polish court. The prince and the bishop succeeded in establishing Christianity in Eastern Pomerania in 1124–25, in Western Pomerania in 1128. The success of this great crusade was crowned by the inauguration of a new bishopric at Wollin for the western region, the eastern region being placed under the diocese of Kujawia. It was this eastern province of Pomerania which was destined, despite many vicissitudes, to give Poland an outlet to the sea, to preserve a remnant of its Slav population, the Kashubes, and to possess in the village of Gdańsk a centre which was to become, by German enterprise under Polish protection, the great port of Danzig. Boleslav's campaigns in the West were cut short by events in Hungary (1132–1135) which brought him into relations with the Emperor Lothar III, to whom at Merseburg in 1135 he did homage for Pomerania and Rügen.

The firm rule of Boleslav maintained order in Poland, while his zeal for the Church resulted in certain improvements in ecclesiastical organisation and encouraged the growing influence of the Church on education and morality. His chaplain, Martin Gallus, wrote the first Polish chronicle. Foreign trade began to transform such castles as Wroclaw (Breslau) and Cracow into cities, and a great advance in civilisation was made during his reign. No ruler of Poland did more for his country than Boleslav III. A great warrior, almost invariably victorious, he also spread the Christian religion both in Poland and among the pagan Slavs. He sowed the seeds of Western culture in his backward country, and shewed how the deepest respect for the ideas and institutions of Western Europe could be combined with a glowing patriotism and a firm resolve to resist the encroachments of his western neighbours. Before his death in 1138, Boleslav drew up a will to determine the succession to the throne, which effected a great change in the internal constitution of the State. Hitherto, while the succession as determined by the will of the dying prince had usually involved a division of territory among his sons, in practice one son, by personal prestige or after civil war, had obtained the sole power.

Boleslav III had been convinced by the long civil war with his own brother that, in order to avoid future dissension among his numerous sons, it would be best to divide the country among them. By his will, therefore, he bequeathed Silesia to his eldest son, Vladyslav, Mazovia and Kujawia to Boleslav, Greater Poland to Mieszko, and Sandomierz to Henry, the youngest son Casimir being too young to receive a principality. In order to preserve the unity of the State, he established out of Cracow, Sieradz, and Lenczyca a suzerain principality, which, together with the tribute from Pomerania and the Oder district, was to be held by the eldest Piast, who was invested in this way with the *Seniorat* or suzerain power over the younger members of the dynasty. The capital was no longer to be at Gniezno (Gnesen), the chief city of Greater Poland, but at Cracow, the chief city of the new suzerain principality. Such was the scheme. But the circumstances of the time combined to carry Boleslav's project not only far beyond the decentralisation which he had intended, but almost to the complete and permanent disruption of the Polish State. The immediate success of the scheme depended on the altruism and enlightenment of his sons, and it was soon apparent that these qualities were lacking in them.

But more fundamental factors were working against the unity of Poland. In the first place, the administration of so large a country by one prince, with the scanty resources and inadequate machinery of a backward State in the early Middle Ages, was only practicable with a ruler of extraordinary energy and ability. Secondly, not only had traditions of tribal separation in the great provinces never died out, but there was now a class of magnates, growing up in each province and holding estates there, to voice the old claims. For instance, the Pomeranian wars had brought both military glory and fresh territory to Greater Poland, but they had brought no gain to the rising aristocracy of Cracow and Sandomierz, which was by class interest opposed to the enhancement of the monarchy and was directed by political interests to the neighbouring Russian principalities. Still less did such wars affect Mazovia, where the people were backward, half pagan, and resembled more their barbarian neighbours the Prussians than they did the Westernised magnates of Greater Poland or Silesia. At this time ethnographical boundaries were not sharply defined, and the border population of Silesia had much in common with the Czechs, just as there was a population half Polish and half Russian on the Wieprz and San. Thus the foreign relations of one province did not concern the other provinces. Moreover, the magnates found it easier to deal with several princes than with one prince, and the establishment of several courts, each with its own hierarchy of officials, gave them wider opportunities for advancement. All these factors combined to intensify the division of Poland, and so for nearly two centuries Poland was split up into a number of provinces—Greater Poland or Wielko-Polska, Silesia, Kujawia, Mazovia, Sandomierz, and others, each with its own prince, its Wojewoda and other officials, its own army, and its own customary law. The only surviving factors of unity were the nominal suzerainty of the prince at Cracow and the influence of the Church, the head of which continued to reside at the ancient capital Gniezno.

The partition of Poland designed by Boleslav III proved extraordinarily permanent. The descendants of Vladyslav continued to rule Silesia till the middle of the seventeenth century. The line of Mieszko ruled Greater Poland till its extinction in 1296. On the death of Boleslav his son, and Henry, their principalities passed to the youngest son Casimir, one of whose grandsons founded the Mazovian line which lasted till 1526; the other inherited Kujawia and became the ancestor of the later kings. For some time after the death of Boleslav the princely power remained as strong as before. Vladyslav II (1138–1146), the first Grand Prince, held Cracow as well as his own province of Silesia, the suzerainty over Pomerania, and other sovereign rights such as the nomination of the archbishop, direction of foreign affairs, and command of the common army. The new prince, at the instigation of his Austrian wife Agnes, attempted to reunite all the provinces under monarchical rule, but the magnates and clergy stood firmly by the Partition and supported his younger brothers against him. After a long struggle, in which Vladyslav made use of Russian allies and even called in the Prussians and Jadźwings, he was defeated, and the senior throne passed to his brother Boleslav IV (1146–1173). The exiled prince succeeded in enlisting the support of the King of the Romans, Conrad III, whom he accompanied on his Crusade. Conrad's intervention in Poland was fruitless, but his powerful successor, Frederick I, invaded Poland, penetrated as far as Poznań, and forced Boleslav to submit. By the peace of Krzyszkowo in 1157 a Polish prince—for the last time—admitted the ancient claim of the Emperor to overlordship, promising to pay him tribute, to appear at his court, to furnish 300 knights for his Italian campaigns, and to make peace with his brother. These promises were not all kept, and Boleslav, in refusing to admit a prince who was forced on Poland by German influence, was supported by the magnates and, in spite of a papal interdict, by the clergy. Vladyslav died in exile in 1159 and not till some years later was Silesia restored to his sons, whose pro-Germanism became a permanent feeling in the Silesian branch of the Piast dynasty. At this time the German Marks were carrying out a rapid expansion in the Elbe and Oder lands. Under Henry the Lion and Albert the Bear, not only were the Obotrites and Lyutitzi finally subdued, but in 1181 the Pomeranian princes of Stettin became vassals of the Empire. These Slav lands were quickly settled with German colonists, and the Mark of Brandenburg began that career of steady conquest and assimilation of the Western Slavs which made it an aggressive and dangerous neighbour to Poland. Of

GENEALOGICAL TABLE OF THE DESCENDANTS OF BOLESLAV III OF THE PIAST DYNASTY

(*Grand Princes or Kings of Poland italicised*)

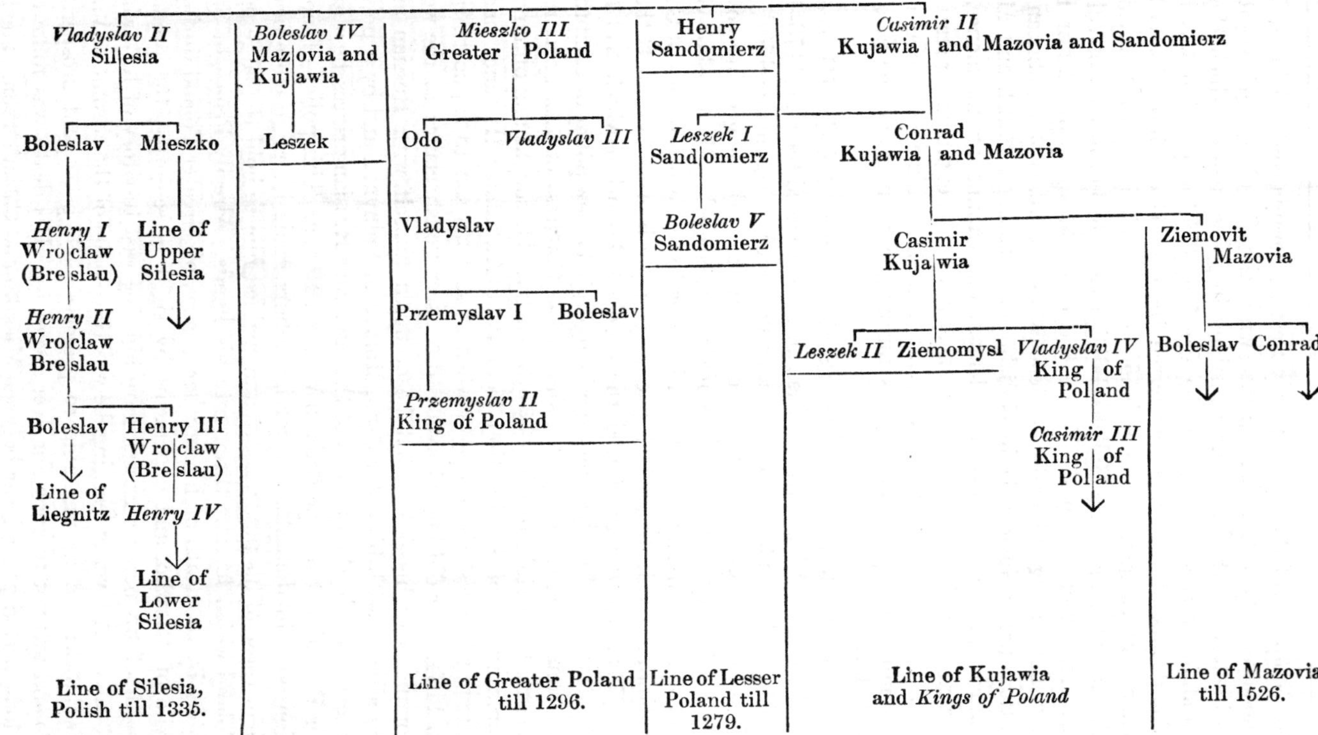

the conquests of Boleslav III, only East Pomerania continued to recognise the suzerainty of the Polish prince, while the crusading spirit spent itself in ineffective attacks on the Prussians, in the course of which Henry of Sandomierz was killed. On the Russian side the position was better. The decline of Kiev had transferred the main strength of Russia to the remote north-east, so that Poland only had relations with Volhynia and the new principality of Halich (Galicia) which had grown out of Volodar's principality of Przemysl. While the more distant provinces of Russia were developing autocratic tendencies (as in Suzdal) or republican institutions (as in Novgorod), in Halich, partly through Polish and Magyar influence, a strong aristocratic element was gaining predominance. The struggles of this class with its princes gave the neighbouring states constant opportunities for intervention. But the weakness of Poland made her military expeditions far less formidable than under the first three Boleslavs.

On the death of Boleslav IV, the third son of Boleslav III succeeded to the Grand Principality as Mieszko III surnamed the Old (1173–1177), a man of lofty ideals and a staunch upholder of the monarchical traditions of his house, who attempted in vain to curb the growing power of the aristocracy. The magnates of Cracow, headed by their Bishop Getko, rose against him, forced him to withdraw to his own province of Greater Poland, and called to the throne his younger brother Casimir II the Just (1177–1194), who renounced the obsolete despotism which had led to the downfall of his brothers and inaugurated a new policy of compromise. He conciliated the magnates, and at the Congress of Lenczyca in 1180 he granted certain privileges to the clergy. He sought and obtained the confirmation of his position from Pope Alexander III, and made no attempt to resist the Emperor when he sent his son to support Mieszko in 1184. Nor did he endeavour to reassert Polish claims to the western conquests of his father, but he occupied himself with Russian affairs. By alliance with his sister's son, Roman of Volhynia, and by a policy of intervention in the quarrels of the numerous Russian princes, he obtained for Poland a strong position in Western Russia. This policy of moderation both in domestic and foreign affairs made his reign more peaceful than those of his predecessors, and enabled him to hold the large part of Poland which fortune threw into his hands. Already Prince of Sandomierz by the death of his brother Henry, of Greater Poland during the exile of Mieszko, and of Cracow by right of seniority, the premature death of his nephew Leszek gave him the vast territory of Kujawia and Mazovia. A lover of learning, he was the patron of the chronicler Vincent Kadlubek; and he was able to preserve such peace and prosperity as Poland was not to know for over a century. His death was followed by a long period of civil war between Mieszko and Casimir's son. The latter was supported by the nobles, but it was not till the death of Mieszko that he finally came to the suzerain throne as Leszek I the White (1202–

1227). Following his father's policy of an alliance with the Church, he managed to obtain the consent of the Pope to a fundamental change which destroyed the principle involved in the will of Boleslav III. This was the transformation of the suzerain principality of Cracow together with his own province of Sandomierz into a new principality to be hereditary in his own family, his younger brother receiving Kujawia and Mazovia. This new province, the ancient territory of the Vistulan tribe, which came to be known as Lesser Poland, Polonia Minor or Malo-Polska, to distinguish it from Greater Poland, thus ceased to be a transferable principality. The affairs of the Church bulked largely in the history of Poland at this time. Hitherto the Polish ecclesiastics had been prominent in Polish internal affairs rather as magnates than as representatives of the Western Church. Several of their leaders, in particular Henry Kietlicz, Archbishop of Gniezno, now began to support Pope Innocent III in his efforts to introduce into Poland the ecclesiastical organisation and discipline which were already universal in Western Europe. In 1215 a synod was held at which the clergy swore to maintain celibacy. But only reluctantly did the princes surrender their sovereign power. Gradually, in the different principalities, ecclesiastics were released from the jurisdiction of the civil courts, the right of the chapters to elect their bishops was conceded, and various other curtailments of princely prerogatives were made in Poland, while externally Leszek formally placed his country under the power of the Holy See. The most important external event of Leszek's reign was the extinction of the dynasty of Volodar in Halich, whereupon the Polish prince followed his father's policy of supporting Roman, who united Halich to his own principality of Volhynia and thus established a powerful State which maintained its independence till 1340. Roman, however, refused to pay the homage which Leszek had demanded, and during an invasion of Poland was defeated and killed at Zawichost in 1205. In the long civil wars which ensued, the diplomacy and arms of Hungary triumphed over those of Poland, but, after a short period of Hungarian rule, the principality was ultimately regained by Roman's son Daniel. The death of Leszek in 1227 was followed by a new war of succession. His son was too young to reign and was placed by the magnates of Lesser Poland in charge of Henry, Prince of Wroclaw, who, after a struggle with Conrad of Mazovia made himself Grand Prince as Henry I the Bearded (1234–1238). Grandson of Vladyslav II, in his own right prince of Lower Silesia, guardian of the princes of Upper Silesia, master by right of conquest of Cracow and Greater Poland, Henry was the eldest, the most powerful, and the ablest of the Piasts of his time. So great was his prestige that he was able to hand down Silesia and Cracow without opposition to his son Henry II the Pious (1238–1241), who inherited many of his father's qualities. Unfortunately, the reigns of these two princes were too short to allow them to effect the permanent reunion of the Polish provinces.

But their careers mark a first effort to restore the dignity of the monarchy and nearly resulted in the restoration of a Polish State with its main strength in Silesia, a development which was abruptly terminated by the calamity of the Mongol invasion.

During the thirteenth century, the acts of the Grand Princes of Poland are overshadowed by two events of primary importance for Central Europe—the settlement of the Germans in Prussia, and the Mongol invasion and its consequences. After the conversion of the Pomeranians, the only large group of pagans left in Central Europe were the tribes of the Letto-Lithuanian stock—a race quite distinct from the Slavs, but brought into contact with them from the earliest times. With the Lettish tribes on the Dvina Poland had in the Middle Ages no connexion. The Lithuanians, dwelling in the dense forests of the river Niemen and its tributaries, had relations with the Russians from an early date, but were not an aggressive people before the thirteenth century and were little known to the Poles. The western members of the group, however, the Prussians and the Jadźwings or Yatvags, their fierce and restless neighbours on the north and north-east, had long presented a difficult problem for Poland. All attempts to conquer or convert the Prussians, from the time of St Adalbert and Boleslav I, had failed. Stubbornly pagan, fierce plunderers of their neighbours, inaccessible in their marshes from the Vistula to the Niemen, they had long been the terror of the Kujawian and Mazovian borderlands. The Jadźwings, who occupied the vast forest of Belovezh from Grodno on the Niemen to Brest on the Bug, a people whose ethnic origin is still a matter of debate, were quite unknown to history, save as barbarous and persistent raiders of Mazovia, Sandomierz, and the Russian province of Volhynia. Mazovia had suffered so much from the continual ravages of these barbarians, that it had lagged behind the other provinces of Poland in civilisation and had become a sort of Polish Ukraine or borderland with a half-wild population habituated to irregular warfare. Conrad of Mazovia, the brother of Leszek I, was seized with the ambition to emulate the conqueror of Pomerania, and to convert the Prussian pagans to Christianity and make them Polish subjects. Innocent III supported him with apostolic zeal, and when a monk named Christian succeeded in converting the Prussians of Chelmno, he made him Bishop of Prussia *in partibus*. A crusade was preached not only in Poland but in Germany, but the campaigns of 1219 and 1222 were fruitless and the borderlands suffered more than ever. Conrad then followed the example of the Bishop of Riga, who had established an Order of Knights to conquer the Letts, and founded the Dobrzyn Brotherhood. When the Brotherhood was almost annihilated in 1224, Conrad and Christian resolved to call to their aid the Teutonic Knights of St Mary.

This Order, which had fought in Palestine and for a short time in Transylvania, was granted the districts of Chelmno or Kulm and Nieszawa on the northern borders of Kujawia in return for assistance against the pagans. The Grand Master, Herman von Salza, hastened to obtain from the Emperor Frederick II and from the Pope the confirmation of Conrad's donation and to place the Order under imperial and papal suzerainty with the right to the ownership of all territory to be won from the pagans. In 1230 the Knights settled in their new lands and began a systematic occupation of Prussian territory, founding castles at Torun, Chelmno, Marienwerder, Elbing, and Braunsberg. The first campaign under the leadership of Conrad himself was successful; and a great crusade in 1234, in which, besides the Order, many Polish princes, the Prince of Pomerania, and the Margrave of Meissen participated, culminated in a decisive victory at Sirgun which won for the Order the whole region of Chelmno and a part of Western Prussia. The Order incorporated in 1234 the Dobrzyn Knights and in 1237 the Livonian Knights of the Sword, and soon conquered the greater part of Prussia. Warriors from all parts of Europe flocked to Prussia to join in this popular crusade, including such an illustrious monarch as Ottokar II of Bohemia after whom Königsberg received its name. For most of the century the Polish princes co-operated zealously with the Order, and contributed no small part to its triumph, which was so sweeping that in 1283 the last Prussian leader Skurdo fled in despair to Lithuania. The Prussians were soon exterminated or assimilated and their lands were colonised by Polish and German settlers. The chief result of the Crusade was the establishment on the borders of Poland of a new German Power, a danger which was only realised by Sventopelk, Prince of Pomerania, who waged a long and desperate war (1241–1253) against the combined forces of the Knights and the Poles. His intervention, however, failed to avert the doom of the Prussians, who vanished from history leaving their name to their German conquerors. Only a thin strip of Pomerania now separated the German settlers in Prussia from the Neumark, which the rulers of Brandenburg were just forming out of newly annexed lands on the Lower Warta and Noteć.

Poland was threatened, too, on another side by the rise of Lithuania—a further result of the conquest of Prussia. The united Orders, having occupied all the lands of the Prussians and Letts, began to threaten Lithuania itself on both sides. The small tribes of Lithuania, menaced with foreign conquest and stirred by the fate of their kinsmen the Prussians, who poured into their country as refugees, began to combine. Under their able prince Mindowe or Mendog (1219–1263) they had annexed part of the Russian borderlands and formed a State with its capital at Novgorodok, which speedily became a centre of resistance to German and Pole alike and a serious danger to the princes of Russia. Lithuanians took an increasing share in the raids of the Jadźwings on Poland. The Poles, while assisting the Knights against Prussians and Lithuanians, co-operated with Daniel of Halich against the Jadźwings. They were so far successful that by a victory at Zawichost in 1264 they broke the power of these barbarians, who disappeared as a people at the same time as the Prussians. Their land, which came to be known as Podlasia, was colonised by Russian settlers from Volhynia and Poles from Mazovia. During the lifetime of Mendog, Lithuania was always formidable, although on his death its military strength was for a time wasted in civil dissension. Poland thus saw a powerful new nation formed on her eastern borders at a time when a still more terrible foe was attacking her from the south-east.

The Black Sea steppes had been occupied for two hundred years by the Kipchak Turks, known to the Russians as the Polovtsy, to Western Europe as the Cumans. The valour of Russian and Magyar arms had protected Europe from all fear of these nomads. But a more organised nomad power was now to fall on Europe—the Mongol Empire of Jenghiz Khan, which in 1224 conquered the Kipchaks and defeated the Russians. Batu Khan, who in the years 1237–1240 had swept over Russia and devastated the whole country, proceeded to invade Central Europe. In 1241 the Mongol host invaded the kingdom of Halich and poured into Poland, devastating just those parts of the country which had not suffered from the raids of the Prussians. The only serious resistance offered was at Liegnitz, where Henry the Pious fell, valiantly fighting, with ten thousand Polish knights. The Mongols retreated, leaving Poland free, but they kept Russia under their direct rule and became the neighbours of Poland, which they continually plundered, in one raid in 1259 working more havoc than in their first invasion. The half century following the Mongol invasion is the darkest period in Polish history. During the reigns of Boleslav V the Chaste (1243–1279) and Leszek II the Black (1279–1288), internal dissensions rendered impossible any attempt to resist German aggression or to check the terrible raids of the Mongols and Lithuanians. Further, Daniel of Halich made an agreement with the Pope, was crowned king in 1254, and increased his power by a close alliance with the successors of Mendog. Thus on all sides of Poland there were powerful States ready to take advantage of her weakness.

An important result of the devastation committed by the Mongols was a great immigration into Poland of German colonists. This movement had begun some time before. German mass-colonisation had long since crossed the Oder and begun to invade not only Pomerania, but Silesia and Greater Poland. The Piast princes of Silesia from the time of Vladyslav II had welcomed German settlers. By the middle of the thirteenth century all the Polish princes were anxious to receive settlers who would cultivate their lands, ruined and depopulated by the persistent raids of the Prussians and Lithuanians and by the still more terrible depredations of the Mongols. Such peasants Germany was sending forth in large numbers in the years when the decline of the central authority made the life of the lower classes far from secure. Consequently, the immigration of Germans took on enormous proportions and became more and more a danger to Polish nationality, since they came not as individuals but in groups, which by treaty with Polish princes established themselves with their own institutions in Poland. This great wave of immigration poured both into the towns and over the countryside. One group would settle in a town, after making an agreement with the prince to form an autonomous community, not under Polish, but under that German law which came to be known as Magdeburg law from the city which was its model and to which such a community had a right to appeal. Such a town governed itself through a Council under its own elected head and possessed its own law courts. It was free from all burdens except the payment of rent to the prince on whose land it was settled. Not only were new German towns founded in this way, but the old Polish towns, too, became Germanised and received privileges under Magdeburg law. Wroclaw in 1241 became German Breslau, while Poznań (Posen), Cracow, Sandomierz, and Lublin were similarly transformed. In the same way German peasants formed village communities with full autonomy and were free of all the burdens which fell on the Polish peasants. Such was the widespread penetration by Germans that it appeared as if Poland, already a political nonentity, would soon disappear as a nation. Parts of the country such as Lower Silesia became definitely German at this time, and the new communities all over Poland, particularly in the towns, soon revealed themselves as a political element which, if not actively in alliance with the enemies of Poland, was decidedly indifferent to Polish national interests. With the Germans there came a considerable Jewish population which received wide concessions such as the Charter of Boleslav V in 1264.

But this influx of German settlers was not altogether an evil. Besides enabling the Poles to repopulate the devastated areas and even to reclaim marshland and forest that had never been tilled, and so revive the economic prosperity of their country, the German element was valuable both because of its own qualities and also as a model for the Poles. The German peasant brought with him the iron plough, the three-field system of agriculture, methods of clearing forest and reclaiming marsh quite unknown to the backward Pole, who soon began not only to imitate his methods, but to envy his liberty and to claim similar privileges. Soon the Polish princes and magnates were granting to the Poles all the privileges of the Germans, and by these concessions the whole position of the Polish peasantry was transformed, and a period of peasant freedom and prosperity began which lasted for two hundred years. Further, the new settlers began to spread Western ideas not only in the courts of princes and magnates, but in the towns and villages. Such foreign communities as the religious Orders were encouraged to settle in Poland, and some of them, particularly the Cistercians, contributed greatly to the social, moral, and economic advance of the country. The towns such as Breslau, Poznań (Posen), and Cracow became important centres of trade, and industry was organised by the new gild institutions. So rapid was the growth of population that the Poles themselves began to spread beyond their ethnographic frontiers, especially the enterprising Mazovians, who colonised the greater part of the Jadźwing country and the south of Prussia, while the Lesser Poles colonised the Lublin plateau and advanced over the Wieprz, the Bug, and the San from Brest to the Carpathians. The Kujawians and Greater Poles made an advance down the Vistula and into South Pomerania. All these movements, though they did not attain their full power till later, began in the later years of the thirteenth century. Even the political disintegration of Poland was not without its advantages. It enabled the local prince and his magnates to devote their resources exclusively to the development of one small area. The different provinces began to display different tribal qualities and to express each its own individuality. The superior education and political sense of the inhabitants of Greater Poland were in striking contrast to the wealth and rude turbulence of the freedom-loving magnates of Lesser Poland or to the restless enterprise and poverty of the backward Mazovians. Such an expression of tribal independence was an inevitable preliminary to any real centralisation of Polish institutions.

Communities absorbed in their own local affairs could learn only from long experience the necessity for combination; and that such a lesson was being learned was obvious towards the end of the thirteenth century. On the death of Leszek II in 1288 a host of claimants appeared, but after the short reign of Henry Probus (1289–1290), Prince of Breslau, a Germanised ruler who recognised the overlordship of the Empire and was elected by the support of the German elements in Poland, three strong candidates emerged—Przemyslav of Greater Poland, Vladyslav of Kujawia, and Wenceslas, King of Bohemia. Wenceslas received support from the Germanised princes of Silesia and certain elements in Cracow, and was able to occupy the capital. But Przemyslav was supported by the patriotic Poles of his own principality, and by Vladyslav who nobly withdrew his candidature. His personal possessions were enhanced by East Pomerania, which was bequeathed to him by its last prince, Mszczuj II, and which he snatched from the grasping hands of Brandenburg. Supported by the revival of national feeling in Greater Poland, especially among the clergy, Przemyslav II made a determined effort to save Poland from foreign domination and, with the consent of the Pope, had himself crowned at Gniezno (Gnesen) as king in 1295. This new attempt to reunite Poland, emanating from Greater Poland instead of Silesia, was frustrated by the assassination of the king in the next year at the instigation of the Margrave of Brandenburg. The magnates of Greater Poland at once proclaimed Vladyslav king, but Wenceslas, already in occupation of Lesser Poland, began to seize the other provinces, and, forcing Vladyslav to flee, had himself crowned in Gniezno (Gnesen) as King of Poland (1300–1305), thus making Poland once more a vassal State of the Empire. At the beginning of the new century the national revival in Greater Poland had failed, and that province began to fall under the influence of the princes of Silesia, while Pomerania was left to its fate, and Mazovia, backward and indifferent, was subdivided into a number of small principalities. Only in Vladyslav of Kujawia did a spark of hope survive. On the extinction of the Hungarian house of Árpád in 1301, all Central Europe seemed to fall into the hands of the Přemyslids of Bohemia, but the death of Wenceslas in 1305, followed by the murder of his only son in the next year, left the question of the succession in Poland, as in Bohemia and Hungary, once more open.

The "partitional period" is marked by rapid and sweeping changes in the constitution of the Polish community. The eleventh century had witnessed the steady development of a monarchy intent on its great task of welding the scattered clans into a State. By the end of the century the disruption of the clans was complete. The aristocratic elements had been attracted to the prince's court; the other enterprising individuals had acquired estates all over the country. The weaker clans or weaker elements in the clans had sunk to a position of dependence on the prince, on the Church, or on the knights on whose estates they worked. The centre of the prince's local administration was the *Gród* or castle under his deputy, the *Kasztelan.* The *Gród* was both a fortress and a centre of the prince's domain. Round it were grouped the peasants in their Hundreds and Tens—an organisation which lasted till the thirteenth century—or in the later territorial units, the *Opola.* To this large class of dependants must be added the slaves. The prince's administration had become supreme. The power of the clans gave way to the *Ius ducale.* In the twelfth century, however, the prince found himself forced to extend his resources to meet the requirements of his wider commitments. To secure the co-operation of the Church—his partner in the work of unification—to obtain more officials and soldiers, he was compelled to make wide concessions, at first to individuals and institutions, then to whole groups. Such concessions took the form of a *Przywilej* or charter, by which the prince not only conferred land, exemption from taxation, and other "immunities," but also defined the status of the individual, institution, or group in question, and so gave up part of his sovereign power. The period from the end of the twelfth century to the death of Casimir the Great is distinguished by the transformation of the community on the basis of such individual privileges. Thereafter the monarch had to deal with definite classes, which were in process of formation in the thirteenth and fourteenth centuries. As the charters conferred tended to conform to certain types, so the individuals receiving them tended to combine into groups with common interests. Such groups crystallised into fixed classes.

The first group to benefit by such privileges was the Church. Not only were charters granted to ecclesiastical landowners, but monastic communities received large grants of land. The Cistercians received a charter in 1140, the Dominicans in 1223; above all the Teutonic Order obtained wide privileges. Besides the clergy, the townsmen and peasants received considerable "immunities" under German law and formed new and important groups. More complex and more important was the evolution of the upper class. We have seen alongside the magnates, or *nobiles*, the rise of a group of *milites* who tended to be identified with the former in status, if not in wealth or influence. After the acquisition of an hereditary estate and the attainment of extensive rights over his dependants, a *miles* desired to make his position secure by some outward symbol. Coats of arms were used in Poland in the twelfth century, in imitation of Western Europe, but were at first temporary marks of individual prowess. In the thirteenth century, however, such arms tended to become hereditary. Now the Polish knights were distinguished from the knights of other Western countries in that they had only recently emerged from the clan stage. Instead of the adoption of a coat of arms by one family, the knights of a whole district, in which the bond of clanship was still strong, adopted a common coat of arms. Further, the war-cry or slogan which along with other clan traditions was rapidly sinking into desuetude, was revived and used along with the coat of arms. Thus, a Polish *miles* was distinguished by his Christian name and the name of the slogan, which he shared with other members of his clan. Only much later did he begin to adopt a surname, almost invariably taken from the name of his estate. It is premature to speak of the *Szlachta* or gentry as a class in the thirteenth century, but it was in process of crystallisation, and its connexion with the earlier clan system is an important factor in the evolution of a class which was to be relatively more numerous, more independent of authority, and more provincially-minded than the knighthood of any other State.

With the multiplication of princely courts, the Polish knights, and particularly the magnates, found a wide field for their energies, and by their numbers and their growing tendency to combine, they became a power to be reckoned with by the princes, and the local officials became rather territorial magnates than officers of the prince. Thus the *Wojewoda* became the head of the province rather than the agent of the ruler, and the *Kasztelan* ceased to function as a royal official, like the counts and barons of the West. The prince began to seek a new class of officials more like the French *bailli*. Such officials were established by the Czech King Wenceslas. The new office of *Starosta* was adopted in Poland as an institution separate from the old territorial hierarchy. But it was inevitable that the growing power of the magnates should find some means of expression. The prince in order to seek advice and support was accustomed to call together a *Wiec* or council, at first simply composed of the officials. Gradually he began to summon the territorial magnates from time to time to discuss questions of policy, and continued to do so even after the *Starosta* had superseded the older officials. But such a *Wiec* was limited to one province. As yet there was no common council for all Poland. There was a *Wiec* for Greater Poland, another for Lesser Poland, another for Mazovia. The different principalities were, in fact, separate States bound together loosely by a common dynasty and a common Church. The very name of Poland was little used and generally meant Greater Poland, while the princes strove to obtain "the throne of Cracow," not of Poland. At the beginning of the fourteenth century the Poles were rapidly assimilating Western ideas; although hopelessly weak politically, they were learning to combine under one ruler; but of the consolidation of the separate provinces into one organic whole there could be no immediate hope.

(C.)

HUNGARY, 1000–1301

THE Magyars of Ural-Altaic stock established in the midst of the Slav nations were bound of necessity to feel the influence of these settled neighbours, who had reached a higher stage in Christian and European civilisation than they had themselves. Two words which still exist in Hungarian political vocabulary will suffice to prove this influence: "liberty" is called *szabadsag*, which represents the Slavonic *svoboda*; the "king" is *Korály*, from the Slavonic *kral*, which itself represented the Germanic name of Karl (Charlemagne, the king *par excellence*), just as in Russia the title of Tsar perpetuated the name of Caesar. The conversion to Christianity introduced the use of Latin among the upper classes; this facilitated closer relations in intellectual matters with the non-Magyar peoples, and up to the Reformation there is no question of linguistic conflicts in medieval Hungary.

The official entry of the Magyars into the family of Christian nations dates from the end of the tenth century. It was a Czech, Vojtěch, otherwise called Adalbert, who, in the town of Gran (Esztergom), baptised the son of Duke Géza, destined to be canonised under the name of St Stephen.

Stephen I reigned from 997 to 1038[1]. He brought Christian Hungary into relations with the neighbouring states, with Poland and with Venice. After the heathen chieftain Árpád, it is in Stephen that the Magyars see the second founder of their nation. Up to the most recent times the crown of Hungary has been called the crown of St Stephen. The prince carried on an energetic struggle against a heathen prince, Kopány, who saw serious danger in the introduction of a new faith. As skilful in diplomacy as he was valiant in war, Stephen entered into direct negotia-

[1] Cf. for St Stephen's reign *supra*, Vol. IV, pp. 214–15, and for his relations with Germany Vol. III, Chaps. X, XI and XII.

tions with the Pope to obtain the exemption of Pannonia from the claims of the German bishops of Lorch and Salzburg, and sent an embassy to Rome to place Hungary under the protection of the Papacy. The latter, in after years, shewed its gratitude by admitting him to the number of the saints.

The Pope cordially welcomed the homage laid at his feet, granted to the king the crown of which we have just spoken, and authorised the establishment of an archbishopric at Gran, and of any bishoprics which the king might wish to set up. Thus Hungary achieved ecclesiastical independence of Germany. He bestowed on the king, in addition, the privilege of having the cross carried before him, as a symbol of the apostolic power with which he was invested.

On 15 August 1000, Stephen was crowned at Gran with the crown which the supreme pontiff had sent to him. In this connexion we may mention a detail which deserves notice. The crown which is still shewn to-day, and which bears the name of St Stephen, is not the crown sent by the Pope. It is a Byzantine work, the gift of the Byzantine Emperor Michael Ducas, who reigned from 1071 to 1078.

Stephen was the first organiser of political life in the kingdom. The kingdom was completely unified and was not divided up into appanages. Latin was the language at once of the Church and of the administration. The king, the supreme overlord, was surrounded by a body which the authorities call sometimes *regalis senatus*, sometimes *regale* or *commune concilium*. From the political point of view the country was divided into counties under counts (*föispán*). This word is derived from the Slavonic (*župan*), as are many other words in the language of politics and administration. We need only cite the word *udvornik*, which designates the intermediate class between noble and serf (from *dvor*, a court or dwelling-place). The same word supplied the name of the chief official of the kingdom, analogous to the Anglo-Norman justiciar, the count-palatine, vice-president of the royal court (*nador*, Slavonic *na dvor*). Christian customs in these primitive times were in certain respects in accord with the barbarous system of ancient days. The loss of a limb by violence was compensated by the loss of a similar limb. It is the application of the old biblical precept; an eye for an eye, a tooth for a tooth. All freemen served in the army. To muster all the warriors, it was enough to send a blood-stained sword through every county.

Stephen had drawn up for his son Emeric a book of instructions, some of which are very remarkable. He notes that Hungary is not inhabited solely by Magyars, but also by "strangers," *hospites*. "Be kindly towards these strangers," he writes, "for they bring knowledge and light into thy country. They are the ornaments of the throne. The kingdom in which a single language and a single set of customs prevail is weak."

From the religious point of view the kingdom was divided into ten dioceses, dependent on the diocese of Gran. Their sees were Kalocsa,

Veszprém, Pécs (Ipek), Borcs (Borsa), Raab, Erlau, Csanád, Nagy-Várad (Grosswardein), and Fehérvár in Transylvania. In the early twelfth century, however, a second province was formed under the archbishopric of Kalocsa. Stephen also founded abbeys to which Benedictine monks were summoned. Schools were built in these abbeys. The religious edifices were built by Italian and Byzantine architects.

Among the inhabitants of certain towns, particularly old Buda, Gran, Raab (of which the Magyar name is Györ, and the Latin name Arrabona), we early find a large number of German *hospites*. The towns enjoyed municipal self-government under the supervision of the *föispán* (count) or the bishop.

At the beginning of Stephen's reign private property did not exist. No property was known but that of the state or the tribe. The king suppressed tribal property and ordained that every citizen might retain and bequeath to his children the possessions which he might have acquired personally or received as a gift from the sovereign.

An aristocratic caste began to be formed, and seems to have been divided into two classes. The first includes the counts, the bishops, the higher officers of the army, probably the descendants of the chieftains of the tribes which once invaded the plain of the Danube. The second was more specially made up of knights. The common people possessed no landed property.

The king was the supreme fountain of justice and in certain cases acted personally as judge. The great ecclesiastical, civil, or military dignitaries appeared before the royal court, which was presided over by the sovereign, or, in his absence, by the count-palatine. The royal court served as a court of appeal against judgments delivered by the *comites* from the bishoprics, the towns, or the villages. Single combat was admitted as a judicial test. Penalties were very severe. The man who sowed dissension among the king's subjects was condemned to lose his tongue. The right of asylum in the churches was refused to a conspirator against the king or against the kingdom. Some crimes were punished according to the social position of the offender. A count who murdered his wife paid her family fifty head of cattle; a knight, in similar circumstances, ten.

The immediate successors of St Stephen are of little interest[1]. But special mention should be made of Ladislas (László) I, who was also surnamed the Saint (1077–1095). This prince had the skill to make himself independent equally of the Pope and of the Emperor. He obtained from the court of Rome the canonisation of Stephen and of his son Emeric. He fought successfully against the foreign peoples who were, besides, blood relations of the Magyars—the Cumans and the Patzinaks—caused

[1] For the history of Hungary during this period see *supra*, Vol. III, Chap. XII, especially pp. 281, 303–4; for relations with Byzantium, see *supra*, Vol. IV, references in the Index; for relations with the Papacy and Germany under Henry IV, see *supra*, Vol. V, references in the Index.

them to settle in his kingdom, and converted them to the Christian faith. By forcing Croatia to accept a Magyar prince, his nephew Almos, son of King Géza I, Ladislas prepared the way for the union of that country with Hungary. He took severe measures against those of his subjects who returned to paganism, and against those who committed theft or acts of violence.

At a great assembly held at Szabolcs in 1092 he promulgated laws upon religious matters. They authorised the marriage of priests, contrary to the traditions of the Roman Church, regularised the collection of tithes, and enacted rigorous penalties against serfs who worked on Sunday. The Church, which from the king's successor secured the revocation of the permission of clerical marriage, grateful for his zeal, made Ladislas a saint.

He was succeeded by Koloman, who reigned from 1095 to 1114[1]. Like his father, this prince was a reforming monarch and a champion of justice and order. His "Great Road" (*Magna Via*), which was long a main artery, shews his appreciation of the value of commerce. When the crusaders passed through Hungary, he entered into relations with Godfrey of Bouillon, and succeeded in preserving his kingdom from the excesses of troops not noted for their discipline. The most important event of his reign was the acquisition of Croatia. This Slavonic province, which to-day forms part of the Jugo-Slav state, had up till that time been an independent kingdom. Koloman succeeded in obtaining his own recognition as king and was crowned King of Croatia in the town of Bielegrad (Zara Vecchia), which to-day is no more than a wretched hamlet south of Zara but was in those days the seat of a bishopric. This Bielegrad has nothing but its name in common with the present capital of Jugo-Slavia. The word means "the white castle," and is found no less than five times in Slavonic countries. At that period, we cannot too often insist upon it, the use of Latin entirely obscured the difference between the Ural-Altaic Magyar tongue and the Slavonic Serbo-Croatian language spoken by their neighbours of Croatia and Dalmatia. Koloman, at a diet held near Zara in 1108, had to swear to allow no Magyar to enter the Croatian countries without the permission of the natives. The Venetians at that time occupied part of the eastern coast of the Adriatic. Koloman took from them the towns of Split (Spalato), Zadar (Zara), Trogir (Traù); it was only for a time, it is true, for they were lost again to the sea-power within a generation[2].

Henceforward the destinies of the Croatian nation were associated with those of the Magyar state; but they were never confounded with them. In virtue of the agreement of 1108 Croatia preserved the right to control its own internal constitution, its national army, and its financial system.

[1] For the relations of Koloman and his successors till 1197 with Byzantium and the Serbs, see *supra*, Vol. IV, and with Germany, Sicily, and the Crusades, Vol. V, references in the Index.

[2] See *supra*, Vol. IV, pp. 406, 409–11.

The reign of Géza II (1141–1161) is marked by an event no less considerable than the union with Croatia for the growth and prosperity of the Hungarian monarchy: the arrival of Saxon colonists in northern Hungary and Transylvania. The colonists obtained a guarantee of what was, in effect, self-government. They had a national assembly which was called *universitas nationis Saxonicae.*

The reign of Béla III (1173–1196) brought his country into closer connexion with Western Europe. He married princess Margaret of France, sister of Philip Augustus and widow of prince Henry of England. On the occasion of this marriage he caused an inventory of the revenues of his kingdom to be compiled, perhaps a trace of the influence of the English Domesday Book. The struggles in which he engaged against his neighbours the Russians of Kiev extended Hungarian ambitions north of the Carpathians into Galicia (Halich). The relations of Hungary with foreign countries began to multiply. King Louis VII of France and Conrad III, King of the Romans, had passed through the kingdom in 1147 on their way to the Crusades. Magyar students travelled to Paris to enrol themselves at the university there.

In the reign of Andrew II (1203–1235)[1] the Golden Bull of 1222, which is the Magna Carta of Hungary, was promulgated. At the head of this document the sovereign takes the titles of hereditary King of Hungary, Dalmatia, Croatia, Rascia (or Serbia proper), Galicia, and Lodomeria (which preserves the name of a Russian prince called Vladímir). The Golden Bull contains thirty-one articles, of which the following are the most important. The king promises to summon a diet every year at the town of Székes-Fehérvár (Alba Regia, Stuhlweissenburg), to imprison no noble without previous trial and condemnation not before himself but before the count-palatine, to levy no taxes upon the estates of the nobles and ecclesiastics, and henceforward to receive tithes in kind and not in money. Foreigners are forbidden to possess landed property. While the provisions were undoubtedly in the interest of the nobles, that is the free landholders, as a whole, they also, in accordance with the strong State-tradition of Hungary, checked the rise of feudalism proper, for it was definitely decreed that, like other great officers of the Crown, the counts (*föispán*) should be removable for misconduct and not be hereditary in tenure, thus providing another analogy in their position to the English sheriffs.

Seven copies of the great charter were engrossed, and these were placed in the hands of the Pope, of the king, of the chapters of the cathedrals of Gran and Kalocsa, of the Knights Hospitallers, of the Templars, and one in charge of the count-palatine, whose special duty it was to watch over the observation of this fundamental law. If the king were to violate it,

[1] For the relations of Hungary with Byzantium and the Balkans from 1197 to 1301, see *supra,* Vol. IV, references in the Index.

the bishops and nobles were empowered to resist *sine nota alicuius infidelitatis*. This article has often been invoked in the history of Hungary. It is similar to the provision for resistance, if the king infringes his concessions in Magna Carta. During the year 1231 an article which forbade Jews and Mohammedans to fill public offices was added to the text of the charter. Taken as a whole, the Golden Bull testifies to a remarkably early development of constitutional and parliamentary rights only paralleled in Spain and England in the thirteenth century. The tumultuary diet, formed by the attendance in person of the nobles, both greater and lesser, was the most archaic of such assemblies, but proved quite capable of concerted action, and of limiting the absolutism of the monarchy. Like John Lackland of England, Andrew II attached his name to a document of the highest importance, but he was himself essentially a mediocre and characterless ruler.

His son Béla IV (1235–1270) saw Hungary laid waste by a terrible plague, the invasion of the Mongols[1]. These Mongols belonged originally to the same race as the Magyars. But the latter had become Christians and Europeans. They had ennobled their primitive stock by inter-marriage with neighbouring peoples. The Ottoman Turks, relations of the Mongols, founded a state which represents, all in all, some degree of civilisation. The Mongols, however, at least in Europe, could only massacre, pillage, and destroy. They were led by a Khan named Batu. They brought with them fire-arms, the use of which they had learned from the Chinese, and powerful siege-engines. They were admirably disciplined. Their arrival was the signal for an appalling panic. The bloodstained sword which was to call the whole population to arms was sent through the villages. The Cumans who formed the advance-guard of the Magyar armies were unable to check the invaders. The Mongols succeeded in capturing the town of Vács (Waitzen) on the left bank of the Danube; its population was entirely destroyed, and had to be replaced later by German colonists. It was formerly the residence of the first princes of the Arpád line. A single ally offered his help to Béla to stem the plague, his neighbour, Frederick, Duke of Austria. The Cumans were accused of treason, and a certain number were put to death. In some districts the people, in exasperation, joined the invaders.

The Magyar army came into contact with that of the invaders in 1241 at Mohi on the banks of the Sajo, a tributary of the Theiss, but only to meet with a disastrous defeat. A hundred thousand men were slain, according to some accounts; others say sixty thousand. *Fere extinguitur militia regni Hungariae*, wrote the Emperor Frederick II. Pesth and Várad fell, Csanád was destroyed. The invasion was only checked by the Croats on the field of Grobnok not far from Fiume on the coast of Dalmatia.

[1] See for the Mongol invasions *supra*, Vol. IV, pp. 637–8, and Vol. VI, pp. 103–4, 437, 458.

King Béla, in terror, fled to Austria. Duke Frederick made him pay for his hospitality by the cession of three border counties. The fugitive vainly begged shelter from the Emperor Frederick II, whose vassal he offered to become, and had to seek refuge in the islands of Dalmatia. Fortunately for him, the invaders, recalled to Asia by circumstances of which we know little, suddenly retreated towards the countries from which they had come. Possibly they had heard of the death of the Great Khan, or possibly they feared that they would perish of starvation, since they had destroyed and ravaged everything.

The Magyar state was not as yet sufficiently civilised to have lost much in this period of torment. But one thing could not be replaced: the lost man-power. The gaps in the population were filled by German colonists.

We have related above how the unchivalrous Frederick of Austria had profited by the wretched situation of his neighbours to extort from them three counties. He was to be punished for this mean action. Béla, freed from the Mongols, demanded the return of his possessions, and fought a battle against Frederick on the banks of the stream which formed the boundary of the two states, that same Leitha which afterwards divided the two halves of the two-fold Austro-Hungarian monarchy. Frederick was killed in the battle, and Bohemia and Hungary disputed his succession. The quarrel was decided in favour of Bohemia. Her king, Přemysl Ottokar II, proved himself generous. He had no wish, he said, by once more weakening Hungary, to lay open to the Mongols access to both kingdoms. He even married a daughter of the King of Hungary, the princess Constance.

During the very brief reign of Béla's successor, Stephen V (1270–1272), a personage who was cleverly to exploit the rivalry between the two countries came on the scene. This was the King of the Romans, Rudolf of Habsburg. He secured an alliance with the young King of Hungary, Ladislas IV, called the Cuman (1272–1290), and pitted him against his rival the King of Bohemia, Přemysl Ottokar II (1253–1278). Hungary, in striving to destroy Bohemia, was paving the way, little as she knew it, for the fortunes of Austria. Fifty-six thousand Hungarians and Cumans took part in the battle of Dürnkrut on the Marchfield, in which the fortunes of Přemysl Ottokar were dashed to the ground (1278). Rudolf, in his letters, shewed himself full of gratitude and affection towards the Magyars, "his dearly beloved children, flesh of his flesh and bone of his bone." Twelve years later he vainly attempted to instal his son Albert as their king on the ground that Hungary was a fief of the Empire.

Ladislas the Cuman, in spite of this victory, was far from popular among the Magyars. He made himself hated on account of the favour he shewed towards the race from which he derives his surname. In 1239 his predecessor Béla IV had received into the kingdom forty thousand representatives of these nomads and had settled them between the Danube and the Theiss. Ladislas, whose mother was a Cuman, remembered too well her race, and the Cumans presumed upon his predilection for them. At last the king was forced to take military measures against them; and they ended by murdering him. It was not until the following century, during the reign of Louis the Great, that they allowed themselves to be completely assimilated and were converted to Christianity. To this day their name is attached to two Hungarian counties: Great and Little Cumania (Nagy-Kunság, Kis-Kunság).

Ladislas IV left no male child. He had adopted a grandson of Andrew II, who was crowned by the name of Andrew III. The court of Rome, which favoured the house of Anjou, refused to recognise him. Charles Martel of Anjou invaded Croatia, and had himself crowned by the papal legate at Zagrab (Agram) in 1290; but he died in 1295, and the death of Andrew III, which took place during the year 1301, produced a new war of succession, for with him ended the dynasty of Arpád.

The princes of the line of Árpád created, in broad outline, the framework within which the Magyar nation was henceforth to develop. This framework included peoples of varied race, Slovaks related to the Czechs, Serbocroats, Roumanians, who all allowed themselves to be absorbed into a unity which, if not Magyar, was at all events Latin. The native languages did not count in public life. The idea of nationality or of historical right did not as yet exist. Right was created by conquest. Time and again the rulers of Hungary undertook military expeditions against the neighbouring peoples, and assumed the titles of King of Serbia, of Rama (Bosnia), of Galicia, of Lodomeria, and even of Bulgaria. But these ephemeral titles never represented an effective and lasting sovereignty. For the most part the occupation was very brief.

The only important acquisition made by the dynasty of Árpád was Croatia. This province, which is to-day a part of the Jugo-Slav kingdom, had in early days formed an independent State lying between the republic of Venice and the Byzantine Empire. Its rulers bore the title of king. One of the most notable of its kings was Peter Kresimir (1059–1073). In 1076 Zvonimir was crowned by the papal legate, and received from him the standard, sword, and sceptre. In return for these good offices he recognised the overlordship of the Pope, and promised him an annual tribute of 200 gold bezants. He married Helen, sister of King Ladislas I of Hungary. In 1103–1108 Koloman, King of the Magyars, profiting by the anarchy which reigned in Croatia, laid hands, as we have seen, upon Croatia and the sea-coast of Dalmatia, although his successor, Stephen II (1114–1131), could not in the end retain all the latter acquisition.

Under the rule of the Magyar kings, the Croatian districts retained the name of Slavonia, which revealed clearly enough their ethnographic character. The kings held the title *Dalmatiae, Croatiae rex*. They had as their lieutenants two officials called *Bans*. This title, which seems to be eastern in origin, continued to be employed for the viceroy of Croatia until the collapse of the Austro-Hungarian State. There were as a rule two *bans*, one for Croatia, the other for Dalmatia. The latter had his residence at Knin. The diets met now in one town, now in another. Up till the fifteenth century the Croats were not represented in the diet of Hungary proper.

The Hungarian Church was in communion with Rome; but it was divided into two sections by districts and liturgical language: the Latin section, which followed the Latin liturgy of the Roman Church, and the Slavonic (Glagolitic) section which employed the Latin liturgy in the Slavonic tongue. The alphabet they used differed from that employed in the Russian, Bulgarian, and Serbian churches, which was called Cyrillic, from the name of the apostle of the Slavs[1].

Transylvania, on the eastern borders of the kingdom of St Stephen, like Croatia on the west, had a clearly defined individuality both from the ethnographical and political point of view. This district, composed mainly of mountains and forests (its Latin name, Transylvania, alludes to the forests which surround the country, while its Magyar name Edily comes from Erdö, a forest), had been occupied successively by the Dacians, the Huns, the Gepids, the Avars, the Slavs, and the Magyars; there were still to be found Roumanian inhabitants, like their kinsmen in Wallachia and Moldavia, and the frontier guards, a Magyar tribe, the Szekels, called in Latin Siculi, in German Szekler, whose native name seems to mean "guardian." The origin of these Szekels is wrapped in mystery, and cannot here be discussed; they were always distinguished by certain peculiarities from the rest of the population. In the first centuries of history the situation of Transylvania as regards Hungary was this: Hungary was the *caput*, Transylvania the *membrum*.

We have just explained the name of this province as an allusion to its vegetation. In German it has another name, Siebenbürgen (in Slavonic Sedniskradsko), which seems to mean the province of the seven castles (Gyuba-Fehérvár or Alba Transylvana, Hunyad, Küküllö, Torda, Kolozs, Doboka, and Szolnok), and has nothing to do with forests or mountains. It is not, however, certain that the name Siebenbürgen was not simply taken from that of the town called in Latin Cibinium, in Roumanian Sibenium, and in Magyar Nagy-Szeben, the population of which was made up of Germans, Roumanians, Magyars, and Jews. Each of these interpretations has its supporters. But we can at all events agree that at the time of the invasion a Magyar tribe occupied the province and there encountered the remnants of an ancient Roumanian civilisation.

Like the rest of Hungary, Transylvania was divided up into counties. We find in its provincial history three clearly marked groups of political importance: the Magyars, who form the nobility, the Szekels, and the

[1] Cf. *supra*, Vol. IV, pp. 225, 229.

colonists who came from Germany, the Saxons. The Magyar group had at its head a *voievode*; the colonists, whose centre was at Nagy-Szeben, a count called in German *Sachsengraf*. The German colonists had come from Flanders, or from the Saxon provinces. In 1224 a royal privilege of Andrew II had gathered them into a single group subject to a single tribunal (*unus populus sub uno iudice*), the *universitas Saxonum de Sibino*. The special organisation under which the Saxons lived was to acquire considerable importance in the period after 1526 when the province of Transylvania formed an independent principality.

CHAPTER XIV.

COMMERCE AND INDUSTRY IN THE MIDDLE AGES

During the ninth and tenth centuries the decay of the Carolingian Empire and the raids or conquests of Northman, Saracen, Bulgarian, and Magyar had hindered the economic consolidation of new peoples and checked intercourse both among Mediterranean lands and between those lands and the North. Byzantium—the great city, the luxurious capital—remained the depositary, and as yet unrivalled elaborator, of the industrial and commercial traditions of the ancient world. But Byzantium faced East; though she conducted an active trade with her Muslim neighbours, and trade of a kind with the inchoate peoples of the North and West, her economic influence westward and northward was, as it were, involuntary. Her chiefest luxuries might not be exported, and she allowed Italian seamen to fetch what they were permitted to take. Her direct influence on Italy, above all on Venice, in the tenth and subsequent centuries was great; though the lines of its action are not always easily traced. At least equally great was the direct influence of Italy on the lands over the mountains. It would therefore be possible to resolve the history of European trade and industry in the Middle Ages into a series of tableaux illustrating the outward spread of Byzantine and Italian influences. But that history cannot truly be so resolved; although it would be distorted, and some of its most significant features would be obscured, were it painted with a Northern rather than a Southern light. In matters economic, as in much else, the homes—even the pillaged homes—of the older culture usually led, and very often they gave; but the newer peoples also were really, if rudely, creative.

What little is known of the intricate commercial and industrial life of tenth-century Byzantium provides, for the most part, rather contrasts with simpler contemporary conditions and subsequent growths elsewhere than suggestions as to the roots from which those growths may have sprung. But, if only for the contrast's sake, that little should not be overlooked. It is drawn mainly from the so-called Prefect's Edict of Leo the Wise, which, though it deals only with the greater organised trades and professions, over which the State exercised a special control, still throws some light into the streets and shops and counting-houses of the city. These State-dominated trades are the bankers (τραπεζῖται), notaries, jewellers, dealers in raw silk, silk-throwers, silk-weavers, dealers in silken garments, linen-dealers—who buy for money in Pontus and Thrace and by way of barter from the Bulgarians—dealers in unguents who buy from the East, dealers in wax, in soap, general dealers, leather-workers, and all the trades connected with the food-supply of a great capital. Other trades, such as marble-workers, painters, and carpenters, are mentioned; but whether or not they were organised into gilds or colleges is uncertain and immaterial. They shew clearly enough a complex subdivision of labour and trade in the service of a luxurious community. The organised trades, though subject to rigid government control, are yet not in the almost servile position once occupied by the *collegia* under the declining Empire of the fourth and fifth centuries. Moreover they are developing in ways unknown to the classical *collegium.* The beginnings of an apprentice and journeyman system; rules for testing the qualifications of new members; attempts on the part of government to prevent prosperous traders from making gain in more than one line of business; and provisions for purchases by whole "gilds" collectively, anticipate familiar aspects of the gild-life of the West in the high noon of the Middle Ages.

There may have been—in Italy there almost certainly was—a measure of continuity between late imperial "gilds," whether of the Byzantine or of some other type, and those "gilds" of traders or craftsmen which come into being—or into the light—throughout Europe, from the latter part of the eleventh century onwards. Ravenna, where evidence of such continuity would most naturally be sought, supplies a series of references to technical *scholae* and their officials—in the sixth century the bakers; in the ninth and tenth the notaries and merchants; in the eleventh the fishers and victuallers. Rome had her *schola* of gardeners early in the eleventh century, and there are similar isolated references from Naples and elsewhere, until the blacksmiths' community of Brescia appears as a well-organised body in 1101. Of the industrial life of these *scholae* in the dark ages really nothing is known, and the continuity, if continuity there were, in Italy or possibly in parts of Gaul, is of little real significance; for there is no reason to suppose that either these *scholae* or those of Byzantium were deliberately copied by other communities in Italy, still less by transalpine communities. What is of great significance is the mere existence of any such "gild" at a given time or place, proving, as it does, commercial or industrial specialisation and suggesting the existence of wide markets.

Though commercially Byzantium faced East, her own lands and the Levantine territory of the Crescent attracted Italian seamen and merchants even in the most perilous days of the tenth century. By the close of the century, Venetians constantly visited all the ports of the Eastern Empire. Venetian slave-traders, and Venetian salt or timber merchants, were in Greece and Egypt certainly in the ninth and possibly in the eighth century. In the early days of Venice, Amalfi, which recognised the suzerainty of the Eastern Emperors down to 1075, had been a serious rival; but by about the year 1000 Venice was undisputed mistress in the Adriatic. She had, also, regular trade relations with Germany and was sending over the Alpine passes the luxuries of the East into the as yet but imperfectly Germanised frontier-provinces of the Empire. It was probably by way of Venice and Mayence that the "men of the Emperor" procured the pepper which they paid to Canute to maintain their trade footing in England. Yet though merchants went to and fro and the worst days were past, Venice and all other Italian towns, at the close of the tenth century, were little better than villages, or encampments among the ruins, when compared with Byzantium's population of at least a hundred thousand and her diversified industrial and commercial life. It is true that from the ninth and even from the eighth century onwards faint reports come through to us of manufacturing industries of more than local importance, in one or other of these Italian towns, of cloth made in Florence, of silk woven and cloth and gold wire made at Lucca, or of rich vestments bought—and possibly made—in Rome. But these are only obscure beginnings or struggling survivals—one cannot tell which—very different from the industries of the great city which had never been pillaged.

Though war may waste the fields, and conquests change and change again the legal and social status of the cultivator, so long as men must be fed there is less chance of widespread technical retrogression in agriculture and the rural crafts, during ages of trouble, than in those urban industries which depend on effective communications and an extensive or wealthy circle of consumers. Therefore, although whole districts went out of cultivation in what had been the home provinces of the Empire between the fourth and the seventh centuries, scattered evidence from the seventh to the tenth—evidence coming mainly from the Exarchate, the Patrimonium Petri, and the South—proves at least the existence of regular leases, arable land owned by small cultivators, enclosed vineyards and oliveyards, rents paid in money, and other rents which just because they were paid in kind reveal a very varied and, so to say, civilised agriculture, an agriculture in sharp contrast with the primitive simplicity of the contemporary Celtic, Teutonic, and Slavonic North; where neither the relics of an old civilisation nor the agricultural specialisation that commerce brings with it had as yet affected systems of tillage, which in any case—owing to climatic reasons—could never attain to the variety of the South.

One force, it is true, must have worked steadily, even during the darkest ages, in the North—the slow growth of population or the slow spread of a dominant race, as in England, over the whole territory available for conquest and settlement. Land was being won from moor and forest and sea; pastoral or semi-pastoral life was giving way to agriculture. The ploughman, "the grey-haired enemy of the wood" of the Anglo-Saxon poet, was everywhere carrying on his slow feud, conquering those forests from which, as King Alfred wrote, "many a home may be built and many a fair 'town' stockaded, wherein men may dwell in peace and quiet." The free peasants of eastern Flanders, of the Campine, and of Frisia, were laboriously attacking the heath and the marshes round about their scattered homesteads. In such districts individual initiative had the freest play; but it was only in later centuries that they became homes of serious technical progress in agriculture. Throughout the greater part of Northern Europe settlement was by villages, and agricultural holdings, whatever the exact status of the holder, were scattered over the open fields and subject to a common routine which, once fully established, proved extraordinarily incapable of change.

It is uncertain over how wide an area what was, generally speaking, the final step in the development of that routine had been taken by the close of the tenth century; but the evidence now available suggests that the area was not very wide. That step was the introduction of the familiar three-field system, in which each of the great village fields was cropped in a regular rotation of winter grain, summer grain, fallow. It was first taken apparently, in a few districts, soon after the final settlement of the Northern peoples. The three-field system was certainly known and practised in the Empire of Charles the Great, to whom legend ascribes an order for its general use. But the less economical two-field system, in which half the arable lay fallow each year, survived in parts of Germany, the Mosel-land in particular, far into the Middle Ages. The two-field rotation was common in such a progressive French province as Normandy during the thirteenth century, and in Central and South-Western France it was universal centuries later; although there one can speak of a two-field rotation, but hardly of a two-field system, because population was more scattered and agriculture less communal than in the North. The two-field system was common too in almost all parts of England in the Middle Ages, and it survived into modern times far more widely than was at one time supposed. All this suggests that the three-field rotation won its way very slowly.

The two-field system itself was only one of several growths from that most primitive form of agriculture in which fields have no permanent existence, but revert periodically into rough pasture or, it may be, into woodland. All over Europe remnants of this earliest system survived to modern times, side by side with remnants or variants of perhaps its most important offshoot other than the two and three-field systems: that is the system in which an "infield" near the village or homestead is permanently cultivated, while a series of "outfields" are cropped in turn so long as they will bear, and are then allowed to revert to the waste. In the tenth century the primitive system of shifting fields, or its first modifications, must have been widespread. It was the typical agriculture of Wales as revealed in her earliest laws; it became a permanency in many parts of Norway. In its "infield" and "outfield" form it remained the basis of Scottish agriculture down to the eighteenth century, and left traces on the agriculture of many English counties. It was long the dominant system in most of the Alpine valleys; it has a modern history in the lowlands of the North Sea coast. Owing to the very flexibility of its rude practice it proved less obdurate, when a stimulus to improvement was forthcoming, than the relatively perfect and very rigid organisation of the two or three-field system; but in the earlier centuries of the Middle Ages it must still have been a mere unprogressive barbarism.

During the dark centuries, the old cities of the Western Mediterranean and of Southern "France" had fallen even lower than those of Italy. In Northern "France" and in England, where the perfected city-life of the old world had never come into being, as in the greater part of Germany, in Scandinavia, and in the Slavonic lands, where there had never been city-life at all, the humble beginnings of that life in its medieval form had to face every kind of difficulty. But around court, cathedral, or monastery, at the nodal points of roads and waterways, and at the chief harbours, a scanty industrial life had persisted through the times of trouble or was coming into existence as society became once more accustomed to a measure of security, so that population, and that luxury among the great which has so often been the cause of industrial specialisation, had once more chances of growth. Even in the ninth century a small Frankish monastic town had its streets of the merchants, the smiths, the armourers, the saddlers, the bakers, the shoemakers, butchers, fullers, furriers, wine-merchants, and inn-keepers; in the tenth century scribes made copies of technical treatises; and at the beginning of the eleventh the reeve, or lord's bailiff, on a great estate in England controlled, ideally and perhaps in fact, a plumber and a mill-wright besides the more primitive types of artisan. But a street need neither be long nor full; a treatise may be copied yet not much read; and the industrial dependents of a great ecclesiastical or lay establishment were not a new social phenomenon.

The raids and conquests of the Northmen had stimulated commerce and town life both directly and indirectly. Themselves great traders, though also great destroyers, their inroads extended both the range and the intensity of European commerce. In the ninth century they joined hands with the East, behind the back of Europe as it were, securing political control of the old trade route down the Dnieper to the Black Sea, and of its profitable commerce in furs, honey, wax, and, above all, slaves. Treasure and Eastern wares came up the route to the Baltic, so that the influence of this "Arab" trade can be clearly traced in Western Germany during the tenth century. Their ships and settlements brought the whole of the British Isles, and to some extent the remote lands of the North-West, into close relations with the continent. In or about the year 1000, York is described as "full of merchants from every quarter especially from the people of the Danes." And though their raids had so wasted the Flemish and Frisian shores that, about the same date, the land beside the mouths of the Rhine and the Meuse was almost uninhabited, yet the needs of self-defence had called into being there, as in other regions subject to their depredations, strong places—stockaded boroughs in the English Danelaw, or fortified monasteries, like the *castrum coenobium Gandense* of St Bavon—which were to become in time centres of urban civilisation.

To these new centres, as to the old, came the wandering merchants of many races whom every great Northern ruler of these centuries, an Otto or an Alfred, appreciated and encouraged. Moving usually in groups, in their ships or with their caravans, through lands which as yet for the most part had no organised commercial life, they seem often to have travelled farther than did their successors of the thirteenth and fourteenth centuries; though few can have rivalled those ninth-century Jews who are said to have journeyed constantly from Frankland to China, sometimes by the coasting routes of Southern Asia, sometimes overland from the Levant, finding at innumerable points of the great journey communities of their own people to aid and protect them. Among these wandering merchants, men bound to no soil and by the law of no single community, there grew up habits of co-operation and a custom of the merchants which was to become the Law Merchant of later centuries.

The developments and changes in transport and intercourse, between the dark earlier centuries and the age (*c.* A.D. 1250–1350) for which information is comparatively abundant, and with which this chapter is mainly concerned, were affected more profoundly by political events than by technical achievement of any kind. True, the trade of Bruges in her great days owed much to the mighty artificial waterway to the sea at which Dante marvelled; the pass of the St Gothard might have remained only a second or third rate Alpine highway, and the federation of the Forest Cantons might not have acquired so great an economic and political importance, had not some nameless engineer—about the year 1225—hung "the bridge of spray" in the gorge of the Reuss above Göschenen; improvements in seamanship, by the fourteenth century, rendered the long voyage from Italian ports to the Channel an ordinary rather than an extraordinary occurrence. But such technical gains were to some extent offset by corresponding losses—an undoubted decay of Roman highways, as for instance in England; siltings up of harbours and waterways with which medieval engineering was unable to cope; lost memories of possible trading routes, such as those revealed by the more distant explorations of the Northmen. And in any case these technical gains had not economic significance comparable—to take examples from varied spheres—with that of the political consolidation of England or of France; the cutting off of Russia from the Black Sea, and the Mediterranean, to which Russian ships had penetrated in the tenth century, by the invasion of the Patzinaks from Asia during the eleventh; the counter-offensive of Genoa and Pisa against Muslim piratical sea-power in the Mediterranean which preceded the First Crusade; the destruction of the sea-going trade of Ferrara by Venice early in the thirteenth century, which marks an important stage in the concentration of the trade, and so of the industry, of north-eastern Italy in the territory of St Mark; the creation of the Mongol empire which opened the overland routes to the Far East for Marco Polo, routes which had been so well trodden by 1315 that Pegolotti the Florentine could write of one of them—which started from the northern shores of the Black Sea—"è sicurissimo, e ciò lo dicono tutti i mercanti che l'hanno usato." Within a generation political events closed them again, and the lands of the "Grand Cham" became lands of fable.

There is one major exception to this general conclusion. The technique of the warehouse and the counting-house, of the money-changer's table and of the moneyer's art, made notable progress with the growing volume and complexity of commerce and the growing capacity of governments to protect and encourage it. This progress, unlike that in the means of transport and the opportunities for trade, is not counterbalanced by any parallel retrogression. It can best be examined in connexion with the spread of commercial influences from Italy. But before any such examination is attempted, the fundamental industry of agriculture, as it had come to be practised in the thirteenth and fourteenth centuries, claims attention—not merely because the Middle Ages were essentially agricultural, but because important problems, connected with the accumulation and distribution of wealth and with the relations of urban and rural industry, must first be viewed, as it were, from the fields.

In its broad outlines the agriculture of Europe changed but little between the eleventh and the fourteenth centuries. Not till the end of the thirteenth century was the agricultural occupation of their territory by the Northern nations approximately complete, a process of which the Villeneuves, the Newtons, and the innumerable villages created by the Germans in the process of their colonisation southward and eastward, are the permanent record. To what extent the creation of new villages was accompanied by improvements in the laying out of the fields in France or England is not yet known; though the planning of new towns can be studied in the French *bastides* of the thirteenth century, or in Edward I's "*bastides*" in North Wales, at New Winchelsea, and at Hull. In Germany, it is possible to trace with some certainty the effect of the constant creation of villages and towns on the arts both of town and of village planning. The semi-agricultural towns of the North and East, such for instance as Breslau, have a systematic rectangular ground-plan which recalls Roman or American colonial enterprise. Modern field-maps of the villages beyond the Elbe, as compared with those of the older settled territory further West, often shew a forethought and system which must have contributed to agricultural efficiency. The directors of the various colonising movements were men who understood their business. They brought to their aid specially qualified pioneers. The marsh lands about Bremen, for instance, began to be settled and laid out with an admirable regularity and efficiency by expert peasants from Flanders and Holland early in the twelfth century. These Low-German and other West-German colonists carried their skill as far eastward as Hungary; and it is not unlikely that the agriculture—together with the industries—of England profited by the close relations with Flanders which followed the Norman Conquest.

The gradual adoption of the three-field system, already referred to in connexion with an earlier period, is an English parallel to this technical progress during the German colonial age. A corresponding development in Western Germany is the progress from a two-field to a four-field system which is found in the valley of the Mosel. It was a distinct technical advance for, whereas under the two-field system half the land lay fallow yearly, of a four-field system it is written *seminabunt agros illos tribus annis et quarto vacabunt.* The same thing happened in some English two-field villages; but the change is hard to date.

The pressure of population in old-settled districts had furnished both colonists and some incentive to the adoption of the less wasteful forms of agriculture. Towards the end of the thirteenth century the business of village-making slackened throughout Germany, and in the fourteenth century it ceased. Forests, which in the twelfth century had been valueless or even a burden, began to be protected systematically, first by the lords and subsequently by the customary law of village or mark. Great numbers of villages were even deserted in various parts of Germany; though how far this was due to war and pestilence, and how far—as has been argued—to the actual inability of a now redundant population to maintain itself on poor land, it is impossible to determine. Had the rural population, in any part of Europe, grown during the two closing centuries of the Middle Ages, fundamental adjustments in technique would have been inevitable. But plague—especially the great visitation of 1349—warfare, and possibly the more subtle social causes which tend to preserve the balance between population and resources, rendered anything of the kind unnecessary. Indeed, what large-scale adjustments took place were often in the opposite direction, as a result of the temporary fall in population, due in England to the Black Death, or in France to the Death and the Hundred Years' War.

Such progress in agriculture as had occurred up to the fourteenth century was not absolutely confined to the mere conquest of wood or waste, and the reproduction on land thus gained of slightly improved forms of the old village life. The transforming power of nearness to the young towns, or of facilities for the production of some luxury or necessity which could enter into commerce, can everywhere be traced, most readily and most extensively in the agriculture of the Mediterranean lands. Throughout Northern Europe special crops could not easily be fitted into the corn-producing routine of the open arable fields; whereas in the South the climatic facilities for the production of such crops—the grape, for instance, and the olive—had maintained a varied and relatively elastic agriculture since ancient times. The gradual extension of crops other than corn, in the Teutonic or semi-Teutonic North, was facilitated by the fact that much land which was cultivated directly by or for the greater "proprietors" either had always lain outside the intermixed acres of the open fields, or was gradually consolidated—extracted from the fields as it were—at some time before the fourteenth century. Whether such land was tilled by a more or less servile peasantry, under the direction of the lord's agents, or was in some fashion farmed, is from the present point of view immaterial. The fact that an intermixture of property was a technical disadvantage had been early recognised. Documentary evidence of such recognition is naturally rare, but a few cases have come to light, such as the exchange effected between two ecclesiastical landowners of South-West Germany in 1158, on the ground that "ex tali permixtione diversarum proprietatum saepe molestiae fiebant et querimoniae." There is little reason to think that, in Germany or any other country, this recognition, with the resulting re-arrangements, affected peasant lands before the fourteenth century.

The peasantry, however, had always controlled some scraps of land outside the fields, and the progressive absorption of waste land had added to the supply. In the earlier centuries land newly won must have often been assigned piecemeal to its first cultivators and subjected to the ordinary arable routine; but when once that routine was set, the new acquisitions—the *essarts* of English agrarian history—often provided opportunities for a more individual agriculture than was possible in the fields, whatever the system of tenure.

The closes of the lord's demesne and the *essarts* in peasant hands, to adopt the English terminology, might be turned into specially well-cared-for meadows, into vineyards or orchards; they might be cropped with flax or hemp, hops or woad; or they might be used as garden ground for pease, cabbages, and small sowings of the finer grain crops. Wherever climate and circumstances favoured, there was a steady addition to the land thus set aside for crops that required special attention. Here and there, in the thirteenth century, whole districts were dominated by some special crop, though this was, of course, exceedingly rare. The high valley of Aquila, in the Abruzzi, grew saffron "for half Europe"[1]; and as its second staple industry was pasture, it drew its corn and oil from other parts of the Regno. In the near neighbourhood of Bordeaux, wine-growing for distant markets controlled agricultural life. South-western

[1] Probably a mere popular judgment. At the close of the Middle Ages there were many other important sources of supply. The Aquila crop in 1493 was 100 mule-loads. Schulte, A., *Ges. der Grossen Ravensburger Handelsgesellschaft*, 1923, I, p. 258, II, pp. 151 sqq.

France was a region in which the closely-articulated and therefore relatively indestructible Teutonic type of open-field husbandry had never existed; so it is not surprising to find that the solvent influence of a commercial agriculture had produced an "entirely individualistic rural economy," in which vines, olives, and wheat were grown by an almost free peasantry on "small, exceedingly subdivided plots, without any communal connexion between them." In a more northerly wine-producing district, that of the Mosel, where vines were grown on demesne land or on land newly won from the waste, the social effects of a specialised agriculture are also to be seen, in the freer forms of tenure, and consequently greater subdivision of property in the peasant vineyards than in the manorially regulated *Hufen* (peasant holdings) of the common fields.

Thirteenth and early fourteenth-century Flanders furnishes the extreme instance north of the Alps of the reaction of an industrial city-life on rural conditions, though wherever towns grew strong some of the results which were general in Flanders were likely to occur sporadically. The great Flemish estates of the Cistercians, and many of those belonging to the nobility, produced for the towns; towards the end of the thirteenth century such estates were let out to *métayers* or rent-paying farmers, since throughout Flanders serfdom was decadent and agricultural capital was accumulating. Polders were multiplying rapidly; some of them still bear names which are probably those of the "undertakers" of the thirteenth century. Inland heaths and marshes were also laid under contribution. Intensive agriculture was already driving out the system of regular fallowing. The urban demand for meat, milk, and cheese enabled the cultivator to keep much live-stock; the climate was favourable to pasture-farming; and so manure was abundant. Agriculture was becoming to some extent specialised locally; there were cattle districts, corn districts, woad districts. Commons had almost disappeared, except the scanty common of the highway side or the dyke bank. There were fed the beasts of the agricultural labourers, the *coppers*, who, like the labourers of eighteenth-century England, had at most a scrap of land attached to their cottages, and supplemented their earnings with those of their wives and children, who span wool for the urban manufacturer.

Languedoc also was a land of towns, and that much earlier than Flanders; but its town life was, for the most part, less industrial. Nevertheless, rural conditions in Languedoc indicate an urbanised rather than a feudal society. In the twelfth, and even in the eleventh century, the Toulousan peasant was but little burdened with services or servile dues. He had inherited a diversified agriculture. He was, it would appear, some sort of *métayer*, paying to his lord usually a quarter of the produce of his plough-land and a half of that of his vineyards, orchards, and nut-trees.

In Northern and above all in Central Italy the *mezzadria* system had become very common by the close of the thirteenth century, as the result of the victory of a rich urban over a poor feudal society. The businesslike landowners, while able and ready to advance capital for the development of their estates, were not prepared to part with their share in the increment, as did the feudal lord when—in France for instance—he granted land to the peasantry in return for a fixed *cens*. Therefore the Italian stipulated for his share of the produce. The typical townsman of Italy despised and bullied the *contadini*; but it was to his interest to promote drainage, irrigation, the rational use of the land, and that diversified agriculture which was necessary to meet the luxury and the varied industrial demands of the cities. As communities also, the cities of the thirteenth century are found applying business principles to land. About Bergamo common pastures were rented out to cattle-owning associations. Brescia let its pastures at auction to the highest bidder, instead of regulating their use by tradition as a contemporary English town might have done. Como sold much of its common land out and out. The constantly recurring prohibition of such sales in urban legislation during the whole century, and also the constant acquiescence in the permanent though irregular occupation of common land by individual citizens, shew how strong the tendency to alienation was in an individualistic society. With the fourteenth century, agriculture in Tuscany, Lombardy, and the other Italian homes of active civic life had taken its place in definite economic subordination to the capitalism of the towns.

The roots of medieval Italian capitalism are buried in and beneath the commercial revival of the eleventh century. It has been argued that medieval trade—at any rate before the thirteenth century—was such a peddling affair, so limited in scope and outlook, that it could not of itself beget accumulated capital, whose immediate origin, so the argument runs, must be sought in the surpluses—the true unearned increments—accruing to the burgess owners of urban real property, during the age of town growth from the tenth to the thirteenth century; and whose ultimate sources were the surpluses which the governing classes in Church and State drew from their control over the springs of rural wealth, and spent in the towns. No doubt ground-rents were a true cause of accumulation; in some parts of Europe, above all in the North, they may well have been a chief cause; but that they were the sole or even a prominent cause in those places where accumulation was earliest, most rapid, and most conspicuous, cannot be maintained. However much the growth of the early medieval town, and so of its ground-rents, may have been promoted by the dispersal of agrarian surpluses through the households of king and count, bishop and abbot, trading wealth and the employment which it brings must be regarded as both cause and consequence of town growth, not as consequence only.

In Italy, where urban history before the thirteenth century is most significant and urban wealth greatest, no such simple connexion between agrarian surpluses and commercial capital can be accepted. The salt-trade, and the earnings of her traffic with Byzantium and the East, laid the foundations of Venetian wealth at a time when her citizens were not lords of the *terra firma*, and when the rental of the Rialto can have been but small. No doubt, in many other towns, accumulations of wealth are found at an early date in the hands of a class which corresponds to the land-owning patriciate of the towns of Northern Europe. But care must be taken in drawing conclusions from this fact. It is on record, for instance, that Genoese noblemen, owners of urban real property, provided capital for the wars of St Louis; but there was no gulf between nobleman and merchant at Genoa, and it is possible that the wealth invested in land had been won by their predecessors in trade. As merchants, shippers, bankers, the nobles of Genoa in the twelfth and early thirteenth centuries took a leading part in the commercial life of the town. They risked, and no doubt also gained, wealth in trading partnerships *en commandite*. A will which has survived from the year 1236 shews clearly the varied, if somewhat modest, investments of one such Genoese trading gentleman. Perhaps his initial capital came from the land; it certainly grew in trade.

There is, however, both in Southern and Northern Europe, and throughout the whole medieval period, one certain connexion between feudal land-ownership and commerce—the lord might himself become a trader or an organiser of trade. The trading lord was most often the head of an ecclesiastical corporation, but not infrequently he was a king. A familiar instance of monastic commerce is the wool trade of the English Cistercians. Monastic houses were the chief traders, shipowners, and money-lenders of Scotland in the twelfth and thirteenth centuries. The early Benedictine houses of the continent had regularly employed a *negociator ecclesiae*, who was charged with the sale of the surplus produce of their lands and of the monastic artificers. In the ninth century the abbey of St Martin of Tours had secured extensive trading privileges from Louis the Pious, and in the eleventh those of St Wandrille, Jumièges, and Fécamp could undersell the other wine-merchants owing to their exemption from tolls. In the twelfth century the government of Richard I carried through some profitable "deals" in tin; in the thirteenth Henry III—or his agents—utilised the royal prerogative to help the sale of wine from the royal vineyards in Gascony; in the fourteenth the Black Prince made profit out of his tin "blowing houses" at Lostwithiel and shipped salt fish for sale to Bordeaux[1].

But nowhere was royal trading so early or so fully developed as in the kingdom of Sicily. The Norman administrative genius, which had not hesitated to tabulate English swine and "otiose beasts" in the Domesday

[1] It has been shewn, however, that some late medieval trading operations in a king's name were made by a king's factors on their own behalf. See E. E. Power, *The English Wool-trade in the reign of Edward IV*, *Cambridge Hist. Journ.*, II, (1926), p. 22.

survey, and had made the Duchy before the year 1200 "the most advanced and self-sufficient country in Europe," found an outlet in the kingdom of Sicily in the organisation of government monopoly and trade. Perhaps the Normans were influenced by the example of Byzantium and stimulated by the congenial Italian commercial atmosphere. In the twelfth century the Crown monopolised the commerce in iron, steel, and pitch; it sold the surplus corn and cattle of its vast domains to merchants from Venice and the northern towns; it conducted an extensive grain trade with Africa. Under Frederick II the agricultural resources of the kingdom were developed systematically, numerous fairs were established, internal customs were abolished, weights and measures were standardised. But royal trade proper attained its greatest extension under the Angevin dynasty. To the corn and cattle trades Angevin administrators added trade with the Venetians in cheese, butter, and oil. Crown agents bought, warehoused, and resold silks, cottons, flax, and spices. Retaining the old monopolies of iron, steel, and pitch, they established a monopoly in salt. Royal ships were not allowed to rest unproductive, but were hired out when not wanted—often to corsairs. This government business was not all sound: the Angevin fiscal greed constantly threatened the prosperity of the kingdom, and the whole commercial development depended too much on the enterprise, and latterly on the capital, of traders from the commercial cities farther north, especially Florentines. Yet government business continued under the Aragonese dynasty; it was imitated by the barons, and it grew rank in the congenial atmosphere of the fifteenth century. At the close of the Middle Ages, King Ferrante's son was speculating in the Genoese oil trade, and there were barons who forbade their people to buy even food except from themselves.

It was by means of capital early accumulated in trade that Italy, from the twelfth to the fourteenth century, exerted her most direct economic influence on Northern and Western Europe. How the Crusading age developed the Levant trade of the Italian cities and brought the princes of the North into financial relations with the Lombards is well known. The Italian trader, long a familiar figure over all the Mediterranean littoral, is found constantly north of the Cévennes, though not often north of the Alps, from the early years of the twelfth century. His chief places of resort were the great fairs in Champagne—the two of Provins; the two of Troyes; those of Lagny-sur-Marne and Bar-sur-Aube. His trade was both in money and in merchandise; but it is only towards the close of the century that his characteristic financial activities can be traced with certainty. Somewhere about the period 1150–75 the Champagne fairs had become such convenient meeting-places for Frenchmen and Germans, Spaniards, Provençals, Catalans and Italians, Flemings, Englishmen and men of Brabant, that the practice of making "international" debts payable among the booths of their money-changers was well established by the close of the century. Each of the six great fairs ran for six weeks and no two overlapped; so trade could be carried on almost all the year round with that full liberty which was only possible during the Middle Ages at the fair. Documents stipulating for the settlement of debts at one or other of these fairs have survived from the late twelfth century; and from the beginning of the thirteenth century Champagne becomes for a time the clearing-house of Europe. In 1202, for example, Baldwin of Flanders is undertaking to repay certain noblemen of Venice—Venetians, by the way, were rarely seen in Champagne—at the fair of Lagny. Or again, from 1213 onwards there are records of a whole series of borrowings by the archbishop and the city of Cologne, the lenders being always Italians, the place of payment always Champagne. The example of Cologne was followed by many other bishops of Southern and Western Germany. As the loans to bishops across the mountains were often made to facilitate payments due from them to the Holy See, and were often arranged with a visiting bishop in Rome itself, the Curia might be induced to use its influence in support of the creditors: "we must get letters from Rome," write the agents of Italian houses when they find their debtors obstinate.

Various types of Italian financiers are to be found in the North. There are humble usurers who wander over France and Germany, doing a little buying and selling, but occupied mainly, like some of their Jewish predecessors and competitors, in lending to small folk who pawn their household goods to get advances at the well-known usurer's rate, 43½ per cent. The Germans called such people Kawerschen (Cahorsins), and some may have come from Cahors in Languedoc; but most of those trading in Germany apparently came from Asti. The men of Asti were among the first to migrate in considerable numbers beyond the Alps, and with them migration seems to have become a habit. According to their own chronicler it was "in the year of Our Lord 1226" that they "began to lend and practise usury in France...beyond the mountains." Sometimes they handled the high as well as the low finance. In the two Burgundies, where they were particularly numerous, they engaged in every form of profitable and unpopular commerce—corn speculation, toll-farming, farming the revenues of ducal domains, and ordinary village usury. They were followed into the Burgundies, France, and Germany by traders and financiers from most of the West Lombard and Tuscan towns, besides men of Genoa, Venice, and Rome.

The financial supremacy of the Florentines dates from about 1250 and endured for a century. They owed much, in the long run, to the quality of Florentine gold money; but they had won their position before the *fiorino d'oro* was first struck in 1252. England admirably illustrates the progress of their influence. John, a stay-at-home king, borrowed of an Italian house in the early years of his reign, but the house was from Piacenza. About a quarter of a century later, Florentines appear, together with Sienese, Lucchese, and Pistoians, on the borrowing list of Henry III.

Henry's son also made use of the Genoese; but by his time the great Florentine firms, led by the Frescobaldi, a house whose head became a member of Edward II's council, were indisputably supreme. So they were also at the court of Philip the Fair, where "Mouche et Biche," that is to say Musciatto and Biccio Guidi of the company of the Frescobaldi and the Franzoni, gained wealth and unpopularity. Under Edward II the Frescobaldi, who after alternations of good and bad fortune abandoned English business in 1312, gave way to the Bardi and Peruzzi. Italian financial operations were already declining in England and would probably have dwindled away, in the course of the fourteenth century, owing to the growing wealth of native merchants and the increasingly difficult economic situation in Florence itself, quite apart from Edward III's notorious act of bankruptcy.

These Italian firms were normally companies, with a family nucleus. In the firm of Peruzzi, for example, about the year 1300 more than half the capital belonged to members of the Peruzzi family, but some sixteen other families were interested in it. There were five or six Directors (direttori); the house had regular representatives in Naples, Avignon, Paris, Bruges, London, Cyprus, Rhodes, and Tunis, to name only the more important centres; and there was an army of travelling agents, identifiable by their *tessera*—the family badge—scattered over the whole commercial field. The business of such firms was varied. Custody of the deposits of private individuals, gilds, churches, and other corporate bodies, formed a large part. This was the home business. More familiar, but not more important, were the loans to crowned heads and the business of remitting funds to Rome—as when in 1317 the papal collector in Hungary *timens maris pericula feci(t) cambium cum sociis societatis Bardorum*, who undertook to pay over at Rome in Florentine money what he had gathered in a great variety of currencies.

Such widespread and intricate transactions required an elaborate business organisation, detailed accounts, drawing of bills (*lettere di pagamenti*) by the scattered agents on the head office, and an infinite knowledge of currencies and exchange. Even primitive forms of the bank-note and the cheque can certainly be traced in the fifteenth century; and the former, if not the latter, appear to have existed much earlier.

The coining of the gold florin in 1252 marks the return into the currencies of Europe of an effective gold unit. Since Charles the Great struck his new (silver) money there had been no regularly renewed gold coinage west of the Adriatic. The golden bezant, continuously struck and used in the Eastern Empire, was known throughout Christendom. In the West, golden coins had been struck from time to time—with some regularity at Genoa from the middle of the twelfth century—but they had not become current money with the merchant. Frederick II, that hardy innovator, issued a golden *augustale* after his return from the East in 1225; but his need became so great that it could not be kept up: once he was reduced to the issue of leather money. So the *augustale* has no history. Twenty-four years after it came the florin, which has a great history. Before the close of the century it had been widely imitated and, owing to its reputation, Florentines had been called in to manage the mints, not only in other Italian towns, but at Hall in Swabia and even in London; though they were not everywhere required to arrange for the striking of gold. The credit of Florence rested on the excellence and abundance of her gold; and her government of traders, who were very willing to strike overrated silver for paying wages by the Arno, maintained the quality of the florin with the honesty of self-interest.

Gold once known and struck with some regularity throughout the West, the currency history of Europe entered its late medieval phase. The gold was mainly a money of commerce, favoured by the great lenders and borrowers, buyers and sellers, because of its portability, its noble aspect and universal welcome. From the first, its use was encouraged by the Papal Curia. But even in Florence silver was the standard money for domestic trade. Now, owing to ignorance, abuse of the royal prerogative, the diversity of moneys, and the defects of medieval minting, the legal ratio of exchange between coins of the two metals was always fluctuating, and only by the merest accident might two countries employ the same ratio at the same time. So governments constantly discovered that one or other metal was undervalued and tended to leak out abroad, in spite of ferocious currency laws. To remedy this evil the legal ratio might be altered or coins made of the undervalued metal might at the next issue be lightened. In the fourteenth century alone the official ratio of the metals was altered a hundred and fifty times by the King of France, with or without alterations in the metallic content of the coins. As, over and above the lightenings thus undertaken to rectify the evils of a crude bimetallism, new coinage was sometimes lightened in order that it might not differ too much in weight from tokens of the same face value which had borne the heavy burden of a medieval circulation, and sometimes because it suited the convenience of kings to lighten it, the metallic content of the European currencies fell steadily from 1300 to 1500. In these two centuries the English silver penny fell from 22 to 12 grains, the gold equivalent of 6/8 from $128\frac{4}{7}$ to 80 grains; and this fall of something like forty per cent. is representative.

Advantageously situated as were the Italian towns for the development of the machinery of commerce, their political independence and animosities accentuated among them, with unfortunate results, that particularism which was characteristic of medieval urban life. Their distinct currencies were only an outward sign of distinct and often conflicting economic policies, policies which produced such trade-wars as that between Venice and Ferrara[1], or industrial wars like that waged by Florence with Vol-

[1] See *supra*, p. 479.

terra about an alum-mine, which was essential to the Florentine wool industry. In countries which possessed a measure of political unity, some of the economic drawbacks of the Italian urban civilisation were mitigated. Flanders is a case in point. The Flemish towns, though not technically independent, were almost autonomous from the twelfth century onwards. But they were subjects of a single ruler, and not the least important of the many causes of Flemish economic development was the care with which the Counts of Flanders maintained the currency, which had a reputation for excellence and uniformity as early as 1100. To uniformity of coinage was added, as time went on, a uniformity of weights and measures exceedingly rare in the Middle Ages; "e lo peso e la misura di Bruggia, e di Guanto, e di Lilla, e di Ipro, e di Doagio sono tutt' uno, salvo le misure del blado," wrote Pegolotti in his merchants' handbook with evident admiration. To most countries, even to most towns, might have been applied his note on London: "in Londra d'Inghilterra si ha di più maniere pesi e misure." Diverse as were her measures, England in Pegolotti's day had at least a more uniform, if a more old-fashioned, coinage than any considerable European country. The excellence of her silver was well known in Italy in the thirteenth century, though she had no gold money of international, or even of domestic, significance until a much later date.

In this matter of the gold currency there can be no doubt that transalpine governments consciously imitated those of Italy. And it is probable that in connexion with many private commercial institutions there was more or less conscious imitation, though proof in such cases is not likely to be forthcoming. That half-public and half-private institution, the gild, commercial or industrial, in its innumerable forms, whatever its ultimate origin or origins, cannot be included among the borrowed institutions; although, as has been already pointed out, the earliest definitely economic gilds of the Middle Ages are to be found south of the Alps. But the commercial company, as employed for instance by the Florentine bankers, was certainly first perfected in Italy, under the influence of Roman law, and made known by Italians in many other parts of Europe. An institution which has its roots in the family, or the simple association of those who "eat the same bread," is not of necessity sprung from any one law or from any one land; and company trading was well developed among the Hanse merchants in the late thirteenth century, without any demonstrable Italian influence. Yet, whereas the first traces of trading companies in Germany go back only to the opening years of that century, in the Italian towns such companies are found a hundred years earlier. They might be extended family partnerships or wider organisations such as that of the Peruzzi. The individual company was usually referred to in legal documents as the *Societas A. B. et sociorum.*

These firms were essentially private partnerships, not primitive joint-stock companies. Not until the middle of the fourteenth century do the beginnings of joint-stock organisation appear at Genoa. Such things remained exceptional, even in Italy, down to the close of the Middle Ages; and they were nowhere imitated.

Older than the company are the sleeping partnership (*commenda*) and the loan to a merchant for a trading venture overseas, which have their roots in Roman Law and Byzantine practice. At Genoa and Marseilles in the twelfth century many varying methods of employing the *commenda* can be traced. The sleeping partner is not however, at this time, a permanent associate of his active colleague. As a rule he hands over his capital only for some specific enterprise; so that in practice such partnerships are not very different from the loans for a venture beyond the sea. The latter, however, provided opportunities for more speculative undertakings. In the form which they assumed in Mediterranean commerce, *commenda* and shipping loan spread northwards; though primitive forms of such obviously natural institutions must have been known to Teutonic traders in very early times. When Burning Flosi, in the Saga of Burnt Njal, was fitting out a ship to leave Iceland, it is said that "he was so beloved by his men that their wares stood free to him to take either on loan or gift, just as he chose"; his men, in short, were prepared to speculate in their chief's half piratical venture.

Nor is it difficult to trace, in very early Northern gild regulations, the beginnings of certain kinds of mutual insurance. Every gild, social, religious, commercial, or industrial, insured its members in some degree against accidents of life, death, or immortality. The suggestive clause which declares that "at a house burning" brethren shall contribute a penny occurs in the rules of the Exeter gild of late Anglo-Saxon times. In the twelfth, and possibly in the eleventh century, the Icelandic Repp, an association of neighbours for mutual protection, and the somewhat similar Danish frith-gild, took special cognisance of losses by fire. But systematic commercial insurance, based on the regular payment of premiums, is first found in Italy at the beginning of the fourteenth century. There is no reason to suppose that it existed before that date; nor can the splitting of risks connected with loans for trading ventures be properly described as insurance. From documents which run back to 1318 it is evident that the Bardi accepted insurance risks, on consignments of cloth despatched overland, in return for definite premiums. From about the middle of the fourteenth century the history of insurance at Genoa is continuous; and before the century closes re-insurance and the subdivision of insurance risks begin to appear. A Genoese trader was concerned in the first demonstrable case of insurance at Bruges—the first in all Northern Europe—which happened in 1370; and, for many decades after that date, insurance business with which Italians have no connexion is rare even in the busiest commercial centres by the North Sea. Premiums for the insurance of human life also begin in Italy in the fourteenth century; but, even in Italy, life insurance only occurs sporadically and in relation to specified risks—those of the sea, for example, or those of childbed.

There is reason to think that commercial insurance was, in part at least, an ultimate product of the condemnation by the Church—about 1230—of contracts for the payment of fixed interest on loans for distant ventures. The growing difficulty which faced the speculating merchant in finding lenders who would share his risks without any certain returns made some means of reducing these risks desirable. Only an isolated canonist here and there ever criticised insurance by way of premiums This episode in the history of the ecclesiastical campaign against usury in the thirteenth century illustrates the fact that, by this date, the campaign was a forlorn hope; because the payment of interest, certain guaranteed interest, was no longer, as in primitive rural communities, merely the sin of detested village usurers but was a part of everydav business-life in Italy and, to a much less degree no doubt, throughout Europe. Innocent III was perhaps hardly exaggerating when he wrote to the Bishop of Arras in 1208 that, if all usurers were really to be shut out of the Church, "omnino claudi ecclesias prae multitudine oporteret.' That was at a time when the Italian money-lenders were extending their operations swiftly and successfully beyond the mountains. Nor did they go to lands where usury was unknown, although they did bring fresh supplies of loanable capital and highly-trained commercial intelligence. Quite apart from Jewish money-lending (which is dealt with elsewhere[1]), outside even of the Jews' range, the loan of money at interest had long been practised in societies which are sometimes conceived of as living in ignorance of how money breeds. It may be that the denunciations of usury by English and Carolingian Church councils in the eighth and ninth centuries were to some extent imitative; but it can hardly be doubted that they were aimed at a real, though perhaps uncommon, evil. Throughout Europe, from very early times, rich monasteries and individual churchmen had committed usury on a large scale. In the thirteenth century the Templars and the Teutonic Knights carried on the old monastic tradition; though their contracts may not have been technically usurious. Much of the lending by religious corporations, during and after the Crusading Age, is connected with the Mediterranean commercial developments of that era, a connexion which further illustrates the size of the problem with which the stricter moralists of the thirteenth-century Church tried to deal. The references to "money out at interest" in Njal's Saga may reflect the environment of the thirteenth-century Icelandic scribe rather than that of his tenth-century hero; but even so they are significant.

The methods of the ordinary Christian usurer, who carried on what he knew to be a doubtful trade, were much the same in all times and places.

[1] See *infra*, Vol. VII.

His devices as described early in the thirteenth century by Raymond of Peñaforte, whose experience was presumably gained in Catalonia, have their parallels in England and Normandy, Italy and Germany. He buys standing crops at impossible prices; he exacts ruinous compensation for delay in repayment, having fixed the date of repayment so that delay is certain to occur; he takes out his interest in the labour of his debtor or, "imitating the Cahorsins," takes it frankly in money; he hides loan and interest behind a fictitious sale and repurchase at an impossibly high price by the debtor—a device which still troubled English legislators in early Tudor times. Whether the pilloried Cahorsin was an Italian or not, his frank acceptance of interest in money reflects Italian practice and Italian law as they existed before the middle of the fourteenth century when, under the influence of Baldus and Bartolus, the prohibition of interest found its way into secular legislation. Fifteen per cent. was a legal rate of interest at Milan in 1197 and twelve per cent. in 1216. The right to a fixed return without risk—the very essence of usury as conceived by the Christian casuist—was publicly admitted in connexion with the debts of Italian city republics. Genoa led both in the creation and in the consolidation of such debts; her consolidated debt of 1274, which still, as has been said, lives on in the national debt of unified Italy, was the first of its kind. Venice was also an early borrower, and she was followed by Florence, Pisa, Bologna, Siena, Novara, Vercelli, and Como. The clash of the doctrine of usury with the habits of a commercial society is well seen in fourteenth-century Florence. In the course of the century every Florentine gild forbade usury; yet all the time the gilds themselves, like the State, both gave and took interest, either frankly "after the manner of the Cahorsins," or under cover of one of the recognised subterfuges.

In societies less radically commercialised than those of the Italian towns, certain types of contract for fixed gains survived the elaboration in the thirteenth, and the legal adoption in the fourteenth century, of the completed canonist doctrine of usury, just because they had so long been familiar. Of these the sale and repurchase of lands and the purchase of rents are the most important. A borrower could sell land cheap, leaving the fruits to the lender as a handsome interest; and the repayment of the loan would appear as a repurchase. Though the sale and resale of chattels came everywhere to be treated as a usurious contract, the principle was never applied to real property. As for the purchase and sale of ground-rents—one of the oldest types of investment—that was never seriously criticised. Rent purchases were always a favourite monastic investment. The sale of urban ground-rents might provide the trader with very necessary capital, or—though less frequently—the rural landowner with funds for improvement and colonisation. In thirteenth-century Germany such transactions were conducted on an average basis of 10 per cent. Latterly they were often fictitious, that is to say undertaken without reference to specified properties; and so they became indistinguishable from ordinary usurious loans at fixed interest. Taking all these various lines of investment into account, it may well be doubted whether at any time in the Middle Ages capital, where it existed, lacked remunerative employment, with risks which—medievally judged—were not great.

Accumulation of capital, as has already been pointed out, was always possible for the landowner, more especially the corporate landowner, and for the successful trader. Whatever may have been the case at an earlier date, by the year 1300 some merchants of weight and wealth were to be found in all parts of Europe. They were of course far more numerous and wealthy in Italy than, for instance, in England; but even the English merchants of the thirteenth century were not such men of straw as has sometimes been suggested. Light is thrown on the comparative scale of Italian and English business operations, in one important branch of commerce, by the records—imperfect but not so far as they go untrustworthy—of the wool export from England in 1273. In that year various persons connected with the house of Scotti in Piacenza shipped at least 2100 sacks of wool, and the Bardi at least 700. (For comparison it may be borne in mind that, sixty years later, 30,000 sacks was a burdensome national grant to Edward III for his French wars). There were twenty Englishmen each of whom exported more than a hundred sacks; of these the two most important were together responsible for a larger export than the Bardi. They were William le Pessuner and John Durant, both of Dunstable. The total amount exported by Englishmen exceeded that exported by foreign merchants. In estimating a merchant's opportunities for profit and accumulation, the fact that he was not necessarily confined to one line of business must not be overlooked. In thirteenth-century London "most of the aldermen were wool-mongers, vintners, skinners, and grocers by turns or all at once." And the capital gathered in trading could be increased from the rentals of urban property, or by customs-farming and other profitable work for the Crown.

But when all has been said, the number of those who, by any or all of these means, were on the road to wealth was singularly small in the average North European town of the early fourteenth century—mainly because of the smallness of the towns themselves. There were, by that time, several Italian cities which approximated in size, and in the variety and splendour of their economic life, to the Byzantium of the tenth century; and it has been maintained that Paris had a population of 200,000, though some would reduce the figure by at least one-third. A better founded estimate gives Bruges 50,000 in 1292. But London can hardly have risen above 20–25,000. Cologne, and rather later Lübeck, were perhaps in the same class as London. Even towards the close of the fourteenth century, really important towns, such as Frankfort, Nuremberg, or Hamburg, York, Norwich, or Bristol, may be assigned from 6–12,000. Such towns were few. More representative of fourteenth-century England is a town like Liverpool, which in 1375 had about 1,000 inhabitants. In Germany it is probable that, at the end of the medieval period, the very great majority of the towns had less than 5,000 inhabitants. Two centuries earlier their position would be still more modest. In such communities the commercial or industrial roads to wealth were few and strait. The five fishmongers, the four drapers, the four bootmakers, and the two tailors, who formed the trading population of Liverpool at the date mentioned, had not the opportunities of a London alderman in the days of Edward II, or of Antonio Frescobaldi who sat on Edward's Council. It is not often possible to draw a satisfactory line between commercial and industrial activities; the typical medieval craftsman was also a shopkeeper, and in the larger towns his interests and outlook were those of the dealer rather than those of the maker; but it is certain that the more purely commercial pursuits gave far greater opportunities for accumulation than those which were primarily industrial. If anyone in fourteenth-century Liverpool became rich it would be the fishmonger rather than the bootmaker.

The difficulties of communication; the dominance of handicraft in the strict sense of the term; the great extent to which townsman and countryman alike provided for their domestic needs by the labour of their own families; the simplicity of those needs and the scanty population both in town and country—these and many like causes tended to keep the scale of industry small, quite apart from the general absence of expensive mechanical appliances, apart too from those definite attempts to prevent any craftsman from rising above his fellows which are so commonly found in the gild regulations of the fourteenth and fifteenth centuries. The ordinary picture of medieval industrial life, drawn from industries working with primitive appliances for a narrow market, is therefore broadly true—true of all the industries in an average town; true of many industries even in the greatest towns of Italy or Flanders. Taking all trades together, it has been argued that even in Paris, say in 1300, there were as many masters as men. For the towns of Germany many scattered instances, from the fourteenth and fifteenth centuries, shew that the majority of master craftsmen employed at any rate three or four assistants—apprentices and journeymen; but, when the minority is taken into account, this does not yield a result which differs much more from the Parisian estimate than the later date of many of the records would lead one to expect. Throughout Europe, in many crafts, the master was very often only a jobbing workman called in to handle materials supplied by his customers. In occupations such as carpentering, in which the master sold not goods but services, he was paid only about 20 per cent. more than his mate in fourteenth-century England, a difference which may be taken as a rough measure of the distance between employer and employed over a large part of the industrial field in Europe. It is not therefore surprising to find that the Parisian *Livre des métiers* (1261–70) contemplates the possibility of masters reverting to the status of journeymen, "through poverty or because they choose to do so." In the gilds of Prussia, at the beginning of the nineteenth century, for every hundred employers there were barely fifty-six employed; and although the petrifaction of the German gild system in early modern times, and the multiplication of masters, who had secured their position—in the English phrase—by patrimony, may in part account for these figures, it can hardly be supposed that the average position in the Middle Ages was more favourable to the employing class, if such a term be not an anachronism.

But an arithmetical statement of this kind by no means exhausts the facts. In the few centres of active industrial life we can discern—as industrial conditions come into the light of fourteenth-century documents—certain significant tendencies: a tendency for the journeyman to become an outworker doing jobs for several masters; a tendency for masters, in some minor industrial craft, to become subordinated economically to the shopkeeper or merchant of an allied commercial occupation; or a similar tendency to differentiation within a trade, the handworking master taking work from his more commercial colleague. From Siena to York, gilds are found laying down the rule that the journeyman shall work for one master only, a rule whose universality is only explicable on the assumption that there was a general tendency in the opposite direction, a tendency favourable to inequality among the masters; for the powerful employer would control a disproportionate share of the trained labour in his town, if he were permitted to secure even some part of the services of men employed primarily by his weaker neighbours. In those towns or trades—and they were very many, especially in Germany—where the industrial gild spirit, with its jealous desire for equality of opportunity among masters, most completely prevailed, the tendency towards inequality was counteracted during the fourteenth century. But it survived and had freer scope elsewhere.

The equally widespread group of rules, limiting the numbers whom any single master might employ, is a further indication of the state of things against which the systematised gild life of the fourteenth century was a reaction or a safeguard.

The growing economic subordination of craft to craft, or of the handworking to the trading element within a single craft organisation, is conspicuous in fifteenth-century London. A marked decline in the number of distinct craft organisations during the century is one evidence of the former process: glovers, pursers, pouchmakers are absorbed constitutionally into the Company of Leathersellers, the master-glover becoming, if not exactly a wage-earner, at least to some extent dependent on the trader through whom alone his wares can reach the consuming public. In the Goldsmiths' Company the process of differentiation between working and trading masters is very well marked. These instances are taken from the eve of modern times, but they illustrate tendencies which, even in England, can be traced back to the thirteenth century and may well have existed in the twelfth. In Bristol, for example, there can be seen in the fourteenth century two distinct species of tailor, the "merchant tailor" and the small master working on commission for him. In London, the thirteenth century reveals a still more modern phenomenon, not the dependent small master but the "server," who could never aspire to the mastery. The ordinances of the Cordwainers of the year 1271, one of the earliest trade-codes extant in any country, shew that the cordwainer's prentice was expected to pay a premium far beyond the means of an ordinary worker in that or any other trade. That there were opulent tradesmen—goldsmiths, weavers, bakers, clothworkers, pepperers—in twelfth-century England the heavy payments made by their associations for privileges from the Crown, and recorded in the early Pipe Rolls, are sufficient testimony. The business organisation which yielded this wealth escapes us; but it can hardly have been that of humble masters barely distinguishable from those who served them.

On the Continent, as in England, only the documents of the later thirteenth and early fourteenth centuries justify any confident account of industrial organisation; but, in certain great towns and in a few trades which produced *articles de luxe* for export, that organisation is so complex, so capitalistic, that its growth must have been a matter of generations, possibly of centuries. It is closely allied, in its most important homes, Italy and Flanders, with the contemporary organisation of commerce, of which it is to a great degree a product. Its directors are men of commercial antecedents and commercial instincts, whose thoughts and whose wares are far away in foreign parts.

At Florence there are early twelfth-century records of the import of fine cloth from Byzantium and of rough unfinished cloth, Frisian and so forth, by way of the fairs of Champagne. In the thirteenth century these "ultramontane" fabrics were dyed and finished for export in cloth-working shops by the Arno, belonging to, or working for, the merchants of the Arte di Calimala. Probably the cloth was exported mainly to the Levant, though early in the fourteenth century it is certain that consignments went back over the Alps or by sea to Marseilles, to supply the Northern markets. Very little was consumed in Florence, so that this industry, relying on imports for its material and on export for its success, was liable to seasons of bad trade, with all their familiar modern accompaniments in the world of labour.

More interesting than the Arte di Calimala is its successful rival the Arte della Lana, which, when it comes into the full light of the documents (1293–1301), is already the organ of a group of manufacturers who like the merchants of the Calimala use foreign raw material—at this date wool from England—and produce mainly for export. A humbler "art" had to do with the making of rough cloth for home use. The

English wool, which for the most part came via the Garonne and Aigues-Mortes, was cleansed and prepared for spinning in the warehouse of the *Lanaiuolo.* The spinning was done on commission for the Lanaiuolo by a distinct group of tradesmen, the *Stamanioli*, who employed village spinners, mere country folk kept in order by their priests, who had instructions from the city government to preach regularly against yarn stealing and bad workmanship, and to excommunicate in case of need. Sometimes the Stamaniolo himself supplied the yarn, but as the fourteenth century went on, the Stamanioli became simply paid agents of the Lanaiuoli. Weavers, working by the piece for the Lanaiuolo, made the cloth on looms which were usually rented from their employer. The master dyers, who in the twelfth century had an "art" or gild of their own, were in a more independent position; they owned their vats and appliances and sometimes employed ten or more hands; but they too worked on commission for the Lanaiuoli. Fulling was mostly done in rural mills; the various finishing processes—teazing, shearing, pressing, and the like—in little urban workshops. Throughout the long series of operations, the Lanaiuolo retained full ownership of the growing cloth, and his gild controlled all the groups of commission workers. The gild was wealthy and enterprising; it imported scarce raw materials; as a partner *en commandite* it subsidised technical experiments; it managed alum-mines and a woad warehouse; it owned ships, a court of justice, and a jail. In all its decisions, the interests of the Lanaiuoli were paramount. The Lanaiuolo was of the same class, often of the same family, as the great financiers; and the State, controlled by these "capitalists," absolutely forbade combinations among the workpeople.

To find in Florence industries in which there was a fair chance that the average prentice would rise to become a really independent working master, one must descend to the lesser arts, butchers, saddlers, bakers. Here the limitation of the numbers that a master might employ, and the other familiar regulations for safeguarding equality of opportunity, suggest the outlook of the typical North European burgess, rather than that capitalistic outlook which the Lanaiuoli shared with the members of the commercial "arts." The art of silk alone, among the manufacturing arts proper, developed an organisation similar to that of the export cloth industry; but it did so only gradually in the course of the fourteenth century.

Approximations to the position of the Florentine Lanaiuoli are to be found in the textile industries of several Italian towns during that century Occasionally records from the early part of the century suggest that such an organisation was of old standing. This is the case with the Lucchese silk industry, as reflected in the regulations of 1308, an industry which sent its goods to the Champagne fairs and even to London. The business undertaker was a merchant, who bought silk and had it put through the various processes for him by groups of dependent domestic workers.

In thirteenth-century Venice, the actual manufacture of silk was in the hands of small master weavers, who bought the raw material from importing merchants and sold silks to dealers and exporters. As a result, it is conjectured, of a migration of manufacturers from Lucca, the Lucchese type of organisation finally prevailed, in spite of the struggles of the weavers, who however succeeded in retaining more independence than the wool-weavers of Florence. The wool industries in Venice and Pisa, as also the "Art of foreign wool" at Bologna, also supply evidence—though in no case so striking and complete as that furnished by the Florentine Arte della Lana—of a group of manufacturers economically and socially dominant over their workpeople.

A similar, though not identical, class can be discerned in the thirteenth and fourteenth centuries among the cloth-working towns of Flanders and the adjacent districts. Frisian cloth, as has already been noticed, was the first manufactured product of a Northern land which became a staple article of European trade. Already in the eleventh century, Flanders was importing wool for the use of an industry that had outgrown its old homes, the peasant's hut and the manorial or monastic workroom, and was maintaining a class of specialised craftsmen. By 1200 the industry was complex and its products of an almost infinite variety. During the following century, in such towns as Ghent, Ypres, and Bruges, operations were directed by the *drapyer* (the clothier) who, like the Lanaiuolo of Florence, himself bought the wool and gave it out to the master weaver, dyer, fuller, and the rest, beneath whom again was the true proletariat of "cnapen," the "blue-nails," living in suburbs of wretched huts, often paid in truck, hired by the week, and liable to dismissal during those times of slack trade which the constant wars and the resulting difficulties of communication produced with distressing frequency. The drapyer was as a rule a member of the old urban aristocracy, a *poorter*, who owned urban property and was in a position to accumulate rents. Apparently he had no direct connexion with the manufacturing processes; so far as is known he did not own looms, like the Florentine Lanaiuolo; nor did his gild, in this case *the* Gild, the Merchants' Gild, take any but a regulative part in the business of manufacture. The craftsmen who worked for him never admitted his supremacy, though forced to accept it; and the economic hatreds which the system produced were among the causes of the social upheavals of the fourteenth century.

Analogous to the position of the Flemish merchant drapyer, was that of the Parisian silk mercer, who bought the raw material and had it spun by wage-earning *filaresses*; but in this case the weaver was an independent craftsman, to whom the mercer sold yarn. More strictly analogous is the English "clothier that doth put cloth to making and sale," as an Elizabethan statute describes him, a type which rose to great prominence with the rapid growth of the English export trade in cloth towards the close of the Middle Ages, but first comes clearly into the light in the fourteenth century. How closely the emergence of this type of entrepreneur was associated with production for a wide market is shewn by the history of the *drapiers* at Brussels. The class came into being in the thirteenth century, and was at the height of its power in the fourteenth. Side by side with it there always existed a class of independent master weavers, who sold their own fabrics instead of working for the *drapier* like their weaker fellows. In the fifteenth century when, owing to commercial and political changes, the cloth export from Brabant declined, these small masters (*lakenmakers*) increased in numbers while the merchant *drapiers* dwindled. Meanwhile the development of the linen trade was calling into existence a class of linen manufacturers who, like the *drapiers*, supplied material to weavers, themselves superintending only the mercantile side of the business. By that time this type of organisation was widespread in the textile industries of Europe, perhaps the most notable instance, besides those already referred to, being the fustian industry of South Germany, in which the Fuggers of Augsburg made their earliest fortune.

The clothier type has not exactly the same history in any two regions. The relations of the clothiers to gild organisations are particularly varied. The early Flemish *drapyer* belonged to an urban aristocracy and an old established Merchants' Gild, a gild which would not admit those who worked for him; the Florentine Lanaiuolo, also connected with a socially dominant class, had his dependent workers regimented in the lower grades of his own "art"; the English clothier, and others of the same type elsewhere in the fifteenth century, often employed rural weavers and tended to operate outside or across the boundaries of gild regulation. But, with certain minor qualifications, all represent the same grade of economic organisation and the dominance of the commercial over the industrial factor. This dominance is not confined to the textile industry; it is noticeable, though not at so early a date, in mining and metallurgy. In the English lead and tin mining of the fourteenth century, for example, the getting of the ore was in the hands of small men; but these small men were often dependent on advances from the merchants; and the merchants came into direct contact with the actual work of production by their control of the business of smelting. In the great mining industries of the German lands the situation is complicated by the special and changing relations between the various governing powers and mining enterprise, especially in the silver mines of Styria and the Harz. During the earlier centuries, in many cases, work had been carried on under the direct superintendence of a lord's agents, by more or less servile labour. From the twelfth century onwards these servile labourers are succeeded—though no one generalisation will cover all the facts—by groups of free working miners. But differentiation sets in among members of the groups almost from the start: the more successful copartners employ day-labourers; their claims can be worked in their absence; where heavy expenditure on the workings becomes necessary only they, or if they fail, the lord of the mine, can make the necessary advances. As time goes on many of these richer shareholders are otherwise occupied: they direct smelting operations, are minters, money-changers, merchants. Yet they control the mines, though working miners may still share with them; for in hardly any case was a complete separation between "capital" and "labour" brought about. The nearest approach to it occurred where the lord of the mine, by making the necessary advances himself, had exchanged his primitive political and proprietary control of the miners for a control that was more purely economic. Like the Duke of Cornwall at Lostwithiel, he became a kind of industrial capitalist[1].

The business undertaker in the various industries which have been discussed—and in the discussion attention has been concentrated on the thirteenth and fourteenth centuries—may fairly be described as a capitalist. But if, in modern terminology, his circulating capital was relatively large, the fixed capital of the industry—tools, appliances, buildings—belonged for the most part, at any rate in the textile industries, to those who took work from him; and they had no greater supply of these things than had the ordinary self-dependent craftsman. Once more the nearest approach to modern conditions is to be found in Italy. The Florentine Lanaiuolo had a large warehouse (*fondaco*), with a staff of bookkeepers and clerks, and accommodation for workpeople who washed, sorted, and prepared the wool for the spinners, or inspected the yarn and cloth as they were brought in at the various stages of the manufacture. He had much capital "fixed" in the looms which his weavers hired from him. The clothiers of Northern Europe must also have had warehouse accommodation. There are records or suggestions that some of them owned looms, dyehouses, or finishing shops. But, on the whole, their fixed capital would seem to have been less; nor were they united into corporations with capitalistic activities like the Arte della Lana.

Generally speaking, there was little in the plant or machinery requisite for medieval industry to encourage large scale operations of the familiar modern type. There was abundant use of "power," but rarely on a large scale. The water-mill for grinding corn, which spread over Europe—how, no one knows—between the fourth century and the consolidation of the new peoples, was a decisive innovation. Medieval society in the West would be hardly recognisable to the modern student without the mill and the miller. Water-power was subsequently adopted for other industries; but its technique hardly varied. From the twelfth century comes evidence of its use in Italy for fulling, at a time when the fuller of Northern Europe was still a "walker," who stamped the cloth till it

[1] See *supra*, p. 484.

thickened and felted. Later the fulling mill spread into the north, being manorialised like the corn mill. Water-power was used during the fourteenth and fifteenth centuries in metallurgy, for driving furnace-bellows, tilt-hammers, and even wire-mills[1]; for grinding operations other than corn-milling; and for sawing. But, until the fifteenth century, iron and steel were produced by very primitive methods and in very small establishments. The high blast-furnace and cast iron were unknown. The smelting forge (*Anglice*, bloomery) in which the roughly prepared ore was worked into "blooms" of metal, and the smithy which turned out rods or shoes, were both so small as to be easily moveable—the *fabricae errantes* of the Forest of Dean in the thirteenth century. Steel was made in tiny quantities, and in few places, in equally small "catalan" forges. The nearest medieval approach to a modern power-equipped factory is a water-mill for silk-throwing, said to have been erected at Bologna in 1391, whose machines could "do the work of four thousand spinners." Others of the same type were subsequently erected by the commune and rented out to manufacturers. As the reputed designer of this medieval factory was a man from Lucca, it is possible that the capitalistic silk industry of that town was familiar with such labour-saving devices at an earlier date. The wind-mill spread slowly from about the time (1190), when, at Bury St Edmunds, *Herbertus decanus levavit molendinum ad ventum super Hauberdun*; but it remained very rough and imperfect.

There can be little doubt that the nearest approach to modern conditions was to be found, neither in the textile industries, nor in mining, nor in metallurgy; but in the shipyards of the seafaring nations, especially those of Byzantium, Genoa, and Venice. In the ninth century large ships began to be built at Venice on Byzantine models. By the close of the eleventh century Byzantium was outstripped; and early in the twelfth, Ordelafo Falier being Doge, the national shipyard was organised. The scale of operations and the rapidity of work at Venice are suggested by the contract made by the republic with the Emperor Isaac Angelus in 1188, to prepare a fleet of from 40 to 100 galleys within six months; but this is doubtful evidence and does not necessarily apply to the government yard alone. From the time when Dante compared the pitch of Malebolge with that which boiled all winter in the Arsenal, information becomes more specific. A detailed account of the operations in the fourteenth century shews that, apart from repairs, 40 galleys could be built in the year, and that the whole body of workpeople connected with the Arsenal may have been numbered in thousands.

Even in the middle of the twelfth century Genoa was able to send out a fleet of 63 galleys and 163 other ships against the Moors of Spain. During her great days in the thirteenth century the orders of the government for galleys suggest a very highly organised ship-building industry,

[1] The wire-mill however is first heard of, as a wonderful innovation, in the late fifteenth century at Nuremberg.

probably superior to that of contemporary Venice. In 1207 the government orders 20 galleys to be built at home and 2 abroad; in 1242 the order is for 40, and in 1282 for no less than 50 galleys. From the scanty records of navies elsewhere, as for instance in England or in Naples, it may be concluded that government ship-building in the thirteenth or fourteenth century, backed as it was by the whole financial power of the State, involved everywhere a great outlay of capital and a considerable organisation of labour, though only the sustained and well-considered naval policy of Venice could produce a continuous government industry at all comparable with the ship-building industries of the modern world.

Like the building of ships, the building of castles, palaces, churches, and monasteries was largely dependent on the resources of the State, or on those of corporations no less durable and not always less wealthy. The scale of building operations in the Middle Ages was certainly not small. Unfortunately the organisation of medieval building is one of the most obscure sections of economic history. For the centuries from which no documentary evidence survives we are occasionally told, and can generally assume, that there was some amount of compulsory service in all the rougher work connected with building. The carrying dues, which peasants so generally owed, were available for this purpose; and for castle-building in conquered districts the subject population might be drawn upon. Voluntary and unpaid labour on the fabric of churches and monasteries is also not infrequently recorded. The slowness of the operations, in almost all religious and in most civil buildings, put the industry as a whole into a class distinct from that of the building of ships of war and of fortifications, in which time might be an object. In cathedral and other records, from the thirteenth century onwards, the deliberate accumulation of materials and the leisurely process of construction can sometimes be traced. There can be no doubt that these instances are typical. Every large foundation had its permanent staff of repairing masons and other craftsmen, who served as a nucleus round which migratory workers might be grouped when some great piece of building was undertaken. Owing to the slowness of the work, it would not as a rule be necessary to call in outsiders in very large numbers at any one time. Besides the ordinary working mason or carpenter, experts were often summoned from great distances. Such a man was Estienne de Bonnueil, mason, who went from Paris to Upsala in 1287; or William of Hurle, master carpenter, who worked for Edward III at Westminster, Windsor, and the Tower, and whose consulting fee put a strain on the resources of Ely; or the German masters, to secure whose advice Gian Galeazzo Visconti sent letters and even embassies over the Alps, to such famous architectural centres as Strasbourg, Cologne, and Prague. Sometimes these experts brought trained subordinates. Estienne de Bonnueil had a band of "compagnons" and "bacheliers." John of Gloucester and at least six "of his men" came to cast the bells of Ely in 1341–2; Johann Nexemsperger of Graz brought a staff of thirteen to help him in a series of difficult problems at Milan. For a much earlier period, the affiliation of architectural styles throughout Europe proves, or suggests, the influence of such experts: we know how even in the seventh century Benedict Biscop brought foreign masons to Jarrow.

Whether attention is fixed on the expert and his subordinates or on the humbler migratory artisan, the medieval building industry in its prime furnishes an important instance of true mobility of labour. In combating the undue stress sometimes laid upon the stagnant character of medieval life, care must be taken not to exaggerate the mobility which undoubtedly existed. Yet even when Crusade and pilgrimage, the wandering scholar and the international Churchman, are put on one side together with all permanent migrations, a great amount of economic movement of the modern kind can everywhere be discerned. The larger towns, created by this movement, continued to be fed from the country or from other towns. Bücher has shewn how the majority of the people admitted as burghers at Frankfort and Cologne, in the fourteenth and fifteenth centuries, had been born elsewhere; many came from the near neighbourhood, but many from distant towns and villages. Less exact English evidence points in the same direction. In a list of 59 master cordwainers, and in another of 128 tailors, of York, from the latter part of the fourteenth century, the great majority are named after Yorkshire towns and villages, from Bridlington to Skipton. The lists include also a number of place-surnames from other counties, of which the most remote is that of Robert de Bristowe. That movement between town and town was common in England is further shewn by the widespread type of gild regulation providing for the admission of competent strangers.

England never developed that systematised migration of journeymen which produced the "*tour de France*" of the French *compagnon* and the compulsory *Wanderjahre* of the German *Geselle*. This is a late medieval development in both countries, and cannot be traced with any certainty before the latter part of the fourteenth century. It is connected with the growing exclusiveness of the gilds, which called into existence journeymen's associations to resist the tyranny of the masters in possession, and is contemporary with considerable migrations of German and Flemish labour into Italy and England. But, whatever special causes may have come into operation during this later period, with which the present chapter is not directly concerned, it is certain that compulsory wandering could hardly have developed had not the industrial life of an earlier age been tolerably familiar with voluntary wandering.

That the commercial classes were mobile needs no proof, and has been illustrated extensively in the foregoing pages. The records of every fair in Europe provide additional evidence. Nor need such evidence be taken from the great central fairs, from Troyes or Paris or Frankfort. Between 1270 and 1329 the visitors to the English fair of St Ives (Huntingdon) include traders from Ghent, Bruges, Douai, Ypres, and Lille; from St Omer, Caen, and Dinant; they include also Florentines, Scotsmen, Germans, and Spaniards.

A few scraps of evidence, from different parts of Europe, suggest that in the fourteenth century and perhaps earlier, even the peasant was not everywhere so completely immobilised as the conditions of medieval agriculture are often held to imply. The reference is not to movements from the country to the town, which were very common, nor to movements of half-nomadic herdsmen, such as those who accompanied the wandering flocks of Spain or the flocks which moved year by year from the Abruzzi into Apulia, but to recurring migrations of agricultural labourers. Wends travelled regularly from Lusatia and elsewhere to help in the woad-harvests of Thuringia in the fourteenth century; and in the fifteenth Polish harvesters helped to get in the crops about Breslau. The descent of labourers from the Alps and the Apennines, to earn a living in the plains, was probably no new thing when it comes to light at the beginning of modern times. This probability is increased by the evidence of a clause in Edward III's Statute of Labourers, which provides for the continued movement of harvesters from the hill districts of England—Staffordshire, Derbyshire, Lancashire, Craven, and the Welsh and Scottish Marches—into the richer agricultural counties. For how long these movements had existed is not known; but a habit so well established as to secure preferential treatment from legislators whose object was to check what they regarded as improper migrations can hardly have been of recent growth.

CHAPTER XV

NORTHERN TOWNS AND THEIR COMMERCE.

THE Roman Empire, as a whole, had, in all respects, constituted a Mediterranean unity. Even from the confines of the most distant provinces there gravitated towards this central sea not only civilisation, but also political and economic activity. All commerce was attracted thereto. Hence all the cities were more or less affected by the Mediterranean, according to the share they took in general commerce. The Germanic invasion in the fifth century did not, as is generally supposed, put an abrupt end to this traditional position. Only England—or to use the Roman term, Britain—after her occupation by the Anglo-Saxons, ceased to form part of this great union of the ancient world whereto she had been affiliated by the conquest of Caesar. As to Gaul, neither the establishment of the Visigoths and the Burgundians, nor that of the Franks and the Alemanni, brought about a similar result. The situation remained unchanged when Clovis and his successors united the whole of Gaul under one ruler. Throughout the Merovingian period, her civilisation remained much more Roman than is usually admitted. The disturbance and desolation from which she suffered at the hands of the barbarians did not succeed in erasing the principal characteristics of the state of affairs introduced by the Empire. It was not only the Catholic organisation which survived the invasions; a similar position may be found in many branches of the civil administration. Here it will be enough to note that the financial system and the monetary system of the Merovingians were evidently mere survivals of Rome. And it is even more striking to observe that all the existing commerce was carried on through the Mediterranean ports. Until the middle of the eighth century, Marseilles continued to maintain active maritime relations with Syria, Egypt, and Constantinople. The goods landed on her quays were exported even to the extreme north of Gaul. In many cities oriental merchants were to be found side by side with native traders. Urban life still continued active. It may be said without exaggeration that there still existed not only a municipal organisation but a municipal population.

This survival of Roman and Mediterranean civilisation, which, in Merovingian Gaul, had not been interrupted by the Germans, was destroyed by Islām. From the day when the irresistible expansion of the Muslims subjugated all the regions bordering on the Mediterranean basin from Lebanon to the Pyrenees, from the day when they established themselves in the Balearic Islands, Malta, and Sicily, Western Europe was cut off from Eastern Europe, and the Mediterranean no longer remained a great commercial artery but became a barrier; while the links which still bound

Gaul to the unity of culture and the economic unity of the Roman world were severed. This great event reached its full development in the middle of the eighth century, *i.e.* at the time when by the usurpation of Pepin the Short (751) the Merovingian dynasty was replaced by that of the Carolingians. And it is obvious that what then occurred was not merely a political revolution, or rather, that the political revolution was accompanied by a profound social and economic change.

When, by the Muslim invasion, the Frankish kingdom found itself debarred from access to that Mediterranean Sea by which it had hitherto communicated with the outer world, it was faced by entirely new conditions of life. It henceforth ceased to gravitate towards the South. During the Merovingian period, the wealthiest and busiest districts were to be found south of the Loire, and particularly round Marseilles. These now found themselves becoming depopulated and impoverished. When maritime trade disappeared, all the activity which it had entailed vanished likewise. The class of professional merchants which it had supported ceased to exist. Under the Carolingians, there began a historical period during which, in marked contrast to the previous period, society was based essentially on rural economy. The most characteristic feature of this economy is the self-supporting estate, the products of which, instead of being intended for the markets, were used only for the consumption of the owner and the men living on his land. An estate of this kind formed a little closed world, which required no outlets. The population nourished therein was attached to the soil: serfdom became a normal condition; personal liberty was only retained when it was to the advantage of the great landowners. As a general rule, the population consisted only of peasants, and these peasants were so essentially a class of serfs that the word used to describe their profession (*rusticus*) became synonymous with the word which described their legal status (*servus*).

Amidst a civilisation such as this, it is idle to seek any vestiges of urban life. The "cities" of Merovingian Gaul were still more or less trading resorts, and it is only necessary to read Gregory of Tours to realise that trade contributed largely to the support of the municipal population. There was nothing of this left in the Carolingian period. In documents we still find the words *civitas*, *urbs*, *municipium*, *oppidum*, but the localities to which they are applied were no longer anything like a city. They were mere fortified enclosures, protecting either the cathedral church of a diocese, or a monastery. Moreover, in most cases, these enclosures were only old Roman walls constructed in the third century to afford the population some protection against barbaric invasions. Wherever in the Merovingian period a city had existed, there was still one to be found in the Carolingian period, and at first sight it seems as though nothing had changed. But appearances are deceptive. That which had formerly been the distinctive mark of the "city" had disappeared. Merchants were no longer to be found there, and the city was no longer the trading resort and economic centre of the surrounding country. Its inhabitants did not present any municipal character. They consisted of priests, clerics, and monks attached to the service of the churches or abbeys round which were grouped the most indispensable servants and artisans. A small market was held once a week to which the peasants of the surrounding districts came to sell small quantities of the common articles of consumption, and where occasionally a wandering pedlar appeared. Commerce and industry played no part therein and did not contribute to the livelihood of any one as a regular profession. The Carolingian "cities" therefore appear to the historian as the headquarters of ecclesiastical circumscriptions in a purely rural country. The bishop or abbot therein established maintained the clergy and the servants surrounding him on the produce of the estates which he possessed elsewhere, which produce was brought to the city at fixed periods by his serfs. Instead of being a centre of municipal life, it was therefore really only the centre of a large estate, or, if it included several churches, the centre of several great estates. The population living within the shelter of its walls differed neither in its manner of life nor in its social and legal conditions from those living in the country. A town of the Carolingian period was thus merely a concourse of people collected within walls. It is not surprising that in current language it became increasingly common to describe such towns by words which meant fortress—whether of Latin derivation such as *castrum* and *castellum*, or of German origin such as *burgus.*

There was an extraordinary increase in the number of these "castles" and *bourgs* during the period of political disintegration and foreign invasion which began at the middle of the ninth century. In order to repel the invasions of the Normans in the west, those of the Saracens in the south, and those of the Slavs in the east, it was necessary everywhere to build strongholds, whither the peasants could betake themselves in case of alarm. The feudal princes, who seized the opportunity offered by the increasing weakness of the royal power to usurp sovereign rights in their domains, and on whom devolved henceforward the protection of the population, were particularly active in founding these walled enclosures. After the Danish invasions in England, the Anglo-Saxon kings did the same. All Western Europe became covered with a mushroom growth of *bourgs* suitable for military purposes. In each of these was established a permanent garrison of knights (*milites*); and the surrounding population was obliged to work at the construction and maintenance of ramparts behind which they took refuge in times of peril. Similar precautions were naturally taken in the old "cities." During the period of insecurity and anarchy which overwhelmed Europe from about 850 until 1000 it was an urgent necessity that men should be able to count on a place of refuge in case of need. The social utility of the *bourgs* is clearly seen in all the history of the period. The part they played may be compared to that played by the forts and blockhouses built by the white population of America in the seventeenth and eighteenth centuries along the Indian frontiers. The security they afforded naturally caused them to become not merely defensive centres for the surrounding country, but also centres of government. The rulers took up their residence there, and transported thither the storehouses and barns wherein was accumulated the produce of their estates; they built churches there and assembled there the courts of justice of their territories; they appointed officials (*castellani*, *praepositi*, *notarii*) to whom were entrusted the command of the local garrison, the presidency of the law-courts, the execution of sentences, and the levying of the various fines and taxes which pertained to the local ruler. In short, it may be said that in all parts the function of the *bourgs* was, like strong armour, to protect against attacks from without the essential organs not only of the religious but also of the economic and administrative life of the period. Like the "cities," they display no traces of urban characteristics. Their population of knights, clergy, officials of the demesne, legal functionaries, and serfs attached to their service, lived on the produce of the soil, or on contributions levied from the external population; they produced nothing themselves, and, from an economic point of view, must be regarded merely as consumers. Moreover they possessed nothing which could be regarded as autonomy or self-government. The *bourg* which contained them was not the object of their activities; it did not exist for itself, but for the surrounding district. It constituted a kind of centre for the local population, who came to it, but who did not live therein. The peasants who brought thither the harvest of their lords, the *scabini* who came there to try cases, did not reside within its walls. They came from the surrounding country and they returned thither after they had fulfilled their mission, so much so that the *bourg* appears to us only a place of transit, provided with a certain number of warders stationed therein.

Nevertheless, though the cities and *bourgs* of the ninth and tenth centuries cannot be regarded as centres of urban life, they possessed an essential importance in the history of the towns. It was these, in fact, which established the sites of the towns of later days; which thus fixed the localities for the commercial and industrial groups which were the ancestors of the bourgeoisies; and to these spots they almost always gave the names which they still bear.

We said above that Carolingian society was essentially based on rural economy. Land formed the only recognised source of wealth, agriculture the only permanent and general form of work. We must not, however, deny that they had some form of trade. The organisation of the estate or domain, so characteristic of this period, inevitably involved a certain amount of commercial activity. For the large domains were nearly always composed of estates, some of which were a considerable distance away from the principal centre, and it was therefore necessary that their harvests should be transported thither, sometimes from afar. Moreover, certain churches were so overwhelmed with gifts by the piety of kings or nobles that their income by far exceeded their needs, and they were consequently obliged to dispose of the surplus. Finally, the small markets of the cities or *bourgs* gave rise to business transactions which, although doubtless of little importance, were regular. There was therefore some trade. What was lacking, and what had disappeared, was the class of merchants by profession, *i.e.* men whose occupation was to buy and sell. The *mercatores*, or *negociatores*, referred to in contemporary texts were not strictly speaking merchants, but only occasional buyers and sellers. The term was applied to servants employed by the abbeys to dispose externally of the excess of their produce; to the adventurers who followed the armies, or who carried on a dubious traffic in arms and slaves on the Slav frontier. In the ninth century the only individuals exhibiting the distinctive features of merchants were the Jews and the Italians who seem at that time to have devoted themselves, under conditions about which little is known, to the hawking of spices and oriental textiles which they transported, no doubt with much difficulty, from Venice across the Alpine passes. All this maintained a certain amount of commercial activity, especially by boats on the navigable rivers during the summer. And even this transport by boat does not seem to have been at all vigorously carried on except in Northern Gaul. We first hear of the Frisians (in whose country were linked together the courses of the Rhine, the Meuse, and the Scheldt) as really enterprising boatmen in the reigns of Charlemagne and his immediate successors. It was because the cloth woven in Flanders was transported by them that in contemporary documents it is referred to as *pallia fresonica.* And it may be presumed with much probability that, during the reigns of Charlemagne and Louis the Pious, the Frisian boatmen had established busy settlements at Mayence, Maestricht, and Valenciennes. They probably also frequented the ports of Dorestad (on the lower Rhine) and Quentovic (near Étaples), by which the northern part of the Carolingian Empire kept up some intercourse with England and the Scandinavian regions.

Towards the middle of the ninth century the Norman invasions interrupted the growth of this commercial movement. The rivers on which this trade had been plied were now for about fifty years used by the invaders as routes along which to penetrate the interior and to remove their booty. When tranquillity was restored, there had been such great changes in Western society that it was impossible for trade to resume its former conditions. Monarchical power, which had been established on too slight foundations, had crumbled. Under cover of the general anarchy, the more powerful officials of the Crown had succeeded in usurping sovereign rights in their territories. The old administrative counties had everywhere been superseded by principalities which were independent of their suzerain except for the simplest bonds of feudal vassalship. These nobles had led the resistance against the Northmen with great energy, and the services they had thus rendered to the population had still further increased the authority they had usurped.

In all parts they had constructed new strongholds (*castra, castella, burgi*), alike to repel the invaders and to afford a refuge to the people on their lands. They had made these strongholds the economic centres of their domains, and had placed therein garrisons of knights and stewards (*castellani*), to whom were entrusted both the defence of the fortress and the business of administering the government and justice of the surrounding district. The different forms assumed by this organisation in different countries cannot conceal the fact that everywhere they possessed the same essential characteristics. This similarity is obvious not only in Continental Europe but also in England. The boroughs (*burhs*) of the Anglo-Saxon Kingdoms undoubtedly appertain to the same type as the *bourgs* of the territorial principalities which had arisen from the dismemberment of the Carolingian Empire.

The Northmen's invasions had not resulted merely in the accumulation of ruins. The Vikings were pirates whose chief aim was to enrich themselves. Their booty enabled them to carry on a kind of barbaric trade on all the coasts of the North Sea and the Baltic. After the close of the ninth century, the settlements established by the Swedes in Russia along the Dvina and Dnieper reaped extraordinary profits from this trade. By this means they actually came into contact with the Byzantine and Muslim lands in the basin of the Black Sea. Henceforward the Scandinavians abandoned the career of pillage by which they had at first terrorised the whole of Europe during the ninth and part of the tenth century; they now appeared specially addicted to maritime and commercial life. It was owing to them that, by way of Russia, Northern Europe regained contact with the much more highly developed civilisation of the Byzantine Empire and the Caliphate of Baghdad.

Almost at the same time it was restored by another route. In spite of the Muslim invasion, Venice, at the head of the Adriatic, had never ceased to maintain an increasingly active trade with the sea-boards of the Greek Empire and with Constantinople. Her enterprising genius had not even hesitated to open early relations with the Muslim ports on the Mediterranean, with results profitable enough to stifle religious scruples. In the tenth century Venice was already a great port whose activities became extended to its Italian hinterland, soon arousing there a new economic life. At the beginning of the eleventh century, Genoa and Pisa began to shew signs of their future greatness and, after bitter struggles with the Saracenic fleets, succeeded in reopening for themselves that sea which had been closed by the great Muslim invasion of the eighth century.

Thus on the one side by the action of the Scandinavians, on the other by that of the Venetians, two trading centres revived at the two ends of Europe. It would be too far removed from our subject to shew the wide extent of both influences on the interior of the Continent. We must be content to state as a self-evident fact, although details are too often lacking, that, under this influence, economic life quickly revived in all parts of the coast and thence spread increasingly towards the interior by means of river-valleys, the natural routes which the conformation of the land imposed, until the day when, about the beginning of the twelfth century, the Northern traffic and that of the South brought about mutually a real economic revival which gradually affected all Western Europe.

We must here only consider one of these centres of economic renaissance, that of the North. The earliest symptoms of the influence it exercised became apparent in the course of the tenth century. At this time there appeared significant manifestations of commercial activity along the same rivers which had been navigated by Frisian boatmen in the time of Charlemagne. Navigation revived on the Rhine, Meuse, and Scheldt. On the coast Bruges, which at that time communicated with the open sea by the gulf of Zwin, soon surpassed in activity Quentovic and Dorestad, which had until then been pre-eminent. It became a centre of attraction for Flanders and Northern France, as farther west Rouen was to the basin of the Seine, or eastward Cologne to that of the Rhine. Moreover, about the year 1000, many other places sprang up elsewhere as more or less important centres of transit. We may mention Paris, Verdun, Huy, Liège, Ghent, St Omer, Cambrai, Valenciennes, and this catalogue is significant, for it is noteworthy that it includes only places connected by natural channels with the sea.

The essential feature of trade at this period is its wandering character. The merchants devoted to it were travelling merchants, collecting in parties and travelling either by boat or by road to transport wheat, wine, wool, or cloth to distant places. The spectacle they presented was, *mutatis mutandis*, very similar to that offered by caravans in Asia at the present day. Everything suggests this comparison: the length and danger of the journeys, the discipline and mutual help required from every member of the party, the community necessitated in buying and selling, the combination of all participants enabling them, in spite of the small amount of individual capital, to carry out wholesale transactions. This combination, indispensable to travelling commerce, is referred to in contemporary texts by names whose variety is of little importance: *gild*, *hanse*, *carité*, or *confrérie*.

In the tenth and eleventh centuries these merchants appear to us as undoubtedly forming a class of professional merchants. To them trade was not an adventitious and occasional occupation, but a habitual, regular, and normal one. With them, that class of individual whose livelihood came, not from the possession or cultivation of land, but from barter and sale, the class which had disappeared since the close of the Merovingian period, now resumed its place in modern society.

Whence came these merchants? In the absence of any definite evidence, we are obliged to resort to hypothesis in answering this question. Probably we must assume that the first were bold and intelligent adventurers, sprung from that unhappy class of society which, having no land, was compelled to live from hand to mouth by bodily labour, hiring themselves out at harvest-time or engaging as mercenary soldiers. In other words, it seems highly probable that the *mercatores* of the earlier Middle Ages were at first drawn from floating elements of agricultural life which the texts call *pauperes*. The recrudescence of commercial activity afforded to many of them an opportunity of employment and of amassing a fortune. Then their example attracted a large number of young men. The increase in population attested in the tenth century must also have tended to swell their numbers by diverting thereto the unemployed surplus of the rural population.

This point of view necessarily implies that the merchant class in the Middle Ages started without capital. And there is no objection to this. Credit undoubtedly played a great part in the beginning of commerce. Many merchants certainly transported goods which did not belong to them. The proceeds of the sale were divided between them and the owner. And there is no doubt that profits were often considerable. The scarcity of goods kept prices at a high level. The chief cause of commercial profits was above all the frequency of famines, and we know that contemporary merchants were skilful in taking advantage of these. An easy way to fortune was found by transporting a few sacks of corn to those districts threatened by famine.

Every kind of trade necessarily implies the existence of certain points of concentration, which are determined by the configuration or contours of the land, inasmuch as they correspond to the necessities of the social organisation and the development of means of communication. The ends of gulfs, the mouths of rivers, the confluence between two rivers, the spot at which a stream ceases to be navigable, are places designed by nature for halting-places in transit. But in the society of the early Middle Ages, it was moreover necessary that the merchants should find at these places at least a minimum of settlement and a minimum of security. Therefore we can easily imagine that they must at once have been attracted by the cities and *bourgs* whose geographical positions were particularly favourable to the exercise of their profession. They betook themselves to the old Roman cities, or to the fortresses of later date which were situated on the natural commercial lines of communication. Those which were too far off, even if like Thérouanne they were the seat of a bishop, or like Stavelot and Cluny that of celebrated monasteries, did not exercise on them the slightest attraction. They only repaired to those places where they found alike convenience of transit, the social protection of established authority, and the material protection of solid walls. These localities were not very numerous and the list was soon exhausted. It is certainly a mistake to believe that the early centres of municipal life were widely spread throughout Western Europe. During the tenth and eleventh centuries it is clearly obvious that they were all included in the region between the Rhine and the Seine. Even within this region, there were none to be found beyond the point where the rivers cease to be navigable. There were none on the Meuse above Verdun, on the Scheldt beyond Cambrai. The centre and east of France, as also the shores of the Atlantic Ocean, did not include any. It was especially in Flanders and the hinterland of its rivers that they abounded, and this fact is enough to prove the intimate relation which existed between the recrudescence of commercial life and the origin of towns.

The establishment of merchants in cities and *bourgs* came to pass under conditions whose details are unknown to us. It may be assumed that at first they settled within the walls. But almost always the small extent of the enclosure did not leave enough room at their disposal and they were obliged to settle outside the walls. There sprang up consequently outside the *bourg* an exterior *bourg*, *i.e.* a *faubourg* (*forisburgus*, *suburbium*). From documents of the tenth century, we learn of the existence of *faubourgs* of this kind at many places, Verdun, Dinant, Huy, Liège, Bruges, Laon, St Omer, etc.

In the Netherlands, and especially in Flanders, we find a particularly characteristic expression to describe them—that of *portus*, borrowed from Low Latin, where it was applied to a warehouse or wharf, and it retained that meaning during the Merovingian and Carolingian periods. Its application to the *faubourgs* of the eleventh century therefore definitely proves the character of the latter. It shews with perfect clearness that they were permanent commercial centres and it would be enough to refute the opinion which attaches the origin of towns to fairs and markets. Markets and fairs in reality only occurred on certain days in certain places. They were the periodical meeting-places of merchants. Moreover we find markets and even fairs in places which never became towns. This was the case for instance in Flanders, where Thourout and Messines were the homes of very ancient and very important fairs, but nevertheless they remained mere villages throughout the Middle Ages. The *portus*, on the other hand, was a business centre, established as a place of residence, a permanent collection of merchants and merchandise. In every place where it is found it implies the existence of a population living by the exercise of commerce, *i.e.* a population which already presented the essential features of an urban population. And this is so true that, in Anglo-Saxon England, the word *portus* frequently appears in the glosses of the tenth century as a synonym for *civitas*.

It follows from what has been said that the origin of medieval towns can be attributed to a combination of two elements differing in their age and in their nature. The first and older was the *bourg* (borough), consisting of a fortified enclosure dating either from the Roman or from the feudal period, and inhabited by a population of clergy, knights, and serfs, living on the produce of the land. The second and more recent was the *faubourg* or *port*, arising from the cohesion of a population of individuals devoted to trade. Between these two elements there were many contrasts, which must be recognised if we wish to understand how the former became subordinated to the latter.

We must at once observe that the *bourg* did not develop. In reality the necessities which it served remained stationary: there was no need to increase the garrison of knights, nor the number of clergy serving its church. Established for the defensive and administrative needs of a purely agricultural population, to the *bourg* naturally was communicated the same stationary character.

The *faubourg*, on the other hand, was constantly growing. As commercial activity increased in intensity, so newcomers were attracted to the settlement in ever-increasing numbers. We are thus concerned with a colony in course of continual development. And the more the importance of the settlement became evident, the greater became its attraction to the surrounding districts. There are many indications to prove that the suburban population was much larger in the eleventh century than it had been in the tenth, and it continued to increase until towards the end of the thirteenth. During the twelfth in many localities it had already surrounded the *bourg* to such an extent that the latter had, so to speak, shrunk into merely a central quarter.

The contrast between the *bourg* and *faubourg* is not less striking if we consider the legal condition of their inhabitants. In the *bourg* only the clergy and the knights were free; the servants round them were in the position of serfs. On the other hand, the merchant and other immigrants to the *faubourg* alike participated in freedom. No doubt their freedom was not original, for all, or almost all, of them were undoubtedly descended from peasant serfs. But who knew the secret of their birth? They were strangers from afar; no one knew their origin, and as medieval law did not presume servitude, they were perforce treated as freemen, since it was impossible to prove them otherwise. They had thus been *practically* enfranchised by the kind of life they led. Even if they had not been born free, they had deserted their native soil, uprooted themselves, and broken all links with the land and with the lord to whom they belonged. They were therefore subject neither to the personal duties nor to the private jurisdiction which resulted from the property of men in men. They had no need to demand freedom, nor to fight for it. They enjoyed it naturally as a consequence of their position as foreigners.

But the liberty accorded to them only affected their persons. It did not involve any right to self-government, nor the enjoyment of any peculiar jurisdiction nor special law. And this inevitably led to a series of conflicts.

For the organisation of the *bourgs* was evidently ill-adapted to the needs of the merchants. It only met the requirements of a rural and feudal society, whose administrative and military centres they were. The law exercised therein had been formulated for an agricultural population subject to a seignorial government of a patriarchal and authoritative character. Liberty of land-tenure was as restricted as personal liberty. All kinds of charges weighed as heavily on the land as they did on the individual. Marriage, inheritance, and the transmission of land-tenures were subject to hereditary taxes and levies either in money or in kind. The political administration likewise bore the character of direct exploitation of man. Taxation properly so-called was unknown. It operated only in the form of levies, or "exactions," on the various manifestations of the primitive economy of the locality. We need only recall the feudal dues on bakehouses, breweries, and mills, the tithes and "champarts" on the harvests, and especially the *tonlieu* (*teloneum*), which confiscated for the use of the lord or territorial ruler part of all merchandise transported by land or water. Finally, it must be added that legal procedure remained faithful to a strict formalism, and that oaths, ordeals, and duels were still regarded as the only means of trial.

It can easily be understood how such a state of things must even from the beginning have irritated the merchants who came to settle in its midst. The greater the difference between the life they led and that hitherto in use, the more they suffered. There was the greatest possible contrast between them and the society in which they had to find a place. The latter was based entirely on the ownership and possession of land, and had no regard for personal property which they represented. It was adapted to a sedentary population, and they were mobile, to a servile population and they were free. Numerous difficulties arose owing to this opposition between past and present. The merchants could not tolerate the brutal methods whereby the *tonlieu* was levied, nor the delays and uncertainties of legal procedure, nor the countless obstacles which old customs offered to all the manifestations of their activities. They demanded, not as a natural right but as a primary need of their profession, the suppression of all the burdens which had hitherto weighed unnoticed on an economic life much simpler than their own. They claimed the enfranchisement of the land on which they had come to dwell, and on which they had built houses, thus investing it with a value hitherto unknown. Being mostly unmarried and obliged to marry girls belonging to serf families, they required for their wives and children the freedom which they themselves enjoyed. In short, it was evident that, to enable them to exist and develop, the legal condition of society must be altered to suit the economic conditions requisite for them. And it was impossible to arrive at this transformation unless by granting to those who desired it that autonomy by which alone they could attain their aims.

Moreover, this autonomy was at once attained by the merchant population of the *faubourgs* to a certain extent. The social authorities in fact allowed them to supply their most essential necessities. It does not seem that they took any steps to regulate their settlements. It was impossible for them to do so as they were devoid of any means or competence for this object. The merchant settlements of the tenth and eleventh centuries were therefore regulated by the initiative of the immigrants. As no one troubled to help them they provided for themselves, and gradually created by spontaneous efforts the buildings, resources, and institutions which they found indispensable.

The rapid growth of the commercial *faubourgs* involved the provision of certain public works. It soon became necessary to build one or more churches, construct bridges, lay out wharves, and, most important of all, erect a palisade or wall for protection against pillagers. At first it seems that these works were undertaken by private enterprise, which is a very interesting fact. Rich merchants generously expended their wealth in the interests of their fellow-citizens. Such was probably a certain Lambert who built a parish church at St Omer in 1043; such was certainly Werimbald, who, a little later, redeemed the toll on one of the gates at Cambrai and provided for the maintenance of a bridge. But public benefactors could naturally only act in restricted and exceptional circumstances. The real driving-force was, as it has always been in all ages with social settlements in course of formation, the force of combination.

We have already stated that the merchants on their journeys combined in corporations called gilds, hanses, or confraternities. These corporations were not dissolved on their return. They constituted permanent bodies binding their "brothers" one to the other. In each locality these bodies, which included the leading merchants, very soon appear to have undertaken to supply the needs of the settlements. Without either official title or mandate, the members of each local gild improvised for themselves, so to speak, a public authority. Their interests were at one with the interests of their fellow-citizens, and they were given a free hand. In the eleventh century we find the gild of St Omer financing the erection of a *gild'halle* and devoting part of their income to the construction of defensive works round the town. In many other localities similar instances must have occurred, and the corporation of merchants seems to have acted as a semi-official municipal administration. The title *comtes de la hanse*, which the treasurers of the city of Lille retained throughout the Middle Ages, is enough to prove, in the absence of old documents, that there also the leaders of the voluntary association of merchants used the funds of their confraternity for the benefit of their fellow-citizens. In any case it must be assumed that the rudiments of a financial organisation were elaborated as necessity arose in the *ports* and *faubourgs*. The construction of a wall round the settlement involved too heavy an expenditure not to have entailed taxing every one for whose advantage it was undertaken. The first tax, properly so-called, must have been for the erection of the *firmitas*. It is characteristic to find that at Liège up to the close of the Ancien Régime the communal tax was always called the *fermeté*.

Thus, it may be affirmed that in the localities most in favour with merchant immigrants, the earliest features of a municipal organisation appeared at the middle of the eleventh century. The new term of *bourgeois* dates from this very period. We find the earliest mention of it at St Omer in 1048, then a little later at Huy in 1066 (*burgenses*). The ancestors of these bourgeois were undoubtedly merchants such as we have hitherto been discussing. But henceforth it was no longer by their profession but by their residence that they are described. The new population, like the old one, had become fortified. The new *bourg* became amalgamated with the old one, and already at this date it was considered much more important than its ancestor, because the name of *burgenses* was reserved for its inhabitants. These burghers of the middle of the eleventh century were still very far from possessing a real municipal organisation. Much progress had still to be made before they could obtain complete realisation of their programme, and before the town was endowed with all essential attributes, and before the medieval burghers succeeded in establishing themselves as a privileged legal class.

When we consider the attitude of the rulers towards the infant bourgeoisies we find a phenomenon which, at first sight, is rather surprising. As a general rule, lay princes were inclined to regard them with favour, while they almost invariably encountered open hostility from ecclesiastical superiors. This difference of attitude can, however, easily be explained. The lay rulers had nothing to fear from the bourgeoisie. On the contrary it was to their advantage to favour and protect them. It was obvious that the more prosperous the bourgeoisie, the greater the advantage to the ruler. The development of trade by enriching the town must inevitably end in also enriching the ruler, as it afforded him the opportunity of levying substantial taxes. Moreover, the lay rulers had no fixed residence. They moved constantly from one place to another in their territory. Consequently they were not in permanent contact with the burghers and causes of offence were reduced to a minimum.

But it was otherwise with the bishops, who perforce remained stationary in the cities in which, ever since the Roman period, the sees had been established, and who wished to preserve their authority intact. The interests of the Church, as well as their personal interest, made them regard the bourgeois claims with suspicion. It seemed to them with reason that urban autonomy must diminish their position and might at the same time imperil the rights and revenues of the clergy. They were all the more suspicious because this autonomy was demanded by merchants. For the Church had an invincible objection to trade. It considered that trade endangered the salvation of souls, it accounted desire for gain as avarice, and in most commercial transactions it detected various forms of usury. The open hostility, which ever since the Carolingian period it had increasingly shewn to the practice of money-lending, was also extended to trading. In fact, the bishops had a social scheme and theory which necessarily made them defend the traditional order of things against the reformers who attacked it.

It is therefore not surprising to find that, during the latter half of the eleventh century, there were insurrectional movements in episcopal cities, and that they were so numerous as to prove that they arose not from local causes but from some common factor. The earliest mentioned occurred at Cologne in 1074; two years later in 1076 one broke out at Cambrai. Then about 1080 there followed a revolt at St Quentin, one at Beauvais in 1099, one at Noyon in 1108–1109, one at Amiens in 1113, one at Laon in 1115. There is no doubt that this tendency to revolt was fomented by the merchants. The important part they played is definitely proved at Cambrai and Cologne; at Beauvais the insurrection movement was led by the cloth-merchants. The subsequent insurrections at Noyon and Laon present a slightly different character. Here it seems that we are concerned with an agitation less obviously provoked by the merchant class. Serfs and even priests were involved in this rebellion. And there is nothing surprising in this. At every time of social unrest irritation is contagious. The initiative taken by the most active and most directly interested class soon becomes communicated to all malcontents who, had they not been roused, would probably not have acted. It therefore remains true to say that the primary and deeper reason for the early municipal insurrections must be sought in the need for reforms which, as we have seen above, were inevitably demanded by the merchant class.

These insurrections were not mere riots roused by sudden passion and giving way to brutal excesses. On the contrary it is obvious that they aimed at a definite object and had been long prepared. The merchants who fomented them wished to use them for the realisation of their desires. They were determined to shake off the old laws and monetary exactions, the weight of which became more onerous in proportion as they themselves increased in numbers and in wealth, and they aimed at seizing the government and substituting their influence for that of the bishop. They collected round them all those who groaned under the system to which they objected themselves, and they bound themselves by mutual sworn agreements, and, with this support at the decisive moment, they proclaimed the commune in a revolutionary manner. In fact, in all the above-mentioned towns, the triumphant burghers established or attempted to establish communes.

What is the meaning of this celebrated word? The commune was, strictly speaking, the association of burghers, constituted by oath, who seized the municipal power and undertook to defend both corporate and individual liberty against all attacks. It was the result of a conjuration and it sometimes even bore the name of Conjuration. Its members were conjurors (*coniurati*), and the same name *iuratus* or *juré* was adopted by the magistrates appointed at their head. It was thus essentially revolutionary, and it never appeared except in towns where self-government was gained as the result of a keen struggle. For this reason it is characteristic of episcopal cities, and especially of episcopal cities in Northern France.

Its aim was to replace seignorial law and jurisdiction by a law and jurisdiction which it would exercise itself. It not only made innovations, but it also unified. As soon as its success was achieved, all the inhabitants of the city not only had a similar personal status, but were subject to the same courts and were governed by the same council, all recruited from among its members. Thereby the city became a distinct judicial territory, alike as regarded private and public law. It thus formed what has often been called a "collective seignory," but it differed greatly from the feudal seignories in being a community with exceptional rights, in fact, a privileged territory.

The revolutionary origin of the communes did not prevent them from attaining a legal existence. Although several were very soon crushed, many succeeded in obtaining from their overlord or from the king a charter guaranteeing the organisation they had set up for themselves. During the course of the twelfth and thirteenth centuries this organisation became general. As the economic conditions of Europe changed under the influence of the renaissance of trade, an ever-increasing number of localities were moved to join in the new life, and commercial centres became multiplied. The older ones communicated their activity to their neighbours; and the bourgeoisies, which had at first collected in certain places particularly favoured by their position, soon spread in all directions. It became not only impossible but dangerous to oppose so general a movement. The opposition originally offered to it had no longer either any reason or any chance of success. It was better to accept the inevitable and to recognise a state of affairs which seemed quite natural in the society now in course of evolution. Princes and overlords now lightly conceded what had at first been wrung from them. Charters of communes, based on those which had been conceded after the insurrection in the eleventh century, were freely granted to many towns during the following century.

Besides the towns which established sworn communes, there were very many others which did not resort to this insurrectionary proceeding. As we have said, the lay rulers had not the same reasons as the ecclesiastical for resisting the attempts of the early burghers to attain autonomy. They were usually much more conciliatory in their methods. The county of Flanders, which was particularly remarkable for the number and activity of its towns, offered a characteristic example in this matter. From the beginning of the twelfth century, we find the count granting privileges as regards justice and finance at the request of the burghers. It seems that, even before the troubles which broke out in this county in 1127 after the murder of Charles the Good, most of the cities were already in possession of their own jurisdiction and administration. The part they took in the struggle between the rival claimants, William of Normandy and Thierry of Alsace, inevitably increased and definitely established their autonomy. The oldest charter of a Flemish city extant, that of St Omer, dates from that very period—1127.

The sworn or insurrectional commune was therefore not absolutely indispensable for securing urban autonomy. It was only one means of establishing it. There existed no essential difference between the towns which had recourse to it and those which did not. In fact, both these constitute communes in the legal sense of the word, *i.e.* they were collective persons recognised by public authority. Every medieval town thus formed a commune despite the difference which may have existed between the origin of one or the other. Only those inhabitants shared in urban rights and obligations who had taken the communal oath before the municipal magistrate.

Nevertheless urban law was not merely personal. It did not affect only the members of the commune. As it was recognised by the public power it also acquired a territorial character. All those dwelling within its enclosure, *infra murum villae*, were subject to it, whether they had taken the communal oath or not. Therefore the city formed a legal state, a real immunity in the midst of the country surrounding it. As soon as its gates were passed, one found oneself in quite a different legal sphere, just as to-day on crossing the frontier of another state. Or rather, it was a transition from the domain of common law to that of privileged law.

In order to appreciate the position of the medieval burgher, it must be realised that he belonged to a privileged class just as much as the cleric or the noble. Just as the privileges of the Churchman were derived from his sacerdotal functions, and those of the noble from his military duties, so the burgher enjoyed his on account of his special economic importance, *i.e.* because he belonged to a class devoted to commerce and industry. It was this condition which constituted the bourgeoisie a special order, the Tiers État: it was this which raised the burgher, like the cleric and the noble, above the mass of the common people.

With the establishment of the bourgeoisie, medieval society finally assumed the characteristic appearance which it henceforth retained, and which in many countries persisted until the end of the Ancien Régime. Like the two older orders, the bourgeoisie consisted of a minority of privileged individuals, and it was because of this that, in all European countries, it shared in the political constitution of the State from the day when the rulers were obliged to concede to it a place in their councils or in their parliaments.

The origin of the towns and of the bourgeoisie can everywhere in Western Europe be attributed to the same general causes; on closer examination, however, it is obvious that there were profound differences between various towns. As we have already said, municipal institutions did not originally (*i.e.* in the eleventh and early twelfth centuries) develop except in a comparatively small number of localities. These localities were those in which the action of economic causes considered above was particularly effective. Without exception the expansion of municipal law followed exactly the expansion of commerce and industry. Just as in the Mediterranean basin Lombardy was alike the most ancient centre of merchant activity and municipal activity, similarly near the North Sea the Flemish region presented the twofold character of enjoying an older and more fully developed economic life and of possessing a larger number of more highly developed towns than any other region. It is obvious that different local conditions must have determined the form of the institutions which sprang up in the early centres of municipal organisation. They developed in various manners according to whether they had to struggle with their ruler or not, whether they were more particularly devoted to this or to that trade, and whether the territorial institutions in the midst of which they had developed were at all compatible or not with their needs. In certain cases the town obtained complete autonomy, in others—and this was much more usual—autonomy was not attained, while elsewhere again the burghers did not even attempt to deprive the ruler or the lord of the rights which he exercised therein. Generally we find that the state of affairs was that of a compromise between the rights of the ruler and the autonomy of the urban commune. The latter usually shared in the domain of real communal administration and jurisdiction, while the higher courts continued to be controlled by the officers of the public power. In certain towns special magistrates exercised joint authority, some representing communal interests, others princely authority. This was for instance the case in many towns in France, the Netherlands, and Germany, where a council of sworn men (*iurati*, *geswornen*, *geschworenen*) with communal authority existed contemporaneously with a council of échevins (*scabini*, *schepenen*, *schoeffen*, etc.) with public powers. But it also happened that the rights of the commune and of the prince were exercised together by the same magistrature. In Flanders, for instance, the échevins were échevins both of the town and of the count. The greater or lesser degree of autonomy attained by a town consequently depended on varying causes and was affected by the political circumstances in which it had arisen; it did not necessarily reflect her wealth or power. The Flemish towns, which were distinguished by the rapidity and exuberance of their development, were satisfied with a municipal independence less complete than many much smaller places in France and Germany. And this doubtless arose from their very power. The counts did not wish to provoke a dangerous conflict with them. They were content to share an authority which they were prudent enough not to render onerous. But it is obvious on the other hand that wherever the overlord felt strong enough to prevent the towns from shaking off his authority, he did not fail to restrict their autonomy to limits compatible with his power. We find this to be the case in France in the towns within the royal domain, especially in Paris, and it is equally obvious in England, where no town ever escaped, or sought to escape, from monarchical supremacy.

Between the urban constitutions of one region we generally find an apparent kinship which enables them to be grouped together. In the Netherlands we easily distinguish a Flemish type, a Brabançon type, a Liégeois type, and a Hollander type. It often happened that towns not very close to each other received or adopted the charter of an older town. Thus, for instance, the institutions of Rouen were copied by many localities in Poitou, Orléanais, and Gascony.

During the course of the twelfth and thirteenth centuries urban institutions became extended to a large number of villages or *bourgs* of rural character. In order to attract men to their lands, the kings, princes, or local seigneurs promised to extend to immigrants who contemplated settling there the advantages of autonomy and municipal liberties. We are here referring to the *villes neuves*. This name was applied to villages possessing a charter of franchise liberating their inhabitants from the former rigid domanial law, and granting them a communal organisation to a greater or lesser degree. Several of these charters enjoyed a wide diffusion. That of Lorris (1155) was for instance extended throughout the royal domain in France, that of Beaumont (1182) throughout Champagne, Lorraine, and Luxembourg, that of Prisches throughout Hainault. We know too that the charter of the Norman *bourg* of Breteuil was adopted by many cities in England, Wales, and even Ireland.

It must not, however, be supposed that the *villes neuves*, or *bourgs* enfranchised by charters, can be absolutely classed with towns properly so called. It is obviously very hard to explain the difference, and in certain cases almost impossible. But it is certain that between a city like Bruges or Ghent, and a village like Prisches or Beaumont, or even a *bourg* like Breteuil, or between London and Rhuddlan, the contrast is too great to allow complete assimilation. The *ville neuve* and enfranchised *bourg* had actually received only a minimum of such urban institutions as were applicable to rural populations. Almost always, the essential part of the franchise granted to them was restricted to fixing conditions affecting persons and tenures. The latter were often governed by the system of *bourgage*, which was liberty when compared with the old tenures of seignorial law, and which was obviously copied from urban tenures. But this would not justify us in regarding the burghers of the *villes neuves* as equal to the burghers of towns. To prove this we need only recall the fact that at least in Normandy we find mention of rural *bourgeois* given with their land. Elsewhere we find that the inhabitants of *villes neuves* were still subject to forced labour in aid of their lord, and even to certain dues of servile origin. Moreover the degree of communal government and liberty which they exercised never reached a high level. All that can be said is that they were *quasi-bourgeois*, just as the *ville neuve* or enfranchised *bourg* was a quasi-town, if we may coin the word, very different from a town with full rights.

In reality the medieval town in the true sense of the word only existed in places where urban law, *i.e.* a law established for a population essentially devoted to commerce and industry, became developed to a point when the town became a clearly defined legal person. A definition, summarising the essential characteristics which it presented and which have been considered in the preceding pages, is not easy to formulate. Perhaps it would be possible to risk the following definition: a medieval town was a community under the aegis of a fortified enclosure, living by the exercise of commerce and industry, and enjoying exceptional judicial and administrative rights which constituted it a privileged body.

It now remains to describe shortly the municipal government, such as it developed in its essential features from the time when towns were formed. This subject is of great interest. For it may be said that this government demonstrates the first attempt made since the days of antiquity to organise public affairs, to establish a *commonwealth*. And it must be added that in the Middle Ages, when the Church and the State constantly blended, it was moreover the earliest example of a purely lay organisation.

Its essential object was the common weal of the bourgeoisie, or the municipal *respublica*. Now as the bourgeoisie was a new class in medieval society, a number of new problems arose, which demanded fresh solutions. The gravest of these problems were of the economic and financial order. For the bourgeoisie which lived on commerce and industry depended on external sources for the food necessary for their existence. It was therefore essential for their maintenance and development that they should first of all attend to commissariat. But it was just as important to organise defences against attacks to which their defenceless wealth was exposed; and the first necessity was to protect themselves by a solid system of moats or walls. This twofold necessity entailed considerable expenditure. It was therefore essential to establish a financial system capable of meeting the heavy expenses, without which the very existence of the bourgeoisie would become impossible.

We are unfortunately ill-informed as to the initial measures taken by the urban magistrates to meet the inevitable calls upon their resources. It is only from the thirteenth century onwards that we possess sufficiently abundant or precise documents concerning municipal administration to enable us to describe it in detail. But there is no doubt that what is then apparent had been preparing during the course of the previous century. Influenced by experience, impelled by practical necessity, and supported by civic sentiment, they arrived pretty quickly at an organisation perfectly adapted to meet the problems confronting it, and which in its chief features was common to all the towns.

In fact in all of them there soon (twelfth century) appeared a municipal tax, differing greatly from the dues, the taxes, or tallages hitherto levied by kings or nobles. This tax, the object of which was exclusively to meet public expenses, was either a direct tax affecting the property of the burghers, or an indirect tax (*assise*) levied on the foodstuffs or merchandise entering the town and on the sales in the market. If it was insufficient, they resorted to a loan, either an internal loan, floated within the town itself, or an external loan, contracted in the neighbouring towns. Already, by the close of the twelfth century, we find the first traces of a communal counting-house and financial audit, although the earliest accounts we possess only date from a century later.

The greater part of the town's financial resources was devoted to what may be termed the budget of its defence. Until the close of the Middle Ages, the construction and maintenance of the surrounding walls and moats, and the purchase of engines of war and arms for the burghers, never failed to reach a figure amounting to eight-tenths of the communal receipts. The growth of the urban population depended on the security offered by its ramparts, but although this growth increased the receipts of the town it also increased expenditure. The space within the walls soon became inadequate and new quarters had to be built, and consequently, at great expense, new walls had to be erected and new moats constructed round them. For instance, by 1169 Ghent had enclosed within her walls much surrounding land, and in 1213 a fresh addition was undertaken, soon followed by a series of other increases, the last of which was in 1299.

Other public works were necessitated by commercial needs. In the eleventh century, we find the cities building markets, planning wharves for their merchandise, and paving streets and market-places.

The provision of food for the bourgeoisie was undoubtedly the most urgent problem which the municipal organisation had to solve. There is no doubt that even in the eleventh century the population of the commercial centres was already too large to be fed on local produce. The foodstuffs required for their consumption were derived partly from wholesale trade, partly from the surrounding country. But it was indispensable to regulate the arrival of these foodstuffs and to prevent arbitrary increase in their cost. Measures were taken at an early date to prevent traders from combining to the detriment of the consumers, and to suppress middlemen between buyers and sellers. The general principle of urban economy was to bring the importer of foodstuffs into touch with the buyer, so as to ensure cheapness of living. This was attained by a minute regulation of commerce and of markets. The theory of the *iustum pretium* which was formulated by the great schoolmen of the thirteenth century undoubtedly corresponded with the practice soon developed in the towns.

Industry, in its turn, demanded the intervention of municipal power. It was not only necessary to supply raw materials, but also to ensure their fair division among the artisans, and finally to supervise the quality of the goods produced so that they should be satisfactory. The first signs of the establishment of craft-gilds (*métiers*, *mysteries*) appeared at the end of the eleventh century, in the most highly developed urban centres. We find artisans of the same craft combining together to buy raw materials and combat foreign competition. Municipal authority rendered obligatory these associations, formerly voluntary, appointing their leaders and regulating their proceedings. The craft-gild, as established in the course of the twelfth century, is undoubtedly the most interesting and most original creation of bourgeois civilisation in the Middle Ages. It provided a solution of the labour-problem admirably adapted to the conditions of a period in which currency and capitalism were still in their infancy. Its great merit was that it ensured alike the economic independence of the producer and the interests of the consumer. It only produced its full effect, however, in its application to the local markets, *i.e.* as far as it was applicable to the industries working for the urban population. The exporting industries, such as, for instance, the weaving industry in the large towns of Belgium and Northern France, were not so successful in adapting themselves. The international markets for which they worked, and the substantial capital they required, did not permit them to submit to a system created for a restricted market and for small producers equal among themselves; this system was incapable of averting conflicts between capital and labour, which first appeared in all their gravity during the course of the thirteenth century. But these were quite rare exceptions. They do not prevent us from regarding the industrial organisation of medieval towns as a masterpiece of its kind. We know with what persistence it survived throughout the centuries, and with what tenacity it resisted in modern times the inevitable changes which resulted from the improvement in communications, in technique, and in capitalism, until the time when the revolutionary movement at the close of the eighteenth century destroyed it, perhaps, too violently.

As we have seen, the activity of urban administration is essentially explicable by the economic problems which it had to face. These problems moreover determined alike the internal and the external policy of the towns.

Internally, it naturally happened that municipal power was exercised by that class of merchants whose trade had formed the nucleus of the town, and who remained the mainstay of its prosperity. In Flanders, in France, England, and the Rhineland of Germany, we everywhere discover until the beginning of the thirteenth century, and sometimes much later, that the members of the Merchant Gild or the Confraternities exercised in actual fact the local government. In all parts, magistrates were elected from the wealthy class which contemporary documents refer to as *maiores*, *divites, homines hereditarii, boni homines, bonnes gens, hommes héritables*, etc., to whom modern historians, by a very inexact parallel with antiquity, have assigned the name of patricians. In short, the political system prevailing in medieval towns began everywhere by being a plutocratic system. As it progressed, this system naturally and increasingly exhibited all the characteristics of class government, of which it possessed not only the virtues but also the vices. These vices occasioned the opposition which it eventually aroused, which towards the close of the thirteenth century almost always culminated either in its complete overthrow, as in Flanders, Brabant, and the territory of Liège, or in its transformation in a greater or lesser degree. It is nevertheless true that these patricians for long shewed themselves worthy of the task they had undertaken. They offered a magnificent spectacle from the middle of the twelfth century to the end of the thirteenth by their intelligence, their diligent activity, and their capacity for business. They devoted themselves to the public weal with a single-heartedness which commands our respect. It may be said that urban civilisation under their government assumed those characteristics which distinguished it to the end. They created municipal administration in all its details, and endowed it with the various public services which we have endeavoured to describe above.

The external policy to which the townsmen always remained faithful was also inaugurated by them. This policy was moreover imposed by the very nature of the bourgeoisie. To understand it we must realise that the bourgeoisie constituted a privileged class of society. Its manner of life, necessitated by the requirements of its commerce and industry, demanded that it should enjoy the highest possible degree of autonomy, that it should be in a position to protect its interests in the most efficacious manner, and consequently that it should be freed as completely as possible from all external interference. The ideal of every town was—as was said by Guy de Dampierre, Count of Flanders, at the close of the thirteenth century—to be a "world apart." In other words, it was to become an independent republic, a "free town," guardian and sovereign over the rights of its burghers. Whether from the Church or from the territorial ruler, it demanded complete autonomy. It wished to escape both from their jurisdiction and from their taxation. It unceasingly strove to obtain, or to seize, additional privileges. Hence so many conflicts with one or the other, so many excommunications launched by the bishops, and so many law-suits or armed conflicts with the lay princes. In most of Europe, the towns did not attain the goal at which they aimed in spite of all their efforts. In England the monarchy maintained its authority over the towns all the more easily because they had never been very powerful. In France, the kings at first supported the communes, but at the close of the twelfth century, when royal power had increased, this policy was reversed. In the Netherlands—Flanders, Brabant, and the district of Liège—the rulers, although almost always obliged to yield to the demands of their towns, still retained their right of suzerainty, either by pitting one town against another, or by summoning quite early representatives from them to their councils. In fact, it was only in Germany and Italy that the anarchy or weakness of the holders of territorial power enabled the cities to become municipal republics, *i.e.* to become states. In all other parts, in spite of every effort, the towns remained within the framework of the state. And by continuing to form part of the national community, they not only enabled the latter to profit by their energy, but exerted a profound influence on the nature of the national civilisation.

CHAPTER XVI

THE DEVELOPMENT OF ECCLESIASTICAL ORGANISATION AND ITS FINANCIAL BASIS.

The attempt will be made in this chapter to trace the medieval system of Church administration from its beginning in the legislation of the Roman Empire and in the custom of the Teutonic tribes, down to the time of its full development under the great Popes of the thirteenth century. The system was in most ways so uniform, at any rate on paper, that illustrations from one region will serve as well as those taken from another, and for the present purpose English examples will be preferred, where they can be found. For the general course of the history it will be necessary that we should limit ourselves to those central countries of Europe where the scheme of government was worked out under the influence of Carolingian monarchs and of Popes; comparatively few words can be said of the peculiarities of outlying regions. There is, indeed, little that is abnormal in any part of Western Europe. Italy had been under Teutonic influence from the time of the Goths and Lombards. Spain was recovered from the Moors at the very time when the medieval system was reaching maturity, and its institutions were modelled on those of Aquitaine and Provence. The lands to the east of Germany borrowed their Church discipline from that country, and the Scandinavian lands from Germany and England, while Anglo-Norman influence gave a new shape to the Churches of Scotland and Ireland. And, in an enquiry which will concern itself chiefly with revenues and their effect upon organisation, it will be necessary to ignore voluntary and occasional donations, however considerable, and to confine attention to endowments consisting in, or derived from, landed property.

The bishop, under the system of the Christianised Roman Empire, was an autocrat. His position was assimilated to that of the governor of a civil area, and the boundaries of his territory were the same as those of the governor's. He was regarded as responsible for the discipline, the doctrine, and the administration of his diocese; and often enough if he displeased the Emperor he was dismissed as though he were a secular official. He was the sole dispenser of the revenues of the diocese, and of the liberal imperial benefactions. He was the sole authorised recipient of endowments which soon began to be generously bestowed, often in the form of lands which might lie outside the bounds of the diocese, or even, especially in the case of the Roman see, be in distant provinces. No endowments for local purposes existed; everything passed through the hands of the bishop, the one responsible officer of the Church. To his central fund the clergy looked for subsistence, and were the more tightly bound in that they were confined to the diocese of their ordination. But the bishop was bound to maintain them, though he could at his discretion increase or diminish their allowance, and they had no appeal against his decision. The dependents on the church, widows and virgins and poor persons on its roll, were supported from the same fund, which also paid for the training of the clergy and for the cost of building churches; a heavy burden when Christians were rapidly increasing in number. This episcopal control was explained and justified by the fact that it was the bishop who had admitted every Christian into the Church and so was responsible for him. To this day in many Italian cities no baptism has been administered save in the bishop's baptistery.

The system might work while Christianity was a religion of the town. It broke down when the faith spread over the country parts, as it did through the efforts of such men as St Martin of Tours in the last generations of the Western Empire. In fact, a complete system of bishoprics had hardly been established in the Western provinces when conditions were altered by the German invasions. When the storm came the bishop might exercise a magnificent liberality, perhaps from accumulated funds, to meet the distresses of the time. He might even, as government grew weak, become practically the ruler of his city. But this could not help him in regard to his rule over the population which lay outside his "Christianity," as the city and its environs were sometimes called.

Two partial attempts had been made to meet the need before the invasions. The bishops themselves had raised a certain number of churches at scattered points some distance apart, where priests of their own appointment ministered. Their choice of place was limited to possessions of their own, for such priests received as their maintenance *precariae*, or revocable grants of land to be enjoyed during their tenure of office; there was no thought of security of tenure. These priests, whose position was that of the clergy officiating at what were called "the old minsters" in the first phase of the conversion of England, were the most important persons, after the bishop, in the work of the diocese; they were often styled "cardinal priests." For they, as the bishop's delegates, had the power of baptising, and every official act of theirs was as effective as his; for in fact it was his. But such churches were never numerous. In his diocese of Tours the great missionary St Martin established six, his successor five, and the work afterwards proceeded slowly.

It was hastened, or rather in a sense frustrated, by the independent action of the laity. The *possessores* took the task in hand. The land within the Empire had fallen into few hands; great estates with almost servile *coloni* covered the provinces. Some of these had been bestowed on the bishops, and in places outside their dioceses. It was natural that they should promote Christianity; they built churches and maintained the clergy. The question arose in the fifth century as to the jurisdiction over such churches. It was claimed by the bishop in whose diocese they lay.

But he had contributed nothing to the building or to the ministry; the bishop who owned the land maintained his rights as a *possessor*. There was no definite solution of the problem. The ultimate result was the existence everywhere of a multitude of "peculiars," such as those which belonged to the Archbishop of Canterbury or the Bishop of Durham till the nineteenth century. Within such areas the bishop whose jurisdiction surrounded them had no authority. The lay *possessor* claimed no less right than the episcopal. He might be, like Sulpicius Severus or Paulinus of Nola, himself in orders but his patrimony was secular property. He built his church and supported his ministry, and resolutely excluded the bishop from an institution to which he had contributed nothing. A compromise was reached. The bishop insisted on his right of supervision, but the great man might have his church—it is even spoken of as his *parochia*—on condition that he endowed it, to secure its permanence. Here was a new thing—ecclesiastical property not vested in the bishop, and over the administration of which, provided there were no scandal, he had no control. How numerous such autonomous churches were we do not know; probably they were more in number than the bishop's own, but they were far from providing a complete parochial system. To these lay foundations we must add those that were erected on the lands with which monasteries were liberally endowed. They had an equal claim to exemption, for it was the generosity of the monks that provided them; and monks as yet were usually laymen, and in any case no monastery was, as such, subject to episcopal authority.

Thus there came to be a great practical diminution of the bishop's authority: numerous parishes with which he and his central fund had nothing to do. And the popular belief of the time justified this exclusion. The cult of saints became universal in the sixth century, and the saint in the eyes of his votaries was thoroughly alive to his own interests. He was owner of the property dedicated in his honour, and would defend it by miracle against aggression. Thus the local, as against the diocesan, interest was still further fortified. On the other hand, there was the danger that local control might be abused. Pope Gelasius I did his best to secure the authority of the bishops, but his injunctions soon came to be a dead letter; and it was in vain that Gregory the Great insisted that the founder of a private church should have no rights unless he provided an endowment, for the endowment itself often reverted to the descendants of the giver.

There was the special difficulty that there was no uniformity of endowment, no right or property that normally belonged to the clerical incumbent, and from the absence of which it might be presumed that he had been unjustly treated. This normal endowment was bestowed by Teutonic paganism upon Christianity in the form of glebe. The Christian priest is the heir of his pagan predecessor. The evidence is ample that the head of the village community was originally its priest, that the temple was his, that in course of time he delegated his priestly office to a nominee of his own, retaining the ownership and, more notably in Scandinavia than elsewhere, taking a share of the profits derived from the worship. The community was incomplete without priest and temple, and its members were bound to attend the services, just as they were bound to fulfil their other customary duties. Thus when the community, following the example of its lord, became Christian, there was an obvious source of maintenance for the priest of the new worship. Men would not be less generous to him than to his pagan predecessor. They would support him in the same way, and choose him in the same manner. Thus from paganism the Church inherited ecclesiastical patronage and glebe land, and also a burdensome load, which gradually dwindled and disappeared, of rights over the church-building and its services. How complete those rights were in the later Anglo-Saxon period in England is shewn in the alliterative description, handed down in the *Textus Roffensis*, of the conditions whereby a churl could rise to the rank of thegn. He must have five hides of land, church and kitchen, bell-house and manor-court, seat and office of his own in the king's hall. The church is his property in the same sense as the kitchen.

In certain regions, however, what seems a more primitive system existed. In Lombardy and also in Norway, regions where there is in various respects a similarity of institutions which must be due to affinity of race, election to the benefice was often, if not always, in the hands of the parishioners; in Norway of the "hundred." It is quite possible that in the English Danelaw and indeed in other parts where, though the case was exceptional, men not subject to a lord had constituted their community as a parish by means of an endowment contributed by themselves, the same case might be found of a village in which the land-holders elected their priest.

If the priest was normally in many ways in a position of dependence, he had at any rate a definite status within his community. He had a fixed customary proportion of the cultivated area. With the lord's share he had nothing to do, but while each full member, under the lord, held an equal single share with the others, the priest had a double portion. To take that frequent case in England of a community with five hides, or twenty yard-lands, it had eighteen lay partners, and the two remaining yard-lands were held by the priest. So, when Charles the Great conquered and settled Saxony, it was ordered in his capitulary that the Christian priest should have two *hufen*; no doubt his pagan predecessor had occupied the same area. The continuity is shewn by a strange and general custom, in which there is nothing specifically Christian. The ecclesiastical tenure was burdened with a servitude, universal from Scandinavia to the Tyrol, that is certainly older than the conversion of the Teutonic tribes. The priest was obliged to provide male animals for the service of the flocks and herds of his parishioners, though not for those of the lord. In England the rule was that he must furnish bull and boar; elsewhere stallion and ram were often required. Usually two or three of these animals, varying without apparent cause from place to place, were specified, and, as in England, were supplied till quite recent times. But the priest was free from any servile rendering of labour. He was secure in his tenure, the equal of his congregation, and inferior only to his lord, who could exact such share as he would from the offerings of the temple but could not seize upon his priest's right in fields and commons.

This landed right was the origin of what in England has come to be called, by a strange development from the original status, the parson's freehold. But the profits of the church itself, its dues and offerings, gave the lord manifold opportunities. The bishop in his own churches had dictated what proportion of such revenue should be transmitted to himself, what retained by the minister of the place. In Gaul in the sixth century the bishop received two-thirds of the oblations, if the canon of the council of Orleans in 511 were observed; but at Braga in 572 this was expressly forbidden. At the same council, held during the brief rule of the Sueves in Galicia and Portugal, it was also enacted that he who builds a *basilica* not from devotion but from greed, in order to divide the oblations of the people equally with the clergy because he has built it on his own land, shall not have his church consecrated by a bishop.

This is proof that the abuse existed, though the motive of the builder is misrepresented. He was claiming the same right that his pagan predecessor had enjoyed. The evidence from all parts of the Teutonic world for the exercise of this right by the lord is convincing. As the density of settlement increased, the land came to be uniformly studded with churches built on these terms, and the earlier private churches, raised before the barbarian conquest, seem to have fallen into line with the later both as to customary endowment and as to the rights claimed by the lord; in the latter respect, indeed, there was no difference between churches on lay and on ecclesiastical lands. The bishops regarded themselves as landlords, and preferred that the churches on their estates should be held of themselves by the same tenure as the clergy held theirs of lay lords. They would have the customary rights of patronage and superiority rather than the more strictly ecclesiastical authority of an earlier time. Thus the feudal conception, and with it the technical feudal terms *benefice* and *advowson*, came into use for the definition of the position of the clergy.

This revenue inevitably had a secular aspect. It was derived from land, and was granted to the beneficiary by the lord of lands on terms that inevitably suggested a feudal relation. How thoroughly this view of the case was accepted in England appears most clearly in the practice whereby all disputes about advowsons fell under the cognisance, not of ecclesiastical, but of royal courts. If the position of the clergy was to satisfy their self-respect, they needed another source of income that should be purely spiritual. Some were to find it in tithe. This among Christians had a double origin, homiletical and exegetical, of which the latter, and later, came to be the more important. From the beginning attention was drawn to the religious practice among the Jews of paying tithe, and believers were exhorted to follow the example. It was, however, a matter of morals, not of discipline; tithe is never mentioned in the canons of the classical councils, promulgated in the fourth and fifth centuries, though they decide points of every kind that arose in the practical working of the Church. Still, tithe being a matter for the personal conscience, preachers and writers thought well to offer guidance, and it was usual to advise that those who felt the duty to give in this proportion should distribute their alms as the oblations were already given, viz. dividing them between the bishop, the local clergy, the poor, and the building or repair of churches. And this scheme of distribution continued from time to time and in various regions to be inculcated even after the new teaching had come to discredit it.

This teaching was that the Christian ministry in its three grades of bishop, priest, and deacon corresponds to that of the high priest, priest, and levite of the older dispensation, and that it is therefore the duty of the Christian to provide for his clergy by the same charge upon his income as had been paid by the Jew. Tithe is a due which must, at the risk of his soul, be paid by every believer. This piece of exegesis, whoever was its author, began to be generally accepted about the year 400, and St Ambrose was its most impressive advocate. It applied to income from every source; Abraham's offer to the priest Melchizedek of tithe from the spoil of Eastern kings was especially noted. Thus it was not a specifically local endowment, though his local priest was an obvious beneficiary if a rich man were seeking an appropriate person to receive the due proportion of his revenue. But, so long as the recipient was in holy orders, the duty was fulfilled; any cleric, or body of clerics, above minor orders satisfied the condition, and we shall see that in fact a great deal, probably the major part, of tithe failed to reach the hands of the holder of the glebe, or at any rate was in course of time withdrawn from him. But these two sources of endowment exerted a reciprocal influence; on the one hand glebe attracted tithe so that the two in combination came to form the complete benefice of the *persona* of a church, and on the other when the tithe of the lands of a parish passed to some religious corporation it tended to draw the glebe, at any rate in part, after it, and the vicar had no more than a minor share in either.

The process was gradual by which the earlier conception of tithe faded out and was displaced by the notion of an express obligation towards the clergy. At first the teaching was only homiletical. Preachers like Caesarius of Arles and numerous councils, beginning with that of Mâcon in 585, impressed the moral duty of obedience and the spiritual danger of defiance. Excommunication was threatened, and Penitentials taught the sinfulness of neglecting the law. Thus the custom of payment became general, and it was an easy step to turn a duty which was generally recognised into a universal obligation. But as yet the earlier conception prevailed; the payment was to be for religious purposes and not specifically for the support of the clergy, nor was attention as yet fixed upon the land and its produce as the source of tithe. Whether or no it could be enforced in practice, on paper all income was equally bound to pay its tenth. So Pepin, the father of Charlemagne, ordained in 765 that "every man, will he or nill he, must give his tithe," and this example was quickly followed in England, where the Legatine Council of 787 in its seventeenth canon first cites commandments of the Old Testament and then proceeds, "Therefore we earnestly enjoin that all men be zealous to give tithes of all that they possess, for this is the peculiar property of the Lord God; and let him live for himself on the nine parts and bestow his alms." The distinction between the two duties of tithe-paying and almsgiving is clearly drawn, and it may be inferred, though it is not said, that tithe has appropriate recipients other than those on whom alms are bestowed. But all is left deliberately vague, and in this ambiguous form the law was accepted for their several kingdoms by the three chief monarchs in England, those of Mercia, Wessex, and Northumbria. It is reasonable to assume that such a law would not have been promulgated, unless it gave voice to a general sense of duty and made universal (at any rate in theory) a practice that was commonly followed. For such a feeling to grow up must have taken time, and it is not unlikely that in England the practice first established itself, and that it was from England that it passed into the Frankish Empire, as a charge on land.

For tithe was, for practical purposes, to take this form, while other tithe was to lapse into insignificance, as having no specific source for assessment or collection. And payment of the fruits of the earth was familiar throughout the Roman Empire. There was a land-tax of a tenth, and a tenth was also a customary rent paid by *coloni*, the largest class of cultivators under the later Empire. When, in disastrous times, Charles Martel granted out Church lands on military tenure to soldiers whom he could not otherwise remunerate, he softened the blow to injured bishops and monasteries by charging what had hitherto been their own land with a payment of two-tenths to its former holders. They were to receive one-tenth, and also one-ninth of the remaining nine parts. It was a purely secular arrangement, based on the familiar payment of a tenth; but it was paid to clergy and in thought came to be associated with the doctrine of clerical right to tithe, to which precision was given by this specific charge upon land.

From 751 onwards this notion spread, in spite of the fact that the burden lay as yet, not on lands in general but on certain lands only, and as an equivalent for the loss of their enjoyment; and also in spite of the fact that a double tenth was imposed. But Charlemagne was to complete his grandfather's work, by making tithe from land universal throughout his dominions. The resumption of Church lands into the hands of the sovereign and their grant under military tenure had continued, and become so general that an equally general compensation had become necessary. It may well be that it was at the suggestion of Alcuin and in obedience to English precedent that this provision was made for the clergy; for what clergy was not specified. And when Charlemagne conquered and organised Saxony he extended the law to his new acquisition. Not only did he provide the clergy with glebe on the customary Teutonic scale, as we have seen, but also with tithe. All holders of land, the king included, were to pay tithe *ecclesiis et sacerdotibus*. Though the clergy who are to benefit are yet undefined, still the tithe is for clergy, and for clergy only. No other recipient is mentioned; the exegesis of St Ambrose has triumphed. From this time tithe, so understood, has a continuous history throughout Western Christendom; it was introduced into the Spanish peninsula as this was gradually recovered from Mohammedan rule, and farther north it was from the first demanded as a right.

We have dealt hitherto with two general sources for the maintenance of the clergy. Neither glebe nor tithe was due to individual gifts; they were a universal provision, and it does not seem that anywhere was there a considerable addition to this revenue. No doubt in the aggregate special benefactions to the local clergy were numerous; in England, for instance, it is not uncommon to find benefices with the additional endowment of a "rectory manor," as at Welwyn in Hertfordshire. In such cases, some lord, probably soon after the Norman Conquest, has bestowed a parcel of his own rights, and till quite recently the rector has had copyhold tenants of his own. Yet, in the main, glebe and tithe have been the maintenance of the beneficed, and their history is that of a diminution rather than an increase of their rights.

When we turn to bishops and monasteries we find persons and institutions who have no original share in these revenues, but have in course of time largely engrossed them. The bishop, while the Christian Empire survived in the West, was subsidised by the State, whose minister he was for ecclesiastical purposes. But for an independent income of his own he had to await the generosity, which was for the most part testamentary, of the wealthier members of his flock. Their benefactions in land might, and often did, lie in quarters distant from his diocese, and we have seen the consequence in the origin of "peculiar" jurisdictions. But the bishops had also exercised a considerable delegated authority on behalf of the Emperor, and under the disorderly Merovingian rule none could take their place. For civil purposes they were a necessary instrument. Thus it was natural that they should be regarded as royal officers, bearing the same relation to their king and patron as the priest of the private church bore to his lord; and also, when royal power grew weak, that the same superiority over bishops should be claimed by local magnates. Theodoric V, who died in 534, is the first king who is known to have sold bishoprics.

But even if the king did not sell, he habitually gave; and when he allowed canonical election his approval had to precede consecration. The number of sees increased, especially in southern France, though important dioceses, such as Laon, were established elsewhere. These actually received their estates from the sovereign, and it was natural that the older dioceses should be assumed to hold by the same tenure. As the kingdom extended eastward, the bishoprics, designed to fulfil a political as well as a religious purpose, were endowed in the same way; and the feudal conception of the relation of bishop to king, which first established itself in the Gallic provinces, became universal. To this superiority of the king there is one striking exception. In the Laws of Aethelberht, committed to writing soon after the conversion of Kent, the rights of "God and the Church" receive a twelve-fold protection, those of the bishop are eleven-fold; king and priest must content themselves with a nine-fold. In Kent the highest claim could only be that of Canterbury, and Rochester was the only bishopric. Ninety years later, in 696, the Laws of Wihtred for the same kingdom, and those of his contemporary, Ine, for Wessex, put Church and king on an equality, and afterwards we find no estimation so high set upon the rights of an English prelate. No doubt the enthusiasm of converts led Aethelberht and his Witan to this exaggeration, and the hope that dignity would give strength to enforce Christianity and morality. The Alemannian laws put the bishop on the level of the duke; but though a duke of Swabia was a potentate more important than any English king before Offa, he was definitely subordinate to the Frankish king. English bishops had been reduced to a much lower estate in the days of Alfred. Under 897 the *Chronicle* records in a disastrous year the deaths of two bishops and of a number of leading laymen, aldermen of shires and others; they are all classed together as "king's thegns."

The grants of land which led to this dependence on the Crown were given in the Frankish Empire with the express intention that the bishop should administer on the monarch's behalf a definite portion of his kingdom. On this side of their activities the bishops' status was the same as that of the immediate lay feudatories, and till the French Revolution some of them continued in Germany, as the sole survivors of the class, to exercise their original function within their original bounds. Where royalty was stronger, the bishoprics were less independent. The French kings had more control over the great sees than over the lay fiefs; and in some cases the laity were in actual possession, by grant which cannot have been voluntary, of Church lands. The county of Champagne was to a great extent held, not directly of the Crown, but of a bishop. In Italy, the bishops, while more powerful in government, were poorer in possessions. And in England, while they were well endowed with lands, they held a national rather than a territorial position. There seems no reason to suppose that their estates were so placed as to facilitate the visitation of their diocese, save in the case of Winchester, where the bishop held manors at the distance of a convenient day's march westward from Southwark into the county of Somerset. When the diocese was divided these continued to be attached to the original see.

Before considering the relation of the bishops to king and clergy under the Franks, it is necessary to recall the first phase of Teutonic Christianity. This was Arian, not by any preference on the part of the German tribes, but because, at the time of the conversion of the first among them, Arianism was the official creed of the Roman Empire, and the example was followed by others even after the Empire had reverted to orthodoxy. Being out of contact with normal Christianity, the tribes were obliged, even in matters not pertaining to their peculiar doctrine, to work out an ecclesiastical system for themselves. They were unaffected by the momentous decree of Valentinian III in 445 that the whole Western Church must be subject to the authority of the Roman see, and by the vigorous exertion of this authority on the part of Leo the Great, for they did not recognise the Pope, and they had little respect for the canonical legislation of the Empire. They struck out a line of their own, and there is reason to think that they were influenced by their hereditary paganism. We have seen how the pagan priest was the predecessor of the Christian incumbent; in the same way the pagan king seems to have had his chief priest, who represented the sacred aspect of kingship, and in some ways anticipated the office of the Christian bishop who succeeded him. In Bede's famous story of the conversion of Northumbria, King Edwin has his pagan *primus pontificum*[1], who is a member, and so far as we know the only priestly member, of his Witenagemot. In the Anglo-Saxon translation of Alfred's time he is called the senior, or chief bishop, so close did the analogy seem between his and the Christian office. As religious representative of the king, he would be nominated by him, as the local priest was by the local lord; and it cannot be a mere coincidence that the Arian bishop was the nominee of the Gothic king, and that his attachment was rather to the king than to the diocese. The court bishop of the Middle Ages seems to be following the Arian example. So when the Norwegians were converted, though it was not to Arianism, their bishops were the king's bishops, and accompanied him on his progresses. Their function was exercised over the whole of his realm, and their position that of the earlier Arian prelates who had been known as "bishops of the Goths." There was no diocesan system in Norway till Hadrian IV organised the Scandinavian churches in the twelfth century. Similarly, English bishops, by their constant attendance upon him before the Norman Conquest, shewed the closeness of their association with the king. This idea, ultimately Arian, was engrafted upon Catholic orthodoxy by Clovis. He found Arianism established in Gaul as a working system, and had no quarrel with its administrative side. In fact, since it was prevalent in the more civilised parts of his

[1] *Hist. Eccl.* II, 13.

kingdom, it was natural that he should extend it to the rest. Its advantages were obvious; the Arian kings had used their orthodox bishops as instruments of government over their Roman subjects, and so might he, and therefore he must control and choose them.

With this Teutonic conception of the relation of bishop to king the orthodox system, accepted on paper at any rate, had to be reconciled. That system had grown up in lands where the church was an institution of the town, and clergy and congregation had jointly chosen their bishop. It was expressed in the canons of councils which were for the most part composed in Greek, though they were familiar, and regarded as authoritative, in Latin translations throughout the West. Their provision for a share of the laity in election could not have been carried out in dioceses like those of the Franks, where the town was insignificant in comparison with the rural area, and where there was no method of collecting the laity for the purpose. On occasion the laity of the town took matters into their own hands, and acclaimed a candidate who then presented himself for approval to the king. On occasion also the clergy of the town ventured upon the same step, with or without lay concert. But these were exceptional cases, and when they occurred it was not the clergy of the diocese at large that made the choice, but the bishop's own staff. We meet here with the origin of the chapter's claim to elect the bishop.

But normally the matter lay in the hands of the king. There were two reasons for this. The Byzantine system, with its assumption of divine right for the monarch, was in existence and offered a principle as well as a precedent for imitation, and the Frankish king did so much for the bishop that he expected a corresponding return. Whatever the sees had lost by confiscation had been largely returned; monasteries, which, like those of England in the time of Bede, were fulfilling no religious purpose, were given to the bishops in compensation for their losses. But for this a return was demanded. Lands, if they were not to be secularised, must do service, and especially military service, to the state. So secular did the bishop's office grow that it became customary, as we shall see, to divide the estates of the diocese that part of them might be devoted to ecclesiastical purposes, while the remainder, under the bishop, served the Crown. The cathedral chapter has its origin in this precaution. But not military service only was required of the bishops. They served as *missi dominici*. In 819 a capitulary speaks of "our *missi*, whether bishops, abbots, or counts." Bishops thus were in the exact position of the episcopal "king's thegns" of Alfred. Cathedrals and great abbeys were *regales ecclesiae*; during the vacancy of a see its revenues lapsed to the Crown. And as the endowment was magnificent and the terms on which it was held the same as those on which nobles held their fiefs, it was natural that nobles should be chosen for the post and that usually the bishop came not from the cathedral but from the court. Such was the position of the Frankish bishop; a position which Alcuin did not venture to criticise in his correspondence with Charlemagne his master, though he vigorously exhorted English bishops to resist such aggression against the rights of the Church. There is no reason to think that they were less submissive than those of Gaul and Germany. In the following generation Louis the Pious revived, on paper, the right of the clergy and laity to elect the bishop. We need not suppose that this concession had any general effect.

The clergy concerned in such an election came to be limited, though not universally until the twelfth century, to those who were in the bishop's immediate service. Early in the Frankish period there seem to be instances in which the clergy of the see-town exercised the right. This would have been natural when the city was the essential or predominant part of the diocese; but where the great majority of the clergy were not only at a distance from the city, but were dependent, not on the bishop but on their lords, no part in the election of the bishop could fall to them. Not even the bishop's own clergy, stationed at outlying places to minister baptism and other needs to the people, were called in to share the election. And the city clergy themselves came to be excluded, not only from the election but from any control of the general affairs of the diocese. This was concentrated in the hands of a corporation of the bishop's own resident assistants, who came to be called the cathedral chapter, and stood to the bishop in the same relation, *mutatis mutandis*, as the fellows of a college in the older English universities to the head of their house. The other clergy of the city were excluded. This body consisted of clerks and monks. It must be remembered that till the time of Louis the Pious in the Frankish Empire, and even later in England, a monk was not necessarily Benedictine; probably those who followed that rule were a minority among monks. The connotation of the term was vague; it meant that he who bore it professed to be aiming at the perfect life. The clerks of the cathedral were usually canons, so called from the canon, or rotation of the Psalter, which it was their duty to sing; but others had for their function to execute the orders, whatever they might be, of the bishop. Originally, no doubt, they had, whether monks or seculars, for the most part served as missionaries, and all had this in common that their home was within their precinct, away from which they could have no permanent settlement. Thus, when private churches in lay ownership became general, their diocesan usefulness was at an end, and they came to exist only for their cathedral. This did not lessen the closeness of their connexion with the bishop. He and they formed one society. As late as 1020 Aethelnoth, "monk and dean in Christ Church," was consecrated Archbishop of Canterbury. He had been the resident head, as his predecessors had been since the days of St Augustine, of a corporation containing both monastic and secular elements; though by his time the idea of a pure Benedictine community had become prevalent, and it was believed that cathedral bodies of that type had existed from their foundation. We must think of these mixed societies as considerable in the number of their members and loose in their organisation. As one body with the bishop they were partners with him in an undivided estate; the bishop could perform no act of importance in relation to it without the consent of his colleagues. In the old canons the bishop had been bidden to give account of his transactions to his clergy; St Benedict had enjoined upon the abbot that in important matters he should take counsel with the senior monks. Both these precedents carried weight; even after the separation of interests, to which we shall come, there were cases, as at Verden and Hereford, where, till the end of the Middle Ages and later, the acts of neither were valid unless confirmed by the seal of the other member of the partnership. Such control was irksome. This was first felt by chapters which found that the burdens, often military, imposed by the state upon their bishop left him without sufficient resources to maintain his cathedral. The only remedy was that there should be a division of properties; the bishop's promise of a share of the income would have been an insufficient security, for he might have been powerless to fulfil it. The earliest known example of such a division is at Sens in 822; it was copied at Nevers in 849, and at Cologne in 866, where the collegiate churches subordinate to the see, the original baptismal churches or "old minsters" as they were called in England, also received a specific endowment from the properties of the see. In such cases the perpetuity and independence of the foundation was further secured by fixing the number of the beneficiaries and giving them at least the rudiments of a constitution. The separation was welcomed as a measure of religious reformation, since it removed the chapter from the dangers of the world. The development of the cathedral system into its complete shape must be considered hereafter.

In regard to the parishes, the Carolingian period saw a serious encroachment. We have seen that the parish church and the lordship of land hung together. The lords had their churches, the bishop had his, and it came to be usual, if not universal, for the bishop in his capacity as landholder to put himself into a feudal, instead of a directly episcopal, relation to the clergy upon whom he had conferred benefices. But it was a new thing that churches should be separated from the land and bestowed on a bishop or a monastery. They were so given, from the seventh century onwards, in increasing numbers. This was not merely a transference of patronage, creating advowsons in gross, to use the technical English term; the churches, as a source of income, were bestowed. This threw upon the new proprietors the responsibility of providing the local ministrations, together with the enjoyment of the revenues after paying the necessary expenses. As yet there was no thought of vicars with security of tenure. When the see of Würzburg was founded in 741, the bishop received twenty-five churches situated on royal lands from the king, as well as lands for himself on which churches had been established, or might be as population spread. In the same generation the monastery of St Gall was similarly endowed with churches, and the example was followed in all countries, chiefly in favour of religious houses. They were able to turn such gifts to profit, especially if the tithe were annexed to the benefice, while the donor lost no income by his generosity. But a still more serious obstacle to the establishment of an independent clergy was set up when Otto the Great in 948 endowed the dioceses of Brandenburg and Havelberg, which he was founding with a view to the conversion of the Wends, with the whole of the tithes. This was for the support of the bishops, who were but poorly furnished with lands by the founder. In fact, the whole history, in France to greater excess than elsewhere, was to be one of a steady diminution of the resources available for the parish clergy, and a corresponding lowering of their status.

For the supervision of the clergy the immediate local authority, under the bishop, was the rural dean or archpriest, sometimes also called, in the earliest period, the cardinal priest or the bishop's dean, or, again, the dean of Christianity. *Decanus* is a word of general use from the fourth century onwards for the lowest officer, military, monastic, or other, who has men under him. The number ten which it indicates can never have been strictly adhered to when it came into general use. There is reason to think that both in England and in Germany the hundred of civil administration was the area of the original rural deanery, and that the deaneries sometimes retain boundaries older than those of the hundreds of the later Middle Ages. It may be only an accident that no record remains of rural deans in England before the Norman Conquest, but it is perhaps more likely that the office was imported by Lanfranc, for "rural dean" was the name borne in the province of Rouen. In the Frankish kingdom, the office is found even in the sixth century and had become universal in the ninth; and since it was as yet the only local office within the diocese its importance tended to increase till it was eclipsed by the archdeaconry. The rural dean or archpriest—one or other of these names came to prevail in different regions—had definite duties of supervision over clergy and laity such as were afterwards engrossed by the archdeacon, and he had a seal of office. But his office was never a benefice. It lost its importance because of the inevitable inefficiency of amateur judges in moral and ecclesiastical causes, whose sphere of duty was so narrow that it was impossible for them to provide trained assistance. Yet the deanery as an area of administration was maintained in existence, and it is said that in Germany it had a revival of importance towards the end of the Middle Ages, the bishops favouring officers dependent on themselves as against archdeacons who had attained independence. But there were cases in which there was an interchange of name between archdeacons and rural deans. In the diocese of Halberstadt there were thirty archdeacons, rural deans with a higher title, while the diocese of Grenoble was under four archpriests, archdeacons with a humbler designation.

The name of archdeacon both in Latin and Greek dates from the fourth century. Custom required that every priest, and *a fortiori* every bishop, should be accompanied in the discharge of his duties by a deacon. The bishop's deacon had a position of peculiar importance; he was sometimes specifically called deacon of the town over which his bishop presided. As representative of the bishop he exercised a wide general supervision of the clergy, which the council of Chalon in the middle of the seventh century describes as coercive. He also administered the central finances of the diocese and the bishop, but he did so without security of tenure. He was archdeacon so long as the bishop chose, and no longer. Nor was he locally connected with any part of the diocese, but exercised the functions entrusted to him throughout its whole extent. In spite of these limitations his office was so important that at Rome, where election to the see was a reality, the archdeacon was often chosen as successor to the bishop. He was necessarily in deacon's orders; it is not till the twelfth century that it became usual for a priest to hold an archdeaconry, and even then protests were made, though without avail, against the innovation.

In the Frankish period two considerations were effectual to give a new position to the bishop. The Roman imperial idea of the divine right of the monarch was accepted as valid for the Teutonic king; and the Church was regarded as national. From 511, the date of the first council of Orleans, councils were summoned by the king, who presided in them. Archbishops and bishops sat side by side as equals, for all were equally the men of the king by whose grant they held their lands. The archbishoprics were but nominal, for they had no provincial jurisdiction, and provincial boundaries were disregarded, as when the historical connexion of Augsburg with Aquileia and of Chur with Milan was disregarded. They were treated simply as bishoprics within the Frankish State, whatever their ecclesiastical associations. Similarly in England, where unity in the Church preceded unity in the State, it is difficult to discriminate between Church and lay assemblies. In the latter, ecclesiastical ordinances were passed, while, in the former, kings and leading laymen were present and attested the record of the proceedings. And both in England and under the Franks, bishops, as royal officers, took an active share in public affairs. In England, from early in the ninth century, bishops fought and fell in battle, and the military duty of Frankish bishops during the same period became one of their most conspicuous functions.

In contrast with this national and feudal conception of the bishop's office was the papal. The policy of the Popes was to make the provincial system a reality, and to govern the Church through the archbishops. These must be strong, yet not strong enough to claim independence. The ineffectual struggles of Arles against Roman domination, though complicated by the fact that the metropolitan had accepted the office of papal vicar for Gaul, are proof of the seriousness with which this Roman claim was urged, and of success in keeping the archbishops in subjection. But the Popes had as yet no success in raising them to the headship of a subordinate hierarchy. One such attempt, political as well as ecclesiastical, was made when in 716 the Duke of Bavaria undertook to establish an effective province for his dominions, so withdrawing his bishops from the Frankish councils and entering into connexion with Rome. But this was frustrated by Charles Martel. The scheme had papal approval; the next effort was made by a Pope. The English St Boniface was a devoted servant of the Papacy, who regarded his commission from Rome as his authority to preach the Gospel. He received it, before he began his work, from Gregory II, and kept in constant relation with his papal patrons. The position assigned him was that of an archbishop without a see, but with a general superintendence over his converts to the east of the Rhine. He was never Archbishop of Mayence, an office not created till after his death, but archbishop by papal nomination and papal legate, holding simultaneously the bishopric of Mayence. He made effective use of his authority, assembling synods and making his province a reality. He thus prepared the downfall of the Frankish system, which came as soon as the Empire grew weak and the Pope advanced a theory and established a system which displaced the Carolingian.

But till after the death of Charlemagne the imperial theory and practice held their ground. In a society comparatively simple it seemed possible that one authority, divinely appointed, could regulate all the affairs of men. The tenure by which the Pope held his estates was exactly the same as that of a duke of Aquitaine or Bavaria, and to the monarch he seemed to belong to the same class as other prelates of his dominions. The sovereign held himself the possessor of authority in regard to the administration as well as the doctrine of the Church; and in the eyes of Charlemagne, in whom this phase of ecclesiastical theory found its full expression, papal authority was inferior to his own whenever he chose to exercise his rights.

Nothing but continuous success could have made such claims plausible. When the Carolingian Empire began to be overwhelmed by calamity and incompetence, it was inevitable that papal claims to occupy the vacant seat of authority should be put forward. This was done, when the Empire was at its lowest point in efficiency and morality, by Nicholas I (858–867). Profoundly convinced of the justice of his claims, he asserted that he was a divinely appointed autocrat over the Church, from whose judgment there is no appeal. Bishops bear rule as his delegates, and when the great Hincmar of Rheims shewed signs of independence which might have made his metropolitan office a reality he was promptly humiliated. Metropolitans were to be the Pope's agents for the supervision of their provinces and nothing more. Councils were only to be held when sanctioned by the Pope; thus the Frankish system of councils of the Empire, held by the Emperor's authority, was condemned. Charged with functions so high, the Pope could have no earthly superior, nor even equal, and therefore (though this conclusion was not so bluntly drawn as in later times) the Emperor must be subordinate to him. In the development of this argument the Pseudo-Isidorian Decretals are quoted for the first time. It must remain an open question whether Nicholas knew that they were forgeries; their primary purpose was certainly rather that of weakening the French metropolitan than of magnifying the office of the Pope. But they served the Pope's purpose, and there is no reason to think that his standard of honesty was higher than that of his and the succeeding centuries. Every important church constructed or profited by forgeries such as were produced by Lanfranc in the strife between Canterbury and York, and at an earlier date by Bremen to the prejudice of Cologne. The authors, rightly or wrongly, were convinced of the justice of their claim, and counted it no wrong that they should take a short cut towards their end by advancing pleas likely to satisfy those whom it was their object to persuade.

But as yet such claims could not be made effectual. They were not to be withdrawn, but in rivalry with them the Empire, when new and stronger dynasties arose, was to maintain its ascendancy, and in time was to develop a theory of its own in justification of its practice. Meanwhile under the Ottos the Crown recovered its position in Germany. Like Charles the Great the kings chose the bishops, the semblance of canonical election being maintained but the reality frustrated, for the election was held either in the monarch's presence or at his court. The bishops did service for their fiefs by an active life of statesmanship; one Archbishop of Cologne was also Duke of Lorraine. All sees were held directly from the Crown, in contrast to the practice of France, where the great nobles, such as the Duke of Normandy, were patrons of bishoprics in their dominions as fully as the king was in his. To this rule there were, however, exceptions, and the fact that among the twelve traditional peers of France were six bishops, whose sees in some cases lay outside the direct domain of the king, is evidence of a special connexion between him and them. But the sovereign not only wielded authority over existing sees. The extension of German influence was promoted under the Ottos by the foundation, without reference to Rome, of sees in Denmark and to the east of the Elbe. Imperial control of the bishoprics was maintained till Frederick Barbarossa gave the patronage of those in Lower Saxony to Henry the Lion, with the view of strengthening the defenders of the north-eastern frontier. After Henry's fall the immediate authority of the Emperor over those sees was resumed and maintained. As the Empire grew weaker several of the eastern sees fell under the control of local princes; and when some small dioceses were carved out of Salzburg the advowson of them was vested in the archbishop. But in Germany the general tendency was an increase of secular independence on the part of the bishops. In France the appointment of see after see passed by conquest or inheritance to the king, the process not becoming complete till in 1714 Louis XIV deprived the Duke of Nevers of his patronage of the small see of Clamecy, on no other ground than that it was unfitting that a French bishopric should be in other hands than those of the king. In England, some attempts were made by marcher lords to obtain control of the Welsh bishoprics by entry on their possessions during vacancy or by efforts to dictate elections, but they had no success; and the last traces of the ancient superiority of Canterbury over Rochester disappear in the thirteenth century. Mediate bishoprics never existed in England.

This feudal relation of bishop to king carried with it incidents of feudal tenure. Royal investiture, and the struggles against it, are part of general history, as is the compromise by which an apparent victory was won by the Pope, while substantially kings and Emperors lost nothing of their practical influence over the choice of bishops. Standing in feudal relation to the grantor of their lands, these were bound to fulfil the duties, whether of giving counsel or military support, in return for which the grant was made. If the office were vacant, the service could not be rendered, and it seemed equitable that, as with a lay fee when the heir was a minor, the revenue should lapse to the Crown till a successor capable of discharging the duty should be appointed. Hence the abuse of prolonged vacancies, as in the time of William II in England. But a reasonable interval was assumed, as in the Statute of Westminster of 1275. The right included, and still includes, that of presentation to benefices in the gift of the vacant see, which the new occupant recovers after paying homage. In England this is the sole right now exercised by the Crown. Elizabeth was the last sovereign to abuse the traditional privilege. In France the royal right to the profits of the see was exercised till the Revolution, though in certain dioceses the claim to patronage was unsuccessfully disputed. In Germany the power of the Crown was insufficient to maintain such a claim.

If the Papacy failed to detach the bishops from their dependence on the sovereign, it was successful in establishing a system of provincial and diocesan councils which were effective in creating uniformity and centralisation, and also in averting the danger of national Churches. In England it was only on the rare occasions of a legatine council that the two provinces met together, while in France the assembling of the first States General in 1302, at which the whole clergy of France was represented, was one of the measures of opposition to Boniface VIII taken by Philip the Fair. This provincial system, completed for Western Europe by the Scandinavian legation of the future Pope Hadrian IV and by the Synod of Cashel, drew the Church together, promoted uniformity and the corporate sense, and also linked the several provinces with Rome. Thus accustomed to act as a class, the clergy withdrew from secular courts and organised an exclusive system of their own. This was sanctioned for England by the undated ordinance of the Conqueror, which forbids a bishop or archdeacon to hold pleas concerning "episcopal laws" in a hundred court. The bishop is to hear the case and pass judgment at the seat of his bishopric or other place of his choice, in accordance with the canons and episcopal laws. No sheriff or other officer of the king nor any layman is to intrude in the matter, but contempt of the bishop's court is to be punished by the king or sheriff.

Thus the clergy tended to become a close corporation, the constitution of which inevitably became feudal. The relation of the beneficed clergy to the bishop resembled that of the bishop to the king. No longer is the parish priest the man of the lord who appointed him; he becomes the bishop's man. Perhaps Lanfranc's canon of 1076, whereby no more service is to be rendered for a benefice than had been paid in the time of King Edward, is evidence that patrons (to use the later term) were giving a feudal interpretation to their relation to the beneficed, for the wording of the canon is so general that it can hardly be limited to endowments granted on a secular tenure. But in any case it is a reference to an expiring conception. After the Conquest the tenure was so thoroughly feudalised that the essential element in institution to a benefice was an act of homage followed by a grant. And the same obligation lay upon the grantee as in the case of a lay fee. The beneficed clergy had on special occasions, such as a visit of the bishop to Rome, to defray his necessary expenses, just as the tenants of a lay lord gave an aid on such occasions as the knighting of his eldest son. This burden survived the Reformation, for under Elizabeth bishops such as Aylmer of London and Bentham of Lichfield demanded it with success. It must be borne in mind that this feudal duty was compensated by a feudal protection. The security of tenure was actually increased by the obligation laid upon the bishop of maintaining the rights of his man.

But the medieval bishop too often neglected his duties. A substitute was found in the *chorepiscopus*, a title found in the Eastern canons and adopted though not always understood in the West. The office seems to have been introduced from the East by Theodore of Canterbury as a regular institution. In England it did not gain much importance, though "county bishops" without diocese are found in the tenth century who are exactly what "chorepiscopus" indicates, and though archbishops of Canterbury had assistants, sometimes called by this name, down to the reforms of Lanfranc. But on the Continent, when the work of such men as Willibrord and Boniface spread, they were faced by the difficulty that the canons, framed in a town-bred Christianity, made no provision for dioceses in townless lands. So where sees could not be founded, chorepiscopi were multiplied. They were kept in subordination; a diocesan would speak of "my bishop," and as a sign of inferiority such assistants were usually, and not only in cases of necessity, consecrated by the diocesan alone. But useful as they were in the missionary stage, they became an abuse when secular bishops, even in regions of established Christianity, employed them to discharge their proper duties, and when sees were left indefinitely vacant for a monarch's profit, with the excuse that a chorepiscopus was doing what was needful. Thus there was a serious evil, which was combated by the usual method of forgery. Beside the respectable chorepiscopi whom Theodore had brought in, there had been in the East ambiguous officers bearing the same name, against whom many canons had been framed. They had not been bishops, but delegates for quasi-episcopal functions, who had often exceeded their commission. It was now assumed that the Western chorepiscopi were of this unsatisfactory class, and a campaign was started against their very existence, as condemned by the canons. Pseudo-Isidore and his predecessors made early Popes denounce them, and Nicholas I assented, though somewhat faintly. The result was a compromise at a Council at Metz in 888. They were recognised as bishops, but must not take the place of a diocesan. They might not consecrate a church, though they might ordain a priest. An absentee bishop was not tempted to employ an assistant so limited, and the class died out, surviving last in England. Such assistant bishops as subsequently appear are absentees from dioceses of their own, and they are nowhere numerous. But with the failure of the Crusades a multitude of sees in the East became nominal, yet it seemed unworthy of Christendom to confess to failure. The occupants found work as assistants to European diocesans, and as they died out the names of their sees were bestowed on men who were never expected to visit their diocese. But the forms were scrupulously carried out. A bishop would be consecrated to Gallipoli, for example, and would promise canonical obedience to his Metropolitan of Heraclea, whose see was as shadowy as his own. He would then, as if with surprise, discover that the unbelievers made it impossible for him to live at Gallipoli, and that no income could be drawn from that place. He would therefore petition the Pope to let him retain the abbey or other preferment he had held, and this would be granted; and till he could obtain possession of his see he was allowed to assist any Catholic bishop who desired his aid. He would then, if he were well endowed, settle down for life as assistant bishop in the diocese whence his revenues were drawn; if he were less fortunate, he might live a wandering life as temporary helper in several successive dioceses. Unsatisfactory as this system was, it was a real and practical reform, for from the latter half of the thirteenth century onwards there was no failure of consecrated bishops to perform the spiritual functions of the office according to the standard of the age.

There had been no failure in regard to the business side of the episcopal office, but it largely passed into new hands. The archdeacon ceased to be the servant of the bishop; his office became a benefice. It seems impossible to fix the dates or to discover the process by which this change was effected in the various countries; it was, to the thought of the times, a natural development. It began, about the tenth century, in the assignment to the archdeacon of a definite region in which he should represent the bishop. This grant was regarded as for life: and so a new authority, independent in practice, came into being. In the thirteenth century archdeacons in Germany were describing themselves as "archdeacon by the grace of God." Being no longer in that relation to the bishop which had been indicated by their membership of the order of deacons, they regarded themselves as released from limitation to that order. From the tenth century archdeacons in priest's orders are to be found; yet as late as St Anselm's council of Westminster in 1102 a canon was passed that archdeacons should be deacons. This however was only a protest, and an ineffectual one, against a well-established practice. By his time most of the English counties had their archdeacons, though local archdeaconries had been unknown here before the Conquest. In England, as elsewhere, archdeaconries varied widely in importance. The larger they were, and the more remote from an episcopal centre, the greater their powers. For instance, in the immense archdeaconry of Richmond the institution to benefices and the nomination of rural deans belonged to the archdeacon, not to the Archbishop of York. The value of an archdeaconry consisted largely in legal profits, drawn chiefly from the proving of wills. It needed therefore, as soon as canon law developed, a legal training. But since archdeacons were often appointed without regard to this, and were frequently absentees, they came to delegate their work to expert officials. The bishops took the same step, regularly appointing vicars-general and officials commissioned to discharge their administrative and litigious tasks. These officers, who never obtained a beneficed position and therefore were dependent on the bishop, maintained his interest in the rivalry which inevitably rose between him and the archdeacon. The latter, however, was made conscious of his subordination by the power of visitation which the bishop regularly exercised over him, in person or by proxy, and during which the archdeacon was suspended from the exercise of his office.

A reason for the archdeacon's independence was that he belonged to a corporate body from which it was the desire of the bishop to detach himself. We have seen that a division of interests between bishop and chapter was carried out in the Frankish Empire in the interest of religious observance. The group of men who were charged with the maintenance of cathedral worship could not be assured of continuity except by a complete separation from the bishop; his revenues were charged with political and military burdens, and he could only provide for his cathedral by detaching a definite proportion of his revenues, and also of his rights; for he could not maintain his control, if he wished it, over a corporation whose finances were no concern of his. Thus his concern with the internal affairs of the cathedral were limited to a visitation, not regularly performed and often disputed. Since there were no diocesan duties, except for archdeacons, when the diocese was fully provided with clergy, the great church came to exist for its own services as much as did that of any monastery. Only when the bishop used it on official occasions did it serve the purpose for which it had been founded; though traditional visits to the mother church by its parochial daughters were prescribed, they were not always fulfilled. This detachment from the diocese was encouraged by benefactions which often were extra-diocesan. To take an English example, Salisbury was endowed with churches and estates scattered over the country from Grantham to the neighbourhood of Plymouth, and few cathedrals had no distant sources of income. In England the separation from the bishop was accomplished soon after the Conquest; in some cases the deed of severance has been preserved, the most noteworthy being that executed by St Osmund of Salisbury. In the division of interests the bishop usually surrendered not only estates and churches but jurisdictions. The cathedral body received episcopal rights, such as that of institution and deprivation, over specified places. Jurisdiction was regarded as a source of income; a striking parallel is to be seen in the creation in 1098 of the Apostolic Legateship for the Count of Sicily by Urban II[1].

So complex a property as that of a well-endowed cathedral could not be managed by medieval methods of accountancy, and the major part was broken up into separate prebends, each member of the corporation having his separate revenue. In great cathedrals these might number fifty or more. To a few prebends definite duties were attached. As for the remainder, they became simply sources of income without cure of souls. Originally the members had performed every function, but, when they came to regard their office as a sinecure, inferior officers were introduced, to sing the services and serve as choirmen, who were not members of the corporation, but often formed subsidiary corporations of their own, so gaining in their turn a secure tenure. But the feeling arose that some of the large number of prebendaries should be resident, to attend the services and conduct the affairs of the cathedral. This smaller number, usually elected from their own ranks by the prebendaries, themselves nominated by the bishop, received a further endowment. This was just, for they had not the same liberty as their brethren, who might be royal clerks, Italian absentees, or otherwise employed. But a further custom arose that the residentiaries should reside in turn, it being regarded as sufficient that one should be on duty at a time. Furthermore, the whole body, now that the bishop had left it to its own devices, needed a head. This was the dean, who was elected by the body over which he was to preside. In some of the greatest German cathedrals there was also a provost, who superintended the secular affairs of the foundation, and tended to become a magnate without part in its inward life.

The history of the cathedrals was also that of the larger collegiate churches. That in neither case was there any hostile criticism appears from the frequent foundation of additional prebends by benefactors who knew that they would be an endowment charged with no duties. On the constitutional and administrative side the history of the monasteries was

[1] See *supra,* vol. v, p. 184.

similar to that of the great secular churches. No distinction need be drawn between those of the Benedictine and the Augustinian rule. Both had begun as congeries of isolated houses, only connected in so far as they followed the same rule; though joint houses of monks and regular canons are found abroad in the ninth century, nor is it likely that in England this combination was confined to the cathedrals. All, till some gained exemption, were subject to the bishop. They stood also in a permanent subordination to the founder and his successors. This might be a bishop who had dedicated certain of his lands to the purpose; it might be a sovereign whose ancestors had founded it, or to whom the fundatorial rights had fallen by escheat or forfeiture; it might be some private nobleman. The rights, like any other advowson, might be sold or otherwise transferred. They passed with the rest of the estate to a new purchaser, or might be given to some religious house, perhaps of a different order. Thus the Benedictines of Durham held the patronage of more than one house of canons. The founder's power included that of granting *congé d'élire* on a vacancy of the headship, though this was not usually, at least in England, accompanied by a letter nominating the successor. During the vacancy the founder's officers entered into possession of the revenues, though in practice this came to be limited to those which were appropriated to the headship. And, finally, the founder had the right of charging the monastery with pensioners, who held for life "corrodies" within it. The division of the abbot's interest from those of his convent began at the same time, and with the same motive, as that between bishop and chapter. The abbacy was so wealthy a post, and one so detached from the daily life of the community, that it tended to become secularised. This was less the case in England than elsewhere, though abbots, as great tenants-in-chief, sat in Parliament. But in France the system of *commendams* made many abbotships purely nominal, while in Germany, when ecclesiastical principalities arose, the feudal bond, being personal, brought the military tenants into relation with the abbot, not with the abbey, as their lord.

As a means of reform it came to be desirable that abbeys should be released from the control of military bishops. In the long run this meant that they would become immediately subordinate to the Pope, or, if he failed to supervise them, that they would be left to their own devices. The remedy for the last evil was to be sought in the concentration of authority, and three great experiments were to be made, starting from Cluny, Cîteaux, and Prémontré, the last being an effort to organise regular canons, while the other two were reformations of Benedictine monachism. Cluny had been founded in 910 by William, Duke of Aquitaine, who granted all his rights over it to the Church of Rome. Thus the house had no patron, and by an extension this was also a privilege of all monasteries which joined the Cluniac congregation. For under the rule of strong and saintly abbots Cluny became not only a pattern, whose peculiarities in life and worship were widely followed in monasteries which maintained their independence, but also the head of a multitude of dependencies. These were under the autocratic rule of the abbot of Cluny, who appointed their abbots or priors, and sent visitors to them at his discretion. Moreover, a monk could not become a full member of the corporation unless he were admitted at Cluny, and by the abbot himself. English and other distant Cluniacs rarely made the journey, and so were excluded from the privilege. The permanent success of this reform depended on the standard maintained by Cluny and its abbots, and the fierce attack of St Bernard shews that by 1125 there had come a certain decline, which must have affected the dependent houses, the legal status of which in England was that of alien cells. During the Hundred Years' War with France they were compelled to purchase denization in order to escape suppression. The Cistercians combined unity with equality; all their houses were abbeys with full rights, whose heads were summoned to the annual chapter at Cîteaux. But there was a further bond of mother and daughter houses, those which had swarmed off in the days of original enthusiasm from an older abbey remaining under its supervision. No patrons were recognised, and the whole Order became directly under the Pope and exempt from episcopal jurisdiction. The contemporary Order of Prémontré followed the same lines, and in its turn was to be copied by the Dominicans. These three Orders were international, and all were to have difficulty in maintaining the central control over the more distant abbeys. The Premonstratensians, especially, tended to division. It may be noted that the purely English Gilbertine Order was also centrally governed, the rule and the property throughout the Order being vested in the Master of Sempringham.

But outside orders or congregations which had been deliberately centralised lay the great mass both of monks and canons, though certain efforts had been made to organise them in part. It remained for Innocent III in the Fourth Lateran Council of 1215 to model them after the Cistercian pattern, and for Benedict XII by bulls of 1336 and 1339 to complete the task. They were to be grouped together by ecclesiastical provinces—in England the Benedictines of Canterbury and York formed separate bodies, the Augustinians of both formed one—and were to hold regular assemblies and arrange for visitation by members of their Order. They had power of taxing themselves for corporate purposes. But the plan was imposed from above and was not heartily accepted. Obscure houses were often overlooked, important houses resisted visitation, abbots refused to attend the general chapters, and taxes remained unpaid.

It remains to notice monasteries which were cathedral. The case of England is exceptional. Save Monreale in Sicily, where the Normans were under English influence, there was no Benedictine chapter outside this country. But cathedrals of regular canons were numerous in France and Spain, while to the east of Germany Premonstratensian chapters at

Riga and elsewhere did much to extend Christianity and civilisation. These last, though with some desire of a release from Prémontré, were effectually members of their Order, but many of those which belonged to the laxer union of Austin Canons instituted by Innocent III may have held but loosely to the association. The Chapter of Carlisle, however, established by Henry I when he founded the see, was represented at the assemblies of the English Austin Canons. In Scotland St Andrew's, on the reconstruction of the see under Norman influence, was made Austin. There were no other cathedrals of the Order in Great Britain. It must be mentioned that St John Lateran, the true cathedral of the Popes, became in the eleventh century the head of a congregation of Austin Canons, which still subsists, though the Lateran has left it. Here again the earlier associations, though weakened by the attempt of Innocent III to force all Austin Canons into an effectual Order, succeeded in thwarting his purpose. These congregations, two of which, the French Arroasians and Victorines, had English members, were unable in face of the Order created in 1215 to maintain a vigorous existence of their own, though they checked its vitality.

The twelfth century saw the general assignment of tithe to permanent owners. We have seen that, when the doctrine prevailed that tithe must be paid to persons in orders, among whom nuns ranked for this purpose, the payers still had liberty to choose their beneficiaries, and if they chose to make the benefaction permanent it rested with themselves to do so. No episcopal sanction was as yet required. Though in England this process did not go so far as in other countries, a proportion of tithe passed thus to monasteries soon after the Norman Conquest, for the invaders were little disposed to sacrifice the lands they had won. Tithe they must pay, and they had the gratification of endowing some favourite shrine, often in France, without increased expense to themselves. This went on till the middle of the twelfth century. And meanwhile, as was natural, in most places the lord had given his tithe to the parish of which he was patron. Hence a new problem arose. The tithe was now annexed to the glebe, and equally attached to the benefice; so much so that the idea spread that the incumbent was of right the possessor, and held tithe by the same tenure as glebe.

But the desire still prevailed to benefit the monasteries, and where this annexation had taken place it could only be done by a grant of the church. The monastery should be patron and incumbent, with power to receive the whole revenue in return for a performance of the services. This performance was usually by a hired chaplain, without security of tenure and often ill-paid; though the Austin and Premonstratensian canons had, and used, the right of settling members of their houses as "revocable" incumbents in churches which they held. While there, they enjoyed the revenue, and in their later years often retired to their abbey. The Benedictines and Cistercians of Germany followed the same practice, but it never seems to have prevailed among them in England. Here also the reform by which perpetual vicarages were instituted was carried out more fully than elsewhere. There are instances earlier than 1200, but the thirteenth century was the period when, by the energy of such bishops as Grosseteste of Lincoln, vicarages became the rule. In France the old abuse continued, and the poverty-stricken parish clergy only gained security of tenure in the eighteenth century, to lose it again by the concordat of 1802. Scotland, before the Reformation, seems to have followed the French example, the abbeys doing little, or even nothing, for the parishes of which they held the endowments. In Italy the strength of the communal movement was such that it involved the parish. The priest came to be regarded as the servant of the community, and it might enter into contract with him for his services, with provision for his dismissal at its will. This was probably better for the parish clergy than the French *portio congrua*, doled out by the appropriator.

The division of interests, as carried out in England, between the monastic patron and the vicar, allotted the great tithes, those on corn, to the former, and the small tithes, on wool, orchards, and the like to the latter. Often there was also a division of the glebe; sometimes the whole of this was taken, leaving but the house and the small tithe to the vicar. But the variations are infinite from place to place, though the maintenance of the chancel by the appropriator of the great tithe is universal. Minor burdens, pensions or portions, were often laid upon a benefice without altering its status. Nothing was more common than for a bishop, as the price of his consent to the conversion of a rectory into a vicarage, to impose a small annual pension for his own benefit upon it. Still, the lot of the beneficed clergy was happier in England than in other countries, for the inroads of the monasteries were fewer and the proportion of benefices with an income above the level of the peasant's was much larger; and this in spite of the fact that there were other than monastic encroachments on the rectories. Bishops would find a revenue for their personal officers by instituting a vicarage in a benefice of their gift, and creating a sinecure rectory out of the residue. And when Henry I founded the see of Carlisle he endowed it with valuable rectories in Derbyshire and Lincolnshire, which the bishop could turn to account by ordaining vicarages; there was, however, the justification that border revenues, which also were supplied, were precarious.

At the head of the whole system was the Pope, confronted in his claim to universal authority by a rival claim to unlimited rule. Both drew from Justinian, and each borrowed arguments from the other. As the Emperor derived strength from the feudal theory of a single head under God, so did the Pope; each made the same demand for military support to be rendered as a duty, claimed the same power of taxation in accordance with his need, exercised the same prerogative of bestowing dominion. In the strife the papacy was inevitably secularised, and the turning-point towards decay may be dated from the reign of Innocent IV. The most prominent symptom, perhaps the principal cause, of this decay was the canon law as it developed from the *Decretum* of Gratian to the books of the *Decretals*. The attempt to arrange a chaotic and often inconsistent mass of existing practices into a coherent legislation opened the way to profitable abuses which were too attractive to be resisted. But always there was a theory to explain and justify the procedure, and to base further claims upon it. An example of aggrandisement attempted through inference is that of Peter's Pence in England. Whatever was the origin of this payment to Rome, whether it began with Ine or Offa, at any rate Aethelwulf made a donation of the annual sum of 300 marks, which became traditional. In the laws of Alfred every Christian throughout England must pay the *Romfeoh*. Naturally in troubled times the payment was made irregularly, though it was never forgotten at Rome. But its voluntary character was forgotten, or ignored. It was assumed on feudal principles that a regular payment was a confession of inferiority, the acknowledgment for a favour conferred. When the Pope in 1059 made Robert Guiscard Duke of Apulia, he was granted a payment from every yoke of oxen in those lands. This was not only a return for the gift of territory, but a public admission of the lord's rights over his tenant. So Gregory VII interpreted the Peter's Pence which William the Conqueror was ready to pay; but William denied the inference that he or his predecessors held England by papal grant. To follow on with the history, the Pence were regularly collected. If a legate were in England (and a legate always had a financial side to his commission) he received them; at other times the Archbishop of Canterbury or some bishop nominated by the Pope; Henry II sometimes bade his sheriffs collect. But the sum of 300 marks was stationary, though wealth and population might increase. It was vain for Popes to protest, or complain that more was levied than was remitted; Innocent III charged the English bishops with collecting 1000 marks and sending 300. This sum, reduced in practice to 299 (£199. 6*s*. 8*d*.), perhaps on the analogy of forty stripes save one, was distributed between the dioceses in a traditional proportion, from Lincoln which paid £42 to Ely which paid £5. In the later Middle Ages, when a resident papal collector received the Pence, the cost of collecting from house to house, if it was ever carried out, must have been too expensive, and probably the payment was made by bishops out of their own revenues. The antiquity of the charge appears from the exemption of Durham, Carlisle, and the Welsh dioceses from the impost. This was laid, after the English pattern, by the English Cardinal Nicholas, afterwards Hadrian IV, upon Sweden and Norway when he organised those Churches. It was unknown in the rest of Western Europe.

We have seen that, on the evidence of the Pence, superiority over England had been claimed. Had it been admitted, it would have enabled the Pope to call on the king for aid against his enemies; and doubtless this, and other claims of the same kind, were designed to enlist worldly aid against the Emperors. In some cases the condition was clear, as when Urban II confirmed Apulia to Duke Roger and Sicily to Count Roger, and Hadrian IV consolidated these grants in 1156 in favour of King William I. Feudal service was recognised as due. So in Spain, when the Count of Barcelona recovered Tarragona from the Moors, he offered his conquest and also his inheritance to the Pope, and received both back as fiefs; though it is very doubtful whether for Barcelona he was not bound to do service to the King of France. When Spanish princes wished to secure their position, it was to the Popes that they surrendered their crowns; other instances can be adduced from Poland, Hungary, and Denmark. Always the grant was made on condition of an annual tribute (*census*), small in itself, but significant of the claim upon loyalty of which the proffer and acceptance of the tribute were tokens. The bargain made between John of England and Innocent III was more substantial. On the surrender of his kingdom of England and lordship of Ireland to the Pope, he received them back on feudal terms, binding himself and his successors to pay annually 700 marks for the one and 300 for the other, and taking as full an oath of fealty as any tenant would take to him. It is needless to say that payment was irregularly made, certainly by Edward I, and that in 1366 Parliament repudiated the transaction. But at first it was a solid and valuable gain, and Pandulf, the legate who carried the transaction through, seized the opportunity of a minor profit of the same kind. Reginald, King of Man, also surrendered and received back his kingdom, over which he declared that there was no earthly superior; an assertion which the Kings of Norway and Scotland, and perhaps the King of England, would have denied. Reginald may have thought that if his assertion were registered at Rome and remained, as it might well do, uncontradicted, it would gain validity from its presence in so respectable a record; and the Pope might gain a little dignity, and possibly some advantage, from a speculative transaction, the financial gain of which was twelve marks a year. So eager was the papal search for such acquisitions that the legislators of Castile and Jerusalem thought it necessary in their codes to assert that the Pope had no temporal authority in those kingdoms. The last victory of Boniface VIII, won in the year of his death, was the surrender of Albert of Austria, who admitted those full papal claims to superiority against which his predecessors in the Empire had been striving for two centuries.

Papal superiority was not limited to secular sovereignties. The Popes became supreme lords of religious houses and their lands, which became detached portions of their territory. When the abbey of Vézelai in Burgundy was founded in the time of Charles the Bald, the founder, with the Emperor's consent, gave full possession to the Pope. In the weaker days of Charles the Simple the founder of Cluny gives, and the Pope accepts, the abbey, free from all royal or other power. The grant stood, though the consent of Charles had not been asked. In such a case the Pope did not expect to draw more than a moderate *census* from the monastery, but he was rewarded by its loyalty for his protection; a protection which was usually extended to its spiritual condition, for he would relieve it from episcopal control. Where, as in England, full sovereignty could not be secured, an exempt abbey, such as St Edmunds, would be free from the bishop, having its own archdeacon; it would also be free not from the king but from the king's officials. Its own officers would execute the writs which elsewhere were sent to the sheriff, and would receive the profits of the king's jurisdiction exercised upon its exempt lands. As to its relation to the local bishop, this might be null as in the rare case of an *abbatia nullius*, like Monte Cassino, where the abbot kept a bishop under his orders to perform any episcopal office; more often he might call in any bishop he would; in other cases he was obliged to request the diocesan to consecrate churches, confirm, and give the annual chrism. In England the fullest exemption released an abbey from visitation, not only from the archbishop as such, but also from him in his capacity of legate. St Augustine's at Canterbury and others must open their doors to a legate *a latere* and to none other. The question might even be raised whether they need admit him if their name were not explicitly mentioned in his commission. Glorious as this exception was, it had one onerous consequence. None but a Pope could admit the abbot of such a house to his office, and the costs of his confirmation were enormous.

All dioceses which lay outside recognised provinces, such as those of Scotland and the isolated diocese of Man, enjoyed the privileges and bore the burdens of immediate subjection to the Pope. He also had power where Christendom was expanding, as in Spain, of shaping new provinces at his will, and retaining such portions as he would under himself. At the other end of Christendom he exercised a special authority. The bishops of the mission which grew into the province of Riga were exempted from the authority of Bremen by Innocent III, and were to hold the temporalities of their sees from the Pope. There was even an attempt to impose the rule of a legate upon the Knights of the Teutonic Order and of the Sword, and so to give the Popes a sovereignty that should threaten Germany. But little came of all this. There were also cases of isolated dioceses which enjoyed exemption, more or less complete, from the authority of metropolitans, with the symbol of the *pallium*, though they were not archbishoprics. The most conspicuous of these were Pavia in Italy and the royal foundation of Bamberg in Germany. There was none in England. Political considerations prompted these exemptions, but there was also the motive that a *census* was the recompense, as in the case of a privileged abbey. And to the abbeys which were granted exemption were soon added a number which the Pope could not profess to regard as exempt from territorial or ecclesiastical superiority, but to which he granted his special protection, always in return for a *census*. This was also paid by many ambitious houses which asked and received the honour of the mitre for their heads. It was granted with various restrictions in place and time of wearing; and in England mitred abbots must not be confused with the smaller class of abbots summoned to Parliament.

In 1192 the Papal Chamberlain (*i.e.* Treasurer) Cencio, the future Pope Honorius III, compiled the *Liber Censuum*, a business-like account of all these payments that were due up to that date; a list more important as a record of claims the Pope could make upon loyalty than as a statement of the income he enjoyed. It was a catalogue of tributes, not of the ordinary sources of revenue, feudal or ecclesiastical. The latter was of ever increasing importance, since fees for the confirmation of bishops and abbots, varying according to the value of the benefice, were being systematically collected, and the profits of litigation, always a chief source of medieval revenue, were steadily increasing. At the same time Honorius III himself was the first to use ecclesiastical revenues throughout Europe as a means of relieving himself of the cost of administration. His officials held benefices everywhere, and needed no salary from their master. By an improvement on this, Innocent IV was to use such benefices for the endowment of his family and friends, and so to set a standard from which Rome was rarely to fall during the following centuries.

This claim to benefices abroad might be justified on two grounds. If the patron were a bishop or an abbey whose head had been admitted by the Pope, he was the Pope's man, and bound to recognise the fact by submitting to a demand of his lord, just as an English bishop, after taking the oath of canonical obedience to the archbishop, shewed that he was his man by giving up to him as his "option" the first benefice—not necessarily the first that fell vacant—that the archbishop should choose out of the bishop's patronage. But Popes were not content with one option; bishops like Grosseteste were broken-hearted at the unworthy or illiterate or youthful presentees whom they might not reject, and who were forced upon them in spite, not only of remonstrances, but of definite promises, such as that one Italian should not immediately follow another in the same post. The Pope was justified, not only feudally but canonically, for canon law was regarded as of papal origin, and an equal authority might override it. It was not contrary to the laws of God or of nature that a child should hold a benefice, and therefore the Pope could admit him. But lay patrons were less submissive. Matthew Paris tells with pride how Robert Thweng, a northern knight, when a foreigner was intruded into his Yorkshire rectory of Upleatham, raised a riot, burned the barns of alien ecclesiastics, rifled their goods and gave them to the poor. Henry III refused to convict him, and sent him to Rome with letters of commendation from himself and his brother Richard of Cornwall, where Gregory IX admitted the justice of his claim to the patronage, deprived the intruder, and promised in future to respect lay rights. They seem, at any rate, to have been less disregarded than those of ecclesiastics.

But the Crusades first gave the Popes occasion to tax Christendom at large. At first kings taxed their realms for this purpose, and with the consent of the Pope taxed their clergy. Direct papal taxation begins with 1199, when Innocent III issued his mandate to all bishops to levy a fortieth of their year's income from all the beneficed of their diocese. The exempt Orders were also assessed. For the carrying out of this taxation it was necessary that benefices should be valued. For England the first valuation of which some fragment remains was made in 1217. It was followed by another in 1229, of which also not many details are known. Then came the Norwich valuation of 1254, of which large portions survive, and finally in 1291 that of Pope Nicholas III, which remains complete, and was the standard by which the clergy were assessed on their official revenues for both papal and royal taxation till the time of Henry VIII. The tax consisted of firstfruits and tenths, the former being the assumed annual value, which was due on entry into the benefice, the other being the annual payment of one tenth of the same sum. In each of these successive valuations the income had been assessed at a higher level; yet there is no reason to doubt that, decided as it was by the oath of neighbours, it was equitable. Small benefices were exempt, so that in the taxation of Pope Nicholas they are unfortunately not recorded, unless the holder were a pluralist, in which case all the items of his revenue are entered. In the bitter strife between Frederick II and successive Popes, he was denounced as worse than a Muslim, and taxation was levied against him on the plea that a crusade was being waged. This was first done by Gregory IX in 1225. The frequency with which the clergy had been taxed for crusading purposes rendered them, and the Popes, so familiar with such imposts, that in the fourteenth century firstfruits and tenths became regular and undisputed sources of papal revenue throughout the West.

For the purpose of gathering in the manifold sums drawn from each country, there had come to be resident papal collectors before 1300. These not only received money, but had power to grant dispensations of many kinds in return for payments. In England, where the Popes were carefully watched, they were obliged on entering upon their office to take oath of fealty to the king. Yet of all countries England was the most carefully observant of ecclesiastical rules. For instance, by canon law tithe could not be redeemed nor alienated from Church uses. Only in England was this obeyed. On the Continent men were less scrupulous. In Germany land was often given in redemption of tithe, and in France it was often in the market and in lay hands. St Louis was a tithe-owner. But everywhere, when the high ideals of the Middle Age became tarnished and distorted by the financial interests which came to dominate the Papacy and, through it, the Church, there was the same spirit of revolt, not to be satisfied till the old system had been purged in the lands of the Counter-Reformation as well as in those which rejected the authority of Rome.

CHAPTER XVII

THE MEDIEVAL UNIVERSITIES

THE revolution—intellectual, moral, and spiritual—which took place in the European world about the middle of the vast period usually comprised in the term "Middle Ages" was at least as decisive and momentous as either of the two later movements which have somewhat overshadowed its importance in popular estimation—that is to say, the Renaissance and the Reformation. The period which immediately followed the completion of the barbarian inroads and the cessation of the Western Empire was a really dark age—an age of violence, confusion, and general ignorance broken only by the dim light of a few isolated scholars who, after all, did little more than conserve some scanty remnants of ancient secular culture and patristic theology. It is difficult to date the beginnings of improvement. For a moment the little circle of learned men who adorned the Carolingian court seemed to herald an era of enlightenment, but the hopes which it suggested were not destined to immediate realisation. The tenth century, at least till towards its close, was as dark as any that went before it. The year 1000 will fairly represent the turning-point. The eleventh century was an age of improvement; the twelfth century one of rapid progress, in some ways even of the most brilliant intellectual activity which the Middle Ages ever knew. The universities were the product of this earlier twelfth-century Renaissance. And it was the universities which kept alive the permanent results of that movement. There was no doubt a popular literature with which the universities had little to do, but on the whole it was due to the universities, more than anything else, that the later Middle Age was not an age of darkness but of high culture and high civilisation—of a kind.

During the Dark Ages, whatever learning and education survived the barbarian cataclysm had their home almost exclusively in the monasteries and the cathedrals[1]; and during this period the monastic schools were perhaps slightly in advance of the secular. The period has been called the Benedictine age. In the cathedrals themselves some of the best known teachers had been pupils of the monks. A marked feature of the intellectual new birth which took place in the twelfth century was the transference of the intellectual primacy from the monastic schools to those of the secular clergy. In the North of Europe the universities were an outgrowth of the cathedral schools, not of the monasteries. Anselm of Bec was one of the last great monastic teachers; the great Abelard—the introducer of a new era in the scholastic philosophy, the true father of

[1] See *supra*, Vol. III, Chaps. XIX, XX; Vol. V, Chap. XXII.

the scholastic theology, out of whose teaching, though not in his lifetime, the University of Paris may be said to have grown—was a secular who lectured in the schools of the cathedral, though accidentally, as it were, he ended his days as a monk. At a later date, regulars played a great rôle in connexion with the universities, but the universities themselves were essentially secular, *i.e.* non-monastic, institutions. In Italy culture was never so completely the monopoly of the clergy as it came to be in the dark ages of northern Europe. The lay professions of law and medicine were never wholly extinguished; and, when the intellectual revival came, the movement was not so closely connected with the Church. And the universities to which it gave birth, though, like all medieval institutions, they had close relations with the Church, may be looked upon as, on the whole, not only secular but lay institutions. This was one of the great differences which from first to last distinguished the universities of northern Europe from those of the South, or at least of Italy. In the northern universities—the universities of which Paris was the type and mother—the scholar was *ipso facto* regarded for many purposes as a clerk; he wore, or was supposed to wear, the tonsure and the clerical habit, while the Master was still more definitely invested with the privileges and subject to the restrictions of the ecclesiastical life, including the obligation to celibacy. In Italy the teacher was more often a layman than an ecclesiastic; the scholar was not necessarily a clerk, and the control which ecclesiastical authorities exercised over the universities was only of the kind which they exercised in all spheres of medieval life.

Corresponding with this difference of origin, and the differences of organisation which were more or less connected with it, was a difference between the favourite studies of the two regions. The great revival of intellectual life in northern Europe centred in the teaching of Theology and Philosophy. If the revived study of the Classics was prominent in the earliest phase of the movement—the phase represented by such teachers as Bernard of Chartres and such writers as John of Salisbury—these studies were never prominent at Paris, and were everywhere thrown into the background by the re-discovery of the lost works of Aristotle at the beginning of the thirteenth century. In Italy the movement, though it began with a revival of literary study, and of Roman Law as a branch of ancient literature, soon concentrated itself on a study of Law which became increasingly scientific and professional. Broadly speaking, Paris was the home of scholastic Philosophy and Theology; Bologna was the great school of Law, and, in a subordinate degree, of Medicine. The contrast must not be over-stated: there was a large body of canonists at Paris; Philosophy was studied at Bologna—though chiefly as a preparation for Medicine rather than for Theology. And Medicine was studied in both; as a place of medical study, Bologna was inferior only to Salerno, which was exclusively a Studium of Medicine. From a period considerably before the actual birth of the university organisation, these three places—

Paris, Bologna, Salerno, stood forth as the three great homes of the highest culture. By the twelfth century they had come to be known as *Studia Generalia*, a term which at first meant simply places of study resorted to by students from all parts. The organisation of Salerno stands by itself. At Paris and Bologna there grew up two different and strongly contrasted types of university organisation; and all later universities were an imitation of one or other of these types or represented a compromise between them. One, however, of these imitations was so ancient, was struck off by the parent university at so early a date and developed on such original lines, that it may almost be said to represent a distinct type of university organisation. Oxford became and was expressly called a *Studium Generale* at almost as early a date as Paris and Bologna. The development of these two types of university organisation must now be traced separately, though we shall have frequent opportunities of observing the curious and complex ways in which they reacted upon one another.

Before entering upon the history of this development in detail, the most salient point of difference may be stated in advance. The word *universitas* meant originally "a whole": it might be applied to any body of men, even to one so comprehensive as all Christian people, who are often addressed by Popes as "universitas vestra," the whole of you; more technically it is the equivalent of the Roman law-term *collegium*, a legally recognised corporation. It is frequently applied to town councils or chapters or trade-gilds. The twelfth century was a period during which a great movement towards associations of one kind or another was going on all over Europe. Men of the same calling aggregated themselves into merchant-gilds, trade-gilds, craft-gilds; or, if in some regions of Europe such associations could claim some kind of continuity from the *collegia* of the old Roman world, it was at this time that they renewed their life, and began to figure prominently in the political organisation of cities and states. The university, in its scholastic sense, was simply a particular kind of trade-gild—an association of persons following a common occupation for the regulation of their craft and the protection of their rights against the outside world. The word *universitas* is, in the earlier part of our period, never used absolutely. The phrase is always "*universitas scholarium, universitas magistrorum, universitas magistrorum et scholarium*" or the like. These gilds were of two kinds. The Universities of Paris, Oxford, and (with the partial exception of Scotland) of northern Europe generally were universities of masters. Those of Italy—and to some extent of southern Europe generally—were gilds of scholars, though the ascendancy of the scholars over the masters was not in all cases so complete as in the parent University of Bologna.

Before entering on the history of Paris and Bologna, however, a few words must be said about the completely isolated Studium of Salerno. During the greater part of its history it was a Studium of Medicine only.

As a health resort and as a place celebrated for the skill of its physicians, Salerno was already famous in the tenth century; in the first half of the twelfth its school of medicine is already spoken of by Ordericus Vitalis as "existing from ancient times."[1] Situated at the meeting-place of Greek, Latin, Arabic, and Jewish culture, it became the focus of a revived study of medicine which slightly preceded the general revival of culture and education of which mention has already been made. It is difficult, if not impossible, to make a comparative estimate of the share of Arabic, Jewish, and Greek-Latin writers respectively in this progress, for the earliest authors shew traces of them all. The Hebrew element was probably strong.

Latin translations of the works of Hippocrates and Galen were indeed the basis of the later teaching of the *Civitas Hippocratica* as of medical scholarship generally, but Jewish writers, especially Isaac Judaeus (Abū-Ya'qūb Isḥāq ibn Sulaimān al-Isrā'īlī, *ob.* 953), were largely used by the best known of the early Salerno writers, Constantinus Africanus. The Studium flourished early and decayed early; isolated and out of touch with the rest of Europe it appears to have exercised no constitutional influence upon other universities. Of its internal organisation almost nothing is known save that it was a College of Doctors and not a university of students, and that it had a Praepositus (afterwards called Prior) at its head.

In 1231 the Emperor Frederick II, who had founded a university at Naples seven years previously, came to its rescue by requiring all medical teachers and practitioners to obtain a licence from the King's Court, only awarded after an examination conducted by the Masters of Salerno. This was followed, as elsewhere, by the usual Inception or *Conventio*.

Many legends have attached themselves to the school, especially one making it the earliest home of women practitioners and teachers, but this together with the eleventh-century authorship of the popular *Regimen Sanitatis Salerni* and its dedication to Robert, Duke of Normandy (1054–1135), as "King of the English," lacks satisfactory proof. The university seems to have maintained a nominally continuous existence until its abolition by an edict of Napoleon in November 1811[2].

The secular schools of the Dark Ages were everywhere connected with some cathedral or other great church. They were placed under the government of some capitular dignitary—sometimes of the archdeacon, sometimes of a special official bearing the title of *Scholasticus*, sometimes (as at Paris) of the Chancellor. At first this official was himself the principal, perhaps the only, teacher. Gradually, as education developed, a custom grew up by which the Chancellor or Scholasticus granted a licence to teach to other

[1] *Hist. Eccles.* P. ii, l. iii, 11. (An. 1059.)

[2] The account of the University of Salerno has been revised since Dr Rashdall's death in order to harmonise it with recent research. *Edd.*

masters. A synod at Westminster in 1138 forbade the growing practice of re-selling such licences, while in 1179 the Lateran Council required the authorities to grant a licence to any properly qualified teacher. There was now no obstacle to the multiplication of masters wherever the fame of some illustrious teacher caused an increase of scholars who desired more teaching than the great man himself could give, and many of whom desired eventually to become masters themselves. The growing respect for learning generated an ambition on the part of scholars to obtain the honours attaching to the teacher's chair, even when they had no intention of devoting themselves, or at least of devoting themselves permanently, to the teacher's career. The title Master, Doctor, or Professor—originally synonymous—became one which even bishops and cardinals did not scorn to prefix to their names. Out of the groups of duly licensed masters who began to multiply in the great centres of education, the gilds of masters arose.

Paris was not a very ancient, or at first a very famous seat of medieval learning. The stories which connect the origin of the university, or even of the schools of Paris, with Charles the Great—a monarch who does not appear to have visited that city twice in the whole course of his life—may be dismissed as mere legends. The schools of Paris are for the first time mentioned at the end of the ninth century. But William of Champeaux (*c.* 1070–1121) is the first master of the Cathedral School who gave it any particular distinction; and it was not till the time of his more famous pupil, Peter Abelard (1079–1142), that Paris rose to a leading position among the schools of northern Europe. But in his time there was no university. The masters obtained their licences from the Chancellor of the cathedral church, and opened schools, sometimes on the crowded island round its walls, sometimes on or near the bridges which connected it with the southern bank (we hear of an Adam de Petit-Pont and an Adam de Grand-Pont), sometimes on the southern bank itself, in the neighbourhood and within the jurisdiction of the great collegiate church—from 1147 the abbey—of Ste Geneviève. Abelard himself at one time taught in "the mount" of Ste Geneviève. But, though at an early period some of the schools were situated within the jurisdiction of the abbey, the Studium was originally the outgrowth of the cathedral school and of that alone.

Though there was no university or formal gild of masters in Abelard's time, we can discover in the course of his career traces of certain scholastic customs out of which the university of masters ultimately grew. It was naturally expected that no one should assume the functions of a master without having passed a certain number of years under a properly licensed master in the study of the subjects which he proposed to teach, and it was almost equally natural that he should obtain the consent of his teacher to that step. When masters began to multiply, it became usual for them to welcome the new master into their fraternity by some sort of initiation—accompanied by feasting at his expense—and to assist at his inaugural lecture. It may be inferred that some such customs existed in the time of Abelard, for, when the already famous master of the liberal Arts betook himself, after only a short period of study under the aged theologian Anselm of Laon, and without that teacher's consent, to the teaching of Theology by lecturing on the difficult book of Ezekiel, the act was regarded as an unheard-of piece of audacity, and is made a distinct article of charge against him at the Council of Soissons in 1121. It may be presumed that among the much larger and younger body of Masters in Arts the custom of inception—as it was called—was in a still more developed condition. This simple custom contained in itself the germ of the whole institution. It came to be considered that the "licentiate" —the scholar who had received from the Chancellor licence to teach (*licentia docendi*)—was not a full master until he had also been made free of the magisterial gild by the ceremony of inception, duly performed, with the concurrence of the whole society, by his ancient master. The University proper consisted of those who had thus been admitted into the masters' gild by inception. And the trade-union rapidly acquired a monopoly of higher education: membership of the University became, by a custom which hardened into law, as necessary for teaching of the higher type as the Chancellor's licence. The trade-gilds and the craft-gilds had no doubt originated in much the same way. Another important medieval institution —the institution of Chivalry—arose from the transference of the same idea to the professional army. The young soldier did not become a full soldier or knight (*miles*) until he had been admitted to the brotherhood of arms by the touch of the veteran's sword. The blessing of the priest occupied in the knight's initiation a position somewhat analogous to the Chancellor's licence in the scholastic career. The term Bachelor was used in connexion with both professions. The soldier who had as yet no others serving under his banner was known as a Knight Bachelor (*Bachelier*, *Baccalaurius*). The same term—originally conveying both the notion of youth and that of apprenticeship—was applied to the young scholar who was on probation for the mastership, and was already permitted to act as a subordinate teacher. In the fully developed University, admission to this position was given in a formal manner by the Rector or other head of the university after examination or other preliminary tests, and became a definite *step* towards the mastership (*gradus ad magisterium*). The term degree (*gradus*) began apparently with this inferior stage in the academical career, and was later applied to each of the steps or stages in the scholastic hierarchy—Bachelor, Licentiate, Master or Doctor. Master, Doctor, and Professor, it may be repeated, were originally synonymous. The English usage, by which the term Doctor was appropriated to the higher faculties and that of Master to Arts, was of later growth and did not obtain universally. Professor was occasionally used in the same sense, especially in the faculty of Theology, in which the letters S.T.P. (*Sanctae Theologiae Professor*) are still occasionally employed. The custom by which the term

Professor has come to be confined to the occupants of endowed chairs had scarcely begun at the close of the Middle Ages.

The idea of the inception—in its developed form—involved two elements. In the first place there was the idea derived from the Roman Law that no one was fully in possession of a magistracy or other office until he had actually performed its duties and the inception was the formal assumption of the teacher's functions; in the second place it was an admission into the gild of teachers by an existing member of it who invested the candidate with the *insignia* of his office in the presence of the rest. The new Master, after taking the proper oaths of obedience to the officers and statutes of the university, was solemnly seated in the magisterial *cathedra*; the characteristic book of his faculty (in Arts a work of Aristotle) was placed in his hands; a ring was put upon his finger in token of his marriage to learning; a cap (*biretta*) was placed on his head, partly as one of the insignia of mastership, partly (after the analogy of the emancipated slave) as a token of his enfranchisement from the subordination of pupilship. The incepting master then left him with a kiss, in token of his admission to the brotherhood, and he proceeded to give his inaugural lecture or disputation. A banquet followed, at the expense of the candidate or candidates. This simple and very human desire to drink the health of a new colleague at his expense may be regarded as the ultimate *raison d'être* of the whole ceremony with all its momentous historical consequences. The origin of one of the greatest and most characteristic of the institutions which the Middle Age has bequeathed to the modern world has grown out of the schoolboyish desire to make the newcomer "pay his footing." The institution was everywhere imitated by the students. The masters, who at first tried to suppress, though they eventually sanctioned, the coarse and brutal initiations and demands of entertainment (*bejaunia*) from the freshman (*bejauni* or *bejani*, from *bec jaune*, a yellow-bill or unfledged bird), were probably unconscious of the large part that the same elementary human instinct had played in the building up of their own universities.

When can we definitely trace the formation of such a gild of masters at Paris? The first indication of any more definite organisation than is implied in the vague customs of Abelard's age—the first definite proof of the existence of a university anywhere in Europe—is to be found in the life of Johannes de Cella, Abbot of St Albans[1]. Matthew Paris tells us, over half a century later indeed, that the subject of his biography studied at Paris and "merited to attain the society of the elect masters" (*ad electorum consortium magistrorum meruit attingere*)[1]. This must have been about the year 1170, but we must beware of exaggerating the degree of organisation which the notice implies. It is not till after the beginning of the following century that the society had a sufficiently

[1] *Gesta Abbatum* in *Mon. S. Alban.*, ed. Riley (Rolls Series), I, p. 217.

definite existence to elect common officers, to use a common seal, or to attempt corporate action of a legal character; even then its right to do so was not undisputed.

The university, like all the greatest institutions, was not founded but grew. It soon, however, began to obtain recognition, privileges, and charters from civil and ecclesiastical authorities. The first documentary recognition of the University of Paris is a charter granted by Philip Augustus in 1200. This earliest "privilege," like so many of its successors, was granted as a solace to the scholars after a defeat—a tavern-brawl, culminating in a riot, wherein they had suffered severely at the hands of the townsmen, headed by the leader of the municipal body (if at this time it can be so called), the Provost of Paris. The then Provost was severely punished, and his successors were required in future to take an oath to respect the privileges of the scholars in the presence of the masters assembled in one of the churches of Paris. This originated the Provost's position as "Conservator of the royal privileges of the University." But even this document[1] only recognises the existence of the University as such in so far as it treats the assembly of masters as a definite body of persons in the habit of holding meetings. The privileges are conferred, not on the Society as such but on the masters and scholars as individuals, the chief privilege being that of surrender to the ecclesiastical judge for trial, which the scholars already enjoyed by custom as "clerks." A clause protecting from "arrest" at the hands of secular justice the *capitale Parisiensium scolarium* was long supposed to mean the Rector, and was even by Denifle taken to mean any master of the university. It really refers to the seizure of a scholar's chattels; in English we still talk of "arresting" a ship. It may safely be affirmed that no official of the university or of any section of it existed at this time; a reference to the scholars of "different provinces," long supposed to prove the existence of the Nations about the year 1170, implies nothing of the kind. The University Statutes—three very simple ones, evidently new—are only heard of in 1209[2]. By a bull of about the same date the university is allowed to elect a "proctor" (*i.e.* a *procurator ad litem*) to act for it in legal transactions[3].

The need for such a proctor arose out of a great litigation in which the university was already engaged with the Chapter and Chancellor of Paris. One of the matters in dispute was precisely the right of the masters to form a corporation, to "sue and be sued" in a corporate capacity. The university was still being treated, just as the earliest trade-unions were treated by the English Courts for a century after their *de facto* existence, as an unlawful society, a "conspiracy" (the word is expressly used) of the masters against their lawful superiors—the Bishop,

[1] *Chartularium Universitatis Parisiensis,* ed. Denifle and Chatelain, Tom. I, No. 1.
[2] *Ib.* I, No. 8.
[3] *Ib.* I, No. 24.

Chapter, and Chancellor of Paris. By the aid of successive papal bulls the "conspiracy," however, succeeded. Already since 1212 the Chancellor had been forbidden to exact an oath of obedience to himself from the masters whom he licensed; and he was required to license gratuitously all candidates presented to him. By the end of the century he had lost the power of imprisoning scholars and practically all judicial powers. The Bishop, not the Chancellor, became the *iudex ordinarius* of scholars. His power was, in fact, reduced to little more than the ceremonial function of granting the licence and to a share in the appointment of examiners[1]. It is in the course of this great struggle on the part of the university for emancipation from the authority which the Chancellor had hitherto exercised over masters and scholars that the necessity for electing common officers was first felt. By the year 1219 masters had elected certain officers "for the avenging of injuries," and for the collection and administration of funds with a view to the prosecution of their suit against the Chancellor[2]. There can be no doubt that these officials were the Proctors of the four Nations into which the Masters of Arts had now divided themselves—probably in imitation of the four universities of students which had already been established at Bologna. The Nations consisted of Masters of Arts only. At first there was no common Head of the Faculty of Arts, but only the four Proctors of the Nations, originally, it is probable, also styled "Rectors." By 1245 we hear of a separate head of the whole Faculty of Arts, and to that official the title of Rector was soon appropriated[3]. The Masters of Theology, Canon Law, and Medicine formed separate groups outside and independent of the Masters of Arts. The word Faculty (*facultas*, the accepted Latin equivalent of δύναμις) meant originally an art or branch of knowledge. It gradually came to be applied also to the body of persons professing such a branch, and particularly to the organised groups of teachers of a particular subject in a university town. The study of the Civil Law, it may be added, was forbidden at Paris in 1219—probably to prevent the extinction of theological study in its most famous home; so that after this date the Law Faculty consisted mainly of Canonists. The fact that few of the most famous universities at the height of their fame possessed all the possible faculties ought, by itself, to have prevented the mistake of supposing that a Studium Generale meant a Studium in which all subjects were taught.

Thus, by about the middle of the thirteenth century, the University of Paris had gradually organised itself into a federal corporation of four distinct bodies, of which one—the Faculty of Arts—was further subdivided into four Nations: France[4], Normandy, Picardy, England. The

[1] *Ib.* I, No. 16.
[2] *Ib.* Nos. 30, 31. Cf. Nos. 41, 45.
[3] *Ib.* No. 137.
[4] *I.e.* at first, roughly the modern Île de France.

names of the four Nations were those of the nationalities which then predominated at Paris, but every country of Europe found itself allotted to one of these bodies. All southern Europe was assigned, for instance, to France; Germany was included in England, and eventually, when English masters at Paris had become few, the Nation was styled German. Each nation had its head or Proctor, elected every three months; the whole Faculty of Arts was presided over by the Rector. Each superior faculty was presided over by a Dean. The Rector was at first merely the head of the Faculty of Arts. But from the first he acted as a representative of the whole university, which, since it energetically repudiated the headship of the extraneous Chancellor, was otherwise without a head, and he practically presided during the common meetings of the four Faculties[1]. It was not till after a long series of struggles that the Rector fought his way to the headship of the university, and the fighting was very literal fighting; on several occasions it assumed the form of a physical encounter in church between the partisans of the Rector and those of the Dean of Theology. At Congregations of the whole university the voting was "by Faculties"; and the discussions took place only in the separate meetings of the whole university. The vote of the Faculty of Arts was taken by nations: a single English master was thus at one time endowed with a voting power equivalent to the whole body of French masters. The principle of majority-voting was at first not universally recognised, even in the separate assemblies of the Faculty or Nation. The proceedings of these bodies frequently illustrate Maitland's now famous generalisation: "the medieval assembly legislated only by unanimity." It was by a still more gradual process of constitutional evolution that it was settled that the whole university was bound by the decision of a majority of Faculties, and that of the Faculty of Arts by a majority of Nations. There was one moment in the history of Europe when an ecclesiastical problem of immense difficulty was solved by an imitation of the Parisian university constitution. Such ecclesiastical reforms as the Council of Constance actually succeeded in accomplishing were made possible by adopting the system of voting by nations, which enabled the small bodies of English and German prelates to hold their own against the swarm of curialist *episcopelli* from petty Italian sees.

One peculiar feature of the Parisian university organisation remains to be noticed. How far the schools on the south bank of the river

[1] The following scheme may make these complicated arrangements clearer.

<table>
<tr><td colspan="2">Superior Faculties of Theology (Dean)</td><td rowspan="7">RECTOR.</td></tr>
<tr><td colspan="2">" " " Canon Law "</td></tr>
<tr><td colspan="2">" " " Medicine "</td></tr>
<tr><td rowspan="4">Inferior Faculty of Arts divided into Nations of</td><td>France (Proctor)</td></tr>
<tr><td>Normandy (Proctor)</td></tr>
<tr><td>Picardy (Proctor)</td></tr>
<tr><td>England (Proctor)</td></tr>
</table>

maintained a continuous existence from the time when Abelard taught in "the mount" may perhaps be doubtful; but, at all events soon after the beginning of the thirteenth century, schools began to multiply in what is now known as the "quartier latin" of Paris, *i.e.* the quarter opposite Notre Dame on the south of the Seine. There teachers found themselves outside the jurisdiction of the Chancellor of Paris, and within that of the Abbot of Ste Geneviève. The masters got their licences from the Abbot of Ste Geneviève or (by 1255) from a separate chancellor appointed by the abbot[1]. The existence of this separate licensing authority was a fact of great importance to the university in its early struggle with the cathedral authorities. If the Chancellor of Paris or his examiner were troublesome, candidates would go to Ste Geneviève. The university thus possessed two chancellors, and the Faculty of Arts two separate examining bodies. The Chancellor of Ste Geneviève never extended his licensing authority to the superior faculties. It may be added that, down to the latest medieval period, the expression "Chancellor of the University" was unknown at Paris, though (when the office was initiated in other universities) that expression was freely used.

It is impossible within our limits to give any adequate account of the great struggle by which the university gradually acquired its autonomy and its privileges. On two great occasions at least the university resorted to the heroic remedy of decreeing a "dispersion." In 1229 this remedy was attempted against the Provost of Paris whose police had killed some students in the course of a riot; the intervention of Pope Gregory IX not merely procured the redress of the university grievances, but led to the issue of the university's chief papal privilege, the bull *Parens Scientiarum* of 1231, which established the independence of the university against the chancellor[2]. A more important war was waged by the university in 1251–7 against the pretensions of the Friars, who wanted to occupy university chairs without submitting to the university discipline. In this case the university resorted not merely to a temporary "dispersion," but to an actual "dissolution." But here the Papacy was on the side of the university's enemies. The university was compelled to recognise in a qualified form the claims of the Mendicant and other regular Doctors of Theology, though the Masters of Arts always managed to exclude them from their Faculty[3]. These conflicts deserve to be mentioned, even in a passing way, because they illustrate the real meaning of the institution, and of the process by which the universities became the powerful corporations that they were in the late Middle Ages. It was in the course of these struggles, and for the purpose of carrying them on,

[1] *Chartul. Univ. Paris.* I, Nos. 55, 260.

[2] *Ib.* No. 79. For other authorities cf. Rashdall, *The Universities of Europe in the Middle Ages*, I, p. 335 sq.

[3] Rashdall, I, pp. 369–392.

that the University of Paris perfected its own organisation and discipline. It was just this power of temporarily or permanently suspending its own existence or transferring itself to another place which formed its most powerful weapon of offence. The universities as such possessed in their earlier period no buildings of their own and practically no endowments. They met in some borrowed church or chapter-house—the University of Paris in the Mathurine convent or the Bernardine chapter-house, its Faculty of Arts in the little Norman Church of St Julien-le-Pauvre off the Rue de Fouarre, which still survives. Its lecture-rooms were hired rooms in or near this famous street—so called from the straw with which the floors of the otherwise unwarmed schools were strewn. The mobility which this poverty secured enabled a university at any moment to transfer itself to another town, or by suspending its lectures to attract the attention of authorities who were not anxious to see the suspension culminate in a final dispersion or a gradual dropping away of students to other universities. In all the more ancient universities wholesale "migrations" or "secessions" of discontented minorities were of common occurrence. But while these migrations generally succeeded in procuring a redress of grievances, they often weakened the parent bodies by leading to the establishment of permanent rivals. Half the universities of Europe originated in migrations of this kind from older universities.

From the organisation we must turn to the studies of the University. In the dark ages of European history the normal secular instruction of the schools was represented by the traditional classification of human knowledge into the *Trivium*—grammar, rhetoric, dialectic or logic—and the *Quadrivium*—arithmetic, geometry, music, and astronomy. The authors in whom these subjects were studied were chiefly the writers who had occupied themselves with reducing to compendiums the surviving relics of ancient science and learning, more especially Boëthius and Martianus Capella. Of Aristotle himself nothing was generally known in Western Europe but Boethius' translation of the *De Interpretatione* and an abridgement of the *Categories*. The rest of the *Organon* was known only through the commentaries of Boethius[1]. Nevertheless, the Logic of Aristotle formed the most important and stimulating element in the secular education of the Dark Ages, and determined the direction assumed by the great educational and intellectual revival of the twelfth century. At first, indeed, the renewal of interest in the Classics was a formidable rival to Logic and the new tendency to apply the weapons of Logic to the field of theological controversy. But the study of the Classics never attained any great importance at Paris, and the gradual recovery of nearly all the now extant works of Aristotle threw into the shade the literary studies which in eleventh-century France shewed every prospect of an-

[1] Cf. *supra*, Vol. v, Chap. xxiii.

ticipating the movement commonly associated with Italy and the fourteenth century. John of Salisbury, the pupil of Abelard, had before him the whole *Organon* of Aristotle. By the beginning of the thirteenth century other works of Aristotle began to find their way to Paris—translated, some from the Arabic which came into northern Europe through the contact of Latin scholars with the Arabic Aristotle in Spain, some in translations directly from the Greek which were due to Latin scholars and were, perhaps, a direct result of the capture of Constantinople by the Fourth Crusade in 1204. Eventually, soon after the middle of the century, nearly the whole surviving Aristotelian corpus was available for the use of the Parisian master in translations made direct from the Greek[1]. The new Scholasticism did not conquer without a struggle. Aristotle did not, indeed, originate that great wave of heresy which began to pass over Europe, starting from the south of France, towards the end of the twelfth century. But there were tendencies in the *Metaphysics* of Aristotle—and still more in the commentaries of Averroës and other Arabian philosophers which came to Paris at about the same time—which coincided with the pantheistic tendencies of men like Amaury of Bène, condemned at Paris in 1207, and David of Dinant whose works were burnt in the year 1210[2]. The Parisian synod, by which this last execution was ordered, also forbade the reading of Aristotle's "books on natural philosophy and his commentaries." The first body of university Statutes in which subjects of study are mentioned—that drawn up by the legate, Robert de Courçon, in 1215[3]—forbade the reading of the "physical and metaphysical works of Aristotle," and the prohibition was renewed in 1231 and in 1263[4]. But in spite of this we find the prohibitions removed or practically ignored[5], and the great Dominican thinkers, Albert the Great and St Thomas Aquinas, found a better way of combating such heresies as "the eternity of the world" and "the unity of the active intellect" than by mere prohibition. They had begun the task of creating a great system of Aristotelian Philosophy and Theology in which whatever in Aristotle was orthodox or capable of an orthodox twist was woven into the very woof and fibre of the Church's teaching[6]. From this time onwards Aristotle represents the sum and substance of a medieval education in the Faculty of Arts. A knowledge of Latin, and the rules of Latin Grammar are, indeed, presupposed and exacted in the university examinations, and this

[1] A leading authority on the subject is Amable Jourdain, *Recherches critiques sur l'âge et l'origine des traductions latines d'Aristote*. Paris, 1843. Cf. also Haskins, *Mediaeval Science*, and the literature there quoted.

[2] Caesarius Heisterbacensis, *Dialogus Miraculorum*, ed. Strange (Cologne, 1851), I, pp. 304–5. Other authorities in Rashdall, I, 356.

[3] *Chartul. Univ. Paris.* I, No. 20.

[4] *Ib.* No. 79.

[5] *Ib.* No. 246. Rashdall, I, p. 358.

[6] On this subject, cf. *supra*, Vol. V, Chap. XXIII.

knowledge was acquired by the reading of a few Latin books, especially Ovid and Virgil. But the teaching of these authors was for the most part left to the grammar school, which the student left at an increasingly early age—often before he was fourteen. There is also some rather perfunctory recognition of the other subjects embraced in the *Trivium* and the *Quadrivium*, and of the authors in which they were learned. But Aristotle and the Boëthian commentaries upon him were the main subject of instruction. By 1366[1] the following is the list of books "taken up for the schools" at Paris, *i.e.*, books which the student was required to have "heard," and in which he was examined:

For B.A.-Grammar—The *Doctrinale* of Alexander de Villa Dei and the *Grecismus*.
Logic —The *Organon* and *De Anima* of Aristotle with the *Isagoge* of Porphyry, the *Principia* of Gilbert de la Porrée, the *Divisions* and *Topics* of Boëthius.

For the Licence —Aristotle's *Physica, De Generatione et Corruptione, De Caelo et Mundo, Parva Naturalia,* and *Liber Metaphysicae,* together with "certain mathematical books" (possibly such books as are prescribed in other universities: the first six books of Euclid, the *Almagestum* of Porphyry, the *De Sphaera* of Johannes de Sacrobosco, the *Perspectiva communia* of John of Pisa).

The "greater part" of Aristotle's *Ethics* and part of the *Meteorics* were to be "heard" between licence and inception. The book of Aristotle which exercised the most profound influence on medieval thought was the *Metaphysics*, which was already lectured on in 1254, and was required at Oxford in the fifteenth century.

This course of study occupied at least five or six years. Every secular student of theology and every intending physician had to take the whole of this course, culminating in the M.A. degree, before he began the study of his own "higher faculty"; for students of Law a degree in Arts was not necessary, though it is probable that many or most of them began their university course with a period of study in Arts. But it is certain that for the great majority of medieval university students—most of whom were intended for the priesthood—this course, regarded as the essential foundation for the study of Theology, remained a foundation without a superstructure. Two-thirds, as is shewn by actual names and numbers at many German universities, never graduated at all; less than half of those who had the B.A. degree proceeded to M.A. And of these last only a small number proceeded to the study of Theology. This fact should be borne in mind as a partial explanation of the gross theological ignorance of the average secular priest at the time of the Reformation. The bishop's examination for orders did nothing to rectify the deficiency. The candidate was examined, so far as appears, chiefly in Latin grammar and in reading or construing some portion of the missal.

[1] *Chartul. Univ. Paris.* III, No. 1319.

In the Faculty of Theology[1] the only books actually lectured upon were the Bible and the *Sentences* of Peter the Lombard—the only one of the numerous attempts made in the twelfth century to elicit an organised system of theology out of the unsystematic and often conflicting utterances of the Fathers which had the good fortune to pass into the position of an authorised text-book. The full theological course was of enormous length and was divided as follows. For four years the student attended lectures on the Bible, and for two years on the *Sentences*. After these six years of study (if he had attained the age of twenty-five) he might be examined and, if passed, be admitted by the Dean to his "first course." By this step he became a Bachelor of Divinity or Bibliary. For two years he lectured successively on the two books of the Bible. At the end of nine years of study he might be admitted to the reading of the *Sentences*, and lectured as a *sententiarius* for a year, on the completion of which he became a *Baccalaurius formatus*. Three or four years more elapsed before he could present himself for the Chancellor's licence. This was followed, after the interval of about a year, by the actual inception, which made him a full Doctor of Theology. The whole course, therefore, occupied a period of twelve or thirteen years; but it would appear that, during the later years of the theologian's course, continuous residence was not insisted upon.

The course of Canon Law at Paris did not differ materially from that of the corresponding faculty at Bologna, and had best be spoken of in connexion with the university which was the especial home of legal study. Nor can we linger on the details of the medical curriculum further than to say that Galen is here more prominent than Hippocrates, and that the Arabic Medicine is less prominent than at Bologna.

In all the faculties quite as much importance was attached to disputations as to lectures and examinations—most of all, perhaps, in the theological faculty. It would involve too much detail to enumerate the various disputations in which the candidate had to respond at different periods of his career. Whether looked upon as a method of education or as a method of examination, the disputations shared the advantages and the disadvantages of the scholastic method with which they were inextricably bound up. In whichever light it is considered, the efficiency of the institution declined with the general decline and corruption of the philosophy with which it was so intimately connected. Long before the close of the medieval period the tendency of the disputation to degenerate into a piece of mere routine had reached such a point that, in 1426, a Bachelor of Theology, refused his licence owing to the character of his performances, actually brought an action in the Parlement of Paris against his examiners, and pleaded that the faculty had no right to refuse it to anyone who had gone through the proper "exercises," no matter how he had acquitted himself.

[1] Rashdall, I, pp. 462 sq.

The students of Paris, as of all other medieval universities, originally lived in the town, where and how they pleased. In point of fact the usual way of living was for a party of students to take a house together, in which they formed a small self-governing community. These establishments were at Paris usually called *hospitia*, at Oxford halls (*aulae*). The young nobleman might hire a house of his own for himself, with his own tutor and a numerous retinue; the poorest students could not afford the expense of a regular *hospitium*, and lodged in a garret or a tradesman's house. But the great majority were members of some *hospitium*. One of the *socii* (as members of the same student-household were called) gave security for the rest of the house, collected their contributions, and generally presided over the establishment. The Principal was at first elected by the community, or at least owed his authority to the consent of those who agreed to join his society. Gradually, however, through the support given to his authority by the university and possibly through the influence of the endowed societies of which we shall proceed to speak, this extremely democratic regime gave way to a more autocratic one. The change is symbolised by the fact that the societies—at least those in which younger students lived—came to be generally known as *paedagogia* and the head of them as *paedagogi*. At an early period in the history of the university it entered into the minds of charitable persons to provide endowments for the assistance of poor scholars. The earlier of these foundations were merely appendages to some larger establishment. Such was the body of scholars afterwards known as the Collège des Dix-huit, which was founded in 1180 and at first occupied a single room in the Hôtel-Dieu. Half-a-dozen small foundations of this character were established before the middle of the thirteenth century. An altogether new conception of a college was introduced by St Louis' chaplain, Robert de Sorbon, who in 1258 began the establishment of a college no longer (like the earlier endowments) for Grammarians or Artists, but for students in Theology. The age and maturity of the students naturally brought with it a larger measure of autonomy, though to the last the Parisian colleges enjoyed rather less independence than the corresponding foundations at Oxford and Cambridge. They were generally, for instance, filled up by the appointment of some outside authority—often the bishop or some cathedral dignitaries of the founder's diocese; and in some cases a Provisor, who occupied a position half-way between that of an English Visitor and that of an English Head, exercised considerable control over the Master (as the resident presiding official was generally called) and the members of the society. A still more extensive establishment was the College of Navarre, founded in 1314 by Joan I, Queen of Navarre, consort of Philip the Fair, which provided for twenty students in Grammar, thirty in Arts, and twenty in Theology, each with a separate Master, Hall, and collegiate establishment, the chapel alone being common to all three sections of the community. Over sixty colleges were established before the year

1500[1], and (contrary to a prevailing impression in England) they played quite as prominent a part in the life of the university as they did in Oxford and Cambridge. At first the colleges boarded and lodged only their foundation-members, and whatever teaching was given in them was simply private instruction supplementary to that which their students received in the public schools of the university. But from the end of the thirteenth century the college occasionally took in paying boarders to be educated with their own foundation-members. There is no reason to believe that this custom prevailed to any great extent before the fifteenth century, but by the middle of that century the great mass of students lived either in colleges or in regular *paedagogia*; and the majority lived in college. In 1445 we even find the university declaring that "almost the whole university resides in the colleges." In 1457 the university forbade residence out of a college or paedagogy. The superior discipline of the college increased the desire of parents to send their sons to them, and helped forward the changes by which the autonomous *hospitium* of the thirteenth century transformed itself into the strictly disciplinal master's boarding-house of the fifteenth. Those who are familiar with the wild license and disorder which might be illustrated from every page of the earlier university records will probably be of opinion that the change was a step in the right direction. In the thirteenth century the boy-student of thirteen or fourteen had been free to choose his own residence, migrate from it to another if his Principal's rule was too exacting; he attended lectures or neglected them, wandered about the town at all hours, drank, gambled, quarrelled, and fought as he pleased. By the end of the fifteenth century he was almost reduced to be the inmate of a boarding-school—disciplined, regulated, and even whipped at the discretion of the Principal.

The change in the position of the colleges was connected with another still more momentous. The fundamental defect of the medieval university was the absence of any pecuniary provision for competent teaching. Every doctor or master had the right to teach. In the higher faculties the teaching was largely left to the bachelors, who were obliged to lecture as a condition of proceeding to a higher degree. Every Master of Arts was compelled to lecture for a year after admission to his degree. This was called his "necessary Regency." At the end of the year he could continue to lecture as long as he pleased; and only so long as he did so could he exercise the full rights of membership in his faculty. Study or teaching in a university was by Canon Law a ground of absence from a canonry or a parochial benefice; and it was only the system by which such non-residence was encouraged—and especially the systematic preferment of university graduates by papal provision—which kept up the supply of Regent Masters or Doctors in the university. But even so the system was a bad one. Especially in the Faculty of Arts the teachers were a body of

[1] List in Rashdall, I, pp. 514 sq.

mostly young, inexperienced, and constantly changing men, who had satisfied no test but the totally inadequate requirements of the university examiners, supported (if unbeneficed) by the scanty and precarious fees of the students. As boarders multiplied in the colleges, the masters came to be assisted by paid Regents. The more efficient teachers were naturally snapped up by the colleges. And the system was rendered more efficient by the practice of sending the students in the *paedagogia* and smaller colleges for lectures and exercises to the larger ones, which came to be known as *collèges de plein exercice*, in each of which a systematic course of study was provided by an adequate staff of Regents. The lectures of the public schools dwindled into a dreary routine and ultimately ceased altogether. Ramus, the revolutioniser of the traditional Logic, records the recent death of the last Regent who had lectured in the Rue de Fouarre[1]. This silent revolution not only made for efficiency but materially helped forward the transformation of the medieval programme of studies into that which we associate with the Renaissance. The Classics could not be taught efficiently—at least to boys in their early stages—by way of formal lecturing. Smaller classes, compulsory preparation, construing in class, the correction of written tasks, individual attention, became possible in the colleges as they had not been in the university schools. How far the increased demand for classical teaching was the cause and how far the effect of the increased importance of college-teaching, it is hard to say; but it is certain that the two movements were closely connected.

If we look back upon the changes which had taken place in the government and constitution of the university since its early days, we shall find that a change had been effected closely analogous to that with which we are familiar in the history of Oxford and Cambridge. The university had transformed itself for practical purposes into a federation of colleges. The change was not so complete as at Oxford. The university exercised more control over the colleges than was the case at Oxford; and the superior faculties maintained a much more independent existence. But even in the Faculty of Theology there was a close connexion between the faculties and certain colleges. The theologians held their disputations in the hall of the Sorbonne, which admitted many theologians outside its endowed members to a kind of honorary membership; and in post-medieval times the theological faculty came to be popularly spoken of as "the Sorbonne." The parallel with the constitutional development of Oxford and Cambridge might be carried farther if our limits of time permitted. In the seventeenth century the turbulent academic democracy of the Middle Ages was practically superseded by an oligarchic "Tribunal of the University," consisting of the Rector, the three Deans, and the four Proctors—to an even greater extent than it was supplanted at Oxford by the "Hebdomadal Board," which consisted of the Vice-Chancellor, Heads of Colleges, and the two Proctors.

[1] Ramus, *Procem. reform. Par. Acad.* (*Scholae in lib. Artes, c.* 1116.)

Northern Italy participated to the full in the great intellectual new birth of the twelfth century. But the movement here took a characteristically different direction. Here, as in northern France, the movement was at first largely literary—a revived study of Latin literature; it was followed, not as at Paris by an outburst of speculation, but rather by a revived interest in Law. The predominant interests of the Italian mind were practical, social, civil. Even the ecclesiastic was more interested in Church Law than in Theology. Scholasticism of course reached Italy; but the study of Aristotle was abandoned for the most part to the physicians, and that of Theology to the Friars—in each case to a class whose studies were directed to the ends of practical life rather than to those of theory. If some of the greatest schoolmen were born in Italy, they were seldom genuine Italians, and they taught chiefly outside Italy. Thomas Aquinas was a Norman; Bonaventura was hardly a great thinker, and he taught at Paris. Though the scholastic method was not without its marked influence upon the study of Law, the legal renaissance of Italy arose chiefly out of a literary interest in the monuments of ancient jurisprudence, and was developed in response to political and social rather than purely intellectual needs.

The story—long accepted on the authority of Gibbon, in spite of his sceptical foot-note—that the origin of the legal renaissance is to be found in the accidental discovery of a copy of the *Pandects* at the capture of Amalfi by the Pisans in 1135 may be dismissed as a pure myth. Roman Law had never been dead in Italy. So long as it was known, it was always supposed to be the law of the tribunals, at least for the conquered Roman and for the ecclesiastics; and the profession of lay lawyers—*iudices, advocati, notarii*—had never ceased to exist. Law as a branch of rhetoric was even included in the school curriculum of the Dark Ages; Lanfranc of Pavia studied, his biographer tells us, "in the schools of the liberal arts, and of the secular laws, according to the custom of his country." But both teaching and practice were based upon the *Institutes*, the *Code*, and the *Breviarium* rather than upon the *Pandects*. Even the *Pandects*, or *Digest*, were not absolutely unknown in the time of Irnerius, with whose fame the rise of Bologna is traditionally connected, nor was Bologna the earliest scientific school of Law in Italy. There are vague traces of some such school, or at least a traditional study of Law, at Rome in the eleventh century. There was a flourishing school of Lombard Law at Pavia at about the same date, while all through the Dark Ages Ravenna was the centre of Roman law-teaching in Italy, and remained so till it was superseded by the growth of the school of Bologna. Bologna was already famous as a school of the liberal arts in 1000[1], and the name of one famous pre-Irnerian law-teacher has been preserved to us, a certain Pepo, who is mentioned in a document of 1076 which expressly quotes the *Digest* as a ground for its

[1] ASB., Jun. I, p. 229.

decision[1]. It is probable, in fact, that in a sense the teaching and practice of the Roman Law existed continuously from the days of the old Roman Empire down to the time of Irnerius. And the revival had begun a generation or two before Irnerius; but there can be no doubt that roughly the traditional view is justified which connects the rise of a great school of Law in Bologna and a consequent revolution in the study of Law in Italy and throughout Europe with the name of that doctor. Irnerius taught at Bologna probably in the earliest years of the twelfth century. His name is first mentioned as a *causidicus* in a document of 1113, and there is reason to believe that his activity as a teacher began still earlier[2].

The new teaching centred in the systematic study of the *Digest*, from which alone of all the *Corpus Iuris* an adequate insight into the true spirit and genius of Roman Law is to be obtained. It seems that the movement was connected, in a more dramatic way than is usual in such movements, with a datable event—the actual arrival of a copy of the Roman Law at Bologna, not from Amalfi but from Ravenna. And the work arrived in sections, a fact which left permanent traces in the traditional divisions of the *Corpus Iuris*. The earliest section, known as the *Digestum Vetus*, arrived perhaps in the time of Pepo. Other sections of it arrived later, and continued to be known as the *Tres Partes*, the *Infortiatum*, and the *Digestum Novum*. The arbitrariness of the divisions between them—the *Tres Partes* actually begins in the middle of a paragraph—testifies to their accidental character. The *Old Digest* and the *Code* were "ordinary" books—the subjects of the earliest lectures at Bologna—the other books of the *Corpus Iuris* (which were introduced later) were "extraordinary." The ordinary books were reserved for doctors and for the best hours of the day, *i.e.* the morning, and the distinction eventually spread (with modifications) to other faculties and other universities, and originated by a long and complicated evolution the still surviving distinction between ordinary and extraordinary professors[3].

The position which Irnerius holds in the annals of the Civil Law was taken in the history of the Canon Law by Gratian, a monk of the Camaldulensian monastery at Bologna. He was not, however, a teacher but a writer—the first who succeeded in reducing to the form of a code, or rather of a text-book, the confused mass of conciliar canons, patristic *dicta*, and papal decretals from which the law of the Church had hitherto been gleaned. Burchard of Worms, Anselm of Lucca, and Cardinal Deusdedit had been before him; but the *Decretum* of Gratian, which appeared about the year 1142, superseded all its predecessors. From

[1] Savioli, *Annali Bolognesi*, Vol. I, Pt. ii, p. 123.

[2] *Ibid.* Vol. I, Pt. ii, p. 151. Cf. Rashdall, I, pp. 118 sq. Cf. on this subject *supra*, Vol. V, Chap. XXI.

[3] For authorities see Rashdall, I, pp. 122 sq. Cf. *supra*, Vol. V, Chap. XXI.

that time, if not before, the Canon Law—derived in part from the Civil Law and reduced to a system in imitation or rivalry of it—became as important an element in the studies of Bologna as the jurisprudence of ancient Rome. The Doctors of the Canon Law now became a body distinct alike from the Theologians and from the Civilians, though much more closely connected with the latter than with the former. The subject of the earlier Canonists' studies was simply the *Decretum*, which occupies in that faculty much the same position as the *Sentences* of Peter the Lombard in the theological schools. To these were gradually added the successive collections of Decretals authoritatively issued by successive Popes—the five books of Decretals put forth by Gregory IX, the "Liber Sextus" by Boniface VIII, and the "Clementines" by John XXII. These together formed the *Corpus Iuris Canonici*[1].

All through the twelfth century Bologna was the home of a succession of eminent jurists who attracted swarms of students from all parts of Europe. In fact, the fame of Bologna and its jurists was never higher than it was in the days of the "four Doctors"—Bulgarus, Martinus, Jacobus, Hugo—who belong to the generation after Irnerius. Bologna was fully established in European opinion as a Studium Generale. But, as there was no "University" at Paris in the days of Abelard, so there was none (so far as we know) at Bologna in the time of Irnerius and his first successors. The forged charter of Theodosius II—forged, it is curious to note, as early as the thirteenth century—belongs to the legendary history of the Studium. It has often been the habit to speak of the famous "Authenticum" *Habita*, issued by Frederick I in 1158, as a foundation charter, or at least as the first official recognition of the university[2]. But, though it was no doubt issued primarily for the benefit of the Bologna doctors and scholars, not only does it involve no official recognition of any organised scholastic body, but the privileges which it confers are not restricted to Bologna. It was a charter of privilege for the student-class throughout the Empire, giving them among other privileges the right of having their causes—whether civil or criminal—tried at their own option either by the bishop or their own doctor. In later days the right of trial by a bishop was limited to the case of clerks; the right of trial by the student's own doctor, while theoretically admitted, was practically superseded by the growth of the university and the jurisdiction of the Rectors. But, though the Authentic directly recognises no academic body whatever, it indirectly supplies a presumption that some sort of process of graduation, implying the existence in a shadowy form of a doctoral society, already existed. The Emperor would hardly have conferred a legal jurisdiction upon a body of teachers completely self-chosen and self-styled like our modern "Professors" of dancing or of legerdemain. An inception or (as it was called in Italy) a

1 Rashdall, I, pp. 128–143. Cf. *supra*, Vol. V, Chap. XXI.
2 See for its text MGH, *Constitutiones*, I, 249.

"conventus" at least as formal, and a society at least as much organised, as we have seen to have existed among the Masters of Paris at just about the same time, may therefore be presumed to have existed in Bologna in the year 1158. In the year 1215 we read of the grammarian Boncompagno reading his *Rhetorica Antiqua* before the "University of Professors of the Civil and Canon Law."[1] What definiteness of organisation the two Colleges of Doctors—one of the Civil, the other of the Canon Law—had obtained by this date it is impossible to say; but it is certain that long before that day a regular system of examination and graduation must have existed at Bologna, and the degrees must have been conferred by the doctors themselves, for the simple reason that there was no one else to confer them. No traditional control of education by the Church was then in existence. But the powerful analogy of Paris seemed to suggest that some authority more public and more formal than that of the doctors was required to confer a distinction to which so much prestige was now attached; and in 1219 a bull of Honorius III conferred the "right of promotion," as it was styled, upon the archdeacon of Bologna. The share which the archdeacon took in the conferment of the degree was purely formal, and he never attempted to make it more. The real test, or "private examination," was conducted by the doctors beforehand; the "public examination" or "conventus" (answering to the Parisian inception) was a mere ceremony. At a much later date the archdeacon was popularly spoken of as the "Chancellor of the University"; but he is never so called in the Middle Ages. When, however, in other universities similar authority was given to some high ecclesiastic, generally the bishop, he was always styled Chancellor of the University.

At Bologna, as at Paris, the doctors formed a gild, or rather a number of faculty-gilds, which regulated the conditions on which members might be received into their body, and made other statutes for the government of their members. But at Bologna it was not the doctors but the students themselves who formed what came to be known as the University, or rather, the Universities. In the northern Studia attempts on the part of the students to organise themselves into a society were sternly repressed, and in most cases successfully; at Bologna they succeeded in completely dominating the Studium, getting all real power (except only the conduct of graduations) into their own hands, and reducing the professors into the position of their obedient, humble servants. The date at which these gilds began to be formed can be fixed with greater precision than the beginnings of the doctoral colleges. Towards the close of the twelfth century the jurist Bassianus, in commenting upon the title *De Collegiis*, disputes the right of the students to elect a rector[2]. It was probably the last quarter—perhaps the last decade—of the twelfth century which saw the

[1] Rockinger, *Sitzungsberichte der bay. Akad. zu München*, 1861, p. 135: Rashdall, I, p. 148.

[2] Sarti, *De claris Archigymnasii Bononiensis Professoribus*, pt. 1 (1888), p. 89.

birth of the first university of students. Although this was later than the first beginnings of the society of Masters at Paris, the further steps towards organisation at Paris—the formation of "Nations," the election of Proctors and Rectors and the like—were no doubt imitations by the Parisian Masters of Arts of the organisation already established by the students of Bologna.

From about the middle of the thirteenth century there were at Bologna two universities of jurists—a Universitas Ultramontanorum and a Universitas Citramontanorum; but the analogy of other universities known to have been founded by migration or secession from Bologna make it almost certain that at one time there were four; while more direct evidence points to the conclusion that the Cismontane University arose from a federation of three smaller societies. In later days these smaller "Nations"—Roman, Tuscan, and Campanian—remained as subdivisions of the Cismontane University, and they were further subdivided into *Consiliariae*—bodies of students coming from the same locality and electing one councillor a-piece. The Ultramontane University had nothing corresponding to these large national divisions, but was divided into fourteen *Consiliariae* only. Though each university was governed by its own Rector, the alliance between them was more than federal. There were no separate congregations of each university, but a single congregation jointly presided over by the two Rectors. As may well be imagined, this enormous and cosmopolitan body of law-students which assembled in the great Dominican church, or (it may be) in the square outside, was incapable of direct legislation; it met only for electoral purposes. Its statutes were made by eight specially appointed *Statutarii*; and as in the ancient Greek and the medieval Italian republics, statute-making was not a matter of every-day occurrence: statutes were supposed to be permanent. In the Bologna universities they could be revised every twenty years. The ordinary executive business of the corporation was carried on by the rectors and the *Consiliarii*; from the judicial decisions of the rector there was an appeal to the *Consiliarii*. The constituent Nations or *Consiliariae* had, at least in some cases, separate meetings of their own—chiefly for festive and ecclesiastical purposes. The German Nation in particular enjoyed peculiar privileges and manifested a special degree of corporate life. One of the earliest and most complete records of the kind which we possess is the accounts of the German Nation beginning in the thirteenth century. The receipts consist chiefly of the payments by its members upon matriculation, the amount being assessed according to the wealth of the students; the expenditure is chiefly upon candles for the corporate services and wine for the festive gatherings. An unusual expenditure upon the latter object is usually followed by an item "pro vitris fractis." The Italian universities themselves, it may be remarked, were somewhat aristocratic bodies. Not only poor students who could pay no fee upon matriculation, but all who lived "at others' expense"—

that is to say, the large body of students who were sent to the university not by their own relations but out of charity by rich ecclesiastics and others—had no vote in the university congregations.

The original object of the student universities was not primarily to direct studies or to appoint teachers, but to protect themselves against, or to secure favourable treatment from all manner of authorities and corporate enemies—and especially the city-government, the virtual republic, of Bologna. In cosmopolitan Paris, the bulk of the masters themselves had no special connexion with Paris: many of them were foreigners, all were ecclesiastics; and ecclesiastics in the twelfth and thirteenth centuries were citizens of the world. Here, therefore, we find masters and scholars uniting to protect themselves against the outside world—whether the provost and citizens on the one hand, or the chancellor and the chapter on the other. At Bologna the doctors, in the period during which the universities grew up, were actually citizens of Bologna. Consequently they were incapable of becoming even members of the academic commonwealth. Students who were natives of Bologna shared the same disfranchisement. But, though excluded from the privileges of university membership, the professors were by no means exempt from its authority. By the use of its powers of combination, boycotting, and "collective bargaining," the trade-union of students managed to reduce the professors to a most humiliating state of servitude. The professors had to swear obedience to the student-rectors and the student-made statutes; and these regulated the conduct of the professor with the utmost severity. He was fined if he was a minute late for lecture, if he went on beyond the time for closing, if he skipped a difficult passage, or failed to get through in a given time the portions of the law-texts provided by the universities. A committee of students—the *denunciatores doctorum*—watched over his conduct and kept the rectors informed of his irregularities. The doctor might not leave the town even for a day without leave of the rectors, lest perchance he should be bribed away by some tempting offer on the part of a neighbouring university. If he wanted to be married, a single day of absence was graciously allowed him, but no honeymoon.

In the earliest days of the university, the doctors of Bologna lived on the fees of their students. It was their custom to carry on the process of collective bargaining through the mediation of a student; and we find the learned Odofred, for instance, publicly commenting in the course of his lectures upon the niggardliness of his payments: he should give, he announces, this year no "extraordinary" lectures (which were optional) because his students were not "good paymasters"; "volunt scire, sed nolunt solvere," he complains[1]. After the neighbouring cities had succeeded in setting up rival Studia and attracting eminent doctors to these,

[1] From Odofred *in Dig. Vet.* (Lyons, 1550), T. II, f. 192: Rashdall, I, p. 211.

the city-government found it expedient to offer *salaria* to some of the doctors. The election to the salarial chairs at first belonged to the students, and the election was only for a year at a time. As, however, the amount of the salaries increased, the city—through a committee known as the *Reformatores Studii*—gradually established a more and more complete control over the appointments. This system was everywhere adopted in the Italian universities, and did more than anything else to differentiate their subsequent history from that of such universities as Paris and Oxford. The teaching came to be practically confined to the holders of salaried chairs, though a certain amount of rather perfunctory lectures were given by bachelors as exercises for the doctorate. And these professors were adequately paid. It was in these universities, in fact, that a professoriate in the modern sense was first established. The doctor as such practically lost the right of teaching. The decay of university teaching which we have already noticed at Paris and at Oxford never took place in Italy; and the colleges never undertook the functions which properly belonged to the university. A good many colleges were founded at Bologna and in other southern universities; but residence in them was confined to their foundation-members; and they never exercised any special influence upon the life of the universities. One of these colleges—the College of Spain, founded by the will of the great Cardinal Albornoz (once Archbishop of Toledo and afterwards papal legate at Bologna)—still survives and is used as a place of education for members of the Spanish diplomatic service. It is curious to observe how the democratic spirit of Bologna made itself felt even in the government of the colleges. Here and in southern universities generally the rector of the college was elected by the students and that for a short period only.

In spite of their completely subordinate constitutional position, the doctors of Bolognese origin contrived to keep in their own hands the solid advantages of their rank. Even the domineering students of Bologna did not interfere with the exercise of the doctors' inherent right to control the admission of candidates to doctoral degrees, *i.e.* to the membership of their own gild. And this right was practically restricted to an inner circle of doctors. The two Colleges of Doctors—one of the Canon, the other of the Civil Law—were reserved for Bologna citizens. The doctor's degree—originally and still in name an admission to the gild of teachers—practically ceased to carry with it either the right to teach or the right of membership in the doctoral colleges and participation in the handsome fees demanded by them for graduation. With bachelors' degrees, it may be remarked, neither the archdeacon nor the doctoral colleges had anything to do; they were conferred by the rectors. Not content with restricting the solid privileges of the doctorate to their own fellow-citizens, the grasping doctors of Bologna continued, to a great extent, to confine both the colleges and the more important chairs to members of their own families. This change took effect at about the middle of the thirteenth century. The experiment of a hereditary professoriate was hardly a success, and the fame of Bologna as a school of law rapidly declined from this time onwards and was supplanted by that of younger universities, such as Padua and Siena, largely founded by secessions of doctors or migrations of students from Bologna itself, where similar restrictions on the choice of the best professors were never reproduced.

So far we have confined our attention entirely to the Law universities. But Bologna was by no means a place of legal education only. The fame of its schools of the liberal arts, from which the Faculty of Law had originally differentiated itself, never entirely departed from it; and, in close connexion with the study of Arts, a medical school attained, at a somewhat later date, a fame rivalling that of Salerno and Montpellier. In spite of this fact, however, these schools long remained in a state of curious subservience to the masterful universities of Law. It was the universities of jurists who had taken the initiative in forming student-clubs and electing rectors. And at first these rectors claimed, and succeeded in asserting, a jurisdiction over all grades and kinds of students in Bologna down to the youngest grammarian, though none but law-students were admitted to the jurist universities. The origin of the separate organisations for doctors and for students of these other subjects is obscure. Regular inceptions in Arts took place at Bologna at least in 1221, and in Medicine at about the middle of the century, when the famous Florentine physician Thaddeus was laying the foundation of its reputation as a school of Medicine. A college of doctors in Medicine and Arts and a university of students in these faculties probably existed at this time or soon afterwards, but it was not until the year 1306 that their rector succeeded in completely establishing his own independent jurisdiction and throwing off the yoke of the dominant jurists. Want of space compels us to pass over the contribution which the Italian Faculties of Medicine made to the earliest triumphs of science. It must suffice to remark that Galileo and most of the early Italian men of science were students of Medicine.

At Bologna and in Italy generally Aristotle and Philosophy were looked upon chiefly as preparation for the study of Medicine; Dante would hardly have acquired his profound knowledge of Aristotle and his medieval disciples had he not started life as a student of Medicine. Hence the close association of the two Faculties in the organisation of the university and the college. But, though the university extended its protection and its authority over students of Arts and even grammar-school boys, the medical students alone voted in the university Congregations. The College of Doctors included Doctors of Medicine and full Doctors of all the Arts, but we hear at Bologna of a distinct graduation in several of the separate subjects embraced under "Arts"—Doctors of Philosophy, of Astronomy, of Logic, and of Grammar, and of salaried

Doctors or Professors in all those subjects. Grammar and Rhetoric were taken much more seriously than in the North of Europe. As early as 1321 we hear of Antonio di Virgilio obtaining a large salary for lecturing upon Virgil, Statius, Lucan, and Ovid, and at about the same time a salaried Professor of Rhetoric lectured upon Cicero. Facts like these recall the striking remark of Ozanam that in Italy the period which intervened between the intellectual day-light of antiquity and the Renaissance was but "une de ces nuits lumineuses où les dernières clartés du soir se prolongent jusqu'aux premières blancheurs du matin."[1]

In Italy the study of Theology was practically abandoned to the Friars. There were organised studies of Theology of a university type in some of the Convents (*Studia Generalia Ordinis*); but if the friar-theologians wished to graduate, they had to go to Paris or Oxford for their degrees. It was part of the deliberate policy of the Holy See to keep up the monopoly of granting such degrees enjoyed by Paris, Oxford, and a very few other universities. But after the outbreak of the Schism, and the adhesion of France to the Avignon Papacy, the Roman Pontiffs desired rather to weaken than to strengthen the great school of the rival "obedience." Already in 1352 a bull had been issued by Innocent VI creating a Faculty of Theology at Bologna, and the example was freely imitated in universities which had hitherto been without such faculties, and in new universities founded after this date. But the change produced little effect in the Italian universities. They remained primarily universities of Law, secondarily of Medicine, while the Faculties of Arts and Grammar were treated as preparatory studies to some extent of the lawyers, but especially of the physicians. It was not by Theology but by Law that Rome ruled the Churches of the West; the study of Theology always contained in it the seeds of rebellion and reform. Secular culture rather than Theology or Philosophy was Italy's contribution to the progress of the human mind.

The story, no longer taken seriously, about the foundation of Oxford by Alfred the Great is now known to rest upon a passage impudently forged and inserted into Camden's printed edition of *Asser Menevensis* by no less a person than the illustrious Camden himself. Even of the city nothing is known till a century after Alfred. Nor is anything heard of any schools whatever at Oxford till the beginning of the twelfth century. The first Oxford teacher whose name has come down to us is one Theobaldus Stampensis (of Étampes in Normandy) who left Caen and came to teach in Oxford in about the year 1110. A short but violent attack upon the monks (*improperium in monachos*)[2] and five letters, in some of which he is styled doctor of Caen (Cadomensis), in others doctor of

1 *Documents inédits pour serv. à l'hist. litt. de l'Italie* (1850), p. 78.

2 MS. Bodley 561: partly printed by Prof. E. T. Holland in *Collectanea* (*Oxf. Hist. Soc.*), II, p. 153.

Oxford (Oxenefordensis)[1], represent the whole literary remains of the first Oxford teacher. By a rare chance we know the approximate number of his students. In a reply to the *improperium* an anonymous monk remarks: "You are said to teach at Oxford as a master sixty or a hundred scholars, more or less."[2]

In or about the year 1133 a far more famous person, Robertus Pullus, has been said to have taught Theology in Oxford[3]. Pullus was the author of one of the books of "Sentences" eventually superseded by Peter the Lombard, and afterwards became a Cardinal and Chancellor of the Roman Church. In 1149 Gervase of Canterbury tells us that the distinguished Italian jurist Vacarius taught the Civil Law in Oxford[4]. It is certain that Vacarius was in England at this time, that he taught somewhere in England, and that at some time in the course of his life he taught at Oxford; it is not quite certain that the teaching at Oxford was as early as 1149. But, in any case, the names of three teachers at most—one at a time—represent absolutely all that we hear about the schools of Oxford till about the year 1170. So far there is nothing to differentiate the schools of Oxford from any of the more famous cathedral or other schools of about the same period. These Oxford schools clearly possessed some repute, but so did the schools of Lincoln, of Salisbury, and of Hereford. In about the year 1170 the allusions to the Oxford schools begin to multiply. We hear of famous persons who came from a distance to study here, of an extensive trade in books, of sermons specially addressed to scholars. In 1185 Giraldus Cambrensis tells us that he publicly read his newly-written *Topographia Hibernica* to a numerous body of masters and scholars in Oxford, "where clergy in England chiefly flourished and excelled in clerkship."[5] By this time, in fact, Oxford has become a Studium Generale; in 1190 it is expressly called a *commune studium*, which is a synonym for *studium generale*[6]. By the year 1209 its students are set down by a contemporary historian at 3000[7].

What caused the sudden rise of Oxford into this position about a decade or so after 1170? Doubtless it might have been owing to the fame of a particular teacher (though at this time we hear of no such person) or to many other imaginable causes. But the development was very rapid; and the mere fact that, when it was complete, the schools are found to be

[1] MPL, CLXIII, col. 759.

[2] Holland, *op. cit.* p. 156.

[3] *Oseney Chron.* (*Ann. Monast.* IV.), pp. 19, 20. Cf. Rashdall, II, p. 335.

[4] *Actus Pontificum Cantuar.* ed. Stubbs (Rolls Series), II, p. 384. Cf. Rashdall, II, p. 335.

[5] Giraldus Cambrensis, ed. Brewer (Rolls Series), I, pp. 72, 73.

[6] *Emonis Chron.* MGH, *Script.* XXIII, p. 467. There is much other evidence for the existence of a considerable Studium in the years 1170–1200 for which see Rashdall, II, pp. 342 sq.

[7] Authorities in Rashdall, II, p. 348.

under the government of no local ecclesiastic but of a Chancellor appointed in recent times, *ad hoc*, solely for the government of the scholars, suggests the probability that the Oxford Studium did not emerge into greatness by a gradual process of evolution, but owed its existence to a cause known in numerous other cases to have occasioned such a sudden development—that is to say, to a scholastic migration. And there is not a little positive evidence which supports that conjecture. In the year 1167 the exiled John of Salisbury speaks in one of his letters of a prophecy that in this year the votaries of Mercury (*Mercuriales*, *i.e.* scholars) should be "depressed," and adds that in point of fact they were now "so depressed that France, the mildest and most civil of nations, has expelled her foreign scholars."[1] At about the same date or a little after we hear of an edict by Henry II—directed against the supporters of the exiled Becket in France—forbidding the "transfretation" of clerks, and calling upon all clerks already abroad who possessed "revenues" to return promptly "as they loved their revenues."[2] More definite still are the words of a contemporary in a letter: "The King wills that all scholars shall be compelled to cross the sea (*transfretare*)" *i.e.* to return to England[3]. Hundreds of English masters and scholars, it is probable, were studying in the schools of Paris. There is every reason to believe that many of them "loved" their revenues or benefices. And at all events the way to the continent was now closed for English scholars. Whether the "expulsion" alluded to by John of Salisbury is a rhetorical way of expressing this voluntary exodus, or whether the expulsion and the voluntary exodus are distinct events, both the "expulsion" and the edict of Henry II would equally conduce to the same result—the return of a great body of Parisian masters and scholars to England in or about 1167–1168, a body which would necessarily grow owing to the impossibility of studying abroad[4]. Nobody who knows anything of the habits of the medieval scholar will doubt that somewhere in England—at one place or in several—in some ancient and more or less famous place of study or in a new one, the Parisians would settle down and resume their interrupted studies, in the old way and under the old masters. In one or more of these places a Studium Generale would be *de facto* established by their presence. As a matter of fact we hear of nothing approaching such a Studium Generale anywhere in England at this time or for long afterwards, except at Oxford. At Oxford we do hear of a Studium Generale, and within a very few years of the presumed migration, while there is nothing to shew the existence of such a Studium before that date. It is probable, there-

[1] *Materials for the Hist. of Thomas Becket*, ed. Robertson (Rolls Series), VI, pp. 235–236.

[2] *Ibid.* I, pp. 53, 54. The exact date of these Ordinances is uncertain.

[3] *Ibid.* VII, p. 148.

[4] [But on this question see Salter, H. E. in *History*, XIV (1929), pp. 57–8.]

fore, that the rapid emergence of Oxford into a Studium Generale may be set down as chiefly due to this Parisian migration.

In the Paris of 1170 we know of the bare existence of a society of masters, constituted by the fact of inception and existing chiefly for the conduct of these inceptions—a customary society without charter or privileges, common officers or common seal, legal recognition or written statutes. A similar society would be at once reproduced at Oxford—there is no reason for supposing that it existed before—by the immigrants. The language of Giraldus suggests some such organisation; at all events, he speaks of a plurality of masters—one of the notes of a Studium Generale. Nothing is known of the organisation of the Studium in the previous period. Theobaldus Stampensis may have taught under some sort of authority from St Frideswyde's monastery; but there was no cathedral in Oxford, which then formed part of the enormous Lincoln diocese; and after St. Frideswyde's church passed into the hands of the regular Canons —perhaps in 1120—there was no secular collegiate church whose chancellor or other scholastic official could claim to grant licences or exercise a jurisdiction over scholars. At this period it is possible that no regular licences were granted. After the migration, it may be that new masters incepted without a licence, or that the licences were granted by the masters themselves, or that the masters ventured on electing an official to grant the licences. There are some traces of an official known as the Rector of the Schools before the year 1214. But, whatever may have been the case before, it is in that year that we hear for the first time of a chancellor. A riot in which two or three scholars were hanged by the townsmen occurred in 1209—during the interdict and the general persecution of clerks throughout the kingdom by King John. A "dispersion" followed: 3000 scholars are said to have abruptly left Oxford—some for Cambridge (this is the first we hear of schools at Cambridge), some for Reading. John's submission to the Papacy at last made it necessary for the townsmen of Oxford also to make their peace with the ecclesiastical authorities. An ordinance issued by the papal legate in 1209 imposes a public penance—a bare-foot procession to the victims' tombs—on the actual offenders, and an annual disbursement of forty-two shillings by the townsmen at large —for ever[1]. It went on to provide that scholars arrested by the townsmen should be at once surrendered upon the demand of "the bishop or of the archdeacon or his official, or the chancellor, or whomsoever the Bishop of Lincoln shall depute to this office." In a later clause this officer is spoken of as "the chancellor whom the Bishop of Lincoln *shall* set over the scholars therein."

From this time onwards the Chancellor of Oxford became the undisputed head of the Oxford schools. His office was obviously an imitation of the Parisian Chancellor; but from the first he was in a totally different

[1] *Munimenta Academica,* ed. Anstey (Rolls Series), I, pp. 1 sq.

position from his prototype. He belonged to no hostile corporation; on the contrary, he represented the rights and independence of the scholars alike in their conflicts with the town and their relations to the bishop and other ecclesiastical authorities. He derived his authority from the bishop, but from the first he seems to have been elected—originally the election was biennial—by the masters from their own body. The necessity for confirmation by the bishop was done away with in 1368 [1], and eventually the Chancellor shook himself free altogether from episcopal and even archiepiscopal authority. By successive bulls, charters, and privileges from Pope and King he acquired an extensive jurisdiction—civil, spiritual, criminal—not only over the scholars but over the burgesses of Oxford. But there was nothing in these privileges to awaken the jealousy or suspicion of the university; rather they were welcomed as so many weapons of offence and defence against the outside world. From the first the Chancellor was regarded as the head of the university as well as the bishop's judge and representative. He conferred the licence, but he also presided over the University Congregations. He was, in fact, the Parisian Chancellor and the Parisian Rector in one—and a good deal more besides.

Every step in the evolution of the university constitution at Paris was imitated at Oxford; but at every turn the constitution of Oxford was modified by a difference of circumstances—especially the different position of the Chancellor. There are traces during the first half of the thirteenth century of four Nations and four Proctors at Oxford; but by about 1248 there were only two—a Northern and a Southern Nation; and in 1274 (after an unusually violent faction-fight between North and South) the university solemnly resolved that there should in future be no Nations at all. The national unity—earlier achieved in England than in any other European country—thus symbolised itself in the suppression of the separate Nations in its oldest university, though this by no means extinguished the faction-fights between North and South, or between the Welsh and Irish students, who belonged constitutionally to the South, and the Northern Nations which included the Scottish. There were still a Northern and a Southern Proctor, but there were no separate meetings of the Nations.

At Oxford there was no room for the growth of a single rector. At Paris the rectors were essentially the representatives of the masters—more strictly, of the Regent Masters of Arts; but, just as the Parisian Rector grew into the head of the whole university, the Proctors became, almost from the first, the executive of the whole university. This position of theirs was connected—whether as cause or effect—with the fact that the superior faculties here possessed no Deans and very little separate organisation. It is very rarely that we find the separate faculties acting as

[1] Wilkins, *Concilia*, III, p. 75; cf. Salter, *Snappe's Formulary* (*Oxf. Hist. Soc.*), p. 86.

independent bodies. There are, indeed, traces of "voting by Faculties' (the Non-Regents here counting as a separate section of the university); but this system disappeared by the fifteenth century. All through its history and down to the present day the distinctive character of the university—in ways more important than mere constitutional organisation—has been affected by the almost entire absence of distinct faculty organisation, especially in the superior faculties; and this almost carried with it the ascendancy of the predominant Faculty of Arts. In the Middle Ages this ascendancy was secured by a peculiar feature of the Oxford constitution—the existence of "previous" or "black" Congregation. This body was composed of the Regent Masters of Arts only; its meetings were held in the church of St. Mildred's, and were presided over by the two Proctors. It claimed the right of previously considering and (if it pleased) vetoing a proposed statute, though eventually it was considered sufficient that the statute should be "promulgated" in the Black Congregation. There were thus at Oxford three distinct Congregations or Convocations: (1) the Black Congregation, (2) the Congregation of Regents of all Faculties, held first at St Mary's, afterwards in the adjoining Convocation House, in which all the ordinary executive business of the university was transacted, and (3) the Great Congregation, held in St Mary's Church, which was only assembled on solemn occasions, such as the making of permanent statutes. It is only in this assembly, so far as appears, that there was any "voting by Faculties."

The colleges of Oxford were originally just what they were at Paris—boarding-houses for students, accommodating only their foundation-members and at most supplementing the teaching of the public schools by providing additional private tuition, especially for their younger members. The revolution by which the colleges to a large extent supplanted the university took place at Oxford later than at Paris. It is not till the dawn of the Renaissance period that we find college teaching keeping pace with the waning efficiency of the university Regents, and it is not till after the Reformation that the bulk of the university began to reside in the colleges, nor till a still later period that an oligarchy of Heads of Colleges practically to a large extent supplanted the medieval Congregations as the really supreme university authority.

The original universities had grown into Studia Generalia by a spontaneous process. Originally, their "licences" to teach were, from a legal or canonical point of view, worth no more than any other licences of the local ecclesiastical authority north of the Alps or of any other Italian college of doctors. The validity of the licence could not extend beyond the jurisdiction of the authority which conferred it. But, practically, the "licences" of certain Studia had acquired an ecumenical prestige; a master who had been licensed at Paris and gone through his inception there would be acknowledged as a master and allowed to teach anywhere in Europe. Such Studia were at first very few in number. The position of the four Studia which we have already mentioned was beyond dispute. The ancient medieval University of Montpellier was perhaps almost equally well recognised as a Studium Generale. A few others which had arisen by migration from one of the old schools might claim to be Studia Generalia with more or less success. One of the earliest of these was Cambridge, which originated (as has already been seen) in a migration from Oxford in 1209, and which almost exactly reproduced the Oxford constitution, and developed along parallel lines. Another was that of Padua, which owed its existence to a migration from Bologna in 1222. The earliest Spanish Universities, Palencia and Salamanca, which date from the beginning of the thirteenth century, were also perhaps regarded as "general" from the first. But even when the conception of the Studium Generale received an official recognition through the conferment upon the clergy of the right to be absent from their benefices for the purpose of studying in Studia Generalia, the question which Studia were general was still incapable of precise determination. The original notion of the Studium Generale was simply one which *de facto* attracted in large numbers students from all parts; to which was generally added the restriction that at least one of the superior faculties must be taught and studied there. At first, as we have seen, there was no necessary connexion between the idea of the Studium Generale and that of the Universitas. But in practice a certain organisation of the type or types which we have already examined grew up in all the Studia which were recognised as general, and rarely existed in an equally developed form in a Studium Particulare; hence a Studium could hardly be recognised as general which did not possess this organisation, so that practically the Studium Generale and the University of Masters or Scholars were formed into a single institution. This institution was emphatically one which in its earliest form grew and was not made. But about the middle of the thirteenth century both the two powers which could claim to confer privileges of ecumenical validity—the Pope and the Emperor—almost simultaneously, for purposes of their own, conceived the idea of giving by the fiat of authority to certain new institutions the privilege which the old had acquired by spontaneous evolution. The idea originated with the Emperor Frederick II, who established a Studium Generale at Naples in 1224 in order to withdraw students from Bologna and the other cities of Lombardy, against which he was on the point of declaring war. In 1230 the Pope erected a Studium Generale at Toulouse, as a manœuvre in his campaign for the suppression of the Albigensian heresy; and shortly afterwards (1237) conferred upon those who had received its licence the right to teach anywhere "without any previous examination." In 1244 or 1245 the same privilege was conferred upon the University of the Court of Rome, a migratory university which was to follow the Curia in its wanderings, and find employment for the idle ecclesiastics who flocked to it in quest of benefices. Other monarchs, cities, or prelates who wished to foster the growth of Studia within their jurisdictions now began to ask for and obtain similar bulls from Pope or Emperor; and before the close of the century it came to be an acknowledged principle of public law that no new Studium Generale could be set up without such a bull. In 1292 even the two most illustrious of the ancient Studia—Paris and Bologna—thought it well to procure similar bulls, and henceforth conferred their licences "apostolica auctoritate." But some of these Studia—such as Oxford—had been so fully recognised as "general" by universal consent that it was impossible for legal theory to dispute their status. These were called Studia Generalia *ex consuetudine*. By the jurists of the fourteenth century it was definitely laid down that a Studium Generale was a Studium which by papal or imperial bull or by ancient custom—which practically meant a custom dating from at least the thirteenth century—enjoyed the right of conferring the *ius docendi hic et ubique terrarum*.

The merest sketch of the rapid multiplication of universities which now set in is all that is here possible. We have already noticed the foundation of Cambridge by the Oxford migration of 1209. It is not certain that it maintained its existence after the return of the Oxford students in 1214. We hear little more about it till in 1229 it received a contingent of the Parisian scholars dispersed in that year in consequence of the great quarrel with the Friars. It claimed to be and was recognised as "general"—at least in England—from the first, though till quite the close of the Middle Ages it had no pretensions to the world-wide fame of Oxford. It is one of the few universities which succeeded in getting recognised as entitled to confer the licence in all the faculties, including Theology, without a papal bull; and yet there was so much doubt about its position that in 1318 it thought it well to obtain a bull from John XXII, which is worded exactly in the usual form of a foundation-bull for a new university, conferring the *ius ubique docendi*. The constitution of the university so nearly follows the Oxford model that in view of the necessary limits of this chapter its further growth must not be traced. Putting aside short-lived attempts of seceders from Oxford and Cambridge to establish new universities at Northampton, Salisbury, and Stamford, Oxford and Cambridge continued to be the only English universities till the foundation of Durham in 1837.

It is not surprising that Italy, with its powerful, almost independent cities and the acute rivalries between them, should have taken the lead in the multiplication of universities. Short-lived Studia Generalia were established by secessions from Bologna at Reggio before the end of the twelfth century, and at Vicenza in 1204. A similar law-school was established at Arezzo by a discontented Bolognese doctor in 1215, which (unlike all other North-Italian universities) was controlled by a magisterial university; but it did not outlive the middle of the thirteenth century, and imperial bulls in 1355 and 1456 failed to effect any permanent revival. The first migration from Bologna which gave rise to a permanent and famous university was the already mentioned migration to Padua in 1222, a university which, after the decline of the law-school of Bologna, began to rival, and ultimately to surpass, the fame of its parent university as a home both of legal and of medical studies. The origin of Naples (1224) has already been mentioned; it was governed despotically in a quite unique fashion by a royal Chancellor, and never played any considerable part in the intellectual life of the Middle Ages. A secession from Padua established itself at Vercelli in 1228, the city undertaking in a formal contract with the student-universities to provide no less than 500 empty houses for the immigrants; but it did not long maintain itself as a Studium Generale. A Studium, which called itself general, arose at Siena by migration from Bologna in 1246. This is the last attempt to establish a Studium Generale in Italy without a bull, and it is interesting as a limiting case. In 1275, when the Bologna immigrants had long since returned, the town council talked of reviving their Studium Generale; but in spite of later immigrations from Bologna, it never quite succeeded in getting recognition as general till it procured an imperial bull from Charles IV in 1357.

All later Italian universities were founded by bull, the initiation proceeding either from the city or the "tyrant" by whom it was governed. Piacenza got a bull for itself in 1248. After 1398 Gian Galeazzo Visconti attempted to make it a university of the Milanese, but the attempt was never very successful, and in 1414 was abandoned, and the university practically transferred to Pavia. The Studium at Rome (quite distinct from the *Studium Curiae*, established in 1245) was founded by Boniface VIII in 1303, Perugia in 1308, Treviso in 1318, Pisa in 1343, Florence in 1349, Pavia in 1361, Ferrara in 1391, Turin in 1405, and Catania in 1444. Thus by the close of the Middle Ages almost every considerable Italian State had acquired a university of its own. An attempt was often made to fill their schools by forbidding the subjects of the State to study elsewhere. In these circumstances the size, efficiency, and reputation of the Studium largely depended on the size and wealth of the State to which it ministered; but it is worthy of notice that universities prospered best in cities not of the largest size and where rents were lower—especially the conquered cities which were often systematically turned into university towns by their conquerors. Towards the close of the Middle Ages the most famous universities of Italy (apart from Bologna with its traditional prestige) were Padua, the university of the Venetian dominions; Pavia, the university of the Milanese; and Pisa, the university of the Florentine dominions, a separate university at Florence having ceased to exist in 1472. The constitution of the universities—with one or two exceptions—was closely modelled on that of

Bologna, with the removal of one of the two anomalies due to its peculiar history, such as the double Rectorship in the jurist university. The Chancellor in the Italian universities, except at Bologna, was always the bishop.

The earliest university of Spain was the first university in Europe to be founded by a definite act of authority. The University of Palencia was founded in 1212–14 by King Alfonso VIII of Castile, who invited a certain number of masters—perhaps from Paris and Bologna—and offered them salaries to teach in Palencia. In 1220 his successor, Ferdinand III, obtained from Pope Honorius III permission to use for the payment of the masters a fourth part of that third of ecclesiastical property of the diocese which in Spain was applied to the maintenance of the fabrics. Similar taxes on ecclesiastical property became in Spain the usual method of supporting universities. The Studium of Palencia came to an end about the year 1250; and, while it lasted, it would hardly have been regarded as more than what afterwards came to be called by the jurists a *Studium Generale respectu regni*. Before it closed its brief career the University of Salamanca was founded by Alfonso IX of Leon about the year 1220, but this university did not begin to flourish till the time of Alfonso X the Wise, who conferred upon it a regular charter in 1254, entrusting the right of promotion and an extensive jurisdiction over scholars to the Scholasticus of the cathedral. In 1255 Pope Alexander IV granted it many privileges, including the right of its graduates to teach anywhere except at Paris or Bologna. Apart from the power and importance of the Scholasticus, the university was organised rather on the Bolognese than on the Parisian model, with a Rector and *Consiliarii* elected by the students, though the doctors were not here excluded from the university congregation. The model there set up was followed by most of the Spanish universities. The Studium of Valladolid had come to be looked upon—at least in Spain—as a Studium Generale by about the middle of the thirteenth century, though it only obtained the *ius ubique docendi* from Pope Clement VI in 1346. The rival State of Aragon and Catalonia obtained its first university by the foundation of Lérida in 1300. It started with a charter from James II of Aragon and a bull from Pope Boniface VIII, and its statutes are known to be an exact copy of the early code of Bologna. The county of Roussillon—now annexed to Catalonia—obtained its university by the erection of Perpignan in 1349, not a successful attempt; while a new university for Aragon proper was set up at Huesca in 1359. A university was erected at Barcelona in 1450, chiefly owing to the efforts of the municipality. Saragossa (in Aragon), founded by a bull of Pope Sixtus IV in 1474, is the only instance of an undoubted Studium Generale in the Faculty of Arts alone. It is doubtful how far the University of Palma in Majorca can claim any continuity with the school set up in that place by the eccentric Raymond Lull[1]; as a regular university it owes its existence to a charter of Ferdi-

[1] See *supra*, Vol. v, Chap. ix, p. 325.

nand the Catholic in 1483. Siguenza (in Castile), founded in 1489, was the first instance of a college endowed with the privileges of a university—a model frequently followed in Spain at a later date. An older Studium at Alcalá in Castile became a Studium Generale in 1499, and a Studium long supported by the municipality at Valencia acquired a similar position from the Valencian Pope Alexander VI in 1500.

While the original division of Spain into many kingdoms naturally brought about the existence of many universities, the unity and independence of Portugal is proclaimed by the fact that throughout its history (if we except a later Jesuit university at Evora) it has had but one university—the university which was originally founded at Lisbon in 1290, and was transferred to Coimbra (in consequence of troubles with the citizens) in 1308–9. In two subsequent periods (1338–1355 and 1377–1537) the university was transferred back to Lisbon, but since 1537 it has remained at Coimbra.

In spite of the superlative reputation of medieval Paris, France possessed from an early period several universities of European reputation. The exclusion of the Civil Law from the studies of Paris left room for the growth of legal universities elsewhere, and Paris never obtained the highest reputation as a home of scientific Medicine. It is a curious fact—due partly to the prominence of Law and partly to the close connexion of southern France with Italy—that most of the French universities were modelled rather upon Bologna than upon Paris or exhibit a combination which may be described as a compromise between the two.

Montpellier as a place of medical study had become a formidable rival to Salerno before the middle of the eleventh century. It possessed a regular University of Medicine by 1220 under a Chancellor appointed by the bishop, and occupying a position very much like that of the Chancellor at Oxford, with two Proctors elected by the Masters, except that the licences were here conferred by the bishop himself. The university was at first purely magisterial, though the students acquired some small share in its government at a later date. Montpellier had also an ancient school of Law; and a regular jurist university, quite distinct from that of Medicine, came into existence about the year 1230. After much collision both with the bishop and the masters, the Law students succeeded by 1334 in acquiring the recognition of a modified student university. Orleans was from an early date famous as a Studium both of the Liberal Arts and of Law. It gradually grew up in the course of the thirteenth century, but its rights—against the bishop and the cathedral Scholasticus—were not fully recognised till it obtained a bull from Pope Clement V in 1306. It remained throughout the Middle Ages the most famous university of Law in France and one of the most famous in Europe. Angers was also an ancient cathedral school which gradually acquired the status of a Studium Generale, at about the time of the great migration from Paris in 1229. The foundation of Toulouse in 1230 has already been mentioned.

Toulouse also was a famous Studium of Law. The other French and Burgundian universities were: Avignon (1303), Cahors (1332), Grenoble (1339), Orange (1365), Aix (1409), Dôle (1422), Poitiers (1431), Caen (1437), Bordeaux (1441), Valence (1459), Nantes (1460), Bourges (1464).

The older French universities are interesting as being among the few which developed spontaneously without having the complete Parisian or Bolognese organisation transplanted to them by an act of authority or a sudden migration. Orleans and Angers emerged much more gradually than Paris from a state of tutelage to the bishop and his representatives, and the cathedral Scholasticus to the last retained more authority than the Parisian Chancellor, and the universities were much later in acquiring even a right to elect a Rector. The organisation of the students in Nations under Proctors of their own—ten at Orleans, six at Angers—was here of ancient and spontaneous growth, but they only succeeded, and that very gradually, in acquiring a modified share in the government of the universities in conjunction with the doctoral colleges. Most of the other French universities likewise exhibit a type of constitution mid-way between that of Paris and that of Bologna. A few universities of the Midi—such as Aix and Valence—approximate more closely to the Bologna model. Caen, which was deliberately instituted to take the place of Orleans during the English domination, alone reproduces the Paris constitution.

Of all the greater countries of Europe, Germany was the last to be seized with the desire to have universities of its own instead of sending its most advanced students to foreign schools like Paris and Bologna for education. The first German university (if it can be called German) was set up by the Emperor Charles IV in 1348 in Prague, the capital of his own hereditary kingdom of Bohemia. It was mainly on the model of Paris, though eventually (1372) the Law-students were allowed to set up a separate university of their own more or less on the Bologna model. A university was founded at Vienna in 1365 by Duke Rudolf IV. Erfurt was an important Studium of Arts from a very early period. It even set up a claim to be a *Studium Generale ex consuetudine*, but it did not succeed in making good its pretensions to full university rank till 1379 when, inspired no doubt by the desire to rival Prague and Vienna, it procured a bull from the Pope at Avignon, Clement VII. When once the example had been set, the ambition to possess a university in their own dominions rapidly spread through the princes and great cities of Germany. The University of Heidelberg dates from 1385, Cologne from 1388, Würzburg from 1409. Leipsic owes its origin to a great quarrel between the German and the Czech students at Prague, which led to a great exodus of German students in 1409, of whom a large body came to Leipsic and established a university of their own. The remaining universities of medieval Germany are: Rostock (1419), Louvain (1425), Trèves (1454), Greifswald (1455–6), Freiburg-im-Breisgau (1455–6), Basle (1459),

Ingolstadt (1459, now transferred to Munich), Mayence (1476), Tübingen (1476–7).

The endowments of the German universities were largely provided by the annexation of prebends in cathedral or collegiate Churches to university chairs. In many cases, too, one or more colleges—especially for the Faculty of Arts—were erected at the same time as the university, the fellowships of which were from the first intended to supply maintenance for the university Regents. College and university were often, in fact, so closely connected as to form a single institution. Thus in Germany an endowed professoriate existed from the very foundation of its universities, and the colleges, as places of residence for students, could gradually disappear without the extinction of university teaching.

As regards the other countries of Europe it must suffice to mention that Poland acquired a university by the foundation of Cracow in 1364. In Hungary three universities were founded in medieval times—Pécs (Fünfkirchen) (1367) which did not long survive, Buda (1389), and Pressburg (1465–7). The first Swedish university was Upsala, founded in 1477. The one Danish university—Copenhagen—dates from 1478. In Scotland three universities were erected in the course of the fifteenth century—St Andrews (1413), Glasgow (1450), and Aberdeen (1494). The Scotch universities were nominally modelled on Bologna rather than Paris or Oxford, and (though the rights of the students were practically very small) the annual election of a Lord Rector by the students of these universities represents the last relic in all Europe of the democratic student-universities which played so important a rôle in the academical system of southern Europe.

The influence of the universities upon the medieval world was exercised in three distinct ways. An adequate treatment of the subject would involve a discussion of three questions: (1) their influence as corporations having close relations both with Church and State but possessing considerable independence in relation to each; (2) the intrinsic value of the learning, knowledge, and thought of which they were the homes; (3) the value of the education which they imparted, and the effects of that education upon the world. A very few remarks are all that can be made within the limits of this chapter.

(1) It was chiefly in the North of Europe that the universities as corporations exercised an important influence upon national and international politics. In Italy the individual doctors played a leading part in the public life of the city republic. At the Diet of Roncaglia in 1158 for instance, it was the famous "four Doctors" of Bologna who are named by Rahewin as giving the opinion regarding regalian rights upon which the Emperor Frederick I acted when he asserted his almost forgotten prerogative against the Lombard cities; and other doctors were prominent members of the aristocratic party in that city. But just

because the Italian doctors were citizens, while the universities were composed of students only, the Italian universities could not well aspire to the kind of influence which the great corporations of learned ecclesiastics, especially the University of Paris, exercised in the North. At Paris the University became a great organ of public opinion at a time when public opinion had few such organs, which could and did make itself felt both in the domestic affairs of France and in the ecclesiastical politics of Europe. The Theology of the Western Church was largely shaped at Paris. In the celebrated question of the "retardation of the heavenly vision" Pope John XXII himself apologised to the University for expressing an opinion on a theological matter though he was not a doctor of Theology. The ecclesiastical law of Europe was moulded at Rome or at Bologna under Roman influence; in matters of pure Theology, Paris led the way and Rome followed.

To mention all the occasions on which the university figured in French politics would involve a long review of the history of France, especially during the confused faction-fights of the fourteenth and early fifteenth centuries. It must suffice to mention the most conspicuous occasion on which the university asserted the position sometimes claimed for it by medieval writers as the third of the great powers or "virtues" by which the European commonwealth of Nations was united and controlled—France's equivalent for the Italian Papacy and the German Empire. It was chiefly through the activity of the university—in alliance with the Emperor and other secular princes—that the termination of the Great Schism was forced upon the rival claimants to the Papacy. For such a task its constitution was extraordinarily well adapted. Its semi-ecclesiastical character covered what was really an extreme measure of interference by the rival powers with religion: its cosmopolitan composition and the close intercourse which it kept up with other universities enabled it to form and to express a kind of European concert; while the secular, anti-monastic, anti-curialist Theology which had grown up in the schools supplied the speculative basis that was required for so startling a measure as the deposition of the Pope by a General Council. The Council of Constance (1415—1418) represents the fleeting triumph of Gallicanism in the Western Church at large. The university long continued to be the home of Gallican Theology, but it was never again able to impose that Theology upon the world with so much effect. The very success of the university in terminating the Schism strengthened the Papacy which it had to some extent purified, and the growing power of centralised monarchies restricted the influence of the great scholastic democracy. In France an age of Concordats succeeded to the age of Councils, and the universities everywhere had to limit such influences as they could still wield in secular and ecclesiastical politics to the internal affairs of their respective countries.

(2) The nature and value of the scholastic Philosophy and Theology

form the subject of other chapters[1], and must therefore be passed over here. But it is important to remark that the scholastic system, though the most characteristic, represents by no means the sole intellectual output of the medieval universities. The study of Law was the predominant study of all the southern universities; and it was at least as prominent as the more speculative branches of knowledge even in northern France and England. The most direct practical influence which the universities exercised over the world was perhaps the influence exercised through this study. The scientific development which the universities gave to the Canon Law was one of the great instruments by which the Papacy succeeded in dominating the Church, and by which the Church and its courts succeeded in dominating the world. And everywhere, except in England, the practitioners and the judges of the secular courts were trained in Roman Law at the universities. Wherever the Law was practised by such lawyers, the substance of the Law that they administered was sure in time to be more or less Romanised. Thus it was through the influence of the university faculties that Roman Law practically took the place of the Teutonic codes in the courts of Germany and largely modified the customary laws of those parts of France in which the *loi écrite*, as such, did not prevail. English historians have dwelt strangely little upon the importance of the fact that in England—alone in all Europe—the legal practitioners were trained in separate schools of the national law. It was the early growth of the Inns of Court which reduced to a minimum the influence of Roman Law upon the substance, the procedure, and the tradition of English Law.

Our space will only allow one glance at the influence of the medical faculties. The actual Medicine and Surgery of Salerno and Montpellier and Bologna were less contemptible than the popular view of them is apt to suggest; and it is seldom remembered to how large an extent modern science had its birth in the medieval schools of Medicine and of Astrology, which was then closely connected with Medicine, owing to the supposed necessity for the physician to know the "critical days" of his patient. It is curious to reflect that but for this superstition the medical student Galileo might have ended his days in a lucrative practice and never been diverted to the studies which revolutionised the thought of the world.

(3) The efficiency of the education given by the medieval universities is not quite the same question as the intrinsic value of the learning which they imparted. Even if we adopt Macaulay's characteristically philistine doctrine that in the Middle Ages the human mind ceased to advance but only marked time, marking time is at least a form of gymnastic. Looked at in that light, it may be questioned whether the intellectual exercise involved in the study of Aristotle, in familiarity with the technicalities of scholastic Logic and in the practice of scholastic disputation, was not at least as valuable a training for the intellectual work of practical life

[1] See *supra*, Vol. v, Chap. xxiii, and *infra*, Chap. xix.

as the later education which consisted in intimate acquaintance with a very small number of Latin classics, a much slighter study of Greek, and unlimited practice in the art of writing Latin verse. For that large body of medieval students whose chief study was Law, the intellectual effects of their study must have been exactly the same as those of a purely legal education at the present day, with the addition of a very thorough acquaintance with the Latin language and an important branch of Latin literature. Except for the almost entire absence of any sense of history, in this as in all other departments of medieval thought, the medieval student studied the very subjects which form at least half of the occupation of a law-student in most European countries, nor was there any very marked difference in the methods of that study.

It would be quite beyond our present scope to insist upon the deficiencies of medieval science and philosophy, and the intellectual limitations which they involved in the persons brought up in them. It is more to the purpose to point out how largely the superiority of the educated man to the uneducated is independent of the subject-matter on which the education is based. The most direct influence which the medieval universities exercised on the world was due to the fact that they put the direction of public and private affairs of all kinds very largely into the hands of highly educated men, "men who had devoted a considerable portion of their lives to severe and exacting mental labour." They did not educate "the people," though a far larger proportion of the population got an elementary, or something more than an elementary, education in the innumerable grammar schools by which the universities were fed[1]. But a very large proportion of those by whom public affairs were directed—the ecclesiastics, the statesmen, the lawyers and other professional men, the men of business who directed the households of great nobles—were for the most part university-trained students. It was chiefly through the universities that poor men of ability, or even younger sons of noble families, could rise to positions of power and influence. In the late Middle Age even princes and great nobles received their education in the universities. And on this side the influence of the universities increased as time went on. The most brilliant period in the history both of medieval Law and of medieval Scholasticism was over before the universities had become numerous; in some ways we may even say that the intellectual history of Europe—at least of northern Europe—from the middle of the thirteenth century to near the end of the fifteenth is a history of progressive decline; but the multiplication of universities went on diffusing the possibilities of education, and the proportion of educated men to the whole population was probably greater at the close of the Middle Ages than it had ever been before.

The actual number of students in the medieval universities has, indeed, been grossly exaggerated. Tradition—often very early tradition—speaks

[1] Cf. *infra*, Vol. VIII, Chap. XXIII.

of 30,000 at Oxford and at more than one other university. But in nothing is the medieval chronicler so untrustworthy as in his numbers. Such documentary evidence as we possess as to the earliest universities make such stories quite incredible. But the very large numbers, often many hundreds, sometimes two thousand, of students revealed by the surviving matriculation-books of smaller universities in the fourteenth and fifteenth centuries suggest that before the multiplication of Studia Generalia there may well have been some 4000 or 5000 students at Paris and some 2000 or 3000 at Oxford. When all allowances have been made for medieval exaggeration, it is probable that a larger proportion of the population received a university education at the close of the Middle Ages than is now the case in modern countries. Certainly that was the case as regards England. Doubtless these crowds of students included thousands whose proper place would have been at a secondary school, but it must be remembered that in those days men went to the universities later as well as earlier than now. High ecclesiastical dignitaries of mature years were found seated on the benches of the schools side by side with mere boys. When all allowances are made for the mixed motives which drew men to the universities, when we have allowed for the coarseness and brutality of the life that was lived in them, when we have admitted to the fullest extent the intellectual deficiencies of their most brilliant products, the very existence of the universities is evidence of a side of the Middle Ages to which scant justice has often been done—their enormous intellectual enthusiasm. The popular conception of the Middle Ages is far too favourable on the side of Religion and of Morality, far too grudging and unappreciative on the intellectual side. The universities represent one of the greatest achievements of the medieval mind, not only on account of the value of their intellectual products, but as pieces of institutional machinery. And the institution has outlived a very large part of the culture which it originally imparted. Through all the changes which have taken place in the subject-matter and the methods of the education regarded as the highest from the twelfth century down to the present time, that education has continued to be given through the machinery supplied by a distinctively medieval institution—an institution which still, even in the minute details of its organisation, continues to exhibit its continuity with its two great thirteenth-century prototypes, medieval Paris and medieval Bologna.

CHAPTER XVIII.

POLITICAL THEORY TO *c.* 1300.

Nowhere is the part assigned to philosophical speculation in the conduct of life less easy to define than precisely at the point where the contact of theory and practice would seem to be inevitable and direct. To discuss the importance of logic or metaphysics is the privilege of philosophers, but at all times the business of government must be carried on, and at all times there will be room for disputes about the equity of laws, the worth of institutions, or some other momentous question involved in the exercise of sovereign power. On merely *a priori* grounds, therefore, the reflections of the "political animal" on his collective destiny might have been expected to find almost continuous expression in literary form. No such anticipation, however, would be justified by the facts. Among the Greeks, as we know, political speculation was slow to arise and swift to disappear. Before Socrates there was little or none of it, while, after Aristotle, concentration upon the problem of conduct served only to dissolve the union between morals and politics, and to make it ever more and more improbable that worthy successors to the *Republic* and the *Politics* would appear. The Roman philosophers, such as they were, produced no distinctive theory of the State, nor yet the Neo-Platonists; and when at last we begin to approach the Middle Ages, we find at the gateway one imposing work, the *De Civitate Dei* of St Augustine, but thereafter have to travel for many centuries before we light upon any deliberate contribution to the development of political thought.

Whatever reasons may be offered for this paucity of material, we cannot attribute the silence of philosophers to any stagnation in the current of political events. On the contrary, the transformation of Europe by the rise of the Macedonian Empire, by the prodigious expansion of Rome, and finally by the triumph of the medieval Church, was on a far grander scale than anything in the fortunes of Athens and Sparta, by which Plato and Aristotle had been moved to compose their immortal books. There were, however, certain definite reasons, in the centuries following upon the decline of the City State, for a severance between the quest of moral perfection and the ambition to make laws for mankind. The philosophers themselves, beginning with Zeno, were often Hellenes rather by intellectual adoption than by racial descent. They were heralds of a new civilisation, of a cosmopolitan society wherein the traditional antagonism of Greek and barbarian could no longer survive. At the same time their doctrines were delivered primarily to men deprived of the old civic activities, and forced to choose between political lethargy at home and a life of adventurous intrigue at the court of some foreign prince. What wonder, then, if the inward life began to prevail over the outward, or if philosophy learned to care less for the reformation of government than for the house that wisdom could build for herself?

In this sense there was a long preparation in Greek philosophy for the antithesis of the Church and the World, and therefore the student who would search antiquity for the first premonition of medieval ideas must be prepared to distract his attention between the teaching of philosophers and the actual remodelling of the world by policy and arms. If there was indeed any political theory distinctive of the Middle Ages, it can only be because a new form of society had come into being; but again, no form of society can be genuinely new unless it embodies an idea beyond the capacity of the old. The true preface, therefore, to our subject is contained in the simple question, why did the City State no longer suffice for the needs of the world? To reply that it was swept away by military empires is little more than an evasion. Alexander would probably have admitted the truth of Aristotle's contention, that the πόλις alone could realise the aptitude of man for enjoyment of the highest good. The Romans in their turn were reluctant to part with their faith in a local citizenship, barely to be imparted even to the neighbouring Italians. When the Empire was established, for every one who hailed the dawn of a new era there doubtless were fifty who bewailed the death of liberty and the triumph of force. The old ideal of urbanity still lingered on, and centuries later a poet could compliment an Emperor in the words—"urbem fecisti quod prius orbis erat."

For us, however, it is impossible to look upon the creation of Empire as merely a violent subversion of a higher form of the State. Whatever the motives of an Alexander or a Julius, men such as these were in effect the authors of a political fabric more august than the Aristotelian city because it provided at last a fit habitation for an idea beyond the range of the Philosopher's vision. The one prophetic anticipation in the older Greek philosophy of the larger world to come is to be found in Plato's *Republic*. The picture of the philosopher-king does at least signify one fact of supreme importance, that no society can finally solve the problem of government unless it can rise above opinion to knowledge and derive its laws from eternal truths. When Aristotle excluded the energy of contemplation from the human life of the State, when he set a limit, as it were, to the "political" instinct, he seemed to be forsaking dreams for realities, but in fact the illusion was his. *All* ideas, or all that can unite two or three in pursuit of an object, are political ideas, and every such union can produce the essentials of a political society, such as the recognition of rules and authority, with the demand for just so much autonomy as is required for the realisation of the common end. What the eventual significance of any given society is to be will depend on the scope of its intention and the breadth of its appeal. In the end there can be but one autonomous society, the one that embodies the autonomous idea. If Aristotle supposed that this ultimate independence could be realised in the City State, we cannot marvel at his mistake. A mistake it was, nevertheless, and for this sufficient reason, that the City State was not cemented by the deepest bonds of political union, except in a local and transient form. Its religion was the cult of gods who preferred Athens to Megara; its "good" was reserved for the cultivated Hellene, and denied to the barbarian and the slave. Whenever, therefore, there should arise a society knit together by a philosophy or religion of universal significance, the doom of the City State must shortly be pronounced. It was not the armies of imperial conquerors that made Athens obsolete, but the birth of a more comprehensive idea.

Where and how the new birth was to be manifested was the vital question for the Graeco-Roman world. By successive conquests the body politic was enlarged to gigantic dimensions; what then remained was to inspire it with a soul. For this more serious task, unfortunately, the Roman genius was not adequately endowed. The instruments most evidently at the disposal of the Emperors were the diffusion of citizenship and the erection of a single system of law. Now it belonged to the very nature of ancient citizenship that diffusion must lower its quality and almost destroy its original meaning. Long before the final largess of Caracalla (in A.D. 212) the last vestige was obliterated of the old idea, that the citizen was one who took an active part in governing the State. What survived, and what indeed was to gain a new significance under Roman dominion, was the majesty and universality of law. If man could live by law alone, there would have been no decline and fall of the Roman Empire, at least within the kingdom of the mind. But great as were the treasures of Roman jurisprudence, more was needed for the welding into a single community of peoples as diverse as those who acknowledged the Roman sway. A single creed, a single object of worship, some common appeal to the deepest instincts of human nature, was the indispensable condition of success. But to this end the religious tradition of Rome provided almost nothing. As the *ius gentium* had grown up outside the *ius civile*, so, no doubt, was there always a larger precinct, beyond the *pomoerium*, where alien gods could hire a lodging and enjoy their appropriate honours. Yet the difference between the Roman law and the Roman religion lay just in this fact, that the law, with some aid from philosophy, could expand, so to speak, into a monotheistic system, while the religion could do nothing of the kind. Under the Empire the old failure of the local gods to resist invasion persisted with startling results. Every eastern cult, brought home with the spoils of war, or imported by wandering quacks, now began to find a home on the banks of the Tiber, submerging the relics of ancient piety, but failing, none the less, to animate the horde of citizens with any single purpose or belief.

The one promising expedient devised or adopted by the Emperors was the deification of the genius of Rome in themselves. The mere notion of apotheosis was no alarming innovation. Neither for Greeks nor for Romans were gods and demigods divided by an impassable gulf from mankind; but for that very reason the sanctification of the Emperor was never likely to arouse either the enthusiasm or the hatred commonly associated with the founding of a new religion. As a form of policy, the Romans borrowed deification (we may fairly assume) from the successors of Alexander, and it was perhaps in the Eastern half of the Empire that the new cult was most likely to flourish. This at least is certain, that the more the status of the Emperor was magnified, the more clearly would Rome begin to assume a place in the oriental tradition. What definitely belonged to the East was, not apotheosis, but the imperial diadem and the notion of universal monarchy, a thing wholly different in character from the kingship depicted in the early history or legends of Greece and Rome. When, therefore, we recognise in Empire the form of government that came to supplant the City State, we should also understand that the whole perspective of history was thus altered, so that later generations, looking backwards along the vista of the past, would barely glance at the republican glories so belauded in our modern tradition, but would pass from Caesar to Alexander, and thence to the remoter dynasties of Persia and Babylon. This vision of Empire it was that for so many centuries was to enchant and bewilder the medieval mind.

Meanwhile in Italy itself, and everywhere within the circle of Hellenic culture, the steady divergence of spiritual and political activity was fatally weakening the ability of Rome to undertake the government of the world. Religion belonged to the apparatus of the State, theology to the philosophical school. Few historical judgments, therefore, are more misleading than the common assertion that Church and State were identical in the ancient world. Before two things can be identified it is necessary that they should first have been conceived as distinct. Now there is no such thing as a Church without a theology, and of theology, in any considerable sense of the word, the City State had none. The only theology (apart from the Jewish) that has shaped the destiny of Europe was invented by Greek philosophers, and from them was taken over by the Church. Thus when we remark the drift of speculative thought towards a spiritual monotheism, or when we applaud the fine cosmopolitan sentiments of the Stoics, we may be inclined at first to marvel that Pagan Rome could not make a stouter resistance to the gospel of the Christian Church. But in truth there is here no matter for surprise. Because the City State was Aristotelian not Platonic, because philosophers were not kings but lecturers, the doctrines which might have remoulded society into an ecumenical whole were never absorbed into the organic life of the State, and thus were never available as instruments of policy to combat the new society. All that imperial Rome could offer to its vast miscellany of subjects the Church could provide in a shape more vivid and real: a common citizenship, with no distinction of Greek and barbarian, of bond and free; a common law, which was likewise the charter of liberty; a common fatherhood of God, presented, not in the dubious guise of a Caesar, but in the life of the Incarnate Son. Against such an array of forces the Roman State could avail nothing, the Graeco-Roman philosophy not much. The Stoic might cast his net more widely than the Platonist or the Aristotelian, but the common folk still slipped through the meshes. The double appeal of the Christian message, to the intellect of the wise and to the heart of the simple, was beyond the competence of the philosophical schools.

At whatever date, then, we choose to place the beginning of the Middle Ages, the characteristic medieval problem is seen to arise from the impending collision of the Roman Empire and the Catholic Church. For two such societies to flourish in mutual disregard was wholly impossible. What concealed this truth from the primitive Christians, and still, it would seem, obscures it for some modern critics, was the spirituality of the Gospel and the flat repudiation of the claim to earthly power: "Regnum meum non est de hoc mundo." Rather than summon many legions of angels the Master had yielded himself to a handful of swords and staves. With this supreme example before it, how could the Church aspire to universal dominion except in a spiritual sense? The exception, however, was more than enough. At no time was the issue to depend on the conflict of armies; what impelled the Church towards its medieval destiny was simply the need of realising what we have called the autonomous idea. Pledged to convert the world to a single allegiance, to control every human activity, to define the boundaries of right and wrong, the new society was forbidden by its very nature to allow the final authority of any sovereign power outside itself. Far from avoiding the crisis by the profession of otherworldliness, it was solely by its preference of the celestial *patria* to this present world that the Church became a revolutionary force. The authority of the keys, the power to bind and loose hereafter, will easily vanquish (so long as men believe in it) every jurisdiction which looks no farther than the grave.

If such was the medieval problem, the uniform character of the political theory properly belonging to the Middle Ages should be readily foreseen. What in fact imparted variety to speculation was, first, the ever-changing phases of the political situation, secondly, the reluctance of statesmen and theologians to admit the impossibility of a division of provinces between the temporal and the spiritual power. In the age of the New Testament, and indeed for some while afterwards, the disparity between Church and Empire was so manifest that the attitude of passive obedience, tempered by martyrdom, seemed alone to be practicable. Most of that early period we are compelled to pass over, but it is impossible to ignore the work of St Augustine, who made the first great survey of the arena in which the protagonists of medieval controversy were to meet.

Not the least remarkable fact about the *De Civitate Dei* is its date. A hundred years after the Edict of Milan, when Christian Emperors had long been enthroned, and when the defeat of Julian's policy might well have removed the fear of reaction, Augustine bases his whole argument on the assumption that the Empire is essentially a heathen power. The eventual fate of Rome he hesitates to prophesy, but he does not believe that the recent capture of the city is the beginning of the end. With sound historical instinct he treats the invasion of Alaric as only one of a series reaching far into the past. On previous occasions the *imperium* had been *afflictum potius quam mutatum*, and there is no reason now to despair. He does not himself desire a general catastrophe, and is far from suggesting that it is the business of the Church to work for that end. The two great misconceptions of empire, he thinks, are to ascribe it to the beneficence of heathen gods and to count it the supreme reward of goodness. Like everything else, earthly dominion is within the control of Providence, but it is given, as God wills, to the just and the unjust, whereas true felicity is reserved for the just. That the Roman virtues, as described in Virgil's famous lines, do qualify a people for the task of earthly government Augustine does not deny. He does, indeed, remark a certain decadence in the Roman character, a descent of the scale from *libertas* to *gloria*, and from *gloria* to *dominatio*, but the gist of his criticism is that the acquisition of empire, no matter by what virtues, is a wholly false ideal. The Church can never be a competitor with Rome for terrestrial sovereignty. The *Civitas Dei* is an eternal society, of which a portion, represented first by the Jews and then by the Catholic Church, is obliged to accomplish a pilgrimage on earth. The *civitas impiorum*, on the other hand, was founded in iniquity by the hand of the murderer Cain. "Gratia civis sursum, gratia peregrinus deorsum"; Abel founded no city, but Cain was driven by his crime to fashion a new society, from which had descended the long succession of Empires—Assyrian, Persian, Macedonian—with Rome (itself the work of the fratricide Romulus) as last of the line. That the Church was now appointed to inherit from Rome the burden of empire was a thought wholly foreign to the mind of Augustine. The Jews alone were the spiritual ancestors of the Christians, and even they had forfeited their birthright by their disposition to seek in terrestrial form the kingdom not to be enjoyed by the saints until the world has passed away.

The Church, then, is essentially a *societas peregrina*, set over against the *societas impiorum*. Open hostility, however, between the two Augustine neither expects nor desires. While there is no room in his theory for a distinction of Church and State within the Divine Society, it is expedient for the true *civitas* to make use of the false. The great function of empire is the establishment of peace. This has to be effected, in the first instance, by war, and thereafter by imposition on the conquered of laws respected by the conqueror himself. This is what Augustine styles the *pax Babylonis*, differing from the *pax caelestis* inasmuch as it always requires the prelude of war. Nevertheless the Church can profit by the inferior kind of peace, and to disturb the public order by wanton opposition would be wrong. During its pilgrimage on earth the heavenly *civitas* summons its citizens from every race, caring nothing for diversity of tongues, institutions, or laws; "nihil eorum rescindens nec destruens, immo servans et sequens."[1] So long as its religious freedom is unhindered, it can co-operate with the earthly *civitas* in every other respect.

Augustine sets forth his position with admirable clearness, but when we proceed to scrutinise it more closely we are compelled to admit that his foresight was limited and his grasp of the problem incomplete. What he does understand to perfection is the fundamental difference between the terrestrial and the celestial ideal. What he fails to see is that the difficulty of mutual adjustment had been enormously increased by the conversion of the Empire to the Faith. How great the complications of the future were likely to be we may learn by considering a little further his luminous contrast between the two *civitates*. Strictly speaking, there is, to Augustine's mind, only one genuine *civitas*. In a well-known passage[2] he observes that *res publica* means *res populi*, quotes the trite Ciceronian definition of *populus* as "coetus multitudinis, iuris consensu et utilitatis communione sociatus," and then declares that the Roman State fails to satisfy the definition. For *ius* is nothing without *vera iustitia*, and true justice there cannot be without service of the one true God. Only in an inferior sense, as a "coetus multitudinis rerum quas diligit concordi communione sociatus," are the Romans a *populus*; the fuller qualifications belong to the *Civitas Dei* alone. Much needless surprise has been caused by this famous declaration. Augustine, it should be superfluous to add, is neither denying the respect of Rome for her own system of law and justice, nor suggesting that any heathen State could exist without such a system. His repudiation of the Roman claim belongs, nevertheless, to the very essence of his thesis. Moreover, he enunciates here a political principle of the highest order and of indisputable truth. In language transformed, indeed, by the movement of history, yet identical in meaning, he revives the Platonic doctrine that the nature of Justice must be hidden until the truth about the first and last things is revealed. Justice, as defined by positive law, there may be in any society, and some part of that law may coincide with the dictates of the *lex divina*. Yet so long as the meaning of right and wrong depends ultimately upon the meaning of the universe (or, as Christians would say, upon the will of God), the Justice of a society that walks in darkness can only be the shadow of a name. To expect from Augustine any doctrine but this is to bid him abandon his deepest convictions and reconstitute the substance of his

[1] *De Civ. Dei*, XIX, 17. [2] *Ib.* XIX, 21 and 24.

mind. At the very least it is to thrust upon him the anachronism of a distinction of Church and State within the Christian Society, from which his own antithesis of the two *civitates* is immensely remote. The real weakness of his theory lies in his failure to suspect that the problem of the temporal power would begin to look insoluble only when the *civitas impiorum*, already moribund, should have ceased to exist.

If it be granted that the distinctive character of medieval politics, as contrasted with ancient, arose from the conception of a society devoted to the pursuit of a celestial ideal, yet constrained to regulate the behaviour of man in his terrestrial condition, we may briefly enumerate the possible theories of the relation between spiritual and temporal power. There would appear to be three, namely, (1) identification, (2) direct opposition, (3) distinction within an area defined by common first principles. Now the first of these, identification, as we find it, not in the City State but perhaps in the society of Islām, was never compatible with the Christian aspiration. Even in the most materialistic phases of the Church's history, the note of otherworldliness never entirely ceased to sound. The Pope could not be Caesar; the kingdom was not of this world. On the other hand, the period of direct antagonism could not be indefinitely prolonged. In the mind of an Augustine it could survive the official conversion of the Empire, but in effect what remained for Christendom was only the last of our three alternatives, to discover, if possible, a scheme for amicable compromise, on the hypothesis that both temporal and spiritual functions must be exercised by the *civitas Dei*, so long as its earthly pilgrimage endured.

Less than a hundred years after the appearance of Augustine's book the elements of the new situation were presented in the celebrated letter of Pope Gelasius I (*ob.* 496) to Anastasius: "duo quippe sunt, imperator auguste, quibus principaliter mundus hic regitur; auctoritas sacrata pontificum et regalis potestas. In quibus tanto gravius est pondus sacerdotum quanto etiam pro ipsis regibus hominum in divino reddituri sunt examine rationem." It was not, however, on the Byzantine Emperors that the task of interpreting these portentous words was laid. The Rome that became an oriental despotism, and made the last utterance of its original genius in the work of Justinian, lies outside our subject. The "Donation of Constantine," one is tempted to say, was the supremely historical fact upon which the edifice of medieval Europe was built. Long anticipated by the decline of imperial power in the West, the fatal moment arrived only when a Pope was driven by the pressure of the Lombards to summon a Christian Prince to his aid. The policy of Ultramontanism was then invented, and its firstfruits were "the translation of the Empire," with the coronation of Charles the Great.

One abiding consequence of that strange and spectacular event was the creation of an artificial atmosphere, in which the drama of the present was perpetually disguised in the garments of the past. The actual importance of the Empire as a political force varied in relation to the competence of the successive holders of the office; but at all times the political nurture of the Emperors was (to speak roughly) Teutonic, while the imperial crown was a symbol but dimly understood by themselves. Meanwhile the whole intellectual tradition, embalmed in the names of old institutions, in the doctrines of jurisprudence, or in fragments of political thought, was Italian, Roman, or even Hellenic, but in any case was a thing apart from feudalism and all the political inventions proper to the barbarians of the north. Hence to modern interpreters of the medieval period the difficulty is to disentangle the study of political speculation from the study of political movements; a difficulty augmented by the fact that many of the institutions and customs most rich in their promise of modern developments occupied little or no place in the conscious theories of medieval authors. It is with theory, however, that this chapter is concerned. Ideas incorporated only in social institutions, and never rising to the level of conscious expression, we can scarcely pretend to examine. For much the same reason it is well, too, to admit at once that the greater part of the arguments employed in medieval controversies were weapons of expediency forged to meet some passing crisis rather than serious products of philosophical reflection. The struggle about Investiture, for example, has played a notable part in our political histories, but in relation to the progress of political thinking we may venture to doubt whether it has any importance at all. At the most it was only a noisy illustration of the wider problem, how to define the place of secular power within the economy of the Church.

As compared with the Papacy, the medieval Empire was a fiction, but there was nothing fictitious in the distaste of powerful monarchs for submission to sacerdotal authority at the expense of their own. A lively and typical example of the conflicts incidental to the new alliance of Papacy and Empire is exhibited in the treatise of Hincmar of Rheims (*ob.* 882), "De Divortio Lotharii regis et Tetbergae reginae." Marriage being admittedly a sacrament, divorce did not provide very favourable ground for the assertion of royal independence, but the controversy served to elicit some expressions of opinion with a reference wider than the particular dispute. The plea of the royal advocates, Hincmar tells us, was that the king derived his office (with the aid of hereditary succession) from Divine authority and owed submission to no laws but those of God. In reply to this pretension the archbishop refuses to admit the necessity of any kingdom but the *unum regnum* which is also the "una ecclesia sub uno rege et sacerdote Christo." If any enjoy the kingly title with special reference to government of the people, they, no less than priest or prophet, will rightly forfeit their office whenever they fail to perform the duties annexed to its possession. After appealing to the Gelasian doctrine and to Scriptural and modern precedents for the submission of kings to priests, Hincmar revives an old definition of *rex* (by Isidore of Seville), as one "qui bonos in viam rectam dirigit, malos autem de via prava in viam rectam corrigit." Such an one, he says, is indeed subject to no laws but those of God, for laws are binding on the unjust, not on the just; nay, there are no *leges*, as distinct from arbitrary decrees, "nisi illae quae Dei sunt, per quem reges regnant et conditores legum iusta decernunt." As to the hereditary claim, this in itself has no peculiar sanction. Kingship has been bestowed, under Providence, in many ways, varying from immediate Divine appointment to tyrannical acquisition by force. As no one of these is outside the Divine economy, so, assuredly, the virtues of a father cannot authorise the vices of a son. Were any king exempted from the jurisdiction of a synod, or from the penalty of excommunication, the rule of Scripture and the canons against "acceptance of persons" would be broken and the integrity of Justice impaired.

From Hincmar himself, or from his contemporaries, it would be as easy to multiply similar pronouncements as it would be difficult to prove that any writers of the ninth century had a clear conception of the problem in which they were actually involved. They were too much engaged in the politics of the hour, and too little versed in philosophical thinking, to detect the gravity of their own dilemma. They could not, in point of fact, resign all secular power to the *civitas impiorum*; for the Emperor was now the authorised defender of the Church, himself not unworthy to enjoy the title of *Vicarius Dei.* They could not, on the other hand, allow that regal authority was derived from God without sacerdotal mediation; for that would have been to rend the seamless garment and to set up a double sovereignty within the kingdom of Christ. They professed, therefore, to uphold the dual authority, to render Caesarian things to Caesar and divine things to God; but how to distinguish the one from the other they did not, and could not, explain. Nor must we look for any superior insight in the minds of those who supported the royal pretensions against the sacerdotal. To declare the king emancipated from all laws but those of God has a lofty sound; but, unless it was thereby implied that the royal conscience enjoyed a special illumination, and a special commission to interpret the truths revealed to the Church, the declaration would amount in the end to very little. Kings and Emperors, in fact, were caught in the same dilemma as Popes and priests. As Catholics they could not repudiate their subjection to the law of Christ; and again, they could not (at least in the ninth century) claim for their own laws a Divine sanction with which the See of Peter had properly no concern. In a word, the perpetual hindrance to mental clearness in the great medieval controversy was simply the fact that in all their first principles and radical assumptions the two parties were perfectly agreed. Precisely for that reason, they could not, or would not, face the logical consequences of their common hypothesis. They merely lost their way, and usually their temper, in an endless series of particular conflicts, of which the divorce of Lothar, with the commentary of Hincmar, is a casual example.

The real question, whether the secular power had any place whatever in the *civitas Dei*, except as a survival of the *civitas impiorum*, was constantly evaded. To make a division of specific functions was comparatively easy. A layman could not say mass; a priest could not (or should not) wield the sword of the warrior or the sceptre of the king. Yet as soon as the argument passed from office to jurisdiction, or to any question touching the source of authority, the delineation of provinces became an almost impossible task. For if, as Hincmar protested, there were no *leges* but those of God, the authority of the civil magistrate could not be independent or final. To recognise it, within certain limits, might be highly expedient, but in essence it could not be more than a delegation from the higher authority of the Church. The conclusion demanded by these premisses it was exceedingly difficult for the Emperors to resist. They were bound to admit the inferiority of the temporal to the spiritual, and with that admission their case was as good as lost. The Popes, however, were prevented by circumstances, as well as by lack of logic, from enjoying the full advantage of their superior claim. Often reduced by lack of military force to virtual dependence on the secular arm, they damaged their position still more fatally by their method of fortifying it, and obscured their right to govern a united Christendom by insisting on the distinction between the layman and the priest.

As many writers have explained, it was common in the Middle Ages to understand by "liberty" a right of exemption from some particular jurisdiction. In accordance with this principle it was natural enough for the Church to aim at withdrawing from secular authority all persons invested with the clerical status. Two kinds of persons, two kinds of legal offence, two kinds of court. Such was the dualism that had somehow to be reconciled with the medieval belief in the unity of Christendom. Unfortunately, the result of claiming legal privileges for the clergy was to suggest at once that a large class of persons, outside one special caste, were properly amenable to civil jurisdiction. But why? Were the laity, then, not Christians? Did not they too belong, as Hincmar would say, to the *regium genus*? And then the issue was further confounded by the distinction between two kinds of offence or case. Upon certain matters (*e.g.* marriage) the Church demanded sole jurisdiction over all persons, lay or clerical; while others were allowed to be within the competence of civil courts. Was it, then, to be inferred that some departments of human life, involving questions of right and wrong, were beyond the scope of the law of God? The full development of these perplexities does not belong to the age of Hincmar. Yet all are latent in the character of his argument, and all arise from the perpetual vacillation of medieval thinkers between two traditions of almost equal authority, one pointing to the condemnation of all secular power as an invention of the devil, the other towards unqualified submission to civil rule, on the ground that all authority must in some way descend from God. To find a middle course between these extreme opinions was the problem that grew at once more urgent and more insoluble as the conception of Christendom became better defined.

One theoretical compromise, relating to government in general and to many social institutions, can be traced to both sacred and secular origins. As the Biblical narrative began with the Garden of Eden, so did the Pagan poets look back to a golden age of innocence, when there was no private property, no violence, no injustice, and therefore no demand for the strong arm of the law. Pagan philosophers, too, could be quoted in favour of the doctrine that government was, at best, a necessary evil, and Justice a convention, whether devised by the few for the oppression of the many or, on the contrary, embraced by the many for protection against the few. Augustine's notorious question, "remota iustitia, quid sunt regna nisi magna latrocinia?" is an echo of ancient philosophy which barely misses the cynical innuendo that the function of government is to authorise robbery in the name of the law. By reserving that criticism for the *civitas impiorum* he had left it open for his successors to believe that the true Justice could be established under the patronage of Christian kings. Yet along with this later view there persisted the tradition that even the best of human institutions were only remedies for sin. The need of the remedies being admitted, many incidental evils were then to be tolerated, on the ground that maladies rooted in the structure of the body politic could not be eradicated without danger to the whole. The failure to abolish slavery, for example, has astonished and incensed many critics of the Church only because they have lost touch with the Christian point of view. As long as the Church was regarded as a *societas peregrina*, the slave was sufficiently emancipated by conversion to the faith. The only liberty that counted for happiness was then in his possession; his status under earthly dominion was but a passing affliction to be cheerfully endured. It is true, however, that the difficulty of tolerating slavery was magnified in proportion as the *civitas impiorum* theory ceased to be tenable. The Christian conscience was plainly troubled by this degradation of human beings, and one writer of the ninth century, Smaragdus, goes so far as to beg the Emperor to forbid enslavement within his realm, and demands that Christians should give liberty to their slaves. As a rule, however, this and other evils were regarded as bound up with the general nature of the social fabric. Ideally, the condition of the slave was wrong, but so was all inequality, economic or social. To jump from these academic premisses to revolution or communism would have been at least as hasty in the Middle Ages as now.

A casual survey of medieval literature might indeed give the wholly false impression that doctrines familiar in modern revolutionary propaganda were commonly held by the intellectual class. Aristotle's penetrating analysis of the term "nature" fell into disregard at an early date, and with it his questionable defence of the "natural slave." The "natural" condition of man, no longer understood as an ideal to be realised only in the highest form of community, was taken to mean the original manner of life, before positive law and convention had done their deadly work. Hence the way was opened for those apparently immortal commonplaces which assert the natural equality and liberty of mankind. "Omnes namque homines natura aequales sumus," says St Gregory, and Ulpian announces the same truth in the more technical phrase, "quod ad ius naturale attinet, omnes homines aequales sunt." This alleged equality was not, in fact, a Christian discovery, but it could easily be interpreted in a specially Christian sense. The slave was as well qualified for salvation as his master, nor was it possible to pretend that the social and economic gradations of human society would be recognised in the kingdom of heaven. The question was, however, whether the doctrine of spiritual equality was to be understood as a solvent of the established social order, or merely as a reminder to Christians that worldly advantages were less precious than the treasure laid up in heaven. The answer was seldom, if ever, in doubt. When writers of the ninth century, like Jonas of Orleans and Agobard of Lyons, revive the patristic declaration of liberty; or when the legal renaissance of the eleventh or twelfth centuries brings the *ius naturale* once more into prominence, we may reasonably look for certain ethical consequences, such as the better treatment of slaves and dependants, but to anticipate anything like political revolution is totally to misapprehend the point.

The same caution must be observed in interpreting medieval utterances about the institution of private property. The influence of doctrines belonging to Jurisprudence was here predominant, and much depended upon the conception of the *ius naturale* and its relation to other kinds of *ius*. Ulpian had extended this "natural right" to other animals besides men, while Gaius, by restricting the term to human life, had come near to identifying it with *ius gentium*. A reflection of this difference perhaps affected the medieval discussions of property. If natural right belonged to all animals, a certain rough mode of *possessio* would indeed be a natural institution, but there could be no opening for private property in the ordinary human sense. Hence the assertion that in the state of nature all things were common could have no political significance whatever. On the other hand, when *ius naturale* was taken to mean the rules or customs dictated by reason, to declare that private property was, or was not, thus authorised might be to open a dispute of genuine importance. In the Middle Ages, however, there was so much vagueness about *ius naturale*, and so much agreement in the sanction of property by the *ius gentium*, that the doctrine of an original communism had only the same kind of academic status as the similar doctrine of an original equality. Isidore of Seville, whose juristic maxims were always influential, had placed *communis omnium possessio* under the head of *ius naturale*. The phrase is rather ambiguous, but it was usually understood in the communistic sense, and (without pretending even to summarise the evidence) we may say with tolerable accuracy that this was the prevalent medieval opinion. Nevertheless, it would be a mere blunder to infer that there was any taste for communism, or any inclination to condemn private property as immoral.

For a clear and considered verdict on the whole question it may be convenient to digress for a moment from the earlier Middle Ages to the more mature thought of St Thomas Aquinas[1]. After a general division of *ius* into *naturale* and *positivum*, Aquinas explicitly follows Ulpian in his definition of *ius naturale*, with the result that *ius gentium* is to be regarded as one species of *ius positivum*, though it is none the less "naturale homini secundum rationem naturalem." In this way he finds it possible to reconcile Aristotle's theory of the natural slave with the common doctrine that slavery was created by the *ius gentium*. As to property, the only "natural" possession of things is seen in the dominion of man over other creatures, which does not involve any *distinctio possessionum*. The right of appropriation is established by the *ius gentium*, and for excellent reasons. It is not even opposed to the *ius naturale*, "sed iuri naturali superadditur per adinventionem rationis humanae." In a word, property is rational, and whatever is rational is natural and right for man. Aquinas makes, however, a valuable distinction between the legal and the ethical aspect of the case. The *potestas procurandi et dispensandi* is secured to individuals by law, but the *usus* of wealth should not be regarded as private; for a man should be ready to communicate what he has for assisting the needs of others. In this doctrine we find the clue to the real position of the medieval Church. The treatment of the slave and the use of private property were ethical questions, and the doctrine of natural equality, in social status or wealth, was a reminder of certain ethical duties. Only when the Christian attitude was giving way to secularism did it become possible to translate the same doctrine into an instrument of political revolution.

On the whole, then, we are obliged to conclude that the inclination to look back to an age of innocence, or a state of nature, when coercive government and social institutions were not yet required, contributed little or nothing to a solution of the general problem relating to the secular power. At first sight there is a great difference between regarding the power of rulers as a natural invention of reason and denouncing it as a consequence of sin. Yet even in theory the two views were compatible, and in either case the practical application was obscure. In the first century of the revived Empire ecclesiastical writers had good reason to extol the greatness of the royal office. With sincere conviction men like Sedulius Sestus and Smaragdus urge the Emperor to remember that he is *Vicarius Dei*, that his business is to act *pro vice Christi*, that he must scrutinise the conduct of all classes, and admonish all who fail in their Christian duty. Rebellion against his authority is freely condemned;

[1] *Summa Theol.*, *Secunda Secundae*, LVII, 3, LXVI, 2, *Prima Secundae*, XCIV, 5 ad 3.

a voice in ecclesiastical matters, such as the appointment of bishops, is allowed him; it is not impossible that he may even be called upon to reprove a Pope. Nevertheless, the Gelasian doctrine is always in the background. The Emperor is constantly warned to beware of meddling with what does not concern him and to remember his own responsibility to the Church. Obscured though it often was by the language employed, the true movement of thought was always towards the high sacerdotal position. The Emperor was God's representative precisely because, and in so far as, he was the champion and servant of the Church. An attempt to extricate him from that subservience, without loss of his Christian character, was eventually made, but not by the amiable clergymen of the ninth century, who called him *Vicarius Dei* because they desired him to act as the sword of the Church.

While there was no continuous development of political theory in the ninth and following centuries, the main problem was further elaborated in two ways, by active collisions between Popes and Princes and by certain intellectual events. Our interest being confined to theory, the details of the political struggles can be omitted, but we must examine, first, the legal conceptions formulated by civil lawyers and canonists, secondly, the revival of philosophy, which culminated in the recovery of Aristotle's writings.

Much of the work accomplished by the medieval jurists is interesting only or chiefly to lawyers, and many of the disturbances arising out of the conflict of Roman with other usage were more important in their bearing on national development than in their theoretical aspect. A general survey of the philosophical principles bound up with the legal renaissance of the eleventh and twelfth centuries reveals, however, one remarkable distinction between the medieval and the modern point of view. For whereas the modern democrat is prepared to respect a law in so far as he can regard himself as its author, medieval obedience was founded on the opposite sentiment, that laws were respectable in so far as they were not made by man. And here once more there was a broad agreement in principle between the sacred and the secular tradition. The Church looked back to a Law of God which the Saviour had come not to destroy but to fulfil. The *lex nova* had abolished the ceremonial parts of the *lex vetus*, but had preserved the moral precepts as a necessary preface to the more spiritual teaching of the Gospel. In course of time the Scriptures had been supplemented by the decisions of Councils and Popes and by the growth of a body of custom, authoritative, not because it was human convention, but because it was believed to represent the inspiration of the Church. The *Corpus Iuris* could not, indeed, lay claim to so exalted a sanction as this, but it was permeated by the belief that Justice was an eternal fact, and that human law owed its moral validity to its derivation from a Law of Nature binding, as Kant would say, on all rational beings. Whatever differences of opinion there were about the meaning of *ius naturale*, it certainly pointed to the existence of a Justice neither made by man nor alterable by his arbitrary will. The political consequences, perhaps, were somewhat ambiguous. For if the authority of rulers was often strengthened by the belief that law was, or might be, much more than a forcible imposition, it was weakened, on the contrary, whenever there was room for the contention that positive law was discordant with natural. Among lawyers this difficulty took shape in disputes upon the relation of *aequitas* to *lex*; in the wider field of politics it might open the way for rebellion, tyrannicide, or any other excursion of conscience. Apart, however, from the risk of those extravagances, the effect of belief in an authoritative law beyond human caprice was beneficial as a restraint on the absolutism which could so easily be extracted from the maxim, *princeps legibus solutus*, by lawyers favourable to the imperial pretensions. The position of the Emperor, as we shall see, was by no means free from ambiguity, but it will be convenient to glance first at the other great legal system which grew up side by side with the renewed enthusiasm for civil law.

The progressive stages in the organisation of Canon Law, and the labours of many eminent scholars, such as Ivo of Chartres, Burchard of Worms, and Cardinal Deusdedit, we are compelled to pass over. As regards the general conceptions of law which affected political theory, it is not unfair to take the systematic work of Gratian as representative of the main tradition. The *Decretum*, composed about the middle of the twelfth century, was not issued under authority, but its later embodiment in the *Corpus Iuris Canonici* is a testimony to its peculiar importance. In estimating the quality of Gratian's teaching we have to beware of attributing his unquestionable support of papal and ecclesiastical claims to any radical difference in principle from the civil lawyers. The sources of his legal conceptions were, and could be, none other than Ulpian, Gaius, and whatever masters of Jurisprudence had supplied the theoretical foundations of Justinian's stupendous work. More directly, no doubt, he often draws upon the *Etymologies* of Isidore of Seville. But while the exact relation of Isidore to the great Pagan jurists is uncertain, his general acceptance of their principles is not doubtful. Here, as always, nothing can be more misleading than to assume that Christian writers are bound to differ from Pagan in their legal and moral conceptions. On the contrary, the guiding thread to the main line of thought in the Middle Ages is the passage in the Epistle to the Romans[1] which teaches that the Gentiles, though they did not enjoy the explicit revelation granted to the Jews, yet did by nature the things that were after the Law. Whether or no St Paul actually derived this thought from Stoic teachers, it needs no argument to prove its close affinity to the notion of the *ius naturale*. What Christian writers did (though, once more, there were Pagan antecedents) was to emphasise the connexion or identity of the Law of

[1] Romans, ii, 14.

Nature with the Law of God. The appearance of the "canon" as a special kind of law not recognised by pre-Christian jurisprudence is a new complication, which does not, however, involve any radical alteration in the philosophical principles belonging to the legal tradition.

"Ius naturae," we read at the opening of the *Decretum*, "est quod in lege et evangelio continetur"; or, in the words of Isidore, "divinae leges natura, humanae moribus constant." Gratian finds, however, that the distinction between divine and human law cannot be accurately represented by *fas* and *ius*; for *ius* contains many species, and the chief of these, the *ius naturae*, is in fact the *lex divina.* The mention of *evangelium*, we must notice, does not imply the whole revelation of the Gospel. The *ius naturale* contains only the general precepts of morality, revealed in some measure to all men, more explicitly (as in the Decalogue) to the Jews, and finally, in a more spiritual form, to the disciples of Christ. "Thou shalt love thy neighbour as thyself" is a brief summary of the whole. On this general hypothesis, Gratian proceeds, like any other lawyer, to discuss the meaning of *ius naturale*, *ius gentium*, and *ius civile*; of *lex* (defined as *constitutio scripta*) and *consuetudo*, with various disputable questions arising out of their mutual relation. In the third *Distinctio* he arrives at the "canon," and defines it as *constitutio ecclesiastica*, to be distinguished from *constitutio civilis.* But while the recognition of ecclesiastical laws, with the whole hypothesis of the Church behind them, places Gratian and all the Decretalists in a historical atmosphere unknown to Pagan lawyers, it does not cut them adrift from the system formulated under the Christian authority of Justinian; much less does it imply their invention of a new philosophy of Jurisprudence. There was, in fact, no such new philosophy; there was only a renewed and increased attention to the divine origin and sanction of natural law.

The canonists are often remarkably elusive at the very point where we require precise instruction. For what, after all, is the place of the canons in the great hierarchy of laws? Are they definitely divine or human, or somehow in a class by themselves? Had it been Gratian's intention to mark, by the distinction between divine and human law, the exact frontier between ecclesiastical and secular jurisdiction; had he, in other words, identified the divine law with the canons, the position would have been comparatively simple. But clearly he intended nothing of the kind. The divine law, which means in effect the *ius naturale*, is the common source of all laws, ecclesiastical or secular, and the common test of their validity. True, it is in the power of man to make laws which fail to satisfy the test, and in that case they cannot claim obedience. But the *ius gentium* (assuredly a part of "human" law) is a derivation from the *ius naturale*, while the *ius civile*, though more variable, is not necessarily opposed to it. And again, the canons, whenever they go beyond the plainest rules of Scripture, are the work of man, and therefore liable to deviation from the *ius naturale.* Hence Gratian finds it necessary to say (under the eleventh canon of the ninth *Distinctio*), "constitutiones ergo vel ecclesiasticae vel seculares, si naturali iuri contrariae probantur, penitus sunt excludendae." In other words, a canon, no less than a secular law, may fail in its claim to the superior sanction.

Briefly, then, the position is this. The *ius naturale* is divine, and therefore unalterable. The only exception is that the ceremonial directions of the *lex vetus* are now to be taken as *mistica* and to be interpreted *secundum moralem intelligentiam.* From the moral precepts of the natural law all human laws are, or ought to be, derived. Of these laws some are adapted to secular, others to ecclesiastical purposes, and for both the art of interpreting the divine injunctions is required. The canons, in Gratian's opinion, are superior in authority to secular laws, not only because they deal with spiritual matters, but because the gift of authoritative interpretation belongs to the Church. Princes, in fact, may err, but Rome does not. Nevertheless, the *ius gentium,* and also such part of the *ius civile* as is not opposed to the *ius naturale,* should command human obedience, and for the same ultimate reason as the canons, namely, because the divine or natural law is binding upon all. It is, therefore, erroneous to identify Canon Law with the *lex divina,* and equally erroneous to suppose that secular laws can boast no more than a human sanction. The frequent conflict between the two jurisdictions was not a conflict of first principles; it arose out of the application of common principles to particular cases. There was only one philosophy of Jurisprudence, acknowledged and professed by civilians and canonists alike. In this way it becomes intelligible that Canon Law, as such, should have no distinctive place even in the masterly exposition of the nature and species of law by Thomas Aquinas. His treatment of the subject[1] is far superior in breadth, lucidity, and precision to anything produced by the lawyers, but in all his minute analysis of the laws derived in successive gradations from the original *lex aeterna* there is no mention of Canon Law.

We must now return to another aspect of the political theory connected with the revival of Roman law. The old republican tradition, that laws could be made, and the *imperium* conferred, by the people alone by no means perished with the birth of the Empire. The conservatism of lawyers, often backed by the Emperors themselves, had made it possible to infer from the *Corpus Iuris* that sovereignty belonged of right to the people, and that the power of the Emperor, however absolute in practice, was only the power of a representative person. What was really the opinion of the ancient jurists we need not stay to enquire. It is enough that the same question was revived in the Middle Ages, with consequences not to be disregarded because of the artificial tone of the arguments employed. In the first epoch of the legal renaissance an attempt was made to enlist the different schools on opposite sides. Ravenna having developed the case against Gregory VII, the great

[1] *Summa Theologica, Prima Secundae,* XC–CVIII.

Matilda proposed to use the learning of Bologna on behalf of the Pope. The lawyers, however, were not content to be thus divided into camps of partisans. Their own political opinions could not be smothered, and their own scientific interest in their subject conduced to independence. If, on the whole, the study of Justinian was bound to magnify the Emperor at the expense of the Pope, the same study could not fail to renew the old difficulties about the *populus Romanus.* The suggestion of popular sovereignty, once made, was full of possibilities. It could be used by the peoples over whom the Emperor actually reigned, or it could be conveniently adapted by ecclesiastics to their special business of depreciating the imperial rights. We have in any case to disengage a view of "the people" which belonged to the future from academic reminiscences of the past.

Irnerius and other medieval lawyers—as a high authority has told us—"reason as if the Lord Justinian was still holding sway over Italy." The same artificiality of language and reasoning is yet more remarkable in all that concerns the position of the people. For if the Roman Emperor in the Middle Ages was something of a fiction, the *populus Romanus* was a myth. Theoretically the name might denote anything from the whole assemblage of peoples within the unity of *latinitas* to the degenerate inhabitants of Rome, who occasionally amused themselves with reviving the Senate and other republican dreams. In effect it meant nothing at all, or nothing that had any genuine connexion with Rome. The arguments of lawyers on constitutional questions affecting the Emperor owed their importance, not to the shadowy *populus Romanus*, but to the existence of similar questions in a practical form among the various peoples of Europe. The feudal system and the whole Teutonic tradition of kingship were opposed to absolutism. The divine right of dynasties to govern, and to behave as they pleased, was not a medieval idea. On the other hand, the growth of the modern national State depended largely on the ability of kings to establish a central government, with a jurisdiction prevailing over minor lordship and special immunities. Hence theoretical disputes, ostensibly relating to the *populus Romanus*, could receive a new interpretation from the actual conditions of medieval life. And although the people's claim to sovereignty might in the end be found to conflict with the notion of deriving all authority from a superhuman law, the two suggestions united to delay the appearance of the absolute sovereign, whose ominous figure was afterwards depicted by the master hand of Hobbes.

However ancient, however momentous in its effects, had been the alliance of law with philosophy, it had never been the duty of lawyers to generate political theories, nor even, perhaps, to analyse the whole implication of the philosophical conceptions most serviceable to Jurisprudence. While it would scarcely be fair to hold Ulpian and Gaius responsible for medieval confusions of mind, it is true that medieval writers before the thirteenth century suffered greatly from lack of acquaintance with a political philosophy detached from legal associations. From the ninth century to the twelfth, philosophers were mainly interested in the development of dialectic and in the relation of reason to faith. Canon Law itself —with *concordantia discordantium canonum* as its goal—belongs at least as much to the history of dialectical method as to the history of political science. Meanwhile the masterpieces of ancient thought, the *Republic*, the *Laws*, and the *Politics*, were unknown except through the fragmentary evidence of Latin authors. Even the Arabic tradition, when it began to affect the Latin world, failed to bring fresh material. For the Muslim philosophers were not politically minded, and the *Politics* remained unknown to Paris and Oxford until it was translated from the Greek by William of Moerbeke about the year 1260. In the preceding century, however, we find one writer, John of Salisbury, whose political doctrines it is profitable to examine.

Devout Christian and loyal ecclesiastic as he was, John was also in some sense a sceptic. No man was better versed in the politics and the culture of his day; few held stronger opinions upon certain disputed questions, or expressed them with greater decision. Yet he never was afraid to criticise what he revered, and never imagined that the rights of Pope and Emperor, the destinies of peoples and kings, could be determined by the formalities of logic and law. It is not that he escapes from the legal atmosphere, or disdains the learning of his friend Placentinus; but when we encounter in the *Policraticus* any of the familiar legal arguments, we do at least observe them in contact with other ideas, and feel that they have passed through the mind of one who could frame the question, "quid sit salus universalis et publica," in the spirit of a philosophical observer of life. Without being a profound or original thinker, John of Salisbury was capable of critical reflection on the mutual support of various intellectual disciplines, the relation of knowledge to conduct, and the characteristics of good government, whether exercised by layman or priest. *Agnitio veritatis cultusque virtutis* is his brief description of the road to public and private welfare. He has heard of the Socratic demand for philosopher-kings, and he quotes with high approval the saying, "rex illiteratus est quasi asinus coronatus."

Among his political doctrines two are prominent, the distinction of the legitimate *princeps* from the *tyrannus*, and the subordination of imperial to sacerdotal authority. "Tyrannum occidere non modo licitum est sed aequum et iustum"[1] is a remarkable declaration in the mouth of one who, far from commending fanaticism, is blessed with a cool and judicial temper. We need not discuss the ethics of tyrannicide, but we must credit John of Salisbury with the sincere conviction that a real danger to the public weal was to be apprehended from the attempt to set the monarch above the law. This unwarrantable claim he meets by

[1] *Policraticus,* III, 15, cf. VIII, 20.

exalting to the utmost the reverence due to the legitimate Prince. "Est ergo, ut eum plerique definiunt, princeps potestas publica et in terris quaedam divinae maiestatis imago. Qui ergo resistit potestati, Dei ordinationi resistit."[1] Yet the right to occupy this sublime position depends, to John of Salisbury's mind, upon the further contention, that the *princeps* differs from the *tyrannus* simply because he does respect the law. To be more precise, the supreme authority belongs to *aequitas*, and of this Equity or Justice the interpreter is *lex*. The assertion that the Prince is *legis nexibus absolutus* can be accepted, therefore, only as meaning that the Prince should be one "qui non timore poenae sed amore iustitiae aequitatem colat." Only if he acts always as "publicae utilitatis minister et aequitatis servus" can his will be said to have the vigour of law; for no man is *legibus solutus* as regards the laws of God.

Thus far, indeed, John does not in principle go beyond the doctrine acknowledged by civil lawyers. He takes a more decisive step when he proceeds to declare that the whole authority of the Prince is received from the Church. "Hunc ergo gladium (the sword of Justice as distinct from the sword of blood) de manu Ecclesiae accipit princeps"; and again, as though to remove all doubts about the inferiority of temporal power, "est ergo princeps sacerdotii quidem minister, et qui sacrorum officiorum illam partem exercet quae sacerdotii manibus videtur indigna." The glory of the Emperor thus fades away into a pale reflection. To be the image of the Divine Majesty is well enough, but when it rests with another human being to confer or withhold that image the pride of the representative is seriously abated. It follows, too, that John will not allow the validity of any claim to rule by hereditary right or by popular acclamation. At the most these are constitutional devices agreeable to custom. The bestowal and transference of royal power remains a Divine prerogative, of which the appointment of Joshua by Moses is a typical illustration. On that occasion the people were invited to be present, but the act of ordaining a leader was performed only by God's representative. "Hic autem plane nulla est populi acclamatio, nulla consanguinitatis ratio, nulla propinquitatis habita contemplatio est."[2] When a dynasty is favoured by God, it is wrong to set up a rival; but that favour will not be continued if kings persist in error; they have no hereditary right to do wrong.

In this passage, and through a large part of the fifth and sixth books of the *Policraticus*, John of Salisbury writes under the influence of a work which he calls the *Institutio Traiani*, and which he supposes to have been sent to Trajan by Plutarch. From this source he draws a rather elaborate comparison of the body politic to the human body, and enlarges upon the duties and needs of various classes in the State.[3] The armed hand is the soldier, the unarmed is the magistrate, the feet are the tillers of the soil

[1] *Policraticus*, IV, 1–4. The text at the close is from Romans xiii, 2.

[2] *Ib.* V, 6.

[3] *Ib.* VI, 1–8.

and all kinds of craftsmen. Assuming the necessity of war, John of Salisbury is at pains to present a lofty picture of the soldier's office and duty. The two things that make a soldier are *electio* and *iuramentum.* Without these he is an enemy of the law; with them he is ordained to his own kind of service as truly as the priest to his. The allotted function of the soldier is to guard the Church, to venerate the priesthood, to protect the poor from injury, to shed his own blood for his brethren, and, if necessary, to lay down his life on their behalf. In a later chapter, John insists on the importance of the humbler classes, the *pedes reipublicae,* whose harmonious co-operation with the higher members is essential to the general health. When the people is depressed and afflicted, the Prince, he says, is suffering from the gout![1]

Throughout this part of his book John of Salisbury reveals himself in the character of an Englishman with genuine national feeling and with a keen eye for the dangers and needs of his country. With the same clearness of vision he admits the harm done by clerical rapacity, and tells us how frankly he once expressed to his friend Hadrian IV the common opinion that the Roman Church was *noverca* rather than *mater* to her children. The Pope, it seems, was delighted with his candid friend, but defended the clergy by the fable of the stomach and the other members of the body. The stomach, he said, is voracious but it diffuses nourishment throughout the other organs: "tale est, frater, si recte attendas, in corpore reipublicae, ubi, licet plurimum appetat magistratus, non tam sibi quam aliis coacervat."[2] The moral, that we must put up with the failings of our governors, John is on the whole prepared to accept. Enough has been said, perhaps, to prove that men of culture, like John of Salisbury and his friends, were ready to discuss political problems in a liberal spirit without restricting themselves overmuch to the legal point of view. More than this it is impossible to claim for the *Policraticus.* There is no striking novelty in material or method, and certainly no departure from the ecclesiastical view of the State. The question is, however, whether it was possible, unless by a revolt against the whole medieval conception of the Church, to construct a case for a really independent secular power. The most celebrated attempt to do so was made by Dante at the very end of the period covered by this chapter, and his treatise on Monarchy may fairly be taken as a summary of the best arguments that could be advanced on the imperial side.

Dante has puzzled his commentators, and not without reason, by his statement, on the first page of the *Monarchia,* that the theory of temporal monarchy is *ab omnibus intentata.* We must remember, however, that he could not in any case have avoided discussion of many familiar arguments, especially those habitually advanced on the papal side. There was, after all, a real novelty in the attempt to construct a theoretical defence of the Empire on the basis of a philosophical survey of human life. With all its

[1] *Policraticus,* VI, 20. [2] *Ib.* VI, 24.

limitations, the *Monarchia* belongs to the same class of literature as the *Politics*, the *Leviathan*, or the *Contrat Social*; and that is more, probably, than could be asserted of any other work composed between the fifth century and the middle of the thirteenth. How far Dante supposed himself to be borrowing new weapons from Aristotle it is difficult to say. References to the *Politics* and other works are numerous, and to Dante it was, presumably, less obvious than to ourselves that Aristotle would have repudiated very warmly the ideal of a Monarch with universal jurisdiction. The belief that the City State was the apex of human development was naturally incredible to medieval writers. Already in St Augustine we hear of a progression from *domus* and *urbs* to *orbis*, and now Dante, with greater detail, declares that the *propria operatio humanae universitatis* cannot be realised in *domus*, in *vicinia*, in *civitas*, or in any *regnum particulare*, but only in the *Monarchia* or *Imperium* to which no territorial or legal bounds are prescribed. If his arguments, in the first book, for perfect unity or government, on the model of the Divine Monarchy, are too logical to convince modern readers, that is chiefly because we have abandoned the hypothesis from which Dante set out. Before the publication of any catholic philosophy or religion, good reason for a plurality of States could be given. And again, the modern acceptance of plurality has grown ever more intelligible in proportion to the increasing secularisation of the State. But in the age of Dante, when profession of a certain creed was admittedly the supreme political bond, the argument for a simple Christian commonwealth, as against a multiplicity of independent units, was difficult to resist. It was not there that the medieval difficulty lay, but rather in the question whether the Catholic unity of government was not adequately secured by the organisation and spiritual sovereignty of the Church.

Thus when the three disputable problems of the *Monarchia* are propounded—whether Temporal Monarchy is necessary for human welfare, whether the Roman people has acquired the Monarchy *de iure*, and whether the monarchical authority depends immediately upon God, or mediately upon some Vicar of His—the first need not be contentious, the second is (in Dante's time) comparatively simple, but the third is the real ground of conflict. As an illustration of medieval thought, and of Dante's mind in particular, the second book is, however, at least as important as the third. The conception of history there unfolded differs profoundly from Augustine's. The *civitas impiorum* has vanished, and the Romans, from the earliest dawn of their history, are presented as a chosen people, not indeed in the manner of the Jews, but as the "populus ad imperandum ordinatus a natura," predestined by the Divine Will to win and hold the palm of victory which a Ninus, a Cyrus, or an Alexander had snatched for a little while. In the medieval style Dante summons Virgil and other poets to appear as historical witnesses. Aeneas is revealed as the man of destiny, who unites in his lineage the ancestral claims of all the continents and carries the imperial heritage to Rome. The providential career of the sacred city, adorned with miracles and wondrous deeds, is then traced through republican days to the fuller manifestation of the Empire, and Dante (though he never could forgive Brutus and Cassius) is as ready to applaud the Cato who gave his life for liberty as the Caesar who ordained the sacrifice and appointed the victim. For later chapters of the story, when Constantine *si fece Greco* and the Roman eagle flew to the eastern mountains, there to linger awhile before returning to its proper home, we have to go to the vivid narrative of *Paradiso VI.* In the *Monarchia* the supreme historical moment is reached in the reign of Augustus, when universal peace is established and the Saviour is born.

The evidence of history Dante supplements by various legal arguments, including the maxim, "quod per duellum acquiritur de iure acquiritur," and culminating in the strange contention that the sin of Adam could not have been expiated in the person of Christ unless Pilate had represented the legitimate jurisdiction of Rome over the entire human race. We have seen already how the study of Civil Law had revived the pretensions of the *populus Romanus*, without furnishing any definition of that term which could hold good in the medieval world. The whole of Dante's plea for the monarchical rights of Rome is steeped in the same confusion. What the *populus Romanus* might happen to be, and where it could be found in the thirteenth century, he never offers to explain. Nor does he attempt to reconcile his real enthusiasm for Italy as a nation with his pressing invitation to a foreigner to take possession of the imperial throne. Precedents for a Roman Emperor who was not a Roman could indeed have been found in abundance, but Dante is not influenced by these. He moves always in the strange world of his imagination, stored with antique and poetical figures, where visions of the past and of the future combine to obscure his insight into present affairs.

When finally Dante addresses himself to the great controversy of the day, he dismisses with contempt the class of opponents whose motive is merely *cupiditas*, and passes on to the *Decretalistae.* The authority of the canons, he says, is venerable, but their professional exponents are "Theologiae ac Philosophiae cuiuslibet inscii et expertes." Their motto is *traditiones Ecclesiae fidei fundamentum*, but the relative importance of the Scriptures, the Church, the Councils, and the Decretals, they do not understand. There remains, then, only the class of men who are moved by an honest zeal for the Power of the Keys. These Dante treats with consideration, giving, on the whole, a fair account of their arguments, and never lapsing into disrespect for the spiritual supremacy of the Pope. It is remarkable, too, that he reserves for the Pope the title of *Vicarius Dei* or *Vicarius Christi*, and does not imitate the earlier writers who had described in those terms the office of the Emperor. His object is only to prove that Pope and Emperor have each their peculiar *ratio*; that each enjoys supremacy, but for different ends, which must not be confused.

The arguments based on metaphors and allegorical interpretations it is perhaps superfluous now to discuss. We notice, however, that Dante deals, in this connexion, very freely with the character and position of St Peter, and there are other incidental points of interest, such as the statement that both *regimina*, the spiritual and the temporal, are *remedia contra infirmitatem peccati*, necessitated only by the lapse from original innocence. Common as this opinion was—at least as regards temporal dominion—it is curious to find it combined with a professedly Aristotelian account of the origin of the State. From allegory Dante passes to history, and attacks the arguments drawn from the reputed Donation of Constantine. "Constantinus alienare non poterat Imperium," he says, "nec Ecclesia recipere." The foundation of the Church is Christ, of the Empire *ius humanum*. The exact sense of *ius humanum* he does not define, but he adds that *iurisdictio* is always prior to the *iudex*, whence it follows that the Emperor had no power to abrogate any of the inherent rights. Moreover, the Church could not have accepted the Donation, because she is forbidden to possess silver and gold. The Emperor could assign material goods *in patrocinium Ecclesiae*, but even so the Pope would not possess them; he would only have the privilege of dispensing them for the benefit of the poor. Passing on from Constantine to Charles the Great, Dante dismisses the story that the Pope had then conferred the imperial dignity with the maxim *usurpatio iuris non facit ius*. To this he adds that historical incidents might equally well be quoted to prove the imperial right of appointing or deposing Popes.

As against the papal version of history Dante could, in fact, hold his own without difficulty, while his own suggestions, that the Empire was in some sense earlier than the Church, and that St Paul had recognised the Emperor's jurisdiction by his appeal to Caesar, could not easily be set aside. Yet there still remained the graver difficulty of constructing an argument to prove that the Emperor derived his office immediately from God. That "the kingdom was not of this world" was generally acknowledged, but why should it follow that there must also be a kingdom, occupied only with terrestrial felicity, which no Pope was empowered to give or take away? The temporal functions of government, all of them subordinate to the great imperial aim of preserving peace on earth, could surely be discharged by a layman in the interests of the *civitas Dei*, without assuming a direct appointment of the Emperor by God.

The papal case, as judged by medieval standards, was in truth too strong for most of Dante's arguments. At the close of the *Monarchia* there is, however, one passage of unusual interest, in which Dante proposes an analogy between the political problem of the two powers and the distinction of two *beatitudines*, one to be achieved by *philosophica documenta* with the moral and intellectual virtues, the other by the exercise of Faith, Hope, and Charity under the guidance of theological truth. In a general sense Dante here reflects the teaching of Aquinas, whose steadfast aim it had been to vindicate the independence of human reason without diminishing the rights of theology or dividing truth against itself. Aquinas, indeed, had no intention of opening the way for a political theory strongly opposed to his own. Yet Dante does, perhaps, succeed, by his political bias rather than by conscious criticism, in exposing a weak point in the Thomist position. For if reason was at liberty to pursue the path of science and to regulate moral conduct, a corresponding freedom in the political field might easily be demanded. The result, however, would not be to justify the imperialism of Dante, but to formulate the eventual dilemma of Christendom, that is to say, the choice between submission to papal authority and the proclamation of the secular State. For the latter alternative Dante was as little prepared as Aquinas. The effect of his division of provinces is only to reveal his imperfect foresight and, incidentally, to shew that not even a Thomas Aquinas could establish a *duplex veritatis modus* without subordinating one mode to the other. As there cannot be two finalities in the sphere of truth, so is it impossible to accept Dante's theory of the two *fines* proposed by Providence. There is only one *finis*, and in the Middle Ages no other could be recognised but the celestial *finis* proper to the *civitas Dei.*

On the papal side a mass of literature extending over many centuries displays a certain monotony of colour. The commission to St Peter, the Gelasian manifesto, and the evidence of historical examples for the ascendency of priests over kings are produced again and again; and, though the style in which Popes addressed Emperors might be modified by circumstances, all were bound to maintain in principle the subordination of temporal to spiritual power. But did this mean that the lower was itself an inferior function of the higher authority? Some care is needed here in distinguishing between two positions. The Popes might well have argued that the earthly kingdom, once recognised as a fact by Christ and the apostles, had now been finally absorbed into the spiritual realm. This was not, however, the common form of the argument. Even when all European princes were orthodox Catholics, something of Augustine's feeling about the *civitas impiorum* lingered on in the papal attitude, with the result that a definite claim to exercise temporal power in one sense could be combined with an equally definite repudiation of it in another. Gregory VII, for example, will assert without hesitation that kings are among the sheep committed to his charge, and will deny the right of any secular power to be independent of his own jurisdiction. "Quod si sancta sedes apostolica, divinitus sibi collata spirituali potestate, spiritualia decernens diiudicat, cur non et saecularia?" But though this claim is alleged by Gregory many times in various language, he does not mean that the Vicars of Christ have simply taken over the secular power as it existed in a secular world. Like their Master, they despise the "saeculare regnum unde filii saeculi tument." The very existence of that kingdom can be denounced in scathing words, as when Gregory declares that kings and potentates have their origin in ignorance of God, in blind ambition instigated by the devil. The humblest exorcist, he says, can wield a higher kind of *imperium* than any layman, though the layman be a prince.

Gregory's position is neither abnormal nor unintelligible. What he rejects is secularism; what he claims is the right of the spiritual power to exercise temporal functions as part of its business on earth. Nevertheless, the situation was embarrassing, and it was not easy to avoid some confusion of thought. The divine ordination of temporal power had somehow to be recognised. More than one inconvenient text of scripture could be quoted, and these, perhaps, could be dealt with most ingeniously by allowing the existence of a province with which ecclesiastical authority would not, as a rule, interfere. Thus when Innocent III is confronted with the apostolic commendation of obedience to rulers, he is content to admit the supremacy of the Emperor over all "qui ab eo suscipiunt temporalia," and to add that the superiority of the *pontifex* in spiritual matters is not thus diminished. It is an answer that settles nothing whatever, but it was common enough to pass as effective.

Of rather exceptional importance among papal pronouncements is the famous *Unam Sanctam* of Boniface VIII (1302). Whether it was Matthew of Aquasparta or someone else who actually penned this document, the author certainly knew his business. Boniface was prepared to style himself *Imperator*, and in the general sublimity of his pretensions he is thought to have outdone all his predecessors. To some extent this impression is due less to any real change of principle than to his concise and lucid statement of the case. Of the "two swords," for example, he writes: "uterque ergo est in potestate ecclesiae, spiritualis scilicet gladius et materialis. Sed is quidem pro ecclesia, ille vero ab ecclesia exercendus. Ille sacerdotis, is manu regum et militum, sed ad nutum et patientiam sacerdotis."[1] No summary could be more admirable, no statement of a familiar thesis more direct. But what raises the argument to an unusual level is a brief reference to first principles just before the conclusion of the Bull. The spiritual power, says Boniface, judges all and is judged of none. "Quicumque igitur huic potestati a Deo sic ordinatae resistit, Dei ordinationi resistit, nisi duo, sicut Manichaeus, fingat esse principia, quod falsum et haereticum esse iudicamus." In this allusion to Manichaeism (to which there are parallels in two or three other writers) we seem at last to arrive at the point. For unless we believe in the irreducible antagonism of two *principia*, there cannot be room for two final authori-

[1] It will be noticed how this phraseology goes back to St Bernard (*De Consideratione*, IV, 3 § 7. MPL, CLXXXII, 776), and had already appeared in a letter of Gregory IX to the Greek Patriarch Germanus (Matth. Paris, *Chron. maj.* (Rolls Series) III, 467).

ties in the government of mankind. Translated into modern language, this means that the State is either secular in essence or a minor department of the Church. Had medieval writers more frequently appreciated the force of this dilemma, we might have been spared the perusal of many arguments devoted chiefly to skilful evasion of the point. Here, too, is the answer to Dante, when he proposes to found the Empire on human right and reason, leaving the theological basis to the spiritual power.

More interesting than any official statement of the papal case is the treatise *De Regimine Principum*, of which the first book and a few chapters of the second are ascribed to Thomas Aquinas, the remainder to Ptolemy of Lucca. Taken as a loosely constructed whole, this book is remarkable for its combination of traditional points of view with anticipations of a later type of political theory. The aim of Aquinas is to set forth the advantages (together with the dangers) of monarchical government, to explain the true function of kingship, and to insist on the superiority of the sacerdotal office. He does not examine the ecumenical claims of the Empire, but discusses kingship as the best form of government for the "perfect community," which he names *civitas vel provincia*. Without disputing Aristotle's opinion, that among corrupt constitutions democracy is the most tolerable and tyranny the least, he holds to his preference for monarchy, and regards the single ruler, on the analogy of the organism, as "intra membra corporis aut cor aut caput." As to tyranny, there is a modern sound as well as an ancient reminiscence in his weighty observation, "in dominio plurium magis saepe contingit dominium tyrannicum quam ex dominio unius."[1] With equal sagacity he adds that rebellion against tyranny may cause more evils than it removes; whence he denies the right of tyrannicide to private persons and urges that only public action should be taken against corrupt rulers. The tyrant himself he admonishes with the words, "timor autem est debile fundamentum," and bids him note that even in worldly advantages he is likely to come off worse than constitutional kings.

The first duty of the king is to secure unity and peace. Should it fall to him to institute a new kingdom, the model of the Divine government is there for his imitation. In any case the functions of *gubernatio* will be his, such as the coercion of iniquity, the defence of his country against foreign enemies, the guidance of his subjects in the way of virtue, and the provision of an ample supply for their bodily needs. Ultimately, however, the mode of government depends on the *finis* of human life; and since this is "per virtuosam vitam pervenire ad fruitionem divinam," there is a special ministry, committed, not to earthly kings, but to priests, and particularly to the Successor of Peter and Vicar of Christ, to whom all kings and peoples should be subject as to Christ himself. Among the Gentiles, St Thomas allows, the subordination of priests to kings was expedient, but under the new law the *sacerdotium* is on a higher plane[2].

[1] *De Reg. Princ.* I, 5.
[2] *Ib.* I, 14.

The argument of the last three books is much more than the completion of an unfinished scheme; it is the work of an original and independent mind. In the first place, there is a notable advance on the conventional doctrine that all government is a consequence of the Fall. Making a broad distinction between *dominium politicum* and *dominium despoticum*, the author is prepared to regard tyranny as the fruit of corruption, but civic order and political government (briefly defined as *dominium plurium*) would have existed, he says, in the state of innocence, because men are naturally unequal, and therefore require authoritative direction[1]. All the Aristotelian reasons for the genesis of the State can thus be accepted, and Scriptural evidence is ingeniously adapted to the same purpose. Still more instructive is the handling of St Augustine. For while the influence of the *De Civitate Dei* is often conspicuous, the testimony from that source is modified just enough to alter its colour, as for example in reference to the story of Cain. Augustine had used this to prove that the earthly *civitas* was born of iniquity, but Ptolemy, without palliating the guilt of the first murderer, clearly acquits him of bad motives in founding the State, and takes his act as an illustration of the thesis that only in a *civitas* can man live a decent life[2]. In a word, Ptolemy is a genuine Aristotelian—far more so than Dante—and he barely conceals his contempt for the old commonplaces about the primitive innocence and equality of men, and their ability to dispense with subjection to rulers.

In his further exposition of the two kinds of dominion Ptolemy is more (or less) than Aristotelian; he comes near to reminding us, now of Hobbes, now of Machiavelli. He resembles Hobbes because, without reading too much between the lines, we can guess that he thinks lightly of the antithesis between the tyrant and the king. He does, indeed, explain the distinction in the manner of the *Politics*, and he understands the common dread of despotic power. Nevertheless, the true antithesis for him is *despoticum* and *politicum*, and when *regale* is offered as a third alternative, he is ready to point out that kings subject to constitutional restrictions properly fall under the head of *dominicum politicum*[2]. A limited monarch, in fact, is not the sovereign. If, then, the only vital distinction is between absolute sovereignty and administration controlled by law, which does Ptolemy himself really prefer? He balances the arguments with tolerable fairness, and has no academic preference for either. As a theologian he is influenced by the example of the Divine Monarchy, but in the main he treats the problem as human and believes that the style of government should vary in accordance with the natural disposition and historical traditions of various peoples. Disposition, he thinks, depends upon climate and physical causes. Certain parts of the world have always been *aptae ad servitutem*, others *aptae ad libertatem*. Among the peoples capable of liberty, at least in their earlier days, were the Romans, and

[1] *De Reg. Princ.* III, 9. [2] *Ib.* IV, 2, 3. [3] *Ib.* IV, 1.

therefore the kings were expelled. On the other hand, tyrants are brought forth by the habit of insubordination: "interdum enim, dum populus non cognoscit beneficium boni regiminis, expedit exercere tyrannides quia etiam hae sunt instrumentum divinae iustitiae: unde et quaedam insulae et provinciae secundum quod historiae narrant, semper habent tyrannos propter malitiam populi, quia aliter nisi in virga ferrea regi non possunt."[1] Here we have an interesting combination of old elements with new. For if the thought of the tyrant as an instrument of Divine Justice carries us back to the patristic tradition, the sentiment of the passage as a whole would be not out of place in the *Prince*.

The same appreciation of varying circumstances is displayed in Ptolemy's distinction between *civitas* and *provincia*. The constitutional polity admired by Aristotle is suitable, he says, to *civitates* (cities), "ut in partibus Italiae maxime videmus," but the larger *provinciae* require royal government; an historical judgment which he qualifies, however, by the admission that republican Rome, and also some modern cities, have succeeded in governing provinces in the "political" style. Machiavellian, again, is his reflection on the character of ministers, which must, he says, conform to the character of the State—"unde regimen politicum ministros requirit secundum qualitatem politiae. Propter quod hodie in Italia sunt mercenarii, sicut et domini; et ideo agunt sicut mercede conducti, non ad utilitatem subditorum sed ad lucrum suum, praestituentes in mercede finem."[2] On the whole it would appear that Ptolemy is sceptical about the advantages of constitutional government. Legal restriction is good for inferior rulers, and laws (here he quotes Cicero) deduce their authority from the *ius divinum* by way of the *ius naturae*. Yet the rigidity of laws is their weakness, and when the *prudentia principis* is not free to amend them, human government thus far fails to imitate the divine.

Up to this point Ptolemy has left untouched the relation of spiritual to temporal power. His remarkable theory of the Papacy and the Empire is preceded by a recognition of *cultus divinus* as a function of kingship, and by a declaration that the king is a Vicegerent of God on earth, whose religious character is proved by the anointing with oil. This is followed by various arguments to shew that all dominion is derived from God, and by a discourse on the fitness of Rome for governing the world, broadly modelled on the parallel discussion in the *De Civitate Dei*. Nothing, however, could be less Augustinian than the view of Empire which Ptolemy proceeds to elaborate. Dominion, he says, is fourfold, "(1) sacerdotale et regale similiter, (2) regale solum, sub quo imperiale sumitur, (3) politicum, (4) oeconomicum."[3] The combined sacerdotal and regal power belongs only to the Church. It is the direct outcome of the *Tu es Petrus*, and the pretence that spiritual power alone is covered by the commission must be flatly rejected. "Sicut ergo corpus per animam habet esse, ita et temporalis iurisdictio principum per spiritualem Petri

[1] *De Reg. Princ.* II, 9, III, 11. [2] *Ib.* II, 10. [3] *Ib.* III, 10.

et successorum eius." The real novelty of Ptolemy's position does not however, appear until he begins to examine the imperial power. This he describes as "medium inter politicum et regale." It is more universal than kingship, and it is invested with most of the royal prerogatives. On the other hand, it is "political" because it is not dynastic. Election, though sometimes suspended (as in the Carolingian age), is its principle, and the dominion expires with its holder. Then follows the really startling contention, that the Church, or, to be more precise, the kingdom of Christ, *is* now the Empire. There were four earlier stages, the Assyrians, the Medes and Persians, the Macedonians, the Romans. Then came the "fifth monarchy," which began with the birth of Christ; "et haec quinta monarchia, quae successit Romanis, secundum veritatem omnibus antecellit."[1] Choosing to live a humble life on earth, Christ allowed the Roman Emperors to exercise His dominion until His own kingdom was ready to appear. The hour of manifestation arrived with Constantine, since whose reign the imperial crown, belonging of right to the Papacy, has been worn by Emperors, but only as delegates selected in whatever manner has seemed expedient to the Popes.

In this proclamation of the "fifth monarchy" we see at last the logical clearness and courage so conspicuously lacking in most medieval discussions of the temporal power. As a practical solution of the European problem Ptolemy's theory may have been useless, but at least it states a conclusion not finally to be avoided when once Augustine's alternative, the *civitas impiorum*, had passed away. The medieval imperialists proposed an impossible dualism. To the Emperor of Dante there succeeded in due time the "Christian Prince" of Hobbes, whose sovereignty was to be made absolute by absorbing the papal functions into itself. But a sovereign of that kind was in fact no more than a prelude to the invention of the secular State. The same disdain for traditional subterfuges may be briefly noted in Ptolemy's economic teaching. He remarks that *dominium oeconomicum* would require a separate treatise, but he does include many suggestive observations, especially on the subject of Communism. Incidentally he refuses to credit Aristotle's report of the Socratic communism of wives, and notes that Aristotle had long enjoyed a bad reputation for unfairness to his predecessors. As to communism of goods, he declines to regard this as an ideal which had to be sacrificed when sin put an end to the age of innocence. Private property, he says, is a consequence of the natural inequality of man, and to insist on equality of goods is to destroy the *ordo in rebus*. He adds that personal possessions are needed "propter ipsorum amoenitatem ad refocillationem animae"; and again (borrowing here a hint from Aristotle) he argues that endowment of the clergy is required to give them leisure for the cultivation of science and art[2]. Thus in some ways the *De Regimine Principum* is almost as modern in spirit as it is medieval in outward form and style.

[1] *De Reg. Princ.* III, 12, 13.

[2] *Ib.* IV, 4, 9, 12.

It need scarcely be said, however, that this mixture of medieval and modern elements is far from uncommon. For the most part the sketch of political theory in this chapter has been conceived from a deliberately limited point of view. By attending chiefly to the political institutions and movements which brought about the transformation of the medieval into the modern world, it would have been possible to convey a very different impression of the facts. To concentrate upon the Papacy and the Empire, rather than upon the Feudal System and the forces destructive of that system, such as the rise of independent communes and the growth of national sentiment, is certainly to distort the medieval picture. Even as regards explicit political theory it would be possible to lay emphasis on the more modern line of thought, which began to find expression, at the beginning of the fourteenth century, in the writings of John of Paris, Peter du Bois, John of Jandun, and Marsilio of Padua. It is not merely a question of dates; for Peter du Bois was born about ten years before Dante, and Marsilio only about five years after him. If, then, we include the *Monarchia* in our survey, but exclude the *Defensor Pacis* and other writings of the same period, the best reason for this discrimination is just that Dante was out of date. In other words, he was medieval in a sense that some of his contemporaries were not. For the same reason, interpreted more widely, it is legitimate to hold that political theory is distinctively medieval only so long as it is engaged with a certain problem in relation to Christendom as a whole. That problem was, in the language of Gelasius, the problem of "auctoritas sacrata pontificum et regalis potestas"; or, more briefly, of the relation between *sacerdotium* and *regnum*. At no time was the essence of the dispute bound up with the existence of the Empire; and when the Empire was virtually displaced by national kingdoms the dispute by no means came to an end. Nevertheless, the irregular boundary between the medieval and the modern is crossed as soon as the conception of Christendom, embodied for Dante in the Roman Empire, gives way to the belief that the largest autonomous community should be the territorial or national State. The City State, the Empire, and the Nation have been the three characteristic stages, and only the second of the three is properly to be regarded as productive of medieval thought.

CHAPTER XIX

MEDIEVAL DOCTRINE TO THE LATERAN COUNCIL OF 1215.

The body of constitutions published by Innocent III at the Fourth Lateran Council in November 1215 marks the completion of that achievement which, by slow degrees and through many vicissitudes, subordinated the Western Church to the spiritual authority of the Roman pontiff. The confession of faith with which it opens has thus a peculiar importance as a clear exposition, through the voice of the greatest of the Popes, of the mind of the Church upon fundamental doctrines which had assumed this irreducible form through centuries of controversy. While it summed up concisely the standpoint which had been reached at a moment when the papal monarchy was able to proclaim itself without contest the supreme interpreter of ecclesiastical law and dogma, it also fixed the foundation upon which subsequent declarations and definitions of articles of faith were to be based. In framing the statement, Innocent had the refutation of special heresies in view, with the result that its emphasis is confined to certain prominent aspects of the creeds and sacraments; but its implications involve the whole body of medieval doctrine. Its text therefore is a necessary starting-point for a survey of the development of those theories which were crystallised into dogmatic expression as the orthodox faith of Western Christendom.

We firmly believe and simply confess, that there is one only true God, eternal, without measure and unchangeable, incomprehensible, omnipotent and ineffable, the Father, and the Son, and the Holy Spirit: three persons indeed, but one simple essence, substance or nature altogether; the Father of none, the Son of the Father alone, and the Holy Spirit of both alike, without beginning, always and without end; the Father begetting, the Son being born, and the Holy Spirit proceeding; consubstantial, and co-equal, and co-omnipotent, and co-eternal; one principle of all things; the creator of all things visible and invisible, spiritual and corporal; who by His omnipotent virtue at once from the beginning of time established out of nothing both forms of creation, spiritual and corporal, that is the angelic and the mundane, and afterwards the human creature, composed as it were of spirit and body in common. For the devil and other demons were created by God; but they became evil by their own doing. But man sinned by the suggestion of the devil.

This Holy Trinity, undivided as regards common essence, and distinct in respect of proper qualities of person, at first, according to the perfectly ordered plan of the ages, gave the teaching of salvation to the human race by means of Moses and the holy prophets and others His servants.

And at length the only-begotten Son of God, Jesus Christ, incarnate of the whole Trinity in common, being conceived of Mary ever Virgin by the co-operation of the Holy Spirit, made very man, compounded of a reasonable soul and human flesh, one person in two natures, shewed the way of life in all its clearness. He, while as regards His divinity He is immortal and incapable of suffering, nevertheless, as regards His humanity, was made capable of suffering and mortal. He also, having suffered for the salvation of the human race upon the wood of the cross and died, descended to hell, rose again from the dead, and ascended into heaven; but descended in spirit and rose again in flesh, and ascended to come in both alike at the end of the world, to judge the quick and the dead, and to render to every man according to his works, both to the reprobate and to the elect, who all shall rise again with their own bodies which they now wear, that they may receive according to their works, whether they be good or bad, these perpetual punishment with the devil, and those everlasting glory with Christ.

There is moreover one universal Church of the faithful, outside which no man at all is saved, in which the same Jesus Christ is both the priest and the sacrifice, whose body and blood are truly contained in the sacrament of the altar under the species of bread and wine, the bread being transubstantiated into the body and the wine into the blood by the divine power, in order that, to accomplish the mystery of unity, we ourselves may receive of His that which He received of ours. And this thing, the sacrament to wit, no one can make (*conficere*) but a priest, who has been duly ordained, according to the keys of the Church, which Jesus Christ Himself granted to the apostles and their successors.

But the sacrament of baptism, which is consecrated in water at the invocation of God and of the undivided Trinity, that is of the Father, and of the Son and Holy Spirit, being duly conferred in the form of the Church by any person, whether upon children or adults, is profitable to salvation. And if anyone, after receiving baptism, has fallen into sin, he can always be restored (*reparari*) by true penitence.

Not only virgins and the continent, but also married persons, deserve, by right faith and good works pleasing God, to come to eternal blessedness.

I

No definition of the authority of the legislator is included in the matters of faith set forth in this statement, nor does it contain any assertion of the necessity of the Roman primacy as a consequence of the apostolic character of the Church and as the visible guarantee of its unity. In the circumstances, however, these points were self-evident. The confession of faith was uttered as the *ipse dixit* of the successor of Peter; it was registered by the approval of the sacred council without discussion, as the preliminary to a series of constitutions issued, not as matters for further debate, but as pronouncements of a supreme tribunal. At the root of doctrinal development throughout the Middle Ages lies the acceptance of the principle that the visible Church, one, holy, catholic, and apostolic, was also Roman, that the ultimate decision in questions of faith and order depended upon the judgment of the Roman see, that the primacy of Peter among the Apostles had been inherited by his successors. It is true that the continuous chain of historical testimony which was needed to connect this theory with the age of the Apostles was wanting; the foundation of the Roman episcopate by Peter was a received tradition which had probability, but rested upon no certain historical proof. But it is equally true that the tendency of the Church to look to the see of Peter for guidance in matters of difficulty was of early growth, and that it is impossible to determine whether this arose from an implicit belief in its claims to supreme authority, or whether those claims took their origin in the growth of custom, which at any rate did much to strengthen them and encourage their dogmatic expression.

It is always hard to draw a precise line of division between the spiritual and temporal aspects of human affairs where politics and religious belief come into contact, and the political element in the history of the Papacy, the growth of its temporal dominion and of its influence upon secular business, is closely interwoven with the expansion of its spiritual monarchy. Its association with Rome was a source of strength which, even without the background of apostolic tradition, could not have failed to give the bishop of the imperial city a place of singular significance in the councils of his brethren. After the fall of the Empire in the West, the survival of the Papacy in Rome kept alive the memories of the period in which Rome had ruled the world; amid the strife of the barbarian invaders of Italy and the rise and fall of their principalities, the head of the Christian Church in Rome remained the trustee and the symbol of imperial power, the champion of the Roman republic against the invader, and the link between classical antiquity and the new world which was in process of formation. As the hold of the Eastern Emperors upon Italy grew weaker, the influence of the Popes naturally increased. Their firm statesmanship preserved the continuity of Rome as the capital of the West, even in an isolation in which from time to time it was threatened with extinction; and when, faced with menaces against which they were unable to contend alone, the Popes called the Frankish kings to their aid, they surrendered their trusteeship of empire, not as a tribute exacted from them by a foreign conqueror, but as a free gift at their disposal, bestowed upon their defender as a reward to be held with filial gratitude.

Nevertheless, the prestige of Rome was insufficient of itself to give the Papacy its unique position. The reverence which Rome excited in the new nations which were coming into being in Europe was not a matter of historical imagination or romantic sentiment. It depended upon the fact that, in the city whose secular princes had abandoned it after a long period of decline and anarchy, the chief ruler founded claims to a spiritual authority, extending far beyond the limits to which the political influence of Rome had shrunk, upon the possession of privileges granted by the Founder of the Christian Church to His Apostles, and specially committed to that one of their number to whom the settlement of Christianity in Rome was generally attributed. It was upon this basis that the Popes themselves, from the date at which authentic documents are found, established the source of their authority. Its assertion became emphatic when for the first time the see of Constantinople, hitherto obscure, laid claim to the second place among the patriarchates on the express ground that Byzantium was New Rome. On the part of a see which could make no pretensions to apostolic foundation until that credit was given to St Andrew long after, this amounted to a declaration that the Roman episcopate was purely political in origin. To this there could be only one answer from Rome. Leo the Great and his successors took their stand upon the literal interpretation of Christ's commission to Peter as a charge delivered to an individual person, not merely as a representative, but as the chosen head of the apostolic body. It was our Lord's will that evangelic truth should be communicated to the world through the Apostles. But He so ordained that the gifts which they were to use should be vested in the person of Peter, as a head from which they were to be imparted to the other members. Peter was the rock on which the Church was built; the fabric of the eternal temple stood fast in the solidity of Peter, and to depart from that firm foundation was to incur exile from the unity of the Church. It was not that this doctrine was put forward for the first time in opposition to the dangerous ambition of the Byzantine patriarchs; its asseveration could be traced back as far as Cyprian and the age of the persecutions. But with Leo the Great, in the age of the Council of Chalcedon, it began to assume an emphatic and peremptory form. At the close of the fifth century a decretal of Gelasius expressed it in the clearest terms. The holy Roman Church, catholic and apostolic, owes its primacy, not to the constitutions of any synod, but to the voice of our Lord Himself in His words to Peter. The apostle Paul, indeed, shared the honour with Peter of consecrating it to the Lord's service and crowning their joint work with simultaneous martyrdom; but the see was the see of Peter, and in this consisted the primacy of Rome, a Church not having spot or wrinkle or any such thing.

Until the time of Gregory the Great, however, the supremacy of Rome over local churches outside the geographical area of her immediate influence was a pious theory rather than an established fact; and Gregory himself made the power of Rome felt less by dogmatic assertion than by his statesmanlike exercise of patriarchal jurisdiction. If, by his dealings with the bishops of the Frankish kingdoms and the metropolitan see of Ravenna, by the value which he set upon the grant of the pallium as a papal privilege, by his maintenance of the superiority of Rome to the see whose holder claimed the title of ecumenical patriarch, and by the mission which introduced Roman Christianity into Britain, he extended the authority of his Church and left the Papacy far greater than he found it, it was not by formulating extravagant claims to obedience. In his arguments against the pretensions of Byzantium, he even allowed himself cautiously to ascribe to the patriarchal sees of Antioch, founded by Peter, and Alexandria, founded directly from him by Mark, a preeminence closely parallel to that of Rome. While stating, with special reference to Constantinople, the right of the Roman see to prohibit unlawful courses to its subordinate Churches, he professed himself ready to learn from and imitate them in good things. In his instructions to Augustine, he reminded him that he had been brought up in the customs of the Roman Church, but advised him to use his judgment in borrowing freely from those of other Churches, if, after careful examination, he found anything in them that was better. His assumption of the title *servus servorum Dei* was in keeping with the moderation with which he exerted his sway, and represented a genuine ambition to rule as one who served the Church. At the same time, there was policy in such humility. The Churches of the West could profit by the salutary contrast between their patriarch's pride in service and the jealous obstinacy of Constantinople. With similar motives he rejected the title of universal bishop, with which Leo the Great had been acclaimed at Chalcedon, arguing that the appropriation of this title to a single prelate detracted from the honour of the episcopate of the universal Church. That honour was his own; its virtue lay in the collective strength of his brethren, and to isolate him from them was to endanger the unity and charity which he sought to maintain in the Church.

The position which Gregory secured for the Roman Church by his prudence and moderation was strengthened by the rigid orthodoxy of its pontiffs, as opposed to the heresies which from time to time appeared in the East and gradually alienated it from communion with the Churches of the West. Further, their readiness to sanction missionary enterprise among the heathen tribes of Europe was a valuable evidence to their fitness to fill the post of guardians of the central fount of episcopal jurisdiction. The relations which Boniface, during his apostolate in Germany, established with Gregory II, Gregory III, and Zacharias placed his mission under the direct patronage of Rome. If, face to face with his converts and the problems arising from such contact, he occasionally found it expedient to take a line of his own, this did not affect his conviction that the approval of the Roman see was necessary to the validity of his work. While Christianity made its way in Northern Europe under papal auspices, the political tie between Rome and the Frankish rulers was cemented. The legation of Boniface was an important link in the chain of events which led to the revival of the Western Empire and the bestowal of the temporal crown upon Charles the Great as the reward and earnest of his defence of the spiritual power. With all his confidence in the theocratic character of his monarchy, Charles asserted the absolute obedience due in spiritual matters to the see of Peter. Rome was the mother of the priestly dignity, and consequently the mistress of ecclesiastical order; her commands, even when they laid a heavy tax upon human endurance, should be piously obeyed.

The authority thus ascribed to Rome by the first Frankish Emperor was enhanced, within no long time of his death, by the appearance of the False Decretals. It is now generally conceded that this compilation had its origin in the Frankish realm, and that its object was to limit the absolutism of local metropolitans by exalting the prerogative of the papal see. Its authors had in view a danger which was near at hand, and aimed at safeguarding their liberty by maintaining the existence of a single jurisdiction which, more remote than that of the provincial primate, could yet be used as an effective check upon his aggressions. If any excuse can be made for the manufacture of the evidence produced for this purpose, it may be found in the disorganised state of the Frankish dominions and the menace of civil war and feudal anarchy to the unity of the Church. Amid these perils, with non-Christian foes invading the frontiers of the distracted kingdoms, such pious frauds might be justified on the ground of motive. More than one collection of decrees and canons appeared about the middle of the ninth century in the district on the borders of Neustria and Austrasia; but of these the most important, which in process of time obtained universal acceptance, was that ascribed to Isidore Mercator. The author, professing to act upon the instigation of many bishops and others, founded his work upon a supposed collection made by Pope Damasus in the later part of the fourth century, containing decretals of Popes from the sub-apostolic age to the days of Constantine. This was supplemented by genuine acts of councils and by more decretals, partly forged and partly authentic, which carried the continuous chain of evidence as far as the first quarter of the eighth century. Earlier in origin than these, however, and probably proceeding from a quarter more near to Rome, was the document known as the Donation of Constantine, by which the Emperor, after his alleged healing and conversion by Pope Sylvester, was represented as bestowing upon the Popes his imperial dignity in the West, with a spiritual principate above all other patriarchs and local Churches. In this edict, which was included in the collection of the pseudo-Isidore, the papal supremacy was stated in an unqualified form. The Pope is set as a prince exalted above all the priesthood of the entire world, and all arrangements for the advancement of the worship of God and the establishment of the Christian faith are placed at his disposal. In view of the later assumption by the Popes of the title Vicar of Christ, it may be noted that the Donation of Constantine, while stating that Peter seems to have been appointed the earthly vicar of the Son of God, refers to his successors as the vicars of the prince of the Apostles.

It cannot be argued that the Forged Decretals enunciated an entirely new doctrine. At most, they gave a legal form to conclusions which could be drawn from a collation of the actual utterances of Popes during the four preceding centuries. They amplified existing canons with material which was to hand in a floating form and was now digested into a code of ecclesiastical law. The possibility that the Roman primacy was as old as the Church itself was assumed as a certainty. Its continuity was asserted by the bold expedient of assigning the documents thus fabricated to Popes whose names were accepted by common tradition. There is no sign that the Forged Decretals in any other way took advantage of the uncritical spirit of the age. Their principal end, the recognition of the Roman see as a final court of appeal for Christians, had already won the sanction of custom; they laid emphasis upon obedience to that court as a divinely appointed duty. There is, further, no definite ground for supposing that the Roman see itself had anything to do with their production, or took advantage of them till a much later period. On the one hand, they were no doubt accepted more readily because their doctrines tallied with the increasingly positive assertions which emanated from Rome. On the other, those assertions were independent utterances upon which the Forged Decretals became a local gloss.

The events of the pontificate of Nicholas I (858–67) put the primacy of Peter in the foreground of controversy. The long strife between Rome and Constantinople culminated in the schism of Photius, and, although the final breach was delayed for two centuries longer, there could be no hope henceforward of lasting union. The conflict was embittered by the claims of the two patriarchates to the allegiance of the Bulgarian Christians. While the arguments and mandates of Nicholas failed to restore unity, they were delivered with an assurance which impressed, if it did not convince. Urging the cause of his see with unwavering consistency and with a minute knowledge of the acts and pronouncements of his predecessors, he strengthened in the West that authority which the East refused to recognise. His letters and decretals reiterate, with all the force of a strong personality, formulas which summed up and confirmed all preceding claims. The Church of Rome was the principal Church, the possessor of privileges which were the gift of Christ Himself for the building up of religion and the restoration of peace and concord to disputants who approached its tribunal. Its rulers were the vicars of Peter, charged with the care of the Lord's sheep, endowed with the gift of clear perception of dangers which might lead the flock astray. They were the source of doctrine, the champions of the integrity of the faith, the ultimate resort of the penitent sinner whose heart the grace of God had touched, the interpreters of ecclesiastical order in whose custody the canons of the Church and the decrees of councils remained inviolable. Their sanctions were law, against which private judgment was of no avail. Councils and synods were means employed for the general propagation of their directions, at which they submitted to the consent of many those matters for which their own authority was sufficient. The whole episcopate was thus dependent upon the see of Peter: the metropolitans of provinces, the bishops in provincial cities, were agents by whose means the cure of the universal Church was concentrated in that single see, the head to which the unity of the body was necessary. In appeal to its decision lay the essential solution of all disputed points; without its consent no debate could be settled. Finally, the claims of Nicholas, while asserting primarily the supremacy of the Roman see over the clergy, involved propositions which his successors extended to all estates of men.

In a letter addressed to the metropolitan Hincmar and the bishops of the kingdom of Charles the Bald, Nicholas set forth at length the causes and progress of his quarrel with the Eastern patriarch, and took occasion to refute, for the benefit of the faithful, the argument that the transference of empire to Constantinople involved the transference of the privileges of the Roman Church. It is noteworthy that such a letter contains no allusion either to the Donation of Constantine or to the spurious authorities which were already current in those regions; nor does it make any reference to that new Empire which the Papacy had brought into being. It relies solely upon the tradition derived from Peter, the consistent maintenance of the faith by his successors, and the permanence of his see as the transmitter of its institutions and doctrine to all younger Churches, of which the relations of Nicholas with the Bulgarian Church were a recent example. The influence which Nicholas exercised in the West was due to his single-minded advocacy of the purely spiritual foundation of his claims to obedience; the extreme form which they took was fearlessly urged without the intrusion of political considerations, and in his correspondence with kings, with Charles the Bald and the erring Lothar as with the Emperor Michael, his voice was that of the father in God, charged with the authority to exhort and rebuke without respect of persons.

The view which Nicholas I held of his office remained firm amid the vicissitudes through which the apostolic see passed during the next two centuries. Political causes contributed to maintain it, for it was to the advantage of the Saxon and Franconian Emperors to uphold the dignity of the spiritual monarch from whom they received their temporal crown. The reforming energy of the German kings placed the Papacy in a position which eventually enabled it to defy their successors and oppose the solid fact of the head of the Church, with his see in the old capital of the world, to the shadowy claims of the temporal monarch who was no longer necessary to its defence. The accession of Leo IX in 1048 marks the point at which the Papacy entered into the full and uninterrupted exercise of its dominion. It was a German bishop, the nominee of a German Emperor, his kinsman, who brought to the Papacy methods of administration learned in the imperial service, and so gave it the efficiency which it needed to carry out the task of ecclesiastical reform. The theories which had been enunciated clearly by Nicholas I were brought fully into practice: the Pope, exercising the universal cure of souls, was the supreme ordinary of the Church, whose duty it was to ordain, rule, and correct universally the churches subject to his apostolate. At the synod of Mayence in 1049, Leo declared that Christ, in raising him to the dignity of the apostolic see, had granted him, as head of the Christian body, the power to remove the defects and scandals of the Church by decrees promulgated in such assemblies. The supremacy of Rome was treated as an obvious fact which required no proof, even in distant parts of the Church. Thus the archbishop of Carthage was called the first archbishop and chief metropolitan of Africa after the Roman pontiff; this privilege, once granted to him by the Roman see, was one of which nothing could deprive him, and of which he would stand possessed for ever.

The lasting controversy with Constantinople reached its last stage under Leo IX. Like Nicholas I in his correspondence with Photius and the Emperor Michael, so Leo, writing to the patriarch Michael Cerularius and his ally the Bulgarian archbishop, admitted no compromise with regard to the supremacy and orthodoxy of his Church. Coming from the district in which the Forged Decretals were composed and had been accepted as genuine, he used their material without question as evidence for his assertions, and quoted the Donation of Constantine at length in this connexion. But his most forcible protest against the presumption of the Eastern prelates was founded upon the unshaken orthodoxy of Rome, the Church founded by Peter, in which St Paul found nothing to correct, but was full of praises of its faith, a faith to which countless martyrdoms had since borne witness. In his grief at the recalcitrance of Constantinople, he turned with relief to the confession of orthodox faith which he received from the patriarch of Antioch. A letter which congratulated this prelate upon his loyalty to the Roman see, and ends with a profession of faith in the same terms, contains a remarkable statement of the inviolable primacy of Rome.

> This is the declaration of all the venerable councils and of human laws, this is confirmed by the Holy of holies, the King of kings and Lord of lords Himself, that the reverend head of the principal dignity and of the entire discipline of the Church is, in its preeminence of splendour and excellence, in that place where Peter, the very summit and cardinal member of the apostles, waits for the blessed resurrection of his flesh in the last day.

The doctrine of the Papacy as the supreme judge of faith and order, whose decrees, in themselves final and without appeal, were made public to the whole Church through the approbation of councils, was thus firmly fixed upon the eve of that struggle on which it was about to enter with the temporal power during the pontificate of Gregory VII. By the Popes themselves it had been held with little change for centuries; what was positively expressed by Nicholas I and, with increased dogmatism, was reasserted by the Popes of the Hildebrandine age was the logical development of the position taken by their predecessors. With the growth of the recognition of a permanent tribunal of appeal at Rome, overriding the decisions of metropolitans and superior to the claims of the declining patriarchates of the East, the grounds of its authority were formulated more boldly; and the Forged Decretals, concocted without aid from Rome and with the intention merely of providing a remedy against local tyrannies, served the purpose of implanting that authority in districts where the welfare and unity of the Church were threatened by civil anarchy. Rome, it is true, by her failure to propitiate the jealousy of the Eastern Empire and its patriarch, severed communion with a large section of Christian believers; in the dispute, each side argued systematically from a different standpoint, and the inevitable result was a complete deadlock. But the assertions which were rejected by the Eastern Church gained credence throughout the whole Western patriarchate. While the legend of the Donation of Constantine, accepted and included in the armoury of papal evidences, gave immense strength to the encroachments of the Papacy, as time went on, upon temporal dominion, the real influence of Rome over the minds and wills of its spiritual subjects lay in the mere reiteration of the powers conferred upon Peter by the Founder of the Catholic Church; and to this the confirmation of spurious documents was a subsidiary matter.

The single-minded fearlessness of Gregory VII in the contest which he waged with kings, in spite of the checks and apparent defeats which he suffered, raised the Papacy to an eminence for which the work of his predecessors had been but a preparation. It is too much to say that, during the twelfth century, the holy see was always consistent in its defence of the Church against the encroachments of the temporal power or disregarded policy by throwing caution to the winds. In the quarrel between Henry II and Becket, Alexander III shewed no superfluous energy on the side of the champion of clerical privilege. The same Pope, in the encouragement which he afforded to the cities of the Lombard League in their war against German feudalism, was actuated quite as much by the menace of imperial supremacy in Italy to his own temporal dominions as by the abstract love of liberty. But, amid the disorder of the age, the Papacy represented a stable element with which were associated ideas of order and righteousness. To the Papacy was due the inception and recurrent revival of the crusading movement which bound together the races of Europe in one common object of pious endeavour. Its orthodoxy kept vigilant note of the progress of heresies which threatened the union of the Church; its administrative system penetrated into every diocese of the West. In its repeated enforcement of the truce of God and the ban which it placed on tournaments, it exercised an influence which counteracted the lawlessness of feudal society, while the example which it presented of a spiritual monarchy uniting the nations under its dominion was the very opposite of that anarchy which unrestrained feudalism produced in temporal affairs.

At the close of the twelfth century, the force of character and the determination of Gregory VII were revived in the person of Innocent III, with higher qualities of statesmanship. Through the eighteen years of his pontificate he was indefatigable in the assertion of the rights of his see and successful in the employment of the spiritual censures by which he secured their recognition. The immense mass of material which his official correspondence contributed to the Canon Law is the standing testimony to the untrammelled exercise and lasting influence of his authority. From these documents passage after passage might be quoted which reiterates the sovereignty inherited from Peter by the Roman pontiffs. It is a sovereignty which brings the whole episcopate under their jurisdiction; once elected and confirmed by the holy see, a bishop cannot be released from the bond which unites him to his diocese without papal permission. The episcopate is subject to Peter, to whom the Lord gave charge of his sheep; the pall, the symbol of metropolitan jurisdiction, is bestowed by the Pope alone, and, while its grant confers upon the recipient the plenitude of his office and the right to wear it in the church from which his jurisdiction is derived, the Pope alone possesses that plenitude of ecclesiastical power which enables him to wear it *semper et ubique*. How deeply such a theory penetrated the smallest details of ecclesiastical jurisdiction is seen in the almost innumerable cases which came before Innocent for decision from the dioceses of distant lands. The unique position claimed for his see was supported by picturesque figures drawn from Scripture. The throne described in the Revelation of St John is the apostolic see, the seat of the Lamb, of Him who liveth for ever and ever; the four beasts round about it are the four patriarchal Churches—this was after the Latin conquest of Constantinople, and that troublesome patriarchate is allowed the fourth place in the quartet—which stand like daughters in its family, and like servants round about it. The occupant of this exalted seat is at the apex of the Christian hierarchy; his power is felt in every grade of it, transfusing itself into every part of the organisation.

Soon after he ascended the papal throne, Innocent III began to use the phrase Vicar of Christ in connexion with his office. It had not been used before his time, and the implication that the successors of Peter were not his deputies, but received their commission, as he did, immediately from Christ, is significant of the conviction upon which the policy of Innocent was founded. At the end of his life, he was the spiritual lord of the Christian world; and his last act of importance was the summoning of the council which should crown his achievements by proclaiming the orthodox faith of the Church, putting an end to irregularities within its borders, and repelling the heresies which attacked it from outside. The assertions of Innocent III went far to establish the Papacy in the possession of semi-divine honours; but his ideal was a monarchy wielded by the earthly representative of Him who said that His kingdom was not of this world, and his interference with kings and princes was guided by their attitude as sons of the Church to him as its head. Nevertheless, his own position as master of a temporal principality and his treatment of the southern Italian kingdom as a fief of the Church shewed another side of the case on which his successors were not slow to enlarge. The idea that the two swords which Peter offered to Christ in the garden were in the hands of Peter's successor and represented the spiritual and temporal powers, both at his disposal, received expression at the opening of the fourteenth century in the bull of Boniface VIII *Unam sanctam*, with the corollary that it was altogether necessary to human salvation that every creature should be subject to the Roman pontiff. These were extensions of the lofty claims advanced by Innocent, and, when they were formulated, forces were at work to hinder them from obtaining the easy acceptance which Innocent had won for his conception of the papal sovereignty.

II

The acknowledgement of Rome as the source of ecclesiastical law and order and of the definition of doctrine was thus complete. Metropolitans might issue statutes in provincial councils, but such statutes constituted no provincial code; they were founded on and enforced papal law, and, generally speaking, quoted freely from the language of papal decrees. After the time of Gratian, who used the authority of papal utterances copiously in the *Decretum*, side by side with quotations from the Fathers and the decrees of councils, the books added to the received code of Canon Law consisted of collections of papal pronouncements, with a few canons of early councils thrown in here and there. Similarly, liturgical practice looked for its model to Rome, and, long before the time of Innocent III, in spite of the prevalence of provincial and diocesan uses, the Roman liturgy had become the norm which was at the foundation of all these, and their peculiarities of ritual were minor matters of local custom.

There were two main and distinct forms of liturgy in the West which for a time prevailed in different areas. The Roman rite assumed its special form in Rome itself and in the Italian dioceses that constituted the papal province. Outside this area, at any rate from the fourth century, a rite was adopted with local variations to which the name Gallican is usually given. Probably of Eastern origin—it has been conjectured to be the liturgy of the Church of Ephesus—it was established at one of the great diocesan centres of the West, according to the older theory at Lyons, but more probably at Milan. It spread to the West, to Gaul and Spain and to the Celtic communities of the west and north of Britain. It even shewed signs of spreading into the Roman area, so that, as early as 416, Innocent I warned the Bishop of Gubbio that the only traditions which the Church ought to observe were those derived from the example of St Peter, and that, if he needed information about rites and ceremonies, it was his duty to come to Rome and observe the practice there. The Pope, in support of this, stated that it was clear that no Church had been founded in Italy, Gaul, Spain, Africa, and Sicily by anyone who had not received ordination from the prince of the apostles. Nevertheless the Gallican rite had free course in the western countries, and, after it had been superseded in Gaul, survived in the strongly local custom of the Church of Spain under the Visigothic monarchy.

The ultimate victory of the Roman rite is primarily to be ascribed to the missions sent out to the tribes of the North under papal protection.

Augustine brought the Roman liturgy with him to England, and, though in Northumbria its acceptance was delayed by the influence of Celtic missionaries, it eventually won its way. To Boniface, an Englishman trained in Roman traditions, the authority and practice of the holy see were of first-rate importance, and through him Roman customs found their way into the Frankish kingdom, just at the period when the Merovingian dynasty was in its final stage of decay and the sovereign power was in the hands of the great mayors of the palace. In the reorganisation of the Gallican Church under the new rulers, Rome was the natural source of advice, and the bonds between Rome and the new dynasty were knit closely by the appearance of the Frankish kings as champions of the Church. At the request of Charles the Great, Hadrian II sent to him a copy of the Sacramentary ascribed to Gregory the Great, comprising the ordinary of the mass with the proper of the seasons and the forms for the ordination of bishops, priests, and deacons. In the form in which this Sacramentary has come down to us, through manuscripts used in France, it is clearly of Roman origin, and the proper collects are distinguished by rubrics naming the various stations or basilicas in Rome appointed for the chief service on the several feast-days; but, as such, much of it is subsequent to the age of Gregory the Great, and it received considerable supplements in Gaul from the hands of Alcuin and others. The similar collection, which received the title of the Gelasian Sacramentary from its supposed origin in the *sacramentorum praefationes et orationes* attributed to Gelasius I by the *Liber Pontificalis*, had appeared in Gaul at an earlier date. The still earlier Leonine book, of which a single manuscript exists, was equally Roman in origin, but is a private compilation which had no official currency. Consequently, the Gregorian and Gelasian books, both of a later date than that of their alleged compilers, while supplying the earliest complete forms of the Roman rite, have reached us through Gaul. Here the Gallican liturgy was superseded, and the rite which took its place was appropriated and amplified in the course of the Carolingian period.

The dissemination of the Roman liturgy was achieved simply by the provision of copies of Sacramentaries, such as that given by Hadrian to Charlemagne, while others may have been brought from Rome by visitors from Gallican churches. Those which we possess very probably had their origin in books arranged for the Pope's use in officiating at the Roman stations. Similarly the *Ordines Romani* of various dates, with their ritual directions, refer to Roman ceremonies, and for the most part to those, such as the visits to the stationary basilicas, in which the Pope took the chief part. These also were used in Gaul as models for ritual. Thus, from the eighth century onward, the old Gallican books were discarded, and, in the kingdom to which, with the favour and help of the Roman pontiffs, the imperial dignity of the West had passed, Roman practice was acclimatised in the services of the Church and the papal authority consequently strengthened.

From these considerations we pass to the development of doctrine which accompanied the growth of the papal supremacy. The survey may be divided into three main portions, dealing (1) with the relations between God and man involved in the doctrine of the creation and fall and the allied subjects of predestination and grace; (2) with the work of salvation manifested in the Incarnation and Passion, and in the operation of the Holy Spirit; and (3) with the doctrine of the Sacraments, especially as regards the important subjects of the Eucharist and penance.

III

The course which medieval dogma was to take was determined by the overpowering influence of St Augustine upon religious thought. That influence, proceeding from a mind incessantly and profoundly active, which expressed itself in a style of wonderful fluency and variety, as sensitive to the casual impressions of a fervent imagination as it was emphatic in recording the permanent convictions implanted by a peculiar intensity of religious experience, not only provided a basis for orthodox doctrine, but suggested lines of argument also of which in process of time impugners of orthodoxy were ready to avail themselves. In his controversies with the Pelagians Augustine laid down the formulas which guided the medieval conception of the relations between God and man, between the omnipotent will which did all things as it would in heaven and earth and the will of man to choose between good and evil; he gave lasting shape to the fundamental principles of the evil of human nature, rooted in original sin, and the counteracting effects of the free grace of God. The Donatist controversy brought out his theory of ecclesiastical polity, of the visible Church possessed of a valid ministry, entrusted with the dispensation of the Word and Sacraments, the divinely appointed means of grace. But between these two main aspects of Augustine's teaching there was a certain degree of incompatibility. On the one hand, his doctrine of grace, founded upon his conviction of the immutability of God's omnipotent will, confined the operation of the free gift to a few persons in comparison with the multitude of human beings born in sin. To such persons, chosen from eternity to salvation by the unchangeable counsels of God, there came, whether they were willing to receive it or not, the grace of God through Christ, disposing them to faith, producing in the unwilling the will to believe, and in those who were willing directing the will aright. Thus, by the working of prevenient grace, the soul predestined to salvation accepted or was prepared to accept the call of God. The soul's progress through the stages of faith which followed the call, with the assistance of cooperating grace, culminated in justification, the attainment of righteousness in the sight of God through the gift of the Holy Spirit and the consequent suffusion of faith by the love in which God became the one object of man's desire. But still there was necessary to the final enjoyment of union with God the gift of final perseverance; and with those to whom this was granted grace was irresistible. The grace of God worked undisturbed in their hearts, and their freedom to will anything but good was entirely supplanted by this principle.

While this theory limited salvation to a small minority of mankind, the visible Church, on the other hand, appeared to be the guarantee of God's will that all men should be saved. The taint of original sin was washed away in the sacrament of baptism, where the Holy Spirit moved upon the face of the regenerating waters. The means of grace with their ensuing benefits were open to all baptised Christians. In the Eucharist they were refreshed by the body and blood of Christ with their saving virtue; in the ministry of penance and reconciliation they made atonement for actual sin committed after baptism. This did not imply, of course, that all who took advantage of the means of grace offered by the Church were saved from perdition thereby. It did not exclude the probability that the ultimate benefit of these gifts was restricted to a small circle, known only to God as the chosen recipients of His grace. But it could not be overlooked that the theory of the bestowal of free grace upon a chosen few in accordance with God's unchangeable purpose made the sacramental system of the Church of secondary importance. The action of grace upon the soul of the true believer was a spiritual experience of whose immediate efficacy the sacraments were at best signs and tokens; the heart swayed by irresistible grace had achieved its mystical union with God and was independent of any mediate connexion. The doctrine of election by grace, by which man's free will was entirely subordinated to the absolute will of God, could be only imperfectly reconciled with a doctrine by which the errors of man's will were continually repaired and the will itself kept in a right direction by resort to the means of grace furnished by the Church.

Thus, while Augustine's doctrine of grace had immense influence upon the development of orthodox dogma, it raised problems which were unfavourable to its complete acceptance. His doctrine of original sin, of the complete corruption of man's nature as the consequence of the fall of Adam, of the transmission of Adam's sin to all his descendants, and of the necessity of spiritual regeneration to counteract the hereditary taint of man's natural birth, remained firmly implanted in religious thought, allowing for diversities of theory with regard to the origin of the individual soul, whether as coming into being with the sinful body, or as the result of an independent act of creation. But the Augustinian doctrine of grace, taking form as an express denial of the Pelagian insistence upon the power of man's unaided free will to determine his destiny, took away from man all liberty of choice between good and evil. Such freedom of choice was open to man before the Fall, while he was in a state of righteousness approaching, though still capable of further, perfection. But the choice of evil had rendered the human will incapable of good. Grace alone could quicken it, and, so quickened, it was no longer man's will, but became simply absorbed in the divine will. So far as any free will was left to man, it was to do evil and follow the lusts of the flesh; and, as the saving power of grace communicated itself merely to the chosen, the predestined few selected from the mass of perdition composed of the whole human race, it followed that man's will, if it could still be called his own, was irrevocably set towards destruction. Augustine did not deny free will, but he confined it to a groove in which there was no alternative to its action; and, although this could be attributed to the natural weakness of the will of fallen man and its impotence for good without the prompting and support of grace, it also opened the way to more severe conclusions. The tendency of man to evil might imply a total loss of free will, with the argument that, as part of the human race was predestined to eternal life, so the vast residue was predestined to damnation.

The distinction between God's foreknowledge with the act of volition implied by His predestination of the elect, and the position that, as evil was merely the privation of good, God, whose will was entirely good, could not be conceived as predestining man to a course of evil, did not remove the difficulty of the narrow limit set to man's free will by the Augustinian doctrine. Yet the groundwork of this doctrine, the universal incidence of original sin and the necessity of grace to initiate good in fallen man, were left undisputed by the orthodox. Semi-Pelagianism is an unsatisfactory term for a system which was more strongly opposed to the Pelagian theory of an untrammelled free will than to strict Augustinianism, and was in fact an attempt to harmonise the strict doctrine with a theory which allowed the human will a wider scope. It combined the acknowledgement that God's grace was independent in special cases of man's will with the principle that the will, though weakened by sin, could work in the right direction and be rewarded by the gift of grace so as to become actively good. It admitted a degree of good implanted in the soul by God so as to counteract the natural tendency to evil; while God in His foreknowledge predestined special persons to salvation, yet His will was that all men should be saved. The theory of irresistible grace, compelling the elect to final perseverance irrespective of any effort of will, was rejected: final perseverance was achieved by the continual efforts of the will aided by grace.

While semi-Pelagianism in various forms was condemned by the Council of Orange in 529, that assembly nevertheless committed itself to a modification of Augustinian doctrine which allowed the sacramental system of the Church an active share in the work of grace which was hard to reconcile with a theory of grace absolute and unconditionally bestowed. The community of original sin to soul and body alike was upheld, excluding any possibility of innate virtue in the soul; but the cleansing of the soul in baptism from the inherited taint was the beginning of the operation of grace which it was open to all men to receive or reject in the sequel. Thus the will was recognised as cooperating with the grace which supported it in its weakness, and without which it could do nothing of itself; and thus irresistible grace, with its negation of the human will, was implicitly denied. Further, while the scheme of a twofold predestination, general and special, was condemned, it was laid down that God had predestined no one to damnation. His eternal purpose was the salvation of mankind, and His predestination was exercised only with that object. These general propositions represent an attitude which, avoiding extreme conclusions, gained ground with orthodox believers as a rational statement of a mystery whose complete solution was beyond the power of man; and the same line of thought, followed by Gregory the Great at the end of the same century, permanently affected the doctrine of the Church on this point.

The admiration of Gregory for Augustine is a remarkable example of the dependence of one great teacher upon another for the material of his thought. It is specially remarkable because the cast of mind of the two men was so different. The genius of Augustine, trained in philosophy and the traditions of pagan learning, and profoundly affected by an experience of the grace of God as startling and convincing as that which had befallen the Apostle of the Gentiles, was exercised upon theological speculations with a fertility which the inheritors of his labours found it impossible to exhaust, and with an insight into mental and spiritual processes which remained unrivalled. Of intellectual originality Gregory had little or nothing. His acuteness of mind was that of a lawyer and administrator, engaged in bringing into order and coherent system the diverse elements which he found ready to his hand. As theologian, he initiated no new theory and produced no connected scheme of thought. His position as a doctor of the Church was the outcome of a practical piety which, in the task of ruling Western Christendom, was confronted, not indeed with controversies such as had called out the full powers of Augustine, but with the need of meeting obscurity and ignorance with fixed statements of doctrine. That such statements are unsystematic in form, and that a full estimate of Gregory's thought can be gathered only by collating passages scattered widely throughout his works, are circumstances due to his preoccupation with the direction of the visible ecclesiastical system, the central object of his practical activity. It is no doubt true that he introduced a coarsening element into the dogmatic teaching of the Church by the readiness with which he availed himself of popular superstition in its service: the marvellous tales of the *Dialogues*, the inculcation of belief in miracles, in the efficacy of the relics of the saints, in the ordered hierarchies of good and evil angels, worked upon the credulity and fear of contemporaries whom only visible signs or the assurance of supernatural wonders could keep within the fold of the Church. Such teaching, appealing to the least spiritual elements of human imagination, brought Christian doctrine down from the heights of Augustine's thought to a prosaic level. But, whether for good or ill, the influence of Gregory, as a supplement to that of Augustine, giving plain form to lofty abstractions and modifying their difficulties in the process, dominated the medieval attitude to religion. Just as he laid the foundation of the power of the see which he ruled, so the development of its authority in matters of doctrine was affected by his example; and he is primarily responsible for that habit of mind which, throughout the Middle Ages, regarded the supernatural, not without awe, but at the same time with a matter-of-fact familiarity.

It cannot be said that Gregory's views upon the doctrine of grace were completely consistent with his opinions upon the fundamental subject of predestination. He was powerfully swayed by the Augustinian dogma that God had chosen a definite number of persons for salvation without respect to His foreknowledge of any merit which they might acquire by the right use of their will. The natural consequence of this is the denial that the will can be so used without the constraining power of grace; grace is all-powerful, man's will is nowhere, and all such merit as man may acquire is the work of grace. On the other hand, Gregory could not accept this annihilation of free will. The will was not merely impaired by the Fall, as the semi-Pelagians taught; it was chained by sin. But it still existed, and the application of grace freed it, so that it became capable of cooperating with grace in the work of salvation. While this did not reconcile the Augustinian with the semi-Pelagian view of predestination and grace, but rather left the contrast between the two unhealed, it at any rate provided a half-way house between them on the subject of the will, admitting its powerlessness without prevenient and cooperating grace, but rejecting the irresistible action of grace upon the justified soul.

The importance thus given to free will, coupled with the general admission that no man, however far advanced in the spiritual life, could be certain that he was chosen to salvation in the eternal counsels of God, put the question of the method of predestination into the background. It was not until the ninth century that this question was seriously raised in controversy. In 829 Gottschalk, a monk of Fulda, appealed to the Archbishop of Mayence for release from his vows, on the ground that he had been devoted to the monastic life as a boy, before he was capable of using his own will. Although his appeal was granted, his abbot, the famous Rabanus Maurus, intervened and obtained a decree from Louis the Pious, as the result of which Gottschalk was relegated from Fulda to the monastery of Orbais. Here he consoled himself with studies which led him to embrace the doctrines of Augustine and Fulgentius on predestination with a fervour and a passionate self-assertion which soon brought him into trouble with his superiors. He appears to have escaped from the monastery after several years of durance, when he entered on a wandering life, having obtained ordination to the priesthood by means which laid him open to the charge of irregularity. His advocacy of a theory of a double or twin form of predestination, to life on the one hand and to damnation on the other, led to his condemnation by a synod under the presidency of Rabanus, who had recently become Archbishop of Mayence, in 848, and to his expulsion from the German kingdom. On his return to northern France, he was summoned by Hincmar of Rheims to a synod at the royal vill of Quierzy, where he is said to have behaved with insane violence, and was punished by flogging and sent into imprisonment at the monastery of Hautvillers, near Épernay. Here he died twenty years later in 869, maintaining his position to the end. In addition to his predestinarian views, he developed an attack upon Hincmar for the alteration of the phrase *trina Deitas* in the hymn *Te trina Deitas unaque poscimus* into *summa Deitas*, as implying the denial of the triune Godhead. On his deathbed he refused to sign a recantation of his doctrines prepared in harmony with Hincmar's views, and died without the sacraments of the Church.

The case of this recalcitrant monk, whose obstinacy was by no means quelled by captivity, provoked remarkable interest at a period when theological controversy was much in the air. Hincmar, Rabanus Maurus, and Ratramnus of Corbie, more famous in connexion with the contemporary dispute on the Eucharist, entered into the strife with treatises; Johannes Scotus came forward with novel arguments on behalf of the orthodox view, which themselves came under suspicion of heterodoxy. The opinions of Gottschalk came under the notice of Pope Nicholas I, to whom he sent an appeal from Hautvillers in 859, without ultimate effect, as Hincmar took no definite action for the relief of his troublesome prisoner. Of the two documents in which these opinions have come down to us, a brief summary of his main position, and the *Confessio Prolixior*, in which it is developed with fuller detail, the second, written in the form of a prayer in obvious imitation of Augustine's *Confessions*, contains clear evidence of the mystical ardour and fanatical insistence upon the absolute truth of his theories which made Gottschalk's life a misery to himself and a perplexity to those who came in contact with him. His point of view was perfectly definite. God foreknew all things, whether good or evil, but His predestination was confined to what was good, that is, He could not be the author of anything that was evil. It assumed two forms: on the one hand, He bestowed the benefits of grace, on the other, the judgments of His justice. Free grace was conferred unconditionally upon the elect; eternal punishment was the doom of the reprobate and the reward of those ill deserts which God foresaw from everlasting. The argument rested upon a conviction of the changelessness of God; it was impossible that His knowledge and purpose should be obedient to the fluctuating conditions of time and space. What He knew and willed once, He willed and knew always. It postulated also the total inability of man to acquire grace by merit. Punishment was incurred deservedly; grace was given freely, without any motion on the part of man.

The greater part of Gottschalk's *Confessio Prolixior* is a string of citations from Scripture, followed by references to Augustine, Fulgentius, and Gregory, whose utterances on predestination he regarded as at one with those of the two elder writers. Throughout the document he passionately asserts his own orthodoxy and condemns the opposite opinion as heretical, and in one extraordinary passage he prays God to give him the opportunity of vindicating his belief in public before the king and the whole hierarchy in a national assembly by an ordeal of fire. It cannot be said that anything in the belief on which he set so high a value was new; its key-note, the phrase *gemina praedestinatio*, was derived from Isidore of Seville. The sincerity with which he defended his tenets was marred and rendered suspect by his pertinacity and vanity; his persistence in controversy was spurred on by his resentment against the authorities who kept him under surveillance, and he took a bitter pleasure in arraigning them of heresy. But it is a tribute to his power of expounding his theories, and a testimony to the influence exercised by them, that he became the centre of a conflict which agitated the rulers and theologians of the Frankish Church for more than twenty years.

Of the two lengthy dissertations *De Praedestinatione Dei* in which Hincmar refuted Gottschalk, only the second remains. The long and involved arguments brought forward to elaborate the points in which Gottschalk could be shewn to differ from his master Augustine, and the reasoning applied to the proposition arising from the premises of the controversy that Christ died for all men, and not merely for the elect, are preceded by an historical survey of the growth of the theory of a dual predestination, and include a somewhat broken narrative of the relations between Gottschalk and his superiors. The work was dedicated to Charles the Bald, in whose presence Gottschalk had been flogged at Quierzy, and to whom Ratramnus had addressed a treatise in explanation of Gottschalk's position. Hincmar found an ally in Scotus, whose book *De Divina Praedestinatione* decisively rejected dual predestination and defended the orthodoxy of Augustine. But Scotus introduced a speculative element into his work which was in itself a source of danger. His attempt to merge theology in philosophy, his free treatment of the literal meaning of Scripture and Augustine to suit his own philosophical theories, and his insistence upon the divine origin of free will and the ability of man to choose the good, went beyond the bounds of strictly orthodox opinion; and Hincmar himself, who had invited Scotus to write and received the dedication of his book, hesitated to endorse its conclusions.

A synod held at Quierzy in 853 passed four decrees under the influence of Hincmar which summed up the orthodox attitude upon the controverted points. (1) The complete unity of divine predestination was asserted. The gift of grace and the retribution of God's justice were two aspects of the same thing. Man was created in paradise without sin and with free will. But, by the abuse of free will, he fell, and so the whole human race became a mass of perdition. God, in His goodness and justice, chose out of this mass according to His foreknowledge those whom He predestined through grace to life, and to these He predestined eternal life.

The residue were left in the mass of perdition by the judgment of justice, but, although God foreknew that they must perish, He predestined, not them to eternal punishment, but, because He is just, eternal punishment to them. (2) The loss of free will in Adam was recovered for man by Christ. With the prevention and aid of grace, man has free will to good; but, abandoned by grace, his will is to evil. Grace frees the will and heals it from the corruption of sin. (3) God wills that all men should be saved without exception. It does not follow that all are saved; but some are saved by the gift of the Saviour, while those who perish receive their due reward. (4) Christ adopted human nature without respect of persons and died for the redemption of every man. If all are not redeemed, it is because they are without faith or are deficient in the faith that works through love. The cup of human salvation, in which human weakness is mingled with divine strength, is for all men to drink; but without drinking there is no healing from sin.

While the decrees of Quierzy were issued by a local synod in the course of a dispute which affected a limited, though by no means small area, they represented the general mind of the Church upon the debated points. The medieval Church as a whole, while founding its doctrine of predestination and grace upon Augustine, interpreted his view of man's free will in a more humane sense than a perfectly logical exposition could allow it to bear, and refused to admit that predestination to destruction was a consequence of his teaching. Such an admission, even safeguarded by the proviso that the righteous judgments of God were inseparable from His goodness and were part of a single Divine purpose, opened the way to the Manichaeism which, after Augustine had escaped from it, had still left some trace upon his conception of the antithesis between good and evil. The heresies of the Cathari and Albigenses, in the twelfth and thirteenth centuries, reviving the Manichaean tenet of a duality of good and evil principles, induced the theory of two distinct forms of predestination, a *praedestinatio duplex* or *bifaria* which depended on a less intricate argument than the *gemina praedestinatio* advocated by Gottschalk. But the orthodox mind recognised a sharp distinction between the predestination and the foreknowledge of God. In scholastic language the elect are *praedestinati*, the reprobate *praesciti*. In both classes of men free will exists, weakened and corrupted by sin; but with the reprobate it is merely a will to evil. In the elect it is powerless to act until awakened by grace. The work of grace delivers it to the enjoyment of the full freedom in which man is able by its exercise to obtain merit in the sight of God, who has called it to cooperate with His free gift.

At the same time, the abstract discussion of the process of grace was overshadowed by the visible organisation of the Church and the benefits offered by it in the sacraments. The elect and reprobate were known only to God, but the means of grace entrusted to the Church were open to all its members. Baptism was not merely the rite of admission to the company of professing Christians; it removed original sin by the operation of the Holy Spirit, and was the necessary preliminary to the saving work of grace. The mystery of the dispensation which allowed infants, incapable of actual sin, to die unbaptised was a constant topic with writers on predestination. Although opinions might vary with regard to the degree of punishment allotted to them for the sin inherited from Adam, there was no escape from the conclusion that they were part of the mass of perdition to which baptism alone could open the gate of salvation. Speculations upon the uncovenanted mercies of God could not alter the fact that the Church possessed only one means of entry to the way of eternal life, without which the infant was as helpless as the unbaptised adult whose apparent virtues were but *splendida vitia*.

The official teaching of the Church, therefore, laid all its emphasis upon the use of the means of grace. It will be noted that the Lateran confession of faith in 1215 laid down no explicit doctrine of predestination. It assumed the existence of the elect and the reprobate who, at Christ's second coming, would receive judgment according to their works. But the only guarantee of salvation was membership of the visible Church, with its crowning benefit of union with Christ through the sacrament of His body and blood. Its initial rite, baptism, was profitable to salvation for all, children and adults alike; and for those who fall into sin after baptism the Church provided a means of recovery in the sacrament of penance. Of that progress in faith and attainment of love which are the offspring and accompaniment of the work of grace nothing was said; of the inner spiritual life God was the sole judge. The criterion which the Church applied to man's approach to salvation was perseverance in good works, initiated, aided, and continually repaired by the grace communicated through the sacraments according to her recognised forms.

IV

As has been shewn, the question of the saving work of Christ arose necessarily out of the predestinarian controversy; for, on the strictest interpretation of the Augustinian doctrine, its benefits applied to the elect alone. The part, however, which this question played in the dispute was subordinate to the principal subject of discussion; by both sides in the controversy the method by which the salvation of man, whether as a whole or in part, was achieved was taken for granted. The Catholic doctrine of the two natures of Christ, divine and human, coexistent in one person, had been laid down, once and for all, at Chalcedon in 451: through the Eternal Word, incarnate by the Holy Ghost of the Virgin Mary, suffering in human form, risen and ascended in His glorified body, the prospect of everlasting life was opened to mankind. Early in the seventh century, however, a new problem in Christology was raised in the East, which was not settled until the beginning of the eighth. The acknowledgment of the two natures of Christ implied the coexistence in Him of two wills directing two modes of operation, distinct but in perfect agreement. Sergius, Patriarch of Constantinople (610–38), professing to rely upon a phrase attributed to his predecessor Mennas (536–52), brought forward the theory that in the two natures there was only one will and one operation, the divine will working through the human instrument. The Monothelete controversy, originating in this way, might have died out early, had it not been for its entanglement with politics. Acceptance of the theory afforded a basis for reconciliation with the Monophysite sects, disaffected subjects of the orthodox Empire; and, as the century advanced and the conquests of Islām absorbed three of the Eastern patriarchates, the need of such a basis became all the more urgent. But the object of its defenders was rather to procure its tacit recognition by stifling public discussion than to assert it openly; and in this they failed, owing to the passionate championship of the opposite cause by orthodox enthusiasts. The Ecthesis of Heraclius (639), who was prompted to support the Monothelete party for the reasons of state already mentioned, imposed silence on both sides, but at the same time shewed an obvious bias in favour of the heresy. In 648 the Type of Constans II renewed the prohibition of debate with a more impartial attitude; but the implied alternative of two opposite doctrines was even more distasteful to the orthodox than the partial pronouncement which the Type superseded.

The historical importance of the Monothelete controversy lies in the severance which it produced between the Churches of the West and the East, temporary indeed, but the beginning of wider divergences which led to ultimate separation. The theory, made in Constantinople, was admitted at Rome by Pope Honorius I, but by him alone of the Popes. At the Lateran Council of 649, held under Martin I, the Ecthesis and the Type were alike condemned, together with the writings of the Monotheletes, as heretical. The somewhat ambiguous term "theandric energy," borrowed by Cyrus of Alexandria from Dionysius the Areopagite to express the operation of the one will in Christ, was explained in the opposite sense, and the doctrine of the two wills and two operations was formulated as that of the Church. The result of these decrees was a persecution of the orthodox by the Emperor Constans. In 653 the Pope was taken prisoner to Constantinople and died in exile; Maximus of Chrysopolis, who had succeeded Sophronius, Patriarch of Jerusalem, as the most ardent defender of the two united wills in the East, died a martyr to his cause. The policy of Constans, however, was reversed in the sequel, and the decrees of the Lateran Council were upheld by the council summoned by Constantine Pogonatus in 680, which met in the hall of the imperial palace called Trullus and was attended by the deputies of Pope Agatho. Here the rival doctrines were again threshed out, with the result that the council confessed the presence of two natural wills and two natural operations in Christ, without division or confusion. The heretics were again condemned, and with their names was joined that of Pope Honorius. Monothelism was not wholly stamped out in 681, when the sixth general council concluded its sittings, nor did the improved relations between Rome and Constantinople lead to permanent cordiality. Agatho, who made his influence felt in 680–681, rejected the disciplinary canons passed ten years later by the "Quinisext" council which met again in the Trullus. But in the condemnation of Monothelism the East and West were at one, and its supporters dwindled. The attempt of the Emperor Philippicus to revive the doctrine in 712 was followed by his overthrow in the following year, and, although it lingered among the Maronites until the close of the twelfth century, it had no vogue outside that limited and remote sect.

The Monothelete dispute, indeed, was wholly forgotten in the fresh excitement of the Iconoclastic controversy of the eighth century, which renewed the breach between Rome and the imperialist Church of Constantinople. From the doctrinal point of view, the significance of a religious warfare which, under the leadership of Leo the Isaurian and Constantine Copronymus, was eminently political, is its bearing upon the doctrine of the Incarnation. On the details of the degree of veneration due to images there were cross-currents of opinion in the West, which reflected to some extent the sharp distinction in the East between Iconoclasts and the defenders of image-worship. When the second Council of Nicaea in 787 put an end to the long conflict and formulated, in re-establishing the use of images, the difference between the *προσκύνησις* due to them and the service of *λατρεία* due to God alone, the council of the Frankish kingdom at Frankfort in 794, acting upon the statement of the case put forward in the *Libri Carolini*, rejected its decrees, distinguishing between the employment of images as an aid to devotion and the payment of worship or service to them. Fundamentally, the controversy turned upon the propriety of pictorial or graven representations of Divinity; the most celebrated incident in its progress is the removal of the image of the Saviour, known as the Ἀντιφωνήτης, in 730 from its position above the Brazen Gate of the palace at Constantinople. It was argued that such representations, picturing the divine in human form, were heretical; the council which condemned them in 754 argued that they encouraged the principal heresies which in time past had denied the Godhead of Christ or confounded His divine with His human nature. The only visible image of Christ which the council allowed to be lawful was the elements in the Holy Eucharist; here, by the union of divine grace with material objects, the union of Godhead with humanity was presented to the eyes of the faithful. This view of the Eucharist was rejected at Nicaea in 787, conflicting as it did with the doctrine that the elements were the very body and blood of Christ. But the theory at the foundation of the defence of images was that the prohibition of the use of images under the old dispensation was annulled by the Incarnation, and that the appearance of God in human shape legalised representations which brought the memory of their originals before the minds of worshippers and deserved the honour that was paid to those originals through their medium.

The Monothelete and Iconoclastic controversies, and especially the second, were to some extent affected by the growth of Mohammedanism, with its unitarian conception of divinity and its prohibition of images and pictures in worship. The opposition of the council of Frankfort in 794 to the decrees of Nicaea, and its denial of the payment of *adoratio* or *servitus* to images, sprang rather from the dread of the idolatry which flourished upon the northern and eastern outskirts of the Frankish kingdom. At the same time, it was faced by a new heresy with regard to the Incarnation which had come into being upon the southern limits of western Christendom, close to the frontier of the Arab caliphate and in a district in which Arianism had long prevailed. Felix, Bishop of Urgel (c. 783–99), was the author, or at any rate the transmitter, of the theory that the humanity of Christ was not derived directly from the Divine essence, but was merely adopted by the Father. He found an energetic supporter in Elipandus, the metropolitan of Toledo, and their propagation of the doctrine was warmly contested by the orthodox prelates of the Spanish Church in their efforts to keep alive the embers of a faith almost extinguished by the victory of Islām. Felix did not deny the divinity of Christ, but recognised a double form of sonship: as divine, He was the true Son of God, as human, the adoptive son. The opinion was condemned in a council of twenty-six bishops, held at Narbonne in 791, at which Felix himself was present. In the following year, it received a second condemnation at Ratisbon, and Felix was sent to Rome, where he confessed and recanted his heresy before Hadrian II. But, like Berengar at a later date, he was no sooner back in familiar surroundings than he renewed his teaching. The orthodox answer to a doctrine which specially threatened Frankish Christianity came from Alcuin, who by correspondence and a formal treatise combated the confusion of ideas into which the Adoptionists had fallen. The gist of his argument was that the sonship of Christ depends, not upon a question of nature, but of person; the two natures are united without division in the single person of the Son. The idea of the son of man, made by adoption and grace the Son of God, was therefore inadmissible. Meanwhile the condemnation of Felix and Elipandus was placed in the forefront of the canons passed by the council of Frankfort, and in 799 Felix was deprived of his see. At Aix-la-Chapelle he was confronted by Alcuin, whose arguments led him to retract his opinions once more; but he was sent into retirement under the supervision of the Archbishop of Lyons, and his final perseverance in orthodoxy is at least doubtful. Although the Adoptionist heresy was weakly defended, and its fate was sealed by the condemnation of Felix, it was still maintained by the aged Elipandus, whose talent for vituperation was more remarkable than his theological ability, until shortly before his death in 808.

Adoptionism was also opposed in writing by Paulinus, Patriarch of Aquileia, and condemned at a council over which he presided at Cividale in 796. But the strength of the heresy, such as it was, lay in the region of its origin, the Aquitanian march which, as the Middle Ages advanced, became notorious as a breeding-ground of heterodoxy. Like the Monophysite and Monothelete controversies, however, the Adoptionist dispute was concentrated upon a single aspect of the Incarnation, the nature and person of the Incarnate Being. The effect of the Incarnation upon the relations between man and God did not enter into it, save in so far as the assumption of humanity by Christ implied a consequent change in those relations as they concerned the whole human race. It has been already shewn that in the discussions which were waged round the subject of predestination the effect of the Incarnation was presupposed as assuring the salvation of man; the question at issue was whether this effect was particular or general. The work of grace, begun in baptism, brought man within reach of the benefits obtained for him by the life and death of Christ; whether in this state he was capable of acquiring merit for himself by good works, or whether his justification depended entirely upon his faith in the merits of Christ's passion, was a consequent alternative to which there was no very certain answer, although the view that salvation was open to the whole of mankind swayed the balance in favour of the first of these opinions. But, apart from the general agreement that Christ, by taking upon Himself our nature uncontaminated by sin, broke the dominion of sin over the world, no theory had as yet explained the Incarnation as a necessary means for the re-establishment of the relationship between God and man which had been forfeited by the sin of Adam, and it was not until the end of the eleventh century and the early days of scholastic theology that a proof of this hypothesis was furnished.

The weight of St Augustine's teaching had fallen upon the sinfulness of mankind and the inability of man to rise to the state of grace by any merits of his own. Christ by the merits of His life and passion restored union between God and man; the death of the perfect Man was a sacrifice for human sin. Thus the Incarnate Son is the mediator who makes Himself responsible for the sin of man and reconciles him to the God whom he has offended by removing him from the dominion of sin. But, side by side with the view that the voluntary sacrifice of Christ delivered man from his natural sinfulness, the theory, derived through Origen, gained ground that man, as a consequence of the Fall, had been subjected to the power of the devil, and that the sacrifice of Christ was demanded to free him from this thraldom to a personal master. It was an act of redemption, a payment made by God to the devil for the ransom of a slave. Such a payment could be made only in the person of one who was sinless and therefore free from the devil's power. On the other hand, it was inconceivable that the devil would accept a sinless ransom; this would be payment without an equivalent. It was necessary therefore that he should enter into the bargain without certainty of the true nature of the offering from which he expected to obtain compensation, and in the hope that Christ was a man liable to succumb to temptation to sin. The Incarnation was thus designed to deceive him and keep him in suspense, and of this successful deception the death of Christ was the climax. This once achieved, the work of redemption was completed; when once the devil witnessed the triumph of Christ over death, he knew himself defrauded where he had expected to get the full advantage of the transaction.

Grotesquely inconsistent with the righteousness of God as this theory seems, it won acceptance; it was at least reasonable to suppose that the arch-deceiver could be conquered only by the use of weapons similar to his own. Augustine, never wholly freed from the notion of the dualism of good and evil which his early Manichaeanism had left behind, represented the devil as caught in a mouse-trap; Gregory, who enriched the idea with much detailed and imaginative treatment, likened the Incarnation to a hook baited for Behemoth, who, seeking to devour the humanity of Christ, was pierced by the sharp point of His divinity. If all writers did not indulge in such images, yet the general view of the sacrifice of Christ was that it was a ransom paid by God to the arch-enemy.

From another point of view, however, the righteousness of God was regarded independently of His will to win back sinful man to Himself. By falling into sin, when, in his paradisal condition, he still possessed the power to refrain from sin, man had offended God and provoked His wrath; and, though God in His love was willing to restore him to favour, yet His justice required satisfaction, a payment of an adequate penalty. This idea, founded upon a legal conception of justice, alternates in Gregory's writings with the ransom-theory; fostered by the penitential system of the Church, it eventually superseded it. The sin of man was so great that man himself could pay no satisfaction which could meet the case. Therefore, in perfect union with the will of the Father, the Son became man and gave Himself as the sinless offering. But the development of this theory left room for the question whether it was by this means alone that satisfaction could have been found, although no other act could have proved more signally the union of mercy with justice in the Divine mind.

Until Anselm, in the treatise *Cur Deus Homo?*, produced the argument which profoundly affected the theology of the Incarnation for centuries after his day, it was generally held that God, in His omnipotence, might have chosen some other means for the redemption of the world. Anselm set out to prove, in the form of a dialogue between himself and a pupil, the necessity of the assumption of human nature by God Himself for this purpose. In themselves, the analogy between the entry of death into the world through man's disobedience and the restoration of life by the obedience of a man, between the sin of Eve and the birth of the Saviour from Mary, between the tree of the garden and the tree of the cross, were merely picturesque unless this necessity could be demonstrated. The idea, however, that God could have restored man to the dignity for which He intended him by means of an angel or some man created without sin, might be rejected; for in that case man, the servant of God and equal to the angels, would have become the servant of a redeemer who was not divine. Anselm further decides against the popular theory that the Incarnation was the means of ransoming man from the power of the devil; the devil had no claims over man which demanded a legal ransom. The writing against man which was blotted out by the death of Christ was not a deed to which the devil was a party; it was the confirmation of the righteous judgment of God, by which man, having sinned of his own will, was condemned to sin and to its punishment.

The foundation of Anselm's argument is his definition of sin as the failure to render to God the honour which is due to Him, the withholding of a just debt. For this satisfaction is necessary, and this implies not merely the payment of the thing withheld, but further compensation for the wrong done. If God were to leave sin unpunished, this would be contrary to His justice and would introduce disorder into His kingdom. In God's order of things there is nothing so intolerable as the subtraction of due honour from the Creator by the creature. That honour must be paid, or punishment must follow; otherwise we must conclude that God is unjust to Himself or unable to exact either alternative. Anselm's view of punishment for sin was that it is a payment forced upon an unwilling debtor; he who withholds from God what is His has to forfeit something of his own. By removing from the sinner that happiness which depends upon obedience to the Creator, God repairs His offended honour and asserts His lordship; not that His honour is affected in itself by the disobedience of angels or men, but such disobedience is an attempt to disturb the order of the universe, and cannot be overlooked by the will from whose domination it endeavours to escape. From these premises Anselm proceeded to discuss the creation and fall of man. In creating man without sin, the intention of God was to fill the gap left by the fall of the rebellious angels and to perfect their number. But the sin of man made it impossible for him, if it were left unpunished, to take his place among the good angels who had never sinned. To recover the blessedness which he lost by sin, he must make satisfaction, and satisfaction must be proportionate to the offence for which it is paid. No atonement for sin which man can make by his own efforts is a sufficient equivalent, for it is merely the payment of the duty which he owes to God, not the restoration of a debt, and there is nothing in it which can outweigh the enormity of a single sin. If man, in the state in which it was in his power to avoid sin, succumbed of his own will to the temptation of the devil, and so frustrated God's purpose of perfecting human nature, how can he now, born in sin and weakness, conquer the devil and render to God His due? His weakness is no excuse for him, for it is the result of deliberate disobedience; his inability to pay the debt is as much a fault as his failure to pay it. To assume, then, that God is ready to forgive man the debt which man should voluntarily render Him, simply because man cannot pay it, is to reduce God's mercy to an absurdity, the forgiveness of a bad debt which He cannot recover. Punishment would be forgone, and man would achieve through sin that blessedness which his sin has made it impossible for him to attain without satisfaction.

Nevertheless, if there were not some means by which the debt could be paid, the mercy of God would be utterly overcome by His justice. Hitherto, the argument has been confined to the relations between an all-powerful and offended God and powerless and sinning man; ignorance of Christ and His work has been expressly supposed. But it has been proved that man cannot pay the debt and so restore himself to his lost blessedness. It follows of necessity that the prospect of salvation assured him by the Christian faith, with its emphasis upon the mercy of God, depends upon Christ. Thus, by the development of the theory of satisfaction through a negative form of reasoning, Anselm arrived at the positive argument for the necessity of the Incarnation, which is worked out in the second book of the treatise.

God created man with a rational nature which could choose between good and evil, and made that nature righteous, so that it could attain blessedness in the enjoyment of the highest good, which is God Himself. If man had not sinned, he would not die: as it is, his perfect restoration to blessedness must be accompanied by the resurrection of the dead in their incorruptible human bodies, for God will perfect the noble work which He has begun and cannot have made in vain. But, as has been shewn, full satisfaction for sin is indispensable to this consummation, and this man cannot pay. In one sense of the word, there is no necessity for God to perfect His creation, for He is bound by no compulsion, and the good which He does is entirely of His grace. On the other hand, the unchangeableness of His nature makes it necessary that His goodness should bring to an end what it has begun. This, however, cannot be achieved without the payment of a satisfaction for sin greater than everything which is not God; and it follows that the person who makes this payment must possess this superior greatness. Now, there is nothing greater than everything which is not God but God Himself. Therefore the payment must be made by God; but, since the satisfaction is due from man, it must be given by a God-man, in whom the two natures, divine and human, are not converted from one into the other or confused, but are both perfect and coexistent in one person. It is further necessary that, as the human race sinned in Adam, so its restoration should be effected by one who should take humanity from the seed of Adam; and, as sin entered the world through the act of a woman who was previously sinless and was made of man without woman, so that humanity which redeems sin should come into the world as the offspring of a pure virgin.

Thus God became man in the person of the Incarnate Word, for the unity of the human person could not combine the three persons of the Godhead, and the son of the virgin could be none of the three but the eternal Son of God, to whom further the act of intercession for man with His Father is proper. Being Himself God and without sin, He could not undergo a mortal death as a debt incurred by the sin of Adam, who, in his perfect state, would not have died. His death was a voluntary offering to God's honour, which He had it in His power to give or withhold, and which God could not exact from Him. Man had alienated himself from God to the uttermost by his sin; the satisfaction made by the Redeemer took the form of the uttermost payment, the laying down of His life. This voluntary death, undergone by the Almighty whom no necessity could bind, and by the sinless One who owed no debt to God, prevailed over the sins of the whole world.

Cur Deus Homo? is the most important of a series of treatises in which Anselm discussed the question of sin and redemption in its various aspects, and it remains one of the great theological classics of the Middle Ages. The theory of the satisfaction due to God for sin eventually superseded the crude notion of the ransom paid by God to the devil. All that was due to the devil from God was punishment; all that man owed him was conquest in return for the victory which he had gained at the Fall. But that conquest was actually the payment of a debt demanded by God. It would be inappropriate in an historical survey to enter into the merits and defects of a theory which has been subjected to searching criticism by modern theologians. Two points, however, may be remarked. In the first place, the whole line of argument was determined by the legal character of Anselm's mind. The working of the free grace of God in the deliverance of man from sin was entirely subordinated to the idea of the penalty due to an offended God and the method of satisfaction by which punishment could be averted. Whether Anselm merely transferred the ecclesiastical conception of the reconciliation of the sinner to the Church by penance to the fundamental question of the redemption of humanity from the sin of Adam, or whether he combined with that conception the secular principle of the wergild, is not a matter of great importance. But the inevitable tendency of the opposition, as in a court of law, between the offended judge and the impotent sinner, and the voluntary interposition of the mediator, was to establish a distinction between the justice and the mercy of God; and, though Anselm himself strove to reconcile these, yet the impression of justice as the peculiar property of the Father, and mercy as that of the Son, was bound to have its influence upon popular thought, especially as the work of the third Person of the Trinity in the Incarnation was hardly considered. Secondly, the stress of the argument was laid entirely upon the act of satisfaction, with the result that the idea of the Incarnation became subordinate to that of the atonement for sin by the death of Christ which was its ultimate object. It is true that Anselm dealt incidentally with the example which the whole life of Christ affords to man, but merely in demonstration of the sinlessness which gave unique value to His death as the expiation of the sin of the world.

The importance of Anselm's work did not appeal noticeably to his contemporaries; it was not until a later generation that its influence was manifest. The old idea of the ransom of man from the power of the devil still held the field. Among the doctrines of Abelard condemned at Sens in 1141 was the proposition, no less strenuously expressed by Anselm, that the devil had never any legal claim upon man, but was merely, by the permission of Divine justice, his gaoler, and that therefore the object of the Incarnation was not the deliverance of man from his yoke. At the same time, while Abelard was under the influence of more than one theory of the Incarnation, he saw in it conspicuously a manifestation of the love of God, exhibited in the life and teaching of Christ and consummated by His death. The plan and purpose of the Incarnation were that God should enlighten the world by His wisdom and kindle it to His love. Its effects are subjective: man is justified and redeemed by the love which the passion of Christ implants in his heart, not only freeing him from the slavery of sin, but admitting him to the liberty of the sons of God, casting out fear and filling him with the sense of the boundless grace which could make such a sacrifice. This view was echoed by Abelard's disciple Peter Lombard, who, at the opening of his discussion of the work of redemption, represented the death of Christ as a pledge of the love of God by which man is excited and kindled to love Him and is thus justified. Nevertheless in the sequel Peter demonstrated what he had actually taken as his hypothesis, that the real effect of the passion is redemption from the devil and the bonds of sin in which he had enchained mankind, and, swayed consistently by the authority of Augustine, accepted the theory of the deception of the devil by God, quoting the famous "mouse-trap" passage. Of the theory of satisfaction he had nothing to say; his only approach to it was the statement that without the cooperation of the penalty paid by Christ the penalty in which the Church binds her penitents would be insufficient.

This being the attitude of the theological text-book which established its authority in the schools, it is not surprising that the permeation of the Anselmic theory was gradual, and that older doctrines still held their own beside it. A century after Peter Lombard, Aquinas presented several parallel views of the purpose of the Incarnation, in which the traditional doctrine of ransom from the devil was included, though without its more grotesque elements of the act of deception and the justice of the devil's dominion. There was thus no definite dogmatic position upon this point. The Lateran Council, which forms the limit of our period, produced no formula to bind speculation with regard to it. Its statement of the doctrine of the Incarnation merely amplified the clauses of the creeds. The Incarnation was represented as the fulfilment of God's eternal plan, by which, for the salvation of the world from the sin into which it had fallen, the Son of God, immortal and incapable of suffering as regards His Divinity, assumed human nature and suffered as a mortal man, to rise again in His glorified body, and return from heaven as the judge of mankind at the last day.

Thus the Incarnation is a cardinal fact of Christian belief, the explanation of which was the ultimate cause of the various controversies amid which medieval doctrine assumed a fixed shape. To this all discussion came back in the end, whether it concerned the foreknowledge of God, the origin of evil, or the question most intimately associated with the assumption of manhood by God, the nature of the Trinity. Upon this last subject the Lateran Council declared the existence of the three Persons, with unity of being, substance, and nature. With regard to the third Person, it affirmed the double procession of the Holy Spirit from the Father and the Son. Of this little need be said, for the history of the doctrine is of political rather than theological significance. The earliest definite statement of the double procession came from regions of Arian controversy, and was made by the bishops of the Spanish Visigothic kingdom at the council of Toledo in 589. But their incorporation of the *Filioque* clause in the text of the Nicene creed represented an orthodox opinion which was a natural consequence of the doctrine of unity of substance, and was intended primarily to avoid all ambiguity of thought which its omission might produce. Subsequently, the hesitation with which the clause was regarded by the orthodox was due, not to any doubt upon the point, but to the question whether it was advisable or necessary to make an addition to the words of the creed. Its gradual acceptance by the councils of the Western Church might have passed unnoticed, had it not been for the attack made upon it by Photius in his encyclical letter to the Eastern patriarchs in 867, in which its admission was placed in the forefront of the heresies attributed to the Latins. From that time, not only its position in the creed, but its doctrinal propriety, came into dispute, and with its introduction into controversy began the irreconcilable division between the West and East which culminated in 1054. The West was forced to make dogmatic assertion of the necessity to orthodoxy of a phrase which the East rejected as heretical.

As a rider to its confession of faith, however, the Lateran Council of 1215 produced a lengthy statement of the doctrine of the Trinity, arising from opinions contained in the works of Joachim, the celebrated Abbot of Flora in Calabria, who had died thirteen years before. The influence of this remarkable mystic upon the thought of his day was exercised mainly through his prophetic writings, in which he announced the approaching end of the present dispensation and the appearance in the world of that final state to which he gave the name of "the everlasting gospel." It was not, however, upon this ground that his views were condemned; and, indeed, he and the small congregation of monasteries which he founded were expressly exempted from censure in the second canon of the Lateran Council, as no fault could be found with his personal profession of faith, the obedience with which he had submitted his works to the sanction of the holy see, and the regularity of the religious life led by him and his followers. Nevertheless, his impatience of the rigid system of definition applied by scholastic theology to the mysteries which occupied his fervent brain had led to an attack upon the doctrine of the Trinity enunciated by Peter Lombard in the *Sentences*. The distinction between the unity of the Godhead and the separate properties of the three Persons appeared to Joachim to convert the Trinity into a quaternity, composed of the three Persons, begetting, begotten, and proceeding, and the common substance of which none of these qualities could be predicated. The refutation by the council of this strange attempt to fasten the stigma of heresy upon a book of unimpeachable orthodoxy, which had devoted a long series of chapters to the proof of the consubstantiality of the three Persons, was singularly elaborate, with its citation of passages from Scripture and its appeal to the analogy of the union of many earthly members in a single Church. The fame of Joachim, however, gave a passing importance to his scruples with regard to the use of terms in the theological manual which had become the text-book of the schools, and the prevalence of heresies which set at naught, not only received doctrines, but the efficacy of the whole ecclesiastical system, demanded the vindication of its formulas from all suspicion of unsound teaching.

V

The final paragraphs of the Lateran confession, following its definition of the Triune Godhead and its statement of the plan of salvation and its fulfilment in Christ, are devoted to the visible Church and the means of grace which it affords to the faithful. There is no enumeration of sacraments, and of two, Confirmation and Unction, no mention is made. Holy Order is touched upon only in so far as it is a necessary condition to the celebrant of the Eucharist, and Marriage only in a brief clause intended to protect its sanctity against the assertions of sectaries who assailed it. The chief emphasis of this part of the canon is laid upon the Holy Eucharist as the central function of the life of the Church, and the paragraph in which this is treated is followed by the declaration of the Church's belief with regard to the two other sacraments essential to the spiritual life of every Christian—Baptism, in which the stain of original sin is washed away and he is brought into membership with the Church, and Penance, by which post-baptismal sin is cleansed and the privileges which it forfeits are restored.

The ecclesiastical doctrine of the sacraments assumed a fixed form with the development of scholastic theology. Until that period the use of the term sacrament, though tending to be confined to certain special rites, was somewhat loose. Augustine's definition of the word, *sacrae rei signum*, could be and was constantly applied to any religious symbol, whether act or concrete object. All doctrine, in the words of the same authority, is concerned either with things or with signs; and, where the mystical temperament was strong, analogies between visible tokens and unseen realities could be discovered indefinitely. But, while there was no strict limitation of its employment, the word acquired a special significance in connexion with those mysteries which were the outward signs of the believer's fellowship with the Church and his union with its Head. Enumerations of these, where they were attempted, differed; but from an early date Baptism and the Eucharist stood out prominently as the two sacraments of the gospel necessary to salvation. To Gregory the Great they had this preeminence over the multitude of lesser ritual observances which could be described as sacraments. A special importance was also attached to the consecration of the holy chrism, from which was derived the ultimate conception of Confirmation and the Unction of the sick as distinct sacraments. As long, however, as the purely general use of the term prevailed, individual writers were at perfect liberty to ascribe it to as many or as few rites as they pleased, or to represent the various forms of one rite, such as the profession and consecration of different classes of religious persons, as separate sacraments.

The technical limitation of the sacraments of the Church to seven in number does not appear before the twelfth century, and the first categorical statements of the number are found in the *Sentences* of the future Alexander III and in the more famous work of Peter Lombard. In the formulation of the scholastic doctrine of the sacraments, however, Peter Lombard was anticipated by Hugh of St Victor, who died in 1141, in his *Liber de Sacramentis*. The number of seven, which Hugh implied rather than stated, was no doubt, as in so many other cases, influenced by mystical reasons, and chiefly by its association with the gifts of the Holy Ghost; at the same time, the establishment of the number itself depended upon the recognition of the principle that, while every sacrament is a sign of an invisible thing, not every such sign is a sacrament. Sacraments are visible forms of invisible grace; as such, they wear the likeness of the realities of which they are tokens, as the water in Baptism signifies the mystical washing of the soul by the Holy Spirit, and the bread and wine in the Eucharist signify the spiritual food which is there partaken. Further, they actually contain by consecration and convey those realities, or at any rate possess and impart their effect, to the recipient; they are the means by which grace communicates itself directly to the soul, as remedies against original and actual sin. As means of grace, their institution was deferred until the coming of Christ, which was the beginning of the work of grace. Marriage, indeed, existed before that time as a sacrament and as a duty; but it was not until the gospel dispensation that it acquired the essential character of a remedy for sin. The old law had its sacraments, circumcision preceded Baptism. But these were merely promises of salvation, while those of the new law actually give it.

Peter Lombard points to three reasons for the institution of the sacraments. They were intended to encourage our humility and obedience to God, by the reverence with which man is commanded to regard the inanimate instruments used as outward signs of God's grace. They are for our instruction, because through them man, blinded by sin, learns to recognise the divine things which he cannot see unaided. They are also given for our exercise, so that by their diligent use the soul may be built up and temptation avoided. In Hugh of St Victor we find the triple distinction between their likeness to the thing signified, their significance, and their efficacy. The first is natural, the work of the Creator, the second is the result of their institution, which was referred to Christ, and the third arises from their consecration by the priest. Further, there are two necessary constituent parts of a sacrament. These are defined by Peter Lombard as *verba* and *res*, the words by which consecration is effected or the grace of the sacrament is bestowed, and the material which is used. In this connexion, we must distinguish between the use of *res* and its application to the inward reality which the sacrament betokens and veils. The latter is, properly speaking, the *res sacramenti*, and, as the doctrine became more fully systematised, *verba* and *res* were supplanted by the terms *forma* and *materia*, the form and matter of the sacraments.

These are the principal points of a doctrine whose full implications, together with the multitude of questions which they suggested, were, at the time of the Lateran Council, still awaiting discussion by the theologians of the thirteenth century. The doctrine was formulated in Paris, the heart of theological teaching in Europe; its contents were still speculative and open to argument in an age distinguished by extreme subtlety of dialectic. Although the seven sacraments were generally accepted, no authoritative pronouncement of their number was made until 1439. While, with regard to certain sacraments, and especially Baptism and the Eucharist, it was easy to define the form and matter, either the form or the matter, or both, of others were more open to discussion. But, while there was room for fluidity of opinion on details and for the debate of numerous problems dependent on or emerging from the main subject, the ground-work of the doctrine of the sacraments was settled in the twelfth century. The task of formulating their theological basis marked no fresh starting-point in the history of ecclesiastical practice or popular belief; it was a necessary outcome of the gradual process by which, as Christianity and, with it, social order advanced, the dispensation of the benefits of the Incarnation of Christ was regarded as vested in the ordained ministry of the Church. The recognition of the special distinction which separated Baptism and the Eucharist from all minor acts that could be considered as having a sacramental character was an obvious consequence of their importance in the life of every Christian, who in the first was restored to the favour of God and by the second was maintained in His grace. The same universal application belonged to the two sacraments of chrism, the one with its renewal of grace to the child who took upon himself the responsibility of the vows made for him in Baptism, the other with its means of defence against the temptations that assailed the deathbed of the Christian. The admission of Marriage to the number of the sacraments gave specially needed sanctity to a bond upon whose maintenance the orderly character of Christian society depended. The requisite of repentance from sin as a condition of the worthy reception of the Eucharist gave significance to Penance as the means by which pardon from actual sin was secured. Finally, the general invalidity of the sacraments, unless dispensed by a ministry consecrated for their exercise, emphasised the peculiar gifts bestowed upon a special class by the rites of ordination, and set apart Holy Order from those acts of consecration to certain offices and conditions of life to which some writers, chiefly those who saw in the spread of monasticism the most fertile method of filling up the number of the elect, were inclined to ascribe sacramental virtue.

VI

The most original feature of the statement of faith issued by the Fourth Lateran Council was its definition of the doctrine of the Holy Eucharist. With the idea of the Catholic Church, the body of the faithful, membership of which is essential to salvation, was closely united the idea of the eternal priesthood of its Founder and Head, whose sacrifice of Himself upon the Cross was commemorated and its redeeming merits imparted in the continually repeated celebration of that sacred feast which He instituted on the eve of His passion. Here, as in so many other cases, the versatile mind of Augustine had anticipated the chief problems which beset this subject and influenced both of those opposite currents of opinion in whose conflicting course the sacrament of peace and unity became a source of division and warfare. At the root of his thought was the conception of the rite of the Eucharist, the partaking of the elements of bread and wine by the Christian congregation, as the mystery of unity, in which the bread, composed of many grains, and the wine, pressed from clusters of many grapes, were the visible symbols of the unity of the members of the Christian body, who, by the act of partaking, were incorporated in mystical union with their Head. They became the Lord's bread; His life was diffused through the whole body, which was one in Him. This was the most striking and definite aspect of Augustine's teaching with regard to the Eucharist. On the other hand, his conception of the elements of bread and wine as the body and blood of Christ was less consistent and uniform. If in certain passages he assumed their objective identity with the body and blood, and was at one with the clearly expressed statements of St Ambrose that the consecration of the elements by the recital of the words of institution is the act of Christ Himself, by which they are changed into His body and blood, he also used language which implied that faith in the recipient was an antecedent condition to that feeding upon Christ in the sacrament which, connected with our Lord's words in the sixth chapter of St John's Gospel, is the safeguard of eternal life to the believer. The sacrament is the outward sign; the elements upon the altar signify the inward virtue of the sacrament, the body and blood which are offered to the faithful partaker. All, worthy and unworthy, partake of the sacrament, and the unworthy run the certain risk which attends the misuse of holy things; but the virtue of the sacrament is confined to the worthy. They alone, fortified by faith, receive the *res sacramenti*; the rest are partakers merely of the *species*, for the *res sacramenti* is life to all who receive it, and cannot involve the privation of spiritual life which is the consequence of unworthy reception. The phrase *crede et manducasti*, in which Augustine summed up the essential conditions in which the virtue of the sacrament is effective, points to his conclusion that, whatever change might take place in the species after consecration, the ultimate test of the presence of Christ in the Eucharist was in the heart of the believer. Further, although the doctrine of an objective change in the elements may be inferred from Augustine, he nowhere defined the exact method of such a change; and, taken into account with his fervent acceptance of the principle "the Spirit quickeneth, the flesh profiteth nothing," his literal use of the words body and blood was qualified by the suggestion of a figurative and mystical interpretation.

While, on the one hand, the nature of the presence of Christ in the Eucharist is the question which stands first in the history of the development of Eucharistic dogma, the sacrificial aspect of the sacramental rite was doctrinally of equal importance. Here again the Fathers of the fourth and fifth centuries, while teaching that the Eucharist was a sacrifice, supplied no precise definition of the general statement. It was an offering to God, in which Christ, through His own words, was the true priest and consecrator. If St Ambrose and the nearly contemporary author of the *Liber de Sacramentis*, in asserting the operation of the Heavenly Word in the consecration of the elements, did not speak of the *confectio sacramenti* as a sacrifice, this is nevertheless the logical inference from their language; to them the visible officiant was the priest (*sacerdos*) who offers the sacrifice of the new Law for the people. Augustine, speaking of the pre-Christian sacrifices, defined the sacrifice which was offered as the visible sacrament, the sacred token, of the sacrifice which was invisible. It was offered for sin; its invisible significance was the sacrifice of a broken and contrite heart. He transferred this offering of the heart and will to the sacrifice of the Christian dispensation. Every work which has for its end the abiding relationship of man to God in holy fellowship is true sacrifice. By such works, which are works of mercy exercised with the object of delivering ourselves or our neighbours from misery, the whole fellowship of the redeemed is offered as an universal sacrifice to God by the great High Priest, in union with His offering of Himself in His passion. This is the fact which is celebrated by the faithful in the sacrament of the altar; in the oblation offered there, the Church itself is offered to God. The true Mediator, who, as God, receives the sacrifice, offered Himself in the form of a servant. Thus He is Himself at once priest and oblation. According to His will, the sacrament or sacred sign of His offering is the daily sacrifice of the Church, which, being the body of which He is the Head, thus learns to offer herself through Him.

The ruling thought of these statements is that the Eucharist is a corporate act in which the Church, relying upon the merits of the one sacrifice, presents herself as a living sacrifice to God. It follows that the remembrance of the death and passion which were the consummation of that one sacrifice must be prominently before the minds of the faithful in this connexion. It follows also that the perpetual presentation of the sacrifice on earth is closely allied with the perpetual mediation of the risen Lord in heaven. The act of communion, by which the Christian, receiving the hallowed elements, becomes a partaker of the body and blood of Christ and so unites himself with God, is the consummation of his part in the sacrifice. The idea of sacrifice is thus inseparable from the visible oblations which are the food of the faithful and, offered upon the altar, become by consecration the body and blood of Him who is both priest and sacrifice. If these aspects of the sacrament emerge from the writings of Augustine and his contemporaries without being consistently formulated, more than one of them are summed up in the earliest form in which part of the canon of the Roman mass has come down to us, the quotations which occur in the *De Sacramentis*, a work probably composed in northern Italy about 400.

> Therefore, mindful of His most glorious passion and of His resurrection from the dead and His ascension into heaven, we offer unto Thee this spotless offering, this holy bread and cup of eternal life; and we pray and beseech Thee to receive this oblation on Thine heavenly altar by the hands of Thine angels, as Thou didst deign to receive the gifts of Thy righteous servant Abel and the sacrifice of our patriarch Abraham and that which the high priest Melchizedek offered unto Thee.

It was in the emphasis which he laid upon the sacrificial character of the Eucharist that Gregory the Great made his contribution to the teaching of the Church on this subject. His observations upon the presence of Christ in the elements amount to little more than an assertion of his belief that the bread and wine in the sacrament are, by an undefined process of conversion, the body and blood of Christ. In one place, indeed, he represents the feeding of the redeemed upon the flesh of Christ as the object of the passion. The reception of His flesh and blood avail to salvation. Here we come to the essential point of Gregory's teaching. The victim, the daily oblation of Christ's body and blood, saves the soul from eternal ruin. It renews (*reparat*) through a mystery the death of the Only-Begotten to ourselves; although He has risen and by His rising has conquered death, yet, while in Himself He lives immortally and without corruption, He is sacrificed for us again in the mystery of the sacred oblation. This sacrifice for our absolution perpetually imitates His passion.

> What faithful person can doubt that, in the very moment of the offering, the heavens are opened at the voice of the priest, that in that mystery of Jesus Christ the choirs of angels are present, the lowest things are united to the highest, things earthly are joined to things divine, and the visible and invisible become one?

In his belief in the efficacy of the offering for the living and the dead, and of the application of its benefits to all circumstances in the life of the believer, Gregory prepared the way for much that is characteristic of medieval doctrine on the point. The stress laid upon the perpetual repetition of the oblation as a means of securing eternal life, the extension of its virtue to the dead who cannot partake of it, led naturally to an objective and mechanical theory in which the idea of the sacrifice, the imitation of our Lord's passion enacted at the altar before the eyes of the faithful, became dissociated from the idea of the sacrifice as an act of communion in which the whole Church shared. At the same time, while Gregory's language unquestionably tended to promote this change of view and was guarded by insufficient qualifications which may pass almost unnoticed, he nevertheless coupled with his veneration for the sacrifice on the altar a recognition of the necessity of personal sacrifice on the part of the believer to the full efficacy of the sacrament. Without the faithful heart and good works, the sacrament is incomplete; it must be received, not merely by the mouth of the body, but by the mouth of the heart; and to the evil recipient it brings no profit. Thus, if we can discover in Gregory the beginning of a divergency from the spiritual and subjective view of sacrament and sacrifice inculcated by Augustine, the attitudes of the two Fathers were not contradictory or greatly different. Where Gregory seems to depart from Augustinian tradition, he was moved by the desire to put his case clearly in unambiguous terms, and in so doing concentrated himself upon a single aspect rather than upon the whole subject with the variety of implications arising from it.

Not even in Gregory, however, did the doctrine of the Eucharist go beyond the general statement of certain outstanding principles. The elements after consecration become the body and blood of Christ, at any rate to the faithful partaker. The sacrament is in some sense a sacrifice. It is an offering made by the Church through its Head, the great High Priest; as such, it is united with His passion and His risen life of eternal intercession. It is also in some sense a memorial and an imitation of His passion. But as yet nothing was subjected to strict definition; the construction put upon these conclusions was not uniform, but varied considerably according to the temperament of the individual mind. Nor was there an approach to a connected theory of the Eucharist until a later date, when controversy was aroused and each side examined the grounds of its belief. The tendency of pious opinion to crystallise into dogma in this connexion appears earlier in the East than in the West. The belief in the operation of the Holy Spirit in effecting the change in the elements, which is found in the Eastern liturgies, established a parallel between the mystery of the Eucharist and the Incarnation. The epiclesis of these liturgies, which is found also in some of the early Gallican liturgies, invokes the descent of the Holy Spirit upon the elements. To this the recital of the words of institution is merely preliminary; the change in the elements is effected by the invocation. In the West, on the other hand, this change from an early date had been associated with the words of institution; the invocation which followed those words took, as in the passage already quoted from *De Sacramentis*, the form of a prayer that the consecrated gifts might be presented at the heavenly altar by the angels, or, as in the form assumed by the canon of the mass in the Sacramentaries of the sixth and subsequent centuries, by the Angel of God, that is, the Angel of the Covenant. While there is this difference between East and West with regard to the point in the service at which the change takes place, the Eastern theologians also employed more definite language with reference to the change itself. It is *metapoiesis*, a transmaking analogous to that by which natural food is incorporated in the body and blood of the eater. Further, the parallel with the mystery of the Incarnation and the analogy derived from natural processes suggest that the body and blood of Christ into which the bread and wine are thus transmade are literally His incarnate body and blood.

The Eastern doctrine was strongly influenced by the iconoclastic controversy of the eighth century. The position taken by the iconoclasts and formulated at Constantinople in 754 was that the Eucharist was the only image by which Christ's incarnation could be represented. To the elements, the image of His body, divinity was imparted by consecration through the descent of the Holy Spirit. In answer to this, orthodox belief, expressed in its clearest form by St John of Damascus, rejected the application of the terms image or figure to the consecrated elements. These were the body and blood of Christ; the terms antitype, image, and figure, which had been used by earlier writers, could apply only to the bread and wine before consecration. The effect of this acknowledgement that the unconsecrated elements were the image of Christ's body and blood was to give them a special sanctity and invite for them a veneration which marks a further difference between Eastern and Western thought. Under such influences the general tendency of Eastern theology at this period was to assert an objective presence of Christ in the sacrament. While orthodox exposition was devoted mainly to the effect of consecration, the idea of the Eucharist as a sacrifice in which the consecrated bread and wine are offered to God was taken for granted by both parties. To the orthodox it was the bloodless sacrifice, the memorial at once of Christ's passion and of His whole work as redeemer and mediator.

The position at which the Eastern Church arrived at this period remained fixed with little subsequent variation, and it was in the West that the work of definition, though beginning later and affected little, if at all, by the influence of a Church with which the bond of unity was broken, was carried on. An epoch in the history of the doctrine was marked by the appearance of the treatise *De Corpore et Sanguine Domini* by Paschasius Radbertus, a monk of Corbie in Neustria. Written about 831 at the request of Warinus, Abbot of the daughter house of Corvey on the Weser, it was revised and presented to Charles the Bald by its author after he had become Abbot of Corbie in 844. Starting from the premise that to the omnipotent will of God nothing is impossible, he laid down the positive statement that, by God's will, the body and blood of Christ in the Eucharist are very flesh and very blood, although they remain in the figure or species of bread and wine, and further that they are the flesh and blood which were born of Mary, suffered on the cross, and rose again the third day from the tomb. Faith is necessary to the perception of the reality under the species, just as faith alone could see that it was God who died on the cross in the form of a servant; the difference between the reality and the outward form is a test of the faith which is unto righteousness. In the visible sacrament Divine virtue works invisibly, sustaining the worthy partaker, and uniting him with the heavenly Word whose flesh is given for the life of the world.

> If He dwells in us, in order that we, the members of His body, may abide in Him, it is just, because we are in Him, that we should live of Him, and therefore do we feed upon the flesh of the Word and drink His blood.

The important point of Paschasius' doctrine was his definite assertion of an objective change, wrought at the consecration of the elements by the word of Christ and through the operation of the Holy Spirit. Like the Greek theologians, he pressed the parallel between this mystery and the manifestation of God in the flesh through the same operation. For the nature of the change he had no special or exclusive term. The visible sacrament is made or created (*conficitur*, *efficitur*, *creatur*) the body and blood of Christ, or is transferred (*transfertur*) into these invisible realities. But the species, the *res sensibilis*, remains; and the essential question which Paschasius endeavoured to answer was whether the mystic change is wrought in very truth or merely figuratively. The fact that the sacrament is mystical, that no apparent change takes place, makes it impossible to deny that it is in one sense a figure of the truth. But it is at one and the same time a figure and the truth itself, a figure as regards the impression of the outward senses, the truth as regards the understanding and belief of the inward heart.

In affirming the necessity of a lively faith as the essential condition of worthy communion, Paschasius safeguarded his teaching against a merely carnal or mechanical interpretation. The sacrament indeed is received by all, and by some ignorantly or unworthily. But it is the believer alone who partakes of its truth, the virtue of the sacrament; the unfaithful recipient, not discerning the Lord's body, receives judgment to himself. The spiritual nature of the feast is strongly emphasised; the flesh and blood of Christ are not converted into our body and blood, but raise us above fleshly things and make us spiritual beings. They nourish that which is born in us of God, not that which is born of flesh and blood. Thus, while Christ Himself is present beneath the species of bread and wine, the operation of the sacrament is wholly transcendent and spiritual; the gift of eternal life promised to those who feed upon the flesh of the Son of Man and drink His blood is restricted to the worthy partaker. In one place Paschasius adds stress to this doctrine by enlarging upon the fatal presumption of the unworthy who dare, like Judas at the Last Supper, to violate the holy mysteries. They do not understand that the flesh of Christ is never rightly received, unless from His own hand and from the heavenly altar where He, the High Priest of good things to come, is present on behalf of all men. This is proved by reference to the epiclesis at the beginning of the offering of the consecrated gifts, where they are committed to the Angel of God for presentation on high.

Here we meet the doctrine of the Eucharistic sacrifice. The gifts hallowed on the earthly altar by the ministry of the priest are presented through a mystical transference by Christ Himself at the heavenly altar, where He pleads continually for the sins of the world. The sacrifice of His death has been offered once, but its effects are eternal. Man still sins daily through his mortal infirmity, but a means of reparation is provided by the mystical daily sacrifice; by the mystery of His body and blood, the continual memorial of His passion, He who by dying once conquered death never ceases the work of releasing man from his constant transgressions

> Not only did He wash us from our sins in His own blood, when He gave His blood upon the cross for us, or when each one of us was washed in the mystery of His most holy passion and by the baptism of water; but every day He takes away the sins of the world, and washes us daily from our sins in His blood, when the memory of His blessed passion is repeated at the altar, when the creatures of bread and wine are translated into the sacrament of His body and blood by the ineffable sanctification of the Spirit.

Although there was no ambiguity in the form which Paschasius gave to his spiritual conception of the virtue of the sacrament, his identification of the consecrated bread and wine with the incarnate body and blood of Christ was a hard saying which provoked controversy. Rabanus Maurus, while asserting that the real body and blood of Christ are received in the sacrament, condemned Paschasius' explicit definition by raising the objection that the incarnate body in its glorified state could not be thus received. Thus the reality of the body and blood must imply their presence in some special state dependent upon consecration, in which their virtue is conveyed to the believer. Charles the Bald, on reading the work of Paschasius, felt some doubt about it and committed it for examination to Ratramnus, a monk of Corbie, who reported upon the opinions of his abbot in a carefully argued tract *De Corpore et Sanguine Domini*, without personal reference to Paschasius. His actual conclusions are somewhat obscure, and elaborate pains have been taken to shew that they are actually in harmony with those of Paschasius; but the use made of the book at a much later date by convinced opponents of the doctrine of transubstantiation is against the complete validity of this view. At any rate, in his discussion of the distinction between *figura* and *veritas*, on which his whole argument turns, he leaned strongly to the figurative interpretation of the sacrament as an image or mystery of the body and blood of Christ, and his acknowledgement of an objective presence as the result of consecration is at least doubtful, although it is not definitely rejected. His work is shorter than that of Paschasius and is free from any employment of pious anecdote such as Paschasius used to illustrate his case. It discusses two questions, whether the body and blood of Christ received in the sacrament are merely a figure or actually His true body and blood, and whether that which is received is identical with His incarnate body.

To the first question he answers in terms which are generally in accordance with the language of Paschasius. The sacrament is a mystery, the meaning of which implies the necessity of a significant figure. Although a change takes place at the words of consecration, it is not a visible change; the figure of Christ's body and blood, the visible species, remains. The change is spiritual; as in baptism, the senses perceive one thing, and faith receives another. The operation of faith is promoted by the visible figure, for, if only the true body and blood remained after consecration, there would be no need of faith. Bodily, then, the elements are bread and wine; spiritually they are the mysteries of the body and blood of Christ which are received by believers. It is the working of the Spirit which gives them their life-giving power, and without which they would be of no avail to feed the soul. Further, the distinction between *figura* and *veritas*, or the equivalent distinction between *sacramentum* and *res sacramenti*, is not mutually exclusive. The sacrament is given the name of the *res sacramenti*, the body and blood, because it bears a likeness to it; it is called by the name of the truth of which it is a figure. So far in detail Ratramnus shows a strong inclination to stress the permanence of the figure. When, by Christ's command, we use the terms body and blood, we mean that elements made of the fruits of the earth are sanctified and become a sacrament by the invisible operation of the Spirit. The result is a transposition, by which the Word of God, the living bread existing invisibly in the sacrament, recreates the souls of the faithful. Therefore the body and blood of Christ in the sacrament are figures according to the visible species but, with reference to the invisible substance, which is the power of the Divine Word, they are truly the body and blood of Christ. The visible species feeds the body, but the virtue of the sacrament feeds and sanctifies the soul. Thus, in spite of his repugnance to an unqualified use of the term *veritas*, so as to induce the idea that the figure of the truth is superseded, he arrives practically at the same conclusion as Paschasius. Similarly, his references to the sacrament as a sacrifice shew no striking difference of view. It is the daily commemoration of the passion; what Christ did once, He now celebrates daily. On the other hand, the sacrifice is treated without detailed exposition, and the thought which is brought out prominently is not its effectual operation for the sins of the world, but the example which this memorial affords to the faithful of their duty to be partakers in the sufferings of Christ.

The discussion of the second point is fortified by frequent references to Ambrose and other Fathers. The antithesis between *figura* and *veritas*, which had been reconciled in the previous conclusion, is renewed when the presence of Christ's incarnate body is in question. In the sacramental bread there is a life unapparent to the bodily eye, but seen by faith. The flesh in which Christ died and was buried was not a mystery, but a natural verity. On the other hand, the flesh which now contains its likeness in a mystery is not flesh in species, but sacramentally. The bread is the body of Christ and the wine His blood, but not in a corporal sense. The sense in which the phrase must be understood is spiritual; the body which is said to be the mystery of God is spiritual, and therefore neither visible nor palpable. Now, the body which Christ took of Mary remained visible and palpable, and in its glorified state the body of the risen Lord is incorruptible, eternal, impassible. On the other hand, the species in the sacrament, which is all we can see, is corruptible, temporary, subject to material change. It is obvious that the species is not the body and blood; how then, in face of its corruptibility, can we speak of *veritas rei*, which implies the actual manifestation of the incarnate and glorified body? What we see is not *ipsa res*, but *imago rei*, a pledge of eternal life and a sacramental image, both of which must disappear when the *veritas rei* is manifest. Therefore in the sacrament the truth is present only in a mental and spiritual sense. When we speak of the presence of the body of Christ, we mean that the Spirit of Christ, the power of the Divine Word, is present in the mystery of the sacrament, not only feeding the soul, but cleansing it. The summing up of the argument is that the bread and the cup are a figure, because they are a mystery. The mystical body differs from the actual body, in which there is no figure or signification, but the thing itself is evident. Moreover, the body is mystical and spiritual in the sense in which the bread is a figure of the Church, the whole body of the faithful. Finally, the sacrament is the figure or memorial of the Lord's death, so that, being made mindful of His passion, we may be made partakers of the divine gift. When we come to the actual vision of Christ, we shall no longer need these similitudes or instruments.

It would be a mistake to interpret Ratramnus' work as an attack upon the doctrine of his abbot. Its object was, however, to clear away the possibility of a loose employment of terms which might lead to a material conception of the sacrament and a confusion between the visible outward form and the hidden reality. Already the stories with which Paschasius had garnished his treatise, to say nothing of earlier reports of marvels, gave some excuse for insistence upon the spiritual nature of the mystery. But, while Ratramnus found some followers, and his doctrine was echoed in England more than a century later by the homilist Aelfric, he failed to dislodge the theory which had been enunciated by Paschasius with less precision, but with more display of fervent emotion. His authorship of the treatise was forgotten, and in the eleventh century it appears to have been assigned to Johannes Scotus Eriugena. Scotus at all events was the authority appealed to by Berengar of Tours in the controversy which, beginning about 1045, lasted for some thirty-five years; and the book of Scotus which was publicly burned at Vercelli in 1050 was probably the treatise of Ratramnus.

Berengar, archdeacon of Tours, had studied in the cathedral school of Chartres under Fulbert, whose views upon the mystical nature of the gift in the sacrament may have had some influence in directing his line of thought. Holding his archdeaconry with the office of *scholasticus* at Tours, his teaching upon the Eucharist, in or shortly after 1045, acquired some notoriety and provoked expostulations from Hugh, Bishop of Langres, and Adelman, the *scholasticus* of Liège, some three or four years later. These private representations seem to have encouraged him to a public profession of his doctrine in a letter to Lanfranc, then at the height of his reputation as a teacher of theology at Bec. Berengar may have chosen his correspondent with the desire to pit the learning of the secular cathedral schools against monastic scholarship. The letter was at any rate a challenge to Lanfranc to explain his support of the doctrine of Paschasius and his rejection of that of "Scotus" as heretical. Berengar's own view was strongly on the opposite side; if the opinions of Scotus were heresy, then the Fathers on whose statements they were founded—incidentally, those whom Ratramnus had quoted in support of his thesis—were heretics. Lanfranc made no immediate reply, but took steps to clear himself of any suspicion of unorthodox teaching at Rome. At the synod there in 1050 Berengar was excommunicated. He met with hard treatment, for, when summoned to defend his opinions at Vercelli later in the year, he was imprisoned by royal order, and, being thus prevented from appearing, his judgment went by default. The synod condemned the view that the sacrament was a figure or pledge of Christ's body and blood, and the book attributed to Scotus from which this was derived was burned. The condemnation was repeated at a synod held shortly afterwards in Paris under the presidency of the French king, whose conduct to Berengar seems to have been influenced by unwillingness to allow him to answer for his heresy before a synod held outside the realm, although in a monastery of which the king himself was lord and patron. He is said also to have appeared at a council held at Brionne by William of Normandy, which was equally adverse to him. At Tours, however, in 1054, he made a solemn profession on oath before the legate Hildebrand, in which he denied the charge of holding that the consecrated bread of the altar was merely bread, and stated that the elements after consecration became the real body and blood of our Lord.

This, however, did not wholly solve the difficulty, for the charge was put in a crude form, which could easily be denied by a convinced supporter of the spiritual view of the mystery advocated by Ratramnus, while the assent demanded was not incompatible with that theory. Berengar's teaching after 1054 laid itself open to renewed objection, and, at a synod held in 1059 at Rome under Nicholas II, a profession of belief was apparently forced upon him by the Burgundian cardinal Humbert, in which the doctrine of the Eucharist was stated in a frankly material form.

I Berengar, an unworthy deacon of the church of St Maurice of Angers, recognising the true, catholic, and apostolic faith, anathematise all heresy, and chiefly that of which I have hitherto been defamed, namely that which endeavours to establish that the bread and wine which are set upon the altar are after the consecration only the sacrament, and not the very body and blood of our Lord Jesus Christ, and that they cannot be handled by the hands of the priests, or broken, or crushed by the teeth of the faithful with the senses (*sensualiter*) but only in a sacramental manner (*in solo sacramento*). And I assent to the holy Roman church and the apostolic see, and with my mouth and heart profess that, with regard to the sacrament of the Lord's table, I hold the same faith which the lord and venerable Pope Nicholas and this holy synod, by evangelic and apostolic authority, have delivered to be held, and have confirmed to me: to wit, that the bread and wine which are set upon the altar are after consecration not only the sacrament, but also the true body and blood of our Lord Jesus Christ, and that with the senses, not only sacramentally but in very truth, these are handled by the hands of the priests, are broken, and are crushed by the teeth of the faithful.

This statement was confirmed by Berengar's oath and declaration of anathema against contrary opinions. He also burned his writings and acknowledged that any return to another form of teaching would expose him to canonical penalties.

On returning to France, Berengar appears to have disregarded the binding power of an oath taken under compulsion, to have complained of his treatment at Rome, and to have reasserted his old heresies. In or after 1063, Lanfranc entered the lists against him with a book *De Corpore et Sanguine Domini*, in which extracts from a letter of protest and recantation which Berengar had circulated were produced and combated. Lanfranc's legal training and natural subtlety of intellect made him a dangerous and persuasive adversary; with some scorn for his opponent's inconsistency, he was also convinced that he himself was arguing upon behalf of the catholic faith against its enemy. His own position and the authority by which it was supported are stated as a preliminary to the arguments with which the treatise concludes.

We believe therefore that the earthly substances, which are divinely consecrated at the Lord's table through the priestly mystery, are, by the ineffable, incomprehensible, wondrous operation of heavenly power, converted into the essence of the Lord's body, while the appearance and certain other qualities of the same realities remain behind, in order that men should be spared the shock of perceiving raw and bloody things, and that believers should receive the fuller rewards of faith. Yet at the same time the same body of the Lord is in heaven at the right hand of the Father, immortal, inviolate, entire, without contamination or injury; so that it may truly be said that we receive the same body that was taken of the Virgin, and yet not the same. The same, as regards its essential being, and the property of its true nature and its virtue; but not the same, if we take into account the species of bread and wine and the other qualities included in the preceding statement. This is the faith that the Church, which, being spread through the whole world, is called catholic, has held from ancient times and holds to-day.

It need hardly be pointed out that the question at issue was not one of change in the species of the elements, for both parties were agreed that the species of bread and wine remained after consecration. But the change which Lanfranc asserted was a material change in which the essential being of bread and wine was superseded by that of the Incarnate Word, whole and entire in every particle. On the other hand, while Berengar was careful to explain in his answer to Lanfranc, the book *De Coena Domini*, that his actual teaching was different from the crude doctrine attributed to him, and that he recognised that the consecration effected a change, he nevertheless held that this change was purely spiritual and did not annihilate the material bread and wine. The controversy was not stilled, and eventually in 1079 Berengar once more came to Rome, and, after protracted discussion of his case, signed a second profession of faith, to the effect that the elements were substantially converted by the mystery of the sacred prayer and the words of Christ into His very flesh and blood, and so were the incarnate body and blood, not figuratively and virtually, but in their own proper nature and true substance. This form of words, less strict than the form of twenty years before, allowed more latitude of construction, and Berengar is said to have accepted it in the first instance with the mental reservation that the phrase "substantially converted" might be taken to imply that in the process of conversion the substance of the elements was retained. In the end his orthodoxy was admitted in accordance with the terms of this form, and the final act in the long dispute was his presentation of an apparently satisfactory statement of his belief at a council held at Bordeaux in 1080, eight years before his death.

The result of the Berengarian controversy was the vindication of the Paschasian doctrine of the Eucharist as the official faith of the Church. The material change in the elements which Paschasius had implied was now specifically stated. To this doctrine, which, difficult and mysterious as it was in detail, was nevertheless definite in its general form, Berengar, like his prototype Ratramnus, could oppose no clear-cut theory. Unwilling to commit himself to the bare theory of the Eucharist as a communion of hallowed bread and wine, the Berengarian might be conceived as holding either that consecration imparted to the elements a spiritual efficacy which they had not possessed before, or that it involved an actual Divine presence which did not displace, but permeated the bread and wine. This second theory owes the name "impanation" to Witmund of Aversa, a pupil of Lanfranc and one of the most distinguished theologians who attacked Berengar. Witmund also combated theories which upheld a partial presence of Christ in the elements, akin to the later doctrine of consubstantiation, and an entire presence which, in the case of unworthy reception, is reconverted into material bread and wine.

To the casual observer this controversy seems merely an acute renewal, with bitterness of feeling on both sides, of the dispute in which Paschasius and Ratramnus had been amicable protagonists. Both parties, however, on this occasion, were provided with weapons which were not within the reach of the monks of Corbie. The terms of scholastic philosophy and theology, which were hardening into systems with a scientific terminology of their own, gave precision to definitions of belief and enabled distinctions, other than the familiar antithesis between *figura* and *veritas*, to be applied to possible modes of the presence of Christ in the Eucharist. In this connexion there came into being the convenient word which defined the material change expounded by Lanfranc. We have seen that the second profession of belief submitted to Berengar in 1079 referred to this change as a substantial conversion, meaning that it affects the substance beneath the species, the invisible matter clothed in the visible form. Some years earlier, a treatise upon the canon of the mass, attributed to St Peter Damiani, who died in 1071, had employed the word Transubstantiation to signify the character of the change. The substance of the elements is transubstantiated; a new substance, that of the body and the blood, fills its place. The word did not pass at once into general use, nor was it adopted in official language until the promulgation of the Lateran formula in 1215; but its introduction marks a noteworthy epoch in the progressive shaping of doctrine on this point into a compact and permanent form.

The quotation already given from Lanfranc is a concise statement of the orthodox view of the presence of Christ in the Eucharist; and from the time of Lanfranc onwards this view, although lending itself to some variety of expression and to expansion in certain directions, remained as a stable element of Eucharistic doctrine. The services of Lanfranc to this side of medieval theology were less remarkable, from the point of view of constructive imagination, than the contribution of Anselm to the doctrine of the Incarnation; he simply applied clear definition to the theory for which he contended, and in so doing provided a firm foundation for future argument. In both instances, however, the trained legal mind of an Italian scholar brought order into the floating conceptions of Gallic theologians and controversialists and substituted dogma for tentative opinion. The controversy was not finally settled; Abelard, who included opposite pronouncements upon the doctrine in *Sic et Non*, recognised the permanence of antagonistic theories. The Berengarian heresy, however, was checked for the time being, until, at the close of the Middle Ages, it manifested itself with a strength nurtured by a long period of repose.

The controversy which has been reviewed gave prominence to a special aspect of the Eucharist. Diversity of view upon the nature of the gifts offered necessarily implies some difference of opinion upon the doctrine of the sacrifice and its effects. The disputants, however, did not proceed to discuss this point; and there was no serious discrepancy of thought upon it. To both sides the Eucharist was the memorial of the passion, in which the sacrifice upon the cross was presented before God. In the liturgy common to both the presentation of the gifts at the heavenly altar simultaneously with their consecration upon the earthly altar was explicitly recognised; the question was the nature of the form in which they were given back to be partaken by the faithful. But the general acceptance of the doctrine of the objective substantial presence of Christ had two results which profoundly influenced the medieval conception of the Eucharist. In the first place, it directed the attention primarily to the incarnate body present on the altar as an object of adoration, and loosened, save in minds predisposed to mystical interpretation, the symbolic analogy between the elements and the life of the Church, knit together with its Head by the mystery of unity. Secondly, the idea of the Eucharist as a propitiatory sacrifice for sin, which, if not actually a daily repetition of Christ's vicarious sacrifice, was a continuation of it, obscured the idea of the oblation of the Church as a living sacrifice to God. The consummation of the sacrifice was shifted from the act of communion, upon the importance of which early writers had insisted, to the act of consecration, from the self-devotion of the believing member of the Church to the visible hallowing of the gifts. The act of communion ceased to be an essential part of the rite, so far as the majority of those who took part in it were concerned. The union of the Church with Christ was effected vicariously by the communion of the officiating priest, in which the faithful participated only on special occasions. The Eucharist thus became a mystical drama enacted before a body of worshippers, who recognised in it, according to their powers, a continual representation of Christ's saving work, culminating in the moment of consecration, when, beneath the veils of bread and wine, the eternal Priest and Victim manifested Himself for the worship of His people and, without interval of time or change of place, presented Himself at the throne of God as the living offering for their sins.

Thus the real presence of the incarnate Christ, effected by the process of transubstantiation of the elements, formed the centre of the official Eucharistic teaching of the Church. The theologians of the twelfth century, after the Berengarian controversy was over, continued to search for rational explanations of the mystery; but in their acceptance of the main dogma they were generally agreed. Such crude phrases as had been used for the sake of clearness in the profession uttered by Berengar in 1059 needed to be guarded from misunderstanding. If Christ's body was said to be broken or pressed by the teeth of the faithful, this implied no division of the substance; in its glorified state, His body was incorruptible, immortal, impassible, and, in the sacrament, it was received entire by each partaker. The distinction between the incarnate body before the passion and after the resurrection needed constant emphasis and raised subsidiary questions. Thus Alger of Liège, whose *De Sacramentis Corporis et Sanguinis Dominici* takes a high place among early twelfth-century treatises on account of the precision of its language and its detailed refutation of heterodox opinions, touches upon the nature of the gift conveyed to the disciples at the Last Supper, before the Passion, and concludes that, just as our Lord manifested Himself in the Transfiguration in a form anticipatory of His glorified state, and after the Resurrection shewed the wounds of His passible body to His followers, so the body and blood which He then gave for meat and drink were by anticipation those with which He rose from the grave and ascended into heaven.

With the doctrine of the entirety of Christ's body and blood in the Eucharist was also connected the question whether the body and blood were separate in several species or were concomitant with one another. The obvious answer was that, as Christ was received entire in both, they were necessarily concomitant. The Eucharist was instituted under a double species in order to signify the assumption by Christ of a human body and soul and the liberation of body and soul wrought by Him. Christ therefore is received whole in both species, neither more in both or less in one. At the same time, the operative change does not convert the bread into blood or the wine into flesh; the blood, however, is concomitant with the first, the body with the second, and in both species there is only one sacrament. The important consequence of this theory was the gradual exclusion of the laity from communion in both kinds, which was effected during the twelfth century; the practice of the reservation of the sacrament in one kind for the sick was extended to all ordinary communions apart from that of the officiating priest. Where it was held that Christ was present entire in either kind, the benefit to the communicant was not lessened by the withdrawal of the chalice, while the risk of accidents in the administration of the latter was removed.

The subject of the Eucharist was treated concisely by Peter Lombard in the *Sentences*, with his customary apparatus of running citations from Augustine and other Fathers, including the most important of those standard passages which were collected by early canonists and were brought together in a more or less consecutive form in the second part of the title *De Consecratione* in Gratian's *Decretum*. The Eucharist, says Peter Lombard, is a source of spiritual refreshment, not merely a token of virtue and grace, but a sacrament in which the fountain and origin of all grace is received. By the words of consecration, which are those of the Heavenly Word, a conversion takes place of bread and wine into the substance of Christ's body and blood. The species of both remain, and thus the reality of the sacrament, the body and blood of the Lord, is at once signified and contained in the mystery. But the sacrament also signifies, though it does not actually contain, the mystical unity of the faithful. He proceeds to distinguish between sacramental communion, in which good and bad are alike sharers, and the spiritual communion which is the privilege of the good alone: to the good the body of Christ brings salvation, while to the unworthy it is condemnation. The figurative theory is then discussed, with severe criticism of those who measure God's power by the modes of nature, and the conversion of the elements reasserted at length. This is followed by an enquiry into the mode of this conversion. Formal it cannot be, because the species are unchanged. The substantial theory seems to be the true answer. An objection may be raised to it, that this implies the constant addition of substantial matter to the body of Christ, as it were, a daily incarnation and creation of a new substance. But this is not so. If priests are said to make (*conficere*) the body and blood of Christ, it is because by their ministry the substance of bread is made the body of Christ, and the substance of wine His blood, without addition or increase. Faith refuses to investigate the matter further, but acknowledges the will and power of God. Certain explanations of the change are examined and rejected, the annihilation or resolution into prejacent matter of the substance of bread and wine by substitution of substance, and the hypothesis of impanation. After dealing with the double species and the entirety of Christ in both, and the mingling of water with the wine as a symbol of the people redeemed by the passion, Peter Lombard turns to the question of accident and subject, introducing terms which indicate how far means of discussion had advanced since the days of Paschasius and Ratramnus. What is the subject, the fundamental matter, of the accidents which remain after consecration, the species, their savour and weight? He concludes that they exist without subject, for the only substance which is there is that of the body and the blood, which is unaffected by these accidents. They therefore subsist independently for the purposes of the mysterious rite and to be tasted as an assistance to faith, while the body of Christ, having its own form and nature, is covered by them.

In this passage the formula *accidens sine subiecto*, which became the orthodox solution of this problem, is put forward tentatively, to be worked out more fully by Aquinas in the next century. The fraction of the bread is treated at some length, with reference to the admissions made by Berengar with regard to the nature of the body consumed. On the other hand, the sacrificial aspect of the sacrament is very briefly dismissed. No reference is made to the heavenly offering. That which is offered and consecrated by the priest is called sacrifice and oblation, because it is the memorial and representation of the true sacrifice and holy immolation made upon the altar of the cross. Christ was sacrificed once; the daily sacrifice is sacramental, a remembrance of what was done then once and for all. Much more space is given to the final topic, which had long exercised the minds of theologians, the validity of the sacrament when celebrated by unworthy priests. Consecration, it is answered, depends not on the merit of the officiant, but on the word of the Creator; the virtues of a good priest cannot enhance the value of the sanctifying influence of the Spirit, nor can the faults of a bad priest diminish it. Only the heretic or schismatic can affect its validity.

The teaching of the standard theological text-book of the Middle Ages may well conclude this summary of the development of Eucharistic doctrine. By the theologians of the eleventh and twelfth centuries, with their command of a language whose terms for abstract conceptions were being multiplied and stereotyped in the schools, elements of thought which were inherent in Eucharistic literature from the early days of the Christian Church were harmonised into a compact doctrine. In the Lateran confession of faith this doctrine was summed up with careful attention to its essential components. In the catholic Church, Christ is both priest and sacrifice, offering and offered in its central rite, the sacrament of the altar. In this His body and blood are truly present, by a process of transubstantiation divinely effected, so that the mystery of unity between Head and members may be duly accomplished, and that God may give back to man that flesh and blood which He took from him and glorified by raising it to the clouds at God's right hand.

VII

The whole stress of the clauses of the Lateran canon which deal with the sacraments was laid upon the Eucharist. In this rite the Head of the Church is both sacrifice and priest, and here the unity of the Church is shewn forth. It is added that for its celebration is necessary the ministry of a priest who has received the apostolic commission in due form. The sacrament of Holy Order is thus alluded to, so far as it concerns the all-important matter of the Church's central ceremony. Beside this, Baptism is secondary. As Peter Lombard had pointed out, Baptism, although its effect was to renew the heart and justify the sinner, nevertheless was of no more effect than its predecessor circumcision in opening the kingdom of heaven to the believer; that was the result of the sacrifice of Christ alone, and the efficient means whereby that result was ensured were the sacrament of His body and blood. The traditional doctrine of Baptism was so well known and universally received that there was little occasion for Innocent III to refer to the part of the sacrament in the scheme of salvation. He made the simple statement that it was profitable to salvation, without dwelling upon its power to remove sin; but the words of the canon were directed mainly to the points which constitute the validity of the rite. In view of the stirrings of heresies, with rites of initiation which deviated from the orthodox model, it was important to affirm the fixed rule of the Church with regard to the matter and form of the sacrament. Two points were also laid down. Baptism is open to infants and adults alike, and the ceremony may be performed by anyone, provided that the essentials prescribed by the Church are duly observed.

These are points intimately connected with the indispensable character of the sacrament as a preliminary to the Christian life; it was necessary that all men should receive it, and the need for its reception in individual cases was so pressing that its dispensation could not be confined to the hands of a limited class, or even to those whose personal orthodoxy was beyond doubt, although normally its proper dispensers were the ordained ministers of the Church. But to these clauses was added another which dealt with the question of actual sin committed after baptism. The sacrament provides the remedy for original sin, but for subsequent lapses a further remedy is needed. As we shall see, another canon of the Lateran Council was especially concerned with this remedy; in the general confession of faith it is simply said that post-baptismal sin can be removed by *vera poenitentia.* The ambiguity of the word *poenitentia*, which is equally applicable to repentance and to the technical term penance, makes this statement by itself seem extremely vague, and, apart from the fact that the existence of a remedy for sin implies its sacramental character, the clause contains no more than a hint that the sacrament of penance is implied.

The history of the penitential system of the Church exhibits a development in doctrine and practice of which the Council of 1215 was actually the climax. The theory which traced the institution of the sacraments to Christ Himself relied upon the power of binding and loosing given to the apostles as the origin of the sacrament of penance; but the revelation of the transmission of this power from the apostles to the whole priesthood of the Church was long in coming. In the early Church the act of penance for sins committed after baptism had a purely judicial significance. Public confession of sin was followed by a long and severe course of penance, extending over a considerable period. The act of reconciliation by which the penitent was restored to communion was his formal readmission to the privileges of the Church from which he had been excluded; it was not an act of absolution from sin. His pardon was left to God. Moreover, such penance was a single solemn act which could not be repeated if he subsequently relapsed into sin. It is obvious that this practice, possible in small and struggling communities to which strictness of discipline was essential, was bound to receive modification with the growth of the Church. In any case, the sins which it affected were of a specially grievous character; it was a remedy for crime which left trifling sins out of account. In process of time, the practical inconvenience of dealing with voluntary confessions in the presence of the whole congregation, aided by the natural repugnance of sinners, especially if they were people of importance in the community, to expose themselves to public humiliation, led to the introduction of private confession. Although this in time entirely superseded the public act, yet public confession of sin still remained the ideal of the Church. Nowhere is this more clear than in the long survival of the practice in those societies whose object was the strict observance of the Christian life; although the solemn and unique confession, incapable of repetition, disappeared, yet public confession, followed by the imposition of penance, continued to form a regular feature of the proceedings of monastic chapters, and, even as late as the twelfth century, was the only method of this kind definitely prescribed in religious houses.

Even with the beginning of private confession, the main idea was still that the penitent desired to make his peace with the Church by less obtrusive means than were implied by the public act. Naturally, penance itself acquired a less openly humiliating form; the performance of good works was an effective equivalent for the self-abasement imposed upon the penitent under the older system. But the theory that confession and penance were a direct method of obtaining God's forgiveness did not appear at once. While the mind of the Church was so deeply imbued with predestinarian doctrine, even in modified forms, the idea that an act of absolution could convey assurance of pardon to the sinner whose destiny lay hidden in the counsels of God was inadmissible; grace, which lay at the absolute disposal of God, could not be forced by the act of man. For a sure pledge of God's grace, the mind naturally turned to the Eucharist and its worthy reception. There was the further circumstance that the restoration of communion with the Church, which was the object of confession and penance, lay solely with the bishops; they alone could pronounce the declaration which freed the offender from the Church's ban. Upon the meaning of the gift of the keys to Peter and the apostles there was more than one construction; but the general practice in this matter indicates the prevalent belief that, in the transmission of the keys from the apostles to the Church, their custody was reserved to the episcopate. It is remarkable that the earliest form of ordination which is known, that in the Hippolytean canons, contains, in the case of priests as well as of bishops, the formula from St John xx. 22, 23, conveying the gift of the Holy Ghost and the power of binding and loosing. But this is merely a local and isolated instance. It was not until the middle of the twelfth century that the words found their way into the ordination of priests according to the Latin rite, and it is noteworthy that in the False Decretals, which reflect the opinions and practice of the Frankish Church in the ninth century, the power of binding and loosing from the censures of the Church was treated as an exclusive possession of bishops.

The extension of this episcopal privilege to the priesthood was powerfully affected by that career of missionary enterprise on which the Church embarked under the influence of Gregory the Great. In the work of pushing forward the frontiers of Christendom, individual missionaries were always in contact with converts, from whom confession of sins and signs of repentance were required as preliminaries to baptism. It was in these outposts of the Church's influence, and especially in the Frankish kingdoms, that the practice of private confession as a binding duty was systematised. The assurance of the Church's pardon, for which in the circumstances personal resort to the tribunal of the bishop was generally impossible, was delegated almost as a matter of course to priests. As a purely delegated power it long remained; indeed, it may be said to have continued to be such in theory until the imperative formula was inserted in the ordinal for priests. The variety of sins with which priests in this position were confronted demanded some variety of treatment, and missionaries were constrained to seek guidance from their superiors, as Augustine, faced with this difficulty in England, sought the advice of Gregory. With this special object Penitentials were compiled as authoritative guides to confessors, enumerating forms of sin and assessing equivalent penances. Thus, under legal influence and embodying ideas familiar to people living under laws which prescribed fixed penalties in compensation for wrongs committed, penance assumed the character of satisfaction for sin. Its original character of outward humiliation, betokening heart-felt repentance, and of a state of probation by which the sinner qualified for the recovery of lost privileges, was thus exchanged for that of an act of compensation, by which the sinner paid an equivalent for his sin, and received pardon in return. How profoundly the theology of the Church was influenced by its penitential system has been seen already in the discussion of Anselm's theory of the Incarnation. The satisfaction which, according to that theory, man owes to God for the insult done to His honour is, on an infinitely larger scale, the obligation which the individual sinner incurs in proportion to his guilt.

As the theory of the power of the keys advanced in strength and the authority delegated to the priesthood became everywhere the normal manifestation of its working, the positive conception of absolution from sin as an accompaniment to satisfaction displaced the older idea of reconciliation to the Church as the end of penance. The satisfaction, though it may involve compensation for injury to a fellow-man, is paid to God; its payment demands the assurance of God's pardon. Accordingly, confession of sin to a priest, made with sincere purpose of amendment and satisfaction, was followed by the pronouncement of absolution. At first, such pronouncement took a declaratory form in which merely the assurance of God's pardon was contained. Just as, when the value of the prayers of the saints was first recognised, the circuitous method was adopted of asking the Creator to authorise the prayers of His elect creatures, so in this case the Church hesitated to put an indicative formula of forgiveness into the possession of its priesthood. Nor was it actually laid down that the penitent who had received absolution was thereby freed from his sin. On this point the evidence of Gratian is clear. The *Decretum* was compiled towards the close of the first half of the twelfth century. The first chapter of the distinction *De Poenitentia* contains a large number of citations, illustrating on the one hand the view that confession is merely a manifestation of repentance, not a means of obtaining pardon, and on the other hand the directly contrary opinion that confession and satisfaction are the avenue to pardon, and that pardon for sin cannot be obtained without them. In his comments, Gratian treats the matter with perfect impartiality. It is an open question, the solution of which he leaves to the judgment of the reader. Both sides are supported by wise and religious men; and a final quotation, which Gratian and other canonists referred to the Penitential of Theodore, by an apparent confusion with Theodulf of Orleans, is given to shew that, while God forgives sins which are confessed to Him directly, He also uses the ministration of priests for this purpose.

The same difference of opinion was discussed at length by Peter Lombard, with an attempt at reconciliation. Three elements constitute the sacrament of penance, contrition or compunction of heart, confession with the mouth, and satisfaction in deed. Contrition by itself, manifested to God, is met by God's forgiveness. But satisfaction is necessary, and for this reason confession to a priest has been instituted; the priest sits as a judge to decide upon the appropriate penalty, and by confession the penitent learns humility and caution. This, however, is not all. It is agreed that the priest possesses the power of the keys. There are two keys, one of which is the key of knowledge and discernment, the other the key of judgment, or of binding and loosing. It is clear that the priest can bind the penitent by imposing satisfaction upon him; but, if God can forgive sin without the aid of the priest, in what does the sacerdotal power of loosing consist? The answer is, that this power lies in the remission of the penalty and the restoration of the penitent to the benefit of the sacraments of the Church. When Christ cleansed the lepers, He told them to shew themselves to the priest; when He restored Lazarus to life, He gave him to the disciples to be loosed from his grave-clothes. The parallel is obvious: the function of the priests of the old law, who certified the bodily cleansing of the lepers, is analogous to that of the priests of the new, who judge of the spiritual cleansing of the sinner. The man justified from sin by contrition of heart must still look to human ministry for complete freedom from the bonds in which he has been held. Thus the exercise of the sacrament of Penance by the Church through confession and absolution is rationalised, and its necessity to the penitent is inferred.

Numerous questions, of course, arose in this connexion. There was, for example, the question of the validity of confession to laymen, which appeared to be sanctioned by the general precept of confession in the epistle of St James. This might cover merely venial sins; but for graver offences the ministry of the priest was necessary, save in extreme cases where no priest might be had. There was, again, some doubt with regard to the power of the keys; for it was patent that to some priests the key of knowledge and discernment was denied, and it might be suspected that the other key may not be given to all alike. We may conclude, however, that all possess it, though not all in a right and worthy manner; and the unworthiness of a priest is no bar to the efficacy of the satisfaction which he enjoins. There was the question of death-bed repentance, when there was no opportunity for the penitent to make satisfaction. There was the obscure problem of the recurrence of forgiven sins, when the penitent relapses into his old sin or one similar to it. Finally, there was the difficulty of distinguishing between the sacrament and the *res sacramenti*, the outward sign of repentance and the inward penitence of heart which accompanies and generally precedes it. But these were academic questions ancillary to the main points of the doctrine. Penance is a sacrament consisting of three parts, for the perfect fulfilment of which the agency of the priest, as the judge appointed by God, is necessary. From the actual sin and its guilt God, approached by the contrite sinner, absolves; the absolution given by the priest after confession removes the punishment which is due to sin and is atoned for by works of satisfaction which lie at the discretion of the priest.

It remained for a later age to develop the doctrine in a direction which gained for the power of the keys a less qualified authority and claimed for priestly absolution a share in the remission of the guilt as well as the penalty. We have not yet arrived at the distinction between the attrition, or mere sorrow of heart, which precedes the saving work of contrition, or at the complete identification of the contrite sinner's confession to God with the oral confession made to the priest. But the essentials of the doctrine were fixed, and it is significant that the age of Gratian and Peter Lombard was the period at which the formula bestowing the gift of the Holy Ghost and the *potentia iudicandi* became a normal part of the ordination of priests. Long before the middle of the twelfth century, the sacrament of Penance had become a regular part of the Church's ministrations. Public confession, except in monasteries, was obsolete; the tribunals of bishops and their delegates dealt with spiritual crimes by regular legal procedure, and the public penances which they enjoined had no sacramental character. The *forum internum*, in which the priest sat as judge of the sin-laden soul and ordained satisfaction for sin, was completely distinct from the *forum externum* in which the local ordinary pronounced excommunication upon transgressors or reconciled them to the Church. Nevertheless, the general acknowledgment that sacramental penance was a salutary medicine for the soul, which every Christian could use with advantage, did not yet extend to the recognition of its obligatory character; and a momentous step was taken when, in the twenty-first canon of the Council of 1215, resort to Penance was imposed upon every Christian as a duty.

The canon *Omnis utriusque sexus* directed that every person who had arrived at years of discretion should make full private confession of his sins to his own priest at least once a year, and endeavour to perform the penance enjoined upon him. Confession was made a necessary preliminary to the reception of the Eucharist, for which Easter was prescribed as the statutory time unless the priest should determine otherwise. Neglect of this order was visited with suspension from entering church for the living, and by denial of Christian burial to the dead. Stress was laid upon the jurisdiction of the parish priest: if the penitent wished to confess to anyone else, he had to obtain the licence of his own priest; otherwise, no other priest had the ability to bind or loose him. Discretion and caution were enjoined upon the priest himself. He was the skilled physician, pouring oil and wine into the wounds of his patient, diagnosing the disease by diligent enquiry into the sin and its circumstances, and so discovering what remedy to apply. He must be careful to preserve what was afterwards known as the seal of confession, avoiding any word or sign which might betray his penitent; and, if he found it desirable to call in another judgment, his statement of the case must be general without mention of names. To violate this prohibition was to incur deprivation of his priesthood and perpetual penance in a strict monastery.

This order was not altogether revolutionary. Its obvious intention was to regularise existing practice and to bring those who neglected the tribunal of Penance into line with the faithful, while it sought to remove those irregularities to which experience had shewn that the sacrament was liable. By making Penance a requisite of communion, it safeguarded the most important of the sacraments from the abuse to which its reception was open in an unruly age. But, by imposing privacy upon priest and penitent alike, and by its insistence upon the control of the sacrament by priests vested with local jurisdiction, it put into the hands of the Church, in her struggle with the temporal power, a weapon of extraordinary effectiveness. The salutary discipline of penance was converted into a compulsory test of fitness for a share in the full privileges of membership of the Church, without which man was debarred from the hope of eternal salvation. Within the narrow area of his jurisdiction, the parish priest became the judge of sin and its penalty, with powers that were of greater ultimate importance than the judgments of temporal courts. The system, it need hardly be said, imposed a burden upon him for which few parish priests in practice were adequate; and, by the reservation of a large number of sins, subjected to scientific distinction, to higher jurisdictions, his power was limited by the superior authority of his diocesan, while this in turn was itself restrained by the supreme authority of the holy see. This, however, was a consequence of the establishment of the general principle, and its development belongs to later history. The fact remains that, at the close of the period in which the greatest of the Popes had successfully vindicated the claims of the Church as the guardian of man's spiritual liberty from feudal dominion, she asserted, by an action in itself perfectly logical, her right to assume complete control of his spiritual life and to withhold the means of grace from those who would not submit to her sacramental discipline.

At this date the scholastic doctrine was still in the making, and Peter Lombard's theories by no means represent the last word upon the subject; in process of time, indeed, they were held to be erroneous in their recognition of pardon of sin by God as antecedent to priestly absolution. The distinction between the pardon of guilt and the remission of its penalty is not touched in the Lateran canon which made confession to a priest obligatory. Already, however, definitions were being formed which connected the work of the minister with more than the treatment of the penalty for sin by the injunction of satisfaction, and made the full distinction between satisfaction and punishment. In the theory enunciated by Richard of St Victor the view of Penance which eventually became prevalent in the medieval Church was clearly foreshadowed. While God's forgiveness alone can remove the guilt of sin and deliver the sinner from eternal perdition, there yet remains the temporary punishment of purgatory after death, and for the remission of this the priest cooperates with God. Thus confession, absolution, and the performance of the satisfaction prescribed remit for the sinner the endurance of pains which, though not lasting, were possibly as severe as those of hell. The doctrine of purgatory, in the earlier centuries a pious opinion falteringly expressed with complete uncertainty of the degree of sin which merited punishment in this intermediate state, developed side by side with the doctrine of penance; and the intimate connexion between the two appears in the treatise *De Vera et Falsa Poenitentia*, a late compilation falsely ascribed to Augustine on which Peter Lombard and his contemporaries placed much reliance. As a matter of fact, Augustine in his genuine writings had said no more than that the opinion that, between death and the final judgment, the soul suffered purgatorial fire, was perhaps true, and it was long before this opinion shewed more than a tendency to crystallise into a general belief. Its progress was aided by the practice of prayers for the dead and its close connexion with the intercessory virtue of the sacrifice of the mass. But, if purgatory was taking its place in the eschatology of the Church, there was no early consensus of opinion either with regard to its certainty or the actual time at which the soul was to be submitted to this trial, whether after death or after the last judgment. Gregory the Great strongly influenced future doctrine by inculcating belief in purgatory as a state into which the soul entered after death; but in his view it was intended as a remedy merely for those small sins which did not merit the punishment of hell, but precluded the sinner from immediate entrance into heaven. It was only, however, with the growth of the sacramental theory of penance that the temporary punishment of purgatory assumed its real importance. Purgatory now, for the sinner who used the way of repentance provided by the Church, whether his sins were mortal or venial, entirely superseded hell, which was no longer to be feared; and over against the pains of purgatory was set the satisfaction which was the final condition of penance.

The whole conception of satisfaction was also modified with the growth of time. The legalism of the Penitentials had strictly assessed the satisfaction in proportion to the gravity of the sin, and the severity of their scale of punishment was hardly less than that of the arduous process through which penitents had to pass to obtain reconciliation in the early centuries of the Church. It was admitted, however, that, if the penitent shewed real progress in his performance of the penance enjoined, the priest had power to remit part of it. The obvious method was, after a certain time, to enjoin the performance of some work of piety in commutation of the remainder of the penance. Such partial remission was in fact an indulgence granted in consideration of good conduct; and, while there was no suggestion that it did anything to remit sin or do more than mitigate severity, the custom opened the way to the introduction of indulgences as a supplementary element in the development of the theory of penance.

Although in theory the strictness of the penalties prescribed by the Penitentials was not relaxed, the character of penance was altered as its injunction became subject to the discretion of the individual confessor. Even in the age which produced the Penitentials, the rigidity of their directions was met by means of commuting or redeeming inconvenient sentences. In place of fasting and other works of expiation, alms were offered to and received by the Church in the person of the priest. Thus in 747 the council of Clovesho condemned this easy way of lessening or transforming satisfaction by a money payment. A century later Hincmar of Rheims forbade such transactions as simoniacal. In spite of these warnings, the commutation of penance had the effect of relaxing its seriousness. Light penances were reduced to forms which involved little or no trouble to the penitent; for the satisfaction of mortal sins which demanded heavy penalties were substituted pious works which drew upon the sinner's worldly substance. The impetus which this gave to the foundation of monasteries by powerful laymen, whose lives were inevitably stormy and irregular, is clear; and this movement rose to its height amid the political turbulence of the twelfth century. It is easy to see how expensive benefactions of this kind, undertaken as a substitute for penance, were regarded as bringing about remission of sin. Not only were they amends for the sins of the founders themselves; they were offered also on behalf of the members of their family and the friends who contributed to them, and not only for the remission of the sins of the living, but those of the dead as well. Further, the express object of the life which was led in these foundations was continual intercession for the founders in life and after death, and to the actual founders was added a whole crowd of benefactors who from time to time made offerings at their altars and at the shrines of the saints in whose special honour they were established. The Books of Life preserved upon the high altars of monasteries recorded the names of such benefactors, and, like the surviving books of Durham and Hyde, were augmented as the centuries passed. They bear witness, not to mere disinterested gratitude, though that doubtless played its part, but to the substantial gifts by which the applicant earned his right to become a partaker in the benefits of the prayers and other good works wrought in the house, and was admitted into its fraternity as an honorary associate. At the root of the pious transaction was the desire to obtain forgiveness of sin and remission of the penalty due to it by the easiest means of satisfaction.

In the importance attached to the help afforded by the intercession of others there is involved the admission that satisfaction can be performed by vicarious means. A parallel has been sometimes drawn between the custom of offering single combat in the person of a professional champion retained for the purpose and that of relying upon the prayers of others for the fulfilment of the satisfaction owed by oneself; and the first custom may certainly have had some influence upon the second. In general the performance of penance by substitutes became an admitted practice; just as personal service in warfare was commuted by the equipment of persons in proportion to the responsibilities of the military tenant, so penance redeemed by the obligation to go on a pilgrimage could be satisfied by deputy. The movement of the crusades brought this to a climax. The advantages offered to those who took the cross could be obtained by meeting the expenses of a substitute; and the transition from this to the direct payment of a sum of money for the object of the crusade without further action was an obvious consequence.

The crusades mark an epoch in the history of penance. At the Council of Clermont in 1095, Urban II, in order to stimulate the zeal of the faithful for the first crusade, proclaimed that to all who confessed their sins the journey to the Holy Land should be reckoned as taking the place of all penance. This large grant, the first example of a plenary indulgence on record, assured full pardon of sin and eternal salvation to those who died on the journey. While the principle involved was the familiar idea of commutation of penance, the indefiniteness of the concession and its far-reaching character differentiated it from ordinary grants made to individuals. Before this date, the custom of granting indulgences in the form of remissions of limited periods of penance had emerged out of the practice of such individual relaxations. Bishops and abbots encouraged the faithful to give of their substance to pious objects, such as the building of churches, by promising them remission for a stated time of the penances enjoined upon them by their priest. It is difficult to trace the exact beginning of this custom, which has been obscured by the citation of spurious instances and by the admission of ordinary examples of remission of penance within the wider sphere of the indulgence. But, while plenary indulgences such as that of 1095 were entirely exceptional, and in the nature of things could proceed only from the highest ecclesiastical authority, partial indulgences increased in number throughout the twelfth century and became general towards its end. By such grants places of pilgrimage, especially Rome and Compostela, benefited, churches and hospitals swelled their fabric funds, and minor works of a quasi-religious nature, such as bridge-building, profited. The principle of redeeming penance by the payment of money as nominal alms was, in fact, extended to the need of money for pious objects, to be collected from the faithful by the sale of assurances of spiritual compensation.

The full theory of the resources which were drawn upon for these grants was not formulated until the thirteenth century; but Urban II's plenary grant was prefaced by the statement that it was made with full trust in the mercy of God and of the apostles Peter and Paul. Belief in the communion of saints and in a common fund made up of their merits, which could be transferred to supply the defects of contrite sinners, influenced the contributions to religious foundations which, as we have seen, were repaid by the prayers of the communities so endowed. The doctrine of the illimitable treasury of the merits of Christ and the saints, however, which produced such an effect upon the grant of indulgences as time went on, that their wide and unqualified assurances put confession and penance altogether in the shade, was not yet understood, though it existed in embryo. The value of the merits and prayers of the saints to those who invoked their help, and the virtue exercised by their relics were of course matters of common belief; and no one had such an influence upon promoting the veneration due to them as Gregory the Great. But it was not for centuries after his day that their merits were explicitly recognised as a vast capital sum which could be used to any extent by constituted authority for the removal of sin and the remission of the pains of purgatory. As this doctrine advanced, the indulgence, still regarded theoretically as an equivalent for the penance enjoined by the confessor, assumed the character of a means of liberation from sin as well as from its penalty, and the satisfaction which atoned for that penalty was superseded, at any rate in popular thought, by release from the penalty itself.

Thus the indulgence was capable of a construction which weakened the effect of the sacrament of Penance. Confession of sin and absolution were in fact reduced to a formality which qualified at best for the receipt of an indulgence; and indulgences, freely put on sale in the hands of licensed traders, became a formidable bar to the proper working of the penitential system of the Church. The Lateran Council, in its insistence upon the duty of confession and penance, foresaw the danger of the unlimited grant of indulgences, and, in two of its canons, the sixtieth and the sixty-second, attempted to put it under restriction. The first of these condemned the encroachments of abbots upon the episcopal authority, and mentioned their injunction of public penances and their grants of letters of indulgence. These were forbidden in future. The second alluded to the extravagant promises made by itinerant preachers who collected alms for special purposes, and required them to establish their mission by exhibiting letters from the Pope or from the bishop of the diocese, composed in the customary form issued by the apostolic see. The form, which was given in full, enjoined the giving of alms for the special object *in remissionem peccatorum*, so that by these and other good works, done by the inspiration of God, the giver might attain eternal bliss. While it contained no mention of confession and penance as a preliminary requisite for the benefit to be derived from alms, the phrase *in remissionem peccatorum* was purely indefinite, and the question at issue was the authorised collection of alms, not the sale of indulgences. In fact, the terms of the letter prescribed the limit of the prospect of profit which such preachers should hold out to their hearers. But the canon, while authorising the grant of such letters by the diocesan, went on to censure the "indiscreet and superfluous indulgences which some prelates of churches are not afraid to grant, whereby the keys of the Church are made contemptible and the satisfaction of penance is deprived of its force." Henceforward indulgences granted at the dedication of a church, whether one or more bishops were present, were not to be granted for a longer period than a year, and those at the anniversary of the dedication for not more than forty days. Such indulgences were explicitly qualified as remissions of penances enjoined. The effect of this decree was to restrain indulgences from taking a direction in which they would become a substitute for penance, whether in the incautious utterances of irresponsible mendicants or in the excessive liberality of prelates. The allusion to the multiplication of indulgences, when several prelates took part in a ceremony, is noticeable. A further safeguard against the reckless granting of indulgences was provided by the prescription of the observation of the example furnished by the holy see. The beggars' letters were to follow the form employed in the papal chancery. The customary forty days' indulgence was ordered as the period to which the Pope usually limited his own grants. Nevertheless, the anxiety of Innocent III to check indulgences in the interests of penance did not bind his successors. In the emphasis which the twenty-first canon of the Council laid upon the sacrament of Penance he had asserted the claims of the Church over the souls of all its members; it is not too much to say that the enforcement of penance upon the faithful was the consummation of the policy with which he had consistently upheld the supremacy of the Church in human affairs. In the development of the system of indulgences he rightly recognised a force which weakened the hold of the Church upon the individual conscience. But, in putting them under papal control with the best intentions, he hardly foresaw the extent to which the holy see would turn them to profit in the future and so defeat his own ends.

VIII

In tracing these aspects of the progress of Christian doctrine, we see that their development passed almost uniformly through the same stages. The period overruled by the ardent imagination of Augustine, open to the most diverse impressions and providing a bewildering variety of suggestions, supplied the framework for later thought. Here the medieval conception of the Church found its origin, and the most characteristic of its doctrines were foreshadowed or casually anticipated. The far different intellect of Gregory the Great, working upon the heritage of Augustine without conspicuous originality, but with the clarity necessary to one who is primarily an expositor, prepared the way for dogmatic statement of doctrine; in this respect, and especially in the definiteness with which he elaborated the relation between man and the supernatural world, his influence was hardly less important than in the administrative sphere. It was not, however, in Rome that further progress was to take place. The centre of activity in religious thought was shifted to the Carolingian kingdom, the seat of those controversies in which fluid opinion was hardened into fixed form. To this transitional period succeeded the growth of scholasticism. While the influence of Anselm, and in a less degree of Lanfranc, legally minded Italians, made contributions of high significance to the beginnings of scholastic theology, its foundation lay in the schools of Paris. Here argument was applied to give a rational basis to the mysteries of the faith, and isolated dogmas were moulded into systematic form. With the Lateran Council we leave this work uncompleted. The reign of Innocent III saw the rise of the Dominican and Franciscan orders, whose doctors were to produce the highest achievements of scholastic reasoning. The work of crystallisation of doctrine, however, was fully in progress, and the twelfth century was the epoch to which medieval dogma owed its consistency and its characteristic shape.

One point remains to be noticed. The final clause of the first canon of the Lateran Council, at first sight a somewhat irrelevant postscript, asserted the possibility of salvation for married persons. The object of inserting this clause in a confession of faith was to safeguard the sacrament of Marriage against the attacks of heretics who regarded it as a mere licence for the satisfaction of carnal desires. The various shapes which were taken by contemporary heresy do not belong to our subject; but the need for authoritative declarations upon essential matters of faith was urged by periodical outbreaks of Catharism and by the stubbornness of the Albigensian movement, which had been condemned by the Lateran Council of 1179 and was now the object of a crusade for which plenary indulgences were offered. To such departures from the faith, involving the rejection of the means of grace offered by the Church, or substituting for the sacraments rites of initiation and spiritual communion derived from infidel sources, the council gave no quarter. We have seen how its second canon condemned the opinion of Joachim of Flora on a matter which affected the orthodoxy of an accredited exposition of the Church's doctrine of the Trinity. Another clause of the same canon condemned the heresies of Amaury of Bène, who taught a form of pantheism under which the Christian revelation was merely a detail in a uniform Divine scheme, and a doctrine of the progressive manifestation of the Trinity through three successive periods. The inclusion of Amaury with Joachim of Flora was possibly due to the superficial resemblance of this latter opinion to Joachim's prophetic assertion of the three states of the world which preceded the imminent advent of the everlasting gospel. The third canon dealt comprehensively and at great length with all heretics, pronouncing anathema and excommunication against them, delivering them over for punishment to the secular power, and declaring secular lords who favoured them to be deprived *ipso facto* of their estates. The centre of the system of belief to which the council gave its assent was the unity of the visible Church and the impossibility of salvation outside its boundaries, and to its positive proclamation of the essentials of dogma the condemnation, with the severest penalties, of all who wilfully departed from that unity and impugned its symbols was an inevitable corollary.

CHAPTER XX

HERESIES AND THE INQUISITION IN THE MIDDLE AGES, *c.* 1000–1305

In the eleventh, twelfth, and thirteenth centuries the Medieval Church was at its greatest and most powerful; yet these centuries witnessed the appearance of various heresies, which in certain parts of Europe were a serious menace to the Church's hold upon the people. While some of the heterodoxies of the period were essentially philosophic and academic, others there were which made a wider appeal direct to the masses; and while the former may have been potentially as dangerous to the Church, it was the latter that inspired most apprehension and that were consequently most vigorously repressed.

While less metaphysical than the heresies of the early Church, those of the later Middle Ages had certain broad characteristics in common with them. Thus the dualism of the Cathari was Marcionite, the anti-sacerdotalism of many of the Waldenses was Donatist, the mystic enthusiasms of Ortlieb, Marguerite de la Porète, and their followers was Gnostic, the ascetic zeal of the Fraticelli was Montanist. This rather obvious parallelism constitutes one of the difficulties in studying the later heresies, for it clouds the evidence. Thus, Catholic writers, convinced that the Albigenses were Manichaeans, were content to go to the works of St Augustine against the Manichaeans and to attribute indiscriminately to the Albigenses all the errors enumerated in those pages. Such a procedure, not necessarily adopted in any spirit of conscious unfairness, was so obviously unscientific that it makes it difficult to use the evidence of these writers with any confidence. In addition to this there is a fundamental difficulty in dealing with any of the great popular heresies of the Middle Ages in the fact that nearly all our knowledge of them is derived in one way or another from their adversaries—either from the treatises of hostile theologians or from confessions and depositions recorded in the archives of the Inquisition. With the academic heretics it is quite a different matter. They have left their own writings behind them, and we can come into direct contact with their thought unclouded by the gloss of the hostile commentator.

The great popular heresies of the Middle Ages constitute so remarkable a phenomenon that they call for a general explanation. It is undoubtedly true that the popularity of heresy was due in considerable measure to the Church's failure to satisfy certain instincts and aspirations in a period which was essentially restless and curious. The crude violence of the time quickened Utopian visions, which were not only hopes of a better future but criticisms of an evil present. A sense of disappointment, or even of disillusion, is apparent after the failure of the earlier crusades. Genuine spiritual fervour had been aroused, it seemed, to no purpose, and no new stimulus to the spiritual imagination presented itself. The exalted mysticism of a Hugh of St Victor or a Peter the Venerable possessed no popular appeal, and it was not until the appearance of St Francis with his extraordinary personal magnetism that the Church was able to provide a powerful answer to the urgent demand for religious inspiration. The saint and the ascetic invariably attracted veneration in the Middle Ages, when the ordinary priesthood, if lacking in personal holiness, only elicited fear, indifference, or dislike. There could be no more prolific encouragement to heresy than clerical abuses. This was clearly the opinion of Innocent III, who, while seeking to eradicate heresy in southern France, also delivered a tremendous indictment against the conduct of the clergy there. St Dominic ascribed the success of the Albigenses to what he regarded as their affectation of holiness and of evangelical poverty which misled the people. And quite clearly the people of Languedoc drew a forceful comparison, all to the advantage of the heretics, between their zeal, simplicity, and austerity, and the wealth, ostentation, and love of temporal power displayed by the accredited envoys of a God who had been poor, humble, and despised. Anti-sacerdotalism is a marked feature, as it was often a predisposing cause, of medieval heresy. Some of the heresies were to begin with not doctrinal at all, but distinctively evangelical, arising from dissatisfaction with existing conditions in the Church, and aiming at a higher standard of faith and conduct.

For the forms which heresy assumed the East was largely responsible. It is but a partial view of medieval history which focuses attention solely upon the purely indigenous aspects of European civilisation and fails to appreciate the force and the significance of the impress upon Europe of the oriental world, the influence of the great trade-routes into Asia as disseminators not only of wealth but of ideas. The intercommunication, already fostered by the merchant and the traveller, was quickened still further by the Crusades. The Christian warriors set forth vowed to hold no other intercourse with the infidel but that of the sword. Yet the later crusaders were not of the temper of those whom the eloquence of Urban II and his coadjutors first enlisted, of those who had pursued their Muslim enemies into the Temple itself with relentless slaughter when they captured the Holy City. Frederick II's crusade of 1229 was the expedition of a diplomatist, not of a warrior, and it was characterised by the friendliness of its leader's relations with the Sultan of Egypt. To the vivid imagination of Frederick the culture of Baghdad made a powerful appeal; the religion of Islām, the speculations of Arabian philosophers, were to him a matter of intense intellectual curiosity, not of abhorrence; and an atmosphere of rationalism prevailed at a court where Greek, Jew, or Arab were all alike welcome. So it was that Gregory IX could with a certain plausibility assign to his abhorred imperial enemy the authorship of the famous blasphemy, that the world had been deceived by three impostors, Moses, Mahomet, Christ. Increasing acquaintance with, and knowledge of, the religion of the Koran made possible at any rate an elementary comparative study of religions, a realisation of their common elements, and such a conception of religious toleration as we find suggested in Boccaccio's famous tale of *The Three Rings*, or in the pseudo-gospel of Barnabas, a strange conglomeration of the Koran with the four canonical gospels, the essential feature of which is a latitudinarian conception that God's message of salvation is for all. "As God liveth, even as the fire burneth dry things and converteth them into fire, making no difference between olive and cypress and palm; even so our God hath mercy on every one that worketh righteously, making no difference between Jew, Scythian, Greek, or Ishmaelite."[1] The possibility of an unholy sympathy between the Christian and the infidel was the basic idea of the dreadful allegations brought against the Templars, whatever their origin in fact may have been. Among the indictments was the charge of practising a ceremony of initiation which included the worship of a black cat, or Baphomet, which is but another name for Mahomet. But it was not necessary to go outside Europe to come into contact with oriental influences. The East had penetrated into Europe; the culture of the Caliphate had been planted in Andalusia, and mainly from Cordova and Toledo its influence was disseminated abroad through Sicily and southern France—its architecture, its medicine, its mathematics, its philosophy. Long after the extinction of the glories of the Umayyad Caliphate of Cordova, the splendour of Moorish learning remained, and in the twelfth century Muslim Spain still eclipsed Catholic Europe in the arts and sciences. There was a certain Moorish element in that brilliant exotic civilisation of Languedoc, where the problem of heresy became most acute. In such a soil any hostility to the Catholic Church, any dissatisfaction with its ministrations, was likely to generate alien doctrine. The heresy of Languedoc was not Moorish, but it was certainly of oriental origin, coming through the Balkans out of Asia.

In the days of the Carolingian Empire, if we except the predestinarian opinions of Gottschalk and the pantheism of the amazing Irish genius, John Scotus Eriugena, there was little heresy of consequence. But it is clear that as a popular force it must have been quietly growing, probably among the common people for the most part, before the opening of the eleventh century. It had already become a serious danger before the Papacy, immersed in other cares, had awakened to its gravity. It is significant that certain heretics were condemned at Orleans, in 1017, for holding Docetic views, and that these ideas were traced to Italy. We hear of the execution of heretics in 1022 at Toulouse, in 1051 at Goslar

[1] L. and L. Ragg, *The Gospel of Barnabas* (London, 1907), p. 184. It is possible that the Gospel was *invented* in 1595, but there is good internal evidence giving grounds for ascribing its origin to the first half of the fourteenth century.

in Saxony. It is not easy to establish the identity of these early heretics. Medieval chroniclers are not exact in their nomenclature. We find a large variety of designations in use. Thus the Cathari are variously known as Albigenses, Albanenses, Bagnolenses, Bagnaroli, Bulgari, Publicani, Patarini, Textores[1]; the Waldenses as Humiliati, Pauperes de Lugduno, Leonistes. Thus the term Albigenses is used in Languedoc, the terms Patarini[2], Albanenses, Concorricci in Italy, *textores* and *texerantes* in Germany. But the words Bulgari or *bougres* are used indiscriminately in France to mean heretics generally, though their derivation as indicating one particular type of heretic is obvious enough. The two dominant heresies were Catharism and Waldensianism, but a number of minor contemporary heterodoxies, having some element or other in common with these, were apt to be closely associated or confused with them, at all events in the popular mind. Thus the Arnoldists, following Arnold of Brescia, from being originally simple opponents of the Pope's temporal power in Rome, developed into opponents of the secularism of the Church as a whole, and so came to have much in common with the Waldenses. Again, the adherents of Peter de Bruys, whose teaching was that there was no efficacy in images, the symbol of the Cross, or in paedobaptism, were liable to identification with the Cathari, for these were also Catharan doctrines. Henry of Lausanne combined the principles of the Arnoldists and the Petrobrusians. The devastation wrought among the faithful of southern France by this heresiarch was the despair of St Bernard at a time when Catharism and Waldensianism were also rampant in the same district. In short, all attacks upon the Catholic Church, however different their origins and however discrepant their fundamental theses, were likely to have a certain affinity and to give a very similar impression to the ordinary undiscerning observer. Among other early twelfth-century heretics were some who were zealots, either partly or wholly insane. Such were Tanchelm of Antwerp, who, starting with the Donatist theory that the sacraments had lost their efficacy owing to clerical degeneracy, is said later to have claimed for himself a divine nature equal with Christ's; and Éon de l'Étoile, who, discovering a reference to his own name in the words of Scripture, "Per *Eum* qui venturus est judicare vivos et mortuos," declared himself to be the Son of God.

Donatism is perhaps the most notable doctrinal feature of these essentially anti-hierarchical minor heresies. In Catharism there is something much more revolutionary. The connexion between the Cathari of Western Europe and the Bogomiles and Paulicians of the Balkan peninsula can be said to have been established. The use of the term Bulgar as synony-

[1] The terms *textores, texerantes (tisserands),* or weavers, seem to be due to the occupation of weaving to which the Humiliati especially devoted themselves.

[2] It is noteworthy that the name of Patarine, which in the eleventh century was applied to the extreme supporters of Church reform at Milan, in the thirteenth and fourteenth centuries denoted Catharan heretics.

mous with heretic in the common parlance of France is significant; so also is the fact that Bulgarian delegates attended a great representative council of Cathari held in 1167 near Toulouse; and so again is the close resemblance of the brief Albigensian ritual which has come down to us, namely, the Ritual of Lyons, with that of the Bosnian Patarini, and with the more elaborate manual of the Paulician Church in Armenia, known as *The Key of Truth*. Matthew Paris tells us of a complaint made in 1233 by the papal legate Conrad, of the direct relations existing between the Albigenses and the Armenian Paulicians, and Rainerius Saccho, a Catharan apostate, writing a little later, states that the Catharan churches in other parts of the world were the offspring of a parent Church in Bulgaria. The ancient Paulicians of Armenia, holding themselves to be the one true Church, were adoptionists—*i.e.* they considered that Christ had been born a man but, having fulfilled all righteousness, had at the time of his baptism in Jordan been chosen by God as Messiah and as the eternal Son of God. They rejected paedobaptism, the idea of purgatory, the invocation of saints, the use of images, the doctrine of the Trinity. Between the eighth and tenth centuries this Greek sect had crossed over in large numbers into Thrace. Leo the Isaurian, and later Theodora, attempted their extirpation, but they were protected by John Tzimisces, in whose reign some hundred thousand of them migrated northward into the region of the Danube. Here they seem to have attempted the conversion of the Bulgars, and here also the pure doctrine of Paulicianism would appear to have become adulterated by an infiltration of Manichaeism, or at all events of ideas of a gnostic and dualist character; and hence arose the sect of the Bogomiles. The connexion between the Paulicians and the western Cathari is clear; but it is probable that the corrupted Paulicianism of the Bulgarians, rather than the original Paulicianism of Armenia, was the origin of western Catharism, and that, helped no doubt by the agencies of the scholar, the merchant, and the crusader, the heresy travelled from Bulgaria, Bosnia, and Dalmatia into Hungary and Italy. It found an easy settlement in Apulia and Lombardy, but an even more favourable atmosphere in France, especially south of the Loire[1].

The new creed clearly possessed a strong attraction for common people desirous of a novel spiritual stimulus, and for a pleasure-loving nobility, such as existed notably in the south, who were only too glad to seize an excuse for despoiling the wealthy Catholic hierarchy. In the comforting rejection of the doctrine of purgatory, and the convenient distinction

[1] The question of the connexion between the Cathari and the Paulicians and Bogomiles is discussed in S. R. Maitland, *Facts and Documents illustrative of the History...of the ancient Albigenses and Waldenses* (1832); C. Schmidt, *Histoire et Doctrine de la Secte des Cathares ou Albigeois* (1848), pp. 7–28; K. Müller, *Theologische Litteraturzeitung* (1890), p. 355; F. C. Conybeare, *The Key of Truth* (1898), introd. pp. cxxx–cli; J. Guiraud, *Cartulaire de N.-D. de Prouille* (1907), vol. I, ch. IX.

drawn between the fully initiated and the simple adherent, Catharism seemed to offer an easier road to salvation than did the Catholic Church, while, at the same time, the zeal and energy of the preachers of this gospel established factories and workshops, where apprenticeship to craft or trade was combined with instruction in the Catharan faith. The fulminations of ecclesiastical councils such as those of Toulouse in 1056 and 1119 were fruitless, and missionary enterprises were no more successful. In 1165 Catholic clergy had to submit to the humiliation of entering into a joint synod with Albigensian representatives. The general Catharan congress of 1167, already mentioned, met undisturbed. Particularly during the reign of William IX, Duke of Aquitaine, the heretics enjoyed full protection, if not positive encouragement, from the secular authority.

To the faithful Catholic, Catharism no doubt appeared to be a body of belief wholly foreign to Christianity, and in the points of similarity between the Catharan ritual and that of the Catholic Church he could discern nothing better than an impious mockery. Nevertheless, in so far as its origin was Paulician, the story of this heresy takes us back into that early era of Christianity prior to the definite formulation of Catholic dogma and the full establishment of the great organisation which we know as the Catholic Church, to the period when it was as yet uncertain to what extent foreign, yet not wholly alien, systems, Neo-Platonic and Gnostic, might be assimilated to Christian theology, and similarly uncertain how far the Church would be prepared to make terms with the world, as represented by the Roman Empire. In this formative period, when Christian doctors were seeking for philosophical explanations of the Gospel revelation and of the relation of Christ to the Godhead, Marcion, in an endeavour to free Christian theology from the taint of Judaism by a reaffirmation of what he conceived to be the message of the Pauline epistles, issued a work called the *Antithesis*, in which an elaborate distinction was drawn between the God of the Old Testament, the God of the Law, on the one hand, and on the other the God of the New Testament, the God of reconciliation. While there is certainly enough dualism in St Paul to warrant this line of argument, on the other hand the features of resemblance between such an explanation of the Christian theophany and an entirely non-Christian dualist system like the Mazdeist rendered possible such a hodge-podge of Marcionitism and Persian magism as the mystic theology of Mani, and also rendered later adherents of Marcionitism liable to corruption by non-Christian influences of that type. It is thus easy to understand how any heresy which unduly stressed the dualist element in Christian dogma was exposed to the imputation of Manichaeism. There were, no doubt, wide theological divergencies between different branches of the Catharan community—some of them more akin to the original Paulicians, others more tainted by Gnostic and exotic influences; yet to the Catholic of the twelfth century all would appear one and the same, manifestly Manichaean.

To the Catharan, as to the Catholic, human existence was a struggle between the opposing forces of good and evil, in which the person of Christ alone provided salvation, but the Catharan laid excessive emphasis upon the inherent evil of the material world. The several picturesque variants of the fundamental Catharan conception are relatively unimportant; what is essential is the idea of a contest between an evil potentate, who ruled over the material universe, and who was sometimes identified with Jehovah, the violent sanguinary deity of the Old Testament, and his adversary, the God of the New Testament, the God of mercy and forgiveness, whose kingdom is not of this world, but a wholly spiritual kingdom. While not entirely rejecting the Old Testament—the Lyons ritual quotes the Book of Solomon—the Cathari repudiated all portions of it which presented matter in a favourable light. The whole purpose of earthly existence they held to be the overcoming of the evil god or Satan. Inasmuch as the material world and the flesh were the dominion of the Devil, nothing worse was imaginable, and there was therefore no hell or purgatory. The object of Christ's work was to reclaim the soul from the thraldom of the flesh, and his servants were the Cathari, who alone had kept the true baptism, which is of fire and of the spirit. There was no such thing as the resurrection of the body. He that had become reconciled with God through membership of the Catharan church was enabled at once to leave his corporeal integument and enter into the celestial body which awaited him in heaven. The soul of the unreconciled passed into another material body, generally that of the animal to which in its human existence it had borne the closest resemblance. The mortal sin was worldliness, because it was devotion to those essentially transitory and evil things which are Satan's. This asceticism had one curious and extreme consequence. The chief weapon in the Devil's armoury was the propagation of the species, because that meant the continuance of his power. Sex was his device. "O Lord," runs the Lyons ritual, "judge and condemn the sins of the flesh, have no pity upon the flesh born in corruption, but have pity on the spirit which is imprisoned." The love of the sexes, whatever its nature, had the same consequence and was service of Satan. Marriage was no better than adultery and incest—indeed by some Cathari it was regarded as worse, being lasting and viewed with complacency instead of temporary and viewed with shame. Because of their belief in metempsychosis the Cathari were necessarily vegetarians, abjuring all meats, eggs, cheese, and milk. They would use nothing for food that was sexually begotten; the exception made in favour of fish being due to the current belief that they were generated in some other way. It is significant that a suspect summoned before the Inquisition of Toulouse on a charge of Catharism vigorously protested against so unwarranted an imputation, seeing that he had a wife and children, ate meat, lied and swore, and was a faithful Christian.

So intense was their conviction of the sanctity of the imprisoned human spirit that the Cathari shewed with regard to the shedding of blood the same uncompromising consistency as they did in the matter of sex, condemning both the judge who pronounced sentence of death and the soldier who slew his enemy in battle as no better than murderers. On the other hand, suicide—regarded as a legitimate hastening of the time of his deliverance from the bondage of the flesh by the fully initiated, and known as the *Endura*—would appear to have been allowed, if not indeed encouraged. It has to be remembered in partial explanation that the *Endura* was practised in days of relentless persecution, when voluntary self-destruction might well seem preferable to falling into the hands of ruthless crusader or inquisitor.

Austerity is the outstanding characteristic of the Catharan existence, but then it was practised only by the "perfected," or *boni homines*, whose ranks were small. The severe asceticism enjoined upon the perfected, the arduous nature of the period of preparation, the menace of persecution, which rendered the postponement of initiation to the last possible moment a measure of security—seeing that the mere *credens* could lawfully disavow membership of the community—all these factors combined to restrict the numbers of the perfected. The simple adherent or *credens* was not required necessarily to order his life on strict Catharan principles; he might even eat meat and marry. His sole obligation was to venerate the "perfected." In the reverence which had to be paid to the initiated by the mere believers, or *auditores*, there is a point of resemblance to Manichaeism, as there is also in certain features of the all-important Catharan rite, the ritual of initiation, known as the *Consolamentum*. This was exceedingly simple, and in other features is reminiscent of the primitive Church. It may be said to have been a combination of the Christian baptism, ordination, eucharist, and absolution, all in one. The Lord's Prayer was explained to the postulant, sentence by sentence; he then renounced the works of Satan and the "harlot" Catholic Church, made confession, and received pardon. One of the elders next explained what the life of the *bon chrétien* involved—the abjuration of the flesh in every way and of the shedding of blood, the modelling of life on the principle of turning the other cheek to the smiter. The precise act of *Consolamentum* was the placing of the gospel and of the hands of the *boni homines* present upon the head of the novice, who was thereby admitted into the ranks, in token whereof he was lastly girt with a sacred thread round his naked body and invested with a black gown.

Catharism was clearly a strange amalgam of asceticism and laxity, of some lofty ideals with aberrations which were perverse and unhealthy. We cannot wonder that the Catholic, ever prone to suspect the heretic of immoral practices, should do so with conviction in the case of a sect whose fanatical attitude towards material existence was plainly inconsistent with the elementary facts of life. We enter a purer atmosphere when we turn from the Cathari to the Waldenses. The origin of the name and of the sect has been disputed, but it is probably safe to attribute both to a certain rich merchant of Lyons, named Peter Waldo, a man of no learning but of native goodness of heart, who started a crusade in 1170 for the furtherance of the law of Christ, which seemed nowhere to be obeyed. Distributing his wealth among the poor, he began to preach the gospel in the streets and in private houses, and he soon obtained a following, who came to be known as the Poor Men of Lyons. At first their work had papal approval, their vow and their preaching being expressly commended by Alexander III, with the proviso that they secured the sanction of the clergy in their districts for whatever ministering activities they undertook. In course of time this condition came to be disregarded. The Poor Men used to inveigh zealously against the low moral standard of the clergy. This naturally gave umbrage to the clergy, who refused any longer to countenance the movement, which was formally condemned by the Council of Verona in 1184. The result was that a sect which had originally been perfectly orthodox tended to become heretical. To the two characteristic doctrines that poverty is the true way of life for the sincere Christian and that Holy Scripture is an infallible guide in matters of religion, they added the essentially heretical tenet that every good man is inherently competent to preach and expound Holy Writ. The right of preaching being denied them, they embraced the theory that personal merit avails more than the rite of ordination, and they proceeded to appoint ministers among themselves, thus becoming schismatics. Like other opponents of the Catholic hierarchy, they soon developed Donatist ideas. Uniformity and conservatism of doctrine, which might have been continued in the main by the preservation of a close organisation, tended to disappear when persecution destroyed central control.

Although Bernard Gui brings charges of immorality against them, the purity of the lives of the Waldenses was generally manifest. Even from inquisitorial sources testimony is forthcoming to their simple piety and goodness, and it is noteworthy that Walter Map, while repeating in lurid detail the usual stories of gross immorality brought against the Albigenses—similar to those narrated by Caesarius of Haisterbach—speaks with obvious respect of the Poor Men, with some of whom he came in contact at Rome, being indeed deputed to examine them. He seems to have thought their zeal rather ridiculous, but their austerity admirable.

The name Poor Men or Humiliati is also applied to a sect which seems to have had a separate origin from the Poor Men of Lyons, but which in course of time came to be identified with the followers of Waldo, and whose habitation was Lombardy. The Humiliati of Provence and those of Lombardy applied for Alexander III's approval at the same time; they held a joint conference in 1217, and there came to a general agreement in doctrine. But subsequently they tended to drift apart in matters of dogma, the Italian party becoming more unorthodox in their views. Waldensianism soon became widespread, penetrating into Spain, Hungary, Germany, Bohemia. The original adherents of southern France suffered together with the Cathari in the thirteenth century, and many were driven into the Piedmontese valleys. But Waldensianism was never suppressed as Catharism was. The zeal of authority against the more pernicious and dangerous Albigenses was outside Languedoc a protection. In Piedmont, in spite of the massacres of the seventeenth century, they have lingered to the present day, and the leaven of Waldensianism in central Europe helped the rise of Anabaptism and Hussitism.

Peter Waldo's persuasion that the law of Christ was nowhere obeyed and that radical reformation was needed was shared by a remarkable contemporary, Joachim of Flora, whose surprising expositions of Scripture and still more surprising vaticinations introduce us to a series of heresies of a different character. In 1254 appeared the extraordinary work known as *The Everlasting Gospel*, consisting of Joachim's authentic works together with exegetical notes and a lengthy introduction, the author of which was either John of Parma, or, more probably, Gerard da Borgo San Donnino—in either case a Franciscan. The burden of Abbot Joachim's prophetic message had been that the world would pass through three eras—that of the Father or of the Law, that of the Son or of the Crucifixion, that of the Holy Ghost or of Love. The first had been a period of obedience; the second a period of study and wisdom; the third would be one of mystic comprehension and ecstatic contemplation. But while Joachim only claimed to be an interpreter of the Scriptures, the author of the *Introductorius* discovered in this conception a new evangel, as much in advance of the gospels as they were in advance of the Old Testament, so that Joachim figured as the apostle of the final era of human history. It was computed that the third cycle would commence in the year 1260; it would be inaugurated by a new mendicant order. Clearly the startling feature of the book was the assumption that the Christian dispensation was not complete in itself, that a new and a higher revelation of the Divine nature was necessary for the salvation of the world. Such a theory rested upon a profound conviction of the corruption of the time and the insufficiency of the Catholic Church. Like all Utopian visions it was essentially a criticism of the existing order.

The revolutionary idea of a new dispensation of the Holy Ghost evidently made a strong appeal to certain types of mind. Among its consequences was one of the most extraordinary instances of medieval credulity—the discovery of more than one incarnation of the Holy Ghost. Thus there was established in Milan the worship, after her death, of a certain very pious woman named Guglielma, who had during her lifetime repudiated in vain any supernatural powers, but who was subsequently acclaimed by a certain Maifreda to have been the Holy Spirit in female form. More dangerous was the appearance in the fateful year 1260 of a very ignorant madman of Parma, by name Segarelli, who aimed at outdoing St Francis in the literal reproduction of the life of Christ. His followers were mainly peasants and swineherds, but they soon spread beyond Italy into Germany. This enthusiast dreamed of proselytising the entire world, but he was seized in 1300 and executed. Yet the mischief was by no means over. Fra Dolcino, fanatic or charlatan, to whom Dante in the *Inferno* conceives Mahomet sending a warning message as to a companion spirit, perceived in the original appearance of Segarelli in 1260 the fulfilment of the prophecies of *The Everlasting Gospel*, and by 1304 he had collected a considerable following in Milan, Brescia, and other northern Italian cities, and in the Italian Alps. In 1305 Clement V organised a crusade against this "son of Belial," and after a desperate resistance these self-appointed emissaries of the Holy Ghost were overcome, their leader being subsequently put to death with the acme of cruelty.

To the followers both of Segarelli and of Dolcino the term Fraticelli is sometimes applied; it came indeed to be used to denote any unauthorised or irregular brotherhood; for, as Salimbene tells us, "all who desired to found a new rule borrowed something from the Franciscan rule, the sandals or the habit." Thus a name derived from St Francis came to be associated with many heretical sects. The author of the *Introductorius ad Evangelium Eternum* was certainly one of the Spiritual Franciscans, those members of the Minorite order who would hear of no compromise with the complete austerity of the founder's system, and who saw in the possession of property of any sort a repudiation of the essential principles of their communion. To a minority consisting of intense enthusiasts, who felt that the whole cause and life-work of St Francis were betrayed by the worldly attitude of the conventual party on the subject of Poverty, *The Everlasting Gospel* appeared as a direct reference to themselves, the only true disciples of that saint, surely somewhat more than man, upon whom the marks of Christ had been imprinted. When in course of time the Papacy declared in favour of the moderate party, mystical and exalted conceptions of the place of Francis in human history were encouraged, and the man who, by enlisting his extraordinary spiritual power and attractiveness on the side of the Church, did more than any other to save the medieval Church against the assaults of heresy, became himself the inspiration of heresies of a pantheist and "illuminist" character. The two principal leaders of the Spirituals in France and in Italy, Pierre Jean Olivi, a brilliant and a beautiful character, regarded by some as the successor of Joachim and of Francis, and the Catalan Arnold of Villanova, denouncing the worldliness of the clergy with as much energy and eloquence as any Waldensian, became suspect of heresy, and after their deaths their followers were vigorously persecuted in the pontificate of John XXII, in whose days the Spirituals generally were in frank revolt, and they were dealt with as manifest heretics. The poet Jacopone da Todi delighted to draw a glaring contrast between the corrupt and carnal Church presided over by the Popes and the true spiritual Church, wed to the principle of poverty, between a Church of mere outward show and one of inward reality.

There were mystics, to whom the term Fraticelli is applied, much more extreme in their views than the Spiritual Franciscans. Whether Francis' own conception of the worship of God in nature was more than lyrical or not, it contained at all events a suggestion of pantheism, and some of the independent communities which adopted one feature or another of the Minorite rule, even if only the outward semblance, were certainly pantheists. In the thirteenth century, inspired by the mendicant idea, there sprang up a number of brotherhoods devoted to religious contemplation and to such good works as the care of the sick and attendance on the dead. While these voluntary associations had no necessary connexion with the Grey Friars, beyond perhaps spiritual sympathy, they came to be regarded as Fraticelli. To such brotherhoods or sisterhoods the words Beghards and Beguines are sometimes applied. The term beguinage is older than the mendicant orders. Pious associations of laymen under that name had existed in the twelfth century, enjoying virtually complete autonomy until the inauguration of Innocent III's movement of centralisation. Large permanent houses, named beguinages, were established in such cities as Paris, Cologne, and Ghent for the protection of widows and orphans. Such houses could be controlled by proper authority, but it was otherwise with the later vagrant associations of beghards or beguines. Over these it was not possible to maintain discipline; neither could their intellectual atmosphere be controlled, and irregular views were apt to flourish in associations which were unauthorised. The medieval vagrant had ever a tendency to become a rebel against authority, as well doctrinal as political; witness the wandering students of the *Carmina Burana*.

Two tendencies developed in the fourteenth century. Heretics of illuminist and pantheist views took to wearing the beghard's garb; beghards adopted illuminist and pantheist doctrines. Among them were the so-called Brethren of the Free Spirit, the disciples of Ortlieb of Strasbourg, who taught that men must be guided solely by the inner light within them. The Brethren held that all sacred history was but the record of their communion. Adam had founded it, Noah had built his ark expressly to preserve it, and after a period of obscurity Christ had re-established it. The sect were sometimes called Luciferans, because they held that Satan was included in the Divine essence. Holding such a theory as this, they were perhaps inevitably—though probably with no justification—credited with devil-worship and the perpetration of horrid obscenities at the ceremony of initiation into their confraternity. Pantheism and antinomianism are often allied. Another of the medieval pantheists, Marguerite de la Porète, held that the soul overwhelmed in love of its creator can and indeed ought to give to nature whatsoever it craves for or desires without the rebuke of conscience or remorse. The illuminist movement was particularly strong in Germany, where the great Dominican, Master Eckehart—predecessor of Tauler, Nicholas of Cusa, and Giordano Bruno in the history of modern mysticism—explained that in the eyes of the Deity sin and virtue were alike. Thus mysticism, normally one of the most powerful forces of which the Church was possessed, its greatest security against the onslaughts of the heterodox, was capable of itself assuming a heretical shape: in the same way that the perfectly orthodox belief in the efficacy of the scourge as a means and an outward sign of repentance could degenerate into a depraved and animal delight in self-torture, combined with a mystic and wholly unlawful belief that flagellation was not only a sacrament but the only effective sacrament. Bands of flagellants, who when they first made their appearance about 1260 were regarded with ecclesiastical approval and popular veneration, in the following century were anathematised as manifest heretics.

Alike in their extravagant and often fanatical mysticism, all the sectaries to whom the term Fraticelli was applied and other similar mendicant associations were alike also in their vagrancy. Sooner or later such roamers in the Middle Ages were apt to become suspect, to be regarded as undesirables; perhaps their unchartered liberty was productive of wild and ecstatic speculations which authority could but regard as dangerous to the faith and to the constitution of the world order.

While Catharism and Waldensianism were essentially popular creeds, whose chief importance lay in their anti-sacerdotalism, the interest of the illuminist heresies lies largely in their philosophic aspect. It is here, in their possession of a common mystical element, that the popular and academic heresies meet. The record of the latter belongs most appropriately to that of the anti-scholastic movements in the history of medieval thought; but at the same time they cannot be omitted from any general consideration of medieval heresy. Philosophy and theology have a natural inclination to invade each other's territories, and while the scholastic philosophers endeavoured to keep them apart, being aided in this by the largely formal pattern of their dialectic, still there arose from time to time venturesome spirits whose philosophic speculations ran counter to correct theology. Hugh of St Victor and, later, Abelard's pupil Peter Lombard were able with great success to utilise philosophy as the handmaid of religion, to glorify God by the rational justification of faith; Anselm, requested by his pupils for a rational explanation of Christian doctrine, duly gave one, premising however that while the Catholic faith could be made clear to the eye of the intellect, it was not dependent upon its reasonableness for its claim to acceptance. On the other hand, Abelard, also endeavouring to use philosophy as a *theodicaea*, exposed himself to the suspicion of heresy. Combating the tritheism of Roscellinus, he seemed to some of his critics to run into the opposite error of Sabellianism. But it was his whole habit of thought that was wrong in their eyes. He could deliberately make a jumble of the contradictions of the Fathers—as he did in *Sic et Non*—in a way most disturbing to a simple belief in their uniform inspiration. His cast of mind was that of the free-thinker. The basis of his reasoning was the conviction that it is by doubting that we are led to inquiry, by inquiry that we perceive the truth. Such a point of view was an abomination to St Bernard with his magnificent affirmation: "Faith is not an opinion, but a certitude." When the appeal to the reason, even for the elucidation of truth, led to a deification of man's finite understanding, devout minds, such as those of Bernard and Peter Damiani, could find in philosophy only an enemy of the faith. He who uses the eye of the intellect overmuch may overcloud the far keener vision of his spiritual sensitiveness; his preference for the former is no better than profane arrogance. It is precisely this attitude, the inclination to trust to the fallible judgment of the individual, in a word self-will, that constituted in the eyes of the pious Catholic of the Middle Ages the heinousness of heresy[1].

Just as Eriugena, who had pronounced the superiority of reason over authority, had proved that this was the path of error by himself falling into pantheism, so Berengar of Tours, a reckless dialectician like Abelard, in the eleventh century found that his reason could not accept the doctrine of Transubstantiation, on the ground that the continuance of such properties as colour, form, and taste in the bread and wine after the consecration could not exist without permanence of substance. So again the reliance of Roscellinus upon fallible reason led to his rejection of the doctrine of the Trinity—there was not one God, but three Gods, sharing, however, a common will and purpose. Philosophy, then, was not always the handmaiden of true religion!

The thirteenth century witnessed a revival of interest in the earlier pantheists, and Eriugena's *De Divisione Naturae* was resurrected. Already Amaury of Bène had been propounding the thesis that all things are one, because whatever is is God, that God is immanent in all creation. He had also been maintaining the antinomian principle that no man filled with the Holy Ghost can sin, because sin is of the flesh, whereas the Holy Ghost is spirit. These opinions Amaury retracted before his death *c.* 1207; they were formally condemned by a council of the ecclesiastical province of Sens held at Paris in 1210. This same council, it is interesting to note, at the same time prohibited the use of the recently discovered works of Aristotle or of his commentators on pain of excommunication. The capture of Constantinople in 1204 had brought Latin Europe more closely into contact with Greek thought than heretofore; still Western Europe knew Aristotle best in the Arabic version and in the expositions of his Saracen interpreters, especially Averroës. Probably the Averroïsts were never very numerous or widely influential; yet in the thirteenth

[1] Cf. *supra*, Vol. v, Chap. xxiii, pp. 799–800.

century they presented to the Church a problem of no little intricacy, raising in an acute degree the question of the relations between philosophy and theology. Catholic theology had been able to make abundant use of Plato from the earliest days of the Church onwards; the medieval discovery of Aristotle brought the query how far it could go in absorbing the peripatetic philosophy too. The newly-discovered writings on the physical sciences contained conceptions of the eternity of matter and the unity of the intellect, which made God only the primordial element in creation and denied the immortality of the individual soul. It soon became apparent that intellectual curiosity was too keen to be repressed by such a prohibition as that of the council of 1210. It became obvious that Aristotle must not be tabooed, but turned to account. Gregory IX, accordingly, ordered the examination and expurgation of the peripatetic philosophy, and in 1255 the two prohibited books, the *Physics* and the *Metaphysics*, were definitely prescribed for the Arts course of the University of Paris. In 1261 Thomas Aquinas and William of Moerbeke, under papal commission, commenced the great undertaking, which lasted eight years, of making a translation and a commentary upon Aristotle. This labour exposed St Thomas to criticism from two opposed quarters: on the one hand he was accused (by the Franciscans) of being an Averroïst, on the other of misinterpreting Aristotle because he was not one. The Dominicans as a whole were accused by their Minorite rivals of being too purely scientific and intellectualist, but the attempt to discredit Aquinas by identifying him with the Averroïsts, whose interpretation of Aristotle was definitely declared heretical, completely failed, and the successful separation of Aristotle from Averroës, the capture of the Aristotelian scientific method for the service of orthodoxy, must be accounted one of the greatest achievements of the scholastics[1].

The view that Albertus Magnus and Aquinas, in seeking to reconcile the wisdom of Aristotle with revealed religion, were simply perverting their original was championed in the University of Paris, the centre of all these academic contentions, by a certain Siger of Brabant and his associate Boëthius of Dacia. Averroës, while honouring religion, had poured contempt on theology. Religion was a genuine thing, a matter for the soul and for the emotions; theology was a hybrid, endeavouring with lamentably poor results to apply the methods of exact science to the sphere of the spiritual imagination. Aristotle, the supreme thinker of all time, had taught the eternity of matter and the unity of the intellect; there could be no equivocation about these principles—they were true. They were contrary to Christian truth, was the orthodox retort, and in 1270 Stephen Tempier, Bishop of Paris, solemnly condemned thirteen Averroïst propositions as erroneous. Undismayed, the Parisian Averroïsts, having come into conflict with the rector of the university, organised

[1] Cf. *supra*, Vol. v, Chap. xxiii, pp. 817 sqq.

themselves into a separate community apart from the rest of the Arts faculty. But in 1277, under papal injunction to search out dangerous errors in doctrine, Tempier tabulated no fewer than 219, and pronounced the penalty of excommunication against those who harboured any of these heresies. Shortly afterwards Siger and Boëthius were cited to appear before the Inquisitor of France, from whom they apparently appealed on the ground of their university privilege. Later they seem to have set off for Rome to defend themselves, to have been tried before the Tuscan Inquisition, and to have been condemned to perpetual imprisonment[1]. The nature of their defence against the charge of heresy is interesting, because it was a pure equivocation. There is, they declared, such a thing as a double truth. What is true in philosophy may not be true in theology and vice versa; they exist on entirely different planes. They had no quarrel with the Church's teaching, no desire to impugn its authority, to embarrass its ministers; on the other hand, they were not prepared to abandon, as philosophers, theories of whose truth they were convinced, simply because they clashed with current theology. They stood in reality for the cause of intellectual freedom, seeking to escape from the embarrassments of a world unable to accept that principle by a subterfuge which they hoped might satisfy the scruples of the Church. For the Church was not hostile to speculative thought as such, but only stipulated that it should be shewn not to be opposed to the essential tenets of the Christian faith.

But in refusing to countenance the Averroïst contention the Church stood on firm ground. The denial of absolute truth, of any correspondence between the concepts of philosophy and of theology, either meant that philosophy was reduced to a mere mental gymnastic, or else was a fundamental cynicism. A man's sincere belief regarding ultimate reality constitutes his religion and is bound to affect his conduct. Acceptance of the Aristotelian theory of matter and of the active and passive intellect was bound to colour a man's ethical ideas as well. It is notable, for example, that the Averroïst Farinata degli Uberti was also an Epicurean, holding that the soul perishes with the body and that human felicity is confined to this temporal world.

Despite the fate of Siger, Averroïsm still continued to exist throughout the fourteenth century, its most outstanding exponent in Paris being John of Jandun; but its most important centre became Padua, where the leader was Peter of Abano. As a rule the Averroïst was unpopular, some like Raymond Lull seeing in him a dangerous corrupter of Christian truth by Muslim impurities, others like Petrarch and Gerson hating him for his self-confident dogmatism. Like the Italian humanist after him, the Averroïst seldom fell into serious trouble; he had not the slightest desire to apostatise or to criticise the Church in any way; he would

[1] Cf. on Siger of Brabant *supra*, Vol. v, Chap. xxiii, pp. 821–2.

cheerfully subscribe to each and every article in all the creeds; his interests and his influence were confined to the class-room. Thus he was seldom regarded as dangerous, though the whole tenour of his teaching might inherently be as destructive of orthodox doctrine as that of the most fanatical Albigensian or Fraticello.

Heresy was defined by Grosseteste as "an opinion chosen by human sense, contrary to Holy Scripture, openly taught, pertinaciously defended." There was never any doubt in the medieval Church as to its culpability; but there was at first difference of opinion as to its appropriate punishment. The early fathers could be quoted, some in favour of leniency, others of severity. The Emperors Theodosius II and Valentinian II had decreed exile and confiscation of property with loss of civil rights for heretics generally, but death for disturbers of the public peace, under which designation Donatists and Manichaeans were included. It is noteworthy that, when Priscillian was executed by the Emperor Maximus, St Leo, though declaring that the Church must never put a heretic to death, still confessed that the severity of Christian princes was to be welcomed, because the fear of punishment won some heretics back to the faith. The Church's own penances at this time were those of flogging and imprisonment.

At the opening of the eleventh century we find the secular arm meting out the punishment of death. In 1022 in the presence of Robert II of France thirteen Cathari were burnt at Orleans; in 1051 other Cathari were hanged in the presence of the Emperor Henry III at Goslar. Neither in France nor in the Empire was there a secular law prescribing the death penalty for heresy, but the executions evidently had public approval. Sometimes indeed the people acted on their own authority. There are cases of this in 1076 at Cambrai, in 1114 in the diocese of Strasbourg, in 1144 at Liège, in 1163 at Cologne. In one instance we are told that the crowd burnt the heretics through fear of clerical leniency. Clearly the greatest zeal against heretics in this period came from the populace; clearly also they were persuaded that the stake was the appropriate retribution. Ecclesiastical councils of this century, while adjuring the secular authority to apprehend heretics, speak only of excommunication as their punishment. As to the desirability of the Church's handing over heretics to the State for drastic treatment, opinions differed. Wazo, Bishop of Liège (1042–48), disapproved of this, his successor Theoduin favoured it. St Bernard preferred the method of persuasion to coercion, yet ominously quoted with reference to heretics the words of St Paul, "For he beareth not the sword in vain." In 1157 a council at Rheims, in calling upon the secular arm to award life-imprisonment to Cathari, seems also to hint at the punishment of death in the vague phrase, "nisi gravius aliquid fieri debet visum." Hugh, Bishop of Auxerre (1183–1206), took upon himself the task of expelling or burning heretics as seemed best in particular cases, and about the same time the Archbishop of Rheims co-operated with the Count of Flanders in stamping out heresy in his diocese by means of the stake. Clearly during the twelfth century there was a tendency towards increasing severity in the Church's attitude.

The evolution of the Canon Law is largely the explanation. In a treatise possibly by Ivo of Chartres, *De edicto imperatorum in dampnatione haereticorum*, part of a law of Justinian meting out death to the Manichaeans is incorporated. At this time the Cathari were universally regarded as Manichaeans. Although the *Decretum* of Gratian does not mention the death penalty for heretics, certain of his commentators state that impenitent heretics may be put to death. The earliest secular law in the Middle Ages relating to heresy is the *Assize of Clarendon*, which orders that any house in which heretics have been harboured is to be destroyed. Shortly before this two Cathari brought before Henry II at Oxford had been whipped, branded, and banished. In 1184 Pope Lucius III and Frederick Barbarossa had a momentous meeting at Verona, at which it was arranged, on the one hand, that bishops should make diligent inquiry for heretics and excommunicate the obdurate, while, on the other hand, the secular authority should enforce the penalties of the imperial ban, namely, exile, infamy, the demolition of tainted houses, the confiscation of property. In 1194 the Emperor Henry VI reissued these instructions, adding the penalty of a fine on any individual or community neglecting opportunities for the apprehension of heretics. The first undoubted instance of the death penalty occurring in medieval secular legislation against heresy appears in an edict of Peter II of Aragon in 1197[1], prescribing banishment for all heretics, but the stake for any that might remain in defiance of the edict. This legislation is important, but it relates only to Aragon and the death penalty is only contingent.

At the best, the measures taken against heretics up to the close of the twelfth century had been half-hearted and spasmodic. It does not appear that the decrees of Verona had been effectively carried out. Emperors and Popes had been in the main so much absorbed in their quarrels that they had not given serious attention to the problem of heresy. Then in 1198 came the accession to the papal throne of Innocent III, at once a lawyer and a man of action. In the first capacity, in a letter addressed to the magistrates of Viterbo, he propounded a most important analogy between heresy and treason, for which the just requital was death. Though he did not here draw the conclusion, the logical outcome of the argument is that treason to Jesus Christ is worthy at least of death. Innocent was

[1] Unless the evidence for one in 1194 be accepted. In a letter written in the year 1211 by the municipality of Toulouse to the King of Aragon it is stated that Count Raymond V had issued an edict in 1194 ordering that any heretic found in the town or suburbs of Toulouse should be put to death. There is no other trace of this edict, but the letter is genuine.

much perturbed by heresy in certain Italian cities—Viterbo itself, Orvieto, Verona. But even worse was the open prosperity of Catharism in the lands of Raymond VI of Toulouse. It was a challenge to the new Pope's masterful spirit. His first remedy was the sending of special missionaries, armed with legatine powers. Their total failure and the murder of one of them, Peter de Castelnau, were the signals for the adoption of his second remedy—the crusade. The Albigensian wars are the most notorious example of sustained and successful persecution in history[1]. But they represent only the first stage in suppression. Catharism was rooted out because they were followed up by the unremitting labour of inquisitors for generations after. To the method of indiscriminate slaughter succeeded procedure by means of an efficient tribunal, specially fitted for the task.

Though the Inquisition may be said to have started soon after the Albigensian wars, it did not arise directly out of them; its origin takes us further back. Heresy, being essentially a spiritual offence, had always come within the purview of every diocesan, like any other ecclesiastical offence. But heresy cases became in the eleventh and early twelfth centuries so numerous that it proved impossible for the bishops to deal adequately with them and at the same time carry on their multifarious other duties with efficiency. When experience shewed this to be undeniably the case, a special new machinery was created—a court existing expressly for the trial of heresy cases, namely, the Inquisition. This process would have taken place even had there never been any Albigensian crusades.

The peculiar features of inquisitorial procedure arose largely from the difficulty experienced in a heretic-infested country in securing evidence. The ordinary methods of initiating a prosecution in a spiritual court, just as in a civil court, were those of *denuntiatio* and *accusatio*. By the former the archdeacon introduced a case from his own personal knowledge; by the latter proceedings were taken upon evidence proffered by an individual informer. The archdeacon having many other duties to attend to, the Church had in the main to rely upon the second method. But when heresy was popular and protected by those in high places, it was not easy to induce private persons to play the part of *delator*. The Council of Verona (1184) suggested another system. It directed that bishops should make periodical circuits of their dioceses with the express purpose of inquiring into, of ferreting out, heresy; that they should compel trustworthy persons to denounce all those whose manner of life differed from that of good Catholics, and that they should take judicial action based upon the common report or *diffamatio* of the locality obtained in this manner. The system thus mapped out is an inquisitorial system. It is a supplement to the usual methods of originating a judicial action, intended to surmount the particular difficulty of securing evidence in cases of heresy.

[1] Cf. *supra*, Chaps. I and IX.

But there is as yet no suggestion of the setting up of a new tribunal. Cases of heresy are still tried by the bishop in the ordinary episcopal court.

The Councils of Avignon (1209) and Montpellier and the Fourth Lateran Council (1215) recommended the same procedure. It was not found to be sufficiently effective, and in 1227 the Council of Narbonne endeavoured to improve upon it by the device of entrusting certain persons described as *testes synodales* with the duty of making diligent inquiry concerning the heretics of their several neighbourhoods. These synodal witnesses—though the term is new—may be merely the trustworthy persons referred to by the earlier Councils, but in any case they are now allotted a new task. They have not merely to denounce, they have to search out. In the literal sense of the word these witnesses are local inquisitors. In the creation of an organised system of delation one characteristic feature of inquisitorial practice has now been evolved, although the tribunal known as the Holy Office has not yet come into existence.

But the new devices of collecting together the material for the creation of a *diffamatio* and of launching judicial proceedings for heresy upon a *diffamatio* still left the machinery of persecution inadequate. Experience seemed to shew that there was something inherently defective for the trial of heretics in the existing spiritual courts, and that it was desirable to entrust both the process of thoroughly organising the search for heretics and that of actually trying them to experts specifically appointed and exclusively employed in that work. Delegates expressly nominated by the Pope to combat heresy, entrusted with special powers and more or less independent of ordinary episcopal authority, there had already been—such, for example, as Peter de Castelnau, Arnold of Cîteaux, and St Dominic himself. Dominic has indeed been hailed as the first inquisitor, though the Inquisition properly speaking was not founded till ten years after his death. But neither in the wider sense of a simple investigator nor in the more technical sense of a judge in cases of heresy is it true that St Dominic was a pioneer. In the wider sense all the envoys employed to combat the errors of the Albigenses and to bring the culprits to justice may be called inquisitors. The conversion of the haphazard and occasional papal delegation in matters of heresy into a properly organised and permanent system was the work of Gregory IX, who may therefore be legitimately accounted the founder of the tribunal of the Inquisition. He was responsible for the institution of the permanent judge-delegate for heretical causes, who, at first acting as advisory colleague to the bishop, in course of time came to oust the bishop from effective control in these cases.

The first and perhaps the most notorious delegate selected by Gregory IX was Conrad of Marburg, the brutal torturer of St Elizabeth of Hungary, who harried the heretics of Germany with the utmost vigour. Another was Robert le Bougre, an apostate Catharan, appointed Inquisitor of

France in 1235[1]. But, generally speaking, the Pope found that members of the two great Mendicant Orders were best fitted for his purpose. Both had already rendered most zealous and conspicuous service in combating heresy; they were, moreover, bound by peculiar ties to the Holy See and could therefore be appropriately used for work which to a large extent must involve the supersession of ordinary episcopal authority. Accordingly from the outset there was a close association between the Friars and the Inquisition. The inauguration of the new system may be taken as dating from April 1233 when Gregory addressed two bulls, the first to the bishops, the second to the Dominicans, of southern France. In the first he refers to the bishops as being "engrossed in a whirlwind of cares, scarce able to breathe in the pressure of overwhelming anxieties." Their burdens must be eased, and he has therefore decided to help them by sending the Preaching Friars against the heretics of France. He therefore orders the bishops, as they reverence the Holy See, to receive the friars kindly, to treat them well, and to give them all possible assistance in the fulfilment of their office. In the second bull the friars are empowered to proceed against all, laymen and clerks, without appeal, calling in the aid of the secular arm when necessary and coercing opposition, if need be, by the censures of the Church. It is possibly true that in publishing these bulls Gregory did not intend to create a new tribunal, that he did not envisage the matured system which was undoubtedly the direct consequence of his action; it is also unquestionably true that he did not contemplate relieving the bishops of their existing authority in cases of heresy—indeed next year he is found angrily threatening the bishops of the province of Narbonne with his serious displeasure if they do not shew greater energy against the heretics. But whatever may have been Gregory's ultimate intentions, certain it is that the bulls of 1233 were decisive in virtually inaugurating the career of the Holy Office. In the subsequent development of its organisation and procedure the greatest part was taken by Innocent IV, Alexander IV, Urban IV, Clement IV, Clement V, and John XXII, aided by the rules of a number of ecclesiastical councils, from that of Béziers in 1233 to that of Albi in 1254.

To begin with, the friars-inquisitors were itinerant, just as their predecessors had been, but gradually, as the advantages of regularly employing the Mendicants in the war against heresy became more and more obvious, the practice was evolved of partitioning different countries and districts between them, and so of instituting permanent local tribunals. Thus in the West, Provence, Dauphiné, and Savoy were allotted to the Franciscans; northern France, Lorraine, and Flanders to the Dominicans. Germany became a Dominican sphere; Bohemia and Dalmatia Franciscan. In theory the inquisitors continued to co-operate with the bishops—in the middle of the thirteenth century Innocent IV still regards the bishops as

[1] Cf. *supra*, Chap. IX, p. 347.

the judges, the friars only as expert assistants; but as time went on and heresy was recognised as being a constant, not merely a passing, menace, and as the inquisitor became more and more experienced, more and more skilled, so the presence of the inquisitor in any heresy trial became indispensable, that of the diocesan purely formal and perfunctory. There is abundant evidence of much episcopal jealousy and of a good deal of friction between bishop and inquisitor, which, in view of the special privileges and immunities of the latter, is not surprising. Released from obedience to provincials and generals, inquisitors could not be interfered with even by papal legates. At first their commissions were regarded as expiring with the life of the Popes who issued them; from 1267, however, they were regarded as being continuously valid. While some medieval inquisitors were looked upon as wantonly cruel even by their contemporaries and appear to a more liberally-minded age as monsters, as a whole they were picked men, and high qualities of courage, probity, zeal, and sagacity were repeatedly demanded by the Popes. Bernard Gui's description of the model inquisitor is a very fine one, even according to modern standards.

In addition to bishop and inquisitor there were present at all heresy trials the notary and certain councillors, known as *viri boni* or *viri periti*. The notary was an official of importance, as all the proceedings of the court were minutely recorded. It often happened that evidence which was irrelevant and unimportant, so far as concerned the case actually being tried, proved to be of the utmost value in some other case, perhaps in a different country and many years later. The sinister and dreadful reputation that the tribunal acquired, the impression of its inexorable, unescapable power, was due largely to the fact that it was secret and ubiquitous, but also in no small measure to the fact that its records were exact and elaborate. The *viri periti* might be either clerks or laymen; quite frequently they were civil lawyers. There might be as many as twenty or thirty of these councillors present at a trial. The inquisitor was under no obligation to accept their advice, and often no doubt their presence was merely formal; the fact remains that the system did provide these assessors—a sort of consultant jury—often consisting of expert civil lawyers, who kept a watch upon the proceedings and were at least a potential check upon arbitrary action. Others who accompanied the inquisitor and might be present in the tribunal were the inquisitor's vicar or lieutenant, who sometimes acted as his deputy and customarily assisted in the examination of witnesses, and the inquisitor's *socius*, who appears to have had no official functions, but only the social duty of attending upon the inquisitor on his journeys. More important were the familiars, a band of petty officials, ever tending to become more numerous, who acted as a personal body-guard for the inquisitor, visited prisons, officiated at *autos-da-fé*, and often played the part of special agents and spies.

Casuistry tended to flourish in a tribunal existing for the trial of an offence which was specifically *in intellectu*, a matter of wrong thinking and believing, not necessarily revealed by any overt act. The manuals of inquisitors abound in nice and subtle distinctions, such as were apt to be produced by an attempt to deal consistently and scientifically with an offence by its very nature complex. A careful classification was made of various types of heretic. *Affirmative* were those who openly avowed their errors, *negative* those who denied or prevaricated; *perfected* heretics were those who not only held erroneous opinion but modelled their lives in accordance with it, *imperfect* those who simply held the opinion but did not conform their behaviour to it. In addition to undoubted heretics the court took cognisance of those who had in greater or less degree exposed themselves to *suspicion* of heresy. Thus, to have saluted a heretic or listened to his discourse on a single occasion was to become *lightly* suspect; to have done so twice or thrice to become *vehemently* suspect; to have done so often to become *violently* suspect. The idea was that for a good Catholic to have acted in such a way as to have incurred the bare suspicion of heretical contamination was in itself a misdemeanour, for which penance must be imposed. Fautorship or the defence of heretics, either in the shape of positive aid or even the most trivial kindness or courtesy or in the shape of neglect to bring them to justice when opportunity offered, was a more serious offence. Sometimes a crime which was not primarily one of heresy was dealt with by the Inquisition, because it resulted from some erroneous belief. Usury, adultery, clerical concubinage did not come under inquisitorial cognisance as such; only if the guilty persons committed those offences with the heretical opinion that they were not sinful. In the fifteenth century much of the tribunal's attention was occupied by cases of sorcery and witchcraft. Alexander IV had exhorted inquisitors not to be deflected from their proper work by such cases; but Bernard of Como in 1250 championed the view that the magic arts were a form of heresy, and this interpretation easily prevailed.

The commencement of inquisitorial proceedings was preceded by the announcement of a time of grace, and a promise of mild treatment for those who voluntarily surrendered themselves before its expiration, and the promulgation of an edict of faith, calling upon good Catholics to denounce the guilty. The actual trial resolved itself largely into a prolonged interrogatory of the accused either by the inquisitor himself or his vicar. If the accused did not at once make confession and throw himself upon the mercy of the court, he had to try to explain away the *diffamatio* against him. This was no easy matter. To invalidate the *diffamatio* it was necessary to prove that the witnesses were actuated by mortal enmity, for it was assumed that no motive less strong could induce any one to launch so terrible a false accusation. As the accused was never confronted with the witnesses, and was never informed who had defamed him, all he could do was to give a list by guess-work of his possible enemies. These disabilities to the defence existed for the protection of informers against the chance of vengeance. The Inquisition was quite indiscriminate in its acceptance of evidence, readily accepting the depositions of one heretic against another (though never in his favour), of husband against wife, of child against parent, of servant against master. Even the evidence of murderers, proved perjurers, and excommunicates was not excluded. At first this type of evidence had not been allowed, but in 1261 Alexander IV declared it to be valid in heretical causes. The interrogatory based on such testimony was apt to be long, baffling, and involved. Seeing that heretics were credited with great acuteness, begotten of the evil one, it was held to be perfectly legitimate to harass the accused with the most intricate and disconcerting examination. The inquisitor, piously regarding himself as engaged in a holy warfare against the powers of darkness, felt he had to put forth all his energy in opposing the craft and subtleties of the Devil. No doubt some heretics had such knowledge and dialectical skill as to put the examiner upon his mettle, but in the majority of cases the duel of wits was quite unequal, the accused, an illiterate man, too much scared to make full use of such faculties as he possessed. At one time defending counsel were allowed, but as inquisitors, such as Bernard Gui, were apt to take the view that the defence of one suspect of heresy rendered the advocate open to the charge of fautorship, such assistance was hard to get, and the ruling of the Council of Albi (1254) that advocates were not to be allowed was soon generally adopted.

If the interrogatory did not by itself suffice to secure what the inquisitor was always aiming at—voluntary confession—torture was employed. Technically foreign though it was to the Canon Law, the use of torture came in with the study of Roman Law and the prohibition of the ordeal. It was sanctioned by the Lateran Council of 1215 and definitely ordered by the great bull of Innocent IV published in 1252, *Ad extirpanda.* At first it was laid down that the actual infliction must be carried out by the civil authority, but this salutary rule being found irksome, Alexander IV in 1256 permitted inquisitors and their officers to absolve one another for such canonical irregularities. Another salutary rule was that torture could be administered to a prisoner only once. This restraint also was found troublesome and it was easily evaded by another subterfuge. While torture could not be *repeated*, it was argued that it might be *continued.* This convenient verbal distinction made it possible to torture a prisoner repeatedly without contravening the letter of the law. A third awkward regulation was that a confession was only valid when voluntary. The device adopted to overcome this difficulty was to have the confession which had actually been wrung by pain confirmed three days after the torture had been applied, not in the torture chamber, and officially to regard the confirmation as the true confession. Clement V endeavoured to moderate the use of torture in a number of canons published among the *Clementines* (1312), which Bernard Gui complained of bitterly.

Strictly speaking, the Inquisition did not punish; it only inflicted penances. Those meted out for a trivial case of *suspicion* might be light enough—the hearing of so many masses for example. But even for the mere suspect the penalty was usually more serious than this. One of the most frequent forms of penance was that of pilgrimage, either to a shrine in the penitent's own country in mild cases or to far distant ones in a foreign country in more serious cases. Long absence from home, loss of employment, and considerable hardship on the journey might be involved. Flogging inflicted with due ceremony publicly in church, often as an interlude during the celebration of mass, was another penance. Another infliction—one originally suggested by St Dominic—was the compulsory wearing of crosses or some other emblem emblazoned in saffron on front and back. This penance was one of the hardest to bear, as it exposed the sufferer to the jeers and sometimes the violence of the mob, and its evasion was often attempted. At length it became clear that some measure of protection for cross-wearers was needful, and the Council of Béziers (1246) ordained that they were not to be subjected to ridicule or driven away from their business. Pecuniary penalties were often exacted. From the point of view of the penitent, the payment of a fine was perhaps preferable to other forms of penance, but the temptation to extortion is obvious, and in 1249 Innocent IV is found denouncing inquisitors for their exactions. Confiscation of property was not a penalty in itself, but the automatic outcome of a conviction of actual heresy; nor was the Inquisition strictly responsible, for the secular authority stepped in and sequestrated the property. But the Inquisition aggravated what had been the rule of Roman Law, that the heretic's possessions should pass to orthodox sons, and made the confiscation absolute. The division of the proceeds varied in different countries. Part went to the prince, part to the Church; but sometimes a portion went to the heretic's immediate lord, and sometimes, as latterly in France, the Crown took all. Confiscations made heretic-hunting profitable to the State, and undoubtedly they formed a strong inducement to the lay power to be zealous. Nevertheless, it is an error to ascribe medieval persecutions to mere cupidity. Most heretics belonged to the poorer classes. The most severe of all penances was imprisonment, often employed as the recompense for failure to carry out some lighter penance, and on those who failed to surrender themselves during the time of grace, but who made voluntary confession of their iniquity afterwards. Imprisonment might be comparatively tolerable, or it might be very terrible. The form termed *murus largus* allowed of the prisoner's leaving his cell at certain intervals and holding converse with other prisoners similarly privileged and with friends from the outside world; *murus strictus* on the other hand meant rigorous solitary confinement. The penalty of perpetual imprisonment in a dark and noisome cell was probably more frightful even than death at the stake.

Nevertheless, it is the spectacular burnings that are associated most vividly in the popular mind with the Inquisition. That being so, it is important to realise that in proportion to the total number of inquisitorial sentences that of relaxation to the secular arm was relatively very small. An analysis of the sentences of Bernard Gui extending over a period of seventeen years shews that out of a total of 613 there were 307 of imprisonment, only 45 of *relaxation*. This penalty was reserved for only two types of offenders—the obdurate who refused to recant and those who after reconciliation relapsed. The Church did not desire the death of the heretic. The martyr does infinitely less damage to his cause than the apostate. Thus relaxation to the secular arm, with its inevitable consequence—the stake—was always a confession of failure. The inquisitor was above all things a missionary, a father-confessor, ready to welcome back truant sheep to the fold, only requiring as the price of forgiveness a confession of sin and the performance of penance as proof of sincere contrition.

In handing over the impenitent and the relapsed to the secular arm, the Inquisition invariably made use of a formula praying that the death or mutilation of the prisoner might be avoided[1]. This adjuration was invariably disregarded, and the Church knew that it always would be. The formula freed the Church from the irregularity of being responsible for the shedding of blood; but moral responsibility is not so easily evaded. The secular authority certainly had seldom any qualms about putting the heretic to death. Apart from the edict of Peter II of Aragon, there are the more important constitutions of Frederick II. In the constitution published at Catania for Lombardy in 1224 the punishment for heresy was declared to be the stake or (at the discretion of the judge) loss of the tongue; in the constitutions of Melfi, which applied to Sicily, there is no mention of an alternative to the stake; in 1238 this regulation was extended to the whole Empire. The use of the stake was customary in France during the contemporary reign of St Louis and it was recognised as legal in the *Établissements* of 1270. When heretics perished in the flames they perished in accordance with civil, not canon, law. But it is clear that the Church approved. Heresy was primarily a spiritual offence, investigated in a spiritual court; the State's appreciation of its enormity was due to clerical exhortations, which likened heresy to treason. There is evidence that Frederick II's constitutions had ecclesiastical influence behind them, that of 1224 the influence of Albert, Archbishop of Magdeburg, that of 1231 the influence of the two Spanish Dominicans, Guala, Bishop of Brescia, and Raymond of Peñafort, confessor to Gregory IX and later general of the Predicant Order. Both these men were exceedingly energetic in the campaign against heresy. In 1229 the very important Council of Toulouse (using language which occurs in Frederick's constitutions and which was repeated by the subsequent Council of Arles in 1234) ordered that all heretics should be brought

[1] This formula ran: "De nostro foro ecclesiastico te proiicimus et tradimus seu relinquimus brachio seculari ac potestati curie secularis, dictam curiam secularem efficaciter deprecantes quod circa et citra sanguinis effusionem et mortis periculum sententiam suam moderetur."

before the lay or the ecclesiastical authority *ut animadversione debita puniantur*, and added significantly that those who *through fear of death* or other cause returned to the faith should be imprisoned to prevent their contaminating others. The phrase "merited penalty" clearly means death, and is used by Gregory IX in his bull *Excommunicamus*, when, while mentioning every other kind of requital for various degrees of guilt short of obduracy, he orders that the impenitent should be handed over to the secular arm for punishment; it is also used by the Senator Anibaldi when introducing the imperial constitution into Rome, which he ruled under the Pope's authority and where in the same year several obdurate heretics were executed. In 1245 Innocent IV included Frederick's constitutions *verbatim* in a bull *Cum adversus haereticam pravitatem.* In a later bull of 1252, addressed to the secular rulers of Italy, *Ad extirpanda de medio populi Christiani pravitatis zizania*, the duty of doing their part in uprooting heresy was forcibly enjoined upon those princes by Innocent, under pain of their being accounted fautors of heretics in case of non-compliance. All civil magistrates were commanded to co-operate with the friars in bringing heretics to justice. With slight modifications this bull was reissued by Alexander IV in 1259 and by Clement IV in 1265. Failure to co-operate with the Church and to carry out its own legislation involved the secular authority in the pain of excommunication. It was easy to justify the Church's attitude towards the death penalty, as Thomas Aquinas did, by the argument of analogy —one of his theses is that the falsification of true doctrine is worse than the issue of false coin, yet the coiner justly merits death. It could also be defended from Scripture—did not Christ speak of the branch that is gathered, cast into the fire, and burnt? So thoroughly did the Church believe in burning as the right fate for the heretic, that when a man's heresy was discovered only after his death, it ordained that his bones should be exhumed and solemnly burnt.

The Inquisition did not penetrate much beyond the central and western parts of Europe. It found no home in the British Isles or in Scandinavia and it made small headway east of the Adriatic, though there was the original home of Catharism. The papal arm rarely stretched so far with effect. Dominicans penetrated into those lands, but with disappointing results, and there were massacres of the Black Friars in Bosnia. After the coming of the Ottoman Turks, Cathari were converted to Islām, never to Christianity. In Germany the tribunal was most vigorous in its earliest days—those of Conrad of Marburg and Conrad Tors. Thereafter there came a lull. It became more influential in the fourteenth century, but the papal schism caused a great reduction in its authority. In Bohemia, though there was much activity against heretics, it appears to have been that of the ordinary episcopal courts, not of the Inquisition. In Italy the legislation of Frederick II and Gregory IX introduced an era of persecution in which the Papacy shewed a marked tendency to translate

Ghibelline into heretic, finding the Inquisition a very useful weapon in waging war against the rival faction. On the other hand, certain Ghibellines, such as Ezzelin da Romano, deliberately supported heretics in order to embarrass the Papacy. The Church was able to enlist a considerable amount of lay enthusiasm in support of the inquisitors, for example in the organisation of the Crocesegnati and the Compagnia della Fede which Peter Martyr, a great hammer of heretics, raised in Florence. In southern Italy the Inquisition was not very active. Charles of Anjou established it in Sicily, but when the island after the Sicilian Vespers passed into the hands of the house of Aragon persecution ceased.

Spain, most intimately associated in later days with the Inquisition because of the activities of the tribunal as it was organised in close touch with the monarchy by Ferdinand and Isabella, was not inherently a specially intolerant country—the reconquered Muslim population was well treated in the main—and the medieval Inquisition does not play an important part in the country's history. In the reign of James I and during the powerful influence of Raymond of Peñafort the Inquisition flourished in Aragon, and a thorough system of persecution was established by the decrees of the Councils of Tarragona of 1232 and 1242. But it had fallen on evil days before the end of the fourteenth century and was sadly lacking in funds, as its great inquisitor, Nicholas Eymeric, laments. In Castile and Portugal the tribunal was practically unknown. It was in France that the Inquisition was most active and most efficacious, not only in the south-east but also north of the Loire. But bitter complaints of the cruelties and extortion of inquisitors reaching his ears, Philip the Fair chose to adopt the cause of the complainants, especially during his quarrel with Boniface VIII, when he took the drastic step of removing on his own authority the two inquisitors most bitterly aspersed, and deprived inquisitors generally of the power to make arbitrary arrests. When King and Pope became reconciled in 1304, a compromise was arranged, whereby the aid of the secular arm was unreservedly placed at the disposal of the friars, but it was stipulated that royal officials were to visit their prisons to prevent abuses. In doing its work so zealously and thoroughly, in bringing Languedoc into complete subjection to the Papacy, the Inquisition had also brought the country into subjection to the King of France. It had, in so doing, helped the aggrandisement of the French monarchy and indirectly enabled it to look on inquisitors as little more than State officials, on the tribunal as but a profitable piece of State machinery.

CHAPTER XXI

THE MENDICANT ORDERS

THE "Four Orders" were (1) the Dominicans or Friars Preachers, often called Black Friars in England and Jacobins in France; (2) the Franciscans or Friars Minor, called in England Grey Friars, in France Cordeliers, and in Germany Barefoot Friars; (3) the Carmelites or Order of the Blessed Virgin of Mount Carmel, or White Friars; (4) the Austin Friars or Order of the Friars Hermits of St Augustine. Many smaller Mendicant Orders also sprang up in the thirteenth century, but were suppressed, *i.e.* forbidden to receive any more novices, by the Second Council of Lyons in 1274.

Each of the four Orders had a separate origin and distinct characteristics. All were alike in rejecting more or less completely permanent endowments and living a life of voluntary poverty, in being world-wide and centralised bodies, independent of the local diocesan and parochial organisation, and in including the service of man in the service of God.

The reconciliation of the religious with the secular life, the possibility of which was revealed by the Crusades, found its first expressions in the institution of the Regular Canons and of the Military Orders and was later more fully realised by the Mendicant Friars, who served God in the world, devoting themselves to the saving of souls by their example and preaching.

Many independent movements at the end of the twelfth century shew the same characteristics as the Franciscan Order—men and women band together to lead a life of poverty and self-sacrifice and active well-doing in conscious imitation of Christ. Examples will be found in the Beguines and Beghards of the Low Countries, the Humiliati of Italy, the Poor Men of Lyons. Between the latter and the followers of St Francis there is a close similarity; but the Poor Men of Lyons, repudiated by the official Church, were turned into heretics, while the Franciscans, authorised by the official Church, became a religious order.

St Francis was born at Assisi in 1181 or 1182. His name no doubt was suggested by the country with which his father, Pietro Bernardone, a rich cloth-merchant, traded—the country of the fairs of Champagne, of the *langue d'oïl* and the "chansons de geste." Francis, though associated in his father's business, had no taste for a merchant's career. Open-handed and open-hearted, with the gaiety and ambitions of a high-spirited youth and an attractive personality which was later to draw all men to him, he early became the leader of the young men of Assisi.

His first idea was, of course, to be a soldier. In one of the little skirmishes between the rival towns of Assisi and Perugia he was taken captive; and an illness contracted in the prison at Perugia seems to have turned his mind in other directions. But his definite "conversion" may be dated from his meeting with the leper, as he was riding through the Umbrian plain. The young gallant, who had been in the habit of holding his nose if he saw the houses of lepers a mile away, dismounted and kissed him. From this day to the end of his life the care of the lepers became a sacred duty. Later, when praying before the crucifix in the ruined chapel of St Damian, he heard a voice saying, "Francis, go and repair my house, which you see is falling into ruins." Interpreting the command literally, Francis took some goods from his father's shop, rode to Foligno, sold horse and stuff, and offered the money to the priest of St Damian. This led to the final breach with his father and the renunciation of his home.

For some time he went on with the work of repairing with his own hands the deserted chapels round Assisi—St Damian's, St Peter's, St Mary of the Angels or the Portiuncula. He assumed the garb of a hermit and thought no doubt of leading the life of a solitary—a life which always had attractions for him. It was in the church of the Portiuncula —probably on 24 February 1208—that his true vocation was revealed to him in the words of the gospel for the day (Matt. x): "As ye go, preach, saying, The kingdom of heaven is at hand. Heal the sick, cleanse the lepers, raise the dead, cast out devils: freely ye have received, freely give. Provide neither gold, nor silver, nor brass in your purses, nor scrip for your journey, neither two coats, neither shoes, nor yet staves: for the workman is worthy of his meat." "This is what I want," cried Francis. He followed the gospel precept at once and literally, going barefoot, and preaching repentance in "words that were like fire, penetrating the heart."

With the language and ideals of the gospel were interwoven in the mind and life of St Francis the language and ideals of chivalry. The Lady Poverty became the mistress of his heart. His friars were sometimes "his Knights of the Round Table," sometimes "minstrels of the Lord, lifting up the hearts of men and moving them to spiritual gladness." He himself "would often break forth into a French song of joyous exulting. At times he would pick up a stick from the ground and setting it upon his left shoulder would draw another stick after the manner of a bow with his right hand athwart the same as athwart a viol, and making befitting gestures would sing in French of our Lord Jesus Christ. But all this show of joyance would be ended in tears and in pity of Christ's passion." "Let the friars," he said in an injunction incorporated in the early Rule, "take care not to appear gloomy and sad like hypocrites, but let them be jovial and merry, shewing that they rejoice in the Lord, and becomingly courteous." "Courtesy is one of the qualities of God Himself, who, of His courtesy, giveth His sun and His rain to the just and the unjust: and courtesy is the sister of charity, and quencheth hate and keepeth love alive." Francis himself was courteous to all alike, even to thieves and robbers. He never felt himself superior to others, was never condescending. "More than a saint among saints," says Thomas of Celano, "he was among sinners as one of themselves."

The same sympathy united him with all nature, animate and inanimate, and gave him power over beasts and birds. This sense of kinship with all created things received its highest expression in the Praises of the Creatures, or Song of the Sun, which he composed at the end of his life, with its final verse of praise for "our sister Death." He loved especially "Brother Fire" for his beauty and strength; the worm because it typified the lowliness of Christ.

The people of Assisi had first hooted Francis as a madman; their scoffing soon turned to veneration, and others began to follow his example. The first to join him was the rich Bernard of Quintavalle, who forthwith gave all his goods to the poor. The second was Peter de Cataneo, canon of the cathedral. A few days later these were joined by Giles, who in his bold adventures in the service of Lady Poverty, as well as in his mystic devotion, remains the ideal of the Franciscan friar. With him Francis made his first missionary journey, tramping through the March of Ancona and preaching repentance. When the number of friars reached eleven, Francis drew up a simple rule of life, consisting apparently of a few passages from the gospels inculcating poverty, and "the penitents of Assisi" set out for Rome in the summer, probably of 1210, to ask for papal approbation. Innocent III raised difficulties: the life was too hard, it was impossible to live without possessions, they would do better to join some existing Order. But, argued the Cardinal John of St Paul, "if anyone says that to observe the gospel and to take a vow to do so is something new or irrational or impossible, he is convicted of blasphemy against Christ, the author of the gospel." Innocent knew the danger of driving religious men into heresy. He gave a verbal sanction to the rule, and authorised Francis and his companions to preach repentance. He also ordered the Cardinal of St Paul to confer on them the ecclesiastical tonsure. Francis seems to have submitted to this with some misgivings. "Take care," he used to say to the barber, "that you do not make me a large tonsure. For I want my simple brethren to have a share in my head."

The friars—now called Friars Minor, either after the *minores* or lower classes, or in reference to the gospel (Matt. xxv. 40–45)—had as their principal rendezvous, first the old leper-house of Rivo Torto, and then the Portiuncula, where they built a few small huts of wattle, mud, and straw, surrounded by a hedge. Here they assembled every year at Whitsuntide for the general chapter, when new brethren were received into the fraternity by Francis. Here in the Lent of 1212 they were joined by Clara, a young heiress of Assisi, who, moved by the preaching of Francis and by his personal admonitions, left her father's house in the dead of night and devoted herself to a life of poverty. Francis eventually established her and those who joined her at St Damian's, giving the Poor Ladies a brief "formula vitae." Clara (probably in 1216) obtained from Innocent III the "privilegium paupertatis" authorising her and her sisters, or the Poor Ladies of St Damian, to live without possessions; the privilege was without precedent in the Roman Chancery, and the Pope drew up the minute of the document with his own hand. The enforcement of the strict *clausura* imposed on the nuns of St Damian by the Rule of Ugolino (afterwards Gregory IX) in 1219 made the observance of absolute poverty increasingly difficult, and though St Clare in her own convent maintained her principles till her death in 1253, the Order generally had already by that time become an endowed Order.

Jacques de Vitry, writing in October 1216 of what he had seen at the papal court at Perugia in July of that year, says: "One comfort, however, I found in those parts: many people of both sexes—rich people of the world—having left all for Christ, were fleeing from the world, who were called Friars Minor. They were held in great reverence by Pope and cardinals. These people give no heed to temporal things, but with fervent desire and impetuous energy labour every day to withdraw perishing souls from the vanities of the world and lead them with them. And already, by the Grace of God, they have borne much fruit and gained many....They live after the model of the primitive Church....By day they go into cities and villages that they may gain some, living the active life: at night they return to the desert or solitary places, devoting themselves to contemplation. The women live together in different hostels near the cities; they receive nothing, but live by the work of their hands. But they are much grieved and distressed because they are more honoured by clerks and laymen than they would wish. Once a year the men of this religion assemble...at a fixed place to rejoice in God and feast together, and by the advice of good men they make and promulgate their holy institutions, which are confirmed by the Pope. After this for the whole year they are dispersed through Lombardy and Tuscany and Apulia and Italy."

The chapter of 1217 witnessed the first attempts to organise the great fraternity and to extend its activities beyond Italy. Provinces were instituted and provincial ministers elected, and missions were sent beyond the Alps and overseas to the Saracens, Giles going to Tunis and Elias and others to Syria. Francis himself, who had already made two attempts to reach Mohammedan lands, determined to go to France. Cardinal Ugolino of Ostia, who met him in Florence, forbade him to go and rebuked him for sending his brethren to die of hunger in distant lands. "Do you think, my lord," replied Francis, "that the Lord has sent the brethren only for these provinces? I tell you in truth that God has chosen the brethren for the profit and salvation of the souls of all mankind, and not only in the lands of the faithful, but also in the lands of the infidel they shall be received and shall save many souls." Francis, however, remained in Italy and sent to France Brother Pacifico, "the King of Verses."

In 1219 missions to Christian countries beyond the Alps were organised on a large scale—to France, Germany, Hungary, Spain. The Albigensian crusade was still smouldering, and the friars in France and Germany, though furnished with papal letters of commendation, were taken for heretics, whom they resembled in their way of life; in Hungary they were ill-treated and robbed of their clothes, and thus in most countries the first missions failed and the friars returned to Italy.

Meanwhile, Francis fulfilled his desire of going to the Saracens. With Peter de Cataneo he joined the crusading army before Damietta (August 1219) and preached before the Sultan, who received him courteously and sent him back to the Christian camp under military escort. He afterwards crossed to Palestine, where he received news which called him home.

During his absence his vicars had called a chapter of *seniores* (probably 29 September 1219) and prescribed the observance of further fasts among the friars, while Brother Philip, Visitor of the Poor Ladies, procured a papal bull authorising him to excommunicate their enemies; both these movements were inconsistent with the ideals of Francis: the former tended to change the free wandering life of the friars as strangers and pilgrims, having no fixed abode, living on alms and the work of their hands, into a regular life resembling that of the monastic Orders; the latter was contrary to the Franciscan spirit, which was opposed to the use of force and the authority of the law.

On his arrival at Bologna, early in 1220, Francis found a further development, which contravened the ideal of poverty—a house of the brethren built for permanent occupation. Francis ordered the friars to leave the house. But feeling himself unable alone to cope with the new situation, he appealed to the Pope to appoint Ugolino, Cardinal-bishop of Ostia, as his adviser, "with whom I can discuss my affairs and those of my Order." That Ugolino was a real admirer both of St Francis and of his ideals there can be no question; but he was above all things a prince of the Church: he would reform the Church by giving to Franciscan friars authority; Francis would reform the world by the power of love and humility.

Ugolino was present at the general chapter in May 1220 and acted as intermediary between Francis and the provincial ministers. The latter urged the cardinal to persuade Francis to let himself be guided by the advice of wise brethren, and instanced as models the rules of St Benedict, St Augustine, and St Bernard. In other words, they demanded a regular constitution and settled way of life. Francis refused in burning words to depart from "the way of humility and simplicity" which the Lord Himself had shewn him. Yet some ordered constitution was necessary. United solely by the personality of the founder, the Order could hardly survive his death. Francis was "not minded to become an executioner" and to attempt to enforce his will by punishment; he resigned the government to Peter de Cataneo and the ministers, and henceforth devoted himself to shewing by his example what the life of a Friar Minor should be, "and at the end his spirit did therein find rest and comfort." In August 1224 he retired to La Verna to fast and meditate on the passion of Our Lord; during his sojourn here he beheld the vision of the Seraph, after which there appeared on his body the stigmata or five wounds of Christ "which he had long borne in his heart."

A change was made in the character of the fraternity by a bull of Honorius III (22 September 1220), which imposed a year's noviciate on the friars and forbade any to leave the Order after making profession. This decree was incorporated in the Rule at the chapter of 1221, together with other ordinances defining the constitution of the general chapter and the powers of ministers. In this chapter Brother Elias, who had been appointed acting head of the Order, probably by Ugolino, after the death of Peter de Cataneo, presided, and successful missions were sent out to Germany and other parts of Europe. Before the death of St Francis 13 provinces had been formed, the last being England, founded in 1224. These were subsequently increased to 32, and ultimately (before 1272) to 34 provinces, of which 17 were Cisalpine and 17 Transalpine. The chapter of 1221 was probably the last of the great popular chapters, which were attended by thousands of friars encamped in huts of wattle round the church of the Portiuncula. Henceforth the general chapter met every three years and contained normally (besides the minister-general) the provincial ministers, each with his *socius*, one *custos* elected by the heads of the custodies in each province, and one *discretus* elected by the provincial chapter.

It is impossible to determine the exact part which Francis took in drawing up the Rules—the earlier and the later—as we know them. It is clear that some things were omitted, some inserted, against his wish, and also that Ugolino was largely responsible for the final form which was confirmed by Honorius III on 29 November 1223. In substance, the two Rules do not differ in essentials. Both insist on the observance of absolute poverty and on begging. More stress is laid on the duty of labour in the early Rule than in the later; and the care of the lepers which is referred to in the early Rule receives no mention in the later. To both these points St Francis reverts in his Testament, written shortly before his death. The Testament cannot, however, be regarded as a "revocation of the Rule," but as a protest against the tendencies in the Order to establish permanent houses and to seek or accept papal privileges; the friars "should not dare to ask any letter in the Roman Curia, neither for a church nor for any other place, nor under pretext of preaching nor on account of their bodily persecution, but wherever they are not received, let them flee to another land to do penance, with the blessing of God." The policy of the Roman Curia in encouraging the Mendicants to have their own churches and in protecting them against local opposition led inevitably to the quarrel between them and the secular clergy; the friars became rivals instead of helpers of the parish priests.

St Francis died at the Portiuncula on 3 October 1226; he was canonised in 1228 by Gregory IX, who in 1230 expounded the Rule and declared the Testament to have no binding force. The Pope modified the Rule by allowing the friars to employ an agent to receive and expend money for their immediate necessities and by permitting them the use of furniture, books, and other movables (though it was not made clear to whom these goods strictly speaking belonged), and of houses and places, which remained the property of the donors. The declaration of Innocent IV in 1245 went further, permitting recourse to money through an agent, not only for necessities but also for the convenience of the brethren, and making the Holy See owner of the lands, houses, and goods used by the friars, where ownership was not expressly reserved for the donors. In England lands and houses were often given to the community of the town for the use of the friars.

The election of Elias as general minister in 1232 was a triumph of the supporters of the new movement, who did not regard poverty as an end in itself, but adhered to it only so far as it served the great practical object of the Order—the conversion of souls—and for this object learning seemed more valuable than simplicity, great houses in the towns more suitable than hermitages in the mountains. Those who upheld the primitive ideals (later known as "spiritual" friars) were forced to withdraw more and more from a life of fruitful activity and to seek refuge in ecstatic contemplation, and were driven to reply to persecution by bitter controversy. Elias, however, soon roused the opposition of others besides the extremists. He lived like a prince. He exercised despotic control over the whole Order; he called no general chapters; he sent visitors armed with absolute powers to the provinces and reduced the authority and prestige of the provincial ministers. While promoting learning, he favoured the lay element against the clerical in the government of the Order. A revolt, led by Haymo of Faversham, was organised in the University of Paris and the provinces of England and Germany. Gregory IX summoned a general chapter to Rome (1239), and, yielding to the universal demand, deposed Elias. The Franciscan Order now adopted with some modifications the form of government set forth in the Dominican constitutions. The general minister was now subordinated to the general chapter. Albert of Pisa, provincial of England, was elected successor to Elias; he was the first priest to hold this position; and under his successor, Haymo of Faversham, the clerical element was further strengthened by a decree excluding laymen from the holding of office in the Order. The declaration of the Rule by Innocent IV led to a division in the Order; the stricter party demanded and were for a time able to secure its rejection. The temporary triumph of this party is shewn in the election to the office of general of John of Parma (1247–1257), who set free a number of "zealots" or "spiritual" friars, imprisoned by his predecessor in the March of Ancona. John of Parma, throughout his life a devoted upholder of poverty, did not belong to the extreme section of the spiritual friars; he had been lecturer at Paris and held that "knowledge and good morals were the two walls out of which the Order was built"; on the other hand, like the spirituals and indeed many of the finer minds in the Order, he was powerfully attracted by the mystical doctrines of Joachim of Flora.

Joachim had proclaimed the advent of the Kingdom of the Holy Ghost. "Spiritual men," who have entered into direct communion with God through poverty, contemplation, and love, will preach to all the world the Gospel of the Spirit, or Eternal Gospel, as it is called, in contradistinction to the Gospel of Christ and the Apostles, which is "transitory and temporal in what touches the form of the sacraments, but eternal for the truths which they symbolise." A spiritual Church will arise in which the Eastern and Western Churches will be merged, and the religion of Christ, purified by the Spirit and freed from the letter which killeth, be established for ever. The belief that St Francis was the angel of the new revelation was widespread in the Franciscan Order, especially among the spiritual friars. This was proclaimed by Friar Gerard of Borgo San Donnino in his "Introduction to the Eternal Gospel," issued at Paris in 1254. But with an amazing misunderstanding of Joachim's teaching, Gerard interpreted the phrase "Eternal Gospel" as meaning not the inspiration of the Holy Spirit, but the works of Joachim himself. Whether this misconception was general or confined to a few is not clear. But it placed a powerful weapon in the hands of the University of Paris in their struggle against the Mendicant Orders. Gerard's book was condemned by the Pope; and the community of the Order freed themselves from the suspicion of heresy by sending the offending brother to perpetual imprisonment and by deposing the general minister, John of Parma. Fra Salimbene, who had been a Joachite, "entirely abandoned that doctrine and resolved to believe only what he saw."

Bonaventura was now elected general and held office for seventeen years. He made no attempt to return to the primitive conditions; in his Life of St Francis, and in the decree of the general chapter of 1266 that all previous lives of the Founder should be destroyed, an endeavour was made to obliterate the memory of the early traditions so far as these were in conflict with the present ideals of the Community of the Order. Bonaventura accepted and defended the privileges which the Popes had granted to the friars. "If we were never to abide in parishes but by the priest's will, then we should scarce ever be able to stay long; since, whether of their own motion or at others' instigation, they would eject us from their parishes sooner than heretics or Jews." He advocated large houses in the towns as better both for discipline and for work, though they were inconsistent with the observance of primitive poverty. And he gloried in the learning of the Order: "I confess before God that it is this which has made me most of all to love the life of St Francis, that it is like the beginning and the consummation of the Church, which first began from simple fishermen and then advanced to the most famous and most learned doctors: this same development you will see in the religion of St Francis."

On the other hand, he endeavoured with little success to check the acknowledged abuses in the Order. Thus, the friars were in the habit of going about attended by a servant who carried the money-box and collected the coin which the friars might not touch. Begging had become so importunate that people feared to meet a friar as they feared to meet a robber. Magnificence in buildings, luxury in dress, greed for legacies, were among the evils denounced by the general. Some houses in Italy were beginning to acquire permanent revenues and endowments in land; and the observance of poverty was reduced to a legal technicality—the lax brethren enjoying the advantages without the responsibilities of wealth.

When the Council of Lyons, in 1274, was suppressing many of the lesser Mendicant Orders, a rumour spread that the Pope, Gregory X, had decided to compel the Orders that remained to accept property in common. The rumour was the signal for a renewed outbreak of hostilities between the spirituals and the community, which had smouldered during the generalship of Bonaventura. The spirituals in the March of Ancona repudiated the supposed papal decree. The provincial chapter sentenced the recalcitrants to imprisonment, and the following years witnessed a fierce persecution of the spirituals at the hands of their laxer brethren in the March, in Tuscany, and in Provence. In vain Nicholas III, for long Protector of the Order, attempted to restore peace by a stricter definition of poverty in the Decretal *Exiit qui seminat* (1279); the spirituals wanted the Rule and the Testament, not papal glosses. In vain Celestine V sought an escape from the difficulty by authorising the spirituals to form a separate Order, in which they might observe to the letter the Rule and Testament of St Francis; Boniface VIII annulled all the acts of his predecessor. At the Council of Vienne a commission of theologians not connected with the Order examined the arguments of both sides (the spirituals being represented by the ex-general Raymund Gaufredi and by Ubertino da Casale); and in 1312 Clement V approved the constitution *Exivi de Paradiso*, forbidding the holding of lands or permanent endowments and insisting on the "usus pauper" in some cases, the "usus moderatus" in others. This neither satisfied the consciences of the spirituals nor stopped their persecution by the community. In Provence the spirituals resisted by force. John XXII, to whom they appealed, ordered them to return to their obedience and handed the recalcitrants over to the Inquisition; four were burnt at Marseilles in 1318 and many more in the next few years throughout southern France. Others in Italy formed a separate Order under Angelo da Clareno as general, and managed to survive in spite of Pope and community; and other groups known under the name of Fraticelli were a constant source of trouble to the ecclesiastical authorities well into the fifteenth century. The community had got rid of the irreconcilable spirituals in 1318, but a new crisis arose in 1322, when the community itself was ranged in battle against the Pope.

In 1322–23 John XXII issued two decretals. The first withdrew from the Franciscans the right of holding property in the name of the Holy See. The second declared the Franciscan doctrine of the poverty of Christ and His Apostles to be heretical. The first shewed that the Franciscans were not true to their ideal in practice; the second asserted that the theoretical basis of their ideal was heresy. The revolt of the Order was led by the general minister, Michael of Cesena, who with his followers joined the Emperor Louis of Bavaria in his struggle with the Papacy, and perhaps the most permanent result was the political writings of William of Occam, which took their origin from this theoretical controversy. The majority soon accepted the situation, and many houses made no scruple about owning permanent endowments. The general decline in religious fervour and discipline was accelerated by the great pestilence and the papal schism. The deaths of friars reported in the general chapters of 1351 and 1354 reached the number of 13,883. The loss of so many old members, followed as it was by a rapid accession of new recruits, involved a breach with old traditions; but the old traditions were bad as well as good, and the breach with the past might lead to a spiritual growth, no less than to an increase of worldliness in the Order.

The beginnings of a new movement can be traced from 1334 when Friar Giovanni Valle received from the minister-general permission to found a hermitage near Foligno. The aim of the new reformers was to acquire small houses, generally at first hermitages, in which they could observe the Rule strictly without raising any doctrinal questions; hence their name of Friars of the Strict Observance, while the laxer portion of the community, who lived in larger convents, became known as Conventuals. The movement, originally lay and eremitical, received a great extension and new direction from St Bernardino of Siena (1380–1444), who made the Observant Friars the most influential religious force in Italy. The relations between Conventuals and Observants were a constant source of disputes, until in 1517 Leo X decreed their separation into two distinct Orders. It was natural that the Observant Friars should make most headway in countries where the Conventuals had departed most from the primitive traditions. In England, where few Franciscan houses held landed property, transferences of Conventual houses to the Observants were few, and the new Observant houses established were royal foundations.

The Dominican Order, both in its origin and internal development, offers a strong contrast to the Franciscan; and such conflicts as arose within it were neither so violent, persistent, nor so radical as those which divided the followers of St Francis.

Dominic was born at Caleruega in Old Castile in 1170. His parents were well off, but there is no conclusive evidence that either of them belonged to the noble family of Guzman. Educated first in the household of his maternal uncle, the arch-priest of Gumiel de Izan, he was sent at the age of fourteen to the schools of Palencia, where he studied arts and then theology for ten years. In 1191 during a famine he is said to have sold all his goods, including his books, to feed the starving. After finishing his studies he was made Canon of Osma, where the Bishop Martin de Bazan was reforming his chapter according to the Augustinian Rule and with the help of Diego de Azevedo. Diego, on his election as bishop in 1201, appointed Dominic as sub-prior. Being sent on a royal mission, he took the sub-prior with him, and at Toulouse Dominic had his first controversy with an Albigensian heretic, at whose house he lodged. At Montpellier Diego advised the papal legates and Cistercian abbots who had come to convert the heretics to give up their luxuries and imitate the simple and self-denying life of their opponents. Dominic adopted the life of voluntary poverty and went about on foot preaching and disputing. He found that the daughters of poor noble families were being entrusted by their parents to heretics, who maintained and educated them. He founded in 1206, with the help of Fulk, Bishop of Toulouse, a house at Prouille where such girls could be sent. The institution by degrees changed its character and became the first monastery of Dominican nuns. Dominic remained in the country for ten years (1205–1216) till the death of Simon de Montfort, often in personal danger after the outbreak of the war in 1208. He had no fear: "I have not yet deserved a martyr's death." He received from the papal legate the power to reconcile to the Church converted heretics, and all the acts recorded of him at this period are acts of reconciliation. Whether this office also implied the power to hand over obstinate heretics to the secular arm is not clear. Dominic is only once mentioned expressly as present at a burning of heretics, and then according to Theodoric of Apoldia he saved one of the victims from the flames.

Dominic by degrees collected a small band of preachers round him, among the first being Peter Cellani, or Seila, a wealthy citizen of Toulouse, who in 1215 gave his house to Dominic. From Simon de Montfort he received the castle of Cassanel. Bishop Fulk in 1215 granted formal recognition to "Brother Dominic and his companions, as preachers, to extirpate heresy," and allotted for their maintenance one-sixth of the tithes of the diocese, together with several churches. In this year Dominic accompanied Fulk to the Lateran Council, and laid before Innocent III his plan for the establishment of an Order of Preachers who should not be confined to any diocese, but should take the whole world as their sphere of action and be subject immediately to the papal see. The Council passed a decree prohibiting the foundation of new Orders. The Pope approved Dominic's plan, but recommended him to adopt one of the existing Rules. In consultation with his followers, now numbering sixteen, at Prouille, Dominic chose the Rule of St Augustine. It was the Rule under which he had lived as Canon of Osma; it was also so vague that those who adopted it were free to choose any organisation; and the Rule was immediately supplemented by a body of *consuetudines*, which were mostly borrowed from the constitutions of Prémontré and regulated the ascetic and canonical life of the friars. Innocent III and Dominic complied with the letter of the conciliar decree. The Dominicans were nominally Austin Canons; in reality they were a new Order of preachers, attached to no particular house, bound by no vow of stability, and owing obedience to the head of their Order and to the Pope. They were a powerful instrument in making the Pope the universal bishop.

Honorius III, on 22 December 1216, "expecting that the brethren will be champions of the faith and true lights of the world," solemnly confirmed and took under his government and protection the Order of "Master Dominic and the Friars Preachers," with all their lands and possessions. Hitherto, the friars had confined their activities to the Albigensian land and their only monastery was at Toulouse. Dominic now dispersed his small band, sending some to Paris, some to Spain, while he himself returned to Italy. The opposition of the bishops to the new preachers was met by a papal bull (11 February 1218), commanding all prelates to assist them. Seven friars reached Paris on 12 September 1217, under Matthew of France, and lived for some months in a house belonging to the hospital of Notre-Dame in great poverty. John de Barastre, dean of St Quentin (who had been appointed by the Pope theological lecturer to the friars), and the University of Paris granted them a house originally founded for poor strangers under the patronage of St James. Here they removed on 6 August 1218, and from this house they derived their popular name of Jacobins. In the same year the friars settled at Bologna, where their rapid success, especially among masters and students of the university, was due to the fiery eloquence of Reginald of Orleans, formerly dean of St Aignan. "All Bologna boiled over." Proffered endowments, accepted by Reginald, were, however, rejected by Dominic (1219), who wished that his sons should have no property but should live by alms—a decision adopted with some hesitation by the first general chapter of the Order held at Bologna in May 1220. This chapter drew up the constitutions which regulated the organisation of the Order. Dominic had recently met Francis and was probably influenced by the example of the Franciscan Order in adopting the vow of absolute poverty. But while to Francis poverty was essential to personal holiness, Dominic adopted it as a means of increasing the influence of the preacher. Another proposal of Dominic, that the whole temporal administration of the convents should be entrusted to lay brethren, was rejected by the chapter. In the chapter of 1221 Dominic commissioned thirteen friars to establish the province of England.

Dominic died at Bologna on 6 August 1221, exhorting his sons "to have charity, guard humility, and possess voluntary poverty." He was canonised in 1234. Of his courage, self-confidence, zeal for the salvation of souls, there is no question, nor of his capacity as a ruler. He was willing to learn from his enemies—both his institutions of poor preachers and of nuns being suggested by the example of the heretics. His brethren laid stress on his kindness and gentleness. He had great influence over women and understood their difficulties. He admitted to Jordan of Saxony that he liked talking to young women better than to old women—a passage that was deleted from Jordan's *Life of St Dominic* by command of the general chapter in 1242. He made the Dominican nuns an integral part of the Order of Preachers, subject like the friars to the master and the decrees of the general chapters. In the Institutions which he drew up for them, generally called the Rule of St Sixtus, he provided that at least six friars should be attached to every nunnery, as spiritual directors and temporal administrators. The increase of nunneries made the obligation very onerous. John the German, fourth master-general, secured a bull from Innocent IV in 1252 freeing the friars from the duty of governing the nuns, except those of St Sixtus and Prouille. The sisters, however, agitated against this decree with such success that it was finally abrogated by Clement IV in 1267, and henceforth the Dominican nuns remained incorporated in the Order of Preachers. In Germany, where most of the nunneries were situated, the learned friars who instructed the sisters—such as the famous Master Eckehart—developed strong mystical tendencies, and the Dominican nunneries became the homes of German mysticism.

The Dominicans excelled as organisers. The earliest extant Constitutions of the Order date from 1228 in the generalate of Jordan of Saxony. They are divided into two parts, the first containing the *consuetudines* of 1216, the second the constitutions of 1220. A re-arrangement on more logical lines was undertaken by the third master-general, Raymond of Peñafort (1238-1240), the famous canonist, whose version formed the basis of all subsequent redactions.

The constitutions, though in the main based on the statutes of the Premonstratensian Canons, contain features new to medieval life. The first is the definite statement of the practical object for which the Order was founded: "Our Order was instituted principally for preaching and the salvation of souls." The second is the importance attached to study "All the hours in church shall be shortened, lest the friars lose devotion and their study be at all impeded." The Friars Preachers were the first religious Order to give up manual labour as one of the essential duties of the religious life and to put intellectual work in the forefront. A third feature, closely connected with the first two, was the authority vested in the superior of every convent, "to grant dispensations whenever he may deem it expedient, especially in regard to what may hinder study or preaching or the profit of souls." This gave a peculiar elasticity to the Order, but was liable to abuse and led to a more or less open division between the active and the ascetic elements in it. The fourth feature is the large share assigned to elected representatives in the government.

The "definitors," or effective part of the general chapter (which met every year till 1370), consisted for two years out of three of elected representatives of the twelve provinces, with the master-general; in the third year, of the provincial priors. Any proposal, before it became law, had to be approved by the majority in three successive chapters. A "capitulum generalissimum" (a very rare assembly), and a general chapter called expressly for the election of a master-general, contained both the official and the elected elements. The business of the "definitors," whether elected *ad hoc* or official, was "to decide all things." They not only managed the legislative business of the chapter, but could call to account, punish, suspend, and even depose the officers.

In each province a yearly provincial chapter was held; this consisted of the provincial prior, the conventual priors, and one elected representative of each convent, and the general preachers; four definitors were elected by the assembled chapter and had within the province much the same powers which the "definitors" of the general chapter had within the Order. The provincial chapter elected the provincial prior and the visitors; the convent elected the conventual prior. In fact, all administrative officers were elected by a simple majority of authorised electors.

No other Order entrusted to elected representatives so much power. Thus the general chapter of definitors without officers remained a peculiarity of the Dominicans. The Franciscans adopted the definitors, but the definitors of their general chapter were always the provincial ministers with one friar elected *ad hoc* in each provincial chapter. The general ministers and provincial ministers were elected by their respective chapters. But the custodians (*i.e.* heads of the groups of houses into which each Franciscan province was divided for administrative purposes) and guardians (*i.e.* heads of houses) were appointed by the provincial minister and definitors in chapter, after consultation with some of the friars of the custody or house. On the other hand, in the Franciscan Order, custodians and guardians formally tendered their resignations every year in the provincial chapter. The Franciscans generally attached great importance to the temporary character of office, and held that "frequent change of prelates keeps religious Orders in health." Among the Franciscans the constitution of provincial chapters was not defined by the general chapter, but left to the determination of the different provinces.

In the fourteenth and fifteenth centuries the Dominican Order was agitated by constitutional and disciplinary controversies. The constitutional problems concerned the relations between the Order and the provinces, the general and provincial chapters, and centred round the rival claims of these bodies to appoint lecturers in the universities. More fundamental was the general decay of discipline and the common life. In the first half of the fourteenth century not only did most Dominican houses own some property in common, but individual friars were allowed to have private incomes for life. It was apparently after the Black Death that the practice was adopted of farming out "termini" or "limites" to individual friars: that is, the friar paid a fixed rent to his convent for the exclusive rights of preaching and hearing confessions and taking the resulting emoluments in a definite area, and kept the surplus revenue for his own requirements. Sometimes these areas were put up to auction; generally the most distinguished members of the convent had first choice. It is clear that a successful preacher could make a very good living out of a wealthy district; he had his private residence and servants and rarely came to his convent. A tentative reform was introduced by Raymond of Capua (master-general, 1380–1399), who had been confessor of St Catherine of Siena: he established in each province one house (under the direct control of the master-general), in which friars who desired to do so might observe the constitutions; but his authority was limited to that section of the Order which adhered to the "Roman obedience." After the Great Schism the reform movement spread; and groups of Observant houses were formed under vicars. But the Dominican Observants were not champions of absolute poverty. Among their most famous houses was the convent of San Marco at Florence, which within twenty years of its foundation obtained a papal dispensation to hold property. And the whole Order received with enthusiasm the bull of Sixtus IV in 1475, which authorised every convent to own permanent endowments and expressly abrogated all constitutions, rules, and ordinances to the contrary.

After the first period of intense religious enthusiasm which marked the beginnings of the Orders, there followed a period of about a century in which the Mendicant Friars supplied Europe with most of its leaders of thought and learning. The rise of the friars coincided with the time of great intellectual activity which was called forth by the rediscovery in the Western world of the philosophical works of Aristotle. The Church regarded the new learning with suspicion, the more so as it first reached the West through Arabian commentators; and after an outbreak of heretical teaching at Paris, lecturing on the books of Aristotle on natural philosophy was prohibited in the university by papal decrees (1215, 1231). The reconciliation of Aristotle with Christian theology was the work especially of the Dominicans.

The Dominicans were from their beginning a learned Order: their first houses in Italy, France, and England were founded in places of learning, and it was in the university towns that Jordan of Saxony, that "fisher of men," made his most successful "catches." The Jacobin convent in Paris was the intellectual centre of the Order. The number of friars there increased from 30 in 1219 to 120 in 1224. Every province had the right of sending students to Paris; their maintenance soon became a pressing problem. The question of providing for students came in some form or other before every general chapter, and a system was gradually worked out to the minutest details. But the Paris house was heavily in debt in the thirteenth century, and it was probably owing to the financial difficulties that the English Dominicans resisted for many years (1248–1261) the elevation of Oxford to the position of a *studium generale* in the Order.

At first the Friars Preachers were restricted to the study of theology. "They shall not learn secular sciences or the liberal arts, except by special dispensation." Though this decree of the early constitution was not abrogated till 1259, the dispensing power was evidently freely used and a more liberal policy soon prevailed. By the middle of the century an elaborate system of schools was being established in the Dominican provinces. While in every convent theological lectures were held which all the friars attended, special provision was made for those who shewed aptitude for learning. These were sent, on the report of the visitors, to a *studium artium*, which served a group of convents; here they studied logic for two years. Thence promising students were passed on to the next grade of school—the *studium naturalium*, where the course lasted three years and included the works of Aristotle on natural philosophy and ethics. The third grade of school was the *studium theologiae*, which might be either *particulare* if it drew its students normally from one province, or *generale* if it drew its students from the whole Order. A general school of theology was usually established in connexion with a university, but not always. Thus, there was a Dominican *studium generale* at Cologne (where both Albert the Great and Thomas Aquinas taught) but no university. Great care was taken in the selection of students in the *studium generale*. According to the statute of 1305, "No one shall be sent to a *studium generale* unless he has made adequate progress in logic and natural philosophy, and has attended lectures on the *Sentences* for two years in a *studium particulare*."

The two greatest thinkers of the Dominican Order had, however, passed their student days before this elaborate system of schools was developed. They were Albert the Great and Thomas Aquinas. Albert (*c.* 1200–1280), who belonged to a noble Swabian family, entered the Order *c.* 1223, lectured in the principal Dominican schools from 1228 to 1245, and became their regent master in Paris, 1245–6; the latter part of his life, except some eight years devoted to administrative work as provincial of Germany and Bishop of Ratisbon, was spent in teaching, writing, and preaching at Cologne. He was the most learned man of his age, and his knowledge extended to the natural sciences, in which he made independent investigations. His chief aim was "to make Aristotle intelligible to the Latins." He wrote paraphrases and commentaries on all Aristotle's works, and was probably all the more stimulating in that he often advanced and defended inconsistent views, and failed to evolve a coherent system of philosophy. This was the work of his pupil Thomas Aquinas.

Thomas, a son of the Count of Aquino, was born about 1225, and went to Frederick II's university at Naples, where he joined the Dominican Order in 1244. He studied under Albert at Paris and Cologne from 1245 to 1252, when he was recalled to Paris to lecture as bachelor and then as master of theology, being finally admitted as master in 1257; about 1260 he became master of the schools at the papal court, and was again lecturing in Paris from 1268 to 1272; he died in 1274 at the age of forty-nine. He had not the vast range of interests which marked Albert, but was far above him in clearness of thinking. He was recognised by his contemporaries as an innovator; the fundamental change which he introduced into scholastic philosophy was the assertion of the primacy of the intellect over the will, of the true over the good, in opposition to the hitherto accepted Augustinian doctrines. He probably came nearer than any other thinker before or after him to establishing harmony between reason and religion and reconciling the rival claims of philosophy and theology.

Even in his lifetime he was accepted as an "authority" in the schools, and the Dominican general chapter in 1286 ordered all the friars to promote and defend his doctrine, and decreed suspension from office for any lecturers who did the contrary. This did not encourage intellectual freedom. The Friars Preachers were distinguished by industry and learning, not originality. They produced about the middle of the thirteenth century a number of co-operative works—in the preparation of which groups of friars collaborated; the chief of them were the revision of the text of the Vulgate, the Biblical Concordances (especially that compiled by the English Dominicans), and the great encyclopaedia, or *Speculum maius* edited by Vincent of Beauvais.

St Francis opposed the forces which made the Franciscans a "student Order." "Tantum homo habet de scientia quantum operatur." Learning, he held, would be destructive of the simplicity and poverty of the friars and his only concession to the new movement was a somewhat grudging authorisation which he gave to Anthony of Padua to lecture on theology "provided that the brethren do not, owing to this study, extinguish the spirit of prayer and devotion." The same view was taken by his immediate disciples, such as Giles, to whom Paris seemed like the Jerusalem which destroyed the prophets: "Paris, Paris, thou that destroyest Assisi!" Yet the development was inevitable and rapid. It was necessary that the friars as teachers and preachers should take part in the intellectual life of the time; and the example of the Dominicans, the settlement of Franciscans in university towns, the entry of learned men into the Order, the policy of Elias as general minister, and the consistent encouragement of the Papacy, all helped to hasten the change.

Two events of decisive importance in the intellectual history of the Order occurred in 1231: Alexander of Hales entered the Order at Paris; Robert Grosseteste became lecturer to the Franciscans of Oxford.

The first Parisian house of the Friars Minor was at St Denis and had no direct connexion with the university; but the increase of their numbers, and the accession of students and masters, such as the "great theologian," Haymo of Faversham, *c.* 1223, led them to seek a home in the university quarter. The great convent which they built at "Vauvart" (Jardin du Luxembourg) fell (1229), apparently before it was finished, and the friars moved subsequently to their famous convent of the Cordeliers. The importance of the accession of Alexander of Hales to the Order was two-fold: he was perhaps the most distinguished professor at Paris, and he was at the time regent master in theology. As he continued his courses in the Franciscan convent, the Franciscan school became one of the public schools of the university, and the friars obtained the right to have one of their members among the regent masters in theology.

The fame of Alexander of Hales, "the master and father" of the Franciscan School, as Bonaventura calls him, rests on his *Summa*, which, based in general on the *Sentences* of Peter Lombard, was the first attempt on a large scale to incorporate in Christian theology the newly-discovered Aristotelian philosophy. The work, which Bacon describes as a "horse-load," was unfinished at his death (1245), and was soon superseded by the works of later theologians, who built on the foundations which he had laid.

Grosseteste, who was undoubtedly the most influential man at Oxford, and probably the greatest scholar of his time, was induced by Agnellus, provincial minister of England, to lecture to the Franciscans at Oxford. He was a whole-hearted supporter of the movement in favour of learning in the Order, and used to say that "unless the brethren devoted themselves to study, the same fate would befall us as had befallen the other religious, whom we see, alas, walking in the darkness of ignorance." He exercised a profound influence on Franciscan learning, and became the founder of a new school of thought, whose chief representatives were Adam Marsh, the first Minorite to become regent master at Oxford (*c.* 1248), and Roger Bacon.

The characteristics of this school were independence of judgment, the use of the experimental method, the study of mathematics and physics, of languages, and of the text of the Scriptures in preference to the *Sentences*. Dependence on authority is placed by Bacon first among the obstacles to the progress of true philosophy, which is defined as the effort to "arrive at a knowledge of the Creator through knowledge of the created world." For dependence on authority he would substitute first-hand knowledge derived from direct observation and experiment. Especially he insists on this in two departments of knowledge—grammar (including the study of languages and textual criticism) and physics. In order to understand the Scriptures and Aristotle a thorough knowledge of Hebrew and Greek was necessary, and Bacon himself compiled grammars of these two languages. The basis of physics he shews to be mathematics. His theory is that all natural phenomena are the result of force acting on matter, and force is invariably subject to mathematical law. It follows that the method of investigation in natural philosophy is essentially deductive; but he is never weary of insisting on the necessity of what he calls "experimental science," "the queen of all the sciences," which is in truth a method rather than a science. The results arrived at "by argument" must always be tested and verified by observation and experiment.

It is important to realise that the more fruitful of the ideas advocated by Roger Bacon were not peculiar to a more or less isolated and suspected genius, but were derived from Grosseteste and were taught to several generations of students in the Franciscan house at Oxford; and during this period the Oxford house supplied teachers to Franciscan schools not only throughout England but in France, Germany, and Italy. Survivals of the Grosseteste-Bacon tradition may be traced into the fourteenth century, but on the whole the attempt to remedy the great defect of scholasticism by widening the bases of knowledge was a failure. On the other hand, the Oxford Franciscan school continued to be prolific of new ideas; and the diversity of views represented by Roger Bacon, Duns Scotus, and William of Occam is evidence of a spirit of liberty. No single teacher in the Franciscan Order acquired the oppressive intellectual predominance which was accorded to Thomas Aquinas among the Dominicans.

Duns Scotus (who was a Scot, not an Irishman) was born about 1270, and studied and taught chiefly at Oxford till 1302. Here he lectured as B.D. on the *Sentences*; from 1302 to 1308 he was at Paris, where he became master of theology; in 1308 he was sent to Cologne and died the same year at the age of about thirty-eight. The "subtle doctor" was rather critical than constructive, and was the destroyer of systems. He attacked especially the system of Thomas Aquinas. It has been well said that while "Aquinas takes the *doctrines* which are to be proved, Duns takes the *proofs* of those doctrines, as the peculiar subject of study." And proofs when they are arranged to lead up to a preconceived conclusion seem much more convincing than when they are examined for themselves and followed out to their natural conclusion. Hence Duns shewed that the harmony between theology and philosophy established by Aquinas was largely illusory. The Franciscan was more of a Realist than the Dominican, and attributed some measure of objective reality to the concepts of the mind. This produced an inevitable reaction, which was led by Occam.

William of Occam lectured as B.D. at Oxford, *c.* 1320–1324, when his academic career was suddenly cut short by a summons to Avignon to answer charges of heresy. While at Avignon he turned his attention to the controversy on evangelical poverty; he escaped to the court of the Emperor in 1328 and wrote the great series of treatises against the papal power. The charges of heresy in 1324 had nothing to do with his later anti-papal attitude, and probably arose out of his teaching at Oxford. He went even farther than Duns in emphasising the gulf between philosophy and theology, between reason and revelation, but he distrusted abstractions and brought philosophy down from its speculative heights to common sense, direct observation, and induction. To him "everything that exists by the mere fact of its existence is individual." Occam's influence lasted long after his death in 1348, but he left no successors, and may indeed be said to have given the death-blow to scholasticism.

The materials for the history of education among the Franciscans are far less complete than among the Dominicans. It is probable that the educational organisation of the former was less uniform, and that considerable variety and latitude were allowed in the various provinces. England, which produced more original thinkers and probably more men of learning than any other province, had the most fully developed system of schools, and the credit for establishing this system on a wide and lasting basis belongs above all to William of Nottingham, provincial minister from 1240 to 1254. Later on we find an advanced school of theology in each of the seven custodies into which the English province was divided, and there is evidence of the existence of schools of arts and philosophy.

The schools of the Mendicant Orders were intended mainly for the training of their own members, but they were open to, and during the thirteenth century frequented by, seculars. Thus Innocent IV granted license for non-residence with the right to receive the full income of their benefices to any clerks of the province of Lyons who studied theology in the Dominican and Franciscan houses at Dijon. The University of Paris in 1254 attributed the scarcity of theological students there to the fact that theology was now being taught by the friars in every city, and Roger Bacon bears testimony to the number and popularity of the new schools. Friars were often chosen as lecturers in the schools of secular cathedrals and in Benedictine monasteries; the Cistercians later protected themselves against this tendency by prohibiting the appointment of Mendicant Friars as lecturers in any of their *studia*.

In the universities the friars came into contact and often into collision with a strongly-organised corporation. At Paris the Chancellor of Notre-Dame had the right of conferring the *licentia docendi* or degree of master. But the masters had limited his powers by forming themselves into a union (society or university) and refusing to admit into it any person of whom they disapproved. This union also enabled them to assert their privileges and resist any encroachment whether by lay or ecclesiastical authority; they could in the last resort decree a suspension of lectures and a dispersal of the university: in other words, they could go on strike. A tavern brawl in 1229 led to a violent conflict between the university and the combined civic and cathedral authorities, as a result of which the masters ordered a suspension of lectures and finally the dispersal of the university. The Mendicant Friars were not directly involved in this decree, except that they were no longer able to attend the lectures of the masters and were confined to the private courses delivered in their own convents. But the Chancellor now conferred the *licentia docendi* on the theological lecturer in the Dominican convent, and hence his school became a public school of the university. This was an infringement of the customary rights of the masters and threatened to undermine their union. The point seems to have been passed over in 1231, when peace was made—on terms favourable to the university—and masters and students returned to Paris. But in 1231 two regent masters in theology, John of St Giles and Alexander of Hales, entered the Dominican and Franciscan Orders respectively, and continued as friars the courses of lectures which they had begun as seculars. The Dominicans now had two public schools and the Franciscans one. The latter soon opened a second and there was a prospect of more being added. In 1250 the Pope definitely ordered the Chancellor to confer the license to teach on as many religious as he should consider qualified. The right of the other doctors of divinity to a voice in their admission was ignored; the university was losing all control over the granting of degrees to the friars.

To the constitutional question, which affected the whole university, was added a very practical consideration which affected the theological faculty. The friars were the most popular lecturers; their lecture halls were crowded, while the secular masters complained that they were left sitting at their desks "like sparrows alone upon the house-tops." The secular masters of theology tried to protect themselves by passing a statute that each religious house should be restricted to one master and one school—a provision accepted by John of Parma on behalf of the Franciscans, for the sake of peace. But this neither settled the constitutional question (though it diminished its importance) nor helped to fill the empty lecture-rooms of the secular masters. One need not accept the Dominicans' taunt that the secular masters were stupid and lazy from eating and drinking too much, but it is certain that the Mendicant Orders attracted the finest minds of the time. Among the Mendicant licentiates in theology whom the faculty refused to admit to the Society of Masters in 1256 were Thomas Aquinas and Bonaventura.

The controversy was carried to the papal court, and the leader of the secular masters, William of St Amour, shewed great ability in connecting—or confusing—the university question with the grievances of the secular clergy against the friars, and thus enlisting the support of bishops and parish priests throughout Europe. So powerful was this combination that

Innocent IV seemed on the point of yielding to it, when he died. His sudden death in 1254 was attributed to the prayers of the Dominicans. His successor, Alexander IV, was a strenuous supporter of the friars; in the bull *Quasi lignum vitae* (1255) he asserted the right of the Chancellor to license any regulars whom he considered fit, and ordered the university to admit all such to the privileges of their society. After a prolonged struggle the university was compelled to submit, protesting that the bull was to them a *lignum mortis*.

There was no faculty of theology at Bologna, and at Toulouse theological teaching was entirely in the hands of the Dominicans. A difficulty arose at Oxford in 1253, owing to a conflict between a statute of the university which demanded that none should be admitted to a degree in theology unless he had previously taken a degree in arts, and the custom of the friars which forbade a friar to take the M.A. degree. An agreement was soon come to that the faculty of theology should grant dispensations to properly trained candidates, but it was held that the vote of the faculty must be unanimous; it was thus within the power of a single regent master to prevent a friar from proceeding to a theological degree. A long and bitter struggle ensued at the beginning of the fourteenth century between the university and the friars, especially the Dominicans, who demanded the application of the Parisian customs to Oxford. They failed to secure this; the university retained its control over the granting of degrees to the friars, but accepted the provision that a majority of the votes of the faculty—not a single adverse vote—should be required for the withholding of a dispensation.

The relations of the friars to the secular clergy and the diocesan organisation opened out wider questions. Gregory IX in 1231 exempted the two Orders from episcopal visitation and jurisdiction, and assured to them full rights of self-government. If the friars were free from the control of the bishops, it became all the more necessary to define their relations to the parish priests.

The controversies centred round the claims of the friars to preach, to hear confessions, to receive offerings and legacies, and to bury in their churches persons not belonging to the Orders. The last privilege was peculiarly unfortunate; it led to indecent squabbles over corpses between the friars and rectors of churches and greatly embittered the struggle. It was granted to the Dominicans in 1227, to the Franciscans in 1250. The latter with a sure instinct had hitherto resisted it, "from love of the clergy, desiring to live at peace with them."

The policy of the Papacy between 1250 and 1300 shewed a curious vacillation. In 1300 Boniface VIII issued the bull *Super cathedram*, which remained the law of the Church for the rest of the Middle Ages. The bull provided that: (1) The friars should have full right of preaching to clergy and people in their own churches and in public places—except at certain times. In parish churches they should only preach by invitation of the parish priest or by command of the bishop. (2) They should choose from their members suitable persons to hear confessions and humbly present these to the bishop of the diocese, who should license them—the number of confessors being regulated by the needs of the population. (3) They should have the right to bury in their churches those who desired it. (4) They should give to the parish priest a quarter of all offerings and legacies. Some minor points at issue were left undecided; and the friars persistently declared that they could not live if they gave up the canonical quarter, while rectors of churches were continually bringing actions to enforce their rights. But on the whole the bull provided a statesmanlike and working settlement.

The Lateran Council of 1215 made confession at least once a year to the parish priest compulsory on all Christians. But the parish priests in the greater part of Europe were neither morally nor intellectually fitted for the task imposed on them; the objections to confessing to them were so widespread and so well-founded that it is probable that the habit of making frequent confessions would never have been established without the assistance of the friars. Bishops and clergy at first welcomed their help. Many handbooks for the instruction of confessors were in the thirteenth century issued either by the friars themselves or by bishops who were closely in touch with the friars; bishops employed them as confessors on their visitations, and parish priests referred difficult questions to their judgment. Popes and kings, as well as humbler folk, had friars as their confessors. All the English kings from Henry III to Richard II had Dominican confessors, while their queens favoured the Franciscans. Occasionally, but rarely, it is possible to trace direct influence of the confessional in public affairs. Raymond of Peñafort, the Dominican confessor of Gregory IX, imposed on the Pope as penance the duty of accelerating the causes of poor litigants at the Roman court. But Nicholas de Carbio, the Franciscan confessor and biographer of Innocent IV, gives in his life of the Pope no hint of his influence over his august penitent. St Louis had a Dominican confessor; Philip the Fair had two. Friars were, however, frequently employed both by the Papacy and by the secular governments in diplomatic negotiations.

From the middle of the thirteenth century onwards complaints were loud and persistent about the demoralising influence of the friar confessors. They destroyed the authority of the parish priests; they granted absolution on such easy terms that the confessional became an avenue to sin; any offence could be compounded by an alms to the friars. Plenty of evidence could be found in support of such charges, which were made by secular clergy and are found in contemporary popular literature. There was also another side. In 1290 a conference of French bishops and masters was held at Paris under Cardinal Gaetani, papal legate, afterwards Boniface VIII, to consider the excessive privileges, especially the unrestricted right to hear confessions, granted to the friars by Martin IV. The Bishop of Thérouanne (a secular) vigorously defended the privileges, and the cardinal upheld them on the ground that "we have to consider not what is agreeable to the clergy but what is useful to the world," and that "we have found the friars the only healthy member" of the Church. The report of the conference comes from a Dominican chronicler, but is probably substantially true. English bishops often recommended nunneries to choose mendicants as their confessors in the fourteenth century, and licensed additional friar confessors in times of pestilence. But no secular clerks seem to have defended the Orders against the attacks of Armachanus and Wyclif.

With the coming of the friars popular preaching acquired a new importance, and their churches were designed on a new and simple plan, suitable rather for holding large congregations who came to hear sermons than for liturgical processions. Francis in his Rule exhorted his brethren to make their sermons short, "announcing to the people vices and virtues, punishment and glory." Of his own methods some interesting details have been preserved. Thus, one who saw him preaching in the public piazza at Bologna in 1222 says: "Almost the whole city had assembled there. His text was 'Angels, men, devils.'...His style was not that of a preacher, but of a public speaker. The whole matter of his discourse was an appeal to extinguish enmities and make lasting peace....God lent such power to his words that many bands of nobles were brought back from the savage fury of family feuds to the way of peace." Another auditor—a learned philosopher—stated that, while he could remember every word of the sermons of others, "the words uttered by the holy Francis alone escape me; and if I commit any of them to memory, they do not seem to be the same that he had spoken."

Many books were issued by friars on the training of preachers, such as the elaborate and illuminating work of Humbert de Romans. Still more numerous were the collections of notes for sermons, with illustrative anecdotes or "exempla" to arrest the attention and point the moral. Among the earlier ones which enjoyed a wide popularity may be mentioned the anecdotes of Stephen of Bourbon and the virtues and vices of William Perault, both Dominicans. The earliest extant collection by an English Dominican (*c.* 1250–1260) is notable for the number of exempla derived from the personal experience of the writer and for the absence of references to the Virgin. The earliest collection by an English Franciscan (*c.* 1275) is also drawn to a considerable extent from personal experience and is full of stories inculcating devotion to the Virgin—some of which carry the implication that the performance of religious exercises compensates for an immoral life. The Dominican compilers—such as Robert Holcot—make great use of exempla taken from classical and semi-classical literature; it was remarked that the governing classes were more apt to be influenced by stories of Alexander or Caesar than by the lives of

Christian saints. The Franciscans were more in the habit of taking illustrations from the common things of daily life.

The most instructive sources of information which we possess on the popular preaching of the friars are the sermons of the Franciscans, Berthold of Ratisbon and Bernardino of Siena, because their sermons are preserved more or less as they were delivered.

Berthold died in 1272; he was already famous as a preacher in Germany in 1250, and Roger Bacon declared in 1267 that "he is doing alone greater work in preaching than almost all the other friars of both Orders put together." In these German sermons the elements of the faith are set forth, but the common people are not to probe into the mysteries; that way lies heresy. The theology is of a popular type; the Blessed Virgin intercedes with her Son for men, but though the first of the Saints she is immeasurably below God. The terrors of hell are very present and very real. But the greater part of the sermons is occupied with the duties and sins of ordinary life. The sin which Berthold hated and denounced most is avarice—or we might say, from the wide meaning he gives to the word, selfishness; it is this that makes men most like devils. The style is dramatic. Berthold needs no anecdotes to keep the attention of his hearers. His words are inspired by a moral fervour which still retains its glowing vitality.

Bernardino of Siena began to preach in 1405; by degrees he found preaching to be his special vocation, and concentrated on it to the exclusion, as far as possible, of all other duties. The value he attached to preaching may be estimated from the advice he gave to those who could not come to both mass and sermon, to "let the mass go rather than the sermon....There is less peril to your soul in not hearing mass than in not hearing the sermon." His sermons fall into two classes: written and reported sermons. The written sermons are mostly in Latin and form theological treatises on which the spoken sermons were based. The reported sermons (in Italian) are courses of daily sermons taken down in shorthand as they were delivered in Lent 1424 and 1425 at Florence, and in 1427 in the Campo at Siena. Much of the sermons is occupied with expository matter, and Bernardino's allegorical interpretation of Scripture is as fanciful as any. He observed also the elaborate system of divisions and subdivisions current at the time. But in spite of this, the style is essentially colloquial, and the most interesting and effective sermons are those which deal with the problems of daily life. When he went to a new place to preach, he was careful to make himself acquainted with everything that was going on there, and even to learn up local expressions. He was very sensitive to the moods of his audience, and made full use of exempla to keep their attention alert. He shews an intimate knowledge of many sides of life—children's games, fashions in dress, tricks of trade, and business methods. He was the uncompromising foe of usury (which included almost all forms of interest), and was merciless to witches. For the honest doubter in matters of faith he had respect, pity, and hope. "If God does not see fit to give them back their faith, we must take it that the palm of martyrdom is reserved for them in heaven, since such mental distress is among the most terrible afflictions of this life." The charities which he specially commended to the Sienese were the maintenance of the hospital and the care of prisoners. He often made definite suggestions for the improvement of civic life—some of which were adopted as laws. Like many of the Italian friars, he laboured unceasingly, with only temporary success, to allay the constant quarrels between families, parties, and cities, and endeavoured to substitute for the party emblems, which symbolised and encouraged strife, the sacred monogram (which was primarily intended as an external aid to devotion) as the symbol of peace and unity.

The friars used their influence as confessors and preachers not only to secure benefactions for themselves and their houses, but to promote works of public utility. Franciscans had a share in the foundation of Balliol College, Oxford, and Pembroke College, Cambridge; and not a few English towns owed their first water-supplies to the enterprise of the friars. Franciscans established a hospital for leper women at Lübeck, *c.* 1258, the Foundling Hospital at Venice, *c.* 1335, and the Monti di Pietà in many Italian cities in the latter part of the fifteenth century.

When Gregory IX was developing the Papal Inquisition, he found in the Dominicans his first and most efficient agents. In 1237 he associated with the Dominican inquisitors of Toulouse a Franciscan colleague, who might "mitigate their severity by his gentleness." The desired result was not achieved, and after the massacre of the inquisitors in 1242, the Dominicans prayed the Pope to release them from the dangerous office. Innocent IV refused, but in 1244 he granted to the master and provincial priors full power to remove and supersede all Dominican inquisitors. This privilege was not effective; for not only did the Popes constantly override it in individual cases, but the inquisitors did not scruple to threaten their superiors with accusations of heresy if they tried to interfere with them. The Franciscans tried to keep control over inquisitors of their Order by issuing commissions for a limited period. The practice of employing Dominicans and Franciscans together led to quarrels and scandals, and Clement IV had to forbid the inquisitors to prosecute each other. It was found wiser to define the boundaries of their jurisdictions; thus in Italy the north was assigned to Dominicans, the centre to Franciscans. Both Orders seem to have carried out their duties in the same spirit, but the Dominicans perhaps displayed greater thoroughness and persistence. The best handbook on inquisitorial procedure was compiled by a Dominican, and it was chiefly against Dominicans that outbursts of popular fury were directed.

The Franciscans and Dominicans were active missionaries to lands outside the Roman Church. The conversion of the Saracens was one of the aims of St Francis, and each of the two Franciscan Rules contains a chapter: "On those who go among the Saracens and other infidels." The first Franciscans who volunteered for this dangerous service were probably inspired rather by the desire for martyrdom than by the hope of converting souls, and the story of the five martyrs of Morocco in 1220 (which induced Anthony of Padua to join the Franciscans) was one of the most popular and stirring legends of the Order. The Dominicans, who entered the field somewhat later, adopted more rational methods. About 1250 Raymond of Peñafort established schools for the study of Hebrew and Arabic in which missionaries could be trained, and before the end of the century Raymond Lull instituted a similar school for the Franciscans. In Mohammedan lands the friars could point to a long line of martyrs but to few successful conversions. Their failure does not seem to have been due to lack of intelligence or insufficient preparation. It may be noted that the itinerary of the Irish Franciscan, Simon Simeonis, proves that the writer—a mere pilgrim or tourist rather than a trained missionary—had considerable knowledge of the Koran.

In Prussia and Lithuania the friars came into collision with the political aims of the Teutonic Knights, who opposed the Christianisation of their Slav subjects. The Far East offered a more fruitful field. The Mongol power threatened Europe in 1240, and Gregory IX ordered the friars to preach a Crusade against the barbarians. But the Crusade soon gave way to missions, which had the double object of converting the heathen and of forming an alliance between Christendom and the Mongols against Islām. The Franciscans, John de Plano Carpinis, an Italian, sent by Innocent IV in 1245, and William of Rubruquis, a Fleming, sent by Louis IX in 1253, visited the court of the Great Khan at Karakorum, and gave to the Western world its first knowledge of the Mongol Empire. While the Italian friar gives the more orderly and complete account of the manners, customs, and history of the Mongols, Rubruquis' work shews a power of observation, an insight into the principles of philology and ethnology, and an interest in strange forms of life, which were new to the Middle Ages. Their journeys formed the beginning of a Franciscan mission to China, which endured at least till the overthrow of the Mongols and establishment of the Ming Dynasty in 1368. Chief among the missionaries was John of Monte Corvino (in Apulia), who laboured in the Far East from 1289 to 1328. He was the first Archbishop of Pekin and founder of a number of bishoprics and monasteries in China; he also translated into the Tartar language the New Testament and Psalter, and apparently the Latin Office. Among the friars who joined him was Odoric of Pordenone, who has also left an account of his journeys. The representation of Odoric on his tomb in the cathedral of Udine, clad in Tartar garments and wearing his hair in Tartar fashion, suggests that the Franciscan missionaries (like the Dominicans, according to a licence granted by the Pope in 1226) adopted the way of life of the people among whom they worked. The Great Khan treated John of Monte Corvino as a trusted councillor, and the policy of the Mongol rulers generally was one of toleration. "For they hold this opinion, or rather error," writes Andrew of Perugia, Bishop of Zaitûn, in 1326, "that everyone can find salvation in his own religion. And we are at liberty to preach without let or hindrance. Of the Jews, indeed, and Saracens, no one is converted, but a great multitude of the idolaters are baptised, though many of the baptised walk not rightly in the way of Christianity."

The Dominicans were no less active. At the beginning of the fourteenth century their eastern missionaries were organised into a self-governing community (under a vicar, subject to the general control of the master of the Order), known as the *Societas Peregrinantium propter Christum.* This was not, as generally supposed, a joint society of Dominicans and Franciscans. There is little trace of regular co-operation between the two Orders in the mission field, though their relations seem to have been friendly. John XXII in 1318 allocated to them different spheres of influence by assigning southern Asia—including Greater Armenia, Persia, and India—to Dominican bishops, and northern Asia to Franciscan bishops. But Franciscan missions continued to operate in the Dominican sphere, and Dominican missions in the Franciscan sphere. The Dominicans achieved their most permanent results among the Armenian "schismatics," where they did something towards founding a native pastorate.

The cessation of missionary enterprise in the latter part of the fourteenth century was due partly to political and religious movements in Asia—such as the fall of the Mongols and the rise of the Ottoman Turks—partly to the Black Death, which disorganised the mission stations in the East and dried up the stream of recruits from the West.

No *modus vivendi* between the Latin and Greek Churches was found or sought for. A Dominican missionary, when laying before Philip VI of France a plan for a new crusade against the Muslims, urged him to begin by burning any Latins who had joined the Greek Church, suppressing the Greek monasteries, and forcibly compelling the people to adopt the Catholic faith.

The friars sought to secure lasting results from the enthusiasm which their preaching and example evoked, by encouraging the formation of fraternities of penitence. Such fraternities came into existence in many Italian cities in the early years of the Franciscan movement. They differed from the fraternity or Order of Friars Minor in that their members continued to live in their own houses, did not renounce private or corporate property, and had at first no common or central organisation: they were local religious gilds. The earliest document on the subject dates from 1221, when Francis had already retired from the active government of the Minorite Order; it is a Rule drawn up by Cardinal Ugolino, probably in consultation with Francis and perhaps with Elias.

It provides that brethren and sisters of penitence living in their own houses should dress plainly, eat and drink with moderation, avoid dances and plays, keep certain fasts, observe the canonical hours at home or in church, confess thrice a year, pay their debts and restore any goods which belonged to others, live peaceably, not bear arms, abstain from oaths, contribute to the support of poor or sick members and other poor people, and attend the funerals of deceased members. The general management was in the hands of two ministers, who held office for one year and chose their successors with the advice of the brethren. Disciplinary power was exercised by a visitor who acted on the report of the ministers; but no indication is given as to the status or method of appointment of the visitor. New members were admitted by the ministers, with the approval of some discreet brethren, after promising to observe the conditions and after a year's probation; once admitted, no one might withdraw from the fraternity except to join a religious Order. The defence of the privileges of the brethren against the city authorities—*e.g.* in the question of exemption from military service—was entrusted to the bishop of the diocese. The fraternity met once a month in a church selected by the ministers, and should on these occasions, if it was convenient, be instructed by a religious.

The Rule is remarkable for its omissions: it contains no reference to St Francis or to the Franciscan Order. But Gregory IX in 1230 refers to these fraternities as the "Third Order of St Francis," though in 1235 he implies that the power of visitation and correction was vested in the bishop. The local fraternities claimed and exercised the right of supplementing the Rule, and used their powers sometimes to establish the closest relations with the neighbouring Minorite houses. But it is clear on the one hand that some fraternities were jealous of ecclesiastical influence, and on the other that some sections of the Minorite Order were averse from any close connexion with the Penitents. Thus there was room for much variety in different places, and recent historians have added to the obscurity of the early history of the Third Order by mistaking one of these local variations for a general rule. In 1247, when the "spiritual" John of Parma became minister-general, Innocent IV, acceding to the prayers of the ministers and Brethren of Penitence in Italy and the kingdom of Sicily, entrusted to the Minorite Order the duty of "visiting them, instructing them in regular discipline, correcting and reforming them in head and members"; but in 1248, in answer to a protest from the community of Brethren of Penitence in the province of Lombardy, he rescinded this order so far as the Lombard brethren were concerned and left them under episcopal control. Bonaventura, on behalf of the Minorite Order, repudiated any special responsibility for the Penitents. His reasons are curious. Not only would the demands of the Penitents be too exacting, and bring the friars into conflict with the civic authorities, but the Penitents despised the clergy and had lay teachers like the heretics, and close alliance with them would lay the friars open to charges of heresy. This pusillanimous attitude seems to have been maintained till 1289, when the Franciscan Pope Nicholas IV issued a revised version of the Rule of 1221. In several respects ecclesiastical control over the lay fraternities was now strengthened: thus the Rule of 1221 admitted persons suspected of heresy who had duly purged themselves before the bishop; the Rule of 1289 excluded all persons suspected of heresy, and decreed that, if any such had been admitted inadvertently, they were to be handed over to the Inquisition; further, the Rule of 1289 stipulated that the visitor must in all cases be a priest. The most important addition was the clause that "whereas the present form of living was instituted by St Francis, we advise that visitors and instructors be chosen from the Order of Friars Minor."

The circumstances and motives which led to this change of policy are obscure. Probably the growth of lay fraternities with a strong anti-ecclesiastical bias was the chief reason. It may also be noted that the bull of 1289 was issued during the generalate of Raymond Gaufredi, who as a representative of the "spiritual" friars would be in sympathy with a closer connexion between the Minorites and the Penitents. But the movement was not confined to the Franciscans. The Dominicans about the same time adopted a similar policy. The master-general, Muño de Zamora, 1285–1291, issued a Rule for "the brethren and sisters of Penitence of St Dominic," ordering every such fraternity to accept as "master and director" a Dominican friar priest approved by the master-general or by the provincial prior. This Rule is generally ascribed to 1285, but the date is uncertain, and until it is established it is impossible to determine the relation between the Dominican Rule and the bull of Nicholas IV. Muño's Rule was generally adopted by the Dominican Tertiaries, and was finally approved, with modifications, by the holy see in 1405.

The Tertiaries suffered much persecution at the hands of the inquisitors during the fourteenth century, and the fear of suspicion of heresy probably helped to popularise among them a form of life more closely resembling that of the regular Orders. Houses of Tertiaries were established where they lived the common life—men and women in separate houses—and eventually took the three solemn vows. So far as this tendency prevailed, the Third Order lost its original character.

Our estimate of the influence of the Third Order must depend partly on our estimate of the number of its members. A letter included in the register of Peter della Vigna, the minister of Frederick II, declared that there was hardly a man or woman who did not belong to one of the fraternities called into being by the Dominicans and Franciscans. But recent research[1] has shewn that this letter was not written by Peter, but emanated from the secular clergy in the north of France, *c.* 1245; it is merely the statement of an excited controversialist and so loses much of the importance hitherto ascribed to it. At Bologna the number of men Tertiaries in 1252 was 57,

[1] *Études Franciscaines*, xxxiv (1922), pp. 538–560.

in 1288, 79. At Siena in 1352 a list of women Tertiaries of the Dominican Order contains 100 names. The fraternities seem to have been most numerous in Umbria and Tuscany, but representatives from 24 cities of Northern Italy assembled in 1289 in a general chapter of Tertiaries at Bologna. The Third Order was established in the thirteenth century in many of the Rhenish cities, while in England, on the other hand, it has left few traces. It is probable that in most centres of industry and commerce there were to be found groups of men and women pledged to live an honest, strict, peaceable, charitable, and devout life. Many famous men—among them Louis IX and Dante—have been claimed as members of the Third Order, but the evidence for these claims is rarely conclusive. It must be remembered that membership of the Third Order normally exempted a man not only from military service, but from the duty of undertaking many public offices; the institution, though its conditions were too severe to attract the shirker, appealed rather to retiring natures than to those fitted to play a leading part in human affairs. The most notable members of the Third Order were women, such as Elizabeth of Hungary, Angela of Foligno, Catherine of Siena.

The Carmelites, who claimed Elijah as their founder, took their origin from a small group of hermits established on Mount Carmel about 1155 by a priest named Berthold, probably a native of Limoges. The Order received an eremitical Rule, based on that of St Basil, from the Patriarch of Jerusalem about 1210, and new communities were soon established at Acre, Tyre, Jerusalem, and elsewhere, but most of these lasted only a few years. Owing to the growth of Mohammedan power the brethren resolved to leave the Holy Land, and colonies of them migrated about 1238 to Cyprus, Sicily, Marseilles, and Valenciennes. In 1241–2 William de Vescy and Richard of Cudnor returning from the crusade brought some of them to England, which became for some years the centre of gravity of the Order. The first houses were built in thinly populated districts, but a change was made by the general chapter at Aylesford in 1247, when Simon Stock was elected general prior. The chapter prayed the Pope to modify the Rule, and accordingly Innocent IV in the same year confirmed to the friars of St Mary of Mount Carmel their Rule as revised by two Dominicans; this substituted the community life for the solitary life, mitigated the strictness of fasts and silence, permitted the friars to found houses elsewhere than *in eremo*, and to beg, though they were still allowed to hold property in common. The right to preach and hear confessions was granted to them in 1253.

Simon Stock was successful in founding houses of the Order in cities and especially in university towns, at Cambridge in 1249, Oxford and London in 1253, York in 1255, Paris in 1259, and Bologna in 1260. But in the Order itself his policy roused strong opposition, and on his death in 1265 the upholders of the old tradition were successful in electing as general Nicholas Gallicus, who denounced the dangerous operations of preaching and hearing confessions, and strove to bring back the Order to a purely contemplative life. The reaction was only temporary, and the recognition of the Carmelites by the Council of Lyons in 1274 as one of the four approved Mendicant Orders marks the triumph of the principles of Simon Stock. In 1287 the friars exchanged their mantle of black and white stripes (from which they were known as *Fratres barrati* or *de pica*) for a mantle of white wool, which gave them the popular name of White Friars.

The earliest extant constitutions date from 1324; they are based partly on decrees by which from about 1256 the general chapters supplemented the Rule, but shew Dominican influence. The Order in 1324 was divided into 15 provinces, including those of Ireland and Scotland, which had till 1305 formed part of the English province. At the head of the Order was the prior-general elected by the general chapter, which had power to depose him; at each succcessive chapter he had to resign his seal of office to the definitors and to render an account of his administration; if no serious complaints were made, he was generally confirmed in his office until his death or resignation. He could depose provincial and conventual priors, but the consent of the provincial or conventual chapter was required for the election of their successors. He could send visitors to a province only at the request of the provincial prior or chapter. The general chapter assembled every third year, each province being represented by the provincial prior and two companions elected by the provincial chapter. The provincial chapter chose one of these three representatives to act as definitor in the general chapter—an interesting variation on the Dominican plan. Except in certain circumstances no one could act as definitor in two successive chapters. While all the representatives took part in the election of a general prior, the ordinary business was conducted by the definitors. They received reports from the provinces, decided whether the general prior should be confirmed or released from office, and had the right of deposing provincial priors and appointing others in their place.

The provincial chapter met every year, and consisted of the provincial prior, the local priors, and one elected representative from each house. Each local prior brought with him a report on his convent; the definitors combined the reports into a single document, which the provincial prior took with him on his visitations. The four definitors were elected by the chapter; with the provincial prior they conducted the general business and had full power to depose and appoint local priors. The definitors could depose the provincial only with the consent of the majority of the chapter. The provincial chapter normally elected the provincial, unless he was appointed in general chapter; and the local chapter normally elected the local prior, unless he was appointed in provincial chapter. There was no time-limit to the holding of their offices until the fifteenth century. In England the masters of theology were *ex officio* members of the provincial chapter. England was the largest province and had statutes of its own, especially in regard to academic matters.

The Carmelite constitutions include elaborate arrangements for the organisation of studies. Every convent, except those in which *studia generalia* were established, was bound to set aside a tenth of its total income from all sources, for scholastic purposes; this tenth formed a central fund in each province which was administered by the provincial prior and the definitors of the provincial chapter, and applied primarily to the support of scholars at *studia generalia*, the residue being distributed among the masters, bachelors, lectors, and students within the province. The allowances—estimated in *grossi antiqui* of Tours—ranged from 400 for the regent master at Paris, and 100 for other regent masters, to 30 or 40 for students at universities. Certain provinces were bound to send one or two students to Paris and to pay for each 150 *grossi*, plus 70 *grossi pro vestiario*; these sums were exacted even if the province failed to send its due quota of students.

The *studia* recognised as *generalia* in the Order were Paris, Toulouse, Bologna, Florence, Montpellier, Cologne, London, and the Roman Curia. The absence of Oxford and Cambridge is remarkable. It would appear, however, that the English province kept the control of appointments to lectureships in these universities in its own hands, and chose candidates for degrees in turn from the four "distinctions" into which England was divided. The statutes of the English province, to which allusion is often made and which would probably have thrown light on the subject, are unfortunately lost.

In every university the regent master in theology appointed two friars bachelors to lecture on moral and natural philosophy. And in each province the provincial prior and definitors of the chapter had to provide schools and lecturers for grammar, logic, natural philosophy, and theology. The insistence on the grammar schools suggests that the Carmelite Order admitted younger or less educated persons than the other Orders.

The most notable product of the Carmelite schools was John of Baconthorpe (*ob.* 1346), who was master of Paris and provincial of England, 1329–1333. He appears to have defended the orthodoxy of Averroës and his teaching, and to have maintained the superiority of the kingly to the priestly power in secular affairs—a view which brings him into touch with Occam, Armachanus, and Wyclif. It is remarkable that a man holding such opinions should have become the great glory of the Carmelite Order. Another of the most prominent Carmelites in medieval history was Thomas Netter of Walden, who at Pisa in 1409 defended the rights of the Council, was confessor to Henry V and Henry VI, provincial of England, ambassador to the King of Poland, and strenuous opponent of Lollards and Hussites, against whom he directed his chief works—the *Doctrinale Fidei Ecclesiae Catholicae* and *Fasciculi Zizaniorum*. It is singular that the Carmelites, in spite of their connexion with the East took little part in missionary enterprises during the Middle Ages.

The Friars Hermits of the Order of St Augustine, unlike the other Mendicant Orders, sprang from the union of a number of already existing and hitherto independent groups of hermits. Many such groups came into being in Italy during the last half of the twelfth and the first half of the thirteenth century. The first step towards union was made by Innocent IV, who in December 1243 appointed the Benedictine Cardinal Richard Anibaldi protector of certain hermits in Tuscany, with the object of forming them into one body under the Rule of St Augustine. During the next twelve years the cardinal gradually extended his operations, and succeeded in bringing together early in 1256 a general chapter containing representatives of many groups of hermits, namely (1) the Order of St William of Malevale near Pisa (or rather that section of the Williamites who did not follow the Benedictine Rule), (2) the Order of St Augustine, probably the Tuscan hermits, (3) the friars of John Bonus or Jamboniti, who were founded about 1209, near Cesena, and are probably identical with the Friars Hermits of St Augustine "in Lombardia et Romaniola," (4) the friars of Fabali or Favali, apparently a branch of the Williamites, (5) the hermits of the desert of Brittini in the March of Ancona. Of these, the Jamboniti seem to have been the most numerous and progressive; they had already begun to abandon the eremitical life and to live in cities, and the early settlements of Austin Friars north of the Alps (*e.g.* in England in 1249) probably proceeded from this congregation; from it, too, was elected the first general prior of the united Order, Lanfranc of Milan, formerly prior of Bologna. The difficulties accompanying the union are illustrated by the action of the hermits of Brittini, who resisted the introduction of the common life and the practice of pastoral duties, and eventually seceded from the Order and obtained a bull from Alexander IV in 1260 guaranteeing their eremitical life for ever. Some of the Williamite houses also succeeded in maintaining their independence, and it appears that no attempt was made at this time to include various other Orders in the Order of Austin Friars. The most important of these was the Order of Friars of the Sack, but they were not founded until 1251, when the negotiations for the formation of the Order of Austin Friars had already made some progress, and they took their origin in Provence while the congregations included in the union were all of Italian origin. On the other hand the Austin Friars soon received notable accessions, the most important perhaps being that of the Order of Poor Catholics, founded by orthodox Waldensians.

The arrangements made by Cardinal Richard were confirmed by a bull of Alexander IV, dated 9 April 1256: the Friars Hermits were authorised to live as a Mendicant Order and to cease to carry the staff, the sign of the hermit's life. From this time they were hermits only in name. In

1257 they were exempted from episcopal jurisdiction; and in 1274 they received like the Carmelites a provisional authorisation in the Council of Lyons. The order is said to have been divided at first into four provinces—Italy, Spain, France, and Germany; it eventually numbered 42 provinces. England was probably a separate province by 1261, certainly before 1289. The earliest extant constitutions of the Order—extant in manuscript only—date from 1290. Both in their form and matter they shew Dominican influence. The organisation, with annual provincial chapters and triennial general chapters, closely resembled that of the other Mendicant Orders. The general prior and the provincial priors were elected by their respective chapters; they resigned the seals of office at each chapter, and the definitors determined whether they should be continued or a new election be held. The definitors of the general chapter were chosen on the same method as that already described in the account of the Carmelite Order. New constitutions had to be approved by two successive general chapters. The conventual priors were normally elected by the convent, but the convent might ask the four definitors of the provincial chapter to depose its prior and appoint another, and might submit the names of several suitable candidates.

The provisions made for study should be noticed. Every province had to send one student, chosen by the provincial and definitors of the provincial chapter after due examination, to Paris to study theology for five years. At the end of this time, the province had to supply him with £40 Tours "for books, lest owing to lack of books when he returns to his province his studies should be impeded." The general prior had to institute four *studia generalia* in Italy and a suitable number in the other provinces, and provide lecturers in theology and philosophy, the text of the Scriptures having the most honoured place. "To these *studia* each province shall send one student sufficiently instructed in grammar, so that after five years in such a *studium* he may be found fit to lecture." Priors of convents where such *studia* were founded were bound to promote and not hinder studies, but might in case of need send out students to beg two or three times a month. The provincial prior and definitors appointed lecturers in convents and had to establish schools of logic and grammar for the instruction of "rudes scolares" of the province. If they could not find a friar to teach them, they were to appoint other masters at a competent salary. The Austin Friars made more provision than the other Orders for giving elementary instruction to their ignorant members, and there is some evidence that they taught in secular schools or admitted seculars to their classes. The inhabitants of Breisach are said to have welcomed them to their town (*c.* 1270) in the expectation that they would give good and cheap education to their children. The tradition, however, that the Austin Friars monopolised the teaching of grammar at Oxford rests solely on a misunderstanding of a university statute.

The Austin Friars seem to have been more interested in practical than in speculative questions. Their greatest doctor was Giles of Colonna (or Aegidius Romanus), whom they tried to place on a level with Thomas Aquinas; but the work on which his fame chiefly rested even in the Middle Ages was his *De Regimine Principum* (written for the instruction of Philip the Fair of France)—a treatise on politics or rather on morals. The best known English Augustinian was the historian John Capgrave. The Austin Friars shewed themselves more open to the influences of the Renaissance and the Reformation than any of the other Orders, though no proof has been adduced that they were in any special way devoted to Pauline or Augustinian doctrines before the time of Staupitz and Luther.

CHAPTER XXII

(A)

ECCLESIASTICAL ARCHITECTURE

In the third volume the course of church building was traced up to the twelfth century, and it was shewn that Romanesque architecture is found in all parts of Western Europe. There are of course local peculiarities, but the family likeness is marked in places so far apart as Milan, the Rhine district, Durham, and Santiago de Compostella. In some countries, notably Catalonia and the south of France, the architecture may be described as static. The builders of the twelfth century, and even of the thirteenth, were content to repeat the forms, of structure and ornament, which they had inherited. Plain cylindrical vaults, massive walls and columns, round arches, small windows, were the rule; there was no restless striving after new ideas. In North Italy, however, and in Normandy and England, Romanesque architecture was dynamic. Even as early as the eleventh century it displayed the new spirit which was to culminate in the Gothic architecture of the thirteenth. Many forces were at work to produce that great result, which cannot be wholly understood by isolating any one of them. The most obvious is structural invention. Architecture is a fine art, but it can do nothing if it does not obey the laws of engineering. Building on them, it achieves stability, but it need not therefore sacrifice beauty and grace. In all great periods of art, and certainly not least in the Gothic, the structural cannot be separated from the ornamental; the two form an indivisible whole.

Dealing, then, first with the development of structure, we find the vital principles which transformed Romanesque into Gothic at work in North Italy as early as 1040. The abbey of Sannazzaro Sesia was begun in that year, and Sant' Ambrogio at Milan followed soon after. Durham was in building before the end of the century. These instances are given, as they are among the first where ribbed vaulting, in any vital manner, is found. The plain groined vault, produced by two intersecting cylindrical vaults, had been used in Roman times and before, and was common enough in the eleventh century. The ribbed form may appear to be merely a development, but it is almost a new principle. The extensive wooden centring required for an unribbed vault constituted a grave difficulty, especially in a country like Lombardy, where wood was scarce. "Ribs" are skeleton arches, built first and filled in between afterwards. The system requires much less centring than the other, especially when, as in Lombardy and France, the vaulting cells are generally domical. Concentration of pressure was made a much easier matter by ribbed vaulting, and concentration is the vital principle, as regards the development of structure, which transformed Romanesque into Gothic.

The second principle in the transforming process many would put first: the use of the pointed arch. Much ingenuity has been wasted in accounting for its invention, and scores of theories have been put forward. We are, however, not concerned here with its origin, for it was used, even in ancient Egypt, many centuries before our period. The Saracens knew it well, and it is found in static Romanesque architecture in the south of France in the eleventh century. Early in the twelfth, vaulting had reached the stage where little progress could be made without it, and thus, as in so many other cases, common sense led to the change. The pointed arch, whether in vaulting or elsewhere, has less outward thrust than the round, and is therefore easier to deal with.

The mention of outward thrust naturally leads to the third transforming principle: the use of the flying buttress. The Middle Ages inherited from the fourth century an aisled hall as its chief church plan. For centuries this was covered by a wooden roof, but gradually the difficulties of throwing a stone vault over a wide space were overcome. Even then, however, there was no solution of the problem of supporting a high vault. For dignity and for light it was desired to have a clerestory with a row of windows high above the aisle roofs. Such windows could not be safely inserted as long as cylindrical vaults with continuous pressure were used. But, even when groined vaults had led to concentration, there was no obvious way of meeting the outward thrust. As regards the aisles, it was simple enough to build buttresses against the outer walls, but the clerestory cannot be thus dealt with without blocking up the aisles below. How then is the abutment to be provided? One of the earliest attempts we see in the choir of Durham, where the original vault was finished in 1104. Complete round arches are built under the roof of the triforium to catch the thrust of the vault and to convey it to the outer wall. In the nave, where the vault was built between 1128 and 1133, the more logical half-arch is used in the same position, as it had been at Norwich as early as 1096, though in that case the vault itself was not built. These concealed half-arches were too low to meet the thrust of the high vault properly, and it was only a step to bring them up higher and expose them over the aisle roofs. The earliest examples naturally enough are not very scientific, and it was some time before the importance of a heavy pinnacle was realised, to verticalise the outward thrust and convey it to the ground within the foot of the buttress.

By the end of the twelfth century the three transforming factors in the structure—ribbed vaulting, the pointed arch, the flying buttress—had full sway in the best buildings. The resulting concentration began to shew in all the parts. As early as 1040 at Jumièges there had been shafts from base to roof, even though there was no central vault. Such shafts became organic features binding the whole structure together, and going far to prove the saying that a Gothic church is designed from the vault downward and not from the base upward. The complete logic of the Gothic system was more and more perceived, especially in the Île de France, during the thirteenth century, so that finally a great church appears to rest on pillars and buttresses only, and walls become a mere screen from the weather. Even the walls themselves are largely done away by the huge windows which fill up the whole space between the vaulting pyramids. A comparison between St Sernin at Toulouse or St John's chapel in the Tower of London on the one hand, and Amiens or St Denis on the other, will shew the extraordinary contrast between the Romanesque of the eleventh century and the Gothic of the thirteenth.

The change from massiveness and gloom to delicacy and light is most prominent in the system of building, but it applies to everything else in the church. If the walls become thin the ornamental carving also becomes delicate. Deeply recessed heavy doorways, embellished with axe-cut surface designs, give way to lighter forms with undercut mouldings. The ornament, here and elsewhere, is full of life and grace. Round-headed slits give place to long lancets, and then, by gradual process, to large traceried windows of endless variety. It is true that the laws of engineering had to be obeyed, but the artist was not enslaved by them. He frankly accepted his limitations, but worked within them in such a way that a harmonious whole was produced. Science and art were combined to perfection in the thirteenth century.

The church plan had almost been determined in the Romanesque period. Starting from the basilican form of the fourth century, it had arrived, at the end of the eleventh, at the characteristic monastic development of St Sernin at Toulouse or Norwich. The secular churches followed suit with nave and aisles, transepts, often with aisles, apsidal presbytery, with or without an ambulatory and projecting chapels. A central tower is normal, but there is usually at least one other. The early Gothic builders made no revolutionary change, but developed what they received. The round apse became the polygonal chevet or the square end. Extra aisles and chapels were added, and there may be towers to the transepts as well as to the west front and the crossing. Through all the changes, however, even when the final result is an oblong, the Romanesque plan can generally be discovered.

So far we have been tracing the main current of the Gothic stream. Taking its rise in Lombardy, it spread all over Western Europe and reached its full breadth in the Île de France. In that district, favoured in so many ways and not least by fine building stone, there were erected between 1150 and 1250 a series of churches which have never been surpassed. No two are alike, and the logic of all is not equally complete, but at Paris, Amiens, Chartres, Rheims, Laon, Soissons, Noyon, and many another, we find the same engineering cleverness and the same beautiful clothing. At Beauvais the skill, in its soaring ambition, overtopped itself and disaster followed. It has been called a failure, but it is surely then a splendid failure.

The period with which this volume is mainly concerned is far the most important in the history of Gothic architecture, the late twelfth century and the thirteenth. Nearly all the great churches of France were created at that time. The fourteenth and fifteenth centuries saw many additions and alterations but few complete wholes. The church of St Ouen at Rouen is almost the only building of the first class. Early in the sixteenth century there was a great revival of church building, which before long departed entirely from Gothic precedents. "Flamboyant" detail became richer and richer till the process was stopped by the Renaissance.

Emphasis has been laid on the Île de France, as we have there, in unique degree, the combination of logical completeness and beauty of carving. In other provinces, however, there is no lack of great building, often with strongly marked local peculiarity. To mention only one example, the cathedral church of Albi, in a district where good stone is rare, has the appearance of a great brick fortress. It is Gothic, but could not be mistaken for the Gothic of the neighbourhood of Paris.

England owes as much as France to the great principles which transformed Romanesque to Gothic, but, north of the Channel, they were not carried out with such complete consistency. English vaulting became far more elaborate than French, though there was not always a structural reason for its developments. The fan vaults, at the end of the Middle Ages, are marvels of scientific skill, and combine the continuity of surface shewn in cylindrical vaults with the concentration of pressure which is the main contribution of groining. English churches run to length, and French to height. English transepts are more marked and are sometimes doubled, as at Salisbury. In that noble secular church, built on a new site in the thirteenth century, many of the chief beauties and peculiarities of English work are illustrated. Its great spire, finished a century later, gathers the whole building together and gives an external effect which contemporary Amiens, with its lofty interior, cannot rival. Salisbury, Lincoln, Worcester, Lichfield, Ely, and most other great churches in the same country, have illustrations of "Early English" architecture, with its purity, its grace, and its vigorous life. Sculpture is much less common and less noble than in France, but Wells is a standing monument to the art of the thirteenth century as well as Amiens and Chartres.

The fourteenth century is far more important, comparatively, in England than in France. As a complete scheme Exeter is the typical example, though incorporating earlier work. The nave of York and the choir of Carlisle are splendid rivals, especially in their huge traceried windows. The lantern of Ely modified the characteristic church plan more obviously than any other erection of the Middle Ages. The carving of natural leaves was a prominent feature late in the thirteenth century and early in the fourteenth. The best examples are the earliest, as in the nave of York and the chapter-house of Southwell.

The fifteenth century, like the fourteenth, is a more important period in England than in France. Even before the Black Death in 1348, a new style had been coming in at Gloucester which has generally been called "Perpendicular." It was taken up elsewhere and came to fruition in the reign of Henry VI. The title refers mainly to the window tracery, which consists largely of vertical and horizontal lines, very different from the flowing tracery which preceded it and the contemporary "flamboyant" in France. Foliage became conventional again, of a wreath-like character, especially in Devonshire. Mouldings were thinner, and, in ornament, effect was sought by reproducing structural forms in miniature. Two of the finest features are the towers, especially in Somersetshire, and the open timber roofs. A fifteenth-century spire is rare, whereas the combined tower and spire was normal in the thirteenth century in France and England. The most striking type of roof is the hammer-beam, common in East Anglian churches, but shewing its noblest and earliest example in a secular building, Westminster Hall. No great cathedral or monastic church was wholly built in the fifteenth century, but independent works were carried out at Canterbury, Gloucester, Norwich, Winchester, York. The special glory of the period is the parish churches. No other country can rival these from 1200 to 1500, but the fifteenth century is the most prolific period, especially in Devonshire and East Norfolk, where almost every church was rebuilt at this time.

Gothic architecture is obviously an importation into Scotland, and not a native art. There are, however, some important monuments, notably Glasgow cathedral, dating mainly from the thirteenth and fourteenth centuries. French influence is strong, as might be expected, and the Perpendicular style never took root. The richest of the later buildings Roslyn chapel, is an exotic and has affinities with Spain and Portugal.

The most interesting churches in Ireland are of earlier date than we are concerned with in this volume, and are in some respects unique. In the Middle Ages English influence was paramount within the Pale, as is illustrated in Christ Church and St Patrick's at Dublin. The best Gothic work is generally found in the conventual houses, particularly those of the various orders of friars.

We have travelled far from Italy, where the Gothic movement first got its inspiration in the organic vaulting of Lombardy. The early promise, however, was not fulfilled, for the extensive remains of classical antiquity always brought back the builders to traditional forms. The round arch was quite common all through the thirteenth century, and it can almost be said that the fourteenth is the only Gothic period not dominated by Romanesque on the one hand or the Renaissance on the other. For delicacy and charm few buildings north of the Alps can rival the tower of Giotto at Florence. This delicacy is a marked feature of many a doorway, window, capital, and base, revealed to us so often by the enthusiasm and insight of Ruskin. Colour schemes add greatly to the beauty, as at Siena, especially when exquisite marbles are used. Brick, too, is a common material. When, however, we turn to the structural principles which govern the whole style, we find the Italian builders very deficient in comprehension. It is true that they built high groined vaults in huge square and oblong compartments, but they provided no proper abutments for them. The flying buttress is almost unknown and there is no efficient substitute for it. The consequence is that many Italian vaults would have fallen down if iron rods had not been added to hold the buildings together. These rods are a great disfigurement inside the churches and also in the porches, whose arches usually rest on pillars without buttresses. So normal did they become that they are often added in places where they are not necessary. The churches have far fewer bays than in northern work. Great churches like San Petronio at Bologna and the Frari at Venice do not really impress by their size, owing to the fewness of the parts. Ornamental screens of stone in front of a church are found in all countries with little relation to what is behind them, but the system was carried farthest in Italy. The west front at Orvieto, for example, and the north front at Cremona are architectural shams, giving little indication of the churches behind them. Milan cathedral is the largest medieval church except Seville. It is built throughout of white marble, and the elaboration of detail is excessive. The external proportions are somewhat squat, and the addition of classical detail gives a hybrid effect. The interior is impressive, but it suffers from the sham piercing of the vault and from the non-structural character of the capitals. During the fifteenth century the Renaissance became more and more pronounced, but Gothic forms lingered on, as in the Certosa at Pavia.

In Sicily there is remarkable early Gothic work at Monreale, Messina, and Palermo. Cefalù cathedral has been claimed as the cradle of the style. It was begun in 1132, and shews the pointed arch in the windows and in the ribbed vaulting over the choir and the north transept.

The coast towns of Dalmatia have Gothic as well as Romanesque churches. The most remarkable is the cathedral of Sebenico, dating from 1430, and Italian Gothic in its earlier parts.

The island of Cyprus, as we might suppose from its medieval history, shews western influence in its buildings. There are important Gothic churches of French character at Nicosia and Famagusta.

Church architecture took a different course in Spain than it did in any other country. For centuries there was the disturbing factor of the Moorish occupation, but Saracenic forms are admitted so sparingly into churches that it would appear to have been almost a point of conscience not to use the style of the hated invader. Toledo was recovered as early as 1085, and a mosque became the Capilla del Cristo de la Luz. A twelfth-century synagogue, in Moorish style, was taken from the Jews in 1405 and became the church of Santa Maria la Blanca. There are other Saracenic features in the churches, notably in the triforium of the cathedral and in the tower of Santo Tomé. There are reminiscences of the Moorish style even in the north, as at San Isidoro at León, but it remains true that in most cases ecclesiastical architecture is unaffected by it.

The Romanesque architecture of Spain is of great interest and importance. One of the finest monuments of the style is the cathedral of Santiago de Compostela, which has even been claimed to be earlier than St Sernin at Toulouse. The Romanesque style went on far longer than in the north. For example, the cathedral of Lérida, built between 1203 and 1278, would be thought in France or England to be a century earlier.

The Gothic movement, however, so overwhelming in the north, conquered Spain as well as Italy. Its spread was no doubt hastened by the Cistercians, whose abbots met once a year in general chapter at Cîteaux and would bring back to outlying places knowledge of the pointed arch and other new forms. The great cathedrals of the thirteenth century are closely copied from those of France. Toledo corresponds with Bourges; and Burgos, as far as its thirteenth-century work is concerned, is very French. León is most remarkable of all. For concentration of vault-pressure, scientific abutment, extent of window space, height in proportion to width, it is the rival of Amiens and Beauvais.

It can scarcely be claimed, however, that this Franco-Spanish style was a complete success. In particular, the huge windows, so characteristic of the complete Gothic of the Île de France, are quite unsuited to the Spanish climate. The three great cathedrals, therefore, were scarcely finished when a new movement of quite a different character took its rise in Catalonia, where regionalism has always been a powerful force. The cathedral of Barcelona was begun in 1298. Santa Maria del Mar followed in 1328 and Santa Maria del Pino in 1329. The last-named is aisleless, but even where aisles are built, as in the other two cases, they have not the external prominence we find in the north. This is due to the fact that small chapels are built all along the north and south sides, and that the buttresses are largely internal, dividing one chapel from another. Flying buttresses are not necessary, for the clerestory is low, with small windows, and the aisles are high. In one respect the cathedral of Gerona is still more remarkable. It was Romanesque at first, and in the first half of the fourteenth century an aisled choir, of normal French character, was built. When it was desired to rebuild the nave early in the fifteenth century, aisles were actually discarded and a great vaulted hall was built seventy-three feet in width, the greatest span of any Gothic church. The abutment of the vault is perfectly managed by internal buttresses forming divisions between the chapels. The remarkable plan corresponds with that of Albi, Perpignan, and other churches in the south of France, but it is most marked in this Catalonian style.

It will therefore be seen that Spain is an exception to the medieval rule that, in most countries, there was one great national style, followed inevitably and unconsciously by the builders. Late in the thirteenth century we have three styles, quite apart from the Moorish work in the south: Romanesque surviving, almost pure French Gothic, and the new Spanish Gothic, especially in Catalonia.

In the fifteenth and sixteenth centuries, the close copying of French churches ceased, though of course French influence was still felt. Important works were carried out at Burgos, Saragossa, Segovia, Toledo. In the south no great Christian churches could be built during the Moorish domination. The cathedral of Seville, begun in 1401, is of enormous size. It is almost a parallelogram, with five aisles and side chapels as well. Each aisle, in height and width, is the same as the nave of Westminster Abbey. Cloisters are more numerous in Spain than anywhere else. They are sometimes added to a church evidently with the main object of protecting it from the sun.

The ritual arrangements of Spanish churches are very different from those elsewhere. The most prominent is the position of the choir, nearly always in the nave, and often connected with the presbytery by a long railed corridor. Choir stalls, "retables" over the altars, screens, and other medieval fittings have been far less disturbed than in most countries. Extreme richness, not to say florid exuberance, is their main characteristic, which is even more pronounced in the tombs, such as those in the Constable's chapel at Burgos and in the Charterhouse of Miraflores.

In Portugal we find of course the influence of France and Spain, but also of England, which is most marked in the great church and monastery of Batalha. Belem has a late and richly adorned monastic church with an elaborate cloister. At the end of the Gothic period a purely national style springs up called Manoelino, which has affinities with Moorish and Indian originals.

The Golden Age of architecture in Germany was the Romanesque period, which lasted till the middle of the thirteenth century. Mayence, Spires, Trèves, and Worms are the best examples, and the church of the Apostles at Cologne. The Gothic of Germany is copied from France and was a reluctant importation of the thirteenth century. It is lacking in poetry and charm, but is often of great technical excellence. The most famous monument is the cathedral of Cologne, but only the choir and part of the west front are medieval: the rest was completed in recent times, between 1842 and 1880. Freiburg has the earliest fine Gothic tower in Germany, completed in 1288: it has the characteristic open-work spire, which was copied at Burgos. Ulm has the loftiest tower and spire in existence, 529 feet high. The "hall church" is a prominent German feature, as illustrated at St Elizabeth's at Marburg. The most important church in Austria is St Stephen's at Vienna, with a lofty spire and a great steep roof which covers nave and aisles in one span. The French Gothic style was imported into Bohemia. The fine cathedral of St Vitus at Prague was designed by Matthew of Arras in the latter part of the fourteenth century. St Barbara's at Kuttenberg is more national, with ornate but rather unscientific flying buttresses.

The ecclesiastical architecture of the Netherlands is of less interest than the civic. The finest church is at Tournai, whose Romanesque transepts influenced the form of Noyon and Soissons; the choir is fully-developed Gothic. The cathedrals of Brussels and Antwerp are notable, and the latter is unique in having no less than seven aisles. The church of St Jacques at Liège is one of the finest examples of Flamboyant Gothic to be found anywhere. The great churches of Bruges, St Sauveur and Notre Dame, are of brick. The same material was commonly used along the Baltic and in Holland, where the churches are of less interest than those of Belgium. They are often barn-like structures, and most of their medieval fittings have been destroyed.

In Scandinavia, Gothic architecture is an exotic, even more than in Germany. The most important church in Sweden is the cathedral of Upsala, designed by a Frenchman at the end of the thirteenth century. The cathedral of Trondhjem in Norway dates from the eleventh century onwards; there is much work of the thirteenth and early fourteenth, with excellent details. The most remarkable church in Denmark is at Kallundborg, with no less than five towers and spires. Gotland is of greater interest, owing to its position on a prosperous trade route in early medieval times. Most of the churches are Romanesque, but in the thirteenth and fourteenth centuries a curious type of Gothic was used. Several of the naves are divided into two equal parts by pointed arcades.

There is of course no special connexion between Gothic architecture and the Goths or with Gotland, and we do not know that the people originally came from the island. The adjective was used as a term of reproach at a time when medieval architecture was regarded as barbarian. It may have this suitability that the new style might never have arisen if the Roman Empire had gone on its way untroubled by northern invasions. The term is a difficult one to define, but is generally held to include most of the buildings in Western Europe during the century mainly dealt with in this volume, and the succeeding centuries till the Renaissance. A narrower definition would confine it to those churches where the vital principles of the style are fully carried out, and therefore mainly to the Île de France. However the term is regarded, the most prominent feature of Gothic architecture is the frequent use of the arch rather than the lintel, and especially of the pointed arch.

The connexion of architecture with history is a close one, but one must admit that it is not always obvious. In the period under review we may well suppose that the activity of the thirteenth century in France was partly due to the piety and enthusiasm of St Louis, that the decay of production in the fourteenth and fifteenth centuries was the result of the English wars and the economic distress which accompanied them. Similar remarks may be made about England, though we are surprised that the Black Death gave so little pause to the building activity of Edward III's reign, and that the Wars of the Roses synchronised with the erection of so many fine parish churches. The truth is, as indicated at the beginning of this chapter, that the forces which go to produce great architecture are many in number, and the pressure of external events is only one of them. The main fact in medieval church architecture is the need that was felt for fine buildings, combined with the power, partly inherited and partly developed, to carry them out. The need was there from the fourth century onwards, but the power was often lacking. At a particular epoch, the twelfth century, the principles of arcuated construction, so long groped after, became understood. One experiment after another was made, and, in an incredibly short space of time, the heavy and gloomy Romanesque was transformed into the light and graceful Gothic.

Without the power, then, the need alone would not have produced fine architecture; but it is surely equally true that, without the need, the achievement would have been lacking. Gothic architecture, in its many forms, was a national style, applied even to the humblest barn; but its greatest glories are found in its houses of religion. Religious fervour was a chief reason for it, especially in the earlier part of its period. Haymo, abbot of St Pierre-sur-Dives, tells us that, when Chartres was built in the middle of the twelfth century, men and women of noble birth were bound by straps to carts and dragged the stones and wood in silence, broken only by confession and prayer. The "Cult of Carts" may have been short-lived, but the spirit behind it came out in many forms. Much of the best work of the eleventh and twelfth centuries was due to the monks, whether working with their own hands or not. Even the Cistercians, whose rule did not allow high towers or painted glass or rich ornament, produced a virile style and spread the knowledge of it all over Western Europe. In the thirteenth century, the influence of the layman was more pronounced, but religion and expert knowledge may go together. The sketch book of Wilars de Honecort has come down to us from this period. The drawings are mixed quite naturally with a request to all who labour to pray for his soul and to hold him in remembrance. The form of the church all through the Middle Ages, and much of its decoration, are dictated by the use to which it was put, and could not have been produced outside the Christian faith.

We cannot contemplate the achievements of Gothic architecture without a feeling of awe. They were the work of men of like passions with ourselves, whose motives were as mixed as ours, but the combination of great qualities had never been found before and may never be found again. Gothic architecture cannot be revived, but its spirit need never die. It will remain an inspiration to all who think seriously of art and of religion.

(B)

MILITARY ARCHITECTURE

The history of medieval fortification in Europe is that of the general appropriation of methods which, brought to a high state of efficiency under the Roman Empire, had survived without interruption in the Byzantine east. With the invasion of the west of Europe by the barbarians, these methods had fallen into disuse. Here and there, during the Merovingian and Carolingian epochs, a bishop or lay lord repaired the walls of a city to resist attack from some foe on the frontiers. Where Roman walls remained, they could be utilised as barriers against such enemies as the Saracens on the borders of Spain and on the Mediterranean seaboard: behind them an unwarlike population could find refuge when driven from their farms and fields. During this period, however, scientific methods of defence were in abeyance, and consequently progress in military architecture was at a standstill. It was not until the invasions of the Northmen that signs of forward movement began to appear. In their penetration of Europe, the Northmen came into contact with the traditional usages of Roman warfare and adopted for their own use engines of war which, to be adequately resisted, needed a corresponding strength of defence. If their actual plan of attack, as at the siege of Paris in 885–6, was somewhat deficient in science, they used the *ballista* and battering-ram with formidable effect; and the inevitable result of an offensive conducted with such energy was to stimulate the employment of means by which it might be successfully repelled.

The walled city, the defended habitation of the community, necessarily takes a prominent place in medieval warfare. The typical fortress of the Middle Ages, however, in which the most characteristic features of defence were initiated and brought to perfection, was the private fortress, the castle of an individual lord. The castle was the direct offspring of feudalism; it was the obvious symbol of the dominion of the feudal lord, the stronghold from which he exercised his authority and within which he entrenched himself against his superiors or rivals. This significance of the word *castellum* was gradually acquired, and the use of that word in documents of the Carolingian period is somewhat ambiguous. In 864 the capitulary of Pistes, in ordering the destruction of certain fortresses raised without royal licence, mentions *castella et firmitates et haias*. Probably walls and wooden stockades raised round private dwelling-houses were included in these categories; but the phrase may equally well refer to similar defences constructed by land-owners round the villages in which they dwelt. No actual example of a private fortress can be found until a few years later; and though it may definitely be said that such strongholds took their origin in Neustria and Austrasia as a natural result of the decline of the Empire of Charlemagne and the growth of feudal lawlessness, they were not common until the tenth century was well advanced. The general prevalence of the castle was a consequence of the recognition of the feudal principle.

This fact is illustrated by the late appearance of the castle in England. The early English *burh*, which comes into great prominence during the wars of Alfred and Edward the Elder, was intended for communal defence. It was a garrisoned centre of population, surrounded by timber fortifications with an outer ditch. If it had stone walls, these, as at London in the time of Alfred, survived from the Roman period and were repaired to meet Danish attacks. The Danes, on their side, when they had gained a permanent footing in England, made the *burh* the centre of their operations. Their first fortresses, during the period of invasion, were those temporary camps by the side of rivers to which the Anglo-Saxon Chronicle gives the name *geweorc*—large enclosures of earthwork within which they docked their ships and sheltered their army. These, as their conquests proceeded, were naturally abandoned for the conquered towns, like the five *burhs* of the Danelaw. On neither side is there a hint of any private fortress. The *burh* handed on its name to the borough of later times; and if, in Germany, the name *burg* acquired a less distinctive sense and was applied, as time went on, to the private castle as well as to the town, the *burgs* by which the Saxon Emperors defended their eastern frontier were, like the English *burhs*, the fortified settlements of communities. Until a few years before the Norman Conquest, it is doubtful whether there was such a thing as a castle in England. Meanwhile the Northmen had established their principality in Normandy, and, towards the close of the tenth century, had organised it on feudal lines. As a consequence, the castle, already familiar in the feudalised districts of inland France, made its way into Normandy. During the minority of the Conqueror, his subjects took the opportunity of turning dwelling-houses into fortresses. William himself was able to keep his vassals in check, and to turn castle-building into a powerful weapon of his own sovereignty. The view, however, that the castles of his realm were the monarch's property, held in trust for him by their tenants, could be maintained in practice only under a strong ruler; and the castle itself, in its origin, is a sign of the anarchy which it was the hardest task of a feudal monarch to suppress. The first English castles seem to have been raised, entirely on their own account, by Norman favourites of Edward the Confessor, to overawe their English neighbours We know with certainty of two only; and it is clear at any rate that the systematic castle-building by which William I consolidated his gains in England and repressed rebellion was a novelty in a country which, if economically ripe for feudalism, now found itself for the first time bound to feudalism as a political system. Domesday supplies more than one instance of the supersession of the English *burh* by the Norman castle. At York and Lincoln sections of the cities were laid waste to make room for castles. At Tutbury we read of the *burgum circa castellum*, the *burh* of earlier times lying round about the new castle, which was built less to protect it than to keep it in subjection. The two castles which the Conqueror founded on either side of the Ouse at York still remain; it is a false analogy which hastily compares them to the double *burhs* with which, at Hertford, Bedford, and other places, Edward the Elder protected the crossings of rivers, for these *burhs* were towns, while the castles at York were royal fortresses thrown up within the town, and were quite distinct in character.

The *burh* and the early castle have this so far in common, that their defences, save in exceptional cases, were of timber and earthwork; and it may also be conceded that in all probability the earliest castles were, like *burhs*, simply stockaded enclosures, but surrounding a single house instead of a collection of dwelling-houses. The castle, however, by the time of the Conquest, had assumed a stereotyped form of which the Bayeux tapestry provides several examples, all taken from Normandy and Brittany except the castle built by William on his landing at Hastings. The dwelling-house, a wooden structure in the form of a tower, stood upon an artificial mount of earth, composed of the material dug from the ditch surrounding its base. A second ditch, starting from and returning to the first, enclosed a platform, roughly oval in shape, which formed the bailey or courtyard of the castle in front of the mount. Wooden stockades encircled the upper edge of the mount and the inner bank of earth cast up from the ditch round the bailey. The entrance to the castle was at the end of the bailey opposite the mount, while access from the bailey to the tower was provided by a steeply inclined bridge of timber with ladder-like footholds, crossing the intermediate ditch. The mount was known as *mota* or *motte*, from the sods which composed it; the *ballium* or bailey probably received its name from the upright stakes which formed the principal feature of its surrounding fence, though the precise derivation of the word is obscure. This type of fortress is now usually known as the motte-and-bailey castle. Its outstanding characteristic was the dwelling-house on the mount, which sometimes, as the description of the house built early in the twelfth century for the lord of Ardres shews us, was large and roomy. The numerous mounts which remain, though generally high and steep, vary much in size; the adjacent baileys, which contained stables and other offices, together with some accommodation for the garrison, are sometimes very diminutive. But in all, large or small, the mount, crowned by its wooden tower, was the symbol of the lord's feudal dominion. By transference of the thing signified to the object itself, it became the *dominio*, corrupted into *dunio*; and thus the French donjon and English dungeon took their origin, as names for the stone tower that superseded the earthen mount.

The strategic value of the Conqueror's system of castles is shewn by the permanent survival of the principal castles which he founded. In these the motte-and-bailey plan, generally speaking, formed the nucleus of the stone fortresses which, as time went on, took the place of timber defences. In some of his greater castles, as at Windsor, a plan was followed in which the mount stood at a re-entrant angle between an outer and an inner bailey. This type was adopted by the builders of Alnwick, the greatest castle in the north of England. On the other hand, Warkworth, the other great Northumbrian stronghold which eventually came into the possession of the Percies, is a large motte-and-bailey castle of the normal plan, which was gradually converted into a fortress of stone. But, while the motte and bailey can be frequently traced as the origin of permanent castles, there are numerous examples of earthwork castles which have no history and can be referred to no special date. Some of these may be early castles which were abandoned for more convenient sites; but probably many of them are fortresses hastily raised in a period of feudal rebellion without the sovereign's licence, and destroyed upon the restoration of order. It is difficult to credit the traditional estimates of the number of adulterine castles fortified during the reign of Stephen; but it is certain that these unauthorised strongholds were thickly spread over the country, and that their earthworks, where they were of any size or strength, must have left some traces behind them.

While the ordinary castle of the eleventh and twelfth centuries was a structure of earthwork and timber, stone was also employed where necessary, as in castles built on rocky sites and promontories, where defences of earthwork were impracticable. But a defensive wall of stone offered less resistance to the battering-ram than a stout fence of timber with planks set horizontally between the uprights. The strength of the wooden wall had been proved in Roman warfare, and, so long as its main object was to present an inert barrier to an enemy, it served its purpose well. Its chief danger, the risk of fire, could be minimised by stretching wet hides over its outer surface. Nevertheless, the stone donjon appears at an early date as an alternative for the earthen mount and its wooden tower. The remains of the tower at Langeais in Touraine, which present several points of contrast to the ordinary donjon of the twelfth century, are generally agreed to belong to the castle begun by Fulk the Black in 994. In three at any rate of the English castles founded by William the Conqueror, at London, Colchester, and Pevensey, towers of stone took the place of the motte. No artificial mound could have borne such masses of masonry, and it was very seldom in later days that a motte was used as a foundation for a stone tower. Outer defences of earthwork were combined with these early towers; and where, as at Richmond in Yorkshire, the castle was surrounded from the first with a stone wall, the dwelling-house within was simply a hall built against one side of the bailey. The donjons of the stone castles of Richmond, Ludlow, and Bamburgh are later additions to the plan; and at Richmond and Ludlow they were formed by the transformation and heightening of early gatehouses.

Stone walls, again, rose in certain instances upon earthen banks shortly after the foundation of castles; and, as the ordinary motte-and-bailey castle became the seat of its lord's authority, its wooden defences were gradually removed to make way for defences of stone round the bailey and the upper edge of the mount. The building of a stone gatehouse to protect the entrance was probably the point at which such alterations started. In large *enceintes* the change went forward slowly: portions of the city wall of York were still of timber in the early part of the fourteenth century. While the stone wall, with its parapet-walk and occasional towers, provided a line of active defence which was to become all-important, the dwelling-house still for a time remained the essential point to be considered by the engineer. The primary idea of a castle was that of a strong house; and the stone wall at first was merely the outer line of fortification which protected the great tower or, to use its modern name, the keep. In many instances, as at Windsor, the mount was simply fortified by a ring-wall, forming what has been called a shell-keep. Sometimes, as at Guildford, a square tower was built upon the summit. As a rule, however, the building of a stone tower meant the abandonment of the motte for a more secure foundation; and, though here and there the motte was partially utilised or even included within the new work, the tower, as at Newcastle-on-Tyne, rose on a new site. At Rochester and Middleham old motte-and-bailey fortresses were deserted for new castles, each dominated by its great tower. In France and Normandy the stone tower made progress during the first half of the twelfth century. Advance in England was slower; and, after the Conqueror's towers, already mentioned, the only authentic example of a rectangular stone keep until the reign of Henry II is the huge tower built at Rochester by Archbishop William of Corbeil. Henry II, however, as part of his measures for restoring order, inaugurated an epoch of castle-building of which the characteristic feature is the great tower or donjon. Two varieties are found, one in which there is a single room on each floor, and the other in which the tower is divided from top to bottom by a cross-wall, the top of which formed a gutter between the gabled roofs of the two compartments. The second type is sometimes oblong in plan and sacrifices height to the large area which it covers. Both types, however, have the same characteristic arrangements. They are usually entered by a doorway on the first or second floor, approached by a flight of stairs which is enclosed in a forebuilding or barbican set against a side of the tower. This steep and narrow passage, crossed on its way by one or more doors and protected at its head by a guard-room, was the only means of access from without. The room, entered from it at right-angles, was the great hall or main apartment. Winding stairs in one or more of the corner-turrets led to the lower and upper floors and to the battlements, which rose above and hid the roof and were provided with a parapet-walk. The vaulted basement was the store-room of the building; while additional accommodation was furnished by chambers, large and small, contrived in the thickness of the walls. The tower had its chapel, which was generally situated in the forebuilding: it also had its well, in the basement or with a long shaft from a well-chamber on one of the upper floors. At Rochester the well-pipe is in the cross-wall, with an opening on each floor. No two towers are exactly alike, and their planning shews remarkable variety and ingenuity. As dwelling-houses, even the most spacious must have been dark and uncomfortable: for considerations of safety, the lower stages were lighted with narrow loops, widely splayed on the inner side; and, though light could be introduced more freely higher up, the thickness of the stonework and the employment of the walls for chambers and passages left the main rooms in twilight. The keep is often represented as intended only for a last resource in time of siege, and it is possible that in some castles a hall in the courtyard was normally used as a more convenient residence. But the general appearance of the dwelling-house in the bailey belongs to a later date; and while there are one or two instances in which the tower seems to have served purely military purposes, the domestic aspect of such towers as those of Falaise, Hedingham, Castle Rising, and Bamburgh is obvious. They are not only the culminating points of fortresses, but they are residences whose impregnable strength is the safety of their tenants.

With its massive walls and dangerous entrance, the rectangular donjon could defy attack with success. It was designed to resist the stones cast from the great catapults which were the most formidable siege-engines of the day; its wider openings were beyond the reach of arrows and javelins. Against an enemy at close quarters, using the ram or attempting to undermine the masonry with bores and picks, the faces of the tower could be protected by wooden galleries or hoardings fixed outside the battlements, with holes in the floor through which missiles could be used. On the other hand, the sharp angles offered the foe a sector in which he could work with security at points where the masonry was most vulnerable. As a precaution against this the north-west turret of the great tower at Newcastle, standing at a point which was liable to attack, was built as a polygon with blunt angles between 1172 and 1177. In 1215 one of the square angle-turrets at Rochester succumbed to stone-throwing machines, and was rebuilt on a curved plan. These devices reduced the dangerous sector to a minimum and substituted a surface whose radiating joints withstood the impact of the ram and neutralised the labours of sappers and miners.

Growing familiarity with the fortifications of the East, acquired during the crusades, aided such improvements. Before the end of the twelfth century, the cylindrical donjon began to supersede the older form. The finest examples are to be found in France, and, until its recent destruction, the early thirteenth-century castle of Coucy, in which the enormous donjon, with its own ditch and curtain-wall, took its place as the principal feature of a perfectly-planned *enceinte*, was the most imposing feudal monument in Europe. In England the circular donjon was never more than a passing phase, but it formed a prominent feature in the interesting thirteenth-century castles of Wales. The round keep at Conisborough in Yorkshire, standing at the highest corner of the bailey, with immensely thick walls and a steeply battering base, is an ingenious attempt to combine a curved surface with a system of flanking formed by a series of projecting buttress turrets, left solid through most of their height. Here, however, some flanking has also been given to the wall of the bailey, which has been reinforced at intervals by smaller circular turrets added to its face. Hitherto, towers breaking the line of the curtain-wall had been built, but without any definite idea of systematic flanking. The outer wall, defended by its ditch, had been left to take its chance; the filling-up of the ditch was necessary before a breach could be made or the gatehouse stormed, and the defenders concentrated their efforts on the ultimate resistance of the great tower. When once means were taken to provide the outer wall with a ring of projecting towers, from which a raking arrow-fire could be directed upon the besiegers, the donjon was no longer a necessity. Although in Richard I's great castle, Château-Gaillard, the round donjon, strengthened by a spur-shaped projection upon its inner face, is still a prominent feature of the defences, the most remarkable point in the plan is the wall, consisting of a series of curved projections, which divides the innermost from the middle ward. Here the division of the bailey into a succession of wards, and the care which is taken to strengthen the outer walls and approaches, mark the arrival of the new period, in which the curtain-wall and its towers begin to bear the whole burden of defence.

The donjon never became wholly obsolete. In France its survival was more persistent than in England, and in England, especially in the region exposed to Scottish raids, it is found in and after the thirteenth century. The fourteenth-century tower between the two wards at Knaresborough and the principal tower of which records remain at Pontefract are cases in point. Soon after the building of Dunstanburgh, another castle of the house of Lancaster, in 1313, the gatehouse was blocked up and converted into a donjon; and to this there is a parallel in South Wales at Llanstephan. That most common feature of late military architecture in the north, the peel-tower, reproduces the disposition of a rectangular keep on a small scale. At the same time the donjon loses its primary character as the fortified residence which is the *raison d'être* of the castle. At Coucy and Pontefract the splendid domestic buildings of the castles were sheltered within strongly defended walls. The mansion within the castle, as at Windsor and Ludlow, is the growth of a period in which the actual fortification of the house has been succeeded by the fortification of the wall which encircles it.

The later medieval castle, in its most scientific development, was therefore an enclosure, usually divided by cross-walls into two or more wards, and surrounded by a wall with towers at regular intervals, so planned as to command the whole outer face of the wall between them. The house with its offices, following the normal domestic plan with the hall as its centre, was in the inner ward: the outer ward contained various additional offices, stables, and quarters for the garrison. A path, approached by stairs set against the inner face at intervals, ran along the top of the wall, protected upon its outer side by a parapet and battlements. The battlements or merlons, sometimes pierced by loops covered with hinged shutters, sheltered the archers, who also could shoot through the embrasures between them. The merlons, at first double the width of the embrasures, became of equal width with them at a later date. While the system of fitting hoardings to the parapets in time of siege continued through the thirteenth century, the flanking afforded by the towers diminished the risk which such precautions were intended to meet. But, as a substitute, the parapets were often corbelled out in front of the wall, and holes were left between the corbels through which stones might be thrown or arrows shot down upon the assailants. These machicolations (*mâche-coulis*) are prominent in castles and town-walls of the later fourteenth and fifteenth centuries. The parapet-walk was carried through the upper floors of the towers; but strong doorways guarded their entrances, so that, in a well-defended castle, the wall could be isolated into sections, and, if one part was scaled by ladders or entered from the movable wooden towers which were used for scaling purposes, the rest could be cut off.

In later castles the gatehouse assumed an importance equal to that of the donjon at an earlier date. The gatehouse, to begin with, had been a simple tower with an upper storey above the arched entrance. Now the archway was flanked by projecting towers, semi-circular or polygonal, with guard-rooms on their lower floors. The vaulted roof of the gateway passage was pierced with holes or slots through which intruders could be annoyed by missiles as effective as, and more economical than, the molten lead of popular fiction. The outer doorway, reached by a drawbridge across the ditch or moat, was shielded by an iron portcullis, worked by a windlass from the first floor. In addition, the approach to the drawbridge was strengthened by a barbican or forebuilding, with its own outer ditch and drawbridge, forming a narrow passage in which the defence had a great advantage over the attacking force. The barbicans at Alnwick and Warwick, the noble gatehouses at Pembroke and Lancaster, bear witness to the care with which the main approach to the castle was guarded.

France led the way in scientific fortification, and from the thirteenth to the fifteenth century her engineers applied great variety of skill to the art of defence. England can shew no castle as colossal as Coucy; the walls of York or even those of so regularly and carefully fortified a town as Conway cannot compare in scientific interest with those of Aigues-Mortes, Carcassonne, and Avignon. England, however, produced at the end of the thirteenth century examples of castle-planning which are second to none in interest. The prototypes of the concentric lines of defence, by means of which the outer ward of the castle entirely surrounded the inner, were to be found in Byzantine fortification, as in the triple *enceinte* of Constantinople, and in the strongholds built by the Crusaders in the Latin kingdom of Jerusalem. The concentric castle of the Knights of St John in the Lebanon area, the Krak des Chevaliers, is one of the most complete achievements of medieval military skill. In such a fortress we see a quadrilateral castle with flanking towers encircled by a second and lower wall, so as to enable the defenders of both lines to work together simultaneously and those on the inner wall, from their superior height, to command the field outside the castle and shoot over their comrades' heads. So advantageous was the system that it was applied to alterations of already existing castles. Thus the Tower of London was converted into a regular concentric castle, in which the Conqueror's great tower and the later domestic buildings were withdrawn from active defence within a double line of wall. The outer ward was a narrow passage between the two walls, broken into sections by transverse walls and gateways. The approach to the gatehouse, across a bridge with a barbican at either end, presented an initial difficulty to the enemy, who further was exposed to a triple line of fire from the archers on both walls and from those on the ground-level of the outer ward, for whom arrow-slits were provided in the wall beneath the parapet. The same plan was used for new castles founded in Wales. Caerphilly, on a low and marshy site, was begun in the reign of Henry III and is the most elaborately defended of all, with outworks of immense strength protecting the moat round the main building. Less complicated in design, and conceived with a masterly simplicity, were Edward I's castles at Rhuddlan and Harlech; while at Beaumaris, the latest of his Welsh castles, general simplicity of plan was combined with fertility in devices for rendering a castle on a low and flat site practically impregnable. At Carnarvon and Conway there is only one line of fortification with flanking towers, and the two wards are divided by a cross-wall internally; but the cluster of round towers and the barbican which defends the entrance at Conway, and the great galleried wall at Carnarvon with its two gatehouses and the polygonal tower at its western angle, are unequalled in Britain for strength and grandeur of effect. The capacity of such fortresses for defence was a convincing answer to contemporary methods of attack; while, instead of the inert front which earlier castles had presented to besiegers, the Edwardian castle, with its looped and parapeted walls and its carefully shielded gatehouses, confronted its assailants with every means for an active defence which might be converted into a formidable offensive.

The combination of the castle with the walled town can be seen to perfection at Conway, where the town is virtually an outer ward to the castle, surrounded by a wall flanked at regular intervals by towers which are rounded to the field and left open at the neck on the inner side. This union of town-wall and citadel may be studied on a more imposing scale and with more variety of scientific features at Carcassonne and other foreign towns; and few English towns retain anything like a complete circuit of walls. Where, however, the walls have almost entirely disappeared, their course can often be traced by the survival of the *pomerium* or lane at their back, which separated them from the houses, or by broad streets which mark the line of the outer ditch and still form a noticeable division between the town and its suburban extensions. Town gatehouses have frequently been preserved, in spite of modern traffic. Of fortified bridges across rivers, of which several fine examples, such as the bridge at Prague and the Pont Valentré at Cahors, remain on the continent, there are few relics in England; the small gatehouses of the bridges at Monmouth and Warkworth are insignificant exceptions. In Gascony and Guyenne Edward I's engineers laid out fortified towns with a gridiron arrangement of streets round a central market-place, of which the standard example is Montpazier (Dordogne). This plan can also be traced in the grass-grown enclosure of Winchelsea. These, however, are only occasional examples of the combination of a street-plan with the outer fortifications of a town; and the town within the walls was usually an intricate labyrinth of streets and lanes.

Fortification attained its highest point in the concentric plan of the castle. During the fourteenth century refinements of castle-planning are frequent. The magnificent castle of Saint-André at Villeneuve, on the right bank of the Rhone opposite Avignon, and, on a smaller scale, the castle of Caerlaverock by the Solway, shew triangular plans at the apex of which is set an imposing gatehouse. As late as 1379 the castle of Bodiam in Sussex was built upon a plan derived from that of Villandraut (Garonne). But, while foreign invasions and internal disturbances still maintained the old importance of the castle in the rest of Europe, and while Italian princes still dwelt within feudal castles and even municipalities constructed castles for their own defence as part of their fortifications, the castle entered upon no further period of development. In the contest for supremacy between the methods of attack and those of defence, the first had always pushed the second closely. Castle-builders had succeeded in forcing an enemy to a respectful distance. Against adequately flanked walls and machicolated battlements the cumbrous operations of the battering-ram and the scaling-tower were of little avail, and miners were at the mercy of a watchful garrison. The moat filled with water dammed up from a neighbouring stream was a more difficult obstacle than the dry ditch which had been the habitual outer defence of earlier castles, and gave strength to positions which in themselves had little natural advantage. At the same time, the opportunity of the besieger lay in the improvement of his engines for hurling missiles. The more formidable these became, the less possibility there was of counteracting them. It is true that the machines which propelled great stones by the release of the cords that held back an upright stock with a hollow chamber, or of a counterpoise which, let free, set a sling in motion, and the arbalasts, cross-bows on a large scale which discharged javelins, were clumsy, and that the damage which they inflicted upon stonework was less than their menace to life and to perishable buildings inside the walls. Their use in defence, however, was necessarily limited. The shock of the discharge made their employment upon towers and ramparts dangerous, unless solid platforms which could resist vibration were made for them; from the ground-level behind the walls, even where there was sufficient room to allow for their trajectory, their aim could be only haphazard. It is probable that the invention of gunpowder and the use of cannon worked no very sudden change. The earliest cannon were awkward engines of no great strength. Nevertheless, their capacity for improvement must have been obvious from the first. The force which they brought into play had possibilities far beyond those of the older machines of warfare; and the decline in medieval fortification begins with their arrival in the fourteenth century.

From this period onwards there are two distinct tendencies in castle-building. On the one hand, in districts constantly harassed by war, like the Scottish border, the castle reverts from the walled and flanked enclosure to the state of a fortified house, protected on its most vulnerable side by a walled courtyard. Quadrangular houses with projecting towers at the corners, like Bolton, Lumley, and other northern castles, were built by great noblemen; the ordinary land-owner raised his peel-tower on a less imposing scale, trusting to the thickness of its walls and the immunity of its vaulted ground-storey from fire. On the other hand, in more peaceful districts the castle abandoned its military character. Defensive features were retained, but for ornament rather than use, just as the feudalism of which the castle had been the symbol had lost its reality. Even in some of the castles of the north, such as the tower of Belsay and the tower-house built upon the mount at Warkworth in the fifteenth century, domestic comfort is at least as prominent an object as safety. In the south of England, Hurstmonceaux, with its mimicry of defence, marks the transition from the military stronghold, like Bodiam, to the English manor-house of the next century. The castle of Tattershall in Lincolnshire, provided with elaborate inner and outer moats and dominated by a lofty brick tower with machicolated battlements, is a palace with the semblance of a fortress. Its builder, the treasurer Cromwell, also began the manor-house of Wingfield in Derbyshire, which similarly preserves some of the features of a castle, while laying more stress upon its true purpose as a mansion. In warfare such houses played little or no part. The wars of the Roses were fought in open field, not against castle walls. Elsewhere the same transition is noticeable. Blois and Amboise, gradually transformed into palaces, may be contrasted with the feudal fortresses of Chinon and Loches. Heidelberg, under the Electors-palatine of the sixteenth century, lost all likeness to the hill-fortresses of the feudal lords in Germany. The castle had seen its day as a factor in the evolution of military science, and the future of fortification lay in a return, under new conditions and through gradual processes, to the system of defence by earthwork from which the castle had grown to maturity.

CHAPTER XXIII.

THE ART OF WAR TO 1400.

With the encroachments of the barbarians upon the frontiers of the Roman Empire, a decisive change came over the character of warfare. The Roman army, as reorganised by Diocletian and Constantine, differed greatly from the army of earlier days. The old distinction between the legionary who was a Roman citizen and the auxiliary recruited from the provinces had long disappeared; the employment of mercenary soldiers from the tribes which surrounded the Empire had modified the whole character of the imperial forces; a new regular army came into being, in which novel elements, the Palatine troops which were directly at the Emperor's disposal, and the Comitatenses who could be moved from the interior of the Empire to meet pressure upon any part of the frontier, took precedence of the older legions stationed in garrisons upon its limits. Cavalry and light-armed infantry, to cope with the inroads of swiftly-moving enemies, assumed an importance which tended to supersede that of the heavy-armed foot-soldier, the traditional mainstay of the Roman military power. The barbarian, in contact with the legions, had profited by his experience; the mercenary who had served in the imperial ranks returned to his home with a new knowledge of the art of war and of military equipment. The enemies with whom the Romans of the later Empire had to deal were formidably armed and could fight upon equal terms with their opponents; while the Roman armies themselves, heterogeneous in composition, no longer formed a compact machine which easily submitted to control. Civil war between rival Emperors and the divided interests of East and West hastened the end of what still remained of the old military system amid its transformations.

The defeat of Valens by the Goths at Hadrianople (378) proved that a new force had arrived against which traditional tactics were found wanting. The battle, begun as an attack by the Roman legions upon the barricades of the Gothic camp, was decided by a sudden charge of cavalry, which threw the Romans into confusion and placed them at the mercy of their enemies. Henceforward cavalry took the upper hand in warfare. Under Theodosius the Great a new army took the place of that which had been destroyed at Hadrianople. Foreign chiefs with their bands of personal followers, horsed and armed with lances, were attracted into his service by gifts and promises and gave him their allegiance. With the aid of these *foederati* he repressed the revolt of the western legions, and so established the supremacy of cavalry and the Teutonic adventurer in the West. While, however, Italy was abandoned to the strife of federate leaders and to the invasions of Goths and

Vandals, the Eastern Emperors kept the foreign element in their armies under control. The influence of the *foederati* is seen in the tendency of the army to move in groups attached by ties of personal allegiance to individual leaders; the greatest generals, Belisarius and Narses, were surrounded like any German chieftain by their *comitatus* of picked followers, and the prominence which his officers thus acquired was a source of suspicion and jealousy to Justinian, whose policy was directed to checking the power of individuals by dividing and changing the command. But the army which had adopted this alien custom was still in large part drawn from the confines of the Empire, and from it was evolved a force which gave to medieval Europe an example of highly developed strategic and tactical practice.

Under the successors of Justinian the *foederati* decreased in number and importance, as the prospect of the rewards which had allured them at first declined. The *comitatus* disappeared, and the Byzantine army, as reconstructed by the military reformers of the end of the sixth and beginning of the seventh centuries, was organised under commanders whose authority was derived immediately from the Emperor. The regiments, *ἀριθμοί* or *κατάλογοι*, representing the *numeri* of the older Roman army, ceased to be independent units, and were grouped into *μοῖραι* or brigades, each under its *μοίραρχος*: three *μοῖραι*, each of two to three thousand men, formed a *μέρος* or division. In this army, drawn from within the Empire, the purely alien element was small and well under the control of an imperial officer who commanded the corps of foreign soldiers. The theme (*θέμα*) or army corps became the basis of a system of administration in which civil was subordinated to military government. The civil province was converted into the military theme, ruled by the commander of the corps and staffed by his officers. In this subdivision of the Empire, subject to re-grouping and further partition as time went on, the shrunken body of *foederati* was represented by the Optimatian theme, with its capital at Nicomedia, while the Bucellarian theme, adjoining it to the east, was garrisoned by the foreign members of the imperial guard, which had formed the Emperor's *comitatus*. No regular system of universal military service was developed, in spite of the military basis of government; but there was certainly no difficulty in recruiting forces within the borders of the Empire, or in finding competent officers among members of noble and wealthy families.

The all-important factor in the Byzantine army was its heavy cavalry. Its most formidable enemies were nations of horse-soldiers, to whose swiftness of movement and Parthian tactics it opposed superiority of weight and scientific method. The Byzantine cavalryman, with his close-fitting steel helm and shirt of mail, and his round shield worn on the left shoulder, rode with a long lance and carried broadsword, dagger, and bow and quiver at his saddle-bow. The use of the bow by horsemen was the result of contact with hostile forces whose main arm it was, and the cavalry of the Eastern Empire employed it with skill and effect. Moreover, the experience of warfare against the Goths had shewn that an enemy who confined the use of the bow to his infantry was unable to combine the operations of his horse and foot successfully. In the open field, the Byzantine infantry played a very subordinate part; employed against enemies like the Franks, whose armies fought chiefly on foot, the heavy infantry with foot-archers ranged on its flanks was covered by wings of horsemen, ready to close in upon the hand-to-hand struggle in the centre and administer the *coup de grâce*. Otherwise, the use of infantry was to operate in districts where horsemen were at a geographical disadvantage.

This was the army whose organisation in an era of reform is drawn in the *Strategicon* of Maurice (Emperor 582–602), written about 580. The fruits of its experience are contained in the *Tactica* of Leo VI (886–912), when the Saracens were the principal foes of the Empire. Although the use of infantry is not neglected by Leo, infantry tactics in his day were of small importance. The Saracen was an armed horseman, hardly inferior at close quarters to the cavalry of the Empire, formidable in the crowds of horse-archers with which he could molest less mobile forces. His foot-soldiers, following in the wake of his horsemen, were practically negligible. The strategy and tactics of the Byzantine army were thus directed towards campaigns in which infantry were useful merely upon occasion, and towards battles from which they might be wholly absent, and the most valuable and original sections of Leo's discussion of tactics are concentrated upon the effective use and disposition of cavalry. Similarly, towards the end of the tenth century, when the Saracen menace was far less serious and Nicephorus Phocas (963–969) had taken Antioch and Aleppo, the author of Περὶ παραδρομῆς πολέμου, outlining the conduct of a war against Saracen raiders, treats the cavalry as the main arm in the battlefield, and relegates the infantry to garrison duty on the edge of the mountain district through which the invaders entered the central plateau of Anatolia. At the same time, the use of infantry in the field was not neglected, and Leo gives detailed advice for their co-operation with horsemen.

The preponderance of cavalry forces in the West was reached much more slowly. The battle of Châlons (450), in which Roman and Gothic horsemen combined to check the progress of the horse-bowmen of Attila, belongs to the last days of the Western Empire; the Roman legionary had passed, but the altered tactics of the Western horseman with lance and bow and of his ally, the Teutonic lancer, found no general success outside Italy, where they were the resources of a power in its last decline. The Franks who over-ran north-western Europe were bands of foot-soldiers, who depended upon their speed in movement and their missile weapons, the casting axe and the heavy javelin. At close quarters they fought with sword, shield, and dagger. The use of body armour came slowly, and, while horsemanship came with it, the horse was regarded as a means of locomotion rather than as an aid to battle. Their favourite method of fighting was in a close square, which turned its face to meet successive changes of attack, and, even when the mounted knight was beginning to count as an important element in their host, he still fought on foot when battle was joined. While there were exceptions to this rule, it prevailed as late as the battle of Poitiers (732), where Charles Martel and his Franks were engaged with the hosts of Saracen light cavalry. Here the charge of an insignificant force of armed horsemen would have courted defeat, and the serried infantry formation was justified by complete victory.

Apart from these defensive tactics, the success of which depended upon sheer weight of resistance to a lightly armed foe, the Franks of the Merovingian period developed no systematic art of war. Under the great mayors of the palace they learned discipline; the victory of Poitiers is all the more remarkable because it followed a period of internecine strife, in which the Frankish kingdom had ceased to be a formidable foe. Charles Martel's army, recruited on the principle of the national levy *en masse*, and including numbers of soldiers whose training can have been in the circumstances only indifferent, did credit to his competent generalship. While this battle was won by infantry, it is clear that operations against a mounted enemy were necessarily accompanied by a development in horsemanship, which was further improved by subsequent contact with the Lombard cavalry in Italy. It was not, however, until the area of Frankish conquest was enlarged by Charles the Great that methods of warfare were systematised among his subjects. The use of armour was enjoined by legislation, which prohibited the exportation of mail shirts from the realm. In the campaigns against the Lombards and Avars a host of cavalry was raised under compulsion from the great tenants and their followers. For the ill-organised national levy was substituted a new system of service, founded upon the obligation of property and arranged upon a graduated scale which relieved the poorer land-owner of a disproportionate share in the cost of equipment; efficiency took the place of casual methods. It is true that Charles' care for his army was neutralised by the civil dissensions which destroyed his Empire in the course of the ninth century; but, amid the weakness of his successors and the growth of feudal principalities, the military reforms which he inaugurated bore fruit, and the tactics of feudal warfare were developed upon foundations which he had laid.

Of the personal tactics of Charles in battle the records are somewhat deficient. The destruction of his rear-guard at Roncesvalles was due rather to a lapse in strategic foresight than to a tactical error; the unexpected attack afforded no opportunity for tactical skill. As a strategist, however, this was his one mistake. The success of his campaigns was the work of a mind which carried the map of his realm imprinted upon it and saw the possibilities which lay beyond its extending boundary. If his successors failed to profit by his example in this respect, he at any rate bequeathed a permanent legacy to Western strategy in his establishment of a chain of fortified bases along his eastern frontier, at once a barrier to the invader and a starting-point for fresh offensives. The burg-system of Charles the Great was the prototype, in a general sense, of the *burhs* which Alfred and Edward the Elder opposed to the advance of the Danes in England; it was revived with signal success by Henry the Fowler and Otto the Great. When feudalism brought about the growth of the castle, the strategic employment of the private fortress as a link in a chain of military outposts was fully recognised. The disposition of the Conqueror's castles in England, the line of fortresses which guarded the trans-Jordanic frontier of the kingdom of Jerusalem, and the Edwardian combinations of citadel and walled town in Wales, were later applications of the same principle. Such applications can hardly be ascribed to direct imitation of the exploits of Charles; but of the experience and instinct which dictated them he may claim to be the first representative among medieval generals.

It may be questioned how far, as the Frankish kingdom assumed coherent form and profited by civilisation, the remains of the Roman occupation influenced its military progress. The traditions of Roman practice outside the Eastern Empire were, by the eighth and ninth centuries, too vague to make much impression on the Frank. Similarly in England the Saxon seems to have learned little from the conquered Romano-Briton. His first invasions, like those of the Frank, were made in isolated bands under individual leaders. Of the art of fortification he knew nothing, and it was not until the time of Alfred that any movement was made to repair the walls of Roman cities which the first settlers had left desolate. In the course of the eighth century the use of armour progressed; it is probable that the English profited to some extent by the importation of shirts of mail from France, the traffic which we have seen forbidden by Charlemagne. Horsemanship, however, lagged far behind. The Englishman had to contend with no mounted enemy on the trackless borders of the Saxon kingdoms; the battles of rival tribes were hand-to-hand encounters on foot, in which one army fought the other with spears behind the close "shield-wall" formed by the round linden shields borne by each warrior. In such straightforward conflicts there was no opportunity for tactics; both sides fought until one gave way. The geography of the early wars of Northumbria, Mercia, and Wessex is too obscure to allow the discovery of much strategic capacity; victory probably depended upon superior numbers and good fortune, and the unfortunate campaign which Ecgfrith led against the Picts in 685 seems to have been conducted with a rashness and ignorance which may not have been exceptional. In Alfred, however, strategic genius came to the front; in his wars with Guthrum and Hasting he achieved success by his perception of the advantage of avoiding pitched battles by sudden strokes at the enemy's base of operations, while by his formation of a fleet he supplied his land-forces with an indispensable auxiliary in their contest with a race of seamen.

The enemy whom Alfred and his immediate successors kept in check was, like Frank and Saxon, a marauder bent upon plunder, whose casual attacks upon the coast-line did not develop at once into an organised attempt at occupation and conquest. The settlements which the Northmen effected in England and the Frankish kingdom were formed by the command of rivers along which their open ships penetrated into the interior, and beside which they made their camps. Their heavy axes and swords could be used to purpose in hand-to-hand fight; but it was not until their raids upon undefended country had put them in possession of horses and armour that their military talent appeared. The latest of the invaders of western and southern Europe, they were the readiest to take advantage of the systems which they encountered in their wanderings. From a sea-rover whose methods, when he was obliged to fight on land, were of the simplest, the Northman became the most accomplished soldier in Europe. At the siege of Paris in 886 he was in possession of siege-engines, the use of which he had probably derived from observation of Byzantine methods of war. It is among the Normans, again, that we find the crossbow in use in the eleventh century; this, known to the Roman soldier but long forgotten, was re-invented during this period by a logical application of the principle of the *balista* or javelin-throwing engine to a missile weapon which could be worked by one man. Whether the discovery can be ascribed to the Normans is uncertain, but they, at any rate, were foremost to profit by it.

This advance took place upon the continent, where it kept pace with the advance of feudalism. It was a feudal army, drawn from Normandy and the adjacent provinces, that Harold, accompanied by the hastily-raised force of the English shires, met at Hastings. From a victory in a hand-to-hand conflict at Stamford Bridge, where both sides as usual fought on foot with axe, spear, and sword, he came into a field where his infantry had to face unfamiliar and superior tactics. His forces included large bodies of men armed only with the traditional English weapons, against whom were arrayed armed infantry with bowmen and crossbowmen in their front line. The English had no cavalry; on the other side, the rear was composed of horsemen, ready to alternate with the bowmen and foot-soldiers in attacks upon the solid mass defended by the shield-wall which fronted them. With the advantage of position on their side, and with unfaltering steadiness, Harold's army stood for hours upon the defensive, enduring the flights of arrows and repelling the charges which followed, until the king was slain and their ranks at last were broken. The obstinate tactics which had been proof against the Saracen cavalry at Poitiers were now no guarantee of success, even had all the English host at Hastings been trained and armed warriors; against the scientific combination of foot-archers and spearmen, backed up by horsemen, the inert mass of infantry was of no avail.

In 1071, five years after Hastings, the Byzantine army, the oldest and best trained military force in Europe, was destroyed in battle with the Seljūq Turks at Manzikert in Armenia. The fight was purely one of cavalry, heavily armed horsemen (cataphracts) against hordes of skilful riders who used the bow to harass their enemy without engaging in close conflict. Rashness in venturing into a position where troops were open to flank attack and encircling manœuvres, combined with treachery in the Byzantine ranks, caused the disaster, which was as great a blow to the military organisation as Hadrianople, seven centuries before, had been. The consequent menace of the Seljūq power to Europe was the political cause which, joined with religious enthusiasm, provoked the Crusades.

The conduct of the Crusades, quite apart from the initial difficulty caused by the assemblage of heterogeneous multitudes from rival nations under jealous leaders of very different capacity, was distinguished by singular improvidence. The strategic problems of carrying a large force to Syria through Asia Minor, an unknown country laid waste by its Turkish invaders, and of holding the precarious group of feudal states formed in Syria against an active and dangerous enemy, might well have taxed the genius of the most competent general. The leaders knew nothing of the topography or climate of the country through which they had to pass, nor did their suspicious Greek allies trouble to enlighten them with proper precautions. Insufficiently provisioned, liable to continual annoyance from the bands of Seljūq horsemen who hung upon their progress, and occasionally without adequate weapons to repel their attacks, they reached Syria with forces enormously depleted. In Syria itself the possession of Jerusalem was the engrossing interest, and the systematic conquest which would have secured that position was neglected in favour of holding isolated posts without proper lines of communication. While the navies of the Italian cities held the coast-line which brought them commercial profit, the Frankish counts and barons, with inadequate forces, were unable to control the interior of the kingdom of Jerusalem; and when in 1149 the armies of the Second Crusade had a good prospect of capturing Damascus, the chance was lost by the mutual distrust of the generals.

Had the crusaders profited by the experience of Byzantine tacticians in the open field, their victories would have produced a more permanent result. From Byzantine methods of fortification they learned much: the practice, of which examples were under their eyes in the Eastern Empire, was employed by them with advantage in their Syrian fortresses and was transferred by them to the West, so that the military architecture of the thirteenth century seems a direct inheritance from the Roman period. On the other hand, even if the crusading leaders had possessed the learning necessary for acquaintance with Greek manuals of theory, they might have mistrusted the practical incompetence whieh was unable to avoid wholesale disaster at Manzikert. As it was, left to their own resources in Asia Minor and Syria, they had no local experience to depend upon and were forced to experiment with opportunity. Their tactics were of a haphazard character; and, while the numerous chroniclers who recorded their battles shewed an observation from which it is easy to draw deductions, the Crusades produced no classical hand-book of warfare.

It has already been said that the Turkish strength lay chiefly in large forces of light cavalry, which, operating in an open area, pursued irritating tactics against which an enemy was helpless. To meet them effectively, it was necessary to choose ground on which their outflanking movements could be prevented. Where they closed in upon their opponents without the possibility of encircling them, the mailed horseman of the West had his advantage. In such a position also a combination of infantry with heavy cavalry ensured success to the crusaders; the crossbowmen in the infantry line countered the arrows from the Turkish horse-bows and prepared the way for the cavalry charges which decided the day. The proper observation of these conditions, combined with caution in keeping on the defensive until the attack could be delivered with a certain prospect of victory, led to the blow inflicted by Richard I upon Saladin at Arsūf in 1191, the culminating point of crusading successes which, had full advantage been taken of it, would have re-established the Franks in Jerusalem. Even at Antioch (1098) in the First Crusade, where the army was beset in front and rear, its disposition across the plain between the northern hills and the Orontes was a decisive element in its favour; the two Turkish forces were hindered from uniting, and while the combination of infantry and cavalry put the Turks to flight on the main front, detachments of heavy cavalry engaged the smaller body of horse in the rear with complete success. But, where precautions were disregarded, where, from mere rashness or out of necessity, an unfavourable position was chosen, or where infantry and horse failed to co-operate, only a happy accident could save the day. In the first great battle of the Crusades, at Dorylaeum (1091), defeat was avoided only by the sudden arrival of a lost contingent; at Ḥiṭṭīn (1187), the disaster which gave Jerusalem to Saladin was caused by the choice of an impossible battle-ground, and by the inability of an exhausted infantry to take its part in the ensuing conflict.

Thus, while the Crusades exhibit instances of judicious and even, as in Baldwin II's battle array at Danith (or Hab, 1119), of elaborate tactics, their leaders were liable to the same mistakes at the end as at the beginning. No scientific method of warfare was evolved from them. Even if the deduction could hardly fail to be drawn that the support of infantry was an aid to victory in certain circumstances, the principle was not fully extended to other occasions. Feudal chivalry put its trust in the horse and despised the infantry arm. Moreover, the prevalence of siege-warfare during the twelfth and thirteeenth centuries in Europe delayed systematic improvement in the field and tended to be the preoccupation of the foot-soldier. While the castle and walled town were still of military significance, a campaign resolved itself into a succession of sieges; the defeated side in a pitched battle could prolong a war by taking to its fortresses. Thus battles like Lincoln (1141) were often a diversion from a siege, fought under the walls of strongholds against a relieving force. There seems also to have been little study of enemy tactics apart from the familiarity which might be gained with them in the course of a protracted war. As a consequence, European warfare in the twelfth and thirteenth centuries shews a somewhat bewildering variety of practice behind which lies no constructive idea. It was not until the close of this period that the notion of cavalry as the all-important arm in the battlefield was seriously abandoned; now and then, as at Legnano (1176), confidence in cavalry to achieve a victory may have been shaken, but, whether acting alone or riding in to finish the work prepared by infantry, it was long regarded as the essential element.

It is interesting to trace the details of individual battles during this period, but a comparison of them reveals differences without discovering any co-ordinating principle. The essential distinction between the battles of the Crusades and contemporary battles in Europe lay in the fact that in the second case the cavalry on both sides was fully armed; the fights were not between heavy cavalry and infantry on one side and light horsemen on the other, but between forces whose chief arm was their heavy cavalry, whether supported by infantry or not. Thus the order of battle was different; the cavalry took the front line, with infantry in reserve to meet the enemy's horse with their spears if the front line were broken, or a mass of infantry was brought into the middle of the front line with cavalry on the wings. At Bouvines (1214), where there is some difference of opinion about details, this seems to have been the arrangement adopted on both sides. As usual, the opposing armies were divided into three "battles," each commanded by its own leader; the front line was placed as described, with spearmen and crossbowmen in the middle, covering the central body of cavalry, which, in the middle of the second line, was supported by infantry at the back of the cavalry wings.

While the foot-soldier, though present in large numbers, took a subordinate position in the field, and the mounted knight and man-at-arms were regarded as the decisive factor in battle, there were yet occasions on which the value of infantry to maintain a defensive position, where cavalry failed to stand an onset, pointed a moral which could not be mistaken. At Legnano the shock of Barbarossa's horsemen broke the front line of Italian cavalry, but the attack wore itself out against the firm resistance of the closely-ranked reserve of Milanese pikemen. It is true that here the routed horsemen rallied and materially stiffened the defence, but the credit of a victory which broke the ascendancy of feudalism in Italy belongs to the foot-soldiers of the free cities. In Italy and the Netherlands revolt against feudal lords was accompanied by the development of infantry forces and of a professional soldiery whose experience, at the service of the highest bidder, leavened European practice in war. We see also in some twelfth-century battles the employment of an expedient which had an important influence in the future. The use of dismounted horsemen in a defensive fight was not new. In the Gothic war of 552 Narses at Taginae had formed his centre by dismounting his *foederati*; the defensive square in which the early Frankish armies fought was strengthened by its horsemen, who took their places on foot with the rest. The *amour propre* of the feudal knight, however, was slow to encourage a practice which confounded him with his inferiors, and its systematic employment was long delayed.

In strategy feudal armies displayed even less advance than in tactics. It is obvious that, even where a general was familiar with the main features of the country covered by his manœuvres, his means for detailed knowledge were small, and he had to depend much upon the reports of scouts who could not always be trusted. In an unknown country, as the crusading expeditions through Asia Minor shewed, he moved blindly. Nowhere was this more conspicuous than in the unfortunate campaign of St Louis in Egypt (1250), in which, even without the chaotic disregard of prudence which caused his defeat and capture at Manṣūrah, the impossible route across the labyrinth of the Delta would in any case have meant disaster. The importance also of castles in warfare checked strategic development on broader lines. In England, throughout the twelfth and thirteenth centuries, success in war depended upon the possession and defence of castles, and strategy took the form of devising the best route by which a castle might be surprised or relieved and a battle in the open avoided. Thus the civil wars of Stephen's reign, with their complicated details, were fought round castles without any consistent plan of campaign; the wars of the Plantagenets in Normandy and the Angevin dominions were concentrated upon the reduction or defence of single fortresses; and the decisive fight with the barons and their French allies in the streets of Lincoln (1217) was the result of a cunning attack on a castle which formed no part of a larger scheme. The campaign of Lewes (1264), as conducted by Henry III, was an aimless attempt at the reduction of castles, in which he deliberately threw away his chance of making for a definite objective and left the field clear for his adversary. At Lewes Simon de Montfort shewed brilliant generalship, and it is possible that a year later, had he fathomed the seriousness of his situation in time, he might have saved himself from defeat. His delay, however, in realising the menace of the alliance between Prince Edward and the Earl of Gloucester kept him engaged in minor operations on the Welsh border until the line of the Severn was closed against him, and his subsequent endeavours to extricate himself from the trap into which he had fallen were successfully countered by his opponent until it was too late.

The success of Edward in the campaign of 1265 was the result of strategy exercised against an enemy neglectful of precautions, who, at the crowning movement, found himself bereft of succour in a position where tactics were useless. In the conduct of his wars in Wales (1277–1295) his military skill was at its height. These wars, waged in difficult country where campaigns were necessarily prolonged into the winter, led to changes in the composition of his army, the discussion of which belongs more properly to the history of the legislation in which these years were so fertile. Feudal obligations of military service were modified and transformed by the system of longer service for fixed payment. While in this direction feudal barriers were broken down, the castle, the symbol of feudalism, was employed as the means of controlling the conquered districts; as yet its military importance was unchallenged, and its defensive superiority was for the time being firmly established.

But the Welsh wars brought about a change which, for the present purpose, is of greater moment. The traditions of cavalry battles in which Edward had been reared were of little help in a mountainous country, and reliance had to be placed in a greater degree than usual upon the infantry. Up to this time the foot-soldier's chief weapons had been the pike and crossbow. The use of the bow, as distinguished from the crossbow or arbalast, had been encouraged and even enjoined by legislation; the shortbow, drawn from the breast, had been long familiar, though overlooked in favour of the crossbow, and the longbow, which was aimed from the ear, had made its appearance. From whatever source the longbow in England was derived, its home was in Wales, and it had played its part in the conquest of Ireland by the Norman settlers from South Wales. In the Welsh wars it came for the first time into prominence in the English service; and henceforward, until it was finally displaced by the progress of newer inventions, it remained the characteristic English weapon.

The value of the longbow was tested in the Scottish wars which followed. Here, as in Wales, the English horseman was opposed to squadrons of foot-soldiers on the defensive with but little cavalry support. At Falkirk (1298) the strength of huge masses of infantry in close order to keep cavalry charges at bay threatened defeat to the English, until the archers were brought up and, raining their arrows into the compact "schiltrons" of the enemy, opened the way for the horsemen to do their work. Had such tactics been properly employed at Bannockburn (1314), the English army might have obtained an advantage which it did its best to forfeit; as it was, in the haste and disorder of the attack the archers were deprived of their opportunity. Those who managed to inflict loss upon the Scots were ridden down by a squadron of Scottish horsemen posted on their flank, and the English cavalry failed miserably for the lack of the support which they had denied themselves. The crushing defeat of Bannockburn proves little in itself, for the chances of success from the beginning were entirely in favour of the Scots; but Falkirk had shewn that cavalry, without the aid of a sufficient force of footmen armed with missiles, could only dash itself in vain against a wall of spearmen. Long before, at Hastings, the value of a combined body of horse and bowmen against a mass of infantry had been proved; these later lessons shewed that it was necessary to victory.

That such lessons had been taken to heart is proved by the gradual tendency to adopt an order of battle in which horsemen and archers take the defensive. The experiment of dismounting horsemen to stand a cavalry charge with their spears on foot has been mentioned. It was employed in combination with archery at Boroughbridge (1322), which thus forms a landmark in the change of English tactics, and the practice was again exemplified at Dupplin Muir (1332), where the disinherited barons overwhelmed the Scottish force which, charging on their centre, was thrown into confusion by the archers posted in open order on the wings. Its use in the French campaigns of Edward III met with striking success; tried upon more than one occasion, it was responsible for the victory of Crécy (1346), where the squadrons of English archers, set obliquely outwards on the flanks of each of the three main battles of dismounted horsemen, presented a front like the teeth of a harrow to the French army. The success of the formation was complete: the Genoese crossbowmen who opened the offensive from the French side missed their marks and were impatiently ridden down by the charge of French horsemen, who, after repeated efforts, failed to break the English line and were shot down from the flanks.

The Hundred Years' War continued the advance which under Edward I had put an end to the stationary period in which the supremacy of cavalry had been uncontested. While England, with the development of its archery, established itself as the first military nation in Europe, it also commanded an army raised on the system of commissions of array which had superseded the old feudal levies; an army prepared for long service in the field and led by experienced captains. The fourteenth century witnessed the development of the professional soldier on a large scale. The exploits of mercenary captains and their trained companies, who followed war as a game and went anywhere where there was fighting to be done, fill the annals of the French war; the civil strife of the Italian states produced the *condottieri* whose ability and ambition won principalities and controlled the political situation. At the same time, with this increase in military efficiency, there was little advance in great qualities of generalship. Edward III and the Black Prince, at Crécy and Poitiers, shewed resource at a crisis; but there was no genius in the conduct of the campaigns which preceded those victories. The English campaigns in France were long processions with uncertain objectives, spreading devastation through a hostile country without regard to the necessity of keeping in touch with a base of operations. Both victories were won at moments in forced retreats when the English army was in danger of being cut off from its destination; they were sudden rallies at a point at which fighting was the last resource, and left the victorious side as exhausted as its opponents. They proved the superiority of English arms, at Crécy to a foe which relied upon outworn tactics, at Poitiers to a clumsy plan of attack which shewed that the lesson of Crecy had not been forgotten but had been imperfectly comprehended. While, after Poitiers, the French, under the influence of Bertrand du Guesclin, adopted the expedient of avoiding pitched battles and allowing the enemy to wear themselves out in a ravaged country, the English pursued their familiar marches through the interior. John of Gaunt's parade of his forces in 1373 through northern and central France, and Thomas of Woodstock's expedition to the relief of Charles of Brittany some years later, conducted by routes which were not merely circuitous but went far in the opposite direction to the places aimed at, met with no opposition and had no result other than the thinning of the invaders by famine and disease.

By the close of the fourteenth century, then, strategy among the Western armies was undeveloped, and had little opportunity of improving. But in tactics the temporary superiority of the defensive signally successful at Crécy had altered traditional conceptions of the art of war. We have seen the armed horseman, in the later days of the Roman Empire, proving his capacity to strike a decisive blow at a host in which infantry was the superior arm. The horseman, throughout the period in which the medieval nations were being formed and throughout the epoch of the supremacy of feudal institutions, ruled the course of battle; if he learned the value of co-operation with infantry, it was he who decided the day. The necessity of an infantry force in the line of battle could hardly be overlooked; examples of battles in which a cavalry charge was successful against a mixed army of horse and foot are very exceptional. Nevertheless, it was not until the English archers took the field in formidable numbers that the feudal trust in horsemen was shaken. In their first great success, at Falkirk, they were in action against large bodies of foot-soldiers and were used to ensure the success of a charge of horse. At Crécy they were opposed, with bodies of dismounted horsemen, to the attack of cavalry. At Poitiers they were met by an attack of dismounted horse modelled on the English method of array, and proved how ill this was calculated to break their defence. Finally, in the victory of the Black Prince at Navarrete (1367), the Spanish horse, trained in the lessons of warfare against the Moors, was incapable of meeting this new formation; and later, at Aljubarrota (1385), Spanish chivalry was once more defeated by an order of battle which the Portuguese king had learned from his English allies.

Meanwhile, even in the day of the English archer's triumph, new methods of warfare were beginning to appear. The archer himself, while offering a difficult problem to any attacking force, could not fail to be met with obvious precautions of defence. Plate armour, slowly introduced, was gradually superseding mail, until it became a protection for the whole body against which arrows were comparatively harmless. A new arm was coming slowly into use, at first cumbrous and ineffective, which, used for the defence and attack of strongholds in the fourteenth century, put an end to the importance of the castle, and was to supersede the longbow in the field. The appearance of a new improvement of infantry in the trained warriors of the Swiss cantons, and the development of military science in Italy, were signs of an epoch which had left the traditions of feudal war entirely behind; while, at the very end of the century, on the field of Nicopolis (1396), the last crusaders were defeated by the Eastern power whose victories were to outlast the Middle Ages and bridge the interval between them and the modern world.

CHAPTER XXIV.

CHIVALRY.

Chivalry is a subject which has attracted the attention of writers from its earliest days to the present time. Modern historians hold very different opinions as to its origin and influence, and even as to its meaning. One calls it a feudal dignity, another a military institution, a third says it was less an institution than an ideal, and a fourth describes it as a view of life. Contemporary authorities also give it varied meanings. Monstrelet explains that a victory gained by the Duke of Burgundy over the Liégeois was won by the superior training of the chivalry and nobility, and that the people were over-confident and not so well armed: here it clearly means fighting-men of a higher class. When Joinville says that the second part of his Memoirs of St Louis will speak of his gallant chivalry and deeds of arms, it stands for the qualities considered characteristic of chivalry as a class. Froissart, describing how one of a batch of knights made before an attack on the enemy encouraged his fellows by urging them to shew their new chivalry, uses it as the equivalent of knighthood. Caxton, in his translation of the *Ordre de Chevalerie*, speaks of the rule of the Order, and of gentlemen that intend to enter chivalry, as if it were an institution, and also mentions its exercises and usages. Passages could be quoted to illustrate other interpretations, but enough have been given to shew its many-sided character.

The old French word *chevalerie* and the English "chivalry" are derived from the Latin *caballarius*, from *caballus* a horse, originally a pack-horse and afterwards a war-horse, and the chevalier was literally the man on the horse. In the Latin then in use he was called *miles*, but in the period which elapsed between the reign of Charles the Great and the Crusades horse-soldiers became the superior branch of the army, and grades appeared amongst them. By the later twelfth century the name was, strictly speaking, confined to the upper ranks of this class and was only applied to those who had been invested with the insignia of knighthood[1]. The English word knight (A.-S. *cniht*) acquired the same meaning.

It seems reasonable therefore to assume that the Knight, regarded as the gentleman who served on horseback, developed out of the mounted soldier, but it is not easy to see how the system of knighthood arose. Several theories have been advanced as to its origin, and it has even been suggested that it was inspired by the Romans or the Saracens; but the view most widely accepted now is that it grew out of the custom of the Germanic tribes of solemnly investing their young men with arms when they reached the age of adolescence. In the council of the tribe, says

[1] Oman, *Art of War in the Middle Ages,* 2nd edn, I, pp. 372—3.

Tacitus, one of the chiefs, usually his father or some other near relation, presented the youth with a lance and shield, and from that time he was recognised as a man and a warrior, and considered to belong to the republic, whereas before he had been regarded as a child, belonging only to his home. Selden and Du Cange saw in the adoption of a son by arms, practised by the Goths, a contributory cause of the development of chivalry. When Theodoric adopted the King of the Heruli in this manner, he wrote to him with a gift of horses and arms declaring him his son, but in some cases the adopted was personally arrayed with arms by the adopter. This ceremony was therefore somewhat similar to the Germanic rite, but it was not universally observed.

Some writers think that feudalism was in a large measure responsible for the growth of chivalry, and find a great similarity between feudal and chivalric ceremonies of investiture. Feudalism provided a very suitable environment for chivalry, and life in a feudal castle afforded opportunities for knightly training. Feudal fealty may also have encouraged the growth of chivalric troth, but the two were quite different; one was based on an hereditary system of land tenure, the other was a voluntary obligation, and the vassal should not be confused with the knight. Professor Bury has drawn attention to the interesting fact that generations of frontier warfare between the Greeks and the Saracens developed a type of warrior very similar to the feudal baron, and a chivalrous ideal analogous to, but quite independent of, Latin chivalry.

It is not possible to say exactly when chivalry took definite shape, but the ceremony by which knighthood was conferred in the eleventh century was of a very simple description. William of Malmesbury says that William the Conqueror, when Duke of Normandy, received from the King of France *militiae insignia* (the insignia of knighthood), and that Henry I *sumpsit arma* (assumed arms). Roger of Wendover states that William *Henricum ... cingulo militari donavit*, which gives the impression that girding with the baldrick was the typical feature. In the Empire, the *swertleide*, the ceremonial girding on the sword, was the important point, as seen in the knighting of Frederick Barbarossa's sons. In France, at the end of the twelfth century, after the sword, spurs, and other arms had been put on the new knight, he was given a vigorous blow on the neck or the ear with the palm of the hand, usually accompanied by the admonition, *sois preux*. The blow was called the *colée*; its meaning is not clear, but it has been suggested that it represents the last injury a knight could honourably endure, or that it was to remind him of the buffet given to Christ when He was before Caiaphas, or was merely to impress the occasion on his memory. It was introduced into Germany at a somewhat later date, but in England a light blow with the flat of the sword took its place.

Far more elaborate was the method of initiation employed in the creation of the Knights of the Bath which is described in *De Studio militari* by Nicholas Upton, who wrote in the reign of Henry VI. The squire served the king with one course at dinner, and after he had himself dined, retired to the chamber assigned to him. His head was shaved by the king's barber, and he then went to his bath which was covered with a linen cloth. While he was in it, lords and knights appointed by the king came and gave him his charge, and declared certain points belonging to the Order: he must love God, be steadfast in the faith, uphold the Church, and be true to his sovereign and his word. He must also uphold widows in their rights, and succour them and maidens with his goods if required. He must not sit in any place where judgment is wrongfully given, but must as far as is in his power bring all murderers and extortioners to justice. They thereupon took up some water from the bath, and made the sign of the cross on his left shoulder and kissed it, wishing him "worshipe" in the name of God. After his bath the squire was laid in a bed very grandly arrayed, and when he arose was clad in hermit's garments of Colchester russet, and kept vigil in the chapel all night. In the morning he confessed, heard mass, and offered a taper with a penny in it. He returned to his chamber, and was reclothed in a red coat and mantle, with a white coif and girdle, with a white lace on his breast, and white gloves. He mounted his horse, and, after he had alighted, entered the king's presence, two knights put on his spurs and sword, and the king kissed him and commanded him to be a good knight.

It is not known when the "Order" of the Bath was recognised as a distinct subdivision of the Order of Knighthood. The Wardrobe Accounts record gifts of beds and robes to knights by Henry III and Edward I, and Selden quotes an entry on a Close Roll of the sixth year of King John ordering the sheriff of Southampton to allow Thomas Esturmy a scarlet robe, another of green or brown, and a pair of linen sheets, and other articles, as he was to be made a knight. These were things which Knights of the Bath would need, so it seems possible that we have here some of those creations which ended in the emergence of the "Order."

A little French poem called *L'Ordene de Chevalerie*, written in the thirteenth century, describes similar rites. It purports to be the reply of a prisoner, Hugh of Tabarie (Tiberias), to a question put to him by his captor, Saladin: How is a knight made? It explains the mystical significance of what was done. The squire ought to come from the bath as free from sin as a babe from the font, and by knighthood should be led to win a bed in Paradise. The scarlet gown shewed that he must give his blood in the service of God and the Church, the white belt that he must keep his body pure. His other garments, and his sword and spurs, all had their meaning according to the poem.

Knighthood was generally conferred by the sovereign or by some person delegated by him, such as the commander of his army, but this was not always the case; ecclesiastics could most certainly bestow knighthood. When it was given by a priest, a religious service of consecration was used, which made it almost a sacrament. The first example of this in France was the knighting of Amaury, son of Simon de Montfort, in 1213 by two bishops. The chronicler who narrates it thought it very unusual, but it may have been in use earlier elsewhere, as M. Léon Gautier tells us that there is a manuscript giving the prayers for the ceremony which is not later than 1050, and probably earlier. In the Empire also dignitaries of the Church sometimes conferred knighthood.

The ceremony was generally reserved for some important occasion, one of the great festivals of the Church, or a public function, such as a coronation or a royal wedding. Knighting on the battle-field was always in fashion; it was as simple as possible, and consisted merely of the accolade and a few words pronouncing the squire a knight in the name of God. This method was also sometimes used in time of peace; it was thus that the Duke of Burgundy knighted Jacques de Lalain before his feat of arms with a Sicilian.

The usual age for knighthood was twenty-one, the legal majority, but it was sometimes bestowed on younger persons for special reasons. St Louis knighted the Prince of Antioch when he was only sixteen, but he was very "discreet."

Noble birth was a necessary qualification for knighthood, and was only dispensed with under exceptional circumstances. Chivalry was an extremely aristocratic institution when thoroughly developed, and this tended to foster pride of birth, and a determination to uphold the honour of the Order. In this sense it was very exclusive, but in another it was quite the reverse; it was diffused throughout the whole of Christendom, and its laws were the same in all countries. Consequently difference of nationality was no bar to intercourse among knights, and they formed something very like an international brotherhood. It was by no means unusual for them to visit foreign countries to perform feats of arms, and there was a feeling of comradeship even among enemies. In 1387 the English were fighting on the side of the Portuguese, and the French were assisting their adversaries, the Spaniards, but the French commander made good company with the English, as noble men of arms would, said Froissart, and an Englishman and a Frenchman jousted together before the King and Queen of Portugal and the Duke of Lancaster.

Just as the ceremony of initiation was at first very simple and afterwards became more elaborate, so too the Order itself developed greatly in the course of time. This change was partly due to the growth of civilisation, but there were also special causes for it, and among these we must place the Crusades. They created a demand for an increased number of knights, and the leaders of the expeditions took hired soldiers with them, knights serving for money, but on an honourable footing. Joinville had nine knights in his pay in the Holy Land, and he himself was in the service of St Louis. Failure to pay their wages was inevitably followed by defection, and liberality was a necessary quality in their employers, so perhaps for this reason it ranked high as a knightly virtue. Richard I, who was considered the crown of chivalry, was continually bestowing largesse and gifts, and inciting his young men by promises of reward; he thought the day lost on which he gave nothing.

The Holy Wars afforded a great incentive to courage, the fundamental virtue of chivalry; the desire to win Heaven by conquering the infidel enhanced the knights' natural love of fighting, and rivalry between crusaders of different nations stirred up a spirit of emulation. In active warfare their bravery was magnificent, sometimes almost superhuman, but they lacked self-control, and failed in passive endurance; during the terrible siege of Antioch in 1098 many deserted.

The Crusades should have afforded the Christians good military training, as the Turks were splendid fighters, but few of them learnt much, as they were satisfied with their own methods of fighting and despised strategy as unworthy of knights.

The difference between foot-soldiers and knights was very marked during the Crusades; when Richard I intended to attack the Sicilians he said that if a footman ran away he was to lose his foot, if a knight fled his belt was to be taken from him. Joinville relates that a sergeant who had pushed a knight had to kneel before him in his shirt, crave for mercy, and offer a sword so that the knight might cut off his hand if it pleased him.

The influence of the Crusades upon the ideals of chivalry was quite as important as their effect on its practical development. The crusaders were soldiers of the Cross fighting for the Christian faith, and the knights as leaders of the host were pre-eminently Christian warriors, and henceforth Christianity and chivalry were inseparably connected, at least in theory. When John of Burgundy, the duke's heir, proposed to lead an army against the Turks who were menacing Hungary, Sir Guy of Tremouille and others said that it was time he entered upon the Order of knighthood, and that he could not enter upon it more nobly than by going against the enemies of Holy Church.

In some ways the Crusades were detrimental to the ideals of chivalry: crusaders were taught that it was a sin to shew pity to an infidel; so mercy to the fallen, unless it were profitable, did not become one of its characteristic virtues. The Church must not, however, be held wholly to blame for this, for it was not only the Saracens who were the victims of the crusaders: at Constantinople in 1204, of killed and wounded there was neither end nor measure, says Villehardouin. Nor were the crusaders the only soldiers who indulged in slaughter: when the French were helping the Duke of Burgundy against the rebellious Flemings in 1382, they spared no more to slay them than if they had been dogs.

The doctrines that the Church could absolve men from their vows, and that it was not necessary to keep faith with infidels, were very pernicious, and frequently the Christians broke their promises. Nevertheless, a strong feeling grew up that it was incumbent upon a knight to keep his word, and the Saracens themselves were perfectly satisfied to take the word of St Louis that his ransom and that of his fellow-prisoners would be paid, and required no pledges. The Black Prince would not break his promise even when urged by his council to revoke a covenant, and Egas Moniz, tutor to Affonso Henriques of Portugal, offered his life in atonement when his pupil refused to keep an engagement he had made for him.

The literature of the period[1] had considerable influence on the development of chivalry; itself the outcome of chivalry, it fostered the growth of the force that gave it birth, a process of action and reaction. The *chansons de geste* were epics, and by extolling the great deeds of heroes incited their hearers to perform similar acts. The noblest of them, those which centred round the person of Charlemagne, held up a lofty idea of honour, of sacrifice in the service of God and the Emperor, and a high sense of the value of an oath of fealty. The *Chanson de Roland* also gave a beautiful picture of the devotion of brothers-in-arms. The romances of the Round Table, based on Breton lays of King Arthur and his knights, which became so popular not only in France but throughout Western Europe, were of a different type. Marvellous adventures, undertaken to satisfy mere caprice or a restless longing for change, replaced serious enterprises, and romantic love, especially love *par amours*, became a theme of absorbing interest. These features were reflected in the knight-errantry and gallantry of chivalry.

Devotion to ladies was one of the paramount duties of a knight; it was held that he ought to help them all to the utmost of his power, especially if they had been deprived of their rights, or were in distress of any kind. It was this spirit which made Sir John of Hainault offer himself as the champion of Queen Isabel, the ill-used wife of Edward II. In addition to the service which he owed to all ladies, a knight was expected to choose one as the special object of his affection. He exalted her as the most perfect of all creatures, and delighted to obey her commands however hard. To win her grace, or to enhance her reputation, he sought adventures, and fought for her both in war and tournaments. He frequently sent challenges to other knights for love of her, and Sir John de Vechin in 1402 announced that he had vowed to make a trial of arms, with the help of God and the lady of his affection. Sometimes the lover was content to worship his lady at a distance, but more often he tried to win her love in return for his, with a persistence which made it difficult for her to resist even if she were married. In any case the matter was kept secret if possible, and if he were honourable, he only saw her when a meeting could be arranged without blame falling on her. It was held that love made a man more hardy in deeds of arms, that it drove away fear and made him forget pain, and as a proof the examples of Lancelot and

[1] Cf. *infra* chap. xxv.

Tristan were quoted. It was a great incentive to courage and to courtesy, but as it disregarded marriage ties, it led to much deceit, even if not, as in many instances, to infidelity, and at its best it was a very artificial sentiment. It was, perhaps, an unconscious protest against the material view of marriage set forth by feudalism and the law. It seems to have been carried to the greatest lengths in the south of France and in Germany, and found literary expression in the poems of the troubadours and minnesingers. An extreme example was given in the exploits of Ulrich von Lichtenstein, who even, according to his own account, disguised himself in rags and ate with lepers in order to gain an interview with his lady.

Some writers are of the opinion that in the last half of the twelfth century there were in Languedoc and elsewhere *cours d'amours*, tribunals of ladies, which judged questions of chivalric love submitted to them by some third person on behalf of lovers whose names were carefully kept secret, and laid down rules to govern the art of love. This opinion is based on the writings of the troubadours, and on a book called *De Arte honeste amandi*, by a certain Andrew the Chaplain, who served Innocent IV from 1243 to 1254. Andrew quotes twenty judgments by various ladies, among whom is the famous Eleanor of Aquitaine, wife successively to Louis VII of France and Henry II of England. But it is very unlikely that there was anything in the nature of a permanent court of arbitration, and Andrew's book is so conventional that it has not the value of historical testimony; the judgments do not refer to actual cases judged by *cours d'amours*, but were merely the outcome of society amusements, analogous to the *tençons provençales*, a form of debate very popular at that time, and they ought not to be taken seriously.

A boy destined for knighthood had to undergo a long and careful training. At the age of seven he was taken from his mother's keeping, and sent to the castle of one of the great nobles to be educated with the lord's own children and other high-born boys and girls. Here the duty of loving God and the ladies was at once impressed upon him by the women of the household, whom he served as a page. Masters taught him such book-learning as was considered suitable to his station, and as a rule it included Latin and foreign languages. French, Dr Emil Michael tells us, was greatly spread abroad in court circles in Germany in the twelfth century; no doubt both French and Latin formed good mediums of communication between knights of different nationalities. Some nobles could not write, although they spoke two or three languages; the young Jacques de Lalain spoke, understood, and wrote both Latin and French, but he was particularly well educated. Knowledge of music, singing, and the art of making rhymes was thought very necessary, and great value was placed upon good manners, as courtesy was one of the most essential characteristics of a knight. Lighter accomplishments, such as dancing and playing at chess, tables, and other games, were not despised; a boy who was clever at them could do much to amuse the ladies and the guests entertained by his lord.

Physical culture was, however, the most important part of his training. From the age of fourteen, when he was promoted to the rank of a squire, it became harder and harder. He was gradually taught to use knightly weapons, to bear the weight of knightly armour, to ride, to jump, to wrestle, to swim, to hunt, to hawk, to joust, and to endure the utmost fatigue of all kinds. Marshal Boucicault as a youth accustomed himself to walking and running long distances, and to dancing in a coat of mail. He could spring from the ground on to the shoulders of a man on horseback, and ride astride there holding on by one hand. He could also, in full armour, climb up the under side of a long ladder by means of his hands only, and perform other acrobatic feats.

Duties of many kinds fell to the lot of squires: some attended their lord in his chamber, some served in the hall, tasted his food or bore his cup, and others had charge of his horse and arms. These services were not considered beneath the dignity of nobles; Joinville was carver to the King of Navarre. When squires were quite expert they attended their lords in battle, and took charge of his prisoners. Pages were also allowed in the field, although they did not fight. Froissart relates that at Crécy the life of Johan de Fussels was saved by his page, who followed him all through the battle and "relyved" him when he fell into a ditch; otherwise he would probably have been slain by rascals with knives, who went about killing Frenchmen as they lay on the ground. In some cases young men completed their chivalric education by travelling, going to tournaments, and studying customs in other lands.

Some squires, from motives of economy or other reasons, preferred not to take knighthood upon them, but if they were men of experience and valour they were treated with great respect, and put into positions of trust. Sir James Audley distinguished himself by his courage at the battle of Poitiers, and as a reward the Black Prince gave him five hundred marks of yearly revenues; this gift he immediately handed over to the four squires who had fought with him, saying that it was through their means and by their valour that he had gained honour.

Du Cange and Menestrier draw a distinction between a knight-bachelor and a banneret. The latter, according to them, must be a knight, and must have sufficient revenues to enable him to take a number of men into the field under his banner; but authorities differ as to the exact number required—some say fifty men-at-arms, some only twenty-five. The knight-bachelor carried a pennon; the ceremony of raising the banner, which transformed him into a banneret, took place before a battle, and Froissart gives examples of it. In 1380, when the English were drawn up in battle array before Troyes, Sir Thomas Tryvet brought his banner rolled up to the commander, the Earl of Buckingham, and said that if it pleased him he would that day display it, as he had revenues sufficient to maintain it. The Earl took the banner, said that it pleased him very well, and delivered it to Sir Thomas, praying that God would give him grace to do nobly that day and always. Sir Thomas then displayed the banner. Olivier de la Marche, who describes how Louis de Vieuville raised his banner at Rupelmonde, says that the Duke of Burgundy cut the tail off his pennon before returning it, thus transforming it into the square banner to which the banneret had a right. He adds that the herald stated in support of Louis' claim that he "ysse de ancienne banniere," and holds a "seigneurie" which was "anciennement terre de banniere;" so apparently the right to a banner was sometimes hereditary and attached to certain lands.

Men whose chief business was fighting needed good weapons and armour, and knights who could afford it had the best that could be obtained. The weapons commonly used were the lance, the sword, the battle-axe, and the misericord. Joinville, praising the gallantry shewn by the Christians at Manṣūrah, says that none made use of the bow, crossbow, or other artillery, but the conflict consisted of blows by battle-axes, swords, and butts of spears. The French despised bows and artillery, and thought their employment unworthy of gentlemen. The lance was generally made of ash with an iron head, and a pennon was attached to the top of the wooden part. The sword was the usual weapon for the mêlée; the Germans and Normans liked long swords, and the French short ones. Spain was famous for the manufacture of them, and the best came from Saragossa. The battle-axe was valuable for fighting at close quarters; Richard I did fearful execution with it.

A definite sequence of various kinds of armour developed during the Middle Ages: mail, plate and mail combined, and finally complete plate armour. Improvements were always being introduced, and when it reached perfection in the fifteenth century every part of the wearer was protected, the head, arms, body, legs, even the fingers and the toes. In addition, he had a large shield to ward off blows. Milanese armour was the best, but some came from Germany in the fifteenth century; the Germans borrowed the ideas and then produced a cheaper article; so they obtained the greater part of the industry, which was carried on at Nuremberg and Augsburg[1]. It was very difficult to penetrate medieval plate-armour before the introduction of fire-arms, and a knight was fairly safe unless he fell; then his heavy covering made him helpless, and he could be easily trampled to death, or a dagger inserted between the plates. Under normal circumstances he was not killed, because it was much more profitable to obtain a ransom for him. Large sums of money could be made in this way: the Duke of Anjou computed an adventure he had at Bergerac in 1377 as worth more than three hundred thousand francs, as all the chivalry of Gascony was taken. It was unchivalrous to treat noble prisoners harshly; Froissart praises the English for their generosity in this respect,

[1] R. C. Clapham, *The Tournament*, pp. 38–9.

but the Spaniards, he says, bound their prisoners in chains of iron, and in this lack of courtesy they were like the Almaynes. The hauberk, which covered the body, was by some considered a mark of knighthood, like the baldrick and gold spurs; Joinville says that in 1241 he had not put it on, meaning that he had not been knighted. Over the hauberk a knight wore a surcoat or tabard, and upon it and upon his shield his arms were displayed, so that it was easy to identify him. When the French rode out to meet the Turks under Bāyazīd near Nicopolis in 1396, the lords were all so richly dressed in their "cote armure" that they looked like little kings, which served them in very good stead when they were defeated, as the Turks saved them alive because they thought they would get such great ransoms.

If a knight disgraced himself he was degraded from the Order of chivalry; his spurs were hacked off, his sword broken, his arms reversed, and all his armour and insignia taken from him. In France, in the twelfth century, the proceedings were simple, but at a later date they became quite theatrical; the vigils for the dead were sung while the knight's arms were taken off, and he was afterwards borne on a hearse to church, where the office for the dead was finished.

The Military or Crusading Orders[1] were the outcome of two very different, almost conflicting, forces, chivalry and monasticism, brought together by zeal for combating the infidel; and the knights of these Orders, as long as they were true to their inspiration, embodied the ideal of a Christian soldier as it presented itself to the men of those days. The Templars and the Hospitallers of St John of Jerusalem developed into a permanent force for the defence of the Christian kingdom of Jerusalem. In both, the knights, whose duty it was to fight, became a superior class with distinctive clothing and higher rank. True to the rules of chivalry, they were an aristocratic body; no knight was admitted unless he could prove that he was of noble birth. As soldiers they were invaluable; on many a hard-fought field they shewed true knightly courage, and their discipline was superior to anything the medieval world saw until Charles VII of France formed his *gendarmerie*. Any knight who armed, or disarmed, or left the ranks without leave, was severely punished. In a small affray between the Turks and the French at Bait-Nūbah, in the Third Crusade, a Hospitaller charged the enemy before his companions came up, and he was only pardoned through the intercession of many influential persons. These Orders were not long in becoming wealthy and powerful, and far removed from their earlier austerity. The loss of the Holy Land forced them to leave Palestine; the Templars came to a tragic end, but the Hospitallers continued their war against infidels elsewhere, at Rhodes and then at Malta.

The Teutonic Order[2] first came into prominence at the siege of Acre in

[1] Cf. *supra* Vol. v, chs. viii and xx, and Vol. iv, refs. in Index.

[2] Cf. *supra* Vol. v, pp. 332–3, and *infra* Vol. vii.

1189, when it succoured wounded Germans. It took its statutes from the Templars, with the addition of a few from the Hospitallers. It suffered from the jealousy of the older Orders, and had some difficulty in asserting its independence, but in 1210 Herman of Salza obtained for it all the privileges they enjoyed. It is best known, however, by its crusade against the heathen in the Baltic Provinces. After a fearful war, which lasted fifty years, it succeeded, with the help of the Order of the Sword and various bands of adventurers, in conquering Prussia and setting up a strong government.

Spain and Portugal had military Orders of their own[1], engaged in the continual war they waged against the Moors. The most important in Spain were the Order of St James (Santiago) of Compostela, whose work in safeguarding the passages to the shrine of that saint developed into the general defence of the kingdom, and the Order of the Knights of Calatrava, who undertook the defence of the fortress of Calatrava, the key to Toledo. There was a branch of the Order of Santiago in Portugal, and other Orders which were also renowned for valour. The Order of St Benedict of Avis took charge at first of Evora, and afterwards of the fortress whose name it bore. The Order of Christ defended the fortress of Castro Marino, and made war against the Moors by land and sea.

Very different from these were the Orders of chivalry; they took their origin later, and did not grow up spontaneously in answer to a pressing need, but were deliberately founded by kings or other grandees, ostensibly from love of chivalry, but really in most cases with ulterior motives. Reserved for men of noble birth and irreproachable character, membership became a coveted honour, and was bestowed by the sovereigns, with great political skill, upon those whom they wished to reward or to attach to their interests. One of the most famous of these Orders was that of the Knights of the Garter, instituted by Edward III. There are many stories as to the origin of its name, but no credence can be attached to them. Some writers, following Froissart, give the date of its foundation as 1344; others on the evidence of payments for garters in the wardrobe accounts place it some years later, and the first feast in 1350. Edward sent heralds to publish it in France, Scotland, Burgundy, Hainault, Flanders, Brabant, and the Empire, and offered safe-conducts to any knights who cared to come and take part in the jousts and tourneys which accompanied it. His object was, probably, as Ashmole suggests, to gather round him the most active spirits from abroad and draw them to his party, as he was engaged in war with France. The number of the original knights was twenty-six, including the sovereign, who was the King of England. There were also twenty-six priests, and twenty-six poor knights. Unfortunately the original statutes have perished, and the earliest transcript of them dates from the reign of Henry V. The greater number of the ordinances deal with the election,

[1] Cf. *supra*, Vol. v, pp. 682–83, and Vol. vi, ch. xii.

installation, and clothing of the knights, but one lays down the rule that no knight may go out of the kingdom without the knowledge and licence of the sovereign, a very wise stipulation if he wished to retain them for his own service. Great care was taken to make sure that the knights were worthy of the Order, and Monstrelet relates that Sir John Fastolf was deprived of his Garter because he fled from the battle of Pataye, but it was afterwards restored to him as he made excuses which were considered reasonable. It was bestowed not only upon Englishmen but also upon foreigners of high position; the Count of Ostrevant won a prize at some jousts at Smithfield in 1390, and was afterwards made a knight, which caused great dissatisfaction in France, as it was reported that by taking the Garter he had become the King of England's man, and that none could enter into the Order unless he made oath never to bear arms against the Crown of England.

It was perhaps to counteract the influence of the Order of the Garter that the King of France instituted the Order of the Star in 1351. The knights swore not to accept any other Order without his leave, nor to go on distant journeys without giving him warning. The Order was initiated with great splendour, but the disaster to the French nobility at Poitiers put a stop to its fêtes. It lasted, however, until King Louis XI founded the Order of St Michael to counterbalance the new prestige of the Order of the Golden Fleece.

This celebrated Order, by far the most interesting of the many of a similar nature which were established in many countries in the century which followed the foundation of the Order of the Garter, was created in 1429 by Philip the Good of Burgundy, on his marriage with Isabella of Portugal and Lancaster. He stated that his object was to honour worthy knights and to encourage feats of chivalry, for the reverence of God, the maintenance of the Christian faith, and the honour of knighthood. Some of the rules of the Order were well calculated to excite knightly ardour, but some clearly inculcated loyalty to the duke and his house. Each knight swore on his election to render personal service if any one tried to damage the duke or his successors, to submit all quarrels between himself and other members of the Order to the arbitration of the duke or his deputy, and not to undertake wars or long journeys without his licence. To keep up a standard of conduct worthy of the Order, a stringent examination into the behaviour of each knight was made at meetings of the chapter, and they were all required to give information about their fellows. Any knight guilty of heresy, treason, or flight from the battle-field, was expelled from the Order; for less serious offences lighter punishments were inflicted.

Tournaments formed one of the favourite amusements of knights, and in earlier days played an important part in their education, by giving them practice in mimic warfare. It is impossible to trace their beginning; some late writers say that one was held by Henry the Fowler in the tenth century, while a chronicle of St Martin of Tours ascribes their invention to Geoffrey of Preuilly, who died in 1066. They are mentioned in chronicles of the eleventh century, and probably arose out of the sports and games engaged in by the young men of those days. The name *conflictus Gallici* given to them by Matthew Paris shews that they were believed to have been of French origin. Some rules attributed to Henry the Fowler, but certainly of much more recent date, shew the views held about these matters when chivalry had become mature. No one who had injured the Church, been false to his lord, fled without cause from the field of battle, made a false oath, committed an outrage on a woman, or engaged in trade, was to be allowed to take part in a tournament, and anyone who could not prove his descent from four noble families was to be chased from the lists.

They were at first very rough and dangerous; the Church was horrified at the waste of men, money, and horses, and Pope after Pope issued bulls excommunicating those who took part in them. The Lateran Council of 1179 even denied Christian burial to those killed in tournaments. Secular authorities also disapproved of them because disorders often arose when so many armed men gathered together, and many monarchs forbade them, but neither ecclesiastical nor lay censures seem to have had much effect. Stephen was greatly blamed for allowing them in England, and Henry II put a stop to them. Richard I reintroduced them into this country, because he did not wish French knights to think the English awkward and unpractised in arms, and also, perhaps, because they were a source of revenue, as he exacted payments for tourneying which were graduated according to rank and were payable in advance. They were soon controlled by royal ordinances, and infractions of rules were punished by forfeiture of arms and horses and by imprisonment. After this, although they were sometimes forbidden in troublous times, they were encouraged by the Crown under normal conditions. On the marriage of Edward III great jousts and tourneys were held which lasted three weeks; and John Tiptoft, Earl of Worcester, the Constable of England, by order of Edward IV drew up a list of rules as to the manner of gaining prizes.

From the time of Philip Augustus they were extremely popular in France, especially in the north-east and in the districts bordering on it. John I of Brabant, who was knighted in 1294, is said to have fought in no less than seventy, and to have been mortally wounded in the last. Many brilliant tournaments were held by the Dukes of Burgundy, and after the death of Charles the Bold the traditions of his house passed to the Empire with Maximilian I, who married his daughter Mary. The Germans had always been addicted to tournaments, but in earlier days they were somewhat rough; in the time of Maximilian they became very elaborate, and of almost weekly occurrence.

As civilisation advanced, devices for rendering tournaments less dangerous were introduced. Special weapons were used; a thirteenth-century ordinance directs that the lance should be blunted, and in the fourteenth century it was tipped with a coronal, which could catch on the armour but not pierce it. The swords were pointless, and not too heavy. René of Anjou even suggests that short spurs would be better than long, as they would do less harm in the press. Armour was padded to ward off blows and prevent jarring. A cushion over the chest of the horse acted as a buffer; he was carefully trained and often blindfolded and his ears stopped with wool, so that he might not take fright, swerve, and unhorse his rider.

The tourney proper was an encounter between two bodies of combatants, the joust was a single combat; generally both took place at tournaments in early days. At Chauvency in 1285 eighty couples met in the first two days, and a mêlée began late in the afternoon so that darkness might separate the fighters. By the fifteenth century the joust tended to supersede the mêlée, and when it was fought on horseback in the lists, a barrier was put up to prevent collisions between the horses; at first this was merely a rope hung with cloth, but from about 1430 planks were used. Jousters sometimes fought on foot, and during the last half of the fifteenth century barriers were put up even between them. Jousting at the tilt prevailed in England, but abroad other varieties were practised. Both in England and on the Continent meetings called Round Tables were held, at which the challengers met all comers, and also kept open house for them. A *pas d'armes* was similar, but some particular place was defended. Ladies were always present at tournaments, and were treated with great deference. When prizes came into fashion in the latter part of the thirteenth century, they presented them. These were often of considerable value, a precious stone, a falcon, a horse, or even the hand of an heiress. In addition to this, the conqueror was entitled to the horse and arms of the vanquished, and could also demand a ransom for his person; so tournaments were profitable to those who were highly skilled.

Besides the jousts of peace, as these friendly encounters were called, there were jousts *à l'outrance*; in these, ordinary weapons were used, and one or other of the combatants was often seriously hurt, or even killed. The opponents were not necessarily enemies; they often fought for the honour of their ladies or their country, or to gain renown in arms for themselves. There were also judicial combats, which were a matter of life and death, but they belong to the domain of law rather than to that of chivalry.

Tournaments reached their highest development in the first half of the fifteenth century; by the middle of the century it became customary to combine mummeries and pageants with them, and they began to decline. Mechanical contrivances and humorous devices on the trappings of the horses took all dignity from them, and in the sixteenth century more attention was paid to the pageantry than to the jousts. In spite of their faults they had served some useful purposes: they had done something to inculcate an idea of fair play, for nothing annoyed the spectators more than a foul stroke, and, by encouraging courtesy between knights from many different countries, they had softened national prejudices.

Heraldry was an important adjunct of chivalry; it fostered pride of birth, and acted as a spur to the desire for honour. As signs of nobility heraldic emblems were highly prized, and they were of practical value in enabling a knight to be recognised; on the battle-field his banner and his *cri d'armes* formed rallying points for his followers. Heralds of all countries worked under the same rules, and went freely from one land to another. The use of coats of arms came into existence about the middle of the twelfth century; the science of heraldry was fully developed by the end of the thirteenth, but by the latter part of the fourteenth it had become very elaborate and over-burdened with detail. Finally, it was subjected to royal authority, lost all initiative, and became merely pictorial.

The Court of Chivalry had jurisdiction in all quarrels concerning coat-armour, pedigrees, personal affronts, and other matters touching the honour of gentlemen of which the Common Law did not take cognisance. It had power to authorise combat for the judgment of these affairs, but frequently settled them by arbitration. Its most severe punishment was degradation from knighthood. It was most active in the fourteenth and fifteenth centuries; after that it sank into the position of an heraldic office, and by 1600 it was an anachronism.

All the ceremonies and adjuncts of chivalry were, as we have seen, simple in their early stages, grew more and more elaborate, and at last deteriorated; chivalry itself passed through the same phases. M. Gautier considers that it reached its apogee in the twelfth century and began to decline at the beginning of the thirteenth, but some writers do not detect any signs of deterioration until the end of that century or even later. Something may be due to the taste of the critic; in the twelfth century chivalry was more virile, but it was also ruder; in the thirteenth it was more refined, but more artificial and less serious. Its decline did not progress simultaneously in all countries. In Italy this started very early because the growth of commerce in the towns was not favourable to it. As we have seen, the Emperor Maximilian I tried to revive it in his dominions but without much success. In Spain there was an increase in the practice of chivalry in the fourteenth century, inspired, perhaps, by the visits of the Black Prince and Du Guesclin. In Portugal, after the decline of the Military Orders, its traditions were carried on by individuals, the most famous of whom were Dom Nuno Alvares Pereira, the Constable, and the sons of King John I—men who combined knightly daring and accomplishments with fervent religious faith. Affonso V won the title of the Knightly King in his expeditions against the Moors in Africa. He attracted to his court distinguished foreigners bent on deeds of arms, and many of his subjects visited other lands for the same purpose. Some of the causes of the decline of chivalry were inherent in its nature—its artificiality inevitably ended in lifelessness, the custom of giving largesse led to extravagance which ruined many knights, and the suicidal civil wars in England and France depleted the nobility and lowered their standards of conduct. Other causes were due to extraneous circumstances—the invention of fire-arms rendered medieval armour useless, cavalry ceased to be the dominant arm, and the development of the art of war made chivalric methods of fighting ineffective. The changes which took place in the later Middle Ages, the growth of trade, the rise of the middle class, the spread of education, all tended to produce conditions unsuited to the continuance of chivalry. In the broader sense, as a spirit inspiring men to fight for the right and protect the weak, it is still alive, but as an Order with distinctive characteristics, demanding special training and qualifications, it passed away with the age that gave it birth, leaving behind it, indeed, imperishable monuments of literature, real and fanciful, such works as Froissart's *Chronicles*, the *Mort d'Arthur* and *Amadis de Gaul*, and the mingled satire and ideal of *Don Quixote.*

CHAPTER XXV.

LEGENDARY CYCLES OF THE MIDDLE AGES.

No history of the Middle Ages would be complete without some account of the literature which, while reflecting more or less faithfully the social life, customs, and modes of thought of the period, kindled the imagination of the men of the day, and provided a far from negligible stimulus to their action. The Middle Ages were, in very truth, the ages of Romance, and the tales which enthralled the listeners of the eleventh and twelfth centuries are still potent with charm for the more sophisticated readers of to-day.

A familiar and oft-quoted passage in the twelfth-century *Chanson des Saisnes* by Jean Bodel sums up in a couple of lines the subject-matter of the vast body of medieval romance:

> "Ne sont que trois matières à nul home entendant,
> De France, de Bretagne, et de Rome le grant."

That is, for the Romance-speaking peoples of Europe, whom alone the writer had in mind, the only three subjects worthy of serious attention were the romantic legends which clustered round the figures of Charlemagne, Arthur, and Alexander the Great. Of these three the two first are by far the most important; few outside the circle of professional scholars are to-day interested in the fictitious adventures of Alexander—fact is here far more interesting than fiction—but no amateur of literature can afford to ignore such texts as the *Chanson de Roland*, *Aliscans*, *Syr Gawayne and the Grene Knyghte*, or the *Perceval* and *Tristan* poems.

From the purely literary point of view the Arthurian romances, as a whole, can perhaps claim superiority over the Charlemagne poems. These offer us no such monuments of conscious literary skill as the works of Chrétien de Troyes, the prose of the *Lancelot*, the *Tristan* of Gottfried of Strasbourg, or the *Parzival* of Wolfram von Eschenbach, but regarded as a collection of human documents the epic of Charlemagne and his peers stands alone. We have nothing in literature more poignant than the *Chanson de Roland*, nothing more purely human than the great *Geste* of Guillaume d'Orange.

So far as actual dates are concerned, the historical Arthur preceded Charlemagne by some three centuries, but as a theme for romantic literature the great Frank Emperor has the priority, and in discussing the cycles we may well follow the example of Jean Bodel and begin with the *Matière de France.*

1. The Charlemagne Cycle.

The *corpus* of the Charlemagne cycle consists of some seventy or eighty *Chansons de Geste*, as these poems are generally called, of which only a comparatively small number deal with the personal adventures of that monarch, or with events taking place in his reign[1]. It will be quite understood that, in the narrow limits at our disposal, it is impossible to deal adequately with such a vast body of romance. We can but outline the main themes and indicate the *chefs-d'œuvre* upon them[2].

The writers of the thirteenth century, probably influenced by the passage from Jean Bodel quoted above, classified the poems of the cycle under three headings, the *Geste du Roi*, the *Geste de Doon de la barbe florie*, and the *Geste de Garin de Monglane*; but this description M. Bédier dismisses as artificial, save in the case of the last group, which covers the romances dealing with the feats of *les Narbonnais* and the most famous member of that family, Guillaume d'Orange, a group which really does constitute a distinct cycle.

Of the romances dealing with Charlemagne himself—his *Enfances*, the woes of his mother (*Berthe aux grands pieds*), his persecuted childhood (*Mainet*), his adventures with the chivalric robber of the Ardennes (*Basin*), his supposed journey to the East (*Pélerinage de Charlemagne*), and his conquest of Brittany (*Chanson d'Aiquin*), are all quite fictitious. *Mainet* is based upon adventures of Charles Martel, but the tale of *Berthe* is pure folk-lore, the theme of the substituted bride; and Charlemagne was never in Brittany, and never made the pilgrimage to Jerusalem. The one poem which may be included in the *Geste du Roi*, and which really rests upon a historical foundation, is the *Chanson de Roland*, which, with the possible exception of the *Chanzun de Willame* (only discovered in 1903), is the oldest text of the cycle. It is an historical fact, recorded by the chronicler Einhard in his *Vita Karoli*[3], that, on 15 August 778, on the return march from an expedition against the Moors of Spain, the rear-guard of Charlemagne's army was surprised in a defile of the Pyrenees by the Basques and, according to the chronicler, slain to the last man, among the dead being "Hruodlandus Brittannici limitis praefectus." In this brief notice we have the germ of the *Chanson de Roland*, as told by one Turold, "ci fait la geste que Turoldus declinet."[4]

In the poem the story has been amplified into a classic theme of heroism betrayed and fidelity to death. Roland is the nephew of Charle-

[1] M. Bédier in *Les Légendes Épiques*, Vol. I, p. 1 and Vol. IV, speaks now of seventy or eighty, now of a *centaine* of texts.

[2] The reader who desires a fuller knowledge of the subject should consult the exhaustive study of M. Joseph Bédier, to whose epoch-making theory on the origin of the *chansons* we shall return later. See *Les Légendes Épiques, recherches sur la formation des Chansons de Geste*, 4 vols. Paris, 2nd edition, 1921.

[3] C. IX, SGUS, p. 12.

[4] MS. Oxford, conclusion.

magne, here represented under the traditional aspect of the white-bearded Emperor "à la barbe florie," who has reached the truly patriarchal age of two hundred years. He has warred for seven years in Spain, conquering all the cities save Saragossa, the seat of the Moorish king, Marsile. The Moor, fearing the power of Charlemagne, sends an embassy to solicit peace, promising to follow it himself, with a thousand of his nobles, to receive baptism. The question arises, who of the Emperor's nobles shall act as envoy to settle the terms, a dangerous errand, as no one feels assured of the good faith of the Moors. Roland proposes Ganelon his "parrastre," and the suggestion is unanimously approved, but Ganelon, who suspects Roland of designs upon his life, bitterly resents the choice, and while obeying the commands of his sovereign, vows to be avenged. But Ganelon is no coward, as this scene of protest might lead us to think; on his arrival at the Moorish court he behaves with all the arrogance which might be expected from an emissary of the great Emperor, and the reader is somewhat surprised that he escapes with his life. But he has arranged with the Moors an ambuscade into which the flower of the Christian army shall fall. Ganelon returns to camp, his mission safely accomplished, and Charlemagne prepares for the homeward march. Who shall command the rear-guard, and be responsible for the safety of the army during its passage through the defiles of the Pyrenees? Who, says Ganelon, but Roland, the bravest of all Charlemagne's knights? Roland suspects treachery, but accepts the post. Charlemagne would leave with him half the army, to assure his safety, but Roland proudly refuses: he will have but 20,000 men, but these include the twelve peers, the glory of Charlemagne's court, and Turpin, the valiant Archbishop of Rheims. The main army sets out on its march, and the doomed 20,000 remain on guard. The hills are high, the valleys shadowed, grey are the rocks, fearsome the defiles (*Halt sunt li pui e li val tenebrus, Les roches bises, li destreit merveillus*)[1]. The main army has hardly passed out of sight when the trumpets of the Moors are heard in the distance. Oliver, mounted on a rock, sees the innumerable army of their foes, and warns Roland that they are betrayed; the Paynims number at least 100,000, it is impossible for the French to withstand them. Charlemagne is still within hearing; let Roland sound his horn, and their comrades will come to their aid. Roland proudly refuses; were he to do so he would lose his glory in "douce France"; their foes are doomed to death. Oliver insists, always to meet with the same answer: the French can hold their own, their foes "tuit sunt a mort livret." "Rollanz est pruz, e Oliviers est sages"; before the headlong rashness of his friend the latter finally holds his peace, their foes are near, Charlemagne is now too far, Roland has not deigned to sound his horn, and their comrades must not be blamed for their fate.

[1] Gautier, II, 814–815.

> "Cist nus sunt près mais trop nus est loinz Charles.
> Vostre olifant suner vus ne l'deignastes,
> Fust i li Reis, n'i oüssum damage.
> Cil qui là sunt n'en deivent aveir blasme."[1]

The battle is joined, and at first the Christians hold their own, but their foes are too numerous, and though they fall by hundreds and thousands (Archbishop Turpin deals more than a thousand blows) they still press on. The French hold out during four attacks, but the fifth is fatal; of all the 20,000 but sixty are left alive. Roland's heart misgives him for the result; he appeals to Oliver, what shall he do? How let the Emperor know of their plight? Shall he sound his horn? Now the rôles are dramatically reversed—Oliver retorts on Roland with the arguments the latter had previously employed. He will not hear of a call for help, it will be great shame and reproach to all their folk:

> "Verguigne sereit grant
> E reproviers à trestuz voz parenz
> Iceste hunte durreit à l'lur vivant."[2]

Roland would not sound his horn when Oliver bade him, now it is too late. Roland asks why is Oliver wroth with him? Oliver replies that reasoned courage is not madness, measure is better than rashness, he has slain many by his folly:

> "Kar vasselage par sens nen est folie.
> Mielz valt mesure que ne fait estutie.
> Franceis sunt mort par vostre legerie."[3]

There is nothing left for them now but to die.

The Archbishop intervenes in their dispute: 'tis true that to sound the horn now will not save them, but at least it will bring Charlemagne back to avenge them, and to give their bodies Christian burial, that they be not left to be devoured by wild boars, wolves, or dogs. "'Tis a good word," says Roland, and putting his horn to his lips he blows till the blood streams from his mouth and the veins of his temples are ruptured with the strain. The echoes of the horn reach the ears of the Emperor, but Ganelon treats the summons lightly: they know Roland's pride, he will sound his horn all day for a hare, he is but jesting with his comrades:

> "Pur un sul levre vait tut le jur cornant:
> Devant ses pairs vait il ore gabant."[4]

There is no battle. But the horn sounds again, and Naimes, the wise Duke of Bavaria, intervenes: there is a battle raging, Roland is in danger, he has been betrayed, and by whom but the man who proposed him as leader of the rear-guard, and who would now prevent Charlemagne from going to his aid? In a flash the Emperor sees the truth, he orders

[1] *Op. cit.* II, 1100–1103.
[2] *Op. cit.* II, 1705–1707.
[3] *Op. cit.* II, 1724–1726.
[4] *Op. cit.* II, 1780–1781.

the arrest of Ganelon, and begins the return march in haste. From afar the Moors hear the sound of the French trumpets; 'tis Charlemagne who comes, and they turn in flight. But it is too late: when the Emperor arrives on the scene each step of the way is marked by dead and dying Christians, not a peer remains alive; Turpin lies where he fell, going to the aid of the dying Roland, and Roland himself, under a pine tree, his face turned towards his foes, has ceased to breathe.

The rest of the poem is taken up with the account of the pursuit and defeat of the Moors, daylight being miraculously prolonged for the purpose; the conversion of the Moorish sovereign; and the trial and death of Ganelon.

This is a brief analysis of what is not only the most important text of early French literature, but also one of the best constructed, most human and poignant romances which the genius of the Middle Ages has bequeathed to us.

I have referred above to the cycle of Guillaume d'Orange, the twenty-four romances composing which form the *Geste* of Garin de Monglane, the ancestor of the noble family of the Narbonnais. Garin de Monglane and his sons have a feud with Charlemagne; in the poem of *Girard de Vienne*, the Emperor, hunting the wild boar, becomes separated from his men, and is made prisoner by Girard, his brothers, and nephews. After considerable debate they make peace with their suzerain; Aymeri, still a youth, is the last to yield. When he does so, it is in words which sound the key-note of all the *Chansons de Geste*:

"Tant com vodroiz je serai vostre amis
Et qant vodroiz par le cors St Denis
Je reserai de vostre amor reschis."[1]

He will deal with Charlemagne as Charlemagne deals with him. This attitude of fierce independence, combined with an essential loyalty, is characteristic of all the heroes of the cycle.

Aymeri owes his title *de Narbonne* to the fact that, when Charlemagne offers the lordship of this city to that one of his nobles who will undertake to conquer it from the Saracens, he is the only one who dare accept the gift (*Aymeri de Narbonne*). We meet him again in old age, the proud father of seven gallant sons (*Les Narbonnais*) who, with the exception of the youngest, have already attained the age of knighthood. At the great feast of Easter, Aymeri, gathering his sons around him, bids them not wait for his death for their heritage, they shall have no foot of his land, that he reserves for the youngest; he won Narbonne for himself, they must follow in his footsteps, and in lordly fashion he allots to each what he deems a fitting heritage. The three eldest are to go to the court of the Emperor, where Hernaut shall be chief councillor, Bernard seneschal, and Guillaume standard-bearer, all of which comes to pass.

[1] Cf. Bédier, *Légendes Épiques*, Vol. I, p. 29.

It is with the fortunes of the third son, Guillaume, that the remainder of the cycle is concerned. We find him in *Le Couronnement de Louis* acting as guardian and protector of the young king, rescuing him from the plots formed against him, establishing him firmly on the throne, and marrying him to his sister Aaliz. But Louis is ungrateful; when he distributes lands and honours to his subservient courtiers Guillaume is passed over; in towering indignation the hero upbraids the ungrateful king, recalling, in order, all the services he has rendered, ending each recital with the slightly varying refrain:

"De cest service ne te membra il gaires
Cant sans moi as departis tes marches."

In vain Louis offers him gifts which Guillaume proudly refuses; he will do as his father did before him, and conquer for himself a heritage (*Le Charroi de Nîmes*). He turns south to the lands occupied by the Saracens, conquers Nîmes and Orange (*La Prise d'Orange*), wins and weds the Saracen queen, Orable, who is baptised and receives the name of Guibourc, and as Guillaume d'Orange "le marquis au court nez" (most probably, as M. Gaston Paris suggested and as recent discoveries have confirmed, "au courb nez") becomes famous as the most determined opponent of the Saracens.

Now a new hero comes upon the scene. As Charlemagne had a valiant nephew, Roland, so Guillaume has a no less valiant nephew, Vivien, a true son of his race[1]. On the day he is dubbed knight he takes an oath never to flee a lance's length before the Saracens (*Le Covenant Vivien*), and his fidelity to his vow causes his death. In the famous poem of *Aliscans* the Saracen king, Desramé, with a powerful fleet, lands at Aliscans and ravages the surrounding country. Vivien, with his cousins, attacks him in wholly inadequate force, and, faithful to his vow, prefers death to retreat. He contrives to send a message to his uncle at Orange, and Guillaume, hastening to the field of battle with such men as he can collect, is in time to receive the lad's dying confession, and messages of love to Guibourc, who has been as a mother to him. Guillaume, priest for the nonce, communicates the boy with the *pain bénit*, and sees him die in his arms:

"Dex, recoif s'arme par ton digne commant
Qu'en ton serviche est mors en Aliscans."[2]

But Guillaume himself is in the greatest danger: all his companions are slain, and he only succeeds in escaping disguised in the armour of a dead Saracen. He reaches the gates of Orange, to be denied entry by his wife,

[1] A distinct note of this group is the intense family pride which characterises all the members, male or female; the descendants of Aymeri de Narbonne "bien traient au linage."

[2] Cf. *Aliscans*, II, 786–787.

who refuses to believe that her husband would have returned without the nephews to whom he was so warmly attached. Convinced at last of his identity, Guibourc shews herself a worthy help-mate; she bids Guillaume seek the court of his brother-in-law King Louis, and demand the aid the latter is pledged to render every seven years; she and her maidens, dressed in armour, will keep the enemy at bay, the while from her private treasure she is assembling a fresh army. Guillaume follows her advice, forces aid from the reluctant Louis, and discovers a champion in a gigantic young Saracen, Rainoart, who has been acting as scullion in the royal kitchen, but is, in fact, brother to Guibourc. Thanks to his valour the Saracens are defeated; Guillaume retires to a hermitage, whence he issues once more to combat the enemies of Christianity (*Le Moniage Guillaume*), and where he dies in the odour of sanctity.

In 1903, a hitherto unknown Anglo-Norman poem, *Le Chanzun de Willame*, was privately printed by the anonymous possessor of the manuscript. The text dates from the thirteenth century, but is based upon an earlier French original, which in the opinion of scholars cannot have been written later than the commencement of the twelfth, and probably is as early as the eleventh century—*i.e.* it is contemporary with the *Chanson de Roland*. The author obviously knew the *Guillaume* cycle as we have it; he was familiar with earlier forms of the *Vivien* poems, and their dénouement in *Aliscans*. It is certainly curious that the earliest manuscript of the *Chanson de Roland* and the only extant version of the *Chanzun de Willame* should both be preserved in England.

Another interesting group of the Charlemagne poems deals with the conflicts of the Emperor and his successors with their rebellious vassals. To this group belong the romances of *Ogier le Danois*, *Girard de Roussillon*, and *Renaud de Montauban*; the last, known also as *Les Quatre Fils Aymon*, retains its popularity as a folk-romance to this day.

The above is a very brief summary of an extensive and important body of literature; we may now ask what is the dominant character of the cycle, what was the public to whom it was addressed, and how far may it be held to repose upon genuine historical tradition?

The character of the *Chansons de Geste* is strongly marked; they are all bellicose to a degree. When the heroes, be they who they may, are not fighting against the enemies of Christianity they are at odds with the suzerain lord. The *Chansons de Geste* are *chansons* of Feudalism, and reflect with truth the generally prevailing social conditions. From this point of view they may be rightly deemed historical. Again, certain of the characters who appear in them had their actual historical counterparts. Charles Martel, Charlemagne, and Louis really lived, though the deeds ascribed to each severally are frequently borrowed from the events occurring in the reigns of their predecessors or successors. There was a Roland who died at Roncesvalles, though the agents of his death were the native Basques, and not the Moorish invaders. Ogier (Autcharus) was in actual fact a rebellious vassal of Charlemagne; Guillaume, Count of Toulouse, really warred against the Saracens in Spain and the south of France, wedded a wife named Guibourc, and died a hermit in the valley of Gellone, where his memory is still reverenced as St Guillaume du Désert. M. Bédier has given a list of fifty-five characters of the cycle who have a genuine claim to represent historical prototypes.

It was long held as an article of faith that, taken as a whole, the Charlemagne cycle was a genuine record of contemporary events, enshrined originally in short chants, "cantilènes," which in process of time, becoming linked together, grew into the *Chansons* we possess. The facts that not a single "cantilène" has survived to our day, and that we possess no text of a *Chanson de Geste* of earlier date than the end of the eleventh century, were insufficient to impair the popularity of this theory. It has now, however, been boldly attacked by M. Joseph Bédier in his epoch-making work. The theory of this distinguished scholar, as summed up by him in the concluding pages of his book, is briefly: "Les Chansons de Geste sont nées au XIe siècle seulement." We possess them in what is practically their original form. The historical element preserved in them is to be traced to various monkish chronicles and local legends, exploited by the monks and minstrels on the great pilgrimage routes through Europe. The three main goals of pilgrimage in the eleventh century were the shrine of St James (Santiago) at Compostela, Rome, and Jerusalem, and there were minor centres of popular devotion, such as St Guillaume du Désert and Ste. Marie Madeleine de Vézelai. It is along these routes of pilgrimage that the *Chansons de Geste* are localised: *e.g.* the author of *Ogier le Danois* was perfectly familiar with the great roads leading to Rome. The authors of the *Chanson de Roland* and the poems recording Charlemagne's victories in Spain were equally familiar with the route to Compostela—they had seen the reputed tombs of Roland and Oliver at Blaye, the relics of Roland and Charlemagne preserved at Roncesvalles, and beyond that route they knew nothing of Spanish geography. The *Chronicle of Turpin* is nothing more than a chapter in the *Livre de St Jacques*, otherwise known, from the copy preserved at Compostela, as the *Codex Callixtinus*, a composition designed for the use of pilgrims. Here Charlemagne appears as a veritable knight of St James.

A similar origin is traceable for all the *Chansons de Geste*: they are connected either with the great pilgrimage routes and the various stages upon one or other of them, or with sanctuaries where the faithful flocked to adore the relics of some local saint, or with centres of popular assembly, the great fairs held annually in the *parvis* of some famous church, as at Cambrai or St Denis. The confraternities of minstrels attached to such churches (*e.g.* at Fescamps) collaborated with the clergy in exploiting the local legends—the *Chansons de Geste* are the combined work of clerks and minstrels. As M. Bédier puts it tersely, "If there had been no tomb of Roland at St Romain de Blaye, no hermitage at Gellone, no shrine of Ste. Marie Madeleine at Vézelay, there would have been no *Chanson de Roland*, no cycle of *Guillaume d'Orange*, no *Girard de Roussillon.*" The *Chansons de Geste* are essentially popular romances, composed not in the interests of one class, the nobles and warriors of court and camp, but for a genuine and mixed public, men who took their part in crusade and pilgrimage, and chaffered at the annual church fair. Regarded from this point of view they become exceedingly interesting; they are human documents, throwing a light upon the general life of the period; their themes, zeal for the Christian Faith, loyalty to the sovereign lord, resistance to the arbitrary will of a feudal seigneur, were themes understood of the people, they formed part of their every-day life, and we need be no longer surprised at the extent and volume of the Charlemagne romances, or at the fact that they were popular outside the country of their birth, and were rendered into English, Italian, and Scandinavian translations. The stories made appeal not merely to a French but to a European public, living under like social conditions, actuated by like religious aims. To these people it was "a far cry" to the central authority; there might indeed be an imperial court, with an Emperor who, to those who came in touch with him, was a more or less impressive and awe-inspiring figure, but that central power operated within a restricted radius; the actual authority was the feudal lord—duke, count, or baron—of the district immediately concerned.

The distinguishing feature of the feudal system was the linking up of all grades of society by a chain of reciprocal and clearly understood duties and responsibilities. The nobles owed service to the sovereign from whom they held their fiefs, the sovereign owed protection to his vassals. All down the social scale the principle held good—protection from above, service from below. That the protecting powers were not infrequently guilty of injustice and oppression, that the vassals were independent, frequently rebellious, is undeniable. The feudal system certainly interfered with individual liberty and development, and thus its eventual disappearance was inevitable; at the same time the principle upon which it was based, its recognition of a common interest and reciprocal duties, undoubtedly made for solidarity. At its worst, feudalism produced glaring abuses; at its best, it offered a basis for human society which modern ingenuity has so far not improved upon. A knowledge of the real functioning of the system is essential if we would understand the spirit of the *Chansons de Geste*, whether the central theme be the relation of the hero to the imperial power, as in the *Guillaume d'Orange* romances, or feuds between nobles of practically equal rank, as in *Renaud de Montauban*. The romances are in a very real sense historical documents, preserving for us a vivid and vital record of a period essentially alien to modern conceptions.

Incidentally we may point out that the theory of the origin of the *Chansons de Geste* advocated by M. Bédier agrees in a most interesting manner with modern interpretations of the underlying cause of the conflicts between the Italian towns. The routes of international communication were factors of vital importance in the social, commercial, literary, and artistic life of the Middle Ages.

II. The Arthurian Cycle.

When we turn from the *Matière de France* to that of *Bretagne* we find ourselves at once in a different atmosphere; we have passed from a world of reality to one of pure romance. Exaggerated as the description of the feats of the heroes of the *Chansons de Geste* may be, they are yet, *au fond*, the normal actions of men of that period. They are warriors of flesh and blood, their consorts true women, faithful wives, and devoted mothers (*e.g.* Guibourc, and the mother of the *Narbonnais*). But in the Arthurian cycle we find ourselves in a world of illusion and faërie—the knights war with forces of another world; they are confronted with giants and demons; smitten by darts from invisible hands; they ride on a mystic quest whose goal is life *perdurable*; their councillors are sorcerers; the ladies they woo are of fairy race.

In tholdè dayès of the king Arthour,
Of which that Britons speeken greet honour,
Al was this land fulfild of fayerye.
The elf-queen, with hir joly companye,
Daunced ful ofte in many a grenè mede.

The charm of the Arthurian story is undeniable, imperishable, but as a rule it lacks the human interest which marks the tales of the Charlemagne cycle.

The two are practically contemporary; although we have no text of Arthurian romance earlier than the twelfth century, we know that tales of Arthur and his knights must have been current at a much earlier date, for Signor Pio Rajna has found in Italian documents of the early twelfth century the attestations of witnesses bearing the names of Arthur and Gawain, and such witnesses, to be of an age to testify, could not have been born later than 1080. A carving over the north doorway of Modena cathedral, also dating from the early twelfth century, represents a group of Arthurian characters riding to the assault of a tower, on which stands a female figure. The adventure in which they are engaged cannot be identified with any of the extant texts. Thus the Arthurian legend was not only formed in the eleventh century, but had already travelled far from its native land. When the *Chanson de Roland* was being composed for the edification of the pilgrims to St James of Compostela and the crusaders against the Moors of Spain, Italy was listening to, and recording by the gift of baptismal names, tales of Arthur and his knights. Yet, as we shall see in our final summary, the influence of the two cycles one upon another was extremely slight.

The historical element in the Arthurian cycle is but meagre; scholars now generally agree to accept as genuine the statement in the *Historia Britonum* of Nennius that a chieftain named Arthur played a dominant rôle in the wars waged between Britons and the Saxon invaders during the fifth century; he was, apparently, the British generalissimo, "ipse erat dux bellorum." The fact that Nennius goes on to relate his hunting of the mythic boar Twrch Trwyth, shews that even in his day fiction was busy with the name of Arthur. The suggestion, made by the late Sir John Rhys, that Arthur held a post analogous to that which under the late Roman occupation was known by the title of *Comes Britanniae*, assigned to a general who was commissioned to defend the island wherever attacked, would explain in a satisfactory manner the existence of widely scattered Arthurian localities. If we accept the thesis of a chief who, during the latter half of the fifth century, waged a successful war against the Saxons, was betrayed by his wife and a near relative, son or nephew, and fell in battle, we probably have all that can safely be claimed as historical basis for the Arthurian story. To seek, as in the Charlemagne cycle, for an historical counterpart to the figures of Arthurian romance, would be labour thrown away; Arthur may indeed have had a valiant nephew who was the prototype of our Sir Gawain, even as it is possible that a tradition of actual fact underlies the tragedy of Tristan and Iseult (who, however, do not really belong to Arthurian tradition); farther than that it is doubtful if any scholar would now be prepared to go.

Arthurian romantic *literature*, as distinguished from *tradition*, may be held to have begun with the *Historia Regum Britanniae* of Geoffrey of Monmouth, probably the most successful piece of fiction ever produced. The work was composed about 1135, and is professedly based upon a volume of British traditions which Geoffrey received from Walter, Archdeacon of Oxford. Whether such a book ever existed, or if it did what was its language, Latin or Welsh, it is now impossible to determine. Whatever the source upon which he drew, Geoffrey represents Arthur, not as a mere British chieftain, but as a *Welt-Kaiser*, whose conquests, extending over practically the known world from Scandinavia to Rome, rivalled the Empire of Charlemagne. Indeed, on the basis of romantic tradition there was no room for the simultaneous existence of two such monarchs, a recognition of which, on the part of poets of the day, may account for the fact that these two practically contemporary cycles ignore each other.

Two chroniclers, writing before Geoffrey—William of Malmesbury and Henry of Huntingdon—refer to Arthur as a popular hero, and the words in which the former characterises the British enthusiasm for their national hero, "hodie delirant," shew clearly that popular imagination was already busy with historical fact. Geoffrey's work appeared at the psychological moment, and gave form and impetus to the already existing tendency.

The immediate effect of the *Historia* is most marked in the pseudo-historic texts: the *Brut* of the Anglo-Norman Wace, and its translation into early English by Layamon; but both writers know more of Arthur than we find in Geoffrey, for both know the Round Table, of which there is no mention in the *Historia*. Layamon, in particular, gives a most vivid account of its foundation which obviously reposes upon a very early tradition[1]. He also gives a fine and detailed account of Arthur's reception of the news of Mordred's treachery, and the subsequent tragedy[2], and, further, a unique and picturesque version of the birth of the enchanter Merlin[3].

Apart from the pseudo-historic chronicles and the *Merlin* texts, the Arthurian romances, however, owe little or nothing to Geoffrey, and their number and variety offer eloquent testimony to the contemporary existence of an extensive Arthurian tradition. The existing manuscripts belong exclusively to the latter part of the twelfth and the early thirteenth century, but the writers were obviously dealing with the later stages of a fully-developed legend; in many cases they were handling a situation of which more than one version was known to them; while the existence of an Arthurian tradition in Italy, already referred to, justifies us in the assumption that the end of the eleventh and the early twelfth century had already witnessed what M. Bédier has happily described as "une première floraison des poèmes Arthuriens."[4]

The earlier Arthurian romances were composed in verse; it was not till the appearance of the prose version of Robert de Borron's cycle, at the close of the twelfth century, that an impetus was given to the construction of the elaborate prose romances, which in the final cyclic versions acquired a portentous volume. Of these earlier poems Arthur was not, as a rule, the actual hero, he was the king at whose court the recorded adventures took place; but, as a matter of fact, he is more or less of a lay figure, he lacks the distinct personality of the old Emperor Charlemagne "à la barbe florie." In the romances most directly connected with him he is found closely associated with Merlin, and this latter, enchanter, guardian, and councillor of the young king, is really the dominant figure. The heroes of Arthurian story are the knights of Arthur's court, and their adventures have been related by a group of writers of no mean literary skill. This is especially noticeable in the *Lais* of Marie de France, an Anglo-Norman poetess of the latter half of the twelfth century. Based, as the authoress distinctly states, on Breton originals, these graceful tales, mostly imbued with a strong fairy element, are connected sometimes

[1] Cf. *Brut,* ed. Madden, Vol. II, p. 532.

[2] *Ibid.* Vol. III, p. 117.

[3] Mr Evans Wentz, in *The Fairy Faith in Celtic Countries,* p. 437, gives an account of the birth of the enchanter Myrddin, as told by an old Welshman of Pontrhydfendigaid, which agrees closely with Layamon's version. It would be interesting to know whence this witness derived it.

[4] Cf. *Le Tristan de Thomas,* Vol. II, p. 154.

with the court of Arthur, more generally with that of some unnamed monarch. It is obvious that the writer is working over, in the interest of the popular Arthurian story, tales which were in no way connected with that tradition. But whoever be the king at whose court the action takes place, whether Arthur or another, he is little more than a lay figure.

There is another point in which the two cycles differ. We know the names of the men who composed the principal romances; we have passed from the stage of the anonymous minstrel to that of the court poet; and though there are still minstrels to delight a public with their rhymes, that public is more sophisticated than that of the fairs and common routes, and the minstrel is generally careful to give to his version the authoritative sanction of some well-known name.

The most famous poet of the period was Chrétien de Troyes; the exact date of his literary activity, his precise social status, whether he were a herald, as M. Gaston Paris believed, or a lawyer, as M. Maurice Willmotte has suggested, we do not know, but it is certain that he was a poet of considerable ingenuity and literary skill, and the group of poems we possess from his hand—*Erec*; *Yvain*, or *Le Chevalier au Lion*; *Cligés*; *Le Chevalier de la Charrette*; and *Perceval*, or *Le Conte del Graal*—rank as classics of medieval literature.

It would be out of place here to enter into details of the controversy which has raged over the question of the originality of Chrétien. Was he, as the late Professor Wendelin Foerster maintained, the first to compose an Arthurian romance, and the source whence all subsequent writers derived their inspiration? Or did he stand, as Dr. Brugger believes, at the end, and not at the beginning, of a period of romantic evolution? It must be admitted that Chrétien himself does not claim to be an inventor, but rather a re-teller of tales, as in the case of the *Perceval*, which he declares to be the best story told at a royal court; but whatever the view held of his independence, the excellence of his style is undisputed, and from a literary point of view his works well deserved the success they achieved. The poems of *Erec* and *Yvain* were translated into German by Hartmann von Aue, a writer who in literary skill is little, if at all, inferior to Chrétien. There is an excellent English rendering of the *Yvain*, "*Ywain and Gawain*," by an anonymous writer; and the Welsh *Mabinogion* in *Geraint ap Erbin*, *The Lady of the Fountain*, and *Peredur*, give parallel versions to *Erec*, *Yvain*, and *Perceval*; the precise relation existing between the Welsh and French texts is still a matter of debate.

The same may be said of the German *Parzival*, by Wolfram von Eschenbach, a work of outstanding merit alike in conception and construction, in many ways the most interesting text of the cycle. A considerable section of the poem agrees closely with the *Perceval* of Chrétien; at the same time, in the description of the hero's youth, the German poem retains details of obviously primitive origin which are lacking in the French text. It also gives a lengthy account of the adventures of his father, to which Chrétien has no parallel, and which at the same time betrays a curious familiarity with the history of the House of Anjou. Wolfram himself distinctly states that he is following the version of one Kiot (? Guiot) the Provençal, and criticises Chrétien as having told the story incorrectly. So far no manuscript of Kiot's poem has been discovered, but it is a significant fact that Wolfram connects the *Perceval Grail* story with that of the Swan Knight, and that both Gerbert, one of the continuators of Chrétien, and the anonymous author of *Sone de Nansai*, are also familiar with this development, though neither of them can have known the *Parzival*. There must certainly have existed a French text from which this feature was derived.

The *Perceval* of Chrétien, left unfinished at his death, was continued by three writers, Wauchier de Denain, Gerbert (most probably Gerbert de Montreuil, author of *Le Roman de la Violette*), and Manessier; the two latter wrote after the full cyclic development of the Arthurian tradition, but the first, who lived at the commencement of the thirteenth century, utilised sources earlier than Chrétien, and his text is of paramount importance for the criticism of the cycle. Among his sources was a "minstrel" manuscript, the excerpts from which throw a most interesting light upon the conditions under which these tales were told. Thus, in relating Gawain's adventure with the knight who is slain in his company by an invisible hand, we find a break in the tale—

"Lors s'en va Mesire Gauvains,
Cil remest mort entre ses mains.
A ces parolles doit chascuns
Dire patrenostre aus defuns,
Puis nous ferez le vin donner."[1]

The impression here given is that of a minstrel reciting his romance in a baronial hall, where the "seigneurs" he addresses are seated round the board, and the wine circulates freely; this is not the public of the *Chansons de Geste*.

This manuscript contained a group of tales dealing with the adventures of Gawain, his son, and brother, a group the existence of which is testified to by extant English poems relating parallel adventures, and which obviously belonged to a stage of Arthurian tradition anterior to that of Chrétien's poems, a stage in which the primacy of Gawain as Arthurian romantic hero was unchallenged. This group, to which may be given the tentative title of *The Geste of Sir Gawain*, is of great importance for critical purposes.

Besides the writings of Chrétien de Troyes we have the poems of Raoul de Houdenc, *La Vengeance de Raguidel*, and *Méraugis de Portlesguez*, and the interesting texts relative to the adventures of Gawain's son, *Le Bel Inconnu*, and the English *Sir Libeaus Desconus*, the source of which no

[1] Cf. *Legend of Sir Perceval*, Vol. I, p. 243.

doubt ultimately goes back to the Geste above referred to. The same origin is probably to be postulated for the curious English poem *The Weddynge of Syr Gawayne*, the central theme of which is admittedly of folk-lore origin; and also for the very fine *Syr Gawayne and the Grene Knyghte*, a fourteenth-century poem of unknown authorship, which the late M. Gaston Paris characterised as "the gem" of medieval English literature. Unfortunately the difficulties of the dialect in which it is composed will always be a bar to its enjoyment by the general reader, but the author possessed an exceptional constructive faculty, a power of imaginative description, and a love of nature, which combine to give the poem an enduring charm. Though of late date, as compared with the bulk of the Arthurian romances, it is generally held to be the rendering of a lost poem, probably Anglo-Norman, and its theme, a head-cutting challenge, is one which occurs frequently in Arthurian romance, and was certainly early connected with Gawain.

At the end of the twelfth century the period of Arthurian poetical activity was succeeded by that of prose. Robert de Borron composed a group of romances which, though originally intended to be written in verse, were ultimately cast in a prose form, and became both the basis and the model upon which the later cyclic versions were constructed.

Here we find ourselves faced with an element which, originally foreign to Arthurian legend and only appearing previously in isolated verse texts, subsequently dominated the whole body of prose romance. Borron's romances, *Joseph of Arimathea*, *Merlin*, *Perceval*, are essentially *Grail* romances, and in the final development of the tradition the *Grail*, its origin, its mystery, and the *Quest* in which first the chief heroes of Arthur's court and finally all the Knights of the Round Table are engaged, becomes the dominating theme. For many years controversy has raged round the subject—what was the Grail? Was it originally a Christian relic? Was it merely a folk-lore talisman? Both views have found stalwart champions. Opinion to-day is now pretty well agreed that there is truth in both contentions, that we are here dealing with a combination of the two elements, that the Grail story represents a confused reminiscence of a Nature cult which, in its essence an inquiry into the sources of life by a process of initiation, had early taken on a pseudo-Christian colouring, and, surviving the ban of ecclesiastical censure, was secretly practised in strongholds of the British Isles. In Borron's hands this cult became definitely stamped with the reverence paid to relics of the Passion, reverence to which the crusades had given a strong impetus; the Grail has become the Dish, eventually the Cup, of the Last Supper. As the receptacle for the Blood which flowed from the Wounds of the Crucified Saviour it became a *Saint-Sang* relic, while the associated Lance became identified with the Lance of Longinus. But both retained their pre-Christian features: the Lance still bled into the Cup, the Grail was still a Feeding Vessel, coming and going without visible agency, and assuring to those who sat at its board the choicest food they could desire.

Interwoven with this theme of the Grail are the pseudo-historic events of Arthur's career: his mysterious birth, his connexion with the enchanter Merlin, his wars with the Romans, and his death. To the fact that Borron has not held the balance equal between his themes but, having started with the idea of writing a Grail cycle, has allowed himself to be carried away by the charm of the Arthurian story, is probably to be ascribed certain incoherences in construction which led scholars for a time to deny the Borron authorship of the final sections. Regarded from the point of view of the *Grail* history there are certainly discrepancies, regarded as an *Arthurian* romance the unity of conception between the *Merlin* (which is undoubtedly by Borron) and the *Perceval* is undeniable. That the final section (the *Mort Artus*) is founded upon a verse chronicle, midway between the versions of Wace and Layamon, is beyond dispute.

Another romance, the date of which has been, and still is, a matter of controversy, the *Perlesvaus*, most probably followed closely on Borron's work; the author bases his conception of the Grail upon Borron; he knew and utilised the *Perceval*, and was familiar with the group of *Gawain* stories to which I have referred above. On the other hand, he does not know the final romances of the cycle, which, on their side, shew signs of influence by the *Perlesvaus*.

While the Grail theme was thus gradually transforming the Arthurian story, another development, of equal importance for the final form of the literature, was taking place, namely, the evolution of the *Lancelot* element. As an Arthurian hero Lancelot is of late introduction; he has no place in the pseudo-historic texts, and his appearance in the poems is fitful and spasmodic. Thus in the *Erec*, *Yvain*, and *Cligés* of Chrétien, he is a name and no more, and he is not even mentioned in the *Perceval*. But in *Le Chevalier de la Charrette*, which was written before the *Perceval*, the whole interest of the poem is centred on his *amours* with Guenevere.

In the early years of the thirteenth century the great prose *Lancelot* made its appearance. Most probably Lancelot was at first very loosely connected with the Grail, and the romance of *Perlesvaus*, where he shares the quest with Perceval and Gawain but does not behold the Grail, was probably the first stage in the process of adopting him into this cycle. The final step was the construction of the *Queste* and the invention of Galahad, through whom Lancelot, though as Guenevere's lover he could not aspire himself to the supreme honour of Grail-winner, achieved the quest vicariously in the person of his son.

In the final evolution of the cycle the *Joseph* of Borron underwent expansion and modification, with the view of fitting it to be an introduction alike to the *Lancelot* and the *Queste*. Under the title of *Le Grand Saint Graal*, or *Estoire du Saint Graal*, it became a lengthy record of miraculous conversions, leading up to the final evangelisation of Britain by Joseph of Arimathea, his son Jesephe, and his descendants. The *Merlin* also underwent expansion, partly pseudo-historic, by the introduction of lengthy wars with the Saxon invaders and with minor British kings; partly romantic, by the incorporation of tales the exact source of which is not yet determined. The entire prose cycle consisting of *Grand Saint Graal*, *Merlin*, *Lancelot*, *Queste*, and *Mort Artus*, is of appalling volume. Fortunately, however, the English reader has at hand, in the *Morte D'Arthur* of Sir Thomas Malory, a skilful abridgement of the main branches of the cycle (the *Grand Saint Graal* is not represented), which, knit together by the underlying chivalric conception of the writer and composed in nervous and vivid prose, will always remain a classic of English literature.

A considerable section of Malory's work is drawn from a romance which, although in its latest form connected alike with the Arthurian and the Grail legend, had originally nothing to do with either, the story of *Tristan and Iseult.* This, one of the world's great stories, is best represented by the translations of a poem composed by an Anglo-Norman named Thomas, who wrote at the end of the twelfth century. Only fragments of the original work remain, but we have a fine translation into German by Gottfried of Strassbourg, a Scandinavian prose rendering, and a fourteenth-century English poem, *Sir Tristrem*; from these we are enabled to reconstruct the story. Thomas cites as his authority one Bréri, to whom he attributes a comprehensive knowledge of British tradition, and who is probably to be identified with the Bleheris "né et engenuïs" in Wales, to whom we owe the Gawain stories utilised by Wauchier de Denain, and the Bledhericus, referred to by Giraldus Cambrensis as "famosus ille fabulator." There also exists a fragment of another Anglo-Norman *Tristan* poem, by one Bérol, which corresponds with a German version by Eilhart von Oberge; these texts appear to represent a form of the story rougher and more primitive than that followed by Thomas. We also have isolated "Tristan" *Lais*, notably that of *La Folie Tristan*, which bear witness to the widespread popularity of the story. There can be no doubt that the tale of the tragic loves of Tristan and Iseult exercised a powerful influence upon the development of the story of Lancelot and Guenevere, nor can there be any dispute as to which is the finer tale. Arthur's queen and her lover, with their conventional sighs and swoonings, love trances, and transports of joy, despair, or jealousy, though they gain some life from Malory's vigorous prose, are but lay figures compared with Tristan's "Iseut ma drue, Iseut ma mie, En vus ma mort, en vus ma vie," and Iseult breathing out her life in the last impassioned embrace of her dead lover. The *Tristan* story is perhaps the world's finest love tale; the story of Lancelot and Guenevere is an interesting document of medieval amatory conventions.

In its final form the *Tristan* has been converted into a lengthy prose romance, in which the original incidents of the story have been obscured and distorted by the introduction of foreign elements. The character of Mark has undergone a radical change: the generous, trusting monarch has become a cowardly, treacherous prince, the final murderer of his nephew; in fact all the Cornish knights are held up to ridicule as cowards. Tristan is closely connected with Arthur's court; he is the chosen friend of Lancelot, whose rival he is both in knightly valour and *amour courtois.* Finally we have a lengthy and diffuse version of the *Queste*, in which some scholars have seen the original form of that romance. If the original *Lancelot-Guenevere* story owes its inspiration to the earlier *Tristan* legend, it is equally true that the final form of this latter has been influenced by the prose *Lancelot.* The one really original feature in the compilation is the conception of the philosophically-minded coward, Dagonet, who is always prepared with a good reason for his own unknightly conduct, and with a humorously satirical comment on his friends' extravagances. It was this version which was before Malory; consequently his text cannot be consulted for the genuine *Tristan* story.

The above is a rapid résumé of the principal texts composing the Arthurian cycle; how does this body of literature compare, as a whole, with the cycle previously discussed? The two are, as we saw, practically contemporaneous, and are written in the same language, but there is a wide difference between them. So far as form is concerned, the Charlemagne romances are composed in *laisses*, or sections of varying length, each marked throughout by a single vowel-assonance, not by rhyme. The Arthurian poems are without exception in octosyllabic lines of which each two rhyme, a form faithfully followed by the German translators. The independent *Lais* adopt the same form. The English Arthurian poems, on the other hand, shew a much more elaborate versification; they are mainly alliterative, and are composed in strophes or stanzas. A very interesting specimen is what is known as the Harleian *Morte Arthure*, which was largely drawn upon by Malory for the concluding section of his work, but the English texts are all comparatively late in date. A very curious and unique manuscript of the *Bibliothèque Nationale* (*fonds Franç.* 337), which recounts the earlier years of Arthur's reign, and seems to be an amplification of the *Merlin* based upon a medley of Arthurian tales current at the time, gives extracts from what appears to have been an Arthurian poem composed in the form of a *Chanson de Geste*, but there appears to be no other instance of an Arthurian poem in *laisses.* The romances as a whole betray a literary consciousness foreign to the Charlemagne poems; the authors name themselves, they are at pains to attribute their sources *à tort ou à raison* (very frequently *à tort*) to some well-known writer. They work under distinguished patronage, that of the King of England, the Count or Countess of Flanders, the Countess of Champagne. Their public is the public of courts, royal or seigneurial; some of the writers shew a marked contempt for the folk, "les vilains"; we feel that both those who wrote and those who listened to the poems belonged to a more sophisticated *milieu* than that in which the *Chansons* of Charlemagne and his peers flourished.

Internally the influence of the two cycles, though rare, seems to have been reciprocal. It is more direct in the *Chansons de Geste*, where in *La Bataille de Loquifer* Rainoart is carried off to Avalon, and combats the monster Chapalu in the presence of Arthur; and in *Huon de Bordeaux*, where the hero inherits a kingdom from the fairy king Oberon, to the detriment of Arthur, the rightful heir. Here the evidence is clear and direct. In the Arthurian romances, on the other hand, the influence is slight; in the manuscript referred to above (B.N. 337), we do indeed find the Saxon invaders of Britain riding on elephants, and described in terms which betray the influence of wars against the Saracens, but there is only one of the Arthurian romances the author of which seems to have been directly under the influence of the *Chansons de Geste*. This is the *Perlesvaus*, where the hero throughout comports himself in a manner befitting the heroes of *Les Narbonnais*; he might well be the son of Aymeri rather than of Alain. His one preoccupation is the establishment of the New Law; and he inflicts summary and sanguinary chastisement upon those who hesitate to accept its precepts. We have heathen queens who, like Orable-Guibourc, receive baptism and become exemplary Christians; stalwart knights who become hermits, but are ready to wage war upon the robber bands who infest the surrounding forests, even as Guillaume and Ogier, though monks, still remained valiant warriors. Lancelot, believing himself about to die, communicates himself with three blades of grass, a feature of frequent occurrence in the *Chansons de Geste*. The writer of this romance, whoever he may have been, was certainly imbued with the spirit of militant Christianity rather than that of Celtic Faërie.

Apart from these instances, the two great cycles seem to have run their course side by side, without appreciably affecting one another; a somewhat curious phenomenon, the secret of which may possibly lie in the theory advanced by M. Bédier, which would seem to suggest that while one cycle was composed for the edification of a mixed and fluctuating public, the other made appeal to a special class of less shifting *milieu* and more generally cultivated tastes. Thus we are conscious of a marked divergence in ethos; if the *Chansons de Geste* are inspired by the general spirit of the time, and are instinct with the breath of the feudal system, the Arthurian romances reflect no less faithfully the exclusive and aristocratic spirit of the knightly orders. As remarked above, it is interesting to note the contempt with which a poet like Chrétien de Troyes refers to the "vilain." The feudal system is in force here as in the Charlemagne cycle, the lord still owes protection to his vassals, but such folk, being outside the charmed circle of knighthood, are of a lower order. The introduction of what we may term the "free-masonry" of chivalry lessened the gulf between the sovereign and his nobles, but it widened that between the knight and the ignoble.

It casts a vivid light on the mentality of the time when we find a poet like Wolfram von Eschenbach, who belonged to the class of small land-owners dependent upon the favour of a princely patron, and who makes frequent allusions to the poverty resulting from the absence of such patronage, exalting his claims as a member of a knightly family—"Zum Schildesamt bin ich geboren"—and his feats of arms, above any fame he may win as a poet:

"Swelh'iu mich minnet umbe sanc
Sô dunket mich ir witze kranc."[1]

If he desires the love of a woman, he will win it with shield and spear. He announces proudly that he is ignorant of all book-lore, and knows no letters—"I'ne kan decheinen buochstap." It would be difficult to find another passage in medieval literature which shews us so clearly and emphatically what was the attitude of the knight to all outside the charmed circle of the order of chivalry. Of Wolfram's feats as a warrior no record whatever remains to-day, but we may well endorse the verdict passed upon him by the author of the *Wartburg-Krieg:*

"Herr Wolferam von Eschenbach
Leien munt nie baz gesprach."

Wolfram's compatriots knew better than himself wherein his true fame lay.

In the same way the Arthurian romances reflect a special attitude of mind on the part of the knight's lady. If his outlook was strictly limited by the rules of his order, the lady to whom he paid court was, on her side, the slave of conventions regulating her conduct towards her suitor. Any student desirous of understanding the curious ethos of the period, the *amour courtois* with its strange developments in the Courts of Love, should study the romances dealing with the story of Lancelot and Guenevere, referred to above, the *Chevalier de la Charrette*, and the prose *Lancelot.* History ascribes much of this curious social development to the influence of Eleanor, wife of Henry II, and her daughter, Marie, Countess of Champagne. It was from this latter that Chrétien received the "sens et matière" for his *Lancelot* poem.

Thus, while both cycles are of extreme interest as records of existing social conditions, the *Chansons de Geste* reflect more faithfully the common life of the period; the Arthurian romances were mostly written to be read, and are practically the literature of a caste, to whose standards of life and rules of conduct they perforce adhere.

III. The Matière de Rome.

It is doubtful whether the third group mentioned by Bodel, the *Matière de Rome*, has any claim to be ranked as a legendary cycle, the romances

[1] *Parzival,* Book II, 11, 1697–1698.

of which it is composed having no inherent connexion with each other, nor indeed with Rome. What we must understand by this term are romances based upon classical themes, largely derived from Greek texts of the decadent period, which had been translated into Latin.

Of these the most important is the *Roman d'Alexandre*. The ultimate source of this, and of all the versions of the history of Alexander, is the Greek work known as the *pseudo-Callisthenes*, which was translated into Latin in the fourth century by Julius Valerius; an abridgement of this translation, made in the ninth century, is the basis for most of the medieval compositions. At the same time medieval writers were familiar with certain apocryphal tales of Alexander's adventures, such as his journey to Paradise, entirely unrepresented in the original Greek.

The earliest French poem was composed by Alberic de Besançon, probably in the first half of the twelfth century; of it only a fragment survives, but this is sufficient to shew that it was a work of considerable literary merit. This was followed by a poem in decasyllabics, the author of which is unknown, and by a long and extremely popular *Roman d'Alexandre*, by two collaborators, Lambert le Tort and Alexandre de Paris. In this version the genuine adventures of the hero are "farced" with fantastic tales derived from other sources, such as that of the three miraculous fountains, of which one restores the aged to youth, another the dead to life, while a draught from the third bestows immortality.

At a date previous to the Conquest the tale of Alexander's journey to Paradise had been rendered into Anglo-Saxon prose, and an attempt to provide a more reliable version of the hero's actual deeds was made by a monk of St Albans about the middle of the twelfth century. The French *Roman d'Alexandre* was rendered into English by an ecclesiastic, Eustace of Kent, in the thirteenth century, and this version formed the basis for an excellent English poem, *King Alisaunder*, composed towards the end of the same century, possibly by the author of *Arthur and Merlin*.

The story of Alexander was extremely popular in England, as is shewn by the words of the Monk in Chaucer's Canterbury Pilgrims:

"The storie of Alisaundre is so comune
That every wight that hath discrecioun
Hath herd somwhat or al of his fortune."

It was even more so in Scotland, where a lengthy poem, *The Buik of the most Noble and Vailyand Conqueror Alexander the Great*, was composed in the fifteenth century, possibly by Barbour, the chronicler of the Bruce; and most of the leading Scottish writers of the period refer to him. It may be questioned whether the survival of names of classical origin, such as Alexander, Hector, and Aeneas, found far more frequently north than south of the Tweed, may not testify to the stronger hold which the romances of this group took upon the imagination of the Scottish people. There was of course no reason why Alexander, as an historic character, should be more popular than Charlemagne or Arthur; it was probably the glamour of an unknown civilisation, the awakening of the spirit of wonder, making its appeal to imaginations which, through the Crusades, had been brought more or less closely into touch with Byzantine and Oriental ideas. Certain of the Grail romances witness to this fascination, which, in the words of the late Professor Ker, led the peoples to forget "their own inheritance of tragic fables for the sake of vanities, wonders, and splendours." The popularity of classical themes among a public to whom a knowledge of the classics was a sealed book was probably due to the same cause.

Thus we have another and, from the point of view of comparative literature, even more interesting group, represented by three poems, the *Roman de Troie*, *Roman d'Aeneas*, and *Roman de Thèbes*. Of these the first-named (possibly not the first in date of composition), by Benoît de Sainte Maure, is the most important. In all three texts, the life of the period and the deeds of the heroes are described as conforming to the courtesies and conventions of the twelfth century, and the work of Benoît, dedicated to Queen Eleanor, wife of Henry II, is generally regarded as having given the initial impetus to the composition of the *roman courtois*, of which we have seen the full development in Arthurian romance. The *Roman d'Aeneas*, translated by Heinrich von Veldeck, played the same rôle in Germany, and paved the way for the poems of Hartmann von Aue, Gottfried von Strassburg, and Wolfram von Eschenbach. Benoît was really a poet of no inconsiderable talent, but it is rather for their position in the evolution of romantic literature than for their intrinsic merit that this group of poems is worthy of study.

A distinctive feature to be noted in these two groups is that while the *Alexander* poems are cast in the mould of the *Chansons de Geste*, with their mere assonance prolonged throughout each *laisse*, Benoît de Sainte Maure and the unknown authors of *Aeneas* and *Thèbes* composed their romances in the eight-syllabled rhyming couplet familiar to us through the works of Chrétien de Troyes and other Arthurian writers.

Under the heading of the *Matière de Rome* should also be classed the direct translations and adaptations of Ovid, whose *Metamorphoses* and *Ars Amatoria* were very popular in the Middle Ages. Chrétien de Troyes, in the list of his works prefixed to *Cligés*, tells us that he has translated *L'Art d'Aimer*, also the stories of Pelops (which is but summarily treated by Ovid), and Philomela; of these versions only the last-named survives. The twelfth century also saw versions of *Narcissus*, and *Piramus and Thisbe*, by writers of less literary importance than Chrétien.

Taken in its ensemble, the *Matière de Rome* is, as was said above, of far less importance and interest as literature than that of *France* or *Bretagne*. As artificial and learned as Palladian architecture, as fantastic as Baroque, its hollow marvels can compare neither with the heady tumult of the *Chansons de Geste* nor with the vivid shore and forest of Arthurian romance, the offspring of native life and of spontaneous dreams.

IV. The Germanic Cycle.

Of considerably more intrinsic interest, and not without importance for the study of Romance literature, is the great Northern cycle, the central theme of which, the tragedy of Siegfried and Brünnhilde, has become familiar to the present generation through the medium of Wagner's music-drama, the *Ring der Nibelungen*. Of this fine story three distinct versions exist: the *Volsunga-Saga*, an Icelandic prose compilation, dating from the twelfth century, based upon earlier poems, fragments of which have been preserved in the *Eddas*; the *Thidrek-Saga*, a thirteenth-century German version, which derives its title from the fact that the central hero of this lengthy and diffuse compilation is Dietrich, or Thidrek, von Bern, the historic Theodoric of Verona; lastly, we have the German poem, *Das Nibelungenlied*, which, originally composed towards the end of the twelfth century and subsequently remodelled by more than one hand, presents us with the story in its latest and most conventionalised form.

The exact relation in which these three versions stand to one another is still a subject of debate; briefly stated, the historic kernel of the whole story is the destruction of the Burgundian kingdom by the Huns in A.D. 437, and the death of Attila, on the night of his marriage with Ildico, in A.D. 453. Closely bound up with this, forming the first part of the story, and providing the *motif* for its tragic development, is the account of the life and death of Siegfried, or Sigurd, undoubtedly a semi-mythical figure, in whom many scholars have seen the euhemerised form of the Northern sun-god, Baldr. Whether Siegfried be a Germanic hero, associated *ab origine* with the Rhenish kings whose sister he has wedded, in oblivion of his pledge to Brünnhilde (originally as mythical a figure as himself), or whether we have here the union of two originally independent themes, is a question which may never be finally settled, but the characteristics of the three versions are distinct. The *Volsunga-Saga* gives us the story in a mythical form: we are in a primitive world, where the sons of God behold the daughters of men; the gods take upon themselves a human form; they mingle in human affairs; they beget children, and direct, by more or less immediate intervention, the lives of those in whom they are interested, dealing reward and punishment with lavish hand. Through the mists of antiquity the characters loom gigantic: the race of Volsung, Siegmund, Signy, Sinfjötli—the offspring of brother and sister, the fruit of the latter's deep-laid and relentless plan of vengeance—are among the most imposing figures in literature. The death of Signy has a terrific grandeur before which the fate of her modern counterpart, Sieglinde, pales into insignificance. Brynhild, whether in her own person, or confused with the Valkyr, Sigdrifa, is no mere woman; nor is the character of Gudrun marred by the treachery and vindictiveness of the German Kriemhild. At the same time the occurrence of so obviously Frankish a name as Hjalprek (Chilperic), the confusion in the relations between Sigurd and Brynhild, in the latter of whom two personalities have been incompletely fused, and the existence of distinct variants in the account of Sigurd's birth and death, forbid us to regard this fine version as the decisively original form of the story.

The *Thidrek-Saga*, on the other hand, though loosely constructed, full of *banal* repetitions, and crowded to confusion with characters in no way connected with one another, yet in its version of Siegfried's birth, early youth, and death appears to have preserved an earlier tradition, traces of which are to be detected in the Northern version. But Brynhild retains of her original character only a superhuman strength, and after Siegfried's death disappears from the scene, while Grimhild's (Gudrun's) vengeance on her brothers is repulsive in its savagery, and we feel that her death at the hand of Dietrich is richly deserved.

The *Nibelungenlied* differs from both the other versions in giving no account of Siegfried's early years; he is represented as the son of King Siegmund (of Xanten on the Rhine) and Sieglinde his wife, and first appears on the scene as suitor for the hand of Kriemhild, daughter of the Burgundian king Dankrat, who reigned at Worms. Brünnhild is here, as in the *Thidrek-Saga*, only distinguished by her extraordinary strength, which she employs to the discomfiture of her would-be lovers. The story in its main lines follows the version of the *Thidrek-Saga*, Brünnhild disappearing from the scene after Siegfried's death, and the fate of Gunther and his brothers being brought about by Kriemhild's treachery in revenge for her husband's murder. The notable feature in this, the latest version of the story, is the insistance of the *motif* of *Treue*, reciprocal faith and loyalty. Hagen, who elsewhere is Gunther's (Gunnar's) brother, is here his vassal, and kills Siegfried purely from loyalty to his liege lady, Brünnhild. It is from loyalty to Gunther that he goes to Etzel's (Attila's) court, knowing that he is going to his death, while Gunther on his part is equally loyal, and refuses to purchase his own safety by delivering Hagen to Kriemhild's vengeance. The characters of Dietrich and the Markgrave Rudiger are developed on the same lines; the legend has here become a vehicle for the exposition of certain medieval ethical conventions, and as such the *Nibelungenlied* has an interest other than its presentment of the actual story.

The Northern cycle in its various branches has not escaped the influence of a tendency which, already noticeable in the *Chansons de Geste*, becomes strongly marked in the final stages of Arthurian romance, that of exalting the importance of a given hero by the recital of the deeds of his ancestors or of his descendants, a tendency which led to the glorification of the family rather than of the individual. Both the *Sigurd* and the *Thidrek* Sagas have thus undergone expansion. In the case of Sigurd the tendency has been downward, in the ascription to him of two daughters, the offspring of his relations respectively with Brynhild and

Grimhild (Gudrun). The daughter of the first, Aslaug, after a chequered youth, being brought up by peasants who had murdered her foster-father for the sake of his gold, becomes the wife of Ragnar Lodbrog and the mother of a race of kings; her story will be found in the *Ragnar-Lodbrog-Saga*. Swanhild, daughter of Gudrun, has a more tragic fate. Wedded to King Ermenrich (a very important figure in the *Thidrek* and its dependent Sagas), she is the victim of a false accusation by the treacherous counsellor Bike, or Sibich, who persuades the king that she has betrayed him with his son. Both are put to death, Swanhild being trodden underfoot by horses, after her head has been enveloped in a sack, the piercing glance of her eyes, inherited from her father the Dragon-Slayer, so terrifying the horses that they turn away from her, even as Sigurd's would-be assassin dare not approach till his eyes are closed in sleep.

The story of Dietrich von Bern has been expanded in the other direction; he has been credited with a notable ancestor, Wolf-Dietrich, son of Hug-Dietrich, king of Constantinople. Victim, like Swanhild, of a false accusation brought against her by a treacherous courtier, the wife of Hug-Dietrich is, at her husband's death, exiled with her son, who, on account of his extraordinary strength and fierceness as much as from the doubts as to his parentage, has from his childhood been brought up by the faithful Berchtold of Meran. The story of Wolf-Dietrich, consisting of a series of wildly improbable adventures, is found in two distinct versions; both finally represent the hero as wedding the widow of King Ortnit of Garda, who has been slain by a dragon, and inheriting his kingdom. This story was probably invented to account for the presence of Dietrich (Theodoric the Goth) at Bern (Verona).

The story of *Ortnit*, given in full in the *Heldenbuch*, is interesting: his father is Alberich, the fairy dwarf-king, who is the original of our Oberon. In the *Ortnit* story Alberich appears in a far more picturesque and amiable guise than he does in the later version of the Siegfried story from which Wagner drew his inspiration.

A point that can hardly fail to strike the student of this cycle is the fact that we have here no central authority, as in the *Chansons de Geste* or the Arthurian romances. There is no Emperor like Charlemagne, no king like Arthur. The heroes of the Northern cycle, Volsung, Gunther, Etzel, Dietrich, Ermenrich, are one and all "kings" and, so far as we can judge from the texts, are considered as of equal rank, the difference between them being simply the greater or lesser number of warriors they can respectively bring into the field. Such a text as the *Thidrek-Saga*, loose in construction, ranging practically over the whole field of European polity, is particularly illustrative of this; the number of kings and their relation to one another are confusing to a degree. We realise that we are dealing with memories of a period of tribal wanderings, of indeterminate boundaries, of mutual aggression, attack, and defence. There is no idea of a settled civilisation, of a central authority whose decrees carry weight outside a strictly limited area. The heroes are warriors, bound by ties of fidelity to their chief; the note of *Treue*, as remarked above, is dominant. There is no idea of an abstract code of conduct imposed from without, such as is inherent in the Orders of Knighthood.

In this connexion it is interesting to note that the author of a recent study on Malory detects in the character of Gawain (certainly the oldest of Arthurian heroes) the traces of this primitive conception. Gawain is imbued with the idea of *Sippe* (Kinship), his loyalty is to the family, to the king his uncle, and to his brothers. His feud with Lancelot, which dominates the closing scenes of the cyclic versions, is a blood-feud, arising from the slaying of his brothers by Lancelot in his final rescue of Guenevere. The suggestion is an interesting one, and from the point of view of a comparative study of the cycles, deserving of attention.

Nor, in this Northern cycle, do we find a separate convention for women; they are, like the men, actuated by motives of blood-loyalty, like them inspired by a passion for revenge. Signy avenging the destruction of her family, Brynhild demanding vengeance for Sigurd's unwitting betrayal, Grimhild luring her brothers to their death in revenge for the murder of Sigurd, are figures of another world from that of Guibourc, the mother of the Narbonnais, or Guenevere. So far as the actual transcription of texts at our disposal is concerned there may be little difference of time, but the gulf between the social conditions represented is wide indeed.

The influence of this cycle upon Romance literature has been much less than its essential beauty and importance would seem to merit. There exists no medieval English or French translation of either version. The story must have been known, for we find Brünnhild referred to in *Huon of Bordeaux*, but the borrowings from Northern tradition are of a general rather than an individual character, and have affected the Arthurian rather than the Charlemagne cycle. Features which scholars are generally agreed in referring to Northern influence are: the shape-shifting, which by deceiving Ygerne brings about the birth of Arthur, parallel to the deception of Brynhild; the sword in the block of stone, by the withdrawal of which Arthur proves his claim to the kingdom, similar to the sword of Branstock, which can only be withdrawn by the chosen hero, Siegmund; the resemblance of Morgain and her sisters of the Isle of Avalon, as described by Giraldus Cambrensis, to the Valkyrie; and the revival of slain warriors by a hag provided with a magic ointment, an incident found alike in Gerbert's continuation of the *Perceval* and in the Northern poem *Kudrun*. In each of these cases it will be noted that the parallel is with the Scandinavian, not with the German, version. Again, in the Anglo-Saxon story of *Beowulf*, which, forming no part of the directly cyclic group of Northern romance, can scarcely be said to fall within the limits of this study, we have an account of the combat between the hero and a sea-monster and her son. A similar adventure is attributed to Gawain in the romance of *Diû Krône*.

The resemblance between the stories of Perceval and Siegfried is due to the fact that both are variants of the same original theme, known by scholars as *The Aryan Expulsion and Return Formula*, rather than to borrowing on either side.

The one character of Northern tradition who appears really to have impressed the imagination of romance writers plays no rôle in the *Siegfried* story, though his feats are recounted at length in the early part of the *Thidrek-Saga* (where his son Witig is one of the comrades of Dietrich von Bern)—Weyland the Smith. That the fame of this mythical personage, and his miraculous skill as a forger of weapons, had reached France at a date anterior to the existing versions of his story, is proved by the fact that according to the Chronicle of Adémar de Chabannes the sword of William I, Count of Angoulême, had been forged by Weyland. William reigned from 916–962, Adémar died in 1034, thus if the story be in the original text of the Chronicle, as M. Ferdinand Lot maintains, the tradition must date from the first half of the eleventh century at latest.

In the romance of *Fierabras* a similar origin is ascribed to Charlemagne's famous sword, Joyeuse[1]. An inscription, said to have been inscribed upon the blade of Gawain's sword, runs thus:

> "Je suis fort tranchant et dur
> Galaan me fist par mult grant cure
> Quatorze ans Jhesu Christ
> Quant Galaan me trempa et fist."[2]

It seems not impossible that the mysterious smith of the Grail story, who forged three swords, and whose fate is bound up with that of the third (he must die after reforging it), may be an imitation of Weyland. His name, Trebuchet (from *trebucier*, to stumble, or fall), may well contain a reference to Weyland's lameness. But there can be no question as to the fact that the story of this famous smith was familiar to the romance writers of the twelfth and thirteenth centuries.

English literature also knew Weyland's father, the giant Wade, and no reader of Sir Walter Scott needs to be reminded how, under the name of Weyland Smith, the tradition of the famous forger of weapons lingered on in the north of England.

In the absence of a literary version of the Northern sagas, the evidence points to an oral tradition; the chants and stories of the dreaded Viking invaders must have impressed themselves upon the memory of the French

[1] Cf. Bédier, *Les Légendes Épiques*, Vol. I, p. 68.

[2] First quoted by Sir F. Madden in the notes to his *Syr Gawayne*, from an unnamed MS. of the thirteenth century. It was subsequently given in a practically identical form by Mr R. H. Fletcher, from the *Polistorie* (*Modern Language Assoc. of America*, Vol. XVIII).

and English victims of their raids. That Arthurian romance has been coloured by this tradition is also beyond doubt, but it is noteworthy that such borrowing as can be proved is all on the side of the Romance writers, the *Siegfried* story shewing no trace of contamination with *Chanson de Geste* or Arthurian poem. It is also interesting to note that such historical elements as may exist in the Northern Saga, the tragedy of the Burgundian kings, the character of Dietrich von Bern, find no reflection in English or French romance. It seems as if here the folk, with their appetite for the marvellous, had been the transmitters; a more educated public, a professional *littérateur*, would surely have seized upon the finer elements of the story, the loves of Sigurd and Brynhild, and their tragic fate, a theme worthy to rank beside the legend of Tristan and Iseult. Instead of this we have reminiscences of the impossible feats of the weird and malicious craftsman, Weyland. The whole question of the form in which the Northern epic was communicated to both France and England is one of extreme interest.

For the student of literature it is difficult to say which of the three great cycles stands highest; each has its individual attraction. From the purely literary point of view the cycles of Charlemagne and Arthur may be held to be the most important, but in sheer dramatic force they lack the grip of the fragmentary Eddic Lays, or the rough prose of the *Volsunga-Saga.* The student of medieval literature may well elect to specialise in one field, but he cannot afford to neglect either.

LIST OF ABBREVIATIONS OF TITLES OF PERIODICALS, SOCIETIES, ETC.

(1) The following abbreviations are used for titles of periodicals:

AB. Analecta Bollandiana. Paris and Brussels. 1882 ff.

AHR. American Historical Review. New York and London.

AKKR. Archiv für katholisches Kirchenrecht. Innsbruck. 1857–61. Mayence. 1862 ff.

Arch. Ven. (*and* N. Arch. Ven.; Arch. Ven.-Tri.). Archivio veneto. Venice. 40 vols. 1871–90; *continued as* Nuovo archivio veneto. 1st series. 20 vols. 1891–1900. New series. 42 vols. 1901–21. *And* Archivio veneto-tridentino. 10 vols. 1922–26. *And* Archivio veneto. 5th series. 1927 ff., in progress.

ASAK. Anzeiger für schweizerische Alterthumskunde. Zürich.

ASI. Archivio storico italiano. Florence. Ser. I. 20 v. and App. 9 v. 1842–53. Index. 1857. Ser. nuova. 18 v. 1855–63. Ser. III. 26 v. 1865–77. Indexes to II and III. 1874. Supplt. 1877. Ser. IV. 20 v. 1878–87. Index. 1891. Ser. V. 50 v. 1888–1912. Index. 1900. Ser. VI. Anni 71–81. 20 v. 1913–23. (Index up to 1917 in Catalogue of The London Library. Vol I. 1913, and Supplt. 1920.) Ser. VII. Anni 82 etc. 1924 ff., in progress.

ASL. Archivio storico lombardo. Milan.

ASPN. Archivio storico per le province napoletane. Naples. 1876 ff.

ASRSP. Archivio della Società romana di storia patria. Rome. 1878 ff.

BEC. Bibliothèque de l'École des Chartes. Paris. 1839 ff.

BISI. Bullettino dell' Istituto storico italiano. Rome. 1886 ff.

BRAH. Boletin de la R. Academia de la historia. Madrid.

BZ. Byzantinische Zeitschrift. Leipsic. 1892 ff.

CQR. Church Quarterly Review. London. 1875 ff.

DZG. Deutsche Zeitschrift für Geschichtswissenschaft. Freiburg-im-Breisgau. 1889–98. *Continued as* HVJS. *See below.*

DZKR. Deutsche Zeitschrift für Kirchenrecht. Freiburg-im-Breisgau. 1891 ff.

EHR. English Historical Review. London. 1886 ff.

FDG. Forschungen zur deutschen Geschichte. Göttingen.

HJ. Historisches Jahrbuch. Munich.

HVJS. Historische Vierteljahrsschrift. Leipsic. 1898 ff.

HZ. Historische Zeitschrift (von Sybel). Munich and Berlin.

JB. Jahresberichte der Geschichtswissenschaft im Auftrage der historischen Gesellschaft zu Berlin. Berlin. 1878 ff.

JTS. Journal of Theological Studies. London.

MA. Le moyen âge. Paris.

MIOGF. Mittheilungen des Instituts für österreichische Geschichtsforschung. Innsbruck.

Neu. Arch. Neues Archiv der Gesellschaft für ältere deutsche Geschichtskunde. Hanover and Leipsic.

NRDF (*and* RDF). Nouvelle Revue hist. de droit français et étranger. Paris. 1877–1921; *continued as* Revue hist. de droit français et étranger. Paris. 1922 ff.

QFIA. Quellen und Forschungen aus italienischen Archiven und Bibliotheken. Rome.

RA. Revue archéologique. Paris.

RBén. Revue bénédictine. Maredsous.

RDF. *See above,* NRDF.

RH. Revue historique. Paris.

RHD. Revue d'histoire diplomatique. Paris.

RHE. Revue d'histoire ecclésiastique. Louvain.

RN. Revue de numismatique. Paris.
RQH. Revue des questions historiques. Paris.
RSH. Revue de synthèse historique. Paris.
SBAW Sitzungsberichte der kön. bayerischen Akademie der Wissenschaften. Munich. [Philos.-philol.-hist. Classe].
SKAW. Sitzungsberichte der kaiserlichen Akademie der Wissenschaften. Vienna. [Philos.-hist. Classe.]
SPAW. Sitzungsberichte der kön. preussischen Akademie der Wissenschaften. Berlin.
TRHS. Transactions of the Royal Historical Society. London.
ZDMG. Zeitschrift der deutschen morgenländischen Gesellschaft. Leipsic.
ZKG. Zeitschrift für Kirchengeschichte. Gotha.
ZR. Zeitschrift für Rechtsgeschichte. Weimar. 1861–78. *Continued as*
ZSR. Zeitschrift der Savigny-Stiftung für Rechtswissenschaft. Weimar. 1880 ff. [Each vol. contains a Romanistische, a Germanistische, and after 1911, a Kanonistische Abteilung.]
ZWT. Zeitschrift für wissenschaftliche Theologie. Frankfort-on-Main.

(2) Other abbreviations used are:

AcadIBL. Académie des Inscriptions et Belles-Lettres.
AcadIP. Académie Impériale de Pétersbourg.
AllgDB. Allgemeine deutsche Biographie. *See Gen. Bibl.* I.
ASBen. *See* Mabillon and Achery *in Gen. Bibl.* IV.
ASBoll. Acta Sanctorum Bollandiana. *See Gen. Bibl.* IV.
BAW. Königliche bayerische Akademie der Wissenschaften. Munich.
BGén. Nouvelle Biographie générale. *See Gen. Bibl.* I.
BHE. Bibliothèque de l'École des hautes études. *See Gen. Bibl.* V.
Bouquet. *See* Rerum Gallicarum...scriptores *in Gen. Bibl.* IV.
BUniv. Biographie universelle. *See Gen. Bibl.* I.
Cal.SP. Calendars of State Papers, Close Rolls, Patent Rolls, etc., issued by the State Paper Office, Public Record Office, and General Register House.
Class. hist. Classiques de l'histoire de France au moyen âge. *See Gen. Bibl.* IV.
Coll.doc. Collection de documents inédits sur l'histoire de France. *See Gen. Bibl.* IV.
Coll.textes. Collection de textes pour servir à l'étude et à l'enseignement de l'histoire. *See Gen. Bibl.* IV.
CSEL. Corpus scriptorum ecclesiasticorum latinorum. *See Gen. Bibl.* IV.
CSHB. Corpus scriptorum historiae Byzantinae.
DNB. Dictionary of National Biography. *See Gen. Bibl.* I.
EcfrAR. Écoles françaises d'Athènes et de Rome. Paris.
EETS. Early English Text Society. *See Gen. Bibl.* IV.
EncBr. Encyclopaedia Britannica. *See Gen. Bibl.* I.
Fonti. Fonti per la storia d'Italia. *See Gen. Bibl.* IV.
KAW. Kaiserliche Akademie der Wissenschaften. Vienna.
Mansi. *See Gen. Bibl.* IV.
MGH. Monumenta Germaniae Historica. *See Gen. Bibl.* IV.
MHP. Monumenta historiae patriae. Turin. *See Gen. Bibl.* IV.
MPG. Migne's Patrologiae cursus completus. Ser. graeco-latina. [Greek texts with Latin translations in parallel columns.] *See Gen. Bibl.* IV.
MPL. Migne's Patrologiae cursus completus. Ser. latina. *See Gen. Bibl.* IV.
PAW. Königliche preussische Akademie der Wissenschaften. Berlin.
PRO. Public Record Office.
RAH. Real Academia de la Historia. Madrid.
RC. Record Commissioners. *See Gen. Bibl.* IV.
Rolls. Rerum Britannicarum medii aevi scriptores. *See Gen. Bibl.* IV.
RR.II.SS. *See* Muratori *in Gen. Bibl.* IV.
SGUS. Scriptores rerum Germanicarum in usum scholarum. *See* Monumenta Germaniae Historica *in Gen. Bibl.* IV.
SHF. Société de l'histoire de France. *See Gen. Bibl.* IV.
SRD. Scriptores rerum Danicarum medii aevi. *See Gen. Bibl.* IV.

Abh.	Abhandlungen.	mém.	mémoire.
antiq.	antiquarian, antiquaire.	n.s.	new series.
app.	appendix.	progr.	programme.
coll.	collection.	publ.	published, publié.
diss.	dissertation.	R. / r.	real, reale.
enl.	enlarged.	repr.	reprinted.
hist.	history, histoire, historical, historique, historisch.	rev.	revised.
Jahrb.	Jahrbuch.	roy.	royal, royale.
k.	kaiserlich. / königlich. / koninklijk.	ser.	series.
		soc.	society, société, società.
		stor.	storico, storica.
mem.	memoir.	Viert.	Vierteljahrsschrift.

GENERAL BIBLIOGRAPHY.

I. DICTIONARIES, BIBLIOGRAPHIES, AND GENERAL WORKS OF REFERENCE.

Allgemeine deutsche Biographie. Ed. Liliencron, R. von, and Wegele, F. X (Hist. Commission BAW.) 56 vols. Leipsic. 1875–1912. (AllgDB.)

Annuario bibliografico della storia d' Italia. 1902 ff.

Ballester, R. Bibliografía de la Historia de España. Gerona. 1921. [Select.]

Balzani, U. Le cronache italiane nel Medio Evo. 3rd edn. Milan. 1909.

Below, G. von, and Meinecke, F. *edd.* Handbuch der mittelalt. und neu. Geschichte. Munich. 1903 ff., in progress. (Below-Meinecke.)

Bernheim, E. Lehrbuch der historischen Methode und der Geschichtsphilosophie 5th and 6th enl. edn. Leipsic. 1908.

Biographie nationale de Belgique. Brussels. 1866 ff., in progress. (Acad. Roy. des sciences, des lettres, et des beaux arts.)

Biographie universelle, ancienne et moderne. (Michaud.) 45 vols. Paris. 1854–65. [Greatly improved edn. of earlier work, 1811–28, and supplt., 1832–62.] (BUniv.)

Bresslau, H. Handbuch der Urkundenlehre für Deutschland und Italien. Leipsic. 1889. Vol. I. 2nd edn. enl. 1912.

Cabrol, F. and Leclercq, H. Dictionnaire d'archéologie chrétienne et de liturgie. Vols. I–VIII (in 16 pts.). Paris. 1907 ff., in progress.

Calvi, E. Bibliografia generale di Roma medioevale e moderna. Pt. I. Medio Evo. Rome. 1906. Supplt. 1908.

Capasso, B. Le fonti della storia delle provincie napolitane dal 568 al 1500. Ed. Mastrojanni, E. O. Naples. 1902.

Ceillier, R. Histoire générale des auteurs sacrés et ecclésiastiques. 23 vols. Paris. 1729–63. New edn. 14 vols. in 15. Paris. 1858–69.

Chevalier, C. U. J. Répertoire des sources historiques du moyen âge. Bio-bibliographie. Paris. 1883–8. Rev. edn. 2 vols. 1905–7. Topo-bibliographie. Montbéliard. 1894–1903.

Dahlmann, F. C. and Waitz, G. Quellenkunde der deutschen Geschichte. 8th edn. Herre, P. Leipsic. 1912. [9th edn. in contemplation.]

Dictionary of National Biography. Ed. Stephen, L. and Lee, S. 63 vols. London. 1885–1900. 1st supplt. 3 vols. 1901. Errata vol. 1904. Re-issue. 22 vols. 1908–9. 2nd supplt. 3 vols. 1912. 3rd supplt. 1927. (DNB.)

Du Cange, C. du Fresne. Glossarium ad scriptores mediae et infimae Latinitatis. Edns. of Henschel, 7 vols., Paris, 1840–50, and Favre, 10 vols., Niort, 1883–7.

—— Glossarium ad scriptores mediae et infimae Graecitatis. 2 vols. Lyons. 1688.

Egidi, P. La storia medioevale. (Guide bibliografiche, 8–9.) Rome. 1922. [Italian publications.]

Encyclopaedia Britannica. 11th & 13th edn. 32 vols. Cambridge. London and New York. 1910–26. 14th edn. 24 vols. London and New York. 1929. (EncBr.)

Encyclopaedia of Islam. A dictionary of the geography, ethnography, and biography of the Muhammadan peoples. Ed. Houtsma, M. T., Arnold, T. W., and Basset, R. Leiden and London. 1913 ff., in progress.

Ersch, J. S. and Gruber, J. G. Allgemeine Encyklopädie der Wissenschaften und Künste. Berlin. 1818–90. (Ersch-Gruber.) [Incomplete.]

Giry, A. Manuel de diplomatique. 2nd edn. 2 vols. Paris. 1925.

Giuseppi, M. S. Guide to the Manuscripts preserved in the Public Record Office. 2 vols. London. 1923–4.

Grässe, J. G. T. Lehrbuch einer allgemeinen Litterärgeschichte aller bekannten Völker der Welt von der ältesten bis auf die neueste Zeit. 4 vols. Leipsic. 1837–59.

Gröber, G. *ed.* Grundriss der romanischen Philologie. 2 vols. Strasbourg. 1888–1902. 2nd edn. Vol. I. 1904–6.
Gross, C. Sources and Literature of English History from the earliest times to about 1485. 2nd edn. enl. London. 1915.
Hardy, T. D. Descriptive catalogue of materials relating to the history of Great Britain and Ireland to the end of the reign of Henry VII. 3 vols. in 4. (Rolls.) 1862–71.
Hastings, J. and Selbie, J. A. Encyclopaedia of Religion and Ethics. 12 vols. Edinburgh and New York. 1908–21.
Herre, P., Hofmeister, A., and Stübe, R. Quellenkunde zur Weltgeschichte. Leipsic. 1910.
Herzog, J. J. and Hauck, A. Real-Encyklopädie für protestantische Theologie und Kirche. 3rd edn. 24 vols. Leipsic. 1896–1913.
Holtzendorff, F. von. Encyklopädie der Rechtswissenschaft. 5th edn. Leipsic. 1890. 6th edn. Kohler, J. 2 vols. Leipsic. 1904. Vol. I. 7th edn. 1913. (Holtzendorff-Kohler.)
Jahresberichte für deutsche Geschichte. Ed. Loewe, V., Brackmann, A., and Hartung, F. Jahrg. 1925 ff. Leipsic. 1927 ff.
Jansen, M. and Schmitz-Kallenberg, L. Historiographie und Quellen der deutschen Geschichte bis 1500. 2nd edn. (Meister's Grundriss. *See below.*) 1914.
Krumbacher, K. Geschichte der byzantinischen Literatur. *See below*, v.
Lichtenberger, F. Encyclopédie des Sciences religieuses. 13 vols. Paris. 1877–82.
Lorenz, O. Deutschlands Geschichtsquellen im Mittelalter seit der Mitte des 13 Jahrhts. 3rd edn. 2 vols. Berlin. 1886–7.
Maigne d'Arnis, W. H. Lexicon manuale ad scriptores mediae et infimae Latinitatis. (Publ. by Migne.) Paris. 1858. Repr. 1866 and 1890.
Manzoni, L. Bibliografia statutaria e storica italiana. 2 vols. in 3. Bologna. 1876–92. I. Bibl. d. statuti, ordini, e legge dei municipii. 2 pts. II. Bibl. storica municipale, etc. A–E. [No more publ.]
Meister, A. *ed.* Grundriss der Geschichtswissenschaft zur Einführung in das Studium der deutschen Geschichte des Mittelalters und der Neuzeit. Leipsic. 1906 ff. 2nd edn. 1912 ff., in progress.
Molinier, A. Les Sources de l'histoire de France des origines aux guerres d'Italie (1494). 6 vols. (Manuels de bibliographie historique, III, 1.) Paris. 1901–6.
Monod, G. Bibliographie de l'histoire de France depuis les origines jusqu'en 1789. Paris. 1888.
Nouvelle Biographie générale,...avec les renseignements bibliographiques. Ed. Höfer, J. C. F. 46 vols. Paris. 1854–66. (BGén.)
Oudin, Casimir. Commentarius de scriptoribus ecclesiae antiquae illorumque scriptis tam impressis quam manuscriptis adhuc extantibus in celebrioribus Europae bibliothecis a Bellarmino etc. omissis ad annum MDCCLX. 3 vols. Frankfort-on-M. and Leipsic. 1722.
Paetow, L. J. Guide to the study of Medieval History. (University of California Syllabus Series, No. 90.) Berkeley, California. 1917.
Paul, H. *ed.* Grundriss der germanischen Philologie. 3rd edn. Strasbourg. 1911 ff.
Pirenne, H. Bibliographie de l'histoire de Belgique. Brussels and Ghent. 1893. 2nd edn. 1902.
Potthast, A. Bibliotheca historica medii aevi. Wegweiser durch die Geschichtswerke des europäischen Mittelalters bis 1500. 2nd edn. 2 vols. Berlin. 1896.
Redlich, O. and Erben, W. Urkundenlehre. Pts. I and III. (Below-Meinecke. *See above.*) Munich. 1907, 11.
Rivista storica italiana. Turin. 1884 ff., in progress. [Up to 1921 contained quarterly classified bibliography of books and articles on Italian history.]
Sánchez Alonso, B. Fuentes de la historia española. Vol. I. Madrid. 1919.
Solmi, A. La storia del diritto italiano. (Guide bibliografiche, 10.) Rome. 1922.
Thompson, E. M. Introduction to Greek and Latin Palaeography. London. 1912.
Vacant, A. and Mangenot, E. Dictionnaire de théologie catholique. Paris. 1899 ff.
Victoria History of the Counties of England. London. 1900 ff., in progress. (Vict. Co. Hist.)

Vildhaut, H. Handbuch der Quellenkunde zur deutschen Geschichte bis zum Ausgange der Staufer. 2nd edn. Werl. 1906.
Villien, A. and Magnin, E. Dictionnaire de droit canonique. Paris. 1924 ff., in progress.
Wattenbach, W. Deutschlands Geschichtsquellen im Mittelalter bis zur Mitte des 13 Jahrhunderts. 6th edn. 2 vols. Berlin. 1893-4. Vol. I. 7th edn. Dümmler, E. Stuttgart and Berlin. 1904.
Wetzer, H. J. and Welte, B. Kirchenlexikon oder Encyklopädie der katholischen Theologie. 1847-60. 2nd edn. Kaulen, F. Freiburg-i.-B. 1882-1903. Index. 1903. (Wetzer-Kaulen.) French transl. Goschler, I. 26 vols. Paris. 1869-70.
Whitney, J. P. Bibliography of Church History. (Historical Assoc. Leaflet 55.) London. 1923.

II. ATLASES AND GEOGRAPHY.

Baudrillart-Vogt-Rouziès. Dictionnaire d'histoire et de géographie ecclésiastique. Paris. 1911 ff., in progress.
Droysen, G. Allgemeiner historischer Handatlas. Bielefeld. 1886.
Freeman, E. A. Historical Geography of Europe (with Atlas). London. 1881. 3rd edn. revised and ed. Bury, J. B. 1903.
Kretschmer, K. Historische Geographie von Mitteleuropa. (Below-Meinecke. *See above*, I.) Munich. 1904.
Longnon, A. Atlas historique de la France depuis César jusqu'à nos jours. (Text separate.) Paris. (1885-9.) 1912. [Incomplete.]
Muir, R. and Philip, G. Philip's Historical Atlas, mediaeval and modern. 6th edn. London. 1927.
Poole, R. L. *ed.* Historical Atlas of Modern Europe. Oxford. 1902. [With valuable introductions.]
Putzger, F. W. Historischer Schul-Atlas. Ed. Baldamus, A. and others. 43rd edn. Bielefeld and Leipsic. 1922.
Schrader, F. Atlas de géographie historique. New edn. Paris. 1907.
Shepherd, W. R. Historical atlas. 6th edn. London. 1927.
Spruner-Menke. Hand-Atlas für die Geschichte des Mittelalters und der neueren Zeit. Gotha. 1880. (3rd edn. of Spruner's Hand-Atlas etc. Ed. Menke, T.)

(For place-names:—)

Bischoff, H. T. and Möller, J. H. Vergleichendes Wörterbuch der alten, mittleren, und neuen Geographie. Gotha. 1892.
Deschamps, P. Dictionnaire de Géographie. (Supplt. to Brunet, J. C. Manuel du Libraire.) Paris. 1870. 2nd edn. 2 vols. 1878, 80.
Grässe, J. G. T. Orbis Latinus. Dresden. 1861. Ed. Benedict, F. Berlin. 1909. [Part I only.]
Martin, C. T. The Record Interpreter. London. 1892. 2nd edn. 1910. [For the British Isles.]
See also above, I. Chevalier, Répertoire etc., Topo-bibliographie.

III. CHRONOLOGY, NUMISMATICS, AND GENEALOGY.

(Chronology:—)

L'Art de vérifier les dates et les faits historiques. 2e partie. Depuis la naiss. de J.-C. 3rd edn. Paris. 3 vols. 1783 ff., and other edns. and reprints. Also 4th edn. by Saint-Allais. 18 vols. 1818-19.
Belviglieri, C. Tavole sincrone e genealogiche di storia italiana dal 306 al 1870. Florence. 1875. Repr. 1885.

Bond, J. J. Handybook of rules and tables for verifying dates. London. Last edn. 1875.
Calvi, E. Tavole storiche dei comuni italiani. Pts. I–III. Rome. 1903–7. I. Liguria e Piemonte. II. Marche. III. Romagna. [Also useful bibliographies.]
Eubel, C. Hierarchia catholica medii aevi. Vol. I. 2nd edn. Münster. 1913.
Gams, P. B. Series episcoporum ecclesiae Catholicae. (With supplt.) Ratisbon. 1873, 86.
Grotefend, H. Taschenbuch der Zeitrechnung des deutschen Mittelalters und der Neuzeit. 3rd enl. edn. Hanover. 1910.
—— Zeitrechnung des deutschen Mittelalters und d. Neuzeit. 2 vols. Hanover. 1891, 98.
Janus: ein Datumweiser für alle Jahrhunderte. By Doliarius, J. E. Leipsic. *n.d.*
Lane-Poole, S. The Mohammadan Dynasties. London. 1894.
Mas Latrie, J. M. J. L. de. Trésor de chronologie, d'histoire, et de géographie pour l'étude des documents du moyen âge. Paris. 1889.
Nicolas, Sir N. H. The chronology of history. Revised edn. London. 1838.
Poole, R. L. Medieval reckonings of time. (Helps for Students of History.) S.P.C.K. London. 1918.
Rühl, F. Chronologie des Mittelalters und der Neuzeit. Berlin. 1897.
Savio, F. Gli antichi vescovi d' Italia dalle origini al 1300. Il Piemonte. Turin. 1899. La Lombardia. Pt. I (Milano.) Florence. 1913.
Schram, R. Hilfstafeln für Chronologie. Vienna. 1883. New edn. Kalendariographische und chronologische Tafeln. Leipsic. 1908.
Stokvis, A. M. H. J. Manuel d'histoire, de généalogie, et de chronologie de tous les États du globe etc. 3 vols. Leiden. 1888–93.
Stubbs, W. Registrum sacrum Anglicanum. 2nd edn. Oxford. 1897.
Wallis, J. E. W. English regnal years and titles, hand-lists, Easter dates, etc. (English Time-books. Vol. I). (Helps for Students of History.) S.P.C.K. London. 1921.
(*Note:*—Much information in such works as Gallia Christiana; Ughelli, Italia sacra; for which see IV.)

(NUMISMATICS:—)

Blanchet, A. and Dieudonné, A. Manuel de numismatique française. Vols. I, II. Paris. 1912, 16, in progress.
Corpus nummorum italicorum. Vols. I–XV. Rome. 1910 ff., in progress.
Dieudonné, A. Les Monnaies françaises. (Collection Payot, 34.) Paris. 1925.
Engel, A. and Serrure, R. Traité de numismatique du moyen âge. 2 vols. Paris. 1891, 94.
Grueber, H. A. Handbook of the Coins of Great Britain and Ireland in the British Museum. London. 1899.
Hill, G. F. Coins and Medals. (Helps for Students of History.) S.P.C.K. London. 1920. [Bibliographical guide.]
Luschin von Ebengreuth, A. Allgemeine Münzkunde und Geldgeschichte des Mittelalters und der neueren Zeit. (Below-Meinecke. *See above,* I.) Munich. 1904. 2nd edn. 1926.
Macdonald, G. The Evolution of Coinage. Cambridge. 1916.
Martinori, E. La Moneta. Rome. 1915. [Dictionary of names of coins.]

(GENEALOGY:—)

Cokayne, G. E. Complete Peerage of England, Scotland, Ireland, Great Britain, and the United Kingdom. 8 vols. Exeter. 1887–98. New enl. edn. Gibbs, V. and others. London. 1910 ff., in progress.
Fernandez de Bethencourt, F. Historia genealógica y heráldica de la Monarquía Española, Casa Real, y Grandes de España. Madrid. 1897 ff., in progress.
Foras, E. A. de and Maréschal de Luciane. Armorial et Nobiliaire de l'ancien duché de Savoie. Vols. I–IV. Grenoble. 1863–1902.

George, H. B. Genealogical Tables illustrative of Modern History. Oxford. 1873. 5th edn. rev. and enl. Weaver, J. R. H. 1916.
Grote, H. Stammtafeln mit Anhang calendarium medii aevi. (Münzstudien. Vol. IX.) Leipsic. 1877.
Guasco di Bisio, F. Dizionario feudale degli antichi stati sardi e della Lombardia dall' epoca carolingica ai nostri tempi (774–1909). 5 vols. (Biblioteca della soc. storica subalpina. Vols. 54–58.) Pinerolo. 1911.
Institut héraldique de France. Le Nobiliaire universel. 24 vols. Paris. 1854–1900.
Litta, P. (and continuators). Famiglie celebri italiane. 11 vols. Milan and Turin. 1819–99. 2nd series. Naples. 1902 ff., in progress.
Moreri, L. Le grand dictionnaire historique. Latest edn. 10 vols. Paris. 1759. English version, Collier, J. 2nd edn. with suppIts. and app. 4 vols. London. 1701–16.
Voigtel, T. G. and Cohn, L. A. Stammtafeln zur Geschichte d. europäischen Staaten. Vol. I. Die deutschen Staaten u. d. Niederlande. Brunswick. 1871.
See also L'Art de vérifier les dates (*above*), Lane-Poole, Mohammadan Dynasties (*above*), and Stokvis (*above*).

IV. SOURCES AND COLLECTIONS OF SOURCES.

Achery, L. d'. Spicilegium sive collectio veterum aliquot scriptorum. 13 vols. Paris. 1655(1665)–77. New edn. Barre, L. F. J. de la. 3 vols. Paris. 1723.
Acta Sanctorum Bollandiana. Jan.–Oct. VI. Antwerp, Brussels, and Tongerloo. 1643–1794. Oct. VII–XIII. Brussels, Paris and Rome, Paris. 1845–83. Nov. Paris and Rome, Brussels. 1887 ff., in progress. [The reprint of Jan.–Oct. X. published by Palmé at Paris and Rome, 1863 ff., among other variations, has 3 instead of 2 vols. of Jan., and re-arranges the contents of the 7 vols. of June.] (ASBoll.) [Supplemented by Analecta Bollandiana. 1882 ff. (AB.)]
Amari, M. *See under* Muratori.
Archivio storico italiano. (ASI.) *See List of Abbreviations* (1).
Biblioteca della società storica subalpina. Ed. Gabotto, F. and Tallone, A. Pinerolo, etc. 1899 ff., in progress. [Contains charters and monographs.]
Böhmer, J. F. Regesta Imperii. (New edn. in several parts by various editors.) Innsbruck. 1877 ff. [*See also Gen. Bibl. of Vol.* V, p. 838.]
  V. Regesten d. Kaiserreichs...1198–1272. Ed. Ficker, J. and Winkelmann, E. 3 vols. 1881–1901.
  VI. Regesten d. Kaiserreichs...1273–1313. Ed. Redlich, O. Abtlg. 1. 1898, in progress.
Bouquet. *See* Rerum Gallicarum...scriptores.
Brackmann, A. Germania Pontificia. *See under* Kehr, P. F.
Camden Society. Publications. London. 1838 ff., in progress. (Now publ. by the Roy. Hist. Soc.)
Chartes et diplômes relatifs à l'histoire de France. AcadIBL. Paris. 1908 ff., in progress.
Classiques de l'histoire de France au moyen âge. General editor: Halphen, L. Paris. 1924 ff., in progress. (Class. hist.) [Texts and French translations.]
Collection de chroniques Belges inédits. Brussels. 1836 ff., in progress.
Collection de documents inédits sur l'histoire de France. Paris. 1835 ff., in progress. (Coll. doc.)
Collection de textes pour servir à l'étude et à l'enseignement de l'histoire. Paris. 1886 ff., in progress. (Coll. textes.)
Corpus Iuris Canonici. Vol I. Decretum Gratiani. Vol. II. Decretales Gregorii P. IX etc. Ed. Friedberg, E. Leipsic. 1879, 81. [Critical edition.]
—— (Edition of Gregory XIII.) 3 vols. Lyons. 1584; and other 16th century edns. also. [Contains the medieval glosses.]
Corpus Iuris Civilis. 3 vols. Berlin. [Critical modern edn.]
  Vol. I. Institutiones. Ed. Krueger, P. Digesta. Ed. Mommsen, T. 13th edn. 1920.
  Vol. II. Codex Iustinianus. Ed. Krueger, P. 9th edn. 1915.
  Vol. III. Novellae. Ed. Schoell, R. and Kroll, W. 4th edn. 1912.

Corpus Iuris Civilis (*cont.*). Ed. Gothofredus, D. 3rd edn. 6 vols. Cologne. 1612; and other edns. [Contains the medieval glosses and additions, such as the Libri Feudorum.]
Corpus scriptorum ecclesiasticorum latinorum. Vienna. 1866 ff., in progress. (CSEL.)
Dugdale, W. Monasticon Anglicanum. 3 vols. London. 1655–73. New edn. by Caley, J., and others. 6 vols. in 8. London. 1817–30. Repr. 1846.
Early English Text Society. Publications. London. 1864 ff., in progress. (EETS.)
España Sagrada. Ed. Florez, H. and others. 51 vols. Madrid. 1747–1879.
Fejér, G. Codex diplomaticus Hungariae ecclesiasticus et civilis. (Chronological table by Knauz, F. Index by Czinár, M.) 45 vols. Buda-Pest. 1829–66.
Fonti per la storia d' Italia. Publ. by Istituto storico italiano. Rome. 1887 ff., in progress. (Chronicles, 36 vols. Letters, 6 vols. Diplomas, 7 vols. Statutes, 7 vols. Laws, 1 vol. Antiquities, 3 vols.) (Fonti.)
Gallia Christiana (Vetus). Ed. Sainte-Marthe, S. de, and others. 4 vols. Paris. 1656.
—— (Nova). Vols. I–XIII. Ed. Sainte-Marthe, D. de, and others. Vols. XIV–XVI. Ed. Hauréau, B. Paris. 1715–1865. 2nd edn. Revised by Piolin, P. Vols. I–V, XI, XIII. Paris. 1870–8. Provincia Tolosana. New edn. Vol. I. Toulouse. 1892.
—— (Novissima). Ed. Albanès, J. H. and Chevalier, C. U. J. 3 vols. Montbéliard and Valence. 1895–1900.
Geschichtschreiber der deutschen Vorzeit etc. Ed. Pertz, Wattenbach, and others. New series. Leipsic. 1884, in progress. [German translations.]
Graevius, J. G. and Burmannus, P. Thesaurus antiquitatum et historiarum Italiae etc. 30 vols. Leiden. 1704–23.
—— —— Thesaurus antiq. et histor. Siciliae, Sardiniae, Corsicae, etc. 15 vols. Leiden. 1723–5. [Forms a continuation of the preceding.]
Guizot, F. P. C. Collection des mém. relatifs à l'hist. de France...jusqu'au 13e siècle. Paris. 1823–35. [French translations.]
Haddan, A. W. and Stubbs, W. Councils and ecclesiastical documents relating to Great Britain and Ireland. Ed. after Spelman and Wilkins. 3 vols. Oxford. 1869–78.
Hinschius, P. Decretales pseudo-Isidorianae et Capitula Angilramni. Leipsic. 1863.
Historiae patriae monumenta. *See* Monumenta historiae patriae.
Kehr, P. F. Regesta Pontificum Romanorum.
Italia Pontificia. Ed. Kehr, P. F. Vol. I. Rome. II. Latium. III. Etruria. IV. Umbria etc. V. Aemilia. VI. Liguria. VII. Venetiae et Histria. Berlin. 1906–25.
Germania Pontificia. Ed. Brackmann, A. Vol. I. Salzburg. II, i, ii. Mayence. Berlin. 1910–27. In progress.
Liber Censuum de l'église romaine. Ed. Fabre, P. and Duchesne, L. Vol. I. EcfrAR. Paris. 1889–1910. Vol. II in progress.
Mabillon, J. Annales Ordinis S. Benedicti. 6 vols. Paris. 1703–39. 2nd edn Lucca. 1739–45.
Mabillon, J. and Achery, L. d'. Acta Sanctorum ord. S. Benedicti [A.D. 500–1100] 9 vols. Paris. 1668–1701. Repr. Venice. 1733–40. (ASBen.)
Mansi, J. D. Sacrorum conciliorum collectio. 31 vols. Florence and Venice. 1759–98. Repr. Martin, J. B. and Petit, L. (With continuation, vols. 32–50.) Paris. 1901 ff., in progress. (Mansi.)
Marrier, M. and Quercetanus (Duchesne), A. Bibliotheca Cluniacensis. Paris. 1614.
Martène, E. and Durand, U. Thesaurus novus anecdotorum. 5 vols. Paris. 1717.
Mémoires et documents publiés par l'École des Chartes. Paris. 1896 ff.
Migne, J. P. Patrologiae cursus completus. Series graeco-latina. Paris. 1857–66. 161 vols. in 166. (MPG.) Indices, Cavallera, F. Paris. 1912. *Also* Hopfner, T. Paris. 1928, in progress. [This is the series containing Greek texts with Latin translations in parallel columns. The so-called Series graeca (81 vols. in 85. 1856–67) contains Latin translations only.]
—— —— Series latina. 221 vols. Paris. 1844–55. Index, 4 vols. 1862–4. (MPL.)
Mirbt, C. Quellen zur Geschichte des Papsttums und des römischen Katholizismus. 2nd edn. Freiburg, Tübingen, and Leipsic. 1901. 4th edn. 1924. (Mirbt. Quellen.)

Monumenta Germaniae Historica. Ed. Pertz, G. H., Mommsen, T., and others. Hanover and Berlin. 1826 ff. Index. 1890. [For full list of the different series *see Gen. Bibl. of Vol.* v. pp. 840–1.] (MGH.)

Deutsche Chroniken (Scriptores qui vernac. lingua usi sunt). I–VI. 1892 ff., in progress.

Epistolae saec. XIII e regestis pontificum Romanorum. I–III. 1883–94.

Epistolae selectae. I–IV. 1916 ff., in progress. 8°. (Epp. select.)

Legum sectiones quinque. 4°.

Sect. III. Concilia. 2 vols. in 4. 1893–1924.

Sect. IV. Constitutiones etc. I–V, VI 1, VIII. 1893 ff.

Libelli de lite imperatorum et pontificum (saec. XI, XII.) I–III. 1891 ff.

Scriptores. Vols. I–XXX. Fol. 1826–1928. And 4°. Vols. XXXI, XXXII. 1903, 1913. In progress. (Script.)

Scriptores rerum Germanicarum in usum scholarum. Hanover. 1839 ff. Fresh series. 1890–1920. 8°. (SGUS.) [Contains revised editions of many of Scriptores in Fol. edition.]

Scriptores rerum Germanicarum. Nova Series. I–IV 1, V. Berlin. 1922 ff., in progress. (Script. N.S.)

Monumenta historiae patriae. 19 vols. Fol. 2 vols. 4°. Turin. 1836 ff., in progress. (MHP.)

Muratori, L. A. Rerum Italicarum scriptores. 25 vols. Milan. 1723–51. Supplements: Tartini, J. M., 2 vols., Florence, 1748, 70; and Mittarelli, J. B., Venice, 1771; and Amari, M., Biblioteca arabo-sicula, versione italiana, and Appendix. Turin and Rome. 1880–1, 1889. Indices chronolog. Turin. 1885. New enl. edn. with chronicles printed as separate parts. Carducci, G. Fiorini, V. Fedele, P. Città di Castello and Bologna. 1900 ff., in progress. (RR.II.SS.)

—— Antiquitates italicae medii aevi. 6 vols. Milan. 1738–42. Indices chronolog. Turin. 1885.

Papal Documents.

Epistolarum Innocentii libri undecim. [Bks. I, II, V, X–XVI only.] Ed. Baluze, S. 2 vols. Paris. 1682. Bks. III, V–IX, ed. La Porte du Theil, F. J. G. *in* Diplomata...ad res Francicas spectantia. Ed. Bréquigny, L. G. O. F. de. 2 vols. Paris. 1791. New edn. 1843, 49. These three are repr. in MPL. CCXIV–CCXVII.

Registrum domini Innocentii III super negotio Romani imperii. Ed. Baluze, S. *in* Epistolarum...libri undecim. Vol. I. Paris. 1682. *Also in* MPL. CCXVI. *Facsimile* ed Peitz, W. M. Rome. 1927.

Regesta Honorii Papae III. Ed. Pressutti, P. 2 vols. Rome. 1888, 95.

Registres de Grégoire IX. Ed. Auvray, L. Pts. I–XII. EcfrAR. Paris. 1896 ff., in progress.

Registres d' Innocent IV. Ed. Berger, E. 4 vols. EcfrAR. Paris. 1884–1921.

Registres d' Alexandre IV. Ed. Bourel de la Roncière, C. etc. Pts. I–V. EcfrAR. Paris. 1902 ff., in progress.

Registres d' Urbain IV. Ed. Guiraud, J. 4 vols. EcfrAR. Paris. 1901–6.

Registres de Clément IV. Ed. Jordan, E. Pts. I–V. EcfrAR. Paris. 1893 ff., in progress.

Registres de Grégoire X et de Jean XXI. Ed. Guiraud, J. and Cadier, L. Pts. I–IV. EcfrAR. Paris. 1892 ff., in progress.

Registres de Nicolas III. Ed. Gay, J. Pts. I–III. EcfrAR. Paris. 1898 ff., in progress.

Registres de Martin IV. Pts. I, II. EcfrAR. Paris. 1901 ff., in progress.

Registres d'Honorius IV. Ed. Prou, M. EcfrAR. Paris. 1888.

Registres de Nicolas IV. Ed. Langlois, E. 2 vols. EcfrAR. Paris. 1905.

Potthast, A. Regesta Pontificum Romanorum inde ab anno 1198 ad annum 1304. 2 vols. Berlin. 1874–5.

Record Commissioners, Publications of the. London. 1802–69. (RC.)

Regesta chartarum Italiae. Publ. by K. Preuss. Histor. Instit. and Istituto storico italiano. Rome. 1907 ff., in progress.

Regesta Pontificum Romanorum. *See above under* Kehr, P. F. *and* Potthast, A.

Rerum Britannicarum medii aevi scriptores. (Chronicles and Memorials of Great Britain and Ireland during the Middle Ages.) Published under direction of the Master of the Rolls. London. 1858 ff. (Rolls.) [For convenient list see Gross (Section I, *above*), App. C.]

Rerum Gallicarum et Francicarum scriptores. (Recueil des hist. des Gaules et de la France.) Ed. Bouquet, M. and others. 23 vols. 1738–1876. Vols. I–XIX re-ed. by Delisle, L. 1868–80, and vol. XXIV, 1894. New series. 4°. 1899, in progress. (Bouquet.)

Rymer, T. Foedera. [1101–1654.] 20 vols. (XVI ff. by Sanderson, R.) London. 1704–35. 3rd edn. The Hague. 1739–45. New edn. [1069–1383] by Clarke, A., Holbrooke, F., and Caley, J. 4 vols. in 7 pts. (RC.) London. 1816–69. Syllabus by Hardy, T. D. 3 vols. London. 1869–85. Report (app. A–E only) by Cooper, C. P. (RC.) London. [1836?] Publ. 1869.

Scriptores rerum Danicarum medii aevi. Ed. Langebek, I. and others. 9 vols. Copenhagen. 1772–1878. (SRD.)

Scriptores rerum Germanicarum in usum scholarum. (SGUS.) *See above*, Monumenta Germaniae Historica.

Selden Society. Publications. London. 1888 ff., in progress.

Société de l'histoire de France. Publications. Paris. 1834 ff., in progress. (SHF.)

Stevenson, J. Church Historians of England. London. 1853–8. [Translations.]

Stubbs, W. Select Charters and other illustrations of English Constitutional History to the reign of Edward I. Oxford. 1870. 9th edn. rev. Davis, H. W. C. Oxford. 1913.

Theiner, A. Codex diplomaticus dominii temporalis S. Sedis. 3 vols. Rome. 1861–2

Ughelli, F. Italia sacra. 2nd edn. Coleti, N. 10 vols. Venice. 1717–22.

Vic, C. de and Vaissete, J. J. Histoire générale de Languedoc. New edn Dulaurier, E. 16 vols. Toulouse. 1872–1904.

V. MODERN WORKS.

Altamira, R. Historia de España y de la civilización española. 3rd edn. 4 vols. Barcelona. 1913–14.

Alzog, J. Universalgeschichte der Kirche. Mayence. 1841. Best edn. 10th by Kraus, F. X. 1882. Transl. (from 9th German edn.) Pabisch, F. J. and Byrne, T. S. Manual of Church History. 4 vols. Dublin. 1895–1900.

Baronius, C. Annales Ecclesiastici una cum critica historico-chronologica P. A. Pagii. [–1198.] Contin. by Raynaldus, O. [1198–1565] Ed. Mansi, J. D. Lucca. 34 vols. 1738–46. Apparatus and Index, 4 vols. 1740, 1757–9. New edn. 37 vols. Bar-le-duc. 1864–83. [Not completed.]

Bédier, J. and Hazard, P. *edd.* Histoire de la littérature française illustrée. 2 vols. Paris. 1923–4.

Bibliothèque de l'École des Hautes Études. Paris. 1869 ff., in progress. (BHE.)

Bréhier, L. L'Église et l'Orient au moyen âge. Les Croisades. 5th edn. Paris. 1928. (Bibliothèque de l'enseignement de l'histoire ecclésiastique.) [With bibliography.]

Brown, P. Hume. History of Scotland to the present time. (Library edn.) 3 vols. Cambridge. 1911.

Brunner, H. Deutsche Rechtsgeschichte. 2 vols. Leipsic. 1887, 92. Vol. I. 2nd edn. 1906. Vol. II, ed. Schwerin, C. von. 1928.

—— Grundzüge der deutschen Rechtsgeschichte. 7th edn. Heymann, E. Munich. 1919. [Bibliographies.]

Bryce, J. The Holy Roman Empire. New edn. London. 1906, and reprints.

Cambridge History of English Literature. Ed. Ward, A. W. and Waller, A. R. 15 vols. Cambridge. 1907–27.

Cánovas del Castillo, A. *ed.* Historia general de la España. (By members of R. Acad. de la Hist.) Madrid. 1892 ff., in progress.

Carlyle, R. W. and A. J. A history of Mediaeval Political Theory in the West. Vols. I–V. Edinburgh and London. 1903 ff., in progress.

Coulton, G. G. Five Centuries of Religion. Vols. I, II. Cambridge. 1923 ff., in progress.

Cunningham, W. The growth of English Industry and Commerce. [Vol. I.] Early and Middle Ages. 5th edn. Cambridge. 1910.

Denifle, H. Die Universitäten des Mittelalters bis 1400. Vol. I. Die Entstehung der Universitäten. Berlin. 1885. [No more publ.]

Ebert, A. Allgemeine Geschichte der Litteratur des Mittelalters im Abendland. 3 vols. Leipsic. 1874–87. 2nd edn. of vols. I. and II. 1889.
England, A History of, in seven volumes. Ed. Oman, C. 7 vols. London. 1905–13.
——The Political History of. Ed. Hunt, W. and Poole, R. L. 12 vols. London. 1905–10.
Ficker, G. and Hermelink, H. Das Mittelalter. (Handbuch d. Kirchengesch. für Studierende. Ed. Krüger, G. Vol. I, ii.) Tübingen. 1912.
Fleury, C. Histoire ecclésiastique. 20 vols. Paris. 1691–1720. Continued to end of 18th century under Vidal, O. Many editions. (Orig. edn. to 1414. 4 add. vols. by Fleury to 1517, publ. Paris. 1836–37.)
Gebhardt, B. Handbuch d. deutschen Geschichte. 2 vols. Stuttgart. 1891–2.
Gibbon, E. The History of the Decline and Fall of the Roman Empire. 1776–81. Ed. in 7 vols. by Bury, J. B. London. 1896–1900. Latest edn. London. 1909–14. [Notes essential, especially for bibliography.]
Gierke, O. Das deutsche Genossenschaftsrecht. 4 vols. Berlin. 1868–1913.
—— Political Theories of the Middle Age. Transl. and ed. Maitland, F. W. Cambridge. 1900. [Translation of a section of the preceding.]
Gieseler, J. C. L. Lehrbuch der Kirchengeschichte. Vols. I–III (in 8 pts.). 4th, 2nd, and 1st edns. Bonn. 1844–8; 35–53. Engl. transl. Davidson, S. and Hull, J. W. Vols. I–III. Edinburgh. 1853 ff.
Gilson, E. La philosophie au moyen âge. 2 vols. Paris. 1922. [Bibliographies.]
Gregorovius, F. Geschichte der Stadt Rom im Mittelalter. 5th edn. 8 vols. Stuttgart. 1903–8. (Engl. transl. from 4th edn. by Mrs A. Hamilton. 8 vols. in 13. London. 1894–1902.)
Hampe, K. Deutsche Kaisergeschichte in der Zeit der Salier und Staufer. 5th edn. Leipsic. 1923.
Hanotaux, G. *ed.* Histoire de la nation française. Paris. 1920 ff., in progress.
Harnack, C. G. A. Lehrbuch der Dogmengeschichte. 4th edn. 3 vols. (Sammlung theolog. Lehrbücher). Tübingen. 1909–10. Engl. transl. of the 3rd edn. Buchanan, N. and others. 7 vols. London. 1894–9.
Hartmann, L. M. *ed.* Weltgeschichte in gemeinverständlicher Darstellung.
Vol. IV. Hellmann, S. Das Mittelalter bis zum Ausgang der Kreuzzüge. Gotha. 1920.
Vol. V. Kaser, K. Das späte Mittelalter. Gotha. 1921.
Haskins, C. H. Studies in the history of Mediaeval Science. Cambridge, Mass. 1924.
Hauck, A. Kirchengeschichte Deutschlands. 5 vols. Leipsic. 1887–1920. Vols. I–IV. 4th edn. 1906–13. Vol. V. 2nd edn. 2 pts. 1911, 20.
Heeren, A. H. L., and others, *edd.* Geschichte der europäischen Staaten. Hamburg and Gotha. 1829 ff. Continued as section I of Allgemeine Staatengeschichte. Ed. Lamprecht, K. and Oncken, H. *Cited sub nom. auct.* (Heeren.)
Hefele, C. J. v., contin. Hergenröther, J. A. G. Conciliengeschichte. 9 vols. Freiburg-i.-B. 1855 ff. 2nd edn. 1873 ff. French transl. Delarc, O. 1869. New rev. Fr. transl. Leclercq, H. Vols. I–VIII (in 16 pts.). Paris. 1907 ff., in progress. (Hefele-Leclercq.)
Heyd, W. Histoire du Commerce du Levant au moyen-âge. 2nd edn. (in French transl. by Raynaud, F.) 2 vols. Leipsic. 1885–6. Reprinted. 2 vols. Leipsic. 1923.
Hinojosa, E. de. Historia general del derecho español. Vol. I. Madrid. 1887. [No more publ.].
Hinschius, P. Das Kirchenrecht der Katholiken und Protestanten in Deutschland. Pt. I. System des kathol. Kirchenrechts, mit besonderer Rücksicht auf Deutschland. Vols. I–VI, 1. Berlin. 1869–97.
Historische Studien. Ed. Ebering, E. Berlin. 1896 ff., in progress.
Holdsworth, W. S. History of English Law. 3rd edn. Vols. I–III. London. 1922–3.
Jahrbücher der deutschen Geschichte bis 1250. (Hist. Commission BAW.) Berlin and Leipsic. 1862 ff., in progress.
Kirchenrechtliche Abhandlungen. Ed. Stutz, U. Stuttgart, 1902 ff., in progress.
Köhler, G. Die Entwicklung des Kriegswesen und der Kriegsführung in der Ritterzeit von der Mitte des 11 Jahrhunderts bis zu den Hussitenkriegen. 3 vols. Breslau. 1886–90.

Kraus, F. X. Geschichte der christlichen Kunst. 2 vols. in 4. Freiburg-i.-B. 1896–1908.
Kretschmayr, H. Geschichte von Venedig. Vols. I, II. (Heeren. *See above.*) Gotha. 1905, 20.
Krumbacher, K. Geschichte der byzantinischen Literatur. (527–1453.) 2nd edn. (Handbuch d. klass. Altertums-Wissenschaft. Ed. Müller, I. von. Vol. IX, i.) Munich. 1897.
Lamprecht, K. Deutsche Geschichte. 12 vols. in 16. Berlin. 1891–1909. Vols. I–V. 3rd edn. 1902–6. Suppl ts. 2 vols. in 3. 1902–4.
Langen, J. Geschichte der römischen Kirche. 4 vols. Bonn. 1881.
Lavisse, E. *ed.* Histoire de France jusqu'à la Révolution. 9 vols. in 18. Paris. 1900–11. Vols. I–IV.
Lavisse, E. and Rambaud, A. *edd.* Histoire générale du IVe siècle jusqu'à nos jours. Vols. I–III. Paris. 1893–1896.
Lea, H. C. History of the Inquisition of the Middle Ages. 3 vols. New York. 1887. French transl. Reinach, S., with introdn. by Frédéricq, P. 3 vols. Paris. 1900–2.
—— History of Sacerdotal Celibacy in the Christian Church. 3rd edn. 2 vols. London. 1907.
Lloyd, J. E. History of Wales from the earliest times to the Edwardian Conquest. 2nd edn. 2 vols. London. 1912.
Loserth, J. Geschichte des späteren Mittelalters von 1197 bis 1492. (Below-Meinecke. *See above*, I.) Munich. 1903.
Luchaire, A. Manuel des institutions françaises; période des Capétiens directs. Paris. 1892.
Manitius, M. Geschichte der lateinischen Literatur des Mittelalters. 2 pts. (Handbuch d. klass. Altertums-Wissenschaft. Ed. Müller, I. von. Vol. IX, ii 1, 2.) Munich. 1911, 23.
Merriman, R. B. The rise of the Spanish empire in the old world and the new. Vols. I and II. New York. 1918.
Miller, W. The Latin Orient. (Helps for Students of History.) S.P.C.K. London. 1920. [Contains a Bibliography.]
Moeller, W. Hist. of the Christian Church (A.D. 1–1648). Transl. Rutherfurd and Freese. 3 vols. London. 1892–1900.
Mosheim, J. L. von. Institutionum historiae ecclesiasticae antiquae et recentioris libri IV. 4 vols. Helmstedt. 1755. Transl. Murdock, J., ed. Soames, H. 4 vols. London. 1841. 2nd rev. edn. 1850.
Müller, K. Kirchengeschichte. Vols. I, II. Freiburg-i.-B. 1892.
Muratori, L. A. Annali d' Italia. 12 vols. Milan. 1744–9. Also other editions.
Norden, W. Das Papsttum und Byzanz. Berlin. 1903.
Oman, C. W. C. History of the Art of War in the Middle Ages. 2nd edn. enl. 2 vols. London. 1924.
Oncken, W. *ed.* Allgemeine Geschichte in Einzeldarstellungen. 45 vols. Berlin. 1879–93. *Cited sub nom. auct.* (Oncken.)
Orpen, G. H. Ireland under the Normans (1169–1333). 4 vols. Oxford. 1911–20.
Pertile, A. Storia del diritto italiano dalla caduta dell' impero Romano alla codificazione. 2nd edn. Del Giudice, P. 6 vols. Turin. 1892–1902. Index. Eusebio, L. Turin. 1893.
Petit de Julleville, L. *ed.* Histoire de la langue et de la littérature française. 8 vols. Paris. 1896–1900.
Pirenne, H. Histoire de Belgique. Vol. I. 3rd edn. Brussels. 1909. Vol. II. 2nd edn. 1908.
Pollock, F. and Maitland, F. W. The history of English Law before Edward I. 2nd edn. 2 vols. Cambridge. 1898.
Poole, R. L. Illustrations of the history of Medieval Thought and Learning. 2nd edn. London. 1920.
Previté-Orton, C. W. Outlines of Medieval History. 2nd edn. Cambridge. 1924.
Ranke, L. von. Weltgeschichte. 9 vols. Leipsic. 1881–8. And later edns.
Rashdall, H. The Universities of Europe in the Middle Ages. 2 vols. in 3. Oxford. 1895. [A new edn. is in preparation.]

Reichel, O. J. The elements of Canon Law. London. 1887.
Richter, G. and Kohl, H. Annalen d. deutschen Geschichte im Mittelalter. 3 pts in 5. Halle-a.-S. 1873–98.
Savigny, F. C. von. Geschichte des Römischen Rechts im Mittelalter. 2nd edn. 7 vols. Heidelberg. 1834–51. French transl. Guenoux, C. 4 vols. Paris. 1839.
Schaube, A. Handelsgeschichte der romanischen Völker des Mittelmeergebiets bis zum Ende der Kreuzzüge. (Below-Meinecke. *See above*, I.) Munich. 1906.
Schröder, R. Lehrbuch der deutschen Rechtsgeschichte. 6th edn. Ed. Künnsberg, E. von. Berlin and Leipsic. 1922.
Schulte, J. F. v. Die Geschichte der Quellen und Literatur des Canonischen Rechts von Gratian bis auf die Gegenwart. 3 vols. Stuttgart. 1875–80.
Storia letteraria d' Italia scritta da una società di professori. Milan. 1900 ff.
Storia politica d' Italia scritta da una società d' amici. Ed. Villari, P. Vols. III (Lanzani, F.), IV (Cipolla, C.). Milan. 1882, 81.
Storia politica d' Italia scritta da una società di professori. Vols. III (Romano, G.), IV (Gianani, F.), V (Orsi, P.). Milan. [1900 ff.]
Stubbs, W. Constitutional history of England. 3 vols. Oxford. 1873–8. (Frequently reprinted.) French transl. Lefebvre, G., with notes and studies by Petit-Dutaillis, C. 3 vols. Paris. 1907–27. English transl. of notes, etc. Ed. Tait, J. Studies and notes supplementary to Stubbs' Constitutional History. Vol. I. Transl. Rhodes, W. E. Vol. II. Transl. Waugh, W. T. Manchester. 1908, 14.
Tiraboschi, G. Storia della letteratura italiana. New edn. 9 vols. in 16. Florence. 1805–13. Milan. 1822–6.
Überweg, F. Grundriss der Geschichte der Philosophie. 10th edn. Ed. Heinze, M. and Prächter, K. 4 vols. Berlin. 1904–9. [Bibliography.]
Vinogradoff, P. Roman Law in Mediaeval Europe. 2nd edn. Oxford. 1929. [Bibliographies.]
Viollet, P. Histoire du droit civil français. 3rd edn. Paris. 1905.
—— Histoire des institutions politiques et administratives de la France. 3 vols. Paris. 1890–1903.
Waitz, G. Deutsche Verfassungsgeschichte. Vols. V–VIII. Vol. V. 2nd edn. Zeumer, K. Berlin. 1893; Vol. VI. 2nd edn. Seeliger, G. Berlin. 1896; Vol. VIII. Kiel. 1878.
Weil, G. Geschichte der islamitischen Völker von Mohammed bis zur Zeit des Sultans Selim. Stuttgart. 1866.
Werminghoff, A. Geschichte der Kirchenverfassung Deutschlands im Mittelalter. Vol. I. Hanover and Leipsic. 1905.
Zeller, J. Histoire d'Allemagne. Vols. I–IX. Paris. 1872–91. [No more publ.]

CHAPTER I.

INNOCENT III.

I. SPECIAL BIBLIOGRAPHIES.

Innocent's dealings with the Empire are covered by the Bibliography to chapters II, III, IV *below*; the Fourth Crusade and the establishment of the Latin rite in the East by the Bibliographies to Vol. IV, chapters XIV and XIX; and his relations with Catharism by the Bibliography to ch. XX *below*; and relations with England and France by the Bibliographies to chapters VII and IX *below*.

Chevalier, C. U. J. Répertoire des sources historiques du moyen âge. Bio-bibliographie. *See Gen. Bibl.* I.
Hampe, K. Mittelalterliche Geschichte. Gotha. 1922. [For recent works on the period.]
Hefele-Leclercq. Histoire des Conciles. Vol. v. *See Gen. Bibl.* v.
Luchaire, A. Innocent III. [Vol. VI.] Le Concile de Latran. pp. 191–222. *See below*, IV.
Meyer, E. W. Staatstheorien Papst Innocenz' III. Bonn. 1920.
Potthast, A. Bibliotheca historica medii aevi. *See Gen. Bibl.* I.

II. CRITICISM OF INNOCENT'S REGISTER.

[*See also below*, VI. B. Curia.]

Battandier, A. Un volume dei Regesti di Innocenzo III donato alla Santità di N.S. Leone XIII da Lord Ashburnham. *In* Studi e documenti di storia e diritto. VI. Rome. 1885.
Delisle, L. Mémoire sur les actes d'Innocent III. BEC. XIX. 1857; XXV. 1863.
—— Les registres d'Innocent III. BEC. XLVI. 1885; XLVII. 1886; LVII. 1896.
Denifle, A. Die päpstlichen Registerbände des 13. Jahr. und das Inventar derselben vom J. 1339. *In* Archiv f. Lit. u. Kirchengeschichte. II. 1886.
Elkan, H. Die Gesta Innocentii im Verhältnis zu den Regesten desselben Papstes. Heidelberg. 1876.
Heckel, R. v. Untersuchungen zu den Registern Innocenz III. HJ. XL. 1920.
Luchaire, A. Les Registres d'Innocent III et les Regesta de Potthast. *In* Bibl. de la Faculté de lettres de Paris. XVIII. 1914.
Peitz, W. M. Das Originalregister Gregors VII im Vatikanischen Archiv nebst Beiträgen zur Kenntnis der Originalregister Innocenz III und Honorius III. SKAW. 1911.
—— Die Entstehung des Registrum super negotio Romani imperii und der Anlass zum Eingreifen Innocenz III in der deutschen Thronstreite. HJ. XXVI. 1926.
Winkelmann, E. Zu den Regesten des Papstes Innocenz III. FDG. IX. 1869.

III. ORIGINAL AUTHORITIES: THE REGISTER AND CANONS.

Böhmer, J. F. Regesta Imperii, 1198–1272. *See Gen. Bibl.* IV.
Corpus Iuris Canonici. Ed. Friedberg, E. *See Gen. Bibl.* IV.
Delisle, L. Lettres inédites d'Innocent III. BEC. XXXIV. 1873.
Hampe, K. Aus verlorenen Registerbänden der Päpste Innocenz III und Innocenz IV. MIOGF. XXIII. 1902.
Innocentius III papa. Epistolae. *See Gen. Bibl.* IV *under* Papal Documents.
—— De contemptu mundi; sermones de diversis; sermones de sanctis. MPL. CCXVII.
—— Gesta. Ed. Baluze, S. *in* Epistolarum Innocentii libri XI. Vol. I. Paris. 1682. *Also in* MPL. CCXIV.
—— Prima collectio decretalium. Ed. Baluze, S. *op. cit.* *Also in* MPL. CCXVI.
—— Registrum domini Innocentii III papae super negotio Romani imperii. *See Gen. Bibl.* IV *under* Papal Documents.
Potthast, A. Regesta Pontificum Romanorum. Vol. I. *See Gen. Bibl.* IV.

Quinque compilationes antiquae. Ed. Friedberg, E. Leipsic. 1882. [Compilations III and IV.]
[For Councils, *see* Mansi, J. D. Sacrorum Conciliorum amplissima Collectio. Vol. XXII. *See Gen. Bibl.* IV.]

IV. BIOGRAPHICAL STUDIES.

Brischar, J. N. Papst Innocenz III und seine Zeit. Freiburg-i.-B. 1883.
Delisle, L. Itinéraire d'Innocent III, dressé d'après les actes de ce pontife. BEC. XIX. 1857.
Deutsch, F. Papst Innocenz III und sein Einfluss auf die Kirche. Breslau. 1876.
Domenici, G. Innocenzo III. Rome. 1917.
Gutschow, E. Innocenz III und England. Munich. 1904.
Haller, J. Innocenz III und Otto IV. *In* Papsttum und Kaisertum. Paul Kehr zum 65 Geburtstag dargebracht. Munich. 1926.
Hurter, F. v. Geschichte Papst Innocenz III und seiner Zeitgenossen. 3rd edn. 4 vols. Hamburg. 1841-3. French transl. with introdn., notes, etc. Jager, J. N. and Vial, T. 3 vols. Paris. 1843.
Luchaire, A. Innocent III. 6 vols. Paris. 1905-8.
1. Rome et l'Italie. 2. La Croisade des Albigeois. 3. La Papauté et l'Empire. 4. La Question d'Orient. 5. Les royautés vassales du Saint-Siège. 6. Le Concile de Latran et la réforme de l'Église.
Meda, C. Un grand' assertore del papato. Nel VII centenario della morte di Innocenzo III. Rome. 1916.
Reinlein, F. F. Papst Innocenz der Dritte und seine Schrift De Contemptu Mundi. Erlangen. 1871.
Schwemer, L. Innocenz III und die deutsche Kirche. Strasbourg. 1882.
Serafini, A. Innocenzo III e la riforma religiosa agli inizi del secolo XIII. Rome 1917.

V. THE CHURCH AND SOCIETY.

Baethgen, F. Der Anspruch des Papsttums auf das Reichsvikariat. ZSR. XLI. Kanon. Abt. x. 1920.
Burdach, K. Vom Mittelalter zur Reformation. Berlin. 1913.
Carlyle, A. J. The Development of the theory of the Authority of the Spiritual over the Temporal Power from Gregory VII to Innocent III. *In* Tijdschrift voor Rechtsgeschiedenis. v. Haarlem. 1923.
—— and R. W. A history of Mediaeval Political Theory in the West. Vol. v. *See Gen. Bibl.* v.
—— R. W. The claims of Innocent III to authority in temporal matters. *In* Tijdschrift voor Rechtsgeschiedenis. v. 1924.
Döllinger, J. J. v. Die Papstfabeln des Mittelalters. 2nd edn. Stuttgart. 1890.
Ehrhard, A. Das Mittelalter und seine kirchliche Entwicklung. (Kultur und Katholizismus. Vol. VIII.) Mainz. 1908.
Friedberg, E. Die mittelalterlichen Lehren über das Verhältnis von Staat und Kirche. Pt. I. Leipsic. 1874.
Gierke, O. v. Das deutsche Genossenschaftsrecht. Vol. III. *See Gen. Bibl.* v.
Gumplowicz, L. Geschichte der Staatstheorien. Innsbruck. 1905.
Hampe, K. Deutschland und die päpstliche Weltherrschaft. Leipsic. 1910.
Hauck, A. Der Gedanke der päpstlichen Weltherrschaft bis Bonifacius VIII. Leipsic. 1904.
Langen, J. Geschichte der römischen Kirche. Vol. IV. Bonn. 1893.
Molitor, W. Die Decretale Per venerabilem. Münster. 1876.
Rocquain, F. La cour de Rome et l'esprit de réforme avant Luther. Vol. I. Paris. 1893.
Sägmuller, J. Die Idee von der Kirche als imperium Romanum im kanonischen Recht. *In* Theol. Quartalschrift. Tübingen. LXXX. 1898.
Schnürer, G. Kirche und Kultur im Mittelalter. Vol. II. Paderborn. 1926.
Schwerner, R. Papsttum und Kaisertum. Stuttgart. 1899.

Tangl, M. Die Deliberatio Innocenz' III. SPAW. 1919.
Troeltsch, E. Die Soziallehren der Christlichen Kirchen und Gruppen. 3rd edn. Tübingen. 1923.

VI. JUSTICE AND ADMINISTRATION.

A. Law.

Baier, H. Päpstliche Provisionen für niedere Pfründen bis zum Jahre 1304. Münster. 1911.
Below, G. v. Das ausschliessliche Wahlrecht der Domkapitel. Bonn. 1882.
Bethmann-Hollweg, M. A. v. Der Civilprocess des gemeinen Rechts in geschichtlicher Entwicklung. Vol. vi, pt. 3. Bonn. 1874.
Brys, J. De Dispensatione in Jure canonico praesertim apud Decretistas et Decretalistas usque ad medium saeculum decimum quartum. Louvain. 1925.
Ebers, G. J. Das Devolutionsrecht vornehmlich nach kathol. Kirchenrecht. Stuttgart. 1906.
Esmein, A. Le Mariage du droit canon. Paris. 1892.
Fournier, P. L'Église et le droit romain au XIIIe siècle. BHE. Paris. 1921.
Genestal, R. Le Privilegium fori en France du Décret de Gratian à la fin du XIVe siècle. (BHE., Sciences religieuses, 35.) Paris. 1921.
Hefele-Leclercq. Histoire des Conciles. Vol. v. *See Gen. Bibl.* v.
Hinschius, P. System des kathol. Kirchenrechts, mit besonderer Rücksicht auf Deutschland. *See Gen. Bibl.* v.
Hübler, B. Kirchenrechtsquellen. Urkundenbuch zu Vorlesungen über Kirchenrecht. Berlin. 1898.
Le Bras, G. L'Immunité réelle. Rennes. 1920.
—— The Canon Law. *In* Legacy of the Middle Ages. Ed. Crump, C. G. and Jacob, E. F. Oxford. 1926.
Leitner, M. Lehrbuch des kathol. Eherechts. Paderborn. 1921.
Paulus, N. Geschichte des Ablasses im Mittelalter. Vol. I. Paderborn. 1922.
Phillips, G. Kirchenrecht. Vol. VI. Ratisbon. 1864.
Roland, E. Les Chanoines et les élections épiscopales en France du XIe au XIVe siècle. Aurillac. 1909.
Ruess, K. Die rechtliche Stellung der päpstlichen Legaten bis Bonifaz VIII. Paderborn. 1912.
Sägmuller, J. Lehrbuch des kathol. Kirchenrechts. 4th edn. Freiburg-i.-B. 1925.
Saltet, L. Les Réordinations. Paris. 1907.
Schulte, J. F. v. Die Geschichte der Quellen und Literatur des Canonischen Rechts. *See Gen. Bibl.* v.
Tangl, M. Die Teilnehmer an den allgemeinen Konzilien des Mittelalters. Weimar. 1922.
Tillmann, H. Die päpstlichen Legaten in England bis zur Beendigung des Legations Gualas, 1218. Bonn. 1926.
Zimmermann, H. Die päpstliche Legation in der ersten Hälfte des 13 Jahrhunderts. Paderborn. 1913.

B. The Curia: and the Chancery.

(i) *Original authorities.*

Chronicon Abbatiae de Evesham. Ed. Macray, W. D. (Rolls.) 1863.
Giraldus Cambrensis. De jure et statu Menevensis ecclesiae. Ed. Brewer, J. S. *in* Opera. Vol. III. (Rolls.) 1863.
Ricardus Anglicus. Summa de ordine iudiciario. *In* Quellen zur Geschichte des Römisch-Kanonischen Processes im Mittelalter. Ed. Wahrmund, L. Innsbruck. 1915.
Tangl, M. Die päpstlichen Kanzleiordnungen 1200–1500. Vienna. 1894.

(ii) *Secondary authorities.*

Baumgarten, P. M. Von der apostolischen Kanzlei. Untersuchungen über die päpstlichen Tabellionen und die Vizekanzler der h. Römischen Kirche. Cologne. 1918.

Bresslau, H. Handbuch der Urkundenlehre für Deutschland und Italien. *See Gen. Bibl.* I.
Clark, A. C. The *Cursus* in Medieval and Vulgar Latin. Oxford. 1910.
Ehrle, F. Die Frangipani und der Untergang des Archivs und der Bibliothek der Päpste am Anfang des dreizehnten Jahrh. *In* Mélanges offerts à E. Chatelain. Paris. 1910.
Giry, A. Manuel de diplomatique. *See Gen. Bibl.* I.
Poole, R. L. Lectures on the history of the Papal Chancery. Cambridge. 1915.
—— Léopold Delisle. (Proc. Brit. Acad. Vol. v.) London. 1911.
Sägmuller, J. Die Entwicklung der Rota bis zur Bulle Johannis XXII "Ratio iuris" a. 1326. *In* Theol. Quartalschrift. LXX. 1895.
Santi, A. de. Il cursus nella storia letteraria e nella liturgia. Rome. 1903.
Spaethen, M. Giraldus Cambrensis und Thomas von Evesham über die von ihnen an der Kurie geführten Prozesse. Neu. Arch. XXXI. 1906.
Toynbee, Paget. Dante and the *Cursus*. Dantis Epistolae. Oxford. 1920.
Valois, N. Étude sur le rythme des bulles pontificales. BEC. XIII.

C. Dogma.

Grabmann, M. Die Geschichte der scholastischen Methode. Vol. II. Freiburg-i.-B. 1911.
Harnack, A. v. Lehrbuch der Dogmengeschichte. Vol. III. Freiburg-i.-B. 1910.
Lea, H. C. History of Auricular Confession and Indulgences in the Latin Church. London and Philadelphia. 1896.
Steitz, G. Das römische Busssakrament. Frankfort. 1854.
Stone, D. History of the doctrine of the Holy Eucharist. Vol. I. London. 1909.
Teetaert, A. La Confession aux laïques dans l'Église latine depuis le VIIIe jusqu'au XIVe siècle. Louvain. 1926.
Vacandard, E. Le pouvoir des clefs et la confession sacramentelle. *In* Revue du Clergé français. XVII. 1899.

VII. ROME AND ITALY.

(i) Original Authorities.

[For Chronicle and other Sources see the Bibliography of ch. v.]

Analecta iuris pontificii. XXIII, XXIV. Ed. Chaillot, L. Rome. 1881, 96.
Fabre, P. and Duchesne, L. Le Liber censuum de l'Église romaine. *See Gen. Bibl.* IV.
Ryccardi de Sancto Germano Chronica. Ed. Gaudenzi, A. (Soc. napol. di storia patria. Mon. stor., Ser. I. Cronache.) Naples. 1888.
Theiner, A. Codex Diplomaticus dominii temporalis S. Sedis. *See Gen. Bibl.* IV.

(ii) Secondary Authorities.

(a) Rome.

Boüard, A. de. La suzeraineté du pape sur Rome au XIIIe et XIVe siècle. RH. CXVI. 1914.
Calisse, C. I prefetti di Vico. ASRSP. 1888.
—— Le regioni di Roma nel medio evo. *In* Studi e documenti di storia e diritto. 1889.
Gregorovius, F. Rome in the Middle Ages. Transl. Hamilton, Mrs A. Vol. v. *See Gen. Bibl.* v.
Halphen, L. Études sur l'administration de Rome au moyen âge. (BHE.) Paris. 1907.
Paravicini. Saggio storico sulla prefettura urbana dal secolo X al XIV. Rome. 1900.
Rodocanachi, E. Les institutions communales de Rome sous la papauté. Paris. 1901.
Schneider, Fedor. Rom und Romgedanke im Mittelalter. Munich. 1926.
Schoenian, E. Die Idee der Volkssouveränität im mittelalterlichen Rome. Leipsic. 1919.
Tomassetti, G. La pace di Roma, anno 1188. *In* Rivista internazionale di scienze sociali e discipline auxiliarie. 1896.

(*b*) *Patrimony.*

Ciampi, I. Cronache e statuti della città di Viterbo. *In* R. Dep. di storia patria pei le provincie di Toscana, etc. Documenti. v. Florence. 1872.

Lanzi, L. Un lodo d'Innocenzo III ai Narnesi specialmente per la terra di Stroncone. *In* Bollettino della società umbra di storia patria. Perugia. 1895.

Magistris, A. de. Il viaggio d' Innocenzo III nel Lazio e il primo spedale in Anagni. *In* Studi e documenti di storia e diritto. XIX. 1898.

Pinzi, C. Storia della città di Viterbo. Rome. 1887–9.

Signorelli, G. Il potestà del commune di Viterbo. *In* Studi e documenti di storia e diritto. 1894.

Tomassetti, G. Documenti feudali della provincia di Roma nel medio evo. *Ibid.* XIX. 1898.

—— La Campagna Romana antica, medioevale e moderna, con figure, tavole e piante. Vols. I–IV. Rome. 1910–26.

(*c*) *Italy.*

Baethgen, F. Die Regentschaft Papst Innocent III im Königreich Sizilien. Heidelberg. 1914.

Below, G. v. Die italienische Kaiserpolitik des deutschen Mittelalters. HZ. Beiheft. 1927.

Bonazzi, L. Storia di Perugia. Vol. I. Perugia. 1875.

Darmstädter, P. Das Reichsgut in der Lombardei und Piedmont bis 1250. Strasbourg. 1896.

Davidsohn, R. Forschungen zur älteren Geschichte von Florenz. Vol. I. Berlin. 1896; Vol. IV. 1908.

—— Geschichte von Florenz. Vols. I, II. Berlin. 1896, 1908.

Ficker, J. Forschungen zur Reichs- und Rechtsgeschichte Italiens. 4 vols. Innsbruck. 1868–74.

Hampe, K. Deutsche Angriffe auf das Königreich Sizilien im Anfang des 13 Jahrhunderts. HVJS. VII. 1904.

—— Deutsche Kaisergeschichte in der Zeit der Salier und Staufer. *See Gen. Bibl.* V.

Lenel, W. Der Konstanzer Frieden von 1183 und die italienische Politik Friedrichs I. HZ. 3rd ser. XXXII. 1923. [For Italian background.]

Levi, G. Documenti ad illustrazione del registro del Cardinale Ugolino d' Ostia, legato apostolico in Toscana e Lombardia. ASRSP. XII. 1889.

Overmann, A. Gräfin Mathilde von Tuscien, ihre Besitzungen, Geschichte ihres Gutes von 1125–1230 und ihre Regesten. Innsbruck. 1895.

Pfaff, V. Kaiser Heinrichs höchstes Angebot an die römische Kurie (1196). Heidelberg. 1927.

Prinz, P. Markward von Anweiler. Emden. 1879.

Scheffer-Boichorst, P. Zu den Mathildinischen Schenkungen. MIOGF. IX. 1888; XI. 1890.

—— Zwei Untersuchungen zur päpstliche Territoriat und Finanzpolitik. MIOGF. IV. Erganzungsband. 1893. [Both for territorial background.]

VIII. ALBIGENSIAN CRUSADE.

(i) Original Authorities.

[For Guides, *see* Smedt, C. de. Les Sources de l'hist. de la Croisade contre les albigeois. RQH. XVI. 1874; Molinier, A. Les Sources de l'histoire de France. Vol. III. *See Gen. Bibl.* I.]

Balme, F. *ed.* Cartulaire...de St-Dominique. 3 vols. Paris. 1893–1901.

Barrau, J. J. and Daragon, B. Nouveaux documents sur l'hist. de France au XIe, XIIe, XIIIe siècles; hist. des croisades contre les albigeois. 2 vols. Paris. 1840.

Chanson de la croisade contre les albigeois. Ed. Meyer, P. 2 vols. (SHF.) Paris. 1875, 79.

Garlande, Jean de. De triumphis Ecclesiae. Ed. Wright, T. (Roxburghe Club.) London. 1856.

Guillaume de Puylaurens. Historia albigensium. *In* Bouquet. XIX, XX.

Guiraud, J. Cartulaire de Notre-Dame de Prouille. Vols. I, II. Paris. 1907.
Pierre de Vaux-Cernay. Petri Vallium Sarnaii monachi Hystoria Albigensis. Ed. Guébin, P., and Lyon, E. Vol. I. Paris. 1926. *Full text in* Bouquet. XIX. *Also in* MPL. CCXIII.
Vic, C. de and Vaissete, J. J. Histoire générale de Languedoc. Vol. VIII. Preuves. *See Gen. Bibl.* IV.
Villemagne, A. Bullaire du bienheureux Pierre de Castelnau martyr de la foi. Montpellier. 1917.

(ii) SECONDARY AUTHORITIES.

[*See also* Bibliography to ch. xx, sect. IV. c.]

Besse, G. Histoire des comtes de Carcassonne. Béziers. 1645.
Castillon, H. Histoire du comté de Foix. 2 vols. Toulouse. 1852.
Catel, G. Histoire des comtes de Toulouse avec quelques traités et chroniques anciennes concernant la même histoire. Toulouse. 1623.
Chassanion, J. Histoire des albigeois touchant leur doctrine et religion. Geneva. 1595.
Delpech, H. La Bataille de Muret et la tactique de la cavalerie au XIIIe siècle. Paris. 1878.
Dezazars, L. L'Hérésie des albigeois et la croisade contre les hérétiques. *In* Mém. de la Soc. archéol. du Midi. XII. 1883.
Gay, J. L'Histoire des schismes et hérésies des albigeois. Paris. 1561.
Guiraud, J. Article: Croisade contre les Albigeois *in* Dictionnaire d'Histoire et de Géographie ecclésiastiques. Ed. Baudrillart, A. Paris. 1912.
Jordan, E. La responsabilité de l'Église dans la répression de l'hérésie au moyen âge. Paris. 1907.

IX. INNOCENT AND THE KINGDOMS.

(i) NORWAY AND THE NORTH.

Bugge, A. Norges Historie. Vol. II. Oslo. 1909.
Origines Islandicae. Ed. Vigfusson, G. and Powell, F. Y. Oxford. 1883.
The Saga of King Sverri. Ed. and transl. Sephton, J. London. 1899.
Willson, T. B. History of the Church and State in Norway. London. 1903.

(ii) SPAIN AND PORTUGAL.

Altamira, R. Historia de España. Vol. I. *See Gen. Bibl.* V.
Colmeiro, M. Reyes Cristianos desdes Alfonso VI hasta Alfonso XI. *In* Historia general de la España. Ed. Cánovas del Castillo, A. 1893. *See Gen. Bibl.* V.
Fita y Colome, F. Biographia inedita de Alfonso IX rey de Leon por Gil de Zamora. BRAH. III. 1888.
Gams, P. B. Die Kirchengeschichte von Spanien. Vol. III. Regensburg. 1876.
Herculano, A. Historia de Portugal. Vol. II. Lisbon. 1888.
Merriman, R. B. The Spanish Empire in the Old World and the New. Vol. I. *See Gen. Bibl.* V.

(iii) HUNGARY.

Fermendzin, E. *ed.* Acta Bosniae potissimum ecclesiastica, 925–1752. *In* Monumenta spectantia historiam Slavorum meridionalium. Vol. V. Agram. 1892.
Fraknói, V. Ecclesiastical and political relations of Hungary with the Roman Curia. Vol. I. Buda-Pest. 1900. (In Hungarian.)
Lanczy, G. St Étienne et la papauté. 1901.

(iv) SERBIA AND BULGARIA.

Jireček, C. J. Geschichte der Bulgaren. Prague. 1876.
—— Geschichte der Serben. Vol. I. Gotha. 1911.
—— Staat und Gesellschaft im mittelalterlichen Serbien. Pt. I. *In* Denkschriften des KAW. Phil.-Hist. Kl. LVI. 1912.
Novaković, S. Introduction to Zakonik Stefana Dušana, cara Srpskog 1349 e 1354. Belgrade. 1898.
Theiner, A. Vetera monumenta Slavorum meridionalium. Rome. 1863.
Xénopol, A. D. L'Empire Valacho-bulgare. RH. XLVII. 1891.

CHAPTERS II, III, IV.

GERMANY, 1197—1273.

I. BIBLIOGRAPHIES.

In addition to the standard Bibliographies (Dahlmann-Waitz, Quellenkunde; Potthast, Bibliotheca historica medii aevi; Wattenbach, Deutschlands Geschichtsquellen; Lorenz, Deutschlands Geschichtsquellen; Jansen and Schmitz-Kallenberg, Historiographie und Quellen der deutschen Geschichte bis 1500) for which *see Gen. Bibl.* I, there is a detailed list of authorities for the period in Böhmer's Regesta (2nd edn. Vol. v, pp. lxxxvii sqq. *See Gen. Bibl.* IV). An exhaustive bibliography for the ecclesiastical history of the period will be found in Hauck, Kirchengesch. Deutschlands. Vol. IV. *See Gen. Bibl.* V. A valuable review of recent works (1914–1920) will be found in Hampe's Wissenschaftliche Forschungsberichte: Mittelalterliche Geschichte. Gotha, 1922. For the latest literature on the subject the bibliographies in the Historische Vierteljahrsschrift (HVJS) and other periodicals should be consulted.

II. ORIGINAL DOCUMENTS.

Böhmer, J. F. Acta imperii selecta. Urkunden deutscher Könige und Kaiser mit einem Anhange von Reichssachen. Collected by Böhmer, J. F., ed. Ficker, J. Innsbruck. 1870.
—— Regesta Imperii. Vol. v. (1198–1272.) *See Gen. Bibl.* IV.
Constitutiones et Acta publica imperatorum et regum. Vol. II. Ed. Weiland, L. MGH. Legum Sect. IV. 1896.
Epistolae saeculi XIII e regestis pontificum Romanorum selectae. Ed. Rodenberg, C. 3 vols. MGH. 1883–94.
Huillard-Bréholles, J. L. A. Historia diplomatica Friderici II. 12 vols. Paris. 1852–61.
Innocent III. Registrum de negotio imperii. *See Gen. Bibl.* IV *under* Papal Documents. (A convenient edition of the Register, translated into German and ed. Tangl, G. is published in the series "Die Geschichtschreiber der deutschen Vorzeit." Leipsic. 1923.)
Origines Guelficae. Ed. Scheidt, C. L. 5 vols. Hanover. 1750–80.
Petri de Vineis...Epistolarum libri VI. 2 vols. Ed. Iselius, J. R. Basle. 1740. *Also in* Huillard-Bréholles, Vie et Correspondance de Pierre de la Vigne. Paris. 1864.
Winkelmann, E. Acta imperii inedita saeculi XIII et XIV. Urkunden und Briefe zur Geschichte des Kaiserreichs und des Königreichs Sicilien in den Jahren 1198–1400. 2 vols. Innsbruck. 1880, 85.

III. NARRATIVE AUTHORITIES.

Acta quorundam episcoporum Lubicensium. MGH. Script. xxv.
Aegidii Aureaevallensis Gesta pontificum Leodiensium (1048–1247). *Ibid.* xxv.
Albertus Bohemus. Ed. Höfler, C. *in* Bibliothek des Literarischen Vereins in Stuttgart. XVI, Abt. 2. Stuttgart. 1847.
Annales Egmundani. MGH. Script. XVI.
Annales Halesienses. *Ibid.* XVI.
Annales Hamburgenses. *Ibid.* XVI.
Annales Lubicenses. *Ibid.* XVI.
Annales Marbacenses. Ed. Bloch, H. SGUS. 1907.
Annales Monasterii de Burton. Ed. Luard, H. R. *in* Annales Monastici. Vol. I. (Rolls.) 1864.
Annales Monasterii de Oseneia. *Ibid.* Vol. IV. 1869.
Annales Monasterii de Waverleia. *Ibid.* Vol. II. 1865.
Annales Monasterii de Wintonia. *Ibid.*
Annales Pegavienses (Continuatio). MGH. Script. XVI.
Annales Prioratus de Dunstaplia. Ed. Luard, H. R. *in* Annales Monastici. Vol. III. (Rolls.) 1866.

Annales Prioratus de Wigornia. *Ibid.* Vol. IV. 1869.
Annales Reinhardsbrunnenses. MGH. Script. XXX.
Annales Scheftlarienses Maiores. *Ibid.* XVII.
Annales Scheftlarienses Minores. *Ibid.*
Annales Stadenses auctore Alberto. *Ibid.* XVI.
Annales Wormatienses. *Ibid.* XVII.
Annales Zwifaltenses. *Ibid.* X.
Arnoldi Chronica Slavorum. Ed. Pertz, G. H. SGUS. 1868.
Braunschweigische Reimchronik. MGH. Deutsche Chroniken. II. 1877.
Burchardi Praepositi Urspergensis Chronicon. Ed. Holder-Egger, O. and Simson, B.v. SGUS. 1916.
Caesarii Heisterbacensis Catalogus Archiepis. Coloniensium. MGH. Script. XXIV.
—— Dialogus Miraculorum. Excerpts relating to Otto IV *in* Leibnitz, G. W. Script. rerum Brunsvicensium. II. Hanover.
—— Vita Sancti Engelberti Archiepiscopi Coloniensis (1204–1225). Ed. Böhmer, J. F. *in* Fontes Rerum Germanicarum. II. Stuttgart. 1845.
Chronica Alberici monachi Trium Fontium a monacho Novi-monasterii Hoiensis interpolata. MGH. Script. XXIII.
Chronica Gervasii Monachi Cantuariensis. Ed. Stubbs, W. (Rolls.) 1879.
Chronica Magistri Rogeri de Houedene. Ed. Stubbs, W. 4 vols. (Rolls.) 1868–71.
Chronica Regia Coloniensis. Ed. Waitz, G. SGUS. 1880.
Chronicon Ebersheimense. MGH. Script. XXIII.
Chronicon Montis Sereni. *Ibid.* XXXIII.
Chronicon Thomae Wykes. Ed. Luard, H. R. *in* Annales Monastici. Vol. IV. (Rolls.) 1869.
Conradus de Fabaria. Casus sancti Galli. MGH. Script. II.
Continuatio Admuntensis. *Ibid.* IX.
Ellenhardi Bellum Waltherianum. *Ibid.* XVII.
—— Chronicon. *Ibid.*
Emonis et Menkonis Werumensium Chronica. *Ibid.* XXIII.
Gervasius Tilleberiensis. Otia imperialia. *Ibid.* XXVII.
Gesta Episcoporum Halberstadensium. *Ibid.* XXIII.
Gesta Episcoporum Traiectensium. *Ibid.*
Gesta Innocentii III papae (1198–1216) auctore anonymo coaevo. MPL. CCXIV.
Gesta Treverorum Continuata. MGH. Script. XXIV.
Gotifredi Viterbiensis Continuatio Eberbacensis. *Ibid.* XXII.
Hagen, Meister Gotfrid. Ed. Cardauns, H. *in* Chronikon der deutschen Städte. XII. Leipsic. 1875.
Heinrici Chronicon Lyvoniae. Ed. Arndt, W. SGUS. 1874.
Hermanni Altahensis Annales. MGH. Script. XVII.
Hugonis et Honorii Chronicorum Continuationes Weingartenses. Ed. Weiland, L. *in* Monumenta Welforum antiqua. SGUS. 1869.
Johannis Abbatis Victoriensis Liber Certarum Historiarum. Ed. Schneider, F. SGUS. 1909.
Matthaei Parisiensis Chronica Majora. Ed. Luard, H. R. 6 vols. (Rolls.) 1876.
Monumenta Erphesfurtensia. Ed. Holder-Egger, O. SGUS. 1899.
Narratio de morte Ottonis IV imperatoris. *In* Martène, E. and Durand, U. Thesaurus novus anecdotorum. Vol. V. *See Gen. Bibl.* IV.
Narratio de testamento et morte Ottonis IV imperatoris Anno 1218. *In* Origines Guelficae. Vol. III. pp. 840 sqq. *See above,* II.
Ottonis de S. Blasio Chronica. Ed. Hofmeister, A. SGUS. 1912.
Radulfi de Coggeshall Chronicon Anglicanum. Ed. Stevenson, J. (Rolls.) 1875.
Reineri Annales S. Jacobi Leodiensis. MGH. Script XVI.
Richeri Gesta Senoniensis Ecclesiae. *Ibid.* XXV.
Rogeri de Wendover...Flores Historiarum. Ed. Hewlett, H. G. (Rolls.) 1886–9.
Ryccardi de Sancto Germano Notarii Chronica. Ed. Pertz, G. H. SGUS. 1864.
Schöppenchronik Magdeburger. Ed. Janicke, K. *in* Chroniken der deutschen Städte. VII. Leipsic. 1869.
Vita Odiliae Leodiensis. MGH. Script. XXV.
Walther von der Vogelweide. Ed. Wilmans, W. 2nd edn. Halle. 1883; *also* ed. Paul, H. *in* Altdeutsche textbibliothek. I. Halle. 1894.

IV. MODERN WORKS.

A. General.

Abel, O. König Philipp der Hohenstaufe. Berlin. 1852.
—— Otto IV und König Friedrich II (1208–1212). Berlin. 1856.
Below, G. v. Der deutsche Staat des Mittelalter; eine Grundlegung der deutschen Verfassungsgeschichte. 2nd edn. Leipsic. 1925.
Fournier, P. Le Royaume d'Arles et de Vienne (1138–1378). Paris. 1891.
Gebauer, G. C. Leben und denckwürdige Thaten Herrn Richards erwählten Römischen Kaysers. Leipsic. 1744.
Hampe, K. Deutsche Kaisergesch. in der Zeit der Salier und Staufer. *See Gen. Bibl.* v.
Hauck, A. Kirchengeschichte Deutschlands. Vols. iv–v. *See Gen. Bibl.* v.
Jastrow, J. and Winter, G. Deutsche Geschichte im Zeitalter der Hohenstaufen. Stuttgart. Vol. ii. 1901.
Kantorowicz, E. Kaiser Friedrich der Zweite. Berlin. 1927.
Kempf, J. Geschichte des Deutschen Reiches während des grossen Interregnums 1245–1273. Würzburg. 1893.
Kington [Oliphant], T. L. The History of Frederick II, Emperor of the Romans. 2 vols. London. 1862.
Lorenz, O. Deutsche Geschichte im 13 und 14 Jahrhundert. Vol. i. Die Zeit des grossen Interregnums. Vienna. 1863.
Loserth, J. Geschichte des späteren Mittelalters von 1197 bis 1492. *See Gen. Bibl.* v.
Luchaire, A. Innocent III. 6 vols. Paris. 1905–8. (1. Rome et l'Italie. 2. La Croisade des Albigeois. 3. La Papauté et l'Empire. 4. La Question d'Orient. 5. Les Royautés vassales du Saint-Siège. 6. Le Concile de Latran.)
Meister, A. Deutsche Verfassungsgeschichte. 3rd edn. (Grundriss der Geschichtswissenschaft. Ed. Meister, A. ii, 3.) Leipsic and Berlin. 1922.
Michael, E. Geschichte des deutschen Volkes vom dreizehnten Jahrhundert bis zum Ausgang des Mittelalters. 6 vols. Freiburg. 1897–1915.
Pirenne, H. Histoire de Belgique. Vol. i. *See Gen. Bibl.* v.
Raumer, F. v. Geschichte der Hohenstaufen und ihrer Zeit. 5th edn. 6 vols. Leipsic. 1878.
Schirrmacher, F. W. Kaiser Friedrich der Zweite. 4 vols. Göttingen. 1859–65.
—— Die letzten Hohenstaufen. Göttingen. 1871.
Waitz, G. Deutsche Verfassungsgeschichte. *See Gen. Bibl.* v.
Werminghoff, A. Verfassungsgesch. der deutschen Kirche im Mittelalter. 2nd edn. (Grundriss der Geschichtswiss. Ed. Meister, A. ii, 6.) Leipsic and Berlin. 1913.
Winkelmann, E. Geschichte Friedrichs des Zweiten und seiner Reiche. Vol. i. 1212–1235. Berlin. 1863. Vol. ii, i. 1235–1239. Reval. 1865.
—— Kaiser Friedrich II, 1218–1233. 2 vols. (Jahrbücher d. deutsch. Geschichte.) Leipsic. 1889, 97.
—— Philipp von Schwaben und Otto IV von Braunschweig. 2 vols. (Jahrb. d. deutsch. Geschichte.) Leipsic. 1873, 78.

B. Special.

Aldinger, P. Die Neubesetzung der deutschen Bistümer unter Papst Innocenz IV, 1243–1254. Leipsic. 1901.
Bappert, J. F. Richard von Cornwall seit seiner Wahl zum deutschen König, 1257–1272. Bonn. 1905.
Bloch, H. Die staufischen Kaiserwahlen und die Entstehung des Kurfürstentums. Leipsic. 1911.
Blondel, G. Étude sur la politique de l'Empereur Frédéric II en Allemagne et sur les transformations de la Constitution Allemande dans la première moitié du xiiie siècle. Paris. 1892.
Bonwetsch, G. Neue Beiträge zur Geschichte des Kurfürstenkollegiums und der deutschen Königswahl. *In* Literarische Rundschau. xl. 1914.

Buchner, M. Der Pfalzgraf bei Rhein, der Herzog von Brabant und die Doppelwahl des Jahres 1198. *In* Festgabe Herman Grauert. Freiburg. 1910.
—— Die deutschen Königswahlen und das Herzogtum Bayern. (Untersuchungen zur deutschen Staats- und Rechtsgesch. Ed. Gierke, O. v. No. 117.) Breslau. 1913.
Busson, A. Die Doppelwahl des Jahres 1257 und das römische Königthum Alfons X von Castilien. Ein Beitrag zur Gesch. d. grossen Interregnums. Münster. 1866.
—— Zur Geschichte Conradins I. Eine Stilübung über die Wahl Conradins zum römischen König. FDG. xi. 1871.
—— Zur Geschichte des grossen Landfriedensbundes deutscher Städte 1254. Innsbruck. 1874.
Cartellieri, A. Die Schlacht bei Bouvines im Rahmen der europäischen Politik. Leipsic. 1914.
Caspar, E. Hermann von Salza und die Gründung des Deutschordensstaats in Preussen. Tübingen. 1924.
Deussen, W. Die päpstliche Approbation der deutschen Königswahl. Münster. 1879. [diss.]
Dove, A. Kaiser Friedrich II. *In* Ausgewählte Schriften, vornehmlich historischen Inhalts. Leipsic. 1898.
Egelhaaf, G. Die Schlacht bei Frankfurt am 5 August 1246. *In* Württembergische Vierteljahrshefte für Landesgeschichte. Neue Folge. xxxi. 1925.
Eichmann, E. Die Excommunikation Philipps von Schwaben. HJ. xxxv. 1914.
Engelmann, E. Der Anspruch der Päpste auf Konfirmation und Approbation bei den deutschen Königswahlen, 1077–1379. Breslau. 1886.
—— Philipp von Schwaben und Papst Innocenz III während des deutschen Thronstreites, 1198–1208. Berlin. 1896. [progr.]
Fanta, A. Ein Bericht über die Ansprüche des Königs Alfons auf den deutschen Thron. MIOGF. vi. 1885.
Ficker, A. Herzog Friedrich II, der letzte Babenberger. Innsbruck. 1884.
Ficker, J. Engelbert der Heilige, Erzb. von Köln und Reichsverweser. Cologne. 1853.
—— Vom Reichfürstenstande. Innsbruck. 1861.
—— Über das Testament Kaiser Heinrichs VI. Vienna. 1871.
—— Erörterungen zur Reichsgeschichte des 13 Jahrh. MIOGF. iii and iv. 1882–3.
Folz, A. Kaiser Friedrich II and Papst Innocenz IV. Ihr Kampf in den Jahren 1244 und 1245. Strasbourg. 1905.
Frensdorff, F. Die Rechtsbücher und die Königswahl. *In* Nachrichten von der Gesellschaft der Wissensch. zu Göttingen. Philol.-Hist. Kl. 1926.
Fuchs, W. Die Besetzung der deutschen Bistümer unter Papst Gregor IX (1227–1241) und bis zum Regierungsantritt Papst Innocenz IV (1243). Berlin. 1911.
Geffcken, H. Die Krone und das niedere deutsche Kirchengut unter Kaiser Friedrich II. Jena. 1890.
Gerlich, F. Das Testament Heinrichs VI. (Ebering's Hist. Studien, 59.) Berlin. 1907.
Grieser, R. Das Arelat in der europäischen Politik von der Mitte des 10 bis zum Ausgange des 14 Jahrhunderts. Jena. 1925.
Grotefend, W. Zur Characteristik Philipps von Schwaben und Ottos IV von Braunschweig. Trèves. 1886. [Jena diss.]
Gutbier, E. Das Itinerar des Königs Philipp von Schwaben. Berlin. 1912. [diss.]
Güterbock, F. Eine zeitgenössische Biographie Friedrichs II, das verlorene Geschichtswerk Mainardinos. Neu. Arch. xxx. 1904.
Halbe, M. Friedrich II und der päpstliche Stuhl bis zur Kaiserkrönung. Berlin. 1888.
Haller, J. Innozenz III und Otto IV. *In* Papsttum und Kaisertum. Forschungen zur politischen Geschichte und Geisteskultur des Mittelalters Paul Kehr zum 65 Geburtstag dargebracht. Ed. Brackmann, A. Munich. 1926.
Hampe, K. Kaiser Friedrich II. HZ. lxxxiii. 1899.
—— Beiträge zur Geschichte Kaiser Friedrichs II. HVJS. iv. 1901.
—— Deutsche Angriffe auf d. Königreich Sizilien im Anfang d. 13 Jahrhunderts. HVJS. vii. 1904.
—— Aus der Kindheit Kaiser Friedrichs II. MIOGF. xxii. 1901.
—— Kritische Bemerkungen zur Kirchenpolitik der Stauferzeit. HZ. xciii. 1904.

Hampe, K. Über die Flugschriften zum Lyoner Konzil von 1245. HVJS. xi. 1908.
—— Kaiser Friedrich II in der Auffassung der Nachwelt. Stuttgart, Berlin, and Leipsic. 1925.
—— Kaiser Friedrich II als Fragensteller in Kultur- und Universalgeschichte. *In* W. Goetz zu seinem 60 Geburtstage dargebracht. Leipsic and Berlin. 1927.
Hasse, T. König Wilhelm von Holland. Strasbourg. 1885. [diss.]
Heinemann, L. v. Heinrich von Braunschweig, Pfalzgraf bei Rhein. Gotha. 1882.
Herrmann, W. Alfons X von Castilien als römischer König. Berlin. 1897. [diss.]
Hintze, O. Das Königtum Wilhelms von Holland. Introd. by Weizäcker, J. (Historische Studien. Ed. Arndt, W. etc. No. 15.) Leipsic. 1885.
Hugelmann, K. G. Die deutsche Königswahl im Corpus iuris canonici. (Untersuchungen zur deutschen Staats- und Rechtsgeschichte. Ed. Gierke, O. No. 98.) Breslau. 1909.
—— Die Wahl Konrads IV zu Wien im Jahre 1237. Weimar. 1914.
Husak, G. Review of Bloch, H. Die staufischen Kaiserwahlen und die Entstehung des Kurfürstentums (*see above*). *In* Göttingische gelehrte Anzeigen, 175. 1913.
Kalbfuss, M. Die staufischen Kaiserwahlen und ihre Vorgeschichte. MIOGF. xxxiv. 1913.
Kap-Herr, H. v. Die unio regni ad imperium. Ein Beitrag zur Geschichte der staufischen Politik. DZG. i. 1889.
Kienast, W. Die deutschen Fürsten im Dienste der Westmächte bis zum Tode Philipps des Schönen von Frankreich. Vol. i. Utrecht. 1924.
Kirmse, E. Der Reichspolitik Hermanns I, Landgrafen von Thüringen und Pfalzgrafen von Sachsen, 1190–1217. *In* Zeitschr. d. Vereins für Thüringische Gesch. und Altertumskunde. n.s. Jena. 1920.
Koch, A. Hermann von Salza. Leipsic. 1885.
Koch, H. Richard von Cornwall (1209–1257). Strasbourg. 1888.
Köhler, C. Das Verhältnis Kaiser Friedrichs II zu den Päpsten seiner Zeit. Breslau. 1888.
Köhler, H. Die Ketzerpolitik der deutschen Kaiser und Könige in den Jahren 1152–1254. (Jenaer Historische Arbeiten, 6.) Bonn. 1913.
Krabbo, H. Ottos IV erste Versprechungen an Innocenz III. Neu. Arch. xxvii. 1902.
—— Die Besetzung der deutschen Bistümer unter der Regierung Kaiser Friedrichs II. (Ebering's Historische Studien, 25.) Berlin. 1901.
Krammer, M. Wahl und Einsetzung des deutschen Königs im Verhältnis zueinander. (Quellen und Studien. Ed. Zeumer, K. i, 2.) Weimar. 1905.
—— Der Reichsgedanke des staufischen Kaiserhauses. (Untersuchungen zur deutschen Staats- und Rechtsgeschichte. Ed. Gierke, O. No. 95.) Breslau. 1908.
—— Das Kurfürstenkolleg von seinen Anfängen bis zum Zusammenschluss im Renser Kurverein des Jahres 1338. Weimar. 1913.
Langerfeld, G. Kaiser Otto IV der Welfe. Hann. 1872.
Lemcke, G. Beiträge zur Geschichte König Richards von Cornwall. (Ebering's Historische Studien, 65.) Berlin. 1909.
Liebermann, F. Zur Geschichte Friedrichs II und Richards von Cornwall. Neu. Arch. xiii. 1888.
Lindner, T. Die deutschen Königswahlen und die Entstehung des Kurfürstentums. Leipsic. 1893.
Malsch, R. Heinrich Raspe, Landgraf von Thüringen und Deutscher König. Halle. 1911. [diss.]
Maurenbrecher, W. Geschichte der deutschen Königswahlen vom zehnten bis dreizehnten Jahrhundert. Leipsic. 1889.
Meister, A. Die Hohenstaufen im Elsass. Strasbourg. Mayence. 1890. [diss.]
Meyer, E. W. Staatstheorien Papst Innocenz' III. (Jenaer Hist. Arb., 9.) Bonn. 1920.
Niese, H. Die Verwaltung des Reichsgutes im 13 Jahrhundert. Ein Beitrag zur deutschen Verfassungsgeschichte. Innsbruck. 1905.
—— Zur Geschichte des geistigen Lebens am Hofe Kaiser Friedrichs II. HZ. cviii. 1912.
Nitzsch, K. W. Staufische Studien. HZ. iii. 1860.

Oppermann, O. Untersuchungen zur nordniederländ. Geschichte des 10 bis 13 Jahrh. Pt. 2. Die Grafschaft Holland und das Reich bis 1256. Utrecht. 1921.
Otto, H. Alexander IV und der deutsche Thronstreit. MIOGF. xix. 1898.
Peitz, W. M. Die Entstehung des Registrum super negotio Romani imperii und der Anlass zum Eingreifen Innozenz III in d. deutschen Thronstreit. HJ. xlvi. 1926.
Powicke, F. M. The Loss of Normandy. 1189–1204. Manchester. 1913.
Redlich, O. Zur Wahl des römischen Königs Alfons von Castilien (1257). MIOGF. xvi. 1895.
Reinhold, P. Die Empörung König Heinrichs (VII) gegen seinen Vater. (Leipziger Historische Abhandlungen, 25.) Leipsic. 1911.
Rodenberg, C. Kaiser Friedrich II und die deutsche Kirche. *In* Historische Aufsätze dem Andenken an Georg Waitz gewidmet. Hanover. 1886.
—— Der Brief Urbans IV von 27 August 1263 und die deutsche Königswahl des Jahres von 1257. Neu. Arch. x. 1885.
Rohden, J. Der Sturz Heinrichs (VII). FDG. xxii. 1882.
Scheffer-Boichorst, P. Deutschland und Philipp II August von Frankreich in den Jahren 1180 bis 1214. FDG. viii. 1868.
—— Zur Geschichte des xii und xiii Jahrhunderts. Diplomatische Forschungen. (Ebering's Historische Studien, 8.) Berlin. 1897.
Schirmer, F. Die Kontroverse über eine Anwesenheit Kaiser Friedrichs II in Deutschland im Jahre 1242. (Beiträge zur Geschichte Kaiser Friedrichs II.) Friedland. 1904.
Schirrmacher, F. W. Beiträge zur Geschichte Kaiser Friedrichs II. FDG. xi. 1871.
—— Die Entstehung des Kurfürstencollegiums. Berlin. 1874.
Schwemer, R. Innocenz III und die deutsche Kirche während des Thronstreites von 1198–1208. Strasbourg. 1882.
—— Papsttum und Kaisertum. Stuttgart. 1899.
Seeliger, G. Neue Forschungen über die Entstehung des Kurfürstenkollegs. MIOGF. xvi. 1895.
Steinen, W. von den. Das Kaisertum Friedrichs des Zweiten nach den Anschauungen seiner Staatsbriefe. Berlin and Leipsic. 1922.
Sternfeld, R. Das Verhältnis des Arelats zu Kaiser und Reich vom Tode Friedrichs I bis zum Interregnum. Berlin. 1881.
Stimming, M. Kaiser Friedrich II und der Abfall der deutschen Fürsten. HZ. cxx. 1919.
Tangl, M. Die Deliberatio Innocenz' III. SPAW. liii. 1919.
Weber, F. P. Richard, Earl of Cornwall, and his Coins as King of the Romans. *In* Numismatic Chronicle. 3rd ser. Vol. xiii. 1893.
Weiland, L. Friedrichs II Privileg für die geistlichen Fürsten. *In* Historische Aufsätze dem Andenken an Georg Waitz gewidmet. Hanover. 1886.
Weizsäcker, J. Der Rheinische Bund 1254. Tübingen. 1879.
Weller, K. Zur Organisation des Reichsgutes in der späteren Stauferzeit. *In* Forschungen und Versuche. Festschrift für D. Schäfer. Jena. 1915.
Wenck, K. Die heilige Elizabeth. HZ. lxix. 1892.
Winkelmann, E. Die Wahl König Heinrichs (VII), seine Regierungsrechte und sein Sturz. FDG. i. 1862.
—— Ueber das Testament Kaiser Heinrich VI. FDG. x. 1870.
—— Die angebliche Ermordung des Herzogs Ludwig von Baiern durch Kaiser Friedrich II im J. 1231. MIOGF. xvii. 1896.
Winter, A. Der Erbfolgeplan und das Testament Kaiser Heinrichs VI. Erlangen. 1908. [diss.]
Wissowa, F. Politische Beziehungen zwischen England und Deutschland bis zum Untergange der Staufer. Breslau. 1889. [diss.]
Wolfschläger, C. Erzbischof Adolf I von Köln als Fürst und Politiker (1193–1205). Münster. 1905. [diss.]
Wunderlich, B. Die neueren Ansichten über die deutsche Königswahl und den Ursprung des Kurfürstenkollegs. (Ebering's Hist. Studien, 114.) Berlin. 1913.
Zeumer, K. Geschichte der Reichssteuern im früheren Mittelalter. HZ. lxxxi. 1898.
—— Der deutsche Urtext des Landfriedens von 1235. Das älteste Reichsgesetz in deutscher Sprache. Neu. Arch. xxviii. 1903.
—— Die böhmische und die bayrische Kur im 13 Jahrhundert. HZ. xciv. 1905.

CHAPTER V.

ITALY AND SICILY UNDER FREDERICK II.

I. SOURCES.

A. Documents.

Acta pacis ad S. Germanum anno MCCXXX initae. Ed. Hampe, K. MGH. Epistolae selectae. IV. 1926.

Beltrani, G. B. Documenti inediti dell' imperatore Federico II e di Carlo II d'Angiò. *In* Archivio storico, artistico, archeologico di Roma. Vol. II. 1877.

Böhmer, J. F. Regesta Imperii...1198–1272. *See Gen. Bibl.* IV.

Codice diplomatico Barese. Publ. by Comm. prov. di archeol. e storia patria di Bari. Vols. I–IX. Trani. 1896 ff., in progress.

Constitutiones et acta publica imperatorum et regum. Vol. I. Ed. Weiland, L. MGH. Legum Sect. IV. 1893. [For Henry VI.]

—— Vol. II. 1896. [For Frederick II.]

Constitutiones regum...Siciliae mandante Friderico II imp. per Petrum de Vinea concinnatae, etc. [Ed. Carcani, G.] Naples. 1786.

Ficker, J. Forschungen zur Reichs- und Rechtsgeschichte Italiens. Vol. IV (Urkunden). Innsbruck. 1874.

Flandina, A. Due diplomi inediti dell' imperatore Federico II. *In* Archivio storico siciliano. 1874.

Gabotto, F. Un diploma inedito di Federico II a Manfredi Lancia. *In* Bollettino storico-bibliog. subalpino. III. Pinerolo. 1898. pp. 271–8. Also publ. separately. Pinerolo. 1898.

Genuardi, L. Documenti inediti di Federico II. QFIA. 1909.

Hessel, A. Einer bisher unbekannte Konstitution Friedrichs II vom November 1242. Neu. Arch. 1906.

Huillard-Bréholles, J. L. A. Historia diplomatica Friderici II. 6 vols. in 12. Paris. 1852–61.

Levi, G. Registro del card. Ugolino d'Ostia. (Fonti.) 1890.

Liber Censuum de l'église romaine. *See Gen. Bibl.* IV.

Matthew Paris. Additamenta in Vol. VI of Chronica majora. *See below,* I B.

Morea, D. Chartularium Cupersanense. Monte Cassino. 1892.

Papal Documents.

For the Letters of Innocent III, and the Registers of Honorius III, Gregory IX, and Innocent IV, *see Gen. Bibl.* IV *under* Papal Documents.

For Honorius III, Gregory IX, and Innocent IV, there is the important collection of selected letters *in* MGH. Epistolae saec. XIII e regestis pontificum Romanorum. Vols. I–III. *See Gen. Bibl.* IV.

Peter de Vinea. Epistolarum libri VI. Basle. 1740. *Also in* Huillard-Bréholles, J. L. A. Vie et correspondance de Pierre de la Vigne. *See below,* II B (i).

Potthast, A. Regesta Pontificum Romanorum. *See Gen. Bibl.* IV.

Quaternus de mandato...Friderici II De excadenciis et revocatis Capitanatae. Monte Cassino. 1903.

Regesta chartarum Italiae. Publ. by K. Preuss. Hist. Institut and Istituto storico italiano. 18 vols. Rome. 1907 ff., in progress.

Winkelmann, E. Acta Imperii inedita. Vol. I. Innsbruck. 1880.

B. Chronicles.

Albericus Monachus Trium Fontium. Chronicon. Ed. Scheffer-Boichorst, P. MGH. Script. XXIII. 1874.

Annales Brixienses. Ed. Bethmann, L. C. *Ibid.* XVIII. 1863.

Annales Caesenates. Ed. Muratori. RR.II.SS. 1st edn. Vol. XIV.

Annales Casinenses. (Anonymi Cassinensis Chronicon.) Ed. Pertz, G. H. MGH. Script. XIX. 1866. *Also in* Del Re, G. Cronisti e scrittori sincroni napoletani Vol. I. Naples. 1845.

Annales Cremonenses. Ed. Holder-Egger, O. MGH. Script. xxxi. 1903.
Annales de Dunstaplia. Ed. Pauli, R. *Ibid.* xxvii. 1885.
Annales Florentini II. Ed. Hartwig, O. *in* Quellen und Forschungen zur ält. Geschichte der Stadt Florenz. Vol. ii. Marburg. 1880.
Annales Ianuenses Cafari et continuatorum. Vols. ii, iii. Ed. Belgrano, L. T. and Imperiale di S. Angelo, C. (Fonti) 1901, 23. *Also* ed. Pertz, G. H. MGH. Script. xviii. 1863.
Annales Mediolanenses. Ed. Muratori. RR.II.SS. 1st edn. Vol. xvi.
Annales et Notae Parmenses et Ferrarienses. Ed. Jaffé, P. MGH. xviii. 1863. *Also* ed. Bonazzi, G. *as* Chronicon Parmense. RR.II.SS. New edn. Vol. ix. 1902.
Annales Placentini Gibellini. Ed. Pertz, G. H. MGH. Script. xviii. 1863. *Also* ed. Huillard-Bréholles, J. L. A. *as* Chron. de rebus in Italia gestis, *in* Chronicon Placentinum. Paris. 1856.
Annales Regienses. Ed. Muratori. RR.II.SS. 1st edn. Vol. vii.
Annales S. Justinae Patavini. Ed. Jaffé, P. MGH. Script. xix. 1866. *Also* ed. Botteghi, L. A. *as* Chronicon Marchiae Tarvisinae et Lombardiae. RR.II.SS. New edn. Vol. viii. 1916.
Annales Senenses. Ed. Holder-Egger, O. *in* Neu. Arch. xi. 1886.
Annales Siculi. Ed. Pertz, G. H. MGH. Script. xix. 1866.
Annales veteres Mutinenses. Ed. Muratori. RR.II.SS. 1st edn. Vol. xi. [*See also* Fragmenta Memorialis Potestatum Mutinae, 1204–1248. Ed. Casini, T. *in* Chronicon Mutinense Johannis de Bazano. RR.II.SS. New edn. Vol. xv. 1917, 19.]
Anonymi Vaticani Historia Sicula. Ed. Muratori. RR.II.SS. 1st edn. Vol. viii.
Antoninus archiepiscopus Florentinus. Chronicon. Ed. Maturus, P. 3 vols. Lyons. 1586.
Arnoldus Lubecensis. Chronica. Ed. Lappenberg, J. M. MGH. Script. xxi. 1869.
Astesanus, Antonius. Carmen. Ed. Tallone, A. RR.II.SS. New edn. Vol. xiv. 1912.
Burchardus Praepositus Urspergensis. Chronicon. Ed. Holder-Egger, O. and Simson, B. v. SGUS. 1916.
Cantus triumphales in imp. Fridericum II De Victoria urbe expugnata. Parma. 1858.
Carbio *or* Curbio (Nicolaus de, Niccolò da Calvi). Vitae Innocentii IV Papae. Ed. Pagnotti, F. ASRSP. xxi. 1898. *Also* ed. Muratori. RR.II.SS. 1st edn. Vol. iii.
Chronica Astensia. Ed. Promis, V. *in* Miscell. di storia italiana. ix. Turin. 1870.
Chronica regia Coloniensis. Continuatio II, 1200–1220. Ed. Waitz, G. SGUS. 1880. *Also in* MGH. Script. xxiv. 1879.
Chronicon Brixianum. Ed. Muratori. RR.II.SS. 1st edn. Vol. xii.
Chronicon de rebus Siculis (Breve). Ed. Huillard-Bréholles, J. L. A. *in* Historia diplomatica Friderici II. Vol. i, pt. 2. *See above,* i a.
Chronicon Estense. Ed. Bertoni, G. and Vicini, E. P. RR.II.SS. New edn. Vol. xv. 1908 ff., in progress.
Corpus Chronicorum Bononiensium. Vol. ii. Ed. Sorbelli, A. RR.II.SS. New edn. Vol. xviii. 1911 ff.
Dandolo, Andrea. Chronicon Venetum. Ed. Muratori. RR.II.SS. 1st edn. Vol. xii.
Ernoul (and others). Estoire d'Oultremer. *In* Recueil des historiens des croisades. Historiens occident. ii. Paris. 1859. [French continuations of William of Tyre.]
Galvanus Flamma. Manipulus florum seu Historia Mediolanensis. Ed. Muratori. RR.II.SS. 1st edn. Vol. xi.
Gesta Innocentii III Papae. MPL. ccxiv.
Gregorius IX. Vita. Ed. Muratori. RR.II.SS. 1st edn. Vol. iii.
Griffonibus, Matthaei de. Memoriale historicum de rebus Bononiensium. Ed. Frati, L. and Sorbelli, A. RR.II.SS. New edn. Vol. xviii. 1902.
Ignoti monachi Cisterciensis S. Mariae de Ferraria Chronica. (Soc. napol. di storia patria. Mon. stor., Ser. i. Cronache.) Ed. Gaudenzi, A. Naples. 1888.
Jamsilla, Nicolaus de. Historia de rebus gestis Friderici II, etc. *In* Del Re, G. Cronisti, etc. (*see above,* Annales Casinenses). Vol. ii. 1868.

Johannes de Ceccano. Chronicon Fossaenovae *or* Annales Ceccanenses. *Ibid.* Vol. I. 1845.
Malaspina, Saba. Rerum sicularum libri VI. Ed. Muratori. RR.II.SS. 1st edn. Vol. VIII. *Also in* Del Re, G. Cronisti, etc. (*see above*, Jamsilla). Vol. II. 1868.
Malvecius, Gerardus. Historia de rebus gestis Eccelini tyranni. Ed. Muratori. RR.II.SS. 1st edn. Vol. VIII.
Matthew Paris. Chronica majora. Ed. Luard, H. R. 7 vols. (Rolls.) 1872–83.
Memoriale Potestatum Regiensium. Ed. Muratori. RR.II.SS. 1st edn. Vol. VIII.
Otto de S. Blasio. Chronica. Ed. Hofmeister, A. SGUS. 1912. *Also* ed. Wilmans, R. MGH. Script. XX. 1868.
Parisius de Cereta. Annales (Veronenses). Ed. Pertz, G. H. MGH. Script. XIX. 1866.
Pipinus, Franciscus, Bononiensis. Chronicon. Ed. Muratori. RR.II.SS. 1st edn. IX.
Radulfus de Diceto. Ymagines Historiarum. Ed. Stubbs, W. *in* Works. 2 vols. (Rolls.) 1876.
Rainerius monachus Leodiensis. Continuatio Chronici Lamberti Parvi. Ed. Pertz, G. H. MGH. Script. XVI. 1859.
Ricobaldus, Gervasius, Ferrariensis. Pomerium Ravennatis Ecclesiae. Ed. Muratori. RR.II.SS. 1st edn. Vol. IX.
Rogeri de Houedene Chronicorum continuatio. Ed. Stubbs, W. *as* Memoriale Walteri de Coventria. Vol. II. (Rolls.) 1873. [Extracts ed. Liebermann, F. MGH. Script. XXVII. 1885.]
Rolandinus Patavinus. Cronica in factis et circa facta Marchie Trivixane. Ed. Bonardi, A. RR.II.SS. New edn. Vol. VIII. 1905, in progress. *Also* ed. Jaffé, P. MGH. Script. XIX. 1866.
Ryccardus de Sancto Germano. Chronica. First recension. Ed. Gaudenzi, A. *with* Ignoti monachi...chronica (*see above*). Second recension only. Ed. Pertz, G. H. SGUS. 1864.
Salimbene de Adam. Cronica. Ed. Holder-Egger, O. MGH. Script. XXXII. 1905–13.
Sicardus Cremonensis. Cronica. Ed. Holder-Egger, O. MGH. Script. XXXI. 1903.
Thomas Tuscus. Gesta imperatorum et pontificum. Ed. Ehrenfeuchter, E. MGH. Script. XXII. 1872.
Villani, G. Historie Fiorentine. Ed. Muratori. RR.II.SS. 1st edn. Vol. XIII.

II. MODERN WORKS.

A. General.

Amari, M. Storia dei Musulmani di Sicilia. Vol. III. Florence. 1872.
Caggese, R. Firenze dalla decadenza di Roma al risorgimento d' Italia. Vol. I. Florence. 1912.
Camera, M. Annali della Sicilia. Naples. 1841.
Collenuccio, P. Compendio dell' istoria del regno di Napoli. Naples. 1771.
De Cherrier, C. Histoire de la lutte des papes et des empereurs de la maison de Souabe. Paris. 1858.
Folz, A. Kaiser Friedrich II und Papst Innocenz IV. Strasbourg. 1905.
Gregorovius, F. History of the City of Rome in the Middle Ages. Engl. transl. Vol. v. *See Gen. Bibl.* v.
Hampe, K. Kaiser Friedrich II. HZ. 1899.
Huillard-Bréholles, J. L. A. Preface and Introduction to Historia diplomatica Friderici II. *See above*, I A.
Jordan, E. Les origines de la domination angevine en Italie. Paris. 1909.
Köhler, C. Der Verhältniss Kaiser Friedrichs II zu den Päpsten seiner Zeit. Breslau. 1888.
Lorenz, O. Kaiser Friedrich II. HZ. 1864.
Luchaire, A. Innocent III: Rome et l'Italie. Paris. 1904.
Muratori, L. A. Annali d' Italia [years 1198–1250]. *See Gen. Bibl.* v.
Pirie-Gordon, C. H. E. Innocent the Great. London. 1907.
Raumer, F. von. Geschichte der Hohenstaufen und ihrer Zeit. 5th edn. 6 vols. Leipsic. 1878.

Raynaldus, O. Annales ecclesiastici. *See Gen. Bibl.* v *under* Baronius, C.
Rodenberg, C. Innocenz IV und das Königreich Sicilien. Halle. 1892.
Schirrmacher, F. W. Kaiser Friedrich II. 4 vols. Göttingen. 1859–65.
Sedgwick, H. D. Italy in the thirteenth century. London. 1913.
Winkelmann, E. Geschichte Kaiser Friedrichs des zweiten und seiner Reiche. Vols. I, II, pt. 1. Berlin. 1863–5. [No more publ.]
—— Kaiser Friedrich II. Vols. I, II. (Jahrbücher d. deutsch. Geschichte.) Leipsic. 1889, 97.

B. Special.

(i) *Political History.*

Amati, S. L' Aquilino di Como restituito a Federico II. *In* Bollettino numismatico-sfragistico. 1884–6.
Audisio, G. Sistema politico e religioso di Federico II e di Pier della Vigna. *In* Annali cattolici. 1866.
Bäseler, G. Die Kaiserkrönung in Rom und die Römer von Karl dem Grossen bis Friedrich II. Freiburg-im-Breisgau. 1919.
Baethger, F. Die Regentschaft Papst Innocenz III. Heidelberg. 1914.
Blasius, H. König Enzio. Breslau. 1884.
Bonaini, F. Sopra alcuni diplomi inediti dell' imperatore Federico II, del principe Federico d'Antiochia, e di Enzo re di Sardegna. ASI. 1845.
Calligaris, G. Di tre diplomi di Federico II. *In* Atti della R. Accad. delle scienze di Torino. 1890–1.
De Blasiis, G. Della vita e delle opere di Pietro della Vigna. Naples. 1860.
Del Giudice, G. Riccardo Filangieri sotto il regno di Federico II. Naples. 1893.
Egidi, P. La colonia saracena di Lucera e la sua distruzione. Naples. 1915.
Falco, G. I preliminari della pace di San Germano. ASRSP. Vol. XXXIII. 1910.
Fastenrath, J. El emperador Federico II. *In* Revista contemporanea. Madrid. 1903.
Fedele, P. Un diplomatico dei tempi di Federico II: Tommaso di Gaeta. ASPN. 1906.
Filangieri di Candida, R. Riccardo Filangieri Imperialis Aulae Marescallus e i suoi omonimi. ASPN. 1913.
Fortunato, G. Della Valle di Vitalba nei secoli XII e XIII. Rome. 1895.
—— Notizie storiche della Valle di Vitalba. Trani. 1898 ff.
—— Riccardo da Venosa e il suo tempo. Trani. 1918.
Galatti, G. Ricordi storici su Federico II e l'Italia ai suoi tempi. Messina. 1871.
Graefe, F. Die Publizistik im letzten Kampfe zwischen Friedrich II und Papst Gregor IX. Heidelberg. 1909.
Grumblat, H. Über einige Urkunden Friedrichs II für den Deutschen Orden. MIOGF. 1908.
Guarini, G. B. La modernità politica e il diritto delle genti nei "Regesta" di Federico II. Rome. 1908.
Güterboch, F. Eine zeitgenossische Biographie Friedrichs II (das verlorene Geschichtswerk Mainardinos). Neu. Arch. XXX. 1904.
Hauss, A. Kardinal Oktavian Ubaldini, ein Staatsmann des XIII Jahrhunderts. Heidelberg. 1913.
Heckel, R. von. Das päpstliche und sizilische Registerwesen. *In* Archiv für Urkundenforschung. Leipsic. 1908.
Huillard-Bréholles, J. L. A. Recherches sur les monuments et l'histoire des Normands et de la maison de Souabe dans l'Italie méridionale. Paris. 1844.
—— Vie et correspondance de Pierre de la Vigne. Paris. 1864.
Kehr, P. F. Das Briefbuch des Thomas von Gaeta, Justitiars Friedrichs II. QFIA. 1905. Italian transl. Guarini, G. B. Teramo. 1906.
Merkel, C. Manfredi I e Manfredi II Lancia. Turin. 1886.
Messeri, A. Enzo re. Geneva. 1912.
Niese, H. Materialien zur Geschichte Kaiser Friedrich II. *In* Nachrichten d. k. Gesellschaft der Wissenschaften. Philol.-hist. Klasse. Göttingen. 1912.
—— Die Register Friedrichs II. *In* Archiv für Urkundenforschung. Leipsic. 1913.
Ottendorff, H. Die Regierung der beiden letzten Normannen-Könige Tancreds und Wilhelms III. Bonn. 1899.

Paolucci, G. Il parlamento di Foggia del 1240 e le pretese elezioni di quel tempo. Palermo. 1896.
—— Contributo di documenti inediti sulle relazioni tra Chiesa e Stato nel tempo Suevo. Palermo. 1900.
—— La giovinezza di Federico II di Suevia e i prodromi della sua lotta col Papato. *In* Atti della R. Accad. di scienze, lettere, ed arti. Palermo. 1901.
—— La prima lotta di Federico II di Suevia col Papato. *Ibid.* 1902.
—— Pretese elezioni di giudici al tempo di Federico II di Suevia. *Ibid.* 1903.
Philippi, F. Zur Geschichte der Reichskanzlei unter den letzten Staufern. Münster. 1885.
Picotti, G. B. I Caminesi e la loro signoria in Treviso. Leghorn. 1905.
Pollaci-Nuccio, F. La feudalità, Federico II e i comuni siciliani. *In* Atti della R. Accad. di scienze, etc. Palermo. 1900.
Salzer, E. War die im Jahre 1244 verstossene Gemahlin Ezzelins von Romano eine Tochter Kaiser Friedrichs II? Neu. Arch. 1907.
Scheffer-Boichorst, P. Zur Geschichte des 12 und 13 Jahrhunderts. Berlin. 1897.
Schneider, F. Un atto di politica ecclesiastica dell' imperatore Federico II. *In* Miscellanea d' erudizione. Pisa. 1905.
—— Toscanische Studien. QFIA. 1908.
Schultz-Gora, A. Ein Sirventes von Guilhem Figueira gegen Friedrich II. Halle. 1902.
Semmola, T. Commentario istorico-critico-filologico sopra quattro lettere greche dell' imperatore Federico II. *In* Atti della R. Accad. di archeologia. Naples. 1868–70.
Simeoni, L. Il comune veronese sino ad Ezzelino e il suo primo statuto. Venice. 1920.
Sthamer, E. Studien über sizilischen Register Friedrichs II. SPAW. 1920.
Stieve, F. Ezzelino von Romano bis zum seine Bündnis mit Friedrich II. Leipsic. 1909.
Toeche, T. De Enrico VI Romanorum imperatore Normannorum regnum vindicante. Berlin. 1860.
Westenholz, E. von. Kardinal Rainer von Viterbo. Heidelberg. 1912.
Winkelmann, E. Bischof Harduin von Cefalù und sein Prozess. MIOGF. 1894.

(ii) *Law and Economics.*

Capasso, B. Sulla storia esterna delle costituzioni del regno di Sicilia promulgate da Federico II. Naples. 1869.
Carabellese, F. Sopra vivenza di comuni rurali sotto Federico II di Hohenstaufen ed i suoi successori. *In* Raccolta di scritti storici in onore del prof. G. Romano. Pavia. 1907.
Chone, H. Die Handelsbeziehungen Kaiser Friedrichs II zu den Seestädten Venedig, Pisa, Genua. (Ebering's Historische Studien, No. 32.) Berlin. 1902.
Del Vecchio, A. Intorno alla legislazione di Federico II. Florence. 1872.
—— La legislazione di Federico II illustrata. Turin. 1874.
Faraglia, F. N. Storia dei prezzi in Napoli dal 1131 al 1860. Naples. 1878.
Garufi, C. A. Di una monetazione imperiale di Federico II transitoria fra i tari e gli augustali. *In* Rendiconti della R. Accad. dei Lincei. 1897.
—— La monetazione di Federico II di Svevia, gli augustali e la pubblicazione del codice di Melfi. Turin. 1897.
—— La "defensa ex parte domini imperatoris" in un documento privato del 1227–8. Turin. 1899.
Lagumina, B. Una pregevole moneta di Federico re e Costanza imperatrice. *In* Archivio storico siciliano. 1895.
La Mantia, G. Su l' uso della registrazione nella cancellaria del regno di Sicilia. *Ibid.* 1907.
La Mantia, V. La legislazione di Federico II imperatore illustrata da A. Del Vecchio. Palermo. 1876.
Paolucci, G. La finanze e la corte di Federico II di Svevia. *In* Atti della R. Accad. di scienze, lettere, ed arti. Palermo. 1903.

Sthamer, E. Die Verwaltung der Kastelle im Königreich Sizilien unter Kaiser Friedrich II, etc. Leipsic. 1914.

—— Die Hauptstrassen des Königreichs Sicilien im 13 Jahrht. *In* Studi di storia napoletana in onore di M. Schipa. Naples. 1926.

Winkelmann, E. Ueber die Goldprägungen Kaiser Friedrich II für das Königreich Sicilien und besonders über seine Augustalen. MIOGF. 1894.

Zechbauer, D. Das mittelalterliche Strafrecht Siziliens nach Friedrichs II Constitutiones Regni Siciliae und den sizilischen Staatsrechten. *In* Juristische Berliner Beiträge. Ed. Kohler. 1908.

(iii) *Culture.*

Amari, M. Questions philosophiques adressées aux savants musulmans par l'empereur Frédéric II. Journal Asiatique. Paris. 1853.

Benamozegh. Federico II e le dottrine rabbiniche. *In* Rivista Bolognese. 1867.

Bertaux, E. Castel del Monte. BEC. 1889.

—— Les Arts de l'orient musulman dans l'Italie méridionale. *In* Mélanges d'archéologie et d'histoire. École Française de Rome. Vol. xv. Rome. 1896.

—— Castel del Monte et les architectes français de Frédéric II. *In* Comptes-rendus des séances. AcadIBL. 1897.

—— L'Art dans l'Italie méridionale. Paris. 1904.

Bertaux, E. and Yver. L'Italie inconnue. *In* Le Tour du Monde. n.s. Vol. v. Paris. 1899.

Dehio, G. Die Kunst Unteritaliens in der Zeit Friedrichs II. HZ. n.s. Vol. LIX. 1905.

Delbrück, R. Ein Portrait Friedrichs II von Hohenstaufen. *In* Zeitschrift für bildende Kunst. Leipsic. 1902.

Di Marzo, G. Delle belle arti in Sicilia. Palermo. 1858–9.

Ficker, J. Verordnung gegen Missbräuche an der Universität zu Neapel von 1239. MIOGF. 1880.

—— Der Einfall Reinalds von Spoleto in den Kirchenstaat (1228). *Ibid.* 1883.

Filangieri de Satriano, G. Documenti per la storia, le arti, e le industrie delle provincie napoletane. 6 vols. Naples. 1883–91.

Gaudenzi, A. La costituzione di Federigo II che interdice lo Studio bolognese. ASI. 1908.

Geymüller, H. von. Friedrich II von Hohenstaufen und die Anfänge des Architektur der Renaissance in Italien. Munich. 1908.

Gregorovius, F. Nelle Puglie. Italian transl. from the German. Mariano, R. Florence. 1882.

Haseloff, A. Das Kastell in Bari. *In* Bibliothek d. K. Preuss. Hist. Instituts in Rom. Rome. 1906.

—— Die Bauten der Hohenstaufen in Unteritalien. Leipsic. 1920.

Le Normant, F. À travers l'Apulie et la Lucanie. Paris. 1883.

Niese, H. Zur Gesch. des geistigen Lebens am Hofe Kaiser Friedrichs II. HZ. 1912.

Novati, F. Freschi e minii del dugento. Milan. 1908.

Philippi, F. Das Portrait Kaiser Friedrichs II. *In* Zeitschrift für bildende Kunst. Leipsic. 1903.

Reinhard, D. J. Das Porträt Kaiser Friedrichs II von Hohenstaufen. *Ibid.* 1903.

Robiony, E. Federico II di Svevia e la donna del suo tempo. Naples. 1901.

Salazar, D. Notizie storiche sul palazzo di Federico II a Castel del Monte. Naples. 1875.

—— Storia dell' arco di trionfo con le torri di Federico II, etc. Naples. 1879.

Schipa, M. La fondazione della Università di Napoli e l' Italia del tempo. Naples. 1924.

Schulz, H. W. Denkmäler der Kunst des Mittelalters in Unteritalien. Dresden. 1860.

Sthamer, E. Dokumente zur Geschichte der Kastellbauten Kaiser Friedrichs II und Karl I von Anjou. Leipsic. 1912.

—— Zur Geschichte des Kastells Rocca S. Agata. QFIA. 1913.

Torraca, F. Studi su la lirica italiana del duecento. Bologna. 1902.

—— Pietro Vidal in Italia. *In* Atti della R. Accad. d' archeologia. Naples. 1916.

—— Le origini. L'età sveva. *In* Storia della Università di Napoli. Naples. 1924.

Werner, J. Verse auf Papst Innocenz IV und Kaiser Friedrich II. Neu. Arch. 1907.

Winkelmann, E. Ueber die ersten Staats-Universitäten. Heidelberg. 1880.

CHAPTER VI.

ITALY, 1250–1290.

I.

A. Bibliographies.

Balzani, U. Le Cronache italiane nel medio evo. *See Gen. Bibl.* I.
Capasso, B. Le Fonti della storia delle provincie napolitane dal 568 al 1500. *See Gen. Bibl.* I.
—— Inventario cronologico-sistematico dei Registri Angioini conservati nell' archivio di stato in Napoli. Naples. 1894.
Egidi, P. La storia medioevale. (Guide bibliografiche, 8–9.) Rome. 1922. [Excellent compendium of Italian publications.]
Manno, A. Bibliografia storica degli stati della monarchia di Savoia. Vols. I–IX. Turin. 1884 ff.
Schmeidler, B. Italienische Geschichtschreiber des XII und XIII Jahrhunderts. Leipsic. 1909.
[Regional bibliographies in works such as Caro, Davidsohn, Kretschmayr, etc. *See below,* III B.]

B. Collections of Sources.

Biblioteca della società storica subalpina. *See Gen. Bibl.* IV.
Del Re, G. Cronisti e scrittori sincroni napoletani. 2 vols. Naples. 1845, 68.
Fonti per la storia d' Italia. (Fonti.) *See Gen. Bibl.* IV.
Gregorio, R. Bibliotheca scriptorum qui res in Sicilia gestas sub Aragonum imperio retulere. 2 vols. Palermo. 1791–2.
Monumenta Germaniae Historica. (MGH.) *See Gen. Bibl.* IV.
Monumenta historiae patriae. (MHP.) *See Gen. Bibl.* IV.
Muratori, L. A. Rerum Italicarum scriptores. (RR.II.SS.) *See Gen. Bibl.* IV.

II. SOURCES.

A. Documents, etc.

For the Registers of the Popes (Innocent IV, Alexander IV, Urban IV, Clement IV, Gregory X, John XXI, Nicholas III, Martin IV, Honorius IV, and Nicholas IV) *see Gen. Bibl.* IV *under* Papal Documents.

Böhmer, J. F. Regesta Imperii. V (1198–1272). *See Gen. Bibl.* IV.
Capasso, B. Historia diplomatica regni Siciliae (1250–1266). Naples. 1874.
Carini, I. Gli Archivi e le biblioteche di Spagna, in rapporto alla storia d' Italia in generale e di Sicilia in particolare. 2 vols. Palermo. 1884, 97.
Codex Astensis qui de Malabayla communiter dicitur. Ed. Sella, Q. *In* Atti r. Accad. dei Lincei. Ser. II. Vols. II, V–VII. Scienze morali storiche. 1880–7.
Codice diplomatico Cremonese. Ed. Astegiano, L. MHP. XXI–XXII. 1895–8.
Codice diplomatico della città d' Orvieto. Ed. Fumi, L. (Doc. stor. ital.) Florence. 1884.
Codice diplomatico Laudense. Ed. Vignati, C. 3 vols. (Bibl. hist. ital.) Milan. 1879–85.
Constitutiones. Vols. II, III. Ed. Weiland, L. and Schwalm, J. MGH. Legum Sect. IV.
Del Giudice, G. Diplomi inediti di re Carlo I d'Angiò riguardanti cose marittime. Naples. 1871.
—— Codice diplomatico di Carlo I e II d'Angiò dal 1265 al 1309. 3 vols. (1265–1268.) Naples. 1863–69, 1902.
Epistolae saeculi XIII e regestis pontificum Romanorum. Ed. Rodenberg, C. Vol. III. MGH. 1894.

La Mantia, G. Documenti su le relazioni del re Alfonso III di Aragona con la Sicilia (1285–91). Barcelona. 1909.
—— Codice diplomatico dei re aragonesi di Sicilia. Vol. I. Palermo. 1918.
Levi, G. Registro del card. Ottaviano degli Ubaldini. (Fonti.) 1890.
Liber Iurium reipublicae Genuensis. 2 vols. MHP. VII, IX. 1854, 57.
Liber Potheris communis civitatis Brixiae. MHP. XIX. 1899.
Minieri Riccio, C. Brevi Notizie intorno all' archivio angioino di Napoli, dopo le quali si pubblica per la prima volta parte di quei registri ora non più esistenti. Naples. 1862.
—— —— Studî storici su' fascicoli angioini dell' archivio della regia zecca di Napoli. Naples. 1863.
—— —— Studi storici fatti sopra 84 registri angioini dell' archivio di Stato di Napoli. Naples. 1866.
—— —— Dei grandi uffiziali del regno di Sicilia dal 1265 al 1285. Naples. 1872.
—— —— L' itinerario di Carlo I d' Angiò. Naples. 1872.
—— —— Alcuni fatti riguardanti Carlo I d' Angiò dal 6 di agosto 1252 al 30 di dicembre 1270. Naples. 1874.
—— —— Il regno di Carlo I d' Angiò negli anni 1271 e 1272. Naples. 1875.
—— —— Il regno di Carlo I d' Angiò dal 2 gennaio 1273 al 31 dicembre 1283. ASI. 3rd Ser. XXII–XXVI, 4th Ser. I–V. 1875–1880.
—— —— Il regno di Carlo I d' Angiò dal 4 gennaio 1284 al 7 gennaio 1285. ASI. 4th Ser. VII. 1881.
—— —— Della dominazione angioina nel reame di Sicilia, studii storici estratti dai registri della cancelleria angioina in Napoli. Naples. 1876.
—— —— Memorie della Guerra di Sicilia negli anni 1282, 1283, 1284. ASPN. I. 1876.
—— —— Nuovi studii riguardanti la dominazione angioina nel regno di Sicilia. Naples. 1876.
—— —— Notizie storiche tratte da 62 registri angioini dell' Archivio di Stato di Napoli. Naples. 1877.
—— —— Saggio di Codice diplomatico formato sull' antiche scritture dell' archivio di stato di Napoli. 2 vols. Naples. 1878, 1879–80. Suppl. 2 pts. Naples. 1882–3.
Potthast, A. Regesta Pontificum Romanorum...1198–1304. *See Gen. Bibl.* IV.
Repertorio diplomatico Visconteo. I. Milan. 1911.
Ricordi e documenti del Vespro siciliano nella ricorrenza del sesto centenario. 2 pts. Palermo. 1882.
Silvestri, G. De rebus regni Siciliae (1282–83). Documenti inediti estr. dall' Archivio della corona d' Aragona. *In* Doc. di storia siciliana. Palermo. 1882–92.
Sthamer, E. Die verlorene Register Karls I von Anjou. SPAW. 1923.
Syllabus membranarum ad regiae Siclae archivium pertinentium. Vols. I–III. Naples. 1824–45.
Tallone, A. Regesto dei marchesi di Saluzzo (1091–1340). *In* Bibl. soc. stor. subalpina. 1906.
Terlizzi, S. Documenti delle relazioni tra Carlo I d' Angiò e la Toscana. Pt. I. (Documenti di storia italiana, XII etc.) Florence. 1914 ff., in progress.
Winkelmann, E. Acta Imperii inedita. 2 vols. Innsbruck. 1880, 85.
[For Venetian documents, see the account in Kretschmayr (*see below*, III B); and for Florence the bibliography in Davidsohn (*see below*, III B).]

B. Chronicles, etc.

Alferius, Ogerius. Ed. Combetti, C. MHP. Script. III (with continuation of Gulielmus Ventura).
Andreas Hungarus. Descriptio victoriae a Karolo, Provinciae comite, reportatae. Ed. Waitz, G. MGH. Script. XXVI. 1882.
Annales Cavenses. Ed. Pertz, G. H. MGH. Script. III. 1839.
Annales Forolivienses. Ed. Mazzatinti, G. RR.II.SS. New edn. Vol. XXII.
Annales Ianuenses Cafari et continuatorum. Ed. Imperiale di Sant' Angelo, C. Vols. III, IV. (Fonti.) 1923, 26; *also* ed. Pertz, G. H. MGH. Script. XVIII. 1863.
Annales Placentini Gibellini. Ed. Pertz, G. H. MGH. Script. XVIII. 1863; *also* ed. Huillard-Bréholles, J. L. A. *as* Chronicon de rebus in Italia gestis *in* Chronicon Placentinum. Paris. 1856.

Azarius, Petrus. Liber gestorum in Lombardia. Ed. Cognasso, F. RR.II.SS. New edn. Vol. XVI.

Azzurrini, Bernardinus. Chronica breviora aliaque monumenta faventina. Ed. Messeri, A. RR.II.SS. New edn. Vol. XXVIII.

Bartholomaeus de Neocastro. Historia Sicula. Ed. Paladino, G. RR.II.SS. New edn. Vol. XIII. 1921–2.

Bazano, Ioannes de. Chronicon Mutinense. Ed. Casini, T. RR.II.SS. New edn. Vol. XV.

Cantinelli, Petrus. Chronicon. Ed. Torraca, F. RR.II.SS. New edn. Vol. XXVIII.

Chronicon Estense. Ed. Bertoni, G. and Vicini, E. P. RR.II.SS. New edn. Vol. XV. 1908 ff., in progress.

Chronicon Marchiae Tarvisinae et Lombardiae. Ed. Botteghi, C. A. RR.II.SS. New edn. Vol. VIII. *Also* ed. as Annales S. Justinae. Jaffé, P. MGH. Script. XIX. 1866.

Chronicon Parmense. Ed. Bonazzi, G. RR.II.SS. New edn. Vol. IX.

Chronicon Siciliae. Ed. Gregorio, R. *in* Bibl. script. Aragon. II. *See above,* I B; *also in* Muratori. RR.II.SS. 1st edn. Vol. X.

Corpus Chronicorum Bononiensium. Ed. Sorbelli, A. RR.II.SS. New edn. Vol. XVIII. 1911 ff., in progress.

Dandolo, Andrea. Chronicon Venetum. Ed. Muratori, L. A. RR.II.SS. 1st edn. Vol. XII.

Ferreto de' Ferreti. Historia rerum in Italia gestarum. Ed. Cipolla, C. Vol. I. (Fonti.)

Galvanus Flamma. Manipulus florum seu Historia Mediolanensis. Ed. Muratori. RR.II.SS. 1st edn. Vol. XI.

Godi, Antonio. Cronaca. Ed. Soranzo, G. RR.II.SS. New edn. Vol. VIII.

Griffonibus, M. de. Memoriale Historicum. Ed. Frati, L. and Sorbelli, A. RR.II.SS. New edn. Vol. XVIII. 1902.

Guido de Corvaria. Fragmenta historiae Pisanae. Ed. Muratori, L. A. RR.II.SS. 1st edn. Vol. XXIV.

Iacopus de Varagine. Chronicon Genuense. Ed. Muratori. RR.II.SS. 1st edn. Vol. IX.

Jamsilla, Nicolaus de. Historia de rebus gestis Friderici II, etc. Ed. Muratori. RR.II.SS. 1st edn. Vol. VIII. *Also in* Del Re, G. Cronisti. Vol. II. 1868. *See above,* I B.

Iohannes de Mussis. Chronicon Placentinum. Ed. Muratori. RR.II.SS. 1st edn. Vol. XVI.

Iulianus Canonicus Civitatensis. Chronica. Ed. Tambara, G. RR.II.SS. New edn. Vol. XXIV.

Liber Regiminum Paduae. Ed. Bonardi, A. with Rolandinus Patavinus, *see below.*

Malaspina, Saba. Rerum Sicularum historia. Ed. Muratori. RR.II.SS. 1st edn. Vol. VIII; *and* ed. Gregorio, R. *in* Bibl. Script. Aragon. II. *See above,* I B.

Marchionne di Coppo Stefani. Cronaca fiorentina. Ed. Rodolico, N. RR.II.SS. New edn. Vol. XXX.

Marco Battagli da Rimini. La marcha. Ed. Massèra, A. F. RR.II.SS. New edn. Vol. XVI.

Martin da Canal. La Cronique des Veniciens. Ed. Polidori, F. ASI. VIII. 1845.

Muntaner, Ramón. Cronica catalana. Ed. Bofarull, A. de. Barcelona. 1860. Engl. transl. Goodenough, Lady. 2 vols. (Hakluyt Soc.) London. 1920–1.

Nicolaus de Carbio (Curbio, Calvi). Vita Innocentii IV. Ed. Pagnotti, F. ASRSP. XXI. 1898.

Pipinus, Franciscus. Chronicon. Ed. Muratori. RR.II.SS. 1st edn. Vol. IX.

Ptolomaeus (Tholomeus) Lucensis. Annales. Ed. Schmeidler, B. with Gesta Florentinorum and Gesta Lucanorum. MGH. Script. rer. Germ. VIII. 1930.

—— Historia ecclesiastica. Ed. Muratori. RR.II.SS. 1st edn. Vol. XI.

Rolandinus Patavinus. Chronica...Marchie Trivixane. Ed. Bonardi, A. RR.II.SS. New edn. Vol. VIII. 1905; *also* ed. Jaffé, P. MGH. Script. XIX. 1866.

Salimbene de Adam. Chronica. Ed. Holder-Egger, O. MGH. Script. XXXII. 1905–13.

Sercambi, Giovanni. Le Croniche. Ed. Bongi, S. Vol. I. (Fonti.) 1892.

Sicardi, E. *ed.* Due croniche del Vespro in volgare siciliano (Lu rebellamentu di Sichilia *and* Athanasio di Jaci, La vinuta e lu soggiornu di lu re Japicu). RR.II.SS. New edn. Vol. XXXIV.

Smereglus, N. Annales civitatis Vicentiae. Ed. Soranzo, G. RR.II.SS. New edn. Vol. IX.
Specialis, Nicolaus. Historia Sicula. Ed. Muratori. RR.II.SS. 1st edn. Vol. X; *and* ed. Gregorio, R., *in* Bibl. script. Aragon. I. *See above*, I B.
Stephanardus de Vicomercato. Liber de gestis in civitate Mediolani. Ed. Calligaris, G. RR.II.SS. New edn. Vol. IX.
Villani, Giovanni. Historie Fiorentine. Ed. Muratori. RR.II.SS. 1st edn. Vol. XIII
Vita Gregorii X papae. Ed. Muratori. RR.II.SS. 1st edn. Vol. III.

III. MODERN WORKS.

A. General.

[Certain works on local history of importance for the whole country are starred below in III B.]

Butler, W. F. The Lombard Communes. London. 1906.
Coulton, G. G. From St Francis to Dante. 2nd edn. London. 1907.
Gianani, F. I Comuni, 1000–1300. (Storia politica d' Italia scritta da una società di professori.) Milan. [19...]
Hefele, C. J. v. Conciliengeschichte. *See Gen. Bibl.* v.
Jordan, E. Les Origines de la domination angevine en Italie. Paris. 1909.
Langlois, C. V. Saint Louis, Philippe le Bel. *In* Lavisse, E. Histoire de France. Vol. III, 2. *See Gen. Bibl.* v.
Lanzani, F. Storia dei comuni italiani dalle origini al 1313. (Storia d' Italia scritta da una società d' amici.) Milan. 1882.
Luchaire, J. Les démocraties italiennes. Paris. 1915. [Brief constitutional sketch.]
Manfroni, C. Storia della marina italiana dalle invasioni barbariche al trattato di Ninfeo (400–1261). Leghorn. 1899.
—— Storia della marina italiana dal trattato di Ninfeo alla caduta di Costantinopoli. Pt. 1. Leghorn. 1902.
Muratori, L. Annali d' Italia. *See Gen. Bibl.* v.
Norden, W. Das Papsttum und Byzanz. *See Gen. Bibl.* v.
Raynaldus, O. Annales Ecclesiastici. *See Gen. Bibl.* v under Baronius.
Saint-Priest, A. de. Histoire de la conquête de Naples par Charles d'Anjou. 4 vols. Paris. 1847–9.
Schaube, A. Handelsgeschichte der romanischen Völker des Mittelmeergebiets bis zum Ende der Kreuzzüge. *See Gen. Bibl.* v.
Schirrmacher, F. W. Die letzten Hohenstaufen. Göttingen. 1871.
Sedgwick, H. D. Italy in the thirteenth century. 2 vols. London. 1913.
Villari, P. Italia da Carlo Magno alla morte di Arrigo VII. Milan. 1910. Engl. transl. Hulton, C. Mediaeval Italy from Charlemagne to Henry VII. London. 1910. [General sketch.]

B. Local.

[Works which deal largely with the general history of Italy are starred.]

*Amari, M. La guerra del Vespro Siciliano. 3 vols. 9th edn. Milan. 1886.
Besta, E. La Sardegna medioevale. 2 vols. Palermo. 1909.
Bozzola, A. Un capitano di guerra e signore subalpino, Guglielmo VII di Monferrato. *In* Miscellanea di storia Ital. 3rd ser. XIX. Turin. 1920.
Caggese, R. Un Comune libero alle porte di Firenze nel secolo XIII (Prato in Toscana). Florence. 1905.
—— La Repubblica di Siena e il suo contado nel secolo XIII. *In* Bullettino Senese di storia pat. XIII. Siena. 1906.
—— Storia di Firenze. 3 vols. Florence. 1912–21. [Bibliography.]
*Caro, G. Genua und die Mächte am Mittelmeer, 1257–1311. 2 vols. Halle-a.-S. 1895. [Bibliography.]
Cipolla, C. Compendio della storia politica di Verona. Verona. 1900.
*Davidsohn, R. Geschichte von Florenz. Vols. II, III. Berlin. 1908, 12. [Bibliography.]
—— Forschungen zur Geschichte von Florenz. Vols. II, III. Berlin. 1900–1.

Gabotto, F. Asti e la politica sabauda in Italia al tempo di Guglielmo Ventura. *In* Bibl. soc. stor. subalpina. XVIII. Pinerolo. 1903.
Gallavresi, G. La Riscossa dei Guelfi in Lombardia dopo il 1260 e la politica di Filippo della Torre. *In* Arch. stor. lombardo. XXXIII. 1905–6.
Giulini, G. Memorie spettanti alla storia, al governo, e alla descrizione della città e della campagna di Milano nei secoli bassi. 2nd edn. 7 vols. Milan. 1854–7.
*Gregorovius, F. Geschichte der Stadt Rom im Mittelalter *See Gen. Bibl.* v.
Hessel, A. Geschichte der Stadt Bologna von 1116 bis 1280. (Ebering's Hist. Studien. No. 76.) Berlin. 1910.
Heywood, W. History of Perugia. London. 1910.
Hodgson, F. C. Venice in the thirteenth and fourteenth centuries. London. 1910.
*Kretschmayr, H. Geschichte von Venedig. Vol. II. *See Gen. Bibl.* v. [Bibliography.]
Merkel, C. La dominazione di Carlo I d'Angiò in Piemonte e in Lombardia. *In* Mem. Accad. Torino. n.s. XLI. 1891.
—— Un quarto secolo di vita comunale e le origini della dominazione angioina in Piemonte. *In* Mem. Accad. Torino. n.s. XL. 1890.
Ottokar, N. Il Comune di Firenze alla fine del dugento. Florence. 1926.
Romanin, S. Storia documentata di Venezia. 10 vols. Venice. 1853–61.
Schevill, F. Siena. London. 1909.
Tallone, A. Tomaso I Marchese di Saluzzo (1244–1296). *In* Bibl. soc. stor. subalpina. LXXXVIII. Pinerolo. 1916.
Verci, G. B. Storia degli Ecelini. 3 vols. Bassano. 1779.
—— Storia della Marca Trevigiana e Veronese. Venice. 1786–91.
Villari, P. I primi due secoli della storia di Firenze. 2nd edn. Florence. 1905.
Volpe, G. Lunegiana medievale. (Bibl. storica toscana.) Florence. 1923.
Wurstemberger, J. L. Peter II, Graf von Savoyen. 4 vols. Bern, Zurich. 1856–8.

C. Special.

Arndt, H. Studien z. innern Regierungsgesch. Manfreds. (Ebering's Hist. Studien. No. 31.) Heidelberg. 1911.
Berger, E. Innocent IV und Louis IX. Paris. 1893.
Bergmann, A. König Manfred von Sizilien. Vom Tode Urbans IV bis zur Schlacht bei Benevent. (Ebering's Hist. Studien. No. 23.) Heidelberg. 1909.
Boüard, A. de. Le Régime politique et les institutions de Rome au moyen âge, 1252–1347. EcfrAR. Paris. 1920.
Busson, A. Die Schlacht bei Alba zwischen Konradin und Karl von Anjou. DZG. IV.
Cadier, L. Essai sur l'administration du royaume de Sicile sous Charles I et Charles II d'Anjou. EcfrAR. Paris. 1891.
Cantù, C. Ezelino da Romano. Milan. 1901.
Canz, O. W. Philipp Fontana, Erzbischof von Ravenna. Leipsic. 1911.
Cartellieri, O. Peter von Aragon und die Sizilienische Vesper. Heidelberg. 1904.
Cessi, R. La Tregua fra Venezia e Genova nella seconda metà del secolo XIII. Arch. Ven.-Tri. IV. 1923.
Demski, A. Papst Nikolaus III. Munich. 1902.
Döberl, M. Berthold von Vohburg-Hohenburg. DZG. XII.
Durrieu, P. Les Archives angevines de Naples. 2 vols. EcfrAR. Paris. 1887.
—— Étude sur la dynastie angevine de Naples. Liber Donationum. Rome. 1886.
Egidi, P. La Colonia saracenica di Lucera e la sua distruzione. Naples. 1915.
—— La Communitas Siciliae di 1282. Messina. 1915.
—— Ricerche sulla popolazione dell' Italia meridionale nei secoli XIII e XIV. Lucca. 1920.
Frankfurth, H. Gregorius de Montelongo. Marburg. 1893.
Gittermann, J. M. Ezzelino III von Romano. Freiburg. 1890. [diss.]
Hampe, K. Geschichte Konradins von Hohenstaufen. Innsbruck. 1894.
—— Urban IV und Manfred. (Ebering's Hist. Studien.) Heidelberg. 1905.
Hauss, A. Kardinal Oktavian Ubaldini. Heidelberg. 1913.
Karst, A. Geschichte Manfreds vom Tode Friedrichs II bis zu seiner Kronung. (Ebering's Hist. Studien. No. 6.) Berlin. 1897.

Kopp, J. E. Geschichte der Eidgenossischen Bund. Vol. II. König Rudolf und seine Zeit. II Abt. 2 Hälfte. Des Reiches Verhältnisse in Italien, bearbeitet von A. Busson. Berlin. 1871.
Levi, G. Il cardinale Ottaviano degli Ubaldini. ASRSP. XIV. 1891.
Maubach, I. Die Kardinäle und ihre Politik um die Mitte des XIII Jahrhunderts (1243–1268). Bonn. 1902.
Merkel, C. Manfredi I e Manfredi II Lancia. Turin. 1886.
Minieri Riccio, C. Genealogia di Carlo I d' Angiò, prima generazione Naples. 1857.
—— —— Genealogia di Carlo II d' Angiò, re di Napoli. ASPN. Pt. I. Naples. 1882.
Morghen, R. Il cardinale Matteo Rosso Orsini. ASRSP. XLVI. 1923.
Naldini, L. La "tallia militum societatis tallie Tuscie" nella seconda metà del secolo XIII. ASI. Anno 78. 1920.
Pardi, G. I registri angioini e la popolazione calabrese del 1276. ASPN. n.s. VII. 1922.
Pawlicki, B. Papst Honorius IV. Münster. 1896.
Rhodes, W. E. Edmund, Earl of Lancaster. EHR. XX (1905), 19 sqq., 209 sqq.
Rodenburg, C. Innocent IV und das Königreich Sicilien. Halle. 1892.
Salvemini, G. Magnati e popolani in Firenze dal 1280 al 1295. Florence. 1899.
Salzer, E. Ueber die Anfänge der Signorie in Oberitalien. Berlin. 1900.
Savio, F. Niccolò III. *In* Civiltà Cattolica. 1899.
Schiffer, Z. Markgraf Hubert Pallavicini. Leipsic. 1910.
Schneider, F. Beiträge zur Geschichte Friedrichs II und Manfreds. Rome. 1912.
—— Die Reichsverwaltung in Toscana. Rome. 1914.
Schoepp, N. Papst Hadrian V. (Heidelberger Abhandlungen 49.) Heidelberg. 1916.
Sternfeld, R. Cardinal Johann Gaetano Orsini (Nikolaus III). (Ebering's Hist. Studien. No. 52.) Berlin. 1905.
—— Karl von Anjou als Graf von Provence. Berlin. 1888.
—— Das Konklave von 1280 und die Wahl Martins IV (1281). MIOGF. XXXI.
—— Ludwigs der Heiligen Kreuzzug nach Tunis 1270 und die Politik Karl I von Sizilien. Berlin. 1896.
Sthamer, E. Die Verwaltung der Kastelle im Königreich Sizilien unter Kaiser Friedrich II und Karl I von Anjou. Leipsic. 1914.
—— Die Hauptstrassen des Königreichs Sicilien im 13 Jahrhundert. *In* Studi di storia napoletana in onore di M. Schipa. Naples. 1926.
Stieve, F. Ezzelino von Romano. Leipsic. 1909.
Tenckhoff, F. Der Kampf der Hohenstaufen um die Mark Ancona und das Herzogtum Spoleto von der zweiteren Excommunication Friedrichs II bis zum Tode Konradins. Paderborn. 1893.
—— Papst Alexander IV. Paderborn. 1907.
Trifoni, R. La legislazione angioina. Naples. 1921.
Vitale, V. Il Dominio della Parte Guelfa in Bologna. 1280–1327. Bologna. 1902.
Volpe, G. Movimenti religiosi e sette ereticali nella società medievale italiana. 2nd edn. Florence. 1926.
Zisterer, A. Gregor X und Rudolf von Habsburg in ihren beiderseitigen Beziehungen. Freiburg-i.-B. 1891.

CHAPTER VII.

ENGLAND: RICHARD I AND JOHN.

I. ORIGINAL AUTHORITIES.

A. Records.

See Gross, C. Sources (*see Gen. Bibl.* I), pp. 406–91 passim; Giuseppi, M.S. Guide to the manuscripts preserved in the P.R.O. Vol. I. *See Gen. Bibl.* I.

The importance of this period in the history of English records has been explained in the text. Most of the Chancery records were printed a century or so ago by the Record Commission, and also some of the extant Plea Rolls. Recently publication of the Plea Rolls has been resumed. The numerous records of the Exchequer have not been printed, with the exception of the Chancellor's Roll (a counter roll of the Great Roll of the Pipe) for 3 John, and the Pipe Rolls for 1–6 Richard I. Extracts from the Pipe Rolls relating to the northern counties and to Staffordshire have also been printed.

Of the unpublished records the most important are the Pipe Rolls, which are virtually complete. For the problems presented by the later rolls *see* Mabel Mills, Experiments in Exchequer Procedure, TRHS. 4th ser. VIII (1925). pp. 161–9. The subsidiary rolls, now in the P.R.O., include five Chancellor's Rolls, in addition to the roll for 3 John; two memoranda rolls, classified as L.T.R. Miscellaneous Rolls 1/3 and 1/4; a draft Pipe Roll of the Hampshire account, belonging to 17 John (Exchequer Miscellanea 1/48); and the Prestita Roll, still unpublished, for the years 14–17 John (Exchequer Account 325/2). A Receipt Roll of Richard's reign, and a doubtful fragment of John's reign have also survived (Receipt Rolls 1 and 2), with two rolls of Jewish receipts (Exchequer Account 249/2 and Receipt Roll, 1564). All these, with the exception of the draft roll, only recently discovered (Mills *op. cit.* pp. 163–5), are described by Hilary Jenkinson *in* Financial Records of the Reign of King John *in* Magna Carta Commemoration Essays (*see below,* II B (iii)); *cf.* also Trans. Jewish Hist. Soc. VIII. pp. 19 sqq.

The Norman Pipe Rolls in the P.R.O. have been published by Stapleton (*see below,* A (ii)). Mr Jenkinson first called attention to fragments of the Miscellaneous Rolls of the Norman Exchequer in Exchequer Account 505/4, membranes 7, 8–11, 13–20 (Magna Carta Commemoration Essays, pp. 281–2); these are edited by Professor Packard (*see below,* A (ii)). Another fragment (Exchequer Account 152/1) has been edited by Henri Legras *in* Bulletin des Antiquaires de Normandie, XXIX. p. 21.

The great series of Curia Regis and Assize Rolls begin in this period. For a list *see* P.R.O. Lists and Indexes no. IV (revised edn. 1910), and *cf.* the introduction to F. W. Maitland's edition of Bracton's Note Book. London. 1887. The published rolls are mentioned below. The treasury also contained the Feet of Fines, *i.e.* the official copy of the final concords made, after 1195, in triplicate. These are arranged according to counties in cases and files, and many are indexed in Le Neve's Indexes, preserved in the P.R.O. A large number have been printed or calendared (*see below*).

For the period before enrolments of charters and letters began, collections of original charters and correspondence or of copies are especially important; and it should be remembered that, during the period of enrolments, many documents, such as treaties, correspondence, etc. were not necessarily enrolled, and in some cases have survived. Many legislative acts survive in chronicles; see, for example, the list in Pollock, F. and Maitland, F. W. History of English Law. 2nd edn. Vol. I, p. 170 note (*see Gen. Bibl.* V). Roger of Howden inserted the capitula of the great eyre of 1194 in his chronicle; the capitula of 1208–9 are in the Liber Albus of London. Ed. Riley, H. T. *in* Munimenta Gildhallae Londoniensis. (Rolls.) 1859–62. It would be impossible to describe the collections of charters and correspondence, but reference should be made to the class of Ancient Correspondence (P.R.O. Lists and Indexes no. XV. 1902).

See also:
Ayloffe, J. Calendars of the ancient charters etc. London. 1774.
Bémont, C. Chartes des libertés anglaises 1100–1305. Paris. 1892.
Madox, T. Formulare Anglicanum. London. 1702.
—— History and antiquities of the Exchequer. 2nd edn. 2 vols. London. 1769.
Prynne, W. An exact chronological vindication of our kings' supreme ecclesiastical jurisdiction. [Prynne's Records.] Vol. III. London. 1668; repr. 1670; 1672.
Reports of the Deputy Keeper of Public Records (passim). 1841 ff.
Reports from the Lords' committees...touching the dignity of a peer. 5 vols. London. 1820–9. [Especially the appendices.]
Rymer, T. Foedera. Vol. I. *See Gen. Bibl.* IV.
Statutes of the Realm. Vol. I. (RC.) 1810.
Stubbs, W. Select Charters. *See Gen. Bibl.* IV.
Wilkins, D. Concilia Magnae Britanniae et Hiberniae, A.D. 446–1718. 4 vols. London. 1737.

Collections of Charters.

Delisle, L. Cartulaire normand etc. Paris. 1852.
Round, J. H. Ancient Charters prior to 1200. (Pipe Roll Soc.) London. 1888.
—— Calendar of Documents preserved in France 918–1206. (Rolls.) 1899.
Teulet, A. Layettes du Trésor des Chartes. Vol. I. Paris. 1863.

Among the numerous collections of local charters the most useful is Farrer, W. Early Yorkshire Charters. 3 vols. Edinburgh. 1914–16. Cartellieri, A. has compiled a list of King Richard's acts and charters *in* Philipp II August. Vol. II, pp. 288 sqq. Vol. III, pp. 217 sqq. Leipsic. 1899, 1900.

The enrolled and filed records now available in print or in calendars may be classified as follows. The introductions by Hardy, T. Duffus, Palgrave, F., and others are sometimes of great value.

(i) *Household and Chancery Records.*

Rotuli chartarum 1199–1216. Ed. Hardy, T. D. (RC.) 1837.
Rotuli litterarum patentium 1201–16. Ed. Hardy, T. D. (RC.) 1835.
Rotuli litterarum clausarum 1204–27. Ed. Hardy, T. D. Vol. I. (RC.) 1833.
Rotuli de liberate ac de misis et praestitis regnante Johanne. Ed. Hardy, T. D. (RC.) 1844.
[Liberate Rolls, *i.e.* the first form of Close Roll, for 2, 3, 5 John, the Misae Roll 11 John, and Praestita Roll 12 John. The Misae Roll 14 John and the Praestita Roll 7 John are printed in Cole, H. Documents illustrative of English History in the thirteenth and fourteenth centuries. pp. 231–76. (RC.) 1844.]
Rotuli Normanniae. Ed. Hardy, T. D. (RC.) 1835. [Contains rolls of 1200–5.]
Rotuli de oblatis et finibus. Ed. Hardy, T. D. (RC.) 1835. [Oblate Rolls 1–3 John; Fine Rolls 6, 7, 9, 15–18 John.]

(ii) *Exchequer and Judicial Records.*

Great Roll of the Pipe, 1 Richard I. Ed. Hunter, J. (RC.) 1844.
Pipe Rolls, 2–6 Richard I. Ed. Stenton, D. M. (Pipe Roll Soc. n.s. Vols. I–III, and V.) London. 1925–8. In progress.
Rotulus cancellarii, 3 John. (RC.) 1833.
For editions or translations of the Pipe Rolls for the northern counties (excluding Yorkshire), Dorset, and Staffordshire during the whole or parts of this period, *see* Gross, *op. cit.* pp. 421–2.
Magni rotuli scaccarii Normanniae. Ed. Stapleton, T. 2 vols. (Soc. of Antiquaries.) London. 1840, 44. [Rolls of 1195, 1198, and fragments 1201–3.]
Miscellaneous records of the Norman Exchequer 1199–1204. Ed. Packard, S. R. (Smith Coll. Studies, Vol. XII.) Northampton, Mass. 1927.
Liber Niger de Scaccario. Ed. Hearne, T. 2 vols. Oxford. 1728. 2nd edn. London. 1771.
Liber Rubeus de Scaccario. The Red Book of the Exchequer. Ed. Hall, H. 3 vols. (Rolls.) 1896.
[*See ante* Vol. V. p. 896. Contains lists of fees and serjeanties, compiled from exchequer records 'for fiscal purposes.' *See* Book of Fees. Pt. I. pp. 53–5.]

The Book of Fees, commonly called Testa de Nevill, reformed from the earliest Roll by the Deputy Keeper of the Public Records. Pt. I. (Cal.SP.) 1920. [This displaces the Testa de Nevill, published by the Record Commission 1807.]

Rotuli curiae regis. Ed. Palgrave, F. 2 vols. (RC.) 1835.

[Rolls of 6 and 10 Richard I, 1–2 John. For the early plea rolls *see* Lists and Indexes no. 4; Round, J.H. A Plea Roll of Richard I. EHR. XXII (1907). 290–92, identifying a roll of Hilary term 1196, printed in Pipe Roll Soc. Vol. XXIV (1900); and the Curia Regis Rolls. Vol. I. *See below.*]

Three Rolls of the King's Court, 1194–5. Ed. Maitland, F. W. (Pipe Roll Soc.) London. 1891.

Curia Regis Rolls of the reign of Richard I and John. 4 vols. (Cal.SP.) 1922–9. In progress.

Select Pleas of the Crown. Ed. Maitland, F. W. (Selden Soc. I.) London. 1888.

Select Civil Pleas. Ed. Baildon, W. P. (Selden Soc. III.) London. 1890.

Select Pleas of the Forest. Ed. Turner, G. J. (Selden Soc. XIII.) London. 1901.

Fines sive pedes finium 1195–1214. Ed. Hunter, J. 2 vols. (RC.) 1835, 44.

Feet of Fines 1182–99. 4 vols. (Pipe Roll Soc.) London. 1894–1900.

A Calendar of Feet of Fines relating to the county of Huntingdon. Ed. Turner, G. J. Cambridge. 1913. [The introduction is valuable. For other local calendars and indexes *see* Gross, *op. cit.* pp. 457–63.]

B. Narrative and Miscellaneous Sources.

See Hardy, T. D. Descriptive catalogue of materials relating to the history of Great Britain and Ireland. Vols. II, III. (*see Gen. Bibl.* I.); and the bibliographies in Gross *op. cit.*, Adams, Davis, Ramsay, Cartellieri, and Petit-Dutaillis (*see below*). Refer also to Vol. v. pp. 897–8. Many of the sources are also edited, in part, by Liebermann, F. *in* MGH. Script. Vols. XXVII, XXVIII. 1885, 88.

(i) *Chronicles.*

Annales monastici. Ed. Luard, H. R. 5 vols. (Rolls.) 1864–9.

[The annals of Margam, Burton, and Waverley are the most important.] *Note also*:

Annales Cestrienses. Ed. Christie, R. C. (Record Soc. for Lancashire and Cheshire.) London. 1887.

Annales Stanleienses. Ed. Howlett, R. *in* Chronicles of the reigns of Stephen, Henry II, and Richard I. Vol. II. pp. 506–68. (Rolls.) 1885.

Annales S. Edmundi (to 1212). Ed. Liebermann, F. *in* Ungedruckte Anglo-Normannische Geschichtsquellen. pp. 136–55. Strasbourg. 1879.

Annals of Southwark and Merton. *See* Tyson, Moses *in* Surrey Archaeol. Collections. XXXVI. pp. 24–57, and Petit-Dutaillis, C. Étude sur la vie et le règne de Louis VIII. Paris 1894. pp. 513–15.

Roger of Howden. Chronica Rogeri de Hovedene. Ed. Stubbs, W. Vols. III, IV. (Rolls.) 1871.

Benedict of Peterborough. Gesta Regis Henrici Secundi (to 1192). Ed. Stubbs, W. Vol. II. (Rolls.) 1867.

William of Newburgh. Historia rerum anglicarum. Ed. Howlett, R. *in* Chronicles etc. Vol. II. (Rolls.) 1885.

Gervase of Canterbury. Chronicon and Gesta Regum. Ed. Stubbs, W. The Historical Works of Gervase of Canterbury. 2 vols. (Rolls.) 1879–80.

Memoriale Walteri de Coventria. Ed. Stubbs, W. 2 vols. (Rolls.) 1872–3.

Richard of Devizes. De rebus gestis Ricardi Primi (1189–92). Ed. Howlett, R. *in* Chronicles etc. Vol. III. pp. 379–454. (Rolls.) 1886.

Ralph de Diceto. Imagines Historiarum (to 1202). Ed. Stubbs, W. Opera Historica. 2 vols. (Rolls.) 1876.

Roger of Wendover. Flores Historiarum. Ed. Coxe, H. O. Vol. III. (English Hist. Soc.) London. 1841. [For the text see Stevenson, W. H. *in* EHR. III (1888). 353–60, and for the connexion between Wendover and Coggeshall, Powicke, F. M. *ibid.* XXI (1906). 286–96. Wendover is comprised in Matthew Paris's Chronica Majora. Ed. Luard, H. R. (Rolls.) 1872–84. Matthew added some important, though often tendentious, material. His Historia Anglorum, Ed. Madden, F. 3 vols. (Rolls.) 1866–9; and his Vitae Abbatum, in Walsingham's Gesta Abbatum. Ed. Riley, H. T. Vol. I. (Rolls.) 1867. should also be consulted.]

Ralph Niger. The Chronicles of Ralph Niger. Ed. Anstruther, R. (Caxton Soc.) London. 1851.
Ralph of Coggeshall. Chronicon Anglicanum. Ed. Stevenson, J. (Rolls.) 1875.
Florence of Worcester. Chronicon ex chronicis. (Second continuation.) Ed. Thorpe, B. Vol. II. (English Hist. Soc.) London. 1849.
Chronica maiorum et vicecomitum Londoniarum. *See* Liber de antiquis legibus. Ed. Stapleton, T. (Camden Soc.) London. 1846. pp. 1–4.

(ii) *Biographies, Letters, etc.*

Chronica Jocelini de Brakelonda de rebus gestis Samsonis abbatis. Ed. Rokewode, J. G. (Camden Soc.) London. 1840.
Gerard of Wales. Opera Giraldi Cambrensis. 8 vols. (Rolls.) 1861–91. Notably the De rebus a se gestis (Vol. I) and the De principis instructione (Vol. VIII).
Peter of Blois. Epistolae. Ed. Giles, J. A. *in* Opera omnia. Vols. I, II. London. 1846. [*See* Robinson, J. Armitage. Somerset Hist. Essays. London. 1921. pp. 100–40, and Cohn, E. S. The manuscript evidence for the Letters of Peter of Blois *in* EHR. XLI (1926). 43–60.]
Magna Vita S. Hugonis episcopi Lincolniensis. Ed. Dimock, J. F. (Rolls.) 1864.
Innocent III. Epistolae. MPL. CCIV–VII. [*See* especially Potthast, A. Regesta Pontificum Romanorum. Vol. I. pp. 1–467 (*see Gen. Bibl.* IV.) and for the preceding popes Jaffé, P. Regesta Pontificum Romanorum ad annum 1198. 2nd edn. Vol. II. Leipsic. 1888.]
Epistolae Cantuarienses. Ed. Stubbs, W. *in* Chronicles and Memorials of the Reign of Richard I. Vol. II. (Rolls.) 1865.
Histoire de Guillaume le Maréchal. Ed. Meyer, P. 3 vols. (SHF.) Paris. 1891–1901. [In some ways the most important text on the political and social life of the period.]

(iii) *French Chronicles.*

Histoire des ducs de Normandie et des rois d'Angleterre. Ed. Michel, F. (SHF.) Paris. 1840.
Chronique française des rois de France par un anonyme de Béthune; extracts in Bouquet. XXIV. pp. 750–75. [For a similar work, coming from the same neighbourhood, *see* Petit-Dutaillis, C. Fragment de l'histoire de Philippe Auguste roy de France. BEC. LXXXVII (1926). pp. 98–141. (Text on pp. 111–41.)]

(iv) *Miscellaneous.*

Wharton, H. Anglia Sacra. London. 1691. Diocesan annals etc. [*See* Hardy, T. D. Descriptive catalogue, *see above*, I B. Vol. I. pp. 691–4.]
Wright, T. Political songs of England from the reign of John to that of Edward II. (Camden Soc.) London. 1839.

II. MODERN WRITERS.

A. General Narratives.

Adams, G. B. History of England 1066–1216. (Political History of England. Ed. Hunt, W. and Poole, R. L. Vol. II.) London. 1905.
Davis, H. W. C. England under the Normans and Angevins. 4th edn. (History of England. Ed. Oman, C.W.C. Vol. II.) London. 1915.
Norgate, K. England under the Angevin Kings. 2 vols. London. 1887.
—— Richard the Lion Heart. London. 1924.
—— John Lackland. London. 1902.
Pauli, R. Geschichte von England. *In* Lappenberg, J. M. and Pauli, R. Geschichte. Vols. III–V. Hamburg. 1834–58.
Pearson, C. H. History of England during the early and middle ages. 2 vols. London. 1867.
Ramsay, Sir J. H. The Angevin Empire 1154–1216. London. 1903.
Stubbs, W. The introductions to Diceto, Howden, Benedict of Peterborough, Gervase of Canterbury, the memorial of Walter of Coventry, the Epistolae Cantuarienses, mentioned above (I B).

B. Studies on Special Subjects.

(i) *Administration.*

Adams, G. B. The Origin of the English Constitution. New Haven. 1912.
—— Council and Courts in Anglo-Norman England. New Haven. 1926.
Brooks, F. W. William de Wrotham and the Office of Keeper of the King's Ports and Galleys. EHR. xl (1925). 570–80.
Davis, H. W. C. The St. Albans Council of 1213. EHR. xx (1905). 282–90. [*Cf.* Turner, G. J. *Ibid.* xxi (1906). 297–9; White, A. B. *in* AHR. Oct. 1911, Jan. 1917.]
Formoy, B. E. R. A Maritime Indenture of 1212. EHR. xli (1926). 556–9.
Foss, E. On the Lord Chancellors and Keepers of the Seal in the reign of King John. *In* Archaeologia. xxxii (1847). 83–95.
Levett, A. E. The Summons to a Great Council, 1213. EHR. xxxi (1916). 85–90.
Maxwell-Lyte, Sir H. C. Historical notes on the use of the Great Seal of England. London. 1926.
Mills, Mabel. Experiments in Exchequer Procedure (1200–32). TRHS. 4th ser. viii (1925). 151–70.
Mitchell, S. K. Studies in Taxation under John and Henry III. New Haven. 1914.
Morris, W. A. The medieval English Sheriff to 1300. Manchester. 1927.
Pasquet, D. Essai sur les origines de la Chambre des Communes. Paris. 1914. Engl. transl. Cambridge. 1925.
Petit-Dutaillis, C. Studies supplementary to Stubbs' Constitutional History. *See Gen. Bibl.* v under Stubbs, W. [Vol. ii contains a study of the forest.]
Powicke, F. M. The Loss of Normandy. Manchester. 1913.
Ramsay, Sir J. H. Revenues of the Kings of England 1066–1399. Vol. i. Oxford. 1925.
Reid, Rachel. Baronage and Thanage. EHR. xxxv (1920). 161–99.
Round, J. H. The Oxford Debate on foreign service (1197). EHR. vii (1892). 301; *and in* Feudal England. London. 1909. 528–38.
—— The Great Carucage of 1198. EHR. iii (1888). 501; iv (1889). 105.
—— The Great Inquest of Service (1212). *In* The Commune of London. London. 1899. pp. 261–77.
—— The King's Serjeants and Offices of State. London. 1911.
Stenton, Doris M., *ed.* The earliest Lincolnshire Assize Rolls, A.D. 1202–9. (Lincoln Record Soc., xxii.) 1926. [Introduction.]
Stubbs, W. Constitutional history of England. *See Gen. Bibl.* v.
Tout, T. F. Chapters in the administrative history of medieval England. Vol. i. Manchester. 1920.
White, A. B. Was there a "Common Council" before Parliament? AHR. xxv (1919). 1–17.

(ii) *The Church.*

Gütschow, Else. Innocenz III und England. Munich. 1904.
Hefele, C. J. v. Hist. des conciles. Transl. Leclercq. Vol. v, pt. 2. *See Gen. Bibl.* v.
Hook, W. F. Lives of the Archbishops of Canterbury. 12 vols. London. 1860–76.
Krehbiel, E. B. The Interdict, its history and its operation. Washington. 1909.
Ladenbauer, W. F. Wie wurde König Johann von England Vasall des römischen Stuhles? *In* Zeitsch. für kathol. Theologie. vi (1882). 201–47, 393–437.
Luchaire, A. Innocent III: les royautés vassales du Saint-Siège. Paris. 1908.
Lunt, W. E. The Valuation of Norwich. Oxford. 1926. [For early papal taxation.]
Maitland, F. W. The Deacon and the Jewess; or, apostasy at Common Law. *In* Collected Papers. Vol. i. pp. 385–406. Cambridge. 1911.
Makower, F. The Constitutional History and Constitution of the Church of England. (Transl. from the German.) London. 1895.
Mercati, A. La prima relazione del cardinale Nicolò de Romanis sulla sua legazione in Inghilterra. *In* Essays in History presented to R. L. Poole. Oxford. 1927. pp. 274-89.
Perry, G. G. Life of St. Hugh of Avalon. London. 1879.

Powicke, F. M. Alexander of St Albans, a literary muddle. *In* Essays...presented to R. L. Poole. *op. cit.* pp. 246–60.
—— Stephen Langton. Oxford. 1928.
—— The Bull "Miramur plurimum" and a letter to Archbishop Stephen Langton, 5 Sept. 1215. EHR. XLIV (1929). 87–93.
Robinson, J. Armitage. Bishop Jocelin and the Interdict. *In* Somerset Hist. Essays. London. 1921. pp. 141–59. [Some information on the effects of the Interdict may also be found in medieval texts not mentioned above, *e.g.* the Peterborough Chronicle (ed. Giles, J. A. London. 1845: *see* Gross, *op. cit.*, no. 1747); the appendix to W. D. Macray's edition of the Chronicon abbatiae Rameseiensis, (Rolls.) 1886; the Chronicon abbatiae de Evesham, ed. Macray, W. D. (Rolls.) 1863; the Historia et Cartularium monasterii Gloucestriae, ed. Hart, W. H. (Rolls.) 1863; Geoffrey of Coldingham, in Historiae Dunelmensis scriptores tres, ed. Raine, J. (Surtees Soc.) London. 1839; the Liber Memorandorum Ecclesie de Bernewelle, ed. Clarke, J. W. Cambridge. 1907.]
Stubbs, W. Registrum Sacrum Anglicanum. 2nd edn. *See Gen. Bibl.* III.

(iii) *The Great Charter.*

For the earlier works by Blackstone, Richard Thomson etc., see McKechnie (*below*). See also the works of Adams and Petit-Dutaillis already mentioned (*above*, II B (i)).

Leclère, L. La Grande charte de 1215 est-elle une "illusion"? *In* Mélanges d'histoire offerts à Henri Pirenne. Vol. I. Brussels. 1926. pp. 279–90.
Magna Carta Commemoration Essays. Ed. Malden, H. E. (Royal Hist. Soc.) London 1917.
McKechnie, W. S. Magna Carta. 2nd edn. Glasgow. 1915.
Riess, L. The reissue of Henry I's coronation charter. EHR. XLI (1926). 321–31. [For the Winchester text current in John's reign, *cf.* Liebermann, F. The text of Henry I's coronation charter. TRHS. n.s. VIII (1894). 21–48.]
—— Zur Vorgeschichte der Magna Carta. HVJS. XIII (1910). 449–58. [On the so-called unknown Charter. *See also* Round, J. H. *in* EHR. VIII (1893). 288–94; Prothero, G. W. and Hall, H. *ibid.* IX (1894). 117–21, 326–35; Davis, H. W. C. *ibid.* XX (1905). 719–26; Petit-Dutaillis, *op. cit.*]
Round, J. H. King John and Robert fitz Walter. EHR. XIX (1904). 707–11.
Tait, J. Waynagium and Contenementum. EHR. XXVII (1912). 720–8.
White, A. B. The name Magna Carta. EHR. XXX (1915). 472–5.

(iv) *Municipal and Social History.*

(*a*) (*General.*)

Bächtold, H. Der norddeutsche Handel im 12 und beginnenden 13 Jahrhundert. Berlin. 1910.
Ballard, A. The English Boroughs in the reign of John. EHR. XIV (1899). 93–104.
—— British Borough Charters 1042–1216. Cambridge. 1913.
Bateson, Mary. Borough Customs. 2 vols. (Selden Soc. XVIII, XXI.). London. 1904, 6. [Introduction.]
Gross, C. The Gild Merchant. 2 vols. Oxford. 1890.
Hemmeon, M. de W. Burgage tenure in medieval England. Cambridge, Mass. 1914.
Tait, J. Liber Burgus. *In* Essays in Medieval History presented to T. F. Tout. Manchester. 1925. pp. 79–88.
Vinogradoff, Sir P. The Growth of the Manor. London. 1905.

(*b*) (*History of London.*)

Bateson, Mary. A London municipal collection of the reign of John. EHR. XV (1902). 480–511, 707–30.
Liebermann, F. Ueber die Leges Anglorum saeculo XIII ineunte Londoniis collectae. Halle. 1894. [*Also*: A contemporary manuscript of the Leges Anglorum Londoniis collectae. EHR. XXVIII (1913). 732–45.]
Page, W. London: its origin and early development. London. 1923.

Round, J. H. The Commune of London. London. 1899. pp. 219–60. [*Cf.* Petit-Dutaillis, *op. cit.* pp. 91–106, and Adams, G. B. The Origin of the English Constitution. pp. 355–69. *See above,* II B (i).]
Thomas, A. H. Calendar of the Early Mayor's Court Rolls. Cambridge. 1924. [Useful introduction.]

(*c*) (*The Jews.*)

Caro, G. Sozial- und Wirtschaftsgeschichte der Juden im Mittelalter und der Neuzeit. Vol. I. Leipsic. 1908.
Hyamson, A. M. A History of the Jews in England. London. 1908.
Jacobs, J. The Jews of Angevin England. London. 1893.
Jenkinson, H. The records of Exchequer receipts from the English Jewry. *In* Trans. Jewish Hist. Soc. of England. VIII (1915). 19–54; *cf.* C. G. Crump in EHR. XXIX (1914). 551.

(v) *Miscellaneous.*

Cartellieri, A. Philipp II August, König von Frankreich. 4 vols. Leipsic. 1899–1922.
Green, V. Account of the discovery of the body of King John in the cathedral church of Worcester. London. 1797.
Hardy, T. D. King John's Itinerary, prefixed to the Rotuli litterarum patentium (*see above,* I A (i)) and also in Archaeologia, XXII (1829). 124–60.
Hope, W. St John. The Loss of King John's baggage train in the Wellstream in October 1216. *In* Archaeologia. LX (1906). 93–110.
Jenkinson, A. V. The Jewels lost in the Wash. *In* History. n.s. VIII (1923). 161–8.
Lehmann, J. Johann ohne Land: Beiträge zu seiner Charakteristik. Berlin. 1904.
Malo, H. Un grand feudataire, Renaud de Dammartin et la coalition de Bouvines. Paris. 1898. [Useful for John's financial dealings with his continental allies.]
Petit-Dutaillis, C. Le déshéritement de Jean Sans Terre et le meurtre d'Arthur de Bretagne: Étude critique sur la formation et la fortune d'une légende. Paris. 1925. [The previous literature on this subject is discussed in this essay.]
Poole, A. L. England and Burgundy in the last decade of the twelfth century. *In* Essays...presented to R. L. Poole. Oxford. 1927. pp. 261–73.
Round, J. H. The Coronation of Richard I. *In* The Commune of London. London. 1899. pp. 201–6.
—— The struggle of John and Longchamp. *Ibid.* pp. 207–18.
—— Richard I's change of Seal (1198). *In* Feudal England. London. 1895. pp. 539–51.
—— Some English crusaders of Richard I. EHR. XVIII (1903). 475–82.
Varenbergh, E. Histoire des relations diplomatiques entre le comté de Flandre et l'Angleterre au moyen âge. Brussels. 1874.

CHAPTER VIII.

ENGLAND: HENRY III.

I. SPECIAL BIBLIOGRAPHIES.

Davis, H. W. C. England under the Normans and Angevins. *See below,* III A (i).
Gross, C. Sources and Literature of English History. *See Gen. Bibl.* I.
Tout, T. F. History of England, 1216–1377. pp. 443–64. *See below,* III A (i).
Winfield, P. H. The chief Sources of English Legal History. Cambridge, Mass. 1925.
The lists of works appended in Lunt, W. E., The Valuation of Norwich, pp. 621–36 (*see below,* III B (iii)), White, A. B., The Making of the English Constitution, 2nd edn., pp. xv–xxx (*see below,* III B (i)) and Hemmeon, M. de W., Burgage Tenure in Mediaeval England, pp. 212–17 (*see below,* III B (vi)) are useful.

II. ORIGINAL AUTHORITIES.

A. NARRATIVE SOURCES.

(i) *Guides.*

Bale, J. Index Britanniae Scriptorum. Ed. Poole, R. L. and Bateson, Mary. (Anecdota Oxoniensia IV, 9.) Oxford. 1902.
Hardy, T. D. Descriptive Catalogue of materials relating to the History of Great Britain. Vol. III. *See Gen. Bibl.* I. [Mostly MS. sources.]
Jenkins, C. The Monastic Chronicler and the early School of St Albans. London. 1923.
Plehn, H. Der politische Charakter von Matheus Parisiensis. Leipsic. 1897.
Poole, R. L. Chronicles and Annals. Oxford. 1925.
Powicke, F. M. Roger of Wendover and the Coggeshall Chronicle. EHR. XXI. 1906.
Prefaces of Pauli, R. and Liebermann, F. to Excerpts from English Chroniclers *in* MGH. Script. XXVII, XXVIII, and of Luard, H. R. to Vol. I of Matthew Paris, Chronica Majora. *See below,* II A (ii).

(ii) *The St Albans Group.*

Roger of Wendover. Flores Historiarum. Ed. Hewlett, H. G. Vols. II and III. (Rolls.) 1883.
Matthew Paris. Chronica Majora. Ed. Luard, H. R. Vols. III–V. (Rolls.) 1876–80. [For years 1216–35 an enlarged revision of Roger of Wendover.]
—— Historia Anglorum. Ed. Madden, Sir F. H. Vols. II and III. (Rolls.) 1866–9.
Flores Historiarum. Ed. Luard, H. R. Vols. II, III (with appendix). 1890. [Principal source for the last years of the reign in the five following chronicles.]
Chronica de duobus bellis apud Lewes et Evesham. Ed. Riley, H. T. *in* Walsingham's Ypodigma Neustriae. (Rolls.) 1876.
William Rishanger. Chronica et Annales. Ed. Riley, H. T. (Rolls.) 1865.
John de Trokelowe. Chronica et Annales. Ed. Riley, H. T. (Rolls.) 1866.
Annales Londonienses. *See below,* II A (iii).
Trevet's Annales. *See below,* II A (v).

(iii) *The London Group.*

Additional MS. (B.M.) 5444. [Transcript of a London Chronicle now no longer extant.]
Annales Sancti Pauli Londoniensis. Ed. Liebermann, F. MGH. Script. XXVIII. 1888.

Annales Londonienses. Ed. Stubbs, W. *in* Chronicles of the Reigns of Edward I and II. 2 vols. (Rolls.) 1882–3.

[See especially extracts from the "Barlings Chronicle" published as an appendix to the Introduction to Vol. II.]

Fitz Thedmar, Arnold. Cronica maiorum et vicecomitum Londoniarum. Ed. Stapleton, T. *in* Liber de Antiquis Legibus. (Camden Soc.) London. 1846.

Croniques de London (1259–1344). Ed. Aungier, G. J. (Camden Soc.) London. 1844.

(iv) *The Annales Monastici.*

Ed. Luard, H. R. 5 vols. (Rolls.) 1864–9.

Vol. I. Annales de Margam. Annales monasterii de Theokesberia. Annales monasterii de Burton.

Vol. II. Annales monasterii de Wintonia. Annales monasterii de Waverleia.

Vol. III. Annales prioratus de Dunstaplia.

Vol. IV. Annales monasterii de Oseneia. Chronicon Thome Wykes. Annales prioratus de Wigornia.

(v) *Other Chronicles and Annals.*

Annales Cestrienses (St Werburgh at Chester). Ed. Christie, R. C. (Lancs. and Cheshire Record Soc.) London. 1887.

Annales Stanleienses. Ed. Howlett, R. *in* Chronicles of the Reigns of Stephen, Henry II, and Richard I. Vol. II. (Rolls.) 1885.

Coggeshall, Ralph of. Chronicon Anglicanum. Ed. Stevenson, J. (Rolls.) 1875.

Cotton, Bartholomew de. Historia Anglicana. Ed. Luard, H. R. (Rolls.) 1859.

Coventry, Walter of. Memoriale. Ed. Stubbs, W. Vol. II. (Rolls.) 1873.

Dover Chronicle. *In* Gervase of Canterbury. Gesta Regum Continuata. Ed. Stubbs, W. (Rolls.) 1880.

Hemingburgh, Walter of. Chronicon. Ed. Hamilton, H. C. (English Hist. Soc.) London. 1848–9.

Lanercost, Chronicon de. Ed. Stevenson, J. (Bannatyne Club.) Edinburgh. 1839. Engl. transl. Maxwell, Sir H. *in* Scottish Hist. Review. Vols. VI–X. Glasgow. 1908–13.

Mailros, Chronica de. Ed. Stevenson, J. (Bannatyne Club.) Edinburgh. 1835.

Merton, Chronique de. Ed. Petit-Dutaillis, C. *in* Étude sur la vie et le règne de Louis VIII. *See below,* III B (iv).

Normandie, Histoire de ducs de. Ed. Michel, F. (SHF.) Paris. 1840.

Oxenedes, Johannes de. Chronica. Ed. Ellis, H. (Rolls.) 1859.

Silgrave, Henry de. Chronicon. Ed. Hook, C. (Caxton Soc.) London. 1849.

Southwark and Merton, the Annals of. Ed. Tyson, M. (Surrey Archaeol. Collections, XXXVI.) 1926.

Taxter, John de. Cronica Abbreviata. Ed. Luard, H. R. *in* Bartholomew de Cotton's Historia Anglicana. *See above.*

Trevet, Nicholas. Annales. Ed. Hog, T. (English Hist. Soc.) London. 1845.

Worcester, Florence of. Chronicon (2nd continuation). Ed. Thorpe, B. (English Hist. Soc.) London. 1848.

(vi) *Metrical.*

Histoire de Guillaume le Maréchal. Ed. Meyer, P. Vols. II, III. (SHF.) Paris. 1891–1901.

Political Songs of England from the reign of John to that of Edward II. Ed. Wright, P. (Camden Soc.) London. 1839.

Poem on the death of Simon de Montfort. Ed. Maitland, F. W. EHR. XI. 1896. *Also in* Maitland's Collected Papers. III. Cambridge. 1911.

The Song of Lewes. Ed. Kingsford, C. L. Oxford. 1890.

Robert of Gloucester. Metrical Chronicle of. Ed. Aldis Wright, W. (Rolls.) 1887.

(vii) *Wales.*

Annales Cambriae. Ed. Williams ab Ithel, J. (Rolls.) 1860.

Annales Monastici. Esp. Tewkesbury, Margam, Dunstable, Worcester. *See above* II A (iv).

Annales Cestrienses. *See above,* II A (v).

(viii) *Ireland.*

Annals of the Kingdom of Ireland by the Four Masters. Irish text, with transl., ed. O'Donovan, J. 7 vols. Dublin. 1851.
Annals of Loch Cé. Irish text, with transl., ed. Hennessy, W. M. (Rolls.) 1871.
Annals of Ulster, otherwise Annals of Senat. Irish text, with transl., ed. Hennessy, W. M. Vols. II–IV by MacCarthy, B. Dublin. 1887–1901.
Annales Inisfalenses. Ed. O'Conor, C. *in* Rerum Hibernicarum Scriptores. Vol. II, pts. 2 and 3. Buckingham. 1825.

B. Record Sources.

Only the most useful classes can be indicated here. For the history of the Records the reader is referred to (1) Reports from the Select Committee appointed to inquire into the State of the Public Records of the Kingdom. London. 1800. (2) Report...of the Select Committee of the House of Commons appointed to inquire into...the Record Commission and...the Records of the United Kingdom. London. 1837. (3) The Annual Reports of the Deputy Keeper of the Public Records. London. 1841 ff.

(i) *Guides.*

Giuseppi, M. S. Guide to the Manuscripts...in the P.R.O. Vol. I. *See Gen. Bibl.* I.
Hall, H. Repertory of British Archives. Pt. I. England. London. 1920.
—— Studies in English Official Historical Documents. Cambridge. 1908.
—— *ed.* Formula Book of English Official Historical Documents. 2 pts. Cambridge. 1908–9.
Winfield, P. H. Chief Sources, pp. 103–144. *See above,* I.

(ii) *General Collections.*

Brady, R. Complete History of England. London. 1685. (Continuation, 1700.) [For transcripts of letters patent and close.]
Champollion-Figeac, J. J. *ed.* Lettres de rois, reines, et autres personnages des cours de France et de l'Angleterre, depuis Louis VII jusqu'à Henri IV. 2 vols. Paris. 1839, 47.
Hunter, J. *ed.* Rotuli selecti ad res Anglicas et Hibernicas spectantes. (RC.) 1834.
Michel, F. and Bémont, C. *edd.* Rôles Gascons. Vols. I, II. Paris. 1885, 1900.
Prynne, W. An exact chronological vindication of our kings' supreme ecclesiastical jurisdiction over all religious affairs. [Prynne's Records.] Vol. III. London. 1668; repr. 1670; 1672.
—— A brief register, kalendar, and survey of the several kinds of all parliamentary writs. Pt. I. London. 1659.
Reports from the Lords' committees...touching the dignity of a peer. Vols. I–IV. London. 1816–25.
Rymer, T. Foedera. Ed. Clarke, A. and others. Vol. I, pt. 1. *See Gen. Bibl.* IV.
Shirley, W. W. *ed.* Royal and other historical letters illustrative of the reign of Henry III. 2 vols. (Rolls.) 1862, 66.
Stubbs, W. Select Charters. 9th edn. *See Gen. Bibl.* IV.
Teulet, A. and De Laborde, J. *edd.* Layettes du Trésor des Chartes. Vols. I–III. Paris. 1863–6. coll. 75–81.

(iii) *Chancery Enrolments and Files.*

(*a*) *Guides.*

Dibben, Miss L. B. Chancellor and Keeper of the Seal under Henry III. EHR. XXVII. 1912.
List of Chancery Rolls. P.R.O. Lists and Indexes, XXVII. 1908.
Maxwell-Lyte, Sir H. C. Historical notes on the use of the Great Seal of England. London. 1926.
Powicke, F. M. The Chancery during the Minority of Henry III. EHR. XXIII. 1908.
Tout, T. F. Chapters in the Administrative History of Mediaeval England. Vol. I. *See below,* III B (i).

(*b*) *Enrolments.*

[These are in the Public Record Office. They have been printed or calendared so far as shewn below.]

Close Rolls, printed (1216–1227) *in* Rotuli litterarum clausarum. Vols. I, II. (RC.) 1833, 4; and (1227–1253) *in* Close Rolls. 7 vols. (Cal.SP.) 1902–27.

Patent Rolls. Calendared 1216–1272. 6 vols. (Cal.SP.) 1901–13.

Charter Rolls. Calendared 1226–1272. 2 vols. (Cal.SP.) 1903, 6.

Fine Rolls. Some printed *in* Excerpta e rotulis finium, A.D. 1216–1272. Ed. Roberts, C. (RC.) 1835–6; and (1242) Un Rotulus finium retrouvé. Ed. Bémont, C. Paris. 1926.

Liberate Rolls. Calendared 1226–1240. (Cal.SP.) 1916.

Treaty Rolls.

Gascon Rolls. *See above*, II B (ii) Rôles Gascons.

French Rolls. *See* Carte, T. Catalogue des Rolles Gascons, Normans, et François. 2 vols. London and Paris. 1743.

Supplementary Close Rolls.

(*c*) *Files.*

[In Public Record Office. Calendared as shewn below.]

Inquisitions *ad quod damnum.* 1244–1272. *See* P.R.O. Lists and Indexes, XVII, XXII. 1904, 6.

Inquisitions *post mortem.* 1216–1272. Calendared (to 1236) *in* Calendarium Inq. post mortem. Vol. I. (RC.) 1806; and (including Exchequer Series) Calendar of Inquisitions, Henry III. (Cal.SP.) 1904.

Inquisitions, Miscellaneous. 1219–1272. Calendared. Vol. I (to 1307). (Cal.SP.) 1916.

Warrants for the Great Seal and Writs of Privy Seal. *See* Giuseppi, *op. cit.* Vol. I, pp. 68–9.

(*d*) *Chancery Miscellanea.*

[In Public Record Office.]

See Giuseppi, *op. cit.* Vol. I, pp. 57–62. The Diplomatic Documents are listed by C. Johnson. P.R.O. Lists and Indexes, XLIX.

(iv) *Documents preserved in the Exchequer.*

(*a*) *Guides to Exchequer development and practice temp. Hen. III.*

(*See also* Bibl. of previous chapter.)

[Gilbert (Sir Geoffrey).] A Treatise on the Court of Exchequer. London. 1758.

Hale, Sir Matthew. Treatise touching Sheriffs' Accompts. London. 1683.

Jenkinson, C. Hilary. Exchequer Tallies. *In* Archaeologia. LXII. London. 1911.

—— Medieval Tallies, Public and Private. *Ibid.* LXXIV. 1925.

Madox, T. The History and antiquities of the Exchequer of England. 2nd edn. 2 vols. London. 1769.

On the co-ordination of Exchequer Records *see* Mills, M. H., The Pipe Roll for 1295, Surrey Membrane. Introduction. (Surrey Record Soc.) Guildford. 1924. On the Issue and Receipt Rolls *see* Jenkinson, C. Hilary, Archive Administration, App. v. London. 1922.

(*b*) *Upper Exchequer.*

[In Public Record Office. Calendared as shewn below.]

(1) (*King's Remembrancer's Department.*)

Accounts, Various. *See* Lists and Indexes. XXXV. 1912.

Escheators' Accounts. *See* P.R.O. MS. Index.

Memoranda Rolls. *See* Giuseppi, *op. cit.* Vol. I, pp. 96–7.

Sheriffs' Accounts.

Miscellaneous Books. On the Liber Rubeus (vol. II) and the Liber Niger Parvus, *see* Bibl. to ch. XVII (p. 896) of Vol. v. The most important is the Liber Feodorum, printed formerly as the Testa de Nevill (RC.) 1807, now re-formed, with additions from K. R. Serjeanties and L. T. R. Misc. Rolls *as* Book of Fees. Pts. I, II. (Cal.SP.) 1920 ff., in progress

(2) (*Lord Treasurer's Remembrancer's Department.*)

Accounts, enrolled. Wardrobe and Household, 42–45 Hen. III.

Pipe Rolls, 1218–1272. The roll for 1241–2 has been edited by Cannon, H. L. New Haven. 1918; that for 1230 by Robinson, C. (Pipe Roll Soc. n.s. Vol. IV.) Princeton. 1927.

Foreign Accounts. *See* Lists and Indexes. XI. (1900.)

Memoranda Rolls, 1216–1272. *See* P.R.O. Abstract of L. T. R. Mem. Rolls (in progress).

Miscellaneous Rolls.

Originalia Rolls, 1227–1272. Abstracts in Rotulorum originalium in curia scaccarii abbreviatio. I. (RC.) 1805.

(3) (*Exchequer of Pleas.*)

Jews Plea Rolls, 1218–1272. *See* Rigg, J. M. *ed.* Calendar of the plea rolls of the Exchequer of the Jews, 1218–75. 2 vols. (Jewish Hist. Soc.) London. 1905, 10.

Plea Rolls, 1236, 1259, 1265–8.

(*c*) *Lower Exchequer* (*of receipt*).

Receipt Rolls, 1215–1272.

Issue Rolls, 1221–1272. *See* Devon, F. Issues of the Exchequer. (RC.) 1837.

(*d*) *Treasury of the Receipt.*

Books. Vols. 274, 275. *See* Giuseppi, *op. cit.* Vol. I, pp. 211–12.

Diplomatic Documents. *See* Lists and Indexes. XLIX. 1925.

A valuable repertory of Exchequer documents is Palgrave, F. The antient kalendar and inventories of the treasury of his Majesty's Exchequer. 3 vols. (RC.) 1836.

(v) *Special Collections.*

[In Public Record Office. Calendared as shewn below.]

Ancient Correspondence. *See* Lists and Indexes. XV. 1902.

Ancient Petitions. *See* Lists and Indexes. I. 1892.

Court Rolls. *See* Lists and Indexes. VI. 1896.

Hundred Rolls. The 1255 inquiry for Bucks, Oxfordshire, Salop, and Wilts (Chapter House Series) is printed *in* Rotuli Hundredorum, temp. Hen. III et Edw. I. 2 vols. (RC.) 1812, 18. *See* Cam, H. M. Studies in the Hundred Rolls (*below*, III B (i)).

Ministers' Accounts. General Series. *See* catalogue of, in Lists and Indexes, V (1894) and VIII (1897).

Papal Bulls. *See* Lists and Indexes. XLIX.

(vi) *Legal Records.*

(*a*) *Guides.*

[Bibliographical references in Holdsworth, W. S. History of English Law. 3rd edn. Vols. I–III (*see Gen. Bibl.* V) and Pollock, F. and Maitland, F. W. History of English Law. 2nd edn. *See Gen. Bibl.* V.]

Cam, Miss H. M. On the material available in the Eyre Rolls. *In* Bulletin of the Inst. of Historical Research. Vol. III, no. 9. London. 1926.

Holdsworth, W. S. Sources and Literature of English Law. Oxford. 1925.

Jacob, E. F. Studies in the period of Baronial Reform and Rebellion. (Oxford Studies in Social and Legal History. Vol. VIII.) Oxford. 1925.

Maitland, F. W. Materials for the History of English Law. *In* Collected Papers. II. Cambridge. 1911.

Richardson, H. G. The Year Books and Plea Rolls as sources of historical information. TRHS. 4th ser. V. 1922.

Winfield, P. H. Chief Sources. *See above*, I.

(*b*) *Statutes* (*printed*).

Bémont, C. Chartes des libertés anglaises, 1100–1305. Paris. 1892.

Riess, L. Englische Verfassungsurkunden des 12 und 13 Jahrhunderts. Bonn. 1926.

Statutes of the Realm. Vol. I. (RC.) 1810.

(c) *Plea Rolls.*

[In Public Record Office.]

Curia Regis Rolls, 1218–1272. *See* Lists and Indexes. IV. 1910. [On the earlier differentiation between *placita coram rege* and *placita de banco see* Powicke, F. M. *in* EHR. XXXIX. 1924.]

The principal contemporary selection from the rolls is in

Bracton's Notebook. Ed. Maitland, F. W. 3 vols. London. 1887.

Abstracts *in* Placitorum Abbreviatio. (RC.) 1811. Agarde's Indexes (P.R.O. in MS.), vols. 6, 29, 43.

Excerpts (ed. Wrottesley, G.) *in* W. Salt Archaeol. Soc. Collections. 1st ser. III–XVII. n.s. III, IV, VI. London. 1883–1903.

—— (translated) in Northumberland Pleas. Ed. Thompson, A. Hamilton. (Newcastle-upon-Tyne Records Series. Vol. II.)

Pleas before the Justices of the Bench are printed in Select Civil Pleas. Vol. I. 1200–1203. Ed. Baildon, W. P. (Selden Soc. III.) London. 1890.

Assize Rolls, 1219–1272.

On the types of record *see* Maitland, F. W. Bracton's Notebook. Vol. I, Introd., *and* Giuseppi, *op. cit.* Vol. I, pp. 235–8. On the development of the Chapters of the Eyre, see Cam, H. M. Studies in the Hundred Rolls. *See below,* III B (i).

Excerpts from, printed in

Select Pleas of the Crown. Vol. I. 1200–1225. Ed. Maitland, F. W. (Selden Soc. I.) London. 1888.

Pleas of the Crown for the County of Gloucester before the Justices itinerant, 1221. Ed. Maitland, F. W. London. 1884.

And in local archaeological transactions for the following counties: Derbyshire, Lancashire, Northumberland, Somerset, Yorkshire.

Forest Pleas. Select Pleas of the Forest. [1209–1334.] Ed. Turner, G. J. (Selden Soc. XIII.) London. 1901.

Feet of Fines (pedes finium). Indexes and Calendars have been printed by most County Societies. *See* Index volumes to their Transactions.

County Court Rolls.

Calendar of County Court, City Court, and Eyre Rolls of Chester, 1259–1297. Ed. Stewart-Brown, R. (Chetham Soc.) Manchester. 1926.

Coroners' Rolls. Bedfordshire only, 49–56, 53–56 Hen. III, printed (partly) *in* Select cases from the Coroners' Rolls, 1265–1413. Ed. Gross, C. (Selden Soc. IX.) London. 1896. pp. 1–32.

(d) *Legal Treatises.*

Bracton. De legibus et consuetudinibus Angliae. Ed. Twiss, Sir T. 6 vols. (Rolls.) 1873–8. Ed. Woodbine, G. E. [to f. 159 b]. 2 vols. New Haven. 1915, 22.

[Carpenter, Robert, of Hareslade.] The Court Baron. Ed. Maitland, F. W. and Baildon, W. P. (Selden Soc. IV.) London. 1891.

(vii) *Ecclesiastical Records.*

(a) *Guides.*

Berger, E. Introduction to Les Registres d'Innocent IV. *See Gen. Bibl.* IV *under* Papal Documents.

Fowler, R. C. Episcopal Registers of England and Wales. (Helps for Students of History.) S.P.C.K. London. 1918.

Poole, R. L. Lectures on the History of the Papal Chancery down to the time of Innocent III. Cambridge. 1915.

(b) *General Collections.*

Athona, John de. Constitutiones legatinae d. Othonis et d. Ottoboni. *In* Lyndwood, W. Provinciale. *See below.*

Dugdale, Sir W. Monasticon Anglicanum. Ed. Caley, J. and others. *See Gen. Bibl.* IV.

Gibson, E. Codex Juris Ecclesiastici Anglicani. 1713. 2 vols. 2nd edn. Oxford. 1761.

Lyndwood, W. Provinciale seu Constitutiones Angliae. Oxford. 1679.

Maskell, W. Monumenta ritualia ecclesiae Anglicanae. 2nd edn. 3 vols. Oxford. 1882.

Prynne, W. Records. Vol. III. *See above,* II B (ii).
Wilkins, D. Concilia Magnae Britanniae et Hiberniae. Vols. I and II. London. 1737.

(*c*) *Papal Letters (printed abstracts).*

Calendar of Papal Registers. Papal Letters. Vol. I. (Cal.SP.) 1893.
Potthast, A. Regesta Pontificum Romanorum. *See Gen. Bibl.* IV.
Papal Registers from Honorius III to Gregory X. *See Gen. Bibl.* IV *under* Papal Documents.

(*d*) *Episcopal Registers (printed) and Letters.*

Bath and Wells. Reg. Giffard (1265–1266). Ed. Holmes, P. S. (Somerset Record Soc.) London. 1899.
Exeter. Reg. Bronescombe, 1257–1280. Ed. Hingeston-Randolph, F. C. London. 1889.
Lincoln. Rotuli Hugonis de Welles (1209–1235). Ed. Phillimore, W. P. W. and Davis, F. N. 3 vols. (Cant. and York Soc.) London. 1907–9.
Rotuli Roberti Grosseteste. (1235–1253.) Ed. Davis, F. N. (*Ibid.*) London. 1913.
Roberti Grosseteste Epistolae. Ed. Luard, H. R. (Rolls.) 1861.
Worcester. Register of Bishop Godfrey Giffard, 1268–1301. Ed. Willis-Bund, J. W. (Worcs. Hist. Soc.) 2 vols. Oxford. 1898–1902. [A Calendar.]
York. Register of Walter Gray, Archbishop of York, 1225–1255. Ed. Raine, J. (Surtees Soc.) Durham. 1872.
Register of Walter Giffard, Archbishop of York, 1266–1279. Ed. Brown, W. (*Ibid.*) Durham. 1904.
Northern Registers, Historical papers and letters from. Ed. Raine, J. (Rolls.) 1873.

(*e*) *Material illustrating history of Religious Houses.*

Chronicon Abbatiae de Evesham. Ed. Macray, W. D. Vol. III. (Rolls.) 1863.
Gesta Abbatum Monasterii Sancti Albani. Ed. Riley, H. T. Vol. I. (Rolls.) 1867.
Glastonbury Chronicle. Bodleian Library, Laudian MS. 750.
Liber Memorandorum Ecclesie de Bernewelle. Ed. Clark, J. W. Cambridge. 1907.
Matthew Paris. Additamenta (Chronica majora. Vol. VI). Ed. Luard, H. R. (Rolls.) 1882.
Wharton, H. Anglia Sacra. 2 vols. London. 1691.

Many important Cartularies and Registers throwing light on the period have been published, which cannot be enumerated here. Useful bibliographical references to these are in the Chapters on Religious History in the Vict. Co. Hist. *See Gen. Bibl.* I. A list of unpublished cartularies is in the Guide to the Victoria Histories of the Counties of England. London. 1903.

(viii) *Wales.*

Clark, G. T. Cartae et alia Munimenta quae ad Dominium de Glamorgancia pertinent. 6 vols. Cardiff. 1910.
Daniel-Tyssen, J. R. and Evans, A. C. Royal Charters and historical documents relating to the town and county of Carmarthen, and the abbeys of Talley and Tygwyn-ar-Daf. [1201–1590, with a translation.] Carmarthen. 1878.
Owen, H. Calendar of the public records relating to Pembrokeshire, vol. I: Haverford [1204–1547]. (Soc. of Cymmrodorion, Record Series, No. 7.) London. 1911.

(ix) *Scotland.*

Bain, J. *ed.* Calendar of Documents relating to Scotland preserved in the Public Record Office, London [1108–1509]. 4 vols. Edinburgh. 1881–8.
Palgrave, F. *ed.* Documents and records illustrating the history of Scotland and the transactions between the Crowns of Scotland and England [21 Hen. III–35 Ed. I]. Vol. I. (RC.) 1837.

(x) *Ireland.*

Sweetman, H. S. *ed.* Calendar of Documents relating to Ireland [1171–1307]. 5 vols. (Cal.SP.) 1875–86.
Chartae, privilegia, et immunitates: transcripts of charters and privileges to cities, towns, abbeys, etc., 1171–1395. (Irish Record Commission.) Dublin. 1889.

III. MODERN WRITERS.

A. General Narrative.

(i) *England.*

Davis, H. W. C. England under the Normans and Angevins. 4th edn. (History of England. Ed. Oman, C. W. C. Vol. II.) London. 1915.
Norgate, K. The Minority of Henry III. London. 1912.
Pearson, C. H. History of England during the Early and Middle Ages. Vol. II. London. 1867.
Ramsay, Sir J. H. The Dawn of the Constitution. London. 1908.
Tout, T. F. History of England, 1216–1377. (Political History of England. Ed. Hunt, W. and Poole, R. L. Vol. III.) London. 1905.
Turner, G. J. The Minority of Henry III. TRHS. n.s. XVIII. 1904. 3rd ser. I. 1907.

(ii) *Ireland.*

Curtis, E. Mediaeval Ireland, 1110–1513. London. 1923.
Orpen, G. H. Ireland under the Normans. Vol. III. *See Gen. Bibl.* v.

(iii) *Wales.*

Corbett, J. S. Glamorgan. Ed. Paterson, D. R. (Cardiff Naturalists' Soc.) Cardiff. 1925.
Lloyd, J. E. History of Wales. Vol. II. *See Gen. Bibl.* v.
Morris, J. E. The Welsh Wars of Edward I. Oxford. 1901.
Tout, T. F. Wales and the March. 1258–1267. *In* Historical Essays by members of Owens College, Manchester. Manchester. 1907.

(iv) *Scotland.*

Brown, P. H. History of Scotland. Vol. I. *See Gen. Bibl.* v.
Rait, R. S. An outline of the relations between England and Scotland. London. 1901.

B. Studies on Special Subjects.

(i) *Constitutional and Administrative.*

Adams, G. B. The Origin of the English Constitution. 2nd edn. New Haven. 1920.
—— Constitutional History of England. London. 1921.
—— Council and Courts in Anglo-Norman England. New Haven. 1926.
Baldwin, J. F. The King's Council. Oxford. 1913.
Cam, H. M. Studies in the Hundred Rolls. *In* Oxford Studies in Social and Legal History. Vol. VI. Oxford. 1921.
—— Cambridgeshire Sheriffs. *In* Cambridge Antiq. Soc. Communications. Vol. XXV. Cambridge. 1924.
Chew, H. M. Scutage under Edward I. EHR. XXXVII. 1922. [A valuable sketch of scutage during the thirteenth century.]
Gavrilovitch, M. Étude sur le traité de Paris de 1259. Paris. 1899.
Gilson, J. P. A notice of the battle of Lewes. EHR. XI. 1896.
—— The Parliament of 1264. EHR. XVI. 1901.
Jacob, E. F. Oxford Studies. Vol. VIII. *See above,* II B (vi) (*a*).
—— The Complaints of Henry III against the Baronial Council in 1261. EHR. XLI. 1926.
—— The reign of Henry III. Some suggestions. TRHS. 4th ser. X. 1927.
Lapsley, G. The County Palatine of Durham. New York. 1900.
Lawlor, H. J. An unnoticed Charter of Henry III (1217). EHR. XXII. 1907.
Maitland, F. W. The Constitutional History of England. Cambridge. 1908.
—— History from the Charter Roll. EHR. VIII. 1893.
Mills, M. H. Adventus Vicecomitum. EHR. XXXVI. 1921.
Mitchell, S. K. Studies in Taxation under John and Henry III. New Haven. 1914.
Morris, W. A. The early English County Court. (Univ. of California publications in History. Vol. XIV, no. 2.) Berkeley. 1926.
—— Plenus Comitatus. EHR. XXXIX. 1924.
—— The Medieval English Sheriff. Manchester. 1927.
Niemeyer, N. An Assessment for the Fortieth of 1232. EHR. XXIV. 1909.

Pasquet, D. An Essay on the origins of the House of Commons. Engl. transl. Laffan, R. G. D., with notes by Lapsley, G. Cambridge. 1925.
Pollard, A. F. The Evolution of Parliament. 2nd edn. London. 1926.
—— Plenum Parliamentum. EHR. xxx. 1915.
Poole, R. L. The publication of Great Charters by the English Kings. EHR. xxviii. 1913.
Powicke, F. M. Some observations on the Baronial Council (1258–1260) and the Provisions of Westminster. *In* Essays in Medieval History presented to T. F. Tout. Manchester. 1925.
Ramsay, Sir J. H. The Revenues of the Kings of England, 1066–1399. Vol. i. Oxford. 1925.
Reid, R. R. Barony and Thanage. EHR. xxxv. 1920.
Riess, L. Geschichte des Wahlrechts zum Englischen Parlament. Leipsic. 1885.
—— Der Ursprung des Englischen Unterhauses. HZ. n.s. xxiv. 1888.
Round, J. H. The Revenue of Henry III. EHR. xiii. 1898.
—— The King's serjeants and officers of State, with their coronation services. London. 1911.
Stubbs, W. Constitutional history of England. Vol. ii. *See Gen. Bibl.* v.
Tout, T. F. Chapters in the Administrative History of Mediaeval England. Vol. i. Manchester. 1920.
—— The Communitas bachelerie Angliae. EHR. xvii. 1902.
—— The Fair of Lincoln and the Histoire de Guillaume le Maréchal. EHR. xviii. 1903.
Treharne, R. F. An unauthorised use of the Great Seal in 1259. EHR. xl. 1925.
Turner, G. J. The Sheriff's farm. TRHS. n.s. xii. 1898.
—— Some thirteenth-century Statutes. *In* Law Magazine and Review. 4th ser. xxi, xxii. 1896–7.
—— A newly-discovered Ordinance. *In* Law Quarterly Review. xii. 1896.
White, A. B. Some Early Instances of Concentration of Representatives in England. AHR. xix.
—— The Making of the English Constitution. 2nd edn. New York. 1925.
Whitwell, R. J. Italian Bankers and the English Crown. TRHS. n.s. xvii. 1903.

(ii) *Legal.*

Adams, G. B. Private Jurisdiction in England. AHR. xxiii.
Ault, W. O. Private Jurisdiction in England. New Haven. 1923.
Bolland, W. C. The General Eyre. Cambridge. 1922.
Ehrlich, L. Proceedings against the Crown (1216–1377). *In* Oxford Studies in Social and Legal History. Vol. vi. Oxford. 1921.
Holdsworth, W. S. History of English Law. 3rd edn. Vols. i–iii. *See Gen. Bibl.* v.
—— Legal Education—Its Debt to Bracton. Exeter. 1923.
Joüon des Longrais, F. La conception anglaise de la Saisine du xiie au xive siècle. Paris. 1925.
Maitland, F. W. *ed.* Select passages from Bracton and Azo. (Selden Soc. viii.) London. 1895.
—— Equity, also the Forms of Action at Common Law. Cambridge. 1909.
—— History of the Register of Original Writs. *In* Collected Papers. Vol. ii. Cambridge. 1911.
—— Roman Canon Law in the Church of England. London. 1898.
—— *ed.* Select Pleas in Manorial and other Seignorial Courts. Vol. i. (Selden Soc. ii.) London. 1889.
Pollock, Sir F. and Maitland, F. W. The History of English Law. *See Gen. Bibl.* v.
Vinogradoff, P. Custom and Right. Oslo. 1925.

(iii) *Ecclesiastical.*

Barker, E. The Dominican Order and Convocation. Oxford. 1913.
Chew, H. M. The Ecclesiastical Tenants-in-Chief and Writs of Military Summons. EHR. xli. 1926.
Dehio, L. Innocenz IV und England. Berlin. 1914.
Gasquet, F. A. Henry the Third and the Church. London. 1905.

Graham, Rose. Letters of Cardinal Ottoboni. EHR. xv. 1900.
—— The Finances of Malton Priory, 1244–1257. TRHS. n.s. xviii. 1904.
—— A Papal Visitation of Bury St Edmunds and Westminster in 1234. EHR. xxvii. 1912.
Hudson, W. The "Norwich Taxation" of 1254, so far as it relates to the Diocese of Norwich, collated with the Taxation of Pope Nicholas in 1291. (Repr. from Norfolk Archaeology. xvii.) Norwich. 1908.
Jordan, E. De Mercatoribus Camerae Apostolicae saeculo xiii. Rennes. 1909.
Le Neve, J. Fasti Ecclesiae Anglicanae. Ed. Hardy, T. D. Oxford. 1854.
Luard, H. R. On the relations between England and Rome during the earlier portion of the Reign of Henry III. Cambridge. 1877.
Lunt, W. E. The Valuation of Norwich. Oxford. 1926.
—— The Sources for the First Council of Lyons, 1245. EHR. xxxiii. 1918.
Makower, F. The Constitutional History and Constitution of the Church of England. (Transl. from the German.) London. 1895.
Mengozzi, N. Papa Onorio III e le sue Relazioni con l'Inghilterra. (From Bullettino Senese di Storia Patria. xviii.) Siena. 1911.
Richardson, H. G. The Parish Clergy of the 13th and 14th centuries. TRHS. 3rd ser. vi. 1912.
Salter, H. E. Chapters of the Augustinian Canons. (Oxford Hist. Soc. lxxiv. Oxford. 1922.
Smith, A. L. Church and State in the Middle Ages. Oxford. 1913.
Stubbs, W. Registrum sacrum Anglicanum. *See Gen. Bibl.* iii.
Sweet, A. H. The English Benedictines and their Bishops in the 13th century. AHR. xxiv.
Zimmermann, H. Die päpstliche Legation in der ersten Hälfte des 13 Jahrhunderts. Paderborn. 1913.
Zulueta, F. de. William of Drogheda. *In* Mélanges de droit Romain dédiés à Georges Cornil. Ghent. 1926.

(iv) *Biographical.*

Bémont, C. Simon de Montfort. Paris. 1884. 2nd edn. transl. Jacob, E. F. is forthcoming.
Gebauer, G. C. Leben und Thaten Herrn Richards von Cornwall und Poitou. Leipsic. 1744.
Johnstone, H. A Year in the Life of Henry III. CQR. xcvii. 1922.
Koch, H. Richard von Cornwall. Strasbourg. 1887. Contd. Baffert, J. F. Bonn. 1905.
Mugnier, F. Les Savoyards en Angleterre au xiiie siècle. Chambéry. 1890.
Pauli, R. Simon de Montfort. Engl. transl. Goodwin, U. M. London. 1876.
Petit-Dutaillis, C. Étude sur la vie et le règne de Louis VIII, 1187–1226. Paris. 1894.
Powicke, F. M. Stephen Langton. Oxford. 1928.
Prothero, G. W. The life of Simon de Montfort. London. 1877.
Rhodes, W. E. Edmund, earl of Lancaster [son of Henry III]. EHR. x. 1895.
Stevenson, F. S. Robert Grosseteste. London. 1899.
Wurstemberger, L. Peter der Zweite, Graf von Savoyen. 4 vols. Berne. 1856–8.

(v) *Society.*

Coulton, G. G. The Medieval Village. Cambridge. 1925.
Davis, H. W. C. *ed.* Mediaeval England. Oxford. 1923.
Farrer, W. Honours and Knights Fees. 3 vols. London; Manchester. 1923–5.
Gray, H. L. English Field Systems. Harvard. 1915.
Hudson, W. Eastbourne Manor and the Honours of Mortain and Aquila. Sussex Archaeol. Collections. xliii. 1900.
Jolliffe, J. E. A. Northumbrian Institutions. EHR. xli. 1926.
Kerr, W. J. B. Higham Ferrers. Northampton. 1925.
Lapsley, G. Cornage and Drengage. AHR. ix. 1904.
Maitland, F. W. Northumbrian Tenures. EHR. v. 1890. *Also in* Collected Papers. ii. Cambridge. 1911.
Mallet, C. E. History of the University of Oxford. Vol. i. London. 1925.
Neilson, N. Boon Service on the estates of Ramsey Abbey. AHR. ii.
—— Customary Rents. *In* Oxford Studies. Vol. ii. Oxford. 1910.

Round, J. H. The Rape of Pevensey. *In* Sussex Archaeol. Collections. XLII.
Salzman, L. F. English Industries of the Middle Ages. New edn. Oxford. 1923.
—— English Life in the Middle Ages. London. 1927.
Vinogradoff, P. Villeinage in England. Oxford. 1892.

(vi) *Municipal Life.*

Ballard, A. and Tait, J. British Borough Charters, 1216–1307. Cambridge. 1923.
Bateson, M. Borough Customs. 2 vols. (Selden Soc. XVIII, XXI.) London. 1904, 6.
—— Records of the Borough of Leicester. 3 vols. Cambridge. 1899–1905.
Davis, H. W. C. The Commune of Bury St Edmunds. EHR. XXIV. 1909.
Hemmeon, M. de W. Burgage Tenure in Mediaeval England. Harvard. 1921.
Hudson, W. and Tingey, J. C. *edd.* Records of the City of Norwich. 2 vols. Norwich. 1906, 10.
Loftie, W. J. A. History of London. 2nd edn. 2 vols. London. 1884.
Riley, H. T. *ed.* Munimenta Gildhallae Londoniensis. 3 vols. (Rolls.) 1859–62.
Sharpe, R. R. London and the Kingdom. 3 vols. London. 1894–5.
Stevenson, W. H. *ed.* Records of the Borough of Nottingham. 5 vols. London. 1882–1900.
Tait, J. The Study of early Municipal History in England. (Proc. British Acad. x.) London. 1922.

Valuable bibliographies of municipal records are found in

Gross, C. Bibliography of British Municipal History. New York. 1897.
Humphreys, A. L. A Handbook to County Bibliography. London. 1917.

(vii) *Art.*

Brayley, E. W. The History and Antiquities of the Abbey Church of St Peter Westminster. 2 vols. London. 1818.
—— and Britton, J. The History of the Ancient Palace and late Houses of Parliament at Westminster. London. 1836.
Hope, W. St J. Windsor Castle. 2 vols. and plans. London. 1913.
Kendon, F. S. H. Mural Paintings in English Churches during the Middle Ages. London. 1923.
Lethaby, W. R. Westminster Abbey and the King's Craftsmen. London. 1906.
—— London and Westminster Painters in the Middle Ages. 1912.
Lowe, W. R. L. and Jacob, E. F. *edd.* Illustrations to the Life of St Alban in Trinity College, Dublin MS. E. I. 40. Preface by James, M. R. Oxford. 1924.
Millar, E. G. English Illuminated Manuscripts from the xth to the XIIIth century. Paris and Brussels. 1926.
Westlake, H. F. Westminster Abbey. The old Lady Chapel. *In* Archaeologia. LXIX (1920).
Westminster Abbey. Inventory of the Historical Monuments in London. Vol. I. (Royal Commission on Historical Monuments.) London. 1924.

CHAPTER IX.

THE REIGNS OF PHILIP AUGUSTUS AND LOUIS VIII OF FRANCE.

I. BIBLIOGRAPHIES AND GENERAL TREATISES.

Cartellieri, A. Philipp II August, König von Frankreich. 4 vols. Leipsic. 1899–1922.

Halphen, L. La France sous les premiers Capétiens (987–1226). RSH. xiv. (1907.) 62–88.

Luchaire, A. Louis VII—Philippe Auguste—Louis VIII. *In* Lavisse, E. Histoire de France. Vol. iii, 1. 1911. *See Gen. Bibl.* v.

Molinier, A. Les Sources de l'histoire de France des origines aux guerres d'Italie (1494). Vol. iii. *See Gen. Bibl.* i.

Petit-Dutaillis, C. Étude sur la vie et le règne de Louis VIII (1187–1226). Paris. 1894.

II. RECORDS AND OTHER ORIGINAL DOCUMENTS.

The earliest registers of the royal chancery come from the reign of Philip Augustus. They are three in number: the "Registrum veterius," in the Vatican library (Ottoboni 2796), the "Registrum ad nudos asseres de quercu," and the "Registrum Guarini" in the Archives nationales (JJ. 7 and 26). They are described in the introduction to Delaborde's Actes de Philippe Auguste (*see below*). The history and transactions of the chancery have to be reconstructed from these registers and from the cartularies, collections of charters, and other varied sources. In addition a few financial and military records survive, which are named below and have been described in the text. For guides to the cartularies see the introduction to Delisle, L. Catalogue des Actes (*see below*) and Stein, H. Bibliographie générale des Cartulaires français, Paris. 1907. For the Acts of Henry II see the Bibliography in Vol. v, ch. xvii (ii a); and for the Rotuli Normanniae, the rolls of the Norman Exchequer, and other records important for French history see the Bibliography to ch. vii (*above*).

Audouin, E. Essai sur l'armée royale au temps de Philippe Auguste. Paris. 1913. [Contains with annotations the "prisia servientum" from the Register in the Vatican (A) and extracts from the revenue account of 1202 printed by Brussel, pp. 124–87; also, from Register A, inventories of arms etc. pp. 187–97.]

Bouquet. Vol. xxiii. [Contains the Scripta de feodis ad regem spectantibus (1210–20) from the Registrum Guarini.]

Brussel, N. Nouvel examen de l'usage général des fiefs en France. Paris. 1727. [Important for the text of the lost "compte général des revenus du roy pendant l'année 1202" ii, cxxxix–ccx.]

Champollion-Figeac, J. J. Lettres de rois, reines, et autres personnages des Cours de France et d'Angleterre depuis Louis VII jusqu'à Henri IV. Vol. i. Paris. 1839.

Delaborde, H. F. Recueil des actes de Philippe Auguste, roi de France. Vol. i (1179–94). Paris. 1916. In progress. [See also the same scholar's Étude sur la constitution du Trésor des Chartes prefixed to the Layettes du Trésor des Chartes, Vol. v., and his letter to L. Delisle: A propos d'une rature dans un registre de Philippe Auguste. BEC. lxiv. (1903).]

Delisle, L. Catalogue des actes de Philippe Auguste. Paris. 1856. [An epoch-making book; includes an appendix of documents in full.]

—— Cartulaire normand de Philippe Auguste, Louis VIII, Saint Louis, et Philippe le Hardi. (Mém. de la Soc. des Antiquaires de Normandie. xvi.) Caen. 1852.

—— Le premier registre de Philippe Auguste, Paris. 1883. [Heliotype reproduction of the Vatican MS.]

—— Recueil des jugements de l'Échiquier de Normandie au xiiie siècle. Paris. 1864.

Denifle, H. and Châtelain, E. Chartularium Universitatis Parisiensis. Vol. I. Paris. 1889.

Ordonnances des rois de France de la troisième race. Vol. I. Paris. 1723.

Tardif, E. J. Coutumiers de Normandie. Vol. I. Statuta et consuetudines. (Soc. de l'hist. de Normandie.) Rouen and Paris. 1881, 1903.

Teulet, J. B. A. T. Layettes du Trésor des Chartes. Vol. I. Paris. 1863.

Weiland, L. Constitutiones et acta publica imperatorum et regum. Vol. II. MGH. Legum Sect. IV. 1896.

III. NARRATIVE SOURCES, AND OTHER CONTEMPORARY TEXTS.

See also the Bibliographies to Chapters VII, VIII, and XX. In addition the following are the most important.

Alberic of Trois Fontaines. Chronicon. MGH. Script. XXIII. 1874. *In* Bouquet (extracts). XVIII, XXI.

Annals of St Aubin. *In* Halphen, L. Recueil d'annales angevines et vendômoises. (Coll. textes.) Paris. 1903.

Bertrand of Born. Poésies complètes. Ed. Thomas, A. Toulouse. 1888.

—— Gedichte. Ed. Stimming, A. Halle. 1892.

Chronicle of Andres. *In* Bouquet. XVIII.

Chronicle of Mortemer. *Ibid.*

Chronicle of Penpont. *Ibid.*

Chronicle of Saint Martin of Limoges. *Ibid.*

Chronicon Turonense magnum. *In* Salmon, A. Recueil de chroniques de Touraine. Tours. 1854.

Chronicon Universale anonymi Laudunensis. MGH. Script. XXVI; *also in* Bouquet. XVIII; and more conveniently, ed. Cartellieri, A. and Stechele, W. Leipsic and Paris. 1909. [1154–1219.]

Geoffrey of Vigeois. Chronicon Lemovicense, pars II. *In* Bouquet. XVIII.

Giles of Paris. Carolinus. lib. V. *Ibid.* XVII.

Guy of Bazoches. Chronosgraphia (part of lib. VII). Ed. Cartellieri, A. and Fricke, W. Jena. 1910. For Guy's apologia and letters see Wattenbach, W. *in* SPAW. 1890, 93, and Neu. Arch. XVI. 69–113.

Hélinand, monk of Froidmont. Chronicle (to 1200). MPL. CCXII. [Repr. from Tissier, B. Bibliotheca patrum Cisterciensium. VII. Bonnefont. 1664.]

James of Vitry. Historia orientalis. Books I and III in Bongars, J. Gesta Dei per Francos. Vol. I. Hanover. 1612. French transl. in Guizot, F. Collection des mémoires etc. Vol. XXII. 1825. *See Gen. Bibl.* IV. Engl. transl. Stewart, A. (Palestine Pilgrims' Tract Soc.) London. 1896.

—— Exempla. Ed. Crane, T. F. (Folklore Soc. XXVI.) London. 1890.

Mousket, Philip. Cronique rimée. Ed. Reiffenberg, F. 2 vols. (Collection des chroniques belges.) Brussels. 1836, 38; *partly in* Bouquet. XXII.

Normanniae nova chronica. Ed. Chéruel, A. *In* Mém. de la Soc. des Antiquaires de Normandie. XVIII. 1856. [A composite Rouen chronicle.]

Rigord, monk of St Denis. Gesta Philippi Augusti. Ed. Delaborde, H. F. (SHF.) Paris. 1882.

[Rigord and William the Breton are the main authorities for the reign.]

Robert of Auxerre. Chronicle. MGH. Script. XXVI. (1112–1219). *In* Bouquet (extracts). XVIII.

Roman d'Eustache le Moine. Ed. Michel, F. *in* Romans, lais, fabliaux...inédits des XIIe et XIIIe siècles. Vol. II. Paris. 1834; *also* ed. Foerster, W. and Trost, W. Halle. 1891.

Scriptores rerum Danicarum. Ed. Langebek, I., etc. Vols. II, V, VI. *See Gen. Bibl.* IV. [For texts bearing on the marriage of Philip Augustus and Ingeborg of Denmark.]

Stephen of Tournai. Letters. Ed. Desilve, J. Valenciennes and Paris. 1893; MPL. CCXI.

Vincent of Beauvais. Speculum. Douai. 1624. For parts of the Speculum historiale: MGH. Script. XXIV. *Also in* Bouquet. XXI.

William le Breton. Gesta Philippi regis, and the Philippis. Ed. Delaborde, H. F. 2 vols. (SHF.) Paris. 1882, 85.

IV. MODERN WORKS.

A. THE GROWTH OF THE DOMAIN; FOREIGN RELATIONS.

(*The more important works are starred.*)

Arbois de Jubainville, H. d'. Histoire des ducs et des comtes de Champagne. 4 vols. Paris. 1861–5.
Berger, É. Histoire de Blanche de Castille, reine de France. Paris. 1895.
Boissonnade, P. Quomodo comites Engolismenses erga reges Angliae et Franciae se gesserint et comitatus Engolismae et Marchiae regno Francorum adjuncti fuerint. Angoulême. 1893. [*Cf.* Annales du Midi. VII. 1895.]
*Borrelli de Serres, L. L. La réunion des provinces septentrionales à la couronne par Philippe Auguste. Paris. 1899.
Cartellieri, A. Philipp II August und der Zusammenbruch des angevinischen Reiches. Leipsic. 1913.
—— Die Schlacht bei Bouvines (27 Juli 1214) im Rahmen der europäischen Politik. Leipsic. 1914.
*Davidsohn, R. Philipp II August von Frankreich und Ingeborg. Stuttgart. 1888. [*See* E. Michael *in* Zeitsch. für Kathol. Theol. XIV (1890). 562–9.]
Delbrück, H. Geschichte der Kriegskunst im Rahmen der politischen Geschichte. Pt. III. Berlin. 1907.
Delisle, L. Chronologie historique des comtes de la Marche issus de la maison de Lusignan. BEC. XVII (1856). 537–45.
—— Chronologie historique des comtes d'Eu issus de la maison de Lusignan. *Ibid.* 545–53.
Delpech, H. La Tactique au XIIIe siècle. Paris. 1886.
Deville, A. Histoire du Château Gaillard et du siège qu'il soutient contre Philippe Auguste en 1203 et 1204. Rouen. 1829.
Dubois, G. Recherches sur la vie de Guillaume des Roches, Sénéschal d'Anjou, du Maine, et de Touraine. BEC. XXX, XXXII, XXXIV. 1869–73.
Flach, J. Le Comté de Flandre et ses rapports avec la couronne de France du IXe au XVe siècle. RH. CXV. 1914.
Imbert, H. Notice sur les vicomtes de Thouars. *In* Mém. de la Soc. des Antiquaires de l'Ouest. XXIX. Poitiers. 1864.
Johnen, J. Philipp von Elsass, Graf von Flandern. Brussels. 1910.
* Kern, F. Die Anfänge der französischen Ausdehnungspolitik bis zum Jahr 1308. Tübingen. 1910.
Kienast, W. Die deutschen Fürsten im Dienste der Westmächte. Utrecht. 1924.
König, L. Die Politik des Grafen Balduin V von Hennegau. Brussels. 1904.
La Borderie, A. de. Histoire de Bretagne. Vol. III. Rennes. 1906.
Lecointre-Dupont. Jean-sans-terre ou essai historique sur les dernières années de la domination des Plantagenêts dans l'Ouest de la France. *In* Mém. de la Soc. des Antiquaires de l'Ouest. XII. Poitiers. 1845.
Ledain. Savery de Mauléon ou la réunion du Poitou à l'unité française. *Ibid.* 2nd ser. XIII. 1890.
Leroux, A. Essai sur les antécédents historiques de la question allemande. Paris. 1886.
—— La Royauté française et le Saint Empire Romain au moyen âge. RH. XLIX 1892.
—— Les Conflits entre la France et l'Empire pendant le moyen âge. Paris. 1902.
Longnon, A. Atlas historique de la France. *See Gen. Bibl.* II.
* —— La Formation de l'unité française. Paris. 1922.
* Lot, F. Fidèles ou vassaux? Paris. 1904.
Luchaire, A. Innocent III. [Vol. V.] Les royautés vassales du Saint-Siège. Paris. 1908.
* Malo, H. Un grand feudataire: Renaud de Dammartin et la Coalition de Bouvines. Paris. 1898.
Pabst, L. Die äussere Politik der Grafschaft Flandern unter Ferrand von Portugal (1215–33). Brussels. 1911.
Pirenne, H. Histoire de Belgique. Vol. I. 3rd edn. *See Gen. Bibl.* V.
* Powicke, F. M. The Loss of Normandy. Manchester. 1913.

Richard, A. Histoire des comtes de Poitou, 778–1204. Vol. II. Paris. 1903.
*Scheffer-Boichorst, P. Deutschland und Philipp II August von Frankreich in den Jahren 1180–1214. FDG. VIII. 1868.
Smet, J. J. de. Mémoire hist. et critique sur Baudouin IX, comte de Flandre et de Hainaut (1195–1202). *In* Nouv. mém. de l'Acad. de Bruxelles. XIX. 1845.
Smets, G. Henri I duc de Brabant, 1190–1235. Brussels. 1908.
Vanderkindere, L. Histoire de la formation territoriale des principautés belges au moyen âge. 2 vols. Brussels. 1902.

B. Normandy and the Angevin Fiefs.

For bibliography *see* Powicke, F. M. Loss of Normandy (*above*, IV A); Prentout, H. La Normandie. (Les régions de la France, VII.) Paris. 1910; Sévestre, E. Quelques notes de bibliographie normande. Paris. 1911; Barrau-Dibigo, L. La Gascogne. (Les régions de la France, I.) Paris. 1902.
Beautemps-Beaupré, C. J. Coutumes et institutions de l'Anjou et du Maine. Pt. II. 4 vols. Paris. 1890–7.
Bonnard, L. La Frontière franco-normande entre Seine et Perche (IXe au XIIIe siècle). Chartres. 1907.
Brunner, H. Geschichte der englischen Rechtsquellen im Grundriss. Mit einem Anhang über die normannischen Rechtsquellen. Leipsic. 1909.
Clédat, L. Du rôle historique de Bertrand de Born (1175–1200). Paris. 1878.
Coutil, L. Le Château Gaillard, 1197–8. Évreux. 1906.
Delisle, L. Essai sur les revenus publics en Normandie au XIIe siècle. BEC. 2nd ser. V. 1848–9.
—— Mémoire sur la chronologie des chartes de Henri II. BEC. LXVII. 1906.
Dieulafoy, M. Le Château Gaillard et l'architecture militaire au XIIIe siècle. Paris. 1898.
Fréville, R. de. Étude sur l'organisation judiciaire en Normandie aux XIIe et XIIIe siècles. Paris. 1912. [Repr. from the NRDF.]
Giry, A. Les Établissements de Rouen. 2 vols. Paris. 1883, 85.
Haskins, C. H. Norman Institutions. Cambridge, Mass. 1918.
Lodge, E. C. Gascony under English rule. London. 1926.
Marsh, F. B. English rule in Gascony, 1199–1259, with special reference to the towns. Ann Arbor, Michigan. 1912.
Packard, S. R. King John and the Norman Church. *In* Harvard Theol. Review. XV. 1922.
—— The Judicial Organization of Normandy 1189–1204. *In* Law Quarterly Review. 1924.
Paris, G. La Littérature normande avant l'annexion (912–1204). Paris. 1899.
Travaux de la semaine d'histoire du droit normand (Mai 1923). Caen. 1925.
Valin, L. Le Duc de Normandie et sa cour (912–1204). Paris. 1910.
Viollet, P. Article on the Norman custumals. *In* Histoire littéraire de la France. XXXIII. Paris. 1906.

C. Administrative and Social History.

Audouin, E. Essai sur l'armée royale au temps de Philippe Auguste. Paris. 1913.
Borrelli de Serres, L. L. Recherches sur divers services publics du XIIIe au XVIIe siècle. 2 vols. Paris. 1895, 1904.
Boutaric, E. Institutions militaires de la France avant les armées permanentes. Paris. 1863.
Chénon, É. Le Droit romain à la *curia regis* de Philippe Auguste à Philippe le Bel. *In* Mélanges Fitting. Vol. I. pp. 195–212. Montpellier. 1907.
Delisle, L. Mémoire sur les opérations financières des Templiers. *In* Mém. Acad. IBL. XXXIII. 1889.
—— Étienne de Gallardon. BEC. LX. 1899.
—— Chronologie des baillis et sénéchaux royaux depuis les origines jusqu'à l'avènement de Philippe de Valois. *In* Bouquet. XXIV. 1904.
Géraud, H. Les routiers au douzième siècle Mercadier, Les routiers au treizième siècle. BEC. III. 1841

Giry, A. Documents sur les relations de la royauté avec les villes en France de 1180 à 1314. Paris. 1885.
Guilhiermoz, P. Essai sur l'origine de la noblesse en France au moyen âge. Paris. 1902.
—— Les deux condamnations de Jean Sans Terre par la cour de Philippe Auguste et l'origine des pairs de France. BEC. LX. 1899.
Halphen, L. Paris sous les premiers Capétiens (987–1223). Paris. 1909.
Holtzmann, R. Französische Verfassungsgeschichte. Munich and Berlin. 1910.
Langlois, C. V. Textes relatifs à l'histoire du Parlement depuis les origines jusqu'au 1314. (Coll. textes.) 1888. [For the introduction.]
—— Les origines du Parlement de Paris. RH. XLII. 1890.
Lazard, L. Essai sur la condition des Juifs dans le domaine royal au XIIIe siècle. Paris. 1887.
Lot, F. Quelques mots sur l'origine des pairs de France. RH. LIV. 1894.
Luchaire, A. Les Communes françaises à l'époque des Capétiens directs. 2nd edn. Paris. 1911.
—— Manuel des institutions françaises; période des Capétiens directs. *See Gen. Bibl.* V.
—— L'Université de Paris sous Philippe Auguste. Paris. 1899.
—— La Société française au temps de Philippe Auguste. Paris. 1909.
Martin, O. Histoire de la coutume de la prévôté et vicomté de Paris. 2 vols. Paris. 1922, 26.
Perrichet, L. La grande Chancellerie de France des origines à 1328. Paris. 1912.
Poëte, M. Une vie de cité: Paris de sa naissance à nos jours. Vol. I. Paris. 1924.
Prou, M. De la nature du service militaire dû par les roturiers aux XIe et XIIe siècles. RH. XLV. 1890.
—— Esquisse de la politique monétaire des rois de France du Xe au XIIIe siècle. Paris. 1901.
Stein, H. Pierre Tristan, chambellan de Philippe Auguste. BEC. LXVIII. 1917.
Tuetey, A. Rapport sur une mission à Rome, en 1876, relative au Cartulaire de Philippe Auguste. Paris. 1880.
Viollet, P. Histoire des institutions politiques et administratives de la France. 3 vols. Paris. 1898–1903.
—— Histoire du droit civil français. Paris. 1893.
Vuitry, A. Études sur le régime financier de la France. Paris. 1878.
Walker, W. On the increase in the royal power in France under Philip Augustus. Leipsic. 1888.
Waquet, H. Le Bailliage de Vermandois aux XIIIe et XIVe siècles. Paris. 1919.

CHAPTER X.

SAINT LOUIS.

I. SPECIAL BIBLIOGRAPHIES.

From the seventeenth century onwards there have appeared a large number of important publications on the reign of St Louis, and room is still left for further investigation. *See*:

Molinier, A. Les Sources de l'histoire de France. Vol. III. *See Gen. Bibl.* I.

Chevalier, C. U. J. Répertoire des sources historiques du moyen âge. (*See Gen. Bibl.* I.) Bio-bibliographie. *Sub nom.* Louis IX, Blanche de Castille, Joinville, etc. Topo-bibliographie. *Sub nom.* Croisades, Juifs, Chapelle (Sainte), Parlement, etc.

II. SOURCES.

A. Documents.

(1) *Acta.*

There has not yet appeared a complete collection or a catalogue of the Acta of St Louis or of his Itinerary. Bréquigny, L. G. O. F. de, and Pardessus, J. M. calendared the Acta published up to their time *in* Table chronologique des diplômes. Vols. V and VI. Paris. 1846, 50. The principal recent collections are:

Layettes du Trésor des Chartes. Vols. II–V. Ed. Teulet, A., Laborde, J. de, Berger, É., Delaborde, H. F. Paris. 1866–1909.

Cartulaire normand de Philippe Auguste, Louis VIII, St Louis, et Philippe le Hardi. Ed. Delisle, L. Caen. 1852.

Vic, C. de and Vaissete, J. J. Histoire...de Languedoc. New edn. Vols. VII and VIII. Preuves. 1879. *See Gen. Bibl.* IV.

Several registers of the Trésor des Chartes of the time of St Louis, especially JJ. 26 in the Archives Nationales, are in parts still unpublished, not to mention many other sources not as yet investigated.

(2) *Finance.*

Some documents are to be found ed. Guigniaut, J. D. and Wailly, N. de *in* Bouquet. Vol. XXI. 1855. *See Gen. Bibl.* IV. *Also* ed. Wailly, N. de and Delisle, L. *Ibid.* Vol. XXII. 1865.

Also in Jusselin, M. Documents financiers concernant les mesures prises par Alphonse de Poitiers contre les Juifs. BEC. 1907.

(3) *Administration.*

Enquêtes. Ed. Delisle, L. *in* Bouquet. Vol. XXIV, pts. I and II. 1904.

Les Plaintes de la comtesse de la Marche contre Thibaud de Neuvi, sénéchal de Poitou. Ed. Thomas, A. BEC. 1907.

Correspondance administrative d'Alphonse de Poitiers. Ed. Molinier, A. 2 vols. (Coll. doc.) Paris. 1894–1900.

Documents sur les relations de la royauté avec les villes en France de 1180 à 1314. Ed. Giry, A. (Recueil de textes pour servir à l'étude et à l'enseignement de l'hist.) Paris. 1885.

(4) *Justice.*

Les Olim. Ed. Beugnot, A. A. Vol. I. (Coll. doc.) Paris. 1839.

Actes du Parlement de Paris. Ed. Boutaric, E. Vol. I. Paris. 1863.

Textes relatifs à l'histoire du Parlement (de Paris). Ed. Langlois, C. V. (Coll. textes.) Paris. 1888

Jugements de l'échiquier de Normandie au XIIIe siècle. Ed. Delisle, L. *in* Notices et extraits des manuscrits. Vol. xx, pt. II. Paris. 1862. [*See also* Mém. AcadIBL. Vol. XXIV, pt. II. Paris. 1864.]

Law Books.

Conseil de Pierre de Fontaines. Ed. Marnier, A. J. Paris. 1846.

Livre de Jostice et de Plet. Ed. Rapetti, P. N. (Coll. doc.) Paris. 1850.

[The compilation called *Établissements de St Louis* belongs to the reign of Philip III.]

(5) *The Church, the Inquisition, and the University.*

Journal des visites pastorales d'Eude Rigaud, archevêque de Rouen, 1248–1269. Ed. Bonnin, T. Rouen. 1852.

Documents pour servir à l'histoire de l'Inquisition dans le Languedoc. Ed. Douais, C. 2 vols. (SHF.) Paris. 1900.

Denifle, H. and Chatelain, E. Chartularium Universitatis Parisiensis. Vol. I. Paris. 1889.

(6) *Documents in Foreign Archives.*

The chief collections are:

The Papal Registers, Gregory IX, Innocent IV, Alexander IV, Urban IV, and Clement IV. *See list in Gen. Bibl.* IV *under* Papal Documents.

There are also:

Shirley, W. W. Royal and other historical letters illustrative of Henry III. 2 vols. (Rolls.) 1862, 66.

Rôles gascons. Ed. Michel, F. Vol. I. Supplt. by Bémont, C. (Coll. doc.) Paris. 1885, 96.

B. Narrative Sources.

(1) *Lives, Chronicles, etc.*

Contemporary Lives of St. Louis.

Jehan, Sire de Joinville, Mémoires. [Begun perhaps *c.* 1273, finished in 1305.] Ed. Daunou, F. *in* Bouquet. Vol. xx. 1840. *Also* ed. Wailly, N. de. (Firmin-Didot.) Paris. 1874. 4to. [Important commentary.] Text reprinted in 16° by Hachette. Paris. 1881.

William of St Pathus. Vie de St Louis. Ed. Delaborde, H. F. (Coll. textes.) Paris. 1899. [*See also* Une œuvre nouvelle de Guillaume de St. Pathus. BEC. 1902.]

Geoffrey of Beaulieu. Vita et sancta conversatio...Ludovici, etc. *In* Bouquet. Vol. xx. 1840.

William of Chartres. De vita et actibus...Ludovici, etc. *Ibid.*

[For the religious life of St Louis, miracles attributed to him, and the bull of canonisation *see* Stilting, J. De Sancto Ludovico Francorum rege Commentarius praevius, with the documents annexed, *in* ASBoll. Aug. (die 25) v.

Fragments of the inquest for canonisation, ed. Riant, P. de *in* Notices et documents publiés par la Soc. de l'Hist. de France. Paris. 1884; and ed. Delaborde, H. F. *in* Mém. de la Soc. de l'Hist. de Paris. Vol. XXIII. 1896.]

Contemporary histories of the reign.

Vincent of Beauvais. Speculum historiale. 4 vols. Douai. 1624. (Extracts *in* Bouquet. Vol. XXI. 1855.)

Primat, Chronique de. Translated from Latin by John of Vignay. *In* Bouquet. Vol. XXIII. 1876.

Alberic of Trois-Fontaines. Chronica. Ed. Scheffer-Boichorst, P. MGH. Script. XXIII. 1874.

Philip Mousket. Chronique rimée. Ed. Reiffenberg, F. A. F. T. de. Vol. II. (Coll. des chron. Belges.) Brussels. 1838.

William of Nangis. Gesta Ludovici IX. *In* Bouquet. Vol. xx. 1840. [A non-contemporary compilation, but useful.]

For the Midi.

Guilhem Pelhisso. Chronicon. Ed. Douais, C. *in* Sources de l'Inquisition dans le Midi de la France. 1881. pp. 83–118. [From 1231–1237. Very interesting. By an inquisitor.]

William of Puilaurent. Historia Albigensium. *In* Bouquet. Vol. xx. 1840.

Foreign Chronicles.

The most important is that of Roger of Wendover enlarged and continued by Matthew Paris, ed. Luard, H. R. Vols. III–VII. (Rolls.) 1876–83, especially for the documents in the Additamenta (Vol. VI). Matthew's statements on French affairs must be read with caution. Wendover's Chronicle unaltered is ed. by Hewlett, H. G. 3 vols. (Rolls.) 1886–9.

(2) *Reports and Letters.*

The numerous and important letters on the Egyptian Crusade are listed by Molinier. (*See above* I.) The most notable are St Louis' Letter to his Subjects (August 1250) *in* Duchesne, A. Historiae Francorum Scriptores. Vol. V. Paris. 1649. pp. 428–32; and John Sarrasin's Letter to Nicholas Arrode (June, 1249) *in* Recueil des historiens des Croisades. Hist. occidentaux. Vol. II. AcadIBL. Paris. 1849. pp. 568–71, 589–93.

For William of Rubruquis, Itinerarium, *see* Vol. IV, p. 881, and the bibliography by Chalandon, F. *in* BEC. 1910. p. 383.

C. Historical Poems, Documents on Manners, and Anecdotes.

Paris, P. Romancero français. Paris. 1833.

Leroux de Lincy, A. J. V. Recueil de chants historiques français. Vol. I. Paris. 1841.

Stephen of Bourbon. Anecdotes historiques. Ed. Lecoy de la Marche, A. (SHF.) Paris. 1877.

Thomas of Cantimpré. Bonum universale de apibus. Ed. Colveneere, G. Douai. 1597, and later edns. [*See also* Berger, É. Thomae Cantipratensis Bonum universale de apibus quid illustrandis saeculi decimi tertii moribus conferat. Paris. 1895.]

Récits d'un ménestrel de Reims au XIIIe siècle. Ed. Wailly, N. de. (SHF.) Paris. 1876.

III. MODERN WORKS.

(*a*) *Histories of St Louis' reign or of a period of it.*

Le Nain de Tillemont, L. S. Vie de St Louis, roi de France. Ed. Gaulle, J. de. 6 vols. (SHF.) Paris. 1847–51. [Although Tillemont died in 1698, his work is still most useful to scholars.]

Wallon, H. St Louis et son temps. 2 vols. Paris. 1875. [For the Crusade in Egypt.]

Berger, É. Blanche de Castille. Paris. 1895. [Useful.]

—— Les dernières années de St Louis, d'après les Layettes du Trésor des Chartes. [Forms the introduction to Vol. IV of Layettes du Trésor des Chartes. 1902. *See above*, II A (1).]

Lecoy de la Marche, A. La France sous St Louis et sous Philippe le Hardi. Paris. [1893.]

Langlois, C. V. *In* Lavisse, E. Histoire de France. Vol. III. pt. 2. 1901. *See Gen. Bibl.* V. [Striking summary of the reign.]

(*b*) *St Louis' personality and his family.*

Brachet, A. Pathologie mentale des rois de France, 852–1483. Paris. 1903. [Very interesting.]

Sepet, M. St Louis. Paris. 1898. [Hagiographical apologia.]

Boutaric, E. Marguerite de Provence. RQH. Vol. III. 1867.

(c) *Administration; Justice; Finances.*

[The studies of Wailly, N. de, on St Louis' finances and coinage *in* Mém. AcadIBL. Vol. XXI, pt. 2. 1857 *and in* the introductions of Bouquet, Vols. XXI and XXII. (1855, 65), and of Boutaric, E. St Louis et Alphonse de Poitiers. Paris. 1870, are obsolete. Ducoudray, G. Les origines du Parlement de Paris. Paris. 1902, is confused.]

Borrelli de Serres, L. L. Recherches sur divers services publics du XIIIe au XVIIe siècle. Vol. I. Notices relatives au XIIIe siècle. Paris. 1895.

Chabrun, C. Les Bourgeois du roi. Paris. 1908.

Delisle, L. Mémoire sur les opérations financières des templiers. Mém. AcadIBL. Vol. XXXIII, pt. 2. 1889.

—— Chronologie des baillis et sénéchaux royaux. *In* Bouquet. Vol. XXIV, pt. 1. 1904. [With numerous documents.]

Dieudonné, A. Les Monnaies royales françaises depuis Hugues Capet jusqu'à la Révolution. [Vol. II of Blanchet, A. and Dieudonné, A. *See Gen. Bibl.* III.]

Guilhiermoz, P. Les Sources manuscrites de l'histoire monétaire de St Louis. MA. 2nd ser. Vol. XXV. 1923.

Langlois, C. V. Les Origines du Parlement de Paris. RH. Vol. XLII. 1890.

—— Doléances recueillies par les enquêteurs de St Louis. RH. Vol. XCII. 1906.

Michel, R. L'Administration royale dans la sénéchaussée de Beaucaire au temps de St Louis. Paris. 1910.

Molinier, A. Étude sur l'administration de St Louis et d'Alphonse de Poitiers en Languedoc. *In* Vic, C. de and Vaissete, J. J. Hist....de Languedoc. New edn. Vol. VII. *See Gen. Bibl.* IV.

Perrot, E. Les Cas royaux. Paris. 1910.

Prou, M. Esquisse de la politique monétaire des rois de France du Xe au XIIIe siècle. *In* Entre Camarades, publié par la Société des anciens élèves de la Faculté des Lettres de Paris. Paris. 1901.

Régné, J. Étude sur la condition des Juifs de Narbonne du Ve au XIVe siècle. Narbonne. 1912.

Waquet, H. Le Bailliage de Vermandois aux XIIIe et XIVe siècles. (BHE.) Paris. 1919.

(d) *The French Church; the Inquisition.*

Viollet, P. La Pragmatique sanction de St Louis, examen critique d'un ouvrage de M. C. Gérin. BEC. 1870.

Scheffer-Boichorst, P. Der Streit über die pragmatische Sanction Ludwigs des Heiligen. MIOGF. Vol. VIII. 1887.

Valois, N. Guillaume d'Auvergne. Paris. 1880.

Cordey, J. Guillaume de Massouris, abbé de St Denis, 1245–1254. *In* Bibliothèque de la Faculté des Lettres de l'Université de Paris. Vol. XVIII. 1904.

Besides the general works on the Inquisition by Lea, H. C., Tanon, L., and others cited in the Bibliography to ch. XX, *see*:

Molinier, C. L'Inquisition dans le midi de la France au XIIIe et au XIVe siècle. Paris. 1880.

Douais, C. Les Sources de l'histoire de l'Inquisition dans le midi de la France. Paris. RQH. 1881.

—— Les Hérétiques du comté de Toulouse d'après l'enquête de 1245. Paris. 1891.

—— L'Inquisition, ses origines, sa procédure. Paris. 1906.

Frederichs, J. Robert le Bougre, premier inquisiteur général de France. (Recueil des travaux publiés par la Faculté de Philosophie de Gand, VI.) Ghent. 1892.

Beuzart, P. Les Hérésies pendant le moyen âge et la réforme dans la région de Douai, d'Arras, et du pays de l'Alleu. Paris. 1912.

(e) *Relations with the Nobles.*

Arbois de Jubainville, H. d'. Histoire des ducs et des comtes de Champagne. Vol. IV. Paris. 1865.

Boissonnade, P. Quomodo comites Engolismenses erga reges Angliae et Franciae se gesserint. Angoulême. 1893.
—— Histoire de Poitou. Paris. 1915.
Le Moyne de la Borderie, A. Histoire de Bretagne. Vol. III. Rennes. 1899.
Molinier, A. L'Expédition de Trencavel. *In* Vic, C. de and Vaissete, J. J. Histoire ...de Languedoc. New edn. Vol. VII. 1879. *See Gen. Bibl.* IV.
Petit, E. Histoire des ducs de Bourgogne de la race capétienne. Vols. IV and V. Dijon. 1891, 94.

(*f*) *Relations with the Towns and the Commonalty.*

Bourgin, G. La Commune de Soissons. (BHE.) Paris. 1908.
Giry, A. Les Établissements de Rouen. Vol. I. (BHE.) Paris. 1883
Labande, L. H. Histoire de Beauvais. Paris. 1892.
Lefranc, A. Histoire de la ville de Noyon. (BHE.) Paris. 1887.
Röhricht, R. Die Pastorellen, 1251. ZKG. Vol. VI. 1884. [On the Crusades of the Pastoureaux.]

(*g*) *Changes with regard to the Royal Domain; Wars, Foreign Policy.*

Bémont, C. La Campagne de Poitou, 1242–1243, Taillebourg et Saintes. *In* Annales du Midi. Vol. IV. Toulouse. 1893.
—— Simon de Montfort, comte de Leicester. Paris. 1884. 2nd. edn. transl. Jacob, E. F., is forthcoming.
Berger, É. St Louis et Innocent IV. Paris. 1893.
Daumet, G. Mémoire sur les relations de la France et de la Castille de 1255 à 1320. Paris. 1913.
Duvivier, C. Les Influences française et germanique en Belgique au XIIIe siècle; la querelle des d'Avesnes et des Dampierre. 2 vols. Brussels. 1894.
Fournier, P. Le Royaume d'Arles et de Vienne. Paris. 1891.
Gavrilovitch, M. Étude sur le traité de Paris de 1259. (BHE.) Paris. 1899.
Jordan, E. Les Origines de la domination angevine en Italie. Paris. 1909.
Labande, L. H. Avignon au XIIIe siècle. Paris. 1908.
Longnon, A. La Formation de l'unité française. Paris. 1922.
Régné, J. Histoire du Vivarais. Vol. II. Largentière. 1921.
Schwann, M. Ludwig der heilige von Frankreich und seine Beziehungen zu Kaiser und Papst. *In* Zeitschrift für allgemeine Geschichte. Vol. IV. Stuttgart. 1887.
Sternfeld, R. Karl von Anjou als Graf der Provence. Berlin. 1888.

(*h*) *The two Crusades of St Louis.*

Bréhier, L. L'Église et l'Orient au moyen âge. Les Croisades. 4th edn. [Good bibliography.] *See Gen. Bibl.* V.
Caro, G. Zum zweiten Kreuzzug Ludwigs IX von Frankreich. HVJS. Vol. III. 1898.
Delaborde, H. F. Jean de Joinville. Paris. 1894.
Lane-Poole, S. History of Egypt in the Middle Ages. (History of Egypt. Ed. Flinders Petrie, W. M. Vol. VI.) London and New York. 1901.
La Roncière, C. de. Histoire de la marine française. Vol. I. Paris. 1899.
Sternfeld, R. Ludwigs des heiligen Kreuzzug nach Tunis 1270 und die Politik Karls I von Sizilien. (Ebering's Historische Studien, No. 4.) Berlin. 1896.

(*i*) *Economic, social, intellectual, artistic development.*

For a general account see Lecoy de la Marche, A. *See above*, III (*a*). For artistic activity and the movement of ideas see the remarkable chapters of Langlois, C. V. *in* Lavisse. pp. 380 sqq. *See above* III (*a*).

(*k*) *Maps.*

There are excellent maps in N. de Wailly's Joinville. 4to edn. 1874. *See above*, II B (1), viz:

Carte du royaume de France après le traité de 1259.

Cartes pour l'intelligence de la première et de la deuxième croisade de St Louis; *with* Notes explicatives (app. XXI) by Longnon, A.

CHAPTER XI.

THE SCANDINAVIAN KINGDOMS UNTIL THE END OF THE THIRTEENTH CENTURY.

I. BIBLIOGRAPHIES.

Erichsen, B. and Krarup, A. Dansk historisk bibliografi. 3 vols. Copenhagen 1917–26.
Norsk historisk videnskap i femti år 1869–1919. Christiania. 1920.
Setterwall, K. Svensk historisk bibliografi, 1875–1900. Stockholm. 1907.

II. AUTHORITIES.

(*a*) Denmark.

Annales Danici medii aevi. Ed. Jörgensen, E. Copenhagen. 1920.
Danmarks gamle Provindslove. Ed. Thorsen, P. G. 4 vols. Copenhagen. 1852–3. New edn. Danmarks gamle landskabslove med kirkelovene. Ed. Bröndum-Nielsen, J. 1920 ff., in progress.
Liber census Daniae. Ed. Nielsen, O. Copenhagen. 1873. New edn. by Aakjaer, S. 1926. [*Cf.* Steenstrup, J. Studier over Kong Valdemars Jordebog. Copenhagen. 1874.]
Saxo Grammaticus. Historia Danica. Ed. Müller, P. E. 3 vols. Copenhagen. 1839–58. Also ed. *as* Gesta Danorum. Holder, A. Strasbourg. 1886. English transl. of the first nine books. Elton, O. London. 1894. Complete Danish transl. Olrik, J. Copenhagen. 1908–12. [*Cf.* Olrik, A. Kilderne til Sakses oldhistorie. 2 vols. Copenhagen. 1892, 94.]
Scriptores minores historiae Danicae medii aevi. Ed. Gertz, M. C. 2 vols. Copenhagen. 1917, 22.
Repertorium diplomaticum regni Danici mediaevalis. Ed. Erslev, K. Vol. i. Copenhagen. 1895.

(*b*) Norway and Iceland.

[Separate editions of the Norwegian-Icelandic sagas are in existence (*cf.* the list in Vol. iii, pp. 618–9), but they need not be enumerated here. A series of Icelandic sagas is ed. by Vigfusson, G., with Engl. transl. by Dasent, Sir G. W. 4 vols. (Rolls.) 1887–94.]
Den norsk-islandske skjaldedigtning. Ed. Jónsson, F. 4 vols. Copenhagen. 1912–15.
Diplomatarium Islandicum. [Ed. Sigurdsson, J., and others.] 10 vols. (Islenzka Bókmentafélag.) Copenhagen and Reykjavik. 1857–1921.
Diplomatarium Norvegicum. Ed. Lange, C. C. A. and others. 20 vols. Christiania. 1849 ff.
Monumenta historica Norvegiae. Ed. Storm, G. Christiania. 1880.
Norges gamle Love indtil 1387. Ed. Keyser, R., Munch, P. A., and others. 5 vols. Christiania. 1846–95.
Regesta Norvegica. Ed. Storm, G. Vol. i. Christiania. 1898.
Snorri Sturluson. Heimskringla. Ed. Jónsson, F. 4 vols. Copenhagen. 1893–1901. English transl. Morris, W. and Magnússon, E. 4 vols. London. 1893–1905. [*Cf.* Storm, G. Snorre Sturlassöns Historieskrivning. Copenhagen. 1873.]

(*c*) Sweden.

Corpus juris Sueo-Gotorum antiqui. Ed. Schlyter, C. J. Vols. i–ix. Stockholm. 1827–53.
Diplomatarium Suecanum. Ed. Liljegren, J. D. Vols. i, ii. Stockholm. 1829, 37.
Sverges traktater med främmande magter. Ed. Rydberg, O. S. Vol. i. Stockholm. 1877.

III. MODERN WORKS.

(a) Scandinavia as a whole.

Bugge, A. Vesterlandenes indflydelse paa Nordboernes og saelig Nordmaendenes ydre kultur, levesaet og samfundsforhold i Vikingetiden. Christiania. 1905.
Hertzberg, E. De nordiske Retskilder. Copenhagen. 1890.
Jörgensen, A. D. Den nordiske Kirkes Grundlaeggelse og förste Udvikling. 2 vols. Copenhagen. 1874 78.
—— Historiske Afhandlinger. Vols. I, II. Copenhagen. 1898–9.
Lehmann, K. Der Königsfriede der Nordgermanen. Berlin and Leipsic. 1886.
—— Abhandlungen zur germanischen, insbesondere nordischen Rechtsgeschichte. Berlin and Leipsic. 1888.
Lie, M. H. Lensprincipet i Norden. Christiania. 1907.
Munch, P. A. Samlede Afhandlinger. 4 vols. Christiania. 1873–6.
Ottosen, J. Vor Historie. Vol. I. Copenhagen. 1899.
Phillpotts, B. S. Kindred and Clan. Cambridge. 1913.
Tunberg, S. Studier rörande Skandinaviens äldsta politiska indelning. Upsala. 1911.
Weibull, C. Om det svenska och det danska rikets uppkomst. Lund. 1921.
—— Sverige och dess nordiska grannmakter under den tidigare medeltiden. Lund. 1921.
Weibull, L. Kritiska undersökningar i Nordens historia omkring år 1000. Lund. 1911.

(b) Denmark.

Arup, E. Danmarks historie. Vol. I. Copenhagen. 1925. [Appeared after this chapter was in print.]
Erslev, K. Valdemarernes Storhedstid. Copenhagen. 1898.
Holberg, L. Dansk og fremmed Ret. Copenhagen. 1891.
—— Konge og Danehof. Vol. I. Copenhagen. 1895.
Hude, A. Danehoffet. Copenhagen. 1893.
Jörgensen, P. J. Forelaesninger over den danske Retshistorie. 4 pts. Copenhagen. 1904–8.
Matzen, H. Forelaesninger over den danske Retshistorie. 6 vols. Copenhagen. 1893–7.
Olrik, H. Konge og Praestestand. 2 vols. Copenhagen. 1892, 95.
—— Absalon. 2 vols. Copenhagen. 1908–9.
Steenstrup, J. and Erslev, K. Danmarks Riges Historie. Vols. I, II. Copenhagen. 1897, 1905.

(c) Norway and Iceland.

Amira, K. v. Das altnorwegische Vollstreckungsverfahren. Munich. 1874.
Bugge, A. Studier over de norske byers selvstyre og handel för Hanseaternes tid. Christiania. 1899.
Bugge, A. and Hertzberg, E. Norges historie fremstillet for det norske folk. I, II. Christiania. 1910, 16.
Bull, E. Folk og kirke i middelalderen. Christiania. 1912.
—— Leding. Christiania. 1920.
Gjerset, K. History of the Norwegian People. Vol. I. New York. 1915.
—— History of Iceland. New York. 1924.
Jónsson, F. Den oldnorske og oldislandske litteraturs historie. 3 vols. Copenhagen. 1894–1902. New edn. in course of publication.
Koht, H. Innhogg og utsyn i norsk historie. Christiania. 1921.
Maurer, K. Die Bekehrung des norwegischen Stammes zum Christenthume. 2 vols. Munich. 1855–6.
—— Island von seiner ersten Entdeckung bis zum Untergange des Freistaats. Munich. 1874.
—— Vorlesungen über altnordische Rechtsgeschichte. 5 vols. Leipsic. 1907–10.
Munch, P. A. Det norske folks historie. 6 vols. Christiania. 1852–9.
Sars, J. E. Udsigt over den norske historie. Vols. I, II. Christiania. 1873, 77. Repr. in his Samlede Vaerker. Vol. I. Christiania. 1911.
Taranger, A. Udsigt over den norske rets historie. 2 vols. Christiania. 1898, 1904.

(*d*) Sweden.

Hildebrand, E. Svenska statsförfattningens historiska utveckling. Stockholm. 1896.
Hildebrand, H. Sveriges medeltid, kultur-historisk skildring. 3 vols. Stockholm. 1879–1903.
Montelius, O. and Hildebrand, H. Sveriges historia intill tjugonde seklet. Vols. i, ii. Stockholm. 1903, 5. New edn. Montelius, O. and Tunberg, S. Sveriges historia till våra dagar. Vols. i, ii. Stockholm. 1919, 26.
Schück, H. Svenska folkets historia. Vol. i in 2 pts. Lund. 1914–15.
Westman, K. B. Den svenska kyrkans utveckling från St Bernhards tidevarv till Innocentius III's. Stockholm. 1915.
Westman, K. G. Svenska rådets historia till år 1306. Upsala. 1904.

CHAPTER XII.

SPAIN, 1031–1248.

Some of the books and documents listed in the Bibliography of Vol. III, ch. XVI are also useful for this period.

I KINGDOMS OF LEON AND CASTILE.

A. Bibliographies.

Gayangos, P. de. Obras arábigas que pueden servir para comprobar la cronologia de los reyes de Asturias y Leon. Madrid. 1847.

Catálogo de las colecciones expuestas en las vitrinas del Palacio de Liria. Madrid. 1898. [Some of the documents belong to medieval Spain.]

Indice de los documentos...de los monasterios y conventos suprimidos que se conservan en le Archivo de la R. Acad. de la Historia. Sect. I. Castilla y León. Vol I: Monasterios de Nuestra Señora de la Vid y San Millán de la Cogolla. Madrid. 1861. [No more publ.]

Colección de Cortes de los antiguos reinos de España. Catálogo. Madrid. RAH. 1855.

Colección de Fueros y Cartas-Pueblas de España. Catálogo. RAH. Madrid. 1852.

Ballester y Castell, R. Las fuentes narrativas de la historia de España durante la Edad Media, 417–1474. Palma de Mallorca. 1908.

B. Original Documents.

(i) *Published.*

Mañueco, M. and Zurita, J. Documentos de la Iglesia Colegial de Sta. Maria la Mayor (hoy Metropolitana) de Valladolid. Siglo XIII (1201–1280). Valladolid. 1920.

Hermandad de Córdoba con Jaen, Baeza, Andujar, Arjona y Santi-Esteban e varios caballeros en tiempo del infante D. Sancho. *In* Colecc. de doc. inéditos para la hist. de España. CXII. 1895.

P. P. Benedictinos de Silos. Documentos para la historia de Castilla. I–III. Valladolid. 1906. In progress.

Vignau, V. Cartulario del monasterio de Eslonza. Madrid. 1885.

Colección diplomática de "Galicia Historica." Vol. I. Santiago. 1904. [No more publ.]

Martinez Salazar, A. Documentos gallegos de los siglos XIII al XVI. Corunna. 1911.

Fernández Duro, C. Romancero de Zamora. Madrid. 1880. [With bibliography.]

Delalande, J. Une charte d'Alphonse VI de l'année 1075 (?). *In* Revue hispanique. LIII. 1921.

Martin Minguez, B. Documento *on* Fernando III de León. *In* Nueva Acad. Heráldica. II. 1914.

—— Notas documentales para la hist. de Alfonso IX de León. *In* Rev. de Hist. y Geneal. española. II. 1913.

Muñoz y Romero, T. Colección de Fueros Municipales y Cartas Pueblas...de Castilla, León, Corona de Aragón, y Navarra. Madrid. 1847. [Some of these documents have been republished in more accurate editions. Many others of this kind had been printed in separate editions which supplemented the Muñoz Colección.]

Hinojosa, E. de. Documentos para la historia de las instituciones de León y Castilla, siglos X–XIII. Madrid. 1919.

Paz y Melia, A. Documentos de los siglos XII–XV correspondientes a los reinos de España, excepto Cataluña (Series de los...docs. del Arch. y Bib. del...Duque de Medinaceli, I). Madrid. 1915.

(ii) *Manuscripts.*

Documents on Alfonso VI of Castile. Nat. Lib., Madrid. MSS. Division. Nos. 700, 1376, 5790, 6932, 7472, 7602, 8809, 9194, 13022, 13075, 13093.
Documents on the epoch of Alfonso IX of Leon. *Ibid.* Nos. 6683, 13064.
Documents on the epoch of Ferdinand III. *Ibid.* Nos. 6932, 6761, 18731 and 2.
Documents on Alfonso VII of Castile. *Ibid.* Nos. 773, 5741, 5790, 9194, 13031, 13039, 13073 to 75, 13093 and 4, 13098.
Constituciones de los reyes de León hechas por D. Alfonso VIII en las Cortes de 1178. *Ibid.* No. 11261[39].

C. Original Authorities.

(i) *Published.*

Anales toledanos. I, II, and III (till 1391). *In* España Sagrada. Vol. XXIII. *See Gen. Bibl.* IV.
Cronicón del Cerratense. *Ibid.* II.
Cronicón de Cardeña. I and II. *Ibid.* XXIII.
Menéndez Pidal, R. Primera crónica general de España. Madrid. 1906. [The crónica ends just at Ferdinand III's death.] *See also* La crónica general de España que mandó componer el rey Alfonso X *by the same author.* Madrid. 1916.
Cartagena, A. de. Regum Hispanorum...Granatam. 1545. Another edition *in* Hispaniae illustratae... Frankfort. 1603–4.
Sánchez de Arévalo, R. Historiae hispanicae partes III. Rome. 1470. *Also in* Hisp. illust. *op. cit.*
Huici, A. Las crónicas latinas de la Reconquista. 2 vols. Valencia. 1913. [Includes some of the above mentioned and the chronicle of Alfonso VII. Good edn.]
Cirot, G. Une chronique latine inédite des rois de Castille (1236). *In* Bulletin hispanique. XIV–XV. 1912–13. *See also* Appendices à la Chronique *and* Recherches sur la Chronique. *Ibid.* XIX–XXI and XXV. 1917–23.
Puyol, J. Las Crónicas anónimas de Sahagún. Madrid. 1920.
La Crónica del noble cauallero el conde Fernan Gonzalez. Sevilla. 1507. *See* Menéndez Pidal, R. La leyenda de los infantes de Lara. Madrid. 1896.
Zamora, Gil de. Biografia...de Alfonso IX de León. BRAH. XIII. 1888.
—— Biografias de Sàn Fernando y Alfonso el Sabio. *Ibid.* V. 1885.
Nuñez de Castro, A. Crónicas de los...reyes de Castilla. Madrid. 1665. [The most valuable part is that relating to Alfonso VIII.]
Sandoval, P. de. Chrónica del inclito emperador de España don Alfonso VII. Madrid. 1600.
—— Historia de los reyes de Castilla y de León. Pamplona. 1615.

(ii) *Manuscripts.*

Crónica Segunda general de 1344. 15th cent. MS. Nat. Lib., Madrid. 10814–15. [Like this many of the general Spanish medieval chronicles are unpublished. *See* Menéndez Pidal, R. Crónicas generales de España. Catálogo de la Nat. Bib. Manuscritos. 3rd edn. Madrid, 1918, and his other monographs on this subject.]
Fernandez de Mendoza, D. Novenario Estorial. Roy. Lib., Madrid. 2–C.–5.
Historia del invitissimo Fernán González. Bibl. Nat., Paris. 180, no. 124 of the Catalogue of Morel-Fatio.
Arredondo, G. de. Crónica de Hernán González, Conde de Castilla. Nat. Lib., Madrid. 894.

D. Modern Works.

(i) *General.*

Azevedo, L. G. de. Notas de Historia Medieval. *In* Rev. de Historia. Lisbon. X. 1921.
Berganza, F. de. Antigüedades de España. 2 vols. Madrid. 1719, 21.
Burriel, A. M. Memorias para la vida del Santo Rey Fernando III. Madrid. 1800.
Carreres Zacarés, S. Tratados entre Castilla y Aragón. Su influencia en la terminación de la Reconquista. Valencia. 1908.

Colmeiro, M. De la constitución y del gobierno de los reinos de León y de Castilla. 2 vols. Madrid. 1855.

Cunha Neves and Carvalho Portugal. Memoria acerca do convenio...entre o conde Henrique e...o conde D. Raimão, sobre os Estados do seu sogro commun o Imperador D. Alfonso Sexto. *In* Mem. da Acad. R. das Sciencias de Lisboa. 2nd ser. I, pt 2.

Fernandez de Navarrete, M. Disertación historica sobre la parte que tuvieron los españoles en las guerras de Ultramar o de las Cruzadas. *In* Mem. RAH. v.

Fernández Duro, C. La Marina de Castilla desde su origen y pugna con la de Inglaterra. Madrid. 1893.

Galvão, D. Chronica do mui alto principe D. Alfonso Henrique, rey de Portugal. Lisbon. 1726.

Gama Barros, H. da. Historia da administração publica em Portugal. 2 vols. Lisbon. 1885 ff. [Includes medieval Spanish history.]

Gutierrez Coronel, D. Disertación historica...sobre los jueces de Castilla. Madrid. 1785.

Ibañez de Segovia, G., marquis of Mondejar. Memorias historicas de...Alonso el Noble, octavo del nombre. Madrid. 1783.

—— Memorias historicas del Rei D. Alonso el Sabio. Madrid. 1777.

Lopez Ferreiro, A. Galicia en los primeros siglos de la Reconquista. *In* Galicia Historica. II. 1903.

Martin Minguez, B. Salpicaduras histórico-literarias. Los Condes de Castilla y los Infantes de Lara. Madrid. 1915.

Martinez Marina, F. Discurso sobre el origen de la monarquia y sobre la naturaleza del gobierno español. Madrid. 1813.

—— Ensayo historico-critico sobre la antigua legislación...de...León y Castilla. Madrid. 1808. 3rd edn. 1845. [Mostly on the medieval legislation.]

—— Teoria de las Cortes o grandes juntas nacionales de...León y Castilla. 3 vols. Madrid. 1813.

Mayer, E. Historia de las instituciones sociales y políticas de España y Portugal durante los siglos V a XIV. Spanish edn. 2 vols. Madrid. 1925–6.

Merca, P. A concesão da terra portugalense a D. Henrique perante a historia jurídica. *In* Anuario Hist. Derecho esp. Madrid. 1925.

Merriman, R. B. The rise of the Spanish empire. Vol. I. *See Gen. Bibl.* v.

Paes Viegas, A. Principios del reino de Portugal. Lisbon. 1641.

Puyol, J. Origenes del reino de León y de sus instituciones políticas. *In* Mem. R. Acad. de Ciencias Moral. y Polít. XII. Madrid. 1926.

Risco, M. Historia de la ciudad y corte de León y de sus reyes. Madrid. 1792.

(ii) *Monographs.*

Altamira, R. La Magna Charta y las libertades medievales en España. *In* Rev. de Ciencias jur. y soc. I, 2. Madrid. 1918. This monograph has been published in English *in* Magna Carta Commemoration Essays. (Roy. Hist. Soc.) London. 1917.

Cárdenas, F. de. Calidad y circunstancias de los bandos políticos de España, desde el siglo XIII hasta fines del siglo XV. Madrid. 1872.

Castañeda, V. Libertades medievales. Notas comparativas. Madrid. 1920.

Cedillo, Conde de. Contribuciones e impuestos en León y Castilla durante la Edad Media. Madrid. 1896.

Cirot, G. L'espionage en Espagne au temps de la Reconquête. *In* Bul. hisp. XIX. 1917.

Diez Canseco, L. Notas para el estudio del Fuero de León. *In* Anuario Hist. Derecho esp. I. 1924.

Fernández y González, F. Estado social y politico de los mudéjares de Castilla. Madrid. 1866.

Forma de las antiguas Cortes de Castilla, con algunas observaciones sobre ellas. Madrid. 1823. 1st sheet.

Garcia Rives, A. Clases sociales en León y Castilla (siglos X–XIII). *In* Rev. Arch. Bib. Mus. XLI. 1920.

Hinojosa, E. de. Origen del régimen municipal en León y Castilla. *In* Estud. sobre la Hist. del Derecho esp. Madrid. 1903.

Laiglesia, F. de la. Cortes de los antiguos reinos de León y Castilla. Madrid. 1909.
Merriman, R. B. The Cortes of the Spanish Kingdoms in the latter Middle Ages. AHR. XVI. 1911.
—— Control by national assemblies on the repeal of legislation in the latter Middle Ages. *In* Mélanges d'histoire offerts à C. Bémont. Paris. 1913.
Murguia, M. D. Diego Gelmirez. Corunna. 1898.
Puyol, J. Las Hermandades de Castilla y León. Madrid. 1913.
Sacristan y Martinez, A. Municipalidades de Castilla y Leon. Madrid. 1877.
Salazar de Mendoza, P. Origen de las dignidades seglares de Castilla y León. Toledo. 1618.
Sanchez Albornoz, C. Las behetrias: la encomendación en Asturias, León y Castilla. *In* Anuario Hist. Derecho esp. I. 1924.
—— El "juicio del libro" en León y un feudo castellano en el siglo XIII. *Ibid.*
—— La potestad real y los señorios en Asturias, León y Castilla. Siglos VIII al XIII. *In* Revista Arch. Bib. Mus. XXXI. 1914.
Sanchez de Ocaña, R. Contribuciones e impuestos en León y Castilla durante la Edad Media. Madrid. 1896.
Serrano, L. Los condes de Castilla y su gobierno. *In* Bol. Soc. Castellana Excurs. IV. 1909, 10.
Torreanaz, Conde de. Los Consejos del Rey en la Edad Media. 2 vols. Madrid. 1884–92.

II. THE CID.

A. Documents.

Crónica del famoso caualllero Cid Ruy-Diez campeador. Burgos. 1512. Ed. Huber, V.A., with preface. Stuttgart. 1853.
Nuñez de Guzman, R. Summa rerum admirabilium Cidi Roderici Diez. MS. Nat. Lib., Madrid. N° 1229.
Suma de las cosas maravillosas (Cronica del Cid Ruy Diez, Sevilla, 1498). *In* Rev. hisp. XX. 1909.
Gesta Roderici Didaci Campidocti. Ed. Risco, M. *in* La Castilla y el más famoso castellano. Madrid. 1792. *Also* ed. Foulché-Delbosc. *In* Rev. hisp. XXI. 1909.
Lucas, H. Documents relatifs à l'histoire du Cid. Paris. 1860.
Poema del Mio Cid. Ed. Menéndez Pidal. 2 vols. Madrid. 1908–11. [With very important introdn.] *Also* ed. by the same, with introdn., *in* "Clásicos castellanos," Vol. XXIV. Madrid. 1913.
Menéndez Pidal, R. Autógrafos inéditos del Cid y de Jimena en dos diplomas de 1098 y 1101. *In* Revista de Filol. esp. II, I.

B. Monographs.

Baumgartner, A. Der Cid in Geschichte und Poesie. *In* Stimmen aus Maria-Laach. LIX. 1898.
Bertrand, J. A. Herder et le Cid. *In* Bul. hisp. XXIII.
Canton Salazar, L. Los restos del Cid y Jimena y sus diferentes translaciones. 2nd edn. Burgos. 1883.
Clarke, H. Butler. The Cid Campeador and the waning of the Crescent in the West. London. 1897.
Dozy, R. P. A. Le Cid, textes et résultats nouveaux *and* Le Cid d'après de nouveaux documents. *In* Recherches sur l'hist. et la litt. de l'Espagne. 3rd edn. 2 vols. Leiden. 1881.
Ganniers, A. de. Les cendres du Cid et de Chimène. *In* Le Correspondant. CVIII. 1886.
Giese, W. Cuadros de la cultura en la época del Cid. *In* B. Bib. Menéndez y Pelayo. VIII, 3. 1926.
Hinojosa, E. de. El Derecho en el Poema del Cid. *In* Homenaje a Menéndez y Pelayo. Madrid. I. 1899.
Menéndez Pidal, R. El Cid en la Historia. Madrid. 1921.
Serrano y Sanz, M. Exactitud geográfica del Poema del Cid. *In* Rev. España. LXII.

III. THE ARABS.

(*See also* the Bibliography in Vol. III. ch. XVI.)

A. Documents and Ancient Works.

Abd-El-Wah'id Merrakechi. Histoire des Almohades. Transl. Fagnan, E. Alger. 1893.

Chronique des Almohades et des Afcides, attribuée à Zerkechi. Transl. Fagnan, E. Constantine. 1895.

Anonymous. El anónimo de Madrid y Copenhague. Arabic text, with transl. and introdn. by A. Huici. *In* Anales del Instituto de Valencia. II. 1917. [This book is the most valuable Arabic source on the Almohade period.]

B. Modern Works.

Alcover, A. M. Los Mozárabes baleares. *In* Rev. Arch. Bib. Mus. XLII (1921). *and* Madrid. 1921.

Asin Palacios, M. Origen y carácter de la revolución almohade. *In* Rev. Aragón. V. 1904.

Bel, A. Les Almoravides, les Almohades. Oran. 1910.

Chabás, R. Çeid-abu-Çeid. *In* Archivo. V. 1891.

—— Mochéid, hijo de Jusuf, y Ali, hijo de Mochéid. *In* Homenaje a Codera. Saragossa. 1904. [Both on the Moors of Valencia.]

Codera, F. Decadencia y desaparición de los Almoravides en España. Saragossa. 1899.

—— Familia real de los Benitexufin. *In* Rev. Aragón. IV[1]. 1903.

—— Hamudies de Málaga y Algeciras. *In* Est. crit. de hist. árabe esp. Saragossa 1903.

—— Estudio critico sobre la historia y monedas de los Hamudies de Málaga y Algeciras. *In* Mus. esp. de Antigüedades. VIII. 1877.

—— Los Benimeruan, llamados los gallegos, en Mérida y Badajoz. *In* Rev. Aragón. V. 1904. [The same author has written upon most of the independent Arab kingdoms succeeding the Caliphate.]

—— Mozárabes. Su condición social y politica. Lérida. 1866.

Dozy, R. Recherches sur les Todjibides d'Aragón. *In* Recherches. 3rd edn. Vol. I. *See above,* II B.

—— Histoire des musulmans d'Espagne. Leiden. 1861. Engl. transl. Stokes, F. G. London. 1913.

González Palencia, A. Historia de la España musulmana. Barcelona. 1925.

Martinez y Martinez, M. R. Historia del reino de Badajoz durante la dominación musulmana. Badajoz. 1905.

Prieto y Vives, A. Los Reyes de Taifas. Estudo historico-numismático de los musulmanes españoles en el siglo V de la Hégira (XI de J.-C.). Madrid. 1926.

Romero y Garcia, J. Instituciones jurídicas de los musulmanes en España. Madrid. 1900.

Saavedra, E. de. Los Almoravides. BRAH. LXIX. 1916.

Simonet, F. J. Historia de los Mozárabes de España. *In* Mem. RAH. XIII.

IV. NAVARRE.

A. Bibliographies.

Altadill, J. Indice de los documentos existentes en Simancas que afectan a la historia de Navarra. *In* Bol. Com. Mon. Navarra. IV–XI. Pamplona. 1913–20.

Garráu, C. Catálogo de los documentos históricos referentes a las antiguas Cortes de Navarra, conservados hoy en el Archivo del Ayuntamiento de Tudela. BRAH. XXXV. 1899.

Azcona, J.-Mª. Documentos relativos a Navarra que se conservan en el British Museum. *Apud* the Catálogo of Gayangos. *In* Bol. Com. Mon. Navarra. XII, XIII. 1921–2.

B. Documents.

(i) *Published.*

Arigita y Sasa, M. Colección de documentos inéditos para la historia de Navarra. I. Pamplona. 1900.

Documentos inéditos. [Under this title, or others similar to it, the "Boletin de la Comisión de Monumentos...de Navarra" is publishing by various editors a large number of documents.]

Brutails, J. A. Documents des Archives de la Chambre de Comptes de Navarre (1196–1384). Paris. 1890.

Serrano y Sanz, M. Noticias y documentos históricos del condado de Ribagorza hasta la muerte de Sancho Garcès III (año 1035). Madrid. 1912.

Bulas históricas del reino de Navarra en los postreros años del siglo XII. Ed. Fita, F. BRAH. XXVI. 1895.

Bulas inéditas. Ed. Fita, F. *Ibid.* XXVII. 1895.

(ii) *Manuscripts.*

Crónica navarro-aragonesa. 14th century. Roy. Lib., Madrid. 2–F.–4.

Suma de las Crónicas de Navarra. Roy. Lib. 2-I.–4 and Nat. Lib. 2086, 7078.

Cronicón de Santa Maria de Beruela. Reyes de Navarra. Nat. Lib., Madrid. 18636[45].

Genealogia de los Reyes de Navarra. *Ibid.* 3546.

Genealogia Regum Navarrae a Garcia Sanctio Abarca. Escurial Lib. N.I. 13.

Carbonell, P. Escrituras y feudos del condado de Ribagorza. Nat. Lib., Madrid. 725.

(iii) *Chronicles.*

Viana, Cárlos Príncipe de. Crónica de los Reyes de Navarra. Ed. Yanguas y Miranda, J. Pamplona. 1843.

Ramirez de Avalos, D. Crónica de los muy ecelentes rreyes de navarra. 16th century. Roy. Lib. 2–C.–5.

C. Modern Works.

Barrau-Dihigo, L. Les premiers rois de Navarre. *In* Rev. hisp. XV. 1906.

—— Les origines du Royaume de Navarre. *Ibid.* VII. 1900.

Bladé, J. F. Les comtes carolingiens de Bigorre et les premiers rois de Navarre. *In* Rev. de l'Agénais. 1895–6.

Campión, A. Gacetilla de la historia de Nabarra. *In* Bol. Com. Mon. Navarra. II–V. 1911–14.

Delmar, P. Du Parlement de Navarre et de ses origines. Bordeaux. 1898.

Moret, José de. Investigaciones históricas de las antigüedades del reino de Navarra. Congressiones apologéticas sobre la verdad de las Investigaciones. Annales del Reyno de Navarra. These three works together. 5 vols. Pamplona. 1766.

Oliver y Hurtado, M. Forma, tiempo, y circunstancias en que hubo de verificarse el nacimiento del reino de Pamplona. Madrid. 1866.

Saleta, H. de la. Estado social del reino navarro bajo el gobierno de D. Sancho el Fuerte. *In* Rev. de Hist. y Geneal. esp. IV. 1915.

V. ARAGON.

A. Bibliographies.

Andrés de Uztarroz, J. F. Progresos de la historia en el Reyno de Aragón. Pt. I. Saragossa. 1680. Saragossa. 1878.

Viñaza, C. de la. Los cronistas de Aragón. Madrid. 1904.

Ibarra, E. Bibliografias históricas regionales. Aragón. *In* Cultura Española. 1906.

—— Documentos aragoneses en los Archivos de Italia. Apuntes para un inventario. *In* Anales...Junta para Ampliación de estudios etc. Madrid. 1911.

Rubió, J. Consideraciones generales acerca de la Historiografia catalana medioeval y particular de la "Crónica de Desclot." Barcelona. 1911.

Régné, J. Catalogue des actes de Jaime Ier...concernant les Juifs. *In* Revue des études juives. 1910–14. Also published separately. Paris. 1911–14.

B. Documents (including Chronicles).

(i) *Published.*

Anonymous. Historia de la Corona de Aragón...conocida generalmente con el nombre de "Crónica de San Juan de la Peña." First printed Saragossa, 1876.

Marineus, L. De primis Aragonie regibus: et eorum rerum gestarum...libri. Caesar Augusta. 1509. Spanish transl. Molina, J. de, under the title of Crónica Daragon. Valencia. 1524.

Tomic Cauller, P. Histories e conquestes dels Reys de Arago e Comtes de Barcelona. Barcelona. 1495. Modern edn. Barcelona. 1886.

Capmany, A. de. Antiguos tratados de paces y alianzas entre algunos reyes de Aragón y diferentes príncipes infieles de Asia y Africa desde el siglo XIII hasta el XV. Madrid. 1786.

Chronica o commentari del...rey En Jacme (Jaime Ier). Valencia. 1557. Modern edn. Aguiló, M. Barcelona. 1873 (1905). Spanish transl. Flotals, M. and Bofarull, A. de. Barcelona. 1848.

Muntaner, R. Chronica o descripció dels fets e hazanyes del...Rey Don Jaume...e de molts de ses descendens. Valencia. 1558. Engl. transl. Goodenough, Lady. 2 vols. (Hakluyt Soc.) London. 1920–1.

Procesos de las antiguas Cortes y Parlamentos de Cataluña, Aragón, y Valencia. 8 vols. (Col. doc. inéd. Arch. Corona Aragón, vols. I–VIII.)

Miret, J. Documentos inéditos de antiguos reyes de Aragón. *In* Bol. Acad. Buenas Letras Barcelona. VI. 1911-12.

Ordenanzas para la casa y corte de los reyes de Aragón (siglos XIII, XIV). *In* Cultura española. 1906.

Colección de documentos para el estudio de la Historia de Aragón. 9 vols. Saragossa. 1904–13.

Orderici Vitalis Angligenae...Ecclesiasticae Historiae liber XIII. *In* España Sagrada, X. *See Gen. Bibl.* IV. [Relating to the co-operation given by the French to Alfonso I.]

Miralles, J. and Aguiló, E. Documentos del rey D. Jaime I. *In* But. Soc. arqueolog. Luliana. Palma de Mallorca. 1908.

Gonzalez Hurtebisse, E. Recull de documents inedits del rey en Jaume I. *In* Congrés d'Història de la Corona d'Aragó dedicat a l'alt rei En Jaume I. Vol. II. Barcelona. 1913.

Huici, A. Colección diplomática de Jaime I el Conquistador. Años 1217 a 1253. 2 vols. Valencia. 1916, 19.

Fragmentum chronicae dominorum regum Aragonum et comitum Barchinonensium. *In* España Sagrada. XLV. *See Gen. Bibl.* IV.

Genealogia dels Rey Daragó e de Navarra e comptes de Barchinona. (Bibl. "La Veu de Monserrat," vol. I.)

Ibarra, E. Cristianos y moros. Documentos aragoneses y navarros. *In* Homenaje a Codera. Saragossa. 1904.

(ii) *Manuscripts.*

Flos mundi. Bibl. Nat., Paris. II. [Ends at 1283.]

Crónica universal desde la creación del mundo hasta Alfonso V de Aragon. Bibl. Nat., Paris. 13.

Domenech, J. Resumen historiale o compilación abreviada de les histories quasi de tota Europa...fins...Pere el Quart. Nat. Lib., Madrid. 186.

Pellicer de Ossau, J. Historia de la casa real de Aragón. Nat. Lib., Madrid. 680.

Briz, J. Historia de la fundación...de San Juan de la Peña y de los Reyes de Sobrarve, Aragón y Navarra. Nat Lib., Madrid. 1225.

C. Modern Works.

(i) *General.*

Blancas, J. de. Aragonensium rerum commentarii. Caesaraugustae. 1588. Spanish transl. Hernandez, P. Manuel. Saragossa. 1878.

—— Coronaciones de los...reyes de Aragón. Con dos tratados del modo de tener Cortes. Saragossa. 1641.

Casaus y Torres, A. Nuevas observaciones para la historia general de Aragón, Navarra y Cataluña. Vol. I. Barcelona. 1829. [No more publ.]
Jimenez de Enbun, T. Ensayo histórico acerca de los origenes de Aragón y Navarra. Saragossa. 1878.
Lafuente, V. de la. Estudios criticos sobre la historia y el derecho de Aragón. 3 vols. Madrid. 1884–6.
Miron, E. L. The Queens of Aragon, their lives and times. London. 1913.
Zurita, J. de. Anales de la Corona de Aragón, 711–1510. 6 vols. Saragossa 1562–80.

(ii) *Monographs.*

Apraiz, O. de. Del origen vasco del reino de Aragon. *In* Bol. Com. Mon. Navarra. XI. 1920.
Arco, R. del. El Obispo de Huesca D. Jaime Sarroca, consejero del rey Don Jaime I. *In* Bol. Acad. Buenas Letras Barcelona. IX. 1917.
Baer, F. Studien zur Geschichte der Juden in Königreich Aragonien während des 13 und 14 Jahrhunderts. Berlin. 1913.
Bofarull, F. de. Jaime I el Conquistador y la comunidad judia de Montpeller. *In* Bol. Acad. Buenas Letras Barcelona. 1909–10.
—— Jaime I y los judios. *In* Congrés d'Història de la Corona d'Aragó dedicat a l'alt rei En Jaume I. Vol. II. Barcelona. 1913.
Bover, J. M. de. Memoria de los pobladores de Mallorca despues de la última conquista por D. Jaime I de Aragón. Palma. 1838.
Capmany, A. de. Práctica y estilo de celebrar Cortes en...Aragon...Cataluña y... Valencia. Madrid. 1821.
Carreras, F. Rebelió de la noblesa catalana contra Jaume I en 1259. *In* Bol. Acad. Buenas Letras Barcelona. VI. 1911–12.
—— La Creuada de Jaume I a Terra Santa (1269–70). *In* Miscelanea Hist. Cat. II.
Danvila, M. Las libertades de Aragón. Madrid. 1881.
Delpech, H. La bataille de Muret et la tactique de la cavalerie au XIIIe siècle. Paris. 1878.
—— Un dernier mot sur la bataille de Muret. Montpellier. 1878.
Dieulafoy, M. Simon de Montfort et la bataille de Muret. *In* Mém. AcadIBL. 1897.
Domingo, C. Estudio critico sobre la conquista de Zaragoza por Alfonso I. Saragossa. 1888.
Dozy, R. Sur l'expédition d'Alphonse le Batailleur contre l'Andalousie. *In* Recherches. 3rd edn. Vol. I. *See above*, II B *under* Dozy.
Gazulla, F. D. Jaime I de Aragón y los Estados musulmanes. Barcelona. 1919.
Ibarra, E. El rey y la nobleza de Aragón en los tiempos primitivos. *In* Rev. de Aragón. II. 1901.
Kern, F. Analekten zur Geschichte des 13 und 14 Jahrhunderts. Eduard I von England und Peter von Aragon. MIOGF. XXX. 1909.
Lafuente, V. de la. La constitución politica de Aragón en 1300. *In* Mem. R. Acad. de Ciencias Moral. y Polít. VIII. Madrid. 1893.
—— Las primeras Cortes de Aragón. *In* Rev. Hisp.-Amer. III. Madrid. 1871.
—— Historia de las tres Comunidades de Aragón. Madrid. 1861.
—— El Privilegio general de Aragón. *In* Rev. Madrid. I. 1881.
Lasala, M. Examen histórico-foral de la Constitución aragonesa. 3 vols. Madrid. 1868.
Lecoy de la Marche, A. La croisade de Mayorque, 1229. RQH. LI. 1892.
Longás, P. Ramiro II el Monje y las supuestas Cortes de Borja y Monzón en 1134. Santoña. 1911.
Martinez, B. Sobrarbe y Aragón. Estudios históricos sobre la fundación y progresos de estos reinos. 2 vols. Saragossa. 1866.
Miret, J. Itinerario del rey Pedro I de Cataluña, II en Aragón. *In* Bol. Acad. Buenas Letras Barcelona. 1905–8.
Oliver, B. La nación y la realeza en los Estados de la Corona de Aragón. Madrid. 1884.
Quinto, J. de. Del juramento politico de los antiguos reyes de Aragón. Madrid. 1848.

Quinto, J. de. Del derecho de suceder las hembras a la corona de Aragón. Madrid. 1840.
—— Respuesta...a D. José Morales Santisteban, autor de un folleto intitulado.... *In* Estudios históricos sobre el reino de Aragón. 1851.
Ribera, J. Origenes del Justicia de Aragón. Saragossa. 1897.
Roehricht, R. Der Kreuzzug des Königs Jakob I von Aragonien (1269). MIOGF. XI. 1890.
Salarrullana, J. El reino moro de Afraga y las últimas campañas y muerte del Batallador. Saragossa. 1909.
Sangorrin, D. La Campana de Huesca. Demostración documentada de la falsedad histórica de esta leyenda. Huesca. 1920.
Sanpere, S. Minoria de Jaime I. Barcelona. 1910.
—— La reconquista de Zaragoza. *In* Bol. Acad. Buenas Letras Barcelona. II. 1903–4.
Swift, F. Darwin. The life and times of James the First, the Conqueror. Oxford. 1894.
—— Marriage alliance of the Infante Pedro of Aragon and Edward I of England. 9 Oct. 1273. EHR. v. 1890.
Tourtoulon, C. de. Jacme Ier le Conquérant. 2 vols. Montpellier. 1863, 67.
—— Les Français aux expéditions de Mayorque et de Valence. *In* Rev. nobiliaire. II. 1866.
Traggia, J. Ilustración del reinado de Don Ramiro II de Aragón. *In* Mem. RAH. III.

VI. CATALONIA, MAJORCA, AND VALENCIA.

A. Bibliographies.

Almarche, F. Historiografia valenciana. Catálogo bibliográfico. Valencia. 1919.
Elias de Molins, A. Bibliografia histórica de Cataluña. *In* Rev. crítica de Hist. y Lit. esp., port., e hispano-americanas. VII. 1902.
—— Los estudios históricos y arqueológicos en Cataluña en el siglo XVIII. Barcelona. 1903.
Morel-Fatio, A. Noticia sobre la colección de documentos relativos a la historia de Cataluña por Jerónimo Pujades, conocidos con el nombre de "Flosculi." *In* Rev. Ciencias histor. Barcelona. II. 1880.
Benicio, F. Estudio sobre la Crónica de Berenguer de Puigpardines. *In* Rev. Ciencias histor. II. 1881. [The Chronicle is one of the 12th century, unpublished.]
Moliné, E. Histories de Catalunya. *In* Renaixement. v. 1914.
Valls, F. Els Estudis d'Historia de la Legislació catalana. *In* Rev. Jurid. Catalunya. XXXI. 1925.
Massó. Historiografia de Cataluña en catalán, durante la época nacional. Paris. 1906.
d'Olwer, N. La cronica del Conqueridor i els seus problemes. *In* Estudis universitaris catalans. XI. 1925.

B. Documents, including Chronicles.

(i) *Published.*

Girbal, E. C. Miscelánea histórica. *In* Rev. Gerona. XIII. 1889. [Gives the text of the "Flosculi" of Pujades.]
Chronicon Barcinonense. I and II. *In* España Sagrada. XXVIII. *See Gen. Bibl.* IV.
Chronicon Durtusense, I and II, *and* Chronicon alterum Rivipullense. Publ. *in* Villanueva, J. L. Viaje literario á las Iglesias de España. v. Madrid. 1806.
Feliu de la Peña y Farell, N. Anales de Cataluña. 3 vols. Barcelona. 1709.
Pujades, J. Crónica universal del Principat de Catallunya. Barcelona. 1609. Modern edn. with Pts. II and III added. Barcelona. 1829.
Gesta veterum Comitum Barcinonensium...scripta circa annum MCCXC a quodam monacho Rivipullensi. (Marca Hispanica. Paris. 1688. Modern edn., with Catalan transl. Barcelona. 1925.)
Barrau-Dihigo, L. Fragments inédits des Gesta Comitum Barcinonensium et Regum Aragoniae. *In* Rev. hisp. IX. 1902.

Boades, B. Libre dels feyts darmes de Catalunya. Barcelona. [1873.]
Diago, F. Historia de los victoriosissimos antiguos condes de Barcelona. Barcelona. 1603.
Colecció de documents historichs inedits del arxiu municipal de...Barcelona. 17 vols. published.
Fita, F. Cortes y usajes de Barcelona en 1064. Textos inéditos. BRAH. XVII. 1890.
Miret, J. and Schwab, M. Documents sur les Juifs catalans aux XIe, XIIe, et XIIIe siècles. *In* Rev. juive. LXVIII. 1914.
—— —— Nuevos documentos de los judios barceloneses de los siglos XI y XII. BRAH. LXVIII, LXIX. 1916.
Rubió, A. Documents per l'Historia de la Cultura Catalana Mig-eval. 2 vols. Barcelona. 1908, 21.
Soler, J. Documents catalans à la Biblioteca de Paris. *In* Rev. Asoc. Art. Arqueol. Barcelonesa. 1905.
Coroleu, J. Colección de documentos catalanes históricos y hasta hoy inéditos. I. Documentos del siglo XIII. *In* Rev. Ciencias hist. Barcelona. V. 1887.
Bosch, A. Summari...dels...Titols d'honor de Catalunya, Rosselló, y Cerdanya, y de les gracies, privilegis, inmunitats... Perpignan. 1618.
Repartimientos de los reinos de Mallorca, Valencia, y Cerdeña. (Colec. doc. ined. Corona Aragón. XI.)

(ii) *Manuscripts.*

Pellicer, J. de. Principio de la conquista de Cataluña. Nat. Lib., Madrid. 11146[14].
Caresmar, P. Memorias cronológico-históricas sacadas de varios Archivos de Cataluña. Roy. Lib., Madrid. 2-Y.-5.
Vila, S. R. Genealogia comitum Barcinone. Nat. Lib., Madrid. 1609.

C. MODERN WORKS.

Aulestia, P. and Moliné, E. História de Catalunya. 2 vols. Barcelona. 1922.
Balaguer, V. Historia de Cataluña y de la Corona de Aragón. 5 vols. Barcelona. 1860–3.
Balari, J. Orígenes históricos de Cataluña. Barcelona. 1899.
Beuter, P. A. Primera parte de la Coronica general de toda España y especialmente del Reyno de Valencia. 2 vols. Valencia. 1604. [This first part, relating in some of its chapters to this period, was printed also in Valencia, 1563.]
Bo, I. Marina catalana medieval. *In* Enciclop. Catalana. Vol. XXXII. Barcelona. 1922.
Bofarull, F. de. Reseña histórica del caracter y desarrollo de los municipios catalanes hasta Felipe V. Villanueva. 1888.
—— Antigua marina catalana. Barcelona. 1898.
—— Los Judíos en el territorio de Barcelona (siglos x al XIII). Reinado de Jaime I (1213–1276). Barcelona. 1911.
Bofarull, F. J. Discurso sobre la constitución que dió al reyno de Valencia su...conquistador...Jaime Primero. Valencia. 1810.
Bofarull, P. de. Tabla cronológica de los Condes soberanos de Barcelona. Barcelona. 1833.
—— Los Condes de Barcelona vindicados. 2 vols. Barcelona. 1836.
Botet, J. Condado de Gerona. Los condes beneficiarios. Gerona. 1890.
Calmette, J. Les origines de la première maison comtale de Barcelonne. Rome. 1890.
Capmany, A. de. Código de las costumbres maritimas de Barcelona...llamado Libro del Consulado. Madrid. 1791.
—— Memorias históricas sobre la marina, comercio, y artes de la antigua ciudad de Barcelona. 2 vols. Madrid. 1779, 92.
Carreras, F. Caciquisme politich en lo segle XIII. *In* Bol. Acad. Buenas Letras Barcelona. III. 1905–6.
—— La institucion del castlá en Catalunya. Barcelona. 1905.

Cauvet, E. Étude historique sur l'établissement des Espagnols dans la Septimanie aux VIIIe et IXe siècles. Montpellier. 1898.
Coroleu, J. El feudalismo y la servidumbre de la gleba en Cataluña. Gerona. 1878.
—— Los Fueros de Cataluña y la sociedad politica moderna. Barcelona. 1888.
—— El Feudalismo en la Gran Bretaña y sus analogias con el del Condado de Barcelona. *In* Rev. España Regional. XII. 1892.
—— and Pella, J. Los Fueros de Cataluña. Barcelona. 1878.
—— —— Las Cortes Catalanas...con muchos documentos inéditos del Archivo de la Corona de Aragón y del Municipio de Barcelona. Barcelona. 1876.
—— —— Lo Sometent. Noticias históricas y juridicas de sa organisació. Barcelona. 1877.
Escolano, G. Década primera de la Historia de la...Ciudad y Reyno de Valencia. 2 vols. Valencia. 1610–11.
Fita, F. El principado de Cataluña. Razón de este nombre. BRAH. XXXIX. 1901.
Hinojosa, E. de. Le "jus primae noctis" et le servage en Catalogne. *In* Ann. internat. d'hist. Paris. 1902.
—— Origen y vicisitudes de la pagesia de remensa en Cataluña. Barcelona. 1902.
—— El régimen señorial y la cuestión agraria en Cataluña durante la Edad Media. Madrid. 1905.
Llobet, J. A. Cataluña antigua y moderna. Obra en la que se trata del Comercio de los catalanes en la Edad Media. Barcelona. 1866.
Melchior, G. Les Établissements des Espagnols dans les Pyrénées Méditerranéennes aux VIIIe et IXe siècles. Montpellier. 1919.
Miret, J. La expansión y dominación catalana en los pueblos de la Galia meridional. Barcelona. 1900.
Oliver, B. Historia del Derecho en Cataluña, Mallorca, y Valencia. 2 vols. Madrid. 1876, 79.
Peguera, L. de. Práctica, forma, y stil de celebrar Corts generals en Catalunya y materies incidents en aquellas. Barcelona. 1632.
Pella, J. Llibertats y antich govern de Catalunya. Barcelona. 1905.
Pons, B. La Carta de Franqueza del Rey En Jaime I constituint el regne de Mallorca. Palma. 1917.
Rodón, F. Fets de la marina de guerra catalana, extrets de las Crónicas de Catalunya. Barcelona. 1898.
Rubió, J. Consideraciones histórico-criticas acerca del origen de la independencia del Condado Catalán. *In* Mem. Acad. Bellas Letras Barcelona. IV. 1887.
Sans, J. Memoria sobre el incierto origen de las barras de Aragón, antiguo blasón del Condado de Barcelona. *In* Mem. RAH. VIII.
Valls, F. Notes per a la Historia de la familia comtal de Barcelona. (Ajuntament de Barcelona. Recull de documents i estudis. III.) 1923.
Valls-Taberner, F. and Soldevila, F. Història de Catalunya. Curs superior. Vols. I, II. Barcelona. 1922–3.

ADDENDUM.

Kehr, P. Papsturkunden in Spanien. Vorarbeiten zur Hispania Pontificia. I. Katalanien. i. Archivberichte. ii. Urkunden und Regesten. *In* Abh. d. k. Gesellschaft d. Wissensch. Philol.-hist. Kl. n.s. XVIII, 2. Göttingen. 1926.

CHAPTER XIII.

(A)

BOHEMIA TO THE EXTINCTION OF THE PŘEMYSLIDS.

I. BIBLIOGRAPHY.

Zíbrt, Č. Bibliografie české historie. (Bibliography of Czech history.) Vols. I and II. Prague, 1900, 2. [Most complete and detailed for this period.]

II. SOURCES.

Codex diplomaticus et epistolaris Moraviae. Ed. Boczek, A. (and others). Vols. I–XV. Olomuc (Olmütz). 1836–45. Brno (Brünn). 1850–1903.

Codex diplomaticus et epistolaris regni Bohemiae. Ed. Friedrich, G. Vol. I in 2 pts. Prague. 1904, 7.

Codex iuris municipalis regni Bohemiae. Ed. Čelakovský, J. 2 vols. Prague. 1886, 95.

Cosmas Pragensis. Chronica Boemorum. Ed. Bretholz, B. MGH. Script. N.S. II. 1923.

Fontes rerum Bohemicarum. Ed. Emler, J. 4 vols. Prague. 1873–82.

Henricus de Isernia. Codex epistolaris Primislai Ottocari II Bohemorum regis. Ed. Dolliner, T. Vienna. 1803.

Henricus Italicus. Das urkundliche Formelbuch des königlichen Notars H. J. aus der Zeit der Könige Ottokar II und Wenzel II von Böhmen. Ed. Voigt, J. *In* Archiv für Kunde österreich. Geschichts-Quellen. XXIX. Vienna. 1863. Also publ. separately. Vienna. 1863.

Novák, T. B. Formulář biskupa Tobiáše z Bechyně 1279–1296. (Formulary of the bishop Tobias of Bechyně.) Prague. 1903.

Redlich, O. Eine Wiener Briefsammlung zur Geschichte des Deutschen Reichs und der österreich. Länder...des 13 Jahrht. Vienna. 1894.

Regesta diplomatica necnon epistolaria Bohemiae et Moraviae. Ed. Erben, C. J. and Emler, J. 4 vols. Prague. 1855 ff.

Ulanowski, B. Neues urkundliches Material zur Geschichte Ottokars II von Böhmen. MIOGF. VI.

III. MODERN WORKS.

A. General History of Bohemia.

Bachmann, A. Geschichte Böhmens. Vol. I (to 1400). (Heeren. *See Gen. Bibl.* V.) Gotha. 1899. [A sober and critical work.]

Bretholz, B. Geschichte Böhmens und Mährens bis zum Aussterben der Přemysliden 1306. Munich and Leipsic. 1912. [Superficial and prejudiced, but yet of value.]

—— Geschichte Mährens. Vol. I in 2 pts. (to 1197). Brünn. 1893, 95. [Critical and good.]

Dudik, B. Mährens allgemeine Geschichte. Vols. I–X (to 1306). Brünn. 1860–83. [Very detailed, but often unreliable.]

Lützow, Francis, Count. Bohemia, an historical sketch. London. 1896. Reprinted *in* Everyman's Library. London. 1909; and 1920.

Maurice, C. E. Bohemia from the earliest times to the fall of national independence in 1620. (Story of the Nations.) London. 1896.

Novotný, V. České dějiny. (Czech history.) Vol. I, 1 (to 1034), I, 2 (1034–1197). Prague. 1912–13. [This very detailed and thorough work, supplied with critical apparatus, is in course of publication.]

Palacký, F. Dějiny národa českého. (History of the Czech people.) Vols. I, 1 (to 1125), I, 2 (1125–1253), II, 1 (1253–1333). Prague. 1848–75. [This classic work of the founder of modern Bohemian historiography, the Czech version of which is thoroughly revised and provided with many valuable additions, is in many parts obsolete but retains great scientific value.]

—— Geschichte von Böhmen. Vols. I (to 1197), II, 1 (1197–1309). Prague. 1836, 39.

Šimák, J. V. Kronika československá (Czechoslovakian Chronicle). Vol. I (to 1306). Prague. 1923. [Popular, but sound and critical.]

Šusta, J. Dvě knihy českých dějin. (Two books of Czech history.) 2 vols. Prague. 1917, 19. [An excellent work on the period of 1300–1320.]

Tadra, F. Kulturni styky Čech s cizinou až do válek husitských. (The cultural relations between Bohemia and the foreign countries until the Hussite wars.) Prague. 1897. [Superficial but containing many details of value.]

Tomek, V. V. Děje království českého. (History of the Kingdom of Bohemia.) Prague. 1850. Many reprints. German transl. Prague. 1865. [Thorough and trustworthy although brief and somewhat antiquated.]

—— Dějepis města Prahy. (History of the city of Prague.) Vol. I (to 1346). Prague. 1855. 2nd edn. Prague. 1891. German transl. Vol. I. Prague. 1856. [An important work giving much of the national history.]

B. Legal, Economic, and Social History.

Čelakovský, J. Povšechné české dějiny právní. (Sketch of Czech legal history.) Prague. 1900. [Very brief, but good.]

Jireček, H. Slovanské právo v Čechách a na Moravě. (Slav law in Bohemia and Moravia.) Vols. I (to 1000), II (11th–13th centuries), III (14th century). Prague. 1863–72. German transl. of the first two volumes: Das Recht in Böhmen und Mähren. Prague. 1866. [Antiquated, but valuable for the systematic arrangement of the evidence from the sources.]

Kapras, J. Právní dějiny zemí koruny české. (Legal history of the lands of the Bohemian crown.) Vols. I and II. Prague. 1913. [Taken as a whole a good compilation of the present results of research, valuable for its exhaustive references to the literature.]

Krofta, K. Přehled dějin selského stavu v Čechách a na Moravě. (Sketch of the history of the peasantry in Bohemia and Moravia.) Prague. 1919.

Lippert, T. Die Socialgeschichte Böhmens in der vorhussitischen Zeit. Vols. I and II. Prague, Vienna, and Leipsic. 1896, 98. [Superficial and inexact, but in some ways useful.]

Peterka, O. Rechtsgeschichte der böhmischen Länder. Vol. I. Reichenberg. 1923. [A conscientious compilation.]

Vacek, F. Sociální dějiny české doby starší. (Czech early social history.) Prague. 1905. [Thorough and valuable, although not methodical; it really treats only of the time up to 1200.]

Yasinski, A. N. Padênie zemskago stroya v cheshskom gosudarstvê X–XII vêkov. (Break-up of the constitution of the Bohemian state of the 10th–12th centuries.) Kiev. 1895. [This valuable Russian work really contains a constitutional history of Bohemia from the 10th to the 12th centuries.]

(B)

POLAND, 1050–1303.

I. BIBLIOGRAPHIES.

Finkel, L. Bibliografia Historyi Polskiej. Cracow. 1906.
Potthast, A. Bibliotheca historica medii aevi. *See Gen. Bibl.* I.
Zeissberg, H. Geschichtsschreibung Polens im Mittelalter. Leipsic. 1873.

II. DOCUMENTS.

Akty istoricheskiye. I and II. St Petersburg. 1841–2.
Bandtkie, J. K. Jus Culmense. Warsaw. 1814.
Berger, E. Les registres d'Innocent IV. *See Gen. Bibl.* IV *under* Papal Documents.
Boczek, A. Codex diplomaticus et epistolaris Moraviae. Olmütz (Olomuc). 1836–78.
Böhmer, J. F. Regesta imperii. *See Gen. Bibl.* IV.
Bule i listy dotyczące Polski. *In* Monumenta medii aevi historica. II. *See below.*
Codex diplomaticus Lubecensis. Lübeck. 1843–84.
Codex diplomaticus Misniensis. Leipsic. 1864.
Codex diplomaticus Silesiae. Breslau. 1857–89.
Codex diplomaticus Tinecensis. Lemberg. 1871.
Dobner, G. Monumenta historica Bohemiae. Prague. 1764–85.
Dogiel, M. Codex diplomaticus regni Poloniae. I. Vilna. 1758.
Epistolae Frederici I. *In* Freher, M. Scriptores rerum Germanicarum aliquot insignes. 3rd edn. Struve, B. G. I. Strasbourg. 1717.
Erben, C. J. and Emler, J. Regesta diplomatica necnon epistolaria Bohemiae et Moraviae. I. Prague. 1855.
Fontes rerum Austriacarum. Abteil. I. Diplomata et Acta. (Hist. Commission. KAW.) Vienna. 1849.
Gawarecki, W. H. Przywileje nadania miastom wojewodztwa plockiego. Warsaw. 1828.
Gersdorf, E. G. Codex diplomaticus Saxoniae regiae. Leipsic. 1864–73.
Geschichtsquellen der Provinz Sachsen. Ed. by Hist. Commission der Provinz Sachsen. Halle. 1870 ff.
Grünhagen, C. Regesten zur schlesischen Geschichte. Breslau. 1876–80.
—— and Markgraf, H. Lehns- und Besitzurkunden Schlesiens. Leipsic. 1881–3.
Hasselbach, K. F. W. and Kosegarten, J. G. L. Codex Pomeraniae diplomaticus. Greifswald. 1842–62.
Hennes, J. H. Codex diplomaticus sanctae Mariae Teutonicorum. I. Mayence. 1845.
Heyne, J. Dokumentirte Geschichte des Bisthums und Hochstifts Breslau. Breslau. 1860–4.
Hube, R. Antiquissimae constitutiones synodales provinciae Gnesnensis. St Petersburg. 1856.
Jabczyński, J. Archiwum teologiczne. Poznań (Posen). 1836–7.
Jaffé, P. Bibliotheca rerum Germanicarum. 6 vols. Berlin. 1864–73.
—— Regesta Pontificum Romanorum. 2nd edn. Wattenbach, W., Loewenfeld, S. 2 vols. Leipsic. 1885, 88.
Jura Judeis per Boleslaum ducem anno 1264. Volumina legum. I. Warsaw. 1732.
Kestner, E. Beiträge z. Gesch. d. Stadt Thorn. Thorn. 1883.
Kętrzyński, W. 30 dokumentów katedry plockiej. Lemberg. 1888.
Köhler, G. Codex diplomaticus Lusatiae superioris. Görlitz. 1851–6.
Lelewel, J. Dyplomata 12 i 13 wieku do prawodawstwa. *In* Roczniki, Towarzystwo Warszawskie Przyjaciól Nauk. Warsaw. 1827.
Lites ac res gestae inter Polonos Ordinemque Cruciferorum. Poznań (Posen). 1855.
Lubomirski, T. J. Kodex diplomatyczny księstwa Mazowieckiego. Warsaw. 1862.
Markgraf, H. and Frenzel, O. Breslauer Stadtbuch. Breslau. 1882.
Monumenta Germaniae Historica. Diplomata regum et imperatorum. Vol. VIII. Berlin. 1927.

Monumenta medii aevi historica res gestas Poloniae illustrantia. 12 vols. (Academia Cracoviensis.) Cracow. 1874 ff.
Monumenta Hungariae historica. *See below,* Bibl. to ch. XIII (c), sect. II.
Mossbach, A. Wiadomości do dziejów polskich. Ostrów. 1860.
Najstarszy dokument Torunia 1231. *In* Przeg. bibliot. arch. Warsaw. 1881.
Paprocki, B. Herby rycerstwa polskiego. Cracow. 1584.
Perlbach, M. Preussische Regesten. Königsberg. 1876.
—— Regesten d. Stadt Königsberg. *In* Altpreussische Monatsschrift. XVIII. Königsberg. 1881.
Pflugk-Harttung, J. Acta pontificum Romanorum inedita. Tübingen. 1880.
Piekosiński, F. Codex diplomaticus civitatis Cracoviensis (1257–1506). *In* Monumenta medii aevi historica. V and VII. *See above.*
—— Codex diplomaticus Poloniae Minoris. *Ibid.* III.
—— and Szujski, J. Libri antiquissimi civitatis Cracoviensis. *Ibid.* IV.
Potthast, A. Regesta Pontificum Romanorum 1198–1304. *See Gen. Bibl.* IV.
Publicationen aus den k. preussischen Staatsarchiv. Leipsic. 1878–89.
Raumer, G. W. Regesta historiae Brandenburgensis. Berlin. 1836.
Regesta Konrada Mazowieckiego. Ed. Perlbach, M. *in* Preussisch-polnische Studien. I. Halle. 1886.
Riedel, A. F. Codex diplomaticus Brandenburgensis. Berlin. 1836.
Rudolff. Codex diplomaticus historiae Megalopolitanae medii aevi. Schwerin. 1780.
Rzyszczewski, L. and Muczkowski, A. Codex diplomaticus Poloniae. Warsaw. 1847–58.
—— Codex diplomaticus majoris Poloniae. Poznań (Posen). 1877–81.
Schirrmacher, F. W. Urkundenbach d. Stadt Liegnitz. Liegnitz. 1868.
Starodawne prawa polskiego pomniki. Cracow. 1857 ff.
Stenzel, G. A. Urkunden z. Gesch. des Bisthums Breslau im Mittelalter. Breslau. 1845.
—— and Tzschoppe, G. H. Urkundensammlung zur Gesch. d. Städte in Schlesien und Ober-Lausitz. Hamburg. 1832.
Strehlke, E. Tabulae Ordinis Teutonici. Berlin. 1869.
Stronczyński. Wzory pism dawnych. Warsaw. 1839.
Theiner, A. Vetera monumenta Poloniae et Lithuaniae ex tabulariis Vaticanis Romae. I. Rome. 1860.
—— Vetera monumenta historica Hungariam illustrantia. Rome. 1859–60.
Ulanowski, B. Dokumenty kujawskie i mazowieckie przeważnie w 13 wieku. Arch. Kom. Hist. IV. Cracow. 1888.
—— O założeniu klasztoru św. Andrzeja w Krakowie. Cracow. 1886.
Urkunden d. Klosters Leubus. Breslau. 1821.
Voigt, J. Codex diplomaticus Prussicus. Königsberg. 1836–61.
Volkmer, F. and Hohaus, W. Urkunden und Regesten d. Grafschaft Glatz. Habelschwerdt. 1883.
Voss, G. Gregorii IX acta. Rome. 1586.
Wiernicke, E. J. Geschichte Thorns. Thorn. 1839–42.
Wierzbowski, T. Synopsis legatorum in Polonia. Rome. 1880.
Woelky, C. P. Urkundenbuch d. Bisthums Culm. Danzig. 1884–7.
Wohlbrück, S. W. Geschichte d. Bisthums Lebus. Berlin. 1829.
Wuttke, H. Städtebuch des Landes Posen. Leipsic. 1864.
Zakrzewski, J. Codex diplomaticus Majoris Poloniae. I. Poznań (Posen). 1877.
Zapisy dla kościola katedralnego w Poznaniu. Archiwum teologiczne. Poznań (Posen). 1836–7.
Zeitschrift d. Vereins f. Geschichte und Alterthum Schlesiens. Breslau. 1856 ff.

III. CHRONICLES ETC.

A. Collections.

Monumenta Germaniae Historica. Scriptores. *See Gen. Bibl.* IV.
Monumenta historiae Warmiensis. Ed. Hist. Verein f. Ermland. Mayence. 1860–89.
Monumenta Poloniae Historica. Vols. I–V. Ed. Bielowski, A. and others. Lemberg. 1864–88.

Pistorius, J. Polonicae Historiae Corpus. 3 vols. Basle. 1582.
Scriptores rerum Livonicarum. I and II. Riga and Leipsic. 1848, 53.
Scriptores rerum Prussicarum. Ed. Hirsch, T., Töppen, M., and Strehlke, E. 5 vols. Leipsic. 1861–74.
Scriptores rerum Silesiacarum. I–II. Ed. Stenzel, G. A. Breslau. 1835 ff.
Sommersberg, F. W. Silesiacarum rerum Scriptores. I–III. Leipsic. 1729–32.
Zeissberg, H. Kleinere Geschichtsquellen Polens im Mittelalter. *In* Archiv für österreich. Geschichte. LV. Vienna. 1877.

B. Separate Chronicles.

Annales Cracovienses. *In* Monumenta Poloniae Historica. II–V. *See above*, A. *Also* MGH. Script. XIX.
Annales Gnesnenses. *Ibid.*
Annales Kamenecenses. *Ibid.*
Annales Lubinenses. *Ibid.*
Annales Mazoviae. *Ibid.*
Annales Majoris Poloniae. *Ibid.*
Annales Polonorum. *Ibid.*
Annales Silesiaci. *Ibid.*
Anonymi Belae regis notarii (1131–96), Historia Hungarica. Ed. Schwandtner, J. G. *In* Scriptores rerum Hungaricarum. Vienna. 1746.
Arndt, W. and Roepell, R. Annales Poloniae. Ed. Pertz, G. H. SGUS. 1866.
Cosmas Pragensis. Chronica Boemorum. Ed. Bretholz, B. MGH. Script. N.S. II. 1923.
Gallus, Martinus. Chronicae Polonorum usque ad a. 1113. *In* Monumenta Poloniae Hist. I. *See above*, A. *Also* MGH. Script. IX.
Ipatievsky Lêtopis. St Petersburg. 1871. [The "Hypatian" text of "Nestor."]
Kadlubek, Vincentius. Historia Polonica. *In* Monumenta Poloniae Hist. II. *See above*, A.
Kéza, Simon de. Chronicon Hungaricum. Vienna. 1833.
Mizler de Kolof. Historiarum Poloniae et magni Ducatus Lithuaniae scriptorum Collectio. I–IV. Warsaw. 1761.
Plano Carpini, J. de. Relation des Mongols ou Tartares. Ed. d'Avezac-Macaya, M. *in* Recueil de Voyages. IV. (Soc. de Géogr., Paris.) Paris. 1839.
Polnoe Sobranie russkikh lêtopisey. (Izd. Arkheograf. Kommiss. I–II.) St Petersburg. 1846–63.
Saxo Grammaticus. Historia Danica. Ed. Müller, P. E., and Velschow, J. M. Copenhagen. 1839–58.
Vita Sancti Stanislai. Ed. Kętrzyński, W. *In* Monumenta Poloniae Hist. IV. *See above*, A.

IV. MODERN WORKS.

A. General.

Abraham, W. Organizacya kościola w Polsce do polowy wieku XII. Lemberg. 1890.
Balzer, O. Corpus iuris polonici medii aevi. Lemberg. 1891.
—— Genealogia Piastów. Cracow. 1895.
Bandtkie, R. Die 4 ersten Herzöge von Schlesien. *In* Schlesische Provinzialblätter. XXXV. Breslau. 1802.
Bobrzyński, M. Dzieje Polski w zarysie. Warsaw. 1887.
—— Geneza spoleczeństwa polskiego. Cracow. 1881.
—— Historya prawa niemieckiego wraz z historyą prawa tego w Polsce. Cracow. 1876.
Dargun, L. O źródlach prawa miast polskich. Cracow. 1888.
Dlugosz, J. Opera omnia. Ed. Przezdziecki, A. Cracow. 1863–87.
Dunin, K. Prawo mazowieckie. Warsaw. 1880.
Fabre, P. La Pologne et la Saint-Siège du X au XIII siècle. Paris. 1896.
Gumplowicz, M. Zur Geschichte Polens im Mittelalter. Innsbruck. 1898.
Historja polityczna Polski. Vol. I. Cracow. 1920.

Hoffman, K. B. Przyczyny podzialu monarchii polskiej. Cracow. 1872.
Hube, R. Prawo polskie w wieku XIII. Warsaw. 1875.
—— Prawo polskie w wieku XIV. Warsaw. 1881.
—— Przywilej żydowski. *In* Biblioteka Warszawska. I. Warsaw. 1880.
Hurter, F. Geschichte Papst Innocenz III. Vols. I and II. 2nd edn. Hamburg. 1838.
Inama-Sternegg, K. T. Deutsche Wirtschaftsgeschichte. Leipsic. 1891–9.
Jaffé, P. Geschichte des Deutschen Reiches unter Lothar dem Sachsen. Berlin. 1843.
Kętrzyński, W. Studya nad dokumentami XII wieku. Cracow. 1891.
—— Prusy a Polska przed przybyciem Krzyżaków. *In* Przewodnik nauk. i lit. Lemberg. 1881.
Krajewski, M. D. Leszek Bialy. Cracow. 1806.
Kulawski, W. Henryk II. Pobożny. Cracow. 1835.
Kunisch, J. G. Herzog Heinrich II. Breslau. 1834.
Kutrzeba, S. Historya ustroju Polski w zarysie. Lemberg. 1908.
Lamprecht, K. Deutsches Wirtschaftsleben im Mittelalter. Leipsic. 1886.
Lebiński, W. Materialy do slownika historycznego języka i starożytności polskich. I. Militaria. Poznań (Posen). 1889.
Lelewel, J. Géographie du moyen âge. Brussels. 1850–7.
—— Polska wieków średnich. Poznań (Posen). 1846–51.
Lewicki, A. Wratyslaw II czeski królem polskim. Przemyśl. 1876.
—— Zarys historyi polskiej. 5th edn. Warsaw. 1913.
Maciejowski, W. A. Historya prawodawstw slowiańskich. Warsaw. 1856–65.
—— Polska aż do pierwszej polowy XVII wieku pod względem obyczajów i zwyczajów. Warsaw. 1842.
Malecki, A. Panowanie Boleslawa Krzywoustego. *In* Dodatek Gaz. lwow. Lemberg. 1873.
—— Testament Boleslawa Krzywoustego. *In* Przewodnik nauk. i lit. Lemberg. 1881.
Pawiński, A. O niemieckom pravie v Polshi i Litvi. St Petersburg. 1871.
Perlbach, M. Preussisch-polnische Studien. Halle. 1886.
Piekosiński, F. Ludność wieśniacza w Polsce w dobie piastowskiej. Cracow. 1896.
—— O lanach w Polsce wieków średnich. *In* Rozprawy...Wydz. hist.-fil. Akad. Um. w Krak. XXI. Cracow. 1888.
Potkański, K. O pochodzeniu wsi polskiej. Ognisko. 1903.
Raumer, F. Geschichte der Hohenstaufen und ihrer Zeit. Leipsic. 1823–5.
Reuter, H. Geschichte Alexanders III und der Kirche seiner Zeit. Leipsic. 1860–4.
Roepell, R. Geschichte Polens. I. (Heeren. *See Gen. Bibl.* V.) Hamburg. 1840.
—— Über die Verbreitung des Magdeburger Stadtrechts. Breslau. 1857.
Romanowski, J. N. De Conradi, Ducis Mazoviae, atque Ordinis Cruciferorum conditione. Poznań (Posen). 1857.
Ropp, G. Deutsche Kolonien im XII und XIII Jahrht. (Univ.-Schr.) Giessen. 1886.
Sartorius, G. Geschichte des Hanseatischen Bundes. Göttingen. 1802–8.
Schirrmacher, F. Kaiser Friedrich II. Göttingen. 1859–65.
Semkowicz, A. Krytyczny rozbior dziejów polskich Jana Dlugosza. Cracow. 1887.
—— Walka o monarchię. Lemberg. 1892.
Smolka, S. Henryk Brodaty. Cracow. 1873.
—— Mieszko Stary i jego wiek. Warsaw. 1881.
—— Obraz historyczny cywilizacyi i spoleczeństwa polskiego w wieku XII. *In* Biblioteka Warszawska. III. Warsaw. 1880.
—— Testament Boleslawa Krzywoustego. Cracow. 1881.
Sokolowski, A. Konrad, książe na Mazowszu i Zakon niemiecki. Poznań (Posen). 1873.
Szajnocha, K. Pierwsze odrodzenie się Polski. Szkic historyczny. Lemberg. 1849.
Szelągowski, A. Chlopi dziedzice w wsiach na prawie polskiem do końca XIII wieku. Lemberg. 1899.
Ulanowski, B. Szkice krytyczne XIII wieku. Cracow. 1886.
Wendt, G. Die Germanisierung der Länder östlich der Elbe. Liegnitz. 1884, 89.
Wojciechowski, T. O rocznikach polskich X–XV wieków. Cracow. 1880.
—— Szkice historyczne XI wieku. Cracow. 1904.

B. Special.

Abraham, W. Pierwszy spór kościelno-polityczny w Polsce. Cracow. 1895.
—— Zjazd łęczycki 1180. *In* Kwartalnik historyczny. Lemberg. 1889.
Bachfeld, G. Die Mongolen in Polen. Innsbruck. 1889.
Baliński, M. i Lipiński, T. Slownik geograficzny. Warsaw. 1880–93.
Balzer, O. Walka o tron krakowski. Cracow. 1894.
Cahun, L. Introduction à l'histoire de l'Asie. Paris. 1896.
Czarnkowski, S. Historya handlu. Warsaw. 1881.
Droba, L. Stosunki Leszka Bialego z Rusią i Węgrami. Cracow. 1881.
Friedrich, H. Die politische Thätigkeit des Bischofs Otto I von Bamberg. Königsberg. 1884.
Gorski, K. Stosunki Kazimierza Sprawiedliwego z Rusią. Lemberg. 1875.
—— O wojskowości polskiej za Piastów. *In* Przegląd powszechny. Dresden. 1897.
Gumplowicz, M. Bischof Baldwin Gallus von Kruszwica. SKAW. cxxxii. 1895.
—— Wyprawa pomorska Boleslawa Śmialego. *In* Ateneum. iv. Warsaw. 1899.
Jekel, F. J. Polens Handelsgeschichte. Vienna and Trieste. 1809.
Karbowiak, A. Dzieje wychowania i szkol w Polsce w wiekach średnich. St Petersburg. 1898.
Krüger, G. Friedrich Barbarossa in seiner Beziehung zu Polen. *In* Mittheilungen aus d. hist. Litteratur. (Hist. Gesellschaft, Berlin.) Berlin. 1896.
Krzyżanowski, S. Diplomy i kancelarya Przemyslawa. Cracow. 1890.
Kutrzeba, S. Urzędy koronne i nadworne w Polsce. *In* Przewodnik nauk. i lit. Lemberg. 1903.
Labęcki, H. Górnictwo w Polsce. Warsaw. 1841.
Lelewel, J. Początkowe prawodawstwo cywilne i kryminalne. Poznań (Posen). 1846–51.
Löschke, T. Die Politik K. Ottokars II gegenüber Schlesien und Polen. *In* Zeitschrift d. Vereins f. Geschichte Schlesiens. xx. Breslau. 1886.
Maciejowski, W. A. Historya rzemiosl i rzemieślników...w Polsce. Warsaw. 1877.
Orpiszewski, L. Odlamek z dziejów Lechii. Paris. 1875.
Osterreich, H. Die Handelsbeziehung der Stadt Thorn zu Polen 1232 bis 1577. *In* Zeitschrift d. Westpreuss. Geschichts-Vereins. xxviii. Danzig. 1891.
Palacký, F. Der Mongolen-Einfall. Prague. 1842.
Piekosiński, F. Sądownictwo w Polsce wieków średnich. *In* Rozprawy...Wydz. hist.-fil. Akad. Um. w Krak. xxxv. Cracow. 1898.
Przezdziecki, A. Pawel z Przemankowa. Warsaw. 1851.
—— and Rastowiecki, E. Wzory sztuki średniowiecznej w dawnej Polsce. Warsaw and Paris. 1853–62.
Romanowski, J. N. O zakonie braci Dobrzyńskich. *In* Biblioteka Warszawska. Warsaw. 1856–7.
Salow, W. Lothar II und das Wendenland. Friedland. 1889.
Stawiski, E. Poszukiwania do historyi rolnictwa krajowego. Warsaw. 1853.
Strakosch-Grassmann, G. Der Einfall der Mongolen in Mittel-Europa. Innsbruck. 1893.
Szajnocha, K. Św. Kinga. Szkice hist. i. Warsaw. 1876.
—— Szlak Batu-Chana. Szkice hist. i. Warsaw. 1876.
Ulanowski, B. Drugi napad Tartarów na Polskę. *In* Rozprawy...Wydz. hist.-fil. Akad. Um. w Krak. xviii. Cracow. 1884.
—— O kilku pomnieszych żródlach do dziejów pierwszego napadn Tartarów. *Ibid.* xvii. 1884.
Volckmann, E. Die älteste geschriebene polnische Rechtsdenkmal. Elbing and Stettin. 1869.
Wojcicki, K. Napad Tartarów. *In* Gazeta lwowska. No. 15. Lemberg. 1879.
Wojciechowski, R. Krótki zarys historyi handlu w Polsce. Cracow. 1839.
Wuttke, H. Ueber Erdkunde und Karten d. Mittelalters. Leipsic. 1853.

(C)

HUNGARY, 1000–1301.

[*Cf.* also the Bibliographies to Bohemia and Poland (*above*). For Dalmatia, Croatia, Transylvania, etc., *see also* the Bibl. to chapters xvii–xviii of Vol. iv.]

I. BIBLIOGRAPHIES.

Bibliographia Hungariae. Vol. i. Historica [1861–1921]. Vol. ii. Geographica-politico-oeconomica. (Ungarische Bibliothek. Ed. Gragger, R. Reihe iii. Hefte 1 and 2.) Berlin. 1923, 26.
Eckhart, F. Introduction à l'histoire hongroise. *See below*, iv a. [Very valuable.]
Kaindl, R. F. Studien zu den ungarischen Geschichtsquellen. Nos. i–xvi Repr. from Archiv für österreich. Geschichte. Vienna. 1894–1902.
Kont, I. La Bibliographie française de la Hongrie (1521–1910). Paris. 1913.
Marczali, H. Ungarns Geschichtsquellen im Zeitalter der Árpáden. Berlin. 1882.
Moravcsik, J. Ungarische Bibliographie der Turkologie und der orientalischen Beziehungen, 1914–25. *In* Körösi-Csoma Archivum. 1926.
Sayous, E. Histoire générale des Hongrois. *See below*, iii.
Ungarische Jahrbücher. Ed. Gragger, R. Berlin. 1921 ff.

II. DOCUMENTARY SOURCES AND COLLECTIONS.

Endlicher, S. L. Rerum Hungaricarum monumenta Arpadiana. Sangalli. 1849.
Fejér, G. Codex diplomaticus Hungariae ecclesiasticus et civilis. 43 vols. Buda-Pest. 1829–44. Chronological table by Knauz, F. 1862. Index by Czinár, M. 1866.
Florianus, M. Historiae Hungaricae fontes domestici. Pt. i. Scriptores. 4 vols. Leipsic and Buda-Pest. 1881–5.
Kukuljevič, I. von. Codex diplomaticus regni Croatiae, Dalmatiae, et Slavoniae. Vol. ii. Agram. 1875.
—— Jura regni Croatiae, Dalmatiae, et Slavoniae. Vol. i. Agram. 1862.
Monumenta hist.-juridica Slavorum meridionalium. Vols. i–ix. Agram. 1895 ff.
Monumenta Hungariae historica. (Published by the Hungarian Academy.) In four series. i. Diplomataria. ii. Scriptores. iii. Monumenta comitialia. iv. Acta extera. Buda-Pest. 1857 ff.
Monumenta Hungariae juridico-historica. Corpus statutorum Hungariae municipalium. 5 vols. Buda-Pest. 1885–97.
Monumenta spectantia historiam Slavorum meridionalium. Agram. 1868 ff.
Monumenta Vaticana historiam regni Hungariae illustrantia. Series i. Vols. i–vi. Buda-Pest. 1885 ff. [*See also* Papal Documents in *Gen. Bibl.* iv.]
Pauler, G. and Szilágyi, S. A Magyar honfoglalás kútföi (Sources for the occupation of Hungary by the Magyars). Buda-Pest. 1900.
Schwandtner, J. G. Scriptores rerum Hungaricarum, etc. 3 vols. Vienna. 1746–8.
Smičiklas, T. Codex diplomaticus regni Croatiae, Dalmatiae, et Slavoniae. Vols. i–xiii. Agram. 1904 ff.
Teutsch, G. D. and Firnhaber, F. Urkundenbuch zur Geschichte Siebenbürgens. Vol. i. (Fontes rerum Austriacarum. Abt. ii. Vol. xv.) Vienna. 1857.
Theiner, A. Vetera monumenta historica Hungariam sacram illustrantia. 2 vols. Rome. 1859–60.
Wenzel, G. Codex diplomaticus Arpadianus continuatus. 12 vols. Buda-Pest. 1857.
Zimmermann, F., Werner, C. and Müller, G. E. Urkundenbuch zur Geschichte der Deutschen in Siebenbürgen. Vols. i–iii (1191–1415). Hermannstadt. 1892–1902.

III. NARRATIVE SOURCES.

Albericus monachus Trium-Fontium. Chronica. Ed. Scheffer-Boichorst, P. MGH. Script. XXIII. 1874.
Annales Posonienses. Ed. Arndt, W. MGH. Script. XIX. 1866.
Chronica Hungarorum (Chronicon Budense). Ed. Podhradczky, J. Buda-Pest. 1838. [*Cf.* the edn of Chronicon Dubnicense, ed. Florianus.]
Chronicon Dubnicense. Ed. Florianus, M. *in* Hist. Hungar. fontes domestici. Pt. I. Vol. III. *See above*, II.
Chronicon pictum Vindobonense. *Ibid.* Pt. I. Vol. II.
Chronicon Posoniense. *Ibid.* Pt. I. Vol. IV.
Cosmas Pragensis. Chronica Boemorum. Ed. Bretholz, B. MGH. Script. N.S. II. 1923.
Gallus, Martinus. Chronicae Polonorum. MGH. Script. IX. 1851.
Heinrich von Muglen. Chronik. Ed. Kovachich, M.G. *in* Sammlung kleiner noch ungedruckter Stücke. I. Ofen (Buda-Pest). 1805.
Kéza, Simon de. Chronicon Hungaricum. Ed. Endlicher, S.L. *in* Rerum Hungar. monumenta Arpad. *See above*, II. *Also* ed. Florianus, M. *in* Hist. Hungar. fontes domestici. Pt. I. Vol. II. *See above*, II.
Planctus destructionis regni Ungariae per Tartaros. Ed. Marczali, H. *in* Neu. Arch. II. 1877. *Also in* MGH. Script. XXIX. 1892.
Rogerius magister. Miserabile carmen super destructione regni Hungariae. Ed. Florianus, M. *in* Hist. Hungar. fontes domestici. Pt. I. Vol. IV. *See above*, II. *Also* ed. Heinemann, L. de. MGH. Script. XXIX. 1892.
Thomas Spalatensis archidiaconus. Historia Salonitanorum pontificum. Ed. Schwandtner, J. G. *in* Script. rerum Hungar. III. *See above*, II. *Also in* Mon. spect. hist. Slavorum merid. XXVI. *See above*, II.
Vincentius (Kadlubek) Cracoviensis episcopus. Historica Polonica. *In* Monumenta Poloniae Historica. II. (*See above*, Bibl. to ch. XIII (B), sect. III A.) Extracts *in* MGH. Script. XXIX.
Vita S. Emerici ducis. ASBoll. Nov. (die 4) II. *Also* ed. Endlicher, S. L. *in* Rerum Hungar. monumenta Arpad. *See above*, II.
Vita S. Gerardi episcopi Chanadensis. ASBoll. Sept. (die 24) VI. *Also* ed. Endlicher, S. L. *op. cit.*
Vita S. Ladislai regis. ASBoll. Junii (die 27) V. *Also* ed. Endlicher, S. L. *op. cit.*
Vita B. Margaritae. ASBoll. Jan. (die 28) II.
Vita S. Stephani. MGH. Script. XI.
—— auctore Hartwico. ASBoll. Sept. (die 2) I. *Also in* MGH. Script. XI.
Vita SS. Zoerardi dicti Andreae et Benedicti auctore Mauro. ASBoll. Julii (die 17) IV. *Also* ed. Endlicher, S. L. *op. cit.*

IV. MODERN WORKS.

A. GENERAL.

Acsády, I. A magyar birodalom története (History of the Magyar Empire). 2 vols. Buda-Pest. 1903.
Boldényi, J. La Hongrie ancienne et moderne. Paris. 1851.
Csánki, D. *ed.* Árpád és az Árpádok. Buda-Pest. 1909.
Csuday, E. Die Geschichte der Ungarn. 2nd edn. German transl. Dorvai, M. 2 vols. Berlin. 1899.
Domanovszky, A. Die Geschichte Ungarns. Munich. 1923.
Eckhart, F. Introduction à l'histoire hongroise. (Bibliothèque d'études hongroises, I.) Paris. 1928.
Gelléri, M. Ungarns Millennium. Aus der Vergangenheit und Gegenwart des tausendjährigen Ungarn. Buda-Pest. 1896.
Horváth, M. Magyarország történelme (History of Hungary). Buda-Pest. 1871–3.
Huber, A. Geschichte Österreichs. Vols. I–V. (Heeren. *See Gen. Bibl.* V.) Gotha. 1885–96.

Knatchbull-Hugessen, C. M. (Lord Brabourne). The political evolution of the Hungarian nation. 2 vols. London. 1908.
Kont, G. La Hongrie littéraire et scientifique. Paris. 1896.
Leger, L. La Save, le Danube, et le Balkan. Paris. 1884.
Mailáth, J. G. Geschichte der Magyaren. 2nd edn. 5 vols. Regensburg. 1852–3.
Marczali, H. Ungarische Verfassungsgeschichte. Tübingen. 1910.
Mazuchelli, N. E. Magyarland. 2 vols. London. 1881.
Pauler, G. A Magyar nemzet története az Árpádházi királyok alatt (History of the Magyar nation during the Arpad dynasty). 2nd edn. 2 vols. Buda-Pest. 1899.
Pulszky, F. Magyarország Archaeologiaja (The archaeology of Hungary). 2 vols. Buda-Pest. 1897.
Sayous, E. Histoire générale des Hongrois. 2 vols. Paris. 1876. 2nd edn. Sayous, A. E. and Dolenecz, J. Buda-Pest and Paris. 1900. [The 2nd edn is both abridged and enlarged. Now obsolescent.]
Szalay, L. Geschichte Ungarns. German transl. Wögerer, H. 3 vols. Buda-Pest. 1870–5.
Szekfü, J. Der Staat Ungarn. Stuttgart and Berlin. 1918.
Szilágyi, S. and others. A magyar nemzet története (History of the Magyar nation). 10 vols. Buda-Pest. 1895–8.
Temperley, H. W. V. Essay on the earlier history of Hungary. *In* Marczali, H. Hungary in the eighteenth century. Cambridge. 1910.
Timon, A. V. Ungarische Verfassungs- und Rechtsgeschichte mit Bezug auf die Rechtsentwickelung der westlichen Staaten. German transl. Schiller, A. v. 2nd edn. Berlin. 1909.
Vámbéry, Á. Hungary in ancient and modern times. (Story of the Nations.) London. 1887.

B. Special.

Domanovszky, S. [*i.e.* A.]. A trónöröklés kérdéséhez az Árpádok korában. *In* Budapesti Szemle. 1913.
Eckhardt, A. L'énigme du plus ancien historien hongrois. *In* Revue des études hongroises. III. 1925.
Erdélyi, L. Árpádkori társadalom-történetünk legkritikusabb kérdései (The most difficult questions of Hungarian social history at the time of the Arpad dynasty). *In* Történeti Szemle. 1914–16.
—— Az aranybulla társadalma (Society at the time of the Golden Bull). *In* Fejérpataky-emlékkönyv. Buda-Pest. 1917.
Fest, A. I primi rapporti della nazione ungherese coll' Italia. *In* Corvina. III and IV. Buda-Pest. 1922.
Fraknói, V. A királyi trónöröklés rendje az Árpádok korában. (The order of succession to the throne in the time of the Arpad dynasty). *In* Kath. Szemle. 1913.
Gombocz, Z. Ossètes et Iazyges. *In* Revue des études hongroises et finno-ougriennes. III. 1925.
Hóman, B. Magyar Pénztörténet, 1000–1325 (Numismatic history of Hungary, 1000–1325). Buda-Pest. 1916.
—— A magyarok honfoglalása és elhelyezkedése (The conquest of Hungary by the Hungarians and their settlement). Buda-Pest. 1923.
—— La première période de l'historiographie hongroise. *In* Revue des études hongroises. III. 1925.
Kaindl, R. F. Geschichte der Deutschen in den Karpathenländern. 3 vols. Gotha. 1907–11.
Karácsonyi, J. Halavány vonások hazánk Szent István-kori határairól (Sketch of the frontiers of our country at the time of St Stephen). *In* Századok. (Magyar Tört. Társulat.) Buda-Pest. 1901.
Károlyi, Á. Az Árpádok, mint a magyar nemzeti királyság és társadalom szervezöi (The Árpadians as organisers of the Hungarian kingship and society). *In* Árpád és az Árpádok. Ed. Csánki, D. *See above,* IV A.
Mályusz, E. Turócmegye kialakulása (The formation of the county of Turoc). Buda-Pest. 1922.
Melich, J. Bulgárok és szlávok. *In* Magyar Nyelv. XVII.

Melich, J. Ahonfoglaláskori Magyarország (Hungary at the time of the conquest). Buda-Pest. 1925.
Pais, D. Les rapports franco-hongrois sous le règne des Árpád. *In* Revue des études hongroises. I. Paris. 1923.
Píč, J. L. Ueber die Abstammung der Rumänen. Leipsic. 1888.
Picot, E. Les Serbes de Hongrie. Prague. 1873. [Originally published anonymously.]
Schünemann, K. Die Deutschen in Ungarn bis zum 12 Jahrhundert. (Ungarische Bibliothek. Ed. Gragger, R. Reihe I. Heft 8.) Berlin. 1923.
Szekfü, G. Serviensek és familiarisok (*Servientes* and *familiares*). *In* Magyar Tud. Akad. Értek. Buda-Pest. 1913.
Tagányi, K. Gyepü és gyepüelve (The Hungarian marches). *In* Magyar Nyelv. 1913.
—— A földközösség története Magyarországon (History of the community of lands in Hungary). *In* Gazd. Történeti Szemle. Buda-Pest. 1894.
—— A honfoglalás és a királyi vármegyék (The Magyar conquest and the royal counties). *In*
—— A nemesi önkormányzatu vármegyék megalakulása (The formation of the autonomous counties of the nobles). *Ibid.*
—— Vármegyéink eredetének kérdése (The question of the origin of our counties). *In* Történeti Szemle. 1913.
—— Lebende Rechtsgewohnheiten und ihre Sammlung in Ungarn. (Ungarische Bibliothek. Ed. Gragger, R. Reihe I. Heft 3.) Berlin. 1922.
—— Vázlatok a régibb Árpádkor társadalom történetéből (Sketches on the history of society under the first Arpadians). *In* Társadalomtudomány. 1923.
Teutsch, G. D. Geschichte der siebenbürger Sachsen. Vol. I. 3rd edn. Teutsch, F. Hermannstadt. 1899.
Váczy, P. A királyi serviensek és a patrimoniális királyság (The royal *servientes* and the patrimonial kingship). Buda-Pest. 1928.

On the non-Magyar peoples there may be consulted the great Czech encyclopaedia, Prague, 1888–1909. (Especially the articles "Roumanians," "Slovaks," and "Jugo-Slavs.")

CHAPTER XIV.

COMMERCE AND INDUSTRY IN THE MIDDLE AGES.

The select bibliography given below contains (i) important modern works from which bibliographical information may be procured, (ii) a few older works which have never been superseded, (iii) a limited number of articles from journals dealing with points of special novelty or importance, (iv) a very few original authorities, inserted because quotations from them appear in the text of the chapter. No attempt has been made to include works dealing with countries or aspects of the subject which are not referred to, or are only referred to incidentally, in the text. The bibliography is a bibliography of the chapter, not of medieval economic history.

I. GENERAL.

Avenel, Vicomte G. d'. Histoire économique de la propriété...et de tous les prix... depuis l'an 1200. 4 vols. Paris. 1894–8.
Below, G. von. Probleme der Wirtschaftsgeschichte. Berlin. 1923.
Boissonnade, P. Le Travail dans l'Europe chrétienne au moyen âge. Paris. 1921. Eng. transl. Power, E. E. London. 1927.
Brentano, L. Die Anfänge des modernen Kapitalismus. Munich. 1916.
Bücher, K. Die Entstehung der Volkswirtschaft. Leipsic. 1893.
Cunningham, W. An essay on Western Civilization in its economic aspects. 2 vols. Cambridge. 1898.
Dopsch, A. Die Wirtschaftsentwicklung der Karolinger Zeit. 2nd edn. 2 vols. Weimar. 1922.
—— Wirtschaftliche und soziale Grundlagen der europäischen Kulturentwicklung. 2 vols. Vienna. 1920, 23.
Handwörterbuch der Staatswissenschaften. Ed. Conrad, J., Elster, L., Lexis, W., and Loening, E. 3rd edn. 8 vols. Jena. 1909–11.
Jannet, C. Les grandes époques de l'histoire économique jusqu'à la fin du 16e siècle. Paris. 1896.
Kötzschke, R. Allgemeine Wirtschaftsgeschichte des Mittelalters. Jena. 1924.
Kowalewsky, M. Die ökonomischen Entwicklung Europas bis zum Beginn der kapitalistischen Wirtschaftsform. 8 vols. Berlin. 1901–14.
Pirenne, H. Les Villes du moyen âge. Brussels. 1926. Transl. Halsey, F. D. *as* Medieval cities; their origins and the revival of trade. Princeton. 1925.
Schmoller, G. Die geschichtliche Entwickelung der Unternehmung. *In* Jahrb. für Gesetzgebung etc. n.s. Leipsic. 1890 ff.
Sombart, W. Der moderne Kapitalismus. 3rd edn. 4 vols. Munich and Leipsic. 1919.
—— Krieg und Kapitalismus. Munich and Leipsic. 1913.
—— Luxus und Kapitalismus. Munich and Leipsic. 1913.
Weber, M. Wirtschaftsgeschichte. Munich and Leipsic. 1923.

II. HISTORIES OF COUNTRIES, AREAS, AND TOWNS.

Arias, G. Il sistema della costituzione economica e sociale italiana nell' età dei comuni. Turin and Rome. 1905.
Ashley, W. J. An Introduction to English Economic History and Theory. 2 vols. 1888, 93. [Many later edns.]
Blok, P. J. Geschiedenis van het Nederlandsche volk. Vol. I. The Hague. 1892. English transl. Bierstadt, O. A. and Putnam, R. New York. 1898.
Bonn, M. J. Die englische Kolonisation in Irland. 2 vols. Stuttgart and Berlin. 1906.
Bothe, F. Beiträge zur Wirthschafts- und Sozial-Geschichte der Reichsstadt Frankfurt. Leipsic. 1906.
Brentano, L. Die byzantinische Volkswirtschaft. *In* Jahrb. für Gesetzgebung etc. XLI. Leipsic. 1917.

Brodnitz, G. Englische Wirtschaftsgeschichte. Jena. 1918.
Capmany y de Montpalau, Antonio de. Memorias historicas sobre la marina, commercio, y artes de...Barcelona. 4 vols. Madrid. 1779–92.
Cunningham, W. The growth of English Industry and Commerce. Early and Middle Ages. *See Gen. Bibl.* v.
Davidsohn, R. Geschichte von Florenz. 4 vols. Berlin. 1896.
Doren, A. Studien aus d. florentiner Wirthschaftsgesch. 2 vols. Stuttgart. 1901, 8.
Fagniez, G. Documents relatifs à l'histoire de l'industrie et du commerce en France [au moyen âge]. 2 vols. (Coll. textes.) Paris. 1898, 1900.
Germain, E. Histoire du commerce de Montpellier. 2 vols. Paris. 1861.
Gothein, E. Die Kulturentwicklung Sud-Italiens. Breslau. 1886.
—— Wirtschaftsgeschichte des Schwarzwaldes. Strasbourg. 1882.
Häbler, K. Die wirthschaftliche Blüte Spaniens im 16en Jahrhundert und ihr Verfall. Berlin. 1888.
—— Der hansisch-spanische Konflikt von 1419 und die älteren spanischen Bestände. *In* Hansische Geschichtsblätter. Leipsic. 1895.
Häpke, R. Brugges Entwicklung zum mittelalterlichen Weltmarkt. Berlin. 1908.
Heynen, R. Zur Entstehung des Kapitalismus in Venedig. Stuttgart and Berlin. 1905.
Inama-Sternegg, K. T. von. Deutsche Wirtschaftsgeschichte. 3 vols. Leipsic. 1879–1901.
Kretschmayr, H. Geschichte von Venedig. *See Gen. Bibl.* v.
Lamprecht, K. Deutsches Wirtschaftsleben im Mittelalter. 4 vols. Leipsic. 1886.
Levasseur, E. Histoire des classes ouvrières et de l'industrie en France avant 1789. 2 vols. Paris. 1900–1.
Lipson, E. Economic History of England. The Middle Ages. London. 1915.
Michel, F. Hist. du commerce et de la navigation à Bordeaux. 2 vols. Bordeaux. 1867.
Pirenne, H. Histoire de Belgique. Vols. I, II. *See Gen. Bibl.* v.
—— Les anciennes démocraties des Pays-Bas. Brussels. 1910. Engl. transl. Saunders, J. V. Manchester. 1915.
Sieveking, H. Die kapitalistische Entwicklung in den italienischen Städten des Mittelalters. *In* Viert. für Sozial- und Wirtschaftsgesch. VII. Leipsic. 1909.
Steffen, G. F. Studien zur Geschichte der englischen Lohnarbeiter. 3 vols. Stuttgart. 1901–5.

III. POPULATION.

Andréadès, A. De la population de Constantinople sous les empereurs byzantins. *In* Metron. I, 2. Padua. 1921.
Beloch, J. Die Bevölkerung Europas im Mittelalter. *In* Zeitschrift für Sozial- und Wirthschaftsgesch. III. p. 405. Freiburg-i.-B. 1894.
Bücher, K. Die Bevölkerung von Frankfurt am M. im 14en und 15en Jahrhundert. Tübingen. 1886.
—— Die Frauenfrage im Mittelalter. Tübingen. 1910.
Levasseur, E. Histoire de la population française avant 1789.... 3 vols. Paris. 1889–92.
Pardi, G. Disegno della storia demografica di Firenze. ASI. 1915.
Sée, H. Peut-on évaluer la population de l'ancienne France? *In* Revue d'économie politique. Paris. 1924.

IV. AGRARIAN INSTITUTIONS.

Allard, P. Les Origines du servage en France. Paris. 1913.
Caggese, R. Classi e comuni rurali nel medio evo italiano. 2 vols. Florence. 1907–8.
Delisle, L. Études sur la condition de la classe agricole...en Normandie au moyen âge. Paris. 1903. [Reprint of the edition of 1851.]
Douglas, D. C. The social structure of Medieval East Anglia. (Oxford Studies in Social and Legal Hist. IX.) Oxford. 1927.
Gonner, E. C. K. Common Land and Inclosure. London. 1910.
Gray, H. L. English Field Systems. Cambridge, Mass. 1915.
Jolliffe, J. E. A. Northumbrian Institutions. EHR. XLI (1926). p. 1.
Klein, J. The Mesta, a study in Spanish economic history. Cambridge, Mass. 1920.
Lodge, E. C. The Estates of the Archbishop and Chapter of Saint-André of Bordeaux under English Rule. *In* Oxford Studies in Soc. and Leg. Hist. III. Oxford. 1912.

Maitland, F. W. Domesday Book and Beyond. Cambridge. 1897.
Meitzen, A. Siedelung und Agrarwesen der Westgermanen und Ostgermanen, der Kelten, Römer, Finnen, und Slawen. 4 vols. Berlin. 1895.
Prothero, R. E. [Lord Ernle]. English Farming past and present. London. 1912.
Rogers, J. E. T. History of Agriculture and Prices in England. Vols. I–III. Oxford. 1866–92.
Sée, H. Les Classes rurales et le régime domanial en France au moyen âge. Paris. 1901.
Seebohm, F. The English Village Community. London. 1883.
—— The Tribal System in Wales. London. 1896.
Siebeck, O. Der Frondienst als Arbeitssystem, seine Entstehung und seine Ausbreitung im Mittelalter. Tübingen. 1904.
Stenton, F. M. Types of Manorial Structure in the Northern Danelaw. *In* Oxford Studies in Social and Legal History. Vol. II. Oxford. 1910.
—— Documents illustrative of the social and economic history of the Danelaw. (British Academy.) London. 1920.
Vinogradoff, P. The Growth of the Manor. London. 1905.
—— English Society in the eleventh century. Oxford. 1908.

V. INDUSTRIAL AND URBAN INSTITUTIONS.

Beck, L. Die Geschichte des Eisens. 4 vols. Brunswick. 1891–9.
Bennett, R. and Elton, J. The History of Corn Milling. 4 vols. London. 1898–1904.
Broglio d'Ajano, Count. Die venetianische Seidenindustrie und ihre Organisation bis zum Ausgang des Mittelalters. Stuttgart and Berlin. 1893.
Chapman, F. R. The Sacrist Rolls of Ely. Cambridge. 1907.
Des Marez, G. Les luttes sociales en Flandre au moyen âge. Brussels. 1900.
—— L'Organisation du travail à Bruxelles au 15e siècle. Brussels. 1905.
—— L'Apprentissage à Ypres à la fin du 13e siècle. *In* Revue du Nord. Paris. 1911.
—— La première étape de la formation corporative. *In* Bulletin de l'Acad. roy. de Belgique. Brussels. 1921.
Doren, A. Deutsche Handwerker und Handwerksbruderschaften im mittelalterlichen Italien. Berlin. 1903.
Dunlop, J. and Denman, R. D. English Apprenticeship and Child Labour. London. 1912.
Eberstadt, R. Das französische Gewerberecht...vom 13en Jahrhundert bis 1581. Leipsic. 1899.
Espinas, G. Jehan Boine Broke, bourgeois et drapier Douaisien. *In* Viert. für Social- und Wirtschaftsgesch. II. Leipsic. 1904.
—— La Vie urbaine de Douai au moyen-âge. 4 vols. Paris. 1914.
—— and Pirenne, H. Recueil de documents relatifs à l'histoire de l'industrie drapière en Flandre. 2 vols. Brussels. 1907, 9.
Green, A. S. Town Life in the fifteenth century. 2 vols. London. 1894.
Gross, C. The Gild Merchant. 2 vols. Oxford. 1890.
Heaton, H. The Yorkshire Woollen and Worsted Industries. Oxford. 1920.
Hemmeon, M. de W. Burgage Tenure in Mediaeval England. Cambridge, Mass. 1914.
Lewis, G. R. The Stannaries, a study of the English tin mines. Cambridge, Mass. 1908.
Lipson, E. The History of the English Woollen and Worsted Industries. London. 1921.
Maitland, F. W. Township and Borough. Cambridge. 1898.
Martin-Saint-Léon, E. Histoire des corporations de métiers.... Paris. 1897.
—— Le Compagnonnage. Paris. 1901.
Mispoulet, J. B. Le Régime des mines à l'époque romaine et au moyen âge. Paris. 1908.
Pariset, E. Histoire de la fabrique lyonnaise. Lyons. 1901.
Püschel, A. Das Anwachsen der deutschen Städte in der Zeit der mittelalterlichen Kolonialbewegung. Berlin. 1910.
Salzman, L. F. English Industries of the Middle Ages. Oxford. 1923.
Schmoller, G. Die strassburger Tücher- und Weberzunft. Strasbourg. 1879.
Scott, J. F. Historical essays on Apprenticeship. Ann Arbor. 1914.
Sellers, M. *ed.* The York Memorandum Book. (Surtees Soc.) 2 vols. Durham. 1911, 14.

Stöckle, A. Spätrömische und byzantinische Zünfte. Leipsic. 1911.
Swank, J. M. History of the manufacture of iron in all ages. Philadelphia. 1892.
Tout, T. F. Medieval town-planning. *In* Bulletin of the John Rylands Library. iv. Manchester. 1917.
Unwin, G. The Gilds and Companies of London. London. 1908.
Volpe, G. Montieri: constituzione...e attività economica d'una terra mineraria toscana nel 13 secolo. *In* Viert. f. Sozial- und Wirtschaftsgesch. vi. Leipsic. 1908.

VI. COMMERCE, CURRENCY, AND FINANCE.

Bourquelot, F. Études sur les foires de Champagne...aux 13e et 14e siècles. 2 vols. Paris. 1865.
Byrne, E. H. Genoese Trade with Syria in the Twelfth Century. AHR. xxv (1920). p. 191.
Davidson, J. and Gray, A. The Scottish Staple at Veere. London. 1909.
Gauthier, L. Les Lombards dans les Deux-Bourgognes. Paris. 1907.
Goldschmidt, L. Universalgeschichte des Handelsrechts. Stuttgart. 1891.
Gras, N. S. B. The evolution of the English Corn Market from the twelfth to the eighteenth century. Cambridge, Mass. 1915.
—— The Early English Customs System. Cambridge, Mass. 1918.
Gray, H. L. The Production and Exportation of English Woollens in the fourteenth century. EHR. xxxix (1924). p. 13.
Gross, C. Select Cases in the Law Merchant. (Selden Soc.) London. 1908.
Heyd, W. Histoire du Commerce du Levant au moyen-âge. *See Gen. Bibl.* v.
Hoffmann, M. Die Geldhandel der deutschen Juden während des Mittelalters. Leipsic. 1910.
Huvelin, P. Essai historique sur le droit des marchés et des foires. Paris. 1897.
Kalischer, E. Handelsgeschichte der Klöster. Berlin. 1911.
Mollat, G. La Fiscalité pontificale en France au 14e siècle. Paris. 1905.
Nagl, A. Die Goldwährung und die handelsmässige Goldrechnung im Mittelalter. *In* Numismatische Zeitschrift. xxvi. Vienna. 1895.
Pegolotti, F. B. La pratica della mercatura. *In* Pagnini dal Ventura, G. F. Della Decima. Vol. iii. Lisbon and Lucca. 1766.
Peruzzi, S. L. Storia del commercio e dei banchieri di Firenze. Florence. 1868.
Power, E. E. The English Wool Trade in the reign of Edward IV. *In* Cambridge Hist. Journal. ii. Cambridge. 1926. p. 17.
Rhodes, W. E. The Italian bankers in England and their loans to Edward I and Edward II. *In* Owens College Essays. Ed. Tout, T. F. and Tait, J. Manchester 1902.
Sagher, H. E. de. L'Immigration des tisserands Flamands et Brabançons en Angleterre sous Édouard III. *In* Mélanges d'histoire offerts à H. Pirenne. i. Brussels. 1926. p. 109.
Schaube, A. Handelsgeschichte der romanischen Völker. *See Gen. Bibl.* v.
—— Die Wollausfuhr Englands vom Jahre 1273. *In* Viert. für Sozial- und Wirtschaftsgesch. ii. Leipsic. 1908.
Schulte, A. Geschichte des mittelalterlichen Handels und Verkehrs zwischen Westdeutschland und Italien. 2 vols. Leipsic. 1900.
—— Geschichte der grossen ravensburger Handelsgesellschaft, 1380–1530. 3 vols. Stuttgart and Berlin. 1923.
Shaw, W. A. The History of Currency, 1252–1894. London. 1895.
Simonsfeld, E. Der Fondaco dei Tedeschi in Venedig. 2 vols. Stuttgart. 1887.
Sombart, W. Die Juden und das Wirtschaftsleben. Leipsic. 1911.
Terry, S. B. The financing of the Hundred Years' War. London. 1914.
Unwin, G. *ed.* Finance and Trade under Edward III. Manchester. 1918.
Uzzano, G. di A. da. La pratica della mercatura. *In* Pagnini dal Ventura, G. F. Della Decima. Vol. iv. Lisbon and Lucca. 1766.
Werveke, H. van. Note sur le commerce du plomb au moyen âge. *In* Mélanges... H. Pirenne. ii. Brussels. 1926. p. 653.
Yver, G. Le Commerce et les marchands dans l'Italie méridionale au 13e et 14e siècle. Paris. 1903.

CHAPTER XV.

NORTHERN TOWNS AND THEIR COMMERCE.

I. SOURCES.

There does not exist in any country a complete collection of the sources of Town-Law. The following may be cited:

Ballard, A. British Borough Charters, 1042–1216. Cambridge. 1913.
Gaupp, E. T. Deutsche Stadtrechte des Mittelalters. 2 vols. Breslau. 1851–2.
Gengler, H. G. Deutsche Stadtrechte des Mittelalters. Erlangen. 1852; Nuremberg. 1866.
—— Codex juris municipalis Germaniae medii aevi. Vol. I. Erlangen. 1863.
Giry, A. Documents sur les relations de la royauté avec les villes en France de 1180 à 1314. Paris. 1885.
Keutgen, F. Urkunden zur städtischen Verfassungsgeschichte. (Below-Keutgen. Ausgewählte Urkunden. I.) Berlin. 1899.

II. MODERN WORKS.

[In this bibliography many obsolete works are omitted. The most important of these are described in Pirenne, H. L'origine des constitutions urbaines au moyen âge. RH. LIII. 1893.

For England *cf.* Tait, J. The study of early municipal history in England. *In* Proceedings of the British Academy. x. London. 1922.

Monographs on the history of single towns are not given here. Lists of these are to be found in the bibliographies of the history of the separate countries of Europe. For England *see* Gross, C. Bibliography of British Municipal History. New York. 1897.]

(*a*) Germany.

Below, G. v. Zur Entstehung der deutschen Stadtverfassung. HZ. LVIII, LIX.
—— Die Entstehung der deutschen Stadtgemeinde. Düsseldorf. 1889.
—— Der Ursprung der deutschen Stadtverfassung. Düsseldorf. 1892.
Doren, A. J. Untersuchungen zur Geschichte der Kaufmannsgilden des Mittelalters. Leipsic. 1893.
Gerlach, W. Die Entstehungszeit der Stadtbefestigungen in Deutschland. Leipsic. 1913.
Hegel, K. Städte und Gilden der germanischen Völker im Mittelalter. 2 vols. Leipsic. 1891.
—— Entstehung des deutschen Städtewesens. Leipsic. 1898.
Keutgen, F. Untersuchungen über den Ursprung der deutschen Stadtverfassung. Leipsic. 1895.
Rietschel, S. Die Civitas auf deutschem Boden. Leipsic. 1894.
—— Markt und Stadt in ihrem rechtlichen Verhältniss. Leipsic. 1897.
—— Das Burggrafenamt. Leipsic. 1905.
Sohm, R. Die Entstehung des deutschen Städtewesens. Leipsic. 1890.

(*b*) France.

Blanchet, A. Les Enceintes romaines de la Gaule. Paris. 1907.
Bonvalot, E. Le Tiers État d'après la charte de Beaumont. Paris. 1884.
Espinas, G. La Vie urbaine de Douai au moyen âge. 4 vols. Paris. 1913.
Flach, J. Les Origines de l'ancienne France. Vol. II. Paris. 1893.
Génestal, R. La Tenure en bourgage. Paris. 1900.
Giry, A. Histoire de la ville de Saint Omer et de ses institutions. Paris. 1877.
—— Les Établissements de Rouen. 2 vols. (BHE.) Paris. 1883, 85.

Huvelin, P. Essai historique sur le droit des marchés et des foires. Paris. 1897.
Labande, L. H. Histoire de Beauvais et de ses institutions communales. Paris. 1892.
Luchaire, A. Les Communes françaises à l'époque des Capétiens directs. 2nd edn. Halphen, L. Paris. 1911.
Ottokar, N. Opiti po istorii frantsuzskish gorodov. Perm. 1919.
Prou, M. Les Coutumes de Lorris. Paris. 1884.

(*c*) England.

Ashley, W. J. The beginnings of town life in the Middle Ages. *In* Quarterly Journal of Economics. x. Boston, Mass. 1896.
Ballard, A. The English borough in the twelfth century. Cambridge. 1914.
Bateson, M. The laws of Breteuil. EHR. xv. 1900.
Gross, C. The Gild Merchant. 2 vols. Oxford. 1890.
Hemmeon, M. de W. Burgage tenure in Mediaeval England. (Harvard Hist. Studies. Vol. xx.) Cambridge, Mass. 1914.
Maitland, F. W. Township and borough. Cambridge. 1898.
Petit-Dutaillis, C. L'Origine des villes en Angleterre. Study no. viii in the French transl. of Stubbs, W. Constitutional History. Vol. i. *See Gen. Bibl.* v.
Round, J. H. The castles of the Conquest. *In* Archaeologia. lviii, pt. 1. London. 1902.
Stephenson, C. The origin of the English Towns. AHR. xxxii. 1926.
Tait, J. The Firma Burgi and the Commune in England, 1066–1191. EHR. xlii. 1927.
—— The origin of Town Councils in England. EHR. xliv. 1929.

(*d*) Netherlands.

Blommaert, W. Les Châtelains de Flandre. Ghent. 1915.
Des Marez, G. Étude sur la propriété foncière dans les villes du moyen âge et spécialement en Flandre. Ghent. 1898.
Pirenne, H. L'Origine des constitutions urbaines au moyen âge. RH. liii, lvii. 1893, 95.
—— Villes, marchés, et marchands au moyen âge. *Ibid.* lxvii. 1898.
—— La Hanse flamande de Londres. *In* Bulletin de l'Acad. royale de Belgique. Classe des Lettres. Brussels. 1899.
—— Les Villes flamandes avant le xie siècle. *In* Annales de l'Est et du Nord. Vol. i. 1905.
—— Les anciennes Démocraties des Pays-Bas. Paris. 1910. Transl. Saunders, J. V. *as* Belgian democracy; its early history. Manchester. 1915.
—— Les Villes du moyen âge. Brussels. 1926. Transl. Halsey, F. D. *as* Medieval cities; their origins and the revival of trade. Princeton. 1925.
Vanderkindere, L. La première phase de l'évolution constitutionnelle des villes flamandes. *In* Annales de l'Est et du Nord. i. 1905.
—— La notion juridique de la commune. *In* Bulletin de l'Acad. royale de Belgique. Classe des Lettres. Brussels. 1906.
Van der Linden, H. Les Gildes marchandes dans les Pays-Bas au moyen âge. Ghent. 1896.
Wauters, A. De l'origine et des premiers développements des libertés communales en Belgique. Preuves. Brussels. 1869.

CHAPTER XVI.

THE DEVELOPMENT OF ECCLESIASTICAL ORGANISATION AND ITS FINANCIAL BASIS.

In this bibliography only certain books of special relevance are included. The original authorities will be found in the General Bibliography to each of Volumes I, II, III, and V, and also the chief modern histories, general, constitutional, and ecclesiastical. There are few chapters in the bibliographies of which some books useful for the present purpose are not included. Those which deal with directly ecclesiastical subjects and with the relations between Church and State will be most profitably searched.

Boehmer, H. Das Eigenkirchentum in England. *In* Festgabe für Felix Liebermann. Halle. 1921.

Brilioth, Y. Den påfliga Beskattningen af Sverige intill den stora Schismen. Upsala. 1915.

Dansey, W. Horae decanicae rurales. 2nd edn. 2 vols. London. 1844.

Delannoy, P. La Juridiction ecclésiastique en matière bénéficiale sous l'ancien régime en France. Vol. I. Brussels. 1910.

Dobiache-Rojdestvensky, O. La Vie paroissiale en France au XIIIe siècle. Paris. 1911.

Fabre, F. Étude sur le Liber Censuum de l'Église Romaine. Paris. 1892.

Galante, A. La condizione giuridica delle cose sacre. Parte prima. Turin. 1903.

Gottlob, T. Der abendländische Chorepiskopat. Bonn. 1928.

Hüfner, A. Das Rechtsinstitut der klösterlichen Exemtion. Mayence. 1907.

Jenson, O. The Denarius Sancti Petri in England. TRHS. n.s. XV. 1901. *Ibid.* XIX. 1905.

Künstle, F. X. Die deutsche Pfarrei und ihr Recht zu Anfang des Mittelalters. Stuttgart. 1905.

Laehns, E. Die Bischofswahlen in Deutschland von 936–1036. Greifswald. 1909.

Lathbury, T. A history of the Convocation of the Church of England from the earliest period to the year 1742. 2nd edn. London. 1853.

Leder, P. A. Die Diakonen der Bischöfe und Presbyter und ihre urchristliche Vorläufer. Stuttgart. 1905.

Makower, F. Die Verfassung der Kirche von England. Berlin. 1894. English transl. London. 1895.

Paulus, C. Welt- und Ordensklerus beim Ausgange des XIII Jahrhunderts im Kampfe um die Pfarr-Rechte. Essen. 1900.

Pöschl, A. Bischofsgut und Mensa episcopalis. 3 vols. Bonn. 1908–12.

Schaefer, H. Pfarrkirche und Stift im deutschen Mittelalter. Stuttgart. 1903.

Schreiber, G. Kurie und Kloster im XII Jahrhundert. Stuttgart. 1910.

Schubert, H. v. Staat und Kirche in den arianischen Königreichen und im Reiche Chlodwigs. Munich. 1912.

Stutz, U. Die Eigenkirche als Element des mittelalterlich-germanischen Kirchenrechtes. Berlin. 1895.

Thomas, P. Le Droit de propriété des laïques sur les églises et le patronage laïque au moyen âge. Paris. 1916.

Vendeuvre, J. L'Exemption de visite monastique. Paris. 1907.

Viard, P. Histoire de la dîme ecclésiastique principalement en France jusqu'au décret de Gratien. Dijon. 1909.

—— Histoire de la dîme ecclésiastique dans le royaume de France aux XIIe et XIIIe siècles. Paris. 1912.

Weise, G. Königtum und Bischofswahl im fränkischen und deutschen Recht vor dem Investiturstreit. Berlin. 1912.

CHAPTER XVII.

THE MEDIEVAL UNIVERSITIES.

Only the more important works on the subject as a whole and on large sections of it are given below. No attempt has been made to give a full list of books on particular universities.

For more complete bibliographies the reader is referred to the works of Denifle and Rashdall. *See below,* I. It should be stated that, while most valuable work had been done and collections of documents published for the history of particular universities, no really critical work on the subject as a whole appeared before Denifle's great work, and all special historians of the older universities were consequently more or less at sea as regards the question of the origins.

I. Universities in General.

Denifle, H. Die Universitäten des Mittelalters bis 1400. Vol. I. Die Entstehung der Universitäten. *See Gen. Bibl.* v.

Haskins, C. H. The rise of universities. New York. 1923.

Meiners, C. Geschichte der Entstehung und Entwickelung der hohen Schulen 4 vols. Göttingen. 1802–5. [Quite uncritical.]

Mullinger, J. B. Article: Universities *in* Enc. Br. Vol. XXVII. 1911. [Bibliography.]

Rait, R. S. Life in the medieval university. Cambridge. 1912.

Rashdall, H. The Universities of Europe in the Middle Ages. *See Gen. Bibl.* v.

II. Paris.

Bréchillet Jourdain, C. M. G. Index chronologicus chartarum pertinentium ad historiam Universitatis Parisiensis. Paris. 1862.

Budinszky, A. Die Universität Paris und die Fremden an derselben im Mittelalter. Berlin. 1876.

Chatelain, E. Essai d'une bibliographie de l'ancienne Université de Paris. *In* Revue des Bibliothèques. Vol. I. 1891.

Crévier, J. B. L. Histoire de l'Université de Paris depuis son origine jusqu'en l'année 1660. 7 vols. Paris. 1761.

Denifle, H. and Chatelain, E. Chartularium Universitatis Parisiensis. 4 vols. Paris. 1889–97. [This work supersedes Du Boulay and Jourdain as collections of documents.]

—— Auctarium Chartularii Universitatis Parisiensis. Liber Procuratorum Nationis Anglicanae (Alemanniae) in Universitate Parisiensi. 2 vols. Paris. 1894, 97.

Du Boulay, C. E. Historia Universitatis Parisiensis a Carolo Magno ad nostra tempora. 6 vols. Paris. 1665–73. [Valuable for the immense collection of documents but entirely uncritical.]

Félibien, M. Histoire de la ville de Paris. Ed. Lobineau, G. A. [An abridgement of Du Boulay, but less credulous and uncritical.] 5 vols. Paris. 1725.

Fournier, M. and Dorez, L. La Faculté de décret de l'Université de Paris au xve siècle. 3 vols. Paris. 1895 ff.

Thurot, C. De l'organisation de l'enseignement dans l'Université de Paris au moyen âge. Paris and Besançon. 1850.

III. Other French Universities.

Denifle, H. Les Universités françaises au moyen âge. Paris. 1892.

Fournier, M. Histoire de la science du Droit en France. Vol. III. Paris. 1892.

—— Les Statuts et privilèges des Universités françaises depuis leur fondation jusqu'en 1789. 4 vols. Paris. 1890–4.

IV. Bologna and the Italian Universities.

Acta Nationis Germanicae Universitatis Bononiensis. Berlin. 1887.

Cavazza, F. G. Le Scuole dell' antico studio bolognese. Milan. 1896.

Chartularium studii Bononiensis. Ed. Nordi, L. and Orioli, E. Vols. I–IV. (Commissione per la storia dell' Università di Bologna.) Bologna and Imola. 1909–19.

Chiappelli, L. Lo Studio bolognese. Pistoia. 1888.

Dallari, U. I rotuli dei lettori, legisti, e artisti dello studio bolognese dal 1384 al 1799. 3 vols. Bologna. 1888–91.

Fitting, H. H. Die Anfänge der Rechtsschule zu Bologna. Berlin and Leipsic. 1888.

Frati, L. Opere della bibliografia bolognese. 2 vols. Bologna. 1888–9.

Malagola, C. Statuti delle università e dei collegi dello studio bolognese. Bologna. 1888.

Sarti, M. (continued by Fattorini, M.). De claris Archigymnasii Bononiensis Professoribus. Vol. I, 2 pts. Bologna. 1769, 72. New edn. Albicini, C. Bologna. 1888–96.

Savigny, F. C. von. Geschichte des Römischen Rechts im Mittelalter. *See Gen. Bibl.* v.

Studi e memorie per la storia dell' Università di Bologna. (Comm. p. la storia...di Bologna.) Bologna. 1907 ff.

Tiraboschi, G. Storia della letteratura italiana. *See Gen. Bibl.* v.

V. Universities of Spain and Portugal.

Fuente, V. de la. Historia de las universidades, colegios, y demás establecimentos de enseñanza en España. 4 vols. Madrid. 1884–9.

Reynier, G. La Vie universitaire dans l'ancienne Espagne. Paris and Toulouse. 1902. [Mainly post-medieval.]

VI. German Universities.

Aschbach, J. R. v. Geschichte der Wiener Universität im ersten Jahrhunderte ihres Bestehen. 3 vols. Vienna. 1865–88.

Bezold, F. v. Die ältesten deutschen Universitäten. HZ. LXXX. 1898. pp. 436–67.

Erman, W. and Horn, E. Bibliographie der deutschen Universitäten. 3 vols. Leipsic and Berlin. 1904–5.

Eulenburg, F. Die Frequenz der deutschen Universitäten von ihrer Gründung bis zur Gegenwart. *In* Abh. d. k. sächsischen Gesellschaft der Wissenschaften. Philol.-hist. Kl. Vol. XXIV, no. II. Leipsic. 1904.

Hautz, J. F. Geschichte der Universität Heidelberg nach handschriftlichen Quellen. 2 vols. Mannheim. 1862, 64.

Kaufmann, G. Die Geschichte der deutschen Universitäten. 2 vols. Stuttgart. 1888, 96.

Keussen, H. Geschichte der Universität Köln 1388–1559. (Mitteilungen aus dem Stadtarchiv von Köln. Heft 36–37.) Cologne. 1918.

Namèche, A. J. Jean IV et la fondation de l'Université de Louvain. Louvain. 1888.

Thorbecke, A. Die Anfänge der Universität Heidelberg. Heidelberg. 1886.

—— Geschichte der Universität Heidelberg. Abteil. I. Die älteste Zeit, 1386–1449. Heidelberg. 1886.

VII. Slavonic Universities.

Morawski, K. Historya Uniwersytetu Jagiellónskiego. 2 vols. Cracow. 1900.

Tomek, W. W. Geschichte der Prager Universität. Prague. 1849.

VIII. English Universities.

Anstey, H. Munimenta Academica. 2 vols. (Rolls.) 1868.

Cooper, C. H. Annals of Cambridge. Vol. I. Cambridge. 1842.

Documents relating to the University and Colleges of Cambridge. 3 vols. London. 1852.

Fuller, Thomas. The History of the University of Cambridge. (Publ. with his Church History of Great Britain.) London. 1655. Ed. Prickett, M. and Wright, T. Cambridge. 1840. *Also* ed. Nichols, J. London. 1840.

Grace Book A, containing the Proctors' Accounts...etc. of the University of Cambridge...1454–88. Ed. Leathes, S. M. (Camb. Antiq. Soc., Luard Memorial Series, I.) Cambridge. 1897.
Grace Book B. Part I,...1488–1511. Ed. Bateson, M. (*Ibid.* II.) Cambridge. 1903.
Mallet, C. E. History of the University of Oxford. Vol. I. London. 1924.
Mullinger, J. B. The University of Cambridge from the earliest times to the Royal Injunctions of 1535. Cambridge. 1873.
Oxford Historical Society Publications. Oxford. 1885 ff., in progress.
Peacock, G. Observations on the Statutes of the University of Cambridge. London. 1841.
Statutes of the Colleges of Oxford. [Ed. Bond, E. A.] 3 vols. Oxford. 1853.
Twyne, B. Antiquitatis Academiae Oxoniensis apologia. Oxford. 1608.
Wood, Anthony à. The History and antiquities of the University of Oxford. Ed. Gutch, J. 2 vols. in 3. Oxford. 1792–6.
—— Historia et antiquitates Universitatis Oxoniensis. Oxford. 1674. [A mutilated Latin translation of the above.]

IX. Scottish Universities.

Anderson, J. M. The University of St Andrews. Cupar. 1878.
Coissac, J. B. Les Universités d'Écosse (1410–1560). Paris. 1915.
Innes, Cosmo. Fasti Aberdonenses. (Spalding Club.) Aberdeen. 1854.
—— Munimenta Alme Universitatis Glasguensis. 3 vols. in 4. (Maitland Club.) Glasgow. 1854.
—— Sketches of early Scotch history. Edinburgh. 1861.
Lyon, C. J. History of St Andrews. Edinburgh. 2 vols. 1843.
Rait, R. S. The Universities of Aberdeen. Aberdeen. 1895.
Report of Commissioners to visit the Universities of Scotland. London. 1831. Evidence. Vol. III. 1837.

CHAPTER XVIII.

POLITICAL THEORY TO *c.* 1300.

I. SOURCES AND CRITICISM.

Accursius. Glossa Ordinaria to (Justinian), Institutes. Mayence. 1472; Codex Venice. 1478; Digestum vetus. Venice. 1477; Novels. Venice. 1491.
—— Die Glosse des Accursius und ihre Lehre vom Eigenthum. Landsberg, E. Leipsic. 1883.
Aegidius Romanus. *See* Colonna.
Agobard of Lyons, Saint. MPL. CIV. *Also* MGH. Epist. v.
Aquinas, St Thomas. De Regimine Principum. *In* Opera. Vol. XVI. Parma. 1852–73. His Commentary on Aristotle's Politics. *Ibid.* Vol. XXI. His Theory of Law *in* Summa Theologica. Prima secundae, quaestiones 90–108. Ed. Migne, J. P. 4 vols. Paris. 1858; etc. *Also in* Opera omnia. Rome. 1882 ff.
Augustine, Saint. De Civitate Dei. Ed. Dombart, B. Leipsic. 1877. Ed., with English notes, Welldon, J. E. C. London. 1924. English transl. Dods, M. 2 vols. Edinburgh. 1897.
Augustinus Triumphus. Summa de Ecclesiastica Potestate. Rome. 1582.
Azo. Summa Institutionum *and* Summa Codicis. Basle. 1563.
—— Brocardica. Basle. 1567.
Beaumanoir, Philippe de Remi, Sire de. Les Coutumes des Beauvaisis. Ed. Salmon, A. 2 vols. (Coll. textes.) Paris. 1899.
Bernard of Clairvaux, Saint. De Consideratione. MPL. CLXXXII. English transl. Lewis, G. Oxford. 1908.
Boniface VIII, Pope. Decretals. *In* Corpus Iuris Canonici. Ed. Friedberg, E. Pt. II. *See Gen. Bibl.* IV. The Bull *Unam Sanctam* is printed in Galante. *See below.*
Brachylogus Juris Civilis (Corpus Legum sive). Ed. Böcking, E. Berlin. 1829.
Bracton. Select passages from Bracton and Azo. Ed. Maitland, F. W. (Selden Soc. Vol. VIII). London. 1895.
Burchard of Worms. Decretum. MPL. CXL.
Colonna, Aegidius. De Regimine Principum. Rome. 1482 and 1607.
Corpus Iuris Canonici. Ed. Friedberg, E. *See Gen. Bibl.* IV.
Damian, Peter. Opera. MPL. CXLV. *Also* MGH. Libelli de Lite. Vol. I. 1891.
Dante Alighieri. Opere. Testo critico. Florence. 1921.
—— —— Opere. Ed. Moore, E. Revised by Toynbee, P. 4th edn. Oxford. 1924.
Deusdedit, Cardinal. Die Kanones Sammlung. Ed. Glanvell, V. W. von. Paderborn. 1905.
Dissensiones Dominorum. Codex Chisianus. Ed. Hänel, G. Leipsic. 1834.
Gaius. Gaii Institutionum Iuris Civilis Commentarii. Ed. Poste, E. 4th edn. Whittuck, E. A. Oxford. 1904. English transl. (with the Rules of Ulpian). Muirhead, J. Edinburgh. 1880.
Galante, A. Fontes Iuris Canonici selecti. Innsbruck. 1906.
Gelasius I, Pope. Epistolae et Decreta. MPL. LIX.
—— Epistolae Romanorum Pontificum. Ed. Thiel, A. Braunsberg. 1868.
Gerhoh of Reichersberg. Opera. MPL. CXCIII, CXCIV.
Goldast, M. Monarchia Sancti Romani Imperii. 2 vols. Hanover and Frankfort. 1611, 14.
Gratian. Decretum. *In* Corpus Iuris Canonici. Ed. Friedberg, E. Pt. I. *See Gen. Bibl.* IV.
Gregory VII, Pope. Registrum. Ed. Jaffé, P. Monumenta Gregoriana. (Bibl. rerum Germanicarum. Vol. II.) Berlin. 1865. *Also* ed. Caspar, E. MGH. Epistolae selectae. Vol. II. Berlin. 1920, 23.
Hincmar of Rheims. Opera. MPL. CXXV, CXXVI.

Hincmar of Rheims. De Ordine Palatii. MGH. Legum Sect. II. Vol. II. 1897.
Honorius of Autun. Summa Gloria. MGH. Libelli de Lite. Vol. III. 1897.
Innocent III, Pope. Opera. MPL. CCXIV–CCXVII.
Innocent IV, Pope. Decretals. *In* Corpus Iuris Canonici. Ed. Friedberg, E. Pt. II. *See Gen. Bibl.* IV.
Irnerius. Summa Codicis. Ed. Fitting, H. H. Berlin and Halle. 1894.
——Quaestiones de Juris Subtilitatibus. Ed. Fitting, H. H. Halle and Wittenberg. 1894.
Isidore of Seville, Saint. Etymologiarum Libri xx. 2 vols. Ed. Lindsay, W. M. Oxford. 1911.
(Pseudo-)Isidore. Decretales Pseudo-Isidorianae. Ed. Hinschius, P. Leipsic. 1863.
Ivo of Chartres. Decretum *and* Panormia. MPL. CLXI.
John of Salisbury. Opera. MPL. CXCIX.
—— Policraticus. Ed. Webb, C. C. J. 2 vols. Oxford. 1909.
Jonas of Orleans. Opera. MPL. CVI.
Liber Pontificalis. Ed. Duchesne, L. 2 vols. EcfrAR. Paris. 1886, 92.
Manegold of Lautenbach. Ad Gebehardum. MGH. Libelli de Lite. Vol. I. 1891.
Petri Exceptiones. *In* Savigny, F. C. von. Gesch. des Römischen Rechts. Vol. II. *See Gen. Bibl.* V.
Petrus Crassus. MGH. Libelli de Lite. Vol. I. 1891.
Placentinus. De Varietate Actionum. Mayence. 1530.
Ptolemy of Lucca. De Regimine Principum. *With* Aquinas. De Regimine Principum. *See above.*
Ratherius of Verona. Opera. MPL. CXXXVI.
Regesta Pontificum Romanorum. Ed. Jaffé, P. (Jaffé-Wattenbach-Loewenfeld). 2nd edn. 2 vols. Leipsic. 1885, 88.
Regesta Pontificum Romanorum, 1198–1304. Ed. Potthast, A. *See Gen. Bibl.* IV.
Rufinus. Summa zum Decretum Gratiani. Ed. Schulte, J. F. von. Giessen. 1892.
Sedulius Scotus. Opera. MPL. CIII.
Smaragdus. Opera. MPL. CII.
Stephen of Tournai. Summa zum Decretum Gratiani. Ed. Schulte, J. F. von. Giessen. 1891.
Ulpian. The Institutes of Gaius and the Rules of Ulpian. Transl. Muirhead, J. Edinburgh. 1880.
Vacarius. Liber Pauperum. Ed. Zulueta, F. de. (Selden Soc. Vol. XLIV.) London. 1927. [*Cf.* article in DNB. by Holland, T. E.]

II. MODERN BOOKS.

Bryce, J. The Holy Roman Empire. *See Gen. Bibl.* V.
Carlyle, R. W. and A. J. A History of Mediaeval Political Theory in the West. *See Gen. Bibl.* V.
Dunning, W. A. A History of Political Theories: Ancient and Mediaeval. New York. 1902.
Ficker, J. Forschungen zur Reichs- und Rechtsgeschichte Italiens. 4 vols. Innsbruck. 1868–74.
Figgis, J. N. The Divine Right of Kings. 2nd edn. Cambridge. 1914.
—— The Political Aspects of St Augustine's 'City of God.' London. 1921.
Fisher, H. A. L. The Medieval Empire. 2 vols. London. 1898.
Fitting, H. H. Juristische Schriften des früheren Mittelalters. Halle. 1876.
—— Die Anfänge der Rechtsschule zur Bologna. Berlin. 1888.
Gierke, O. Das deutsche Genossenschaftsrecht. *See Gen. Bibl.* V.
—— Political Theories of the Middle Age. *See Gen. Bibl.* V.
Giesebrecht, W. von. Geschichte der deutschen Kaiserzeit. Vols. I–III, 5th edn. Leipsic. 1881–90. IV, 2nd edn. Brunswick. 1877. V, Leipsic. 1880–8. VI, Ed. Simson, B. von. Leipsic. 1895.
Hearnshaw, F. J. C., and others. The Social and Political Ideas of some great Mediaeval Thinkers. London. 1923.
Holdsworth, W. S. History of English Law. *See Gen. Bibl.* V.

Janet, P. Histoire de la Science politique dans ses rapports avec la morale. 2 vols. Paris. 1887.
Maitland, F. W. *See under* Gierke *and* Pollock.
Pollock, F. and Maitland, F. W. History of English Law. *See Gen. Bibl.* v.
Poole, R. L. Illustrations of the history of Medieval Thought and Learning. *See Gen. Bibl.* v.
Rashdall, H. The Universities of Europe in the Middle Ages. *See Gen. Bibl.* v.
Savigny, F. C. von. Geschichte des Römischen Rechts im Mittelalter. *See Gen. Bibl.* v.
Schaarsmidt, C. Joannes Saresberiensis. Leipsic. 1862.
Seidel, B. Die Lehre des heiligen Augustinus vom Staate. Berlin. 1909.
Stubbs, W. Lectures on the study of Mediaeval and Modern History. Oxford. 1886
Tardif, A. Histoire des sources du droit canonique. Paris. 1887.
Troeltsch, E. Die Soziallehren der christlichen Kirchen und Gruppen. Tübingen. 1923.
Vinogradoff, P. Roman Law in Mediaeval Europe. *See Gen. Bibl.* v.
Wulf, M. de. Philosophy and Civilisation in the Middle Ages. London. 1922.

CHAPTER XIX.

MEDIEVAL DOCTRINE TO THE LATERAN COUNCIL OF 1215.

I. ORIGINAL AUTHORITIES.

(*a*) Ecclesiastical Authority: the Papacy.

Alexander III, Pope. Epistolae et privilegia. MPL. cc.
Bernard of Clairvaux, Saint. De consideratione. MPL. clxxxii. Engl. transl. Lewis, G. Oxford. 1908.
Boniface, archbishop of Mayence. Epistolae. MPL. lxxxix.
Calixtus II, Pope. Epistolae et privilegia. MPL. clxiii.
Corpus Iuris Canonici.
Decretum Gratiani.
Decretales Gregorii P. ix, etc. } *See Gen. Bibl.* iv.
Gregory VII, Pope. Registrum et epistolae. Ed. Jaffé, P. *in* Monumenta Gregoriana. (Bibliotheca rerum German. ii.) Berlin. 1865. Registrum (only). Ed. Caspar, E. MGH. Epp. Select. ii. 1920, 23.
Hincmar, archbishop of Rheims. Epistolae. MPL. cxxvi.
Innocent III, Pope. Opera omnia. MPL. ccxiv–ccxvii.
Ivo, bishop of Chartres. Decretum and Panormia. MPL. clxi.
Leo IX, Pope. Epistolae et decreta pontificia. MPL. cxliii.
Liber Pontificalis. Ed. Duchesne, L. 2 vols. (EcfrAR.) Paris. 1884.
Libri Carolini. Ed. Bastgen, H. MGH. Legum Sect. iii. Concilia ii, Supplt. 1924.
Mansi, J. D. Concilia. *See Gen. Bibl.* iv.
Mirbt, C. Quellen zur Geschichte des Papsttums. *See Gen. Bibl.* iv.
Nicholas I, Pope. Epistolae. MPL. cxix.
Paschal II, Pope. Epistolae et privilegia. MPL. clxiii.
Petrus Damianus. Opera omnia. MPL. cxliv, cxlv.
(Pseudo-) Isidore. Decretales pseudo-Isidorianae et Capitula Angilramni. Ed. Hinschius, P. Leipsic. 1863.
Stephen II, Pope. Epistolae et decreta. MPL. lxxxix.
Urban II, Pope. Epistolae et privilegia. MPL. cli.
Zacharias, Pope. Epistolae et decreta. MPL. lxxxix.

(*b*) Doctrine of the Church and Sacraments, etc.

Augustine, Saint. Opera. (CSEL. Vols xii ff.) Vienna. 1887 ff., in progress. *Also* MPL. xxxii–xlvii.
Bernard of Clairvaux, Saint. Opera omnia. MPL. clxxxii–clxxxv.
Gregory the Great, Saint. Opera. MPL. lxxv–lxxix.
Hugh of St Victor. De sacramentis Christianae fidei. MPL. clxxvi.
Joannes Damascenus. Opera. MPG. xciv–xcvi. MPL. lxxiii.
Peter Lombard, bishop of Paris. Sententiarum libri quatuor. MPL. cxcii.
Peter of Poitiers. Sententiarum libri quinque. MPL. ccxi.

(*c*) Doctrine of Predestination and Grace.

(*See also authors under* (*b*) *above.*)

Anselm, archbishop of Canterbury. Liber de conceptu virginali et originali peccato. Dialogus de libero arbitrio. Tractatus de concordantia praescientiae et praedestinationis. MPL. clviii.
Florus Diaconus Lugdunensis. Sermo de praedestinatione. Adversus Joannis Scoti Erigenae erroneas definitiones liber. MPL. cxix.

Gotteschalcus, monk of Orbais. Confessio, Confessio prolixior, etc. MPL. CXXI.
Guibert, abbot of Nogent. Tractatus de incarnatione contra Judaeos. MPL. CLVI.
Hincmar, archbishop of Rheims. De praedestinatione Dei et libero arbitrio dissertatio posterior. MPL. CXXV.
Joannes Scotus Erigena. De divina praedestinatione liber. MPL. CXXII.
Odo, bishop of Cambrai. De peccato originali libri tres. MPL. CLX.
Prudentius, bishop of Troyes. De praedestinatione contra Joannem Scotum cognomento Erigenam. MPL. CXV.
Ratramnus. De praedestinatione Dei libri duo. MPL. CXXI.

(*d*) CHRISTOLOGY: THE INCARNATION AND ATONEMENT.
(*See also authors under* (*b*) *above.*)

Abelard. Opera. MPL. CLXXVIII. *Also* ed. Cousin, V. 2 vols. Paris. 1849, 59.
Agobardus, bishop of Lyons. Liber adversum dogma Felicis Urgellensis. MPL. CIV.
Alcuin (Flaccus Albinus). De fide sanctae et individuae Trinitatis. Adversus haeresin Felicis. Contra Felicem Urgellitanum episcopum. Contra epistolam sibi ab Elipando directam. MPL. CI.
Anselm, archbishop of Canterbury. Cur Deus homo. MPL. CLVIII.
Benedict, abbot of Aniane. Disputatio Benedicti levitae adversus Felicianam impietatem. MPL. CIII.
Elipandus, bishop of Toledo. Epistolae. MPL. XCVI.
Felix, bishop of Urgel. Confessio fidei. MPL. XCVI.
Heterius and Beatus. Ad Elipandum epistola. MPL. XCVI.
Paulinus, patriarch of Aquileia. Libellus sacrosyllabus contra Elipandum. Contra Felicem Urgellitanum libri tres. MPL. XCIX.

(*e*) THE TRINITY: DOCTRINE OF THE HOLY SPIRIT.
(*See also authors under* (*b*) *above.*)

Alcuin. De processione Spiritus Sancti. MPL. CI.
Anselm, archbishop of Canterbury. De processione Sancti Spiritus. MPL. CLVIII.
Chrysolanus, P., archbishop of Milan. Oratio de Spiritu Sancto ad imperatorem Alexium Comnenum. MPG. CXXVII. MPL. CLXII.
Eterianus, H. De haeresibus quos Graeci in Latinos devolvunt libri tres. MPL. CCII.
Hincmar, archbishop of Rheims. De una et non trina Deitate. MPL. CXXV.
Photius, patriarch of Constantinople. Περὶ τῆς τοῦ ἁγίου Πνεύματος μυσταγωγίας. Epistolarum libri tres. MPG. CII.
Ratramnus. Contra Graecorum opposita Romanam ecclesiam infamantium libri quatuor. MPL. CXXI.
Rupert, abbot of Deutz. De glorificatione Trinitatis et processione Sancti Spiritus. MPL. CLXIX.
Theodulfus, bishop of Orleans. De Spiritu Sancto veterum patrum sententiae quod a Patre Filioque procedit. MPL. CV.

(*f*) BAPTISM, THE EUCHARIST, PENANCE.
(*See also authors under* (*b*) *above.*)

Adelman, bishop of Brescia. De eucharistiae sacramento ad Berengarium epistola. MPL. CXLIII.
Adrevaldus, monk of Fleury. De corpore et sanguine Christi. MPL. CXXIV.
Alger, canon of Liège. Liber de sacramentis corporis et sanguinis dominici. MPL. CLXXX.
Amalarius, Symphosius. De ecclesiasticis officiis libri quatuor. MPL. CV.
Anselm, bishop of Havelberg. Dialogi. MPL. CLXXXVIII.
Berengarius. De sacra coena adversus Lanfrancum liber posterior. Ed. Vischer, F. T. Berlin. 1834.
Columbanus. De poenitentiarum mensura taxanda liber. MPL. LXXX.
Cummianus. De mensura poenitentiarum liber. MPL. LXXXVII.
Durandus, abbot of Troarn. Liber de corpore et sanguine Christi contra Berengarium. MPL. CXLIX.

Egbert, archbishop of York. Poenitentiale. MPL. LXXXIX.
Florus Diaconus Lugdunensis. De expositione missae. MPL. CXIX.
Fulbert, bishop of Chartres. Epistolae et sermones. MPL. CXLI.
Guibert, abbot of Nogent. Epistola de buccella Judae data et de veritate dominici corporis. MPL. CLVI.
Guimundus (Witmund), archbishop of Aversa. De corporis et sanguinis Christi veritate in eucharistia. MPL. CXLIX.
Halitgarius, bishop of Cambrai. De vitiis et virtutibus et de ordine poenitentium libri quinque. MPL. CV. (Including two supplementary Libri Poenitentiales.)
Haymo, bishop of Halberstadt. De corpore et sanguine Domini. MPL. CXVIII.
Hildebert, archbishop of Tours. Epistolae et sermones. MPL. CLXXI.
—— Versus de mysterio missae. Liber de sacra eucharistia. MPL. CLXXI.
Hincmar, archbishop of Rheims. De cavendis vitiis et virtutibus exercendis. MPL. CXXV.
Honorius, bishop of Autun. Sacramentarium seu de causis et significatu mystico rituum divini in ecclesia officii liber. MPL. CLXXII.
—— Eucharistion seu liber de corpore et sanguine Domini. MPL. CLXXII.
Hugh, bishop of Langres. De corpore et sanguine Christi contra Berengarium. MPL. CXLII.
Lanfranc, archbishop of Canterbury. De corpore et sanguine Domini adversus Berengarium liber. MPL. CL.
Leidradus, bishop of Lyons. Liber de sacramento baptismi. MPL. XCIX.
Odo, bishop of Cambrai. Expositio in canonem missae. MPL. CLX.
Paschasius Radbertus, abbot of Corbie. Liber de corpore et sanguine Domini. Epistola de corpore et sanguine Domini ad Frudegardum. MPL. CXX.
Peter of Blois, archdeacon of Bath. Liber de confessione sacramentali. De poenitentia vel satisfactione a sacerdote injungenda. MPL. CCVII.
Rabanus Maurus, archbishop of Mayence. De clericorum institutione...libri tres. MPL. CVII.
—— Poenitentiale. MPL. CX.
—— De videndo Deum, de puritate cordis et modo poenitentiae libri tres. De vitiis et virtutibus et peccatorum satisfactione (Liber tertius). Poenitentium liber. MPL. CXII.
Ratramnus. De corpore et sanguine Domini liber. MPL. CXXI.
Sylvester II, Pope. De corpore et sanguine Domini. MPL. CXXXIX.
Theodore, archbishop of Canterbury. Poenitentiale. MPL. XCIX.

(*g*) LITURGICAL.

Bobbio Missal. Ed. Lowe, E. A. (Henry Bradshaw Soc.) London. 1920.
Gelasian Sacramentary. Liber sacramentorum Romanae ecclesiae. Ed. Wilson, H. A. Oxford. 1894.
Gregorian Sacramentary. Ed. Wilson, H. A. (Henry Bradshaw Soc.) London. 1915.
Gregorian Sacramentary. Sancti Gregorii Magni...liber sacramentorum. *In* Gregorii Magni opera. MPL. LXXVIII.
Liturgia Mozarabica secundum regulam beati Isidori. MPL. LXXXV, LXXXVI.
Missae Gallicanae undecim. MPL. CXXXVIII.
Romani ordines (Antiqui libri rituales sanctae Romanae ecclesiae). *In* Gregorii Magni opera. MPL. LXXVIII.
Vetus sacramentarium. MPL. CLI.

II. SECONDARY WORKS.

(*a*) GENERAL HISTORIES OF THE CHURCH AND DOGMA.

Baronius, C. Annales Ecclesiastici. *See Gen. Bibl.* v.
Baur, F. C. v. Geschichte d. christl. Kirche. 5 vols. Tübingen. 1853–62. Vols. II and III. 2nd. edn. Leipsic. 1863, 69.
—— Lehrbuch d. christl. Dogmengeschichte. 2nd edn. Tübingen. 1858.
—— Vorlesungen über d. christl. Dogmengeschichte. 3 vols. Leipsic. 1865–67.

Carlyle, R. W. and A. J. A history of Mediaeval Political Theory in the West. *See Gen. Bibl.* v.
Duchesne, L. L'Église au sixième siècle. Paris. 1925.
Funk, F. X. Lehrbuch d. Kirchengeschichte. 5th edn. Paderborn. 1907. English transl. ed. Cappadelta. 2 vols. 1910.
Gieseler, J. C. L. Lehrbuch d. Kirchengeschichte. *See Gen. Bibl.* v.
Greenwood, T. Cathedra Petri, a history of the great Latin patriarchate. 6 vols. London. 1856–72.
Hagenbach, C. R. Kirchengeschichte. New edn. 7 vols. Leipsic. 1870–87.
—— Lehrbuch d. Dogmengeschichte. 2 vols. Leipsic. 1840–1.
—— Vorlesungen ü. d. Kirchengeschichte d. Mittelalters. 2 vols. Leipsic. 1860–1.
Harnack, C. G. A. Lehrbuch d. Dogmengeschichte. *See Gen. Bibl.* v.
Hefele, C. J. v. Conciliengeschichte. *See Gen. Bibl.* v.
Knöpfler, A. Lehrbuch d. Kirchengeschichte. 4th edn. Freiburg-i.-B. 1906.
Kurtz, J. H. Lehrbuch d. Kirchengeschichte. 14th edn. Bonwetsch, N. and Tschackert, P. 2 vols. Leipsic. 1906. Engl. transl. Edersheim, A., etc. 5th edn. 2 vols. Edinburgh. 1884.
Loofs, F. Leitfaden zum Studium d. Dogmengeschichte. 4th edn. Halle. 1906.
Maimbourg, L. Histoire de l'hérésie des iconoclastes et de la translation de l'empire aux françois. 2 vols. 3rd edn. Paris. 1679.
—— Histoire du schisme des Grecs. 2 vols. 3rd edn. Paris. 1680.
Moeller, W. History of the Christian Church. *See Gen. Bibl.* v.
Mosheim, J. L. v. Ecclesiastical history. Transl. Maclaine, A. 2nd edn. 5 vols. London. 1768.
Neander, J. A. W. Allgemeine Geschichte d. christl. Religion u. Kirche. 6 vols. Hamburg. 1825–52.
Poole, R. L. Illustrations of the history of Medieval Thought and Learning. *See Gen. Bibl.* v.
Raynaldus, O. Annales Ecclesiastici. *See Gen. Bibl.* v. *under* Baronius.
Reuter, H. F. Geschichte d. religiösen Aufklärung im Mittelalter. 2 vols. Berlin. 1875, 77.
Robertson, J. C. History of the Christian Church. New edn. 8 vols. London. 1874–5.
Schwane, J. Dogmengeschichte. 4 vols. Münster and Freiburg-i.-B. 1862–90.
Seeberg, R. Lehrbuch d. Dogmengeschichte. Vols. I, II. Erlangen. 1895 ff.
Tixeront, J. Histoire des dogmes. 2 vols. Paris. 1905 ff.
Vossius, G. J. Historiae de controversiis quas Pelagius ejusque reliquiae moverunt, libri septem. 2nd edn. Amsterdam. 1655.

(*b*) The Papacy.

Fournier, P. La question des fausses décrétales. NRDF. 1887–8.
—— Etudes sur les fausses décrétales. RHE. 1906–7.
Gregorovius, F. Geschichte d. Stadt Rom im Mittelalter. *See Gen. Bibl.* v.
Grisar, H. Geschichte Roms u. d. Päpste im Mittelalter. Vol. I. Freiburg-i.-B. 1898–1901. Engl. transl. Cappadelta, L. Vol. I. St Louis. 1911.
Mann, H. K. Lives of the popes in the early Middle Ages. Vols. I–XII. London. 1902 ff.
Poole, R. L. Lectures on the history of the Papal Chancery down to the time of Innocent III. Cambridge. 1915.

(*c*) History of Special Dogmas and Ecclesiastical Institutions.

Amort, E. De origine, progressu, valore, ac fructu indulgentiarum, necnon ad eas lucrandas requisitis accurata notitia. 2 pts. Augsburg. 1735–6.
Batiffol, P. Études d'histoire et de théologie positive. Paris. 1907 ff.
Baur, F. C. v. Die christliche Lehre von d. Dreieinigkeit u. Menschwerdung Gottes. 3 vols. Tübingen. 1841–3.
Beringer, F. Die Ablässe, ihr Wesen u. ihr Gebrauch. New edn. Paderborn. 1900. French transl. Abt, E. and Feyerstein, A. 2nd edn. 2 vols. Paris. 1893.
Boileau, J. Historia confessionis auricularis. Paris. 1683.
Bouvier, J.-B., bishop of Le Mans. Traité dogmatique et pratique des indulgences, des confréries, et du jubilé. 10th edn. Paris. 1855.

Gore, C. Dissertations on subjects connected with the Incarnation. London. 1895.
Lea, H. C. History of auricular confession and indulgences in the Latin Church. 3 vols. Philadelphia. 1896.
Lépicier, A. M. Indulgences, their origin, nature, and development. London. 1895.
Morin, J. Commentarius historicus de disciplina in administratione sacramenti poenitentiae. Paris. 1682.
Mozley, J. B. A treatise on the Augustinian doctrine of Predestination. London. 1855.
Ottley, R. L. Doctrine of the Incarnation. 2 vols. London. 1896.
Petavius, D. De potestate consecrandi et sacrificandi...diatriba. Paris. 1685.
Rashdall, H. The idea of atonement in Christian theology. London. 1919.
Schmitz, H. J. Die Bussbücher u. d. Bussdisciplin. 2 vols. Mayence. 1883, 98.
Sirmond, J. Historia poenitentiae publicae. *In* Opera. Vol. IV. Venice. 1728.
Stone, D. History of the doctrine of the Eucharist. 2 vols. London. 1909.
Vacant, J. M. A. Histoire de la conception du sacrifice de la messe dans l'église latine. Paris. 1894.
Watkins, O. D. A history of penance. 2 vols. London. 1920.
Williams, N. P. The ideas of the Fall and of Original Sin. (Bampton Lectures, 1924.) London. 1927.

(*d*) Special Biographies.

Bindemann, C. Der heil. Augustinus. 3 vols. Berlin, etc. 1844–69.
Cunningham, W. St Austin and his place in the hist. of Christian thought. London. 1886.
Dudden, F. H. Gregory the Great: his place in history and thought. 2 vols. London. 1905.
Gfrörer, A. F. Papst Gregorius VII und sein Zeitalter. 7 vols. Schaffhausen. 1859–61.
Hurter, F. v. Geschichte Papst Innocenz III. 4 vols. 2nd edn. Vol. I, 3rd edn. Hamburg. 1841–4.
Kellett, F. W. Pope Gregory the Great and his relations with Gaul. Cambridge. 1889.
Luchaire, A. Innocent III. [Vol. VI.] Le Concile de Latran et la réforme de l'église. Paris. 1908.
Poujoulat, J. J. F. Histoire de St-Augustin, sa vie, ses œuvres, son siècle. 6th edn. 2 vols. Tours. 1875.
Reuter, H. F. Geschichte Alexanders d. Dritten und d. Kirche seiner Zeit. 3 vols. Leipsic. 1860–4.
—— Augustinische Studien. Gotha. 1887.
Schnitzer, J. Berengar von Tours, ein Beitrag zur Abendmahlslehre d. Beginn. Mittelalters. Munich. 1890.

(*e*) Liturgical History.

Batiffol, P. Histoire du bréviaire romain. 3rd edn. Paris. 1911. Engl. transl. Baylay, A. M. Y. London. 1912.
Bäumer, S. Geschichte d. Breviers. Freiburg-i.-B. 1895.
Bishop, E. Liturgica historica: papers on the liturgy and religious life of the Western Church. Oxford. 1918.
Cabrol, F. Introduction aux études liturgiques. Paris. 1907.
Duchesne, L. Origines du culte chrétien. 2nd edn. Paris. 1898.
Probst, F. Die ältesten römisch. Sacramentarien u. Ordines. Münster. 1892.
—— Die abendländ. Messe vom 5 biz zum 8 Jahrht. Münster. 1896.

CHAPTER XX.

HERESIES AND THE INQUISITION IN THE MIDDLE AGES, *c.* 1000–1305.

I. SPECIAL BIBLIOGRAPHIES.

Alphandéry, P. Les idées morales chez les hétérodoxes latins au début du XIIIe siècle. Paris. 1903.
Cauzons, T. de C. Histoire de l'Inquisition en France. Vol. I. Paris. 1909.
Frédéricq, P. *In* preface to the French transl. of H. C. Lea's History of the Inquisition of the Middle Ages. *See below,* IV A.
Guiraud, J. Cartulaire de Notre-Dame de Prouille. Vol. I. pp. CCCXXXIX–CCCLI. Paris. 1907.
Turberville, A. S. Mediaeval Heresy and the Inquisition. London. 1920.

II. MANUSCRIPT SOURCES.

The greatest quarry for the early history of the Inquisition is the Collection de Languedoc, known as the Doat collection, in 258 volumes, in the Bibliothèque Nationale. These include Bernard Gui's *Practica Inquisitionis haereticae pravitatis* in vol. XXX, the *Sentences* of Pierre Cella in vol. XXII, the *Archives of the Inquisition of Carcassonne* in vols. XXVII–XXXVI, *Responsa Prudentum,* vol. XXXVII, *Archives of the bishopric of Albi* in vol. XXXV. There are better MSS of Bernard Gui's *Practica* in the Bibliothèque Municipale of Toulouse, Nos. 98, 196, and in Brit. Mus., Egerton MSS No. 1897. It has been edited by C. Douais (*see below,* III A), and extracts from the other sources have been printed *e.g.* as Pièces Justificatives in his *L'Inquisition: ses origines, sa procédure* (*see below,* III B), in his *Documents pour servir à l'histoire de l'Inquisition dans le Languedoc* (*see below,* III B), and in the appendices to Lea's *History of the Inquisition of the Middle Ages* (*see below,* IV A). In the Bibliothèque Municipale of Toulouse there are Latin MSS. 379, *Summa contra Haereticos*; and 609, the inquisitorial reports of Bernard de Caux and Jean de St Pierre. For a discussion of the MS sources see C. Molinier, *L'Inquisition...Étude sur les sources de son histoire.* Paris. 1881.

III. PRINTED SOURCES.

A. Inquisitorial Treatises.

Eymeric, N. Directorium Inquisitorum cum commentariis F. Pegnae. Rome. 1585; Venice. 1607.
Gui, Bernard. Practica Inquisitionis haereticae pravitatis. Ed. Douais, C. Paris. 1886. Pt. 5 *only is also ed. with* French transl. Mollat, G. *as* Manuel de l'Inquisiteur. 2 vols. (Class. hist.) Paris. 1926–7. *Cf.* Hist. fr. Dulcini. Ed. Segarizzi, A. *See below,* III E.
—— Liber Sententiarum Inquisitionis Tholosanae, 1307–23. *In* Limborch. Hist. Inquisitionis (*see below,* IV A). *See also* Delisle, L. Les Manuscrits de Bernard Gui. *In* Notices des Manuscrits de la Bibl. Nat. Vol. XXVII, 2.

The following are printed in Zilettus, F. Tractatus Universi Juris. Vol. XI, pt. 2. Venice. 1633.

Albertini, Arnaldo. Tractatus de agnoscendis assertionibus Catholicis et haereticis.
Bernard of Como. Lucerna Inquisitorum haereticae pravitatis.
Bzovius, A. Historiae Ecclesiasticae ab anno 1198 cum annotationibus F. Pegnae.
Royas, J. à. De Haereticis eorumque impia intentione et credulitate.

Simancas, J. De Catholicis assertionibus.
Zanchino. Tractatus de Haereticis.

See also:

Carena, C. Tractatus de officio Sanctae Inquisitionis. Lyons. 1669.
Ludovico à Paramo. De origine et progressu officii Sanctae Inquisitionis. Madrid. 1598.
Peña, F. Inquirendorum haereticorum lucerna. Madrid. 1598.

B. DOCUMENTS ON THE INQUISITION.

For Papal Registers of Innocent III, Honorius III, etc. see under Papal Documents in *Gen. Bibl.* IV. For Imperial and Papal Registers see under Böhmer, J. F. in *Gen. Bibl.* IV, and also the earlier edition for 1246–1313. Stuttgart. 1844.

Badouin, M. A. Lettres inédites de Philippe le Bel. Paris. 1886.
Bene, T. del. De officio S. Inquisitionis circa haeresim cum bullis tam veteribus quam recentioribus ad eandem materiam seu ad idem officium spectantibus. Lyons. 1666.
David of Augsburg. Tractatus de haeresi Pauperum de Lugduno, sive potius de inquisitione haereticorum. Ed. Preger, W. *in* Abh. Hist. Classe. BAW. XIV. 1878.
Douais, C. Documents pour servir à l'hist. de l'Inquisition dans le Languedoc. Paris. 1900. [Includes the Sentences of Bernard de Caux and of Jean de Saint Pierre, and the Register of the Notary of the Inquisition of Carcassonne, etc.]
—— L'Inquisition: ses origines, sa procédure. Paris. 1906. [Includes S. Raymond of Peñaforte's directory for the use of Aragonese inquisitors, 1242.]
Échard, J. Scriptores ordinis Praedicatorum. 2 vols. Paris. 1719.
Frédéricq, P. Corpus documentorum Inquisitionis haereticae pravitatis Neerlandicae. 4 vols. Ghent. 1889–96.
Guy Foulquois (Clement IV). Quaestiones quindecim ad inquisitores cum annotationibus Caesaris Carenae. Lyons. 1669.
Huillard-Bréholles, J. L. A. Historia diplomatica Friderici secundi. 12 vols. Paris. 1852–61.
Magnum Bullarium Romanum. Luxemburg. 1730–58. Vols. I–VIII.
Mansi. Sacrorum conciliorum collectio. Vols. XXII–XXV. *See Gen. Bibl.* IV.
Pelhisso, G. Chronicon. Ed. Molinier, C. in appendix to De Fratre Guil. Pelisso veterrimo inquisitionis historico. Paris. 1880. *Also* ed. Douais, C. *in* Les Sources de l'hist. de l'Inquisition. *See below,* IV A.
Potthast, A. Regesta Pontificum Romanorum. *See Gen. Bibl.* IV.
Processus Inquisitionis. *In* Appendix to Vacandard, E. L'Inquisition. *See below,* IV A.
Ripoll, F. T. and Brémond. Bullarium ordinis S. Dominici. 8 vols. Rome. 1737 ff.
Sbaralea, J. H. Bullarium Franciscorum. Rome. 1759–63.
Sousa, A. de. Aphorismi Inquisitorum...cum vera historia de origine inquisitionis Lusitanae. Tournon. 1639.
Vidal, J. M. Bullaire de l'Inquisition française au XIVe siècle et jusqu'à la fin du grand schisme. Paris. 1913.

C. ON MEDIEVAL HERESIES GENERALLY.

[Besides the great collections of chronicles etc. (*see Gen. Bibl.* IV), the following may be noted.]

Archiv für Litteratur- und Kirchengeschichte des Mittelalters. Ed. Denifle, H. and Ehrle, F. 7 vols. Berlin and Freiburg-i.-B. 1885–1900.
Bibliotheca...Patrum et antiquorum scriptorum. Ed. M. de la Bigne and Despont, P. 27 vols. Lyons. 1677. Index. Genoa. 1707.
D'Argentré, C. de Duplessis. Collectio judiciorum de novis erroribus qui ab initio duodecimi saeculi...usque ad annum 1632 in ecclesia proscripti sunt et notati. 3 vols. Paris. 1728.
Döllinger, J. J. v. Beiträge zur Sektengeschichte. 2 vols. Munich. 1890. [Vol. II contains documents.]

Martène, E. and Durand, U. Thesaurus novus anecdotorum. *See Gen. Bibl.* iv.
—— Veterum scriptorum et monumentorum hist. dogm. moral. amplissima collectio. 9 vols. Paris. 1724–33.
Raynaldus, O. Annales Ecclesiastici ab 1198. *See Gen. Bibl.* v *under* Baronius.

D. On the Cathari, Waldenses, and other early sects.

Ademar of Chabannes. Chronicon. Ed. Chavanon, J. (Coll. textes.) Paris. 1897.
Alain of Lille. De fide catholica contra haereticos sui temporis. MPL. ccx.
Amati, G. Processus contra Valdenses in Lombardia. ASI. Ser. iii. 1 and 2.
Anna Comnena. Alexiadis libri xv. Ed. Schopen, L. and Reifferscheid, A. 2 vols. CSHB. 1839, 78.
Bernard of Fontcaude. Contra Waldensium sectam. MPL. cciv.
Bonacursus of Milan. Vitae haereticorum. MPL. cciv.
Caesarius of Heisterbach. Dialogus miraculorum. Ed. Strange, J. 2 vols. Cologne. 1850–1. Index. 1922.
Chanson de la Croisade contre les Albigeois. Ed. Meyer, P. 2 vols. Paris. 1875, 79.
Chronicon Turonense. Ed. Martène, E. and Durand, U. *in* Amplissima Collectio. Vol. v. *See above,* iii c.
Clédat, L. Le Nouveau Testament traduit au xiiie siècle en langue provençale suivi d'un rituel cathare. Paris. 1887.
Coggeshall, Ralph of. Chronicon Anglicanum. (Rolls.) 1875.
Débat d'Izarn et de Sicart de Figueiras. Ed. Meyer, P. *in* Bulletin SHF. Paris. 1880.
Eckbert of Schönau. Sermones adversus pestiferos foedissimosque Catharorum damnatos errores ac haereses. MPL. cxcv.
Ermengaudus. Opusculum contra haereticos. MPL. cciv.
Euthymius Zigabenus. Narratio de Bogomilis. MPG. cxxx.
Geoffroy d'Ablis. Registres. Bibl. Nat. MS latin, 4269.
Guillaume de Nangis. Chronique latine. 1113–1300. *In* Bouquet. Vols. ix, x, xx. *Also in* Guizot, F. P. C. Coll. des mém. relatifs à l'hist. de France. Vol. xiii. *See Gen. Bibl.* iv.
Guillaume de Puys-Laurens. Historia Albigensium. *In* Bouquet. Vols. xix, xx. Transl. *in* Guizot, *op. cit.* Vol. xv.
Hoveden, Roger of. Chronica. Ed. Stubbs, W. 4 vols. (Rolls.) 1868–71.
Hugues de Rouen. Contra haereticos sui temporis. MPL. cxcii.
Katharisches Rituale, Ein. Ed. Cunitz, E. Jena. 1852.
Luke of Tuy. De altera vita fideique controversiis adversus Albigensium errores. *In* Bibliotheca...Patrum. Vol. xxv. *See above,* iii c.
Mapes, Walter. De Nugibus Curialium. Ed. James, M. R. (Anecdota Oxon., Mediaeval Series, xiv.) Oxford. 1914.
Moneta of Cremona. Adversus Catharos et Waldenses. Rome. 1743.
Paris, Matthew. Chronica majora. 7 vols. (Rolls.) 1872–83.
—— Historia Anglorum. 3 vols. (Rolls.) 1866–9.
Passau, Anon. *In* Bibliotheca...Patrum. Vol. xxv. *See above,* iii c.
Peter Cantor. Summa de Catharis et Leonistis seu Pauperibus de Lugduno. *In* Martène and Durand. Thesaurus. Vol. v. *See Gen. Bibl.* iv.
—— Verbum abbreviatum. MPL. civ.
Peter the Venerable. Epistolae adversus Petrobrusianos. MPL. clxxxix.
Pierre de Vaulx-Cernay (Petrus Sarnensis). Hist. Albigensium. MPL. ccxiii; *also in* Bouquet, Vol. xix, *and in* Guizot, *op. cit.* Vol. xiv. *Also* ed. Guébin, P. and Lyon, E. Vol. i. Paris. 1926.
Pilichdorf, Peter de. Contra haeresim Waldensium tractatus. *In* Bibliotheca... Patrum. Vol. xiii. *See above,* iii c.
Rainerius Saccho. Summa de Catharis et Leonistis seu Pauperibus a Lugduno. *In* Martène and Durand. Thesaurus. Vol. v. *See Gen. Bibl.* iv.
Rescriptum haeresiarcharum Lombardiae ad Leonistes in Alemannia. Ed. Preger, W. *in* Abh. Hist. Classe. BAW. xiii.
Tiraboschi, G. Vetera Humiliatorum monumenta. 3 vols. Milan. 1766.
Vic, C. de and Vaissete, J. J. Histoire générale de Languedoc. *See Gen. Bibl.* iv.

E. On the Fraticelli, Averroists, Heretical mystics.

Albertus Magnus. Opera omnia. Ed. Borgnet, A. 38 vols. Paris. 1890-1900. Vols. xxxi, xxxii, xxiii.
—— De Quindecim Problematicis. *In* Mandonnet, P. F. Siger de Brabant. *See below*, iv d.
Analecta franciscana. 5 vols. Quaracchi. 1885-1912.
Aquinas, Thomas. Opera omnia. Rome. 1882-1906. Vols. i, ii, iii.
Bacon, Roger. Opera quaedam hactenus inedita. Ed. Brewer, J. S. (Rolls.) 1859.
Chartularium Universitatis Parisiensis. Ed. Denifle, H. 4 vols. Paris. 1889-97. Vols. i and ii.
Douceline, Vie de Sainte, fondatrice des Béguines de Marseille. Ed. Albanès, J. H. Marseilles. 1879.
Historia fratris Dulcini. Ed. Segarizzi, A. RR.II.SS. New edn. Vol. ix, pt. 5. 1907.
Historia septem Tribulationum ordinis minorum. *In* Ehrle, F. Die Spiritualen. *See below*, iv d.
Joachim of Flora. Concordia novi et veteris Testamenti. Venice. 1579.
—— Expositio in Apocalypsin. Venice. 1527.
—— Psalterium decem Chordarum. Venice. 1527.
Peckham, J. Registrum epistolarum. Ed. Martin, C. T. 3 vols. (Rolls.) 1882-5.
Ruteboeuf. Oeuvres complètes. 3 vols. Paris. 1874-5.
Salimbene. Cronica. Ed. Holder-Egger, O. MGH. Script. xxxii. 1905-13.
Siger of Brabant. Works in appendix to Mandonnet, P. F. Siger de Brabant. *See below*, iv d.
Tocco, F. Alcuni capitoli della Chronaca delle Tribolazioni. ASI. 4th ser. Vol. xvii. 1886.
—— Due opuscoli inediti di Arnaldo da Villanova. ASI. 4th ser. Vol. xviii. 1886.
Wadding, L. Annales Minorum. 25 vols. Rome. 1731-45, 1860.

IV. SECONDARY AUTHORITIES.

A. The Inquisition.

Arnould, A. Histoire de l'Inquisition. Paris. 1869.
Cauzons, T. de. Histoire de l'Inquisition en France. 2 vols. Paris. 1909, 13.
Darwin Swift, F. Life and times of James I, King of Aragon. London. 1894.
Douais, C. La formule *communicato bonorum virorum consilio* des sentences inquisitoriales. Fribourg. 1908.
—— L'Inquisition; ses origines, sa procédure. Paris. 1906.
—— La procédure inquisitoriale en Languedoc au xive siècle d'après un procès inédit de l'année 1337. Paris. 1900.
—— Les Sources de l'histoire de l'Inquisition dans le midi de la France aux xiiie et xive siècles. RQH. 1881.
Esmein, A. Hist. de la procédure criminelle en France et spécialement de la procédure inquisitoire. Paris. 1882.
—— A History of Continental Criminal Procedure. Transl. Simpson, J. Boston, Mass. 1913.
Ficker, J. Die gesetzliche Einführung der Todesstrafe für Ketzerei. MIOGF. 1880.
Flade, P. Das römische Inquisitionsverfahren in Deutschland. Leipsic. 1902.
Fournier, P. Les Officialités au moyen âge. Paris. 1889.
Frédéricq, P. Les récents historiens catholiques de l'Inquisition en France. RH. cix. 1912.
—— Robert le Bougre, premier inquisiteur-général de France. Liège. 1892.
Hansen, J. Quellen und Untersuchungen zur Geschichte des Hexenwahns und der Hexenverfolgung im Mittelalter. Bonn. 1901.
Haskins, C. H. Robert le Bougre. AHR. vii. 1902.
Havet, J. L'Hérésie et le bras séculier au moyen âge jusqu'au treizième siècle. *In* Oeuvres. Vol. iii. Paris. 1896.
Henner, C. Beiträge zur Organisation und Competenz der päpstlichen Ketzergerichte. Leipsic. 1890.

Hoffmann, F. Geschichte der Inquisition. 2 vols. Bonn. 1878.
Kaltner, B. Konrad v. Marburg und die Inquisition in Deutschland. Prague. 1882.
Lacordaire, J. B. H. Vie de St Dominique. 4th edn. Paris. 1852.
Lamothe-Langon, E. L. de. Histoire de l'Inquisition en France. 3 vols. Paris. 1829.
Langlois, C. V. L'Inquisition après les travaux récents. Paris. 1902.
Lea, H. C. A History of the Inquisition of the Middle Ages. 3 vols. New York. 1887. French transl. Reinach, S. Paris. 1900–2.
—— A History of the Inquisition in Spain. 4 vols. New York. 1906–7.
—— Superstition and Force. 4th edn. Philadelphia. 1892.

[For critiques of Lea's work see P. Frédéricq's introduction to the French translation of his *Inquisition of the Middle Ages*; articles by S. Reinach on his *Inquisition in Spain* in Revue critique d'hist. et de litt., May 1906, Oct. 1907, Feb. 1908; F. M. Baumgarten's *H. C. Lea's Historical Writings: a critical inquiry*. New York. 1909; Lord Acton's *The History of Freedom and other Essays*. London. 1909. Recent works on the Inquisition by French Catholic writers are in large measure attempts to answer Lea, *e.g.* Maillet and Moeller. *See below*.]

Limborch, P. Historia Inquisitionis cui subjungitur Liber Sententiarum Inquisitionis Tholosanae ab anno 1307 ad annum 1324. 2 vols. Amsterdam. 1692. Engl. transl. Chandler, S. London. 1731. [The English version does not contain the Liber Sententiarum.]
Llorente, J. A. Histoire critique de l'Inquisition en Espagne. Paris. 1817; 2nd edn. 4 vols. Paris. 1818.
—— Istoria critica de la Inquisicion. 10 vols. Madrid. 1822.

[The first version of this great work was in French. The original Spanish text did not appear till five years later. Only the introduction and the first four chapters relate to the Middle Ages.]

Maillet, H. L'Église et la répression sanglante de l'hérésie. Liége. 1909.
Marsollier, J. L'Histoire de l'Inquisition et son origine. Cologne. 1693.
Moeller, C. Les Bûchers et les Autos-da-fé de l'Inquisition depuis le moyen âge. RHE. XIV. 1913.
Molinier, C. Études sur quelques manuscrits des bibliothèques d'Italie concernant l'Inquisition et les croyances hérétiques du XIIe au XVIIe siècle. In Archives des missions scientifiques et littéraires. 3rd ser. Vol. XIV. Paris. 1888.
—— L'Inquisition dans le midi de la France au XIIIe et au XIVe siècles. Toulouse. 1880.
Nickerson, H. The Inquisition. A political and military study of its establishment. London. 1923.
Percin, F. J. J. Monumenta Conventus Tolosani. Toulouse. 1693.
Robert, A. Les Signes d'infamie au moyen âge. Paris. 1891.
Tanon, L. L'Histoire des tribunaux de l'Inquisition en France. Paris. 1893.
Turberville, A. S. Mediaeval Heresy and the Inquisition. London. 1920.
Vacandard, E. L'Inquisition. 2nd edn. Paris. 1913. Engl. transl. Conway, B. L. London. 1908.
Vidal, J. M. Le Tribunal de l'Inquisition de Pamiers. *In* Annales de St Louis-des-François. 1904–5.
Zurita, G. Anales de la Corona de Aragon. 7 vols. Saragossa. 1610–21.

B. On Medieval Heresies generally.

Alphandéry, P. Les Idées morales chez les hétérodoxes latins au début du XIIIe siècle. Paris. 1903.
Bossuet, J. B. The History of the Variations of the Protestant Churches. Engl. transl. 2nd edn. Dublin. 1836.
Comba, E. I nostri Protestanti. Vol. I. Avanti la riforma. Florence. 1895.
Cunitz, E. Beiträge zu den theol. Wissenschaften. 1852.
Döllinger, J. J. v. Beiträge zur Sektengeschichte. *See above*, III c.
Füsslin, J. C. Neue und unpartheyische Kirchen- und Ketzerhist. d. Mittlern Zeit. 3 vols. Leipsic. 1770–4.

Gieseler, J. C. L. Lehrbuch d. Kirchengeschichte. *See Gen. Bibl.* v. [Vol. III contains extracts from documents.]
Gregorovius, F. Geschichte der Stadt Rom im Mittelalter. *See Gen. Bibl.* v.
Hahn, C. U. Geschichte der Ketzer im Mittelalter. 3 vols. Stuttgart. 1845–50.
Harnack, C. G. A. Lehrbuch d. Dogmengeschichte. *See Gen. Bibl.* v.
Hastings, J. Encyclopaedia of Religion and Ethics. *See Gen. Bibl.* I. [Articles on Albigenses, Bogomiles, Inquisition, Waldenses etc.]
Loofs, F. Leitfaden zum Studium d. Dogmengeschichte. Halle. 1906.
Neander, J. A. W. Allgemeine Geschichte der christlichen Religion und Kirche. 3rd edn. Hamburg. 1856. Engl. transl. Torrey, J. 9 vols. in 10. London. 1850–8.
Reusch, J. H. Index der verboten Bücher. 3 vols. Bonn. 1883.
Reuter, H. F. Geschichte der relig. Aufklärung im Mittelalter. 2 vols. Berlin. 1875, 77.
Tocco, F. L'Eresia nel medio evo. Florence. 1884.

C. On the Cathari, Waldenses, and other early sects.

Albe, E. L'Hérésie albigeoise et l'Inquisition en Quercy. *In* Revue d'histoire de l'Église en France. Vol. I. 1910.
Beausobre, I. de. Histoire critique de Manichée et du Manichéisme. 2 vols. Amsterdam. 1734–9.
Benoist, J. Histoire des Albigeois et des Vaudois. 2 vols. Paris. 1691.
Bérard, A. Les Vaudois, leur histoire sur les deux venants des Alpes du IVe au XVIIIe siècle. Paris. 1892.
Boutaric, E. Saint Louis et Alphonse de Poitiers: Réunion des provinces du midi et de l'ouest à la couronne. Paris. 1870.
Brutails, J. A. Étude sur la condition des populations rurales du Roussillon au moyen âge. Paris. 1891.
Catel, G. de. Histoire des comtes de Toulouse. Toulouse. 1628.
—— Mémoires de l'hist. de Languedoc. Toulouse. 1633.
Chabrand, J. A. Vaudois et Protestants dans les Alpes: recherches historiques. Grenoble. 1886.
Chassanion de Monistrol. Histoire des Albigeois. Geneva. 1598.
Chevalier, J. Mémoire historique sur les hérésies en Dauphiné avant le XIIe siècle, accompagnés de documents inédits sur les sorciers et les Vaudois. Valence. 1890.
Comba, E. L'Histoire des Vaudois d'Italie. Paris. 1898.
—— Waldo and the Waldensians before the Reformation. Transl. Comba, T. E. New York. 1880.
Compayré, C. Études historiques et documents inédits sur l'Albigeois. Albi. 1841.
Conybeare, F. C. The Key of Truth. Oxford. 1895. [The connexion between the Paulicians and the Albigenses is discussed in the introduction.]
Diechkoff, W. Die Waldenser im Mittelalter. Göttingen. 1851.
Douais, C. Les Albigeois; leur origine. Paris. 1879.
—— L'Albigéisme et les Frères Prêcheurs à Narbonne au XIIIe siècle. Paris. 1894.
—— Les Frères Prêcheurs en Gascogne au XIIIe et au XIVe siècle. Paris. 1888.
—— Les Hérétiques du midi au XIIIe siècle. Paris. 1891.
Faber, G. S. An Inquiry into the history and theology of the ancient Vallenses and Albigenses. London. 1838. [Answered by S. R. Maitland. *See below.*]
Gaster, M. Lectures on Greeko-Slavonic Literature. London. 1887.
Gay, J. L'Histoire des schismes et hérésies des Albigeois. Paris. 1561.
Gay, T. L'Histoire des Vaudois refaite d'après les plus récentes recherches. Paris. 1912.
Guiraud, J. L'Albigéisme languedocien aux XIIe et XIIIe siècles. Introd. to Cartulaire de Notre-Dame de Prouille. Vols. I, II. Paris. 1907.
—— Le *Consolamentum* ou initiation cathare; la Répression de l'hérésie au moyen âge. *In* Questions d'Hist. et d'Archéol. chrétiennes. Paris. 1906.
—— St Dominique. Paris. 1901. Engl. transl. Mattos, K. de. London. 1901.

Haupt, H. Waldenserthum und Inquisition im sudöstl. Deutschland. Freiburg-i.-B. 1890.
Hauréau, A. Bernard Délicieux et l'inquisition albigeoise. Paris. 1887.
Hausrath, A. Die Arnoldisten. (Weltverbesserer im Mittelalter. Vol. III.) Leipsic. 1895.
Lombard, A. Pauliciens, Bulgares, et Bon-hommes. Geneva. 1879.
—— Pierre Waldo et les Vaudois du Briançonnais. Geneva. 1880.
Luchaire, A. Innocent III [Vol. II]. La croisade des Albigeois. Paris. 1905.
Mahul, A. J. Cartulaire et archives des communes de l'ancien diocèse...de Carcassonne. 7 vols. Paris. 1857–82.
Maitland, S. R. Facts and documents illustrative of the Albigenses and Waldenses. London. 1832.
Melia, P. The origin, persecution, and doctrines of the Waldenses. London. 1870.
Molinier, C. L'Endura, coutume religieuse des derniers sectaires albigeois. Bordeaux. 1881.
Montet, E. Hist. littéraire des Vaudois du Piémont, d'après des monuments. Paris. 1885.
Müller, K. Die Waldenser. Gotha. 1886.
Muston, A. L'Israel des Alpes: histoire des Vaudois, suivie d'une bibliographie. Paris. 1851. Engl. transl. London. 1852.
Perrin, J. P. Histoire des Vaudois. Geneva. 1619.
Peyrat, N. Histoire des Albigeois. 2 vols. Paris. 1880, 82.
Preger, W. Beiträge zur Geschichte der Waldensier im Mittelalter. *In* Abh. Hist. Classe. BAW. XIII. 1875.
Raeke, F. Bogomili i Patarini. *In* Rad. Vols. VII, VIII, X. (Jugoslav. Akad. Znan. i Umjet.) Agram. 1870.
Schmidt, C. Histoire et doctrine de la secte des Cathares ou Albigeois. Paris. 1848.
Smedt, C. de. Les Sources de l'histoire de la croisade contre les Albigeois. RQH. 1874.
Todd, J. H. The Books of the Vaudois...the Waldensian MSS. London, Cambridge, and Dublin. 1865.
Vacandard, E. Arnaud de Brescia. RQH. XXXV.
Vedder, H. C. Origin and early history of Waldenses. *In* American Journal of Theology. Chicago. 1900.
Vidal, J. M. Les derniers ministres d'Albigéisme. RQH. 1906.
Warner, H. J. The Albigensian Heresy. London. 1922.

D. On the Fraticelli, Averroists, Heretical mystics etc.

Alphandéry, P. Y a-t-il eu un averroïsme populaire aux XIIIe et XIVe siècles? *In* Revue de l'hist. des religions. Paris. 1901.
Asin y Palacios, M. El Averroïsmo teologico de S. Tomas a Aquino. Saragossa. 1904.
Baeumker, C. Die europäische Philosophie des Mittelalters. *In* Die Kultur der Gegenwart. Ed. Hinneberg, P. I, 5. Berlin. 1909.
—— Ein Traktat gegen die Amalricianer aus dem Anfang des XIII Jahrhts. *In* Jahrb. f. Philos. u. spekul. Theol. Paderborn. 1893.
Baeumker, C. and Hertling, G. v. Beiträge zur Gesch. der Philosophie des Mittelalters. Münster. 1891–1909.
Boer, J. T. de. Geschichte der Philosophie im Islam. Stuttgart. 1901. Engl. transl. London. 1903.
Boileau, J. Histoire des flagellants. Amsterdam. 1701.
Callacy, F. L'Idéalisme franciscain spirituel au XIVe siècle. Louvain. 1911.
Carra de Vaux, A. Avicenne. Paris. 1900.
—— Gazali. Paris. 1902.
Delacroix, H. Essai sur le spéculatif en Allemagne au XIVe siècle. Paris. 1900.
Denifle, H. Das Evangelium aeternum und die Commission zu Anagni. *In* Archiv f. Litteratur- u. Kirchengeschichte. Vol. I. Berlin. 1885.
Döllinger, J. J. v. Der Weissagungsglaube und das Prophetenthum in der christl. Zeit. Leipsic. 1871. Engl. transl. ed. Plummer, A. London. 1873.

Douais, C. Essai sur l'organisation des études dans l'ordre des Frères-Prêcheurs. Paris. 1884.
Ehrle, F. Die Spiritualen, ihr Verhältnis zum Franziskanerorden u. zu den Fraticellen. *In* Archiv f. Litteratur- u. Kirchengeschichte. Vols. I–IV 1885–8.
—— John Peckham über den Kampf des Augustinismus und Aristotelismus. *In* Zeitschrift f. Kathol. Theol. 1889.
Feret, P. La faculté de théologie de Paris et les docteurs les plus célèbres. Le moyen âge. Vols. I and II. Paris. 1894, 97.
Fournier, P. Joachim de Flore, ses doctrines, son influence. RQH. I. 1900.
Gardner, E. G. Joachim of Flora and the everlasting Gospel. *In* Franciscan Essays. By Sabatier, P. and others. Aberdeen. 1912.
Gebhart, E. L'Italie mystique; la Renaissance religieuse au moyen âge. 6th edn. Paris. 1908. Engl. transl. ed. Hulme, E. M. London. 1922.
—— Recherches nouvelles sur l'hist. du Joachitisme. RH. XXXI. 1886.
Hallmann, E. Die Geschichte des Ursprungs der belgischen Beghinen. Berlin. 1843
Haupt, W. Die Geschichte des Joachitismus. Gotha. 1885.
Hauréau, B. Histoire de la philosophie scholastique. Paris. 1880.
Heitz, T. Essai hist. sur les rapports entre la philosophie et la foi de Bérengar de Tours et Thomas d'Aquin. Paris. 1909.
Jourdain, C. Recherches sur l'âge et l'origine des traductions latins d'Aristote, et sur les comm. grecs ou arabes employés par les docteurs scholastiques. Paris. 1843.
—— Excursions hist. et philosophiques à travers le moyen âge. Paris. 1880.
—— Sources philosophiques des hérésies d'Amaury de Bène et David de Dinan. *In* Actes AcadIBL. XXVI. 1870–81.
Jundt, A. Histoire du Panthéisme populaire au moyen âge et au XVIe siècle, suivie de pièces inédites concernant les Frères du libre esprit, maître Eckhart, les libertines spirituels, etc. Paris. 1875.
Little, A. The Grey Friars in Oxford. (Oxford Hist. Soc. XX.) Oxford. 1892.
Mandonnet, P. F. Pierre le Vénérable et son activité littéraire contre l'Islam. Paris. 1894.
—— Siger de Brabant et l'Averroïsme latin au XIIIe siècle. 2nd edn. 2 vols. Louvain. 1908, 11.
Mosheim, J. L. v. De Beghardis et Beguinabus commentarius. Leipsic. 1790.
Müller, K. Die Anfänge des Minoritenordens. Freiburg. 1885.
Munk, S. Mélanges de la philosophie juive et arabe. Paris. 1859.
Ogniben, A. I Guglielmiti del secolo XIII. Perugia. 1847.
Owen, J. The Skeptics of the Italian Renaissance. London. 1893.
Paris, G. Siger de Brabant. *In* La Poésie du moyen âge. Paris. 1895.
Poole, R. L. Illustrations of the history of Medieval Thought. *See Gen. Bibl.* V.
Preger, W. Das Evangelium aeternum und Joachim von Floris. *In* Abh.Hist. Classe.BAW. XII. 1874.
—— Geschichte d. deutschen Mystik im Mittelalter. Vol. I. Leipsic. 1874.
—— Meister Eckhart und die Inquisition. Munich. 1896.
Reinach, S. Cultes, mythes, et religions. Paris. 1906.
Renan, E. Averroës et l'Averroïsme. Paris. 1861.
—— Nouvelles études d'histoire religieuse. Paris. 1884.
Schott, L. E. Die Gedanken des Abtes Joachim v. Floris. ZKG. 1902.
Tamassia, N. S. Francesco d'Assisi e la sua leggenda. Padua and Verona. 1906.
Tocco, F. Gli apostolici e Fra Dolcino. ASI. 5th ser. Vol. XIX. 1897.
—— Guglielmina Boema e i Gugliemiti. *In* Mem. della R. Accad. dei Lincei. Cl. filol. VIII. 1899.
Wulf, M. de. Hist. de la philosophie médiévale. 5th edn. 2 vols. Louvain. 1924–5. Engl. transl. Messenger, E. C. 2 vols. London. 1926.

CHAPTER XXI.

THE MENDICANT ORDERS.

I. GENERAL.

Heimbucher, M. Die Orden und Kongregationen der katholischen Kirche. Vol. II. Paderborn. 1907. [Contains valuable bibliographies.]

II. FRANCISCANS.

A. Sources.

(i) *Lives of St Francis, etc.*

Opuscula S. P. Francisci Assisiensis. Quaracchi. 1904. Reprinted 1929.

Boehmer, H. Analekten zur Geschichte des Franciscus von Assisi. Tübingen and Leipsic. 1904.

The Writings of St Francis of Assisi. Transl. Robinson, P. Philadelphia. 1906.

Legendae S. Francisci Assisiensis. *In* Analecta Franciscana. x. Fasc. i–iii. Thomas de Celano, Vitae. Quaracchi. 1927–8.

S. Francisci Assisiensis Vita et Miracula additis opusculis liturgicis auctore Fr. Thoma de Celano. Ed. d'Alençon, E. Rome. 1906. [This has superseded the edition in ASBoll. Oct. (die 4) II.]

The Lives of S. Francis of Assisi by Brother Thomas of Celano. Transl. Ferrers Howell, A. G. London. 1908.

La Légende de S. François d'Assise par Julien de Spire. Ed. Van Ortroy, F. AB. XXI. 1902.

Legenda Trium Sociorum. ASBoll. Oct. (die 4) II. 723–42. Rome. 1866. Ed. Faloci Pulignani, M. Foligno. 1892.

The Legend of St Francis by the Three Companions. Transl. Salter, E. G. (Temple Classics.) London. 1905.

La Leggenda di San Francesco scritta da tre suoi Compagni (legenda trium sociorum). Ed. Civezza, M. da, and Domenichelli, T. Rome. 1899.

[On Legenda Trium Sociorum, *see* Van Ortroy, F. *in* AB. XIX; Sabatier, P. *in* RH. LXXV; Goetz, W. Die Quellen zur Geschichte des hl. Franz von Assisi. Gotha. 1904.]

La leggenda latina di S. Francesco secondo l'anonimo Perugino. Ed. Van Ortroy, F. *in* Miscellanea Francescana. IX. Foligno. 1902.

Speculum Perfectionis seu S. Francisci Legenda Antiquissima, auctore Fratre Leone. Ed. Sabatier, P. Paris. 1898. [A revised edition is being issued by the British Society of Franciscan Studies. *See below*, B. No. 13.]

Documenta Antiqua Franciscana. Ed. Lemmens, L. Quaracchi. 1901.

Description of a Franciscan Manuscript, by Little, A. G. *in* Collectanea. I. (Brit. Soc. of Franciscan Studies. v.) Aberdeen. 1914. *And* Un Nouveau Manuscrit Franciscain. (Opuscules de critique historique. XVIII.) Paris. 1919.

La Legenda Antiqua S. Francisci. Ed. Delorme, F. M. *in* Archivum Franciscanum Hist. xv. Quaracchi. 1922.

Actus S. Francisci in Valle Reatina. Ed. Pennacchi, F. *in* Miscell. Franc. XIII. 1911.

Bonaventura, St. Legendae duae de Vita S. Francisci. Quaracchi. 1898.

—— Opera Omnia. Tom. VIII (Opuscula...ad res ordinis Fratrum Minorum spectantia). Quaracchi. 1898.

Bernard de Bessa. Liber de Laudibus S. Francisci. *In* Analecta Franciscana. III.

Actus B. Francisci et sociorum ejus. Ed. Sabatier, P. Paris. 1902.

I Fioretti del...Santo Francesco e de' suoi frati. Ed. Passerini, G. L. Florence. [1903.] (Many editions and translations.)

Francisci Bartholi de Assisio Tractatus de Indulgentia S. M. de Portiuncula. Ed. Sabatier, P. Paris. 1900.

Dialogus de vitis sanctorum fratrum minorum. Ed. Lemmens, L. Rome. 1902. *Also* ed. Delorme, F. Quaracchi. 1923.
S. Antonii de Padua vitae duae. Ed. Kerval, L. de. Paris. 1904.
[Thomas de Celano.] Legenda S. Clarae. Ed. Pennacchi, F. Assisi. 1910.
Life of St Clare ascribed to Fr. Thomas of Celano. Transl. Robinson, P. Philadelphia. 1910.

(ii) *Franciscan Rules, etc.*

Seraphicae Legislationis Textus Originales. Quaracchi. 1897.
Regula Antiqua Fratrum et Sororum de Poenitentia. Ed. Sabatier, P. (Opuscules de critique hist. I.) Paris. 1901. [*Cf.* Archiv. Franc. Hist. VI, XIV.]
Two Franciscan Rules—"The Thirde Order of Seynt Franceys," and "The Rewle of Sustris Menouresses enclosid." Ed. Seton, W. W. (EETS.) 1914.
Bullarium Franciscanum. Ed. Sbaralea, J. H., de Latera, and Eubel, C. Vols. I–VIII with 2 suppl. vols. Rome and Quaracchi. 1759–1908.
Ehrle, F. Die ältesten Redactionen der Generalconstitutionen Franziskaner-Ordens. *In* Archiv f. Lit. u. Kirchengeschichte. VI. [Also printed in S. Bonaventurae Opera Omnia. VIII. pp. 449–67. Quaracchi. 1898.]
[For other constitutions, general and provincial, *see* Guide to Franciscan Studies by Little, A. G. (S.P.C.K.) London. 1920.]
Firmamentum trium ordinum beatissimi Patris nostri Francisci. Paris. 1512. Venice. 1515.

(iii) *Chronicles, Registers, Letters.*

[Odo Rigaldi.] Journal des visites pastorales d'Eudes Rigaud archevesque de Rouen. Ed. Bonnin, T. Rouen. 1847.
Monumenta Franciscana. Vol. I. Ed. Brewer, J. S. Vol. II. Ed. Howlett, R. (Rolls.) 1858, 82.
[Eccleston.] Tractatus Fr. Thomae vulgo dicti de Eccleston de Adventu Fratrum Minorum in Angliam. Ed. Little, A. G. Paris. 1909.
Jordani, Chronica fratris. Ed. Boehmer, H. Paris. 1908.
Salimbene. Cronica fr. Salimbene de Adam. Ed. Holder-Egger, O. MGH. Script. XXXII. 1905–13.
Lanercost, Chronicon de. Ed. Stevenson, J. Edinburgh. 1839.
Registrum Epistolarum Fratris Johannis Peckham, archiepiscopi Cantuariensis. Ed. Martin, C. T. 3 vols. (Rolls.) 1882–5.
Angelo da Clareno. Chronica Septem Tribulationum. (Portions ed. Döllinger, J. J. I. von *in* Beiträge z. Sektengeschichte des Mittelalters. II. Munich. 1890. Ehrle, F. *in* Archiv f. Lit. u. Kirchengeschichte. II. Tocco, F. Le due prime Tribulazioni dell' Ordine Francescano. Rome. 1908.)
—— Expositio Regulae Fratrum Minorum. Ed. Oliger, L. Quaracchi. 1912.
Chronica XXIV Generalium Ordinis Minorum. *In* Analecta Franciscana. III. Quaracchi. 1897.
Bartholomaeus de Pisa. De conformitate vitae B. Francisci ad vitam Domini Iesu. *In* Analecta Franciscana. IV, V. Quaracchi. 1906, 12.
Bernardini Aquilani Chronica fratrum minorum observantiae. Ed. Lemmens, L. Rome. 1902.
Nicolaus Glassberger. Chronica. *In* Analecta Franciscana. II. Quaracchi. 1887.
Registrum Fratrum Minorum Londoniae. Ed. Kingsford, C. L. *In* The Grey Friars of London. (Brit. Soc. of Franc. Studies. VI.) Aberdeen. 1915.
Monumenta Germaniae Franciscana herausgegeben von Mitgliedern des Franziskanerordens. II Abt.: Urkundenbücher. Bd. I: Urkundenbuch der Kustodien Goldberg und Breslau von P. Chrysogonus Reisch, OFM. I Theil. 1240–1517. Düsseldorf. 1917. [The first volume of a great projected series.]
Bihl, M. De tertio Ordine S. Francisci in Provincia Germaniae superioris sive Argentinensi Syntagma. *In* Archiv. Franc. Hist. XIV–XV, XVII–XVIII. 1921–5, in progress.
Berthold von Regensburg. Vollständige Ausgabe seiner deutschen Predigten. Ed. Pfeiffer, F. and Strobl, J. 2 vols. Vienna. 1862, 80.
Le Prediche Volgari di S. Bernardino da Siena. Ed. Banchi, L. Siena. 1880–8.

B. Societies and Periodicals.

British Society of Franciscan Studies. Aberdeen. 1908 ff., in progress.
1. Liber exemplorum ad usum praedicantium. Ed. Little, A. G. 1908.
2. Fratris J. Pecham Tractatus tres de paupertate. Ed. Kingsford, C. L., Little, A. G., Tocco, F. 1910.
3. Fratris Rogeri Bacon Compendium Studii Theologiae. Ed. Rashdall, H. 1911.
4. Part of the Opus Tertium of Roger Bacon. Ed. Little, A. G. 1912.
5. Collectanea Franciscana. i. Ed. Little, A. G., James, M. R., Bannister, H. M. 1914.
6. The Grey Friars of London. Kingsford, C. L. 1915.
7. Some new sources for the Life of Blessed Agnes of Bohemia. Seton, W. W. 1915.
8. Giles of Assisi. Seton, W. W. 1918.
9. Materials for the history of the Franciscan Province of Ireland. Fitzmaurice, E. B. and Little, A. G. 1920.
10. Collectanea Franciscana. ii. Ed. Kingsford, C. L. 1922.
11. Nicolas Glassberger and his works. Seton, W. W. 1923.
12. The English Minoresses. Bourdillon, C. 1926.
13. Speculum Perfectionis. i. Ed. Sabatier, P. 1928.
14. Roger Bacon. Medical works. Ed. Little, A. G. and Withington, E. 1929.
Extra Series. i. Franciscan Essays. Sabatier, P., and others. 1912. ii. The Grey Friars of Canterbury. Cotton, C. 1924.

Archivum Franciscanum Historicum. Quaracchi. 1908 ff., in progress.
Études franciscaines. Paris. 1899 ff., in progress.
Franziskanische Studien. Münster-i.-W. 1914 ff., in progress.
La France franciscaine. Lille. 1912 ff., in progress.
Miscellanea Francescana. Ed. Faloci Pulignani, M. Foligno. 1886 ff., in progress.
Opuscules de critique historique. Ed. Sabatier, P. Fascicules 1–18. Paris. 1901–19.
Revue d'histoire franciscaine. Ed. Lemaître, H. Paris. 1924 ff., in progress.

C. Later Writers.

Balthasar, K. Geschichte des Armutsstreites im Franziskanerorden bis zum Konzil von Vienne. Münster-i.-W. 1911.
Bryce, W. Moir. The Scottish Grey Friars. 2 vols. Edinburgh. 1909.
Callaey, F. L'Idéalisme franciscain spirituel au xive siècle. Étude sur Ubertin de Casale. Louvain. 1911.
Carton, R. L'Expérience physique chez Roger Bacon.
—— L'Expérience mystique chez Roger Bacon.
—— La Synthèse doctrinale de Roger Bacon.
All in Gilson, E. Études de Philosophie Médiévale. ii, iii, v. Paris. 1924.
Charles, É. Roger Bacon, sa vie, ses ouvrages, ses doctrines. Paris. 1861.
Cuthbert, Fr. Life of St Francis of Assisi. London. 1912. 2nd edn. 1913, and reprints.
Davison, E. S. Some Forerunners of St Francis of Assisi. Columbia University. 1907. [diss.]
Doelle, F. Reformtätigkeit des Provincials Ludwig Henning in der sächsischen Franziskanerprovinz (1507–15). (Franziskanische Studien. Beiheft 3.) Münster-i.-W. 1915.
—— Die Martinianische Reformbewegung in der sächsischen Franziskanerprovinz im 15 u. 16 Jahrht. (*Ibid.* Beiheft 7.) 1921.
—— Die Observanzbewegung in der sächsischen Franziskanerprovinz bis...1529. Münster-i.-W. 1918.
Ehrle, F. Der Sentenzenkommentar Peters von Candia. (Franziskanische Studien. Beiheft 9.) Münster-i.-W. 1925.
Eubel, K. Geschichte der oberdeutschen (Strassburger) Minoriten-Provinz. Würzburg. 1886.
—— Geschichte der kölnischen Minoriten-Ordensprovinz. Cologne. 1906.
—— Die avignonesische Obedienz im Franziskanerorden zur Zeit des grossen abendländischen Schismas. (Franziskanische Studien. i.) 1914.
Facchinetti, V. San Francesco d'Assisi nella Storia, nella Leggenda, nell' Arte. Milan. 1921.

Facchinetti. V. San Francisco de Assís en la Historia, en la Leyenda, en la Arte. 2 vols. Barcelona and Madrid. 1925.
Felder, H. (Père Hilarin de Lucerne.) Geschichte der wissenschaftlichen Studien im Franziskanerorden bis um die Mitte des 13 Jahrht. Freiburg-i.-B. 1904. Transl. Père Eusèbe de Bar-le-Duc *as* Histoire des études dans l'Ordre de S François depuis sa fondation jusque vers la moitié du XIIIe siècle. Paris. 1908.
Ferrers Howell, A. G. St Bernardino of Siena. London. 1913.
Fidentius van den Borne. Die Franziskus-Forschung in ihrer Entwicklung dargestellt. (Veröffentlichungen aus dem Kirchenhistorischen Seminar Muenchen. IV Reihe, Nr. 6.) Munich. 1917. [Bibliographical.]
—— Die Anfänge des franziskanischen Dritten Ordens. (Franziskanische Studien Beiheft 8.) Münster-i.-W. 1925.
Gebhart, E. L'Italie mystique. Paris. 1890.
Gilliatt-Smith, E. St Clare of Assisi. London. 1914.
Gilson, E. La Philosophie de Saint Bonaventura. Paris. 1924.
Goetz, W. Die Quellen zur Geschichte des hl. Franz von Assisi. Gotha. 1904.
Golubovich, G. Biblioteca Bio-Bibliographica della Terra Santa e dell' Oriente Francescano. Vols. I–IV. Quaracchi. 1906–23.
Greiderer, V. Germania Franciscana. Vols. I and II. Innsbruck. 1777, 81.
Gubernatis, D. de. Orbis Seraphicus. Vols. I–IV. Rome and Lyons. 1682–5.
Hefele, K. Der hl. Bernhardin von Siena und die Franziskanische Wanderpredigt in Italien während des XV Jahrhunderts. Freiburg-i.-B. 1912.
Hofer, J. Biographische Studien über Wilhelm von Ockham. *In* Archiv. Franc. Hist. VI. 1913.
Holzapfel, H. Handbuch der Geschichte des Franziskanerordens. Freiburg-i.-B. 1909.
Joergensen, J. Saint Francis of Assisi. Transl. Sloane, T. O'C. New York, London. 1912.
Kleinschmidt, B. Die Basilika San Francesco in Assisi. Vols. I and II. Berlin. 1915, 26.
Knotte, E. Untersuchungen zur Chronologie von Schriften der Minoriten am Hofe Kaiser Ludwigs des Bayern. Bonn. 1903.
Kybal, V. Die Ordensregeln des hl. Franz von Assisi und die ursprüngliche Verfassung des Minoritenordens. (Beiträge zur Kulturgeschichte des Mittelalters. Ed. Goetz, W. XX.) Leipsic. 1915.
—— Ueber das Testament des hl. Franz von Assisi: Quellenkritische Studie. MIOGF. XXXVI (1915). pp. 312–40.
Lemmens, L. Die Anfänge des Klarissenordens. *In* Römische Quartalschrift f. christl. Altertumskunde. 1902.
—— Der hl. Bonaventura. Munich. 1909.
Lempp, E. Frère Élie de Cortona. Paris. 1901.
—— Die Anfänge des Klarissenordens. ZKG. XIII. 1892. XXIII. 1902.
Little, A. G. The Grey Friars in Oxford. (Oxford Hist. Soc. XX.) Oxford. 1892.
—— *ed.* Roger Bacon Commemoration Essays. Oxford. 1914.
—— Studies in English Franciscan History. Manchester. 1917.
—— Introduction of the Observant Friars into England. *In* Proc. British Acad. Vol. X. London. [1923.]
—— The Constitution of Provincial Chapters in the Minorite Order. *In* Essays in Medieval History presented to Professor T. F. Tout. Manchester. 1925.
—— The Franciscan School at Oxford in the thirteenth century. *In* Archiv. Franc. Hist. XIX. 1926.
Longpré, E. La Philosophie du B. Duns Scot. Paris. 1924.
López, A. La Provincia de España de los Frailes Menores. Apuntes históricocríticos sobre los origines de la Orden Franciscana en España. Santiago. 1915.
Macdonell, A. Sons of Francis. London and New York. 1902.
Mandic, P. D. De legislatione antiqua ordinis fratrum minorum. Vol. I. Législation franciscaine 1210–21. Mostor. 1924.
Mandonnet, P. Les origines de l'Ordo de Poenitentia. *In* Compte rendu du IVe congrès scientifique international des Catholiques. Sciences historiques. Fribourg. 1898.

Mandonnet, P. Les règles et le gouvernement de l'Ordo de Poenitentia au XIIIe siècle. (Opuscules de critique hist. IV.) Paris. 1902.
Marcellino da Civezza. Storia universale delle Missioni Francescane. I–VI. Rome and Prato. 1857–81.
Müller, K. Die Anfänge des Minoritenordens und der Bussbruderschaften. Freiburg-i.-B. 1885.
Oliger, L. De origine regularum ordinis S. Clarae. *In* Archiv. Franc. Hist. v. 1912.
Othon de Pavie. L'Aquitaine Séraphique. Auch. 1910.
Ozanam, F. Les Poètes franciscains en Italie au XIIIe siècle. 6th edn. Paris. 1882.
—— Engl. transl. Nellen, A. E. and Craig, W. C. London. 1914.
Papini, N. La Storia di S. Francesco. 2 vols. Foligno. 1825, 27.
P[arkinson], A. Collectanea Anglo-Minoritica. London. 1726.
Pelzer, A. Les 51 articles de G. Occam censurés en Avignon en 1326. RHE. XVIII. 1922. pp. 240–70.
René de Nantes. Histoire des Spirituels dans l'Ordre de Saint François. Couvin. 1909.
Riezler, S. Die literarischen Widersacher der Päpste zur Zeit Ludwigs von Bayern. Leipsic. 1874.
Sabatier, P. Vie de Saint François d'Assise. Paris. 1894.
—— Le privilège de la très haute pauvreté accordé à Sainte Claire. *In* Revue d'hist. franciscaine. I. 1924.
Sbaralea, J. H. Supplementum ad scriptores trium ordinum S. Francisci a Waddingo aliisve descriptos. Rome. 1806. New edn. Pts. I, II. Rome. 1908, 21, in progress.
Schlager, P. Beiträge zur Geschichte der kölnischen Franziskaner-Ordensprovinz im Mittelalter. Cologne. 1904.
Schnürer, G. Franz von Assisi. Munich. 1905.
Seton, W. W. Two fifteenth-century Franciscan Rules. (EETS.) 1914.
—— *ed.* St. Francis of Assisi, 1226–1926. Essays in Commemoration. London. 1926.
Suyskens, C. De S. Francisco confessore. Commentarius Praevius, Appendix ad gloriam posthumam. Analecta. ASBoll. Oct. (die 4) II. pp. 545–683, 799–1004. Rome. 1866.
Tamassia, N. St Francis of Assisi and his legend. Transl. Ragg, L. London. 1910.
Thode, H. Franz von Assisi und die Anfänge der Kunst der Renaissance in Italien. Berlin. 1885.
Tilemann, H. Studien zur Individualität des Franziskus von Assisi. (Beiträge zur Kulturgeschichte des Mittelalters. Ed. Goetz, W. XXI.) Leipsic. 1914.
Tocco, F. Studi Francescani. Naples. 1909.
—— La Questione della Povertà nel secolo XIV secondo nuovi documenti. Naples. 1910.
Underhill, E. Jacopone da Todi. A spiritual biography. London. [1919.]
Wadding, L. Annales Minorum. 2nd edn. Vols. I–XVI. Rome. 1731–6.
—— Scriptores Ordinis Minorum. Rome. 1650. Repr. Rome. 1906. *See also above*, Sbaralea, J. H.
Wauer, E. Entstehung und Ausbreitung des Klarissenordens besonders in den deutschen Minoritenprovinzen. Leipsic. 1906.

III. DOMINICANS.

A. Sources.

(i) *Lives of St Dominic.*

The chief authorities for the life of St Dominic are scattered in various publications: they are:

Dicta testium in inquisitione de vita et miraculis. ASBoll. Aug. (die 4) I. Quétif, J. and Échard, J. Scriptores Ordinis Praedicatorum. I. *See below*, III B. Mamachi, T. M. Annales Ordinis Praedicatorum. I. *See below*, III B.
Epistola inquisitorum Tolosanorum de virtutibus et miraculis. *Ibid.*
Vita auct. Iordane de Saxonia. ASBoll. Aug. (die 4) I. B. Iordanis de Saxonia Opera. Ed. Berthier, J. J. Fribourg. 1891.

Epistula Iordanis de Saxonia. *Ibid.*
Miracula coram Gregorio IX probata. *In* Quétif and Échard. I. *See below*, III B.
Miracula auct. Angelica moniali. *In* Mamachi. I. *See below*, III B.
Vita auct. Petro Ferrandi. AB. XXX.
Vita auct. Constantino Mediceo. *In* Quétif and Échard. I. *See below*, III B.
Vita auct. Humberto de Romanis. *In* Mamachi. I. *See below*, III B. (Excerpts in Quétif and Échard. I. *See below*, III B.)
Vita auct. Theodorico de Appoldia. ASBoll. Aug. (die 4) I.

(ii) *Dominican Rule etc.*

Die Constitutionen des Prediger-Ordens vom Jahre 1228, *and* Die Constitutionen des Predigerordens in der Redaction Raimunds von Peñaforte. Ed. Denifle, H. *in* Archiv f. Lit. u. Kirchengeschichte. I and V. 1885, 89.
Bullarium S. Ordinis Praedicatorum. Ed. Ripoll and Brémond. 8 vols. Rome. 1729–40.

(iii) *Dominican Chronicles, Charters etc.*

Monumenta ordinis Praedicatorum Historica. Ed. Reichert, B. M. Rome. 1897–1904. (Containing Gerardi de Fracheto Vitae Fratrum, Galvagni de la Flamma Chronica, Raymundiana, Chronica et Chronicorum excerpta, Litterae Encyclicae Magistrorum Generalium, Acta Capitulorum Generalium 1220–1844.)
Analecta S. Ordinis Fratrum Praedicatorum seu vetera Ordinis monumenta. Rome. 1893 ff.
Balme, F. and Lelaidier. Cartulaire ou Histoire diplomatique de Saint Dominique. 3 vols. Paris. 1893–1901.
Guiraud, J. Cartulaire de Notre-Dame de Prouille. Vols. I, II. Paris. 1907.
Douais, C. Acta Capitulorum provincialium Ordinis Fratrum Praedicatorum. Toulouse. 1894.
Humberti de Romanis Opera de Vita regulari. Ed. Berthier, J. J. 2 vols. Rome. 1888.
Finke, H. Ungedruckte Dominikanerbriefe des 13 Jahrhunderts. Paderborn. 1891.
Rashdall, H. The Friars Preachers *v.* the University (of Oxford). *In* Collectanea. II. (Oxford Hist. Soc. XVI.) Oxford. 1890.
Vincent of Beauvais. Speculum Historiale. Douais. 1624.
Thomas of Chantimpré (Cantipratanus). Bonum universale de apibus. Douais. 1605.
Martin of Troppau. Chronicon Pontificum et Imperatorum. MGH. Script. XXII.
Bernard Gui. Practica officii inquisitionis. Ed. Douais, C. Paris. 1886. [On the Inquisition see Bibliography to ch. XX.]
—— (Some sections of his history of the Friars Preachers have been printed in Martène, E. and Durand, U. Veterum Scriptorum Amplissima Collectio. VI. Paris. 1739. pp. 397–539; Bouquet. XXI, XXIII; and in some French archaeological societies' publications, *see* Molinier, A. Les sources de l'hist. de France. Vol. III. No. 2511. *See Gen. Bibl.* I.)
Nicholas Trivet (Trevet). Annales sex regum Angliae. Ed. Hog, T. (Eng. Hist. Soc.) London. 1845. [*Cf.* Ehrle, F. Nicolaus Trivet, sein Leben, seine Quolibet und Quaestiones ordinariae. *In* Festgabe Clemens Baeumker. Münster. 1923.]

B. LATER WRITERS.

Altaner, B. Der hl. Dominikus, Untersuchungen und Texte. Breslau. 1922.
—— Die Dominikanermissionen des 13 Jahrhts. Habelschwerdt. 1924.
Barker, E. The Dominican Order and Convocation. Oxford. 1913.
Burgo, T. de. Hibernia Dominicana. Cologne. 1762, 72.
Chapotin, M. D. Histoire des Dominicains de la Province de France. Rouen. 1898.
Cuper, Gul. De S. Dominico confessore. ASBoll. Aug. (die 4) I. pp. 359–541. Rome. 1867.
Douais, C. Essai sur l'organisation des études dans l'ordre des Frères Prêcheurs. Paris. 1884.
Drane, A. T. The History of St Dominic. London. 1891.
Fawtier, R. Sainte Catherine de Sienne. Essai de critique des sources. Sources hagiographiques. Paris. 1921.

Galbraith, G. R. The Constitution of the Dominican Order, 1216–1360. Manchester. 1925.
Gardner, E. G. St Catherine of Siena. London. 1907.
Guiraud, J. Saint Dominique. Paris. 1899.
Gumbley, W. Provincial Priors and Vicars of the English Dominicans. EHR. xxxiii. 1918. *Cf. ibid.* viii. 1893, xxxiv. 1919.
Jarrett, B. The English Dominicans. London. 1921.
Loë, P. v. and Reichert, B. M. Quellen und Forschungen zur Geschichte des Dominikanerordens in Deutschland. Leipsic. 1907 ff. [Containing also documents of interest for the general history of the Order.]
MacInerny, M. H. A History of the Irish Dominicans. Vol. i. Irish Dominican Bishops. Dublin. 1916.
Mamachi, T. M. Annales Ordinis Praedicatorum. Vol. i. Rome. 1756.
Mandonnet, P. La crise scolaire au début du xiiie siècle et la fondation de l'Ordre de Frères Prêcheurs. RHE. xv. 1914.
—— Preachers, Order of. *In* The Catholic Encyclopedia. xii. New York. 1911.
—— Saint Dominique, l'idée, l'homme, et l'œuvre. Ghent. 1921.
Miscellanea Dominicana in memoriam vii anni saecularis ab obitu s. Patris Dominici. Rome. 1923.
Mortier, D. A. Histoire des Maîtres généraux de l'ordre des Frères Prêcheurs. 8 vols. Paris. 1903 ff.
Palmer, R. (Articles on English Dominican houses in the Reliquary and elsewhere: for list *see* Jarrett, B. The English Dominicans. App. iii. London. 1921.)
Quétif, J. and Échard, J. Scriptores Ordinis Praedicatorum. 2 vols. Paris. 1719, 21.
Simon, A. L'ordre des Pénitentes de Sainte Marie Madeleine en Allemagne au xiiie siècle. Fribourg. 1918.

IV. WORKS RELATING TO THE HISTORY OF TWO OR MORE ORDERS.

[*See also* Bibliography to Vol. v, ch. xxiii (Philosophy in the Middle Ages); and Vol. vi, ch. xx (Heresies and the Inquisition).]
Archiv für Litteratur- und Kirchengeschichte des Mittelalters. Ed. Denifle, H. and Ehrle, F. 7 vols. Berlin and Freiburg-i.-B. 1885–1900.
Bierbaum, M. Bettelorden und Weltgeistlichkeit an der Universität Paris. Texte und Untersuchungen. Münster-i.-W. 1920.
Denifle, H. and Chatelain, E. Chartularium Universitatis Parisiensis. 3 vols. Paris. 1889–97.
—— Auctarium Chartularii Univ. Paris. 2 vols. Paris. 1894, 97.
Dugdale, W. Monasticon Anglicanum. New edn. Vol. vi, pt. iii. *See Gen. Bibl.* iv.
Felten, J. Robert Grosseteste. Freiburg-i.-B. 1887.
Finke, H. Acta Aragonensia. Vols. i–iii. Berlin and Leipsic. 1908–22.
Fournier, M. Les Statuts et Privilèges des universités françaises. 3 vols. Paris. 1890–2.
Glorieux, P. Prélats français contre religieux mendiants (1281–1290). *In* Revue d'hist. de l'Église de France. xi. 1925.
Gratien, R. P. Ordres mendiants et clergé séculier à la fin du xiiie siècle. (Études Franciscaines. xxvi.) 1924.
Grosseteste, Robert. Epistolae. Ed. Luard, H. R. (Rolls.) 1861.
Hefele, H. Die Bettelorden und das religiöse Volksleben Ober- und Mittelitaliens im 13 Jahrht. (Beiträge zur Kulturgeschichte des Mittelalters und der Renaissance. Ed. Goetz, W. ix.) Leipsic and Berlin. 1910.
Histoire Littéraire de la France. Vols. xviii–xxxv. Paris. 1835–1921.
Jallonghi, E. La grande discordia tra l'Università di Parigi e i Mendicanti. *In* Scuola Cattolica. Milan. Vols. xiii, 1917, xiv, 1918.
Lea, H. C. History of the Inquisition of the Middle Ages. *See Gen. Bibl.* v.
Lecoy de la Marche, A. La chaire française au moyen âge. 2nd edn. Paris. 1886.
Little, A. G. Educational organisation of the Mendicant Friars in England. TRHS. viii. 1895.
—— Administrative divisions of the Mendicant Orders in England. EHR. xxxiii. 1918.

Little, A. G. The Mendicant Orders. *In* Mediaeval England. Ed. Davis, H. W. C. Oxford. 1924.
—— Measures taken by the Prelates of France against the Friars in A.D. 1289–90. *In* Miscellanea Fr. Ehrle. III. Rome. 1924.
Luchaire, A. Innocent III. 6 vols. Paris. 1905–8. (*Esp.* [II] La Croisade des Albigeois *and* [VI] Le Concile de Latran et la réforme de l'Église.)
Marx, J. L'Inquisition en Dauphiné. (BHE. 206.) Paris. 1914.
Pierron, J. B. Die Katholischen Armen. Freiburg-i.-B. 1911.
Rashdall, H. The Universities of Europe in the Middle Ages. *See Gen. Bibl.* v.
Recueil de Voyages et de Mémoires publié par la Société de Géographie. Vols. IV, X. Paris. 1839, 91.
Seppelt, F. X. Der Kampf der Bettelorden an der Universität Paris in der Mitte des 13 Jahrhts. Breslau. 1907; *and in* Kirchengeschichtliche Abhandlungen. III and VI. Ed. Sdralek, M. Breslau. 1908.
Stevenson, F. S. Robert Grosseteste. London. 1899.
Tanner, T. (Bp. of St Asaph). Notitia Monastica. Ed. Nasmith, J. Cambridge. 1787.
Tiraboschi, G. Vetera Humiliatorum monumenta. 3 vols. Milan. 1766.
Tocco, F. L'Eresia nel medio evo. Florence. 1884.
Vict. Co. Hist. (*See Gen. Bibl.* I.) Articles on Friaries.
Weber, M. Les origines des Monts-de-Piété. Rixheim. 1920.
Zanoni, L. Gli Umiliati nei loro rapporti con l'eresia. Milan. 1911.

V. CARMELITES.

Bullarium Carmelitanum. Ed. Monsignano, E. and Ximenez, I. A. Rome. 1715, 68.
Monumenta Historica Carmelitana. Ed. Zimmermann, B. (5 fasciculi only.) Lirinae. 1905–7.
Acta Capitulorum Generalium Ordinis Fratrum B.V. Mariae de Monte Carmelo. Ed. Wessels, G. Rome. 1912.
Grossus, J. Viridarium O.B.M.V. de Monte Carmelo. Antwerp. 1680.
Daniel a Virgine Maria. Vinea Carmeli. Antwerp. 1662.
—— Speculum Carmelitanum. Antwerp. 1680.
Tritheim, J. De origine progressu et laudibus O. Fr. Carmelitarum. Lyons. 1639.
Villiers a S. Stephano, C. de. Bibliotheca Carmelitana. Orleans. 1752.

VI. AUSTIN FRIARS.

Bullarium Ord. Erem. S. Augustini. Ed. Empoli, L. Rome. 1628.
Brit. Museum MS. Add. 38649 (Constitutiones Generales).
Constitutiones Generales Ord. Fr. Erem. S. Augustini. Rome. 1625.
Vitae *and* Processus Canonizationis of Johannes Bonus. *In* ASBoll. Oct. (die 22) IX. 746–885.
Lubin, A. Orbis augustinianus. Paris. 1659, 1671, 1672.
Pamphilus, J. Chronica Ord. Frat. Erem. S. Aug. Rome. 1584.
Crusenius, N. Monasticon Augustinianum. Munich. 1623.
Kolde, T. Die deutsche Augustiner-Congregation. Gotha. 1879.

CHAPTER XXII.

(A)

ECCLESIASTICAL ARCHITECTURE.

Bond, F. Gothic Architecture in England. London. 1905.
—— An introduction to English Church Architecture from the eleventh to the sixteenth century. 2 vols. London. 1913.
Bowman, H. and Crowther, T. S. Churches of the Middle Ages. 2 vols. London. 1857.
Brandon, R. and J. A. Analysis of Gothic Architecture. 2 vols. London. 1847.
Champneys, A. C. Irish Ecclesiastical Architecture. London. 1910.
Chapuy, N. M. J. and Ramée, D. Le Moyen-Âge monumental et archéologique. 4 vols. Paris. 1840-3.
Choisy, A. Histoire de l'architecture. 2 vols. Paris. 1899.
Colling, J. K. Details of Gothic Architecture. 2 vols. London. 1851, 56.
Dehio, G. and Bezold, G. Die kirchliche Baukunst des Abendlandes. 8 vols. and atlas. Stuttgart. 1884–1901.
Enlart, C. L'Art gothique et la Renaissance en Chypre. 2 vols. Paris. 1899.
—— Manuel d'archéologie française depuis les temps mérovingiens jusqu'à la Renaissance. Vol. I. Architecture religieuse. 2nd edn. Paris. 1917.
Fergusson, J. History of Architecture. 3rd edn. London. 1893.
Fletcher, B. A History of Architecture on the comparative method. 7th edn. London. 1924.
Frothingham, A. L. A History of Architecture. Vol. III. New York. 1915.
Gailhabaud, J. Monuments anciens et modernes. Vols. II, III. Paris. 1850.
Garbett, E. L. Principles of Design. 7th edn. London. 1891.
Hubbard, G. The Cathedral Church of Cefalù, Sicily. *In* Journal of the Royal Institute of British Architects. 3rd ser. Vol. xv, no. 11.
Jackson, T. G. Gothic Architecture in France, England, and Italy. 2 vols. London. 1915.
Johnson, R. J. Specimens of Early French Architecture. Newcastle-upon-Tyne. 1864.
Knight, H. G. Ecclesiastical Architecture of Italy from the time of Constantine to the fifteenth century. Vol. II. London. 1844.
Lampérez y Romea, V. Historia de la arquitectura cristiaña española en la edad media. 2 vols. Madrid. 1908–9.
Lethaby, W. R. Mediaeval Art. New edn. London. 1912.
Macgibbon, D. and Ross, T. The Ecclesiastical Architecture of Scotland from the earliest Christian times to the seventeenth century. 3 vols. Edinburgh. 1896–7.
Michel, A. Histoire de l'art depuis les premiers temps chrétiens jusqu'à nos jours. Vols. I–III, pt. 1. Paris. 1905–8.
Monumentos arquitectónicos de España. Ed. Alvarez, A., and others. 8 vols. Madrid. 1859–85.
Moore, C. H. Development and character of Gothic Architecture. 2nd edn. London. 1899.
—— The Mediaeval Church Architecture of England. New York. 1912.
Parker, J. H. Glossary of Architecture. 4th edn. 3 vols. Oxford. 1845–6.
Porter, A. Medieval Architecture. 2 vols. New York. 1909. New edn. 1912. [This book contains a lengthy bibliography of general and special works. It is concerned more with France than with England.]
Prior, E. S. History of Gothic Art in England. London. 1900.
Rickman, T. Styles of Architecture in England. 7th edn. Oxford. 1881.
Ruskin, J. Lectures on Architecture and Painting delivered at Edinburgh in November 1853. New edn. Orpington. 1891.

Ruskin, J. The Seven Lamps of Architecture. 3rd edn. Orpington. 1880.
—— The Stones of Venice. 4th edn. 3 vols. Orpington. 1886.
Scott, G. G. Lectures on...Mediaeval Architecture. 2 vols. London. 1879.
Scott, G. G., *jun.* English Church Architecture. London. 1881.
Simpson, F. M. History of Architectural Development. Vol. II. London. 1909.
Street, G. E. Some account of Gothic Architecture in Spain. New edn. 2 vols. London. 1914.
—— Brick and Marble in the Middle Ages. London. 1874.
Stroobant, F. Monuments d'architecture et de sculpture en Belgique. Brussels. 1878.
Strzygowski, J. Origin of Christian Church Art. Transl. from the German by Dalton, O. M. and Braunholtz, H. J. London. 1923.
Villa-Amil, G. P. de, and Escosura, P. de la. España artistica y monumental. 3 vols. Paris. 1842–50.
Viollet-le-Duc, E. E. Dictionnaire raisonné de l'architecture française du XIe au XVIe siècle. 10 vols. Paris. 1858–68.
—— Rational Building. (Transl. by Huss, G. M. of the article Construction in the Dictionnaire, *above.*) New York. 1895.
Watson, W. Portuguese Architecture. London. 1908.
West, G. H. Gothic Architecture in England and France. 2nd edn. London. 1927.
Willis, R. Facsimile of the sketch-book of Wilars de Honecort. London. 1859.
—— Remarks on the Architecture of the Middle Ages, especially in Italy. Cambridge. 1835.

(B)

MILITARY ARCHITECTURE.

I. GENERAL.

Clark, G. T. Medieval military architecture in England. 2 vols. London. 1884.
Dieulafoy, M. Le Château-Gaillard et l'architecture militaire au XIIIe siècle. *In* Mém. AcadIBL. XXXVI. 1898.
Enlart, C. Manuel d'archéologie française. Vol. II. Paris. 1904.
Harvey, A. The castles and walled towns of England. London. 1911.
Krieg von Hochfelden, G. H. Geschichte der Militär-Architektur in Deutschland. Stuttgart. 1859.
Mackenzie, Sir J. D. The castles of England, their story and structure. 2 vols. London. 1897.
Thompson, A. Hamilton. Military architecture in England during the Middle Ages. London. 1912.
Viollet-le-Duc, E. Dictionnaire raisonné de l'architecture française du XIe au XVIe siècle. 10 vols. Paris. 1858–68.
—— Essai sur l'architecture militaire au moyen âge. Paris. 1854. Engl. transl. Macdermott, M. Oxford. 1860.
—— Histoire d'une forteresse. Paris. [1874.]

II. EARLY EARTHWORKS AND CASTLES.

Allcroft, A. Hadrian. Earthwork of England. London. 1908.
Armitage, Ella S. Anglo-Saxon burhs and early Norman castles. *In* Proc. Soc. Antiq. Scotland. XXXIV. 260–88.
—— The early Norman castles of England. EHR. XIX (1904). 209–45, 417–55.
—— The early Norman castles of the British Isles. London. 1912.
Hope, [Sir] W. H. St John. English fortresses and castles of the tenth and eleventh centuries. *In* Archaeol. Journ. LX (1903). 72–90.
Neilson, G. The motes in Norman Scotland. *In* Scottish Review. LXIV (1898). 209–38.

Orpen, G. H. Motes and Norman castles in Ireland. *In* Journ. Roy. Soc. Antiq. Ireland. XXXVII (1907). 123–52.
—— Mote and bretesche building in Ireland. EHR. XXI (1906). 417–44.
Round, J. H. English castles. *In* Quarterly Rev. CLXXIX (1894). 27–57.
—— The castles of the Conquest. *In* Archaeologia. LVIII (1902). 313–40.
Westropp, T. J. Irish motes and early Norman castles. *In* Journ. Roy. Soc. Antiq. Ireland. XXXIV (1905). 313–45; XXXV (1906). 402–6.

III. SPECIAL MONOGRAPHS AND DESCRIPTIONS.

Bates, C. J. The border holds of Northumberland. Vol. I. *In* Archaeol. Aeliana. 2nd ser. XIV. Newcastle. 1921.
Bilson, J. Gilling castle. *In* Yorks. Archaeol. Journ. XIX. 105–92. Leeds. 1907.
Bothamley, C. H. The walled town of Aigues-Mortes. *In* Archaeol. Journ. LXXIII (1916). 217–94.
Cooper, T. P. York: the story of its walls, bars, and castles. London. 1904.
—— The history of the castle at York. London. 1911.
Curzon of Kedleston, G. N., Marquess. Bodiam castle. London. 1926.
Hartshorne, C. H. Feudal and military antiquities of Northumberland and the Scottish borders. *In* Mem. British Archaeol. Inst., Newcastle. Vol. II. London. 1858.
Hope, [Sir] W. H. St John. The castle of Ludlow. *In* Archaeologia. LXI (1908), 257–328.
I'Anson, W. M. The castles of the North Riding. *In* Yorks. Archaeol. Journ. XXII. 303–99. Leeds. 1913.
—— Helmsley castle. *Ibid.* XXIV. 325–68. Leeds. 1917.
Knowles, W. H. Aydon castle. Archaeologia. LVI (1898). 71–88.
—— The castle of Newcastle-upon-Tyne. *In* Archaeol. Aeliana. 4th ser. Vol. II. Newcastle-upon-Tyne. 1926.
Lefèvre-Pontalis, E. Le château de Coucy. (Petites monographies des grands édifices de la France.) [1909.]
Mackenzie, W. Mackay. The mediaeval castle in Scotland. London. 1927.
Middleton, Sir A. E. An account of Belsay castle. Newcastle-upon-Tyne. 1910.
Sands, H. Bodiam castle. *In* Sussex Archaeol. Coll. XLVI. 114–33. Lewes. 1903.
—— Some Kentish castles. (Memorials of Old Kent.) London. 1907.
—— The Tower of London. (Memorials of Old London, vol. I.) London. 1908.
Thompson, A. Hamilton. The castles of Yorkshire. (Memorials of Old Yorkshire.) London. 1909.
Viollet-le-Duc, E. La cité de Carcassonne. Paris. 1858.
—— Description du château de Coucy. Paris. [1857.]
See also Clark, G. T. and Mackenzie, Sir J. D. in section I above.

CHAPTER XXIII.

THE ART OF WAR TO 1400.

I. GENERAL.

Delbrück, H. Gesch. d. Kriegskunst im Rahmen d. polit. Geschichte. 3 vols. Berlin. 1900–7. Vols. i, ii. 2nd edn. 1908–9. [Vol. iii deals with medieval warfare.]
Köhler, G. Die Entwickelung d. Kriegswesens u. d. Kriegführung in d. Ritterzeit v. Mitte d. 11 Jahrhunderts bis zu d. Hussitenkriegen. 3 vols. in 5 pts. Breslau. 1886–9. Suppl. pt. 1893.
Oman, C. W. C. History of the Art of War in the Middle Ages. *See Gen. Bibl.* v.

II. ENGLISH WARFARE.

Drummond, J. D. Studien zur Kriegsgeschichte Englands im 12 Jahrhundert. Berlin. 1905.
Fortescue, J. W. A history of the British army. Vol. i. London. 1899.
George, H. B. Battles of English history. 3rd edn. London. 1896.
Grose, F. Military antiquities respecting a history of the English army from the Conquest to the present time. 2 vols. London. 1786, 8. Also 1801, 1812.
Morris, J. E. The Welsh wars of Edward I. Oxford. 1901.
Orpen, G. H. Ireland under the Normans (1169–1333). *See Gen. Bibl.* v.
Ramsay, Sir J. H. The Foundations of England, or twelve centuries of British history, B.C. 55–1154. 2 vols. Oxford. 1898.
—— The Angevin empire, or the three reigns of Henry II, Richard I, and John, A.D. 1154–1216. Oxford. 1903.
—— The Dawn of the Constitution, or the reigns of Henry III and Edward I, 1216–1307. Oxford. 1908.
—— The Genesis of Lancaster, or the three reigns of Edward II, Edward III, and Richard II, 1307–99. 2 vols. Oxford. 1913.
—— Lancaster and York, 1399–1485. 2 vols. Oxford. 1892.
Round, J. H. Feudal England: historical studies of the 12th and 13th centuries. London. 1895. Repr. 1909.

III. SPECIAL BATTLES.

Edwards, J. G. The battle of Maes Madog and the Welsh campaign of 1294–5. EHR. xxxix (1924). 1–12.
Mackenzie, W. Mackay. The battle of Bannockburn, a study in medieval warfare. Glasgow. 1913.
Nicolas, Sir N. H. History of the battle of Agincourt. London. 1827. 3rd edn. 1833.
Prince, A. E. A letter of the Black Prince describing the battle of Nájera in 1367. EHR. xli (1926). 415–18. *See also* Déprez, E. La bataille de Nájera. RH. cxxxvi (1921). 97.
Round, J. H. The commune of London and other historical studies. (iii. Anglo-Norman warfare; xiv. Bannockburn.) London. 1899.
Spatz, W. Die Schlacht v. Hastings. Berlin. 1896.
Tout, T. F. Tactics of the battles of Boroughbridge and Morlaix. EHR. xix (1904). 711–15.
—— Some neglected fights between Crécy and Poitiers. EHR. xx (1905). 726–30.

IV. ARMOUR AND EQUIPMENT.

Ashdown, C. H. Armour and weapons in the Middle Ages. London. 1925.
Clephan, R. C. An outline of the history of gunpowder and that of the hand-gun, from the epoch of the earliest records to the end of the 15th cent. *In* Archaeol. Journn. LXVI (1909). 145–70.
—— The ordnance of the 14th and 15th centuries. *Ibid.* LXVIII (1911). 49–138.
Laking, Sir G. A record of European armour and arms. 5 vols. London. 1920–2.
Meyrick, Sir S. R. A critical enquiry into ancient armour from the Norman conquest to the reign of Charles II. 3 vols. London. 1824. 2nd edn. 1842.
—— Engraved illustrations of ancient arms and armour. 2 vols. London. 1830. Repr. 1854.
Ramsay, Sir J. H. The strength of English armies in the Middle Ages. EHR. XXIX (1914). 221–7.
Round, J. H. The staff of a castle in the 12th century. EHR. XXXV (1920). 90.
Tout, T. F. Firearms in the 14th century. EHR. XXVI (1911). 666–702.

CHAPTER XXIV.

CHIVALRY.

I. AUTHORITIES.

[For the romances of chivalry belonging to the Legendary Cycles see the Bibliography to ch. xxv below.]

Brakelmann, J. Les plus anciens Chansonniers français. Vol. I. Paris. 1891. Vol. II. Marbourg. 1896.

Bretex, Jacques. Les Tournois de Chauvenci. Valenciennes. 1835.

Caxton, William. The Order of Chivalry. Transl. from the French. Ed. Ellis, F. S. London. 1892.

Chartier, Alain. Le Breviaire des nobles. Complainte d'amours. Le Parlement d'amour. *In* Oeuvres de...Chartier. Ed. Du Chesne Tourangeau, A. Paris. 1617.

Curzon, Henri de. La Règle du Temple. (SHF.) Paris. 1886.

Devizes, Richard of. De rebus gestis Ricardi Primi. Ed. Howlett, R. *in* Chronicles of the reigns of Stephen, Henry II, and Richard I. Vol. III. (Rolls.) 1886. Engl. transl. Stevenson, J. *in* Church Historians of England. Vol. V, pt. I. London. 1858. *Also* transl. Giles, J. A. *in* Chronicles of the Crusades. (Bohn's Antiq. Library.) London. 1848.

Dillon, H. A., Viscount. On a MS. collection of Ordinances of Chivalry of the fifteenth century. *In* Archaeologia. 2nd ser. Vol. VII. London. 1900. p. 29.

Du Guesclin, Bertrand. Chronique de Du Guesclin. Ed. Michel, F. Paris. 1830.

Froissart, Jean. Chroniques. Ed. Luce, S. and Raynaud, G. 11 vols. (SHF.) Paris. 1869-99. Engl. transl. Berners, Lord. 1523-5. Introduction by Ker, W. P. 6 vols. (Tudor Translations.) London. 1901-3.

Histoire de Guillaume le Maréchal. Ed. Meyer, P. 3 vols. (SHF.) Paris. 1891-1901.

Histoire de Messire Jean de Boucicaut, Mareschal de France. Ed. Godefroy, T. *in* Petitot, C. B. Collection des mémoires relatifs à l'hist. de France. Sér. I. Vols. VI and VII. Paris. 1819.

Itinerarium Regis Ricardi. Ed. Stubbs, W. *in* Chronicles and Memorials of...Richard I. Vol. I. (Rolls.) 1864. Engl. transl. *in* Chronicles of the Crusades. *See above.*

Joinville, Jehan, Sire de. Histoire de Saint Louis. Ed. Wailly, N. de. Paris. 1874. Engl. transl. Johnes, J. *in* Chronicles of the Crusades. *See above.*

La Marche, Olivier de. Mémoires. Ed. Beaune, H. and d'Arbaumont, J. 4 vols. (SHF.) Paris. 1883-8.

Lefebre, Jean. Seigneur de Saint-Remy. Chronique de J. de Lalaing. [Wrongly attributed to G. Chastellain.] Ed. Buchon, J. A. *in* Collection des chroniques nationales françaises. Vol. XLI. Paris. 1825. *Also* ed. Kervyn de Lettenhove *in* Oeuvres de G. C. Vol. VIII. Brussels. 1866.

Lichtenstein, Ulrich von. Frauendienst. Ed. Bechstein, R. 2 vols. (Deutsche Dichtungen des Mittelalters. Vols. VI and VII.) Leipsic. 1888. Extracts transl. Coulton, G. G. *in* A Medieval Garner. London. 1910.

Lobeira, V. de. Amadis de Gaula. Ed. Lopez, D. U. 2 vols. Madrid. 1837-8. Another edn. 4 vols. Barcelona. 1847-8. Engl. transl. Southey, R. New edn. 3 vols. London. 1872.

Monstrelet, Enguerrand de. Chroniques. Ed. Douët-d'Arcq, L. 6 vols. (SHF.) Paris. 1857-62. Engl. transl. Johnes, T. 2 vols. London. 1840.

L'Ordene de la Chevalerie (Hue de Tabarie). Ed. Barbazan, E. Paris. 1759. Engl. transl. Morris, W. London. 1893.

Raynouard, M. Choix des poésies originales des Troubadours. 6 vols. Paris. 1816-21.

René d'Anjou. Traictie de la Forme et Devis d'ung Tournoy. *In* Oeuvres complètes. Ed. Quatrebarbes, T. de. Vol. II. Angers. 1834.

Villehardouin, Geoffrey de. La conquête de Constantinople. Ed. Wailly, N. de. Paris. 1872. *Also* ed. Bouchet, E. 2 vols. Paris. 1891. Engl. transl. Marzials, Sir F. *in* Memoirs of the Crusades. London. 1908.

II. MODERN WORKS.

(*a*) General.

Batty, J. The spirit and influence of Chivalry. London. 1890.
Chivalry. Ed. Prestage, E. London. 1928. [Bibliographies.]
Cornish, F. W. Chivalry. 2nd edn. (Social England Series.) London. 1908.
Coulton, G. G. Article: Knighthood and Chivalry *in* EncBr. Vol. xv. 1911.
—— Social life in Britain. Cambridge. 1918. Section v.
Du Cange, C. du Fresne. Glossarium...mediae et infimae Latinitatis. *See Gen. Bibl.* i.
—— Dissertations...sur l'histoire de S. Louys écrite par Jean Joinville. *In* Du Cange's edn. of Joinville. Paris. 1668. *Also in* Petitot, C. B. Collection des mémoires relatifs à l'hist. de France. Sér. i. Vol. iii. Paris. 1819.
Fauchet, C. Origines des Chevaliers, Armoiries, et Heraux. Paris. 1600.
Favygn, A. Le Théâtre d'honneur et de chevalerie. Paris. 1620.
Gibbon, E. The...Decline and Fall of the Roman Empire. Vol. vi. *See Gen. Bibl.* v.
Hallam, H. View of the state of Europe during the Middle Ages. Vol. iii. 10th edn. London. 1853.
Honoré, de Sainte-Marie [Vauzelle, B.]. Dissertations hist. et critiques sur la Chevalerie. Paris. 1718.
Lacroix, P. Vie militaire et religieuse au moyen âge. 2nd edn. Paris. 1873. Engl. transl. London. 1874.
La Curne de Sainte-Palaye, J. B. Mémoires sur l'ancienne Chevalerie. Ed. Nodier, C. 2 vols. Paris. 1826.
Meller, W. C. A Knight's life in the days of Chivalry. London. 1924.
Menestrier, C. F. De la Chevalerie ancienne et moderne. Paris. 1683. *Also in* Leber, J. M. C. Collection des...dissertations...relatifs à l'hist. de France. Vol. xii. Paris. 1836.
Mills, C. History of Chivalry, or Knighthood and its times. 2 vols. London. 1826.
Moeller, W. History of the Christian Church. *See Gen. Bibl.* v.
Palgrave, Sir Francis. The Lord and the Vassal. London. 1844.
Segar, Sir W. Honor, military and civill. London. 1602.
—— The Book of Honor and Arms. London. 1590.
Selden, John. Titles of Honor. 3rd edn. London. 1672.
Taylor, H. O. The Mediaeval Mind. 2nd edn. Vol. i. London. 1914. Ch. xxiii.
Upton, N. De studio militari. 4th Book. Ed. Bysshe, Sir E. London. 1654.
Vulson, M. de, Sieur de la Columbière. Le vray théâtre d'honneur et de chevalerie. 2 vols. Paris. 1648.

(*b*) Monographs and Treatises on Separate Countries.

Armour and Weapons.

Clephan, R. C. The defensive armour and the weapons and engines of war of mediaeval times and of the Renaissance. London. 1900.
ffoulkes, C. J. Armour and weapons. 3 vols. London. 1909.
—— The Armourer and his craft from the xiith to the xviith century. London. 1912.
Hewitt, J. Ancient armour and weapons in Europe. 3 vols. Oxford and London. 1855–60.
Meyrick, Sir S. R. A critical inquiry into antient armour. London. 1824.

Courts of Love.

Balaguèr, V. Historia política y literaria de los Trovadores. Vol. i. Madrid. 1878.
Chabaneau, C. Les Biographies des Troubadours. *In* Vic, C. de and Vaissete, J. J. Histoire gén. de Languedoc. Vol. x. *See Gen. Bibl.* iv. *Also* publ. separately. Toulouse. 1885.
Diez, F. Die Poesie der Troubadours. 2nd edn. ed. Bartsch, K. Leipsic. 1883.
Nostredame, J. de. Les Vies des plus célèbres et anciens poètes provençaux. Ed. Chabaneau, C. Paris. 1913.
Paris, G. Mélanges de littérature français. Paris. 1912.
Rajna, P. Le corti d'amore. Milan. 1890.
Rowbotham, J. F. The Troubadours and the Courts of Love. (Social England Series.) London. 1895.

England.

Freeman, E. A. The Law of Honour. *In* Fortnightly Review. London. Dec. 1876.
—— The Reign of William Rufus. Vols. I and II. Oxford. 1882.
Mediaeval England (Barnard, F. P. Companion to English History). Rev. edn. Davis, H. W. C. Oxford. 1924.

France.

Daniel, G. Histoire de la milice françoise. 2 vols. Amsterdam. 1724.
Gautier, L. La Chevalerie. New edn. Paris. 1890. Engl. transl. Frith, H. London. 1890.
Guilhiermoz, P. Essai sur l'origine de la noblesse en France au moyen âge. Paris. 1902.
Guizot, F. P. G. Histoire de la civilisation en France. New edn. Vol. III. Paris. 1846.
Jusserand, J. J. Les Sports et jeux d'exercice dans l'ancienne France. Paris. 1901.
Lacroix, P. L'ancienne France: Chevalerie et les Croisades, féodalité, blason, ordres militaires. Paris. 1886.
Langlois, C. V. La Société française au XIIIme siecle d'après dix romans d'aventure. Paris. 1904.
Luce, S. Histoire de Bertrand du Guesclin. 2nd edn. Paris. 1882.
Luchaire, A. Les premiers Capétiens (987–1137). (*In* Lavisse, E. Histoire de France. II, 2. 1901. *See Gen. Bibl.* v.)
—— La Société française au temps de Philippe Auguste. Paris. 1909. Engl. transl. Krehbiel, E. B. London. 1912.
Martin, H. Histoire de France. Vol. III. Paris. 1878.

Germany.

Buesching, J. G. G. Ritterzeit und Ritterwesen. 2 vols. Leipsic. 1823.
Falke, J. v. Die ritterliche Gesellschaft im Zeitalter des Frauencultus. (Deutsche National-Bibliothek.) Berlin. 1864.
Henne-am-Rhyn, O. Geschichte des Rittertums. Leipsic. 1893.
Michael, E. Geschichte des deutschen Volkes. Vol. I. Freiburg-im-Breisgau. 1897.
Roth von Schreckenstein, C. H. Die Ritterwürde und der Ritterstand. Freiburg-im-Breisgau. 1886.
Schulte, A. Der Adel und die deutsche Kirche im Mittelalter: Studien zur Social- Rechts- und Kirchengeschichte. (Kirchenrechtliche Abhandlungen. Ed. Stutz, U. Nos. 63, 64.) Stuttgart. 1910.
Schultz, A. Das höfische Leben zu Zeit der Minnesinger. 2 vols. Leipsic. 1879–80.
Vedel, V. Mittelalterliche Kulturideale, I. Heldenleben. (Aus Natur und Geisteswelt, 292.) Leipsic. 1910.
Weinhold, K. Die deutschen Frauen in dem Mittelalter. 2 vols. Vienna. 1897.

Heraldry.

Hozier, L. P. d'. Armorial général de la France. 2nd edn. 12 vols. Paris. 1865 ff.
Menestrier, C. F. Nouvelle méthode raisonnée du Blason. Ed. Lemoine, P. C. Lyons. 1780.
Rietstap, J. B. Armorial général. 2nd edn. 2 vols. Gouda. 1884, 87. Suppl ts. and plates. Rolland, V. and H. Paris. 1903–26.
Seyler, G. A. Geschichte der Heraldik. Nüremberg. 1885, 89. [Part of Siebmacher, *see below.*]
Siebmacher, J. Grosse und allgemeines Wappenbuch. Ed. Hefner, O. T. von. Seven sections in many parts. Nuremberg. 1856–1907.
Woodward, J. A treatise on Heraldry, British and Foreign. New edn. 2 vols. Edinburgh and London. 1896.

Italy.

Muratori, L. A. De institutione militum quos cavalieri appellamus, et de insiguiis quae nunc arme vocantur. Dissertation LIII *in* Antiquitates italicae medii aevi. Vol. IV. *See Gen. Bibl.* IV.
Rajna, P. Le origini dell' epopea francese. Florence. 1884.
Salvemini, G. La dignità cavalleresca nel comune di Firenze. Florence. 1896.
Sismondi, S. de. Histoire des républiques italiennes du moyen âge. New edn. Vol. III. Paris. 1840.

Orders.

[*Cf.* also the Bibliography to Vol. v, ch. xx (Monastic Orders), p. 919.]

Anstis, J. Observations introductory to an historical essay upon the Knighthood of the Bath. London. 1725.

Ashmole, E. The Institution, laws, and ceremonies of the most noble Order of the Garter. London. 1672.

Beltz, G. F. Memorials of the Order of the Garter. London. 1841.

Brasier, L. and Brunet, J. L. Les Ordres Portugais. Paris. 1898.

Delaville Le Roulx, J. Les Hospitaliers en Terre Sainte et à Chypre (1100–1310). Paris. 1904.

Lawrence-Archer, J. H. The Orders of Chivalry. London. 1871.

Mottart, F. La Toison d'Or d'Espagne. Brussels. 1907.

Nicolas, Sir N. H. History of the Orders of Knighthood of the British Empire. 4 vols. London. 1841.

Perkins, J. H. T. The most honourable Order of the Bath. 2nd edn. London and Manchester. 1920.

Shaw, W. A. The Knights of England. 2 vols. London. 1906.

Steenackers, F. F. Histoire des Ordres de Chevalerie et des distinctions honorifiques en France. Paris. 1867.

Spain and Portugal, and Saracens.

Ameer Ali, Syed. A short history of the Saracens. London. 1899.

Dozy, R. Spanish Islam: a history of the Moslems in Spain. Transl. Stokes, F. G. London. 1913.

Thomas, H. Spanish and Portuguese romances of Chivalry. Cambridge. 1920.

Viardot, L. Histoire des Arabes et des Mores d'Espagne. 2 vols. Paris. 1851.

Tournaments.

Clephan, R. C. The Tournament; its periods and phases. London. 1919. [Excellent account, with bibliography.]

Duvernoy, É. and Harmand, R. Le Tournoi de Chauvency en 1285. Paris and Nancy. 1905.

Niedner, F. Das deutsche Turnier im 12 und 13 Jahrht. Berlin. 1881.

Various.

[*Cf.* also the Bibliographies to ch. xxii (b) (Military Architecture), ch. xxiii (The Art of War to 1400), and ch. xxv (Legendary Cycles of the Middle Ages).]

Bury, J. B. Romances of Chivalry on Greek soil. Oxford. 1911.

Krey, A. C. The First Crusade. The account of eye-witnesses and participants. Princeton. 1921.

Oman, C. W. C. History of the Art of War in the Middle Ages. *See Gen. Bibl.* v.

Tout, T. F. "Communitas Bacheleriae Angliae." EHR. xvii (1902). 89.

Way, A. Illustrations of Medieval Manners, Chivalry, and Costume, from original documents. *In* Archaeological Journal. Vol. v. London. 1848. p. 258.

CHAPTER XXV.

LEGENDARY CYCLES OF THE MIDDLE AGES.

I. The *Chansons de Geste*.

The *Chansons de Geste* have formed the subject of an extensive literature; apart from editions and studies of the individual romances, we have more than one *travail d'ensemble*, essaying to cover the entire ground: *L'Histoire poétique de Charlemagne*, by G. Paris (Paris, 1865; 2nd edn. Paris, 1905), *L'Épopées françaises*, by L. Gautier (4 vols. Paris, 1878–92); these both repose upon the theory of contemporary *cantilènes* as the source of the extant texts. This theory was attacked by P. Rajna, in his *Origini dell' epopea francese* (Florence, 1884), and it may be said to have received its death-blow in *Les Légendes épiques, recherches sur la formation des Chansons de Geste*, by J. Bédier (2nd edn., 4 vols. Paris, 1914–21). In this comprehensive work each of the *Chansons de Geste* is analysed, the editions of the text and the studies of which it has been the subject noted, and the sources probed. The history of the criticism of the cycle is fully given, with illustrative quotations from the works referred to; the whole work is a monument of minute research and painstaking erudition, and is indispensable to anyone desiring a real knowledge of the cycle. For the convenience of readers it may be noted that the volumes can be purchased separately: Vol. I deals with the cycle of Guillaume d'Orange; Vol. III with the Charlemagne poems and the *Chanson de Roland*, and includes the valuable *Histoire des Théories* on the formation of the cycle in general, and the *Chanson de Roland* in particular. The other volumes deal with the independent poems. The text of the *Chanson de Roland* was edited by L. Gautier (Tours, 1872), and has passed through many editions. That of *Aliscans* was edited by G. Rolin, Leipsic, 1894.

II. The Arthurian Cycle.

The only *travail d'ensemble* dealing with the Arthurian cycle is *The Evolution of Arthurian Romance from the beginning down to the year* 1300, by J. D. Bruce, 2 vols. Göttingen and Baltimore, 1923. This is a work of most painstaking erudition, containing not only a discussion of the texts, but a bibliography listing critical studies, articles, and reviews. As a work of reference it will probably be of permanent value; but the late Professor Bruce's determined adherence to the views of the Foersterian school, denying the existence of a romantic Arthurian tradition previous to Chrétien de Troyes, and his refusal to examine the grounds upon which modern criticism of these views is based, largely deprives his conclusions of value. The book requires to be used with caution.

The Arthurian Legend in the Literature of the Spanish Peninsula, by W. J. Entwistle, London, 1925, is a valuable discussion of a little known branch of the subject.

For the pseudo-historic section the most useful work is *The Arthurian Material in the Chronicles*, by R. H. Fletcher (Harvard Studies and Notes in Philology and Literature, Vol. x), Boston, Mass. 1906. This covers the whole ground from the sixth to the sixteenth century, more than 200 chronicles being examined. For the separate texts, Nennius was edited by T. Mommsen, MGH. Auctores antiq., Vol. XIII (Berlin, 1898), and a study on the authenticity of the text, by H. Zimmer, *Nennius Vindicatus*, appeared at Berlin, 1895. Geoffrey's *Historia Regum Britanniae* was edited by San-Marte [A. Schulz], Halle, 1854; Wace's *Brut* by Le Roux de Lincy, 2 vols. Rouen, 1835, 38; and the *Brut* of Layamon by Sir F. Madden (Soc. of Antiquaries), 3 vols. London, 1847.

The *Lais* of Marie de France have been edited by K. Warnke, Halle, 1900. A new edition by Dr Mary Williams is in preparation. Translations are in *Four Lais of Marie de France*, by J. L. Weston (in *Arthurian Romances unrepresented in Malory*), London, 1900, and *Seven Lais of Marie de France*, by E. Rickert, London, 1901.

Of the poetical works, the poems of Chrétien de Troyes, *Erec* (1890), *Yvain* (1887), *Cligés* (1884), and *Le Chevalier de la Charrette* (1899), have been critically edited in *Sämtliche Werke*, Halle, by the late Professor W. Foerster. The *Perceval* still awaits an editor. It was printed by C. Potvin from the Mons MS. (Soc. des Bibliophiles de Mons), Mons, 1866–71 (6 vols., the first of which contains the *Perlesvaus*). Unfortunately this is the most defective and unreliable of the *Perceval* MSS., nor was Potvin a very skilful editor. Dr Mary Williams is editing the Gerbert continuation in Les Classiques français du moyen âge (Nos. 28, 50, etc.), *La Continuation de Perceval*, Paris, 1922 ff. The *Parzival* of Wolfram von Eschenbach, on the other hand, has been critically edited three times: by K. Bartsch, in the series of Deutsche Classiker des Mittelalters, Leipsic, 1875; by K. Lachmann, 5th edn. Berlin, 1891; finally by E. Martin, Halle, 1903. The *Erec* (3rd edn. 1893) and *Yvain* (3rd edn. 1888) of Hartmann von Aue (ed. F. Bech) are also included in the series of Deutsche Classiker. The poems of Raoul de Houdenc have been edited by M. Friedwagner; *Meraugis de Portlesguez* was published, Halle, 1897, *La Vengeance de Raguidel*, 1909. The English *Gawain* poems were published by Sir F. Madden, under the title of *Syr Gawayne*, for the Bannatyne Club, London, 1839. There is an edition by R. Morris of *Syr Gawayne and the Grene Knyghte* in the EETS. (2nd edn. 1869), and a full rendering into modern verse will be found in *Romance, Vision, and Satire*, by J. L. Weston, London, 1912. The same volume contains a translation of the *Awntyrs of Arthur*. A very important text for the Gawain tradition is *Diû Crône*, by Heinrich von dem Türlin, ed. G. H. F. Scholl, Stuttgart, 1852. *Syr Percyvelle of Galles*, an English rendering of what is probably the earliest version of the *Perceval* story, was published by J. O. Halliwell for the Camden Society in *The Thornton Romances* (London, 1844); a rendering into modern verse will be found in *Chief Middle English Poets*, by J. L. Weston, London, 1923.

Of the *Tristan* poems the *Tristan* of Thomas has been edited by J. Bédier (2 vols. Paris, 1902, 5); the *Tristan* of Berol, by E. Muret (Paris, 1903), both in the series of La Société des anciens textes français. Berol's *Tristan* has also been edited by E. Muret in Les Classiques français du moyen âge (No. 12, 3rd edn.), Paris, 1928. The *Tristan* of Gottfried von Strassburg, ed. R. Bechstein (2 vols. Leipsic, 1869–70), is included in the Deutsche Classiker. The English *Sir Tristrem* was edited by E. Kölbing (Heilbronn, 1882); a modern rendering is in *Chief Middle English Poets* (*see above*).

For the prose romances, the whole cycle has been edited by Dr H. O. Sommer, under the title of *The Vulgate version of the Arthurian Romances*, 7 vols. and index vol. (Carnegie Trust), Washington, 1908–16. This is not a critical edition, and the choice of MSS. reproduced is open to criticism. *Le Grand Saint Graal* was edited by E. Hucher (3 vols. Paris, 1875–79). The third volume gives the text of Borron's *Perceval*, from the Didot MS. The text of the later discovered Modena MS., which is superior to the Didot, though obviously not the original text, is in Vol. II of *The Legend of Sir Perceval*, by J. L. Weston (London, 1909). Borron's original poem is edited by W. A. Nitze, *Le Roman de l'Estoire dou Graal*, in Les Classiques français du moyen âge (No. 57), Paris, 1927. *Le Mort Artus* was edited by Dr J. D. Bruce, Halle, 1910. The same scholar is responsible for an edition of the Harleian *Morte Arthur*, in the EETS. 1903. *Perlesvaus* was published from the Brussels text by C. Potvin in Vol. I of his edition of the Mons *Perceval* (*see above*). There is a fine English translation by the late Dr S. Evans published under the title of *The High History of the Holy Grail* (Everyman's Library), London, 1910. A critical text has long been in preparation by Dr W. A. Nitze, but has not yet appeared. *The Morte Darthur* of Sir Thomas Malory has been reprinted from the original text by Dr H. O. Sommer, 3 vols. London, 1889–91. Vol. II, a study of the sources, is useful, but unfortunately Dr Sommer was not aware of the differences existing between the printed editions of the *Lancelot*, and used an abridged text, with the result that the *Lancelot-Queste* section is open to serious criticism. The *Queste* was published by Dr F. J. Furnivall (Roxburghe Club, London, 1864) from a MS. in the British Museum; a critical text by A. Pauphilet is in Les Classiques français du moyen âge (No. 33), Paris, 1923.

For the Grail Legend, Professor A. Birch-Hirschfeld's *Die Sage vom Heiligen Gral* (Leipsic, 1877), A. Nutt's *Studies on the Legend of the Holy Grail* (London, 1888), with the later essay, *The Legends of the Holy Grail* (London, 1902), in *Popular Studies in Mythology, Romance, and Folk-lore*, and *From Ritual to Romance*, by J. L. Weston (Cambridge, 1920), cover the ground, and shew the gradual evolution of opinion on the subject. A series of *Studies on the Chronology of the Grail Romances* by Dr W. A. Nitze is appearing in *Modern Philology*; so far only the *Perlesvaus* has been treated, but they promise to be of distinct value.

The Welsh *Mabinogion* was published, with an English translation, by Lady Charlotte Guest (3 vols. London, 1849), and with a French translation, by J. Loth, (2 vols. Paris, 1889). There is a re-issue of Lady Charlotte Guest's translation, without the original text, by A. Nutt, London, 1902.

It may be noted that besides the tales referred to in the text the *Mabinogion* also contains the stories of *Kilhwch and Olwen*, and *The Dream of Rhonabwy*, which deal with the Arthurian tradition in a more primitive form, but are of less importance from the critical point of view.

Translations of some of the shorter Arthurian tales may be found in the series of *Arthurian Romances unrepresented in Malory*, J. L. Weston, 8 vols. London, 1898–1907.

Of late years an attempt, notably by American scholars, has been made to establish a direct affiliation between Arthurian romance and early Irish tradition. Both undoubtedly share in the mythical heritage common to all Celtic peoples, but their line of evolution has been independent. Parallels may well exist, but direct borrowing cannot be established. Tales directly connected with Arthur, such as *The Crop-Eared Dog* and *Eagleboy*, ed. and transl. by R. A. S. Macalister (Irish Texts Society, Vol. x, 1908), are demonstrably late in origin, and shew a knowledge of the Arthurian tradition in its latest and least original form.

For a general study of the evolution of the literature the reader may be referred to Dr E. Brugger's introductory study on *L'Enserrement Merlin* (*Zeitschrift für französische Sprache*, Vol. xxix). Dr Brugger's scheme can hardly be accepted in all its details, but it is a valuable attempt at co-ordinating a vast and complicated body of romance. F. Lot published in 1918 an elaborate study on *Le Lancelot en prose* (BHE.), the critical conclusions of which will scarcely win acceptance, but it should not be neglected. The volumes in the Grimm Library, *The Legend of Sir Lancelot*, by J. L. Weston (London, 1901), with an analysis of the Dutch text, and an examination of Dr O. H. Sommer's 'Sources of Malory' (*see above*); the *Legend of Sir Perceval*, by J. L. Weston (2 vols. London, 1906, 9), the first of which gives a detailed description and classification of the existing *Perceval* MSS. and an analysis of the Wauchier continuation of Chrétien's poem, and the second containing the Modena text, are essential for a study of the Perceval romances. A study on *Syr Percyvelle of Galles*, by R. H. Griffith (Chicago, 1911), may also be noted. There are of course innumerable studies and articles which have appeared in such publications as *Romania*, *Le Moyen Âge*, *The Romanic Review*, *Modern Philology*, etc., but the above are sufficient for a reader to obtain a sound first-hand knowledge of the subject matter.

III. The *Matière de Rome*.

The work of P. Meyer, *Alexandre le Grand dans la littérature française du moyen âge* (2 vols. Paris, 1886), still remains the standard work for the *Alexander* romances. The *Roman de Troie* of Benoît de Sainte-More has been published by L. Constans for La Société des anciens textes français (6 vols. Paris, 1904–12). The same scholar is responsible for an edition of the *Roman de Thèbes*, included in the same series (1890). The *Roman d'Éneas* is being edited by J. J. Salverda de Grave in Les Classiques français du moyen âge (Nos. 44, etc.), Paris, 1925 ff. For general in formation on the subject the student may be referred to the latest (6th) edition of G. Paris' *La littérature française au moyen âge* (Paris, *s.a.*), in which the bibliographies have been brought up to date. For the *Alexander* tradition in England and Scotland the reader may consult *English Literature from the Norman Conquest to Chaucer*, by W. H. Schofield, London, 1906.

IV. The Germanic Cycle.

The *Völsunga-Saga*, with the original Lays, has been rendered into English by W. Morris and E. Magnússon (London, 1870). *The Story of Sigurd the Volsung*, by W. Morris (London, 1877), is a very fine poetical version of the story, and follows faithfully the original form. Dr S. Bugge's *The Home of the Eddic Poems*, transl. by W. H. Schofield (Grimm Library, Vol. XI, London, 1911) is now out of print. *The Thidrek-Saga* is included in *Altdeutsche und Altnordische Heldensagen*, transl. by F. H. von der Hagen, re-ed. A. Edzardi, 3 vols. Stuttgart, 1880. A later edition is by H. Bertelsen, Copenhagen, 1905–6. The *Nibelungenlied* (6th edn. Leipsic, 1886) and *Kudrun* (3rd edn. Leipsic, 1874) are both edited by K. Bartsch in the series of Deutsche Classiker des Mittelalters. The later editions scarcely alter the text, so that the older and more easily accessible versions can be safely used. An abstract of all three versions, with a detailed examination of their variants in connexion with Wagner's *Ring des Nibelungen* (where all three have been used), will be found in *The Legends of the Wagner Drama*, by J. L. Weston, London, 1896. A considerable number of studies on the cycle have appeared of late years; among the most important are A. Heusler, *Thidrek-Saga und Nibelungenlied* (Dortmund, 1920), and *Nibelungensage und Nibelungenlied* (Dortmund, 1921). The works of F. Panzer, *Gudrun* (Halle, 1901), *Beowulf* (Munich, 1910), and *Sigfried* (Munich, 1912), treat the subject of origins from the folk-lore point of view. A similar standpoint to that of J. Bédier with regard to the *Chansons de Geste* is assumed by the Dutch scholar, R. C. Boer, in his *Untersuchungen über den Ursprung und die Entwickelungen der Nibelungensage* (2 vols. Halle, 1906, 9), and *Sagen von Ermanrich und Dietrich von Bern* (Halle, 1910). The general handbooks, such as H. Paul's *Grundriss der germanischen Philologie* (*see Gen. Bibl.* I) and W. Golther's *Geschichte des deutschen Literatur* (Stuttgart, 1892), require bringing up to date. A useful summary of the literature of the Icelandic Sagas may be found in *The Edda, the Divine Mythology of the North*, by Winifred Faraday (No. 12 of Nutt's *Popular Studies in Mythology, Romance, and Folk-lore*), London, 1902. The late Professor W. P. Ker's *Epic and Romance* (2nd edn. London, 1908) covers the whole field of medieval romantic literature, and may especially be consulted for a discussion of the structure of *Beowulf*. The texts of *Ortnit*, *Hug-Dietrich*, and *Wolf-Dietrich* may be found in F. H. von der Hagen's *Heldenbuch*, 2 vols. Leipsic, 1855.

CHRONOLOGICAL TABLE

OF

LEADING EVENTS MENTIONED IN THIS VOLUME.

fl. 831 Paschasius Radbertus.
858–867 Pontificate of Nicholas I.
fl. 868 Ratramnus.
950 Bohemia becomes a fief of the Empire.
950–985 Reign of Harold Bluetooth of Denmark.
992–1025 Reign of Boleslav the Great of Poland.
995–1000 Reign of Olaf Trygveson in Norway.
997–1038 Reign of St Stephen of Hungary.
c. 1000 The Christianisation of Scandinavia.
1031 Fall of the Caliphate of Cordova.
1037 Ferdinand I unites Leon and Castile for the first time.
c. 1040 Beginning of the transformation of Romanesque into Gothic.
1050–1100 The earliest *Chansons de Geste* composed.
1054 Schism between the Eastern and Western Churches.
Battle of Atapuerca.
1066 Battle of Hastings.
Death of Geoffrey de Preuilly, reputed inventor of tournaments.
1071 Battle of Manzikert.
1079–1142 Peter Abelard.
1085 Capture of Toledo from the Moors.
1086 Christian defeat at Zalaca by the Almorávides.
Death of Berengar of Tours.
1095–1114 Reign of Koloman in Hungary. Union with Croatia.
1095 (18–28 Nov.) Council of Clermont proclaims the First Crusade.
1099 Death of the Cid.
c. 1100 Irnerius teaches Roman Law at Bologna.
1104 Consecration of the first Scandinavian archbishop (at Lund in Denmark).
1109 Death of St Anselm.
1118 Capture of Saragossa by the Christians.
1124–1128 Establishment of Christianity in Pomerania.
1125 Decline of the Almorávides in Spain.
1127 Earliest Flemish town charter granted (to St Omer).
c. 1130 Beginning of the Wars of Pretenders in Scandinavia.
c. 1135 Geoffrey of Monmouth's *Historia Regum Britanniae.*
1137 Union of Aragon and Catalonia.
1141 The Council of Sens condemns the doctrine of Abelard.
Death of Hugh of St Victor.
c. 1142 The *Decretum* of Gratian.
c. 1145–1150 Peter Lombard's *Sentences.*
1146 The Almohades arrive in Spain.
1147–1149 The Second Crusade.
1152 Norwegian Church settlement.
1157–1182 Reign of Waldemar the Great of Denmark.
1158 Frederick Barbarossa issues the "Authenticum" *Habita.*
1164 Swedish archbishopric founded at Upsala.
The Military Order of Calatrava founded by Alfonso VIII of Castile.
1167 General Congress of Cathari near Toulouse.
1170 Rise of Oxford University to importance.
Birth of St Dominic.
Peter Waldo begins to preach at Lyons.

c. **1170** *fl.* Chrétien of Troyes.
1176 Battle of Legnano.
1177–1194 Reign of Casimir the Just in Poland.
1179 The Third Lateran Council.
1180 (18 Sept.) Death of Louis VII of France: accession of Philip Augustus.
Death of John of Salisbury.
c. **1181** Birth of St Francis of Assisi.
1184–1202 Reign of King Sverre of Norway.
1189–1192 The Third Crusade.
1189–1199 Reign of Richard I of England.
1190 Foundation of the Teutonic Order.
1190–1197 Reign of Emperor Henry VI.
c. **1190** Original composition of the *Nibelungenlied*.
1191 Richard I of England defeats Saladin at Arsūf.
1192 Compilation of the *Liber Censuum*.
1194 Hubert Walter governs England during Richard I's absence abroad.
1196–1213 Reign of Peter II of Aragon.
1196 (18 July) Victory of the Almohades at Alarcos.
1197–1230 Reign of Přemsyl Ottokar I of Bohemia.
1197 (Nov.) Formation of an anti-Imperialist league of cities in Tuscany.
1198 (8 Jan.) Election of Pope Innocent III.
(6 Mar.) Philip of Swabia elected King of Germany.
(17 May) Frederick II crowned King of Sicily at Palermo.
(9 June) Election of Otto IV as anti-king in Germany.
Death of Averroës.
Bohemia finally made a kingdom.
1199 Death of Richard I of England. Accession of John.
Beginning of direct Papal taxation.
1200 (Jan.—Sept.) Pope Innocent III lays France under an interdict.
Charter granted to the University of Paris by Philip Augustus.
The *Deliberatio* of Pope Innocent III.
c. **1200** Most Italian cities are instituting Podestàs.
1201 The Fourth Crusade begins.
(8 June) The Donation of Neuss by Otto IV.
1202–1241 Reign of Waldemar the Victorious in Denmark.
1202 (Apr.) Philip Augustus makes war upon John.
The Bull *Venerabilem*.
Death of Joachim of Flora.
1204 (13 Apr.) Sack of Constantinople by the Crusaders.
Foundation of the Latin Empire of Constantinople.
(24 June) Final loss of Normandy by John.
1205 Death of Archbishop Hubert Walter.
1207 Stephen Langton consecrated Archbishop of Canterbury.
1208 (24 Feb.) His vocation revealed to St Francis of Assisi.
(21 June) Murder of Philip of Swabia.
(11 Nov.) Otto IV unanimously elected King of Germany at Frankfort.
1209 England laid under an interdict.
Crusade against the Albigensians begins.
(4 Oct.) Otto IV receives the imperial crown at Rome.
Excommunication of John.
1210 (Nov.) Excommunication of the Emperor Otto IV.
The Council of Sens prohibits Aristotle.
1211 Diet of Nuremberg offers the crown of Germany to Frederick II.
1212 Christian victory over the Almohades at Las Navas de Tolosa.
The Golden Bull of Bohemia.
1213 John submits to the Pope and receives absolution.
The Golden Bull of Eger.
Battle of Muret: death of Peter II of Aragon.
1214 Battle of Bouvines.
1215 The Great Charter sealed at Runnymede (15 June).

1215 The Fourth Lateran Council.
1216 (May) Louis of France arrives in England.
(16 July) Death of Innocent III. Election of Pope Honorius III.
(19 Oct.) Death of King John.
(28 Oct.) Henry III crowned at Gloucester.
(12 Nov.) Renewal of the Great Charter.
Pope Honorius III confirms the Dominican Order.
1218 Death of Otto IV.
Death of Simon de Montfort, the crusader against the Albigensians.
1219 (Aug.) The Fifth Crusade begins.
Study of the Civil Law forbidden at Paris.
1220 Frederick II issues the *Privilegium in favorem principum ecclesiasticorum.*
Henry (VII) elected King of the Romans.
Frederick II's imperial coronation at Rome.
c. 1220 Death of Wolfram von Eschenbach.
1221 Death of St Dominic.
1222 First appearance of the Mongols in Europe.
The Golden Bull of Hungary.
The University of Padua founded by a migration from Bologna.
1223 (14 July) Death of Philip Augustus.
1223–1226 Reign of Louis VIII of France.
1223 The Franciscan Rule in its final form confirmed by Pope Honorius III.
1224 The University of Naples founded by the Emperor Frederick II.
1226 Formation of the second Lombard League.
(3 Oct.) Death of St Francis of Assisi.
Suppression of the first Rhine league.
1226–1229 Second Albigensian Crusade.
1226–1234 Regency of Blanche of Castile.
1226–1270 Reign of St Louis IX of France.
1227 Death of Pope Honorius III. Election of Gregory IX.
Defeat of Waldemar II of Denmark at Bornhövede.
First excommunication of Frederick II.
End of the minority of Henry III.
1228–1229 Crusade of Frederick II. Recovery of Jerusalem.
1228 St Francis of Assisi canonised by Pope Gregory IX.
1230 Treaty of San Germano between Frederick II and the Papacy.
Pope Gregory IX recognises the Third Order of St Francis.
Settlement of the Teutonic Order in Prussia.
Final union of Leon and Castile under Ferdinand III.
The University of Toulouse founded by the Papacy.
1231 *Constitutio in favorem principum* issued by Frederick II.
Renewal of the Lombard League.
Frederick II promulgates a new code for Sicily at Melfi.
Robert Grosseteste begins lecturing at Oxford.
The Franciscans and Dominicans exempted from episcopal jurisdiction by Pope Gregory IX.
The Bull *Parens Scientiarum* establishes the independence of the University of Paris.
1232 Imperial edict against heretics.
1233 Inauguration of the Inquisition by Pope Gregory IX.
1234 Rebellion of Henry (VII) against his father the Emperor Frederick II.
Canonisation of St Dominic.
1235 Deposition of Henry (VII) of Germany.
1236 Conquest of Cordova from the Moors.
1237 Conrad IV elected King of the Romans.
Frederick II's victory at Cortenuova.
1239 Frederick II again excommunicated.
1241 (Mar.) The Mongols capture Cracow.
(9 Apr.) They defeat Duke Henry of Silesia at Liegnitz.
(21 Aug.) Death of Pope Gregory IX.

1241 Mongols defeat Hungarians at the battle of Mohi.
1243 (25 June) Election of Pope Innocent IV.
1245 The First Council of Lyons deposes the Emperor Frederick II.
Death of Alexander of Hales.
1246–1248 St Louis builds the Sainte Chapelle in Paris.
1246 Henry Raspe chosen as anti-King in Germany.
1247 Death of Henry Raspe. William of Holland chosen to succeed him.
System of circuits of *enquêteurs* established in France.
1248–1254 The first Crusade of St Louis.
1248 (18 Feb.) Defeat of the Emperor Frederick II near Vittoria.
Capture of Seville from the Moors.
1250 Death of the Emperor Frederick II.
The *Primo Popolo* at Florence.
1250–1273 The Great Interregnum in Germany.
1251 (Jan.) Conrad IV enters Italy.
1251 (May) Pope Innocent IV returns to Italy.
1252 Murder of Peter Martyr, the Dominican Inquisitor.
Death of Ferdinand III of Castile.
The Florentine gold florin first coined.
Innocent IV's bull, *Ad extirpanda,* against heresy.
1253–1278 Reign of Přemsyl Ottokar II of Bohemia.
1253 William of Rubruquis sent by Louis IX on a mission to the court of the Great Khan.
Death of Robert Grosseteste.
1254 Death of Conrad IV. Innocent IV invades the Regno.
Formation of the Rhenish League.
Death of Innocent IV.
1254–1261 Pontificate of Pope Alexander IV.
1254 Königsberg founded by the Teutonic Knights.
St Louis returns to France.
Publication of *The Everlasting Gospel.*
1256 Death of William of Holland.
1257 Election of Richard of Cornwall as King of Germany; first appearance of the Seven Electors.
1258 St Louis forbids private wars.
Treaty of Corbeil between Louis IX of France and the King of Aragon.
Provisions of Oxford.
Manfred becomes King of Sicily.
1259 Martin della Torre becomes lord of Milan.
Death of Ezzelino da Romano.
Provisions of Westminster.
Treaty of Paris between England and France.
Death of Matthew Paris.
1260 Florentine defeat at Montaperto.
Appearance of the Fraticelli.
c. 1260 First appearance of the Flagellants.
1261 Treaty of Nymphaeum.
1261–1264 Pontificate of Urban IV.
1261 Recapture of Constantinople by the Greeks: end of the Latin Empire.
William of Moerbeke begins to translate Aristotle from the Greek.
1264 Mise of Amiens.
Victory of the barons at Lewes.
1265–1268 Pontificate of Pope Clement IV.
1265 Clement IV's treaty with Charles of Anjou.
Birth of Dante.
Simon de Montfort slain at the battle of Evesham.
1266 Defeat and death of Manfred at Benevento.
1266–1285 Reign of Charles I of Anjou in Naples and Sicily.
1268 Battle of Tagliacozzo: execution of Conradin.
Constitutions of Cardinal Ottobon.

1268–1271 Three years' interregnum in the Papacy.
1270 St Louis again embarks on Crusade.
(25 July) Death of St Louis.
1270–1285 Reign of Philip III of France.
1271–1276 Pontificate of Pope Gregory X.
1272 Death of Richard of Cornwall.
Death of Henry III of England.
1273 (1 Oct.) Rudolf of Habsburg elected King of the Romans.
1274 Death of St Thomas Aquinas.
Second Council of Lyons.
1277–1280 Pontificate of Nicholas III.
1277 Execution of Averroïsts at Paris.
King Magnus the Law-mender confirms the privileges of the Norwegian Church.
1277-1295 Edward I's campaigns in Wales. Adoption of the longbow.
1278 Defeat and death of Ottokar II of Bohemia.
Fall of the Torriani.
1280 Death of Albertus Magnus.
1281–1285 Pontificate of Martin IV.
1281 Martin IV excommunicates the Greeks.
1282 (30 Mar.) The Sicilian Vespers.
Peter III of Aragon becomes King of Sicily.
Signature of the "Magna Carta of Denmark."
1284 Loria's victory off Naples. Capture of Charles the Lame.
Naval victory of Genoa at Meloria. Fall of Pisa.
1285 Death of Charles of Anjou.
1285–1287 Pontificate of Honorius IV.
1285 Death of Peter III of Aragon.
1288–1289 Pontificate of Pope Nicholas IV.
1289–1328 Mission of John of Monte Corvino to China and the Far East.
1291 Fall of Acre.
Taxatio of Pope Nicholas IV.
1294 Death of Roger Bacon.
1298 Battle of Falkirk.
1300 Boniface VIII's Bull *Super cathedram.*
1301 Death of Andrew III of Hungary: end of the Árpád dynasty.
1302 Boniface VIII's Bull *Unam Sanctam.*
1306 Murder of Wenceslas III, King of Bohemia: end of the Přemyslid dynasty.
1308 Death of Duns Scotus.
1321 Death of Dante.
1322 Battle of Boroughbridge.
1344 Foundation of the Order of the Garter.
1346 Battle of Crécy.
1348 Foundation of the University of Prague by the Emperor Charles IV.
Death of William of Occam.
c. 1348 Beginnings of the Perpendicular style in English architecture.
1365 University of Vienna founded by Duke Rudolf IV.
1385 University of Heidelberg founded.
1429 Foundation of the Order of the Golden Fleece by Philip the Good of Burgundy.
1485 Caxton publishes Malory's *Morte D'Arthur.*

INDEX

Map 57

Ecclesiastical Divisions
of Europe
c. 1250

Cambridge University Press

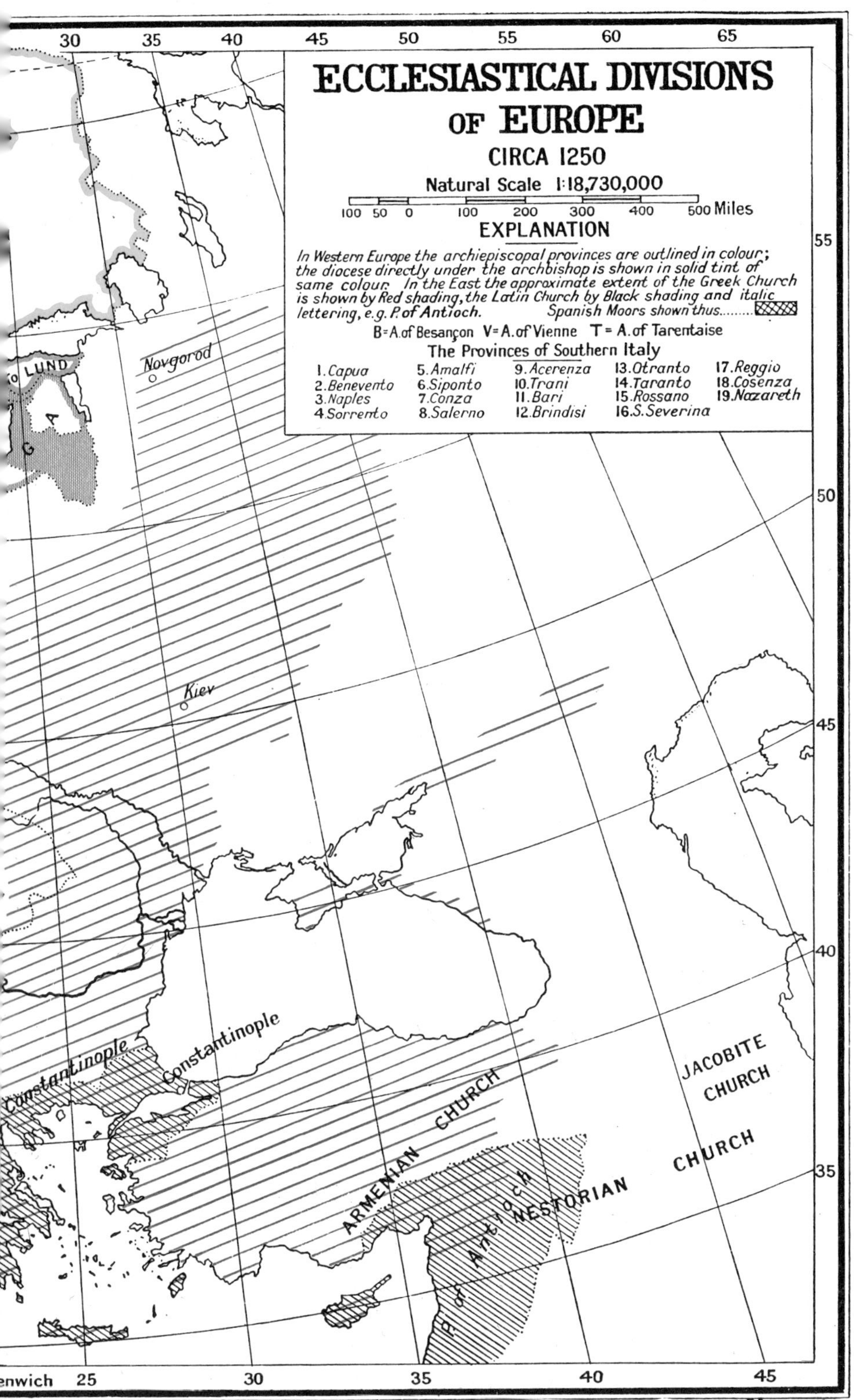
ECCLESIASTICAL DIVISIONS
OF EUROPE
CIRCA 1250
Natural Scale 1:18,730,000
100 50 0 100 200 300 400 500 Miles
EXPLANATION
In Western Europe the archiepiscopal provinces are outlined in colour; the diocese directly under the archbishop is shown in solid tint of same colour. In the East the approximate extent of the Greek Church is shown by Red shading, the Latin Church by Black shading and italic lettering, e.g. P. of Antioch. Spanish Moors shown thus.........
B = A. of Besançon V = A. of Vienne T = A. of Tarentaise
The Provinces of Southern Italy
1. Capua
2. Benevento
3. Naples
4. Sorrento
5. Amalfi
6. Siponto
7. Conza
8. Salerno
9. Acerenza
10. Trani
11. Bari
12. Brindisi
13. Otranto
14. Taranto
15. Rossano
16. S. Severina
17. Reggio
18. Cosenza
19. Nazareth
LUND
Novgorod
Kiev
Constantinople
Constantinople
ARMENIAN CHURCH
JACOBITE CHURCH
NESTORIAN CHURCH
P. of Antioch
enwich

Map 58

France
in 1260

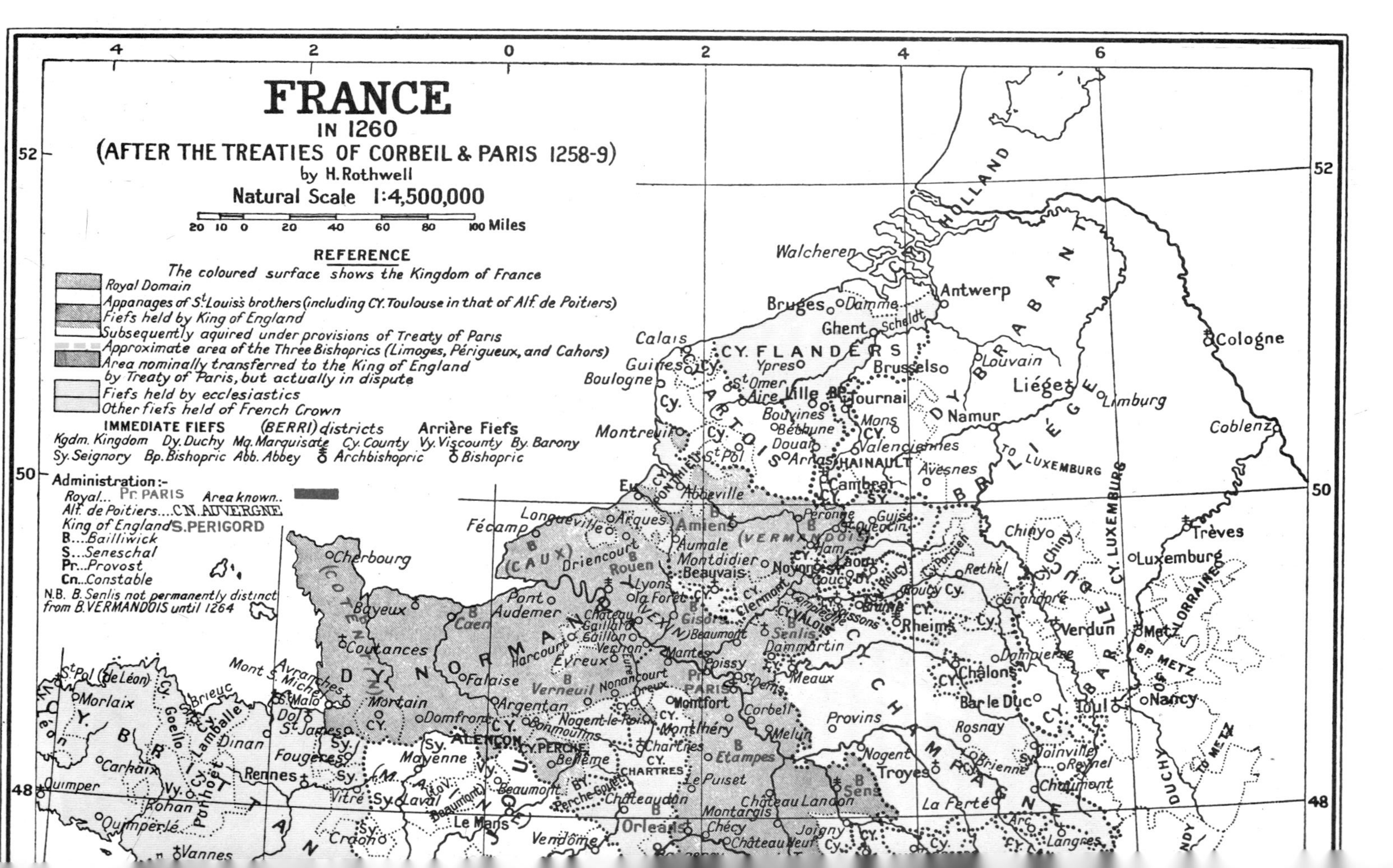

FRANCE
IN 1260
(AFTER THE TREATIES OF CORBEIL & PARIS 1258-9)
by H. Rothwell
Natural Scale 1:4,500,000
20 10 0 20 40 60 80 100 Miles
REFERENCE
The coloured surface shows the Kingdom of France
Royal Domain
Appanages of St. Louis's brothers (including CY. Toulouse in that of Alf. de Poitiers)
Fiefs held by King of England
Subsequently aquired under provisions of Treaty of Paris
Approximate area of the Three Bishoprics (Limoges, Périgueux, and Cahors)
Area nominally transferred to the King of England by Treaty of Paris, but actually in dispute
Fiefs held by ecclesiastics
Other fiefs held of French Crown
IMMEDIATE FIEFS
(BERRI) districts
Arrière Fiefs
Kgdm. Kingdom Dy. Duchy Mq. Marquisate Cy. County Vy. Viscounty By. Barony
Sy. Seignory Bp. Bishopric Abb. Abbey Archbishopric Bishopric
Administration:-
Royal... Pr. PARIS
Area known..
Alf. de Poitiers.... CN. AUVERGNE
King of England's S. PERIGORD
B... Bailliwick
S... Seneschal
Pr... Provost
Cn... Constable
N.B. B. Senlis not permanently distinct from B. VERMANDOIS until 1264

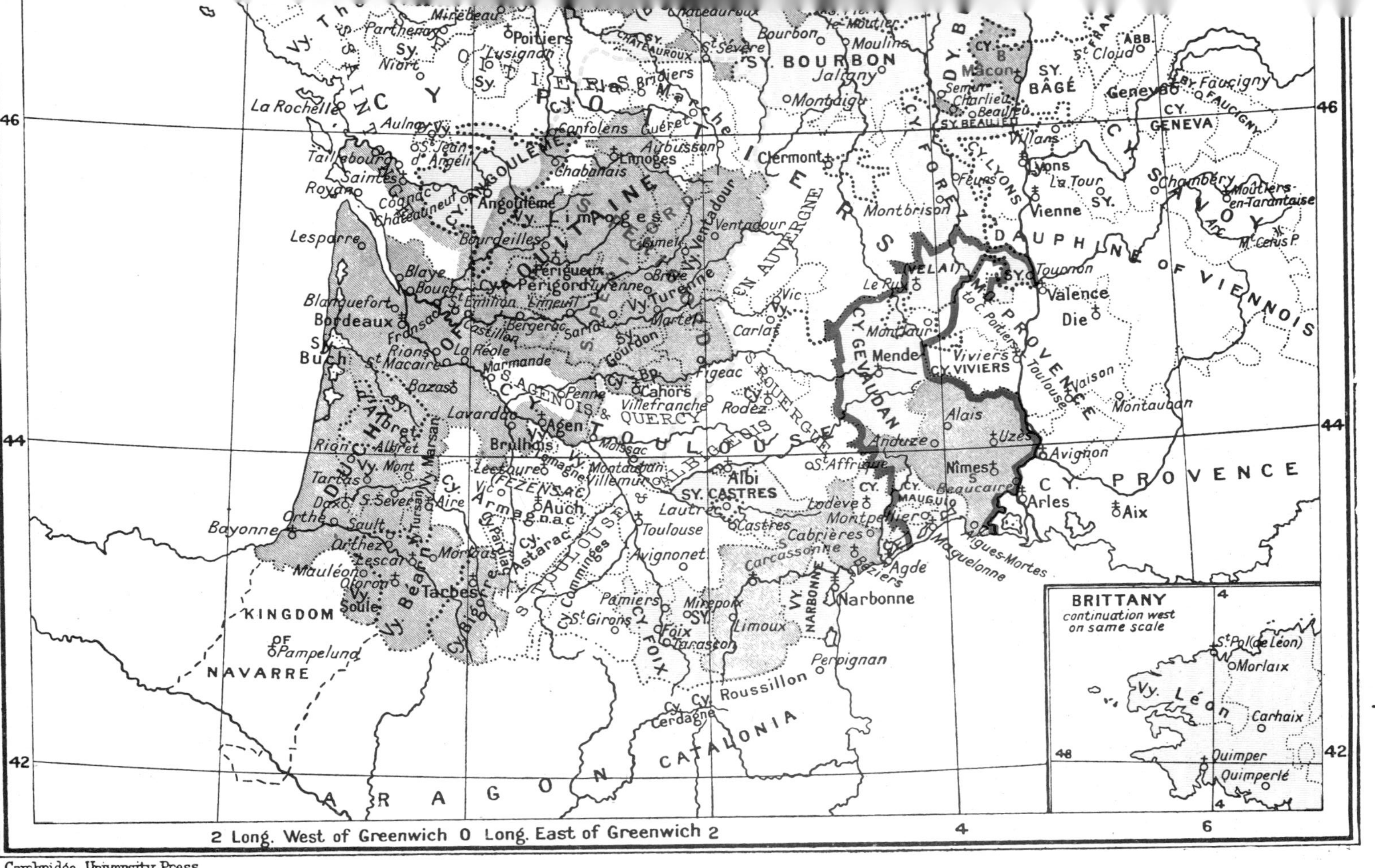
PROVENCE
DAUPHINÉ OF VIENNOIS
SAVOY
CY. GENEVA
CY. GEVAUDAN
CY. FOREZ
CY. LYONS
SY. BOURBON
EN AUVERGNE
AQUITAINE
CY. ANGOULÊME
QUERCY
ROUERGUE
TOULOUSE
ALBIGEOIS
CATALONIA
ARAGON
KINGDOM OF NAVARRE
CY. FOIX
VY. NARBONNE
SY. CASTRES
Roussillon
Perpignan
Narbonne
Béziers
Agde
Montpellier
Maguelonne
Aigues-Mortes
Nîmes
Uzès
Avignon
Arles
Aix
Valence
Die
Vienne
Lyons
Mende
Albi
Castres
Carcassonne
Toulouse
Cahors
Rodez
Agen
Auch
Bordeaux
Bayonne
Tarbes
Pamiers
Limoges
Périgueux
Angoulême
Poitiers
La Rochelle
Saintes
Royan
Niort
Clermont
Moulins
Montbrison
Chambéry
BRITTANY
continuation west
on same scale
St. Pol (de Léon)
Morlaix
Carhaix
Quimper
Quimperlé
Vy. Léon
2 Long. West of Greenwich 0 Long. East of Greenwich 2
46
44
42
4
6
48

Map 59

Germany
in the 13th Century

FRISIA
HOLLAND
UTRECHT
Utrecht
GUELDERS
SAXONY
C. OLDENBURG
Bremen
Verden
Stade
Ratzeburg
Hamburg
Lüneburg
C. HOLSTEIN
WAGRIA
Ditmarschen
BRUNSWICK-LÜNEBURG
Brunswick
Osnabrück
Minden
Hildesheim
Münster
Goslar
Paderborn
Soest
C. Altena
CLEVE
R. Meuse
D. BRABANT
Antwerp
Ghent
FLANDERS
C. LOOS
Maastricht
Neuss
Kaiserswerth
Jülich
Cologne
BERG
Aix-la-Chapelle
Sayn
Liège
Namur
Limburg
C. HAINAULT
Cambrai
Bouvines
Avesnes
R. Somme
Andernach
Coblenz
C. NASSAU
HESSE
Marburg
C. Waldeck
THURING
Wartburg
Eisenach
Fulda
Gelnhausen
Frankfort
R. Rhine
FRANCONIA
BAMBERG
Würzburg
C. LUXEMBURG
Luxemburg
R. Moselle
Treves
Mayence
Worms
C. Falkenstein
C. Leiningen
PALATINATE OF RHINE
C. Hohenlohe
Spiers
Trifels
R. Seine
R. Marne
Verdun
Metz
Weissenburg
Hagenau
D. LORRAINE
Toul
C. Dagsburg
ALSACE
Baden
C. Wurtemberg
Staufen
C. Teck
Strasbourg
SWABIA
Augsburg
C. Andechs
R. Loire
Zähringen
BREISGAU
St. Blaise
C. Pfirt
Basel
Constance
St. Gall
COUNTY OF BURGUNDY
Besançon
Solothurn
Bern
Chur
Lausanne
Trent
Lyons
Longitude
Cambridge University Press

W. & A.K. Johnston Ltd

Map 60

Italy
under Charles of Anjou
c. 1270

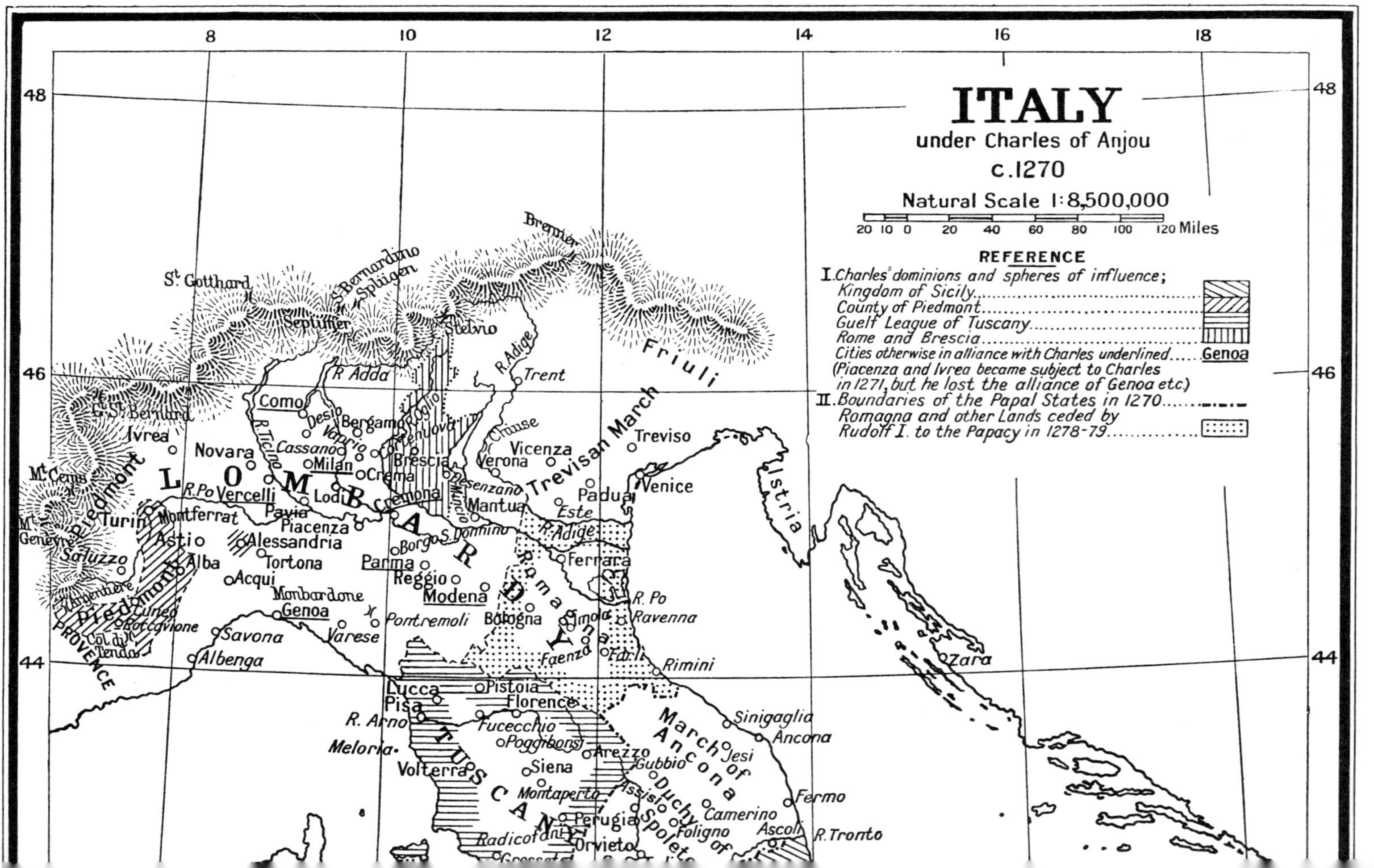

ITALY
under Charles of Anjou
c.1270
Natural Scale 1:8,500,000
20 10 0 20 40 60 80 100 120 Miles
REFERENCE
I. Charles' dominions and spheres of influence;
Kingdom of Sicily
County of Piedmont
Guelf League of Tuscany
Rome and Brescia
Cities otherwise in alliance with Charles underlined
Genoa
(Piacenza and Ivrea became subject to Charles in 1271, but he lost the alliance of Genoa etc.)
II. Boundaries of the Papal States in 1270
Romagna and other Lands ceded by Rudolf I. to the Papacy in 1278-79
8
10
12
14
16
18
48
46
44
St. Gotthard
S. Bernardino
Splügen
Septimer
Stelvio
Brenner
Friuli
G. St. Bernard
Mt. Cenis
Mt. Genèvre
Ivrea
Novara
LOMBARDY
Piedmont
R. Po
Vercelli
Turin
Montferrat
Astio
Saluzzo
Alba
Cuneo
Col di Tenda
PROVENCE
Como
R. Ticino
Desio
Cassano
Vaprio
Bergamo
R. Adda
Milan
Crema
Lodi
Pavia
Piacenza
Alessandria
Tortona
Acqui
Monbardone
Genoa
Savona
Albenga
Varese
Brescia
Cremona
Parma
Borgo S. Domnino
Reggio
Modena
Pontremoli
Bologna
Imola
Faenza
Forli
Ravenna
R. Po
Rimini
Romagna
Ferrara
R. Adige
Este
Padua
Venice
Treviso
Trevisan March
Vicenza
Verona
Chiuse
Desenzano
Mantua
Mincio
R. Adige
Trent
Istria
Zara
Lucca
Pisa
R. Arno
Meloria
Pistoia
Florence
Fucecchio
Poggibonsi
Volterra
Siena
Montaperto
TUSCANY
Arezzo
Gubbio
Assisi
Perugia
Radicofani
Orvieto
Sinigaglia
Ancona
Jesi
March of Ancona
Camerino
Foligno
Duchy of Spoleto
Fermo
Ascoli
R. Tronto

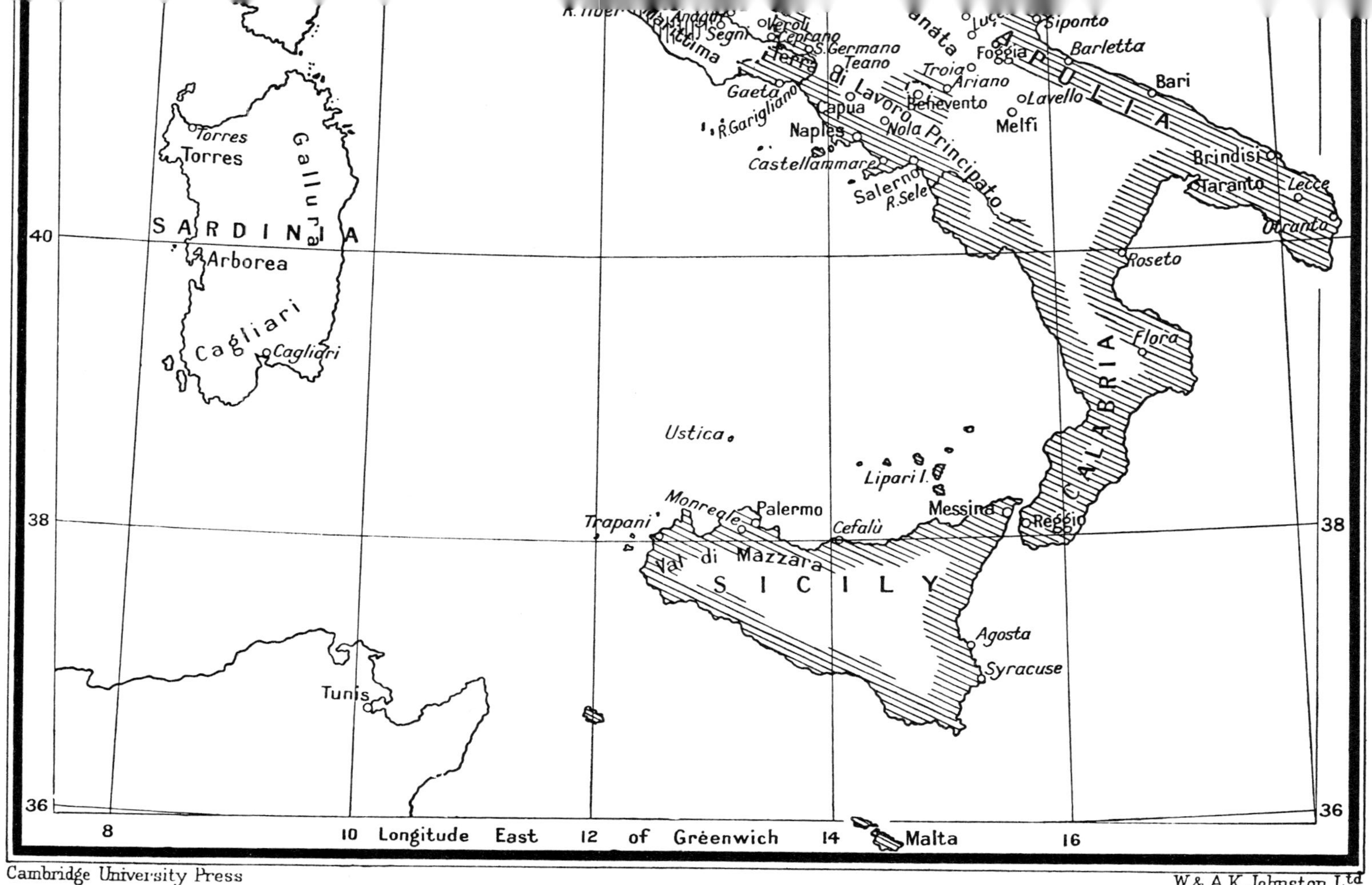
Siponto
Veroli
Ceprano
Segni
S. Germano
Teano
Terra di Lavoro
Barletta
Foggia
APULIA
Bari
Troia
Ariano
Gaeta
Capua
Benevento
Lavello
Melfi
R. Garigliano
Naples
Nola
Principato
Castellammare
Salerno
R. Sele
Brindisi
Taranto
Lecce
Otranto
Torres
Gallura
SARDINIA
Arborea
Cagliari
Roseto
Flora
CALABRIA
Ustica
Lipari I.
Monreale
Palermo
Trapani
Cefalù
Messina
Reggio
Val di Mazzara
SICILY
Agosta
Syracuse
Tunis
Malta
40
38
36
8
10
12
14
16
Longitude East of Greenwich
Cambridge University Press
W & A K Johnston Ltd

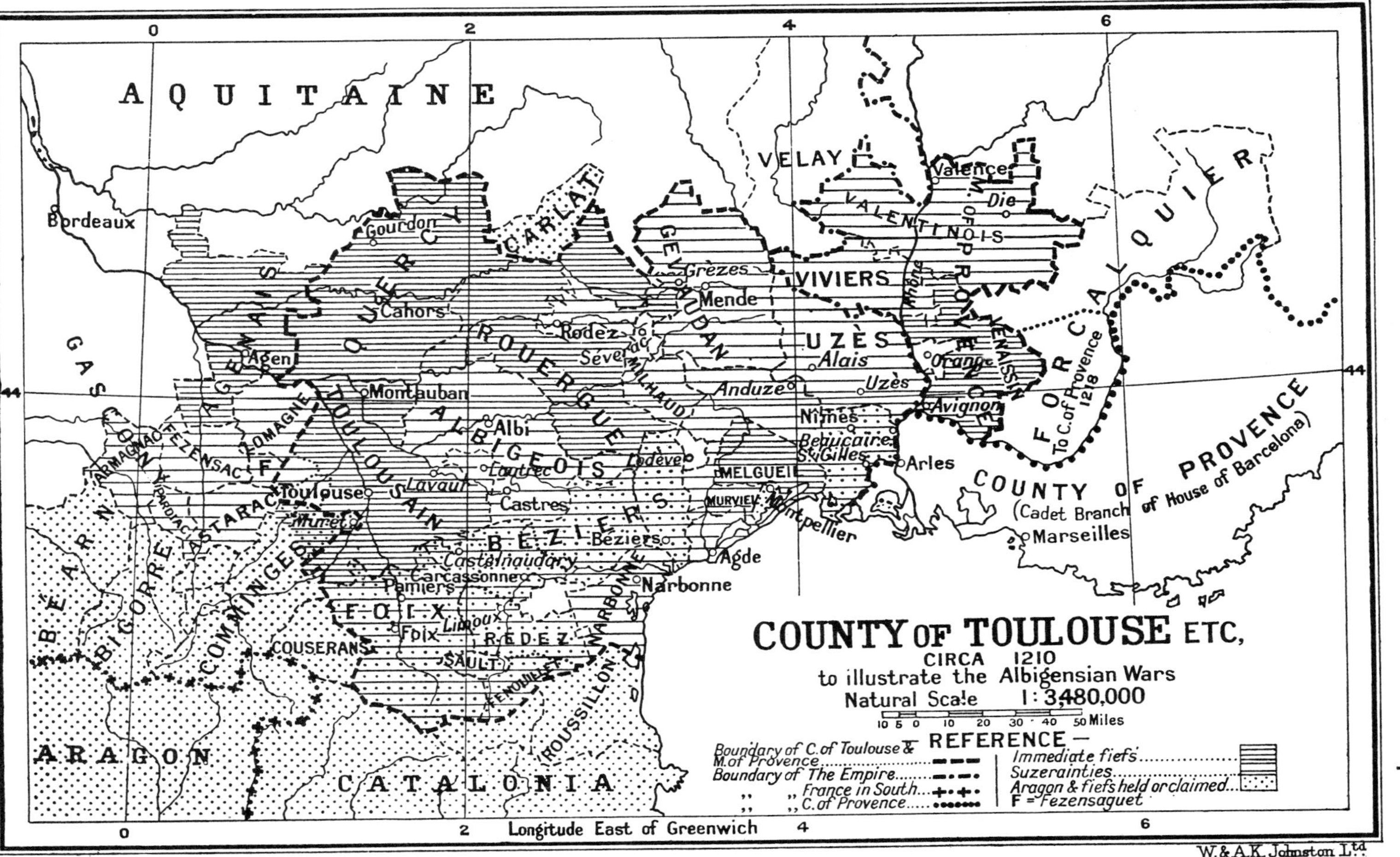
COUNTY OF TOULOUSE ETC,
CIRCA 1210
to illustrate the Albigensian Wars
Natural Scale 1: 3,480,000
10 5 0 10 20 30 40 50 Miles
REFERENCE —
Boundary of C. of Toulouse & M. of Provence
Boundary of The Empire
" " France in South
" " C. of Provence
Immediate fiefs
Suzerainties
Aragon & fiefs held or claimed
F = Fezensaguet
Longitude East of Greenwich
W. & A. K. Johnston Ltd.
AQUITAINE
GASCONY
ARAGON
CATALONIA
VELAY
VALENTINOIS
M. OF PROVENCE
VIVIERS
GEVAUDAN
UZÈS
VENAISSIN
FORCALQUIER
To C. of Provence 1218
COUNTY OF PROVENCE (Cadet Branch of House of Barcelona)
QUERCY
CARLAT
ROUERGUE
MILHAUD
ALBIGEOIS
TOULOUSAIN
AGENAIS
LOMAGNE
ARMAGNAC
FEZENSAC
PARDIAC
ASTARAC
BÉARN
BIGORRE
COMMINGES
COUSERANS
FOIX
RÉDEZ
SAULT
FENOUILLET
ROUSSILLON
NARBONNE
BÉZIERS
MELGUEIL
MURVIEL
Bordeaux
Gourdon
Cahors
Agen
Montauban
Rodez
Séverac
Grezes
Mende
Albi
Lautrec
Lavaur
Toulouse
Muret
Castres
Castelnaudary
Carcassonne
Pamiers
Foix
Limoux
Béziers
Agde
Narbonne
Lodève
Montpellier
Anduze
Alais
Uzès
Nîmes
Beaucaire
St. Gilles
Arles
Avignon
Orange
Valence
Die
Marseilles
Rhône

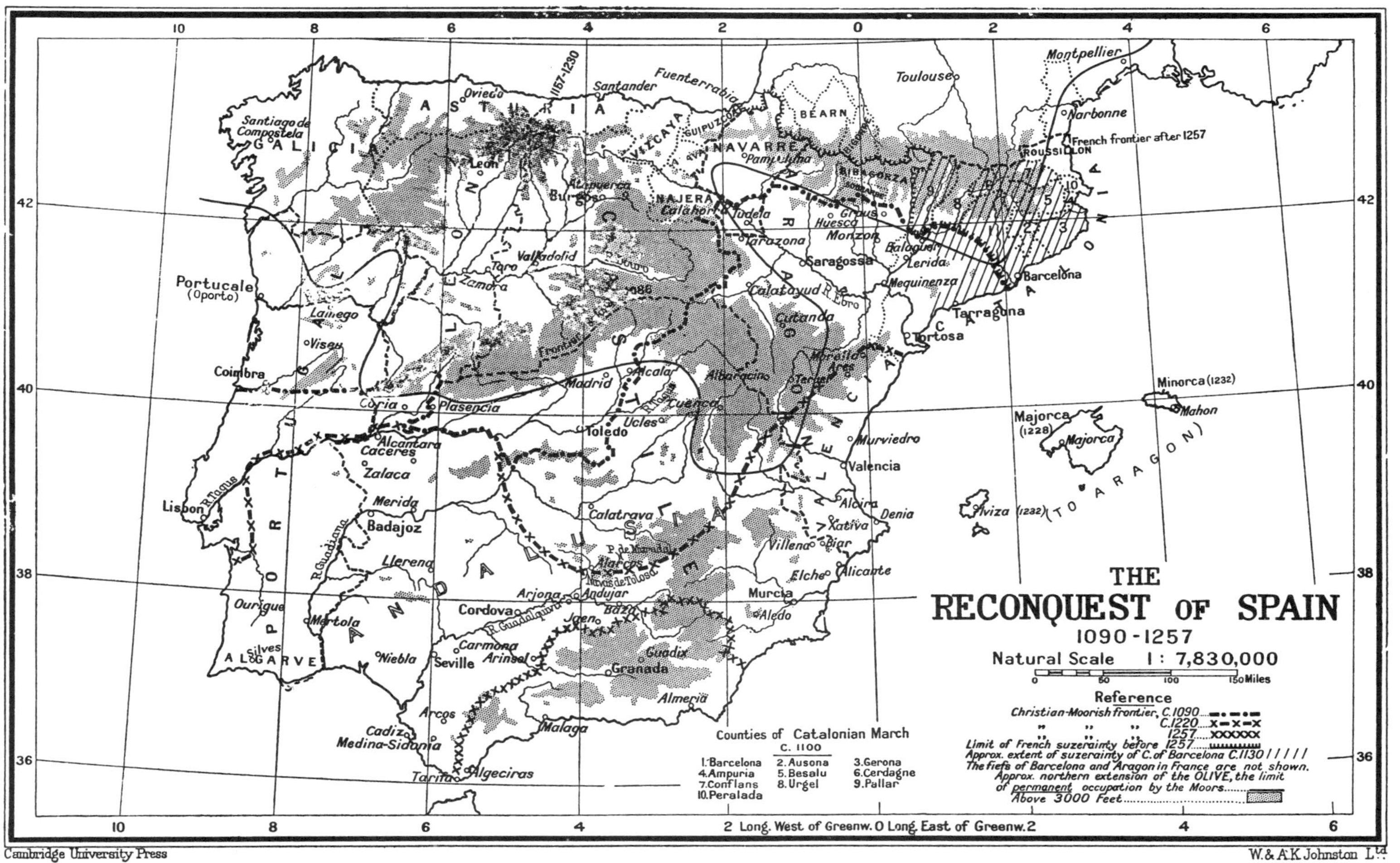
THE
RECONQUEST OF SPAIN
1090-1257
Natural Scale 1: 7,830,000
0 50 100 150 Miles
Reference
Christian-Moorish frontier, C.1090
" " " C.1220
" " " 1257
Limit of French suzerainty before 1257
Approx. extent of suzerainty of C. of Barcelona C.1130
The fiefs of Barcelona and Aragon in France are not shown.
Approx. northern extension of the OLIVE, the limit of permanent occupation by the Moors
Above 3000 Feet
Counties of Catalonian March
C. 1100
1. Barcelona
2. Ausona
3. Gerona
4. Ampuria
5. Besalu
6. Cerdagne
7. Conflans
8. Urgel
9. Pallar
10. Peralada
2 Long. West of Greenw. 0 Long. East of Greenw. 2
Cambridge University Press
W. & A.K. Johnston Ltd
Montpellier
Toulouse
Narbonne
French frontier after 1257
ROUSSILLON
BEARN
NAVARRE
Pamplona
RIBAGORZA
GUIPUZCOA
VIZCAYA
Fuenterrabia
Santander
Oviedo
1157-1230
ASTURIA
Santiago de Compostela
GALICIA
Leon
Burgos
NAJERA
Calahorra
Tudela
Graus
Huesco
Monzon
Tarazona
Saragossa
Balaguer
Lerida
Barcelona
Mequinenza
Tarragona
Tortosa
CATALONIA
Valladolid
Toro
Zamora
Calatayud
R. Ebro
Cutanda
Portucale
(Oporto)
Lamego
Viseu
Coimbra
Madrid
Alcala
Albarracin
Teruel
Morella
Coria
Plasencia
Cuenca
Ucles
Toledo
Alcantara
Caceres
Zalaca
Murviedro
Valencia
Minorca (1232)
Mahon
Majorca (1228)
Majorca
Iviza (1232)
(TO ARAGON)
Lisbon
R. Tagus
Merida
Badajoz
R. Guadiana
Llerena
Calatrava
Alarcos
Navas de Tolosa
Alcira
Denia
Xativa
Biar
Villena
Elche
Alicante
Murcia
Aledo
Arjona
Andujar
Cordova
Jaen
Baza
R. Guadalquivir
Ourique
Mertola
Silves
ALGARVE
Niebla
Seville
Carmona
Arinsol
Granada
Guadix
Almeria
Arcos
Cadiz
Medina-Sidonia
Malaga
Tarifa
Algeciras
PORTUGAL
ANDALUSIA
CASTILE
LEON
ARAGON
VALENCIA

Map 63

Bohemia, Poland and Hungary 1050-1300

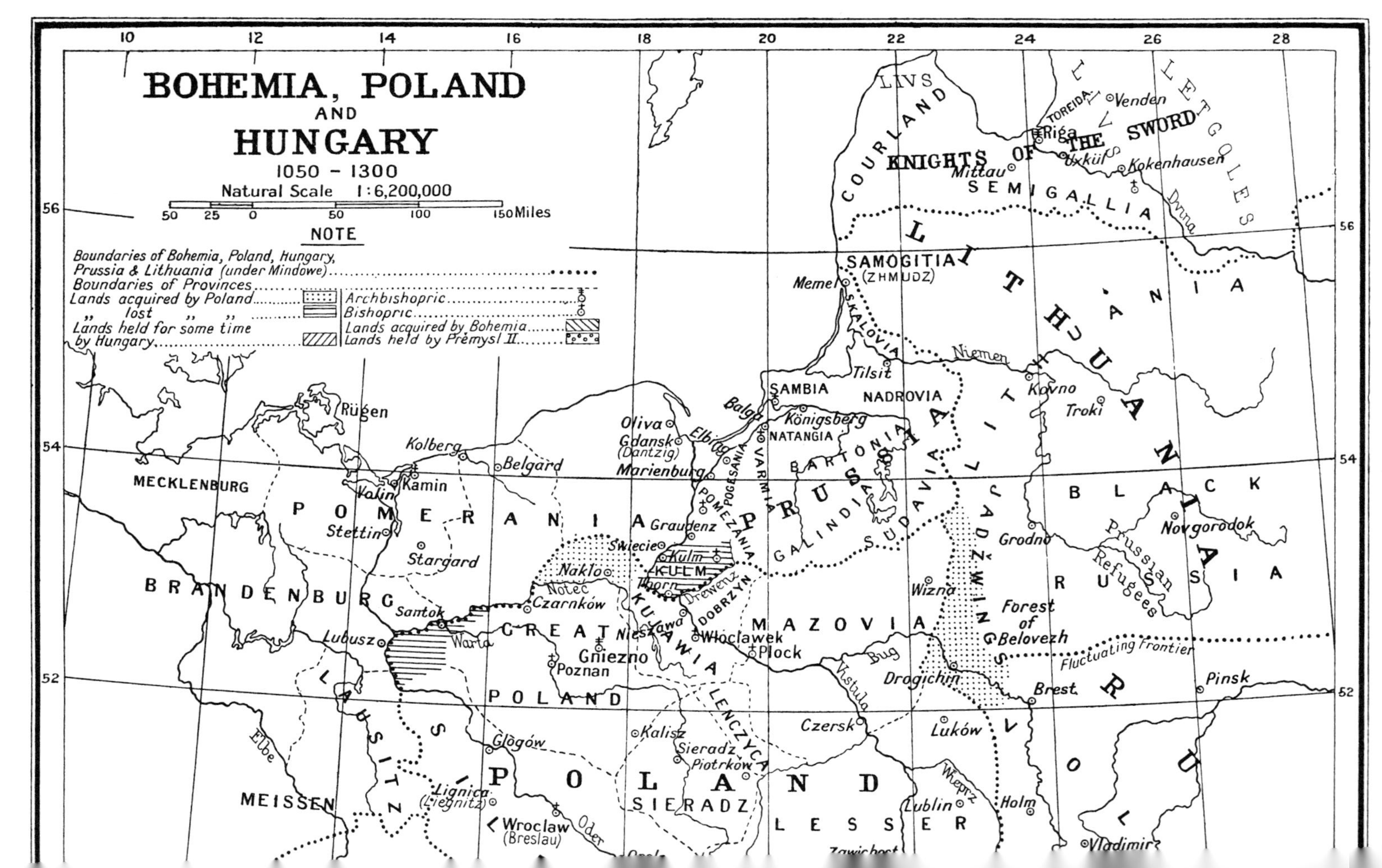

BOHEMIA, POLAND
AND
HUNGARY
1050 – 1300
Natural Scale 1:6,200,000
50 25 0 50 100 150 Miles
NOTE
Boundaries of Bohemia, Poland, Hungary, Prussia & Lithuania (under Mindowe)
Boundaries of Provinces
Lands acquired by Poland
" lost " "
Lands held for some time by Hungary
Archbishopric
Bishopric
Lands acquired by Bohemia
Lands held by Přemysl II
LIVS
COURLAND
KNIGHTS OF THE SWORD
Riga
Venden
Uxküll
Kokenhausen
Mittau
SEMIGALLIA
Dvina
LETGOLES
SAMOGITIA (ZHMUDZ)
LITHUANIA
Memel
SKALOVIA
Tilsit
Niemen
Kovno
Troki
SAMBIA
NADROVIA
Königsberg
NATANGIA
BARTONIA
PRUSSIA
GALINDIA
SUDAVIA
VARMIA
POGESANIA
POMEZANIA
Balga
Elbing
Oliva
Gdansk (Dantzig)
Marienburg
Graudenz
Swiecie
Kulm
KULM
Thorn
Drewenz
DOBRZYN
Naklo
Notec
Czarnków
Rügen
Kolberg
Kamin
Volin
Belgard
Stettin
Stargard
MECKLENBURG
POMERANIA
BRANDENBURG
Santok
Lubusz
Warta
GREAT POLAND
Gniezno
Poznan
KUJAWIA
Nieszawa
Wloclawek
Plock
MAZOVIA
JADŽWINGS
Grodno
Wizna
Forest of Belovezh
Fluctuating Frontier
BLACK RUSSIA
Novgorodok
Prussian Refugees
Pinsk
Brest
Drogichin
Bug
Vistula
Czersk
Luków
Lublin
Wieprz
Holm
Vladimir
LENCZYCA
Kalisz
Sieradz
Piotrków
SIERADZ
LESSER POLAND
Zawichost
LAUSITZ
Elbe
MEISSEN
SILESIA
Glogów
Lignica (Liegnitz)
Wroclaw (Breslau)
Oder
VOLHYNIA
RUS
10 12 14 16 18 20 22 24 26 28
56 54 52

(CECHY)
MORAVIA
Olmütz
Brno (Brünn)
BAVARIA
Danube
AUSTRIA
Dürnkrut
MARCHFELD
Vienna
March
Leitha
Pressburg
STYRIA
CARINTHIA
CARNIOLA
SLOVAKIA
Esztergom (Gran)
Győr (Raab)
Veszprem
Buda
Pesth
Vacs
Szekes-Fehervar
Kalocsa
Pecs
Borcs
Zagreb
HUNGARY
CUMANS
Eger
Sajo
SZABOLCS
Bihar
Nagyvarad
Csanad
Theiss
TRANSYLVANIA
DOBOKA
Gyula-Fehervar
SAXONS
Nagyszeben
ROUMANIANS
(Teutonic Knights)
Roumanian Princes
SZEKELY
Banat of Szörény
Braničevo
Peremysl (Przemysl)
Galich
GALICHIA
SLAVONIA
CROATIA
Drave
Save
Banat of Bosnia
Banat of Mačva
Belgrade
BOSNIA
SERBIA
Morava
Niš
CUMANS
BULGARIA
Danube
DALMATIA
Knin
Split
Zadar
Bielegrad
48
46
44
12
14
16
18 Longitude East 20 of Greenwich
22
24
26
Cambridge University Press
W. & A.K. Johnston Ltd

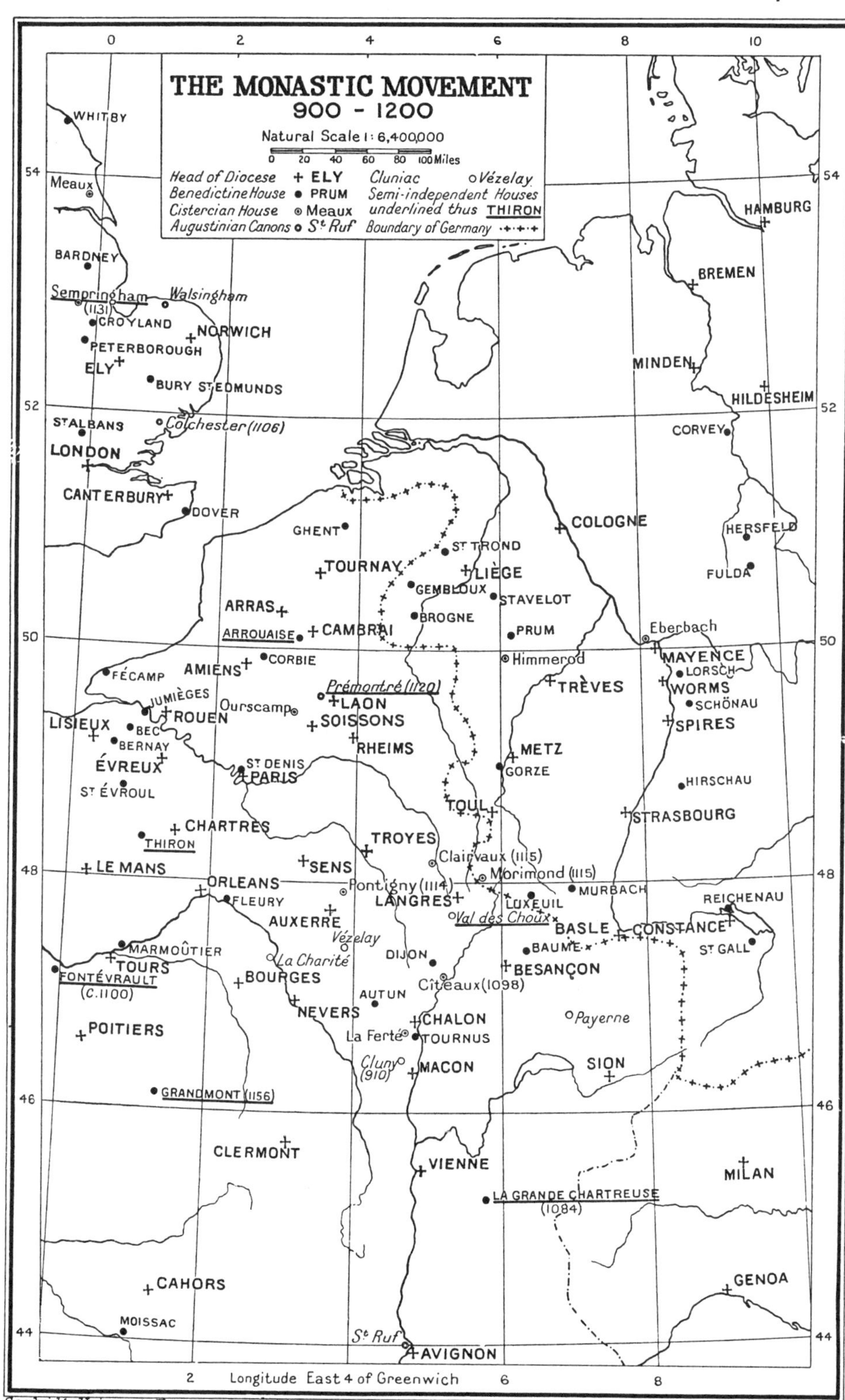

Cambridge University Press
W. & A. K. Johnston Ltd

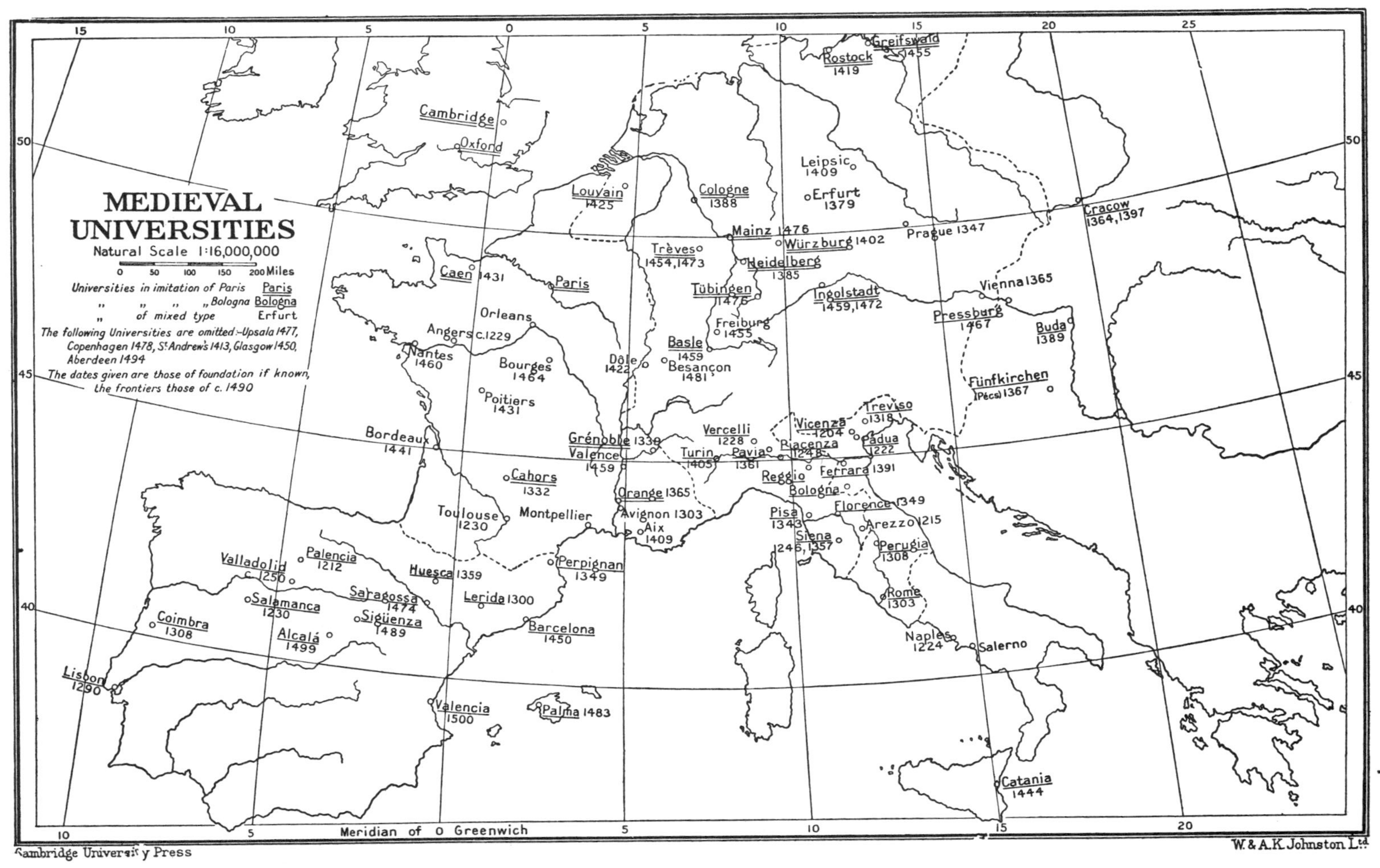
MEDIEVAL UNIVERSITIES
Natural Scale 1:16,000,000
0 50 100 150 200 Miles
Universities in imitation of Paris Paris
" " " " Bologna Bologna
" of mixed type Erfurt
The following Universities are omitted:—Upsala 1477, Copenhagen 1478, St Andrew's 1413, Glasgow 1450, Aberdeen 1494
The dates given are those of foundation if known, the frontiers those of c. 1490
Cambridge
Oxford
Rostock 1419
Greifswald 1455
Leipsic 1409
Erfurt 1379
Louvain 1425
Cologne 1388
Cracow 1364, 1397
Mainz 1476
Würzburg 1402
Prague 1347
Trèves 1454, 1473
Heidelberg 1385
Caen 1431
Paris
Tübingen 1476
Ingolstadt 1459, 1472
Vienna 1365
Orleans
Angers c. 1229
Freiburg 1455
Pressburg 1467
Buda 1389
Nantes 1460
Basle 1459
Bourges 1464
Dôle 1422
Besançon 1481
Fünfkirchen (Pécs) 1367
Poitiers 1431
Treviso 1318
Vicenza 1204
Vercelli 1228
Padua 1222
Bordeaux 1441
Grénoble 1339
Valence 1459
Turin 1405
Pavia 1361
Piacenza 1248
Ferrara 1391
Reggio
Cahors 1332
Bologna
Orange 1365
Florence 1349
Toulouse 1230
Montpellier
Avignon 1303
Aix 1409
Pisa 1343
Arezzo 1215
Siena 1246, 1357
Perugia 1308
Valladolid c. 1250
Palencia 1212
Huesca 1359
Perpignan 1349
Saragossa 1474
Lerida 1300
Rome 1303
Salamanca 1230
Coimbra 1308
Sigüenza 1489
Alcalá 1499
Barcelona 1450
Naples 1224
Salerno
Lisbon 1290
Valencia 1500
Palma 1483
Catania 1444
Meridian of 0 Greenwich
Cambridge University Press
W. & A. K. Johnston Ltd

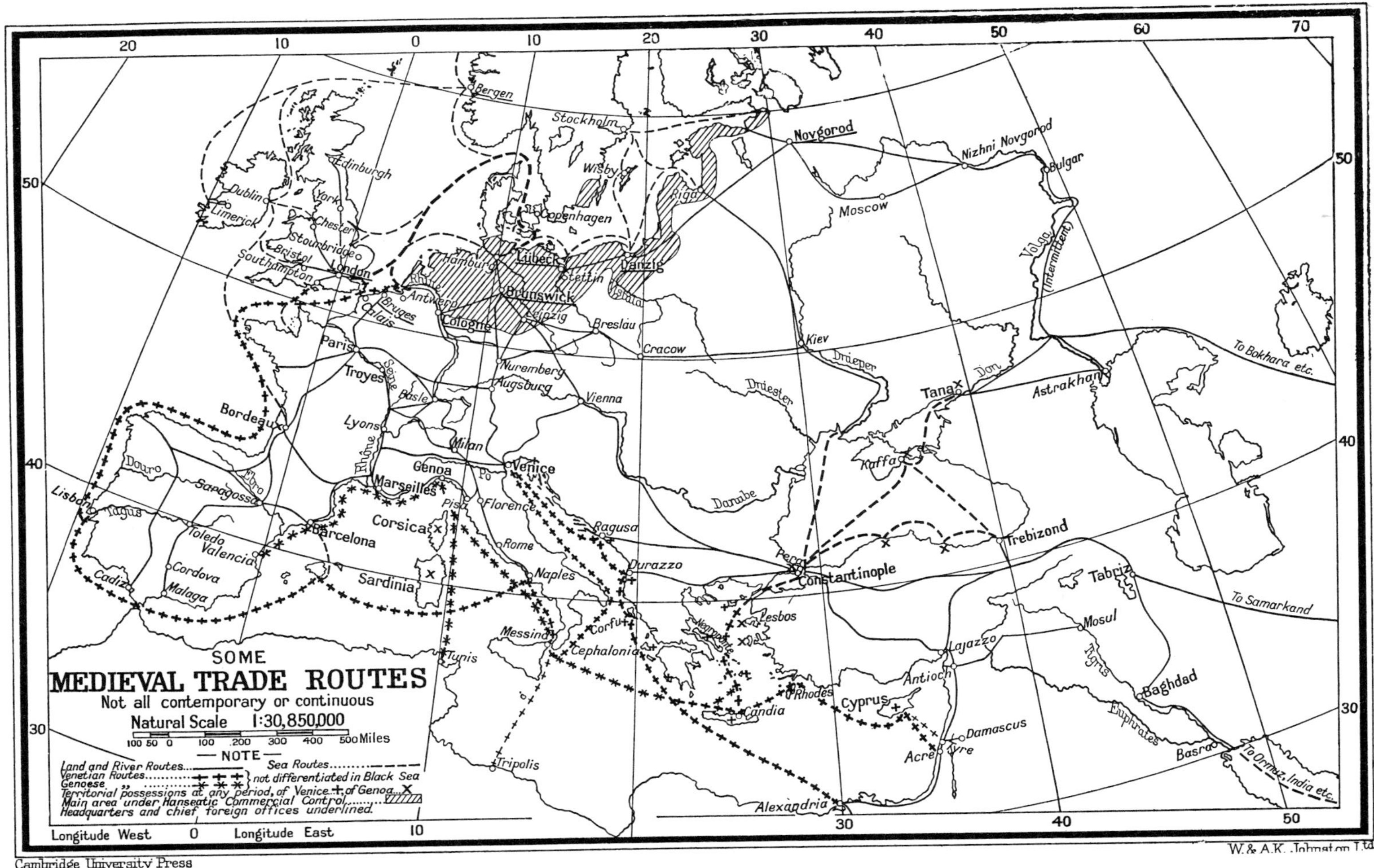
SOME
MEDIEVAL TRADE ROUTES
Not all contemporary or continuous
Natural Scale 1:30,850,000
100 50 0 100 200 300 400 500 Miles
— NOTE —
Land and River Routes
Sea Routes
Venetian Routes
Genoese "
not differentiated in Black Sea
Territorial possessions at any period, of Venice +, of Genoa X
Main area under Hanseatic Commercial Control
Headquarters and chief foreign offices underlined.
Longitude West 0 Longitude East
Bergen
Stockholm
Novgorod
Nizhni Novgorod
Bulgar
Edinburgh
Dublin
Limerick
York
Chester
Stourbridge
Bristol
Southampton
London
Wisby
Copenhagen
Riga
Moscow
Volga
(Intermittent)
Hamburg
Lübeck
Stettin
Danzig
Vistula
Rhine
Antwerp
Bruges
Calais
Brunswick
Cologne
Leipzig
Breslau
Cracow
Kiev
Dnieper
To Bokhara etc.
Paris
Troyes
Seine
Nuremberg
Augsburg
Vienna
Driester
Don
Tana
Astrakhan
Basle
Bordeaux
Lyons
Rhône
Milan
Genoa
Po
Venice
Kaffa
Douro
Ebro
Saragossa
Lisbon
Tagus
Marseilles
Pisa
Florence
Danube
Corsica
Barcelona
Toledo
Valencia
Rome
Ragusa
Trebizond
Cordova
Cadiz
Malaga
Sardinia
Naples
Durazzo
Pera
Constantinople
Tabriz
To Samarkand
Messina
Corfu
Cephalonia
Negropont
Lesbos
Mosul
Tigris
Lajazzo
Tunis
Antioch
Rhodes
Cyprus
Candia
Baghdad
Euphrates
Damascus
Tyre
Acre
Basra
To Ormuz, India etc.
Tripolis
Alexandria
W. & A.K. Johnston Ltd
Cambridge University Press